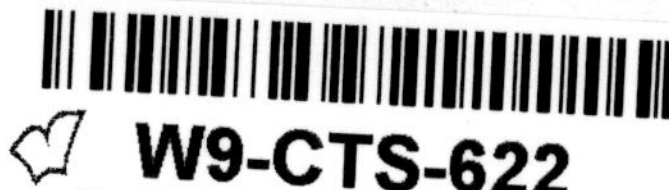
W9-CTS-622

Teacher's Edition

Realidades 1

realidades.com

Digital Edition

Peggy Palo Boyles
OKLAHOMA CITY, OK

Myriam Met
ROCKVILLE, MD

Richard S. Sayers
LONGMONT, CO

Carol Eubanks Wargin

PEARSON

Boston, Massachusetts | Chandler, Arizona
Glenview, Illinois | Upper Saddle River, New Jersey

WE DEDICATE THIS BOOK TO THE MEMORY OF OUR ESTEEMED COLLEAGUE,

Carol Eubanks Wargin.

Front cover, left: Teen boy sitting in park
Center left: Museo Bilbao, Bilbao, Spain
Center right: Girls in Nicaraguan dresses, Miami Arts in the Street, Independence of Central America and Mexico Cultural Integration Day, Miami, Florida
Right: Chac-Mool figure at Cancún, Yucatán Peninsula, Mexico

PEARSON

ISBN-13: 978-0-13-319951-2
ISBN-10: 0-13-319951-7

4 5 6 7 8 9 10 V056 16 15 14

Professional Development Handbook

Realidades 1

realidades.com

Digital Edition

Table of Contents

realidades.com Get started on **realidades.com**!

Now that you have purchased Realidades ©2014, follow these steps to set up a new account:

a. Go to **realidades.com** and click "Register."
b. Select the account type you need.
c. Provide your School Code or use the search tool to find it.
d. Follow directions to complete registration.

For Video Modules and other implementation support, visit:

*my*PearsonTraining.com

- Video Modules and PDFs for product training

Realidades, Research, and the Standards

Topics covered:

- *Realidades* and Research-based Instruction
- Achieving the Standards with *Realidades*

REALIDADES and the Common Core State Standards

The *Common Core State Standards for English Language Arts and Literacy in History/Social Studies, Science, and Technology Subjects* define general, cross-disciplinary literacy expectations to ensure that all students are prepared for success in college or workforce training programs. These Standards contain four strands: Reading, Writing, Speaking and Listening, and Language.

Teachers using *REALIDADES* can be assured that they are supporting the Common Core Standards. Look for the National Standards for Language Learning correlations within a chapter as evidence of support:

- Reading: 1.2, 2.1, 2.2, 3.1, 3.2, 4.1, 4.2, 5.1
- Writing: 1.3, 2.1, 2.2, 3.1, 3.2, 4.1, 4.2, 5.1
- Speaking and Listening: 1.1, 1.3, 2.1, 2.2, 3.2, 4.1, 5.2

You'll also find this icon next to Common Core activities in the *¡Adelante!* section.

Realidades is based on the belief that the purpose of learning Spanish is to communicate with the people who speak it and to understand their cultures. *Realidades* presents a fresh, exciting approach to Spanish by making language learning real for today's students.

Realidades and Research-based Instruction

Realidades reflects the most current research on how students learn languages and what teachers and materials need to do to help them become proficient language users. Let's take a look at some of the basic premises about language and language learning.

Communication

Communication is an authentic exchange of information for a real purpose between two or more people. By this we mean that people tell each other (through speech or writing) something the other person doesn't already know.

Communicating meaning has several aspects. Students need to listen to and read Spanish in order to interpret intended meanings. Students need to express meaning by conveying their own messages for a purpose and to a real audience. They also need to negotiate meaning through the natural give-and-take involved in understanding and making oneself understood. Research tells us that classroom activities must provide students practice in interpreting, expressing, and negotiating meaning through extensive and frequent peer interactions.

Throughout *Realidades,* students are engaged in understanding messages, in sending their own messages, and thus in communicating real ideas and real meanings for real purposes.

Comprehensible input

Research states that students learn best when they have ample opportunities to internalize meanings before they have to produce them. In other words, comprehension precedes production. The term "comprehensible input" suggests that learners acquire language by understanding what they hear and read. Students need many opportunities to match what they hear with visual cues (pictures, video, or teacher pantomime) or experiences (physical actions). Reading input should be supported by a close connection between text and visuals. All these strategies for comprehensible input help students associate meaning with forms.

> "Communication is an authentic exchange of information for a real purpose between two or more people."

In keeping with this research, *Realidades* begins each chapter of Levels 1–3 with a section called *A primera vista*. These four pages of language input give students opportunities to comprehend new language before producing it. The visualized presentation of vocabulary in context, the reading input in the *Videohistoria,* and the listening input in the *A primera vista* video segment provide a wide range of comprehensible input of new language that addresses all students and all learning styles.

Practice activities

Research tells us that students need extensive practice using new language to create and convey their own messages. The *Manos a la obra* section in Levels 1–3 provides a wide range of practice activities. New vocabulary and grammar are first practiced in skill-getting activities that provide concrete practice. This basic practice helps to develop accuracy in using the language and prepares students to transition into more communicative tasks. In the transitional activities that follow the basic practice, students work with a partner or in small groups with information- or opinion-gap activities that are characteristic of real-life communication. Students then continue on to more open-ended, personalized speaking or writing tasks.

Meaningful context in language learning

All effective learning is rooted in a meaningful context. We know from research that information is most likely to be retained when it is connected to other information in a meaningful way. Thus, language learning is most successful and retention more likely when we present new language organized into topics or by situations.

Realidades is organized into themes. All material in a chapter—vocabulary, grammar, culture— is rooted in a context and used meaningfully. Students engage in communicative tasks that are relevant to their lives. Students work with readings, realia, photography, and art that are authentic to the Spanish-speaking world. The video programs and Internet links show native speakers engaged in real-life situations and experiences.

Understanding grammar

Students learn grammar most effectively when it is presented and practiced in a meaningful context and when it connects to real communication needs. Students also benefit when shown how the patterns of grammar work.

In *Realidades,* new structures are foreshadowed through lexical presentation (grammar is presented as vocabulary) in the *Vocabulario en contexto* language input section in Levels 1–3. In addition, early vocabulary activities in the *Vocabulario en uso* section have students work with the grammar lexically. This allows students to see the grammar and work with it in a meaningful context before being formally presented with the rules or paradigms.

Grammar is formally presented with clear explanations and examples in the *Gramática* section in Levels 1–3. Comparisons between English and Spanish grammar are made whenever possible. Students then practice the grammar concepts in a variety of tasks that range from concrete activities that focus primarily on the structures to more open-ended tasks that focus on communication.

To further facilitate the learning of grammar, *Realidades* offers *GramActiva,* a multi-modality approach to grammar that includes grammar videos and hands-on grammar activities. By teaching and practicing grammar through different learning styles, more students will be able to learn grammar.

Building cultural perspectives

The *Standards for Foreign Language Learning* have expanded how culture is taught in today's classroom. We want students to understand the *why* (perspectives) of culture that determines the *what* (products and practices).

The approach to culture in *Realidades* not only teaches students the *what* but asks students to explore the *why*. Cultural products, practices, and comparisons are presented throughout *Realidades* in features such as *Arte y cultura, Fondo cultural, La cultura en vivo,* and *Perspectivas del mundo hispano,* and in *Realidades 3, Puente a la cultura*. Students read information about cultures that offer different perspectives and they are asked questions that encourage them to think and make observations about cultures.

Strategies for Success

Research shows that effective learners know how to help themselves become successful learners. One way they do this is by using specific problem-solving strategies.

Realidades teaches students strategies to be effective communicators whether listening, speaking, reading, or writing. Each reading selection in Levels 1–3 is supported by a reading strategy. Each performance-based task in Levels 1–3 includes a useful strategy that connects to a step-by-step approach that helps students plan, rehearse, and present or publish. Each also includes a rubric so students know how they might be evaluated.

We know more than ever about how foreign languages are learned. *Realidades* is based on solid research in second-language acquisition, on accepted theories about the teaching of culture, and on sound pedagogical practices that are common to all disciplines. We are sure that you and your students will find this an exciting, motivating, and enormously successful approach to learning Spanish.

Achieving the Standards with *Realidades*

The *Standards for Foreign Language Learning* provide an important and useful framework to guide the teaching and learning of foreign languages. This framework should result in a new generation of language learners prepared to meet the demand for competence in other languages that our nation will face in an increasingly interdependent world.

Realidades is based upon the Standards. This means that instruction used in *Realidades* will help students develop the competencies delineated in the *Standards for Foreign Language Learning*. Teachers will find a correlation to the Standards at the beginning of each chapter and with the notes that accompany each activity (if appropriate) in the Teacher's Edition.

Goal 1: Communication

1.1 (Interpersonal): Each chapter provides a wide range of paired and group activities. Students speak with a partner, work in small groups, and interview classmates.

1.2 (Interpretive): *Realidades* builds the interpretive listening skill through the Audio Program. This program in Levels 1–3 supports activities in the Student Edition (input checks, dictations, listening comprehension, and test preparation) and the *Writing, Audio, & Video* section of the *Communication Workbook*. The Video Program also develops listening through the different language, grammar, and storyline mystery video segments.

Realidades provides extensive support for the interpretive reading skill. Students read throughout the chapter: comprehensible input, practice activities, realia, culture notes, and reading selections. Reading is seamlessly integrated with practice and anchored in real-life contexts. Whenever possible, readings are supported by focused strategies.

1.3 (Presentational): Each chapter in Levels 1–2 ends with a performance-based task: in the "A" chapters, a speaking task, in the "B" chapters a presentation writing task. Both presentations are supported by strategies and the speaking or writing process, step-by-step support to help students successfully complete the task.

Goal 2: Culture

2.1 (Practices and Perspectives) and **2.2** (Products and Perspectives): Each chapter in *Realidades* explores a cultural theme through a wide range of practices, products, and perspectives. Students see authentic culture through realia, art, photographs, popular sayings, tongue twisters, rhymes and songs, hands-on projects, readings, and authentic literature. In addition, the unique *Fondo cultural* readings in Levels 1–3 generally include a Standards-based critical thinking question.

Goal 3: Connections

3.1 (Cross-curricular Connections): *Realidades* integrates cross-curricular activities (*Conexiones*) within the *Manos a la obra section* in Levels 1–3. Students make connections to a variety of disciplines through activities that integrate the language of the chapter.

3.2 (Connections to Target Culture): *Realidades* exposes students to perspectives only available within the target culture through art, realia, pronunciation activities, and readings.

Goal 4: Comparisons

4.1 (Language Comparisons): *Realidades* enables students to see comparisons between languages in both the grammar explanations in the text and *GramActiva* videos, and in a unique section called *Exploración del lenguage* in Levels 1–2. Students learn to look for language connections, to understand how language works, and to integrate these new skills as they continue in their study of Spanish.

4.2 (Cultural Comparisons): *Realidades* is rich in cultural comparisons. A unique feature called *Fondo cultural* in Levels 1–3 generally informs students about a cultural product or practice and is followed by a question that challenges students to think critically and make comparisons between cultures.

Goal 5: Communities

5.1 (Outside the Classroom): *Realidades* provides informative features called *El español en la comunidad* and *El español en el mundo del trabajo* in Levels 1–3. These sections help students see how to use Spanish beyond the classroom, in their communities, and in the world of work.

5.2 (Lifelong Learners): For a textbook to help students achieve this goal, it must motivate students to want to communicate and want to learn more about the culture. The core of *Realidades*—real language, real culture, real tasks—motivates students. The video programs and other technology support engage learners in ways that may encourage them to continue their exploration of the Spanish language and cultures.

Standards for Foreign Language Learning

Goal 1: Communicate in Languages Other Than English

- Standard 1.1: Students engage in conversation, provide and obtain information, express feelings and emotions, and exchange opinions.
- Standard 1.2: Students understand and interpret written and spoken language on a variety of topics.
- Standard 1.3: Students present information, concepts and ideas to an audience of listeners or readers on a variety of topics.

Goal 2: Gain Knowledge and Understanding of Other Cultures

- Standard 2.1: Students demonstrate an understanding of the relationship between the practices and perspectives of the culture studied.
- Standard 2.2: Students demonstrate an understanding of the relationship between the products and perspectives of the culture studied.

Goal 3: Connect with Other Disciplines and Acquire Information

- Standard 3.1: Students reinforce and further their knowledge of other disciplines through the foreign language.
- Standard 3.2: Students acquire information and recognize the distinctive viewpoints that are only available through the foreign language and its cultures.

Goal 4: Develop Insight into the Nature of Language and Culture

- Standard 4.1: Students demonstrate understanding of the nature of language through comparisons of the language studied and their own.
- Standard 4.2: Students demonstrate understanding of the concept of culture through comparisons of the cultures studied and their own.

Goal 5: Participate in Multilingual Communities at Home and Around the World

- Standard 5.1: Students use the language both within and beyond the school setting.
- Standard 5.2: Students show evidence of becoming life-long learners by using the language for personal enjoyment and enrichment.

Program Organization

Realidades is a communication-based six-level series with a full range of print and technology components that allow teachers to meet the needs of the different students in today's Spanish classroom.

Middle School

Realidades A and ***B*** are separate middle school books that meet the needs of the younger learners. Each Student Edition provides the same content of ***Realidades 1*** but has been adapted with new art, photographs, and activities that are age-appropriate for the younger learner. Students completing ***Realidades B*** will make a smooth transition into ***Realidades 2***.

High School

Each high school Student Edition provides the complete curriculum for one year of instruction. The spiraling of themes and extensive recycling of content allows for smooth articulation between levels. Students completing ***Realidades 3 and 4*** will have a solid foundation for advanced Spanish study.

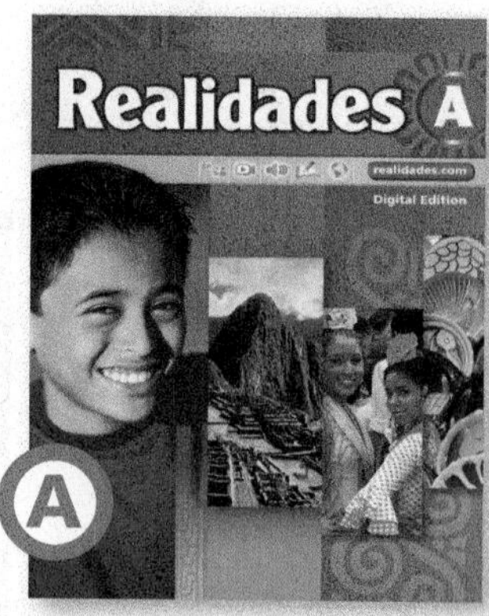

Realidades A
- Introductory section ***Para empezar***
- Temas 1–4

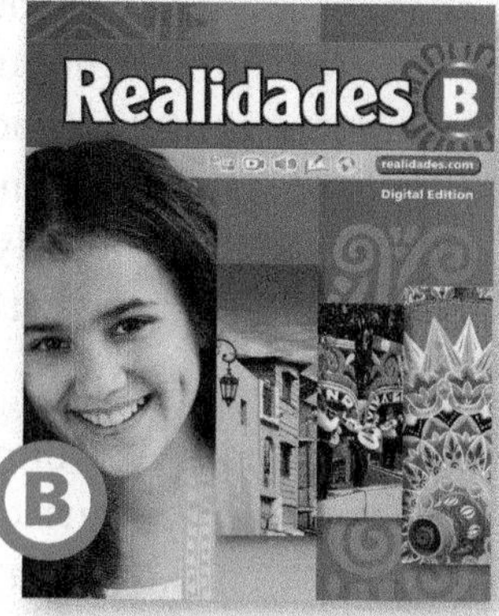

Realidades B
- Review section ***Para empezar***
- Temas 5–9

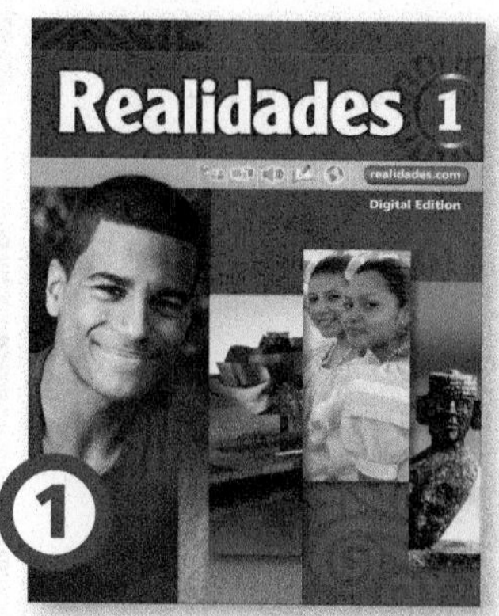

Realidades 1
- Introductory section ***Para empezar***
- Temas 1–9

Realidades 2
- Review section ***Para empezar***
- Temas 1–9

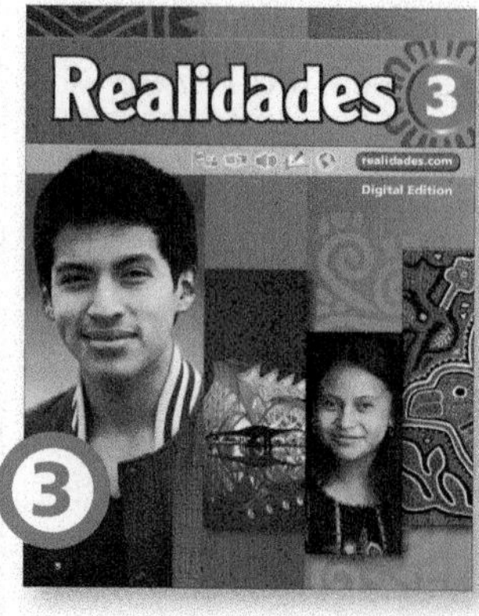

Realidades 3
- Review section ***Para empezar***
- Capítulos 1–10

Realidades 4
- Capítulos 1–12

Chapter Organization

Temas

Realidades 1 begins with an introductory section followed by nine thematic units, called *Temas*. Each *Tema* is divided into two chapters.

Tema	Capítulo A	Capítulo B
Para empezar	**1.** En la escuela **2.** En la clase **3.** El tiempo	
1: Mis amigos y yo	1A: *¿Qué te gusta hacer?*	1B: *Y tú, ¿cómo eres?*
2: La escuela	2A: *Tu día en la escuela*	2B: *Tu sala de clases*
3: La comida	3A: *¿Desayuno o almuerzo?*	3B: *Para mantener la salud*
4: Los pasatiempos	4A: *¿Adónde vas?*	4B: *¿Quieres ir conmigo?*
5: Fiesta en familia	5A: *Una fiesta de cumpleaños*	5B: *¡Vamos a un restaurante!*
6: La casa	6A: *En mi dormitorio*	6B: *¿Cómo es tu casa?*
7: De compras	7A: *¿Cuánto cuesta?*	7B: *¡Qué regalo!*
8: Experiencias	8A: *De vacaciones*	8B: *Ayudando en la comunidad*
9: Medios de comunicación	9A: *El cine y la televisión*	9B: *La tecnología*

Chapters

Each chapter in *Realidades* is built around a clear sequence of instruction.

Chapter Section	Pedagogical support
A primera vista • Vocabulario en contexto • Videohistoria	Provides comprehensible language input for the chapter's new vocabulary and grammar within an authentic context. Input includes words, dialogues, narration, visuals, audio, and video. Students' language production focuses on comprehension and limited production.
Manos a la obra • Vocabulario en uso • Gramática	Provides productive language practice with a variety of concrete, transitional, and open-ended activities. The activities develop all four language skills and focus on relevant language tasks. Many activities build off of authentic documents, *realia,* and photographs.
¡Adelante! • Lectura • La cultura en vivo / Perspectivas del mundo hispano • Presentación oral/escrita • El mundo hispano	Provides culminating theme-based activities that have students apply what they have learned. The section features a culturally-based reading, performance-based speaking or writing tasks, cultural activities, and the storyline mystery video *¿Eres tú, María?*
Repaso del capítulo • Vocabulario y gramática • Preparación para el examen	Provides complete support for the end-of-chapter assessment. One page summarizes what students need to know (vocabulary and grammar). The second page outlines the proficiency and culture sections of the test by describing the task, providing a practice task, and referring students to chapter activities for review.

Realidades 1

Scope and Sequence

Articulation

Realidades offers a completely articulated Scope and Sequence across all levels. The recursive themes allow for the recycling, review, and reteaching of vocabulary and grammar.

Realidades 1

Tema	Capítulo	
Para empezar	• En la escuela: greetings; introductions; leave-takings; numbers; time; body parts • En la clase: classroom, dates, asking for help • El tiempo: weather, seasons	
	A	**B**
1: Mis amigos y yo	**1A ¿Qué te gusta hacer?** **Vocabulary:** activities and expressions for saying what you like and don't like to do **Grammar:** infinitives; making negative statements	**1B Y tú, ¿cómo eres?** **Vocabulary:** adjectives and vocabulary to ask about and describe someone's personality **Grammar:** adjectives; definite and indefinite articles; word order
2: La escuela	**2A Tu día en la escuela** **Vocabulary:** classroom items and furniture; parts of the classroom; prepositions of location **Grammar:** subject pronouns; the present tense of *-ar* verbs	**2B Tu sala de clases** **Vocabulary:** classroom items and furniture; parts of the classroom; prepositions of location **Grammar:** the verb *estar;* plurals of nouns and articles
3: La comida	**3A ¿Desayuno o almuerzo?** **Vocabulary:** foods; beverages; adverbs of frequency; expressions to show surprise **Grammar:** present tense of *-er* and *-ir* verbs; *me gusta(n), me encanta(n)*	**3B Para mantener la salud** **Vocabulary:** food; beverages; expressions to discuss health; expressions to discuss preferences, agreement, disagreement, and quantity; adjectives to describe food **Grammar:** the plural of adjectives; the verb *ser*
4: Los pasatiempos	**4A ¿Adónde vas?** **Vocabulary:** leisure activities; places; expressions to tell where and with whom you go; expressions to talk about when things are done **Grammar:** the verb *ir;* interrogative words	**4B ¿Quieres ir conmigo?** **Vocabulary:** leisure activities; feelings; expressions for extending, accepting, and declining invitations; expressions to tell when something happens **Grammar:** *ir* + *a* + infinitive; the verb *jugar*
5: Fiesta en familia	**5A Una fiesta de cumpleaños** **Vocabulary:** family and parties **Grammar:** the verb *tener;* possessive adjectives	**5B ¡Vamos a un restaurante!** **Vocabulary:** describing people and ordering a meal **Grammar:** the verb *venir;* the verbs *ser* and *estar*
6: La casa	**6A En mi dormitorio** **Vocabulary:** bedroom items; electronic equipment; colors; adjectives to describe things **Grammar:** comparisons and superlatives; stem-changing verbs: *poder* and *dormir*	**6B ¿Cómo es tu casa?** **Vocabulary:** rooms in a house and household chores **Grammar:** affirmative *tú* commands; the present progressive tense
7: De compras	**7A ¿Cuánto cuesta?** **Vocabulary:** clothing; shopping; numbers 200–1,000 **Grammar:** stem-changing verbs: *pensar, querer,* and *preferir;* demonstrative adjectives	**7B ¡Qué regalo!** **Vocabulary:** places to shop; gifts; accessories; buying and selling **Grammar:** preterite of *-ar, -car,* and *-gar* verbs; direct object pronouns *lo, la, los, las*
8: Experiencias	**8A De vacaciones** **Vocabulary:** vacation places; activities; modes of transportation **Grammar:** preterite of *-er* and *-ir* verbs; preterite of *ir*; the personal *a*	**8B Ayudando en la comunidad** **Vocabulary:** recycling and volunteer work; places in a community **Grammar:** the verb *decir;* indirect object pronouns; preterite of *hacer* and *dar*
9: Medios de comunicación	**9A El cine y la televisión** **Vocabulary:** television shows; movie genres; giving opinions **Grammar:** *acabar de* + infinitive; *gustar* and similar verbs	**9B La tecnología** **Vocabulary:** computers; communication; computer-related activities **Grammar:** the verbs *pedir* and *servir; saber* and *conocer*

Scope and Sequence

Realidades A and *B* provide the same Scope and Sequence as *Realidades 1*.

Realidades A covers the same content as the *Para empezar* section and *Temas* 1–4.

Tema	Capítulo A	Capítulo B
Para empezar	• En la escuela: greetings; introductions; leave-takings; numbers; time; body parts • En la clase: classroom, dates, asking for help • El tiempo: weather, seasons	
1: Mis amigos y yo	**1A ¿Qué te gusta hacer?** **Vocabulary:** activities and expressions for saying what you like and don't like to do **Grammar:** infinitives; making negative statements	**1B Y tú, ¿cómo eres?** **Vocabulary:** adjectives and vocabulary to ask about and describe someone's personality **Grammar:** adjectives; definite and indefinite articles; word order
2: La escuela	**2A Tu día en la escuela** **Vocabulary:** classroom items and furniture; parts of the classroom; prepositions of location **Grammar:** subject pronouns; the present tense of *-ar* verbs	**2B Tu sala de clases** **Vocabulary:** classroom items and furniture; parts of the classroom; prepositions of location **Grammar:** the verb *estar;* plurals of nouns and articles
3: La comida	**3A ¿Desayuno o almuerzo?** **Vocabulary:** foods; beverages; adverbs of frequency; expressions to show surprise **Grammar:** present tense of *-er* and *-ir* verbs; *me gusta(n), me encanta(n)*	**3B Para mantener la salud** **Vocabulary:** food; beverages; expressions to discuss health; expressions to discuss preferences, agreement, disagreement, and quantity; adjectives to describe food **Grammar:** the plural of adjectives; the verb *ser*
4: Los pasatiempos	**4A ¿Adónde vas?** **Vocabulary:** leisure activities; places; expressions to tell where and with whom you go; expressions to talk about when things are done **Grammar:** the verb *ir;* interrogative words	**4B ¿Quieres ir conmigo?** **Vocabulary:** leisure activities; feelings; expressions for extending, accepting, and declining invitations; expressions to tell when something happens **Grammar:** *ir* + *a* + infinitive; the verb *jugar*

Realidades B provides a review section called *Para empezar* and continues with *Temas* 5–9.

Tema	Capítulo A	Capítulo B
5: Fiesta en familia	**5A Una fiesta de cumpleaños** **Vocabulary:** family and parties **Grammar:** the verb *tener;* possessive adjectives	**5B ¡Vamos a un restaurante!** **Vocabulary:** describing people and ordering a meal **Grammar:** the verb *venir;* the verbs *ser* and *estar*
6: La casa	**6A En mi dormitorio** **Vocabulary:** bedroom items; electronic equipment; colors; adjectives to describe things **Grammar:** comparisons and superlatives; stem-changing verbs: *poder* and *dormir*	**6B ¿Cómo es tu casa?** **Vocabulary:** rooms in a house and household chores **Grammar:** affirmative *tú* commands; the present progressive tense
7: De compras	**7A ¿Cuánto cuesta?** **Vocabulary:** clothing; shopping; numbers 200–1,000 **Grammar:** stem-changing verbs: *pensar, querer,* and *preferir;* demonstrative adjectives	**7B ¡Qué regalo!** **Vocabulary:** places to shop; gifts; accessories; buying and selling **Grammar:** preterite of *-ar, -car,* and *-gar* verbs; direct object pronouns *lo, la, los, las*
8: Experiencias	**8A De vacaciones** **Vocabulary:** vacation places; activities; modes of transportation **Grammar:** preterite of *-er* and *-ir* verbs; preterite of *ir;* the personal *a*	**8B Ayudando en la comunidad** **Vocabulary:** recycling and volunteer work; places in a community **Grammar:** the verb *decir;* indirect object pronouns; preterite of *hacer* and *dar*
9: Medios de comunicación	**9A El cine y la televisión** **Vocabulary:** television shows; movie genres; giving opinions **Grammar:** *acabar de* + infinitive; *gustar* and similar verbs	**9B La tecnología** **Vocabulary:** computers; communication; computer-related activities **Grammar:** the verbs *pedir* and *servir; saber* and *conocer*

Scope and Sequence

Realidades 2 uses a recursive Scope and Sequence that revisits the themes from *Realidades A, B,* or *1.* This natural recycling allows for important review and reteaching. In addition, students expand their vocabulary, grammar, and cultural understanding as they revisit each theme in greater depth.

Realidades 2

Tema	Capítulo A	Capítulo B
Para empezar	**A.** ¿Cómo eres tú? *Repaso:* describing people; asking for information; nationalities; adjective agreement; the verb *ser* **B.** ¿Qué haces? *Repaso:* leisure activities; seasons of the year; regular *-ar, -er,* and *-ir* verbs	
1: Tu día escolar	**1A ¿Qué haces en la escuela?** Vocabulary: classroom items, activities, and rules Grammar: *(Repaso)* stem-changing verbs; affirmative and negative words	**1B ¿Qué haces después de las clases?** Vocabulary: extracurricular activities Grammar: making comparisons; *(Repaso)* the verbs *saber* and *conocer; hace* + time expressions
2: Un evento especial	**2A ¿Cómo te preparas?** Vocabulary: daily routines, getting ready for an event Grammar: reflexive verbs; *(Repaso)* the verbs *ser* and *estar;* possessive adjectives *mío, tuyo, suyo*	**2B ¿Qué ropa compraste?** Vocabulary: shopping vocabulary, prices, money Grammar: *(Repaso)* the preterite of regular verbs; demonstrative adjectives
3: Tú y tu comunidad	**3A ¿Qué hiciste ayer?** Vocabulary: running errands; locations in a downtown; items purchased Grammar: *(Repaso)* direct object pronouns; the irregular preterite of the verbs *ir, ser, hacer, tener, estar, poder*	**3B ¿Cómo se va . . . ?** Vocabulary: places in a city or town; driving terms; modes of transportation Grammar: *(Repaso)* direct object pronouns: *me, te, nos;* irregular affirmative *tú* commands; *(Repaso)* present progressive: irregular forms
4: Recuerdos del pasado	**4A Cuando éramos niños** Vocabulary: toys; play terms; describing children Grammar: the imperfect tense: regular verbs and irregular verbs; *(Repaso)* indirect object pronouns	**4B Celebrando los días festivos** Vocabulary: expressions describing etiquette; holiday and family celebrations Grammar: the imperfect tense: describing a situation; reciprocal actions
5: En las noticias	**5A Un acto heroico** Vocabulary: natural disasters; emergencies; rescues; heroes Grammar: the imperfect tense: other uses; the preterite of the verbs *oír, leer, creer,* and *destruir*	**5B Un accidente** Vocabulary: parts of the body; accidents; events in the emergency room Grammar: the irregular preterites: *venir, poner; decir, traer;* the imperfect progressive and preterite
6: La televisión y el cine	**6A ¿Viste el partido en la televisión?** Vocabulary: watching television programs; sporting events Grammar: the preterite of *-ir* stem-changing verbs; other reflexive verbs	**6B ¿Qué película has visto?** Vocabulary: movies; making a movie Grammar: verbs that use indirect objects; the present perfect
7: Buen provecho	**7A ¿Cómo se hace la paella?** Vocabulary: cooking expressions; food; appliances; following a recipe; giving directions in a kitchen Grammar: negative *tú* commands; the impersonal *se*	**7B ¿Te gusta comer al aire libre?** Vocabulary: camping and cookouts; food Grammar: *Usted* and *ustedes* commands; uses of *por*
8: Cómo ser un buen turista	**8A Un viaje en avión** Vocabulary: visiting an airport; planning a trip; traveling safely Grammar: the present subjunctive; irregular verbs in the subjunctive	**8B Quiero que disfrutes de tu viaje** Vocabulary: staying in a hotel; appropriate tourist behaviors; traveling in a foreign city Grammar: the present subjunctive with impersonal expressions; the present subjunctive of stem-changing verbs
9: ¿Cómo será el futuro?	**9A ¿Qué profesión tendrás?** Vocabulary: professions; making plans for the future; earning a living Grammar: the future tense; the future tense of irregular verbs	**9B ¿Qué haremos para mejorar el mundo?** Vocabulary: environment; environmental issues and solutions Grammar: the future tense: other irregular verbs; the present subjunctive with expressions of doubt

Scope and Sequence

Realidades 3 offers ten thought-provoking thematic chapters that integrate rich vocabulary groups and a thorough presentation of grammar. Chapter activities combine communication, culture, and cross-curricular content with authentic literature and poetry.

Realidades 3

Capítulo	Each thematic chapter is divided into two sections. Each of these sections (1 and 2) present and practice vocabulary and grammar.	
Para empezar	1. Tu vida diaria *Repaso:* daily routines; school life; leisure activities; present tense verbs; reflective verbs 2. Días especiales *Repaso:* weekend activities; celebrations; special events; verbs like *gustar:* possessive adjectives	
	1	**2**
1: Un día inolvidable	Vocabulary: hiking objects, activities, and perils; weather Grammar: *(Repaso)* preterite verbs with the spelling change *i–y; (Repaso)* preterite of irregular verbs; *(Repaso)* preterite of verbs with the spelling change *e–i* and *o–u*	Vocabulary: getting ready for an athletic or academic competition; emotional responses to competition; awards and ceremonies Grammar: *(Repaso)* the imperfect; uses of the imperfect
2: ¿Cómo te expresas?	Vocabulary: describing art and sculpture; tools for painting; describing what influences art Grammar: (*Repaso*) the preterite vs. the imperfect; *estar* + participle	Vocabulary: musical instruments; describing dance; describing drama Grammar: *(Repaso) ser* and *estar;* verbs with special meanings in the preterite vs. the imperfect
3: ¿Qué haces para estar en forma?	Vocabulary: nutrition; illnesses and pains; medicine; habits for good health Grammar: *(Repaso)* affirmative *tú* commands; *(Repaso)* affirmative and negative commands with *Ud.* and *Uds.*	Vocabulary: exercises; getting and staying in shape; health advice Grammar: *(Repaso)* the subjunctive: regular verbs; *(Repaso)* the subjunctive: irregular verbs; *(Repaso)* the subjunctive with stem changing *-ar* and *-er* verbs
4: ¿Cómo te llevas con los demás?	Vocabulary: personality traits; interpersonal behavior; friendship Grammar: *(Repaso)* the subjunctive with verbs of emotion; *(Repaso)* the uses of *por* and *para*	Vocabulary: expressing and resolving interpersonal problems; interpersonal relationships Grammar: commands with *nosotros;* possessive pronouns
5: Trabajo y comunidad	Vocabulary: after-school work; describing a job Grammar: *(Repaso)* the present perfect; *(Repaso)* the past perfect	Vocabulary: volunteer activities; the benefits and importance of volunteer work Grammar: the present perfect subjunctive; demonstrative adjectives and pronouns
6: ¿Qué nos traerá en el futuro?	Vocabulary: jobs and professions; qualities of a good employee Grammar: *(Repaso)* the future; *(Repaso)* the future of probability	Vocabulary: technology; inventions; jobs in the future Grammar: the future perfect; *(Repaso)* the use of direct and indirect object pronouns
7: ¿Mito o realidad?	Vocabulary: archaeological terms and activities; describing archaeological sites Grammar: the present and past subjunctive in expressions of doubt	Vocabulary: myths and legends; ancient beliefs; pre-Columbian scientific discoveries Grammar: the subjunctive in adverbial clauses
8: Encuentro entre culturas	Vocabulary: architecture and history of Spain Grammar: the conditional	Vocabulary: Spain in the Americas; the encounter between Cortés and the Aztecs; family heritage Grammar: the past subjunctive; the past subjunctive with *si* clauses
9: Cuidemos nuestro planeta	Vocabulary: caring for the environment Grammar: present subjunctive with conjunctions (*mientras, tan pronto como,* etc.); relative pronouns *que, quien, lo que*	Vocabulary: environmental issues; endangered animals Grammar: present subjunctive with other conjunctions (*a menos que, sin que, para que,* etc.)
10: ¿Cuáles son tus derechos y responsabilidades?	Vocabulary: rights and responsibilties Grammar: the passive voice: *ser* + past participle; the present vs. the past subjunctive	Vocabulary: government; the role of government; individual rights Grammar: the past perfect subjunctive; the conditional perfect

Scope and Sequence

Realidades 4 offers twelve thought-provoking thematic chapters that integrate a unique and thorough scope and sequence, careful progression of activities, and a wealth of authentic literature, songs, and paintings by renowned artists from the Spanish-speaking world.

Realidades 4

Capítulo	Each thematic chapter is divided into two sections. Each of these parts (1 and 2) present and practice vocabulary and grammar.	
	Primera parte	**Segunda parte**
1: Esas modas que van y vienen	Vocabulary: fashion trends and fads Grammar: the preterit tense; the imperfect tense	Vocabulary: the influence of fashion on cars Grammar: preterit vs. imperfect
2: La tecnología y el progreso	Vocabulary: environmental issues affecting your world Grammar: uses of *ser, estar*, and *haber;* the future tense	Vocabulary: professions and activities in the future Grammar: the subjunctive in noun clauses
3: Los derechos humanos	Vocabulary: human rights and foreign policy Grammar: indirect commands	Vocabulary: the work of charitable organizations Grammar: direct and indirect object pronouns and the personal *a*; *gustar* and similar verbs
4: El individuo y la personalidad	Vocabulary: personality and routines Grammar: reflexive constructions	Vocabulary: discussing personality Grammar: agreement, form, and position of adjectives; the past participle and the present perfect indicative and subjunctive
5: Las relaciones personales	Vocabulary: styles of communication and relationships with friends and family Grammar: subjunctive vs. indicative in adjective clauses	Vocabulary: feelings and qualities Grammar: the future perfect and the pluperfect tenses; comparisons with nouns, adjectives, verbs, and adverbs; superlatives
6: El mundo del espectáculo	Vocabulary: entertainers and shows Grammar: subjunctive vs. indicative in adverbial clauses	Vocabulary: music, musicians, and musical events Grammar: formal and informal commands; subjunctive with *ojalá, tal vez*, and *quizá(s)*
7: La diversidad humana	Vocabulary: equality of opportunity Grammar: review of the preterit and imperfect; *hacer* and *desde* in time expressions	Vocabulary: ethnic and gender diversity Grammar: *por* and *para;* verbs that require a preposition before an infinitive
8: Las artes culinarias y la nutrición	Vocabulary: foods and their preparation Grammar: the imperfect subjunctive	Vocabulary: foods and nutrition Grammar: the conditional and conditional perfect; the indicative or subjunctive in *si*-clauses
9: Nuestra compleja sociedad	Vocabulary: crime and personal safety Grammar: the pluperfect subjunctive	Vocabulary: social problems and personal excesses Grammar: uses of *se* with impersonal and passive constructions; indefinite and negative expressions
10: El empleo y la economía	Vocabulary: career choices and the interview process Grammar: indirect speech	Vocabulary: talking about finances Grammar: the relative pronouns *que, quien*, and *lo que* and the relative adjective *cuyo/a(s)*; the relative pronouns *el / la cual* and *los / las cuales*
11: El tiempo libre	Vocabulary: outdoor activities and sports Grammar: sequence of tenses with the subjunctive	Vocabulary: what you do in your free time Grammar: uses of definite and indefinite articles; uses of the infinitive and the -ing (*-ndo*) form of the verb
12: Temas que no pasan de moda	Vocabulary: 21st Century advances and challenges Grammar: *se* for unplanned events	Vocabulary: how life will be in the future Grammar: the passive voice; diminutives and augmentatives

Integrating 21st Century Skills in the Spanish Classroom

Spanish teachers recognize the need for students to interact effectively with the many Spanish speakers in the United States and across the globe. Today's world languages curriculum and instruction are based upon the 5Cs (Communication, Cultures, Connections, Comparisons, and Communities) with the goal of building communicative proficiency and cultural understanding. World languages learners are 21st Century Learners.

However, as today's students enter into an increasingly global economy, it is important that they have a diverse range of skills to succeed. The Partnership for 21st Century Skills, a national organization that advocates for 21st century readiness for every student, has developed a Framework for 21st Century Learning. This document fuses the traditinoal 3Rs with what they call the 4Cs:

- Critical thinking and problem solving
- Communication
- Collaboration
- Creativity and innovation

World Languages 21st Century Skills Map

The American Council on the Teaching of Foreign Languages (ACTFL) has worked with the Partnership for 21st Century Skills to create a 21st Century Skills Map that describes the integration of World Languages and 21st Century Skills. This map provides concrete examples of how 21st Century Skills can be integrated into all world language classrooms.

By combining the 5Cs of the National Standards for Foreign Language Learning with the 4Cs from the Partnership for 21st Century Skills, world languages teachers now have a unique opportunity. As schools, districts, and states expand assessment and instruction to focus on 21st Century Skills, we can further prepare students for their future. The 4Cs can be seamlessly integrated on a daily basis within the world languages classroom.

Realidades and the 21st Century World Languages Classroom

Teachers using *Realidades* will easily be able to integrate 21st Century Skills into daily instruction due to the series' pedagogical framework, the alignment of assessment and instruction, and the integration of print and digital resources. In *Realidades*:

- Each chapter is built around thematic instruction based upon real-world tasks and authentic sources.
- Instruction is learner-centered; students take responsibility for the learning and creation of new content.
- Technology is integrated with instruction and assessment to support and enhance learning.
- Instruction and assessment are differentiated to meet the needs of individual learners.
- Assessment is focused on what students can do with the language; students know what they will be asked to do and how they will be assessed.
- Instruction and assessment of culture focuses on the relationship between the products, practices, and perspectives of the target culture as well as comparisons between cultures.
- Students explore opportunities to use the language outside of the classroom.

Realidades and the 4 Cs

Realidades provides a wide range of resources, activities, and assessments that support the 4Cs. At the beginning of each *Tema* in the Teacher's Edition for Levels 1–3, the "b" page contains a chart with recommended activities and assessments in each chapter that build the skills outlined on the 21st Century Skills Map for World Languages.

For further information about the Partnership for 21st Century Skills, please visit their Web site: www.p21.org.

Program Components

Realidades offers a wide range of program components to support the diverse students in today's Spanish classroom! To provide more teaching and learning options, program components are available in three convenient formats: print, DVD, or online at **realidades.com**.

For the Student

Student Edition ONLINE, DVD, PRINT

- eText on DVD-ROM and online contains embedded audio and video files plus flashcards.

Workbooks ONLINE, DVD, PRINT

Leveled Vocabulary and Grammar Workbook

PART 1: GUIDED WORKBOOK

- Vocabulary clip art and study sheets
- Step-by-step grammar activities
- Simplified reading, speaking, and writing activities

PART 2: CORE WORKBOOK

- Focused practice for vocabulary and grammar
- End-of-chapter Crossword Puzzle and Organizer

Communication Workbook with Test Preparation

PART 1: WRITING, AUDIO, AND VIDEO ACTIVITIES

- Additional writing practice
- Student response pages for the Audio Program and *A primera vista: Vocabulario en contexto* video segments

PART 2: TEST PREPARATION

- Thematic readings that prepare students for standardized assessments
- Reading Skills Study Sheets
- Integrated Performance Assessments (IPA)

Realidades para hispanohablantes Workbook

- All-Spanish companion worktext to Student Edition
- Grammar explanations in Spanish
- More practice for language mechanics, usage, vocabulary, grammar, reading, and writing

¿Eres tú, María? Video Workbook **PRINT**

- A variety of activities for language and culture

Readers PRINT

Lecturas

- Sixteen readings per level

Grammar Study Guide PRINT

- Laminated cards summarize grammar for Levels 1–2

realidades.com

Students have complete access to all these digital assets on their account:

Student Edition

- eText with embedded audio and video files plus flashcards

DK Bilingual Visual Dictionary

- eText with over 6,000 vocabulary items organized by topics

DK Reference Atlas

- Complete overview of Spanish-speaking world

Mapa global interactivo

- Links to locations and activities from across the Spanish-speaking world using KMZ files

Videos

Videocultura: Theme-based culture videos

Videohistoria: Video segments that present new vocabulary

GramActiva: Videos that teach grammar using context, humor, and graphics

Tutorials: Grammar videos with comparisons to English

***Videomodelos*:** Videos that model interpersonal speaking tasks

¿Eres tú, María?: 10-episode mystery video (starts in *Capítulo* 5A)

Audio

- All audio for Student Edition and workbooks
- *Canciones de hip hop* (downloadable)

Animations

- Animated Grammar

Assignable content

- Auto-graded activities from eText, Instant Check, and workbooks
- Interactive auto-graded games for fun, end-of-chapter review
- Teacher-graded RealTalk! speaking activities
- Teacher-graded speaking, writing, and culture activities from eText and workbooks

Assignable assessments

- Quizzes
- Quizzes with Study Plans
- Chapter Tests
- Cumulative Tests
- Integrated Performance Assessments

PLANNING AND INSTRUCTION

Interactive Teacher's Edition with Resource Library DVD-ROM DVD

- Interactive Teacher's Editions (TE)
- Point-of-use links in TE to PDF file of resources
- PDF files of resources

Activities and Tools for Interactive Whiteboards ONLINE DVD

- Interactive practice activities for vocabulary and grammar
- Teaching suggestions, extensions, and answers
- Downloadable SMART Notebook Files
- Use with or without a SMART Interactive Whiteboard
- Over 6,000 images from DK Bilingual Visual Dictionary in Image Gallery
- DVD includes DK dictionary eText

PresentationExpress™ Premium DVD-ROM DVD

Presentation tool that includes:

- Vocabulary images and clip art
- Student Edition audio files
- DK Bilingual Visual Dictionary eText
- *GramActiva* videos
- Animated Verbs
- Transparencies

Transparencies (on PresentationExpress™ Premium DVD-ROM) ONLINE DVD

- *Vocabulario en contexto*
- Answer Keys to Student Edition
- Maps, Graphs, Realia, and Rapid Review
- Fine Art Transparencies
- *Videohistoria*
- Answer Keys to Workbooks

Video Programs ONLINE DVD

Video Program

- ***Videohistoria:*** Vocabulary presentation videos
- ***GramActiva:*** Engaging grammar explanations
- ***¿Eres tú, María?:*** Mystery video (starting in *Capítulo* 5A)

Videomodelos Video Program

- Videos model speaking tasks

Videocultura Video Program

- Theme-based culture videos

Audio Program ONLINE DVD

All audio is available on a single DVD organized by chapter using mp3 files or on **realidades.com**:

- *Vocabulario en contexto*
- Communication Workbook Audio activities
- Student Edition *Escuchar* activities
- *Videohistoria*
- *Pronunciación*
- Listening section of *Examen del capítulo*

Teacher's Resource Book ONLINE PRINT DVD

Includes by chapter:

- Components Overview
- Theme Project
- School-to-Home Letter
- Input Script
- Audio and Video Script
- *Lecturas* Teacher's Guide
- Communicative Pair Activities
- Situation Cards
- *GramActiva* Blackline Masters
- Vocabulary Clip Art
- Answer Keys for Workbooks
- 21st Century Skills Rubrics

Pre-AP* Resource Book ONLINE PRINT DVD

- Strategies for building Pre-AP® skills at all levels
- Activities to practice for AP® Spanish Language and Culture Examination

TPR Stories ONLINE PRINT DVD

- Complete support for integrating TPR Storytelling into instruction

ASSESSMENT AND REMEDIATION

Assessment Program ONLINE PRINT DVD

- Use for core assessment

realidades.com

- *Pruebas* for Vocabulary Recognition: auto-graded
- *Pruebas* with Study Plans for Vocabulary Production and Grammar: auto-graded with built-in remediation and retesting
- *Examen del capítulo*: auto- and teacher-graded
- RealTalk! Speaking Tasks: *Presentación oral, Examen del capítulo*, Integrated Performance Assessments

Alternate Assessment Program ONLINE PRINT DVD

- For students needing adapted assessment or retesting

Assessment Program: *Realidades para hispanohablantes* ONLINE PRINT DVD

- For heritage learners

Communication Workbook with Test Preparation ONLINE PRINT DVD

- Integrated Performance Assessments

ExamView® Assessment Suite CD-ROM

- Four editable test banks per chapter: two for core assessment, one for heritage learners, one for Pre-AP® learners
- Test banks available in **realidades.com** Question Library

Getting Started

Students get started in *Realidades 1* with these colorful reference and introductory sections:

- Mapas
- Why Study Spanish?
- Getting Started on realidades.com
- Para empezar

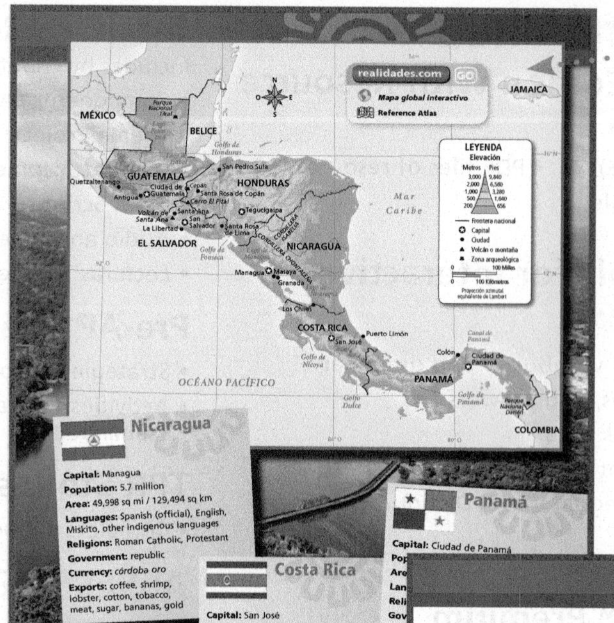

Mapas

Colorful atlas pages support geography skills.

Students can explore more online:

- *Mapa global interactivo*
- Reference Atlas

Getting Started with REALIDADES

Why Study Spanish?

Congratulations on your decision to study Spanish! Did you know that more than 425 million people in Spain, 18 Latin American countries, Puerto Rico, Equatorial Guinea, the Philippines, and the United States speak Spanish? It is the second most common language in the United States and the third most commonly spoken language in the world.

Learn to communicate When you study Spanish, you will be able to communicate with the many people in your community and across the globe who speak Spanish. You can bargain in a market, read information on the Internet, and watch television shows.

Understand culture The Spanish speaking world is rich in music, food, art, literature, and everyday traditions. Learning about culture helps you understand other people's perspectives, patterns of behavior, and contributions to the world at large.

Expand career opportunities In today's increasingly global community, your employment and career options expand greatly when you have the right job skills and proficiency in Spanish.

Improve language skills Studying Spanish improves your first language skills: vocabulary, grammar, reading, and writing. Research shows your test scores may even improve!

v

Why Study Spanish?

Students focus on real-life purposes for learning Spanish.

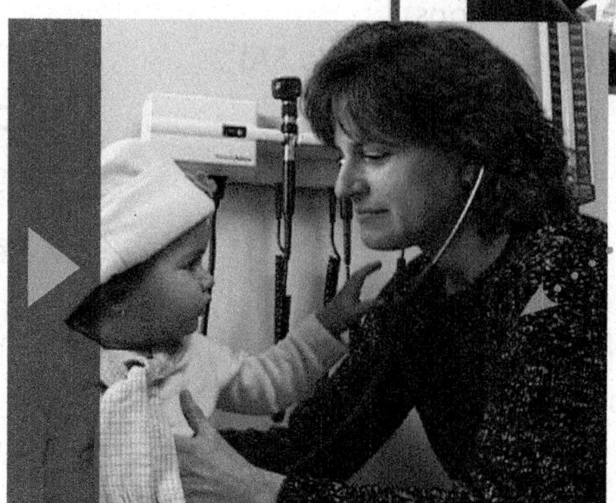

Why Study Spanish? Video

Why Study Spanish? Video

This motivating video introduces students to the Spanish-speaking world and to several people who talk about how speaking Spanish has helped them personally and professionally.

Online Resources with realidades.com

REALIDADES includes lots of online resources to help you learn Spanish! You can easily link to all of them when you log on to your Home Page within realidades.com. Your teacher will assign some activities, such as the ones in the workbooks. Others you can access on your own.

You'll find these resources highlighted on the pages of your print or online Student Edition with technology icons. Here's a list of the different icons used.

Bilingual Visual Dictionary Links to additional vocabulary words presented visually

Reference Atlas Quick links to the countries in the online atlas

Mapa global interactivo Links to GIS showing locations across the Spanish-speaking world

Videos

Videocultura Cultural overview of each theme

Videohistoria Vocabulary video to help present the new vocabulary

GramActiva Grammar explanations to help present the new grammar

Grammar Tutorials Clear explanations of grammar with comparison to English

Animated Verbs Animations that highlight verb conjugations

¿Eres tú, María? A 10-episode mystery video starting in *Capítulo 5A*

Modelo ***Videomodelos*** Video models of speaking activities

Audio Audio files for vocabulary, listening practice, and pronunciation

Canciones de hip hop Songs to help practice new vocabulary and grammar

Flashcards Practice for the new vocabulary

RealTalk! Speak-and-record tool for speaking activities

***GramActiva* Acti** practice for the *Gr*

Más práctica GO **Onl**

Instant Check Short activi your progress right away

Guided Workbook Step-b and grammar practice

Core Workbook Vocabula exercises

Communication Workboo video, and writing activi

Cultural Reading Activity *Lectura* reading

Actividades Questions for

Puzzles End-of-chapter ga

vi

Getting Started on realidades.com

Students get a complete overview of online resources available on **realidades.com.**

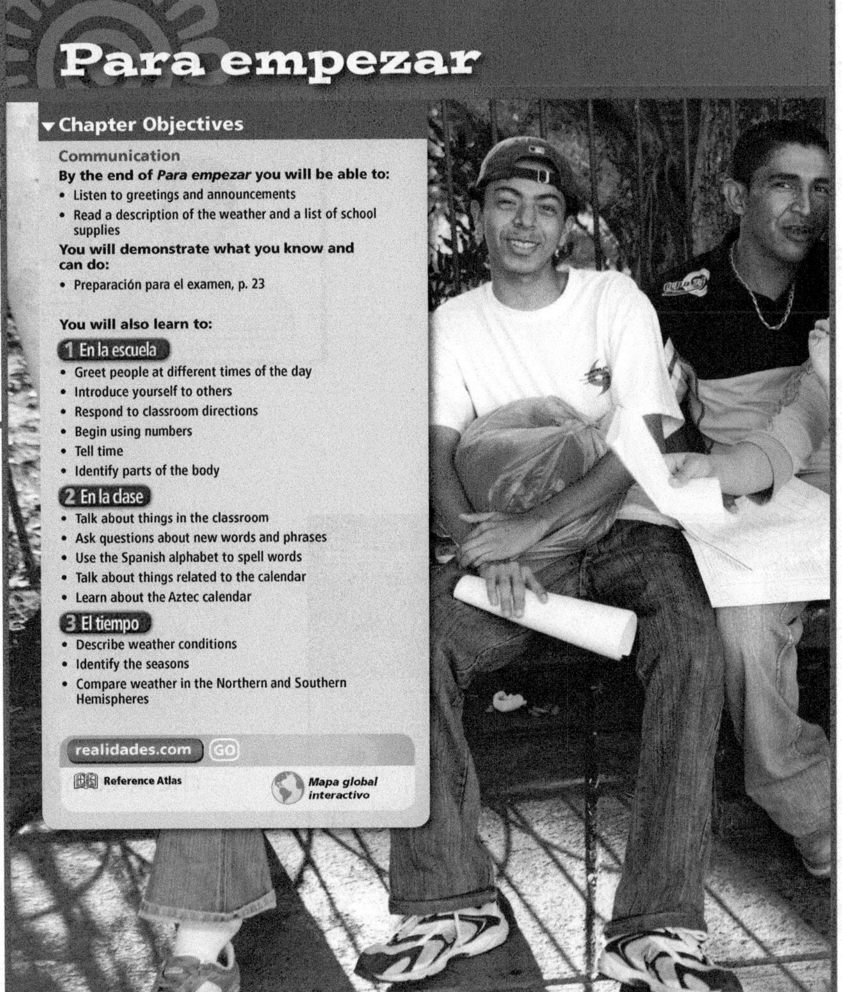

Para empezar

Chapter Objectives

Communication

By the end of *Para empezar* you will be able to:

- Listen to greetings and announcements
- Read a description of the weather and a list of school supplies

You will demonstrate what you know and can do:

- Preparación para el examen, p. 23

You will also learn to:

1 En la escuela

- Greet people at different times of the day
- Introduce yourself to others
- Respond to classroom directions
- Begin using numbers
- Tell time
- Identify parts of the body

2 En la clase

- Talk about things in the classroom
- Ask questions about new words and phrases
- Use the Spanish alphabet to spell words
- Talk about things related to the calendar
- Learn about the Aztec calendar

3 El tiempo

- Describe weather conditions
- Identify the seasons
- Compare weather in the Northern and Southern Hemispheres

realidades.com GO

Reference Atlas — *Mapa global interactivo*

Para empezar

This introductory section gets students started in Spanish. Topics include greetings, classroom items and commands, the calendar and dates, and weather expressions.

Chapter Organization

realidades.com

All content and activities available online.

Chapter Sequence

- Vocabulario en contexto
- Vocabulario en uso
- Gramática y vocabulario en uso
- ¡Adelante!
- Repaso del capítulo

A primera vista

Vocabulario en contexto

This four-page section gives students a "first look" at the new vocabulary and grammar through comprehensible input that integrates visuals and text with audio and video.

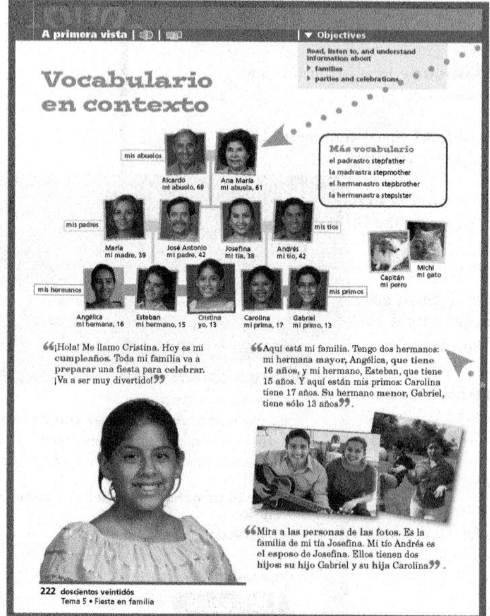

Visualized Vocabulary

New words are presented visually and in context.

Language Input

Input continues with visuals accompanied by narrative. All new vocabulary words and grammar are highlighted in blue.

Chapter opener *Capítulo 5A*

Listening Comprehension

Short listening activities check comprehension.

More Practice

Extra practice is available in the workbooks and online.

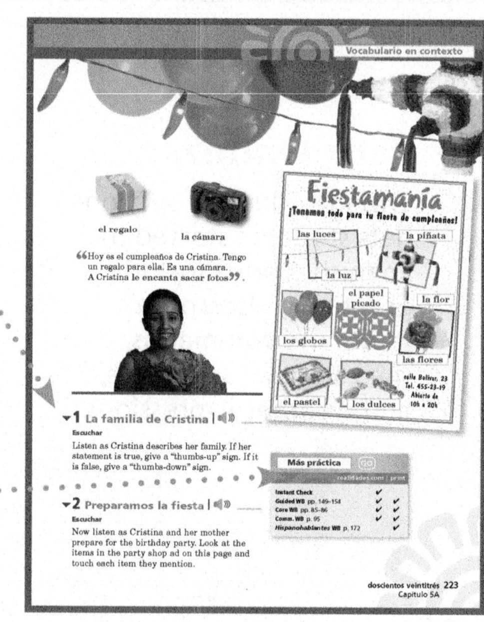

Reading and Language Input

The input of new vocabulary and grammar continues through a short, engaging reading written as a *videohistoria*. This story is based upon the accompanying *A primera vista* video segment.

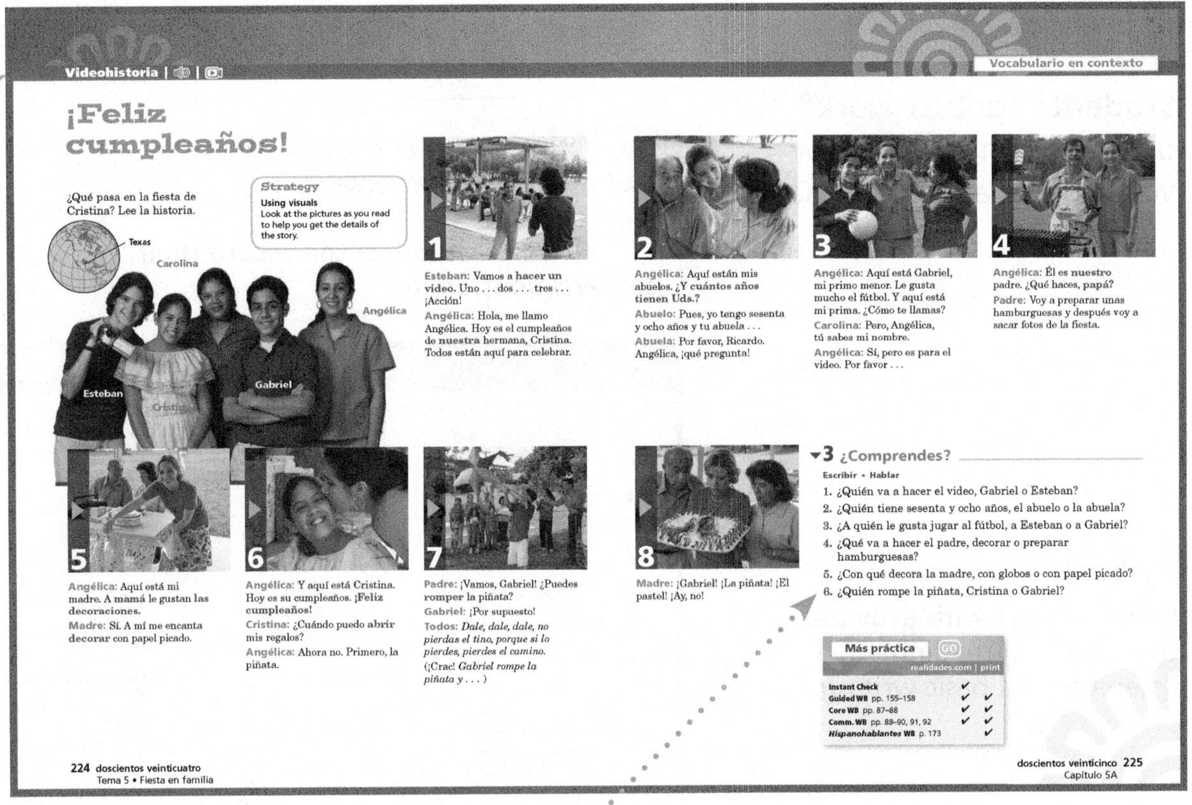

Videohistoria | 🔊 | 🎬

Vocabulario en contexto

¡Feliz cumpleaños!

¿Qué pasa en la fiesta de Cristina? Lee la historia.

Strategy

Using visuals
Look at the pictures as you read to help you get the details of the story.

1 **Esteban:** Vamos a hacer un video. Uno . . . dos . . . tres . . . ¡Acción!
Angélica: Hola, me llamo Angélica. Hoy es el cumpleaños de **nuestra** hermana, Cristina. Todos están aquí para **celebrar**.

2 **Angélica:** Aquí están mis **abuelos**. ¿Y **cuántos años tienen** Uds.?
Abuelo: Pues, yo tengo sesenta y ocho años y tu abuela . . .
Abuela: Por favor, Ricardo. Angélica, ¡qué pregunta!

3 **Angélica:** Aquí está Gabriel, mi **primo menor**. Le gusta mucho el fútbol. Y aquí está mi **prima**. ¿Cómo te llamas?
Carolina: Pero, Angélica, tú sabes mi nombre.
Angélica: Sí, pero es para el video. Por favor . . .

4 **Angélica:** Él es **nuestro padre**. ¿Qué haces, **papá**?
Padre: Voy a preparar unas hamburguesas y después voy a **sacar fotos** de la fiesta.

5 **Angélica:** Aquí está mi madre. A **mamá** le gustan las **decoraciones**.
Madre: Sí. A mí me encanta **decorar** con papel picado.

6 **Angélica:** Y aquí está Cristina. Hoy es su cumpleaños. **¡Feliz cumpleaños!**
Cristina: ¿Cuándo puedo **abrir** mis **regalos**?
Angélica: Ahora no. Primero, la piñata.

7 **Padre:** ¡Vamos, Gabriel! ¿Puedes **romper la piñata**?
Gabriel: ¡Por supuesto!
Todos: *Dale, dale, dale, no pierdas el tino, porque si lo pierdes, pierdes el camino.*
(¡Crac! *Gabriel rompe la piñata y . . .*)

8 **Madre:** ¡Gabriel! ¡La piñata! ¡El pastel! ¡Ay, no!

3 ¿Comprendes?

Escribir • Hablar

1. ¿Quién va a hacer el video, Gabriel o Esteban?
2. ¿Quién tiene sesenta y ocho años, el abuelo o la abuela?
3. ¿A quién le gusta jugar al fútbol, a Esteban o a Gabriel?
4. ¿Qué va a hacer el padre, decorar o preparar hamburguesas?
5. ¿Con qué decora la madre, con globos o con papel picado?
6. ¿Quién rompe la piñata, Cristina o Gabriel?

Más práctica GO

	realidades.com	print
Instant Check	✔	
Guided WB pp. 155–158	✔	✔
Core WB pp. 87–88	✔	✔
Comm. WB pp. 88–90, 91, 92	✔	✔
***Hispanohablantes* WB** p. 173		✔

224 doscientos veinticuatro
Tema 5 • Fiesta en familia

doscientos veinticinco 225
Capítulo 5A

Reading Comprehension

Questions check students' comprehension of the story while practicing the new vocabulary and grammar.

From the *A primera vista* video segment

🎬 Videos and Language Input

The language, characters, and culture of the *Videohistoria* come to life in the *A primera vista* video segment. Each video segment is approximately 5 minutes in length. The videos were filmed in San Antonio, Mexico City, Costa Rica, and Spain (Madrid and Toledo). To help students with language input, each video is shown twice. The first time, key vocabulary is labeled on the screen. The second time, the words are not shown. Additional video activities can be found in the Writing, Audio & Video section of the Communication Workbook.

Manos a la obra

Vocabulario en uso

Students "get to work" using the chapter's new vocabulary and grammar.

Modelo Students can view videos that model the conversation.

Paired students can record their conversations online!

Paired Practice

Students transition to paired practice activities that focus on the new vocabulary.

Focused Practice

Students start with activities that focus on reading, listening, and basic writing.

Integrated Culture

Cultural notes are embedded throughout the chapter.

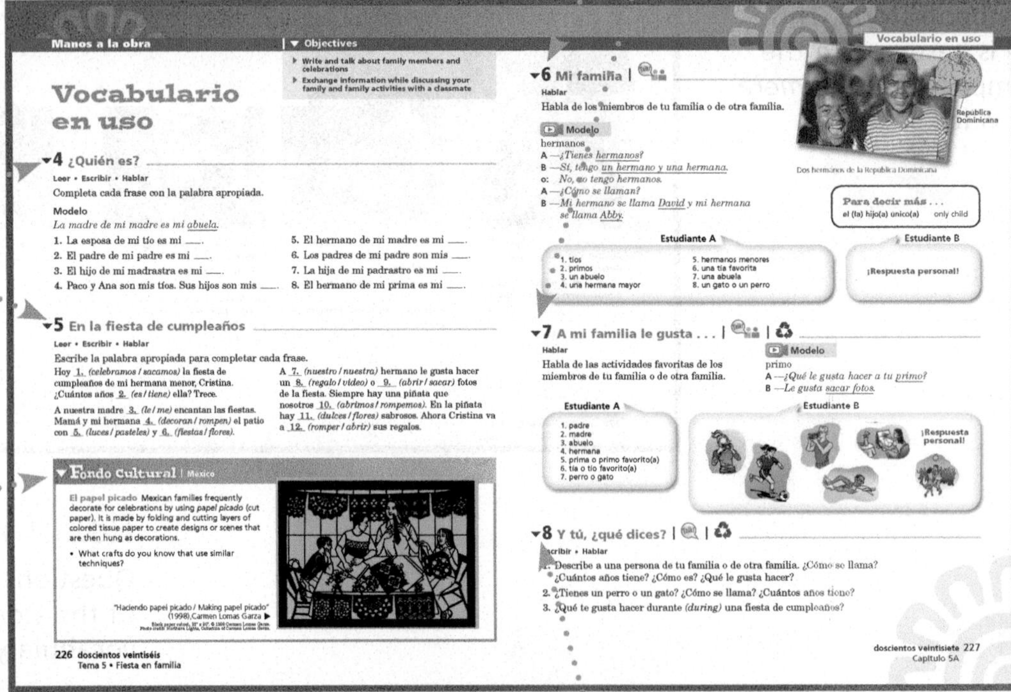

Manos a la obra

Vocabulario en uso

▼ Objectives

- Write and talk about family members and celebrations
- Exchange information while discussing your family and family activities with a classmate

4 ¿Quién es?

Leer • Escribir • Hablar

Completa cada frase con la palabra apropiada.

Modelo

La madre de mi madre es mi abuela.

1. La esposa de mi tío es mi ___.
2. El padre de mi padre es mi ___.
3. El hijo de mi madrastra es mi ___.
4. Paco y Ana son mis tíos. Sus hijos son mis ___.
5. El hermano de mi madre es mi ___.
6. Los padres de mi padre son mis ___.
7. La hija de mi padrastro es mi ___.
8. El hermano de mi prima es mi ___.

5 En la fiesta de cumpleaños

Leer • Escribir • Hablar

Escribe la palabra apropiada para completar cada frase.

Hoy 1. *(celebramos / sacamos)* la fiesta de cumpleaños de mi hermana menor, Cristina. ¿Cuántos años 2. *(es / tiene)* ella? Trece.

A nuestra madre 3. *(le / me)* encantan las fiestas. Mamá y mi hermana 4. *(decoran / rompen)* el patio con 5. *(luces / pasteles)* y 6. *(fiestas / flores)*.

A 7. *(nuestro / nuestra)* hermano le gusta hacer un 8. *(regalo / video)* o 9. *(abrir / sacar)* fotos de la fiesta. Siempre hay una piñata que nosotros 10. *(abrimos / rompemos)*. En la piñata hay 11. *(dulces / flores)* sabrosos. Ahora Cristina va a 12. *(romper / abrir)* sus regalos.

Fondo Cultural | México

El papel picado Mexican families frequently decorate for celebrations by using *papel picado* (cut paper). It is made by folding and cutting layers of colored tissue paper to create designs or scenes that are then hung as decorations.

- What crafts do you know that use similar techniques?

"Haciendo papel picado / Making papel picado" (1998), Carmen Lomas Garza ▶

226 doscientos veintiséis
Tema 5 • Fiesta en familia

Vocabulario en uso

6 Mi familia

Hablar

Habla de los miembros de tu familia o de otra familia.

Modelo

hermanos

A —*¿Tienes hermanos?*
B —*Sí, tengo un hermano y una hermana.*
o: *No, no tengo hermanos.*
A —*¿Cómo se llaman?*
B —*Mi hermano se llama David y mi hermana se llama Abby.*

República Dominicana

Dos hermanos de la República Dominicana

Para decir más . . .
el (la) hijo(a) único(a) — only child

Estudiante A

1. tíos
2. primos
3. un abuelo
4. una hermana mayor
5. hermanos menores
6. una tía favorita
7. una abuela
8. un gato o un perro

Estudiante B

¡Respuesta personal!

7 A mi familia le gusta . . .

Hablar

Habla de las actividades favoritas de los miembros de tu familia o de otra familia.

Modelo

primo

A —*¿Qué le gusta hacer a tu primo?*
B —*Le gusta sacar fotos.*

Estudiante A

1. padre
2. madre
3. abuelo
4. hermana
5. prima o primo favorito(a)
6. tía o tío favorito(a)
7. perro o gato

Estudiante B

¡Respuesta personal!

8 Y tú, ¿qué dices?

Escribir • Hablar

1. Describe a una persona de tu familia o de otra familia. ¿Cómo se llama? ¿Cuántos años tiene? ¿Cómo es? ¿Qué le gusta hacer?
2. ¿Tienes un perro o un gato? ¿Cómo se llama? ¿Cuántos años tiene?
3. ¿Qué te gusta hacer durante *(during)* una fiesta de cumpleaños?

doscientos veintisiete 227
Capítulo 5A

Personal Responses

The sequence of exercises culminates with personalized speaking and writing activities.

Grammar Integrated with Communication

The complete grammar presentation features clear explanations and examples.

Manos a la obra

Gramática

▼ Objectives

- Talk about what people have and have to do
- Interview a classmate and write a description of a classmate's family and their ages
- Read about, identify, and describe the ages of members of the Spanish royal family

The verb *tener*

The verb *tener* is used to show relationship or possession.

Tengo un hermano mayor. — *I have an older brother.*
Tenemos un regalo para Tere. — *We have a gift for Tere.*

Some expressions in Spanish use *tener* where English uses "to be."

Mi primo tiene dieciséis años. — *My cousin is sixteen years old.*
Tengo hambre y sed. — *I am hungry and thirsty.*

Here are all the present-tense forms of *tener:*

(yo)	tengo	(nosotros) (nosotras)	tenemos
(tú)	tienes	(vosotros) (vosotras)	tenéis
Ud. (él) (ella)	tiene	Uds. (ellos) (ellas)	tienen

¿Recuerdas?
You have been using the verb *tener* for several chapters.
- ¿Tienes una bicicleta?
- Tengo que hacer ejercicio.

Más ayuda — realidades.com
- *GramActiva* Video Tutorials: *Tener, Tener que* Animated Verbs
- *Canción de hip hop: Fiesta de cumpleaños*
- *GramActiva* Activity

9 Rompecabezas

Leer • Escribir • Pensar

Escribe la forma apropiada del verbo *tener* para cada frase. Luego *(Then)* resuelve el problema.

El total de las edades *(ages)* de los hijos de nuestra familia es cien. Marta 1. 19 años. Paco y yo 2. dos años menos que Marta. Laura y Eva 3. cinco años menos que Paco y yo. ¿Cuántos años 4. nuestro hermano mayor, Enrique?

10 ¿Qué hay para la fiesta?

Hablar

Pregunta a otro(a) estudiante qué tienen estas personas para la fiesta.

Modelo

Ana

A — *¿Qué tiene Ana?*
B — *Ana tiene la piñata.*

1. David
2. Yolanda
3. tu abuela
4. tú
5. Uds.
6. Juan y Marcos

228 doscientos veintiocho
Tema 5 • Fiesta en familia

Review and Recycling

¿Recuerdas? notes help students remember what they've already learned about the grammar point.

Reinforce Grammar through Videos

GramActiva videos help students "see" how grammar works through humor and graphics.

Gramática y vocabulario en uso

Language and Culture

Culture is woven together with language practice.

Connections to Other Disciplines

Cross-curricular connections are integrated into the language practice.

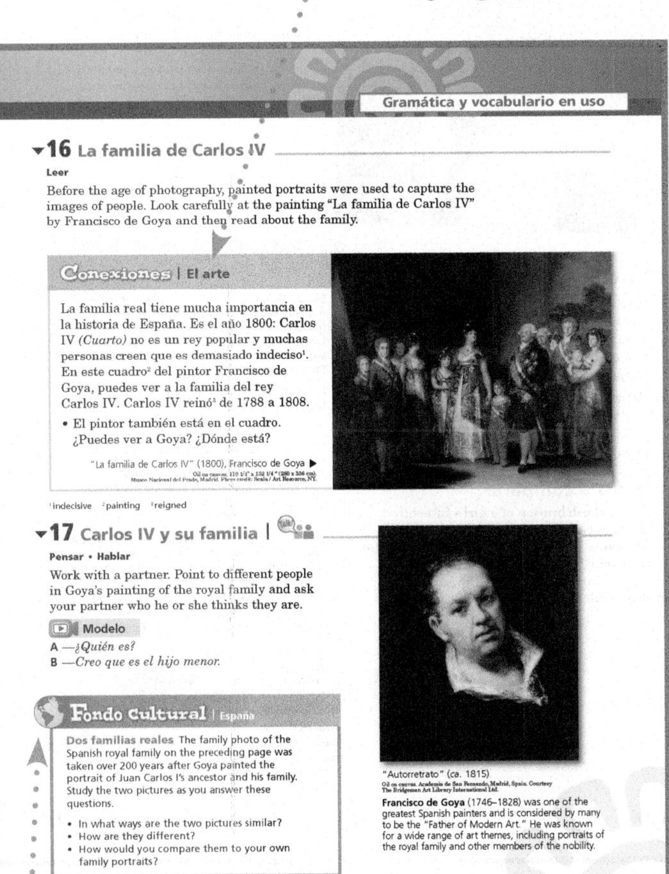

Gramática y vocabulario en uso

16 La familia de Carlos IV

Leer

Before the age of photography, painted portraits were used to capture the images of people. Look carefully at the painting "La familia de Carlos IV" by Francisco de Goya and then read about the family.

Conexiones | El arte

La familia real tiene mucha importancia en la historia de España. Es el año 1800: Carlos IV *(Cuarto)* no es un rey popular y muchas personas creen que es demasiado indeciso[1]. En este cuadro[2] del pintor Francisco de Goya, puedes ver a la familia del rey Carlos IV. Carlos IV reinó[3] de 1788 a 1808.

- El pintor también está en el cuadro. ¿Puedes ver a Goya? ¿Dónde está?

"La familia de Carlos IV" (1800), Francisco de Goya ▶
Oil on canvas, 110 1/4" x 132 1/4" (280 x 336 cm). Museo Nacional del Prado, Madrid. Photo credit: Scala / Art Resource, NY.

[1]indecisive [2]painting [3]reigned

17 Carlos IV y su familia

Pensar • Hablar

Work with a partner. Point to different people in Goya's painting of the royal family and ask your partner who he or she thinks they are.

Modelo

A —*¿Quién es?*
B —*Creo que es el hijo menor.*

"Autorretrato" (ca. 1815)
Oil on canvas. Academia de San Fernando, Madrid, Spain. Courtesy The Bridgeman Art Library International Ltd.

Francisco de Goya (1746–1828) was one of the greatest Spanish painters and is considered by many to be the "Father of Modern Art." He was known for a wide range of art themes, including portraits of the royal family and other members of the nobility.

Fondo Cultural | España

Dos familias reales The family photo of the Spanish royal family on the preceding page was taken over 200 years after Goya painted the portrait of Juan Carlos I's ancestor and his family. Study the two pictures as you answer these questions.

- In what ways are the two pictures similar?
- How are they different?
- How would you compare them to your own family portraits?

doscientos treinta y uno 231
Capítulo 5A

14 La familia de Sofía

Leer • Escribir

Look carefully at the photograph of Sofía's family, the royal family of Spain, as they celebrate her special day. As Sofía describes this family photo, complete the story with the appropriate forms of the verb *tener*.

Me llamo Sofía de Borbón y Ortiz. Mi cumpleaños es el 29 de abril. Nosotros __1.__ muchas fiestas en mi familia. En la foto celebramos un día muy especial para mí. Es el día de mi bautizo. (Yo) __2.__ una hermana mayor que se llama Leonor. Ella __3.__ dos años. También (yo) __4.__ seis primos; dos chicas y cuatro chicos: Victoria Federica que __5.__ siete años y su hermano Felipe. Felipe __6.__ nueve años. Victoria y Felipe son los hijos de mis tíos, la infanta[1] Elena y su esposo, Jaime. Ellos están a la izquierda, en el fondo[2] de la foto. A la derecha, en el fondo, están mis tíos Cristina e Iñaki con su hija Irene que __7.__ sólo cuatro meses más que mi hermana. Yo estoy en los brazos de mi mamá, la princesa Letizia. Mi padre, el príncipe Felipe, está al lado de ella con mi hermana. Mis abuelos, el rey Juan Carlos I y la reina Sofía, __8.__ 69 años. Ellos están a los dos lados de mis padres. Ellos son los reyes[3] de España. ¿ __9.__ tú tíos y primos? Me encanta tener una familia grande.

[1]In the Spanish royal family, *una infanta* is a princess *(una princesa)* who is not heir to the throne.
[2]background
[3]Note that *el rey + la reina = los reyes*

La familia de Juan Carlos I, rey de España

Fondo Cultural | España

La Familia Real *(royal)* **de España** Juan Carlos I and Sofía have been king and queen of Spain since 1975.

- What other countries can you name that have monarchies?

Más práctica GO realidades.com | print

Instant Check	✔	
Guided WB pp. 159–160	✔	✔
Core WB p. 89	✔	✔
Comm. WB pp. 92, 96	✔	✔
***Hispanohablantes* WB** pp. 174–177, 181		✔

15 ¿Quiénes son los miembros de la Familia Real?

Leer • Hablar • Pensar

Work with a partner to identify the members of the royal family. Use the photograph and answers from Actividad 14 to help.

Modelo

A —*Creo que el número uno es el abuelo de Sofía. Se llama Juan Carlos I.*
B —*Estoy de acuerdo.*
o: —*No estoy de acuerdo.*

230 doscientos treinta
Tema 5 • Fiesta en familia

Hands-on Learning

Fun, interactive games help students learn new concepts.

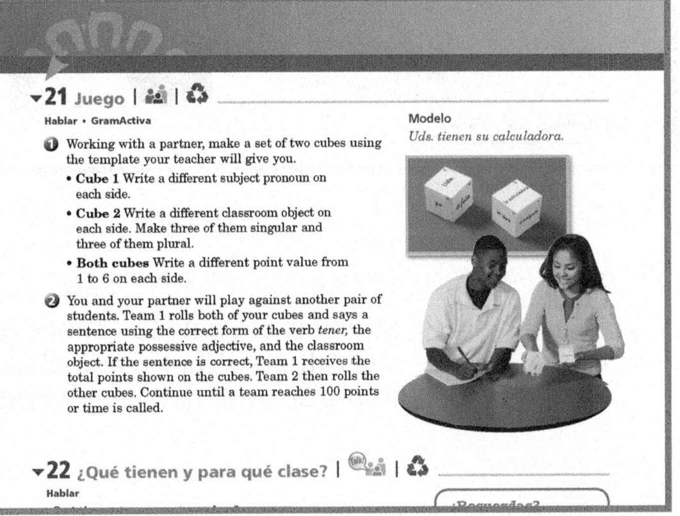

21 Juego

Hablar • GramActiva

1. Working with a partner, make a set of two cubes using the template your teacher will give you.
   - **Cube 1** Write a different subject pronoun on each side.
   - **Cube 2** Write a different classroom object on each side. Make three of them singular and three of them plural.
   - **Both cubes** Write a different point value from 1 to 6 on each side.
2. You and your partner will play against another pair of students. Team 1 rolls both of your cubes and says a sentence using the correct form of the verb *tener,* the appropriate possessive adjective, and the classroom object. If the sentence is correct, Team 1 receives the total points shown on the cubes. Team 2 then rolls the other cubes. Continue until a team reaches 100 points or time is called.

Modelo
Uds. tienen su calculadora.

22 ¿Qué tienen y para qué clase?

Hablar

Interactive Geography

Students expand their geography skills using our online *Mapa global interactivo* activities.

¡Adelante!

Students apply their language skills with culminating activities that include culturally authentic readings, performance-based speaking and writing tasks, a mystery video, and a variety of cultural activities.

Reading Strategies

Reading strategies help students become better readers.

Common Core: Reading

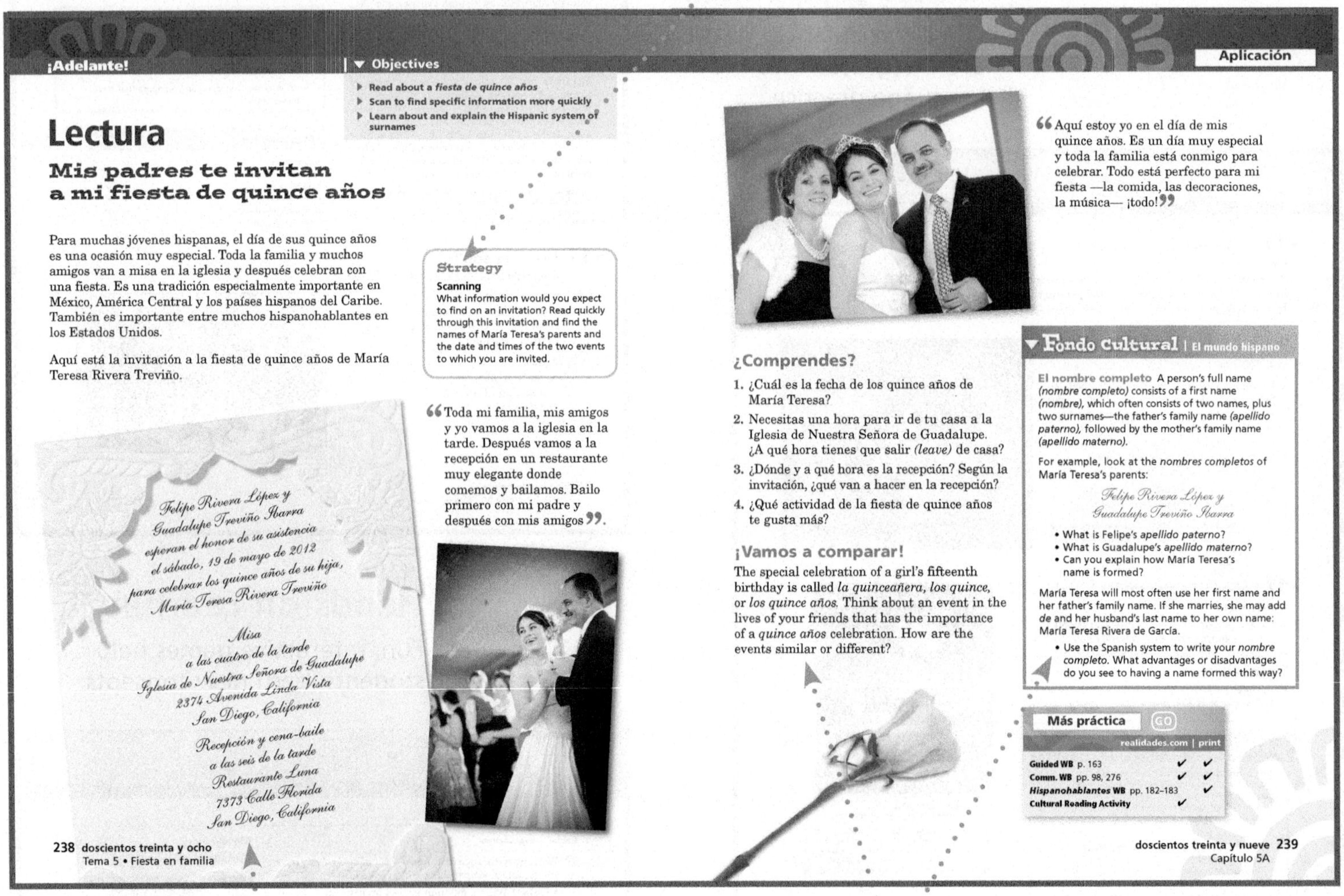

¡Adelante!

▼ Objectives

- Read about a *fiesta de quince años*
- Scan to find specific information more quickly
- Learn about and explain the Hispanic system of surnames

Aplicación

Lectura

Mis padres te invitan a mi fiesta de quince años

Para muchas jóvenes hispanas, el día de sus quince años es una ocasión muy especial. Toda la familia y muchos amigos van a misa en la iglesia y después celebran con una fiesta. Es una tradición especialmente importante en México, América Central y los países hispanos del Caribe. También es importante entre muchos hispanohablantes en los Estados Unidos.

Aquí está la invitación a la fiesta de quince años de María Teresa Rivera Treviño.

Strategy

Scanning
What information would you expect to find on an invitation? Read quickly through this invitation and find the names of María Teresa's parents and the date and times of the two events to which you are invited.

Felipe Rivera López y
Guadalupe Treviño Ibarra
esperan el honor de su asistencia
el sábado, 19 de mayo de 2012
para celebrar los quince años de su hija,
María Teresa Rivera Treviño

Misa
a las cuatro de la tarde
Iglesia de Nuestra Señora de Guadalupe
2374 Avenida Linda Vista
San Diego, California

Recepción y cena-baile
a las seis de la tarde
Restaurante Luna
7373 Calle Florida
San Diego, California

“Toda mi familia, mis amigos y yo vamos a la iglesia en la tarde. Después vamos a la recepción en un restaurante muy elegante donde comemos y bailamos. Bailo primero con mi padre y después con mis amigos”.

“Aquí estoy yo en el día de mis quince años. Es un día muy especial y toda la familia está conmigo para celebrar. Todo está perfecto para mi fiesta —la comida, las decoraciones, la música— ¡todo!”

¿Comprendes?

1. ¿Cuál es la fecha de los quince años de María Teresa?
2. Necesitas una hora para ir de tu casa a la Iglesia de Nuestra Señora de Guadalupe. ¿A qué hora tienes que salir *(leave)* de casa?
3. ¿Dónde y a qué hora es la recepción? Según la invitación, ¿qué van a hacer en la recepción?
4. ¿Qué actividad de la fiesta de quince años te gusta más?

¡Vamos a comparar!

The special celebration of a girl's fifteenth birthday is called *la quinceañera, los quince,* or *los quince años.* Think about an event in the lives of your friends that has the importance of a *quince años* celebration. How are the events similar or different?

▼ Fondo Cultural | El mundo hispano

El nombre completo A person's full name *(nombre completo)* consists of a first name *(nombre),* which often consists of two names, plus two surnames—the father's family name *(apellido paterno),* followed by the mother's family name *(apellido materno).*

For example, look at the *nombres completos* of María Teresa's parents:

Felipe Rivera López y
Guadalupe Treviño Ibarra

- What is Felipe's *apellido paterno*?
- What is Guadalupe's *apellido materno*?
- Can you explain how María Teresa's name is formed?

María Teresa will most often use her first name and her father's family name. If she marries, she may add *de* and her husband's last name to her own name: María Teresa Rivera de García.

- Use the Spanish system to write your *nombre completo.* What advantages or disadvantages do you see to having a name formed this way?

Más práctica GO

	realidades.com	print
Guided WB p. 163	✔	✔
Comm. WB pp. 98, 276	✔	✔
***Hispanohablantes* WB** pp. 182–183		✔
Cultural Reading Activity	✔	

238 doscientos treinta y ocho
Tema 5 • Fiesta en familia

doscientos treinta y nueve 239
Capítulo 5A

Real-world Readings

Students are able to connect to the cultural richness and diversity in the Spanish-speaking world.

Cultural Comparisons

Standards-based questions focus students on cultural perspectives and comparisons.

¡Adelante!

La cultura en vivo

El papel picado

As you've seen in this chapter, *el papel picado* (cut paper) is a well-known Mexican craft. Colored tissue paper is cut into small patterns similar to making paper snowflakes. The cut paper is then hung on string to make a banner to use as decoration at many different celebrations. Here's how to make *papel picado* to decorate your classroom.

Una fiesta con música de mariachi

Materials

- colored tissue paper cut into 12" x 18" sheets
- scissors
- stapler
- string

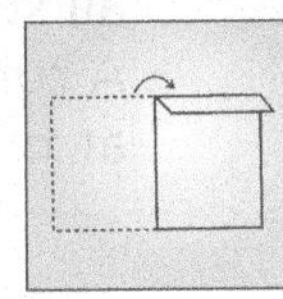
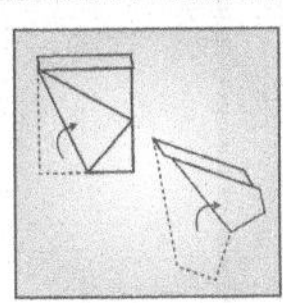

Directions

1 Spread the tissue paper flat. Fold down 1" on the 18" side for making a hanging flap.
2 Fold the paper in half on the 12" side and crease on the fold to make a sharp line.
3 Fold the paper twice, diagonally.
4 Cut out designs along the folded edge. Experiment with snowflake or other geometric designs.
5 Cut a scalloped design on the outside edge.
6 Open the cutout and staple to a string to hang across a room to decorate for a *fiesta*.

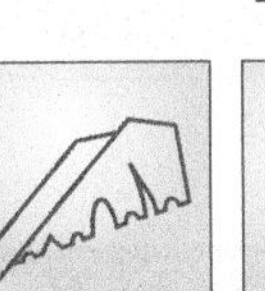
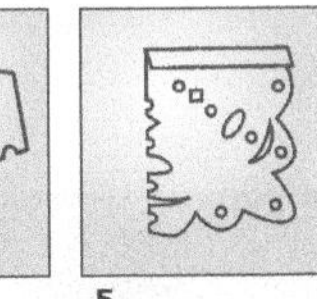
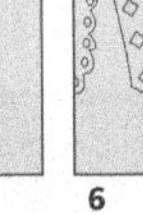
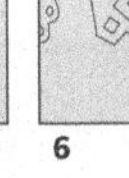

240 doscientos cuarenta
Tema 5 • Fiesta en familia

Hands-on Culture

La cultura en vivo offers a fun, hands-on experience with a wide range of cultural products and practices.

¡Adelante!

Perspectivas del mundo hispano

A la hora de comer

Imagine that you had two hours for lunch every day. Or imagine that every time you ate a meal, you sat down at a table with a friend or family member and had a lengthy conversation. Now imagine that you didn't jump up from dinner as soon as you finished eating. What do these situations have in common?

Una familia en la República Dominicana

In many Spanish-speaking cultures, even ordinary mealtimes are considered social events, a time to spend enjoying food and company. People often take time after a meal to relax, to sit around the table and enjoy a good conversation or just to have a laugh. This custom, called the *sobremesa,* is more important in many cultures than getting to the next appointment or saving time and money by buying a quick meal.

Not surprisingly, most Spanish-speaking countries have very few drive-through restaurants. Since people rarely take food "to go," they might be surprised if you suggested grabbing a sandwich to eat in the car. In fact, many cars don't have cup-holders.

Una familia chilena come al aire libre, Renaca, Chile

Check it out! Figure out how much time you and your family spend at breakfast, lunch, and dinner on days when you're not in school or at work. Compare your results with those of your classmates. Then complete the following statements about practices among families in your community.

Modelo

En mi comunidad, es común *(common)* comer el desayuno en quince minutos.

1. En mi comunidad, es común comer el desayuno en ________ .
2. En mi comunidad, es común comer el almuerzo en ________ .
3. En mi comunidad, es común comer la cena en ________ .

Think about it! What does your research say about the importance of relaxing and enjoying a leisurely meal with friends and family? How does it compare to what happens during meals in Spanish-speaking countries? Consider the two different attitudes towards mealtime. What benefits might each one have?

264 doscientos sesenta y cuatro
Tema 5 • Fiesta en familia

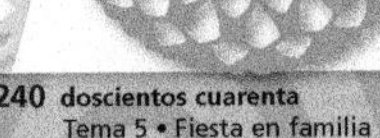
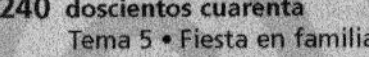

Cultural Perspectives

Perspectivas del mundo hispano provides a thought-provoking overview of a product or practice (and its related perspectives) from the Spanish-speaking world.

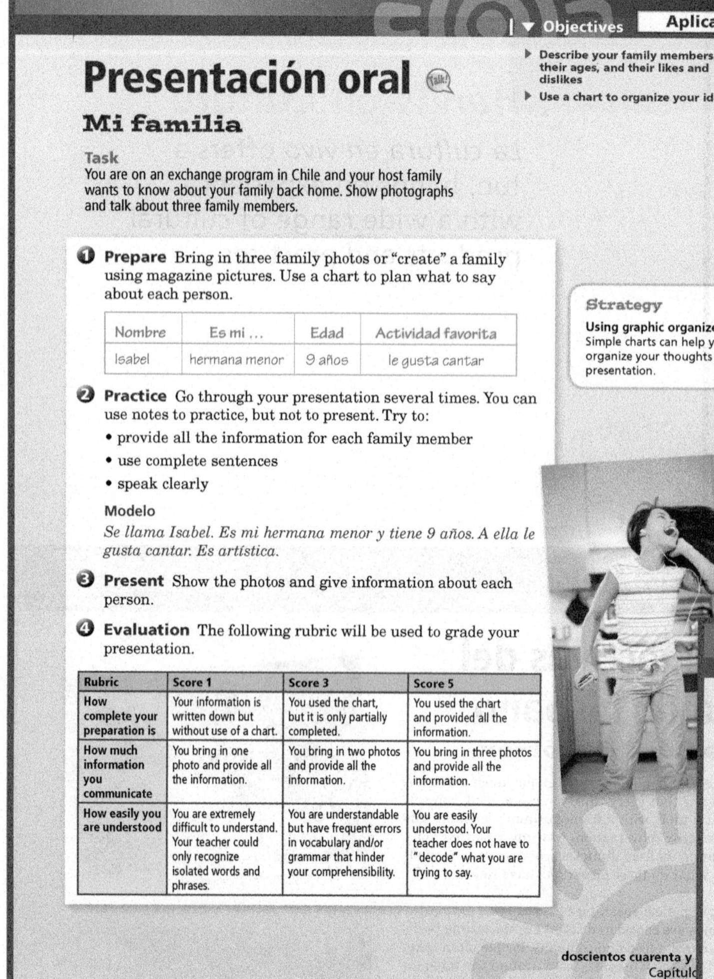

Objectives
- Describe your family members, their ages, and their likes and dislikes
- Use a chart to organize your ideas

Aplicación

Presentación oral

Mi familia

Task
You are on an exchange program in Chile and your host family wants to know about your family back home. Show photographs and talk about three family members.

1. **Prepare** Bring in three family photos or "create" a family using magazine pictures. Use a chart to plan what to say about each person.

Nombre	Es mi ...	Edad	Actividad favorita
Isabel	hermana menor	9 años	le gusta cantar

2. **Practice** Go through your presentation several times. You can use notes to practice, but not to present. Try to:
   - provide all the information for each family member
   - use complete sentences
   - speak clearly

   Modelo
   Se llama Isabel. Es mi hermana menor y tiene 9 años. A ella le gusta cantar. Es artística.
3. **Present** Show the photos and give information about each person.
4. **Evaluation** The following rubric will be used to grade your presentation.

Rubric	Score 1	Score 3	Score 5
How complete your preparation is	Your information is written down but without use of a chart.	You used the chart, but it is only partially completed.	You used the chart and provided all the information.
How much information you communicate	You bring in one photo and provide all the information.	You bring in two photos and provide all the information.	You bring in three photos and provide all the information.
How easily you are understood	You are extremely difficult to understand. Your teacher could only recognize isolated words and phrases.	You are understandable but have frequent errors in vocabulary and/or grammar that hinder your comprehensibility.	You are easily understood. Your teacher does not have to "decode" what you are trying to say.

Strategy
Using graphic organizers
Simple charts can help you organize your thoughts for a presentation.

doscientos cuarenta y
Capítulo

Common Core: Speaking

Performance-based Speaking Tasks

Real-life speaking tasks are supported by strategies and a step-by-step process that helps all students to be successful. A rubric for this task appears at the bottom of the page.

Students can record their speaking using RealTalk!

Objectives
- Write a review of your favorite restaurant
- Use examples to persuade your reader

Aplicación

Presentación escrita

Un restaurante muy bueno

Task
Your school is creating a community guide for Spanish speakers. Your class is writing about restaurants. Write a review of your favorite restaurant.

1. **Prewrite** Think about the restaurant you like best. Copy the word web. Write the name of the restaurant in the middle circle. Write words and expressions associated with each category inside the appropriate circles.
2. **Draft** Write your review of the restaurant using information from the word web. Include information that might persuade others to try the restaurant.
3. **Revise** Read through your review and check for agreement, verb forms, and spelling. Share your review with a partner. Your partner should check the following:
   - Did you provide information about all categories?
   - Did you use the correct forms of the verbs?
   - Do you have any errors in spelling or agreement?
   - Is the review persuasive?
4. **Publish** Write a final copy of your review, making any necessary changes or additions. You may want to add illustrations and include your review in a booklet with your classmates' reviews or in your portfolio.
5. **Evaluation** The following rubric will be used to grade your review.

Rubric	Score 1	Score 3	Score 5
Completion of task	You provide information in three categories from the word web.	You provide information in four categories from the word web.	You provide information in five categories from the word web.
Use of new and previously learned vocabulary	You use very limited and repetitive vocabulary.	You use only recently acquired vocabulary.	You use both recently acquired and previously learned vocabulary.
Accurate spelling/use of grammar	You have many patterns of misspelling and misuse of grammar.	You have frequent patterns of misspelling and misuse of grammar.	You have very few patterns of misspelling and misuse of grammar.
Correct use of verbs	You have many repetitions of incorrect verb forms.	You have frequent repetitions of incorrect verb forms.	You have very few incorrect verb forms.

Strategy
Persuasion
Give specific information and concrete examples to persuade your readers to try a restaurant.

doscientos sesenta y cinco 265
Capítulo 5B

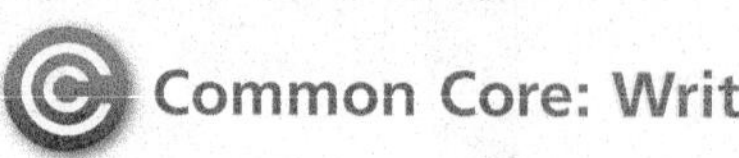

Common Core: Writing

Performance-based Writing Tasks

Students become better writers with real-life tasks that are supported with the writing process and focused strategies. As with the speaking tasks, a rubric has been specially written for each *Presentación escrita*.

Students can submit writing tasks online for easy teacher grading!

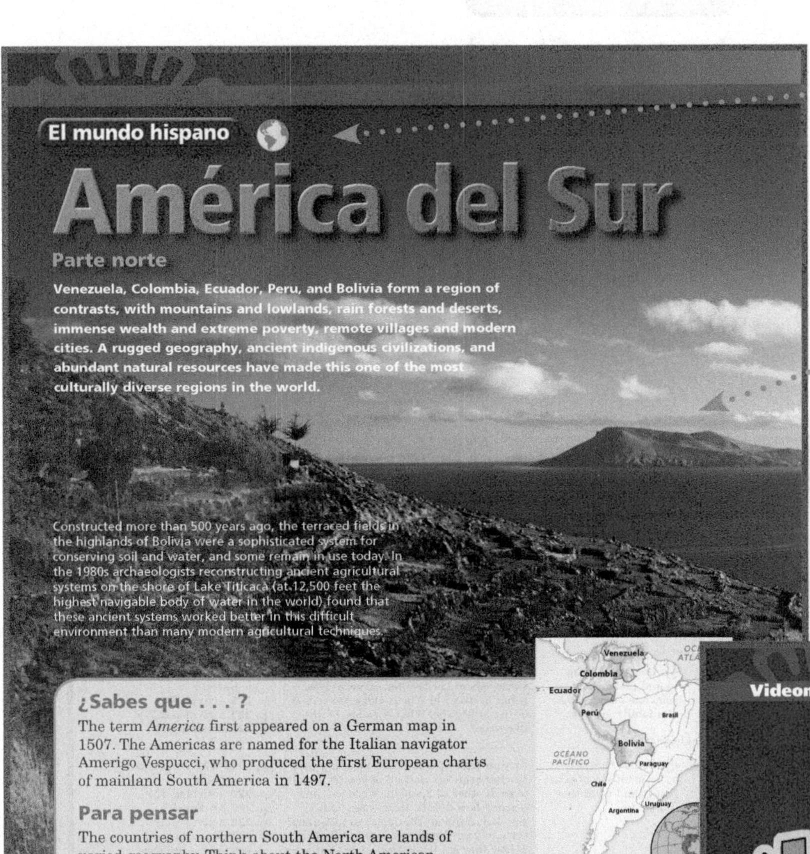

El mundo hispano

América del Sur

Parte norte

Venezuela, Colombia, Ecuador, Peru, and Bolivia form a region of contrasts, with mountains and lowlands, rain forests and deserts, immense wealth and extreme poverty, remote villages and modern cities. A rugged geography, ancient indigenous civilizations, and abundant natural resources have made this one of the most culturally diverse regions in the world.

Constructed more than 500 years ago, the terraced fields in the highlands of Bolivia were a sophisticated system for conserving soil and water, and some remain in use today. In the 1980s archaeologists reconstructing ancient agricultural systems on the shore of Lake Titicaca (at 12,500 feet the highest navigable body of water in the world) found that these ancient systems worked better in this difficult environment than many modern agricultural techniques.

¿Sabes que . . . ?

The term *America* first appeared on a German map in 1507. The Americas are named for the Italian navigator Amerigo Vespucci, who produced the first European charts of mainland South America in 1497.

Para pensar

The countries of northern South America are lands of varied geography. Think about the North American continent. It is also a land of geographical contrasts. In what ways are both regions rich in natural resources, environmentally protected areas, and ancient civilizations?

realidades.com

Mapa global intera

Reference Atlas

142 ciento cuarenta y dos
Tema 3 • La comida

Interactive Geography

Students expand their geography skills using our online *Mapa global interactivo* activities.

Learn About the Spanish-Speaking World

In *Temas 1–4*, the *¡Adelante!* section ends with *El mundo hispano,* where students learn about people, places, and things in the different regions.

Videomisterio

Objective

- Understand the expanding plot of a mystery video set in Spain

Episodio 1

Antes de ver el video

Personajes importantes

Lola Lago, detective

Doña Lupe, portera

Nota cultural In many apartment buildings in Spain, you will find a *portero* or *portera*. In exchange for a small salary and free apartment (in Spain, an apartment is called *un piso*), this person watches over the building and its residents, doing small chores such as taking messages and receiving packages. Because the *portero* or *portera* knows everyone in the building, he or she is often a good source of information about the residents.

Resumen del episodio

Estamos en el piso de Lola Lago, una detective que trabaja en Madrid, la capital de España. Es la una de la mañana. Desde[1] su balcón, ella ve a dos personas hablando enfrente de un edificio[2]. ¿Qué pasa? Más tarde, Lola encuentra[3] algo muy importante en la calle[4]. Al día siguiente[5], doña Lupe, la portera del edificio, entra en el piso de doña Gracia y . . .

[1]From [2]building [3]finds [4]street [5]The next day

Palabras para comprender

investigar	to investigate
las llaves	keys
el periódico	newspaper
el piso	apartment; floor *(of a building)*

242 doscientos cuarenta y dos
Tema 5 • Fiesta en familia

Motivate and Build Confidence with a Mystery Video

In *Temas 5–9,* students join Lola Lago as she solves the mystery of *¿Eres tú, María?* This 10-episode "whodunit" is beautifully filmed in Madrid and is easily comprehensible to first-year students.

Repaso del capítulo

These two pages provide complete review and preparation for the chapter test.

Additional Review

Flashcards, Tutorials, *GramActiva* Videos, Animated Verbs, and *Canciones de hip hop* for this chapter are available online.

realidades.com

Instant Check

End-of-chapter activity provides extra practice.

Review Games

Online interactive games make review fun!

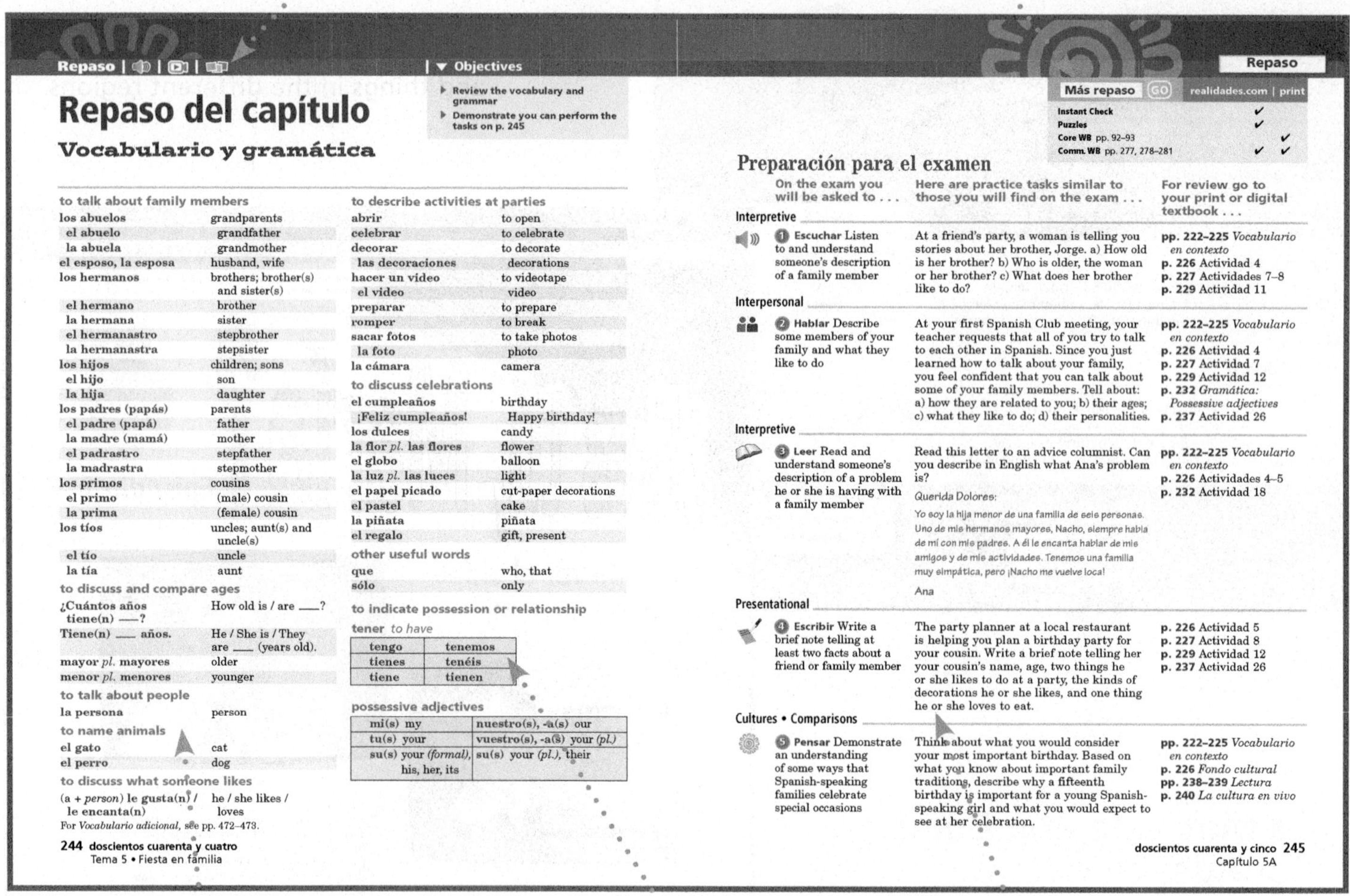

Repaso

▼ Objectives

- Review the vocabulary and grammar
- Demonstrate you can perform the tasks on p. 245

Repaso del capítulo

Vocabulario y gramática

to talk about family members

los abuelos	grandparents
el abuelo	grandfather
la abuela	grandmother
el esposo, la esposa	husband, wife
los hermanos	brothers; brother(s) and sister(s)
el hermano	brother
la hermana	sister
el hermanastro	stepbrother
la hermanastra	stepsister
los hijos	children; sons
el hijo	son
la hija	daughter
los padres (papás)	parents
el padre (papá)	father
la madre (mamá)	mother
el padrastro	stepfather
la madrastra	stepmother
los primos	cousins
el primo	(male) cousin
la prima	(female) cousin
los tíos	uncles; aunt(s) and uncle(s)
el tío	uncle
la tía	aunt

to discuss and compare ages

¿Cuántos años tiene(n) ___?	How old is / are ___?
Tiene(n) ___ años.	He / She is / They are ___ (years old).
mayor *pl.* mayores	older
menor *pl.* menores	younger

to talk about people

la persona	person

to name animals

el gato	cat
el perro	dog

to discuss what someone likes

(a + *person*) le gusta(n) / le encanta(n)	he / she likes / loves

For *Vocabulario adicional*, see pp. 472–473.

to describe activities at parties

abrir	to open
celebrar	to celebrate
decorar	to decorate
las decoraciones	decorations
hacer un video	to videotape
el video	video
preparar	to prepare
romper	to break
sacar fotos	to take photos
la foto	photo
la cámara	camera

to discuss celebrations

el cumpleaños	birthday
¡Feliz cumpleaños!	Happy birthday!
los dulces	candy
la flor *pl.* las flores	flower
el globo	balloon
la luz *pl.* las luces	light
el papel picado	cut-paper decorations
el pastel	cake
la piñata	piñata
el regalo	gift, present

other useful words

que	who, that
sólo	only

to indicate possession or relationship

tener *to have*

tengo	tenemos
tienes	tenéis
tiene	tienen

possessive adjectives

mi(s) my	nuestro(s), -a(s) our
tu(s) your	vuestro(s), -a(s) your (*pl.*)
su(s) your (*formal*), his, her, its	su(s) your (*pl.*), their

244 doscientos cuarenta y cuatro
Tema 5 • Fiesta en familia

Repaso

Más repaso GO realidades.com | print

Instant Check	✔	
Puzzles	✔	
Core WB pp. 92–93	✔	✔
Comm. WB pp. 277, 278–281	✔	✔

Preparación para el examen

On the exam you will be asked to . . .	Here are practice tasks similar to those you will find on the exam . . .	For review go to your print or digital textbook . . .
Interpretive		
1 **Escuchar** Listen to and understand someone's description of a family member	At a friend's party, a woman is telling you stories about her brother, Jorge. a) How old is her brother? b) Who is older, the woman or her brother? c) What does her brother like to do?	**pp. 222–225** *Vocabulario en contexto* **p. 226** Actividad 4 **p. 227** Actividades 7–8 **p. 229** Actividad 11
Interpersonal		
2 **Hablar** Describe some members of your family and what they like to do	At your first Spanish Club meeting, your teacher requests that all of you try to talk to each other in Spanish. Since you just learned how to talk about your family, you feel confident that you can talk about some of your family members. Tell about: a) how they are related to you; b) their ages; c) what they like to do; d) their personalities.	**pp. 222–225** *Vocabulario en contexto* **p. 226** Actividad 4 **p. 227** Actividad 7 **p. 229** Actividad 12 **p. 232** *Gramática: Possessive adjectives* **p. 237** Actividad 26
Interpretive		
3 **Leer** Read and understand someone's description of a problem he or she is having with a family member	Read this letter to an advice columnist. Can you describe in English what Ana's problem is? *Querida Dolores:* *Yo soy la hija menor de una familia de seis personas. Uno de mis hermanos mayores, Nacho, siempre habla de mí con mis padres. A él le encanta hablar de mis amigos y de mis actividades. Tenemos una familia muy simpática, pero ¡Nacho me vuelve loca!* *Ana*	**pp. 222–225** *Vocabulario en contexto* **p. 226** Actividades 4–5 **p. 232** Actividad 18
Presentational		
4 **Escribir** Write a brief note telling at least two facts about a friend or family member	The party planner at a local restaurant is helping you plan a birthday party for your cousin. Write a brief note telling her your cousin's name, age, two things he or she likes to do at a party, the kinds of decorations he or she likes, and one thing he or she loves to eat.	**p. 226** Actividad 5 **p. 227** Actividad 8 **p. 229** Actividad 12 **p. 237** Actividad 26
Cultures • Comparisons		
5 **Pensar** Demonstrate an understanding of some ways that Spanish-speaking families celebrate special occasions	Think about what you would consider your most important birthday. Based on what you know about important family traditions, describe why a fifteenth birthday is important for a young Spanish-speaking girl and what you would expect to see at her celebration.	**pp. 222–225** *Vocabulario en contexto* **p. 226** *Fondo cultural* **pp. 238–239** *Lectura* **p. 240** *La cultura en vivo*

doscientos cuarenta y cinco 245
Capítulo 5A

Vocabulary List

Chapter vocabulary is listed as language functions and with English translations.

Grammar Summary

Chapter grammar is conveniently summarized.

Complete Test Preparation

This page prepares students for the proficiency and culture sections of the chapter test. Students are told how they will be tested, what the task might be like, and how to review.

End-of-Book Student Resources

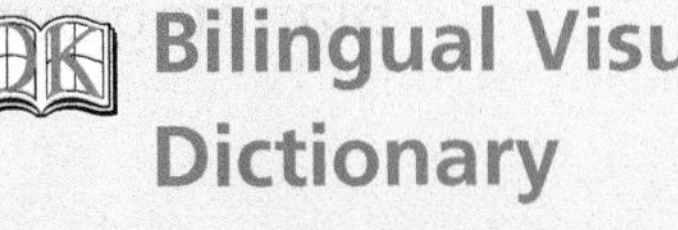

Bilingual Visual Dictionary

Complete e-Text with over 6,000 additional visualized vocabulary words

Vocabulario adicional

472 cuatrocientos setenta y dos
Vocabulario adicional

Additional Thematic Vocabulary

Useful lists provide additional thematic vocabulary.

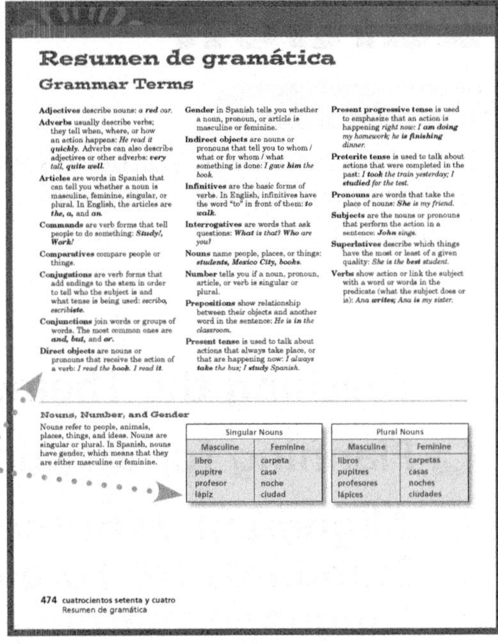

Resumen de gramática

Grammar Terms

474 cuatrocientos setenta y cuatro
Resumen de gramática

Grammar Summary and Charts

This quick reference guide helps students build a strong grammar foundation.

Expresiones útiles para conversar

Greeting Someone

Making Introductions

Asking How Someone Is

Talking on the Phone

Making Plans

Making an Excuse

Being Polite

Keeping a Conversation Going

Giving a Description When You Don't Know the Name of Someone or Something

Ending a Conversation

cuatrocientos ochenta y tres 483
Expresiones útiles para conversar

Expressions for Communication

This handy list can help students become better communicators.

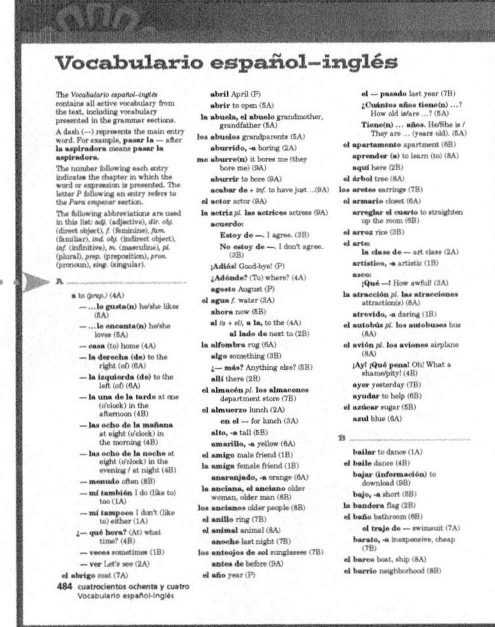

Vocabulario español–inglés

484 cuatrocientos ochenta y cuatro
Vocabulario español-inglés

End Glossaries

Helpful Spanish-English and English-Spanish glossaries are located at the end of the book

Students can listen to pronunciation online.

Using the Teacher's Edition

realidades.com

Use the Lesson Plans, teacher resources, and program content to plan for instruction and assign activities.

- Teaching the Theme
- Planning for Instruction
- Alignment with the Standards for Foreign Language Learning
- Complete Teaching Support

Teaching the Theme

The Teacher's Edition provides complete planning support for teaching the themes.

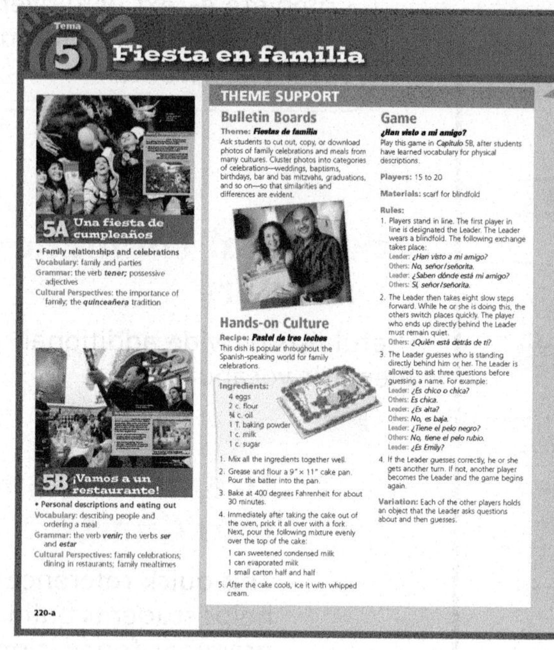

Tema 5 **Fiesta en familia**

5A Una fiesta de cumpleaños

- Family relationships and celebrations

Vocabulary: family and parties

Grammar: the verb ***tener;*** possessive adjectives

Cultural Perspectives: the importance of family; the ***quinceañera*** tradition

5B ¡Vamos a un restaurante!

- Personal descriptions and eating out

Vocabulary: describing people and ordering a meal

Grammar: the verb ***venir;*** the verbs ***ser*** and ***estar***

Cultural Perspectives: family celebrations; dining in restaurants; family mealtimes

THEME SUPPORT

Bulletin Boards

Theme: ***Fiestas de familia***

Ask students to cut out, copy, or download photos of family celebrations and meals from many cultures. Cluster photos into categories of celebrations—weddings, baptisms, birthdays, bar and bas mitzvahs, graduations, and so on—so that similarities and differences are evident.

Hands-on Culture

Recipe: ***Pastel de tres leches***

This dish is popular throughout the Spanish-speaking world for family celebrations.

Ingredients:
4 eggs
2 c. flour
¾ c. oil
1 T. baking powder
1 c. milk
1 c. sugar

1. Mix all the ingredients together well.
2. Grease and flour a 9" × 11" cake pan. Pour the batter into the pan.
3. Bake at 400 degrees Fahrenheit for about 30 minutes.
4. Immediately after taking the cake out of the oven, prick it all over with a fork. Next, pour the following mixture evenly over the top of the cake:
   1 can sweetened condensed milk
   1 can evaporated milk
   1 small carton half and half
5. After the cake cools, ice it with whipped cream.

Game

¿Han visto a mi amigo?

Play this game in *Capítulo* 5B, after students have learned vocabulary for physical descriptions.

Players: 15 to 20

Materials: scarf for blindfold

Rules:

1. Players stand in line. The first player in line is designated the Leader. The Leader wears a blindfold. The following exchange takes place:
   Leader: *¿Han visto a mi amigo?*
   Others: *No, señor/señorita.*
   Leader: *¿Saben dónde está mi amigo?*
   Others: *Sí, señor/señorita.*
2. The Leader then takes eight slow steps forward. While he or she is doing this, the others switch places quickly. The player who ends up directly behind the Leader must remain quiet.
   Others: *¿Quién está detrás de ti?*
3. The Leader guesses who is standing directly behind him or her. The Leader is allowed to ask three questions before guessing a name. For example:
   Leader: *¿Es chico o chica?*
   Others: *Es chica.*
   Leader: *¿Es alta?*
   Others: *No, es baja.*
   Leader: *¿Tiene el pelo negro?*
   Others: *No, tiene el pelo rubio.*
   Leader: *¿Es Emily?*
4. If the Leader guesses correctly, he or she gets another turn. If not, another player becomes the Leader and the game begins again.

Variation: Each of the other players holds an object that the Leader asks questions about and then guesses.

220-a

Theme Support

Time-saving teaching ideas include bulletin board suggestions, games, and other activities.

21st Century Skills

This correlation highlights ways to integrate 21st Century Skills into instruction.

Theme Project

Each theme includes a project divided into manageable steps. The rubric is at the bottom of the page as well as in the Teacher's Resource Book and in the Assessment Program.

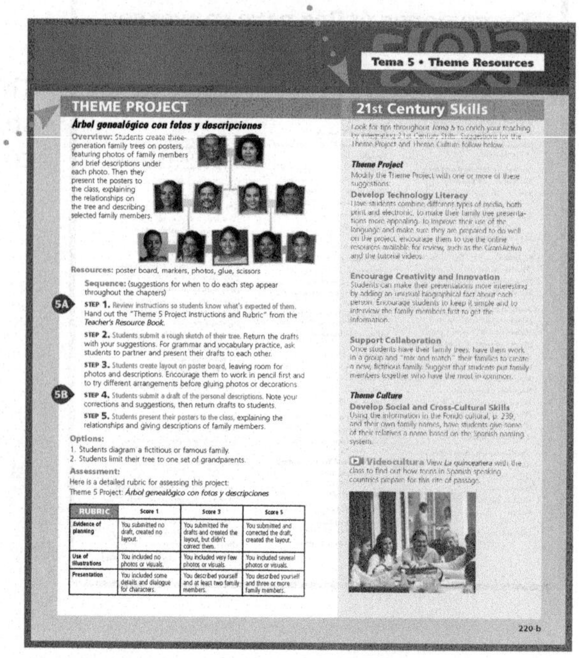

Tema 5 • Theme Resources

THEME PROJECT

Árbol genealógico con fotos y descripciones

Overview: Students create three-generation family trees on posters, featuring photos of family members and brief descriptions under each photo. Then they present the posters to the class, explaining the relationships on the tree and describing selected family members.

Resources: poster board, markers, photos, glue, scissors

Sequence: (suggestions for when to do each step appear throughout the chapters)

5A **STEP 1.** Review instructions so students know what's expected of them. Hand out the "Theme 5 Project Instructions and Rubric" from the *Teacher's Resource Book.*

STEP 2. Students submit a rough sketch of their tree. Return the drafts with your suggestions. For grammar and vocabulary practice, ask students to partner and present their drafts to each other.

STEP 3. Students create layout on poster board, leaving room for photos and descriptions. Encourage them to work in pencil first and to try different arrangements before gluing photos or decorations.

5B **STEP 4.** Students submit a draft of the personal descriptions. Note your corrections and suggestions, then return drafts to students.

STEP 5. Students present their posters to the class, explaining the relationships and giving descriptions of family members.

Options:

1. Students diagram a fictitious or famous family.
2. Students limit their tree to one set of grandparents.

Assessment:

Here is a detailed rubric for assessing this project:
Theme 5 Project: *Árbol genealógico con fotos y descripciones*

RUBRIC	Score 1	Score 3	Score 5
Evidence of planning	You submitted no draft, created no layout.	You submitted the drafts and created the layout, but didn't correct them.	You submitted and corrected the draft, created the layout.
Use of illustrations	You included no photos or visuals.	You included very few photos or visuals.	You included several photos or visuals.
Presentation	You included some details and dialogue for characters.	You described yourself and at least two family members.	You described yourself and three or more family members.

21st Century Skills

Look for tips throughout *Tema 5* to enrich your teaching by integrating 21st Century Skills. Suggestions for the Theme Project and Theme Culture follow below.

Theme Project

Modify the Theme Project with one or more of these suggestions:

Develop Technology Literacy
Have students combine different types of media, both print and electronic, to make their family tree presentations more appealing. To improve their use of the language and make sure they are prepared to do well on the project, encourage them to use the online resources available for review, such as the GramActiva and the tutorial videos.

Encourage Creativity and Innovation
Students can make their presentations more interesting by adding an unusual biographical fact about each person. Encourage students to keep it simple and to interview the family members first to get the information.

Support Collaboration
Once students have their family trees, have them work in a group and "mix and match" their families to create a new, fictitious family. Suggest that students put family members together who have the most in common.

Theme Culture

Develop Social and Cross-Cultural Skills
Using the information in the Fondo cultural, p. 239, and their own family names, have students give some of their relatives a name based on the Spanish naming system.

Videocultura View *La quinceañera* with the class to find out how teens in Spanish-speaking countries prepare for this rite of passage.

220-b

Planning for Instruction

The Teacher's Edition provides four pages of planning support interleaved at the beginning of each chapter.

Chapter Overview

This section gives a quick overview of each chapter.

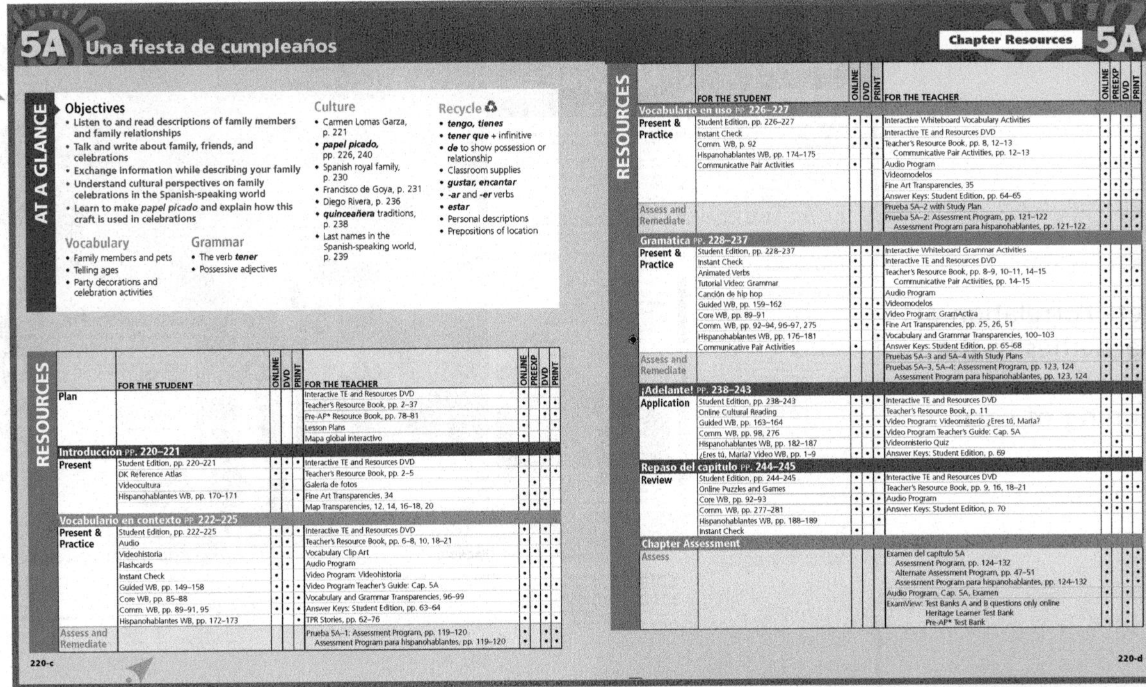

Program Resources

This section shows all the program resources available for this chapter. All resources are conveniently referenced at point of use in the chapter.

Lesson Plans

Lesson Plans are provided for instruction on the regular or block schedule.

Lesson plans are also available on **realidades.com.**

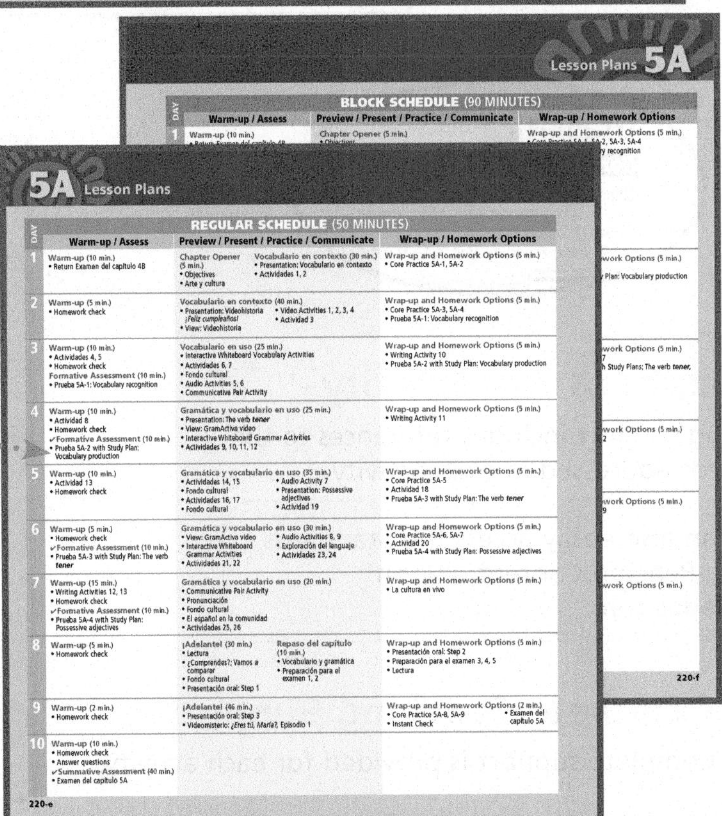

Alignment with the Standards for Foreign Language Learning

Realidades provides complete coverage of the Spanish I standards. Correlations to the standards are provided throughout the Teacher's Edition.

Standards Correlation

A complete correlation of chapter activities to the standards is provided at the beginning of each chapter.

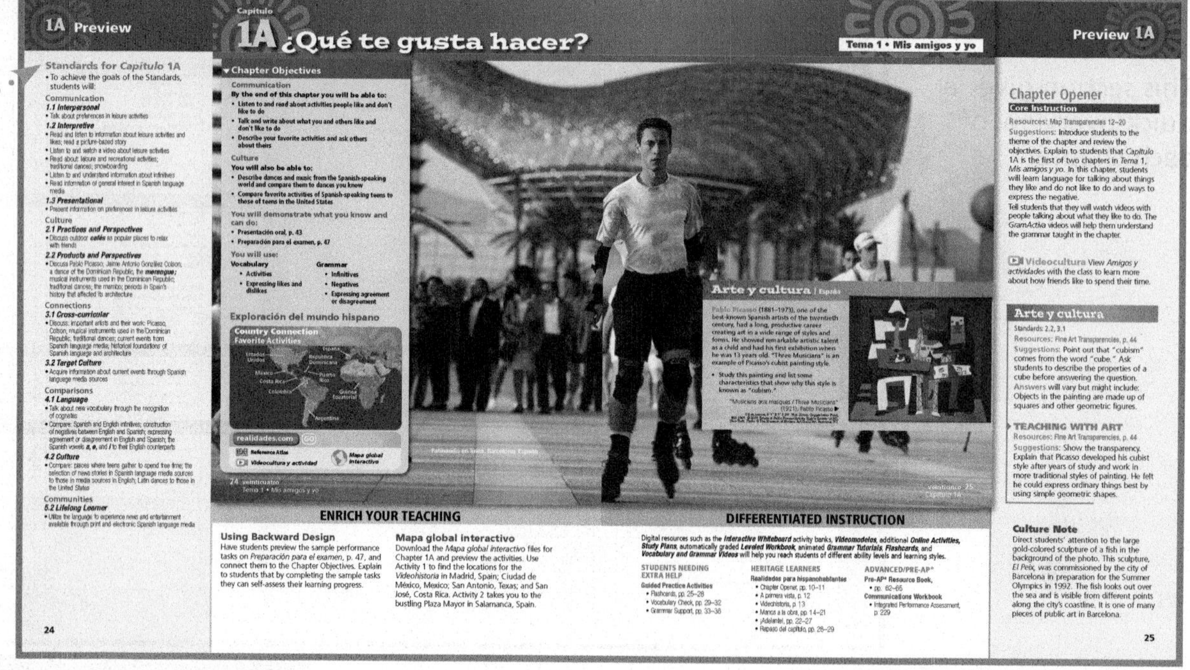

Standards Correlations per Activity

Teaching support includes references to the standards addressed in each activity.

You can also easily access the Standards on the Pearson Content link on **realidades.com**.

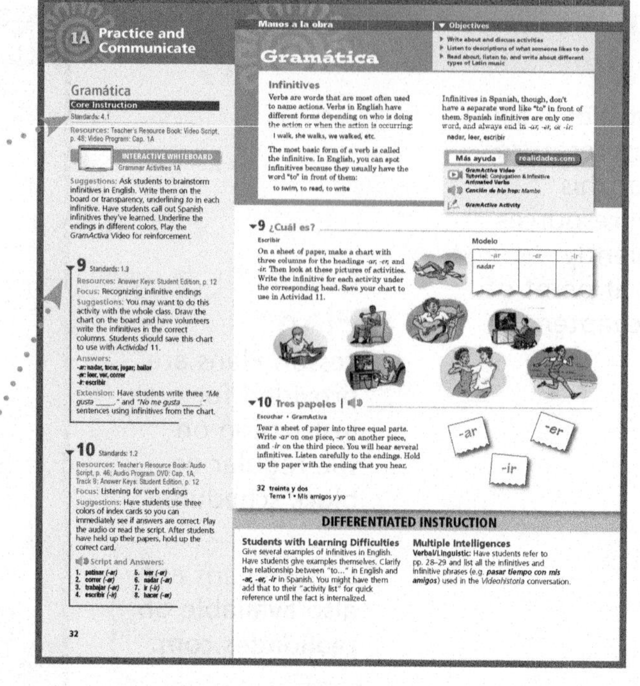

Complete Teaching Support

Complete support is provided for each activity.

Complete Teaching Support

Realidades provides teachers with complete instructional support in both print and technology formats.

Chapter Objectives

Each chapter provides a well-organized structure, clear student outcomes based upon the standards, and a variety of activities that develop all language skills.

Objectives

- Listen to and read about activities people like and don't like to do
- Talk and write about what you and others like and don't like to do
- Describe your favorite activities and ask others about theirs
- Describe dances and music from the Spanish-speaking world and compare them to dances you know
- Compare favorite activities of Spanish-speaking teens to those of teens in the United States

Assessment

Teachers are provided with multiple print and technology tools that measure student progress in listening, speaking, reading, and writing. The program also offers an Integrated Performance Assesssment for each chapter.

ASSESSMENT

Prueba 1A-2 with Study Plan (online only)

Quiz: Vocabulary Production

Prueba 1A-2: pp. 15–16

Más repaso GO

Instant Check
Puzzles
Core WB pp. 20–21
Comm. WB pp. 117, 118–120

Presentación oral

A mí me gusta mucho . . .

Task

You are a new student at school and have been asked to tell the class a little bit about your likes and dislikes.

Differentiated Instruction

Realidades provides teaching suggestions to help all students learn Spanish. Each level also provides differentiated assessment.

DIFFERENTIATED INSTRUCTION

Students with Learning Difficulties
Have students review the *Repaso del capítulo* and create flashcards for any words that they do not know. Pair them with a student who is more confident with the vocabulary to practice. Before the test, provide students with a practice test, so they can become comfortable with the format.

Heritage Language Learners
Have students write a few paragraphs telling about their perfect day: What activities are they going to do? Whom are they going to invite? What activities do they like the most? Encourage them to use as many vocabulary words from this chapter as they can.

DIFFERENTIATED ASSESSMENT

CORE ASSESSMENT
- **Assessment Program:** Examen del capítulo 1A, pp. 19–25
- **Audio Program DVD:** Cap. 1A, Track 23
- **ExamView:** Chapter Test, Test Banks A and B

ADVANCED/PRE-AP*
- **ExamView: Pre-AP* Test Bank**
- **Pre-AP* Resource Book,** pp. 61–65

STUDENTS NEEDING EXTRA HELP
- **Alternate Assessment Program:** Examen del capítulo 1A
- **Audio Program DVD:** Cap. 1A, Track 23

HERITAGE LEARNERS
- **Assessment Program: Realidades para hispanohablantes:** Examen del capítulo 1A
- **ExamView: Heritage Learner Test Bank**

Instructional Planning and Support

Realidades provides complete planning and teaching support. The Teacher's Edition, the Interactive Teacher's Edition and Resources DVD, the PresentationEXPRESS™ DVD, **realidades.com**, and other program components provide time-saving teaching tools to help you teach all your students.

Assessment

Topics covered:

- Assessing Student Progress
- Purposes of Assessment
- Forms of Assessment
- *Realidades* and the ACTFL Performance Guidelines
- Integrating Technology with Assessment
- Assessment Resources in *Realidades*

“Performance assessment does not determine *who* is best but helps learners *do* their best.”
—Challenge for a New Era; Nebraska K–12 Foreign Language Frameworks

An assessment program in a second language classroom should be based on the premise that the main purpose of learning a language is to communicate in a meaningful and culturally appropriate way. As you begin to teach a unit of instruction, you might want to start by asking a few key questions: What do I expect my students to learn? What do I want them to be able to do? How can I assess what I am looking for in student performance?

Assessing Student Progress

The role of assessment in the world languages classroom is to provide both the teacher and students with a measure of progress toward achieving predetermined outcomes. It is an integral and ongoing part of the learning process. Here are key factors to consider as you develop curriculum that aligns assessment with instruction:

- Focus assessment on what students can do in the language (not just what they know).
- Performance tasks should be based upon real-world, authentic activities.
- Consider the principles of backward design to align assessment with instruction: determine outcomes, decide upon the evidence of transfer (performance tasks), and then create the learning activities.
- Give students multiple opportunities to show what they can do with the language that take into consideration cultures, learning styles, languages, and individual abilities.
- Use rubrics to evaluate performance tasks. This tool measures specific criteria against a defined scale. Provide the rubric to students in advance of the performance task.
- Provide students with anchors, or representative samples, of the performance task so that they can better understand the desired outcomes.
- Utilize both formative and summative assessments to provide ongoing feedback to students.
- Provide opportunities for students to self-evaluate and reflect upon their learning and progress.

Purposes of Assessment

The following chart outlines the various purposes for assessment:

Purposes of Assessment	
Entry-level assessment	• Analyzes students' ability to communicate as a basis for placing students at an appropriate level in an established world languages program
Formative assessment	• Provides real-time feedback during the instructional process • Can take many different forms in the classroom • Helps the teacher and student determine the next steps to further learning • Takes place prior to the summative assessment
Summative assessment	• Documents and judges students' learning or success at a point in time such as the end of a unit, chapter, or course of study

Forms of Assessment

Achievement tests determine what students know by evaluating them on specific, previously learned material, such as the names of items of clothing or the conjugation of *-ar* verbs. Students are tested on discrete bits of information. Achievement tests are used to measure the incremental steps involved in learning a second language—for example, to cover what was taught in a specific chapter. Achievement may be quizzed or tested with some frequency as proof of regular progress for both student and teacher.

Performance-based assessment measures what students can do with this knowledge and how well they can perform in the language. These tests do not involve testing specific items; rather they are performance-based, checking how well students integrate what they have learned. Their characteristic open-endedness permits students to use what they know to receive or communicate a message, since the emphasis is on communication needs. Performance-based assessment addresses this question: How well and at what level can the student use the language to receive and express meaningful communication?

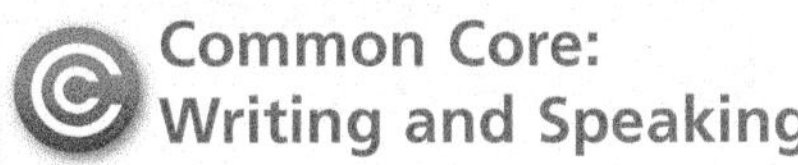

Common Core: Writing and Speaking

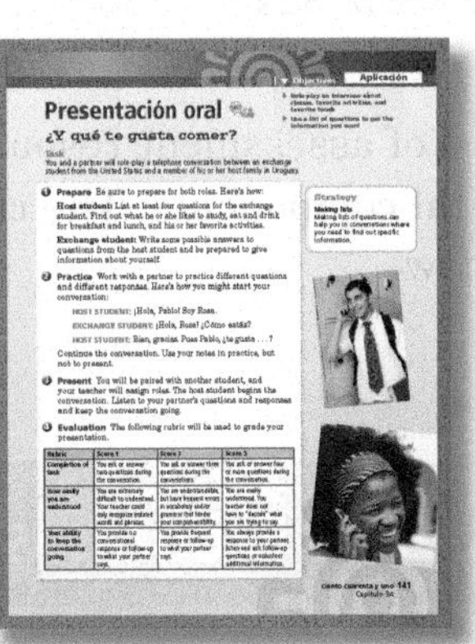

Presentación oral

¿Y qué te gusta comer?

Performance-based speaking task in ***Realidades 1 Capítulo 3A***

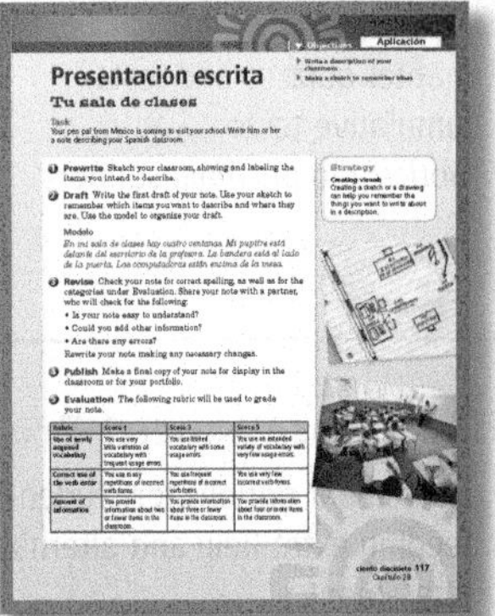

Presentación escrita

Tu sala de clases

Performance-based writing task in ***Realidades 1 Capítulo 2B***

Realidades and the ACTFL Performance Guidelines

The ACTFL Performance Guidelines for K–12 Learners describe the language proficiency of learners in Standards-based language programs such as ***Realidades***. They are organized around three Modes of Communication: Interpersonal, Interpretive, and Presentational and provide for three Benchmark Levels: Novice, Intermediate, and Pre-Advanced.

Realidades has been carefully written to provide activities that develop and assess the Modes of Communication at levels appropriate to the students' proficiency. The last page in each chapter of Levels 1–3, called *Preparación para el examen*, provides an overview of the chapter outcomes and performance tasks organized around the three Modes. The Communication Workbook features an Integrated Performance Assessment (IPA) as an alternate assessment resource.

Assessment Resources in *Realidades*

Realidades offers a wide range of assessment resources found in various print and digital components. The chart on page T37 provides an overview.

Integrating Technology with Assessment

There are many opportunities to use the technology in ***Realidades*** to assess student performance. These include:

RealTalk! Use the RealTalk tool in **realidades.com** to evaluate your students' interpersonal and presentation skills.

Online Games Who says learning can't be fun? Each chapter within **realidades.com** offers three games that help students monitor their learning.

Interactive Whiteboard Activities Get your students talking using the *¡Cuéntame!* and *Encuesta* Interactive Whiteboard Activities.

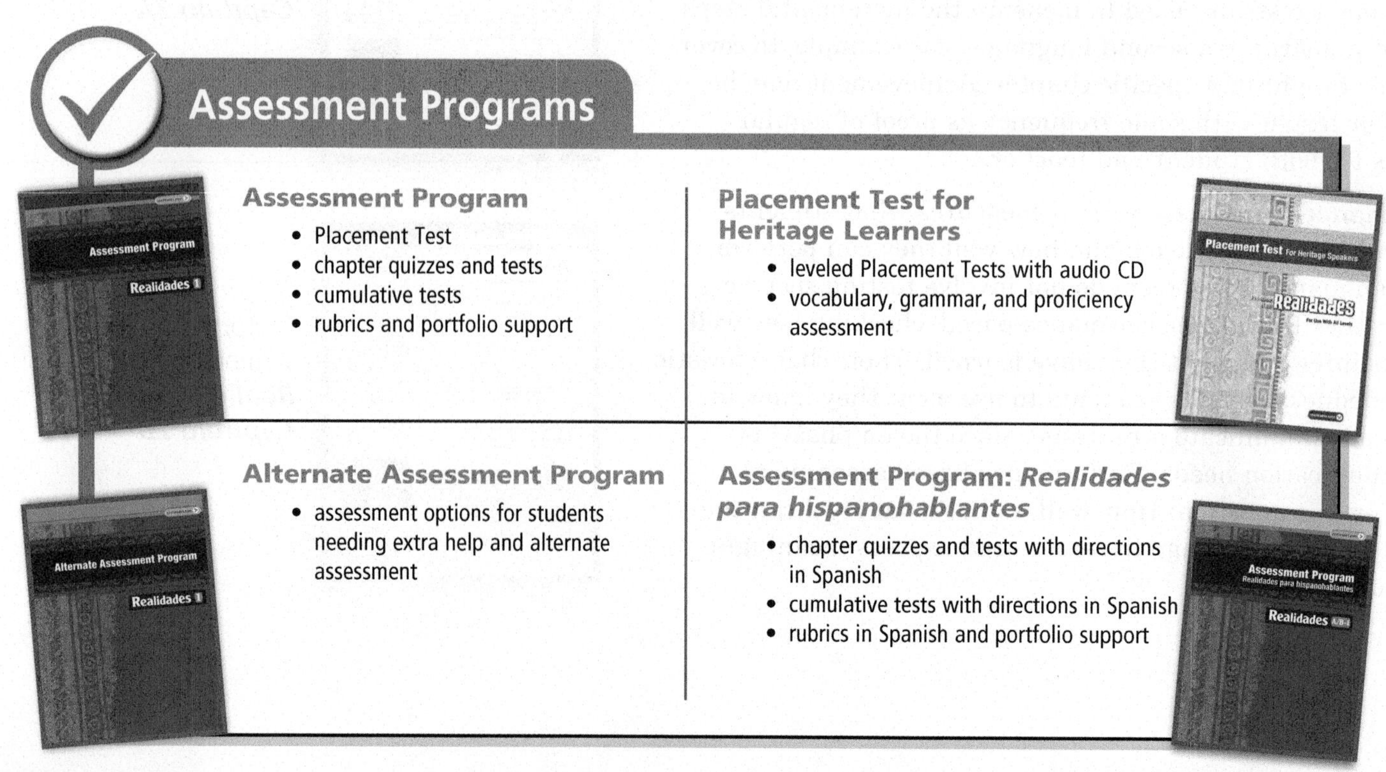

Assessment Resources in *Realidades*

Assessment Resources	Self-Evaluation	Formative	Summative: Achievement	Summative: Performance
Student Edition				
Actividades (various)		X		X
Presentación oral				X
Presentación escrita				X
Preparación para el examen				X
realidades.com				
Actividades with (talk!)	X	X		X
Presentación oral with (talk!)				X
Instant Checks	X	X		
Online Games	X			
Chapter Quizzes with Study Plans		X		
Chapter Tests with (talk!)			X	X
Integrated Performance Assessments with (talk!)				X
Assessment Programs				
Placement Tests				X
Chapter Quizzes		X		
Chapter Tests			X	X
Cumulative Tests			X	X
Rubrics				X
Chapter Checklist and Self-Assessment Worksheet	X			
Communication Workbook				
Audio and Writing Activities		X		
Practice Tests				X
Integrated Performance Assessments				X
Teacher Resource Book				
Communicative Pair Activities		X		
Situation Cards				X
Pre-AP® Resource Book				
Activities				X
Interactive Whiteboard Activities				
Vocabulary and Grammar		X		X
ExamView® Computer Test Generator				
Test Banks			X	

Differentiated Instruction

Topics covered:

- Success in Teaching All Students
- Effective Instructional Strategies
- Teaching Today's Students
- Teaching Spanish to Students with Learning Disabilities
- Accommodating Instruction
- Accommodations for Students with Special Needs
- Accommodation in *Realidades*
- Teaching Heritage Learners
- Teaching Heritage Learners with *Realidades para hispanohablantes*
- Teaching Heritage Learners with *Realidades 1*
- Teaching All Students: Summary

All students are capable of and can benefit from learning a second language. However, today's students bring into the classroom a wide range of needs, interests, motivations, home languages, and literacy levels. This diversity presents heightened challenges to both curriculum and instruction. It should be clearly acknowledged that individual needs of some students require additional specialized support. However, the goal of a comprehensive program remains the provision of teaching all students to develop proficiency in Spanish. All students should have access to a communicative and culturally rich program in addition to whatever specialized intervention may be required. *Realidades* has been developed especially to meet the diverse needs of students in Spanish classrooms.

Success in Teaching All Students

All students are able to access learning when teachers provide curriculum and instruction in ways that allow all learners in the classroom to participate and achieve the instructional and behavioral goals of general education, as well as those of the core curriculum. Success is achieved in classrooms that consistently and systematically integrate instructional strategies that are responsive to the needs of all learners with a special focus on students that need extra help—students with learning difficulties, heritage learners, and students who are eligible for and receiving special education services.

Effective Instructional Strategies

Here are general strategies that deliver effective instruction for all learners in the Spanish classroom.

- **Clarify the objectives for a chapter.** Students need to understand the outcomes for which they will be assessed.
- **Provide "thinking time" before students have to talk.** You may want to ask a question and then count to 10 before expecting a response. If a student is struggling, state that you want him/her to think about it, and indicate that you'll be back for the response in a minute. Move on to another student, and then return to the student for his/her response.

- **Write all assignments on the board.** Assignments given both verbally and visually are clearer to all students.
- **Use visuals throughout the lesson.** Present vocabulary visually. Use charts to present grammar. Use video that provides visual support (such as vocabulary words highlighted on the screen) and grammar videos that visualize grammar patterns. Use graphic organizers whenever possible. Connect communicative tasks to photos, art, and realia.
- **Assist in time management.** When requiring students to complete projects or long-term assignments, provide a calendar that breaks down requirements by due dates. Many students experience significant difficulties in self-managing the time needed to complete complex projects.
- **Build in opportunities for reteaching and practicing vocabulary words and grammar.** Students need many opportunities to learn new concepts and need to practice in a variety of formats.
- **Build vocabulary skills by teaching the patterns of language.** Teach the meaning of prefixes, suffixes, and the role of cognates. Point out connections between English, Spanish, and Latin.
- **Work with students based on their strengths rather than their weaknesses.** Allow students to experience success by using their strengths while working on areas of weakness.
- **Consider alternative means for demonstrating understanding.** Think beyond the common modes of reading and writing. Students could present information orally, create a poster or visual representation of work, record their ideas on an audio file, or act out their understanding.
- **Have students begin all work in class.** Prior to class dismissal, check to ensure that each student has a good start and understands what is expected.

> "All students are capable of and can benefit from learning a second language."

- **Assign work using the Calendar on *realidades.com* or create a class Web page.** Homework assignments could be posted and easily accessed by parents and students outside of school hours.

Teaching Today's Students

The strategies presented on these pages provide an overview of instructional strategies that are effective with all learners. Today's students need instruction that enables them to see how learning is relevant, that helps them organize their time and learning, that provides focus on what is important (either within instructional materials or with classroom activities), that provides multiple opportunities to learn utilizing different modalities, and that assures students know what is expected of them whether in the classroom or for homework.

Teaching Spanish to Students with Learning Disabilities

There are many reasons why students may experience difficulties in learning a second language. In general, these difficulties may be characterized by the inability to spell or read well, problems with auditory discrimination and in understanding auditory input, and difficulty with abstract thinking. Research by Ganchow and Sparks (1991) indicates that difficulties with one's first language are a major factor in foreign language learning difficulties.

It is not always evident which students will experience difficulties with learning a second language. Many times these students are bright and outgoing. They may have experienced reading or spelling problems in elementary school, but they have learned to compensate over time. Ask students what problems they may have experienced with their first language, especially in the areas of reading and dictation.

Accommodating Instruction

Students with learning disabilities can develop a level of proficiency in a second language with some modifications to instruction and testing. These learners benefit from a highly structured approach that teaches new content in context and in incremental amounts. Teach, practice, and assess using multi-sensory strategies. Many students benefit when instruction combines seeing, hearing, saying, and writing. For example, a teacher would first show a visual of a word and say it aloud. This is followed by using the new word in context. The teacher then writes the word on the board. Students would say the word aloud with the teacher. They then write it down and say it aloud again. In subsequent days, many students benefit from frequent reviews of learned auditory materials.

Accommodations for Students with Special Needs

Here are suggestions for instruction for students with special needs. For additional support, see the *Realidades* Alternate Assessment Program.

Hearing impairments

- Help students comprehend oral information or instructions. Provide written directions/materials and/or visual cues to support what is presented orally. Face the students when speaking, repeat as needed, and speak clearly. Seat these students in the front of the classroom. Provide outlines of lectures or oral presentations. Have another student take notes and make copies of notes available to all students. Use the audio and video scripts of the *Realidades* Audio or Video Program. Utilize the close-captioned version of the Video Program.
- Allow students to refer to their textbooks or to other written materials during oral presentations.
- Limit background noises that may distract students. Avoid seating these students where they may hear extraneous noise.
- Change listening activities and assessments to reading/writing activities. In activities that require aural/oral skills, let students demonstrate skills through alternative responses such as writing.
- Provide access to the audio and video materials. Students can download all Student Edition audio material from **realidades.com.** The eText provides pronunciation support for all vocabulary, access to all Student Edition listening activities, and access to the vocabulary and grammar videos.

Visual perception problems

- Help students access information provided visually. Allow for preferred seating in the front of the class, including providing space for a guide dog, if necessary. Avoid seating students where they will be distracted by extraneous auditory or visual stimuli. Give students additional time to review visual input prior to an oral or written task. Highlight important information by providing key words, visuals, and simple outlines.

- Provide support for accessing printed information. Make sure the print is easy to read. The readings should be designed to maximize readability: easy-to-read font, layout, and design. Teach reading strategies that highlight the visual aspects of a selection: text organization, use of visuals, titles and headers, and the use of color. Provide copies of reading selections with additional support: underline key words/sentences/concepts or magnify the text in duplication.
- Teach, practice, and assess using multi-sensory strategies.

ADHD/ADD

- Provide additional support that enables students to focus. Present information in small "chunks." This includes new content, short instructions or directions, and shorter assignments, or break assignments into steps. Limit extraneous auditory and visual stimulation. Provide visual and written support for aural instructions or input. Repeat and explain (again) as needed. Provide outlines of oral presentations. Support readings with strategies similar to those for students with visual perception problems. Use graphic organizers.
- Verify that students "got it." Check that students are looking at you (eye contact) when providing oral instructions. Ask students to repeat what you just told them. Move closer to students to increase attention. Provide preferential seating that allows you to monitor students' focus and attention. Allow extra wait time when students are responding.
- Provide a variety of different learning activities that reach different learning styles. This will also allow for frequent changes of activities within a class. Provide for hands-on activities, vocabulary clip art, and grammar manipulatives.
- Use technology to provide interactive learning. These students will benefit from using the online resources at **realidades.com.**
- Be predictable. Establish a daily routine for managing the classroom and be consistent. Avoid surprises with these students.
- Help students organize themselves and their learning. Ask students to maintain notebooks that are organized by dividers. Provide study guides, summary sheets, and organizers for daily or weekly assignments.

Accommodation in *Realidades*

Realidades 1 **provides a wide range of support for accommodating instruction.**

Student Edition

- clean design and layout of pages
- visualized presentation of vocabulary
- step-by-step scaffolding of activities
- online vocabulary and grammar tutorials and extra practice at **realidades.com**

Teacher's Edition

- Differentiated Instruction article
- Differentiated Instruction suggestions

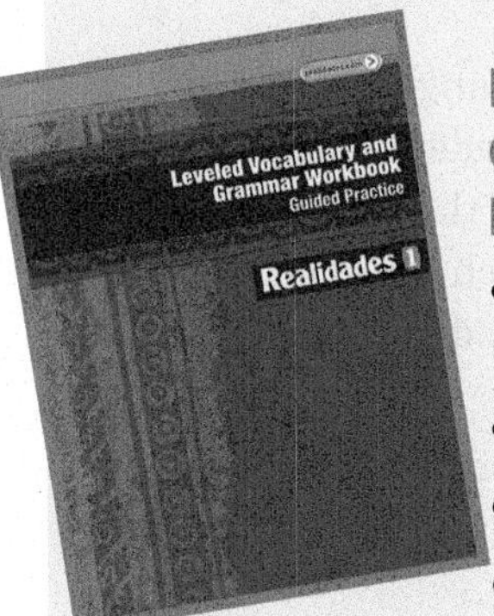

Leveled Vocabulary and Grammar Workbook: Guided Practice

- vocabulary clip art to create flashcards
- focused vocabulary practice
- simplified grammar instruction
- Answer Key in Teacher's Resource Book

Alternate Assessment Program

- additional suggestions for accommodating assessment
- for students needing extra help

Teaching Heritage Learners

A diverse background

Those who have a home language other than English bring a wider range of language abilities to the classroom. These abilities range from minimal functioning in the language to complete fluency and literacy. It is important for teachers to assess the language skills of the different heritage learners in the classroom. This diversity includes:

- Students who are able to understand the spoken language, but are unable to respond in the language beyond single-word answers.
- Students who are able to understand the language and communicate at a minimal level. These students may be able to read some items, but because of their limited vocabulary, they may not comprehend much information. They may write what they are able to sound out, but errors are evident.
- Students who can speak the language fluently but who have little to no experience with the language in its written form.
- Students who have come to the United States from non-English-speaking countries. They can understand and speak the language fluently; however, their reading and writing skills may be limited due to lack of a formal education in their country of origin.
- Fluent bilingual students who can understand, speak, read, and write another language very well and have possibly received formal instruction in that language in the United States or in another country.

Program goals

Heritage learners bring rich home language experiences to the classroom that can serve as a foundation for learning. Because of their language background, these students have the potential to be bilingual, biliterate, and bicultural. Heritage learners need to be exposed to a program that can improve and maintain the home language. Students need to study the grammar and focus on vocabulary development. Emphasis should be placed on building reading and writing skills. It is important that students develop a sensitivity to when standard and non-standard language should be employed and comfortably adjust their language accordingly. In addition, students should be exposed to the diverse cultures within the Spanish-speaking community while developing a sense of pride in their own heritage. Heritage learners need to reach a high level of proficiency and accuracy that will ensure success at the advanced level of language study and testing. These students should also be ready to transition into a focused study of Spanish in specific professional areas.

Focus on individual needs

Due to their diverse backgrounds, heritage learners differ greatly in language skills and may need individualized instruction. In many of today's classrooms, teachers encounter classes that contain a mixture of beginning-level students and heritage learners. These groups need different materials, different instructional approaches, and different objectives. Here are several strategies that may be helpful for heritage learners:

- Build upon their background knowledge. Develop instructional units around themes and topics that relate to their life experiences. Encourage students to use these experiences as the foundation for building language skills through vocabulary development, reading, and writing.
- Help students connect aural with written language. If students don't understand a word in a reading, have them read it aloud or ask a friend or teacher to read it aloud. Often they can recognize the word once they hear it. Allow for opportunities for students to follow along as a story is read aloud.
- Use strategies that are effective in a language arts classroom, such as building schema, teaching language-learning strategies, using graphic organizers, and incorporating pre- and post-reading tasks. Use the writing process to develop good writers.

- Encourage students to begin communicating, especially in writing. Have them write down their thoughts in the way they sound to them. Then have students work with the teacher or another student for corrections. Students can also look through textbooks and dictionaries to assist with error correction.
- Maintain high standards. Require students to focus on accuracy and proficient communication. Many heritage learners experience frustration with reading and writing in the home language when they have good aural/oral skills. Building language skills takes time.

Teaching Heritage Learners with *Realidades 1*

Realidades 1 offers the ideal solution for heritage learners who begin Spanish instruction with a first-year textbook. It is recommended that teachers use *Realidades 1* and the companion worktext, *Realidades para hispanohablantes,* with these students. This gives teachers three options: (1) the student textbook with English support; (2) the companion all-Spanish worktext; or (3) a combination of both.

Teaching All Students: Summary

The diverse needs of today's Spanish students pose a challenge to teachers, curriculum developers, and school administrators as they design programs to ensure that all students develop language proficiency. With *Realidades,* teachers have at their disposal a variety of materials and strategies to enable them to provide access to Spanish for all learners. Clearly, some students will require additional tutoring and specialized services to reach their full learning potential. However, the activities and materials that accompany *Realidades,* coupled with instructional strategies described within this article, constitute a viable framework for reaching and teaching all learners.

Teaching Heritage Learners with *Realidades para hispanohablantes*

***Realidades 1* provides extensive support for teaching heritage learners.**

Student Edition

- focused vocabulary and grammar
- integrated language and culture
- extensive reading and writing

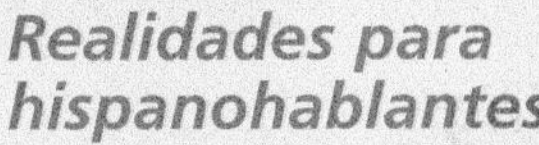

Realidades para hispanohablantes

- all-Spanish companion worktext
- all-Spanish grammar explanations
- companion pages for each section of Student Edition
- increased emphasis on reading and writing
- accompanying Teacher's Guide

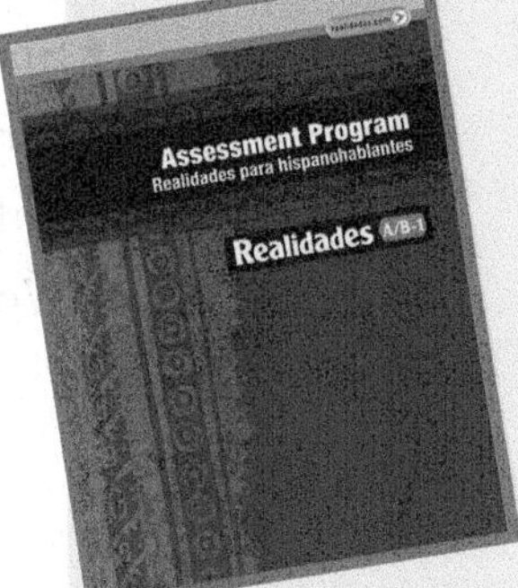

Assessment Program: *Realidades para hispanohablantes*

- direction lines in Spanish
- complete assessment support
- rubrics in Spanish

Placement Test

- leveled Placement Test with audio
- vocabulary, grammar, and proficiency assessment

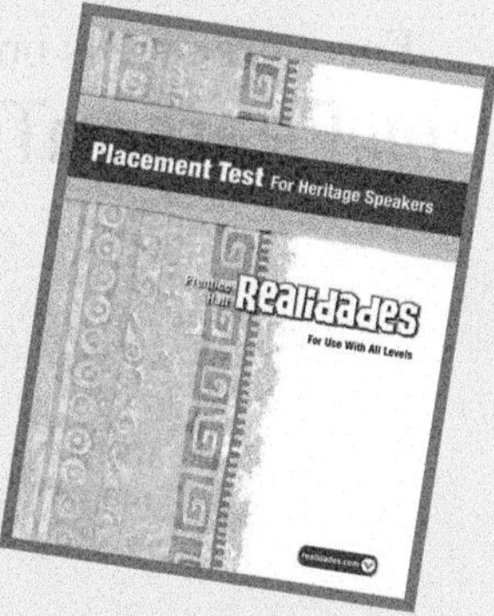

Instructional Planning and Support

Today's Spanish classroom is a vibrant and interactive learning community, integrating language with culture. Teachers are planning for instruction that is communicative, motivating, and real for ***all*** students. They are incorporating a wide range of strategies, activities, and technology to achieve clearly defined teaching objectives. This section provides an overview of instructional strategies that will help teachers achieve these goals.

Topics covered:

- Creating a Communicative Learning Community
- The Role of Grammar in a Communicative Classroom
- Pair and Group Activities in a Communicative Classroom
- Integrating Technology in the Classroom

For more issues online, see
*my*PearsonTraining.com

Creating a Communicative Learning Community

A communicative classroom is built upon activities that enable students to use language in meaningful and purposeful ways. One of the challenges is to get students ready, willing, and able to communicate. Here are several strategies that can be built into communicative tasks to help all students be successful.

Teach and use learning strategies

Research states that successful language students use a wide range of learning strategies. In contrast, unsuccessful students employ fewer strategies and tend to give up quickly. Strategies are inherently student-centered and when employed by learners, allow them to become more independent and more successful. Learning strategies enable students to:

- Learn and recall information more efficiently
- Interpret and comprehend language when reading or writing
- Speak more effectively
- Write more effectively
- Take more risks and be more positive
- Work more cooperatively with others

Use activities based upon multiple intelligences

The Multiple Intelligences Theory tells us that students learn in different ways. If new material is presented in a variety of formats, more students will likely learn and be able to demonstrate proficiency with the new material. Howard Gardner proposed the theory of multiple intelligences in his book *Frames of Mind.* This theory states that a person has many different ways of acquiring and demonstrating intelligence. Some people remember just about anything if learned to the tune of a jingle or chant, while someone else may be able to grasp an idea, concept, or grammatical point if presented as a graph, chart, or picture.

Gardner presents the notion that there is no "general intelligence," but rather that the mind is organized around distinct functional capacities, which he defines as "intelligences." Though each of the intelligences is developed independently of the others over the course of a lifetime, they usually work together and do not often appear in isolation. Gardner has identified and labeled eight main styles of acquiring and demonstrating knowledge; those eight intelligences are:

- Verbal/Linguistic
- Visual/Spatial
- Bodily/Kinesthetic
- Logical/Mathematical
- Interpersonal/Social
- Intrapersonal/Introspective
- Musical/Rhythmic
- Naturalist

In this Teacher's Edition, you will find frequent specific suggestions for accommodating and teaching to the Multiple Intelligences. This is not meant to be construed as a paradigm for labeling every student in your class. On the contrary, they are presented as tools to help more students access content while recognizing that they are intelligent in many ways and that their overall "intelligence" is based upon the sum of all their intelligences.

Scaffolded tasks

Step-by-step support builds success.

19 ¿Qué te gusta más?

Escribir • Hablar

1. A popular magazine has provided this survey to see how much you and a friend have in common. On a sheet of paper, write the numbers 1–7 and then write your preferences.
2. Take turns asking your partner about the survey items. Keep track of your similarities and differences. See how the magazine rates you.

Modelo

¿La comida mexicana o la comida italiana?
A —*¿Qué te gusta más, la comida mexicana o la comida italiana?*
B —*Me gusta más la comida italiana.*
o: —*No me gusta ni la comida mexicana ni la comida italiana.*

Activities that incorporate critical thinking tend to be more interesting for students as they are guided to think differently in ways such as:

- use or apply
- illustrate/sketch/diagram
- compare and contrast
- analyze
- categorize
- create
- organize/prepare
- evaluate
- revise
- value

Provide activities that require critical thinking

All students learn more effectively when activities help them make connections and see and use information in new and different ways. Critical thinking skills can be used as tools for learning and are easily integrated in a variety of tasks beginning in the first year of language study in both communication and culture activities.

Scaffold communicative tasks

Communicating in a second language is a complicated task. There are mental steps that take place as a student attempts to communicate a message. Activities that help students get through these mental steps allow students to be successful. This "scaffolded" support is provided throughout *Realidades.*

For example, in preparing for a speaking task, students think through what they might want to say using a chart. In writing, they might fill out a word web before attempting the first draft. By providing a scaffold that asks students to think, plan, process, and then communicate, more students will become effective communicators.

The Role of Grammar in a Communicative Classroom

In a proficiency-based curriculum, vocabulary and grammar are viewed as tools that students need in order to communicate, rather than as ends in themselves.

Input grammar in context

For students to internalize grammar, it needs to be presented in a meaningful context. For example, students can grasp the concept of the preterite more easily if it is presented within a topic, like shopping. As the teacher presents clothing and store vocabulary, she can tell the class what items of clothing she or another person bought, when it was purchased, and how much was paid. As the teacher points to a picture of a sweater on an overhead transparency or clip art or an actual sweater, she begins with comprehensible input that uses the *yo* form of the preterite: *Ayer, yo fui de compras y compré un suéter nuevo. Y pagué veinte dólares. No es mucho, ¿verdad?* Repetition of the input can continue with other articles of clothing, allowing students to easily deduce and internalize the meaning of *compré* and *pagué.* The teacher then begins to ask students questions using *compraste* and *pagaste* and makes summary comments about what is said in the class, drawing other students into the discussion as she introduces other preterite forms. As students begin to internalize these forms and the chapter vocabulary, they begin to make simple statements or ask questions to a partner about shopping for clothing.

Input grammar in small, manageable chunks

Present new grammar in manageable chunks that can be immediately practiced. In the example above, students can use a few preterite forms of *comprar* and *pagar* as they talk about shopping. Additional *-ar* verbs and other preterite forms can be added as students become comfortable using *comprar* and *pagar.*

Input grammar in readings

Grammar input can also take place through reading. As students read sentences, short paragraphs, and dialogues with supporting contextual and visual cues, they can understand new grammatical forms. Through carefully planned out questions asked by their teacher, students can be led to explain grammatical concepts.

Teach what is needed for the immediate communication objectives

Teach students the grammar needed to accomplish the communicative objective. This allows students to learn the concept in context and practice. For example, if you teach *pensar* or *querer* in connection with a theme, don't give students an additional list of all *ie* stem-changing verbs. Rather, teach additional *ie* verbs in later chapters as they connect to the themes.

Practice grammar in a variety of activities

Just as there are several ways to provide input, there are many useful methods for practicing grammar. This practice can involve hands-on activities and games that let students manipulate grammatical structures. Grammar practice is effectively integrated into communicative activities such as surveys, Venn diagrams, and paired and group activities. In addition, practice can involve activities on **realidades.com** where students can practice grammar again and again at their own pace.

Grammar and communication

Grammar can be successfully integrated in a communicative classroom with activities that deal with grammatical accuracy at different levels. When presented in meaningful contexts, in manageable chunks, and with presentation and practice that incorporate a variety of activities, students will develop increasing accuracy with grammar.

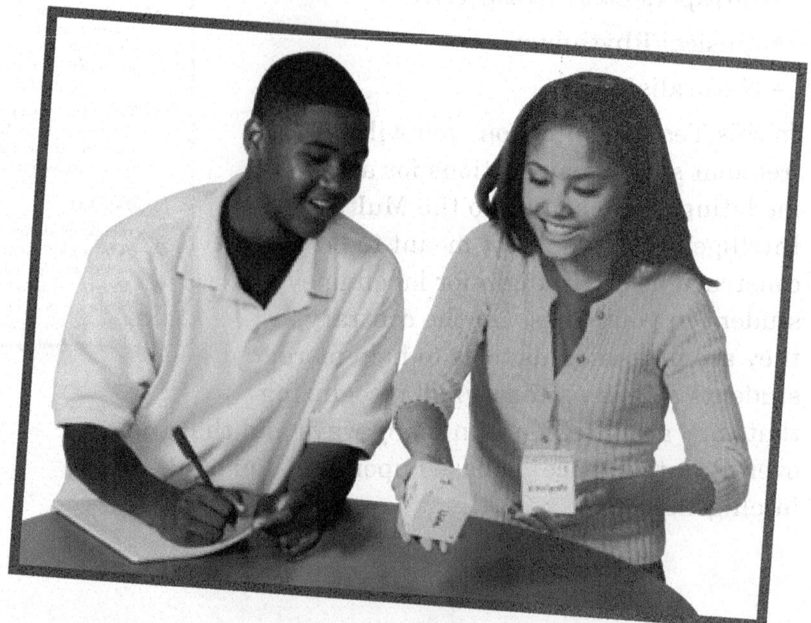

Pair and Group Activities in a Communicative Classroom

Benefits of group work

Effective group work develops a friendly and cooperative atmosphere by giving students a chance to get to know each other better. This sense of camaraderie leads to a more relaxed classroom in which students are more willing to talk and to participate. Group work also allows more opportunity for "student talk," thereby increasing the quantity of student practice in the target language.

Grouping options and techniques

The communicative activities in a Spanish classroom allow for a variety of grouping options.

The most common option is random grouping that includes pairing up two students or creating small groups of three to five students. Some possible ways to randomly group students include:

- Count off by going left to right or up and down in rows.
- Write on pieces of paper vocabulary words (English/Spanish), countries/capitals, opposites, colors, or categories that can be matched up, in a bag. Have students draw a piece of paper and find their partner(s).
- Order students along a continuum by birthday, height, phone numbers, etc.
- Place numbers or a deck of cards in a hat, bag, or box and have students draw.
- Turn to the student to the left or right, front or back.

Another grouping option is to place students by their ability level. Homogeneous grouping allows students of similar ability to work together. In this case, teachers assign tasks based upon the ability level of the group. Advanced students are given a more challenging task. Other students are given tasks that they can successfully complete. Heterogeneous grouping places students of varying abilities together. This allows for stronger students to help weaker students.

Grouping students by interest level is another option to consider. Students could group themselves for an activity or longer project based upon mutual interest.

Planning and facilitating an effective group activity

- Make sure that the task involves a true exchange of information.
- Think through the language functions and content information to make certain students can complete the task.
- Prepare all materials in advance and anticipate questions.
- Explain the task before the students break up into groups. Be sure to model the task if necessary.
- Determine in advance how students will be evaluated and share those criteria with the class.
- Allow adequate time for the task. Make sure at least three quarters of the students at different ability levels can complete it. Tell students how much time they have and stick to the plan.
- Encourage students to stay on task by walking around the class and monitoring the groups.
- Build into your grading system a way to include group participation and staying on task.
- Develop some sort of follow-up upon completion of the task.

Error correction

As students work in groups, they will be making mistakes. Here are strategies that can help students focus on accuracy while doing group work.

- Listen for common errors while monitoring the class. If the error is one of vocabulary usage or grammar, discuss the error with the class and do some focused practice once the task is completed. If the error is one of meaning (very common in beginning writing), have the class work together to determine how best to express the message.
- If you want to correct an individual student error, correct the student only after he or she has spoken. Restate the student's response using the correction in your restatement.

Integrating Technology in the Classroom

For the Teacher

Realidades provides many time-saving digital resources to help teachers plan, teach, assess, and remediate or enrich instruction.

	Teacher Resources	eText	realidades.com	DVD
Planning	• Interactive Teacher's Edition (ITE) with Resource Library		•	ITE with Resource Library
	• Teacher Resources (PDF files)		•	ITE with Resource Library
	• Lesson Plans (PDF files with links)		•	
	• DK Bilingual Visual Dictionary (enrichment)		•	Activities and Tools for Interactive Whiteboards DVD-ROM
Chapter Opener	• *Videocultura* Videos		•	*Videocultura* Video Program
	• Fine Art and Map Transparencies		•	PresentationExpress™ Premium DVD-ROM
Vocabulario en contexto	• Audio	•	•	Audio Program, PresentationExpress™ Premium DVD-ROM
	• *Videohistoria* Videos	•	•	Video Program
	• Transparencies, Clip Art		•	PresentationExpress™ Premium DVD-ROM
	• *Prueba:* Voc. Recognition Quiz		•	ITE with Resource Library
Vocabulario en uso	• Interactive Whiteboard Vocabulary Activities		•	Activities and Tools for Interactive Whiteboards DVD-ROM
	• *Videomodelos* Videos	•	•	*Videomodelos* Video Program
	• Audio	•	•	Audio Program
	• *Prueba:* Voc. Production Quiz with Study Plan		•	ITE with Resource Library
Gramática y vocabulario en uso	• Interactive Whiteboard Grammar Activities		•	Activities and Tools for Interactive Whiteboards DVD-ROM
	• *GramActiva* Videos	•	•	PresentationExpress™ DVD, Video Program
	• Tutorial Videos		•	
	• Animated Verbs	•	•	PresentationExpress™ Premium DVD-ROM
	• *Videomodelos* Videos	•	•	*Videomodelos* Video Program
	• Audio	•	•	PresentationExpress™ DVD, Audio Program
	• Transparencies		•	PresentationExpress™ Premium DVD-ROM
	• *Canciones de hip hop*		•	
	• *Prueba:* Grammar Quiz with Study Plan		•	ITE with Resource Library
¡Adelante!	• *¿Eres tú, María?* Videos	•		Video Program
Repaso del capítulo	• Integrated Performance Assessment		•	ITE with Resource Library
	• Situation Cards		•	ITE with Resource Library
	• *Examen del capítulo*		•	ITE with Resource Library
	• ExamView® Assessment Suite			ExamView® Assessment Suite CD-ROM

For the Student

Realidades is ready for today's digital learner! Through **realidades.com,** students can access a wide array of interactive online activities and multimedia resources. They can monitor their own progress, complete graded assignments and assessments, record speaking tasks, explore the Spanish-speaking world, and much more! Here is a list of the resources available for students on **realidades.com.**

	Student Resources	Auto-graded	Teacher-graded
Chapter Opener	*Mapa global interactivo*		•
	eText *Actividades*	•	•
	Videocultura and *Actividades*		•
	DK Reference Atlas		
Vocabulario en contexto	eText *Actividades*	•	•
	Flashcards	•	
	Videohistoria and *Actividades*	•	•
	Instant Check	•	
	Workbook activities	•	•
	Quiz	•	•
	Additional practice	•	
Vocabulario en uso	eText *Actividades*	•	•
	Videomodelos		
	RealTalk! speaking tasks		•
	Workbook activities	•	•
	Quiz with Study Plans	•	
	Communicative Pair Activities		•
Gramática y vocabulario en uso	eText *Actividades*	•	•
	GramActiva and *Actividad*	•	
	Tutorials, Animated Verbs		
	Canciones de hip hop		
	Instant Check	•	
	Workbook activities	•	•
	RealTalk! speaking tasks		•
	Quizzes with Study Plans	•	
	Additional practice	•	
¡Adelante!	eText *Actividades*	•	•
	Presentación oral		•
	Culture Reading Activity		•
	Workbook activities	•	•
	¿Eres tú, María? and *Actividades*	•	•
	DK Bilingual Visual Dictionary		
Repaso del capítulo	eText *Actividades*	•	•
	Games and Puzzles	•	
	Instant Check and Self-Test	•	
	Workbook activities	•	
	Situation Cards		•
	Integrated Performance Assessment		•
	Examen del capítulo	•	•

Bibliography

realidades.com

Go online for links to state and national professional organizations, regional conferences, Web sites of interest, and Listservs.

Assessment

Boyles, Peggy. "Assessing the Speaking Skill in the Classroom: New Solutions to an Ongoing Problem." *Northeast Conference Reports: Testing, Teaching, and Assessment,* ed. Charles R. Hancock. Lincolnwood, IL: National Textbook Company, 1994.

Cooper, Thomas C., Daniel J. Yanosky II, and Joseph M. Wisenbaker. "Foreign Language Learning and SAT Verbal Scores Revisited." *Foreign Language Annals,* Summer 2008.

James, W. "Formative Assessment: Why, What, and Whether," from *Transformative Assessment*, W. James. Popham, Chapter 1. ASCD Member Book, 2008.

Liskin-Gasparro, Judith. "Assessment: From Content Standards to Student Performance." *National Standards. A Catalyst for Reform*, ed. Robert Lafayette. Lincolnwood, IL: National Textbook Co., 1996.

National K–12 Foreign Language Resource Center. "National Assessment Summit Papers", *New Visions in Action,* Iowa State University, 2005.

New Visions in Action: National Assessment Summit Papers, ed. Marcia Harmon Rosenbusch, National K–12 Foreign Language Resource Center, Iowa State University, 2005.

Pettigrew, Frances and Ghislaine Tulou. "Performance Assessment for Language Students." *Language Learners of Tomorrow: Process and Promise,* ed. Margaret Ann Kassen. Lincolnwood, IL: National Textbook Co., 1999.

Tomlinson, Carol Ann. "Learning to Love Assessment." *Educational Leadership,* Jan. 2008.

Block Scheduling

Blaz, Deborah. *Teaching Foreign Languages on the Block.* Larchmont, NY: Eye on Education, 1998.

Canady, R. L., and M. D. Rettig. *Block Scheduling: A Catalyst for Change in High Schools.* Larchmont, NY: Eye on Education, 1995.

———. *Teaching on the Block: Strategies for Engaging Active Learners.* Larchmont, NY: Eye on Education, 1996.

Culture

Byram, Michael. *Teaching and Assessing Intercultural Competence.* Clevedon, U.K.: Multilingual Matters, 1997.

Fantini, Alvino. "Comparisons: towards the Development of Intercultural Competence." *Foreign Language Standards: Linking Theory, Research, and Practice,* ed. June Phillips. Lincolnwood, IL: National Textbook Co., 1999.

Galloway, Vicki. "Bridges and Boundaries: Growing the Cross-Cultural Mind." *Language Learners of Tomorrow: Process and Promise.* Lincolnwood, IL: National Textbook Co., 1999.

Heusvinkveld, Paula R., ed. *Pathways to Culture*. Yarmouth, ME: Intercultural Press, Inc. 1997.

Koning, Patricia. "Let's Go to the Movies." *The Language Editor,* Vol. 6, Issue 4 (2011): 32–36.

Curriculum and Instruction

ACTFL Performance Guidelines for K–12 Learners. Yonkers, NY: ACTFL, 1999.

"Challenge for a New Era." *Nebraska K–12 Foreign Language Frameworks.* Lincoln: Nebraska Department of Education, 1996.

Chamot, Anna U. "Reading and Writing Processes: Learning Strategies in Immersion Classrooms." *Language Learners of Tomorrow: Process and Promise,* ed. Margaret Ann Kassen. Lincolnwood, IL: National Textbook Company, 1999.

Davis, Robert. "Group Work is NOT Busy Work: Maximizing Success of Group Work in the L2 Classroom." *Foreign Language Annals,* Vol. 30 (1997): 265–279.

Ferguson, Susan. "Breathing Life Into Foreign Language Reading," *Educational Leadership,* Vol. 63 No. 2 (2005): 63–65.

Foreign Language Framework for California Public Schools Kindergarten Through Grade Twelve. Sacramento: California State Department of Education, 2002.

Guntermann, G., ed. *Teaching Spanish with the Five C's: A Blueprint for Success.* New York: Harcourt College Publishers, 2000.

Hall, Joan Kelly. "The Communication Standards." *Foreign Language Standards: Linking Theory, Research, and Practice,* ed. June Phillips. Lincolnwood, IL: National Textbook Co., 1999.

Jackson, Claire, et al. *Articulation & Achievement: Connecting Standards, Performance, and Assessment in Foreign Language.* New York: College Board of Publications, 1996.

Klee, Carol A. "Communication as an Organizing Principle in the National Standards: Sociolinguistic Aspects of Spanish Language Teaching." *Hispania.* Vol. 81 (2) (1998), pp. 339–351.

Krashen, Stephen. *Principles and Practice in Second Language Acquisition.* Oxford: Pergamon Press, 1982.

Met, Myriam, with J. Phillips. *Curriculum Handbook.* Association for Supervision and Curriculum Development, 1999.

———. "Making Connections." *Foreign Language Standards: Linking Theory, Research, and Practice,* ed. June Phillips. Lincolnwood, IL: National Textbook Co., 1999.

Moeller, Aleidine. "Optimizing Student Success: Focused Curriculum, Meaningful Assessment, and Effective Instruction," *The 2005 Report of the Central States Conference on the Teaching of Foreign Languages. The Year of Languages: Challenges, Changes, and Choices,* ed. Peggy Boyles and Paul Sandrock. Eau Claire, WI: Crown Prints. 2005.

National K–12 Foreign Language Resource Center. "A Guide to Aligning Curriculum with the Standards." Ames: Iowa State University, 1996.

———. *Bringing the Standards into the Classroom: A Teacher's Guide.* Ames: Iowa State University, 1997.

Patrick, Paula. "The Keys to the Classroom." *The ACTFL Guide for Professional Language Education.* ACTFL, 2007.

Standards for Foreign Language Learning in the 21st Century: Including Chinese, Classical Languages, French, German, Italian, Japanese, Portuguese, Russian, and Spanish. Lawrence, KS: Allen Press, 1999.

VanPatten, Bill and Wong, Wynne. "The Evidence is IN: Drills are OUT." *Foregin Language Annals,* Fall 2003.

Zaslow, Brandon. "Teaching Language for Proficiency: From Theory to Practice (An Instructional Framework)." Unpublished document. School of Education, University of California, Los Angeles, 2001.

Heritage Learners

Blanco, George. "El hispanohablante y la gramática." *Bilingual Research Journal* 18 (1995): 23–46.

Colombi, Cecilia M. and Francisco X. Alarcón, eds. *La enseñanza del español a hispanohablantes: Praxis y teoría.* Boston: Houghton Mifflin Co., 1997.

Rodríguez-Pino, Cecilia, and Daniel Villa. "A Student-Centered Spanish for Native Speakers Program: Theory, Curriculum Design, and Outcome Assessment." *Faces in a Crowd: The Individual Learner in Multisection Courses,* ed. Carol Klee. Boston: Heinle and Heinle, 1994.

Miller, Barbara L., and John B. Webb, eds. *Teaching Heritage Language Learners: Voices from the Classroom,* ACTFL Series. Princeton: Princeton University, 2000.

Methodology

Hadley, Alice Omaggio. *Teaching Language in Context,* 3rd ed. Boston: Heinle and Heinle, 2001.

Hall, Joan Kelly. *Methods for Teaching Foreign Languages: Creating a Community of Learners in the Classroom.* Upper Saddle River, NJ: Merrill Prentice Hall, 2001.

Hamilton, Heidi E., Crane, Cori, Bartoshesky, Abigal. "Doing Foreign Language: Bringing Concordia Language Villages into Language Classrooms." Pearson Education, Inc. 2005.

Lee, James, and Bill Van Patten. *Making Communicative Language Teaching Happen.* New York: McGraw Hill, 1995.

Oxford, Rebecca L. *Language Learning Strategies: What Every Teacher Should Know.* New York: Newbury House, 1990.

Shrum, Judith, and Eileen Glisan. *Teacher's Handbook: Contextualized Language Instruction.* Boston: Heinle and Heinle, 1994.

Multiple Intelligences

Armstrong, Thomas. *Multiple Intelligences in the Classroom.* Alexandria, VA: Association for Supervision and Curriculum Development, 1994.

Gardner, Howard. *Frames of Mind: The Theory of Multiple Intelligences.* New York, NY: Basic Books, 1983.

Lazear, David. *Seven Pathways of Learning: Teaching Students and Parents about Multiple Intelligences.* Tucson, AZ: Zephyr Press, 1994.

Middle School

Raven, Patrick T. and Jo Anne S. Wilson. "Middle-School Foreign Language: What Is It? What Should It Be?" *Visions and Reality in Foreign Language Teaching: Where We Are, Where We Are Going,* ed. William N. Hatfield. Lincolnwood, IL: National Textbook Co., 1993.

Verkler, Karen W. "Middle School Philosophy and Second Language Acquisition Theory: Working Together for Enhanced Proficiency." *Foreign Language Annals,* Vol. 27 (1994): 19–42.

Differentiated Instruction & Inclusion

Ganschow, Leonore, and Richard Sparks. "A Screening Instrument for the Identification of Foreign Language Learning Problems." *Foreign Language Annals,* Vol. 24 (1991): 383–398.

———, and James Javorsky, John Patton, Jane Pohlman, Richard Sparks. "Test Comparisons among Students Identified as High-Risk, Low-Risk, and Learning Disabled in High School Foreign Language Courses," *The Modern Language Journal,* Vol. 76 (1992): 142–159.

Sax Mabbott, Ann. "An Exploration of Reading Comprehension, Oral Reading Errors, and Written Errors by Subjects Labeled Learning Disabled." *Foreign Language Annals,* Vol. 27 (1994): 294–324.

Sheppard, Marie. "Proficiency as an Inclusive Orientation: Meeting the Challenge of Diversity." *Reflecting on Proficiency from the Classroom Perspective,* ed. June Phillips. Lincolnwood, IL: National Textbook Co., 1993.

Tomlinson, Carol Ann and McTighe, Jay. "Integrating Differentiated Instruction & Understanding by Design." ASCD Publication, 2006.

Treviño, María. "Inclusion in the languages other than English classroom." *LOTE CED Communiqué,* Issue 9. Austin, TX: 2003.

Technology

Moore, Zena T. "Technology and Teaching Culture: What Spanish Teachers Do. *Foreign Language Annals,* Vol. 39, No. 4, pp. 579–593.

Muyskens, Judith Ann., ed. *New Ways of Learning and Teaching: Focus on Technology and Foreign Language Education.* Boston: Heinle and Heinle, 1997.

21st Century Skills

Simplicio, Joseph S.C. *Educating the 21st Century Student.* Bloomington, IN: AuthorHouse, 2007.

Trilling, Bernie and Charles Fadel. *21st Century Skills: Learning for Life in Our Times.* San Francisco, CA: Jossey-Bass, 2009.

Understanding by Design

Wiggins, Grant and McTighe, Jay. *Understanding by Design,* 2nd edition. ASCD Publication, 2005.

Index of Cultural References

D

E

F

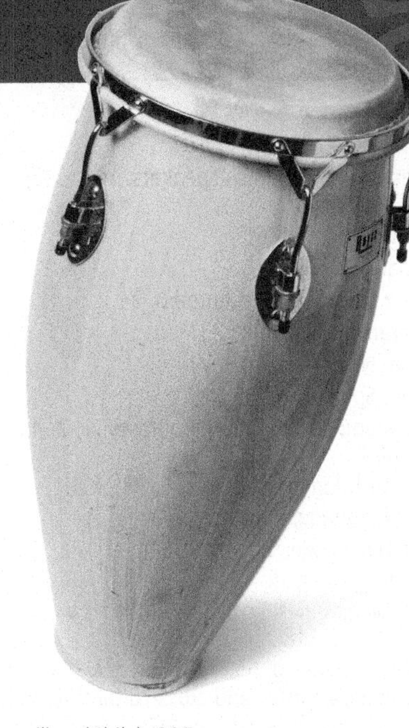

G

Index of Cultural References

P

Q

R

S

realidades.com

Digital Edition

Peggy Palo Boyles
OKLAHOMA CITY, OK

Myriam Met
ROCKVILLE, MD

Richard S. Sayers
LONGMONT, CO

Carol Eubanks Wargin

PEARSON

Boston, Massachusetts | Chandler, Arizona
Glenview, Illinois | Upper Saddle River, New Jersey

WE DEDICATE THIS BOOK TO THE
MEMORY OF OUR ESTEEMED COLLEAGUE,

Carol Eubanks Wargin.

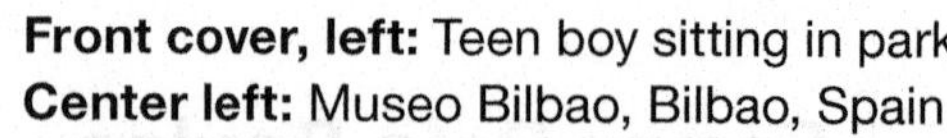

Front cover, left: Teen boy sitting in park
Center left: Museo Bilbao, Bilbao, Spain
Center right: Girls in Nicaraguan dresses, Miami Arts in the Street, Independence of Central America and Mexico Cultural Integration Day, Miami, Florida
Right: Chac-Mool figure at Cancún, Yucatán Peninsula, Mexico

Acknowledgments appear on pages 511–513, which constitute an extension of this copyright page.

ISBN-13: 978-0-13-319965-9
ISBN-10: 0-13-319965-7

PEARSON

5 6 7 8 9 10 V063 17 16 15 14 13

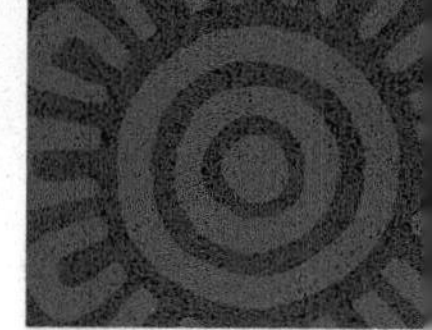

Realidades 1

Digital Edition

Realidades Authors

Peggy Palo Boyles

During her foreign language career of over thirty years, Peggy Palo Boyles has taught elementary, secondary, and university students in both private and public schools. She is currently an independent consultant who provides assistance to schools, districts, universities, state departments of education, and other organizations of foreign language education in the areas of curriculum, assessment, cultural instruction, professional development, and program evaluation. She was a member of the ACTFL Performance Guidelines for the K–12 Learners task force and served as a Senior Editor for the project. She currently serves on the Advisory Committee for the ACTFL Assessment for Performance and Proficiency of Languages (AAPPL). Peggy is a Past-President of the National Association of District Supervisors of Foreign Language (NADSFL) and was a recipient of ACTFL's K–12 Steiner Award for Leadership in K–12 Foreign Language Education. Peggy lives in Oklahoma City, OK with her husband, Del. Their son, Ryan, works at the University of Texas at Arlington.

Myriam Met

For most of her professional life, Myriam (Mimi) Met has worked in the public schools, first as a high school teacher in New York, then as K–12 supervisor of language programs in the Cincinnati Public Schools, and finally as a Coordinator of Foreign Language in Montgomery County (MD) Public Schools. She is currently a Senior Research Associate at the National Foreign Language Center, University of Maryland, where she works on K–12 language policy and infrastructure development. Mimi Met has served on the Advisory Board for the National Standards for Foreign Language Learning, on the Executive Council of ACTFL, and as President of the National Association of District Supervisors of Foreign Languages (NADSFL). She has been honored by ACTFL with the Steiner Award for Leadership in K–12 Foreign Language Education and the Papalia Award for Excellence in Teacher Education.

Richard S. Sayers

Rich Sayers has been an educator in world languages since 1978. He taught Spanish at Niwot High School in Longmont, CO for 18 years, where he taught levels 1 through AP Spanish. While at Niwot High School, Rich served as department chair, district foreign language coordinator, and board member of the Colorado Congress of Foreign Language Teachers. Rich has also served on the Board of the Southwest Conference on Language Teaching. In 1991, Rich was selected as one of the Disney Company's Foreign Language Teacher Honorees for the American Teacher Awards. Rich has served as a world languages consultant for Pearson since 1996. He is currently the Curriculum Specialist Manager for Pearson in the Mountain Region.

Carol Eubanks Wargin

Carol Eubanks Wargin taught Spanish for 20 years at Glen Crest Middle School, Glen Ellyn, IL, and also served as Foreign Languages department chair. In 1997, Ms. Wargin's presentation "From Text to Test: How to Land Where You Planned" was honored as the best presentation at the Illinois Conference on the Teaching of Foreign Languages (ICTFL) and at the Central States Conference on the Teaching of Foreign Languages (CSC). She was twice named Outstanding Young Educator by the Jaycees. Ms. Wargin passed away in 2004.

Contributing Writers

Eduardo Aparicio
Chicago, IL

Daniel J. Bender
New Trier High School
Winnetka, IL

Marie Deer
Bloomington, IN

Leslie M. Grahn
Howard County Public Schools
Ellicott City, MD

Thomasina Hannum
Albuquerque, NM

Nancy S. Hernández
World Languages Supervisor
Simsbury (CT) Public Schools

Patricia J. Kule
Fountain Valley School of Colorado
Colorado Springs, CO

Jacqueline Hall Minet
Upper Montclair, NJ

Alex Paredes
Simi Valley, CA

Martha Singer Semmer
Breckenridge, CO

Dee Dee Drisdale Stafford
Putnam City Schools
Oklahoma City, OK

Christine S. Wells
Cheyenne Mountain Junior High School
Colorado Springs, CO

Michael Werner
University of Chicago
Chicago, IL

National Consultants

María R. Hubbard
Braintree, MA

Patrick T. Raven
Milwaukee, WI

iv

Getting Started with REALIDADES

Why Study Spanish?

Congratulations on your decision to study Spanish! Did you know that more than 425 million people in Spain, 18 Latin American countries, Puerto Rico, Equatorial Guinea, the Philippines, and the United States speak Spanish? It is the second most common language in the United States and the third most commonly spoken language in the world.

Learn to communicate When you study Spanish, you will be able to communicate with the many people in your community and across the globe who speak Spanish. You can bargain in a market, read information on the Internet, and watch television shows. ▶

◀ **Understand culture** The Spanish-speaking world is rich in music, food, art, literature, and everyday traditions. Learning about culture helps you understand other people's perspectives, patterns of behavior, and contributions to the world at large.

Expand career opportunities In today's increasingly global community, your employment and career options expand greatly when you have the right job skills *and* proficiency in Spanish. ▶

◀ **Improve language skills** Studying Spanish improves your first language skills: vocabulary, grammar, reading, and writing. Research shows your test scores may even improve!

v

Online Resources with realidades.com

REALIDADES includes lots of online resources to help you learn Spanish! You can easily link to all of them when you log on to your Home Page within realidades.com. Your teacher will assign some activities, such as the ones in the workbooks. Others you can access on your own.

You'll find these resources highlighted on the pages of your print or online Student Edition with technology icons. Here's a list of the different icons used.

Bilingual Visual Dictionary Links to additional vocabulary words presented visually

Reference Atlas Quick links to the countries in the online atlas

Mapa global interactivo Links to GIS showing locations across the Spanish-speaking world

Videos

Videocultura Cultural overview of each theme

Videohistoria Vocabulary video to help present the new vocabulary

GramActiva Grammar explanations to help present the new grammar

Grammar Tutorials Clear explanations of grammar with comparison to English

Animated Verbs Animations that highlight verb conjugations

¿Eres tú, María? A 10-episode mystery video starting in *Capítulo 5A*

Modelo ***Videomodelos***
Video models of speaking activities

Audio Audio files for vocabulary, listening practice, and pronunciation

Canciones de hip hop Songs to help practice new vocabulary and grammar

Flashcards Practice for the new vocabulary

RealTalk! Speak-and-record tool for speaking activities

***GramActiva* Activity** Extra practice for the *GramActiva* video

Más práctica 

Online practice

Instant Check Short activities that check your progress right away

Guided Workbook Step-by-step vocabulary and grammar practice

Core Workbook Vocabulary and grammar exercises

Communication Workbook Listening, video, and writing activities

Cultural Reading Activity Questions for the *Lectura* reading

Actividades Questions for the *Videomisterio*

Puzzles End-of-chapter games

vi

Getting Started on realidades.com

At the beginning of the year, you'll want to get registered on realidades.com. Your teacher will help you get started. If you log on to realidades.com using a non-school computer, be sure to check out the System Requirements to make sure you are using compatible browsers and have the needed software.

realidades.com Home Page

After you register, you'll land on your realidades.com Home Page. Here you'll be able to access assignments, grades, and study resources. You'll also be able to communicate with your teacher.

You'll find everything that's in the book online as eText.

RealTalk!

You'll be able to record many of your speaking activities using RealTalk! You can use the microphone in your computer or a headset with microphone. If you want, you can download and save your recording.

Mapa global interactivo

Build your geography skills and learn about more locations throughout the Spanish-speaking world. You can download .kmz files from realidades.com and link to sites using Google Earth™ or other geographic information systems.

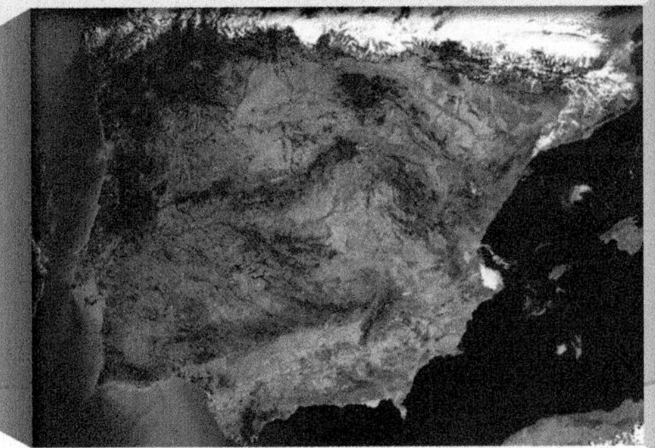

vii

Tabla de materias

Tema 1 Mis amigos y yo

Tema 2 La escuela

Capítulo

2A Tu día en la escuela 72

Capítulo

2B Tu sala de clases 98

Tema 3 La comida

Tema 4 Los pasatiempos

Tema 5 Fiesta en familia

Tema 6 La casa

Capítulo

6A En mi dormitorio 270

Capítulo

6B ¿Cómo es tu casa? 296

Tema 7 De compras

Tema 8 Experiencias

Capítulo 8A De vacaciones 372

Capítulo 8B Ayudando en la comunidad 398

Tema 9 Medios de comunicación

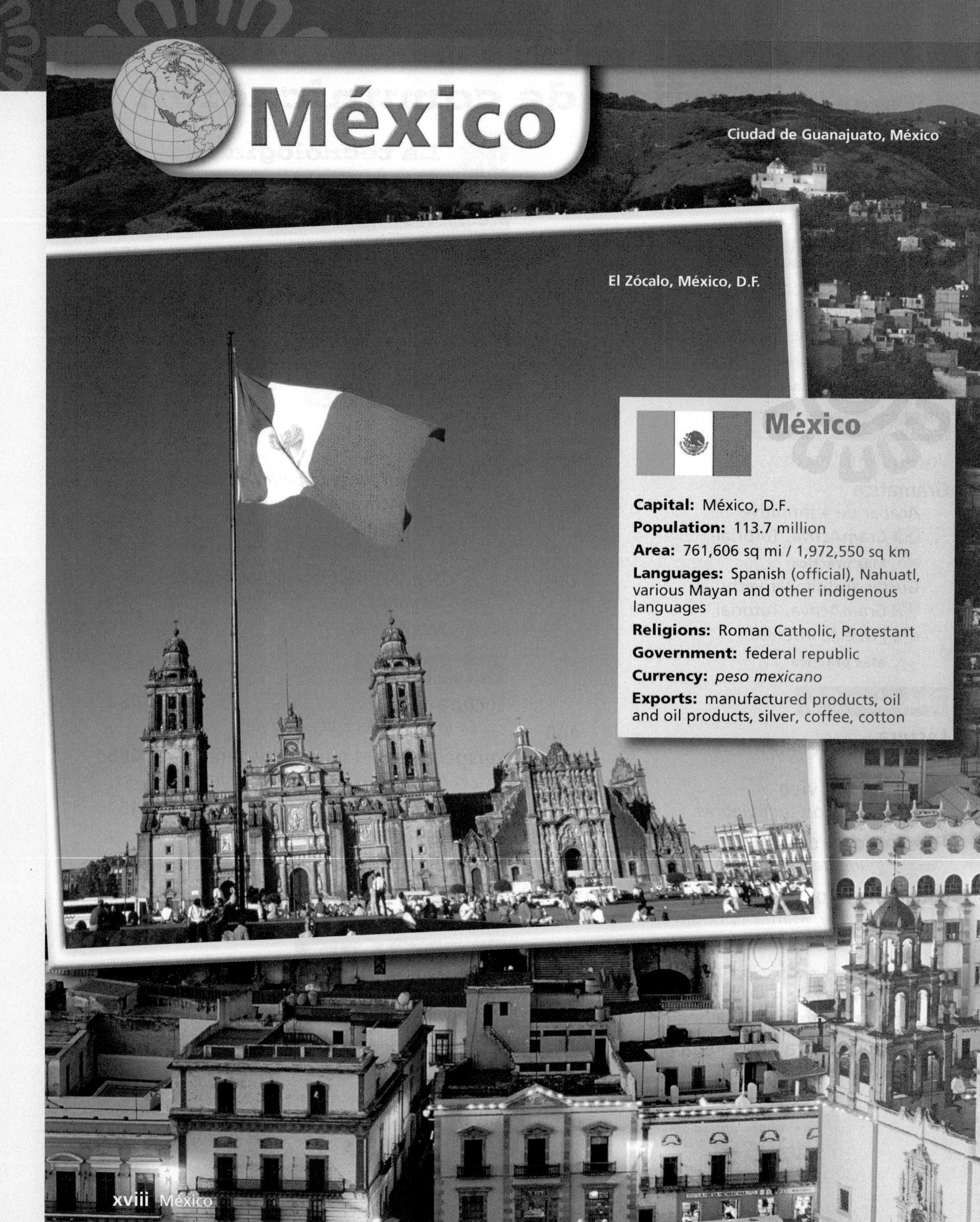

Ciudad de Guanajuato, México

El Zócalo, México, D.F.

México

Capital: México, D.F.

Population: 113.7 million

Area: 761,606 sq mi / 1,972,550 sq km

Languages: Spanish (official), Nahuatl, various Mayan and other indigenous languages

Religions: Roman Catholic, Protestant

Government: federal republic

Currency: *peso mexicano*

Exports: manufactured products, oil and oil products, silver, coffee, cotton

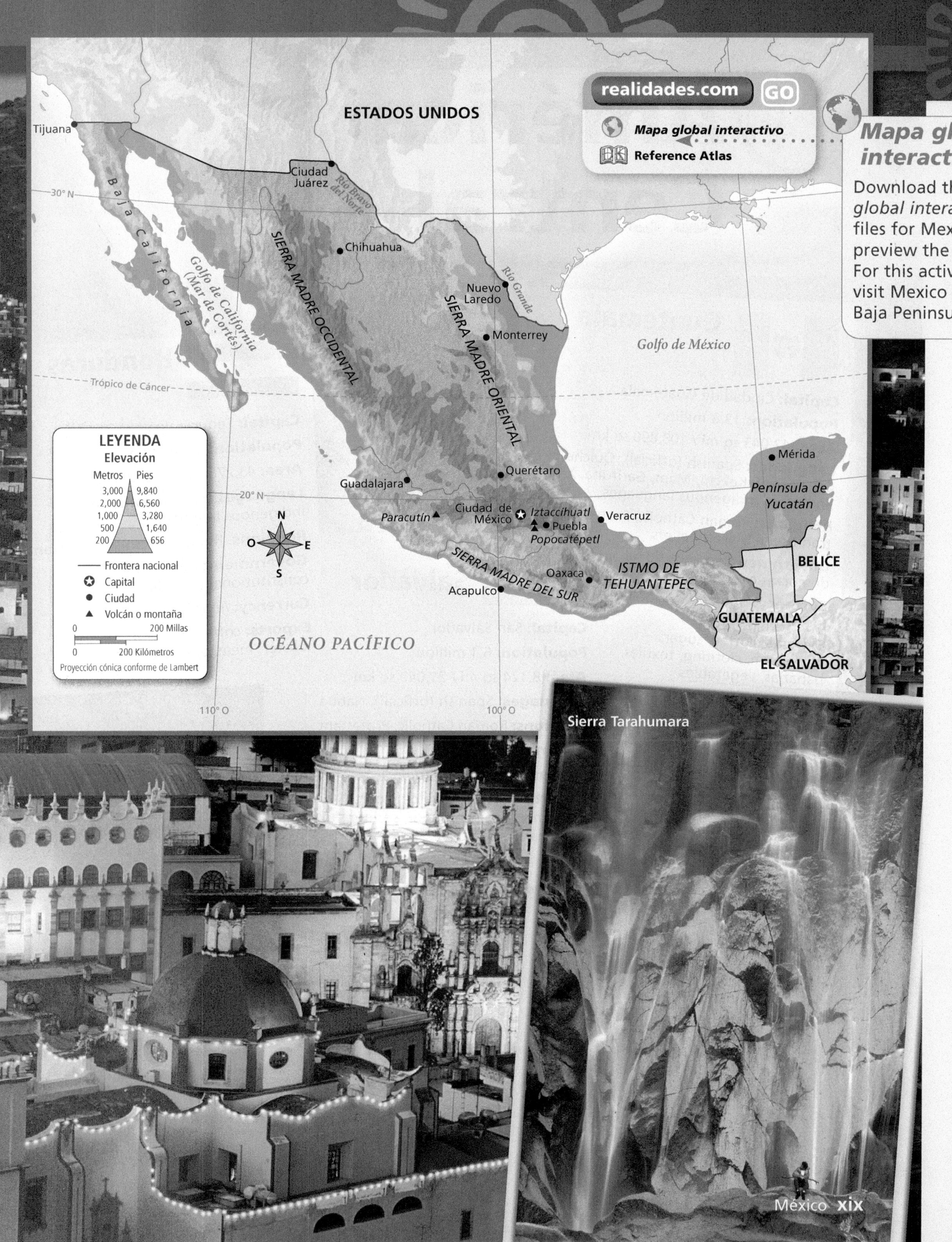

Mapa global interactivo

Download the *Mapa global interactivo* files for Mexico and preview the activity. For this activity, you visit Mexico and the Baja Peninsula.

América Central

Guatemala

Capital: Ciudad de Guatemala

Population: 13.8 million

Area: 42,043 sq mi / 108,890 sq km

Languages: Spanish (official), Quiche, Cakchiquel, Kekchi, Mam, Garifuna, Xinca, and other indigenous languages

Religions: Roman Catholic, Protestant, traditional Mayan beliefs

Government: constitutional democratic republic

Currency: *quetzal*, U.S. dollar *(dólar)*

Exports: coffee, sugar, petroleum, clothing, textiles, bananas, vegetables

El Salvador

Capital: San Salvador

Population: 6.1 million

Area: 8,124 sq mi / 21,040 sq km

Languages: Spanish (official), Nahua

Religions: Roman Catholic, Protestant

Government: republic

Currency: U.S. dollar *(dólar)*

Exports: offshore assembly parts, equipment, coffee, sugar, shrimp, textiles, chemicals, electricity

Honduras

Capital: Tegucigalpa

Population: 8.1 million

Area: 43,278 sq mi / 112,090 sq km

Languages: Spanish (official), indigenous languages

Religions: Roman Catholic, Protestant

Government: democratic constitutional republic

Currency: *lempira*

Exports: coffee, bananas, shrimp, lobster, meat, zinc, wood

El Canal de Panamá

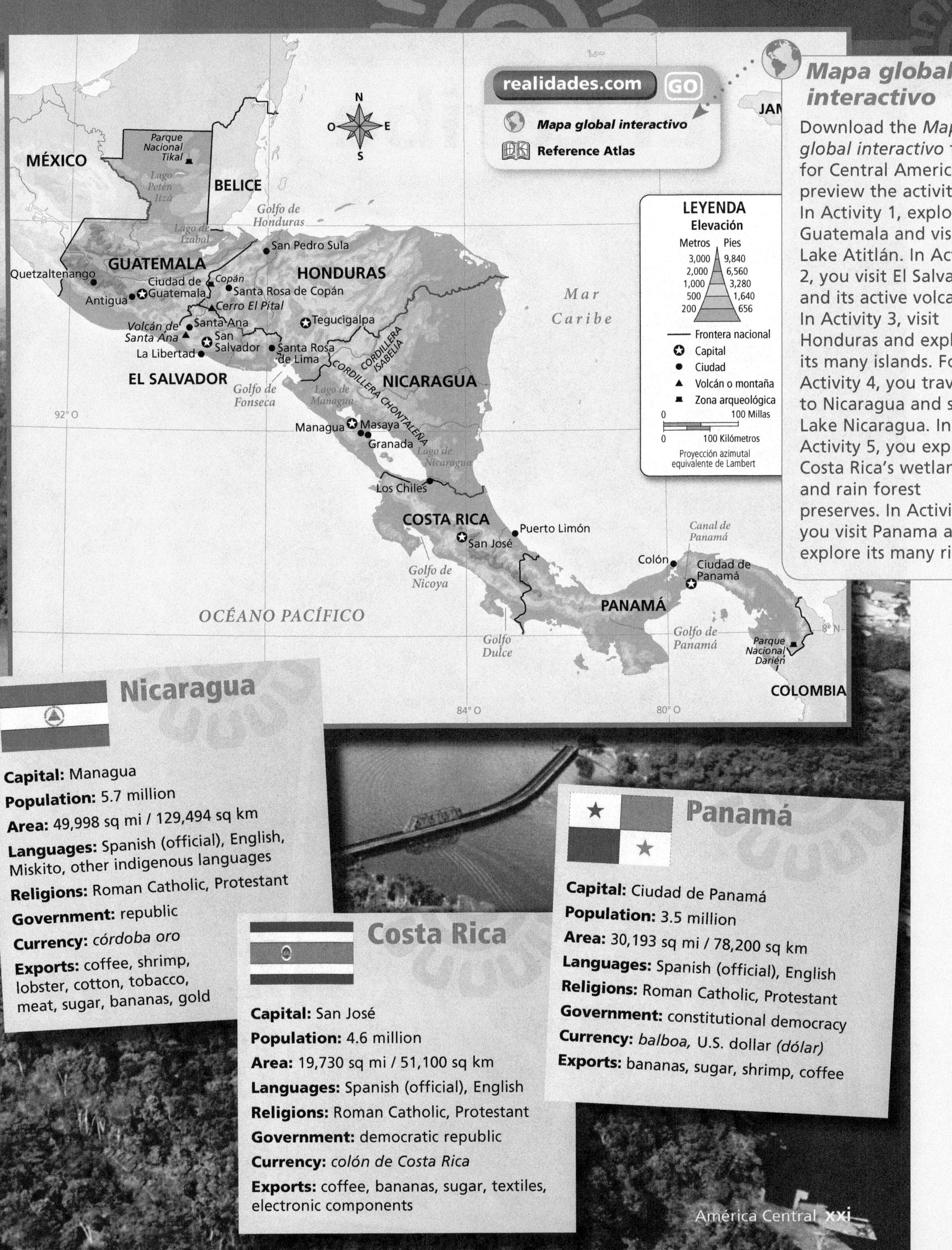

Mapa global interactivo

Download the *Mapa global interactivo* files for Central America and preview the activities. In Activity 1, explore Guatemala and visit Lake Atitlán. In Activity 2, you visit El Salvador and its active volcano. In Activity 3, visit Honduras and explore its many islands. For Activity 4, you travel to Nicaragua and see Lake Nicaragua. In Activity 5, you explore Costa Rica's wetlands and rain forest preserves. In Activity 6, you visit Panama and explore its many rivers.

Nicaragua

Capital: Managua
Population: 5.7 million
Area: 49,998 sq mi / 129,494 sq km
Languages: Spanish (official), English, Miskito, other indigenous languages
Religions: Roman Catholic, Protestant
Government: republic
Currency: *córdoba oro*
Exports: coffee, shrimp, lobster, cotton, tobacco, meat, sugar, bananas, gold

Costa Rica

Capital: San José
Population: 4.6 million
Area: 19,730 sq mi / 51,100 sq km
Languages: Spanish (official), English
Religions: Roman Catholic, Protestant
Government: democratic republic
Currency: *colón de Costa Rica*
Exports: coffee, bananas, sugar, textiles, electronic components

Panamá

Capital: Ciudad de Panamá
Population: 3.5 million
Area: 30,193 sq mi / 78,200 sq km
Languages: Spanish (official), English
Religions: Roman Catholic, Protestant
Government: constitutional democracy
Currency: *balboa*, U.S. dollar *(dólar)*
Exports: bananas, sugar, shrimp, coffee

El Caribe

El Morro, San Juan, Puerto Rico

Un arrecife de coral, República Dominicana

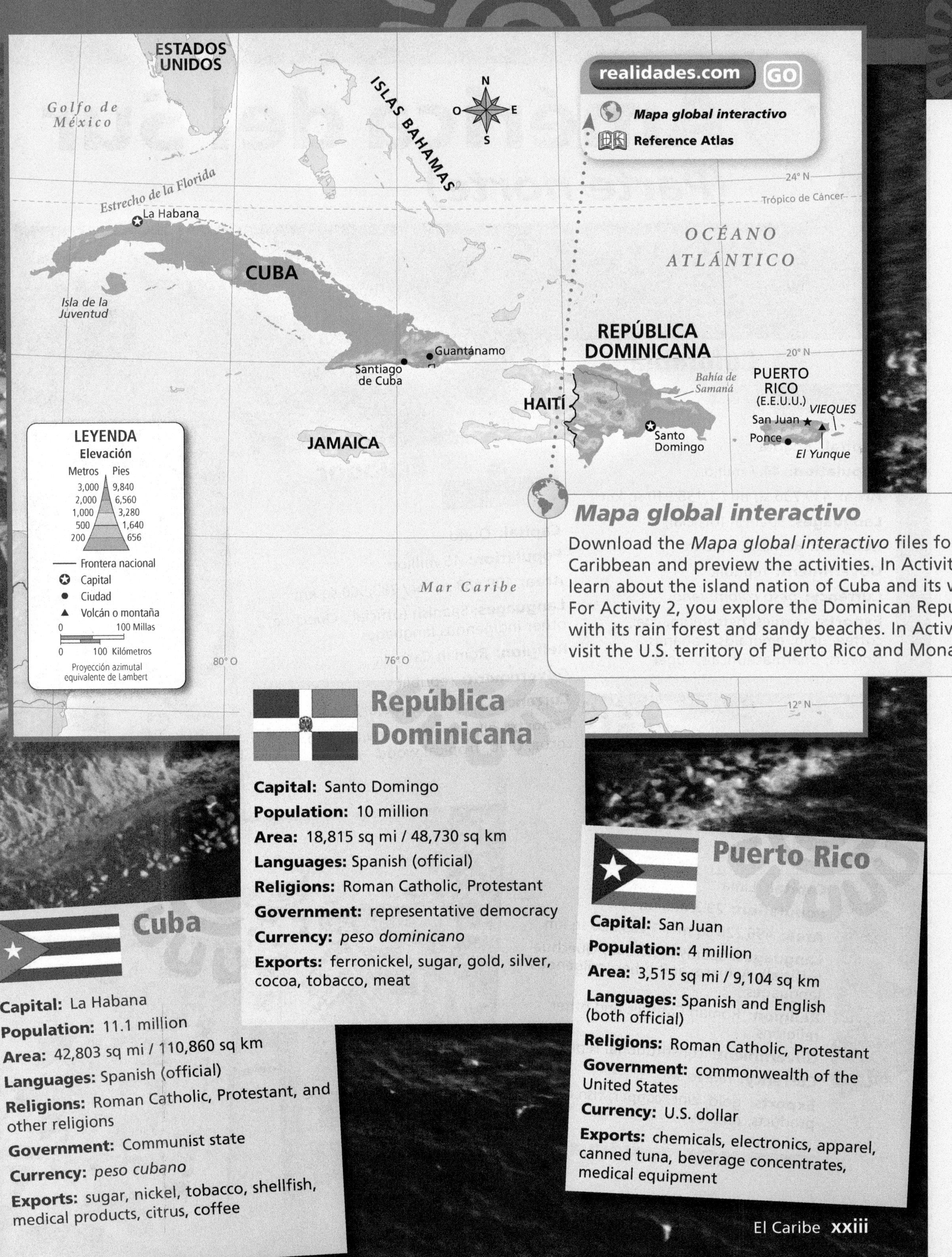

Mapa global interactivo

Download the *Mapa global interactivo* files for the Caribbean and preview the activities. In Activity 1, learn about the island nation of Cuba and its wetlands. For Activity 2, you explore the Dominican Republic with its rain forest and sandy beaches. In Activity 3, visit the U.S. territory of Puerto Rico and Mona Island.

República Dominicana

Capital: Santo Domingo
Population: 10 million
Area: 18,815 sq mi / 48,730 sq km
Languages: Spanish (official)
Religions: Roman Catholic, Protestant
Government: representative democracy
Currency: *peso dominicano*
Exports: ferronickel, sugar, gold, silver, cocoa, tobacco, meat

Cuba

Capital: La Habana
Population: 11.1 million
Area: 42,803 sq mi / 110,860 sq km
Languages: Spanish (official)
Religions: Roman Catholic, Protestant, and other religions
Government: Communist state
Currency: *peso cubano*
Exports: sugar, nickel, tobacco, shellfish, medical products, citrus, coffee

Puerto Rico

Capital: San Juan
Population: 4 million
Area: 3,515 sq mi / 9,104 sq km
Languages: Spanish and English (both official)
Religions: Roman Catholic, Protestant
Government: commonwealth of the United States
Currency: U.S. dollar
Exports: chemicals, electronics, apparel, canned tuna, beverage concentrates, medical equipment

América del Sur
(Parte norte)

Colombia

Capital: Bogotá
Population: 44.7 million
Area: 439,736 sq mi / 1,138,910 sq km
Languages: Spanish (official)
Religion: Roman Catholic
Government: republic
Currency: *peso colombiano*
Exports: textiles, petroleum, coal, coffee, gold, emeralds, bananas, flowers, pharmaceuticals, sugar

Ecuador

Capital: Quito
Population: 15 million
Area: 109,483 sq mi / 283,560 sq km
Languages: Spanish (official), Quechua, other indigenous languages
Religion: Roman Catholic
Government: republic
Currency: U.S. dollar *(dólar)*
Exports: oil, bananas, tuna, shrimp, cocoa, gold, tropical wood

Las ruinas de Machu Picchu, Pe

Perú

Capital: Lima
Population: 29.2 million
Area: 496,226 sq mi / 1,285,220 sq km
Languages: Spanish (official), Quechua (official), Aymara, and other indigenous languages
Religion: Roman Catholic and other religions
Government: constitutional republic
Currency: *nuevo sol*
Exports: gold, zinc, copper, fish and fish products, textiles

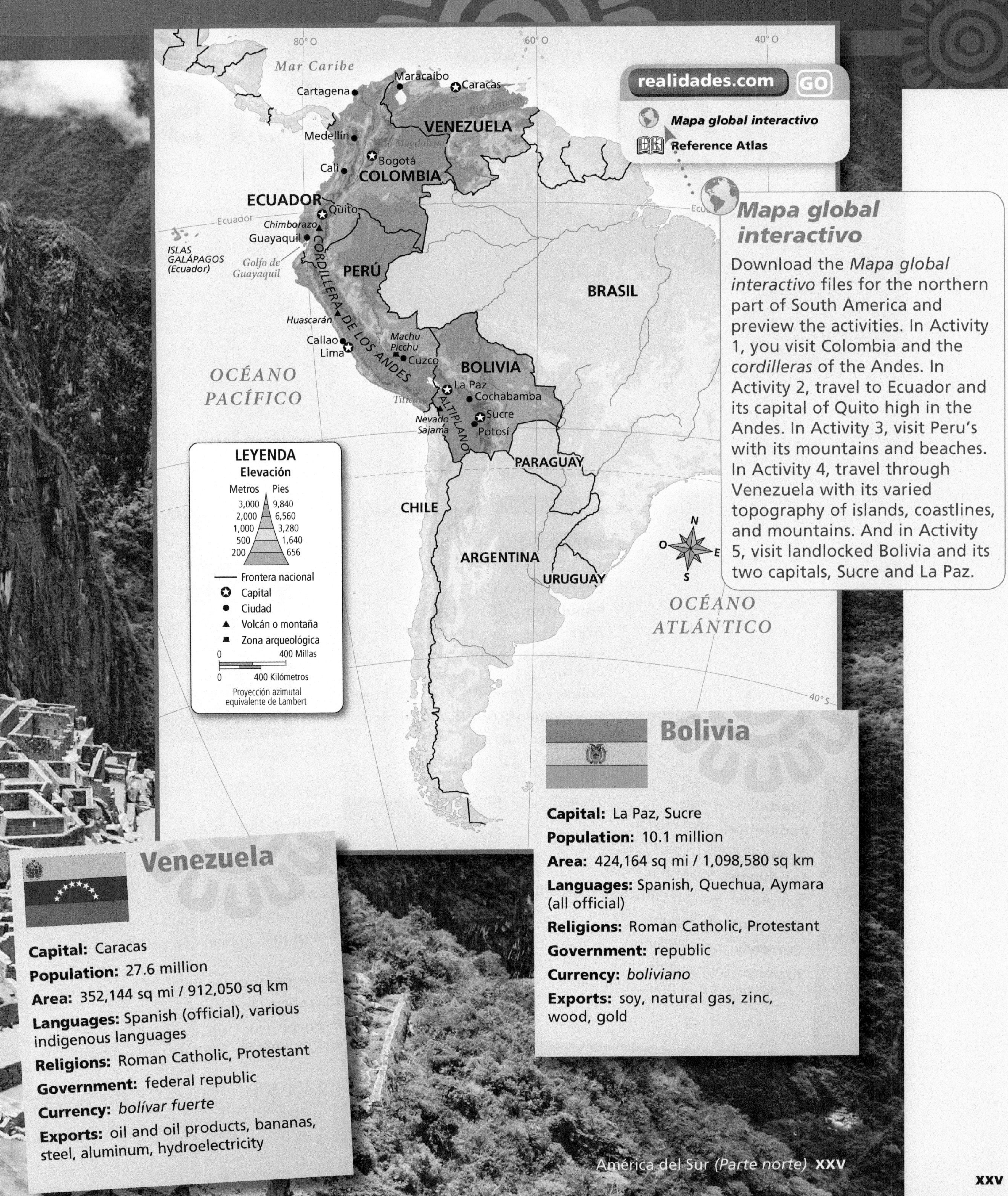

Mapa global interactivo

Download the *Mapa global interactivo* files for the northern part of South America and preview the activities. In Activity 1, you visit Colombia and the *cordilleras* of the Andes. In Activity 2, travel to Ecuador and its capital of Quito high in the Andes. In Activity 3, visit Peru's with its mountains and beaches. In Activity 4, travel through Venezuela with its varied topography of islands, coastlines, and mountains. And in Activity 5, visit landlocked Bolivia and its two capitals, Sucre and La Paz.

Venezuela

Capital: Caracas
Population: 27.6 million
Area: 352,144 sq mi / 912,050 sq km
Languages: Spanish (official), various indigenous languages
Religions: Roman Catholic, Protestant
Government: federal republic
Currency: *bolívar fuerte*
Exports: oil and oil products, bananas, steel, aluminum, hydroelectricity

Bolivia

Capital: La Paz, Sucre
Population: 10.1 million
Area: 424,164 sq mi / 1,098,580 sq km
Languages: Spanish, Quechua, Aymara (all official)
Religions: Roman Catholic, Protestant
Government: republic
Currency: *boliviano*
Exports: soy, natural gas, zinc, wood, gold

América del Sur
(Parte sur)

El Monte Fitz Roy, Patagonia, Argentina

Paraguay

Capital: Asunción
Population: 6.5 million
Area: 157,047 sq mi / 406,750 sq km
Languages: Spanish and Guaraní (both official)
Religions: Roman Catholic, Protestant
Government: constitutional republic
Currency: *guaraní*
Exports: sugar, meat, tapioca, hydroelectricity

Chile

Capital: Santiago
Population: 16.9 million
Area: 292,260 sq mi / 756,950 sq km
Languages: Spanish (official)
Religions: Roman Catholic, Protestant
Government: republic
Currency: *peso chileno*
Exports: copper, fish, iron, iodine, fruit, wood, paper and pulp, chemicals

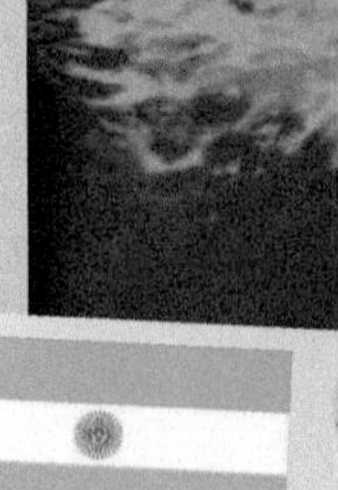

Argentina

Capital: Buenos Aires
Population: 41.8 million
Area: 1,068,302 sq mi / 2,766,890 sq km
Languages: Spanish (official), English, French, Italian, German
Religions: Roman Catholic, Protestant, Jewish
Government: republic
Currency: *peso argentino*
Exports: meat, edible oils, fuels and energy, cereals, feed, motor vehicles

Mapa global interactivo

Download the *Mapa global interactivo* files for the southern part of South America and preview the activities. In Activity 1, you visit Chile and the island of Chiloé. For Activity 2, you travel to Paraguay and explore the Paraná River. Activity 3 takes you to Argentina and its cosmopolitan capital city of Buenos Aires. In Activity 4, visit Uruguay and its beautiful capital city of Montevideo.

Uruguay

Capital: Montevideo
Population: 3.3 million
Area: 68,039 sq mi / 176,220 sq km
Languages: Spanish (official), Portuñol/Brazilero
Religions: Roman Catholic, Protestant, and other religions
Government: constitutional republic
Currency: *peso uruguayo*
Exports: foods, vehicles, meat, rice, timber

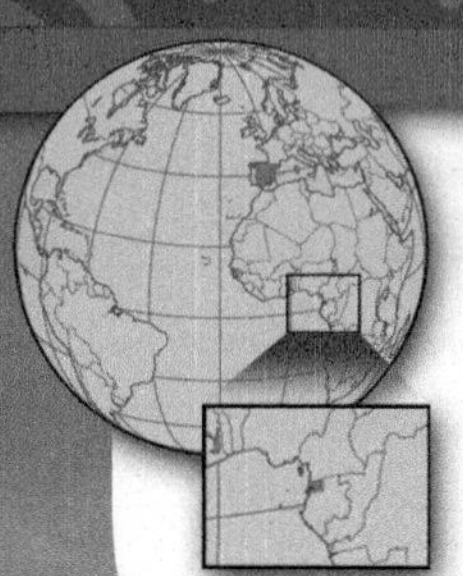

España
Guinea Ecuatorial

España

Capital: Madrid

Population: 46.8 million

Area: 194,897 sq mi / 504,782 sq km

Languages: Castilian Spanish (official); Catalan, Galician, Basque (official regionally)

Religion: Roman Catholic

Government: parliamentary monarchy

Currency: *euro*

Exports: food, machinery, motor vehicles

El Alcázar de Segovia, Segovia, España

realidades.com GO

Mapa global interactivo

Reference Atlas

Mapa global interactivo

Download the *Mapa global interactivo* files for Spain and Equatorial Guinea and preview the activities. For Activity 1, you travel to Spain and the Canary Islands. Activity 2 takes you to Equatorial Guinea, the only Spanish-speaking country in Africa.

Guinea Ecuatorial

Capital: Malabo
Population: 668,225
Area: 10,831 sq mi / 28,051 sq km
Languages: Spanish and French (both official), Fang, Bubi, Ibo, pidgin English
Religions: Roman Catholic, traditional African religions, and other religions
Government: republic
Currency: *franco CFA*
Exports: oil, timber, cocoa, coffee

Playa, Guinea Ecuatorial

Estados Unidos

Estados Unidos

Capital: Washington, D.C.

Population: 313.2 million

Area: 3,717,813 sq mi / 9,631,418 sq km

Languages: English, Spanish, other Indo-European languages, Asian and Pacific Islander languages, other languages

Religions: Protestant, Roman Catholic, Jewish, Muslim, and other religions

Government: federal republic

Currency: U.S. dollar

Exports: motor vehicles, aircraft, medicines, telecommunications equipment, electronics, chemicals, soybeans, fruit, wheat, corn

Las grandes llanuras

Caras estadounidenses

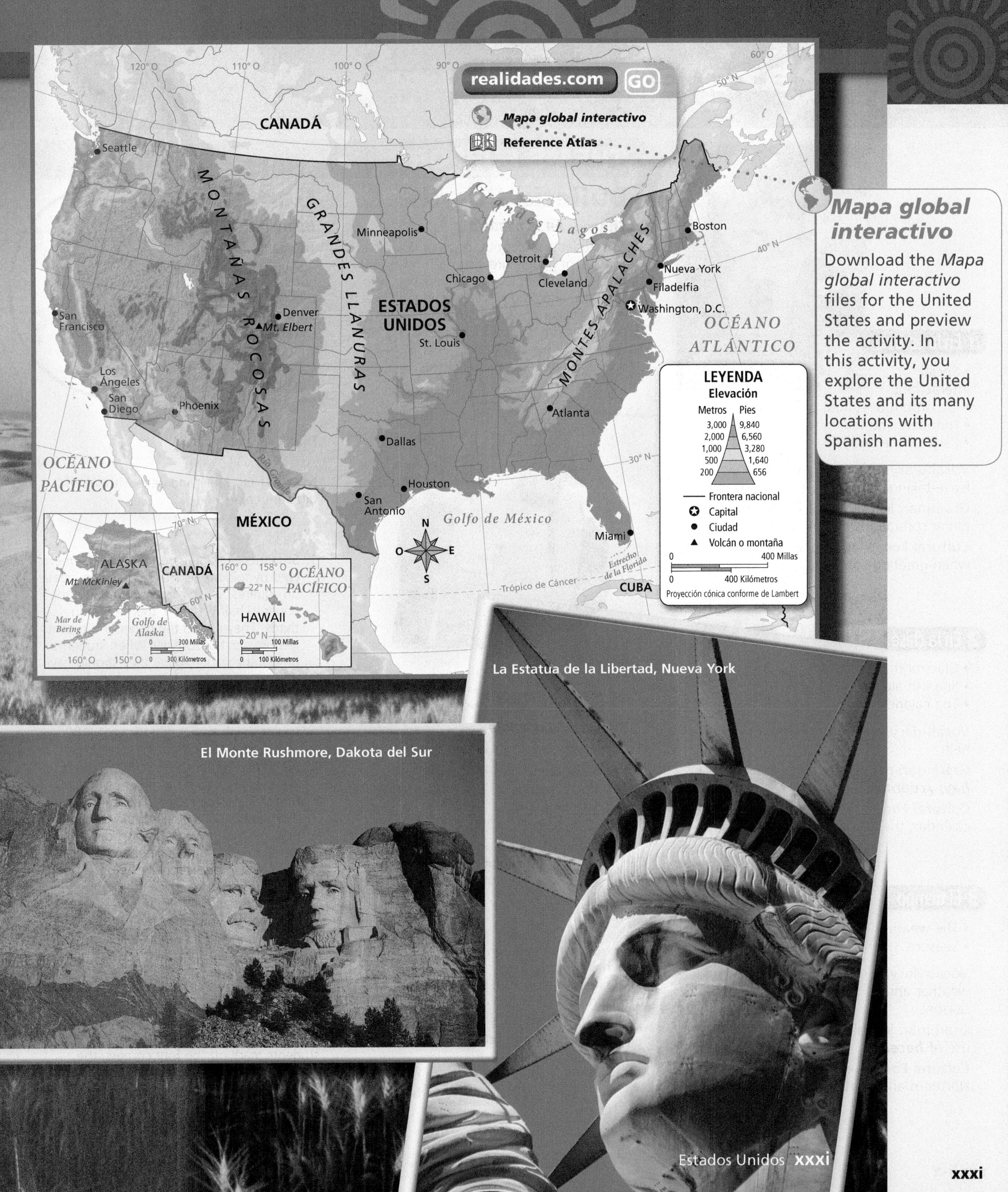

La Estatua de la Libertad, Nueva York

El Monte Rushmore, Dakota del Sur

Mapa global interactivo

Download the *Mapa global interactivo* files for the United States and preview the activity. In this activity, you explore the United States and its many locations with Spanish names.

1 En la escuela

- Social interactions
- Classroom directions
- Numbers and telling time
- Parts of the body

Vocabulary: greetings; introductions; leave-takings; numbers; time; body parts

Grammar: lexical use of ***estar, ser,*** and plural commands

Cultural Focus: appropriate behavior when greeting someone

2 En la clase

- Classroom interactions
- Spanish alphabet
- The calendar

Vocabulary: classroom; date; asking for help

Grammar: nouns; singular definite articles; ***hay; ¿cuántos, -as?***

Cultural Focus: the Aztecs and the Aztec calendar; the Maya and glyphs; holidays

3 El tiempo

- The weather
- Seasons

Vocabulary: weather and seasons

Grammar: lexical use of ***hacer***

Cultural Focus: reversed seasons in the Northern and Southern Hemispheres

THEME SUPPORT

Bulletin Boards

Theme: *En la escuela*

Ask students to cut out, copy, or download pictures of people greeting each other and saying good-bye, teachers interacting with students, and students interacting with each other. Cluster photos according to what the people are doing in each scene: saying hello, saying goodbye, socializing, asking questions, offering assistance, etc.

Hands-on Culture

Recipe: *Guacamole*

Guacamole is a popular dip from Mexico.

Ingredients:

2 ripe avocados
1 small tomato
1 clove garlic, chopped
1 T. of chopped onion juice from 1 lemon
2 T. chopped cilantro
salt

1. Cut the avocados in half, remove the pits, and scoop out the pulp with a spoon.
2. Mash the avocados with a fork.
3. Mix in the garlic, onion, lemon juice, and cilantro.
4. Dice the tomato and fold into mixture.
5. Add salt to taste and serve with tortilla chips.

Game

Número

This game practices numbers and is played like Bingo. Use it toward the end of *En la escuela*, after students have learned numbers 1–100.

Players: entire class

Materials: paper and pens with ink of different colors

Rules:

1. Students each prepare their own ***Número*** card by folding a sheet of paper to create 36 squares. To do this, students fold the paper in half vertically, then fold it in thirds. They unfold the paper and repeat the process horizontally. When students unfold the paper again, they should have 36 squares.
2. Students write ***n-ú-m-e-r-o*** in the top six squares. They then fill in the remaining 30 squares with any number from 1–100. The result should look like a Bingo card.
3. Call out a number from 1–100. Note the number you called on a sheet of paper that students can't see. If students have the number on their card, they cross it out. When a player has marked off an entire row of numbers, either vertically, horizontally, or diagonally, he or she calls out ***Número,*** then reads the numbers aloud in Spanish. If the numbers match the ones you have recorded, that student is the winner. If a number is incorrect, play continues until another student calls out ***Número.***
4. Play again, having students use a pen of a different color to cross out numbers.

Variation: Instead of marking off a row, students mark off the four corners, the borders of the square, or the borders of a smaller square within the card.

THEME PROJECT

Pronóstico del tiempo

Overview: Students write a video script and create maps for a weather forecast for four locations in the Western Hemisphere. They then record their forecast for the class to view.

Resources: poster board, markers, video equipment

Sequence: (suggestions for when to do each step appear throughout the chapter)

STEP **1.** Review instructions so students know what is expected of them. Hand out the "Preliminary Unit Project Instructions and Rubric" from the *Teacher's Resource Book.*

STEP **2.** Students write a rough draft of their weather forecast. They then exchange scripts with a partner for peer editing. Students make corrections based on their partner's comments.

STEP **3.** Students create one or more maps for their forecast on poster board. After completing their map(s), students add drawings or symbols that indicate the weather in each city they plan to talk about and the temperature there.

STEP **4.** Students rehearse their forecast with a partner. Partners give students feedback about the content, accuracy, and presentation of the forecast.

STEP **5.** Students record their weather forecast. Show video to the class.

Options:

1. Students present their forecasts to the class "live" instead of recording them.
2. Students give a presentation on the weather of one location for each season.

Assessment:

Here is a detailed rubric for assessing this project:

Preliminary Unit Project: *Pronóstico del tiempo*

RUBRIC	Score 1	Score 3	Score 5
Evidence of planning	You submitted no written draft.	Your draft was written, but not corrected.	You submitted a corrected draft.
Your use of illustrations	You included no map.	Your map was difficult to read, incomplete, and / or inaccurate.	Your map was easy to read, complete, and accurate.
Your presentation	You did not include the majority of the required elements.	You included some of the following: greeting, name, day, date, weather, and temperature for four locations.	You included all of the following: greeting, name, day, date, weather, and temperature for four locations.

21st Century Skills

Look for tips throughout *Para empezar* to enrich your teaching by integrating 21st Century Skills. Suggestions for the Theme Project and Theme Culture follow below.

Theme Project

Modify the Theme Project with one or more of these suggestions:

Promote Critical Thinking and Problem Solving

Have students research the climates in the four locations they choose and figure out what season it is in the current month. Their maps and weather reports should reflect those seasons. Have students think about the relationship between month and season in those locations, and compare to their own areas.

Foster Media Literacy

Before students use Web sites to learn more about weather and climates in the Western Hemisphere, have them read the handout "Evaluate Web Sites" to help them analyze online materials. Have students think about possible ways to evaluate the accuracy of information in a Web site, and to observe how the material is presented and organized to convey its message.

Encourage Collaboration

Have students working as partners review the four points from the handout "Give an Effective Presentation." Ask them to make sure to include these points in their feedback to their partners as they practice their presentations.

Theme Culture

Develop Social and Cross-Cultural Skills

Have students review their answers to the *Fondo cultural* question on page 1, as well as the information about formal and informal greetings in the chapter. Ask them to discuss in small groups what they have learned so far about differences between their own culture and the culture of Spanish-speaking countries in this respect. Have students imagine they have to explain common forms of greeting in their own culture to a student from a Spanish-speaking country.

PE Para empezar

AT A GLANCE

Objectives

- **Greet people at different times of the day**
- **Introduce yourself to others**
- **Respond to classroom directions**
- **Begin using numbers**
- **Tell time**
- **Identify parts of the body**
- **Talk about things in the classroom**
- **Use the Spanish alphabet to spell words**
- **Talk about the calendar**
- **Describe weather and the seasons**

Vocabulary

- Greetings and leave-takings
- Introductions
- Forms of address
- Ask/tell how you and others are
- Classroom commands
- Numbers 1–100
- Body parts

Grammar

- Nouns
- Singular definite articles
- ***cuántos, -as***
- ***hay***

Culture

- Greetings, pp. 1, 2–4
- First names in the Spanish-speaking world, p. 3
- Mayan glyphs, p. 13
- Mexican holidays, p. 15
- ***Los sanfermines,*** p. 16
- The Aztecs and the Aztec calendar, p. 17
- Reversed seasons in the Northern and Southern Hemispheres, p. 20

RESOURCES

	FOR THE STUDENT	ONLINE	DVD	PRINT	FOR THE TEACHER	ONLINE	PREEXP	DVD	PRINT
Plan					Interactive TE and Resources DVD	•		•	
					Teacher's Resource Book, pp. 1–38	•		•	•
					Pre-AP* Resource Book, pp. 60–61	•		•	•
					Lesson Plans	•			•
					Mapa global interactivo	•			
Introducción PP. **xxxii–1**									
Present	Student Edition, pp. xxxii–1	•	•	•	Interactive TE and Resources DVD	•		•	
	DK Reference Atlas	•	•		Teacher's Resource Book, pp. 2–5	•		•	•
	Hispanohablantes WB, pp. x–1			•	Galería de fotos		•		
En la escuela PP. **2–9**									
Present & Practice	Student Edition, pp. 2–9	•	•	•	Interactive Whiteboard Vocabulary Activities	•		•	
	Audio	•	•		Interactive TE and Resources DVD	•		•	
	Canción de hip hop	•			Teacher's Resource Book, pp. 6–8, 11, 14–15, 17–21	•		•	•
	Instant Check	•			Communicative Pair Activities, pp. 11, 14–15	•		•	•
	Guided WB, pp. 1–10	•	•	•	Vocabulary Clip Art	•	•	•	•
	Core WB, pp. 1–5	•	•	•	Audio Program	•	•	•	
	Comm. WB, pp. 1, 4	•	•	•	Vocabulary and Grammar Transparencies, 21–27	•	•	•	
	Hispanohablantes WB, pp. 4–5			•	Answer Keys: Student Edition, pp. 1–4	•	•	•	
	Communicative Pair Activities	•							
Assess and Remediate					Prueba P–1 with Study Plan	•			
					Prueba P–1: Assessment Program, p. 8	•		•	•
					Assessment Program para hispanohablantes, p. 8	•		•	•

RESOURCES

	FOR THE STUDENT	ONLINE	DVD	PRINT	FOR THE TEACHER	ONLINE	PREEXP	DVD	PRINT
En la clase PP. **10–17**									
Present & Practice	Student Edition, pp. 10–17	•	•	•	Interactive Whiteboard Vocabulary Activities	•		•	
	Audio	•	•		Interactive TE and Resources DVD	•		•	•
	Instant Check	•			Teacher's Resource Book, pp. 6, 8–9, 12–13, 17–21	•		•	•
	Guided WB, pp. 11–18	•	•	•	Communicative Pair Activities, pp. 12–13	•		•	•
	Core WB, pp. 6–8	•	•	•	Audio Program	•	•	•	
	Comm. WB, pp. 2, 5	•	•	•	Vocabulary and Grammar Transparencies, 28–30	•	•	•	
	Hispanohablantes WB, pp. 4–5			•	Answer Keys: Student Edition, pp. 6–8	•	•	•	•
	Communicative Pair Activities	•							
Assess and Remediate					Prueba P–2 with Study Plan	•			
					Prueba P–2: Assessment Program, p. 9	•		•	•
					Assessment Program para hispanohablantes, p. 9	•		•	•
El tiempo, PP. **18–21**									
Present & Practice	Student Edition, pp. 18–21	•	•	•	Interactive Whiteboard Vocabulary Activities	•		•	
	Audio	•	•		Interactive TE and Resources DVD	•		•	
	Instant Check	•			Teacher's Resource Book, pp. 6, 9–10, 17–21	•		•	•
	Canción de hip hop	•			Audio Program	•	•	•	
	Guided WB, pp. 19–24	•	•	•	Vocabulary and Grammar Transparencies, 15–17, 20, 31	•	•	•	
	Core WB, p. 9	•	•	•	Answer Keys: Student Edition, p. 9	•	•	•	
	Comm. WB, pp. 3, 6	•	•	•					
	Hispanohablantes WB, pp. 6–7			•					
					Prueba P–3 with Study Plan	•			
					Prueba P–3: Assessment Program, p. 10	•		•	•
					Assessment Program para hispanohablantes, p. 10	•		•	•
Repaso del capítulo PP. **22–23**									
Review	Student Edition, pp. 22–23	•	•	•	Interactive TE and Resources DVD	•		•	
	Online Puzzles and Games	•			Teacher's Resource Book, pp. 10, 16, 17–21	•		•	•
	Core WB, pp. 10–12	•	•	•	Audio Program	•	•	•	
	Hispanohablantes WB, pp. 8–9			•	Answer Keys: Student Edition, p. 10	•	•	•	
	Instant Check	•							
Chapter Assessment									
Assess					Examen de Para empezar	•		•	•
					Assessment Program, pp. 11–12	•		•	•
					Alternate Assessment Program, pp. 1–2	•		•	•
					Assessment Program para hispanohablantes, pp. 11–12	•		•	•
					Audio Program, *Para empezar* Examen	•		•	
					ExamView: Test Banks A and B questions only online	•		•	
					Heritage Learner Test Bank	•		•	
					Pre-AP* Test Bank	•		•	

DAY	REGULAR SCHEDULE (50 MINUTES)		
	Warm-up / Assess	**Preview / Present / Practice / Communicate**	**Wrap-up / Homework Options**
1	**General Housekeeping (15 min.)** • Chapter Opener • Arte y cultura	**En la escuela (30 min.)** • Presentation: ¡Hola! ¿Cómo te llamas? • Presentation: Los nombres • Exploración del lenguaje • Actividades 1, 2, 3	**Wrap-up and Homework Options (5 min.)** • Core Practice P-1
2	**Warm-up (5 min.)** • Homework check	**En la escuela (40 min.)** • Interactive Whiteboard Vocabulary Activities • Presentation: ¡Hola! ¿Cómo estás? • Exploración del lenguaje • Actividades 4, 5, 6 • Presentation: ¡Atención, por favor! • Actividad 7	**Wrap-up and Homework Options (5 min.)** • Core Practice P-2, P-3
3	**Warm-up (10 min.)** • Homework check	**En la escuela (35 min.)** • Presentation: Los números • Actividades 8, 9, 10 • Communicative Pair Activity • Presentation: ¿Qué hora es? • Actividades 11, 12	**Wrap-up and Homework Options (5 min.)** • Core Practice P-4
4	**Warm-up (5 min.)** • Homework check	**En la escuela (25 min.)** • Presentation: El cuerpo • Actividades 13, 14 • Communicative Pair Activity • Audio Activities 5, 6 **En la clase (15 min.)** • Objectives • Presentation: La sala de clases • Actividad 1	**Wrap-up and Homework Options (5 min.)** • Core Practice P-5 • Prueba PE-1 with Study Plan: En la escuela
5	**Warm-up (10 min.)** • Writing Activity 10 • Homework check **✔Formative Assessment (10 min.)** • Prueba PE-1 with Study Plan: En la escuela	**En la clase (25 min.)** • Actividad 2 • Presentation: Nouns • Actividad 3 • Interactive Whiteboard Vocabulary Activities • Presentation: El alfabeto • Actividad 4	**Wrap-up and Homework Options (5 min.)** • Core Practice P-6
6	**Warm-up (10 min.)** • Actividad 5 • Homework check	**En la clase (35 min.)** • Exploración del lenguaje • Fondo cultural • Actividades 6, 7 • Presentation: El calendario y la fecha • Actividades 8, 9	**Wrap-up and Homework Options (5 min.)** • Core Practice P-7, P-8
7	**Warm-up (10 min.)** • Actividad 10 • Homework check	**En la clase (20 min.)** • Fondo cultural • Audio Activity 7 • Actividades 11, 12 **El tiempo (15 min.)** • Presentation: ¿Qué tiempo hace? • Presentation: Las estaciones • Actividad 1	**Wrap-up and Homework Options (5 min.)** • Prueba PE-2 with Study Plan: En la clase
8	**Warm-up (10 min.)** • Writing Activity 11 **✔Formative Assessment (10 min.)** • Prueba PE-2 with Study Plan: En la clase	**El tiempo (25 min.)** • Interactive Whiteboard Vocabulary Activities • Actividades 2, 3, 5, 6 • Audio Activities 8, 9	**Wrap-up and Homework Options (5 min.)** • Actividad 4 • Core Practice P-9 • Prueba PE-3 with Study Plan: El tiempo
9	**Warm-up (15 min.)** • Writing Activities 12, 13 • Homework check **✔Formative Assessment (10 min.)** • Prueba PE-3 with Study Plan: El tiempo	**El tiempo (5 min.)** • Communicative Pair Activity **Repaso del capítulo (15 min.)** • Vocabulario • Preparación para el examen 1, 2, 3, 4 • Situation Cards • Communicative Pair Activities	**Wrap-up and Homework Options (5 min.)** • Core Practice P-10, P-11 • Instant Check • Examen del capítulo
10	**Warm-up (10 min.)** • Homework check **✔Summative Assessment (40 min.)** • Examen del capítulo		

BLOCK SCHEDULE (90 MINUTES)

DAY	Warm-up / Assess	Preview / Present / Practice / Communicate	Wrap-up / Homework Options
1	**General Housekeeping (15 min.)** • Chapter Opener • Arte y cultura	**En la escuela (70 min.)** • Objectives • Presentation: ¡Hola! ¿Cómo te llamas? • Presentation: Los nombres • Exploración del lenguaje • Actividades 1, 2, 3 • Interactive Whiteboard Vocabulary Activities • Presentation: ¡Hola! ¿Cómo estás? • Exploración del lenguaje • Actividades 4, 5	**Wrap-up and Homework Options (5 min.)** • Audio Activity 1 • Core Practice: P-1, P-2
2	**Warm-up (10 min.)** • Homework check	**En la escuela (75 min.)** • Actividad 6 • Presentation: ¡Atención, por favor! • Actividad 7 • Presentation: Los números • Actividades 8, 9, 10 • Communicative Pair Activity • Presentation: ¿Qué hora es? • Actividades 11, 12 • Presentation: El cuerpo • Actividades 13, 14 • Communicative Pair Activity • Audio Activity 2	**Wrap-up and Homework Options (5 min.)** • Core Practice P-3, P-4, P-5 • Writing Activity 6 • Prueba PE-1 with Study Plan: En la escuela
3	**Warm-up (15 min.)** • Homework check • Review: En la escuela ✔**Formative Assessment (10 min.)** • Prueba PE-1 with Study Plan: En la escuela	**En la clase (60 min.)** • Objectives • Presentation: La sala de clases • Actividades 1, 2 • Presentation: Nouns • Actividad 3 • Interactive Whiteboard Vocabulary Activities • Audio Activity 3 • Presentation: El alfabeto • Actividades 4, 5, 6, 7 • Exploración del lenguaje • Fondo cultural • Audio Activity 4 • Presentation: El calendario y la fecha • Presentation: Los meses del año • Actividades 8, 9	**Wrap-up and Homework Options (5 min.)** • Core Practice P-6, P-7, P-8 • Prueba PE-2 with Study Plan: En la clase
4	**Warm-up (20 min.)** • Fondo cultural • Actividad 10 • Homework check ✔**Formative Assessment (10 min.)** • Prueba PE-2 with Study Plan: En la clase	**El tiempo (55 min.)** • Actividades 11, 12 • Writing Activity 7 • Objectives • Presentation: ¿Qué tiempo hace? • Presentation: Las estaciones • Actividades 1, 2, 3, 5, 6 • Interactive Whiteboard Vocabulary Activities • Audio Activity 5 • Writing Activity 8	**Wrap-up and Homework Options (5 min.)** • Actividad 4 • Core Practice P-9 • Prueba PE-3 with Study Plan: El tiempo
5	**Warm-up (20 min.)** • Writing Activities 12, 13 • Homework check • Review: El tiempo ✔**Formative Assessment (10 min.)** • Prueba PE-3 with Study Plan: El tiempo	**Repaso del capítulo (55 min.)** • Vocabulario • Preparación para el examen 1, 2, 3, 4 • Situation Cards • Communicative Pair Activities • Theme Project: Begin	**Wrap-up and Homework Options (5 min.)** • Practice Workbook P-10, P-11 • Instant Check • Examen del capítulo
6	**Warm-up (15 min.)** • Homework check • Answer questions ✔**Summative Assessment (45 min.)** • Examen del capítulo		**Wrap-up and Homework Options (30 min.)** • Theme Project: Finish

Para empezar

Standards for *Para empezar*

- To achieve the goals of the Standards, students will:

Communication

1.1 Interpersonal

- Greet and introduce themselves to others
- Use correct leave-taking phrases
- Ask how others are
- Provide others with the correct numbers of things
- Ask and provide others the correct time
- Talk about classroom people and objects
- Ask for and provide others the date or day of the week
- Talk about the weather

1.2 Interpretive

- Read and listen to information about appropriate greetings, introductions, and leave-takings
- Read and listen to information about how to ask about how someone is
- Read and listen to information about classroom directions and commands
- Read and listen to information about numbers
- Read and listen to information about telling time
- Read and listen to information about parts of the body
- Read and listen to information about classroom people and objects
- Read and listen to information about the alphabet
- Read and listen to information about the calendar
- Read and listen to information about weather and seasons

1.3 Presentational

- Present information about appropriate greetings, introductions, and leave-takings
- Write the correct numbers of things
- Present information about people and things
- Present information about the Spanish alphabet
- Present information about dates and days of the week
- Present information about seasons and the weather

Culture

2.1 Practices and Perspectives

- Talk about ***los sanfermines***

Connections

3.1 Cross-curricular

- Discuss the hieroglyphics of the Maya
- Discuss the Aztec calendar
- Discuss geography and climatology in the Southern Hemisphere
- Reinforce math and metric conversion skills

Comparisons

4.1 Language

- Explain the difference between ***tú*** and ***usted***
- Discuss that nouns are either masculine or feminine
- Discuss some rules of punctuation and accent marks

4.2 Culture

- Compare customs of greetings and introductions
- Compare festivals in which animals play a role

Chapter Objectives

Communication

By the end of *Para empezar* you will be able to:

- Listen to greetings and announcements
- Read a description of the weather and a list of school supplies

You will demonstrate what you know and can do:

- Preparación para el examen, p. 23

You will also learn to:

1 En la escuela

- Greet people at different times of the day
- Introduce yourself to others
- Respond to classroom directions
- Begin using numbers
- Tell time
- Identify parts of the body

2 En la clase

- Talk about things in the classroom
- Ask questions about new words and phrases
- Use the Spanish alphabet to spell words
- Talk about things related to the calendar
- Learn about the Aztec calendar

3 El tiempo

- Describe weather conditions
- Identify the seasons
- Compare weather in the Northern and Southern Hemispheres

realidades.com 

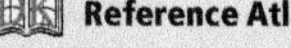

Reference Atlas

Mapa global interactivo

ENRICH YOUR TEACHING

Using Backward Design

Have students preview the sample performance tasks on *Preparación para el examen,* p. 23, and connect them to the Chapter Objectives. Explain to students that by completing the sample tasks they can self-assess their learning progress.

Mapa global interactivo

Download the *Mapa global interactivo* files for *Para empezar* and preview the activities. Use Activity 1 to travel to Mexico and compare Mayan ruins. Activity 2 takes you to the streets of Pamplona, Spain. In Activity 3, you look at North and South America and Ecuador, and you compare weather in the Northern and Southern hemispheres.

Arte y cultura | El mundo hispano Estados Unidos

Greetings Social relations are somewhat more formal in Spanish-speaking countries than in the United States, since new acquaintances usually greet one another with a handshake. Friends, however, greet each other with a hug or a kiss on the cheek.

- How does this compare with the way you greet people in the United States?

Un grupo de amigos en el Parque Darío, Matagalpa, Nicaragua

PresentationExpress™
See pp. xxxii-c–xxxii-d

Chapter Opener

Core Instruction

Suggestions: As you go through the Objectives, ask volunteers to identify in English the ways people might introduce themselves, name common classroom objects, or describe the day's weather. Scan the section with students to help familiarize them with the structure of this unit (which follows a different pattern from the other chapters). Explain that the *Para empezar* is an introduction to their language learning that will help them communicate right away, and that the vocabulary and expressions they learn here will then be recycled throughout the book. The emphasis should be on recognition and limited use, not on mastery.

Arte y cultura

Standards: 4.1

Suggestions: Ask students about the different ways strangers, adults, young people, men, women, and family members greet each other in the United States.

Answers will vary.

TEACHING WITH PHOTOS

Have students look at the teens in the photo. What do they notice about how these young people are dressed? How does it compare with the way they dress?

Culture Note

Young people in the United States have many colloquialisms for greeting each other. *How's it going?*, *What's up?*, and *Hey!* are just a few of them. Teens in Latin America also have informal ways of greeting each other, such as *¿Cómo te va?*, *¿Qué onda?*, and *¿Quehúbole?*

DIFFERENTIATED INSTRUCTION

Digital resources such as the ***Interactive Whiteboard*** activity banks, ***Videomodelos***, additional ***Online Activities***, ***Study Plans***, automatically graded ***Leveled Workbook***, animated ***Grammar Tutorials***, ***Flashcards***, and ***Vocabulary and Grammar Videos*** will help you reach students of different ability levels and learning styles.

STUDENTS NEEDING EXTRA HELP

Guided Practice Activities
- Flashcards, pp. 1, 11, 19
- Vocabulary Check, pp. 7, 15, 21
- Pronunciation, pp. 9, 17, 23

HERITAGE LEARNERS

Realidades para hispanohablantes
- Chapter Opener, pp. x–1
- En la escuela, pp. 2–3
- En la clase, pp. 4–5
- El tiempo, pp. 6–7
- Repaso del capítulo, pp. 8–9

ADVANCED/PRE-AP*

Pre-AP* Resource Book,
- pp. 60–61

Communication Workbook
- Integrated Performance Assessment, p. 226

PE Language Input

Vocabulary Activities PE

¡Hola! ¿Cómo te llamas?

Core Instruction

Standards: 1.2

Resources: Teacher's Resource Book: Input Script, p. 6, Clip Art, pp. 17–21, Audio Script p. 7; Voc. and Gram. Transparency 21; Audio Program DVD: Cap. 00, Track 1

Focus: Presenting different ways to greet friends and adults in the morning, afternoon, and evening

Suggestions: Use the Input Script from the *Teacher's Resource Book* or the stories from the *TPR Stories Book* any time you have new vocabulary to introduce, or use other ideas that work for you. Show the transparencies to introduce the words. Be sure students notice the age differences of the speakers and the different times of day the conversations take place. When students have become familiar with the conversations, ask them to greet you and one another. Point out the *Nota* and explain that these provide additional explanations and useful information.

Exploración del lenguaje

Core Instruction

Focus: Explaining different ways to address others

Suggestions: Write examples on the board such as ***Señor Trujillo*** and then write the abbreviation ***Sr. Trujillo.*** Point out the comparison in English to students. They may be surprised at the relative formality with which adults are addressed in Spanish. Have students identify school personnel with the new Spanish titles.

1 En la escuela

▼ Objectives

- Greet people at different times of the day
- Introduce yourself to others
- Respond to classroom directions
- Begin using numbers
- Tell time
- Identify parts of the body

¡Hola! ¿Cómo te llamas?

—**¡Buenos días, señor!**

—¡Buenos días! **¿Cómo te llamas?**

—**Me llamo** Felipe.

—**¡Buenas tardes, señora!**

—¡Buenas tardes! ¿Cómo te llamas?

—Me llamo Beatriz.

—**Mucho gusto.**

—**Encantada.**

—**¡Buenas noches!** ¿Cómo te llamas?

—**¡Hola!** Me llamo Graciela. **¿Y tú?**

—Me llamo Lorenzo.

—Mucho gusto.

—**Igualmente.**

Nota

A woman or girl says *encantada.*
A man or boy says *encantado.*

▼ Exploración del lenguaje

Señor, señora, señorita

The words *señor, señora,* and *señorita* mean "sir," "madam," and "miss" when used alone. When they are used with people's last names they mean "Mr.," "Mrs.," and "Miss," and are abbreviated *Sr., Sra.,* and *Srta.* Note that the abbreviations are capitalized.

In Spanish you should address adults as *señor, señora,* or *señorita,* or use the titles *Sr., Sra.,* and *Srta.* with their last names.

DIFFERENTIATED INSTRUCTION

Students with Learning Difficulties

If students have problems identifying individual phrases in context, provide them with a list of specific words and phrases that you want them to know. Model different ways in which they can combine the words and phrases for communication.

Advanced Learners

Explain that *¿Cómo te llamas?* and *Me llamo...* do not literally mean "What's your name?" and "My name is...". Use this as an opportunity to demonstrate that languages cannot be translated on a word-to-word basis. Some students may also benefit from further explanation of the *Nota* and of agreement of adjectives.

1 Buenos días

Escuchar

Listen as people greet each other. Then point to the clock that indicates the time of day when the greetings are probably taking place.

a. 

b. 

c. 

2 ¿Cómo te llamas?

Hablar

Your teacher will divide the class in half. Students in one half of the class will introduce themselves and shake hands, and students in the other half will say they are pleased to meet the others. Move quickly from person to person until time is called. Then switch roles.

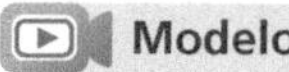

A —*¡Hola! ¿Cómo te llamas?*
B —*Me llamo David. ¿Y tú?*
A —*Me llamo Antonio. Mucho gusto.*
o: *Encantado.*
B —*Igualmente.*

¿Recuerdas?
If you are a girl, you say *encantada.*

3 ¡Hola

Hablar

Work with a partner. Choose a clock from Actividad 1 and greet each other appropriately for the time of day. Then find out your partner's name. Follow the model. Change partners and repeat.

Modelo

A —*Buenas tardes.*
B —*Buenas tardes. ¿Cómo te llamas?*
A —*Me llamo Paco. ¿Y tú?*
B —*Me llamo Lourdes. Mucho gusto.*
A —*Encantado.*

Los nombres

Chicas
Alicia
Ana
Beatriz
Carmen
Cristina
Dolores (Lola)
Elena
Gloria
Inés
Isabel (Isa)
Juana
Luisa
Luz María (Luzma)
Margarita
María
María Eugenia (Maru)
Marta
Teresa (Tere)

Chicos
Alejandro
Antonio (Toño)
Carlos (Chacho, Cacho)
Diego
Eduardo (Edu)
Federico (Kiko)
Francisco (Paco)
Guillermo (Guille)
Jorge
José (Pepe)
Juan
Manuel (Manolo)
Miguel
Pablo
Pedro
Ricardo
Roberto
Tomás

Practice and Communicate

PE

1 Standards: 1.2

Resources: Teacher's Resource Book: Audio Script, p. 7; Audio Program DVD: Cap. 00, Track 2; Answer Keys: Student Edition, p. 1

Focus: Listening to understand greetings

Suggestions: In all *Escuchar* activities, you may either play the *audio* or read the script. Walk around the room to monitor comprehension and check that students are pointing to the correct clocks.

Script and Answers:

1. **—Buenas noches, señor Rodríguez.**
   —Hola, Roberto. *(c)*
2. **—Buenas tardes, Alicia.**
   —Buenas tardes, señora. *(b)*
3. **—Buenos días, señora Gómez.**
   —Hola, Ana. *(a)*
4. **—Buenos días, Pablo.**
   —Buenos días, señor. *(a)*
5. **—Buenas noches, Jorge.**
   —Hola, María. *(c)*
6. **—Hola, Juana.**
   —Buenas tardes, Catalina. *(b)*

2 Standards: 1.1

Focus: Practicing introductions

Suggestions: Model a personalized version of the conversation with a volunteer and go over roles. Students will need to learn how to do paired practice. Point out that the *¿Recuerdas?* boxes will remind students of things they've already learned.

3 Standards: 1.1

Focus: Practicing greetings appropriate to time of day; asking and telling names

Suggestions: If you wish, have students choose Spanish names to use in class. Allow students to repeat the activity with several partners.

ENRICH YOUR TEACHING

Culture Note

In Spain and many other Spanish-speaking countries, ***Buenos días*** is used until noon. ***Buenas tardes*** is used from noon until the evening meal. ***Buenas noches*** is considered both a greeting and a farewell.

21st Century Skills

Communication Remind students of the tools available in **realidades.com,** such as the eText with embedded audio files and the *Videomodelos,* that can help them develop their fluency, including gestures and body language, as they watch and listen to the native speakers in the videos.

Teacher-to-Teacher

Bring in a kitchen timer and set it for the time you want to allot for each paired activity. When the bell rings, stop the activity, review the task with students if necessary, and move on. The timer will help you keep track of the time and will help students focus.

PE Language Input

¡Hola! ¿Cómo estás?

Core Instruction

Standards: 1.2

Resources: Teacher's Resource Book: Input Script, p. 6, Audio Script, p. 7; Voc. and Gram. Transparency 22; Audio Program DVD: Cap. 00, Track 3

Focus: Introducing expressions used to ask and answer how someone is

Suggestions: Use the transparencies and the dialogue to help students guess the meanings of the unfamiliar words in blue type. Direct attention to the *¿Recuerdas?* Play the *audio* or read the conversations beneath the pictures. Then role-play the conversations with students. Draw a rising sun at one end of the board, a noontime sun a little to the right with a dividing line under it, a setting sun a little further to the right, and a moon at the far end. Position pairs of students at various points along the board, and have the class identify whether they would say ***Buenos días, Buenas tardes,*** or ***Buenas noches,*** depending on where they are. Point out that ***hasta*** + **an expression of time** means that you're saying good-bye until that time.

BELLRINGER REVIEW

Show Vocabulary and Grammar Transparency 22. Ask students to prepare a short dialogue with a partner to represent one of the pairs of speakers pictured. (Cover the dialogues on the transparency.)

¡Hola! ¿Cómo estás?

—Buenos días, Adela. **¿Cómo estás?**
—**Bien, gracias,** Sr. Ruiz. **¿Y usted?**
—Bien, gracias.

—Buenas tardes, Sr. Ruiz. **¿Cómo está Ud.?**
—**Muy** bien, gracias. ¿Y tú?
—Bien, gracias.

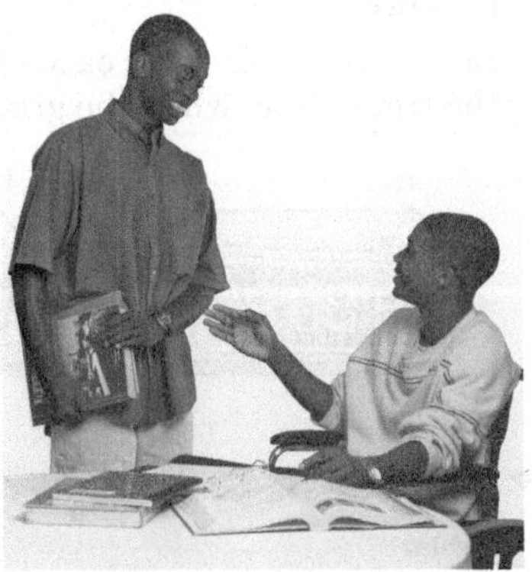

—Buenas noches, Miguel. **¿Qué tal?**
—**Regular.** ¿Y tú, Carlos? **¿Qué pasa?**
—**Nada.**

—**¡Adiós,** Srta. Moreno! **¡Hasta luego!**
—**¡Hasta mañana!**

—¡Hasta luego, Juan!
—**¡Nos vemos!**

¿Recuerdas?

Señor, señora, and *señorita* are abbreviated to ***Sr., Sra.,*** and ***Srta.*** before a person's last name.

DIFFERENTIATED INSTRUCTION

Students with Learning Difficulties

Have students create a section in their notebook for vocabulary and a separate section for grammar. For each chapter, students can enter new vocabulary and grammar concepts into their respective sections. Allow students to accompany vocabulary words with pictures and English translations, as needed.

Heritage Language Learners

Many students who already speak Spanish may have little or no formal experience with the written language. Ask these students to write new versions of the dialogues above, personalizing them in some way. Have them pay special attention to spelling. You can use this exercise to informally assess their written Spanish.

Exploración del lenguaje

Tú vs. *usted*

For most Spanish speakers there are two ways to say "you": *tú* and *usted*. Use *tú* when speaking to friends, family, people your own age, children, and pets. *Usted* is formal. Use it to show respect and when talking to people you don't know well, older people, and people in positions of authority. In writing, *usted* is almost always abbreviated *Ud.*, with a capital *U*.

Would you say *tú* or *Ud.* when talking to the following people?

- your brother
- your teacher
- your best friend
- your friend's mother
- your cat
- your principal
- a new acquaintance who is your age

4 ¿Hola o adiós?

Escuchar

Make a chart on your paper with two columns. Label one *Greeting*, the other *Leaving*. Number your paper from 1–8. As you hear each greeting or leave-taking, place a check mark in the appropriate column next to the number.

Greeting	Leaving
1.	
2.	
3.	

5 ¡Hola! ¿Qué tal?

Hablar

Work with a partner. Greet each other and ask how your partner is. Say good-bye. Then change partners and repeat.

Modelo

A —*Hola, Luisa. ¿Qué tal?*
B —*Bien, Lupe. ¿Y tú?*
A —*Regular. ¡Hasta luego!*
B —*¡Adiós!*

6 Mucho gusto

Leer

Read the conversation and then reply *sí* or *no* to the statements.

Profesor: Buenos días. Me llamo José Guzmán. ¿Y tú?
Estudiante: Me llamo María Hernández. Mucho gusto.
Profesor: Igualmente. ¿Cómo estás, María?
Estudiante: Bien, gracias. ¿Y Ud.?
Profesor: Muy bien, gracias. Hasta luego.
Estudiante: Adiós, señor.

1. The people knew each other.
2. The teacher is a man.
3. We know the last names of both people.
4. The student talks to the teacher in a formal tone.
5. Neither person is feeling well today.

Más práctica GO

	realidades.com	print
Core WB p. 2	✔	✔
Comm. WB p. 1	✔	✔

ENRICH YOUR TEACHING

Culture Note

In Spain, a newborn child is generally given a first name, no middle name, and two surnames — one from each parent. Usually, the father's surname is first and the mother's surname is second. This is different in the United States, where a child is given a first name, perhaps a middle name, and one last name, usually the father's surname.

Teacher-to-Teacher

To keep students on task and speaking Spanish during a paired activity, circulate and place star stickers on the desks of students who are participating. Give the stars a value—three stars equals a bonus point, for example. When using this system, remind students that stars can be taken away for not participating or for speaking English.

Practice and Communicate PE

Exploración del lenguaje
Core Instruction

Standards: 4.1

Resources: Answer Keys: Student Edition, p. 1

Suggestions: Tell students to use ***Ud.*** for anybody that they call by their last name.

Answers: **1. tú; 2. usted; 3. tú; 4. usted; 5. tú; 6. usted; 7. tú**

4
Standards: 1.2

Resources: Teacher's Resource Book: Audio Script, p. 7; Audio Program DVD: Cap. 00, Track 4; Answer Keys: Student Edition, p. 2

Focus: Listening to understand greetings

Suggestions: Draw the chart on the board as a model.

Script and Answers:

1. **Hola, Juan. ¿Qué pasa? *(greeting)***
2. **Adiós, Miguel. *(leaving)***
3. **Buenos días, señor García. *(greeting)***
4. **Hola, Elena. *(greeting)***
5. **Nos vemos. *(leaving)***
6. **Hasta mañana, señor Pérez. *(leaving)***
7. **Buenas noches, señora. *(greeting)***
8. **Hasta luego, Ana. *(leaving)***

5
Standards: 1.1

Focus: Using greetings

Suggestions: Have students switch roles with one asking and one answering.

6
Standards: 1.2, 1.3

Resources: Answer Keys: Student Edition, p. 2

Focus: Reading comprehension

Suggestions: If the answer is "No," have students provide correct information.

Answers:
1. no 2. sí 3. sí 4. sí 5. no

Additional Resources

- Communication Wbk.: Audio Act. 1, p. 1
- Teacher's Resource Book: Audio Script, p. 7, Communicative Pair Activity, p. 11
- Audio Program DVD: Cap. 00, Track 5

¡Atención, por favor!

Core Instruction

Standards: 1.2

Resources: Voc. and Gram. Transparency 23; Teacher's Resource Book: Audio Script, p. 7; Audio Program DVD: Cap. 00, Track 6

Focus: Presenting common classroom commands

Suggestions: Play the *audio* or refer to the text under the pictures. Dramatize the classroom commands while saying them aloud or playing the audio. Have students guess the commands. Then say them again and have the class respond as asked. Try to do as much classroom management in Spanish as possible.

7 Standards: 1.2

Resources: Teacher's Resource Book: Audio Script, p. 7; Audio Program DVD: Cap. 00, Track 7; Answer Keys: Student Edition, p. 2

Focus: Listening and responding to classroom commands

Suggestions: Play the *audio* or read the script. Have students simply listen the first time. Then play or read the script again, having students act out the commands.

Script and Answers:

1. **Abran el libro.** ***(open the book)***
2. **Levántense.** ***(stand up)***
3. **Repitan: Buenas tardes.** ***(repeat)***
4. **Siéntense.** ***(sit down)***
5. **Cierren el libro.** ***(close the book)***
6. **Saquen una hoja de papel.** ***(take out a sheet of paper)***

Extension: Provide additional commands for the students: *Pasen a la pizarra. Trabajen en parejas. Cierren la puerta. Abran la ventana.*

¡Atención, por favor!

—¡Silencio, **por favor!** Abran el libro en la página 10.

—¡Atención! Cierren el libro.

—Repitan, por favor: Buenos días.

—Buenos días.

—Levántense, por favor.

—Siéntense, por favor.

—Saquen una hoja de papel. Escriban los números.

—Entreguen sus hojas de papel.

7 ¡Siéntense! 

Escuchar

You will hear some classroom commands. Listen carefully and act them out.

DIFFERENTIATED INSTRUCTION

Students with Special Needs

For students who find the commands difficult to act out, have them discuss with you other ways they might indicate comprehension of the commands. Depending on the students, these might include simple hand or arm movements.

Advanced Learners

Have students turn to p. 100 in their textbook and then flip through the pages, randomly stopping ten times. They should say or write the page number each time they stop. Point out that the numbers are written out on each page.

Los números

      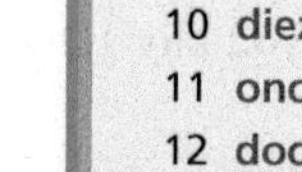  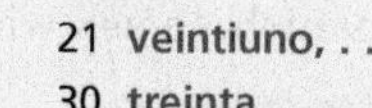

cero uno dos tres cuatro

cinco seis siete ocho nueve

10	diez	21	veintiuno, . . .
11	once	30	treinta
12	doce	31	treinta y uno, . . .
13	trece	40	cuarenta
14	catorce	50	cincuenta
15	quince	60	sesenta
16	dieciséis	70	setenta
17	diecisiete	80	ochenta
18	dieciocho	90	noventa
19	diecinueve	100	cien
20	veinte		

8 Los números | Talk!

Hablar

Supply the missing number. Then read the sequence in Spanish.

1. 1, ___, 3
2. 6, ___, 8
3. 7, ___, 9
4. 10, ___, 12
5. 14, ___, 16
6. 17, ___, 19
7. 23, ___, 25
8. 29, ___, 31

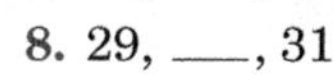

9 Más números | Talk!

Pensar • Hablar

With a partner, provide the missing numbers in each sequence. Then say the number sequence aloud in Spanish.

1. 1, 2, 3, . . . 10
2. 2, 4, 6, . . . 20
3. 1, 3, 5, . . . 19
4. 5, 10, 15, . . . 60
5. 3, 6, 9, . . . 39
6. 10, 20, 30, . . . 100

Más práctica GO

realidades.com | print

Core WB p. 3 ✔ ✔

10 Números y más números | Talk!

Hablar • Escuchar • Escribir

Tell your partner these numbers in Spanish. He or she will write them using numerals, not words. Then check your partner's work.

1. the phone numbers used to dial for information and emergencies
2. the bar code number on the back of your Spanish book
3. your house or apartment number
4. number of minutes it takes you to get from your home to school
5. number of months until your next birthday

Azulejo *(tile)* de cerámica

ENRICH YOUR TEACHING

Teacher-to-Teacher

Give each student a number written large on a piece of paper. Have them tape the numbers to their shirts. Then have the class stand in a circle and clap their hands rhythmically. The student who is *uno* says his or her number and then calls out another number. The student who has that number says it, then calls out another number (e.g., "*¡uno, diez!*"; *diez* then responds, saying "*¡diez, cuatro!*"). All the while, students clap the rhythm. If someone makes a mistake, the person and number are out.

Practice and Communicate PE

Los números

Core Instruction

Standards: 1.2

Resources: Voc. and Gram. Transparency 24; Teacher's Resource Book: Audio Script, p. 8; Audio Program DVD: Cap. 00, Track 8

Suggestions: Have students practice numbers by playing bingo or by rolling number cubes.

8 Standards: 1.1

Resources: Answer Keys: Student Edition, p. 3

Focus: Reading numbers

Suggestions: Have students read the entire sequence, not just the answer.

Answers:

1. dos
2. siete
3. ocho
4. once
5. quince
6. dieciocho
7. veinticuatro
8. treinta

9 Standards: 1.1

Resources: Answer Keys: Student Edition, p. 3

Focus: Practicing with numbers

Suggestions: Make sure students understand that each sequence represents a pattern. They have to identify the pattern before they can provide the missing numbers.

Answers:

1. cuatro, cinco, seis, siete, ocho, nueve
2. ocho, diez, doce, catorce, dieciséis, dieciocho
3. siete, nueve, once, trece, quince, diecisiete
4. veinte, veinticinco, treinta, treinta y cinco, cuarenta, cuarenta y cinco, cincuenta, cincuenta y cinco
5. doce, quince, dieciocho, veintiuno, veinticuatro, veintisiete, treinta, treinta y tres, treinta y seis
6. cuarenta, cincuenta, sesenta, setenta, ochenta, noventa

10 Standards: 1.1, 1.3

Focus: Using numbers

Suggestions: Verify answers using a transparency.

Answers will vary.

Additional Resources

- Teacher's Resource Book: Communicative Pair Activity, pp. 14–15

PE Language Input

¿Qué hora es?

Core Instruction

Standards: 1.2

Resources: Voc. and Gram. Transparencies 25–26; Teacher's Resource Book: Audio Script, p. 8; Audio Program DVD: Cap. 00, Track 9

Focus: Telling time

Suggestions: Show the transparencies for telling time. Ask: *¿Qué hora es?* Point to a clock, and have students tell you the time. Mark different times on the transparency.

Pre-AP* Support

- **Learning Objective:** Interpretive: Audio
- **Activity:** Show Transparency 25. Have students number 1–8 on a sheet of paper. As you point to each clock, make true/false statements. Have students write *C (Cierto)* or *F (Falso)* to respond.
- ***Pre-AP* Resource Book:*** Comprehensive guide to Pre-AP* skill development, pp. 10–57

11 Standards: 1.1

Resources: Answer Keys: Student Edition, p. 3

Focus: Asking and telling the time

Suggestions: Point to the classroom clock and prompt students to say what time it is.

Answers: **1. Son las siete; 2. Son las tres y media / treinta; 3. Es la una y cuarto / quince; 4. Son las dos y veinte; 5. Son las nueve y cuarenta. / Son las diez menos veinte; 6. Son las doce y cincuenta. / Es la una menos diez.**

12 Standards: 1.2

Resources: Teacher's Resource Book: Audio Script, p. 8; Audio Program DVD: Cap. 00, Track 10; Answer Keys: Student Edition, p. 4

Focus: Listening to understand time of day

Suggestions: Repeat the activity and ask volunteers for the answers.

Script and Answers:

1. Es la una y media. *(1:30);* 2. Son las diez. *(10:00);* 3. Son las once y cinco. *(11:05);* 4. Son las doce. *(12:00);* 5. Son las seis y media. *(6:30);* 6. Son las siete y cuarenta y cinco. *(7:45);* 7. Son las nueve y veinte. *(9:20);* 8. Son las tres y treinta y cinco. *(3:35)*

Teaching with Art

Resources: Fine Art Transparencies, p. 16

¿Qué hora es?

In Spanish, to ask what time it is, you say *¿Qué hora es?* Here are some answers:

Es la una.

Son las dos.

Son las tres y cinco.

Son las cuatro y diez.

Son las cinco y cuarto.

Son las seis y media.

Son las siete menos veinte.

Son las ocho y cincuenta y dos.

11 ¿Qué hora es?

Hablar

Work with a partner to ask and answer questions about the time. Use these clocks.

Modelo

A —*¿Qué hora es?*

B —*Son las diez.*

1.

2.

3.

4.

5.

6.

12 La hora

Escuchar

Write the numbers 1–8 on a sheet of paper. Write the times you hear with numerals—1:00, 2:15, and so on.

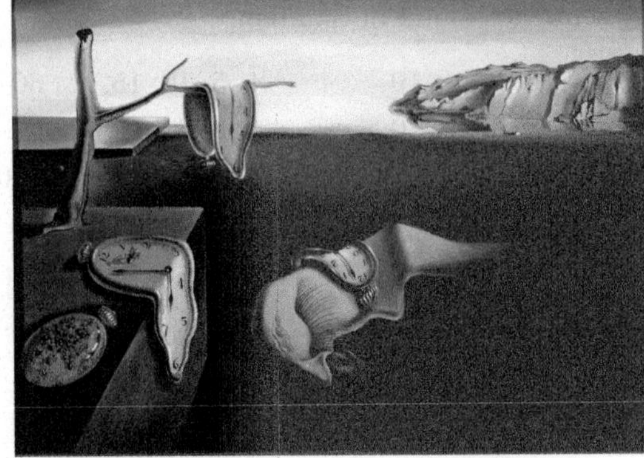

"La persistencia de la memoria / The Persistence of Memory" (1931), Salvador Dalí

Oil on canvas, 9 1/2 x 13 in. (24.1 x 33 cm). Given anonymously. © 2009 Salvador Dalí, Gala-Salvador Dalí Foundation/Artists Rights Society (ARS), New York./A.K.G., Berlin. Photo: Superstock.

DIFFERENTIATED INSTRUCTION

Students with Learning Difficulties

Some students may be unable to read clocks with faces and hands. If so, provide times on digital clocks.

Advanced Learners

Have students write a television program guide with the names and times of their favorite programs. Suggest that they use newspaper or internet listings as a model. Have students exchange program guides. One student will say a time, and the other student will say the name of the program.

El cuerpo

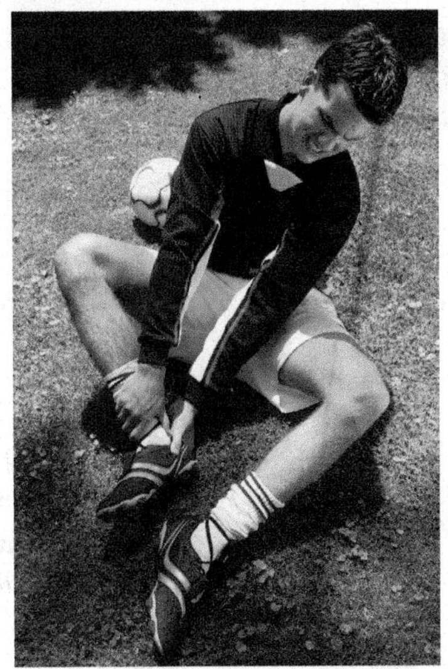

“¡Ay! Me duele el pie”.

13 Señalen

Escuchar

You will hear some commands. Listen carefully and act out the commands. When you hear the word *señalen*, you should point to that part of the body.

14 Juego

Escuchar

Play the game *Simón dice* . . . (Simon Says). Listen and follow the leader's directions. Remember that if the leader does not say *"Simón dice,"* you should not do the action.

Más práctica GO

realidades.com | print

	realidades.com	print
Canción de hip hop	✔	
Instant Check	✔	
Guided WB pp. 1–10	✔	✔
Core WB p. 5	✔	✔
Comm. WB pp. 1, 4	✔	✔
Hispanohablantes WB pp. 2–3		✔

Language Input PE

El cuerpo

Core Instruction

Standards: 1.2

Resources: Voc. and Gram. Transparency 27; Teacher's Resource Book: Audio Script, p. 8; Audio Program DVD: Cap. 00, Track 12

Focus: Presenting the parts of the body

Suggestions: Play the *audio* and show the transparency. Pretend to be in pain and say: *¡Ay! Me duele el pie.* Continue with the rest of the vocabulary. Note that only singular body parts are used. Point out the use of the article to refer to body parts.

13 Standards: 1.2

Resources: Teacher's Resource Book: Audio Script, p. 8; Audio Program DVD: Cap. 00, Track 13

Focus: Listening comprehension of commands

Suggestions: Play the *audio* or read the script twice. Have students listen first and perform the action the second time.

Script and Answers:

1. **Señalen la nariz.** ***(nose)***
2. **Señalen el estómago.** ***(stomach)***
3. **Señalen la mano.** ***(hand)***
4. **Señalen la cabeza.** ***(head)***
5. **Señalen el pie.** ***(foot)***
6. **Señalen el brazo.** ***(arm)***

14 Standards: 1.2

Focus: Listening and responding

Suggestions: Have students take turns playing leader in small groups.

Additional Resources

- Communication Wbk.: Audio Act. 2, p. 1
- Teacher's Resource Book: Audio Script, p. 8
- Audio Program DVD: Cap. 00, Track 11

ENRICH YOUR TEACHING

Teacher-to-Teacher

Have students create a poster of a "creature" using images cut from magazines or newspapers. Their creature can have six arms, four legs, etc. Have them label each of the body parts. Provide plurals as necessary. Display the art in the classroom and ask students true-or-false questions about each one, or have them list the body parts that they see.

21st Century Skills

Initiative and Self-Direction Direct students to use all the tools available in **realidades.com**, including the embedded audio and the Online Games, to learn the new vocabulary. Once they are comfortable with it, have them work in groups of four to write a game, a song, or a poem using the vocabulary on this page (parts of the body).

ASSESSMENT

Prueba P-1 with Study Plan (online only)

Quiz: En la escuela

- Prueba P-1: p. 8

PE Language Input

INTERACTIVE WHITEBOARD
Vocabulary Activities PE

La sala de clases

Core Instruction

Standards: 1.2

Resources: Teacher's Resource Book: Input Script, p. 6, Clip Art, pp. 17–21, Audio Script, p. 8; Voc. and Gram. Transparency 28; Audio Program DVD: Cap. 00, Track 14

Focus: Presenting classroom vocabulary

Suggestions: Use the commands from p. 6 to introduce and practice these vocabulary items, using actual items in your classroom. Combine these with other commands for students to carry out. Tell students that for the rest of the year, if they want to know either the Spanish or English word for something, you will only respond if they use the questions presented here.

1

Standards: 1.2

Resources: Teacher's Resource Book: Audio Script, pp. 8–9; Audio Program DVD: Cap. 00, Track 15; Answer Keys: Student Edition, p. 5

Focus: Listening comprehension of vocabulary for classroom objects

Suggestions: Tell students that if an object is not visible in the classroom, they may point to the picture in the book. Explain the *También se dice...* but tell students that they will not have to remember these words.

Script and Answers:

1. **la hoja de papel** ***(sheet of paper)***
2. **el libro** ***(book)***
3. **la profesora (el profesor)** ***(teacher)***
4. **el pupitre** ***(student desk)***
5. **el bolígrafo** ***(pen)***
6. **el cuaderno** ***(notebook)***
7. **el lápiz** ***(pencil)***
8. **la carpeta** ***(folder)***

BELLRINGER REVIEW

Show Vocabulary and Grammar Transparency 23. Working in pairs, have students alternate saying these classroom commands.

2 En la clase

▼ Objectives

- Talk about things in the classroom
- Ask questions about new words and phrases
- Use the Spanish alphabet to spell words
- Talk about things related to the calendar
- Learn about the Aztec calendar

La sala de clases

1 El libro, el lápiz, . . .

Escuchar

You will hear the names of classroom objects. After you hear each word, hold up the object if you have it on your desk or point to it if it is somewhere in the classroom.

También se dice . . .

In many Spanish-speaking countries or regions, you will hear different words for the same thing. Words like these are highlighted in the *También se dice . . .* sections.

For example, in Spain a classroom is ***el aula,*** while in Mexico, it is ***el salón de clases.***

DIFFERENTIATED INSTRUCTION

Students with Learning Difficulties

The concept of grammatical gender is sometimes difficult for English speakers. Encourage students to always learn a noun with its article as a means of reinforcing the sound and rhythm. If they are copying new vocabulary into their notebooks, have them use a blue and a pink highlighter to color-code the words.

Heritage Language Learners

Ask students if they use any words that are different from the vocabulary in the book, but that mean the same thing. For instance, in Spain, a pen is **el bolígrafo,** but in some other countries, people say ***la pluma.*** Be sure students understand that their words are valid, but that you may make other vocabulary choices for class.

2 ¿Cómo se dice . . . ?

Hablar

Talk with a partner about items and people in your classroom.

Modelo

A —*¿Cómo se dice book en español?*
B —*Se dice libro.*

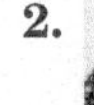

1. 
2. 
3. 
4. 
5. 

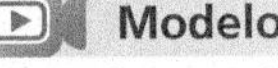

Modelo

mano

A —*¿Qué quiere decir mano?*
B —*Quiere decir hand.*

6. cuaderno
7. hoja de papel
8. cabeza
9. carpeta
10. brazo

Gramática

Nouns

Nouns refer to people, animals, places, things, and ideas. In Spanish, nouns have gender. They are either masculine or feminine.

Most nouns that end in *-o* are masculine. Most nouns that end in *-a* are feminine.

Masculine	Feminine
el libro	la carpeta
el bolígrafo	la hoja de papel

The definite articles *el* and *la* also point out if a word is masculine or feminine. They both mean "the."

Spanish nouns that end in *-e* or a consonant must be learned as masculine or feminine. You should practice them with their definite articles, *el* or *la*.

Masculine	Feminine
el profesor	la noche
el lápiz	la conversación

3 ¿Masculino o femenino?

Pensar • Escribir

Look at these words and decide whether each one is masculine or feminine. Rewrite each word and add the appropriate definite article *(el* or *la)*.

1. pierna
2. nariz
3. cuaderno
4. hora
5. pupitre
6. pie
7. profesora
8. estudiante

Más práctica GO

realidades.com | print

Core WB p. 6	✔	✔
Comm. WB p. 2	✔	✔

ENRICH YOUR TEACHING

Teacher-to-Teacher

Since Spanish nouns have gender, a concept foreign to most native English speakers, students often make overgeneralizations when learning vocabulary. Point out exceptions to the gender rule: ***la mano*** (feminine even though it ends in ***o***) and ***el día*** (masculine even though it ends in ***a***), but stress that in most cases the ***o / a*** rule is accurate. Tell students that they should always learn nouns with the correct article.

Practice and Communicate

PE

2 Standards: 1.1

Resources: Answer Keys: Student Edition, p. 5

Focus: Speaking with a partner about items and people in the classroom

Suggestions: Be sure students understand that they are to use the English word in items 1–5 because they are asking for the Spanish word. In items 6–10, they must use the Spanish word because they are asking for an English word.

Answers:

1. pen / bolígrafo
2. student / estudiante
3. notebook / cuaderno
4. desk / pupitre
5. folder / carpeta
6. cuaderno / notebook
7. hoja de papel / sheet of paper
8. cabeza / head
9. carpeta / folder
10. brazo / arm

Gramática

Core Instruction

Standards: 4.1

Suggestions: Use the various vocabulary transparencies and have students identify the gender of the nouns. Show the grammar transparencies for reinforcement.

3 Standards: 1.3

Resources: Answer Keys: Student Edition, p. 6

Focus: Identifying gender and using appropriate definite articles

Suggestions: Have students identify the genders of nouns ending in ***-o*** or ***-a.*** Point out that ***estudiante*** is tricky, and that ***nariz*** must simply be learned as feminine.

Answers:

1. la
2. la
3. el
4. la
5. el
6. el
7. la
8. el / la

Additional Resources

- Communication Wbk.: Audio Act. 3, p. 2
- Teacher's Resource Book: Audio Script, p. 9, Communicative Pair Activity, pp. 12–13
- Audio Program DVD: Cap. 00, Track 20

El alfabeto

Core Instruction

Standards: 1.2

Resources: Teacher's Resource Book: Input Script, p. 6, Clip Art, pp. 17–21, Audio Script, p. 9; Voc. and Gram. Transparency 29; Audio Program DVD: Cap. 00, Track 16

Focus: Introducing the Spanish alphabet and spelling in Spanish

Suggestions: Develop a rap rhythm for the letters. Ask volunteers to say a letter, quickly moving from one student to the next.

4 Standards: 1.2, 1.3

Resources: Teacher's Resource Book: Audio Script, p. 9; Audio Program DVD: Cap. 00, Track 17; Answer Keys: Student Edition, p. 6

Focus: Listening to letters in a word and writing the word

Suggestions: Allow students to listen more than once.

Script and Answers:

1. **ge-u-ese-te-o *(gusto)***
2. **be-i-e-ene *(bien)***
3. **ere-e-ge-u-ele-a-ere *(regular)***
4. **o-ene-ce-e *(once)***
5. **be-ere-a-zeta-o *(brazo)***
6. **pe-i-e-ere-ene-a *(pierna)***
7. **pe-u-pe-i-te-ere-e *(pupitre)***
8. **ce-a-be-e-zeta-a *(cabeza)***

5 Standards: 1.1, 1.3

Resources: Answer Keys: Student Edition, p. 6

Focus: Speaking and writing letters/words

Suggestions: As students work, monitor their pronunciation.

Answers:

1. **carpeta:** ***ce-a-ere-pe-e-te-a***
2. **cuaderno:** ***ce-u-a-de-e-ere-ene-o***
3. **libro:** ***ele-i-be-ere-o***
4. **pupitre:** ***pe-u-pe-i-te-ere-e***
5. **bolígrafo:** ***be-o-ele-i acento-ge-ere-a-efe-o***

BELLRINGER REVIEW

Show Vocabulary and Grammar Transparency 28. Put on the board: "Have handy two of the items pictured. Be prepared to spell them in Spanish."

El alfabeto

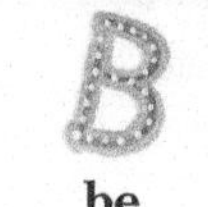

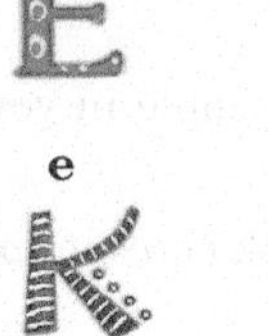
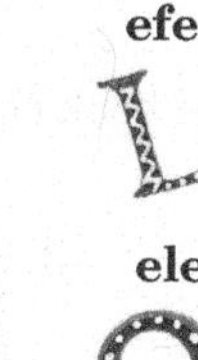
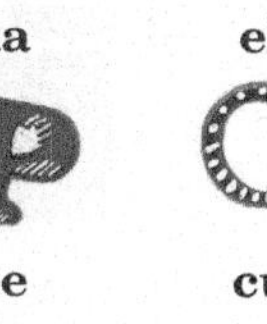

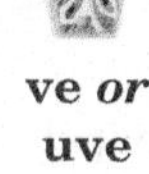

a	**be**	**ce**	**de**	**e**	**efe**
ge	**hache**	**i**	**jota**	**ka**	**ele**
eme	**ene**	**eñe**	**o**	**pe**	**cu**
ere	**erre**	**ese**	**te**	**u**	**ve** *or* **uve**
doble ve *or* **doble u**	**equis**	**i griega** *or* **ye**	**zeta**		

—**¿Cómo se escribe** *libro*?

—**Se escribe** ele-i-be-ere-o.

4 Escucha y escribe

Escuchar • Escribir

On a sheet of paper, write the numbers 1–8. You will hear several words you know spelled aloud. Listen carefully and write the letters as you hear them.

5 Pregunta y contesta

Hablar • Escribir

Work with a partner. Use the pictures to ask and answer according to the model. As Student B spells the words, Student A should write them out. When you are finished, check your spelling by looking at p. 10.

Modelo

A —*¿Cómo se escribe* <u>lápiz</u>?
B —*Se escribe* <u>*ele-a acento-pe-i-zeta.*</u>

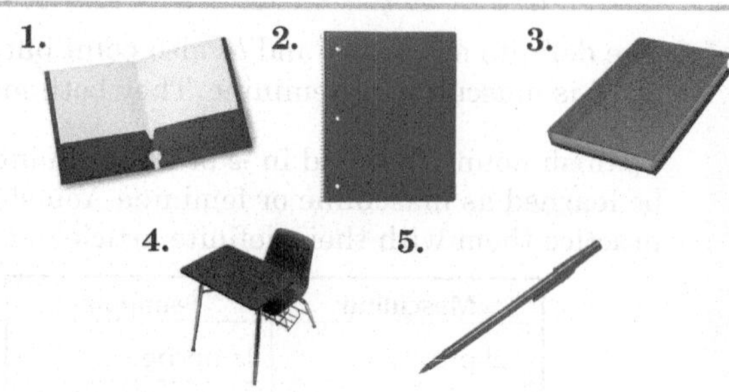

DIFFERENTIATED INSTRUCTION

Heritage Language Learners

Have students look at Spanish newspapers or magazines and write a list of ten words that have accent marks. Then have students spell the words aloud. Remind them to include the accent marks in their spelling.

Advanced Learners

Have students turn to p. 9, make a list of the labeled parts of ***El cuerpo,*** and then write or say the letters for each word.

6 ¿Cómo te llamas? | 

Hablar

Work with a partner. Follow the model to find out each other's names and how they are spelled. Then change partners and repeat.

A —*¿Cómo te llamas?*
B —*Me llamo María.*
A —*¿Cómo se escribe María?*
B —*Se escribe eme-a-ere-i acento-a.*

Strategy

Sustaining a conversation
If you need your partner to spell a word again, say *Repite, por favor.*

Exploración del lenguaje

Punctuation and accent marks

You have probably noticed that in Spanish, questions begin with an upside-down question mark (¿) and exclamations with an upside-down exclamation point (¡). This lets you know at the beginning of a sentence what kind of sentence you are reading.

You have probably also noticed the accent mark *(el acento)* on words like *días* and *estás.* When you write in Spanish, you must include these accents and punctuation marks.

Try it out! Rewrite these sentences and insert the correct punctuation and accents.

Como estas   Que tal   Hasta luego   Y tu

Fondo Cultural | El mundo hispano

Los mayas were among the early civilizations in the Western Hemisphere to develop a form of writing with symbols, known as hieroglyphics *(los jeroglíficos).* Each symbol, or glyph, represents a word or an idea.

- With what other hieroglyphic writing are you familiar?

Jeroglíficos mayas

7 Juego |

Escribir • Hablar • Escuchar

1. Play this game in pairs. Each player makes a list of five Spanish words that you have learned. Don't let your partner see your words.
2. Spell your first word aloud in Spanish. Don't forget any accent marks. Your partner will write the word as you spell it. Then your partner will spell a word for you to write. Take turns until you have spelled all the words on your lists.
3. Check each other's papers. The winner is the player with the most words spelled correctly.

Practice and Communicate PE

6 Standards: 1.1

Focus: Asking partners their names and how to spell them

Suggestions: Direct students' attention to the *Strategy*. Explain that these are tips that will help in language learning. Have students change partners three or four times. When reviewing, call on pairs of students who did not work together to do the dialogue.

Answers will vary.

Exploración del lenguaje

Core Instruction

Standards: 4.1

Focus: Using punctuation and accent marks

Suggestions: If students need help, have them look at p. 4 to review the words. Stress that accent marks are required for correct meaning and pronunciation.

Fondo cultural

Standards: 3.1

Suggestions: Explain that glyphs can be difficult to translate because they are not individual letters that form words, but pictures that represent something—an idea, a person, an action. Glyphs are closer in function to words than letters.

Mapa global interactivo, Actividad 1 Compare ancient Mayan ruins in different locations in Mexico.

7 Standards: 1.2

Focus: Listening to and spelling words

Suggestions: Suggest that students choose vocabulary words from different categories, rather than from a single group. This way, their partner will not be able to guess as easily.

Answers will vary.

Additional Resources

- Communication Wbk.: Audio Act. 4, p. 2
- Teacher's Resource Book: Audio Script, p. 9
- Audio Program DVD: Cap. 00, Track 23

ENRICH YOUR TEACHING

Teacher-to-Teacher

Have students write two sentences about themselves and then create their own hieroglyphs. Tell them to draw pictures that represent the sentences they wrote. Then have students exchange their glyphs with another student and try to read their hieroglyphic system.

Teacher-to-Teacher

In 1994, the Association of Spanish Language Academies eliminated *ch* and *ll* as separate letters from the Spanish alphabet. This simplified dictionaries and made the language more computer friendly. Spelling, pronunciation, and usage are not affected. Some sources treat *rr* as a sound and not a letter of the alphabet. In *Realidades*, the *rr* is listed as a letter.

BELLRINGER REVIEW

Use flashcards or transparencies to quickly drill students on numbers 1–31.

El calendario y la fecha

Core Instruction

Standards: 1.2

Resources: Voc. and Gram. Transparency 30; Teacher's Resource Book: Audio Script, p. 9; Audio Program DVD: Cap. 00, Tracks 18–19

Focus: Reading and speaking the months of the year; asking questions about days, months, and dates

Suggestions: You may want to present this vocabulary in three sets: days of the week, months of the year, and asking and telling the date. Show students a calendar or use the transparency, and explain that in most Spanish-speaking countries, calendars start with Monday. Prompt students to ask you: *¿Qué día es hoy?* Respond and point to the day at the top of the calendar, then ask students: *Y mañana, ¿qué día es mañana?* Repeat this exercise for each of the days of the week.

Use the question *¿Cuántos días hay en el mes de...?* to introduce the months in order. Students answer with a number. As they listen, ask students to raise their hand when they hear their birth month.

Direct attention to the *Nota*.

Use the dialogues to introduce how to ask the date. Practice other dates by flipping through a calendar and pointing to random dates. Direct attention to the second *Nota*, then include ***el primero*** in the practice. Each day at the beginning of class, ask students what the date is.

El calendario y la fecha

—¿Qué día es hoy?
—Hoy es lunes. Mañana es martes.
—¿Cuántos días hay en el mes de agosto?
—Hay treinta y un días.

Los meses del año

enero	febrero	marzo
abril	mayo	junio
julio	agosto	septiembre
octubre	noviembre	diciembre

(Each month: l m m j v s d)

Nota

Notice that the days of the week and the months of the year are not capitalized in Spanish, except at the beginning of sentences.

The first day of the week in a Spanish-language calendar is *lunes*.

DIFFERENTIATED INSTRUCTION

Heritage Language Learners

Have students research and write down the names and dates of three important celebrations in their heritage countries. Give them opportunity to describe the occasion and the festivities that occur during these celebrations. Check their written work for correct spelling, including use of accents.

Advanced Learners/Pre-AP*

Have students make a twelve-month calendar using the Spanish names for months and days of the week. Students should note important days, such as school holidays and classmates' birthdays. You may want students to research and include important holidays in Spanish-speaking cultures. Post the calendars in the room.

—¿Cuál es la fecha?
—Es el 22 de agosto.

—¿Cuál es la fecha?
—Es **el primero** de agosto.

Nota

To say the first day of the month, use *el primero*. For the other days, use the numbers *dos, tres,* and so on.

8 Hoy y mañana | 

Hablar

Ask and answer according to the model.

 **Modelo**

lunes
A —*¿Qué día es hoy?*
B —*Hoy es lunes. Mañana es martes.*

1. martes
2. sábado
3. jueves
4. miércoles
5. viernes
6. domingo

El Cinco de Mayo es un día festivo en México.

9 Días de fiesta

Leer • Escribir

Read the following sentences and rewrite them, making the necessary corrections.

1. El Día de San Patricio es el 14 de enero.
2. El Día de San Valentín es en junio.
3. Janucá es en febrero.
4. La Navidad *(Christmas)* es el 25 de noviembre.
5. El Día de la Independencia de los Estados Unidos *(United States)* es el 4 de junio.
6. El Año Nuevo *(New Year's Day)* es en diciembre.
7. Hoy es el 3 de agosto.

ENRICH YOUR TEACHING

Culture Note

Cinco de mayo commemorates the victory of the Mexican army over the invading French army at the Battle of Puebla in 1862. It is not, as is commonly misunderstood, Mexican Independence Day, which is celebrated September 15 and 16. *Cinco de mayo* has become an occasion for parties and celebration in the United States, even among people of other heritages.

Practice and Communicate PE

8 Standards: 1.1

Resources: Answer Keys: Student Edition, p. 7

Focus: Asking and answering questions about days of the week

Suggestions: Be sure students understand their roles. Have them switch roles and repeat the activity.

Answers:

Student B:

1. **Hoy es martes. Mañana es miércoles.**
2. **...domingo.**
3. **...viernes.**
4. **...jueves.**
5. **...sábado.**
6. **...lunes.**

Extension: Create a spinner with the seven days of the week randomly placed. Have students spin and tell you the day that follows the day shown.

9 Standards: 1.3

Resources: Answer Keys: Student Edition, p. 7

Focus: Writing dates of holiday celebrations

Suggestions: Tell students to first read to identify the errors, then to read again, substituting the correct information before they write their sentences. When students are done, show the answers and have them correct their sentences if necessary.

Answers:

1. **El Día de San Patricio es el 17 de marzo.**
2. **El Día de San Valentín es en febrero.**
3. **Janucá es en diciembre.**
4. **La Navidad es el 25 de diciembre.**
5. **El Día de la Independencia de los Estados Unidos es el 4 de julio.**
6. **El Año Nuevo es en enero.**
7. **Hoy es el *(the current date).***

Teaching with Photos

Direct attention to the photo. Ask: *¿Qué día es?* Have students read the caption and answer. Encourage them to look for and read captions throughout *Realidades,* because they will give important information and will also use new words and structures. Explain how photos can support understanding of unfamiliar words.

10 Standards: 1.3

Resources: Answer Keys: Student Edition, p. 8

Focus: Writing answers to questions about days of the week

Suggestions: Be sure students understand they are to answer based on the calendar in the book.

Answers:

1. **Hoy es el 7 de julio.**
2. **Hoy es lunes.**
3. **Mañana es martes.**
4. **Mañana es el 8 de julio.**
5. **Hay 31 días en el mes de julio.**
6. **Hay 7 días en una semana.**

Extension: Make transparencies of other months and repeat the activity.

Fondo cultural

Standards: 2.1, 4.2

Suggestions: Explain that ***los sanfermines*** dates back to the Middle Ages. There are many other parts of this celebration, including music, dancing, and the Masquerade of the Giants, papier-mâché figures of kings and queens that are paraded through the streets. Stress that the running of the bulls is a very dangerous activity that frequently results in injury or death.

Answers will vary, but may include events such as annual rodeos or the Kentucky Derby.

Mapa global interactivo, Actividad 2 Explore the narrow streets of Pamplona, Spain.

10 El calendario

Escribir

julio

lunes	martes	miércoles	jueves	viernes	sábado	domingo
	1	2	3	4	5	6
7	8	9	10	11	12	13
14	15	16	17	18	19	20
21	22	23	24	25	26	27
28	29	30	31			

hoy (points to 7)

Answer the questions based on the calendar page above.

1. ¿Cuál es la fecha hoy?
2. ¿Qué día de la semana es?
3. ¿Qué día es mañana?
4. ¿Cuál es la fecha de mañana?
5. ¿Cuántos días hay en este *(this)* mes?
6. ¿Cuántos días hay en una semana?

Más práctica GO

realidades.com | print

	realidades.com	print
Instant Check	✔	
Guided WB pp. 11–18	✔	✔
Core WB pp. 7–8	✔	✔
Comm. WB p. 5	✔	✔
***Hispanohablantes* WB** pp. 4–5		✔

Fondo cultural | España

Los sanfermines, or the "Running of the Bulls," is a popular two-week festival in Pamplona, Spain, named for the town's patron saint, San Fermín, who is commemorated on July 7 each year. The celebration includes daily bullfights, but before they begin the real excitement starts! As the bulls are released from their pens and run through the streets, many people run ahead or alongside them to the bullring.

- What festivals are you familiar with in which animals play a role?

La Fiesta de San Fermín, en Pamplona, España

DIFFERENTIATED INSTRUCTION

Advanced Learners

Ask students to research Pamplona and ***los sanfermines.*** Remind them to include information on the other aspects of the two-week-long festival, not just on the running of the bulls. Suggest that they create print or digital visuals to share with the class.

Students with Special Needs

Some students may have difficulty grasping the abstraction of pretending that it is a different date in *Actividad* 10. If so, make a calendar that shows today's date and have them answer the questions on that basis.

11 El calendario azteca

Leer

The Aztecs were a nomadic tribe that finally settled in the valley of central Mexico in 1325. They established their capital, Tenochtitlán, on a swampy lake and built a mighty empire that dominated most of Mexico. The Aztec empire flourished until 1521, when it was defeated by the Spaniards, led by Hernán Cortés.

Conexiones | La historia

One of the most famous symbols of Mexico is the monolith, or huge stone, carved by the Aztecs in 1479. Known today as the Aztec calendar or the Sun Stone, the carving weighs almost 24 tons and is approximately 12 feet in diameter. The Aztecs dedicated it to the sun, represented by the face in the center. The calendar represents a 260-day year.

12 Los símbolos aztecas

Pensar

Here are several glyphs representing days found on the Sun Stone. Match the glyph with the Spanish word. What do you think each of the glyphs represents? Why do you think the Aztecs included those symbols on their calendar?

1. 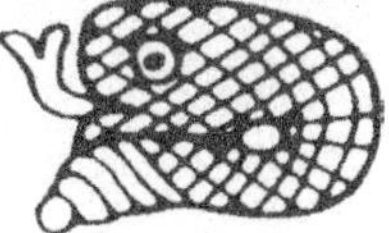
2. 
3. 
4. 
5. 
6. 

a. Jaguar
b. Perro
c. Movimiento
d. Serpiente
e. Cráneo
f. Agua

Practice and Communicate PE

11 Standards: 3.1

Focus: Reading about the Aztec calendar, cross-curricular connection to history

Suggestions: Throughout the program, you will find *Conexiones* activities that link language study with other disciplines. Students are moved into working directly in Spanish as quickly as possible. The *Conexiones* will either include activities and questions or will be followed by a related activity. Ask: Why might a people like the Aztecs abandon a nomadic lifestyle, settle, and develop agriculture? How long did the Aztecs dominate Mexico? What does the Sun Stone suggest about the Aztec culture?

12 Standards: 3.1

Resources: Answer Keys: Student Edition, p. 8

Focus: Speculating about the Aztec glyphs and calendar

Suggestions: Help students define the Spanish words before beginning the activity.

Answers:

1. d 2. e 3. f 4. b 5. a 6. c

ENRICH YOUR TEACHING

Culture Note

After the Spaniards conquered the Aztec city of Tenochtitlán (now Mexico City) in 1521, the Sun Stone was buried. It was rediscovered December 17, 1790, in what is now the ***Zócalo,*** or main plaza, of Mexico City. The Sun Stone now sits in Mexico's National Museum of Anthropology.

21st Century Skills

Social and Cross-Cultural Skills After students have read the *Conexiones: La historia* note on page 17, guide them in a brief investigation about different forms of time tracking and calendar models among Native American tribes in the United States. Have them find information about the importance of the Moon in the formation of calendars among these groups. Compare this to the central role played by the Sun in the Aztec calendar.

ASSESSMENT

Prueba P-2 with Study Plan (online only)

Quiz: En la clase

- Prueba P-2: p. 9

INTERACTIVE WHITEBOARD
Vocabulary Activities PE

¿Qué tiempo hace?

Core Instruction

Standards: 1.2

Resources: Teacher's Resource Book: Input Script, p. 6, Clip Art, pp. 17–21, Audio Script, p. 9; Voc. and Gram. Transparency 31; Audio Program DVD: Cap. 00, Track 21

Focus: Describing weather conditions and identifying seasons

Suggestions: Show the vocabulary transparencies. Use gestures to convey meaning. Bring in clothing or other items associated with each weather condition and use them in presenting and cueing the vocabulary. Have volunteers choose one of the items to hold up and ask their classmates *¿Qué tiempo hace?* Make this a regular question that you ask at the beginning of each class period. After modeling each expression, ask questions like *¿Hace calor en diciembre?* Say the name of a month and a region of the United States, and ask students for possible logical weather conditions.

To introduce the seasons, model pronunciation. Then say the months of a particular season ***(septiembre, octubre, noviembre)*** and ask students to choose which one it is.

3 El tiempo

Objectives

- Describe weather conditions
- Identify the seasons
- Compare weather in the Northern and Southern Hemispheres

¿Qué tiempo hace?

Hace sol.

Hace calor.

Hace frío.

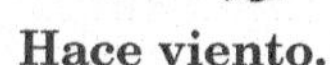

Hace viento.

Llueve.

Nieva.

Las estaciones

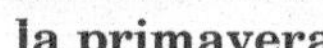

la primavera

el verano

el otoño

el invierno

DIFFERENTIATED INSTRUCTION

Advanced Learners/Pre-AP*

Assign students a city in the Spanish-speaking world, and have them follow the weather for one week. They can find weather conditions on the Internet and summarize their findings for the class. Make a bulletin board to track the weather. Have students provide additional facts about the cities and tell how weather may affect the lifestyle there.

Multiple Intelligences

Bodily/Kinesthetic: Nonverbal cues can often help students retain new vocabulary and expressions. Ask students to work in pairs to pantomime each of the weather conditions and seasons. Have students guess what kind of weather or which season is being represented and say the vocabulary word.

1 El tiempo

Escuchar

You will hear six descriptions of different weather conditions. Write the numbers 1–6 on a sheet of paper. Then, next to each number, write the letter of the photo for which the weather is being described.

a. 
b. 
c. 
d. 

2 ¿Qué tiempo hace?

Hablar

Work with a partner. Ask and answer the questions based on the city and weather information for each item.

Modelo
Miami / julio /
A —*¿Qué tiempo hace en Miami en julio?*
B —*Hace sol.*

1. Denver / enero / 
2. Chicago / octubre / 
3. San Francisco / noviembre / 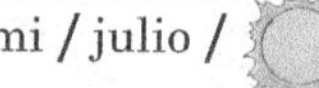
4. Washington, D.C. / junio / 
5. Minneapolis / diciembre / 
6. Dallas / agosto / 

3 Las estaciones

Hablar • Escribir

Answer the questions based on where you live.

1. ¿Qué tiempo hace en la primavera? ¿En el otoño? ¿En el verano? ¿En el invierno?
2. ¿En qué estación hace frío? ¿Calor? ¿Sol? ¿Viento?
3. ¿En qué estación llueve?
4. ¿En qué estación nieva?

Más práctica GO

	realidades.com	print
Canción de hip hop	✔	
Instant Check	✔	✔
Guided WB pp. 19–24	✔	✔
Core WB p. 9	✔	✔
Comm. WB p. 6	✔	✔
Hispanohablantes WB p. 6		✔

ENRICH YOUR TEACHING

Teacher-to-Teacher

Make photocopies of a newspaper weather map. Have students use the symbols on the map or read the weather for various cities and then write a sentence indicating the weather for those cities.

21st Century Skills

Communication Remind students of the various tools available in **realidades.com**, such as eText with embedded audio files and computer-corrected activities. Using these tools on a regular basis will help students develop fluency at a faster rate.

Practice and Communicate PE

BELLRINGER REVIEW

Put these expressions on the board: *Hace calor, hace frío, hace viento, nieva, llueve, hace sol.* Ask students to draw a simple illustration. As a follow-up, have them point to the appropriate illustration as you say the expressions.

1 Standards: 1.2

Resources: Teacher's Resource Book: Audio Script, p. 9; Audio Program DVD: Cap. 00, Track 22; Answer Keys: Student Edition, p. 9

Focus: Listening to and identifying weather vocabulary

Suggestions: Ask students to briefly describe in English the weather they see in each picture. Explain that there are six items, so some of the pictures will be used more than once.

Script and Answers:
1. **Hace calor.** ***(b)***
2. **Llueve.** ***(d)***
3. **Nieva.** ***(c)***
4. **Hace frío.** ***(c)***
5. **Hace viento.** ***(d)***
6. **Hace sol. No hace calor.** ***(a)***

2 Standards: 1.1

Resources: Answer Keys: Student Edition, p. 9

Focus: Asking and answering questions about the weather

Suggestions: Ask students to think about what the weather is like in each city. Be sure they understand which words they need to replace in each item.

Answers:
1. **Nieva. / Hace frío.**
2. **Hace viento.**
3. **Llueve.**
4. **Hace calor. / Hace sol.**
5. **Hace frío.**
6. **Hace calor. / Hace sol.**

Extension: Ask: *¿Qué tiempo hace en* (your town) *en* (month)? Have volunteers ask questions of their classmates.

3 Standards: 1.2, 1.3

Focus: Asking and answering questions about weather and seasons

Suggestions: Have students write this activity in paragraph form, giving it a title such as *El tiempo en* (name of town).

Answers will vary.

PE Practice and Communicate

4 Standards: 1.1, 1.2, 1.3, 3.1

Resources: Voc. and Gram. Transparencies, 15–17, 20; Answer Keys: Student Edition, p. 9

Focus: Speaking and writing about weather in the two hemispheres; cross-curricular connection

Suggestions: Ask students to describe the location of Colorado and Chile. Show the Map Transparencies or a globe. Refer students to the pictures. Be sure they understand the difference between the Northern and Southern Hemispheres. Have students share their answers with the class.

Answers:

1. **En febrero hace calor en Chile.**
2. **En junio hace calor en Colorado.**
3. **Answers will vary.**

Extension: Write on the board the names of ten places in the Northern and Southern Hemispheres and refer students to a world map or globe. Have students identify which hemisphere each place is in and ask them what the weather might be like during ***enero, abril, junio, julio, septiembre,*** and ***noviembre.***

Mapa global interactivo, Actividad 3 Locate the continents of North and South America, the equator, and the country of Ecuador. Then compare weather north and south of the equator.

Teacher-to-Teacher

Using a world map or globe, ask students to follow these instructions: *Señalen dónde hace frío en enero; Señalen dónde hace calor en enero; Señalen dónde hace frío en julio; Señalen dónde hace calor en julio; Señalen dónde nieva en diciembre; Señalen dónde nieva en agosto.* Then have students work in pairs to think of more scenarios and give instructions to classmates.

4 Dos hemisferios

Leer • Pensar • Escribir • Hablar

Read about the seasons in the Northern and Southern Hemispheres and then answer the questions.

Conexiones | La geografía

Did you know that the seasons for the Northern and Southern Hemispheres are reversed? When it's winter in the Northern Hemisphere, it's summer in the Southern Hemisphere and vice versa. So if you want to ski all year round, go from the slopes of the Rockies in Colorado in December to those of the Andes in Bariloche, Argentina in July. Or for a December getaway to a warmer climate, go to one of the coastal resorts at Viña del Mar, Chile.

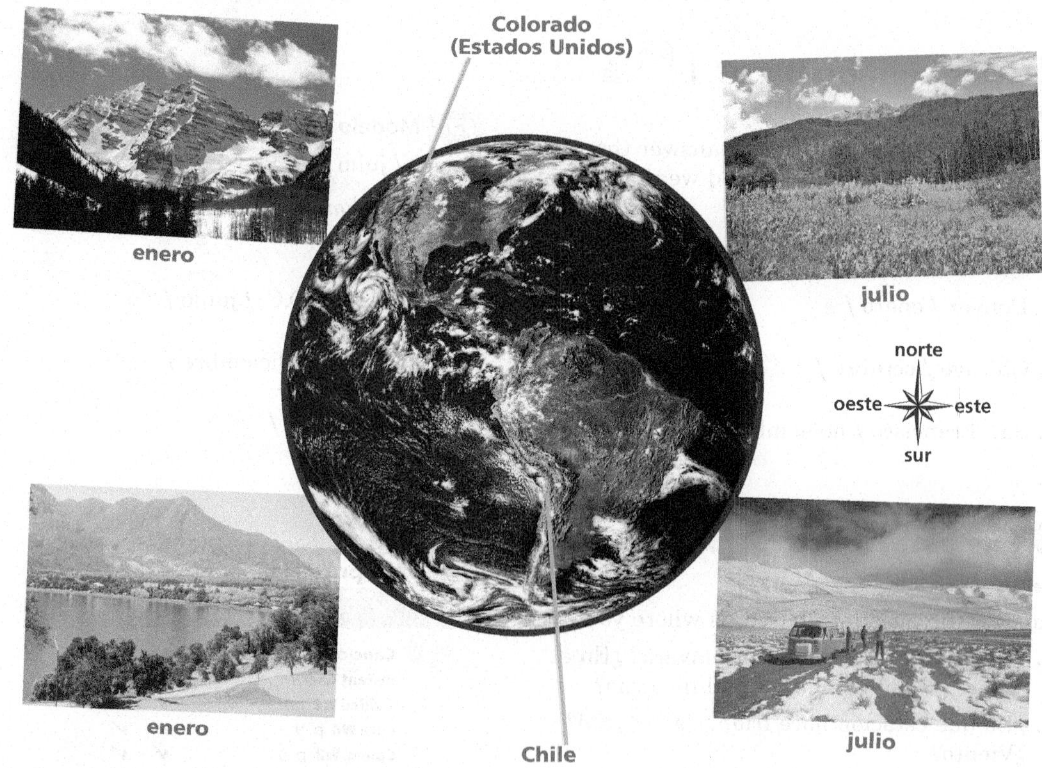

1. En febrero, ¿qué tiempo hace en Chile?
2. En junio, ¿qué tiempo hace en Colorado?
3. En tu comunidad, ¿qué tiempo hace en diciembre? ¿Y en agosto?

DIFFERENTIATED INSTRUCTION

Students with Learning Difficulties

You might need to read this passage with students who struggle with reading. Encourage them to read through the questions at the bottom prior to reading. Converting temperatures might prove a challenge for students; the *Nota* on p. 21 could be an added task not required of all students.

Heritage Language Learners

Have students research the climate and seasons of their heritage countries and write a short paragraph. They should note the country's hemisphere, compare the weather with that of your community, and distinguish the seasons and their temperatures in the two places.

Practice and Communicate PE

Los Ángeles

Tegucigalpa, Honduras

Asunción, Paraguay

ciudad	diciembre	julio
Asunción, Paraguay	85°F / 29°C	75°F / 24°C
Bogotá, Colombia	66°F / 19°C	64°F / 17°C
Buenos Aires, Argentina	78°F / 26°C	50°F / 10°C
Caracas, Venezuela	80°F / 27°C	80°F / 27°C
Chicago	36°F / 2°C	75°F / 24°C
Ciudad de México, México	70°F / 21°C	74°F / 23°C
Guatemala, Guatemala	72°F / 22°C	74°F / 23°C
La Habana, Cuba	76°F / 24°C	82°F / 28°C
La Paz, Bolivia	58°F / 15°C	55°F / 13°C
Lima, Perú	76°F / 24°C	76°F / 24°C
Los Ángeles	67°F / 19°C	88°F / 31°C
Miami	76°F / 24°C	97°F / 36°C
Nueva York	41°F / 5°C	74°F / 23°C
Quito, Ecuador	65°F / 18°C	67°F / 19°C
San José, Costa Rica	78°F / 26°C	78°F / 26°C
San Juan, Puerto Rico	74°F / 23°C	80°F / 27°C
Santiago, Chile	82°F / 28°C	50°F / 10°C
Seattle	41°F / 5°C	66°F / 19°C
St. Louis	36°F / 2°C	81°F / 27°C
Tegucigalpa, Honduras	70°F / 21°C	81°F / 27°C

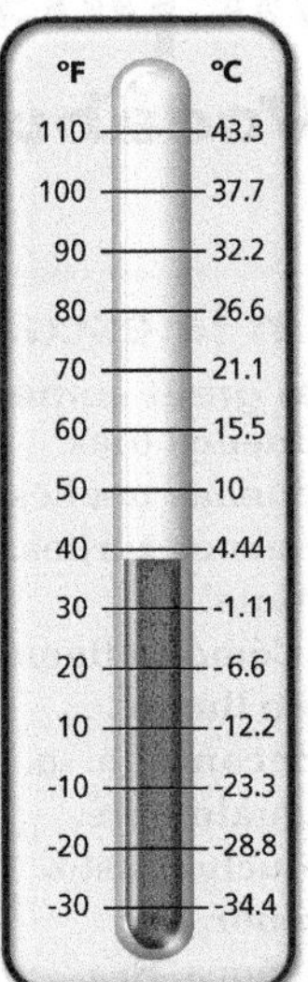

Nota

In most parts of the world, people express temperatures in Celsius. A simple way to convert from Celsius to Fahrenheit is to multiply the temperature by $\frac{9}{5}$, then add 32.

30°C = ? F

$30 \times \frac{9}{5} = 54 + 32$

30°C = 86°F

5 ¿Hace calor o hace frío?

Hablar • Escribir

Work with a partner. Discuss the weather in six different places on the chart.

Modelo

A —*¿Qué tiempo hace en Chicago en diciembre?*
B —*Hace frío.*

6 ¿Y qué tiempo hace en . . . ?

Hablar

Work with a partner. Ask about the temperature in six different places on the chart.

Modelo

A —*¿Cuál es la temperatura en Quito en diciembre?*
B —*Sesenta y cinco grados.*
o: —*Dieciocho grados.*

Para decir más . . .

la temperatura temperature
grados degrees

BELLRINGER REVIEW

Have students turn to p. 7 and review *Los números.*

5 Standards: 1.1, 3.1

Focus: Reading a chart and writing about the weather for cities in the Northern and Southern Hemispheres

Suggestions: Show the map transparencies and help students locate the countries and cities in the chart. Direct their attention to the *Nota*. To internalize the concept, have them practice one or two conversions using a calculator. Have students take turns asking and answering the questions. Both students should write the questions and the answers, indicating the cities they selected and their weather.

Answers will vary.

Extension: Students should point to the map and show the cities they chose.

6 Standards: 1.1

Focus: Talking about temperatures in the Northern and Southern Hemispheres

Suggestions: Point out that the words in *Para decir más....* are helpful for completing the activity but do not have to be memorized.

Answers will vary.

Pre-AP* Support

- **Learning Objective:** Interpersonal Speaking
- **Activity 6:** Students practice informal speaking skills as they ask and answer questions about weather.
- ***Pre-AP* Resource Book:*** Comprehensive guide to Pre-AP* speaking skill development, pp. 39–50

Additional Resources

- Communication Wbk.: Audio Act. 5, p. 3
- Teacher's Resource Book: Audio Script, p. 10
- Audio Program DVD: Cap. 00, Track 24

ASSESSMENT

Prueba P-3 with Study Plan (online only)

Quiz: El tiempo

- Prueba P-3: p. 10

ENRICH YOUR TEACHING

Culture Note

The highest temperature in the continental United States, 134°F (57°C), was recorded on July 10, 1913, in Death Valley, California. The lowest recorded temperature, –70°F (–57°C), was at Roger's Pass, Montana, on January 20, 1954. In South America, the highest and lowest recorded temperatures were in Argentina: 120°F (49°C) at Rivadavia on December 11, 1905, and –27°F (–33°C) at Sarmiento on June 1, 1907. Remind students that the highest and lowest temperatures happen at opposite times of the year in North and South America. Write these dates and have students read them.

PE Review

Review Activities

To greet someone and to say good-bye: Have students practice greetings and leave-takings in pairs.

To ask and tell how someone is: Have students circulate from partner to partner asking and telling how they are doing.

To tell time: Have students list five times and take turns asking *¿Qué hora es?* and answering with different times.

To count up to 100: Have students write the numerals 1–9 on index cards. Shuffle the cards and place them face down. Each player draws two cards and says the number that is formed.

To talk about the body: Have students draw the outline of a person and identify the body parts, referring to p. 9 for help.

To talk about the classroom: Have students use the Clip Art in the *Teacher's Resource Book* to make flashcards to identify classroom items.

To say the date: Have partners ask and answer *¿Qué día es hoy?* and *¿Cuál es la fecha?* while pointing to a calendar.

To ask for help: Have students quiz one another on word meanings using the questions shown.

To talk about the weather: Have students ask each other, *¿Qué tiempo hace?*

To talk about the seasons: Have students identify seasons using transparencies.

Portfolio

Invite students to review the activities they completed in this chapter, including written reports, posters, other visuals, and recordings of oral presentations or other projects. Have them select one or two items that they feel best demonstrate their achievements in Spanish to include in their portfolios. Have them also include the Chapter Checklist and Self Assessment Worksheet.

Additional Resources

Student Resources: Realidades para hispanohablantes, pp. 8–9

Teacher Resources:

- Teacher's Resource Book: Situation Cards, p. 16, Clip Art, pp. 17–21
- Assessment Program: Chapter Checklist and Self-Assessment Worksheet, pp. T56–T57

Repaso del capítulo

Objectives
- Review the vocabulary
- Demonstrate you can perform the tasks on p. 23

Vocabulario

En la escuela

to greet someone

Buenos días.	Good morning.
Buenas noches.	Good evening.
Buenas tardes.	Good afternoon.
¡Hola!	Hello!
¿Cómo te llamas?	What is your name?
Me llamo . . .	My name is . . .
Encantado, -a.	Delighted.
Igualmente.	Likewise.
Mucho gusto.	Pleased to meet you.
señor, Sr.	sir, Mr.
señora, Sra.	madam, Mrs.
señorita, Srta.	miss, Miss

to ask and tell how someone is

¿Cómo está Ud.? *(formal)*	How are you?
¿Cómo estás? *(familiar)*	How are you?
¿Qué pasa?	What's happening?
¿Qué tal?	How are you?
¿Y tú? / ¿Y usted (Ud.)?	And you?
(muy) bien	(very) well
nada	nothing
regular	okay, so-so
gracias	thank you

to say good-bye

¡Adiós!	Good-bye!
Hasta luego.	See you later.
Hasta mañana.	See you tomorrow.
¡Nos vemos!	See you!

to tell time

¿Qué hora es?	What time is it?
Es la una.	It's one o'clock.
Son las . . . y / menos . . .	It's . . . *(time).*
y cuarto / menos cuarto	quarter past / quarter to
y media	thirty, half-past

to count up to 100 (Turn to p. 7.)

to talk about the body (Turn to p. 9.)

En la clase

to talk about the classroom

el bolígrafo	pen
la carpeta	folder
el cuaderno	notebook
el estudiante, la estudiante	student
la hoja de papel	sheet of paper
el lápiz	pencil
el libro	book
el profesor, la profesora	teacher
el pupitre	(student) desk
la sala de clases	classroom

to say the date

el año	year
el día	day
el mes	month
la semana	week
¿Qué día es hoy?	What day is today?
¿Cuál es la fecha?	What is the date?
Es el *(number)* de *(month).*	It's the . . . of . . .
Es el primero de *(month).*	It's the first of . . .
hoy	today
mañana	tomorrow

to say the days of the week and the months of the year (Turn to p. 14.)

other useful words

¿cuántos, -as?	how many?
en	in
hay	there is / there are
por favor	please

to ask for help

¿Cómo se dice . . . ?	How do you say . . . ?
Se dice . . .	You say . . .
¿Cómo se escribe . . . ?	How is . . . spelled?
Se escribe . . .	It's spelled . . .
¿Qué quiere decir . . . ?	What does . . . mean?
Quiere decir . . .	It means . . .

DIFFERENTIATED INSTRUCTION

Students with Learning Difficulties

The *Repaso* page contains a lot of information, and may be too much for some students to absorb and understand at once. Help students take the review section by section. Show them how to focus on things they've not mastered.

Advanced Learners

You may wish to ask students to facilitate review sessions within small groups. Suggest that they write five review questions to share with their group.

Más repaso GO realidades.com | print

Instant Check	✔	
Puzzles	✔	
Core WB pp. 10–11		✔
Comm. WB p. 226	✔	✔

El tiempo

to talk about the weather

¿Qué tiempo hace?	What's the weather like?
Hace calor.	It's hot.
Hace frío.	It's cold.
Hace sol.	It's sunny.
Hace viento.	It's windy.
Llueve.	It's raining.
Nieva.	It's snowing.

to talk about the seasons

la estación	season
el invierno	winter
el otoño	fall, autumn
la primavera	spring
el verano	summer

Preparación para el examen

Interpretive

1 **Escuchar** On the exam you will be asked to listen to and understand people as they greet each other and introduce themselves. To practice, listen to some students greet people in the school halls. Answer these questions about each greeting: Is it morning or afternoon? Was the greeting directed to an adult? How did that person respond?

To review, see pp. 2–5 and Actividades 1, 4.

Interpretive

2 **Escuchar** You will be asked to listen to and understand someone announcing the current date and time. To practice, listen to the message and answer the questions: What is the time of day? What is the date?

To review, see pp. 7–8 and Actividad 12; pp. 14–16 and Actividad 10.

Interpretive

3 **Leer** You will be asked to read and understand a description of the weather for a given day. To practice, read the weather forecast below. Answer the questions: What is the date? What are the high and low temperatures? What is the weather like?

El dos de septiembre
Hoy en San Antonio hace sol. La temperatura máxima es 75 grados y la mínima es 54. No llueve.

To review, see pp. 18–21 and Actividades 2–6.

Interpretive

4 **Leer** You will be asked to read a list of school supplies and identify them. To practice, copy the school supply list below onto a sheet of paper. Please note: *un, una* mean "a" or "an." Then look to see whether you have any of the items on your desk right now. Make a check mark next to each item you have.

un cuaderno	un lápiz	una hoja de papel
un bolígrafo	una carpeta	un libro

To review, see p. 10.

Review PE

Performance Tasks

Standards: 1.2, 1.3

Student Resource: Realidades para hispanohablantes, p. 9

Teacher Resources: Teacher's Resource Book: Audio Script, p. 10; Audio Program DVD: Cap. 00, Tracks 26–27; Answer Keys: Student Edition, p. 10

Note that the test for the *Para empezar* does not ask for active communicative production.

1. Escuchar

Suggestions: Remind students of the greetings for different times of day and for greeting adults versus friends.

Script and Answers:

1. **—Buenas tardes, Sr. Ruiz. ¿Cómo está Ud.?**
   —Bien, señor. *(afternoon; to an adult; he is well)*
2. **—¡Hola, Elena!**
   —Buenos días. Nos vemos en la escuela. *(morning; to a teen; she said good morning)*
3. **—Julio, ¿qué tal?**
   —Regular, ¿y tú? *(either; to a teen; he's so-so)*

2. Escuchar

Suggestions: Play the *audio* or read the script.

Script and Answers:

1. **Muy buenos días. Es el veintidós de septiembre. Son las ocho y media de la mañana. *(morning; September 22)***
2. **Muy buenas tardes. Es el ocho de enero. Son las dos y veinte de la tarde. *(afternoon; January 8)***
3. **Muy buenas noches. Es el cuatro de noviembre. Son las nueve y diez de la noche. *(evening/night; November 4)***

3. Leer

Suggestions: Have volunteers share their answers with the class.

Answers: **September 2; high temperature 75°; the low is 54°; it's sunny and not raining**

4. Leer

Suggestions: Have students try this activity without consulting the vocabulary list.

Answers will vary.

DIFFERENTIATED ASSESSMENT

CORE ASSESSMENT
- **Assessment Program:** Examen de *Para empezar,* pp. 11–12
- **Audio Program DVD:** Cap. 00, Track 28
- **ExamView:** Chapter Test, Test Banks A and B

ADVANCED/PRE-AP*
- **ExamView: Pre-AP* Test Bank**
- **Pre-AP* Resource Book,** pp. 60–61

STUDENTS NEEDING EXTRA HELP
- **Alternate Assessment Program:** Examen del capítulo PE
- **Audio Program DVD:** Cap. 00, Track 28

HERITAGE LEARNERS
- **Assessment Program: Realidades para hispanohablantes:** Examen del capítulo PE
- **ExamView: Heritage Learner Test Bank**

Mis amigos y yo

1A ¿Qué te gusta hacer?

- **Activities you and others like and don't like to do**

Vocabulary: activities and expressions for saying what you like and don't like to do

Grammar: infinitives; making negative statements

Cultural Perspectives: favorite activities of teens

1B Y tú, ¿cómo eres?

- **Personality traits**

Vocabulary: adjectives and vocabulary to ask about and describe someone's personality

Grammar: adjectives; definite and indefinite articles; word order

Cultural Perspectives: opinions about what makes a good friend

THEME SUPPORT

Bulletin Boards

Theme: ***Mis amigos y yo***

Ask students to cut out, copy, or download photos of people from many different cultures engaged in a variety of academic, social, and leisure activities, sports, crafts, and artistic pursuits. Cluster photos according to the types of activities featured.

Game

¿Quién es?

This game is played like Twenty Questions. Use it in *Capítulo* 1B.

Players: entire class

Materials: scraps of paper, pen, a paper bag

Rules:

1. Students write their names on scraps of paper and place them in a paper bag.
2. Shake the paper bag to mix up the names. Then call on a volunteer to come to the front of the class. The volunteer draws the name of a student from the paper bag, then gives the paper to you.
3. Students take turns asking the volunteer yes / no questions in an attempt to determine the identity of the person listed on the scrap of paper.
   Student 1: ¿Es una chica?
   Leader: Sí.
   Student 2: ¿Es deportista?
   Leader: Sí.
   Student 3: ¿Le gusta montar en bicicleta?
   Leader: No.
4. When a student correctly guesses the identity of the person on the paper, he or she becomes the new volunteer.

Hands-on Culture

Craft: ***Maracas***

Maracas are very popular percussion instruments in Spanish-speaking countries. They can be made of many materials.

Materials: newspaper, 2 round balloons, 2 jars, white glue, scissors, foil pan, measuring cup, pin, masking tape, 24 dried beans or small pebbles, 2 paper towel tubes, paint, paintbrush, crepe paper

Directions:

1. Cover work area with newspapers.
2. Blow up balloons to grapefruit size.
3. Place each balloon in the mouth of a jar, with the tied end inside the jar.
4. Cut strips of newspaper 6" × ½".
5. In the foil pan, mix equal amounts of white glue and water (about ½ cup each). Dip newspaper strips in glue mixture and apply wet strips to balloons, criss-crossing them. Use five layers to make the maraca strong. Be sure only the bottom parts of the balloons show through.
6. Let dry overnight. Hold each balloon by the tied end and burst it with a pin.
7. Remove the balloon. Insert 12 beans or pebbles through the hole in each maraca and tape the hole closed.
8. To make handles, cut four parallel slits (about 3" long) into the end of each paper towel tube, running lengthwise. Circle the tubes with tape just below the slits to keep them from splitting further. Spread the slit pieces apart and fit the maraca onto them. Tape the slit pieces firmly to the maraca, taping all the way around and ½ to ¾ of the way up the maraca. Paint and let dry overnight.
9. Cut two strips of crepe paper about 3" wide and 14" long. To make a fringe, cut 1½" slits all along the edge of each strip, about ½" apart. Glue the uncut edge of one strip to the handle of one of the maracas, starting just below the maraca. Wind and glue the strip around the handle.

THEME PROJECT

Álbum de recuerdos

Overview: Students create two pages for a scrapbook featuring photos of their friends and themselves with captions written underneath. They then give an oral presentation of their scrapbook, describing the people in the photos and telling what they like and don't like to do.

Resources: electronic or print photos, image editing and page layout software and/or construction paper, magazines, colored pencils, markers, glue, scissors

Sequence: (suggestions for when to do each step appear throughout the chapters)

1A **STEP 1.** Review instructions so students know what is expected of them. Hand out the "Theme 1 Project Instructions and Rubric" from the *Teacher's Resource Book.*

STEP 2. Students submit a rough sketch of their scrapbook pages. Return the sketches with your suggestions. For vocabulary and grammar practice, ask students to work with a partner and present their drafts to each other.

STEP 3. Students do layouts. Encourage students to try different arrangements before finalizing layouts and writing captions.

1B **STEP 4.** Students submit a draft of their captions. Note your corrections and suggestions, then return the drafts to students.

STEP 5. Students complete and present their scrapbook to the class. They should describe the people in the photos and say what they like and don't like to do.

Options:

1. Students feature fictitious friends in their scrapbook.
2. Students create scrapbook pages only about themselves.

Assessment:

Here is a detailed rubric for assessing this project:
Theme 1 Project: *Álbum de recuerdos*

RUBRIC	Score 1	Score 3	Score 5
Evidence of planning	You provided no written draft or page layouts.	Your draft was written and layout created, but not corrected.	You corrected your draft and layout.
Your use of illustrations	You included no photos / visuals.	Your photos / visuals were included, but your layout was unorganized.	Your scrapbook was easy to read, complete, and accurate.
Your presentation	You included little of the required information for each photo.	You included most of the required information for each photo.	You included all the required information for each photo.

21st Century Skills

Look for tips throughout *Tema* 1 to enrich your teaching by integrating 21st Century Skills. Suggestions for the Theme Project and Theme Support follow below.

Theme Project

Modify the Theme Project with one or more of these suggestions:

Promote Creativity and Innovation
Have students come up with creative ideas for arranging the content of their scrapbooks, such as themes, seasons, favorite places, activities, or people. Encourage them to decide how to choose materials at the outset.

Develop Initiative and Self-Direction
Have students develop their own timeline for accomplishing different stages of the project. They should study the rubric and anticipate which grammar and vocabulary tools they will need. The handout "Solve Problems" can help them develop a plan of action.

Encourage Social and Cross-Cultural Skills
Have students working as partners compare the activities in their scrapbooks with those presented in the chapter. Provide them with the handout "Compare and Contrast" to help them organize their ideas.

Theme Culture

Foster Critical Thinking and Problem Solving
Have students review the *Fondo cultural* notes on pages 31 and 34, comparing responses with a partner's. They can investigate similarities and differences they notice regarding activities in the two countries. What could explain what they notice? Location? Climate?

Videocultura View *Amigos y actividades* with the class to learn more about how friends like to spend their time.

1A ¿Qué te gusta hacer?

AT A GLANCE

Objectives

- **Listen to and read about activities people like and don't like to do**
- **Talk and write about what you and others like and don't like to do**
- **Describe your favorite activities and ask others about theirs**
- **Describe dances and music from the Spanish-speaking world and compare them to dances you know**
- **Compare favorite activities of Spanish-speaking teens to those of teens in the United States**

Vocabulary

- Activities
- Expressing likes and dislikes

Grammar

- Infinitives
- Negatives
- Expressing agreement or disagreement

Culture

- Pablo Picasso, p. 25
- Outdoor cafés, p. 31
- ***La Plaza Mayor*** in Salamanca, p. 31
- The ***güiro*** and rhythm instruments, p. 34
- Jaime Antonio González Colson, p. 34
- Music and dances of different Spanish-speaking countries, pp. 35, 42
- Spanish architecture, pp. 44–45

Recycle ♻

- Accent marks
- *nada*

RESOURCES

	FOR THE STUDENT	ONLINE	DVD	PRINT	FOR THE TEACHER	ONLINE	PREEXP	DVD	PRINT
Plan					Interactive TE and Resources DVD	•		•	
					Teacher's Resource Book, pp. 40–75	•		•	•
					Pre-AP* Resource Book, pp. 62–65	•		•	•
					Lesson Plans	•			•
					Mapa global interactivo	•			
Introducción PP. **24–25**									
Present	Student Edition, pp. 24–25	•	•	•	Interactive TE and Resources DVD	•		•	
	DK Reference Atlas	•	•		Teacher's Resource Book, pp. 40–43	•		•	•
	Videocultura	•	•		Galería de fotos		•		
	Hispanohablantes WB, pp. 10–11			•	Fine Art Transparencies, 44	•	•	•	
					Map Transparencies, 12–20	•	•	•	
Vocabulario en contexto PP. **26–29**									
Present & Practice	Student Edition, pp. 26–29	•	•	•	Interactive TE and Resources DVD	•		•	
	Audio	•	•		Teacher's Resource Book, pp. 44–45, 48	•		•	•
	Videohistoria	•	•		Vocabulary Clip Art	•	•	•	•
	Flashcards	•	•		Audio Program	•	•	•	
	Instant Check	•			Video Program: Videohistoria	•		•	
	Guided WB, pp. 25–32	•	•	•	Video Program Teacher's Guide: Cap. 1A	•		•	•
	Core WB, pp. 13–16	•	•	•	Vocabulary and Grammar Transparencies, 32–35	•	•	•	
	Comm. WB, pp. 7–10	•	•	•	Answer Keys: Student Edition, p. 11	•	•	•	
	Hispanohablantes WB, pp. 12–13			•	TPR Stories, pp. 17–23	•		•	•
Assess and Remediate					Prueba 1A–1: Assessment Program, pp. 13–14	•		•	•
					Assessment Program para hispanohablantes, pp. 13–14	•		•	•

RESOURCES

	FOR THE STUDENT	ONLINE	DVD	PRINT	FOR THE TEACHER	ONLINE	PREEXP	DVD	PRINT
Vocabulario en uso PP. **30–31**									
Present & Practice	Student Edition, pp. 30–31	•	•	•	Interactive Whiteboard Vocabulary Activities	•		•	
	Instant Check	•			Interactive TE and Resources DVD	•		•	
	Comm. WB, p. 11	•	•	•	Teacher's Resource Book, pp. 45–46, 50–51	•		•	•
	Hispanohablantes WB, pp. 14–15			•	Communicative Pair Activities, pp. 50–51	•		•	•
	Communicative Pair Activities	•			Audio Program	•	•	•	
					Videomodelos	•		•	
					Answer Keys: Student Edition, p. 12	•	•	•	•
Assess and Remediate					Prueba 1A–2 with Study Plan	•			
					Prueba 1A–2: Assessment Program, pp. 15–16	•		•	•
					Assessment Program para hispanohablantes, pp. 15–16	•		•	•
Gramática PP. **32–39**									
Present & Practice	Student Edition, pp. 32–39	•	•	•	Interactive Whiteboard Grammar Activities	•		•	
	Instant Check	•			Interactive TE and Resources DVD	•		•	
	Animated Verbs	•			Teacher's Resource Book, pp. 46–48, 52–53	•		•	•
	Tutorial Video: Grammar	•			Communicative Pair Activities, pp. 52–53	•		•	•
	Canción de hip hop	•			Audio Program	•	•	•	
	Guided WB, pp. 33–36	•	•	•	Videomodelos	•		•	
	Core WB, pp. 17–19	•	•	•	Video Program: GramActiva	•	•	•	
	Comm. WB, pp. 12–13, 15–16, 227	•	•	•	Fine Art Transparencies, 24	•	•	•	
	Hispanohablantes WB, pp. 16–21			•	Vocabulary and Grammar Transparencies, 36	•	•	•	
	Communicative Pair Activities	•			Answer Keys: Student Edition, pp. 12–14	•	•	•	
Assess and Remediate					Pruebas 1A–3 and 1A–4 with Study Plans	•			
					Pruebas 1A–3, 1A–4: Assessment Program, pp. 17–18	•		•	•
					Assessment Program para hispanohablantes, pp. 17–18	•		•	•
¡Adelante! PP. **40–45**									
Application	Student Edition, pp. 40–45	•	•	•	Interactive TE and Resources DVD	•		•	
	Online Cultural Reading	•			Teacher's Resource Book, pp. 47, 55	•		•	•
	Guided WB, pp. 37–38	•	•	•	Map Transparencies, 18	•	•	•	
	Comm. WB, pp. 17, 228	•	•	•	Vocabulary and Grammar Transparencies, 37–39	•	•	•	
	Hispanohablantes WB, pp. 22–27			•	Answer Keys: Student Edition, p. 15	•	•	•	
Repaso del capítulo PP. **46–47**									
Review	Student Edition, pp. 46–47	•	•	•	Interactive TE and Resources DVD	•		•	
	Online Puzzles and Games	•			Teacher's Resource Book, pp. 47, 54, 57–59	•		•	•
	Core WB, pp. 20–21	•	•	•	Audio Program	•	•	•	
	Comm. WB, pp. 230–232, 229	•	•	•	Answer Keys: Student Edition, p. 15	•			
	Hispanohablantes WB, pp. 28–29			•					
	Instant Check	•							
Chapter Assessment									
Assess					Examen del capítulo 1A	•		•	
					Assessment Program, pp. 19–25	•		•	
					Alternate Assessment Program, pp. 3–7	•		•	
					Assessment Program para hispanohablan[illegible]	•		•	
					Audio Program, Cap. 1A, Examen				
					ExamView: Test Banks A and B questi[illegible]				
					Heritage Learner Test [illegible]				
					Pre-AP* Test Bank				

REGULAR SCHEDULE (50 MINUTES)

DAY	Warm-up / Assess	Preview / Present / Practice / Communicate		Wrap-up / Homework Options
1	**Warm-up** (10 min.) • Return Examen del capítulo	**Chapter Opener** (5 min.) • Objectives • Arte y cultura	**Vocabulario en contexto** (30 min.) • Presentation: Vocabulario en contexto • Actividades 1, 2	**Wrap-up and Homework Options** (5 min.) • Core Practice 1A-1, 1A-2
2	**Warm-up** (5 min.) • Homework check	**Vocabulario en contexto** (40 min.) • Presentation: Videohistoria *¿Qué te gusta hacer?* • View: Videohistoria	• Interactive Whiteboard Vocabulary Activities • Video Activities 1, 2, 3, 4 • Actividades 3, 4	**Wrap-up and Homework Options** (5 min.) • Core Practice 1A-3, 1A-4 • Prueba 1A-1: Vocabulary recognition
3	**Warm-up** (10 min.) • Actividades 5, 6 • Homework check ✔**Formative Assessment** (10 min.) • Prueba 1A-1: Vocabulary recognition	**Vocabulario en uso** (25 min.) • Actividades 7, 8 • Fondo cultural • Audio Activities 5, 6 • Communicative Pair Activity		**Wrap-up and Homework Options** (5 min.) • Writing Activity 10 • Prueba 1A-2 with Study Plan: Vocabulary production
4	**Warm-up** (5 min.) • Homework check ✔**Formative Assessment** (10 min.) • Prueba 1A-2 with Study Plan: Vocabulary production	**Gramática y vocabulario en uso** (30 min.) • Presentation: Infinitives • View: GramActiva video • Interactive Whiteboard Grammar Activities	• Actividades 9, 10, 12, 13 • Communicative Pair Activity • Audio Activity 7	**Wrap-up and Homework Options** (5 min.) • Core Practice 1A-5 • Actividad 11 • Prueba 1A-3 with Study Plan: Infinitives
5	**Warm-up** (10 min.) • Writing Activity 11 • Homework check ✔**Formative Assessment** (10 min.) • Prueba 1A-3 with Study Plan: Infinitives	**Gramática y vocabulario en uso** (25 min.) • Exploración del lenguaje • Fondo cultural • Actividad 14 • Presentation: Negatives	• View: GramActiva video • Interactive Whiteboard Grammar Activities • Actividades 16, 17	**Wrap-up and Homework Options** (5 min.) • Core Practice 1A-6
6	**Warm-up** (10 min.) • Actividad 15 • Homework check	**Gramática y vocabulario en uso** (35 min.) • Audio Activity 8 • Writing Activity 12 • Communicative Pair Activity • Presentation: Expressing agreement or disagreement	• Interactive Whiteboard Grammar Activities • Actividades 18, 19	**Wrap-up and Homework Options** (5 min.) • Prueba 1A-4 with Study Plan: Negatives
7	**Warm-up** (5 min.) • Review Negatives ✔**Formative Assessment** (10 min.) • Prueba 1A-4 with Study Plan: Negatives	**Gramática y vocabulario en uso** (20 min.) • Audio Activity 9 • Writing Activity 13 • Pronunciación • El español en la comunidad	**¡Adelante!** (10 min.) • Lectura • ¿Comprendes?	**Wrap-up and Homework Options** (5 min.) • Core Practice 1A-7
	Warm-up (10 min.) • [illegible]omework check	**¡Adelante!** (30 min.) • La cultura en vivo • Presentación oral: Steps 1, 2 • El mundo hispano		**Wrap-up and Homework Options** (10 min.) • Presentación oral: Step 2 • Preparación para el examen 3, 4, 5
10	**Warm-up** (1[illegible] • Homework check ✔**Summative Assess**[illegible] • Examen del capítulo 1A	**¡Adelante!** (30 min.) • Presentación oral: Step 3	**Repaso del capítulo** (10 min.) • Vocabulario y gramática • Preparación para el examen 1, 2	**Wrap-up and Homework Options** (5 min.) • Core Practice 1A-8, 1A-9 • Instant Check • Examen del capítulo 1A

BLOCK SCHEDULE (90 MINUTES)

DAY	Warm-up / Assess	Preview / Present / Practice / Communicate	Wrap-up / Homework Options
1	**Warm-up** (10 min.) • Return Examen del capítulo	**Chapter Opener** (15 min.) • Objectives • Arte y cultura **Vocabulario en contexto** (55 min.) • Presentation: Vocabulario en contexto • Actividades 1, 2 • Presentation: Videohistoria *¿Qué te gusta hacer?* • View: Videohistoria • Video Activities 1, 2, 3, 4 • Actividades 3, 4	**Wrap-up and Homework Options** (10 min.) • Core Practice 1A-1, 1A-2, 1A-3, 1A-4 • Prueba 1A-1: Vocabulary recognition
2	**Warm-up** (10 min.) • Actividades 5, 6 • Homework check ✔**Formative Assessment** (10 min.) • Prueba 1A-1: Vocabulary recognition	**Vocabulario en uso** (10 min.) • Actividades 7, 8 • Fondo cultural • Interactive Whiteboard Vocabulary Activities • Audio Activities 5, 6 **Gramática y vocabulario en uso** (55 min.) • Communicative Pair Activity • Presentation: Infinitives • View: GramActiva video • Interactive Whiteboard Grammar Activities • Actividades 9, 10, 12, 13 • Audio Activity 7 • Communicative Pair Activity	**Wrap-up and Homework Options** (5 min.) • Writing Activity 10 • Core Practice 1A-5 • Actividad 11 • Pruebas 1A-2, 1A-3 with Study Plans: Vocabulary production, Infinitives
3	**Warm-up** (10 min.) • Homework check • Writing Activity 11 ✔**Formative Assessment** (15 min.) • Pruebas 1A-2, 1A-3 with Study Plans: Vocabulary production, Infinitives	**Gramática y vocabulario en uso** (60 min.) • Exploración del lenguaje • Fondo cultural • Actividad 14 • Presentation: Negatives • View: GramActiva video • Interactive Whiteboard Grammar Activities • Actividades 16, 17 • Audio Activity 8 • Writing Activity 12 • Communicative Pair Activity	**Wrap-up and Homework Options** (5 min.) • Core Practice 1A-6 • Prueba 1A-4 with Study Plan: Negatives
4	**Warm-up** (5 min.) • Homework check • Actividad 15 ✔**Formative Assessment** (10 min.) • Prueba 1A-4 with Study Plan: Negatives	**Gramática y vocabulario en uso** (35 min.) • Presentation: Expressing agreement or disagreement • Interactive Whiteboard Grammar Activities • Actividades 18, 19 • Audio Activity 9 • Writing Activity 13 • Pronunciación • El español en la comunidad **¡Adelante!** (35 min.) • Lectura • ¿Comprendes? • La cultura en vivo • Presentación oral: Steps 1, 2 • El mundo hispano	**Wrap-up and Homework Options** (10 min.) • Core Practice 1A-7
5	**Warm-up** (10 min.) • Homework check ✔**Formative Assessment** (10 min.)	**¡Adelante!** (45 min.) • Presentación oral: Step 3 **Repaso del capítulo** (25 min.) • Vocabulario y gramática • Preparación para el examen 1, 2, 3, 4, 5	**Wrap-up and Homework Options** (10 min.) • Core Practice 1A-8, 1A-9 • Instant Check • Examen del capítulo 1A
6	**Warm-up** (15 min.) • Homework check • Answer questions **Repaso del capítulo** (25 min.) • Situation Cards • Communicative Pair Activities ✔**Summative Assessment** (45 min.) • Examen del capítulo 1A		**Wrap-up and Homework Options** (5 min.) • Lectura • El mundo hispano

Standards for *Capítulo* 1A

- To achieve the goals of the Standards, students will:

Communication

1.1 Interpersonal
- Talk about preferences in leisure activities

1.2 Interpretive
- Read and listen to information about leisure activities and likes; read a picture-based story
- Listen to and watch a video about leisure activities
- Read about: leisure and recreational activities; traditional dances; snowboarding
- Listen to and understand information about infinitives
- Read information of general interest in Spanish language media

1.3 Presentational
- Present information on preferences in leisure activities

Culture

2.1 Practices and Perspectives
- Discuss outdoor ***cafés*** as popular places to relax with friends

2.2 Products and Perspectives
- Discuss Pablo Picasso; Jaime Antonio González Colson; a dance of the Dominican Republic, the ***merengue;*** musical instruments used in the Dominican Republic; traditional dances; the mambo; periods in Spain's history that affected its architecture

Connections

3.1 Cross-curricular
- Discuss: important artists and their work: Picasso, Colson; musical instruments used in the Dominican Republic; traditional dances; current events from Spanish language media; historical foundations of Spanish language and architecture

3.2 Target Culture
- Acquire information about current events through Spanish language media sources

Comparisons

4.1 Language
- Talk about new vocabulary through the recognition of cognates
- Compare: Spanish and English infinitives; construction of negatives between English and Spanish; expressing agreement or disagreement in English and Spanish; the Spanish vowels ***a, e,*** and ***i*** to their English counterparts

4.2 Culture
- Compare: places where teens gather to spend free time; the selection of news stories in Spanish language media sources to those in media sources in English; Latin dances to those in the United States

Communities

5.2 Lifelong Learner
- Utilize the language to experience news and entertainment available through print and electronic Spanish language media

Capítulo 1A ¿Qué te gusta hacer?

Chapter Objectives

Communication

By the end of this chapter you will be able to:
- Listen to and read about activities people like and don't like to do
- Talk and write about what you and others like and don't like to do
- Describe your favorite activities and ask others about theirs

Culture

You will also be able to:
- Describe dances and music from the Spanish-speaking world and compare them to dances you know
- Compare favorite activities of Spanish-speaking teens to those of teens in the United States

You will demonstrate what you know and can do:
- Presentación oral, p. 43
- Preparación para el examen, p. 47

You will use:

Vocabulary
- Activities
- Expressing likes and dislikes

Grammar
- Infinitives
- Negatives
- Expressing agreement or disagreement

Exploración del mundo hispano

Country Connection
Favorite Activities

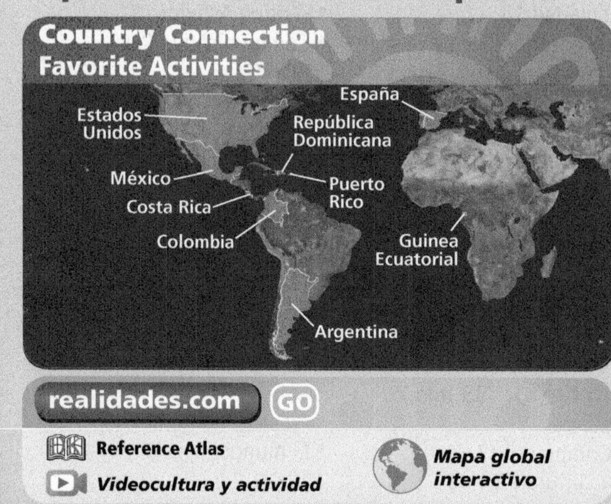

realidades.com GO

Reference Atlas

Videocultura y actividad

Mapa global interactivo

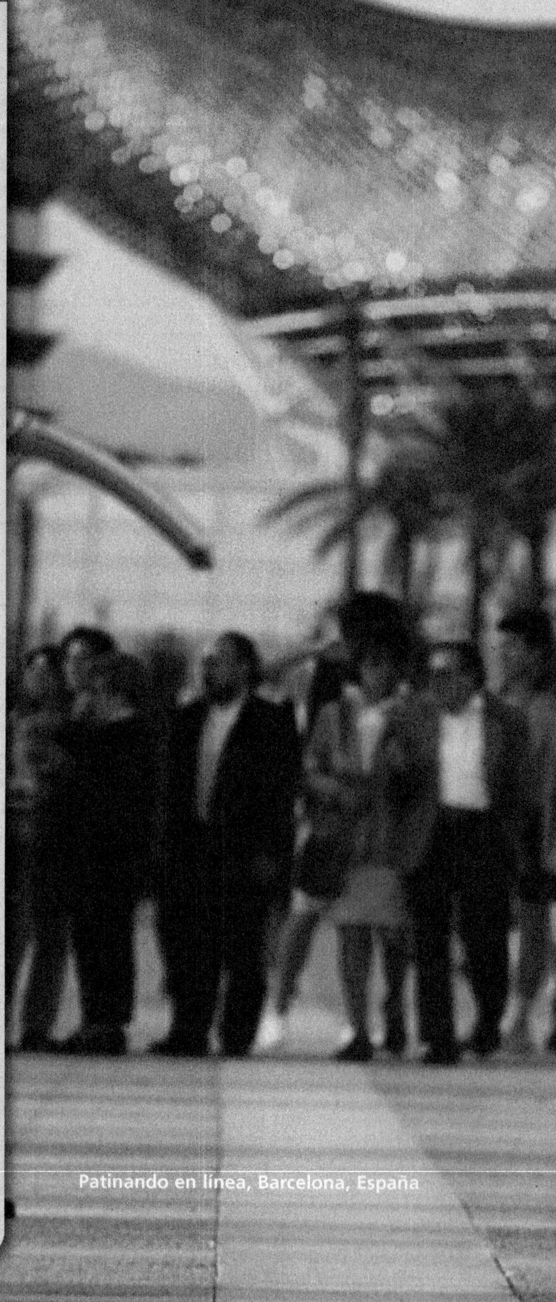

Patinando en línea, Barcelona, España

ENRICH YOUR TEACHING

Using Backward Design

Have students preview the sample performance tasks on *Preparación para el examen*, p. 47, and connect them to the Chapter Objectives. Explain to students that by completing the sample tasks they can self-assess their learning progress.

Mapa global interactivo

Download the *Mapa global interactivo* files for Chapter 1A and preview the activities. Use Activity 1 to find the locations for the *Videohistoria* in Madrid, Spain; Ciudad de México, Mexico; San Antonio, Texas; and San José, Costa Rica. Activity 2 takes you to the bustling Plaza Mayor in Salamanca, Spain.

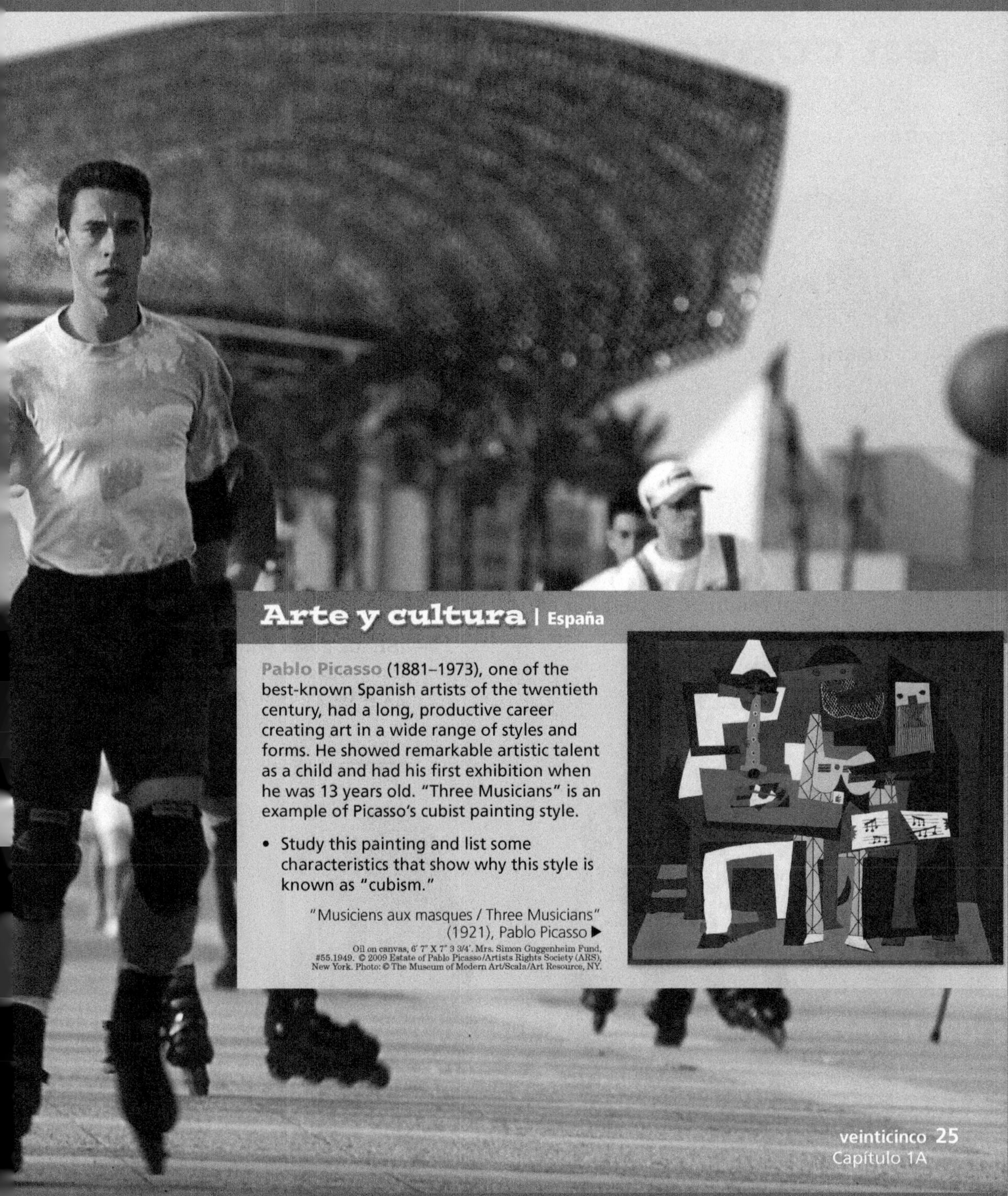

Arte y cultura | España

Pablo Picasso (1881–1973), one of the best-known Spanish artists of the twentieth century, had a long, productive career creating art in a wide range of styles and forms. He showed remarkable artistic talent as a child and had his first exhibition when he was 13 years old. "Three Musicians" is an example of Picasso's cubist painting style.

- Study this painting and list some characteristics that show why this style is known as "cubism."

"Musiciens aux masques / Three Musicians" (1921), Pablo Picasso ▶

Oil on canvas, 6′ 7″ X 7″ 3 3/4′. Mrs. Simon Guggenheim Fund, #55.1949. © 2009 Estate of Pablo Picasso/Artists Rights Society (ARS), New York. Photo: © The Museum of Modern Art/Scala/Art Resource, NY.

DIFFERENTIATED INSTRUCTION

Digital resources such as the ***Interactive Whiteboard*** activity banks, ***Videomodelos***, additional ***Online Activities, Study Plans***, automatically graded ***Leveled Workbook***, animated ***Grammar Tutorials, Flashcards***, and ***Vocabulary and Grammar Videos*** will help you reach students of different ability levels and learning styles.

STUDENTS NEEDING EXTRA HELP

Guided Practice Activities
- Flashcards, pp. 25–28
- Vocabulary Check, pp. 29–32
- Grammar Support, pp. 33–36

HERITAGE LEARNERS

Realidades para hispanohablantes
- Chapter Opener, pp. 10–11
- A primera vista, p. 12
- Videohistoria, p. 13
- Manos a la obra, pp. 14–21
- ¡Adelante!, pp. 22–27
- Repaso del capítulo, pp. 28–29

ADVANCED/PRE-AP*

Pre-AP* Resource Book,
- pp. 62–65

Communications Workbook
- Integrated Performance Assessment, p. 229

PresentationExpress™
See pp. 24c–24d

Chapter Opener

Core Instruction

Resources: Map Transparencies 12–20

Suggestions: Introduce students to the theme of the chapter and review the objectives. Explain to students that *Capítulo* 1A is the first of two chapters in *Tema* 1, *Mis amigos y yo*. In this chapter, students will learn language for talking about things they like and do not like to do and ways to express the negative.

Tell students that they will watch videos with people talking about what they like to do. The *GramActiva* videos will help them understand the grammar taught in the chapter.

Videocultura View *Amigos y actividades* with the class to learn more about how friends like to spend their time.

Arte y cultura

Standards: 2.2, 3.1

Resources: Fine Art Transparencies, p. 44

Suggestions: Point out that "cubism" comes from the word "cube." Ask students to describe the properties of a cube before answering the question.

Answers will vary but might include: Objects in the painting are made up of squares and other geometric figures.

TEACHING WITH ART

Resources: Fine Art Transparencies, p. 44

Suggestions: Show the transparency. Explain that Picasso developed his cubist style after years of study and work in more traditional styles of painting. He felt he could express ordinary things best by using simple geometric shapes.

Culture Note

Direct students' attention to the large gold-colored sculpture of a fish in the background of the photo. This sculpture, *El Peix,* was commissioned by the city of Barcelona in preparation for the Summer Olympics in 1992. The fish looks out over the sea and is visible from different points along the city's coastline. It is one of many pieces of public art in Barcelona.

Vocabulario en contexto

Core Instruction

Standards: 1.2

Resources: Teacher's Resource Book: Input Script, p. 44, Clip Art, pp. 57–59, Audio Script, p. 45; Voc. and Gram. Transparencies 32–33; TPR Stories, pp. 17–23; Audio Program DVD: Cap. 1A, Tracks 1–2

Focus: Presenting new vocabulary about leisure activities and likes and dislikes

Suggestions: Use the *TPR Stories Book* or the Input Script from the *Teacher's Resource Book* as a source of ideas for presentation of new vocabulary and comprehensible input. Keep in mind that *A primera vista* is designed for input of new words and lexical presentation of grammatical structures explained in the *Manos a la obra* section.

Tell students that *A primera vista* means "At first sight." Point out that pictures often help us understand the meanings of unfamiliar words. Show Transparency 32 to guide the presentation. Tell students that the words in heavy blue type are the words they will be responsible for knowing.

Read each conversation and dramatize each sentence as you say it. Use gestures, facial expressions, and tone to convey meaning. Ask students to guess the meaning. When they understand the statements, begin substituting words from the visuals, using the transparencies to highlight the substitution.

Ask students to raise their hands when they hear an activity they like. Ask a volunteer to track the responses and tally them on the board to see which are the most- and least-favored leisure activities.

BELLRINGER REVIEW

Have students practice greeting and introducing themselves to two other classmates.

Objectives

Read, listen to, and understand information about

- activities people like and don't like to do

Vocabulario en contexto

bailar

escuchar música

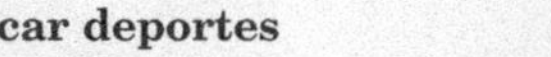

practicar deportes

nadar

correr

esquiar

—¡**Me gusta mucho** bailar!

—**A mí también. Y también me** gusta escuchar música.

—¡Hola, Beatriz! **¿Qué te gusta hacer?** **¿Te gusta** practicar deportes?

—**¡Sí!** Me gusta mucho practicar deportes. Me gusta correr, nadar y esquiar. **¿Y a ti?** ¿Qué te gusta hacer?

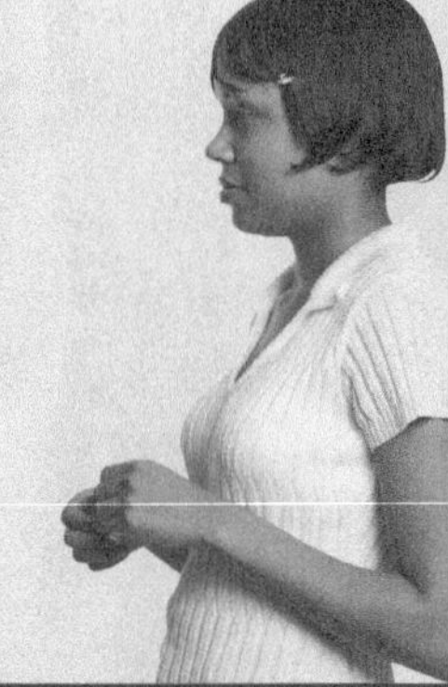

DIFFERENTIATED INSTRUCTION

Heritage Language Learners

Have students identify the leisure activities that are most popular with young people in their heritage countries. Are there any leisure activities preferred by people in Spanish-speaking countries that are not common in the United States? Are there differences in what the activities are called in various countries?

Students with Learning Difficulties

Use the Organizer from the *Practice Workbook* to create a written vocabulary list for easy reference for oral, listening, and writing activities throughout the chapter. The list will help students to succeed with the activities. Encourage them to use their lists whenever they need them.

escribir cuentos

montar en monopatín

dibujar

cantar

—A mí me gusta mucho escribir cuentos y dibujar. **¡No me gusta nada cantar!**

—¡Uy! **A mí tampoco.**

ver la tele

usar la computadora

montar en bicicleta

jugar videojuegos

—**¿Qué te gusta más,** ver la tele **o** montar en bicicleta?

—**Pues, no me gusta ni** ver la tele **ni** montar en bicicleta. Me gusta usar la computadora y jugar videojuegos. Y a ti, ¿qué te gusta más?

1 ¿Te gusta o no te gusta?

Escuchar

You will hear Rosa say what she likes to do and doesn't like to do. Give a "thumbs-up" sign when you hear her say something she likes to do and a "thumbs-down" sign when she says something she doesn't like to do.

2 Me gusta . . .

Escuchar

Listen to what some people like to do. Point to the picture of the activity each describes.

Más práctica GO

realidades.com | print

Instant Check	✔	
Guided WB pp. 25–28	✔	✔
Core WB pp. 13–14	✔	✔
Comm. WB p. 14	✔	✔
Hispanohablantes WB p. 12		✔

ENRICH YOUR TEACHING

Culture Note

Because the climates and cultures of Spanish-speaking countries are so diverse, a variety of leisure activities are available. People in eastern Chile can engage in mountain climbing. In Caracas, Venezuela, free time can be spent surfing and swimming. Throughout Mexico, soccer is a common sport on any open field.

Teacher-to-Teacher

Have students make flashcards using the Clip Art from the *Teacher's Resource Book*. Students can write a Spanish word on one side of each card and paste the picture on the other. For nonvisualized words, have students write the Spanish word.

Language Input 1A

1 Standards: 1.2

Resources: Teacher's Resource Book: Audio Script, p. 45; Audio Program DVD: Cap. 1A, Track 3; Answer Keys: Student Edition, p. 11

Focus: Listening to someone talk about likes and dislikes; indicating comprehension

Suggestions: Demonstrate the "thumbs-up" and "thumbs-down" signs. Play the audio or read the script to the class. Allow students to listen and display the signs several times.

Script and Answers:

¡Hola! Me llamo Rosa y me gusta mucho bailar. (*up*) También me gusta escuchar música y cantar. (*up*) No me gusta ver la tele ni jugar videojuegos. (*down*) Y tampoco me gusta nadar. (*down*) ¡Uy! ¡Me gusta más bailar! (*up*)

Extension: Choose other new vocabulary to vary and extend the activity.

2 Standards: 1.2

Resources: Teacher's Resource Book: Audio Script, p. 45; Audio Program DVD: Cap. 1A, Track 4; Answer Keys: Student Edition, p. 11

Focus: Listening comprehension of leisure activity words

Suggestions: Play the audio or read the script as students point to the pictures. Walk around the classroom and check that they select the correct pictures.

Script and Answers:

¡Hola! Me llamo Sebastián y me gusta mucho montar en monopatín. También me gusta escribir cuentos y ver la tele. (*montar en monopatín, escribir cuentos, ver la tele*) Yo soy Valentina y a mí me gusta bailar, dibujar y montar en bicicleta. (*bailar, dibujar, montar en bicicleta*) Mi nombre es Carmen. Me gusta usar la computadora, escuchar música y esquiar. (*usar la computadora, escuchar música, esquiar*) Yo soy Daniel. A mí me gusta correr, practicar deportes y nadar. (*correr, practicar deportes, nadar*)

Videohistoria

Core Instruction

Standards: 1.2

Resources: Voc. and Gram. Transparencies 34–35; Audio Program DVD: Cap. 1A, Track 5

Mapa global interactivo, Actividad 1
Find the locations for the *Videohistoria*: Madrid, Spain; Ciudad de México, Mexico; San Antonio, Texas; and San José, Costa Rica.

Focus: Presenting additional vocabulary and grammar in visual and story context; previewing the language video

Suggestions:

Pre-reading: Direct attention to the *Strategy*. Have students close their books. Present the transparencies, panel by panel, and ask students to predict who likes to do what.

Reading: Explain that the *Videohistoria* is a reading that introduces more vocabulary and will prepare students for watching a video story in each chapter. The characters will appear throughout *Realidades*. Read the captions with students or use the audio. Using the transparencies and pantomime, help students understand the new words in blue type. Ask students the comprehension questions found on the transparencies.

Post-reading: Complete *Actividad* 3 to check comprehension.

Video

Core Instruction

Standards: 1.2, 4.1

Resources: Teacher's Resource Book: Video Script, p. 48; Video Program Teacher's Guide: Cap. 1A; Video Program: Cap. 1A

Focus: Comprehending new vocabulary and grammar in authentic context

Suggestions:

Pre-viewing: Remind students that they will not understand every word in the video, but that they should listen and watch for overall understanding.

Viewing: Show the video once without pausing; then show it again, stopping to check comprehension. Show it a final time without pausing.

Post-viewing: Have students complete the Video Activities in the *Communication Workbook*.

¿Qué te gusta hacer?

> **Strategy**
>
> **Using visuals**
> Look at the pictures with each postcard to help you understand the meaning of the new words.
> - Can you predict what each student likes to do?

You're going to meet eight students from around the Spanish-speaking world and find out what they like and don't like to do. You'll be able to figure out where they live by looking at the globes on the page.

“Y yo me llamo Ana. A mí me gusta **hablar por teléfono**”.

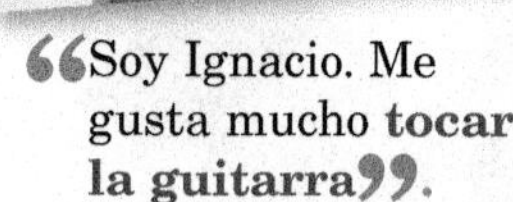

“Soy Ignacio. Me gusta mucho **tocar la guitarra**”.

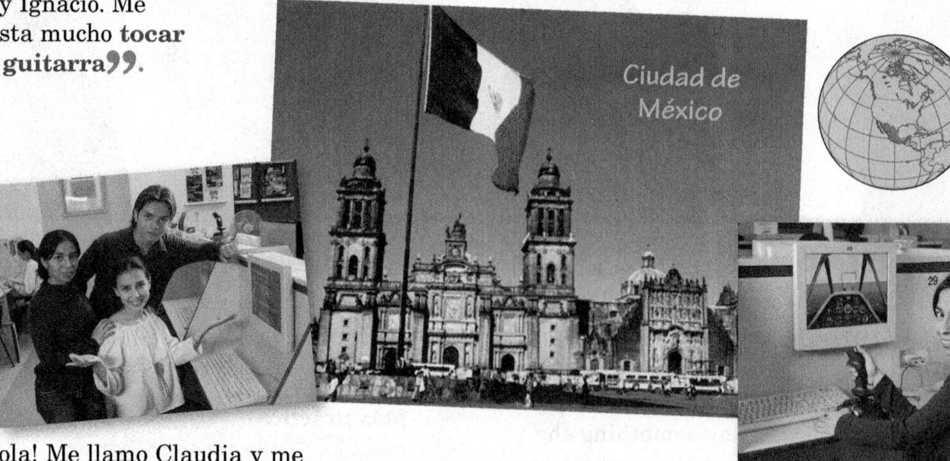

“¡Hola! Me llamo Claudia y me gusta usar la computadora y **pasar tiempo con mis amigos**”.

“Yo soy Teresa. También me gusta usar la computadora, pero **me gusta más** jugar videojuegos”.

DIFFERENTIATED INSTRUCTION

Advanced Learners
Have students choose one of the places named on the postcards and do Internet or other research on the locale's popular places, events, or holidays. Pictures or other graphics showing the city can add visual interest to the written or oral presentation to the class.

Multiple Intelligences
Verbal/Linguistic: Ask students to bring in a postcard or photo of where they live, as well as a photo of themselves. Ask them to use the *Videohistoria* as a model to write a brief caption that tells who they are and what they like to do. Post the photos and captions in the classroom.

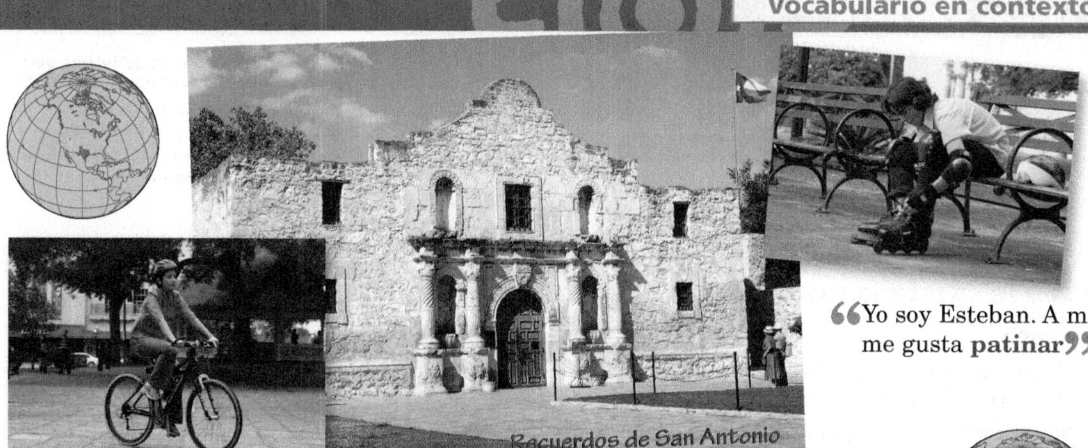

“Yo soy Esteban. A mí me gusta **patinar**”.

“¡Hola, amigos! Me llamo Angélica y me gusta mucho montar en bicicleta”.

“¿Qué tal, amigos? Soy Gloria. A mí me gusta **ir a la escuela,** y también me gusta **trabajar**”.

“Me llamo Raúl. Me gusta ir a la escuela . . . más o menos . . ., pero me gusta más **leer revistas**”.

3 ¿Comprendes?

Leer

On a sheet of paper, write the numbers 1–6. Read the following statements by the characters in the *Videohistoria* and write *C (cierto)* if the statement is true, or *F (falso)* if it is false.

1. **Angélica:** No me gusta montar en bicicleta.
2. **Raúl:** Me gusta mucho leer revistas.
3. **Esteban:** Me gusta patinar.
4. **Claudia:** Me gusta pasar tiempo con mis amigos.
5. **Teresa:** No me gusta usar la computadora.
6. **Gloria:** Me gusta trabajar.

4 Y tú, ¿qué dices?

Escribir • Hablar

Write your answers to these questions.

1. ¿Qué te gusta más, leer revistas o montar en monopatín?
2. ¿Qué te gusta más, jugar videojuegos o bailar?
3. ¿Qué te gusta hacer en junio? ¿Y en diciembre?

Más práctica GO

	realidades.com	print
Instant Check	✔	
Guided WB pp. 29–32	✔	✔
Core WB pp. 15–16	✔	✔
Comm. WB pp. 7–9, 10	✔	✔
Hispanohablantes WB p. 13		✔

3 Standards: 1.2, 1.3

Resources: Answer Keys: Student Edition, p. 11

Focus: Reading for comprehension

Suggestions: Ask volunteers to read the statements and give their answers.

Answers:

1. F
2. C
3. C
4. C
5. F
6. C

Extension: Ask students to find and read at least one statement in *Actividad* 3 with which they personally agree.

4 Standards: 1.1, 1.3

Focus: Writing and speaking about what you like to do in a personalized context

Suggestions: When students have completed the activity, ask volunteers to read the questions and give their answers.

Answers will vary.

Extension: Have students write three more questions using vocabulary from pp. 26–27 to ask classmates.

Pre-AP* Support

- **Learning Objective:** Interpersonal Speaking
- **Activity:** Display Vocabulary and Grammar Transparencies 32-33. Have pairs of students recreate any dialog substituting new vocabulary for actions that you point out.
- ***Pre-AP* Resource Book:*** Comprehensive guide to Pre-AP* vocabulary skill development, pp. 39–50

Additional Resources

- Communication Wbk.: Audio Act. 5, p. 10
- Teacher's Resource Book: Audio Script, p. 45
- Audio Program DVD: Cap. 1A, Track 7

ENRICH YOUR TEACHING

Culture Note

San Antonio has been part of six different nations: Spain, France, Mexico, the Republic of Texas, the Confederate States of America, and the United States of America. The Alamo, built in 1724, was originally part of a Franciscan mission, called Misión San Antonio de Valero. It was fortified in the early 1800s. In 1836, a relatively small group of separatist Texans led by Colonel William Travis, David (Davy) Crockett, and Jim Bowie, defended the Alamo against thousands of Mexican troops for 13 days before they were defeated. The defeat mobilized the movement for independence from Mexico. Today the Alamo remains an important historical symbol to Texans.

ASSESSMENT

Quiz: Vocabulary Recognition

- Prueba 1A-1: pp. 13–14

INTERACTIVE WHITEBOARD
Vocabulary Activities 1A

5 Standards: 1.2, 1.3

Focus: Practicing new vocabulary for activities

Suggestions: Show the transparencies to review visualized vocabulary. Remind students that *¡Respuesta personal!* means they supply their own answers. Leave the transparencies on the projector as a visual reference while students work.

Answers will vary.

6 Standards: 1.3

Focus: Practicing vocabulary for likes and dislikes; writing infinitives

Suggestions: Be sure students understand that the words shown on the chart are models. They do not have to include them in their own charts. Remind them to save their charts for *Actividad* 7.

Answers will vary.

7 Standards: 1.1

Focus: Communicating likes and dislikes to a partner

Suggestions: Help students understand that this is a real conversation, so they will need to listen to their partners carefully. Be sure Student B understands that he or she should answer truthfully.

Answers will vary.

Block Schedule

Give each student at the beginning of a row a blank sheet of paper. Tell them to write a Spanish infinitive and pass the paper to the next person, who will write another infinitive, and so on. Call time. Have a student in one of the rows say one of the infinitives, and tell the rest of the class to pantomime the action. Do this several times.

Vocabulario en uso

Objectives

- Write and talk about activities you and others like and don't like to do
- Exchange information while comparing what you like to do
- Compare how you spend free time to teenagers in Spain

5 ¿Te gusta o no te gusta?

Escribir

Complete the following sentences with one of the activities shown, or with any of the other activities shown on pp. 26–29.

1. Me gusta ___.
2. No me gusta ___.
3. Me gusta mucho ___.
4. No me gusta nada ___.
5. Me gusta ___.
6. No me gusta ni ___ ni ___.

Modelo

Me gusta practicar deportes.

¡Respuesta personal!

6 Me gusta o no me gusta

Escribir

Find four activities on pp. 26–29 that you like to do and four that you don't like to do. Copy this chart on your paper and write the activities in the corresponding columns.

Modelo

Me gusta	No me gusta
correr	cantar

7 ¡A mí también! 

Hablar

Using the information from Actividad 6, tell your partner three activities that you like to do. Your partner will agree or disagree with you. Follow the model. Then switch roles and repeat the activity.

Modelo

A —*Me gusta correr.*
B —*¡A mí también!*
o:—*¡A mí no me gusta!*

DIFFERENTIATED INSTRUCTION

Students with Learning Difficulties

Review *¡A mí también!* and *¡A mí no me gusta!* as the two responses for *Actividad* 7. Students might need an immediate reminder in order to succeed.

Heritage Language Learners

You may want to allow heritage language learners to include additional activities on their lists for *Actividad* 6. Use this as an informal opportunity to assess spelling skills. If you choose this option, pair heritage language learners for *Actividad* 7.

8 ¿Qué te gusta hacer? | Talk!

Hablar

Ask your partner whether he or she likes doing the activities below. Your partner will answer using one of the two responses shown. Then switch roles and answer your partner's questions.

Modelo

A —*¿Te gusta montar en monopatín?*
B —*Sí, me gusta mucho.*
o: —*No, no me gusta nada.*

Estudiante A
¿Te gusta . . . ?

1. 2. 3. 4. 5. 6. 7. 8.

Estudiante B

¡Respuesta personal!

Fondo cultural | El mundo hispano

Outdoor cafés are popular gathering places throughout the Spanish-speaking world. Friends go there to enjoy a snack or light meal, catch up with one another, or just watch people go by.

- Where do you go to spend time with friends or to meet new ones? How does your experience compare with that of the Spanish teens shown here at a café in Salamanca's *Plaza Mayor*?

En el verano, me gusta pasar tiempo con mis amigos en la Plaza Mayor de Salamanca, España.

También se dice . . .

No me gusta nada = No me gusta para nada *(muchos países)*

Practice and Communicate 1A

8 Standards: 1.1

Resources: Answer Keys: Student Edition, p. 12

Focus: Asking about likes and dislikes; practicing with new vocabulary

Suggestions: Review the visualized vocabulary with the class, then role-play the model with a student. When students are paired, remind them that *¡Respuesta personal!* in the Student B bubble means that their answer should express their own opinion. When finished, ask for volunteers to practice for the class.

Answers:

Student A

1. —¿Te gusta hablar por teléfono?
2. —¿Te gusta dibujar?
3. —¿Te gusta bailar?
4. —¿Te gusta pasar tiempo con amigos?
5. —¿Te gusta tocar la guitarra?
6. —¿Te gusta cantar?
7. —¿Te gusta correr?
8. —¿Te gusta escribir?

Student B: Answers will vary.

Common Errors: Students may forget to use proper intonation. Model appropriate intonation for questions and answers.

Fondo cultural

Standards: 2.1, 4.2

Suggestions: Have students study the photo and read the paragraph. Provide other information that you know about plazas and cafés.

Answers will vary but might include malls, fast-food restaurants, school activities, etc.

Mapa global interactivo, Actividad 2 Visit the Plaza Mayor in Salamanca, Spain, and the area that surrounds it.

Additional Resources

- Communication Wbk.: Audio Act. 6, p. 11
- Teacher's Resource Book: Audio Script, pp. 45–46, Communicative Pair Activity, pp. 50–51
- Audio Program DVD: Cap. 1A, Track 7

ASSESSMENT

Prueba 1A-2 with Study Plan (online only)

Quiz: Vocabulary Production

- Prueba 1A-2: pp. 15–16

ENRICH YOUR TEACHING

Culture Note

The *Plaza Mayor* is one of Salamanca's most famous and popular meeting places. Built by order of Felipe V, the baroque-style plaza was completed in 1755 under the direction of the Churriguera family, famous Spanish architects. Ceremonies, festivities, and even bullfights have taken place there. In 1988, UNESCO made the Plaza Mayor of Salamanca a World Heritage Site.

21st Century Skills

Communication Remind students that whenever they do a speaking activity they will always have the opportunity to first watch and listen to native speakers in the *Videomodelos*. This way, they can use a native-speaker model to monitor their own progress.

Gramática

Core Instruction

Standards: 4.1

Resources: Teacher's Resource Book: Video Script, p. 48; Video Program: Cap. 1A

INTERACTIVE WHITEBOARD
Grammar Activities 1A

Suggestions: Ask students to brainstorm infinitives in English. Write them on the board or transparency, underlining *to* in each infinitive. Have students call out Spanish infinitives they've learned. Underline the endings in different colors. Play the *GramActiva* Video for reinforcement.

9 Standards: 1.3

Resources: Answer Keys: Student Edition, p. 12

Focus: Recognizing infinitive endings

Suggestions: You may want to do this activity with the whole class. Draw the chart on the board and have volunteers write the infinitives in the correct columns. Students should save this chart to use with *Actividad* 11.

Answers:

-ar: **nadar, tocar, jugar; bailar**
-er: **leer, ver, correr**
-ir: **escribir**

Extension: Have students write three *"Me gusta ____."* and *"No me gusta ____."* sentences using infinitives from the chart.

10 Standards: 1.2

Resources: Teacher's Resource Book: Audio Script, p. 46; Audio Program DVD: Cap. 1A, Track 8; Answer Keys: Student Edition, p. 12

Focus: Listening for verb endings

Suggestions: Have students use three colors of index cards so you can immediately see if answers are correct. Play the audio or read the script. After students have held up their papers, hold up the correct card.

Script and Answers:

1. **patinar *(-ar)***
2. **correr *(-er)***
3. **trabajar *(-ar)***
4. **escribir *(-ir)***
5. **leer *(-er)***
6. **nadar *(-ar)***
7. **ir *(-ir)***
8. **hacer *(-er)***

Manos a la obra

Objectives

- Write about and discuss activities
- Listen to descriptions of what someone likes to do
- Read about, listen to, and write about different types of Latin music

Gramática

Infinitives

Verbs are words that are most often used to name actions. Verbs in English have different forms depending on who is doing the action or when the action is occurring:

I walk, she walks, we walked, etc.

The most basic form of a verb is called the infinitive. In English, you can spot infinitives because they usually have the word "to" in front of them:

to swim, to read, to write

Infinitives in Spanish, though, don't have a separate word like "to" in front of them. Spanish infinitives are only one word, and always end in *-ar, -er,* or *-ir:*

nadar, leer, escribir

Más ayuda realidades.com

***GramActiva* Video**
Tutorial: Conjugation & Infinitive
Animated Verbs

Canción de hip hop: *Mambo*

***GramActiva* Activity**

9 ¿Cuál es?

Escribir

On a sheet of paper, make a chart with three columns for the headings *-ar, -er,* and *-ir.* Then look at these pictures of activities. Write the infinitive for each activity under the corresponding head. Save your chart to use in Actividad 11.

Modelo

-ar	-er	-ir
nadar		

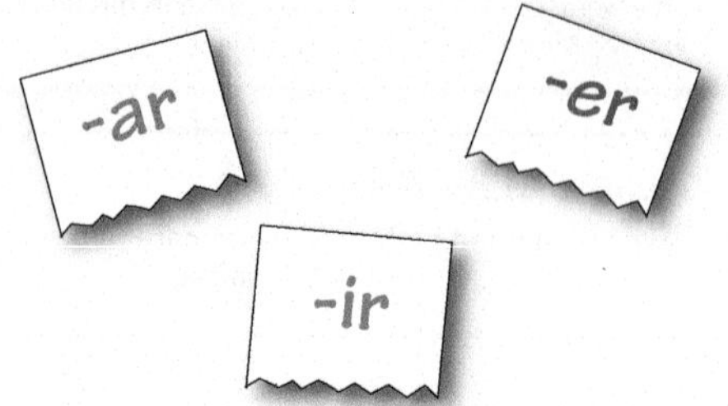

10 Tres papeles

Escuchar • GramActiva

Tear a sheet of paper into three equal parts. Write *-ar* on one piece, *-er* on another piece, and *-ir* on the third piece. You will hear several infinitives. Listen carefully to the endings. Hold up the paper with the ending that you hear.

-ar

-er

-ir

DIFFERENTIATED INSTRUCTION

Students with Learning Difficulties

Give several examples of infinitives in English. Have students give examples themselves. Clarify the relationship between "to..." in English and ***-ar, -er, -ir*** in Spanish. You might have them add that to their "activity list" for quick reference until the fact is internalized.

Multiple Intelligences

Verbal/Linguistic: Have students refer to pp. 28–29 and list all the infinitives and infinitive phrases (e.g. ***pasar tiempo con mis amigos***) used in the *Videohistoria* conversation.

11 El verbo es . . .

Escribir

Here are some verbs in English. Look them up in the English-Spanish glossary at the back of the book and write down the Spanish infinitives on the chart you made in Actividad 9.

to walk   to live   to eat   to study   to have

It's easy to talk about the things you like to do once you know the infinitive, because you just add the infinitive to *Me gusta*. Try writing this sentence in Spanish: *I like to sleep.*

Strategy

Using a dictionary or glossary
When you need to look up a verb, always look under the infinitive form.

12 Encuesta: ¿Qué te gusta hacer?

Escribir • Hablar

1. Ask four classmates to tell you two things they like to do (*¿Qué te gusta hacer?*) and two things they don't like to do (*¿Qué no te gusta hacer?*). Record their names and responses on a chart like this one.

2. Work in groups of four. Add up the results of your interviews to see which activities are the most popular and which ones are the least popular.

3. Share your results with the class.
   1. Las actividades más *(most)* populares:
   2. Las actividades menos *(least)* populares:

Modelo

Nombre	Me gusta	No me gusta
Beto	nadar ir a la escuela	patinar usar la computadora

Actividad	Me gusta	No me gusta
tocar la guitarra	|||	|
cantar	|	|||
trabajar	||	||

13 Escucha y escribe

Escuchar • Escribir

Write the numbers 1–7 on a sheet of paper. You will hear Raúl say seven things that he likes to do. Write them down as he says them. Spelling counts!

¿Recuerdas?

Remember to include any accent marks when you spell a word.

Más práctica GO

realidades.com | print

Instant Check	✔	
Guided WB p. 33	✔	✔
Core WB p. 17	✔	✔
Comm. WB pp. 12, 15	✔	✔
***Hispanohablantes* WB** pp. 14–17		✔

ENRICH YOUR TEACHING

Teacher-to-Teacher

Take time to explain the Glossaries to students. For most, this will be the first time they have used a dictionary with two languages. Point out that there are two sections, one that presents words from Spanish to English, and one that presents them from English to Spanish. Warn of the limitations of using dictionaries and glossaries, especially as this relates to words that have multiple meanings in one language but not the other.

Practice and Communicate 1A

11 Standards: 1.3, 4.1

Resources: Answer Keys: Student Edition, p. 13
Focus: Using the glossary or dictionary
Suggestions: Help students locate the Glossary that starts on p. 496. Show them how to find the first item.
Answers:

1. **caminar**
2. **vivir**
3. **comer**
4. **estudiar**
5. **tener**
6. **Me gusta dormir.**

12 Standards: 1,1, 1.2, 1.3

Resources: Voc. and Gram. Transparency 36
Focus: Surveying likes and dislikes
Suggestions: Using the transparency, have students review infinitives to describe leisure-time activities.
Answers will vary.

13 Standards: 1.2, 1.3

Resources: Teacher's Resource Book: Audio Script, p. 46; Audio Program DVD: Cap. 1A, Track 9; Answer Keys: Student Edition, p. 13
Focus: Listening comprehension and writing accuracy
Suggestions: Read the *¿Recuerdas?* and ask for three words that have accent marks. Play the audio or read the script.

Script and Answers:

1. **Me gusta tocar la guitarra.**
2. **Me gusta ver la tele.**
3. **También me gusta jugar videojuegos.**
4. **Me gusta ir a la escuela.**
5. **Me gusta patinar.**
6. **Me gusta usar la computadora.**
7. **¡Y me gusta mucho escuchar música!**

Additional Resources

- Communication Wbk.: Audio Act. 7, p. 12
- Teacher's Resource Book: Audio Script, p. 46
- Audio Program DVD: Cap. 1A, Track 10

ASSESSMENT

Prueba 1A-3 with Study Plan (online only)

Quiz: Infinitives

- Prueba 1A-3: p. 17

Exploración del lenguaje
Core Instruction

Standards: 4.1

Focus: Understanding cognates

Suggestions: Refer students to the *Strategy*. When they finish *Try it out!*, ask volunteers to identify the cognates. Have them find the cognates on these pages.

Answers: *Try it out!*: ***música, practicar, esquiar, usar, computadora, bicicleta, tele, guitarra***

BELLRINGER REVIEW

Have students refer to the map on p. xxiii and locate the three islands in the Caribbean where Spanish is spoken, and their capitals.

Fondo cultural

Standards: 2.2, 3.1

Resource: Fine Art Transparency 24

Suggestions: Have students read the *Fondo cultural*. Then have students find the Dominican Republic on the map on p. xxiii, or on the transparency. Ask them to identify the musical instruments they see. Have students answer the question and discuss their responses.

Answers will vary.

Teaching with Art

Resource: Fine Art Transparencies, p. 24

Have students examine the painting *Merengue* by Jaime Antonio González Colson. The artist was born in the Dominican Republic in 1901. The indigenous peoples of the Dominican Republic were influenced by both Spanish and African cultures, and its music, dance, and art reflect these influences. Ask students: What words in Spanish do you know that describe the actions in the painting? ***(hablar, tocar, cantar, bailar)***

Exploración del lenguaje

Cognates

Words that look alike and have similar meanings in English and Spanish are called **cognates** *(cognados)*. Here are examples from this chapter:

Spanish	English
popular	popular
usar	to use
guitarra	guitar
computadora	computer

Try it out! Look at pp. 26–29 and make a list of seven cognates from the vocabulary on those pages.

Strategy

Recognizing cognates
Becoming skilled at recognizing cognates will help you understand what you read and will increase your vocabulary.

Fondo cultural | República Dominicana

Jaime Antonio González Colson (1901–1975) was an artist from the Dominican Republic. His works usually focused on the people and culture of his homeland.

The *merengue*, the dance shown in this painting, originated in the Dominican Republic in the nineteenth century. One of the instruments used to accompany it is the *güiro* (shown at the top right), made from a gourd and played by scraping it with a stick.

- What instruments set the rhythms in the music that you listen to?

"Merengue" (1937), Jaime Antonio González Colson ▶
Courtesy of Museo Bellapart, Dominican Republic.

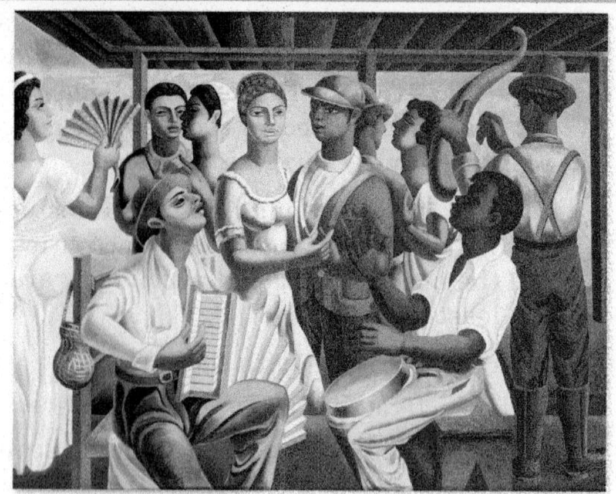

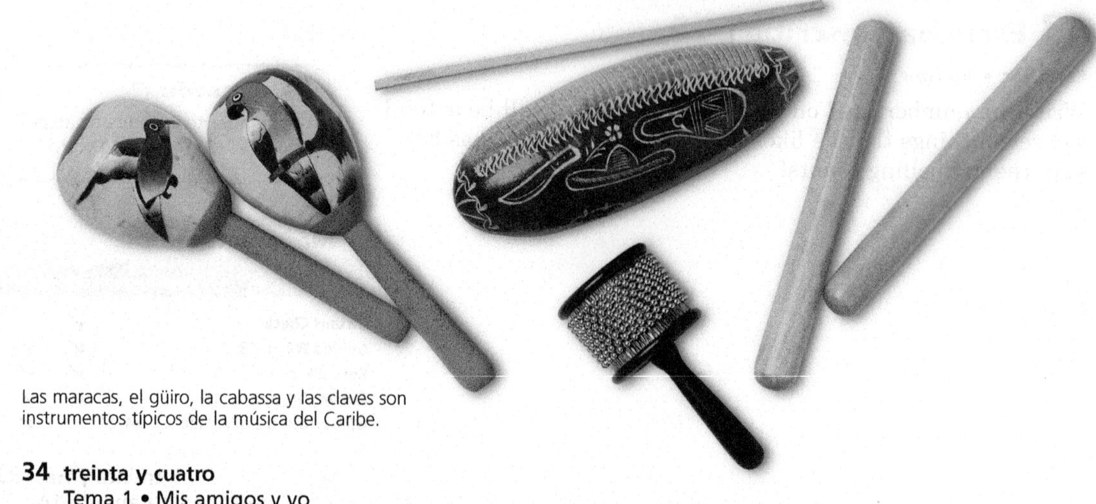

Las maracas, el güiro, la cabassa y las claves son instrumentos típicos de la música del Caribe.

DIFFERENTIATED INSTRUCTION

Heritage Language Learners

Students may have items from Spanish-speaking countries in their homes that they can share with their classmates. Ask if anyone has ***maracas, un güiro, un rascador, una clave,*** or ***una cabassa*** to bring to class. Emphasize, however, that students should not bring valuables or rare items.

Advanced Learners

Have students research artist Jaime Antonio González Colson. Ask them to use the Internet and other resources to find information about his life, other artists who influenced his work, and additional examples of his work. Students can share their research with the class.

14 El baile y la música del mundo hispano

Leer • Escuchar • Escribir

Each country in the Spanish-speaking world has distinct musical styles and traditions. Many of the unique rhythms and dances of Spanish-speaking countries are now popular in the United States. This music features instruments such as guitars, violins, accordions, and various types of percussion such as *güiros,* sticks, cymbals, cow bells, and drums. As you read the captions, see how many words you can understand due to their similarity to English words. After you read, your teacher will play examples of each type of music. Listen for the different instruments used.

Conexiones | La música

El flamenco es un baile típico de España. El instrumento más importante en el flamenco es la guitarra.

En Argentina, el tango es muy popular. Es un baile romántico.

En la República Dominicana, el baile tradicional es el merengue. El merengue tiene muchos ritmos africanos.

En Puerto Rico, la salsa es el baile preferido. El ritmo de la salsa es popular en la música de los Estados Unidos también.

La cumbia es el baile más famoso de Colombia.

- Reread each of the captions and make a list of seven cognates.
- Make a list of instruments you heard in the different songs. You might need to listen to the music again.

ENRICH YOUR TEACHING

Culture Note

Play samples of merengue music by Juan Luis Guerra, the Dominican Republic's foremost contemporary composer of songs with this rhythm. Tango rhythms by Carlos Gardel and Astor Piazzola, and salsa music by Celia Cruz or Tito Puente are good selections. Cumbia musicians Juan Madera, Wilson Choperena, José Barros, and Mario Gareña are also good choices. The local library may have music from Spanish-speaking countries, or you may be able to find short clips on the Internet. Search online with the words **merengue, tango, salsa,** and **cumbia** to read more about the history of these music genres and about how they are being mixed with modern music styles.

Practice and Communicate 1A

14 Standards: 1.2, 2.2, 3.1

Teacher's Resources: Teacher's Resource Book: Audio Script, p. 47; Audio Program DVD: Cap. 1A, Tracks 13–18; Answer Keys: Student Edition, p. 13

Focus: Reading for comprehension using cognates and context; making cross-curricular connections to music

Suggestions: Read through *El baile y la música del mundo hispano* with students. Then have them read each of the captions silently, using cognates, the photos, and the globe locators to help with comprehension. Ask volunteers to share their understanding of the captions. Then have students complete the activity.

Answers:

Cognates: típico, música popular, romántico, República, tradicional, ritmo(s), africanos, preferido, famoso
Instruments: Answers will vary.

Common Errors: Some students may be confused by the general placement of adjectives and adjective phrases after the noun they modify. Explain to students that in Spanish, the noun usually comes first.

Pre-AP* Support

- **Learning Objective:** Interpretive: Print and Audio
- **Activity 14:** Have students read the captions carefully as a homework assignment. In class the next day, read only a portion of the assigned page as a dictation. (A few sentences should be enough.) Have students write what they hear. After they finish writing, point out the selection that you read in the book and have students correct their answers.
- ***Pre-AP* Resource Book:*** Comprehensive guide to Pre-AP* communication skill development, pp. 10–57

Theme Project

Give students copies of the Theme Project outline and rubric from the *Teacher's Resource Book.* Explain the task to them, and have them perform Step 1. (For more information, see p. 24-b.)

Teacher-to-Teacher

Bring to class a recording of merengue music. Although it originated in the 19th century, it is still very popular. If you have time, show students pictures of merengue performers, play a few songs, and have them listen for the rhythm, instruments, and any words they understand.

1A Practice and Communicate

Gramática

Core Instruction

Standards: 4.1

Resources: Teacher's Resource Book: Video Script, p. 48; Video Program: Cap. 1A

INTERACTIVE WHITEBOARD
Grammar Activities 1A

Suggestions: Write on the board the affirmative sentence *Me gusta cantar.* Show students how to make the negative by adding ***No*** in front of ***Me,*** and changing capital *M* to lowercase. Do this with additional examples. Direct attention to the *¿Recuerdas?* Show the *GramActiva* Video to reinforce use of the negative. Note that the video also includes a discussion of ***también*** and ***tampoco,*** so you may want to stop it and use the second part with the grammar presentation on p. 38.

15 Standards: 1.2, 1.3

Resources: Answer Keys: Student Edition, p. 13

Focus: Reading and writing negatives

Suggestions: Have students silently read the conversation between Ana and Tomás and then write the words that belong in blanks 1–5. When they have finished the activity, have two students role-play the conversation for the class. If any of the answers are incorrect, ask the class to provide the correct negative.

Answers:

1. **no**
2. **ni**
3. **ni**
4. **nada**
5. **tampoco**

Block Schedule

Working in pairs, have students write ten infinitives for common activities. Have students use their lists to ask four other students about what they like to do. Students should answer truthfully: *Me gusta mucho bailar* or *No me gusta nada bailar.*

Gramática

Objectives

- Read and write about other people's likes and dislikes
- Ask and answer questions about activity preferences

Negatives

To make a sentence negative in Spanish, you usually put *no* in front of the verb or expression. In English you usually use the word "not."

No me gusta cantar.	*I do not like to sing.*

To answer a question negatively in Spanish you often use *no* twice. The first *no* answers the question. The second *no* says, "I do *not . . . (don't).*" This is similar to the way you answer a question in English.

¿Te gusta escribir cuentos?	*Do you like to write stories?*
No, no me gusta.	*No, I don't.*

In Spanish, you might use one or more negatives after answering *"no."*

¿Te gusta cantar?	*Do you like to sing?*
No, no me gusta nada.	*No, I don't like it at all.*

If you want to say that you do not like either of two choices, use *ni . . . ni:*

No me gusta ni nadar ni dibujar.	*I don't like either swimming or drawing.*
	I like neither swimming nor drawing.

¿Recuerdas?

Did you remember that *nada* has another meaning?

- ¿Qué pasa? **Nada.**

In this case, *nada* means "nothing."

Más ayuda realidades.com

***GramActiva* Video**
Tutorials: Affirmative and Negative, Making a Sentence Negative, Formation of Negative Sentences

***GramActiva* Activity**

15 Una persona muy negativa

Leer • Escribir

Fill in the blanks in the dialogue with one of these expressions: *no, nada, tampoco, ni . . . ni.*

Tomás es un nuevo estudiante en la clase y es una persona muy negativa.

Ana: Hola, Tomás. ¿Te gusta escuchar música?
Tomás: No, __1.__ me gusta.
Ana: Pues, ¿qué te gusta más, jugar videojuegos o usar la computadora?
Tomás: No me gusta __2.__ jugar videojuegos __3.__ usar la computadora.
Ana: ¿Te gusta practicar deportes?
Tomás: No, no me gusta __4.__ practicar deportes.
Ana: Pues, Tomás, no me gusta pasar tiempo con personas negativas.
Tomás: ¡A mí __5.__!

DIFFERENTIATED INSTRUCTION

Students with Learning Difficulties

To help visual learners grasp the pattern for negation, write *No, I don't like to sing.* and *No, no me gusta cantar.* Circle *No* and write the number 1, then circle *don't* and write the number 2. In the Spanish version, circle the first ***No*** and write the number 1, then circle the second ***no*** and write the number 2.

Advanced Learners/Pre-AP*

Have students write a paragraph describing what they like to do, what they do not like to do, and what they do not like to do at all. When you hand back their corrected papers, have them rewrite the paragraphs and display them for the class to read.

16 ¡No, no me gusta!

Hablar

Today you feel as negative as Tomás. With a partner, respond to each question saying that you don't like to do any of these activities.

Modelo

A —*¿Te gusta ver la tele?*
B —*No, no me gusta ver la tele.*

Estudiante A

1. 
2. 
3. 
4.
5. 
6. 

Estudiante B

No, no me gusta . . .

17 ¿Qué te gusta más?

Hablar

Find out what your partner likes more. Then switch roles.

Modelo

A —*¿Qué te gusta más, nadar o esquiar?*
B —*Pues, me gusta más nadar.*
o: —*Pues, no me gusta ni nadar ni esquiar.*

1.  
2.  
3.  
4.  

Más práctica GO	realidades.com	print
Instant Check	✔	
Guided WB pp. 34–35	✔	✔
Core WB p. 18	✔	✔
Comm. WB pp. 13, 16, 227	✔	✔
Hispanohablantes WB pp. 18–19		✔

ENRICH YOUR TEACHING

Teacher-to Teacher

Ask students to brainstorm a gesture for each of the vocabulary words. Then have students work in pairs to give and follow instructions using the vocabulary: Student A says *hablar por teléfono* and Student B acts out the expression. Student A gives instructions until Student B misses one. Then they switch roles.

21st Century Skills

Initiative and Self-Direction Make sure students are aware that the digital tools available for every chapter in **realidades.com** serve different purposes, from presentation and guided practice to remediation. Students should explore which tools best support their individual learning needs and styles, and keep track of the way they use the tools to become more fluent speakers of Spanish.

Practice and Communicate 1A

BELLRINGER REVIEW

Ask students to name the activities shown in the Student A balloon.

1.1
…wer Keys: Student Edition, p. 14
…nd answering questions
…emind pairs that Student … pond in the negative. …inish, have them reverse … the activity.

Tues 10/17 ✓ 7th Thu video Finish Act 16 Do 17

2. montar en bicicleta
3. nadar
4. usar la computadora
5. dibujar
6. ir a la escuela

Extension: Use *Transparencies 32* and *33* to cue additional activities.

17 Standards: 1.1

Resources: Answer Keys: Student Edition, p. 14

Focus: Discussing likes and dislikes

Suggestions: Review the visualized vocabulary with the class. Role-play the *Modelo* with a student. Stress the ***ni ... ni*** to emphasize the negatives. When students have completed the activity, ask several pairs to present to the class.

Answers:

1. ¿Qué te gusta más, leer o cantar? Pues, me gusta más leer. o: Pues, no me gusta ni leer ni cantar.
2. ¿... ver la tele o tocar la guitarra?
3. ¿... jugar videojuegos o montar en monopatín?
4. ¿... hablar por teléfono o pasar tiempo con amigos?

Additional Resources

- Communication Wbk.: Audio Act. 8, p. 13
- Teacher's Resource Book: Audio Script, p. 46, Communicative Pair Activity BLM, p. 52
- Audio Program DVD: Cap. 1A, Track 11

ASSESSMENT

Prueba 1A-4 with Study Plan (online only)

Quiz: Negatives
- Prueba 1A-4: p. 18

Gramática

Core Instruction

Standards: 4.1

INTERACTIVE WHITEBOARD
Grammar Activities 1A

Suggestions: Be sure students understand that they say ***A mí también*** to agree with an affirmative statement and ***A mí tampoco*** to agree with a negative statement. Use the second portion of the *GramActiva* Video on negatives.

18 Standards: 1.1, 1.3

Resources: Voc. and Gram. Transparencies 32–33

Focus: Expressing agreement or disagreement in personalized context

Suggestions: First, ask students to brainstorm leisure activities they like and do not like to do while you write them on the board. Show the transparencies to help them recall the words.

Answers will vary.

19 Standards: 1.2, 1.3, 4.1

Resources: Answer Keys: Student Edition, p. 14

Focus: Reading comprehension

Suggestions: Explain to students that they do not know all these words and should use cognates, and context for overall comprehension.

Answers:

1. Alicia; sometimes
2. Enrique; with his friends
3. Sandra; it's bad for your eyes
4. Answers will vary.

Pre-AP* Support

- **Learning Objective:** Interpersonal Writing
- **Activity 19:** Have students use their responses to the activity's questions to write an email to Alicia, Enrique, or Sandra expressing their personal opinion about videogames.
- ***Pre-AP* Resource Book:*** Comprehensive guide to Pre-AP* writing skill development, pp. 27–38

Gramática

Objectives

- Express agreement and disagreement about what you and others like to do
- Read and write opinions about activities

Expressing agreement or disagreement

To agree with what a person likes, you use *"a mí también."* It's like saying "me too" in English.

Me gusta pasar tiempo con amigos.	*I like to spend time with friends.*
A mí también.	*Me too.*

If someone tells you that he or she dislikes something, you can agree by saying *"a mí tampoco."* It's like saying "me neither" or "neither do I" in English.

No me gusta nada cantar.	*I don't like to sing at all.*
A mí tampoco.	*Me neither.*

18 ¿También o tampoco?

Escribir • Hablar

Write a list of three things that you like to do and three things that you don't like to do. Tell your partner the activities on your list. Your partner will agree or disagree based upon his or her personal preferences. Follow the model.

Modelo

A —*Me gusta mucho bailar.*
B —*A mí también.*
o:—*Pues, a mí no me gusta nada bailar.*
A —*No me gusta nada cantar.*
B —*A mí tampoco.*
o:—*Pues, a mí me gusta cantar.*

19 Opiniones

Leer • Escribir

Read the opinions of three students on videogames and answer the questions.

1. Who thinks that videogames are neither good nor bad? How often does he or she play videogames?
2. Who likes videogames a lot? With whom does this person play them?
3. Who doesn't like videogames? Why not?
4. ¿A ti te gusta jugar videojuegos?

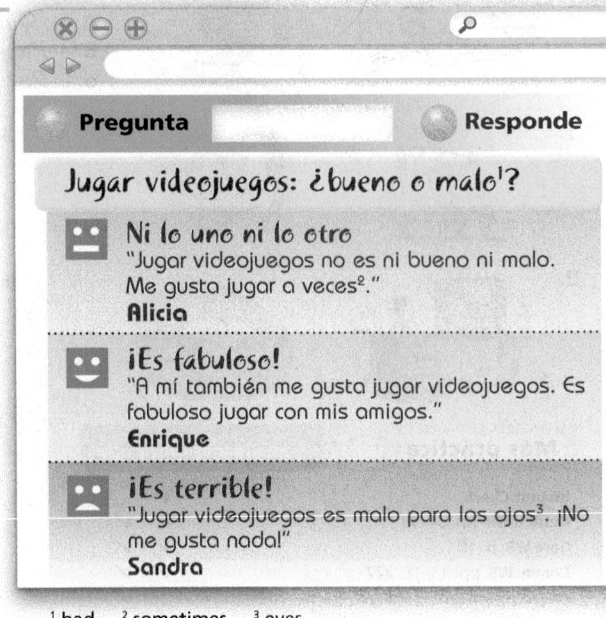

[1] bad [2] sometimes [3] eyes

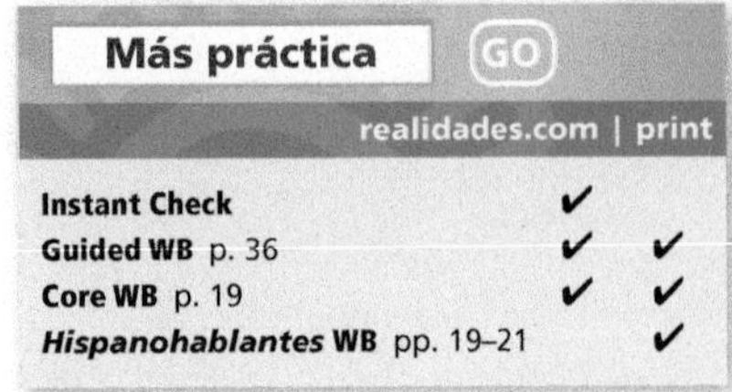

Más práctica GO

realidades.com | print

	realidades.com	print
Instant Check	✔	
Guided WB p. 36	✔	✔
Core WB p. 19	✔	✔
Hispanohablantes WB pp. 19–21		✔

DIFFERENTIATED INSTRUCTION

Students with Learning Difficulties

Some students may have difficulty understanding the two choices in the second model for *Actividad* 18. Explain that the first means that they agree with their partner, and the second means that they disagree. Write the model on the board and label the choices as "agree" and "disagree."

Heritage Language Learners

Have students choose two leisure activities studied in this chapter and use the text in *Actividad* 19 as a model to express written opinions appropriate for their selections. Provide feedback on errors in standard Spanish.

▾ Pronunciación

The vowels *a, e,* and *i*

The vowel sounds in Spanish are different from those in English. In Spanish, each vowel has just one sound. Spanish vowels are also quicker and shorter than those in English.

The letter *a* is similar to the sound in the English word *pop.* Listen to and say these words:

andar	cantar	trabajar
hablar	nadar	pasar

The letter *e* is similar to the sound in the English word *met.* Listen to and say these words:

tele   me   es   Elena   deportes

The letter *i* is similar to the sound in the English word *see.* As you have already seen, the letter *y* sometimes has the same sound as *i.* Listen to and say these words:

sí   escribir   patinar   lápiz   ti   mí

Try it out! Listen to and say this rhyme:

A-E-I El perro canta para ti.
A-E-I El tigre baila para mí.

Try it again, substituting *el gato* for *el perro* and *la cebra* for *el tigre.*

El español en la comunidad

Hispanics in the United States make up approximately 16 percent of the total population and are the fastest-growing minority group. By the year 2050, the Hispanic population is expected to be almost 29 percent of the total U.S. population. Because of this, there are an increasing number of Spanish-language electronic and print media sources—Internet, television, radio, magazines, and newspapers—available throughout the country.

- Make a list of Spanish-language media sources in your community. Try to find local, regional, national, or even international sources, as well as both electronic and print media. If possible, bring in examples. How much can you understand?

These sources will help you improve your Spanish, and you'll learn about Spanish-speaking cultures as well.

ENRICH YOUR TEACHING

Teacher-to-Teacher

Use this tongue twister to teach the vowels ***a, e,*** and ***i:*** *Mi mamá me mima y mimo a mi mamá.* ("My mom pampers me, and I pamper my mom.")

21st Century Skills

Social and Cross-Cultural Skills After students have completed the suggested activity in *El español en la comunidad*, have them work in small groups to compare their findings. Did the Spanish-language examples they found vary much or little in form and content from English media examples they know? Ask them to try to identify specific forms of information in their examples, such as advertisements, public service announcements, etc.

Practice and Communicate 1A

Pronunciación

Core Instruction

Standards: 4.1

Resources: Teacher's Resource Book: Audio Script, p. 47; Audio Program DVD: Cap. 1A, Track 10

Suggestions: Go through the *Pronunciación* with students. Have them pronounce the vowels ***a, e,*** and ***i*** and the example words. Let students work individually to memorize the rhyme. Then ask volunteers to say the rhyme. Use the drawing to identify the animals.

Regional variations in English [illegible]nunciation can affect so[illegible] ch as "pop." [illegible] er words like "fa[illegible]" as exampl[illegible] Draw a [illegible] hree columns, [illegible] ords. Have stu[illegible] ther words the[illegible] n these vow[illegible] he board and [illegible] chart.

El español en la comunidad

Core Instruction

Standards: 1.2, 3.1, 3.2, 4.2, 5.2

Suggestions: Have the class suggest ideas for Spanish-language media sources while you write them on the board. Possible answers include local newspapers, radio and television stations, magazines they've seen on newsstands, etc.

Theme Project

Students can perform Step 2 at this point. Be sure they understand your suggestions. (For more infomation, see p. 24-b.)

Additional Resources

- Communication Wbk.: Audio Act. 9, p. 13
- Teacher's Resource Book: Audio Script, pp. 46–47, Communicative Pair Activity BLM, p. 53
- Audio Program DVD: Cap. 1A, Track 12

BELLRINGER REVIEW

Ask students to explain what cognates are and give examples.

 Common Core: Reading

Lectura

Core Instruction

Standards: 1.2, 1.3, 4.1

Resources: Voc. and Gram. Transparencies 37–38

Focus: Reading about other teens' likes and dislikes

Suggestions:

Pre-reading: Direct attention to the *Strategy*. Have students quickly scan the selection to see if they can identify any cognates. Remind them that cognates can help them to understand the notes as they read them.

Reading: Have students read each note without interruption. They can predict the meaning of the notes from the context and cognates. Stop after each note and ask volunteers to tell what activities were mentioned.

Post-reading: After students finish reading the four notes, review each one with them. Ask a volunteer to read the first note aloud. Ask: What things does Marisol like to do? Let students suggest activities until all volunteers have spoken. Make sure the class agrees on all of the activities and that they are correct. Ask students to explain how they arrived at their understanding. Repeat the exercise with all four notes.

Block Schedule

Divide the class into groups of three or four. Have them write as many cognates as they can in five minutes. Have them agree in their group what cognates are. Call time and ask a representative of each group to give their explanation.

Objectives

- Read about favorite activities of some teenagers
- Use cognates to figure out new words

Lectura

¿Qué te gusta hacer?

Here are some notes that four students have written to a popular teen magazine. All four are looking for e-pals. As you read their notes, think about how their likes and interests compare to yours.

Strategy

Using cognates
Use what you already know about cognates to figure out what new words mean.

Puerto Rico
Marisol, 14 años

"¿Te gusta practicar deportes y escuchar música? ¡A mí me gusta mucho! También me gusta jugar al básquetbol. ¡Hasta luego!".

Colombia
Daniel, 13 años

"Me gusta mucho ver la tele y escuchar música clásica. También me gusta tocar el piano y pasar tiempo con amigos en un café o en una fiesta. ¿Y a ti?".

DIFFERENTIATED INSTRUCTION

Multiple Intelligences

Intrapersonal/Introspective: Have students respond to the four young people from Puerto Rico, Colombia, España, and Guinea Ecuatorial by writing an e-pal note to each one. In their e-mails, students should tell Marisol, Daniel, Silvia, and Pablo about themselves, indicating their own likes and dislikes.

Students with Learning Difficulties

Have students divide a sheet of paper into four equal sections. In each section, have them list what each student likes and doesn't like to do. They may wish to use this list as an aid in answering the questions in the *¿Comprendes?* section.

España
Silvia, 17 años

"Me gusta leer revistas, bailar y cantar. Soy fanática de la música alternativa. También me gusta hablar por teléfono con amigos. ¿Y a ti? ¿Qué te gusta hacer?".

Guinea Ecuatorial
Pablo, 15 años

"Me gusta mucho jugar al vóleibol y al tenis. Me gusta escribir cuentos y también me gusta organizar fiestas con amigos. No me gusta ni jugar videojuegos ni ver la tele. ¡Hasta pronto!".

¿Comprendes?

1. Draw a bar graph. Indicate on the graph how many of the four young people like each of these types of activities: *televisión, música, deportes, pasar tiempo con amigos.* Which are the most popular?
2. Of the four students, with whom do you have the most in common?
3. Write a personal message similar to those in the magazine. Use one of them as a model.

Más práctica GO

realidades.com | print

Guided WB p. 37	✔	✔
Comm. WB pp. 17, 228	✔	✔
***Hispanohablantes* WB** pp. 22–23		✔
Culture Reading Activity	✔	

ENRICH YOUR TEACHING

Teacher-to-Teacher

Using a large wall map, map transparencies, or the maps on pp. xxiii, xxv, and xxix, help students find *Puerto Rico, Colombia, España,* and *Guinea Ecuatorial.* Make sure students understand that *Puerto Rico* is not a country, but *un Estado libre asociado,* a territory—not a state—of the United States.

21st Century Skills

Initiative and Self-Direction Remind students of the tools available for extra reading support in **realidades.com.** Computer-corrected activities use different strategies to help students comprehend the new vocabulary, monitor their learning needs, and progress at their own pace through the reading.

Reading 1A

¿Comprendes? Standards: 1.1, 1.3

Resources: Answer Keys: Student Edition, p. 15

Focus: Demonstrating reading comprehension of the e-pal notes by creating a bar graph and writing a similar note

Suggestions: Make sure students understand how to make a bar graph. Have students complete the activity. Draw the bar graph on the board or use the blank bar graph transparency and ask a volunteer to fill it in. Students can compare their charts with the one on the board, suggest corrections, and check their own. After students write their own messages, have several students share their personal messages with the class by reading them or writing them on the board.

Answers:

1. **Students' bar graphs should indicate: 1 televisión; 3 música; 2 deportes; 3 pasar tiempo con amigos.**
2. **Answers will vary.**
3. **Answers will vary.**

Pre-AP* Support

- **Learning Objective:** Interpersonal Speaking
- **Activity:** Have students create a short conversation, based on the responses of any two of the teens in the reading as models, and substituting their own likes and dislikes.
- ***Pre-AP* Resource Book:*** Comprehensive guide to Pre-AP* speaking skill development, pp. 39–50

Teacher-to-Teacher

If you have the resources, students may enjoy having an e-pal with whom they can practice Spanish. This could take the form of a class-only chat if you have access to a lab or an arrangement with another Spanish class, or with students in a Spanish-speaking country. If Internet access is not available, students may enjoy having a secret pen pal in class. They can draw names and write notes that you collect and distribute.

For Further Reading

Student Resource: Realidades para hispanohablantes: Lectura 2, pp. 24–25

La cultura en vivo

Core Instruction

Standards: 2.2, 3.1

Resources: Teacher's Resource Book: Audio Script, p. 47; Audio Program DVD: Cap. 1A, Track 20

Focus: Reading about ***el mambo*** and learning the dance

Suggestions: Locate in advance some mambo music to play in class. Tell the class that dancing is popular in Spanish-speaking countries and some of the dances have been around for many years. People often learn popular national or regional dances as young children. Direct attention to the diagram. Explain that the dotted line shows the moving foot, and then demonstrate the steps with your back to the students. Have them follow along with you. After a little practice, play the music. Have students listen to the rhythm and the beat. Explain that this music is for dancing the ***mambo,*** a popular dance from Cuba.

Be sensitive to students who do not dance for religious reasons or because of physical limitations. Other students may be hesitant to dance, so create an inviting environment by not putting individuals on the spot. Show that this is fun. Clear a space in the classroom, or move to an open area where students have room to move. Demonstrate the steps slowly. Then, as a class, practice the steps slowly a few times. Try to move more quickly and smoothly each time.

Once students have acquired some proficiency, allow them to practice. Arrange students in pairs with partners facing each other. Have one partner begin the dance with the left foot moving forward and the other with the right foot going back at the same time. After a few minutes have each pair change partners.

Play a mambo tune and allow students to dance. If students have fun and become even mildly proficient, they may enjoy holding a dance contest.

Direct attention to *Think About It!* and have students answer the questions.

Answers will vary.

Additional Resources

Student Resource: Realidades para hispanohablantes, p. 26

La cultura en vivo

¿Te gusta bailar?

Thanks to the worldwide popularity of Latin music, Latin dances have captured the attention of people of all ages. As a result, people all around the United States are learning dances such as the merengue, tango, and salsa. Here is a dance you can learn. It is called the mambo, and it originated in Cuba in the 1940s.

Bailando el mambo

El mambo

Directions

Beat 1 (of the music): Step forward with the left foot and slightly raise the right foot in a rocking motion.

Beat 2: Step back down on the right foot.

Beat 3: Place the left foot next to the right foot.

Beat 4: Hold both feet in place with the left and right feet next to each other.

Repeat the same motion, now moving backwards.

Beat 5: Step backward with the right foot and slightly raise the left foot in a rocking motion.

Beat 6: Step back down on the left foot.

Beat 7: Place the right foot next to the left foot.

Beat 8: Hold both feet in place with the left and right feet next to each other.

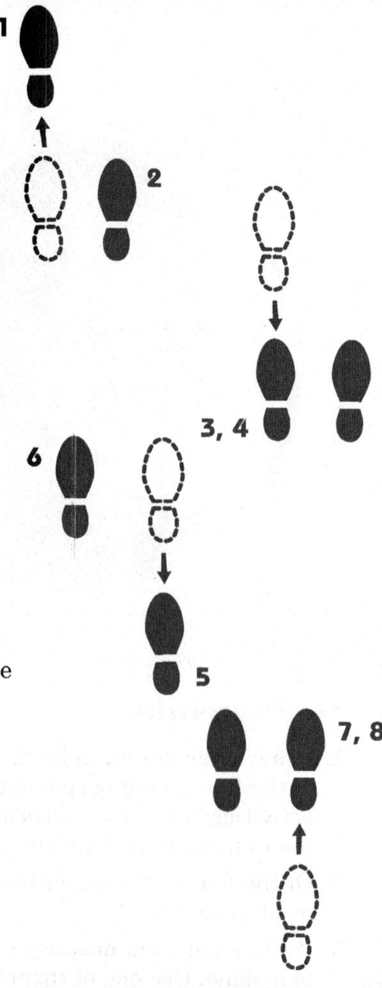

These steps are repeated throughout the music. If partners dance together, then the male should start with his left foot going forward and the female should start with her right foot going backward.

Think about it! How is doing the mambo with a partner different from dances you might do? What dances do you know from the United States that are danced with a partner?

DIFFERENTIATED INSTRUCTION

Heritage Language Learners

Some students may be familiar with the mambo and the music associated with it. If so, allow them to help teach the steps and to share personal experiences if they wish. Others may be familiar with other dances from Spanish-speaking countries and may have interesting stories to share with the class.

Multiple Intelligences

Musical/Rhythmic: If students master the dance quickly, they may find other dances interesting too. Encourage them to research salsa, merengue, or tango and present their findings to the class, preferably demonstrating the dance.

Presentación oral

A mí me gusta mucho . . .

- Talk about your likes and dislikes
- Use a diagram to organize your ideas

Task
You are a new student at school and have been asked to tell the class a little bit about your likes and dislikes.

1 Prepare Copy this diagram, then list at least five activities to include in the three different ovals.

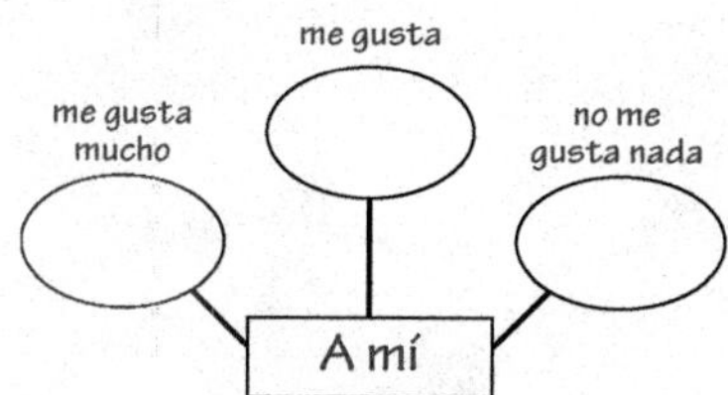

Using your list, create a poster or other visual aid to illustrate the three categories and at least five activities. You can use drawings, pictures from magazines, or photos of yourself doing the activities. Make sure that each activity is easy to identify. You will use this visual as part of your presentation.

2 Practice Rehearse your presentation with classmates. Use your notes the first time or two, then practice using only the visuals.

Modelo
Me gusta mucho . . .
Me gusta . . .
No me gusta nada . . .

3 Present Talk about yourself using your visuals. Look at the Evaluation rubric below to know what to emphasize in your presentation. Begin the presentation with your name, and try to:
- use complete sentences
- use visuals to stay focused
- speak clearly

4 Evaluation The following rubric will be used to grade your presentation.

Rubric	Score 1	Score 3	Score 5
How much information you communicate	You mention one detailed example in each category.	You mention four activities and all three categories.	You mention five activities and all three categories.
How easily you are understood	You are difficult to understand and have many patterns of grammatical errors.	You are fairly easy to understand with occasional patterns of grammatical errors.	You are easy to understand and have very few patterns of grammatical errors.
How clearly and neatly your visuals match what you are saying	You include three visuals that clearly connect to activities.	You include four visuals that clearly connect to activities.	You include five visuals that clearly connect to activities.

Strategy
Creating visuals
Making a diagram can help you organize a presentation.

Speaking 1A

Common Core: Speaking

Presentación oral

Core Instruction

Standards: 1.3

Resources: Voc. and Gram. Transparency 39; Teacher's Resource Book: GramActiva, p. 55

Focus: Communicating about likes and dislikes in a personalized context

Suggestions: Explain the task and the 4-step approach to students. Review the rubric with the class to explain how you will grade the performance task. Do a presentation of your own (an anchor) to model a top-scoring presentation. Have students work through each step of the speaking process.

Pre-

- **Learni**[...]aking
- **Activit**[...]ring likes ar[...]
- ***Pre-AP***[...] guide to [...]ent, pp. 39–5[...]

End 1A Me Poster Project
← Write ID for #s 2-3

Portfo[...]
Make vid[...] of student presentations in class, or assign the RealTalk activity so they can record their presentations online. Include the recording in their portfolios.

Additional Resources
Student Resources: Realidades para hispanohablantes, p. 27; Guided Practice: Presentación oral, p. 38

ENRICH YOUR TEACHING

Teacher-to-Teacher
Display the students' visual presentations for the class. Make time for students to walk around, view each diagram, and take notes or write questions to ask their classmates. Provide time for a class discussion of the diagrams, comments, and questions.

21st Century Skills
Communication Using the *Presentación oral* as a model, find a student you don't know well in Spanish class, greet him or her, and ask about his or her favorite activities. Find one of your friends with an interest in common with the student, introduce them, and mention the interest they have in common.

ASSESSMENT
Presentación oral
- Assessment Program: Rubrics, p. T28

Go over the descriptions of the different levels of performance. After assessing students, help individuals understand how their performance could be improved. (See Teacher's Resource Book for suggestions on using rubrics in assessment.)

El mundo hispano

Core Instruction

Standards: 2.2, 3.1

Resources: Map Transparencies, 18

Focus: Reading about Spain's heritage

Presentation: After students read the opening page, use a world map to point out Spain and the areas that belonged to the Spanish empire. Discuss how over time Spain's colonial territories gained their independence.

Locate Rome on the map. Point out the proximity of Spain and Rome. Since Spain was once a province of the Roman empire, it is easy to understand why Spanish is called a Romance language.

Have students look at the top two photos and read the paragraphs on p. 45. Discuss how Spain still shows traces of other cultures that influenced it. Ask students to point out evidence of this. Locate North Africa on the map and note where the Moors originated. Indicate a path linking North Africa and Spain, so students can visualize how they came to Spain. Entertain ideas about their method of travel. Point out that the Moors, who ruled Spain for nearly 800 years, spoke Arabic and that Spanish today still reflects its influence. On a map of Spain, have students locate Granada and Córdoba, once-important Moorish cities. Help students see that the cities are in southern Spain, the area closest to North Africa. Point out that the Alhambra and other sites dating back to the time of the Moors still exist. Have students focus on the photo of the Retiro. Talk about its original purpose and how it is used now. Locate Bilbao on the map. Point it out as the location of the Guggenheim Museum.

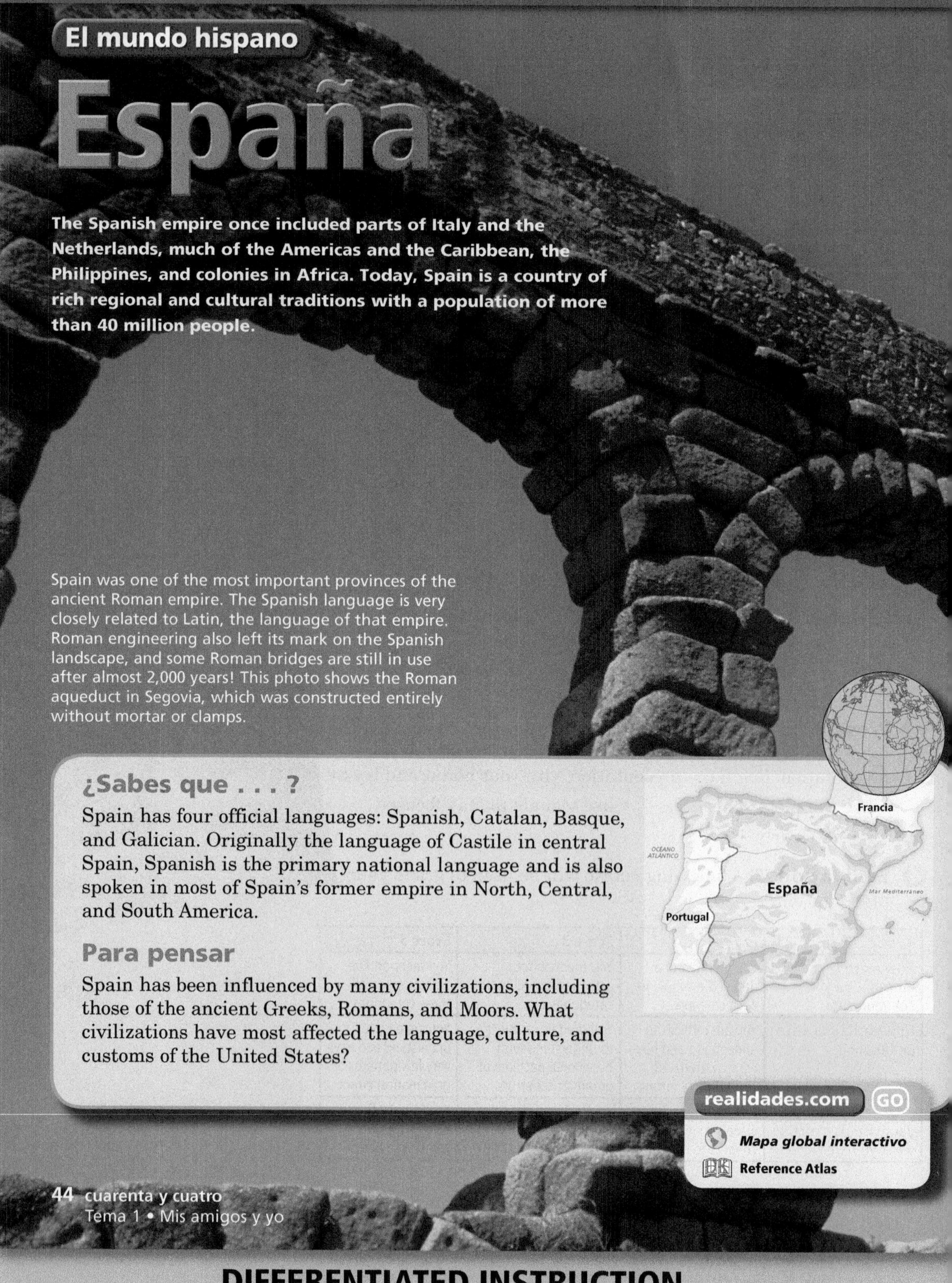

El mundo hispano

España

The Spanish empire once included parts of Italy and the Netherlands, much of the Americas and the Caribbean, the Philippines, and colonies in Africa. Today, Spain is a country of rich regional and cultural traditions with a population of more than 40 million people.

Spain was one of the most important provinces of the ancient Roman empire. The Spanish language is very closely related to Latin, the language of that empire. Roman engineering also left its mark on the Spanish landscape, and some Roman bridges are still in use after almost 2,000 years! This photo shows the Roman aqueduct in Segovia, which was constructed entirely without mortar or clamps.

¿Sabes que . . . ?

Spain has four official languages: Spanish, Catalan, Basque, and Galician. Originally the language of Castile in central Spain, Spanish is the primary national language and is also spoken in most of Spain's former empire in North, Central, and South America.

Para pensar

Spain has been influenced by many civilizations, including those of the ancient Greeks, Romans, and Moors. What civilizations have most affected the language, culture, and customs of the United States?

realidades.com GO

Mapa global interactivo

Reference Atlas

DIFFERENTIATED INSTRUCTION

Advanced Learners

Have students research Spain's monarchy that defeated the Moors in 1492. Have them answer questions such as: Who were the monarchs at that time? What regions were occupied by the Moors? Does the monarchy still exist?

Heritage Language Learners

Have students research the languages that influenced their heritage country. Have them answer the question: Why is Spanish spoken there? Also, have them find some words used in their heritage country that, due to non-Spanish influences, may not be used in Spain.

Originally a royal retreat, the Parque del Buen Retiro is now a favorite place for the traditional Sunday-afternoon *paseo* (stroll). Throngs of people come to enjoy the Retiro's lakes, gardens, and museums, or simply to spend time with friends or family. What are your favorite places to go walking with friends? Why?

Arabic-speaking Moors from North Africa ruled much of Spain for nearly 800 years. Córdoba in southern Spain became one of the most important cities in Islam, and its mosque, the Mezquita, was one of the largest in the world. The Alhambra in Granada (shown above) is a strongly fortified and beautiful complex of palaces and gardens. It was also the last stronghold of the Moors in Spain, falling to Spain's Catholic monarchs in 1492.

The Bilbao Guggenheim Museum opened in October 1997 and houses a collection of modern and contemporary art. The building's titanium-paneled curves and concrete blocks imitate the harbor of Bilbao, a principal seaport and former shipbuilding center in the heart of the Basque country in the north.

Suggestions: Some students may have difficulty understanding the timeline. Spain was part of the Roman empire before the Moors occupied it and later acquired its own possessions in other regions and continents after defeating the Moors in 1492.

Point out how Spain has maintained its history (the buildings from the time of the Moors) while incorporating the very up-to-date (the Guggenheim Museum).

Direct attention to the *Para pensar* section and have students discuss the question.

Answers will vary.

Extension: Have students research the official languages of Spain. Direct them to the *¿Sabes que...?* section and have them find out where in Spain each language is spoken. Note that Spanish (Castillian) was originally the language of Castile.

Theme Project

Students can perform Step 3 at this point. (For more information, see p. 24-b.)

ENRICH YOUR TEACHING

Teacher-to-Teacher

Allow those who did the research described in the Differentiated Instruction sections to present their findings to the class. You may wish to have a physical or electronic bulletin board where students can display photos or reports. This will allow others to review them.

Teacher-to-Teacher

Let students work together to create a map showing Spain as a Roman colony and Spain as a colonial power. Have them display it on a wall or bulletin board in the classroom.

Review Activities

To talk about activities: Have students work in pairs to quiz each other on the vocabulary. Have them create flashcards. Creating and collecting these cards may prove helpful to students throughout the *Realidades* course.

To say what you like and don't like to do: Have students work in pairs and tell each other what they like to do and don't like to do. Students can respond with ***A mí también*** or ***A mí tampoco***.

To ask others what they like to do: Have students interview each other about activities they like to do. Ask students to brainstorm a list of activities and write five questions using ***¿Te gusta...?*** Tell them to interview a different classmate for each question. Encourage students to use the phrases in *Other useful words and expressions* in their responses. After they have completed the interview, ask volunteers: *¿Qué te gusta hacer?*

Portfolio

Invite students to review chapter activities, including written reports, posters or other visuals, and tapes of oral presentations, or other projects. Have them select one or two items that they feel best demonstrate their achievements in Spanish. Include these products in students' portfolios. Have them include this with the chapter checklist and Self-Assessment Worksheet.

Additional Resources

Student Resources: Realidades para hispanohablantes, p. 28

Teacher Resources:

- Teacher's Resource Book: Situation Cards, p. 54, Clip Art, pp. 57–59
- Assessment Program: Chapter Checklist and Self-Assessment Worksheet, pp. T56–T57

Objectives

- Review the vocabulary and grammar
- Demonstrate you can perform the tasks on p. 47

Repaso del capítulo

Vocabulario y gramática

to talk about activities

bailar	to dance
cantar	to sing
correr	to run
dibujar	to draw
escribir cuentos	to write stories
escuchar música	to listen to music
esquiar	to ski
hablar por teléfono	to talk on the phone
ir a la escuela	to go to school
jugar videojuegos	to play video games
leer revistas	to read magazines
montar en bicicleta	to ride a bicycle
montar en monopatín	to skateboard
nadar	to swim
pasar tiempo con amigos	to spend time with friends
patinar	to skate
practicar deportes	to play sports
tocar la guitarra	to play the guitar
trabajar	to work
usar la computadora	to use the computer
ver la tele	to watch television

to say what you like to do

(A mí) me gusta ___.	I like to ___.
(A mí) me gusta más ___.	I like to ___ better. (I prefer to ___.)
(A mí) me gusta mucho ___.	I like to ___ a lot.
A mí también.	I do too.

to say what you don't like to do

(A mí) no me gusta ___.	I don't like to ___.
(A mí) no me gusta nada ___.	I don't like to ___ at all.
A mí tampoco.	I don't (like to) either.

to ask others what they like to do

¿Qué te gusta hacer?	What do you like to do?
¿Qué te gusta más?	What do you like better (prefer)?
¿Te gusta ___?	Do you like to ___?
¿Y a ti?	And you?

other useful words and expressions

ni . . . ni	neither . . . nor, not . . . or
o	or
pues . . .	well . . .
sí	yes
también	also, too
y	and

For *Vocabulario adicional,* see pp. 472–473.

DIFFERENTIATED INSTRUCTION

Students with Learning Difficulties

Have students review the *Repaso del capítulo* and create flashcards for any words that they do not know. Pair them with a student who is more confident with the vocabulary to practice. Before the test, provide students with a practice test, so they can become comfortable with the format.

Heritage Language Learners

Have students write a few paragraphs telling about their perfect birthday celebration: Where are they going to have it? Whom are they going to invite? What food are they going to eat? What kind of music are they going to play? Encourage them to use as many vocabulary words from this chapter as they can.

Más repaso GO realidades.com | print

Instant Check	✔	
Puzzles	✔	
Core WB pp. 20–21		✔
Comm. WB pp. 229, 230–232	✔	✔

Preparación para el examen

On the exam you will be asked to . . .	Here are practice tasks similar to those you will find on the exam . . .	For review go to your print or digital textbook . . .
Interpretive		
 **1 Escuchar** Listen to and understand a description of what someone likes to do	Listen to a voice mail from a student looking for a "match-up" to the homecoming dance. a) What are two things this person likes doing? b) What is one thing this person dislikes doing?	**pp. 26–29** *Vocabulario en contexto* **p. 27** Actividades 1–2 **p. 33** Actividad 13
Interpersonal		
 **2 Hablar** Talk about yourself and what you like and don't like to do and ask the same of others	You agreed to host a student from the Dominican Republic for a week. What can you tell him or her about yourself in a taped message? Include a brief description of what you like to do. How would you ask the student to tell you something about himself or herself?	**p. 30** Actividad 7 **p. 31** Actividad 8 **p. 33** Actividad 12 **p. 37** Actividades 16–17 **p. 43** *Presentación oral*
Interpretive		
 **3 Leer** Read and understand someone's description of himself or herself	Read this pen pal e-mail from a Spanish-language magazine. What types of things does the person like to do? Does this person have anything in common with you? What is it? *¡Hola! A mí me gusta mucho usar la computadora y tocar la guitarra. No me gusta ni ir a la escuela ni leer. En el verano me gusta nadar y en el invierno me gusta esquiar. ¿Y a ti? ¿Qué te gusta hacer?*	**pp. 26–29** *Vocabulario en contexto* **p. 29** Actividad 3 **p. 36** Actividad 15 **p. 38** Actividad 19 **pp. 40–41** *Lectura*, no. 3
Presentational		
 **4 Escribir** Write about yourself with a description of things you like and don't like to do	A school in the Dominican Republic wants to exchange e-mails with your school. Tell your e-pal your name and what you like to do and don't like to do.	**p. 30** Actividades 5–6 **p. 33** Actividad 12 **p. 38** Actividad 18 **p. 41** *¿Comprendes?*
Cultures		
5 Pensar Demonstrate an understanding of cultural differences regarding dancing	How would you describe the Latin dances that have become popular in the United States? With what countries do you associate each dance? With what type of music or rhythms do you associate each dance?	**p. 34** *Fondo cultural* **p. 35** Actividad 14 **p. 42** *La cultura en vivo*

Performance Tasks

Standards: 1.1, 1.2, 1.3, 4.2

Student Resource: Realidades para hispanohablantes, p. 29

Teacher Resources: Teacher's Resource Book: Audio Script, p. 47; Audio Program DVD: Cap. 1A, Track 22; Answer Keys: Student Edition, p. 15

Suggestions: Explain the format of the chapter test to students. The first portion will assess their knowledge of vocabulary and grammar. The second portion is performance-based and will have tasks very similar to those shown here.

1. Escuchar

Suggestions: Play the audio or read the script.

***Script and Answers:**

Pues, ... a mí me gusta practicar deportes y pasar tiempo con amigos. *(This person likes to practice sports and spend time with friends.)* ¿Y bailar? No me gusta nada bailar. ¿Y a ti? *(This person doesn't like to dance.)*

2. Hablar

Suggestions: Allow time for students to work in class. If they have difficulty speaking spontaneously, have them write their messages and practice them until they can say them without notes.

Answers will vary.

3. Leer

Suggestions: Remind students that cognates can help them understand unfamiliar words.

Answers: usar la computadora, tocar la guitarra, nadar, esquiar; answers will vary.

4. Escribir

Suggestions: Have students try this activity without consulting the vocabulary list, notes, or completed activities.

5. Pensar

Suggestions: Ask students to name the various dances. Elicit comments about rhythms, instruments, etc.

DIFFERENTIATED ASSESSMENT

CORE ASSESSMENT
- **Assessment Program:** Examen del capítulo 1A, pp. 19–25
- **Audio Program:** Disc 20, Chap 1A, Track 16
- **ExamView:** Chapter Test, Test Banks A and B

ADVANCED/PRE-AP*
- **ExamView: Pre-AP* Test Bank**
- **Pre-AP* Resource Book,** pp. 62–65

STUDENTS NEEDING EXTRA HELP
- **Alternate Assessment Program:** Examen del capítulo 1A
- **Audio Program DVD:** Cap. 1A, Track 16

HERITAGE LEARNERS
- **Assessment Program Realidades para hispanohablantes:** Examen del capítulo 1A
- **ExamView: Heritage Learner Test Bank**

1B Y tú, ¿cómo eres?

AT A GLANCE

Objectives
- **Listen to and read descriptions of others**
- **Talk and write about your personality traits**
- **Describe your personality to others**
- **Compare cultural perspectives on friendship**

Vocabulary
- Personality traits
- Expressing likes and dislikes

Grammar
- Adjectives
- Definite and indefinite articles
- Word order: Placement of adjectives

Culture
- Frida Kahlo, p. 49
- Simón Bolívar, p. 58
- *huipil*, p. 65
- What makes a good friend in different cultures, p. 66
- Facts about the Caribbean, pp. 68–69

Recycle
- Gender
- Negatives
- *gustar*

RESOURCES

	FOR THE STUDENT	ONLINE	DVD	PRINT	FOR THE TEACHER	ONLINE	PREEXP	DVD	PRINT
Plan					Interactive TE and Resources DVD	•		•	
					Teacher's Resource Book, pp. 76–107	•		•	•
					Pre-AP* Resource Book, pp. 62–65	•		•	•
					Lesson Plans	•			•
					Mapa global interactivo	•			
Introducción PP. **48–49**									
Present	Student Edition, pp. 48–49	•	•	•	Interactive TE and Resources DVD	•		•	
	DK Reference Atlas	•	•		Teacher's Resource Book, pp. 76–77	•		•	•
	Hispanohablantes WB, pp. 30–31			•	Galería de fotos		•		
					Fine Art Transparencies, 33	•	•	•	
					Map Transparencies, 12–17, 20	•	•	•	
Vocabulario en contexto PP. **50–53**									
Present & Practice	Student Edition, pp. 50–53	•	•	•	Interactive TE and Resources DVD	•		•	
	Audio	•	•		Teacher's Resource Book, pp. 78–79, 82, 90–91	•		•	•
	Videohistoria	•	•		Vocabulary Clip Art	•	•	•	•
	Flashcards	•	•		Audio Program	•	•	•	
	Instant Check	•			Video Program: Videohistoria	•		•	
	Guided WB, pp. 39–46	•	•	•	Video Program Teacher's Guide: Cap. 1B	•		•	•
	Core WB, pp. 22–25	•	•	•	Vocabulary and Grammar Transparencies, 40–43	•	•	•	
	Comm. WB, pp. 18–20, 21, 25	•	•	•	Answer Keys: Student Edition, pp. 16–17	•	•	•	
	Hispanohablantes WB, pp. 32–33			•	TPR Stories, pp. 24–28	•		•	•
Assess and Remediate					Prueba 1B–1: Assessment Program, pp. 26–27	•		•	•
					Assessment Program para hispanohablantes, pp. 26–27	•		•	•

RESOURCES

	FOR THE STUDENT	ONLINE	DVD	PRINT	FOR THE TEACHER	ONLINE	PREEXP	DVD	PRINT
Vocabulario en uso P. **54**									
Present & Practice	Student Edition, p. 54	•	•	•	Interactive Whiteboard Vocabulary Activities	•		•	
	Instant Check	•			Interactive TE and Resources DVD	•		•	
	Comm. WB, p. 22	•	•	•	Teacher's Resource Book, pp. 79–80	•		•	•
	Hispanohablantes WB, p. 34			•	Communicative Pair Activities, pp. 84–85	•		•	•
	Communicative Pair Activities	•			Audio Program	•	•	•	
					Videomodelos	•		•	
					Answer Keys: Student Edition, pp. 17–18	•	•	•	•
Assess and Remediate					Prueba 1B–2 with Study Plan	•			
					Prueba 1B–2: Assessment Program, pp. 28–29	•		•	•
					Assessment Program para hispanohablantes, pp. 28–29	•		•	•
Gramática PP. **55–63**									
Present & Practice	Student Edition, pp. 55–63	•	•	•	Interactive Whiteboard Grammar Activities	•		•	
	Instant Check	•			Interactive TE and Resources DVD	•		•	
	Animated Verbs	•			Teacher's Resource Book, pp. 80–83, 86–87, 89	•		•	•
	Tutorial Video: Grammar	•			Communicative Pair Activities, pp. 86–87	•		•	•
	Canción de hip hop	•			Audio Program	•	•	•	
	Guided WB, pp. 47–50	•	•	•	Videomodelos	•		•	
	Core WB, pp. 26–28	•	•	•	Video Program: GramActiva	•	•	•	
	Comm. WB, pp. 23–24, 26–28, 233	•	•	•	Vocabulary and Grammar Transparencies, 2, 40–41, 44–46	•	•	•	
	Hispanohablantes WB, pp. 35–41			•	Answer Keys: Student Edition, pp. 18–21	•	•	•	
	Communicative Pair Activities	•							
Assess and Remediate					Pruebas 1B–3 to 1B–5 with Study Plans	•			
					Pruebas 1B–3 to 1B–5: Assessment Program, pp. 30, 31	•		•	•
					Assessment Program para hispanohablantes, pp. 30, 31	•		•	•
¡Adelante! PP. **64–69**									
Application	Student Edition, pp. 64–69	•	•	•	Interactive TE and Resources DVD	•		•	
	Online Cultural Reading	•			Vocabulary and Grammar Transparencies, 47	•	•	•	
	Guided WB, pp. 51–52	•	•	•	Map Transparencies, 14	•	•	•	
	Comm. WB, p. 234	•	•	•	Answer Keys: Student Edition, p. 22	•	•	•	
	Hispanohablantes WB, pp. 42–47			•					
Repaso del capítulo PP. **70–71**									
Review	Student Edition, pp. 70–71	•	•	•	Interactive TE and Resources DVD	•		•	
	Online Puzzles and Games	•			Teacher's Resource Book, pp. 81, 88, 90–91	•		•	•
	Core WB, pp. 29–30	•	•	•	Audio Program	•	•	•	
	Comm. WB, pp. 235–238	•	•	•	Answer Keys: Student Edition, p. 22	•	•	•	
	Hispanohablantes WB, pp. 48–49			•					
	Instant Check	•							
Chapter Assessment									
Assess					Examen del capítulo 1B	•		•	•
					Assessment Program, pp. 33–40	•		•	•
					Alternate Assessment Program, pp. 8–12	•		•	•
					Assessment Program para hispanohablantes, pp. 33–40	•		•	•
					Audio Program, Cap. 1B Examen	•		•	
					ExamView: Test Banks A and B questions only online	•		•	
					Heritage Learner Test Bank	•		•	
					Pre-AP* Test Bank	•		•	

DAY	REGULAR SCHEDULE (50 MINUTES)		
	Warm-up / Assess	**Preview / Present / Practice / Communicate**	**Wrap-up / Homework Options**
1	**Warm-up** (10 min.) • Return Examen del capítulo 1A	**Chapter Opener** (5 min.) • Objectives • Arte y cultura **Vocabulario en contexto** (30 min.) • Presentation • Actividades 1, 2	**Wrap-up and Homework Options** (5 min.) • Core Practice 1B-1, 1B-2
2	**Warm-up** (5 min.) • Homework check	**Vocabulario en contexto** (40 min.) • Presentation: Videohistoria *Amigos por Internet* • View: Videohistoria • Video Activities 1, 2, 3, 4 • Actividades 3, 4	**Wrap-up and Homework Options** (5 min.) • Core Practice 1B-3, 1B-4 • Prueba 1B-1: Vocabulary recognition
3	**Warm-up** (10 min.) • Homework check ✔**Formative Assessment** (10 min.) • Prueba 1B-1: Vocabulary recognition	**Vocabulario en uso** (25 min.) • Actividades 5, 6 • Audio Activities 5, 6 • Communicative Pair Activity • Interactive Whiteboard Vocabulary Activities	**Wrap-up and Homework Options** (5 min.) • Writing Activity 10 • Prueba 1B-2 with Study Plan: Vocabulary production
4	**Warm-up** (5 min.) • Homework check ✔**Formative Assessment** (10 min.) • Prueba 1B-2 with Study Plan: Vocabulary production	**Gramática y vocabulario en uso** (30 min.) • Presentation: Adjectives • View: GramActiva video • Interactive Whiteboard Grammar Activities • Actividades 8, 9, 10, 11	**Wrap-up and Homework Options** (5 min.) • Core Practice 1B-5 • Actividades 7, 12 • Prueba 1B-3 with Study Plan: Adjectives
5	**Warm-up** (10 min.) • Writing Activity 11 • Homework check ✔**Formative Assessment** (10 min.) • Prueba 1B-3 with Study Plan: Adjectives	**Gramática y vocabulario en uso** (15 min.) • Actividad 13 • Audio Activity 7 • Communicative Pair Activity (10 min.) • Exploración del lenguaje • Fondo cultural • Actividad 14	**Wrap-up and Homework Options** (5 min.) • Actividad 15 • El mundo hispano
6	**Warm-up** (5 min.) • Homework check	**Gramática y vocabulario en uso** (40 min.) • Presentation: Definite and indefinite articles • View: GramActiva video • Interactive Whiteboard Grammar Activities • Actividades 16, 17 • Audio Activity 8 • Writing Activity 12 • Pronunciación	**Wrap-up and Homework Options** (5 min.) • Core Practice 1B-6 • Prueba 1B-4 with Study Plan: Definite and indefinite articles
7	**Warm-up** (10 min.) • Actividad 18 • Homework check ✔**Formative Assessment** (10 min.) • Prueba 1B-4 with Study Plan: Definite and indefinite articles	**Gramática y vocabulario en uso** (25 min.) • Presentation: Word order: Placement of adjectives • Interactive Whiteboard Grammar Activities • Actividades 20, 21 • Audio Activity 9 • Writing Activity 13 • El español en el mundo del trabajo	**Wrap-up and Homework Options** (5 min.) • Core Practice 1B-7 • Actividad 22 • Prueba 1B-5 with Study Plan: Placement of adjectives
8	**Warm-up** (10 min.) • Actividad 19 • Homework check ✔**Formative Assessment** (10 min.) • Prueba 1B-5 with Study Plan: Placement of adjectives	**¡Adelante!** (25 min.) • Lectura • ¿Comprendes? • Fondo cultural • Presentación escrita: Steps 1, 5 • Perspectivas del mundo hispano	**Wrap-up and Homework Options** (5 min.) • Presentación escrita: Step 2 • Preparación para el examen 3, 4, 5
9	**Warm-up** (5 min.) • Homework check	**¡Adelante!** (20 min.) • Presentación escrita: Step 3 **Repaso del capítulo** (20 min.) • Vocabulario y gramática • Preparación para el examen 1, 2	**Wrap-up and Homework Options** (5 min.) • Presentación escrita: Step 4 • Core Practice 1B-8, 1B-9 • Instant Check • Examen del capítulo 1B
10	**Warm-up** (10 min.) • Homework check ✔**Summative Assessment** (40 min.) • Examen del capítulo 1B		

BLOCK SCHEDULE (90 MINUTES)

DAY	Warm-up / Assess	Preview / Present / Practice / Communicate	Wrap-up / Homework Options
1	**Warm-up** (10 min.) • Return Examen del capítulo 1A	**Chapter Opener** (10 min.) • Objectives • Arte y cultura **Vocabulario en contexto** (60 min.) • Presentation: Vocabulario en contexto • Actividades 1, 2 • Presentation: Videohistoria *Amigos por Internet* • View: Videohistoria • Video Activities 1, 2, 3, 4 • Actividades 3, 4	**Wrap-up and Homework Options** (10 min.) • Core Practice 1B-1, 1B-2, 1B-3, 1B-4 • Prueba 1B-1: Vocabulary recognition
2	**Warm-up** (10 min.) • Homework check ✓**Formative Assessment** (10 min.) • Prueba 1B-1: Vocabulary recognition	**Vocabulario en uso** (65 min.) • Interactive Whiteboard Vocabulary Activities • Actividades 5, 6 • Audio Activities 5, 6 • Communicative Pair Activity • Presentation: Adjectives • View: GramActiva video • Interactive Whiteboard Grammar Activities • Actividades 7, 8, 9, 10, 11, 12	**Wrap-up and Homework Options** (5 min.) • Writing Activity 10 • Core Practice 1B-5 • Prueba 1B-2 with Study Plan: Vocabulary production
3	**Warm-up** (5 min.) • Homework check ✓**Formative Assessment** (10 min.) • Prueba 1B-2 with Study Plan: Vocabulary production	**Gramática y vocabulario en uso** (70 min.) • Exploración del lenguaje • Fondo cultural • Actividades 13, 14 • Audio Activity 7 • Communicative Pair Activity • Presentation: Definite and indefinite articles • View: GramActiva video • Interactive Whiteboard Grammar Activities • Actividades 15, 16, 17 • Audio Activity 8 • Writing Activity 11 • Writing Activity 12 • Pronunciación	**Wrap-up and Homework Options** (5 min.) • Core Practice 1B-6 • Pruebas 1B-3, 1B-4 with Study Plans: Adjectives, Definite and indefinite articles
4	**Warm-up** (10 min.) • Actividad 18 • Homework check ✓**Formative Assessment** (15 min.) • Pruebas 1B-3, 1B-4 with Study Plans: Adjectives, Definite and indefinite articles	**Gramática y vocabulario en uso** (40 min.) • Presentation: Word order: Placement of adjectives • Interactive Whiteboard Grammar Activities • Actividades 19, 20, 21, 22 • Audio Activity 9 • Writing Activity 13 • El español en el mundo del trabajo **¡Adelante!** (20 min.) • Lectura • ¿Comprendes? • Fondo cultural • Presentación escrita: Steps 1, 5 • Perspectivas del mundo hispano	**Wrap-up and Homework Options** (5 min.) • Core Practice 1B-7 • Actividad 22 • Presentación escrita: Step 2 • Lectura • Prueba 1B-5 with Study Plan: Placement of adjectives
5	**Warm-up** (5 min.) • Homework check ✓**Formative Assessment** (10 min.) • Prueba 1B-5 with Study Plan: Placement of adjectives	**¡Adelante!** (45 min.) • Presentación escrita: Step 3 • El mundo hispano **Repaso del capítulo** (25 min.) • Vocabulario y gramática • Preparación para el examen 1, 2, 3, 4, 5	**Wrap-up and Homework Options** (5 min.) • Presentación escrita: Step 4 • Core Practice 1B-8, 1B-9 • Instant Check • Examen del capítulo 1B
6	**Warm-up** (15 min.) • Homework check • Answer questions **Repaso del capítulo** (25 min.) • Situation Cards • Communicative Pair Activities ✓**Summative Assessment** (45 min.) • Examen del capítulo 1B		**Wrap-up and Homework Options** (5 min.) • El mundo hispano

Standards for *Capítulo* 1B

- To achieve the goals of the Standards, students will:

Communication

1.1 Interpersonal
- Talk about personality traits
- Talk about themselves and each other
- Talk about activities and personality traits
- Talk about familiar objects

1.2 Interpretive
- Listen to information about personality traits
- Read information about personality traits
- Read a picture-based story
- Listen to and watch a video about personality traits
- Listen to and identify the gender of nouns
- Read a personality quiz based on color association

1.3 Presentational
- Present descriptions of traits of themselves and others
- Use poetry to express and describe themselves

Culture

2.1 Practices and Perspectives
- Explain how friendships are formed and maintained in some Spanish-speaking countries.
- Explain how Spanish in the Caribbean is influenced by the infusion of multiple European and African tongues

2.2 Products and Perspectives
- Discuss Frida Kahlo and her painting
- Discuss how the ***huipil*** reveals facts about its wearer
- Explain how music in the Caribbean is influenced by the musical styles from around the world.

Connections

3.1 Cross-curricular
- Discuss important artists and their work: Frida Kahlo
- Talk about and write a type of poem known as the ***diamante***

Comparisons

4.1 Language
- Talk about vocabulary through the recognition of cognates
- Discuss building vocabulary through the use of root words
- Explain gender-agreement rules with use of adjectives
- Compare cognates that begin with the letters ***es*** plus consonant
- Explain the use of definite and indefinite articles
- Talk about the pronunciation of the letters ***o*** and ***u***
- Talk about the placement of adjectives

4.2 Culture
- Compare Internet-based chat habits of teenagers
- Talk about and compare the influence of Simón Bolívar to other leaders
- Compare clothing choices that reflect personality
- Compare words used to identify friends and acquaintances
- Compare how friendships are formed and maintained
- Compare the African influence on music in the Americas

Communities

5.1 Beyond the School
- Reflect and discuss careers for which bilingualism is an asset

5.2 Lifelong Learner
- Communicate by e-mail in Spanish

Capítulo

1B Y tú, ¿cómo eres?

▾ Chapter Objectives

Communication

By the end of this chapter you will be able to:
- Listen to and read descriptions of others
- Talk and write about your personality traits
- Describe your personality to others

Culture

You will also be able to:
- Compare cultural perspectives on friendship

You will demonstrate what you know and can do:
- Presentación escrita, p. 67
- Preparación para el examen, p. 71

You will use:

Vocabulary
- Personality traits
- Expressing likes and dislikes

Grammar
- Adjectives
- Definite and indefinite articles
- Word order: Placement of adjectives

Exploración del mundo hispano

Country Connection
Describing Yourself and Others

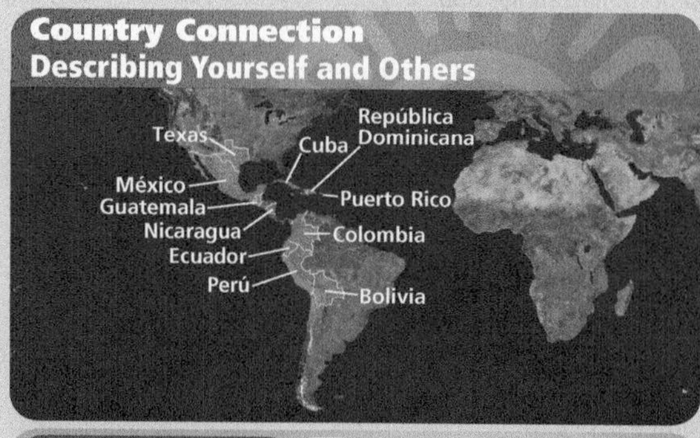

realidades.com GO

Reference Atlas

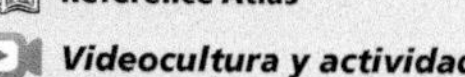
Videocultura y actividad

Mapa global interactivo

Un grupo de amigos, San Juan del Sur, Nicaragua

ENRICH YOUR TEACHING

Using Backward Design

Have students preview the sample performance tasks on *Preparación para el examen,* p. 71, and connect them to the Chapter Objectives. Explain to students that by completing the sample tasks they can self-assess their learning progress.

Mapa global interactivo

Download the *Mapa global interactivo* files for Chapter 1B and preview the activities. In Activity 1, discover artist Frida Kahlo's world in Ciudad de México. Activity 2 looks at the countries Simón Bolívar liberated—Venezuela, Colombia, Ecuador, Peru, and Bolivia. In Activity 3, you explore the islands of Cuba, the Dominican Republic, and Puerto Rico.

Arte y cultura | México

Frida Kahlo (1907–1954) is one of the best-known Mexican painters. In spite of a childhood illness, a crippling traffic accident, and many hospital stays throughout her life, Kahlo was a successful painter and led a very active social life. She used her artwork as an outlet for her physical and emotional suffering.

- Frida Kahlo painted over fifty self-portraits. What is she saying about herself through this painting?

"Autorretrato con mono" (1938), Frida Kahlo ▶

Oil on masonite, 16 X 12 inches. Courtesy of Albright-Knox Art Gallery, Buffalo, NY. Bequest of A. Conger Goodyear, 1966. © 2009 Banco de México, Diego Rivera & Frida Kahlo Museums Trust, México, D.F./Artists Rights Society (ARS), New York.

PresentationExpress™
See pp. 48a–48b

Chapter Opener

Core Instruction

Resources: Map Transparencies 12–17, 20

Suggestions: Explain that students will learn language for identifying personality traits and describing what people are like. (Physical descriptions will be taught in *Capítulo* 5B in the context of family.) The video story focuses on e-mails being exchanged by strangers in two different cities. The *GramActiva* Videos will help students learn to describe things using adjectives.

Videocultura View *Amigos y actividades* with the class to learn more about how friends like to spend their time.

Arte y cultura

Standards: 2.2, 3.1

Resources: Fine Art Transparencies, p. 33

Suggestions: After students have studied the paragraph and the painting, explain that Frida Kahlo chose to wear traditional Mexican clothing and jewelry, and this is reflected in her self-portraits. Have students comment on what the painter is wearing and her facial expression. Ask them what they would include in a self-portrait.

Answers will vary but may include personality traits, or that she displays some pain in the serious tone of the self-portrait.

Mapa global interactivo, Actividad 1 Discover artist Frida Kahlo's world in Ciudad de México.

TEACHING WITH ART

Resources: Fine Art Transparencies, p. 33

DIFFERENTIATED INSTRUCTION

Digital resources such as the ***Interactive Whiteboard*** activity banks, ***Videomodelos***, additional ***Online Activities, Study Plans***, automatically graded ***Leveled Workbook***, animated ***Grammar Tutorials, Flashcards***, and ***Vocabulary and Grammar Videos*** will help you reach students of different ability levels and learning styles.

STUDENTS NEEDING EXTRA HELP

Guided Practice Activities
- Flashcards, pp. 39–42
- Vocabulary Check, pp. 43–46
- Grammar Support, pp. 47–50

HERITAGE LEARNERS

Realidades para hispanohablantes
- Chapter Opener, pp. 30–31
- A primera vista, p. 32
- Videohistoria, p. 33
- Manos a la obra, pp. 34–41
- ¡Adelante!, pp. 42–47
- Repaso del capítulo, pp. 48–49

ADVANCED/PRE-AP*

Pre-AP* Resource Book,
- pp. 62–65

Communications Workbook
- Integrated Performance Assessment, p. 235

Vocabulario en contexto

Core Instruction

Standards: 1.2, 4.1

Resources: Teacher's Resource Book: Input Script, p. 78, Clip Art, pp. 90–91, Audio Script, p. 79; Voc. and Gram. Transparencies 40–41; TPR Stories, pp. 24–28; Audio Program DVD: Cap. 1B, Tracks 1–2

Focus: Presenting new vocabulary about personality traits

Suggestions: Use the story in the *TPR Stories Book* or the Input Script from the *Teacher's Resource Book* to present the new vocabulary, or use some of the suggestions here. Show the transparencies and ask students to tell you in English what trait is represented in each image. Then go back and provide input as you describe each one using the language in the book. Present the *Más vocabulario* using pantomime or exaggerated acting and explain to students that they will be held responsible for knowing these words.

Ask a male student to read the description of ***el chico*** and a female to read ***la chica.*** Explain that many adjectives have different endings depending on whether they're describing a female or a male. Can students begin to deduce the rules? Encourage them to guess meanings of cognates. Can they guess the opposite of ***impaciente?***

BELLRINGER REVIEW

Put these letters for words for personality traits on the board and ask the students to unscramble them: **licoseba; rosie; utidosesa**
(**Answers:** *sociable, serio, estudiosa*)

Block Schedule

Have students bring in pictures that represent the adjectives in this chapter. Have them cut out the pictures, paste them on poster board, and write the appropriate adjectives under each picture. Help students use correct gender endings.

▼ Objectives

Read, listen to, and understand information about
- personality traits

Vocabulario en contexto

“¿El chico? **Es mi amigo. ¿Cómo se llama?** Se llama Marcos. **¿Cómo es?** Pues . . .

la chica

. . . él es **deportista. Le gusta mucho** practicar deportes.

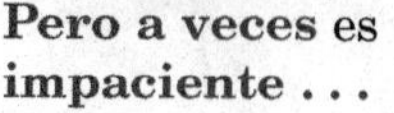

Pero a veces es impaciente . . .

. . . también es **un** chico **desordenado**”.

“Mi amiga Sarita es **una buena** amiga. **Ella** no es **muy** deportista . . .

. . . pero es una chica **artística** . . .

el chico

. . . y muy **ordenada.**

Es una chica muy **inteligente**”.

DIFFERENTIATED INSTRUCTION

Students with Learning Difficulties

Give students English adjective examples that correspond to the Spanish ones shown on this page. Have them copy the list of new vocabulary into the Organizer from the *Practice Workbook.*

Advanced Learners

Have students bring in magazine or newspaper pictures of people in various professions, such as firefighters, judges, athletes, comedians, artists, etc. and write a list of personality traits for each profession. Students can use these as flashcards to review or expand their vocabulary.

Más vocabulario

atrevido, -a	daring
paciente	patient
reservado, -a	shy
simpático, -a	nice, friendly
talentoso, -a	talented

"Hola, me llamo Luz. **¿Yo?** ¿Cómo **soy?** Pues . . .

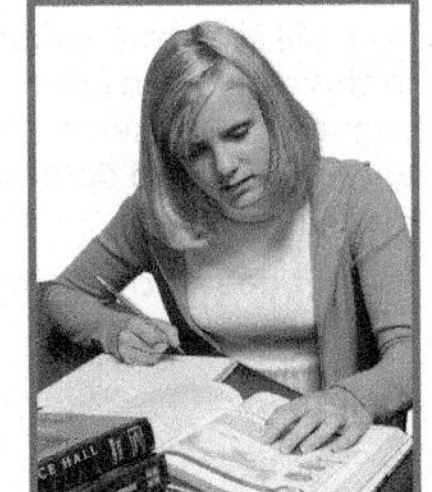

. . . soy **estudiosa** . . .

. . . y **trabajadora** . . .

. . . y también **graciosa** . . .

. . . pero **según mi familia** ¡a veces soy **perezosa!** Y tú, **¿cómo eres?**"

1 ¿Marcos o Sarita?

Escuchar

Look at the pictures of Marcos and Sarita. Listen to the descriptions. If a word describes Marcos, point to his picture. If a word describes Sarita, point to her picture.

2 ¿Cierto o falso?

Escuchar

You will hear some statements about Luz. Give a "thumbs-up" sign if the statement is true, or a "thumbs-down" sign if it is false.

Más práctica GO

realidades.com | print

Instant Check	✔	
Guided WB pp. 39–42	✔	✔
Core WB pp. 22–23	✔	✔
Comm. WB p. 25	✔	✔
***Hispanohablantes* WB** p. 32		✔

ENRICH YOUR TEACHING

Teacher-to-Teacher

Have students draw a series of three pictures of themselves and label the pictures using vocabulary from pp. 50–51. Point out that adjectives usually have different endings when used to describe a female or a male. Ask volunteers to share drawings with the class.

21st Century Skills

Communication After using the eBook with embedded audio files in **realidades.com** to learn and practice the new vocabulary, have students work in mixed pairs (males and females) to describe themselves and each other, using the new vocabulary.

Language Input 1B

1 Standards: 1.2

Resources: Teacher's Resource Book: Audio Script, p. 79; Audio Program DVD: Cap. 1B, Track 3; Answer Keys: Student Edition, p. 16

Focus: Listening comprehension to vocabulary for personality traits

Suggestions: Have students scan the photos and read the captions on p. 50 before beginning the activity. Play the audio or read the script. Pause often to monitor that students are identifying the correct person. Have volunteers say the answers aloud.

Script and Answers:

1. **deportista *(Marcos)***
2. **artística *(Sarita)***
3. **inteligente *(Sarita)***
4. **impaciente *(Marcos)***
5. **ordenada *(Sarita)***
6. **desordenado *(Marcos)***
7. **el chico *(Marcos)***
8. **buena amiga *(Sarita)***

2 Standards: 1.2

Resources: Teacher's Resource Book: Audio Script, p. 79; Audio Program DVD: Cap. 1B, Track 4; Answer Keys: Student Edition, p. 16

Focus: Listening comprehension vocabulary for personality traits

Suggestions: Play the audio or read the script. Be sure students understand that the references are to the girl pictured at the top of p. 51. Tell them that words not included in the pictures should receive a thumbs down.

Script and Answers:

¿Cómo es Luz?
Es estudiosa. *(up)*
Es impaciente. *(down)*
Es muy graciosa. *(up)*
Es ordenada. *(down)*
Es trabajadora. *(up)*
Es talentosa. *(down)*
Pero, según la familia, ¡a veces es perezosa! *(up)*

Videohistoria

Core Instruction

Standards: 1.2, 4.1

Resources: Voc. and Gram. Transparencies 42–43; Teacher's Resource Book: Audio Script, p. 79; Audio Program DVD: Cap. 1B, Track 5

Focus: Presenting additional personality traits vocabulary; extending presentation of contextualized vocabulary and grammar; previewing the language video

Suggestions: Introduce the four new characters by name. Explain that Pedro, who is chatting on the Internet, receives a mystery e-mail from a girl named ***Chica sociable.*** Be sure students understand that the boys are in San Antonio and the girls are in Mexico City, and that they don't know one another.

Pre-reading: Direct students' attention to the *Strategy.* Have them scan the story and write a list of possible cognates. Using the transparencies, ask students to predict the story line: Whom would Claudia like, Pedro or Esteban?

Reading: Go through the captions with students. Using the transparencies, help students figure out the details of the story.

Post-reading: Have students review their list of cognates and discuss their findings. Complete *Actividades* 3–4 and check comprehension.

Video

Core Instruction

Standards: 1.2, 4.1

Resources: Teacher's Resource Book: Video Script, p. 82; Video Program Teacher's Guide: Cap. 1B; Video Program: Cap. 1B

Focus: Comprehension of a story about people describing themselves

Suggestions:

Pre-viewing: Remind students that they will not understand every word in the video, but that they should listen and watch for overall understanding.

Viewing: Show the video once without pausing, then show it again, stopping to check comprehension. Show the video segment a final time without pausing.

Post-viewing: Complete the Video Activities in the *Communication Workbook.*

Amigos por Internet

See what happens when *Chica sociable* sends an e-mail message to Esteban.

Strategy

Using cognates
You will see some unfamiliar words in this story. Many of these are cognates. Use their similarity to English words to determine their meaning.

- What does *sociable* mean?
- What does *ideal* mean?

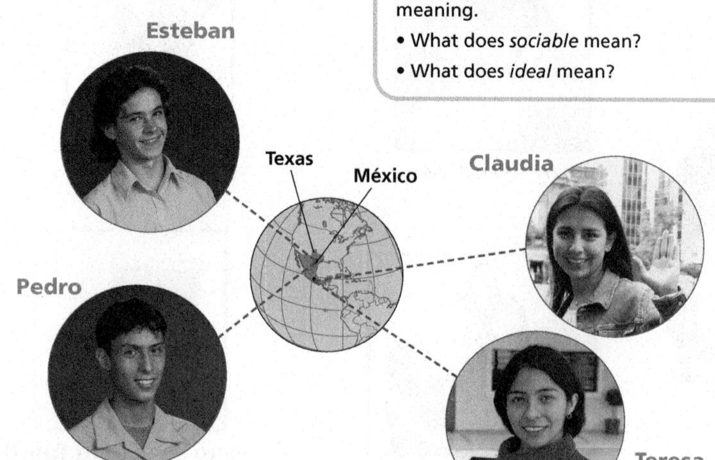

Pedro: Esteban, escucha: "Hola, ¿cómo eres? ¿Qué te gusta hacer? Me gusta mucho hablar con mis amigos. Me llamo ***Chica sociable.*** Escríbeme."

Esteban: ¡Ja! *Chica sociable.* A responder. Escribe, Pedro. . . .

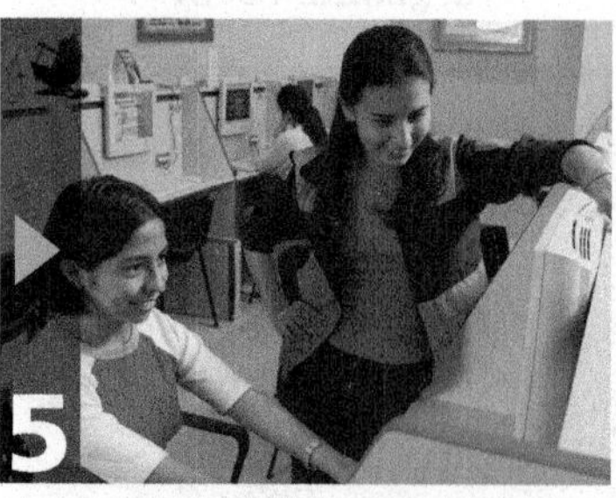

Teresa: "Soy muy desordenada. Me gusta hablar por teléfono. Y no me gusta ir a la escuela. Escríbeme. *Chica sociable*".

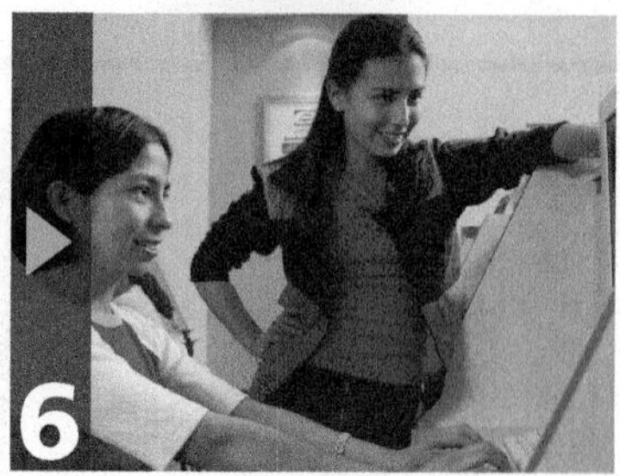

Claudia: Un momento . . . uno más de mí. Escribe. . . "Yo soy *Chica misteriosa*. Soy amiga de *Chica sociable*. Soy muy simpática".

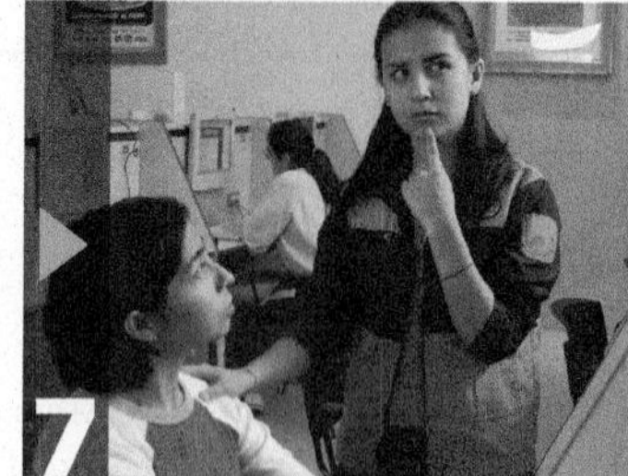

Claudia: "Y me gusta ir a la escuela. Soy estudiosa y trabajadora. Yo no soy tu chica ideal. *Chica misteriosa*".

DIFFERENTIATED INSTRUCTION

Heritage Language Learners

Have students write a paragraph describing the ideal person for ***Chica misteriosa*** or ***Chico sociable.*** Check to be sure they are making appropriate adjective agreements.

Multiple Intelligences

Bodily/Kinesthetic: Ask students to come to the front of the class and role-play the parts of the four students in the video. Encourage them to be dramatic and act out any adjectives they can. Give them a few minutes to practice beforehand.

Pedro: "Hola. Me llamo *Chico sociable*. ¡Qué coincidencia!".

Pedro: "Me gusta pasar tiempo con mis amigos. **No soy** muy **serio.** Según mis amigos, soy gracioso".

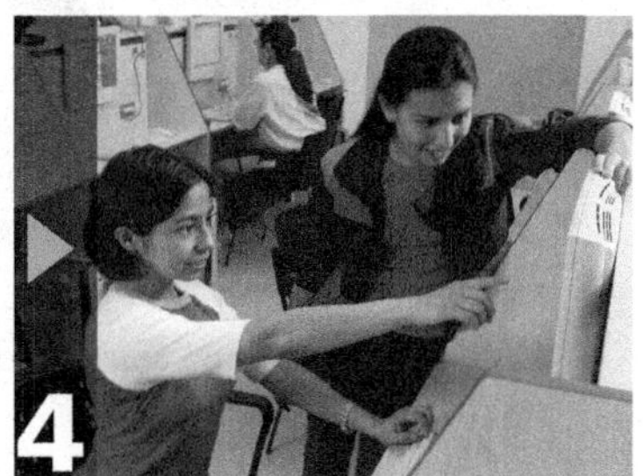

Claudia: ¡*Chica sociable*! ¡Ja!
Teresa: Yo soy *Chica sociable*.
Claudia: ¡No! ¿Tú **eres** *Chica sociable*? ¡¿Mi buena amiga . . . ?!

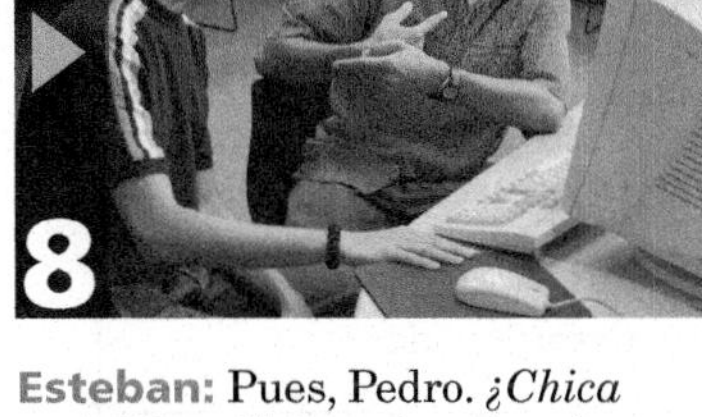

Esteban: Pues, Pedro. ¿*Chica sociable* o *Chica misteriosa?*
Pedro: *Chica misteriosa*. Me gusta la escuela y a ella le gusta la escuela también.
Esteban: Perfecto. A mí me gusta más *Chica sociable.*

3 ¿Comprendes?

Escribir • Hablar

Read each of the sentences below and indicate which character is being described: *Chica sociable* or *Chica misteriosa*.

1. Me gusta hablar por teléfono.
2. Me gusta ir a la escuela.
3. Soy simpática.
4. No soy muy ordenada.
5. Soy trabajadora.

Más práctica GO

	realidades.com	print
Instant Check	✔	
Guided WB pp. 43–46	✔	✔
Core WB pp. 24–25	✔	✔
Comm. WB pp. 18–20, 21	✔	✔
Hispanohablantes WB p. 33		✔

4 Y tú, ¿qué dices? | Talk!

Escribir • Hablar

1. Find five cognates in the *Videohistoria* and write what you think they mean in English.
2. Write an activity that goes with each of these characteristics.
   sociable estudioso trabajador
3. ¿Qué te gusta más, usar la computadora o hablar por teléfono?

3 Standards: 1.2, 1.3

Resources: Answer Keys: Student Edition, p. 17
Focus: Reading comprehension
Suggestions: When students tell you the name of the character being described, have them identify the number of the panel that contains this information.
Answers:
1. Chica sociable (5)
2. Chica misteriosa (7)
3. Chica misteriosa (6)
4. Chica sociable (5)
5. Chica misteriosa (7)

4 Standards: 1.2, 4.1

Resources: Answer Keys: Student Edition, p. 17
Focus: Using cognates
Suggestions: Have students review the *Videohistoria* and scan for cognates. For item 2, point out that they should come up with actions (verbs) from *Capítulo* 1A.
Answers will vary but might include:
1. sociable, responder, coincidencia, serio, teléfono, misteriosa, ideal, estudiosa, perfecto
2. sociable: pasar tiempo con mis amigos; estudioso: ir a la escuela, estudiar, leer libros; trabajador: trabajar, estudiar
3. Me gusta más...

Pre-AP* Support

- **Learning Objective:** Presentational Writing
- **Activity:** Have students choose Pedro, Claudia, Teresa, or Esteban and write a sentence (using several adjectives) to describe him/her.
- ***Pre-AP* Resource Book:*** Comprehensive guide to Pre-AP* vocabulary skill development, pp. 51–57

Additional Resources

- Communication Wbk.: Audio Act. 5, p. 21
- Teacher's Resource Book: Audio Script, p. 79
- Audio Program DVD: Cap. 1B, Track 6

ENRICH YOUR TEACHING

Culture Note

Suggest that students research the cities of San Antonio and Mexico City for pictures and information about their common history and culture. The Southwestern United States was influenced by Spain and Mexico, beginning in the 1500s when the Spaniards explored the region and encountered the indigenous cultures.

21st Century Skills

Collaboration After students have watched the *Videohistoria* embedded in the eBook for these two pages, have them work with a partner to create two additional characters who e-mail each other and present the exchange to the class.

ASSESSMENT

Quiz: Vocabulary Recognition
- Prueba 1B-1: pp. 26–27

INTERACTIVE WHITEBOARD
Vocabulary Activities 1B

5 Standards: 1.2, 1.3

Resources: Answer Keys: Student Edition, p. 17

Focus: Using new vocabulary to complete sentences with adjectives

Suggestions: Point out that students should look at the two adjective choices with each picture as well as at the pictures.

Answers:

1. artística	3. reservado	5. atrevida
2. perezosa	4. desordenado	6. estudioso

Common Errors: Beginning students may forget to use the correct gender ending when they focus on vocabulary meanings.

BELLRINGER REVIEW

Put the following sentences on the board:

1) ___ es un chico ___ y ___
2) ___ es un chica ___ y ___

Have students refer to pp. 50–51 and fill in the blanks to describe classmates.

6 Standards: 1.2, 1.3, 4.1

Resources: Answer Keys: Student Edition, p. 18

Focus: Writing new vocabulary in a story

Suggestions: This is a good homework assignment.

Answers:

1. deportista	4. desordenado	6. trabajador
2. gracioso	5. estudioso	7. bueno
3. sociable		

Additional Resources

- Communication Wbk.: Audio Act. 6, p. 22
- Communicative Pair Activity BLM, pp. 84–85
- Teacher's Resource Book: Audio Script, pp. 79–80
- Audio Program DVD: Cap. 1B, Track 7

ASSESSMENT

Prueba 1B-2 with Study Plan (online only)

Quiz: Vocabulary Production
- Prueba 1B-2: pp. 28–29

▶ Write about what people are like

Vocabulario en uso

5 ¿Cómo es el chico o la chica?

Escribir

Choose the correct word to describe each of the people in the pictures.

Modelo
El chico es
(*impaciente* / *estudioso*).

1. La chica es (*reservada* / *artística*).

2. La chica es (*graciosa* / *perezosa*).

3. El chico es (*reservado* / *deportista*).

4. El chico es (*desordenado* / *atrevido*).

5. La chica es (*artística* / *atrevida*).

6. El chico es (*estudioso* / *desordenado*).

6 Mi amigo José

Escribir

Maritza is talking about her friend José. Read the sentences, then choose the appropriate word to fill in each blank.

Modelo
No es un chico impaciente. Es muy paciente.

trabajador	deportista	bueno
paciente	estudioso	sociable
gracioso	desordenado	

1. Le gusta mucho practicar deportes. Es ___.
2. A veces no es serio. Es un chico ___.
3. Le gusta pasar tiempo con amigos. Es muy ___.
4. No es un chico ordenado. Es ___.
5. Le gusta ir a la escuela. Es ___.
6. No es perezoso. Es un chico muy ___.
7. Es simpático. Es un amigo muy ___.

DIFFERENTIATED INSTRUCTION

Students with Learning Difficulties

Have students study the word bank for *Actividad* 6 before starting the activity to be sure they understand all the words. Some students will benefit from writing the words on their own paper, then crossing them out as they are used.

Students with Special Needs

Students with motor difficulties may find it easier to do *Actividad* 7 if you use colored string or yarn to make ovals on a tabletop. Write the words on index cards for them and have them sort the words into the ovals.

▼ Objectives

- Write about and discuss what you and others are like
- Describe your personality
- Read and write a self-descriptive poem

Gramática

Adjectives

Words that describe people and things are called adjectives *(adjetivos)*.

- In Spanish, most adjectives have both masculine and feminine forms. The masculine form usually ends in the letter *-o* and the feminine form usually ends in the letter *-a*.
- Masculine adjectives are used to describe masculine nouns.

Marcos es ordenado y simpático.	*Marcos is organized and nice.*

- Feminine adjectives are used to describe feminine nouns.

Marta es ordenada y simpática.	*Marta is organized and nice.*

- Adjectives that end in *-e* describe both masculine and feminine nouns.

Anita es inteligente.	*Anita is smart.*
Pedro es inteligente también.	*Pedro is also smart.*

Masculine	Feminine
ordenado	ordenada
trabajador	trabajadora
paciente	paciente
deportista	deportista

- Adjectives whose masculine form ends in *-dor* have a feminine form that ends in *-dora*.

Juan es trabajador.	*Juan is hardworking.*
Luz es trabajadora.	*Luz is hardworking.*

- Some adjectives that end in *-a*, such as *deportista*, describe both masculine and feminine nouns. You will need to learn which adjectives follow this pattern.

Tomás es deportista.	*Tomás is sports-minded.*
Marta es deportista también.	*Marta is also sports-minded.*

Más ayuda realidades.com

***GramActiva* Video**
Tutorials: Adjectives, Adjective clauses

Canción de hip hop: *¿Cómo soy yo?*

***GramActiva* Activity**

▼7 Roberto y Yolanda

Escribir

Copy the Venn diagram on a sheet of paper. Which words from the list below could only describe Roberto? Write them in the oval below his name. Which words could only describe Yolanda? Write them in the oval below her name. Which words could describe either Roberto or Yolanda? Write them in the overlapping area.

artístico	atrevida	deportista	estudiosa
graciosa	impaciente	simpático	inteligente
ordenada	paciente	perezosa	reservado
serio	sociable	talentosa	trabajador

Modelo

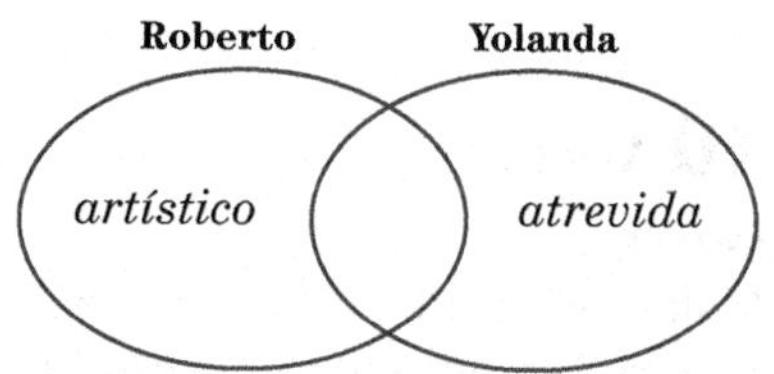

ENRICH YOUR TEACHING

Teacher-to-Teacher

Give each student a blue, a yellow, and a pink index card. As you call out various adjectives, have students hold up the card whose color matches the gender of the word you've said. This allows for a quick check of comprehension.

Teacher-to-Teacher

Have students practice questions and answers with the classmates in their row of desks. Ask the first student in each row: *¿Cómo eres?* That student answers using an appropriate adjective, then asks the second student the same question. Continue until all students have participated.

Gramática

Core Instruction

Standards: 4.1

Resources: Voc. and Gram. Transparency 44; Teacher's Resource Book: Video Script, pp. 82–83; Video Program: Cap. 1B

INTERACTIVE WHITEBOARD
Grammar Activities 1B

Suggestions: Use the *GramActiva* Video as an initial introduction to adjectives or as a follow-up. Write ***gracioso, estudiosa,*** and ***inteligente*** on the board. Ask which one applies to a male, which one to a female, and which one can be applied to either. Use the transparency and the text on p. 50 to demonstrate agreement. Change the genders of the characters and tell the story again. Once students grasp the concept of agreement, introduce invariable adjectives.

7

Standards: 1.3

Resources: Voc. and Gram. Transparency 2; Answer Keys: Student Edition, p. 18

Focus: Recognizing feminine, masculine, and neutral endings

Suggestions: Draw the Venn diagram on the board or use the transparency. Shade Roberto's oval blue, Yolanda's pink, and the overlapping portion yellow. Have volunteers write the answers in the diagram.

Answers: ***Roberto:*** **artístico, serio, simpático, reservado, trabajador;** ***Yolanda:*** **graciosa, ordenada, atrevida, perezosa, talentosa, estudiosa;** ***Either:*** **impaciente, paciente, sociable, deportista, inteligente**

Common Errors: Adjectives ending in ***-ista*** are mistaken as feminine. Remind students that they apply to both genders.

ASSESSMENT

Prueba 1B-3 with Study Plan (online only)

Quiz: Adjectives

- Prueba 1B-3: p. 30

8 Standards: 1.2

Resources: Answer Keys: Student Edition, p. 18

Focus: Asking and answering questions about what people are like

Suggestions: Remind Student B to pay attention to the adjective endings. When they have completed the activity, have students reverse roles.

Answers:

1. **Elena es perezosa.**
2. **Marisol es artística.**
3. **Felipe es gracioso.**
4. **Juan es desordenado.**
5. **Lola es sociable.**
6. **Gloria es atrevida.**

Extension: Have students bring in pictures of famous people and mount them on poster board. Label the pictures with an attribute of each person: *Pete Sampras es deportista.*

9 Standards: 1.2

Resources: Voc. and Gram. Transparencies 40–41

Focus: Asking and answering questions about what people are like; using vocabulary in a personalized context

Suggestions: To provide a word bank, use the *Voc. & Gram. Transparencies.* Tell students not to repeat an adjective. Remind students to use the correct endings.

Answers will vary.

10 Standards: 4.1

Focus: Writing adjectives in a personalized context

Suggestions: Model a chart on the board or overhead that describes you. Be sure students use correct gender endings when they make their charts. Encourage them to use ***muy*** and ***a veces*** when applicable.

Answers will vary.

Extension: Have students create another chart with names of friends and family members at the top. For example, *Mi madre es / no es …, Mi amigo Brent es / no es …*, etc. Have students share their charts with the class. Tell students to save their charts to use in *Actividades* 11 and 12.

8 ¿Cómo es Paloma?

Hablar

Work with a partner to ask and answer questions about the people shown below.

Modelo

Paloma
A —*¿Cómo es Paloma?*
B —*Paloma es trabajadora.*

1. Elena 
2. Marisol 
3. Felipe 
4. Juan 
5. Lola 
6. Gloria 

9 Juego

Hablar

Choose an adjective and act it out for a small group or the class. The other students take turns asking you questions. The first to ask a question with the correct adjective (in the correct form) gets to do the next charade.

Modelo

A —*¿Eres ordenada?*
B —*Sí, soy ordenada.*
o: —*No, no soy ordenada.*

10 Yo soy . . .

Escribir

Make a chart like the one on the right. Write at least two adjectives in each column to say what you are like and are not like. Include *muy* and *a veces* when they are appropriate. Save your work to use in later activities.

Modelo

Soy	No soy
estudiosa	perezosa
muy trabajadora	impaciente
deportista	

DIFFERENTIATED INSTRUCTION

Heritage Language Learners

Ask students to name a famous person from their heritage country or someone they consider a role model and describe that person, using the vocabulary they have learned. Check that they are using appropriate gender endings.

Students with Special Needs

Allow students to refer to their Organizer and / or their flashcards as they complete the activities. Some students may need to have someone transcribe for them. Having a fellow student do this can benefit both students.

11 ¿Eres estudioso(a)? 

Hablar • Escribir

Use your chart from Actividad 10. Talk with your partner about your personality traits. Take notes on what your partner tells you. Make another two-column chart, but with the headings *Es* and *No es*. Fill it in with information about your partner. You will use this chart in the next activity.

Modelo

A —*¿Cómo eres?*
B —*Soy estudiosa y muy trabajadora. También soy deportista. ¿Y tú?*
A —*Soy artístico. Según mis amigos, soy talentoso. No soy perezoso.*

12 Mi amigo(a)

Escribir • Hablar

Use the information from the previous activity to write a short description of yourself and your partner. Read your description to a small group or the class.

Modelo

Me llamo Luisa. Soy estudiosa y trabajadora. Y soy deportista. Mi amiga se llama Susana. Ella es simpática. También es deportista y trabajadora.

Exploración del lenguaje

Cognates that begin with *es* + consonant

Many words in Spanish that begin with *es* + consonant are easy to understand because they have the same meaning as English words. Knowing this pattern helps you recognize the meaning of new Spanish words and learn them quickly.

Try it out! Look at these words, then cover up the *e* at the beginning. Name the English words that come from the same root word.

estudiante	estudioso	escuela	estómago
esquiar	especial	estricto	escena

Es muy estudioso. Le encanta estudiar.

ENRICH YOUR TEACHING

Teacher-to-Teacher

Have students write five names of real or fictional people on a piece of paper, such as Frida Kahlo, Abraham Lincoln, Rosa Parks, Sponge Bob, Superman, or Goldilocks. Then have them write a sentence using an adjective to describe each person or character.

21st Century Skills

Social and Cross-Cultural Skills Work with teams of students to set up an imaginary e-mail exchange with an English class in a Spanish-speaking country. Have your students share with the Spanish-speaking class information about themselves and ask questions about those students' interests, likes, and dislikes.

Practice and Communicate 1B

11 Standards: 1.1, 1.3

Focus: Asking and answering questions about personality traits; listening for comprehension

Suggestions: Show students how to set up the new chart. Use your personal chart and role play the *Modelo* with a volunteer. Remind students to save their answers for *Actividad* 12.

Answers will vary.

BELLRINGER REVIEW

Show Voc. and Gram. Transparency 44 (top). Have students write two sentences using the names of their classmates and the personality traits listed. Model: *María es paciente.* Share with the class.

12 Standards: 1.3

Focus: Writing descriptions of yourself and others

Suggestions: Point out that students should refer to both their ***Soy / No soy*** chart from *Actividad* 10 and their ***Es / No es*** chart from *Actividad* 11.

Answers will vary.

Exploración del lenguaje
Core Instruction

Standards: 4.1

Suggestions: Remind students of the concept of cognates. Have them work individually with the list in *Try it out!* and then have them share their answers.

Pre-AP* Support

- **Learning Objective:** Interpersonal Speaking
- **Activity:** Give each student handouts containing clip art of new vocabulary words to talk about what they and others are like. Have them cut the squares apart. Then, have students work in pairs to play "*Memoria.*" Pairs should mix their clip art cards and put them face down in rows. One at a time, students turn over one picture and try to find a match by turning over a second picture. If a match is made, a student must say the word aloud to add the pair to his or her stack.
- ***Pre-AP* Resource Book:*** Comprehensive guide to communication skill development, pp. 10–57

13 Standards: 1.1

Resources: Answer Keys: Student Edition, p. 19

Focus: Asking and answering personalized questions about what you and others like to do

Recycle: ***Me/te gusta,*** activities vocabulary

Suggestions: Students should answer according to what is true for them. Encourage them to use the *¡Respuesta personal!*

Answers:

Student A:

1. **¿Te gusta trabajar?**
2. **¿... practicar deportes?**
3. **¿... dibujar?**
4. **¿... esquiar?**
5. **¿... pasar tiempo con los amigos?**
6. **¿... cantar?**
7. **¿... ir a la escuela?**

Student B answers will vary.

Fondo cultural

Standards: 4.2

Suggestions: Ask students what can be inferred from the picture about the time period and the person depicted. What is he grasping in his left hand? *(a sword)* Use the map transparency to show where Venezuela, Colombia, Ecuador, Peru, and Bolivia are located.

Answers will vary.

Mapa global interactivo, Actividad 2 Locate the countries that Simón Bolívar liberated: Venezuela, Colombia, Ecuador, Peru, and Bolivia.

Block Schedule

Have students conduct Internet research on Simón Bolívar. Students can work in groups and choose different aspects of his life (family, education, the influence of Napoleon Bonaparte, liberation of Latin America, etc.) and prepare a short report. They can present their findings orally or in poster format.

Additional Resources

- Communication Wbk.: Audio Act. 7, p. 23
- Teacher's Resource Book: Audio Script, p. 80
- Audio Program DVD: Cap. 1B, Track 8

13 ¿Qué te gusta hacer? | 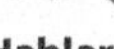 |

Hablar

Trabaja con otro(a) estudiante. Pregunta y contesta según el modelo.

Modelo

A —*¿Te gusta correr?*
B —*Sí, soy deportista.*
o: —*No, no soy deportista.*
o: —*Sí, pero no soy muy deportista.*

Estudiante A

Estudiante B

Fondo cultural | El mundo hispano

Simón Bolívar (1783–1830) liberated the territory that is now Venezuela, Colombia, Ecuador, Peru, and Bolivia from Spanish rule. A daring military commander and statesman, Bolívar is revered in South America as *el Libertador* (the Liberator).

- Name three leaders who had a similar influence on events of their time.

◀ "Simón Bolívar" (siglo xix), Anónimo
Chromolitho. Private Collection / Archives Charmet / Bridgeman Art Library.

DIFFERENTIATED INSTRUCTION

Multiple Intelligences

Intrapersonal/Introspective: Have students choose three or four words to describe themselves. For each of the words, have them write a sentence telling what they like or dislike doing. Example: ***artístico***—*Me gusta tocar la guitarra.*

14 El poema "Soy Elena"

Leer • Escribir

The following poem is called a *poema en diamante*. Can you guess why? After you've read the poem, answer the questions.

Conexiones | La literatura

Soy Elena
En general, soy
reservada y ordenada.
A veces, soy atrevida,
graciosa o impaciente.
No soy ni deportista
ni artística.
¡Yo soy yo!

1. Which activity would you invite Elena to do based on what she has told you about herself?
   dibujar   montar en monopatín   escuchar música
2. Rewrite the poem replacing *Soy Elena* with *Soy Tomás.*

15 Y tú, ¿qué dices?

Escribir

Write *un poema en diamante* about yourself. Choose adjectives that best describe you. Look back at Actividad 10 for some ideas. Substitute your adjectives in the poem above. Be sure to write the poem in the form of a diamond. You might want to use calligraphy or an appropriate font on the computer and add pictures to illustrate your work.

Más práctica GO

realidades.com | print

Instant Check	✔	
Guided WB pp. 47–48	✔	✔
Core WB p. 26	✔	✔
Comm. WB pp. 23, 26	✔	✔
Hispanohablantes WB pp. 34–37		✔

ENRICH YOUR TEACHING

Teacher-to-Teacher

If students enjoy writing poems, you can have them bring photos of friends, family members, celebrities or pictures from magazine advertisements and use them to write similar poems. These should be in the third-person form: *Es* ______. Ask students to decorate their finished poems and present them to the class. The class can vote for the best poem in categories such as ***el más artístico, el más atrevido,*** or ***el más gracioso.*** Display finished poems in the classrooms.

Practice and Communicate 1B

14 Standards: 1.2, 1.3, 3.1

Resources: Teacher's Resource Book: GramActiva BLM, p. 89; Answer Keys: Student Edition, p. 19

Focus: Reading and writing using adjectives

Suggestions: Have students answer item 1 aloud. They can then complete item 2 on a sheet of paper, writing in the ***diamante*** form. Ask volunteers to share their poems with the class.

Answers:

1. ***dibujar:*** **No. Elena no es artística.**
   montar en monopatín: **Sí. Elena es atrevida.**
   escuchar música: **No. Elena no es artística. o: Sí, es reservada.**
2. **Soy Tomás. En general soy reservado y ordenado. A veces, soy atrevido, gracioso o impaciente. No soy ni deportista ni artístico. ¡Yo soy yo!**

BELLRINGER REVIEW

Complete these sentences about two classmates:

______ (Boy) ______ es ______ y ______.
______ (Girl) ______ es ______ y ______.

15 Standards: 1.3, 3.1

Focus: Writing poetry with learned vocabulary

Suggestions: Point out that the title will still be *Soy* ______, and the last line will be *¡Yo soy yo!* Students can review the lesson, make a list of adjectives, and refer to the list as they write their poems. Encourage students to decorate their poems and display them in the classroom.

Answers will vary.

Theme Project

Students can perform Step 4 at this point. Be sure students understand your corrections and suggestions. (For more information, see p. 24-b.)

1B Practice and Communicate

Gramática

Core Instruction

Standards: 4.1

Resources: Voc. and Gram. Transparency: 45; Teacher's Resource Book: Video Script, p. 83; Video Program: Cap. 1B

INTERACTIVE WHITEBOARD

Grammar Activities 1B

Suggestions: Present the new grammar using the transparency and show the *GramActiva* Video as reinforcement. Some students will benefit from further clarification of the terms *definite* and *indefinite*. Direct attention to the *Strategy*. Use flashcards with familiar nouns and have students say ***el*** (or ***un***) or ***la*** (or ***una***) as they say each one.

16 Standards: 1.2

Resources: Teacher's Resource Book: Audio Script, p. 80; Audio Program DVD: Cap. 1B, Track 9; Answer Keys: Student Edition, p. 20

Focus: Listening for definite articles

Suggestions: You may want to bring thick markers to class so that students can write the articles in large, visible letters. Use blue and pink paper or index cards to reinforce the gender relationship and to allow for easy assessment of comprehension. Play the audio or read the script to students.

Script and Answers:

1. **libro *(el)***
2. **carpeta *(la)***
3. **chica *(la)***
4. **profesor *(el)***
5. **escuela *(la)***
6. **chico *(el)***
7. **sábado *(el)***
8. **amiga *(la)***

Block Schedule

Have students write a list of ten nouns, omitting the definite articles. Ask Student A to say a word on the list. Student B repeats the word, and adds the correct definite article. If the article is correct, Student B gets a point. When Student A finishes his or her list, the pair should reverse roles. When both lists have been practiced, the partner with the most points wins.

Gramática

Objective

- Identify and write about people and things at your school

Definite and indefinite articles

El and *la* are called definite articles and are the equivalent of "the" in English. *El* is used with masculine nouns; *la* is used with feminine nouns. You've already seen words with definite articles:

el libro *the book* la carpeta *the folder*

Un and *una* are called indefinite articles and are the equivalent of "a" and "an" in English. *Un* is used with masculine nouns; *una* is used with feminine nouns:

un libro *a book* una carpeta *a folder*

el	the
la	the

un	a, an
una	a, an

Strategy

Learning by repetition
When you learn a new noun, say it aloud, along with its definite article, as often as you get a chance. Eventually, you will find that words just "sound right" with the correct definite article and you will know whether nouns are masculine or feminine.

Más ayuda realidades.com

***GramActiva* Video**
Tutorial: Definite and Indefinite Articles

***GramActiva* Activity**

16 ¿El o la?

Escuchar • GramActiva

Write the word *el* in large letters on a sheet of paper or an index card. Write *la* in large letters on another sheet. You will hear eight words you already know. When you hear a masculine word, hold up the paper with *el*. When you hear a feminine word, hold up the paper with the word *la* on it.

DIFFERENTIATED INSTRUCTION

Students with Learning Difficulties

When teaching articles, provide very concrete examples that students can easily write in their Organizer or on flashcards. Students who struggle with writing might need the information provided on a handout that can be put directly into their notebooks.

Advanced Learners/Pre-AP*

Have students review the *Videohistoria* and list all the nouns and their corresponding articles. Students can exchange lists to compare answers.

17 ¿Qué es? |  | 

Hablar

Tell your partner the names of the things pictured below.

Modelo

A —*¿Qué es?*
B —*Es un brazo.*

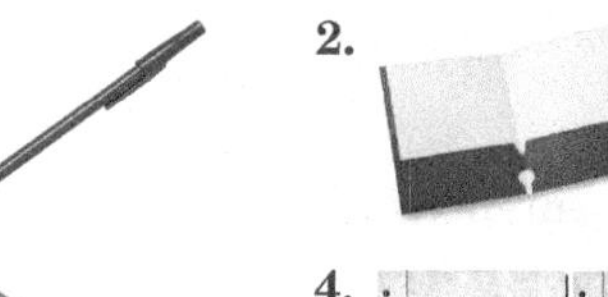

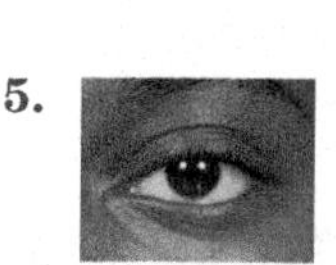

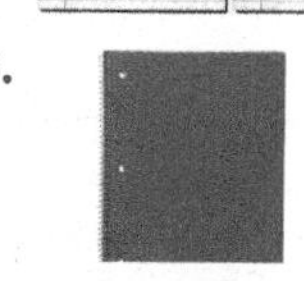

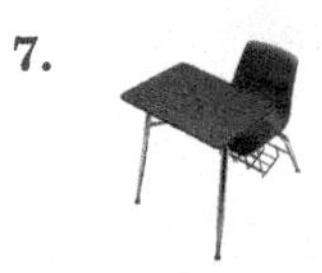

1. 2. 3. 4. 5. 6. 7. 8.

18 La escuela de Diego

Escribir

Diego is talking about people at his school. Read the sentences and complete each one with *un* or *una*.

1. La Sra. Secada es ___ profesora simpática.
2. Alicia es ___ estudiante trabajadora.
3. Juan Carlos es ___ chico perezoso.
4. Germán es ___ chico sociable.
5. El Sr. Guzmán es ___ profesor gracioso.
6. Adriana es ___ chica muy seria.
7. La Srta. Cifuentes es ___ profesora paciente.
8. Arturo es ___ estudiante talentoso.

Más práctica GO

realidades.com | print

Instant Check	✔	
Guided WB p. 49	✔	✔
Core WB p. 27	✔	✔
Comm. WB pp. 23, 27, 233	✔	✔
***Hispanohablantes* WB** pp. 37–38		✔

Pronunciación | |

The vowels *o* and *u*

In Spanish, the pronunciation of the letter *o* is similar to the vowel sound in the English word "boat" but is always cut very short. Say these words, concentrating on making a short *o* sound.

bolígrafo	gracioso	cómo
teléfono	tampoco	otoño

In Spanish, the pronunciation of the letter *u* is similar to the vowel sound in the English word "zoo." Say these words.

mucho	lunes	usted
octubre	estudioso	según

¡Ojo! Careful! Sometimes the words we mispronounce most are the ones that remind us of English words.

Try it out! Pronounce these words, concentrating on the Spanish vowel sounds:

agosto	regular	tropical	música
gusto	universidad	Uruguay	Cuba

El mundo

Practice and Communicate 1B

17 Standards: 1.1

Resources: Answer Keys: Student Edition, p. 20

Focus: Speaking using indefinite articles

Recycle: School vocabulary; body parts

Suggestions: Have students reverse roles when they have completed the activity.

Answers:

1. Es un bolígrafo.
2. Es una carpeta.
3. Es un lápiz.
4. Es una hoja de papel.
5. Es un ojo.
6. Es un cuaderno.
7. Es un pupitre.
8. Es una pierna.

18 Standards: 1.2, 1.3

Resources: Answer Keys: Student Edition, p. 20

Focus: Writing and using indefinite articles

Suggestions: Remind students to read the whole sentence for clues to gender.

Answers:

1. una; 2. una; 3. un; 4. un; 5. un; 6. una; 7. una; 8. un

Pronunciación

Core Instruction

Standards: 4.1

Resources: Teacher's Resource Book: Audio Script, p. 80; Audio Program DVD: Cap. 1B, Track 11

Suggestions: Have students say each word in the *Pronunciación* and in *Try it out!*

Additional Resources

- Communication Wbk.: Audio Act. 8, p. 23
- Teacher's Resource Book: Audio Script, p. 80
- Audio Program DVD: Cap. 1B, Track 10

ENRICH YOUR TEACHING

Teacher-to-Teacher

For homework, have students write two columns with the headings *Masculine Nouns:* ***el / un*** and *Feminine Nouns:* ***la / una.*** Instruct them to list ten objects or people, such as ***un profesor,*** in the appropriate columns. After the homework has been checked, students should keep their lists and add other nouns as they learn them, using this as an ongoing reference.

ASSESSMENT

Prueba 1B-4 with Study Plan (online only)

Quiz: Definite and Indefinite Articles

- Prueba 1B-4: p. 31

Gramática

Core Instruction

Standards: 4.1

Resources: Voc. and Gram. Transparency 46

INTERACTIVE WHITEBOARD
Grammar Activities 1B

Suggestions: Contrast English and Spanish word order by having students give English equivalents of the sentences in the chart. Direct attention to the *¿Recuerdas?* Have students practice making negative sentences by placing the word ***no*** in the sample sentences.

19 Standards: 1.3

Resources: Answer Keys: Student Edition, p. 21

Focus: Using correct word order

Suggestions: Help students identify the various parts of speech before they unscramble the sentences.

Answers:

1. **Marina es una chica artística.**
2. **Tito es un chico perezoso.**
3. **Paquita es una chica deportista.**
4. **Marcos no es un chico reservado.**
5. **Rafael no es un chico estudioso.**
6. **Teresa no es una chica inteligente.**

Extension: Write additional sentences on strips of paper and cut them apart. Have students work together to unscramble them.

20 Standards: 1.2, 1.3

Resources: Teacher's Resource Book: Audio Script, p. 80; Audio Program DVD: Cap. 1B, Track 12; Answer Keys: Student Edition, p. 21

Focus: Listening for comprehension

Suggestions: Play the audio or read the script as many times as necessary. Point out that two of the people described are female and one is male. Remind students to listen carefully and write the correct adjective endings. Have students check their work with a partner.

Script and Answers:

Arturo es un chico atrevido y serio. Le gusta mucho esquiar.
Marta es una chica inteligente, paciente y trabajadora.
Belinda es muy sociable. Le gusta hablar con los amigos.

Objectives

- Write about and describe yourself and others
- Listen to and write a description of three teens

Gramática

Word order: Placement of adjectives

In Spanish, adjectives usually come after the noun they describe. Notice how *artística* follows *chica* in the Spanish sentence.

Margarita es una chica artística. *Margarita is an artistic girl.*

Did you notice that in the English sentence the adjective comes before the noun?

Here's a simple pattern you can follow when writing a sentence in Spanish.

Subject	Verb	Indefinite Article + Noun	Adjective
Margarita	es	una chica	muy artística.
Pablo	es	un estudiante	inteligente.
La Sra. Ortiz	es	una profesora	muy buena.

¿Recuerdas?

To make a sentence negative you place the word *no* before the verb.

- Eduardo **no es** un chico serio.
- **No** me gusta jugar videojuegos.

Más ayuda realidades.com

Tutorial: Position of Adjectives

19 Frases desordenadas

Escribir

Rewrite these scrambled words to create a sentence. Follow the "building-blocks" pattern above and be sure to add a period at the end of each sentence.

Modelo

perezoso Antonio es chico un
Antonio es un chico perezoso.

1. artística es una chica Marina
2. es un Tito perezoso chico
3. deportista chica una es Paquita
4. Marcos chico un es reservado no
5. chico no Rafael es estudioso un
6. no una Teresa chica es inteligente

20 Escucha y escribe

Escuchar • Escribir

You will hear a description of Arturo, Marta, and Belinda. Write what you hear.

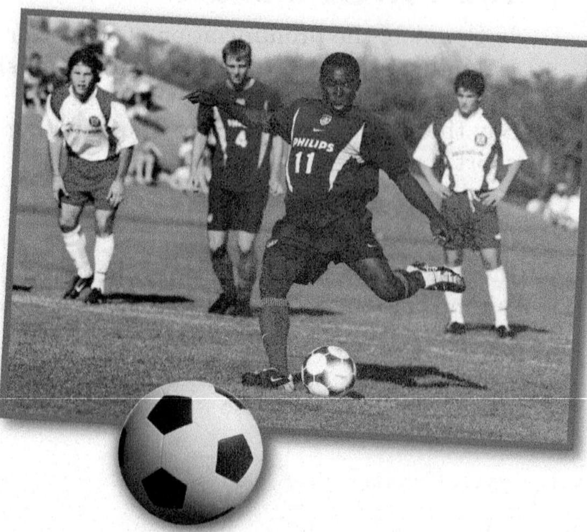

DIFFERENTIATED INSTRUCTION

Students with Learning Difficulties

Have students write female and male names, the verb form ***es,*** the indefinite articles ***un*** and ***una,*** along with appropriate nouns (***chico, chica estudiante***), and adjectives on individual index cards. They can use these cards to practice forming sentences using correct word order. Color-coding can help to reinforce the pattern.

Heritage Language Learners

For homework, have students ask family members to describe the personality of their best friends and write down the description. Have students use different highlighters to mark the various parts of speech.

21 ¿Cómo es . . . ?

Escribir

You are sitting in your school cafeteria with a new exchange student from Costa Rica. Describe the other students based on their activities.

Modelo

Emilia es una chica talentosa.

22 Y tú, ¿qué dices?

Escribir • Hablar

1. Según tu familia, ¿cómo eres?
2. Según tu mejor *(best)* amigo(a), ¿cómo eres?
3. Y tú, ¿cómo eres?

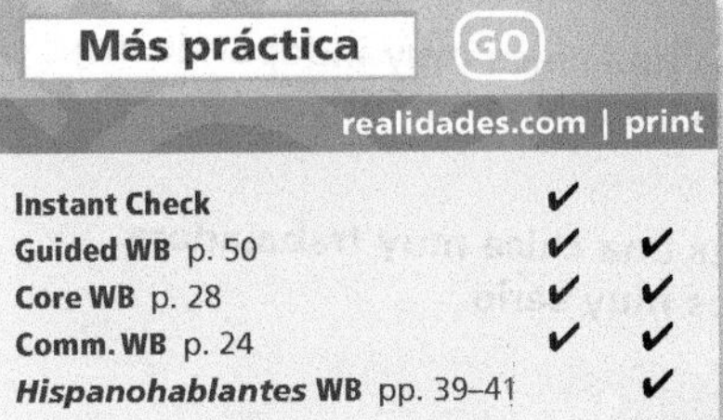

Más práctica GO

realidades.com | print

	realidades.com	print
Instant Check	✔	
Guided WB p. 50	✔	✔
Core WB p. 28	✔	✔
Comm. WB p. 24	✔	✔
Hispanohablantes WB pp. 39–41		✔

El español en el mundo del trabajo

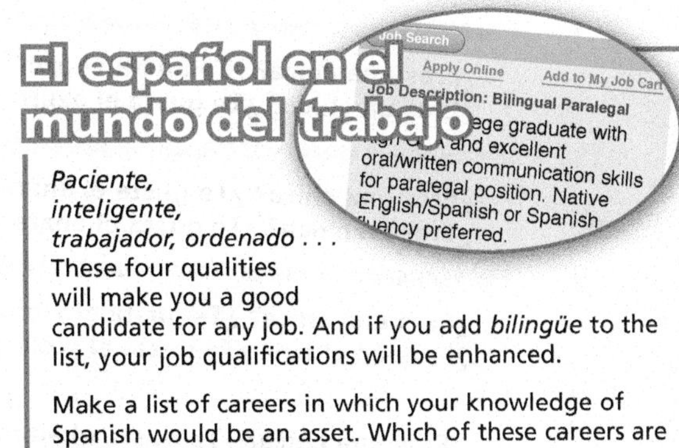

Paciente, inteligente, trabajador, ordenado . . . These four qualities will make you a good candidate for any job. And if you add *bilingüe* to the list, your job qualifications will be enhanced.

Make a list of careers in which your knowledge of Spanish would be an asset. Which of these careers are of interest to you?

Practice and Communicate 1B

21 Standards: 1.3

Resources: Answer Keys: Student Edition, p. 21

Focus: Writing sentences about people

Suggestions: Point out to students that they should write as many adjectives as apply to each person.

Answers will vary but may include:

Carmen es una chica talentosa *(graciosa, sociable).*
Felipe es un chico estudioso *(trabajador, inteligente)*
Also accept negative statements.

Pre-AP* Support

- **Learning Objective:** Interpersonal Writing
- **Activity 22:** Based on their answers to activity 22, have students write an e-mail describing themselves to one of the students pictured in activity 21.
- ***Pre-AP* Resource Book:*** Comprehensive guide to Pre-AP* writing skill development, pp. 27–38

22 Standards: 1.2, 1.3

Focus: Writing and speaking about oneself

Suggestion: In items 1 and 2, point out that *tu* means "your."

Answers will vary.

El español en el mundo del trabajo

Core Instruction

Standards: 5.1

Suggestions: Ask students how else bilingualism might be valuable, in addition to being an asset professionally.

Additional Resources

- Communication Wbk.: Audio Act. 9, p. 24
- Teacher's Resource Book: Audio Script, p. 81, Communicative Pair Activity BLM, pp. 86–87
- Audio Program DVD: Cap. 1B, Track 13

ENRICH YOUR TEACHING

Teacher-to-Teacher

Make "human sentences" to reinforce word order. Give each student a color-coded sheet of paper with a word or phrase on it. Use one color for subjects, one color for verbs, one color for indefinite articles + objects, and one color for adjectives. At your signal, students must place themselves in the correct order so the class can read the sentences that are formed. Have one student be the negative who inserts himself or herself in the various sentences.

ASSESSMENT

Prueba 1B-5 with Study Plan (online only)

Quiz: Word Order

- Prueba 1B-5: p. 31

 Common Core: Reading

Lectura

Core Instruction

Standards: 1.2, 1.3, 4.1

Resources: Voc. and Gram. Transparency 47

Focus: Reading a magazine personality quiz

Suggestions:

Pre-reading: Direct students' attention to the *Strategy* and discuss how visual clues often help in understanding a text. Help them identify the color names. Colors are formally taught in *Capítulo* 6A. You may want to use this as an opportunity to introduce them and demonstrate that color words are adjectives and must agree with the nouns they modify.

Reading: Pair students and have them take turns reading the text to each other. Encourage them to choose their favorite color and see what it reveals about them.

Post-reading: Have students tell what the quiz says about them. Do they agree with the quiz? Have them complete the *¿Comprendes?* to check comprehension.

Theme Project

Students can perform Step 5 at this point. Record their presentations for inclusion in their portfolio. (For more information, see p. 24-b.)

Block Schedule

Colors have different meanings in different cultures. Have students work in small groups to discuss which colors are used to convey messages and feelings in the United States. Each group should summarize their discussion and share it with the class or make a collage showing colors and their cultural significance.

¡Adelante!

Objectives

- Read and understand an article about personality traits
- Use visual clues to understand new words
- Learn how a Mayan item of clothing represents family and community

Lectura

Un *self-quiz*

¿Hay una relación entre los colores y la personalidad? Según un *self-quiz* de la revista *Amigos,* tus colores favoritos revelan perfectamente cómo eres.

Strategy

Using visual clues to get meaning

You have not yet learned the Spanish words for colors, but see if you can figure out what they are from the visual clues in the article.

¿Cómo eres tú? ¡Los colores revelan tu personalidad!

¿Eres una chica? ¿Te gusta el rojo? ¿Eres un chico? ¿Te gusta el rojo?	Eres muy apasionada. Eres atrevido.
¿Eres una chica? ¿Te gusta el verde? ¿Eres un chico? ¿Te gusta el verde?	Eres una chica natural. Eres muy generoso.
¿Eres una chica? ¿Te gusta el azul? ¿Eres un chico? ¿Te gusta el azul?	Eres muy talentosa. Eres un chico sociable.
¿Eres una chica? ¿Te gusta el anaranjado? ¿Eres un chico? ¿Te gusta el anaranjado?	Eres una chica artística. Eres gracioso.
¿Eres una chica? ¿Te gusta el violeta? ¿Eres un chico? ¿Te gusta el violeta?	Eres una chica muy independiente. Eres un chico romántico.
¿Eres una chica? ¿Te gusta el amarillo? ¿Eres un chico? ¿Te gusta el amarillo?	Eres una chica muy trabajadora. Eres muy serio.

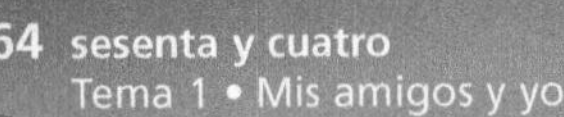

DIFFERENTIATED INSTRUCTION

Advanced Learners

Have students write a brief poem about themselves using the names of colors and other adjectives. Be sure they understand that the words in the poem do not have to rhyme. Students can decorate their papers using corresponding colors and pictures.

Heritage Language Learners

Have students search the Internet to find additional personality quizzes. They can print these out and write summaries of what the tests say about them, changing from the second person to the first person.

¿Comprendes?

1. You probably were able to understand most of the words in the quiz. Write the English meaning for these Spanish cognates from the reading:
   - revelan
   - natural
   - independiente
   - generoso
   - apasionada
   - romántico
2. According to the "self-quiz," what should be the favorite colors of these teenagers?
   a. A Beto le gusta estar con amigos.
   b. A Margarita le gusta dibujar.
   c. A Lorenzo le gusta el trabajo voluntario.
   d. A Lupe le gusta estudiar. Es muy seria.
   e. A Isabel le gusta estar con amigos, pero también le gusta estar sola *(alone)*.
3. Which of the colors in this reading best matches your personality? Why?

Modelo
Amarillo: *Soy una chica trabajadora. Me gusta ir a la escuela.*

Fondo Cultural | Guatemala • México

Huipil is the word for the colorful, hand-woven blouse worn by female descendants of the Maya. The color, design, and style of weaving are unique to each *huipil* and identify the background and specific village of the weaver. Hundreds of designs and styles of weaving have been identified in the Mayan regions, which are located principally in Guatemala and parts of Mexico.

- What do you wear that might represent your personality or likes and dislikes?

Una mujer de Guatemala con huipil

Más práctica GO

realidades.com | print

	realidades.com	print
Guided WB p. 51	✔	✔
Comm. WB pp. 28, 234	✔	✔
***Hispanohablantes* WB** pp. 42–45		✔
Cultural Reading Activity	✔	

ENRICH YOUR TEACHING

Culture Note

Crafting the ***huipil*** is a tradition kept by Mayan women. Other indigenous peoples have similar traditions. The Kuna, who live on small coral islands along the Atlantic coast of Panama, are famous for their ***molas*** (see p. 338)***. Mola*** is the Kuna word for the elaborate embroidered panels that make up the front and back of a Kuna woman's blouse.

21st Century Skills

Critical Thinking and Problem Solving

Have students working in small groups tally their responses to the self-quiz. Was there a favorite color among female students? Among male students? Then, have all the groups compare their results. Was there a favorite color in the class? Ask students if they agree with the suggested relationship between color and personality trait.

¿Comprendes? Standards: 1.1

Resources: Answer Keys: Student Edition, p. 22

Suggestions: Have students share their answers for items 1 and 2. Ask for volunteers to explain their answer for part three.

Answers:

1. **reveal, natural, independent, generous, passionate, romantic**
2. **a) azul; b) anaranjado; c) verde; d) amarillo; e) violeta**
3. **Answers will vary.**

Fondo cultural

Standards: 2.2, 4.2

Suggestions: Bring in photos or actual examples of clothing from various Spanish-speaking cultures. Help students recognize that even if they are purchasing clothing rather than making it, it nonetheless is a reflection of their values and personalities.

Answers will vary but might include t-shirts, team uniforms, particular colors or styles of clothing, etc.

Pre-AP* Support

- **Learning Objective:** Interpretive: Print
- **Activity:** Have students bring to class a picture (from a magazine, the Internet, etc.) of a famous person and attach the picture to a sheet of construction paper that is the color associated in the article with that person's personality. Have them write a sentence below the picture identifying the personality traits.
- ***Pre-AP* Resource Book:*** Comprehensive guide to Pre-AP* reading skill development, pp. 19–26

For Further Reading

Student Resource: Realidades para hispanohablantes: Lectura 2, pp. 44–45

Perspectivas del mundo hispano

Core Instruction

Standards: 2.1, 4.2

Focus: Reading about friendship

Suggestions: Get students thinking about friendship and what it means to them by asking them to think about how many friends they have and the qualities they look for in a friend.

Have students read the page. Talk about the experiences of Marcos and Brianna. Do students feel these experiences are realistic? Have any of them had similar experiences? Ask if they differentiate between a friend and an acquaintance. If so, what terms do they use for this distinction?

Direct students to the *Check it out!* section. After they have completed it, go over the Spanish terms and have students answer the question.

Some students may have personal experiences similar to those described because of having moved to a foreign country or to another city or community. Have students look at the photos and discuss what they see as compared to their own world.

Direct attention to the *Think about it!* section and have students discuss it.

Answers will vary.

Pre-AP* Support

- **Learning Objective:** Presentational Speaking (Cultural Comparison)
- **Background:** This task prepares students for the Spoken Presentational Communication tasks that focus on cultural comparisons.
- **Activity:** Have students prepare a two-minute (maximum) presentation in English on the following topic: Perspectives on friendship can vary between cultures: True or false? Think about the experiences shared by the teens in the reading. Then, compare this to your own experiences, and to perspectives about friendship in your own culture. In your opinion, could location (small town versus large city, for example) influence perspectives on this issue?
- ***Pre-AP* Resource Book:*** Comprehensive guide to Pre-AP* speaking skill development, pp. 39–50

Additional Resources

Student Resource: Realidades para hispanohablantes, p. 46

Perspectivas del mundo hispano

¿Qué es un amigo?

Marcos, a Costa Rican student on an exchange program in the United States writes:

“When I arrived in the United States, I was amazed at all the friends my host brother and sister had. They knew a lot of people. These friends came to the house frequently, and we went out in groups. People were very open when meeting me. We'd spend some time together and get to know each other in a short amount of time. And once you got to know them, you ended up talking about everything!”

Brianna, a United States student on an exchange program in Colombia writes:

“After I spent my year in Colombia, I learned that the concept of friendship is a little different than in the United States. My host brother and sisters spent a lot of time with their family. They knew people at school and from after-school activities, but they had just a few close friends and we'd do things with them. It was definitely a smaller group than I was used to. It seems that it took longer to become close friends with people too”.

Dos amigas estudiando

In Spanish, two expressions are used frequently to describe friendly relationships: *un amigo,* which means “friend,” and *un conocido,* which means “acquaintance.” You already know the word *amigo. Conocido* comes from the verb *conocer,* which means “to meet.” Each expression implies a different type of relationship.

Check it out! In many Spanish-speaking countries you'll find lots of expressions for someone who is your friend: *hermano, cuate (México), amigote (España),* and *compinche (Uruguay, Argentina, España).* Make a list of the expressions for “a friend” that are popular in your community. How would you explain them to someone from a Spanish-speaking country?

Think about it! Compare how the United States perspective on friendship is different from that of a Spanish-speaking country. Use the terms *amigo* and *conocido* as you make the comparison.

DIFFERENTIATED INSTRUCTION

Heritage Language Learners

Students may have first-hand knowledge of the differences in friendships if they have moved from another country. If so, encourage them to share their experiences with the class.

Teacher-to-Teacher

e-amigos: Pair students to be *e-amigos.* Have them use e-mail to send each other short notes like the notes they write for the *Presentación escrita* on p. 67. Have students print out their e-mails or send them to you for your review.

Presentación escrita

Amigo por correspondencia

- Write an e-mail introduction
- Apply the steps of the writing process

Task
Write an e-mail in which you introduce yourself to a prospective pen pal.

1. **Prewrite** To think about and organize the information you want to give, answer these questions:
   - ¿Cómo te llamas?
   - ¿Cómo eres?
   - ¿Qué te gusta hacer?
   - ¿Qué no te gusta hacer?
2. **Draft** Write a first draft of your e-mail answering the questions above. Begin by introducing yourself: *¡Hola! Me llamo . . . .* End with *Escríbeme pronto*. ("Write to me soon.")

   Modelo
   ¡Hola! Me llamo Pati. Soy atrevida y muy deportista. Me gusta mucho nadar y correr, pero me gusta más esquiar. ¡No me gusta nada jugar videojuegos! Escríbeme pronto.
3. **Revise** Revise your first draft and share it with a partner. Ask yourself:
   - Is it well organized?
   - Does it answer the Prewrite questions?
   - Are the spelling and adjective forms correct?
   - Did you include the opening and the closing?

   Decide whether or not to use your partner's suggestions and rewrite your draft.
4. **Publish** Type up your e-mail. You might send it to a pen pal or your teacher, or print it for a classmate to answer.
5. **Evaluation** The following rubric will be used to grade your e-mail.

Rubric	Score 1	Score 3	Score 5
Completion of task	You provide some of the required information.	You provide most of the required information.	You provide all of the required information.
Following the writing process	You provide only the prewrite questions.	You provide the prewrite questions and rough draft.	You provide the prewrite, rough draft, and final product.
Using adjectives correctly	You use only one adjective with grammar errors.	You use two adjectives with some grammar errors.	You use more than two adjectives with very few grammar errors.

Strategy
Using the writing process
To create your best work, follow each step in the writing process.

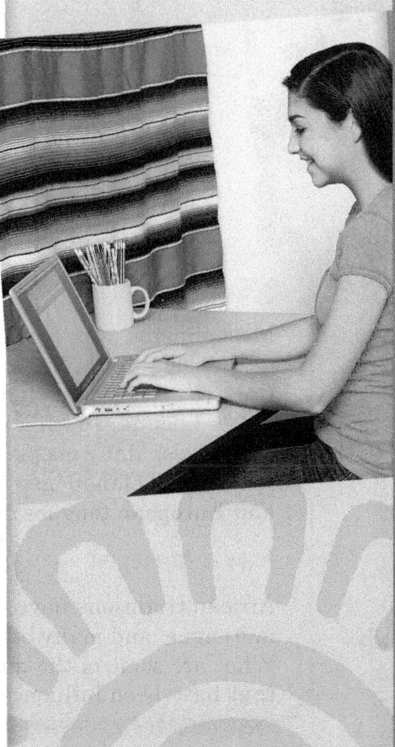

ENRICH YOUR TEACHING

21st Century Skills

Initiative and Self-Direction Before students write their e-mails, direct them to study the third step of the task, Revise. Using these questions as a pre-writing guide will make it easier for them to fulfill the requirements in the rubric for writing a better e-mail and getting a high score on the assignment.

Common Core: Writing

Presentación escrita

Expository
Standards: 1.3

Focus: Writing an e-mail as an introduction to a prospective pen pal

Suggestions: Introduce the *Presentación escrita* to the class and have students review the rubric. Then have them work through each step of the process.

Prewrite: Suggest to students that they make an outline or write a list of facts they want to include in their e-mail. Students should use the questions in Step 1 to guide their thinking.

Draft: Encourage students to be creative when they write their e-mail, but explain that they can use the example in Step 2 to format their own message.

Revise: Tell students to check their e-mail to identify errors or better ways to communicate before sharing it with a partner. When suggestions have been accepted, be sure students know to incorporate them and revise their message.

Publish: Remind students to reread their final copy of the e-mail for typing errors before they send it or give it to someone.

Evaluation: See Assessment below.

Pre-AP* Support

- ***Pre-AP* Resource Book:*** Comprehensive guide to Pre-AP* writing skill development, pp. 27–38

Portfolio

Have students print out their e-mails for inclusion in their portfolios.

Additional Resources

Student Resources: Realidades para hispanohablantes, p. 47; Guided Practice: Presentación escrita, p. 52

ASSESSMENT

Presentación escrita

- Assessment Program: Rubrics, p. T28
  Go over the descriptions of the different levels of performance. After assessing students, help individuals understand how their performance could be improved. (See Teacher's Resource Book for suggestions on using rubrics in assessment.)

El mundo hispano

Core Instruction

Standards: 2.1, 2.2, 4.2

Resources: Voc. and Gram. Transparency 14

Mapa global interactivo, Actividad 3 Explore the Caribbean islands of Cuba, the Dominican Republic, and Puerto Rico.

Focus: Reading about the heritage of the Caribbean

Suggestions: After students read the text, display a map of the Caribbean. Point out the islands mentioned, indicating the Spanish-speaking islands. Explain that Hispaniola is shared by two countries and that only the eastern portion of it, the Dominican Republic, is Spanish-speaking. (The languages of Haiti are Creole and French.)

Discuss the voyage of Columbus, using a map to show how he traveled from Spain to Hispaniola. Have students hypothesize about the origins of the colonists who returned with Columbus to the island on his second voyage.

Direct attention to the top photo on p. 69. Ask students if it looks like other universities they have seen. Have them note that it is the oldest university in the Americas.

Focus on the *¿Sabes que...?* section. Using a map that shows Africa and the Caribbean, indicate how Africans traveled across the ocean to the islands. Discuss the languages spoken, their roots, and how they may have evolved.

Direct attention to the photo at the bottom of p. 69. Guide students to understand that the music of the Caribbean is a fusion of many different cultures. Have them discuss which cultures contributed to this fusion and how it came to be.

Have students locate Puerto Rico on the map. Mention that it is not a state, but a territory of the United States. As a territory, its citizens have rights that are similar to those of a citizen, but not as far-reaching.

Focus on the photo in the middle of p. 69. This observatory remains very important as we continue to explore space and our universe.

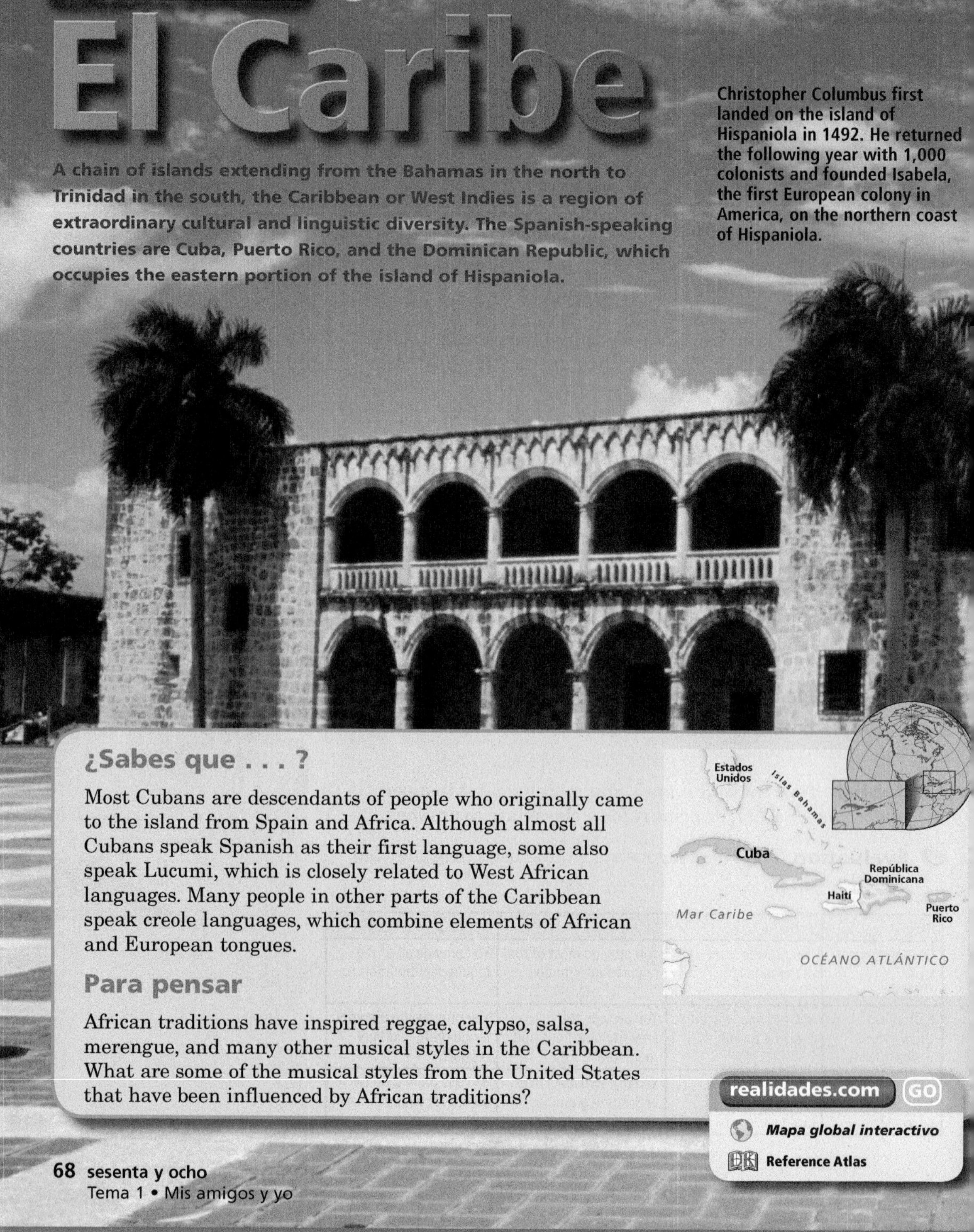

El Caribe

A chain of islands extending from the Bahamas in the north to Trinidad in the south, the Caribbean or West Indies is a region of extraordinary cultural and linguistic diversity. The Spanish-speaking countries are Cuba, Puerto Rico, and the Dominican Republic, which occupies the eastern portion of the island of Hispaniola.

Christopher Columbus first landed on the island of Hispaniola in 1492. He returned the following year with 1,000 colonists and founded Isabela, the first European colony in America, on the northern coast of Hispaniola.

¿Sabes que . . . ?

Most Cubans are descendants of people who originally came to the island from Spain and Africa. Although almost all Cubans speak Spanish as their first language, some also speak Lucumi, which is closely related to West African languages. Many people in other parts of the Caribbean speak creole languages, which combine elements of African and European tongues.

Para pensar

African traditions have inspired reggae, calypso, salsa, merengue, and many other musical styles in the Caribbean. What are some of the musical styles from the United States that have been influenced by African traditions?

DIFFERENTIATED INSTRUCTION

Advanced Learners

Have students research the history of Puerto Rico and its present relationship to the United States. What rights do United States citizens have that Puerto Ricans do not have? Have students include their opinion on whether or not Puerto Rico should become a state.

Heritage Language Learners

Have students choose a Spanish-speaking country in the Caribbean and research the languages spoken there. In what ways have languages other than Spanish influenced the country?

The Universidad Autónoma de Santo Domingo, located in the capital of the Dominican Republic, Santo Domingo, is the oldest university in the Americas. It was founded in 1538—almost 100 years before Harvard—and continues to be one of the most important in the Caribbean.

Opened in 1963, the Arecibo Observatory in Puerto Rico has the largest single-dish radio telescope in the world. Some 200 scientists from around the world conduct research at Arecibo every year. In the early 1990s astronomers at Arecibo discovered the first planets outside our solar system.

The Caribbean is famous for its diverse musical styles that fuse African and European influences. Some groups even combine salsa, rumba, cha-cha-cha, and other Caribbean musical styles with jazz, hip-hop, and rock and roll.

Culture 1B

Suggestions: Bring in, or have students bring in, recordings of the types of music mentioned. Compare their rhythms and the types of musical instruments used. Direct attention to the *Para pensar* section and have students discuss the question.

Answers will vary.

ENRICH YOUR TEACHING

Culture Note

Africans were taken to the Caribbean and enslaved just as they were to the United States. Families were split up and cultural roots broken. People spoke different languages, and many transplanted Africans found themselves unable to communicate. Eventually, however, languages and cultures blended.

Teacher-to-Teacher

Have students research musical instruments of the Caribbean. Have them find out how certain instruments came to be and how they are made, and explore making one in class using simple materials.

Review Activities

To talk about what you and others are like: Have students work in pairs to quiz each other on the vocabulary. They can pantomime the adjectives and have classmates guess the words.

To ask people about themselves or others: Have students walk around the room and ask three people about themselves or another person. Each student should ask and answer three questions.

To talk about what someone likes or dislikes: Have students talk in pairs about what their friends like and dislike, using infinitives from the learned vocabulary in the structure *(No) Le gusta ___.*

To describe someone: Have students work in small groups to describe themselves or another person using *(No) Soy ___.* and *Es ___.* Tell them to use as many adjectives as possible.

To tell whom are you talking about: Have the class write short sentences *(Es un chico...)* using correct verb forms and gender endings to describe themselves or someone else.

Other useful words: Refer students to this section and remind them to practice these expressions as they create sentences.

Portfolio

Invite students to review the activities they completed in this chapter, including written reports, posters or other visuals, and recordings of oral presentations or other projects. Have them select one or two items that they feel best demonstrate their achievements in Spanish. Include these products in students' portfolios. Have them include this with the Chapter Checklist and Self-Assessment Worksheet.

Additional Resources

Student Resources: Realidades para hispanohablantes, p. 48

Teacher Resources:

- Teacher's Resource Book: Situation Cards, p. 88, Clip Art, pp. 90–91
- Assessment Program: Chapter Checklist and Self-Assessment Worksheet, pp. T56–T57

▼ Objectives

- Review the vocabulary and grammar
- Demonstrate you can perform the tasks on p. 71

Repaso del capítulo

Vocabulario y gramática

to talk about what you and others are like

artístico, -a	artistic
atrevido, -a	daring
bueno, -a	good
deportista	sports-minded
desordenado, -a	messy
estudioso, -a	studious
gracioso, -a	funny
impaciente	impatient
inteligente	intelligent
ordenado, -a	neat
paciente	patient
perezoso, -a	lazy
reservado, -a	reserved, shy
serio, -a	serious
simpático, -a	nice, friendly
sociable	sociable
talentoso, -a	talented
trabajador, -ora	hardworking

to ask people about themselves or others

¿Cómo eres?	What are you like?
¿Cómo es?	What is he / she like?
¿Cómo se llama?	What's his / her name?
¿Eres . . . ?	Are you . . . ?

to talk about what someone likes or doesn't like

le gusta . . .	he / she likes . . .
no le gusta . . .	he / she doesn't like . . .

to describe someone

soy	I am
no soy	I am not
es	he / she is

For *Vocabulario adicional*, see pp. 472–473.

to tell whom you are talking about

el amigo	male friend
la amiga	female friend
el chico	boy
la chica	girl
él	he
ella	she
yo	I

other useful words

a veces	sometimes
muy	very
pero	but
según	according to
según mi familia	according to my family

adjectives

Masculine	Feminine
ordenado	ordenad**a**
trabajador	trabajad**ora**
paciente	paciente
deportista	deportista

definite articles

el	the
la	the

indefinite articles

un	a, an
una	a, an

DIFFERENTIATED INSTRUCTION

Students with Learning Difficulties

Cut out magazine pictures of people who could be described using the vocabulary in this chapter. Hold up two of the pictures and give a short description of one of them. Have students tell you which one you are describing.

Multiple Intelligences

Logical/Mathematical: Have students make a word-search puzzle with all the new adjectives mixed in among other letters. Instead of listing the words to search for, have students write clues. For example: *Me gustan los deportes.* ***(Soy deportista.)***

Más repaso GO realidades.com | print

	realidades.com	print
Instant Check	✔	
Puzzles	✔	
Core WB pp. 29–30		✔
Comm. WB pp. 235, 236–238	✔	✔

Preparación para el examen

On the exam you will be asked to . . .	Here are practice tasks similar to those you will find on the exam . . .	For review go to your print or digital textbook . . .
Interpretive		
 **1 Escuchar** Listen to and understand a description of a friend	Listen as a character in a Spanish soap opera describes his ex-girlfriend. What does he think her good qualities are? What does he think her shortcomings are? Can you understand why he broke up with her?	**pp. 50–53** *Vocabulario en contexto* **p. 57** Actividades 11–12 **p. 62** Actividad 20
Interpersonal		
 **2 Hablar** Talk about yourself in terms of how you see yourself	While you're talking to your Spanish teacher, you realize that she doesn't know the "real you." Tell her some things about yourself that would help her understand you.	**pp. 50–53** *Vocabulario en contexto* **p. 56** Actividad 9 **p. 57** Actividad 11 **p. 58** Actividad 13 **p. 63** Actividad 22
Interpretive		
 **3 Leer** Read and understand a description of someone	In a popular Spanish magazine, you see an interview with the actor who plays the part of a teenager, Carlos, in a TV show you have been watching. See if you can understand what he is saying about the character he plays: *¡No me gusta nada el chico! Él es muy inteligente, pero le gusta hablar y hablar de NADA. Es ridículo. Es muy impaciente y perezoso. Él no es ni simpático ni gracioso. Yo soy un actor . . . ¡no soy como Carlos!*	**pp. 50–53** *Vocabulario en contexto* **p. 59** Actividad 14 **pp. 64–65** *Lectura*
Presentational		
 **4 Escribir** Write a short paragraph describing yourself	The first issue of your school's online newspaper is called "Getting to Know You." Submit a brief profile of yourself. Mention what your family thinks of you and list some things you like to do. For example: *Yo soy una chica deportista y muy sociable. Según mi familia, soy graciosa. Me gusta patinar y hablar por teléfono.*	**pp. 56–57** Actividades 10–12 **p. 59** Actividad 15 **p. 63** Actividad 22 **p. 67** *Presentación escrita*
Cultures • Comparisons		
 **5 Pensar** Demonstrate an understanding of cultural perspectives on friendship	Explain the differences between the terms *amigo* and *conocido* in Spanish-speaking cultures. How does this compare to words that we use in the United States?	**p. 66** *Perspectivas del mundo hispano*

DIFFERENTIATED ASSESSMENT

CORE ASSESSMENT
- **Assessment Program:** Examen del capítulo 1B, pp. 33–40
- **Audio Program DVD:** Cap. 1B, Track 16
- **ExamView:** Chapter Test, Test Banks A and B

ADVANCED/PRE-AP*
- **ExamView: Pre-AP* Test Bank**
- **Pre-AP* Resource Book,** pp. 62–65

STUDENTS NEEDING EXTRA HELP
- **Alternate Assessment Program:** Examen del capítulo 1B
- **Audio Program DVD:** Cap. 1B, Track 16

HERITAGE LEARNERS
- **Assessment Program: Realidades para hispanohablantes:** Examen del capítulo 1B
- **ExamView: Heritage Learner Test Bank**

Performance Tasks

Standards: 1.1, 1.2, 1.3, 3.1

Student Resource: Realidades para hispanohablantes, p. 49

Teacher Resources: Teacher's Resource Book: Audio Script, p. 81; Audio Program DVD: Cap. 1B, Track 15; Answer Keys: Student Edition, p. 22

1. Escuchar

Suggestions: Play the audio or read the script. Have students suggest answers.

Script: ¿Cómo es María Elena? Pues... es una chica inteligente y talentosa, pero es muuuy seria. Y no es sociable. Yo soy un chico gracioso y muy sociable. A mí me gustan más las chicas atrevidas.

Answers: Elena is talented and intelligent, but very serious. Her shortcomings are that she is not sociable. He likes more outgoing or daring women.

2. Hablar

Suggestions: For more practice, have students describe themselves as the opposite of what they are like.

Answers will vary.

3. Leer

Suggestions: Remind students to look for cognates. Ask volunteers to point out the phrases that describe personality traits.

Answers:
1. **Es ridículo. Es muy impaciente y perezoso. Él no es ni simpático ni gracioso.**
2. **Él es muy inteligente, pero le gusta hablar de nada.**

4. Escribir

Suggestions: Encourage students to be creative. Tell them they can either describe themselves as they are, or write about a "person" they create as themselves.

Answers will vary.

5. Pensar

Suggestions: Allow students to speak spontaneously or from a short list of their thoughts.

Answers will vary.

Tema

2 La escuela

2A Tu día en la escuela

- **School subjects and schedules**

Vocabulary: class subjects; school activities; school supplies; ordinal numbers

Grammar: subject pronouns; the present tense of ***-ar*** verbs

Cultural Perspectives: comparing schools

2B Tu sala de clases

- **Describing a classroom**

Vocabulary: classroom items and furniture; parts of the classroom; prepositions of location

Grammar: the verb ***estar;*** plurals of nouns and articles

Cultural Perspectives: opinions about school

THEME SUPPORT

Bulletin Boards

Theme: *La escuela*

Ask students to cut out, copy, or download photos of school supplies, classroom items, schools from around the world, and scenes from different school settings. Cluster photos according to these four categories.

Hands-on Culture

Chant for choosing teams

When choosing teams to play a game, students in ***América Latina*** often sing a chant like the one that follows.

Directions:

1. Type out the words to the chant and distribute copies to students.
2. Have students repeat each line of the chant after you to practice pronunciation.
3. Begin the chant, or choose a leader. The entire class responds to the leader.

   Leader: Ambos a dos … Matarile, rile, rile. Ambos a dos … Matarile, rile, rile, ron.

   Class: ¿Qué quiere usted? Matarile, rile, rile. ¿Qué quiere usted? Matarile, rile, rile, ron.

   Leader: Yo quiero un paje. Matarile, rile, rile. Yo quiero un paje. Matarile, rile, rile, ron.

   Group: ¿Qué paje quiere usted? Matarile, rile, rile. ¿Qué paje quiere usted? Matarile, rile, rile, ron.

   Leader: Yo quiero a *(name of a student)*. Matarile, rile, rile. Yo quiero a *(name of a student)*. Matarile, rile, rile, ron.

   Group: Aquí tiene usted su paje. Matarile, rile, rile. Aquí tiene usted su paje. Matarile, rile, rile, ron.
4. The student who is named joins the leader, and the chant begins again to choose the next team member.

Game

¿Tienes...?

This game is similar to Go Fish. Have students play it after you present the vocabulary from *Capítulo* 2B.

Players: 2 to 4

Materials: index cards, colored pencils or markers

Rules:

1. The cards for this game should be prepared ahead of time. Have students draw on the index cards the classroom items listed on p. 120. There should be four index cards for each item, making a deck of 48 cards for each pair or group.
2. One student deals each player five cards, then places the remaining cards face down on the desk or table.
3. Players examine their cards to see whether they have any matching pairs. If they do, they remove the pairs and set them aside.
4. The dealer begins play by asking whether anyone has a card.

   Dealer: Linda, ¿tienes un reloj?
5. If the player has the card that the dealer is asking for, he or she responds affirmatively and gives the card to the dealer. The dealer then sets the pair aside and takes another turn. If the player doesn't have the card, the dealer must draw one from the pile and the next player takes a turn.

   Player: Sí, tengo un reloj.
   No, no tengo un reloj. Toma un naipe *(card)*.
6. The game ends when one player puts down or gives away the last card. All players count their cards. The player with the most pairs wins.

Variation: Have students write the vocabulary words on index cards, then turn them face down on a large table or the floor to play Concentration. Students turn over two cards at a time to find matching pairs.

THEME PROJECT

Página Web

Overview: Students create a Web page for their school featuring the school's name, address, and phone number and at least four symbols or photos that represent different classes. Under each symbol or photo, students write a description of the class represented. Students then present their Web page to the class, describing all the information featured on the page.

Resources: Web creation software (if available), poster board, magazines, colored pencils, markers, glue, scissors, bilingual dictionary

Sequence: (suggestions for when to do each step appear throughout the chapters)

2A

STEP 1. Review instructions so students know what is expected of them. Hand out the "Theme 2 Project Instructions and Rubric" from the *Teacher's Resource Book*.

STEP 2. Students submit a rough sketch of their Web page. Return the sketches with your suggestions. For vocabulary and grammar practice, ask students to partner and present their drafts to each other.

STEP 3. Students create layouts on poster board. Encourage students to try different arrangements before drawing or gluing photos or symbols and writing descriptions. Encourage students to use as much of the vocabulary from *Capítulos* 2A and 2B as possible in the descriptions. Also, encourage them to use a bilingual dictionary for any words they would like to use, but do not yet know.

2B

STEP 4. Students submit a draft of their descriptions. Note your corrections and suggestions, then return the drafts to students.

STEP 5. Students complete and present their Web page to the class, reading and / or describing all the information featured on the page.

Options:

1. Students create a brochure for their school instead of a Web page.
2. Students create a virtual tour of a classroom, describing its contents.

Assessment:

Here is a detailed rubric for assessing this project:

Theme 2 Project: *Página Web*

RUBRIC	Score 1	Score 3	Score 5
Evidence of planning	You provided no written draft or page layout.	Your draft was written and layout created, but not corrected.	You corrected your draft and layout.
Your use of illustrations	You included no photos or visuals.	You included photos or visuals, but your layout was unorganized.	Your Web page was easy to read, complete, and accurate.
Your presentation	You included little of the required information.	You included most of the required information.	You included all the required information.

21st Century Skills

Look for tips throughout *Tema* 2 to enrich your teaching by integrating 21st Century Skills. Suggestions for the Theme Project and Theme Support follow below.

Theme Project

Modify the Theme Project with one or more of these suggestions:

Promote Critical Thinking and Problem Solving

Have students research several Web sites and decide which design features and arrangement of information will be best for their Web site. With help from the teacher, they might also decide what could be added to the site to best represent the values of the school.

Develop Media Literacy

As students examine different Web sites, have them develop criteria that they can use now and in the future to judge the quality of the sites they research. The handout "Evaluate Web Sites" can help them analyze online materials.

Encourage Collaboration

Each student in the group should have a role, and work should be equally distributed. For example, three roles are design, photo/text selection, and site set-up. To better understand collaboration, have students read together and discuss the handout "Work in Teams."

Theme Culture

Foster Flexibility and Adaptability

Have students review the *Fondo cultural* notes on pages 80 and 86 and then draft an e-mail to a U.S. student, pretending to be a Spanish speaker. The writer should discuss school activities that differ from those the U.S. student might be used to.

Videocultura View *Los uniformes escolares* with the class to learn more about different types of uniforms.

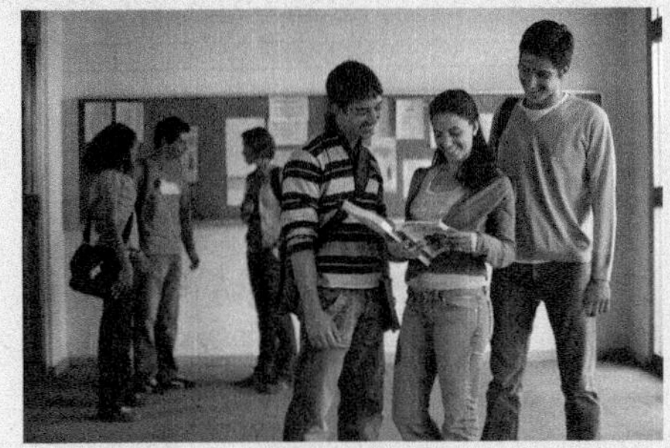

2A Tu día en la escuela

AT A GLANCE

Objectives
- **Listen to and read descriptions of school subjects and schedules**
- **Talk and write about classes, school activities, and likes and dislikes**
- **Exchange information while explaining what classes and activities you and friends have in common**
- **Compare your school day with those of students in Spanish-speaking countries**
- **Compare sports and attitudes towards sports in the Spanish-speaking world and the United States**

Vocabulary
- School subjects and schedules
- School supplies
- Class descriptions

Grammar
- Subject pronouns
- Present tense of ***-ar*** verbs

Culture
- Fernando Botero, p. 73
- Courses students take in Spanish-speaking countries, p. 80
- Romans in Spain, p. 81
- Latin influence on Spanish, p. 81
- ***el recreo,*** p. 86
- The Mayan numbering system, p. 88
- Facts about Costa Rica, pp. 90–91
- The 24-hour clock, p. 91
- Soccer fan chants, p. 92

Recycle ♻
- Titles used with adults
- Infinitives
- Negatives
- ***gustar***

RESOURCES

	FOR THE STUDENT	ONLINE	DVD	PRINT	FOR THE TEACHER	ONLINE	PREEXP	DVD	PRINT
Plan					Interactive TE and Resources DVD	•		•	
					Teacher's Resource Book, pp. 110–143	•		•	•
					Pre-AP* Resource Book, 66–69	•		•	•
					Lesson Plans	•			•
					Mapa global interactivo	•			
Introducción PP. **72–73**									
Present	Student Edition, pp. 72–73	•	•	•	Interactive TE and Resources DVD	•		•	
	DK Reference Atlas	•	•		Teacher's Resource Book, pp. 110–113	•		•	•
	Videocultura	•	•		Galería de fotos		•		
	Hispanohablantes WB, pp. 50–51			•	Fine Art Transparencies, 7	•	•	•	
					Map Transparencies, 12–13, 15, 18	•	•	•	
Vocabulario en contexto PP. **74–77**									
Present & Practice	Student Edition, pp. 74–77	•	•	•	Interactive TE and Resources DVD	•		•	
	Audio	•	•		Teacher's Resource Book, pp. 114–116, 118, 126–127	•		•	•
	Videohistoria	•	•		Vocabulary Clip Art	•	•	•	•
	Flashcards	•	•		Audio Program	•	•	•	
	Instant Check	•			Video Program: Videohistoria	•		•	
	Guided WB, pp. 53–62	•	•	•	Video Program Teacher's Guide: Cap. 2A	•		•	•
	Core WB, pp. 31–34	•	•	•	Vocabulary and Grammar Transparencies, 48–51	•	•	•	
	Comm. WB, pp. 29–30, 31, 35	•	•	•	Answer Keys: Student Edition, p. 24	•	•	•	
	Hispanohablantes WB, pp. 52–53			•	TPR Stories, pp. 29–36	•		•	•
Assess and Remediate					Prueba 2A–1: Assessment Program, pp. 41–42	•		•	•
					Assessment Program para hispanohablantes, pp. 41–42	•		•	•

RESOURCES

	FOR THE STUDENT	ONLINE	DVD	PRINT	FOR THE TEACHER	ONLINE	PREEXP	DVD	PRINT
Vocabulario en uso PP. 78–81									
Present & Practice	Student Edition, pp. 78–81	•	•	•	Interactive Whiteboard Vocabulary Activities	•		•	
	Instant Check	•			Interactive TE and Resources DVD	•		•	
	Comm. WB, p. 31, 239	•	•	•	Teacher's Resource Book, pp. 116, 120–121	•		•	•
	Hispanohablantes WB, pp. 54–55, 60			•	Communicative Pair Activities, pp. 120–121	•		•	•
	Communicative Pair Activities	•			Audio Program	•	•	•	
					Videomodelos	•		•	
					Vocabulary and Grammar Transparencies, 55	•	•	•	
					Answer Keys: Student Edition, pp. 25–26	•	•	•	•
Assess and Remediate					Prueba 2A–2 with Study Plan	•			
					Prueba 2A–2: Assessment Program, pp. 43–44	•		•	•
					Assessment Program para hispanohablantes, pp. 43–44	•		•	•
Gramática PP. 82–89									
Present & Practice	Student Edition, pp. 82–89	•	•	•	Interactive Whiteboard Grammar Activities	•		•	
	Instant Check	•			Interactive TE and Resources DVD	•		•	
	Animated Verbs	•			Teacher's Resource Book, pp. 116–117, 119, 122–123, 125	•		•	•
	Tutorial Video: Grammar	•			Communicative Pair Activities, pp. 122–123	•		•	•
	Canción de hip hop	•			Audio Program	•	•	•	
	Guided WB, pp. 63–66	•	•	•	Videomodelos	•		•	
	Core WB, pp. 35–37	•	•	•	Video Program: GramActiva	•	•	•	
	Comm. WB, pp. 32–34, 36–37, 239	•	•	•	Vocabulary and Grammar Transparencies, 2, 52–54	•	•	•	
	Hispanohablantes WB, pp. 56–59, 61			•	Answer Keys: Student Edition, pp. 26–28	•	•	•	
	Communicative Pair Activities	•							
Assess and Remediate					Pruebas 2A–3 and 2A-4 with Study Plans	•			
					Pruebas 2A–3, 2A–4: Assessment Program, pp. 45, 46	•		•	•
					Assessment Program para hispanohablantes, pp. 45, 46	•		•	•
¡Adelante! PP. 90–95									
Application	Student Edition, pp. 90–95	•	•	•	Interactive TE and Resources DVD	•		•	
	Online Cultural Reading	•			Vocabulary and Grammar Transparencies, 56	•	•	•	
	Guided WB, pp. 67–68	•	•	•	Map Transparencies, 12	•	•	•	
	Comm. WB, pp. 38, 240	•	•	•	Answer Keys: Student Edition, p. 29	•	•	•	
	Hispanohablantes WB, pp. 62–67			•					
Repaso del capítulo PP. 96–97									
Review	Student Edition, pp. 96–97	•	•	•	Interactive TE and Resources DVD	•		•	
	Online Puzzles and Games	•			Teacher's Resource Book, pp. 117, 124, 126–127	•		•	•
	Core WB, pp. 38–39	•	•	•	Audio Program	•	•	•	
	Comm. WB, pp. 241–244	•	•	•	Answer Keys: Student Edition, p. 29	•	•	•	
	Hispanohablantes WB, pp. 68–69			•					
	Instant check	•							
Chapter Assessment									
Assess					Examen del capítulo 2A	•		•	•
					Assessment Program, pp. 47–53	•		•	•
					Alternate Assessment Program, pp. 13–18	•		•	•
					Assessment Program para hispanohablantes, pp. 47–53	•		•	•
					Audio Program, Cap. 2A, Examen	•		•	
					ExamView: Test Banks A and B questions only online	•		•	
					Heritage Learner Test Bank	•		•	
					Pre-AP* Test Bank	•		•	

DAY	REGULAR SCHEDULE (50 MINUTES)		
	Warm-up / Assess	**Preview / Present / Practice / Communicate**	**Wrap-up / Homework Options**
1	**Warm-up** (10 min.) • Return Examen del capítulo 1B	**Chapter Opener** (5 min.) • Objectives • Arte y cultura **Vocabulario en contexto** (30 min.) • Presentation: Vocabulario en contexto • Actividades 1, 2	**Wrap-up and Homework Options** (5 min.) • Core Practice 2A-1, 2A-2
2	**Warm-up** (5 min.) • Homework check	**Vocabulario en contexto** (40 min.) • Presentation: Videohistoria *El primer día de clases* • View: Videohistoria • Video Activities 1, 2, 3, 4 • Actividad 3	**Wrap-up and Homework Options** (5 min.) • Core Practice 2A-3, 2A-4 • Prueba 2A-1: Vocabulary recognition
3	**Warm-up** (10 min.) • Actividades 4, 5 • Homework check ✓**Formative Assessment** (10 min.) • Prueba 2A-1: Vocabulary recognition	**Vocabulario en uso** (25 min.) • Interactive Whiteboard Vocabulary Activities • *Actividades* 6, 7, 8, 9 • Fondo cultural • Audio Activities 5, 6	**Wrap-up and Homework Options** (5 min.) • Writing Activity 10 • Prueba 2A-2 with Study Plan: Vocabulary production
4	**Warm-up** (10 min.) • Communicative Pair Activity • Homework check ✓**Formative Assessment** (10 min.) • Prueba 2A-2 with Study Plan: Vocabulary production	**Gramática y vocabulario en uso** (25 min.) • Exploración del lenguaje • Fondo cultural • Presentation: Subject pronouns • View: GramActiva Video • Interactive Whiteboard Grammar Activities • Actividades 10, 12 • Audio Activity 7	**Wrap-up and Homework Options** (5 min.) • Core Practice 2A-5 • Actividad 11 • Prueba 2A-3 with Study Plan: Subject pronouns
5	**Warm-up** (10 min.) • Writing Activity 11 • Homework check ✓**Formative Assessment** (10 min.) • Prueba 2A-3 with Study Plan: Subject pronouns	**Gramática y vocabulario en uso** (25 min.) • Presentation: Present tense of ***-ar*** verbs • View: GramActiva video • Interactive Whiteboard Grammar Activities • Actividades 13, 14, 15 • Audio Activities 8, 9	**Wrap-up and Homework Options** (5 min.) • Core Practice 2A-6, 2A-7
6	**Warm-up** (15 min.) • Writing Activities 12, 13 • Homework check	**Gramática y vocabulario en uso** (30 min.) • Communicative Pair Activity • Actividades 16, 17, 18, 19 • Fondo cultural	**Wrap-up and Homework Options** (5 min.) • Prueba 2A-4 with Study Plan: Present tense of ***-ar*** verbs
7	**Warm-up** (5 min.) • Review ***-ar*** verbs ✓**Formative Assessment** (10 min.) • Prueba 2A-4 with Study Plan: Present tense of ***-ar*** verbs	**Gramática y vocabulario en uso** (15 min.) • Actividades 20, 21 • Pronunciación • El español en la comunidad **¡Adelante!** (15 min.) • Lectura • ¿Comprendes? • Fondo cultural	**Wrap-up and Homework Options** (5 min.) • El mundo hispano • Lectura, El mundo hispano
8	**Warm-up** (10 min.) • Homework check	**¡Adelante!** (35 min.) • La cultura en vivo • Presentación oral: Step 1 • Situation Cards • Communicative Pair Activities	**Wrap-up and Homework Options** (5 min.) • Presentación oral: Step 2 • Preparación para el examen 3, 4, 5
9	**Warm-up** (5 min.) • Homework check	**¡Adelante!** (30 min.) • Presentación oral: Step 3 **Repaso del capítulo** (10 min.) • Vocabulario y gramática • Preparación para el examen 1, 2	**Wrap-up and Homework Options** (5 min.) • Core Practice 2A-8, 2A-9 • Instant check • Examen del capítulo 2A
10	**Warm-up** (10 min.) • Homework check ✓**Summative Assessment** (40 min.) • Examen del capítulo 2A		

DAY	BLOCK SCHEDULE (90 MINUTES)		
	Warm-up / Assess	**Preview / Present / Practice / Communicate**	**Wrap-up / Homework Options**
1	**Warm-up** (10 min.) • Return Examen del capítulo 1B	**Chapter Opener** (5 min.) • Objectives • Arte y cultura **Vocabulario en contexto** (60 min.) • Presentation: Vocabulario en contexto • Actividades 1, 2 • Presentation: Videohistoria *El primer día de clases* • View: Videohistoria • Video Activities 1, 2, 3, 4 • Actividad 3 **Vocabulario en uso** (10 min.) • Actividad 6 • Fondo cultural • Interactive Whiteboard Vocabulary Activities	**Wrap-up and Homework Options** (5 min.) • Core Practice 2A-1, 2A-2, 2A-3, 2A-4 • Prueba 2A-1: Vocabulary recognition
2	**Warm-up** (10 min.) • Actividades 4, 5 • Homework check ✔**Formative Assessment** (10 min.) • Prueba 2A-1: Vocabulary recognition	**Gramática y vocabulario en uso** (65 min.) • Actividades 7, 8, 9 • Audio Activities 5, 6 • Writing Activity 10 • Exploración del lenguaje • Fondo cultural • Presentation: Subject pronouns • View: GramActiva video • Interactive Whiteboard Grammar Activities • Actividades 10, 11, 12 • Audio Activity 7	**Wrap-up and Homework Options** (5 min.) • Core Practice 2A-5 • Actividad 11 • Prueba 2A-2 with Study Plan: Vocabulary production
3	**Warm-up** (5 min.) • Communicative Pair Activity • Homework check ✔**Formative Assessment** (10 min.) • Prueba 2A-2 with Study Plan: Vocabulary production	**Gramática y vocabulario en uso** (70 min.) • Presentation: Present tense of ***-ar*** verbs • View: GramActiva video • Interactive Whiteboard Grammar Activities • Actividades 13, 14, 15 • Audio Activities 8, 9 • Writing Activities 11, 12, 13	**Wrap-up and Homework Options** (5 min.) • Core Practice 2A-6, 2A-7 • Pruebas 2A-3, 2A-4 with Study Plans: Subject pronouns, Present tense of ***-ar*** verbs
4	**Warm-up** (10 min.) • Homework check ✔**Formative Assessment** (15 min.) • Pruebas 2A-3, 2A-4 with Study Plans: Subject pronouns, Present tense of ***-ar*** verbs	**Gramática y vocabulario en uso** (35 min.) • Communicative Pair Activity • Actividades 16, 17, 18, 19 • Fondo cultural • Actividades 20, 21 • Pronunciación • El español en la comunidad **¡Adelante!** (25 min.) • Lectura • ¿Comprendes? • Fondo cultural • Presentación oral: Step 1	**Wrap-up and Homework Options** (5 min.) • El mundo hispano • Presentación oral: Step 2
5	**Warm-up** (5 min.) • Homework check	**¡Adelante!** (50 min.) • La cultura en vivo • Situation Cards • Communicative Pair Activities • Presentación oral: Step 3 **Repaso del capítulo** (30 min.) • Vocabulario y gramática • Preparación para el examen 1, 2, 3, 4, 5	**Wrap-up and Homework Options** (5 min.) • Core Practice 2A-8, 2A-9 • Instant check • Examen del capítulo 2A
6	**Warm-up** (15 min.) • Homework check • Answer questions **Repaso del capítulo** (25 min.) ✔**Summative Assessment** (45 min.) • Examen del capítulo 2A		**Wrap-up and Homework Options** (5 min.) • Lectura

Capítulo

2A Tu día en la escuela

Standards for *Capítulo* 2A

- To achieve the goals of the Standards, students will:

Communication

1.1 Interpersonal
- Talk about: homework and classes; preferences in school subjects; preferences in activities; people and schedules at school

1.2 Interpretive
- Listen to information: on school subjects, schedules, supplies; about the present tense of ***-ar*** verbs; about activities during ***recreo***
- Read: a picture-based story; information about school subjects, schedules, supplies; information about a language school in Costa Rica
- Listen to and watch a video about school schedules
- Listen to the use of subject pronouns

1.3 Presentational
- Present information about: work, home, and school activities; school subjects, schedules, supplies
- Present school cheers like those in Spanish-speaking countries

Culture

2.1 Practices and Perspectives
- Explain the focus on English language acquisition in Spanish-speaking countries
- Talk about: school sporting event celebrations and traditions; leisure time during school hours
- Explain the concept of Sunday "family time" in Mexico

2.2 Products and Perspectives
- Discuss Fernando Botero and his painting
- Read and talk about school cheers
- Discuss traditional dances of Mexico

Connections

3.1 Cross-curricular
- Discuss Fernando Botero; migration patterns of monarch butterflies
- Build vocabulary through an understanding of mathematics
- Explain influences of Roman Empire history on Spain; similarities between Mayan numbering system and Roman numerals; the impact Spanish exploration had on the Maya

3.2 Target Culture
- Read and recite school cheers

Comparisons

4.1 Language
- Talk about new vocabulary through the recognition of cognates; the present tense of ***-ar*** verbs
- Compare personalized school-related vocabulary
- Explain the use of subject pronouns; the pronunciation of the letter ***c***

4.2 Culture
- Compare: motivations for foreign language learning; leisure periods during the school day; the use of the 24-hour clock to the 12-hour clock; school cheers and sporting event celebrations

Communities

5.1 Beyond the School
- Discuss why English-speakers in the community are interested in learning Spanish

Chapter Objectives

Communication

By the end of this chapter you will be able to:
- Listen to and read descriptions of school subjects and schedules
- Talk and write about classes, school activities, and likes and dislikes
- Exchange information while explaining what classes and activities you and friends have in common

Culture

You will also be able to:
- Compare your school day with those of students in Spanish-speaking countries
- Compare sports and attitudes towards sports in the Spanish-speaking world and the United States

You will demonstrate what you know and can do:
- Presentación oral, p. 93
- Preparación para el examen, p. 97

You will use:

Vocabulary
- School subjects and schedules
- School supplies
- Class descriptions

Grammar
- Subject pronouns
- Present tense of *-ar* verbs

Exploración del mundo hispano

Country Connection
Your Day at School

realidades.com GO

Reference Atlas

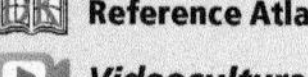
Videocultura y actividad

Mapa global interactivo

Unos estudiantes, San Cristóbal de las Casas, México

ENRICH YOUR TEACHING

Using Backward Design

Have students preview the sample performance tasks on *Preparación para el examen,* p. 97, and connect them to the Chapter Objectives. Explain to students that by completing the sample tasks they can self-assess their learning progress.

Mapa global interactivo

Download the *Mapa global interactivo* files for Chapter 2A and preview the activities. In Activity 1, you visit Segovia, Spain. Activity 2 takes you to Costa Rica, and Activity 3 explores the canals of Xochimilco in Ciudad de México.

Arte y cultura | Colombia

Colombian artist Fernando Botero (1932–) is among the best known and most respected Latin American artists. His works have been exhibited around the world in prestigious museums, galleries, and open-air places. Botero's style is unique and recognizable. Pedrito Botero, shown in the painting, was the artist's son. He died in a car accident when he was four years old.

- Based upon the painting, how could you describe Botero's style?

"Pedrito" (1997), Fernando Botero ▶

PresentationExpress™
See pp. 72c–72d

Chapter Opener

Core Instruction

Resources: Map Transparencies 12–13, 15, 18

Suggestions: Introduce students to the theme of the chapter, school schedules, and subjects by discussing what their school day is like now. Ask students to predict what some of the vocabulary words may be, based on the context. Help students locate the countries featured in the chapter by using the map transparencies.

Videocultura View *Los uniformes escolares* with the class to learn more about different types of uniforms.

Arte y cultura

Standards: 2.2, 3.1

Resources: Fine Art Transparencies with Teacher's Guide, p. 7

Suggestions: Discuss the style in which the artist depicted the child in the painting. You may want to comment on the title of the work, *Pedrito,* and ask students if they notice anything interesting or strange about the proportions of the child: the face, the neck, and the hands.

Answers will vary but may include adjectives such as *strange* or *unrealistic.*

TEACHING WITH ART

Resources: Fine Art Transparencies, p. 7

Suggestions: Remind students that not all artists want to recreate an image exactly. You may wish to give examples of other artists who distort reality, such as Salvador Dalí, Pablo Picasso, or Joan Miró.

DIFFERENTIATED INSTRUCTION

Digital resources such as the ***Interactive Whiteboard*** activity banks, ***Videomodelos***, additional ***Online Activities, Study Plans***, automatically graded ***Leveled Workbook***, animated ***Grammar Tutorials, Flashcards***, and ***Vocabulary and Grammar Videos*** will help you reach students of different ability levels and learning styles.

STUDENTS NEEDING EXTRA HELP

Guided Practice Activities
- Flashcards, pp. 53–58
- Vocabulary Check, pp. 59–62
- Grammar Support, pp. 63–66

HERITAGE LEARNERS

Realidades para hispanohablantes
- Chapter Opener, pp. 50–51
- A primera vista, p. 52
- Videohistoria, p. 53
- Manos a la obra, pp. 54–61
- ¡Adelante!, pp. 62–67
- Repaso del capítulo, pp. 68–69

ADVANCED/PRE-AP*

Pre-AP* Resource Book,
- pp. 66–69

Communications Workbook
- Integrated Performance Assessment, p. 241

Vocabulario en contexto

Core Instruction

Standards: 1.2

Resources: Teacher's Resource Book: Input Script, p. 114, Clip Art, pp. 126–127, Audio Script, p. 115; Voc. and Gram. Transparencies 48–49; TPR Stories, pp. 29–36; Audio Program DVD: Cap. 2A, Tracks 1–2

Focus: Presenting new vocabulary for school subjects, school schedules, school supplies, adjectives

Suggestions: Use the story in the *TPR Stories Book* or the Input Script from the *Teacher's Resource Book* to present the new vocabulary and grammar. Using the transparencies, ask students to describe the schedule they see by answering short questions. (Example: *¿Alicia tiene ciencias sociales o matemáticas en la tercera hora?*) Borrow from fellow teachers textbooks or other items associated with their disciplines and use these objects in your presentation. Arrange them in piles corresponding to different class periods, and tell what classes you have in each period. Then switch the order, and have students tell you in what order the classes fall. Play ***Lotería del horario.*** Give students blank versions of the school schedule shown. Allow them to fill in the schedule with classes however they wish. Call out a class period and a course name. Students mark off the classes as you call them. The first to completely mark a schedule calls out: *¡Tengo mi horario!*

BELLRINGER REVIEW

Review telling time by dictating several clock times. Ask that one student work at the board for confirmation.

Objectives

Read, listen to, and understand information about
- the school day
- subjects and classes
- school supplies

Vocabulario en contexto

El horario de Alicia

"Me gusta mucho mi **horario. En la primera hora, tengo** la **clase de** tecnología . . . ¡es mi clase **favorita!** Es **interesante** y **práctica.** Pero a veces es **difícil**".

primera hora		tecnología
segunda hora		arte
tercera hora		ciencias sociales
cuarta hora		ciencias naturales
quinta hora	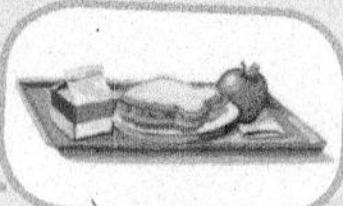	el almuerzo
sexta hora		español
séptima hora		matemáticas
octava hora		inglés
novena hora		educación física

Más vocabulario

décimo, -a — tenth

DIFFERENTIATED INSTRUCTION

Advanced Learners/Pre-AP*

Have students prepare a schedule of their classes like the one above. Have them put their teachers' names under each subject, using ***Profesor*** + (name) and ***Profesora*** + (name). Ask students to write three sentences under their schedule: *Mi clase favorita es* (subject); (Subject) *es difícil;* (Subject) *es fácil.*

Students with Learning Difficulties

Have students write new words into the vocabulary section of their notebooks and encourage them to accompany each with a picture if possible. Have students look at *El horario de Alicia* on p. 74 while they listen to *Actividades* 1 and 2.

“Tengo **mucha tarea** en la clase de inglés”.

“**Estudio** mucho en la clase de español. Para mí, la clase de español es **más** interesante **que** la clase de matemáticas”.

“**Para** la clase de matemáticas **necesito una calculadora** y **una carpeta de argollas**”.

“Para la clase de español necesito **un diccionario**”.

1 ¿Sí o no?

Escuchar

You will hear Alicia make several statements about her school day and schedule. Give a "thumbs-up" sign if what she says is true or a "thumbs-down" sign if what she says is false.

2 El horario de Alicia

Escuchar

Listen to Alicia as she describes her class schedule. Touch the picture of each class as you hear it.

Más práctica GO

	realidades.com	print
Instant Check	✔	
Guided WB pp. 53–58	✔	✔
Core WB pp. 31–32	✔	✔
Comm. WB p. 35	✔	✔
***Hispanohablantes* WB** p. 52		✔

ENRICH YOUR TEACHING

Culture Note

Explain to students that in some parts of Latin America students begin classes at 7 A.M. in order to end the day at 1 or 2 P.M. so they can go home for lunch. Lunch is the main meal of the day, and family members often gather to eat at home.

Teacher-to-Teacher

A great way to get students on task at the beginning of the class is to put a short, written exercise on an overhead transparency. Stand at the door as students enter and hand them papers with questions, so they can begin immediately. Set a time limit, and take attendance or collect homework while students work.

1 Standards: 1.2, 4.1

Resources: Teacher's Resource Book: Audio Script, p. 115; Audio Program DVD: Cap. 2A, Track 3; Answer Keys: Student Edition, p. 24

Focus: Listening to statements about the school day and schedule

Suggestions: Play the audio or read the script to the class. Allow students to listen more than once. Remind students that they should respond based on Alicia's statements about her classes on pp. 74–75.

Script and Answers:

1. **Estudio mucho en la clase de español.** ***(thumbs-up)***
2. **Mi clase favorita es la clase de tecnología.** ***(thumbs-up)***
3. **La clase de tecnología es fácil.** ***(thumbs-down)***
4. **Tengo mucha tarea en la clase de inglés.** ***(thumbs-up)***
5. **Para la clase de español necesito una calculadora.** ***(thumbs-down)***
6. **¡No me gusta nada mi horario!** ***(thumbs-down)***

2 Standards: 1.2, 4.1

Resources: Teacher's Resource Book: Audio Script, p. 115; Audio Program DVD: Cap. 2A, Track 4; Answer Keys: Student Edition, p. 24

Focus: Listening to understand contextualized vocabulary about the school schedule

Suggestions: Use the audio or read the script aloud. Pause in between descriptions to verify that students are indicating the correct picture.

Script and Answers:

Tengo ocho clases.

1. **Mi clase favorita, la clase de tecnología, es en la primera hora.** ***(computer)***
2. **La clase de español es en la sexta hora.** ***(Spanish textbook)***
3. **La clase de educación física es en la novena hora.** ***(athletic shoes)***
4. **La clase de matemáticas es en la séptima hora.** ***(math book)***
5. **La clase de arte es en la segunda hora.** ***(palette and brushes)***
6. **La clase de ciencias sociales es en la tercera hora.** ***("El Mundo" book)***
7. **La clase de inglés es en la octava hora.** ***(English literature book)***
8. **Y la clase de ciencias naturales es en la cuarta hora.** ***(microscope)***
9. **En la quinta hora tengo el almuerzo.** ***(tray of food)***

Videohistoria

Core Instruction

Standards: 1.2

Resources: Voc. and Gram. Transparencies 50–51; Audio Program DVD: Cap. 2A, Track 5

Focus: Presenting additional contextualized vocabulary and grammar; previewing the language video

Suggestions:

Pre-reading: Point out the *Strategy* to the class. Have a student answer the question, guessing what ***enseña*** means with the help of the context. Then have students close their books and look at the transparencies. Go panel by panel and ask students to predict what is going to happen.

Reading: Use the audio and have students follow along in their books. Pause after each panel to check comprehension.

Post-reading: Complete *Actividad* 3 to check comprehension.

Video

Core Instruction

Standards: 1.2

Resources: Teacher's Resource Book: Video Script, p. 118; Video Program: Cap. 2A; Video Program Teacher's Guide: Cap. 2A

Focus: Hearing the new vocabulary in context

Suggestions:

Pre-viewing: Remind students that they will not understand every word in the video, but that they should listen and watch for overall understanding.

Viewing: Show the video once without pausing. Show it again, stopping along the way to check comprehension. You may wish to show the segment a final time without pausing.

Post-viewing: Complete the Video Activities in the *Communication Workbook*.

El primer día de clases

Es el primer día de clases en la Escuela Bilingüe en la Ciudad de México.

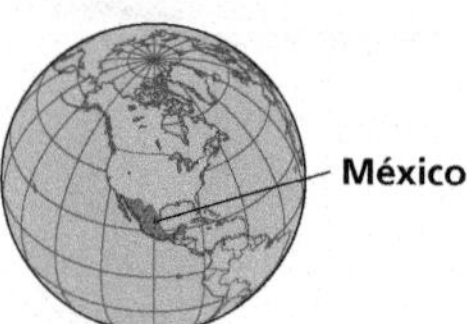

Strategy

Using context clues
You can often guess the meaning of new words by reading the words around them and understanding what the rest of the sentence or paragraph is about.

- Based on the words around it, what does *enseña* mean in Panel 2?

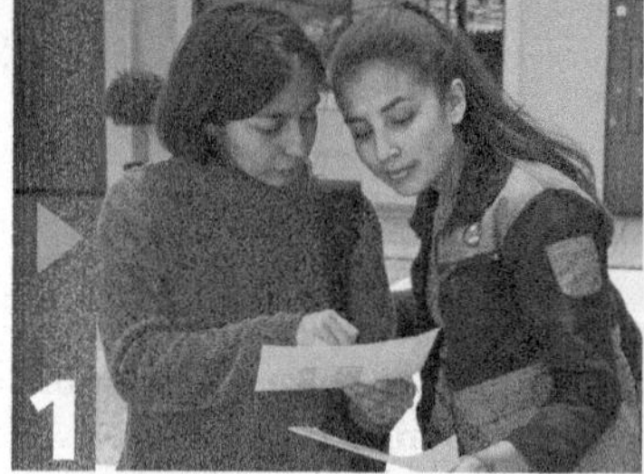

Claudia: Teresa, ¿qué clase **tienes** en la primera hora?

Teresa: Tengo la clase de inglés.

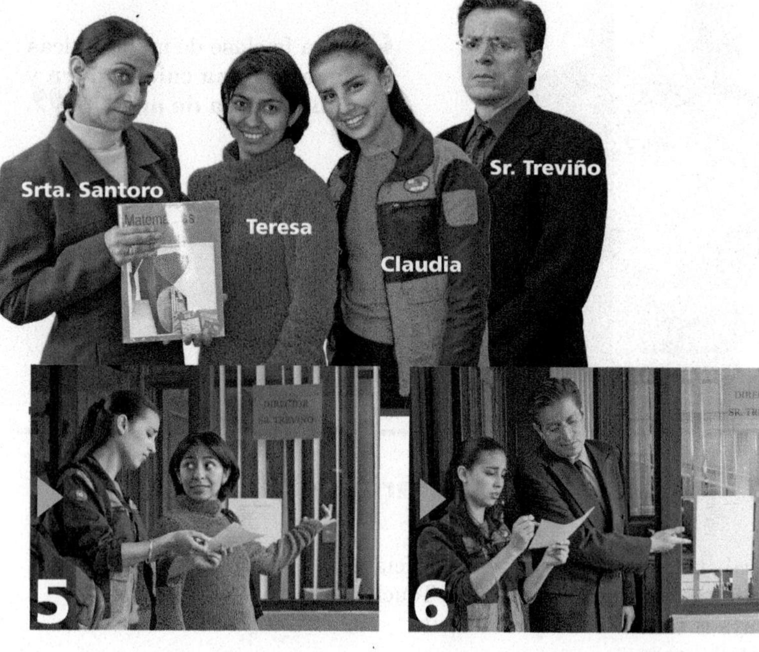

Teresa: **Necesitas hablar** con el señor Treviño, en la oficina.

Claudia: Buena idea.

Claudia: Buenos días, señor Treviño. Necesito hablar con Ud. Tengo la clase de matemáticas . . .

Sr. Treviño: Sí, sí, Claudia, pero ahora no es posible. Mañana.

Srta. Santoro: Buenos días, estudiantes. Las matemáticas son muy interesantes y prácticas, ¿verdad?

Estudiantes: Sí, profesora.

Srta. Santoro: Y es muy importante **estudiar** y trabajar mucho . . .

DIFFERENTIATED INSTRUCTION

Heritage Language Learners

Have students write a letter to an imaginary friend telling about the first day of school. Then have students exchange letters and answer them. When reading and reviewing students' letters, discuss any necessary strategies for improving their writing skills.

Multiple Intelligences

Interpersonal/Social: Have students prepare a short survey to interview their classmates about their opinions on each class. Suggest that they use the words ***interesante, divertida, aburrida, práctica, fácil,*** and ***difícil*** as categories. Have them present the results in a chart, with the adjectives going down the left side and the names of classes going across the top.

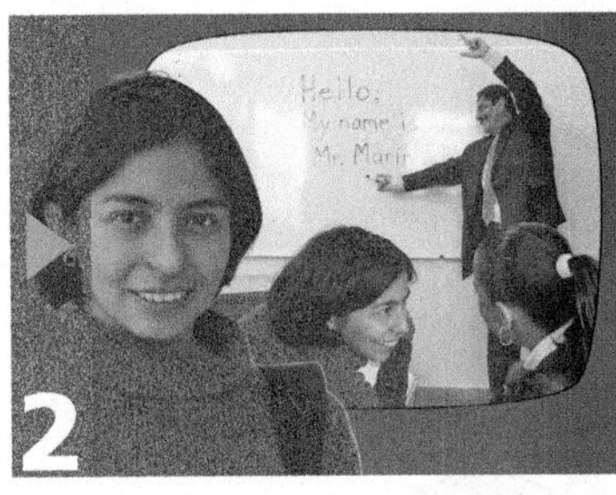

Claudia: **¿Quién enseña** la clase de inglés?

Teresa: El señor Marín. Es un profesor muy **divertido.** ¿Y tú? ¿Qué clase tienes en la primera hora?

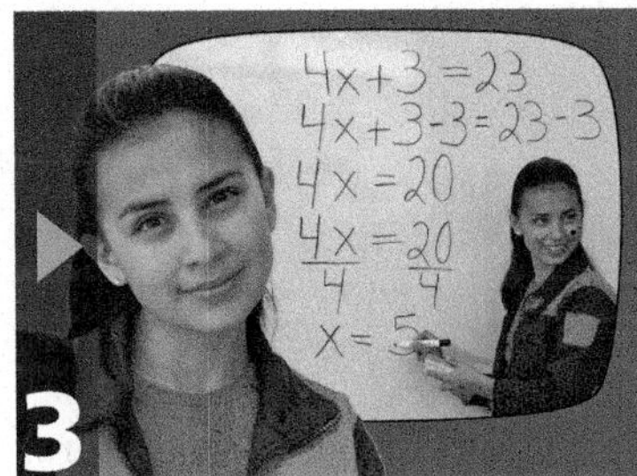

Claudia: Tengo la clase de matemáticas. Me gusta mucho. Para mí es muy **fácil.** Y, ¿qué tienes en la segunda hora?

Teresa: La clase de educación física.

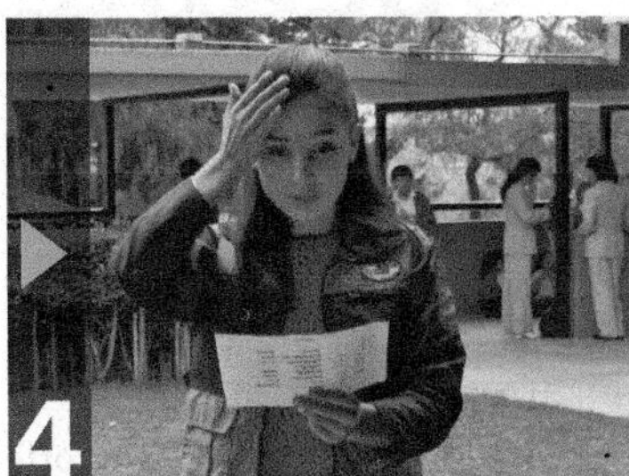

Teresa: Y en la segunda hora, ¿qué clase tienes, Claudia?

Claudia: **A ver . . .** En la segunda hora, tengo la clase de matemáticas. ¡Y también tengo la clase de matemáticas en la tercera, en la cuarta, en la quinta y en la sexta hora!

Srta. Santoro: ¿Claudia?

Claudia: ¡Tengo seis clases de matemáticas hoy!

Srta. Santoro: ¡Seis! Es **aburrido,** ¿no? . . .

3 ¿Comprendes?

Leer • Escribir

Read each sentence. Write *sí* if it is correct or *no* if it is incorrect.

1. Es el primer día de clases.
2. A Teresa le gusta la clase de inglés.
3. Para Claudia, la clase de matemáticas es difícil.
4. Claudia tiene la clase de educación física en la segunda hora.
5. Según la profesora, la clase de matemáticas es muy práctica.
6. En la sexta hora la clase de matemáticas es interesante.

Más práctica GO

realidades.com | print

	realidades.com	print
Instant Check	✔	
Guided WB pp. 59–62	✔	✔
Core WB pp. 33–34	✔	✔
Comm.WB pp. 29–30, 31	✔	✔
Hispanohablantes WB p. 53		✔

3 Standards: 1.2, 1.3

Resources: Answer Keys: Student Edition, p. 24

Focus: Reading and writing to verify comprehension of the *Videohistoria*

Suggestions: Have different students read each statement to the class. When you call on students, ask them to give you the number of the panel in which the information for their answer is presented.

Answers:

1. sí
2. sí
3. no
4. no
5. sí
6. no

Extension: Have students write or say the correct answer for the sentences that were incorrect.

Pre-AP* Support

- **Learning Objective:** Presentational Writing and Speaking
- **Activity:** As a post-viewing activity, have pairs of students rewrite the second and third frames of the story, using the names of their own teachers, classes, and opinions about them in the script. Then, have them act out their new versions of the scene in front of the class.
- ***Pre-AP* Resource Book:*** Comprehensive guide to Pre-AP* vocabulary skill development, pp. 51–57

Additional Resources

- Communication: Audio Act. 5, p. 31
- Teacher's Resource Book: Audio Script, pp. 115–116
- Audio Program DVD: Cap. 2A, Track 6

ENRICH YOUR TEACHING

Teacher-to-Teacher

Have each student write one school-related question such as *¿Qué tienes en la tercera hora?* on a small piece of paper. Put all the papers in a grab bag. Go around the room and have students pull out a question, read it, and call on a classmate to answer. The student who answers picks the next question.

21st Century Skills

Social and Cross-Cultural Skills After students read the captions and are familiar with the story, have them watch the *Videohistoria* in small groups and then discuss together any differences and similarities they see between their school and the school portrayed in the video.

ASSESSMENT

Quiz: Vocabulary Recognition

- Prueba 2A-1: pp. 41–42

INTERACTIVE WHITEBOARD
Vocabulary Activities 2A

4 Standards: 1.2, 1.3, 4.1

Resources: Voc. and Gram. Transparency 55; Answer Keys: Student Edition, p. 25

Focus: Reading and writing about a school schedule in Mexico

Suggestions: Have students review class names, and ask about those they cannot identify. Point out that "the arts" may refer to more than art class: the term includes performing as well as visual arts. Ask specific questions about word meanings, such as ***artes plásticas*** and ***semanales.*** Remind students to use strategies such as prior knowledge and cognate identification.

Answers:

1. **once**
2. **tres horas**
3. **dos—historia universal y educación cívica y ética**
4. **dos—biología e introducción a la física**
5. **danza, teatro, artes plásticas, música**

Extension: Have students design their own list of classes based on Ignacio's. Suggest that they total up the number of hours they spend on each subject. You will need to supply names for some classes. Discuss which classes are important, practical, fun, and interesting.

BELLRINGER REVIEW

Have students work in pairs to tell each other the names of their teachers using *Sr., Sra.,* and *Srta.* as well as what they teach.

5 Standards: 1.3

Focus: Writing about a class schedule in a personalized context

Suggestions: Point out the *¿Recuerdas?* Write the names of several teachers in your school with the appropriate titles, for example: ***el Sr. Hassan, la Srta. Chung, la Sra. McGuire.***

Answers will vary.

Manos a la obra

Vocabulario en uso

Objectives

- Read and write about school subjects and schedules
- Discuss and compare classes and opinions about school

4 Un horario

Leer • Escribir

Read the list of classes offered at a high school in Querétaro, Mexico. This school has a special focus on the arts. Answer the questions about the schedule.

CENTRO DE EDUCACIÓN ARTÍSTICA 
"IGNACIO MARIANO DE LAS CASAS"

PRIMER SEMESTRE	
Español	5 h semanales
Matemáticas	5 h semanales
Historia universal	3 h semanales
Educación cívica y ética	3 h semanales
Biología	3 h semanales
Introducción a la física	3 h semanales
Inglés	3 h semanales
Danza	3 h semanales
Teatro	3 h semanales
Artes plásticas	3 h semanales
Música	3 h semanales
	Total 37 h semanales

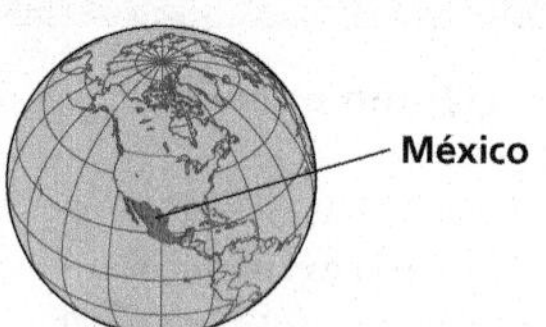

1. ¿Cuántas clases hay cada *(each)* semana?
2. ¿Cuántas horas de inglés hay?
3. ¿Cuántas clases de ciencias sociales hay?
4. ¿Cuántas clases de ciencias naturales hay?
5. Escribe los nombres de las diferentes clases de arte.

5 Mi horario

Escribir

Write out your class schedule. Copy the chart and provide the information for each class.

Modelo

Hora	Clase	Profesor(a)
la primera hora	la clase de inglés	la Sra. Sánchez

¿Recuerdas?

Use *señor, señora,* and *señorita* when talking **to** adults. Use *el* in front of *señor* and *la* in front of *señora* or *señorita* when talking **about** adults.

DIFFERENTIATED INSTRUCTION

Heritage Language Learners

If students have attended school in other countries, ask them to describe any different scheduling and grading procedures. They may mention rotating schedules with different classes each day, and grading with numbers instead of letters. You may wish to discuss these differences with the rest of the class.

Students with Learning Difficulties

When practicing reading comprehension, as in *Actividad* 5, allow students with learning difficulties extra time to use the variety of reading strategies that are accessible. Comprehension may require two or three attempts at reading the questions and text.

6 Mucha tarea | 

Hablar

With a partner, ask and tell if you have a lot of homework in each class.

Modelo

A —*¿Tienes mucha tarea en la clase de matemáticas?*
B —*Sí, tengo mucha tarea.*
o: —*No, no tengo mucha tarea.*
o: —*No estudio matemáticas.*

Estudiante A

Estudiante B

¡Respuesta personal!

7 Me gusta más . . .

Escribir

Write sentences stating which of the two classes you like better and why. Use the list of adjectives to help with your response. Save your paper for Actividad 8.

aburrida	divertida	interesante
difícil	fácil	práctica

Modelo

inglés/español
Me gusta más la clase de español. Es divertida.
o: *Me gusta más la clase de español. No es aburrida.*
o: *No me gusta ni la clase de español ni la clase de inglés.*

1. inglés / español
2. arte / educación física
3. inglés / matemáticas
4. ciencias sociales / ciencias naturales
5. tecnología / música
6. matemáticas / ciencias sociales

Practice and Communicate 2A

6 Standards: 1.1

Resources: Answer Keys: Student Edition, p. 25

Focus: Speaking about homework in a personalized context

Suggestions: Briefly review which subject each object represents. Have volunteers read the model and be sure students understand their options. Have them take turns being Student A and Student B.

Suggestions: Student A:
1. **¿Tienes mucha tarea en la clase de español?**
2. **¿ ... en la clase de inglés?**
3. **¿ ... en la clase de tecnología?**
4. **¿ ... en la clase de ciencias naturales?**
5. **¿ ... en la clase de arte?**
6. **¿ ... en la clase de educación física?**
7. **¿ ... en la clase de ciencias sociales?**

Student B: Answers will vary.

Common Errors: Students often have trouble understanding that ***mucho(a)*** is an adjective and must agree with the noun that follows it. Remind students that ***tarea*** is feminine; they should say ***mucha tarea,*** not ***mucho tarea.***

7 Standards: 1.3

Focus: Writing and comparing class preferences in a personalized context

Suggestions: If students do not take all the classes listed, suggest alternatives. Remind students to save their answers to use in *Actividad* 8.

Answers will vary.

Extension: For homework, have students rewrite their opinions, this time comparing both classes. Provide a model to copy onto their papers. The sentences should be simple, for example: *La clase de inglés es divertida, pero la clase de español es difícil.*

ENRICH YOUR TEACHING

Culture Note

In Spanish-speaking countries, students often address teachers by their title to show respect: for example, ***Profesor Rodríguez, Profesora Millán,*** or simply ***Profesor(a).*** Occasionally, students will address their teacher as ***profe,*** short for ***profesor(a).*** Students in Spain, however, may actually call teachers by their first names.

Teacher-to-Teacher

When students see the words *¡Respuesta personal!* in an activity, encourage them to create phrases beyond what the model suggests.

8 Standards: 1.1

Resources: Answer Keys: Student Edition, p. 26

Focus: Making comparisons using ***más...que***

Suggestions: Remind students to use the information from *Actividad* 7. Point out that instead of using ***me gusta*** in the response, they will use ***es más*** (adjective) ***que*** to explain why they prefer one class to another.

Answers: Student A:

1. **¿Te gusta más la clase de inglés o la clase de español?**
2. **¿ ... la clase de arte o la clase de educación física?**
3. **¿ ... la clase de inglés o la clase de matemáticas?**
4. **¿ ... la clase de ciencias sociales o la clase de ciencias naturales?**
5. **¿ ... la clase de tecnología o la clase de música?**
6. **¿ ... la clase de matemáticas o la clase de ciencias sociales?**

Student B: Answers will vary.

9 Standards: 1.1, 1.3

Focus: Writing and speaking in a personalized context

Suggestions: You may want to have students answer the questions in paragraph format, with the title *Mi clase favorita*.

Answers will vary.

Fondo cultural

Standards: 2.1, 4.2

Suggestions: Tell students that throughout the Spanish-speaking world, learning English is important to success both in school and at work. Students begin to learn English at an early age and by middle school are often quite competent.

Answers will vary.

Additional Resources

- Communication: Audio Act. 6, p. 31
- Teacher's Resource Book: Audio Script, p. 116, Communicative Pair Activity BLM, pp. 120–121
- Audio Program DVD: Cap. 2A, Track 7

8 ¿Qué te gusta más?  

Hablar

With a partner, ask and tell which classes from Actividad 7 you like best and why.

 **Modelo**

A —*¿Te gusta más la clase de inglés o la clase de español?*
B —*A ver . . . Para mí, la clase de español es más divertida que la clase de inglés.*

9 Y tú, ¿qué dices?

Escribir • Hablar

1. ¿Qué clase te gusta más?
2. ¿Cómo es la clase?
3. ¿En qué hora tienes la clase?
4. ¿Quién enseña la clase?
5. ¿Tienes mucha tarea en la clase?

Fondo Cultural | El mundo hispano

Studying English While you're in Spanish class at your school, large numbers of Spanish-speaking students are studying to learn the most popular foreign language worldwide: English. Many children begin to study English in grade school and continue through high school. They often attend a special language school for additional English classes. When visiting a Spanish-speaking country, you might easily find someone who is eager to practice his or her English skills with you in exchange for helping you improve your Spanish.

- Why do you think English is so popular in other countries? Are you studying Spanish for similar reasons?

Estudiantes mexicanos en una clase de inglés

DIFFERENTIATED INSTRUCTION

Heritage Language Learners

Have students compare English and Spanish. Do the languages seem closely related? What specific structures in English are different in Spanish? What expressions are difficult to remember? Follow up your comments with a whole-class discussion on some of the challenges and rewards of learning a second language.

Advanced Learners/Pre-AP*

Assign students a Spanish-speaking country and ask them to use the Internet to find information about the education system in that country. Suggest that they include details such as the format and size of schools, subjects offered, and languages of instruction. Have them share their findings with the class.

Exploración del lenguaje

Connections between Latin, English, and Spanish

Many words in English and Spanish are based on Latin. Seeing the relationship between these words will help expand your English or Spanish vocabulary. Look at the list of Latin root forms for the numbers 1 to 10.

Try it out! For each Roman numeral listed, choose one of the root forms (if more than one is listed) and write down a Spanish or English word you know that is based on that root.

Try it out! The Roman year used to begin with the month of March. Knowing that, can you explain why *septiembre, octubre, noviembre,* and *diciembre* use the Latin root forms for seven, eight, nine, and ten?

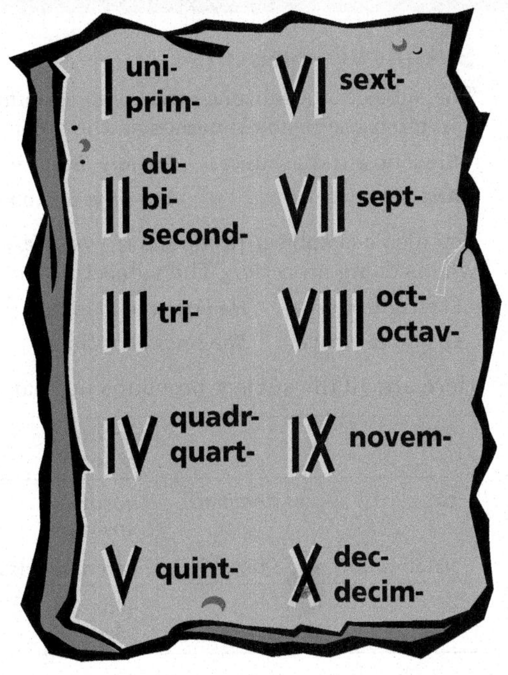

Fondo cultural | España

Many Spanish words are derived from Latin because Spain was once part of the Roman Empire. Rome occupied most of Spain from about 209 B.C. to 586 A.D. During that time, massive public structures, including aqueducts and theaters, were built. Some of these, such as the aqueduct that towers over the modern city of Segovia, are still standing. The Latin name for Spain was *Hispania*.

- Can you see the similarity between *Hispania* and the country's name in Spanish, *España?*

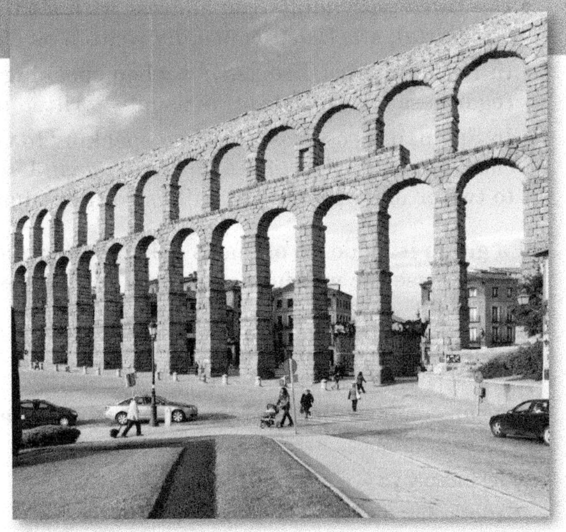

El Acueducto de Segovia

Practice and Communicate 2A

Exploración del lenguaje

Core Instruction

Standards: 3.1

Suggestions: To extend the second *Try it out!*, ask students to come up with other words in English or Spanish that use the roots *sept-, oct-, nov-, dic-* or *dec-*. Have students share their answers with the class.

Answers may include: **unisex, primary, dual, bicycle, secondary, tricycle, quadrant, quarter, quintuplets, sexto, September, *séptimo*, octagon, *octavo*, octave, November, decade, decimal; these months were named using ordinals, so September, October, November, and December were the seventh, eighth, ninth, and tenth months, respectively.**

Fondo cultural

Standards: 3.1

Suggestions: Point out that the historical connection between Rome and Spain goes beyond language. Some of Rome's most successful leaders came from Spain, for example, Trajan (98–117 A.D.)

Mapa global interactivo, Actividad 1 Locate the Roman aqueduct in Segovia, Spain.

Pre-AP* Support

- **Learning Objective:** Interpretive: Print
- **Activity:** Provide students with a short passage in Spanish about some aspect of the historical influence of the Roman Empire in Spain. Encourage students to identify the main idea and supporting details as they read. Clarify the language where necessary. Have students summarize the main ideas of the text and compare their responses.
- ***Pre-AP* Resource Book:*** Comprehensive guide to Pre-AP* reading skill development, pp. 19–26

Teaching with Photos

Point out to students that this structure, like many of the Roman Empire remains, is significant because of its size and complexity. Remind students that lack of modern building tools made construction projects difficult.

ASSESSMENT

Prueba 2A-2 with Study Plan (online only)

Quiz: Vocabulary Production

- Prueba 2A-2: pp. 43–44

ENRICH YOUR TEACHING

Culture Note

Spanish is one of the Romance languages, along with French, Italian, Portuguese, Romanian, and Romansch (one of the official languages of Switzerland). These languages are called "Romance" because they came from the language of ancient Rome, Latin. Spanish is considered the most similar to Latin. More than half of English words are derived from Latin or Greek, though most of these are relative latecomers to the English language.

Search online with the keyword ***Hispania*** to read more about the history of Spain during the time of the Roman Empire. For photos and information on Roman ruins in Spain, search with the keywords ***Segovia*** or ***Merida, Spain.***

2A Practice and Communicate

BELLRINGER REVIEW

Before beginning, define subject pronouns and have students list them in English. Without looking at the chart, can students name Spanish subject pronouns they've seen so far?

Gramática

Core Instruction

Standards: 4.1

Resources: Voc. and Gram. Transparencies 52–53; Teacher's Resource Book: Video Script, pp. 118–119; Video Program: Cap. 2A

INTERACTIVE WHITEBOARD
Grammar Activities 2A

Suggestions: Use the *GramActiva* Video either as an initial introduction to subject pronouns or as a follow-up to your own explanation. Use the transparencies to reinforce the subject pronouns. Remind students of the distinction between ***tú*** and ***usted.*** Use groups of students standing at the front of the class to reinforce the concepts, pointing to them and moving them as necessary. Recall students' English language knowledge to introduce compound subjects in Spanish.

10 Standards: 1.2

Focus: Listening and speaking using subject pronouns

Suggestions: Model this activity for your students, pointing to pre-designated people in the class. You will need to say the subject pronouns aloud. For example, point to yourself for ***yo,*** have students face each other and point for ***tú,*** point to a male or female student when saying ***él*** and ***ella,*** indicate an imaginary circle including yourself when saying ***nosotros,*** point directly to two or more students for ***vosotros,*** and point to a group of male or female students for ***ellos / ellas.*** You might want to draw several adult-like stick figures on the board so students can point to ***ustedes.***

Manos a la obra | **Objective**

- Identify, talk to, and write about different people

Gramática

Subject pronouns

The subject of a sentence tells who is doing the action. You often use people's names as the subject:

Gregorio escucha música. *Gregory listens to music.*
Ana canta y baila. *Ana sings and dances.*

You also use subject pronouns *(I, you, he, she, we, they)* to tell who is doing an action. The subject pronouns replace people's names:

Él escucha música. *He listens to music.*
Ella canta y baila. *She sings and dances.*

Here are all the subject pronouns in Spanish:

yo	I	nosotros nosotras	we *(masc., masc./fem.)* we *(fem.)*
tú	you *(familiar)*	vosotros vosotras	you *(masc., masc./fem.)* you *(fem.)*
usted (Ud.)	you *(formal)*	ustedes (Uds.)	you *(formal)*
él ella	he she	ellos ellas	they *(masc., masc./fem.)* they *(fem.)*

Tú, usted, ustedes, and *vosotros(as)* all mean "you."

- Use *tú* with family, friends, people your age or younger, and anyone you call by his or her first name.
- Use *usted* with adults you address with a title, such as *señor, señora, profesor(a),* etc. *Usted* is usually written as *Ud.*
- In Latin America, use *ustedes* when speaking to two or more people, regardless of age. *Ustedes* is usually written as *Uds.*
- In Spain, use *vosotros(as)* when speaking to two or more people you call *tú* individually: *tú* + *tú* = *vosotros(as).* Use *ustedes* when talking to two or more people you call *usted* individually.

If a group is made up of males only or of both males and females together, use the masculine forms: ***nosotros, vosotros, ellos.***

If a group is all females, use the feminine forms: ***nosotras, vosotras, ellas.***

You can combine a subject pronoun and a name to form a subject.

Alejandro y yo = nosotros　Pepe y tú = ustedes
Carlos y ella = ellos　Lola y ella = ellas

Más ayuda realidades.com

***GramActiva* Video**
Tutorials: Present indicative, Pronouns, Subject pronouns, Subjects

***GramActiva* Activity**

DIFFERENTIATED INSTRUCTION

Heritage Language Learners

Give students a paragraph or list of sentences. Ask them to underline the subjects of the sentences in one color and the subject pronouns in another.

Students with Learning Difficulties

Students often have difficulty substituting subject pronouns for proper nouns. Give students two or three examples in English of how they substitute subject pronouns, and then have them transfer this skill to Spanish. Start with individual nouns, then work up to full sentences.

10 ¡Señala!

Escuchar • Hablar • GramActiva

Your teacher will name several subject pronouns. Point to people in the classroom who represent the pronoun you hear. After you have practiced with your teacher, practice with a partner.

11 ¿Es ella?

Escribir

What subject pronouns would you use to talk about these people?

Modelo
Gloria
Ella.

1. Carlos
2. Felipe y yo
3. María y Sarita
4. Pablo, Tomás y Anita
5. el señor Treviño
6. tú y Esteban

12 ¿Tú, Ud. o Uds.?

Hablar

Tell whether you would use *tú, Ud.,* or *Uds.* with these people.

1. 

2. 
3. 
4. 
5.

6. 
7. 

8. 

Más práctica GO

realidades.com | print

	realidades.com	print
Instant Check	✔	
Guided WB pp. 63–64	✔	✔
Core WB p. 35	✔	✔
Comm. WB pp. 32, 36, 239	✔	✔
***Hispanohablantes* WB** pp. 54–57		✔

Practice and Communicate 2A

11 Standards: 1.3

Resources: Answer Keys: Student Edition, p. 26
Focus: Writing subject pronouns
Suggestions: Refer students to p. 82 to decide which subject pronoun is appropriate. Point out that item 6 has two possible responses.

Answers:

1. **él**
2. **nosotros**
3. **ellas**
4. **ellos**
5. **él**
6. **vosotros / ustedes**

12 Standards: 1.3

Resources: Answer Keys: Student Edition, p. 27
Focus: Choosing socially appropriate subject pronouns
Suggestions: Remind students that ***tú*** is used informally, and ***usted*** is generally used for people who would be addressed by their last name. Point out that students will not use ***vosotros(as)*** in this activity. If you stress ***vosotros,*** however, allow that as an answer.

Answers:

1. **Ud.**
2. **tú**
3. **Ud.**
4. **Uds.**
5. **Ud.**
6. **Uds.**
7. **tú**
8. **Ud.**

Theme Project

Give students copies of the Theme Project outline and rubric from the *Teacher's Resource Book*. Explain the task to them, and have the perform Step 1. (See p. 72-b.)

Additional Resources

- Communication Wbk.: Audio Act. 7, p. 32
- Teacher's Resource Book: Audio Script, p. 116
- Audio Program DVD: Cap. 2A, Track 8

ASSESSMENT

Prueba 2A-3 with Study Plan (online only)

Quiz: Subject Pronouns

- Prueba 2A-3: p. 45

ENRICH YOUR TEACHING

Teacher-to-Teacher

Often, confusion arises when the subject pronouns ***yo*** and ***tú*** are seen in an activity. When given such prompts, students generally should assume that they will stay the same in their answers. When an activity is "talking to" the students (for example, ***Y tú, ¿qué dices?***), they need to change the ***tú*** in the question to ***yo*** in the answer in order to talk about themselves.

Teacher-to-Teacher

Have students prepare three pieces of paper, one labeled ***tú,*** one labeled ***usted,*** and one labeled ***ustedes.*** Have them cut out magazine pictures or download images showing individuals and groups of people whom they would address as ***tú, usted,*** or ***ustedes,*** and mount them on the correct sheet. These can be displayed on the bulletin board.

2A Practice and Communicate

Gramática

Core Instruction

Standards: 4.1

Resources: Voc. and Gram. Transparency 54; Teacher's Resource Book: Video Script, p. 119; Video Program: Cap. 2A

INTERACTIVE WHITEBOARD
Grammar Activities 2A

Suggestions: Point out the *¿Recuerdas?* and remind students that they have seen ***-ar*** verbs before. Present the new grammar using the transparencies, and show the *GramActiva* Video as reinforcement. Give students several examples of how stems are derived. Show them that the stem of a verb carries the basic meaning, while the ending tells "who" and "when." Point out that the same thing happens in English, though the endings are not as helpful—which is why we cannot usually drop the subject. Demonstrate this difference with examples from the two languages: ***canto/ canta*** vs. *I sing/he sings*. Have students identify stems of other infinitives.

13 Standards: 1.2

Resources: Teacher's Resource Book: Audio Script, p. 116; Audio Program DVD: Cap. 2A, Track 9; Answer Keys: Student Edition, p. 27

Focus: Listening for verb endings

Suggestions: Before beginning, direct students' attention to the *Strategy*. Have students refer to the verb chart while doing this activity. Point out that the forms on the left side of the chart are singular (one person doing the action), and those on the right are plural.

Script and Answers:

1. **hablo** ***(one hand)***
2. **enseñan** ***(two hands)***
3. **dibujamos** ***(two hands)***
4. **trabaja** ***(one hand)***
5. **cantas** ***(one hand)***
6. **estudian** ***(two hands)***
7. **necesitan** ***(two hands)***
8. **practico** ***(one hand)***

Common Errors: Students hear the ***-s*** in the ***tú*** ending and think it is a plural. Remind them that the ***-s*** ending makes nouns plural, but not verbs.

Gramática

Objectives

- Write and exchange information about what you and others study and do
- Listen to a description of activities during recess
- Compare the Mayan numbering system to the one you use

Present tense of *-ar* verbs

You already know that the infinitive forms of Spanish verbs always end in *-ar*, *-er*, or *-ir*.

¿Recuerdas?
You already know many *-ar* verbs, such as *cantar* and *bailar*.

The largest group of verbs end in *-ar*. *Hablar* is one of these *-ar* verbs.

You will want to use verbs in ways other than in the infinitive form. To do this, you will drop the *-ar* ending and make changes.

To create the forms of most *-ar* verbs, you first drop the *-ar* from the infinitive, leaving the stem:

hablar → habl-

Then you add the verb endings *-o*, *-as*, *-a*, *-amos*, *-áis*, or *-an* to the stem.

Here are the forms of *hablar:*

(yo)	hablo	(nosotros) (nosotras)	hablamos
(tú)	hablas	(vosotros) (vosotras)	habláis
Ud. (él) (ella)	habla	Uds. (ellos) (ellas)	hablan

In Spanish, the present tense form of a verb can be translated into English in two ways:

Hablo español. — *I speak Spanish.* / *I am speaking Spanish.*

The verb endings always indicate who is doing the action. In this case, they tell *who* is speaking. Because of this, you can often use the verb without a subject:

Hablo inglés. **¿Hablas** español?

Subject pronouns are often used for emphasis or clarification.

Ella habla inglés pero él habla español.

Más ayuda realidades.com

GramActiva **Video**
Tutorials: Subject and verb agreement, Verbs, *-ar* verbs, Singular and plural, Definite and indefinite articles
Animated Verbs

Canción de hip hop: *En la clase*

GramActiva **Activity**

13 ¿Una mano o dos?

Escuchar • Pensar • GramActiva

You will hear eight *-ar* verbs. If the ending tells you one person is performing the action, raise one hand. If the ending tells you more than one person is doing something, raise both hands.

Strategy
Listening for information
Always listen carefully for the endings on verbs to know who is doing the action.

DIFFERENTIATED INSTRUCTION

Multiple Intelligences

Bodily/Kinesthetic: Have students cut out magazine pictures that depict ***-ar*** verbs and paste them on construction paper to make posters. At the bottom of the poster have students write a sentence describing each action.

Heritage Language Learners

Pay special attention to students' verb formation. Depending on their heritage, their pronunciation may vary from the "standard" ways of saying these endings. These differences may result in incorrect spelling or adding the wrong verb ending. Some students may also use forms such as the ***voseo,*** which should be recognized.

Practice and Communicate 2A

14 ¿Qué estudian?

Escribir • Hablar

Look at the pictures and tell what these people are studying.

Modelo
Tomás
Tomás estudia música.

1. Laura

2. Josefina, Elena y yo

3. tú

4. Catalina y José

5. Joaquín y tú

6. yo

15 Juego

Escuchar • Hablar • GramActiva

1. Work with a partner and tear a sheet of paper into eight pieces of equal size. Write a different subject pronoun on each piece *(yo, tú, él, ella, Ud., nosotros, ellas, Uds.)*. Place the subject pronouns face down in a pile.
2. Your teacher will say an infinitive. One partner will select the top piece of paper from the pile, read the subject pronoun, and say the correct verb form. A correct answer earns one point. Place the "used" subject pronouns in a separate pile. Take turns selecting from the pile and answering.
3. When your teacher tells you to stop, shuffle the pieces of paper with subject pronouns and place them in a new pile face down. When the next verb is read aloud, continue playing. The partner with the most correct answers is the winner.

En una escuela en México

Más práctica GO

	realidades.com	print
Instant Check	✔	
Guided WB pp. 65–66	✔	✔
Core WB pp. 36–37	✔	✔
Comm. WB pp. 33–34, 37	✔	✔
***Hispanohablantes* WB** pp. 58–60		✔

14 Standards: 1.3

Resources: Answer Keys: Student Edition, p. 28

Focus: Writing simple sentences with *-ar* verbs

Suggestions: Review the school subjects quickly. Call on students to answer orally.

Answers:

1. **Laura estudia matemáticas.**
2. **Josefina, Elena y yo estudiamos arte.**
3. **Tú estudias inglés.**
4. **Catalina y José estudian español.**
5. **Joaquín y tú estudian (estudiáis) tecnología.**
6. **Yo estudio ciencias sociales.**

Extension: Have students replace the subjects with subject pronouns in the answers for items 1, 2, 4, and 5. Then have them write out all six answers in the negative, with the pronouns.

15 Standards: 1.1, 1.2

Resources: Teacher's Resource Book: GramActiva BLM, p. 125

Focus: Listening comprehension of infinitives; providing forms of verbs

Suggestions: Tell students how much time they will have, and walk around the room to make sure students check their answers.

Teacher's Script:

1. **estudiar**
2. **enseñar**
3. **trabajar**
4. **cantar**
5. **bailar**
6. **patinar**
7. **necesitar**
8. **usar**

Answers will vary.

Additional Resources

- Communication Wbk.: Audio Act. 8–9, pp. 33–34
- Teacher's Resource Book: Audio Script, pp. 116–117, Communicative Pair Activity BLM, pp. 122–123
- Audio Program DVD: Cap. 2A, Tracks 11–12

ENRICH YOUR TEACHING

Culture Note

Look at the picture on p. 85 and point out that students are wearing uniforms. It is common practice to require uniforms in secondary schools in many Spanish-speaking countries. You might also mention that in some places students stay in the same room all day, and the teachers come to them.

21st Century Skills

Initiative and Self-Direction Have students use the many tools available in **realidades.com** to support grammar learning, such as the online text with audio, the *Canción de hip-hop,* and the *GramActiva video,* as well as the online games. Have students track the different tools they use and how effective each is, so they can establish over time what type of learners they are. This will help them in all areas of learning.

ASSESSMENT

Prueba 2A-4 with Study Plan (online only)

Quiz: Present tense of *-ar* verbs

- Prueba 2A-4: p. 46

2A Practice and Communicate

16 Standards: 1.2, 1.3

Resources: Answer Keys: Student Edition, p. 28

Focus: Writing using *-ar* verb conjugations

Recycle: Meanings of *-ar* verbs

Suggestions: Refer students to the *-ar* verb chart on p. 84. Point out that they need both the correct form and meaning to get the right answer. They will not use all of the verbs in the word bank.

Answers:

1. dibujan
2. usas
3. necesito
4. practicamos
5. enseña
6. habla

17 Standards: 1.2, 1.3

Resources: Teacher's Resource Book: Audio Script, p. 116; Audio Program DVD: Cap. 2A, Track 10; Answer Keys: Student Edition, p. 28

Focus: Listening comprehension; writing about school breaktime

Suggestions: Play the audio or read the script more than once.

Script and Answers:

1. Dos amigos y yo hablamos de las clases.
2. Tomás estudia español.
3. Ana canta.
4. Y María escucha música.

Fondo cultural

Standards: 2.1, 4.2

Suggestions: Have students look at the picture of ***el recreo*** and identify what the students are doing and where. Ask them to talk about what they do in the short breaks between classes.

Answers will vary.

Block Schedule

For *Actividad* 16, have students write out the sentences and underline the subjects. Then have them write eight more sentences or questions using the verbs listed. Encourage them to write at least two negative sentences.

16 En la escuela

Escribir

Use the verbs in the list to complete the sentences about what different activities take place during school.

Modelo

Yo <u>estudio</u> mucho en la clase de español.

necesitar	hablar	dibujar
usar	practicar	enseñar
patinar	bailar	

1. Lupe y Guillermo ___ mucho en la clase de arte.
2. Tú ___ la computadora en la clase de tecnología.
3. Yo ___ una calculadora y una carpeta para la clase de matemáticas.
4. Tomás y yo ___ deportes en la clase de educación física.
5. ¿Quién ___ la clase de ciencias naturales?
6. Marta ___ mucho en la clase de español.

17 Escucha y escribe

Escuchar • Escribir

Listen to a student describe this picture of himself and other students during their *recreo.* Write what you hear.

Fondo Cultural | El mundo hispano

El recreo In Spanish-speaking countries, students usually have *el recreo* (recess or break) in the school *patio*. Students take time to relax and spend time with friends, eat a snack, or participate in activities such as a quick game of basketball, soccer, or volleyball.

- How is this similar to your school? How is it different?

El recreo ▶

DIFFERENTIATED INSTRUCTION

Multiple Intelligences

Visual/Spatial: Have students create posters promoting activities that can be done during school free time. Explain that by using the ***nosotros*** form of the verb ***ir,*** minus the subject pronoun, they are expressing the command "Let's." For example, ***¡Vamos a jugar!*** they are suggesting, "Let's play!"

Students with Special Needs

Before starting the *Actividades* for this section, review infinitives and the word bank in *Actividad* 16. Transcribing while listening can be difficult for some students. Have them listen and then discuss what they understood. For *Actividad* 18, review the activities in the word bank. Provide a copy of the Venn diagram graphic organizer.

Practice and Communicate 2A

18 Actividades y más actividades  

Escribir • Hablar

1. Work with a partner. Copy the Venn diagram on a sheet of paper. Label the oval on the left *Yo.* Label the oval on the right with the name of your partner. Label the overlapping area *Nosotros* or *Nosotras.*

Modelo

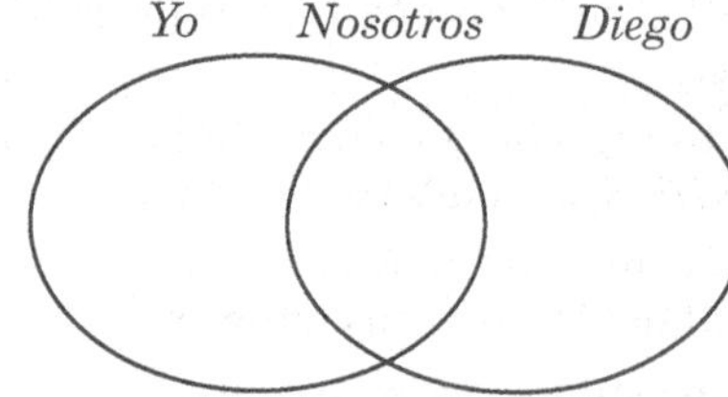

2. From the list below, choose five activities you do a lot. Write your activities in the oval labeled *Yo.* Be sure to conjugate the verb in the *yo* form.

montar en bicicleta	pasar tiempo con amigos	trabajar
hablar por teléfono	practicar deportes	cantar
escuchar música	hablar español	bailar
dibujar	nadar	
estudiar	usar la computadora	

3. Interview your partner. Ask questions to find out the five activities your partner wrote in his or her diagram. When you find out an activity, write it in the right oval of your diagram. Be sure to conjugate the verb in the *él/ella* form. Save your diagram for Actividad 19.

¿Recuerdas?
When you answer in the negative, you often use *no* twice. The first *no* answers the question. The second *no* goes before the verb and means "not."

Modelo

A —*¿Dibujas mucho?*
B —*A ver . . . No, no dibujo mucho.*
A —*Pues, ¿trabajas mucho?*
B —*Sí, trabajo mucho.*

19 Nosotros(as) . . .

Escribir

Compare the two sides of your diagram. Write the activities you and your partner both do in the center. Be sure to use the *nosotros(as)* form. Then use your completed diagram from Actividad 18 to write about what you and/or your partner do. Write at least five complete sentences.

Modelo

Diego y yo trabajamos.
Yo dibujo.

18 Standards: 1.1, 1.3

Resources: Voc. and Gram. Transparency 2
Focus: Writing and speaking using *-ar* verbs in personalized context
Recycle: *-ar* verb meanings
Suggestions: Use the board or an overhead transparency to show students how to fill in the ovals. Point out that students must write the words in the ***yo*** form for Step 2, and in the ***él/ella*** form for Step 3. Have volunteers read the ***Modelo*** for Step 3, and then re-read it, this time personalizing it with their information. Encourage students to use other words besides ***mucho,*** such as ***bien*** or ***con mis amigos.*** Point out that they will not use the ***nosotros*** section of the Venn diagram until *Actividad* 19.
Answers will vary.

19 Standards: 1.3

Focus: Writing using ***nosotros*** forms of ***-ar*** verbs in a personalized context
Suggestions: Encourage students to write negative sentences about actions neither of them do: *Nosotros no dibujamos.* Ask them to then state who does the action and who doesn't. For example: *Diego dibuja pero yo no dibujo.*
Answers will vary.
Extension: Have pairs read a sentence aloud. Then have a third student repeat the information, using the ***ellos/ellas*** form.

Pre-AP* Support

- **Learning Objective:** Interpersonal Writing
- **Activity 19:** Use the information from the center of your diagram to write an e-mail to another classmate, describing what you and your partner do. Be sure to ask your friend at least one question about what he or she does.
- ***Pre-AP* Resource Book:*** Comprehensive guide to Pre-AP* writing skill development, pp. 27–38

ENRICH YOUR TEACHING

Teacher-to-Teacher

Have students bring in action pictures of themselves, family, or friends, or pictures from magazines. They should prepare 3–5 sentences about the actions shown, using more than one picture if needed. The next day, they can present these orally to a partner, or volunteers can present them to the class.

21st Century Skills

Critical Thinking and Problem Solving After using all the tools for *-ar* verbs in this chapter, have students make a connection between the reading they did in Chapter 1B (p. 64) and the activities they learn in this chapter by connecting color preference, personality type, and preferred activities.

ASSESSMENT

Evaluate students on both their written and spoken accuracy on Act. 18 and 19.

20 Standards: 1.1, 1.3

Focus: Writing and speaking about school in a personalized context

Recycle: School subjects; meanings of *-ar* verbs

Suggestions: Before students answer the questions, remind them that the verb forms for the answers will differ from the verb forms in the questions. Suggest that students ask and answer the questions with a partner before reviewing their answers as a class.

Answers will vary.

Common Errors: Students often get confused about which subject to use when answering questions in Spanish. Write this chart on the board for students to copy into their notebooks as a reference. Remind them that this pattern is the same as in English.

Question		Answer
tú/Ud.	→	yo
Uds.	→	nosotros(as)
él/ella	→	él/ella
ellos/ellas	→	ellos/ellas
tú y ____	→	nosotros(as)

21 Standards: 3.1

Focus: Reading about the Mayan civilization's system of mathematics

Suggestions: Make up two or three additional numbers to review with students before having them decipher the ones in the book.

Answers will vary but may include the Roman numeral system.

Extension: Write simple addition or subtraction problems on the board using the Mayan number system. Have students give the answers in both Mayan symbols and Arabic numerals.

20 Y tú, ¿qué dices?

Escribir • Hablar

1. En tu escuela, ¿quién enseña la clase de arte? ¿Quién enseña la clase de educación física?
2. En tu escuela, ¿quién canta muy bien *(well)*? ¿Quién dibuja muy bien?
3. ¿Escuchan tus amigos(as) mucha música? ¿Bailan bien tú y tus amigos(as)?
4. ¿Qué estudias en la primera hora?
5. ¿Qué clase tienes en la tercera hora?

Una estudiante en la clase de español

21 Los números mayas

Leer • Pensar

Long before the Spaniards set foot in the Americas, many different civilizations already existed here. One of these, the Maya, lived in southern Mexico and Central America, where their decendants still make their home. One of the accomplishments of the ancient Maya was the development of a system of mathematics.

Conexiones | Las matemáticas

The Maya used three symbols to write numbers: a dot •, a bar —, and a drawing of a shell. The dot equals 1, the bar equals 5, and the shell equals 0. Mayan numbers were written from bottom to top, not from left to right. Look at the Mayan numbers below.

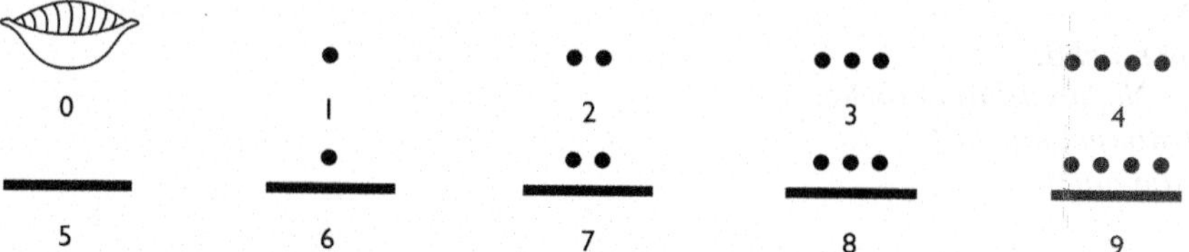

What would these Mayan numbers be in our numbering system?

1. 2. 3.

Now write these numbers in the Mayan system.

4. 13 5. 16 6. 19

Are you familiar with any other numbering systems that remind you of the Mayan system?

DIFFERENTIATED INSTRUCTION

Advanced Learners

Have students use the Internet to do further research on the Mayan number system. They could also explore numbering systems used by other civilizations in the Americas.

Pronunciación

The letter c

In Spanish the pronunciation of the letter *c* depends on the letter that follows it.

When the letter *c* comes before *a, o, u,* or another consonant, it is pronounced like the *c* in "cat." Listen to and say these words:

computadora	cantar	escuela
tampoco	cómo	tocar
correr	practicar	Carlos

When the letter c comes before *e* or *i*, most Spanish speakers pronounce it like the *s* in "Sally." Listen to and say these words:

veces	sociable	gracioso	gracias
hacer	once	doce	trece

Try it out! Listen to this rhyme. Listen particularly for the sound of the letter *c*. Then repeat the rhyme.

0 + 4 = 4
4 + 0 = 4

Cero más cuatro,
o cuatro más cero,
siempre° son cuatro. *always*
¿No es verdadero°? *true*

Say the rhyme again, first replacing *cuatro* with *doce,* then replacing *cuatro* with *trece.* Then say the rhyme quickly several times.

El español en la comunidad

Do you know about opportunities to learn Spanish in your community outside of your school? Do some research using the Internet. Consult the web pages of local colleges, universities, libraries, or language schools to find out about Spanish classes or private lessons offered in your community. Make a list of your findings. Why do you think people in your community want to study Spanish?

ENRICH YOUR TEACHING

Teacher-to-Teacher

If you know of older students who have traveled abroad on an exchange program, invite them to speak to the class describing how their language skills improved during the trip. If you participated in an exchange program yourself, you may want to share your experiences with learning Spanish. This will serve as a good introduction to the reading on p. 90.

21st Century Skills

Social and Cross-Cultural Skills Guide students in a brief investigation about the numbering system developed by the Inca in Perú. Discuss with the class the basic idea of a system of knots tied on strings, as the Inca had no written language. Have students think about the advantages and disadvantages of such a numbering system. Which is more similar to our own, the Mayan or the Incan?

Practice and Communicate 2A

Pronunciación

Core Instruction

Standards: 4.1

Resources: Teacher's Resource Book: Audio Script, p. 117; Audio Program DVD: Cap. 2A, Track 13

Suggestions: You should explain that some Spanish speakers pronounce a *c* before *e* or *i* with a "th" sound. For the *Try it out!*, read the rhyme first, then have student volunteers read it aloud. Have volunteers say the variations with ***doce*** and ***trece.*** Students can compete to say the rhyme the fastest.

El español en la comunidad

Core Instruction

Standards: 1.2, 5.1

Suggestions: Ask if students know of anyone who is taking Spanish classes outside of your school. If so, have them inquire about the courses. Why does the person want to learn Spanish? What methods and activities does the teacher use? What are some of the topics covered? If these answers are available, have students compare the community class with their own class.

Answers will vary but may include:
Spanish classes are offered by adult education centers, community colleges, private language institutes, and private tutors. Reasons for studying Spanish may include for travel, business, and being able to talk with family or friends.

Theme Project

Students can perform Step 2 at this point. Be sure they understand your corrections and suggestions. (See p. 72-b.)

Teacher-to-Teacher

Communities: Invite a Spanish professor from a local community college or university to talk to your students about college courses and class schedules using the words and expressions in this chapter.

Common Core: Reading

Lectura

Core Instruction

Standards: 1.2, 1.3

Focus: Reading about a Spanish-language school in Costa Rica

Mapa global interactivo, Actividad 2 Explore the topography of Costa Rica.

Suggestions:

Pre-reading: Have students look at the title and subtitle and ask them to predict what the reading is about. Direct attention to the Strategy and point out that the photos will help identify the context of the reading.

Reading: Pair students and have them take turns reading the text to each other. Encourage students to deduce the meaning of the passage from context and cognates. Have students share words they could not figure out and write them on the board. Ask volunteers to guess the meanings and explain how they deduced them.

Post-reading: Answer the *¿Comprendes?* questions in class or have students write their answers as homework.

BELLRINGER REVIEW

Put these letters on the board representing the days of the week. Ask that students unscramble the letters as they write the days in correct order.

J M S M V D L

Teaching with Photos

Before reading, have students guess what some of the activities offered by the school, based on the climate and atmosphere depicted in the photos. Brainstorm a list of activities that would be done in such an environment, and then have the class check the list as you review the reading.

Block Schedule

Have students choose a destination in the United States and create a brochure for an English language institute similar to ***La Escuela Español Vivo.*** Have them include a schedule of classes and other possible activities that students can participate in. They may illustrate their piece with drawings or photos.

¡Adelante!

Objectives

- Read about a language school in Costa Rica
- Use photos to help you understand what you read
- Analyze how the 24-hour clock is used in Spanish-speaking countries

Lectura 

Consider what an immersion experience in Spanish would be like for you as you read this brochure from a Spanish language school in Costa Rica.

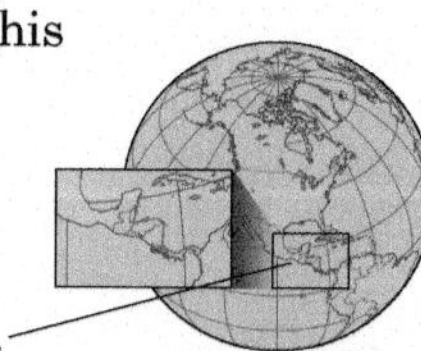

Strategy

Using photos
Look at the photos to help you understand the contents of a brochure or advertisement.

La Escuela Español Vivo

¡Una experiencia fabulosa en Costa Rica!
¡Estudia español con nosotros en la Escuela Español Vivo!

Es verano, el mes de junio. Eres estudiante en Santa Ana, un pueblo en las montañas de Costa Rica.

¿Y cómo es una clase? Hay cinco estudiantes en tu clase. Uds. escuchan, hablan y practican el español todo el día. También usan la computadora.

En la escuela hay estudiantes de muchos países: Estados Unidos, Inglaterra, Francia, Brasil, Canadá, Japón, India, Sudáfrica y otros. ¡Todos estudian español!

90

DIFFERENTIATED INSTRUCTION

Heritage Language Learners

If applicable, ask students to comment on the idea of immersion. If they came from another country, did they know English at all before coming to the United States? If not, or if their English skills were limited, ask them to list the advantages and disadvantages of being immersed in an English-speaking culture.

Multiple Intelligences

Logical/Mathematical: Have students rewrite their own schedules in Spanish, including after-school activities, using the 24-hour clock. Have them use a chart format.

El horario de clases en la escuela es:

hora	lunes a viernes
08:00–10:30	Clases de español
10:30–11:00	Recreo
11:00–13:00	Clases de español
13:00–14:00	Almuerzo
14:00–15:30	Conversaciones
15:30–16:30	Clase de música y baile

¿Por qué la Escuela Español Vivo?

- La naturaleza de Costa Rica en el pueblo de Santa Ana
- Amigos de muchos países
- Mucha práctica y conversación en español
- Clases de música y baile
- Excursiones los sábados y domingos

¿Comprendes?

1. When does the program take place?
2. Describe what a class is like.
3. What activities are offered on the weekends?
4. How many hours are spent on learning and using Spanish each week?
5. Would you like to study Spanish in Costa Rica? Why or why not?

Más práctica GO

	realidades.com	print
Guided WB p. 67	✔	✔
Comm. WB pp. 38, 240	✔	✔
Hispanohablantes WB pp. 62–43		✔
Culture Reading Activity	✔	

Fondo Cultural | El mundo hispano

La hora in Spanish-speaking countries is usually shown using the 24-hour clock on official schedules and timetables. Times in the morning are shown as 00:00 (midnight) through 11:59 (11:59 A.M.), 1:00 P.M. is shown as 13:00, 2:00 P.M. is 14:00, and so on.

- Look at the times in the *horario* from the train station. At what time does the train for Toledo leave?

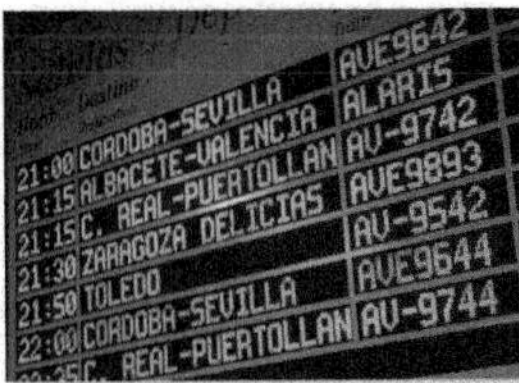

En una estación de trenes de Madrid ▶

Reading 2A

¿Comprendes? Standards: 1.2, 1.3

Resources: Answer Keys: Student Edition, p. 29

Focus: Demonstrating reading comprehension

Suggestions: Have students share their answers for items 1–4. Ask volunteers to explain their answers for item 5.

Answers:

1. In the summer, in June.
2. There are five students in a class. They listen, speak, and practice Spanish all day, and also use the computer.
3. You can visit a volcano or a park, or you can swim in the ocean.
4. Six hours a day.
5. Answers will vary.

Fondo cultural

Standards: 4.2

Resources: Answer Keys: Student Edition, p. 29

Suggestions: Read the text to the class and give students some extra examples of schedules in the 24-hour format. Point out that the 24-hour clock is used in the United States Armed Forces, and therefore is often referred to as military time. Ask students what the benefits are of using this system.

Answers:

The train for Toledo leaves at 21:50, or 9:50 P.M.

Pre-AP* Support

- **Learning Objective:** Interpretive: Print and Audio
- **Activity:** Write on the board the words: *"En la clase"* and *"Los sábados y los domingos."* Read several teacher-made statements indicating where/when the activities usually take place. Students raise their left hand if the answer is *"en la clase"* and their right hand if the answer is *"los sábados y los domingos."* (Ex. *Visitamos un parque nacional.*)
- ***Pre-AP* Resource Book:*** Comprehensive guide to Pre-AP* communication skill development, pp. 10–57

For Further Reading

Student Resource: Realidades para hispanohablantes: Lectura 2, pp. 64–65

ENRICH YOUR TEACHING

Culture Note

In Spanish-speaking countries, the 24-hour clock is used for public events such as concerts, bullfights, sports events, and radio and television schedules, as well as for invitations to private events such as graduations and weddings. It may also be used in ordinary conversation to specify that an event people are talking about is occurring in the evening.

Teacher-to-Teacher

Look at Spanish-language Web sites, newspapers, magazines, or travel guides to find examples of how times of events are listed using the 24-hour clock. Post these scheduled events on a bulletin board.

La cultura en vivo

Core Instruction

Standards: 1.3, 2.1, 2.2, 3.2, 4.2

Focus: Reading cheers for sports teams and creating one

Suggestions: Before reading, poll students to determine their favorite sports. List them on the board and have students arrive at a class favorite. After noting the favorite sport of the class, ask what they think the favorite sport is in the entire world.

Direct attention to the opening paragraph. After students have finished reading, find out if any correctly predicted the world's most popular sport. If your school has a soccer team, talk about it.

Many teams have cheerleaders who cheer the team on enthusiastically, boost spirits, and help create a winning attitude. Have students think about cheers they know and their meaning, if any. Point out those in the book. Read one aloud with enthusiasm. Emphasize the rhythm. Have students repeat after you. Move on to the second and do the same. Direct students to the Try it out! Allow them to work on their cheers and present them another day.

Some students will have no interest in soccer (or perhaps in any sport at all). You may find it helpful to allow them to focus on the rhyme scheme of the cheers. Perhaps grouping them with students who are enthusiastic will help. Also, when working in a group, these students may prefer to record the group's ideas.

Direct attention to the Think about it! section and have students discuss the questions.

Answers will vary.

Teacher-to-Teacher

Have students visit other Spanish classes and present the school cheers they created. Students might want to present their Spanish cheer at a school pep rally or assembly.

Additional Resources

Student Resource: Realidades para hispanohablantes, p. 66

La cultura en vivo

Aficionados al fútbol

El fútbol (soccer) is the favorite sport in most Spanish-speaking countries. In fact, it is the most popular sport in the entire world. It has grown in popularity in the United States over the past years. As with other sports you are familiar with, *fútbol* has loyal fans, cheers, team songs, and sometimes cheerleaders. If you attended a game in Venezuela at the Escuela Secundaria Bolívar you might hear the following chant:

Jugando al fútbol, Rosario, Argentina

Chiquitibúm a la bim bom bam
A la bío
A la bao
A la bim bom bam
¡Bolívar! ¡Bolívar!
¡Ra, ra, ra!

Except for the school name, the words of this chant do not have any meaning.

Here's another cheer:

¡Se ve! ¡Se siente!	**You see it, you feel it!**
¡Bolívar está presente!	**Bolívar is here!**
¡Que sí, que no!	**Oh, yes, oh, no!**
¡Bolívar ya ganó!	**Bolívar has already won!**
¡A la bío, a la bao!	**¡A la bío! ¡A la bao!**
¡El otro está cansao!	**The other team is tired!**

Try it out! In groups of five, select one of the chants and use it for a model to create a chant for one of your school teams. Present it to the class.

Think about it! How are these cheers and fan enthusiasm similar to or different from the cheers at your school?

Aficionados al fútbol, Bogotá, Colombia

DIFFERENTIATED INSTRUCTION

Multiple Intelligences

Bodily/Kinesthetic: Encourage students to make up moves to accompany their cheers. Allow them to present their cheers to the class.

Heritage Language Learners

Some students may be familiar with cheers from their heritage country. Allow them time to ask family and friends about them, and then to bring the information to share with the class.

- Describe your classes and schedule
- Use a chart to organize your ideas

Presentación oral 

Mis clases

Task
Imagine there is a new student from Costa Rica at your school. Tell the student about some of your classes.

1 Prepare Fill in a chart with information about three of your classes. Use this chart to think through what you may want to say about these classes.

Hora	Clase	Comentarios	Profesor(a)
primera	español	me gusta hablar español	la Sra. Salinas
cuarta	arte	difícil	el Sr. Highsmith
octava	ciencias naturales	divertida	la Sra. Huerta

Strategy

Using graphic organizers
Simple charts can help you organize your thoughts for a presentation.

2 Practice Go through your presentation several times. You can use your notes in practice, but your teacher may not want you to use them when presenting. Try to:

- mention the information about your classes and teachers
- use complete sentences and speak clearly

Modelo
En la primera hora tengo la clase de español. Me gusta hablar español. La clase es muy divertida. La Sra. Salinas es la profesora.

3 Present Describe the three classes you selected.

4 Evaluation The following rubric will be used to grade your presentation.

Rubric	Score 1	Score 3	Score 5
How complete your preparation is	You have information written down but without the use of the chart.	You used the chart, but only partially completed it.	You used the chart and provided all the information.
Amount of information you give	You describe three classes but only provide one piece of information about each class.	You describe three classes but only provide two pieces of information about each class.	You describe five classes and include all requested information.
How easily you are understood	You are very difficult to understand, using only isolated words and phrases.	You are understandable but have frequent errors in vocabulary and/or grammar.	You are easily understood. Your teacher does not have to "decode" what you are trying to say.

Speaking 2A

BELLRINGER REVIEW

Use the Transparencies to quickly review the class names and ordinal numbers.

 Common Core: Speaking

Presentación oral

Core Instruction

Standards: 1.3

Resources: Voc. and Gram. Transparency 56

Focus: Speaking about classes

Suggestions: Review the task and the four steps with students. You might want to model a top-scoring presentation. Then, to get students started, have them brainstorm vocabulary they can use to describe classes. Have students practice their presentation with a partner, focusing on fluency and pronunciation.

Portfolio

Make video or audio recordings of student presentations in class, or assign the RealTalk activity so they can record their presentations online. Include the recording in their portfolios.

Additional Resources

Student Resources: Realidades para hispanohablantes, p. 67; Guided Practice: Presentación oral, p. 68

ASSESSMENT

Presentación oral

- Assessment Program: Rubrics, p. T29

Review the rubric with students. Go over the descriptions of the different levels of performance. After assessing students, help individuals understand how their performance could be improved. (See Teacher's Resource Book for suggestions on using rubrics in assessment.)

ENRICH YOUR TEACHING

21st Century Skills

Critical Thinking and Problem Solving Have teams of students come up with a model for a simple brochure for their own school, inspired by the brochure about the school in Costa Rica in the *Lectura*. Encourage students to use the materials for their *Presentación oral,* as well as the information in the reading, to propose the text and layout for their brochure.

El mundo hispano

Core Instruction

Standards: 2.1, 2.2, 3.2, 4.2

Resources: Map Transparency, 12

Mapa global interactivo, Actividad 3
Discover the canals of Xochimilco in Ciudad de México.

Focus: Reading about Mexico's heritage

Suggestions: After students read the text, show a map of Mexico. Have them note that Mexico borders the Gulf of Mexico on the east and the Pacific Ocean on the west. Locate Mexico City and the Yucatan peninsula. Have students identify Mexico's three neighbors. Point out that Belize—once known as British Honduras—is an English-speaking country.

Focus on the first paragraph. Have students hypothesize about the ways in which the United States and Mexico have influenced each other.

Direct attention to the large background photo. Have students identify it. Point out its approximate location on the map. Ask students what advantage there would be in having a port built on a cliff. When discussing the Mayan civilization, highlight its years of existence and its achievements. Have students do the math to get a clearer understanding of how long the civilization flourished. Imagine the conditions and life-style during those years. On a map, indicate the expanse of the Mayan civilization. Remind students that the present borders between countries did not exist at that time. Point out that there are approximately thirty languages that evolved from ancient Mayan.

Direct attention to the photo of Mexico City and to its location on a map. Have students discuss the advantages and disadvantages of its location. Point out that, like the port in the background photo, it was built by indigenous peoples (the Aztecs) before the arrival of the Spaniards. When the Spaniards arrived in 1519, the city was already larger than most European cities. Today it is the largest city in the world.

Focus on the picture of the Ballet Folklórico. Ask students to compare this troupe to what they know about ballet companies in the United States. If necessary, point out the traditional clothing, emphasizing the wide, colorful skirts and the white embroidered blouses.

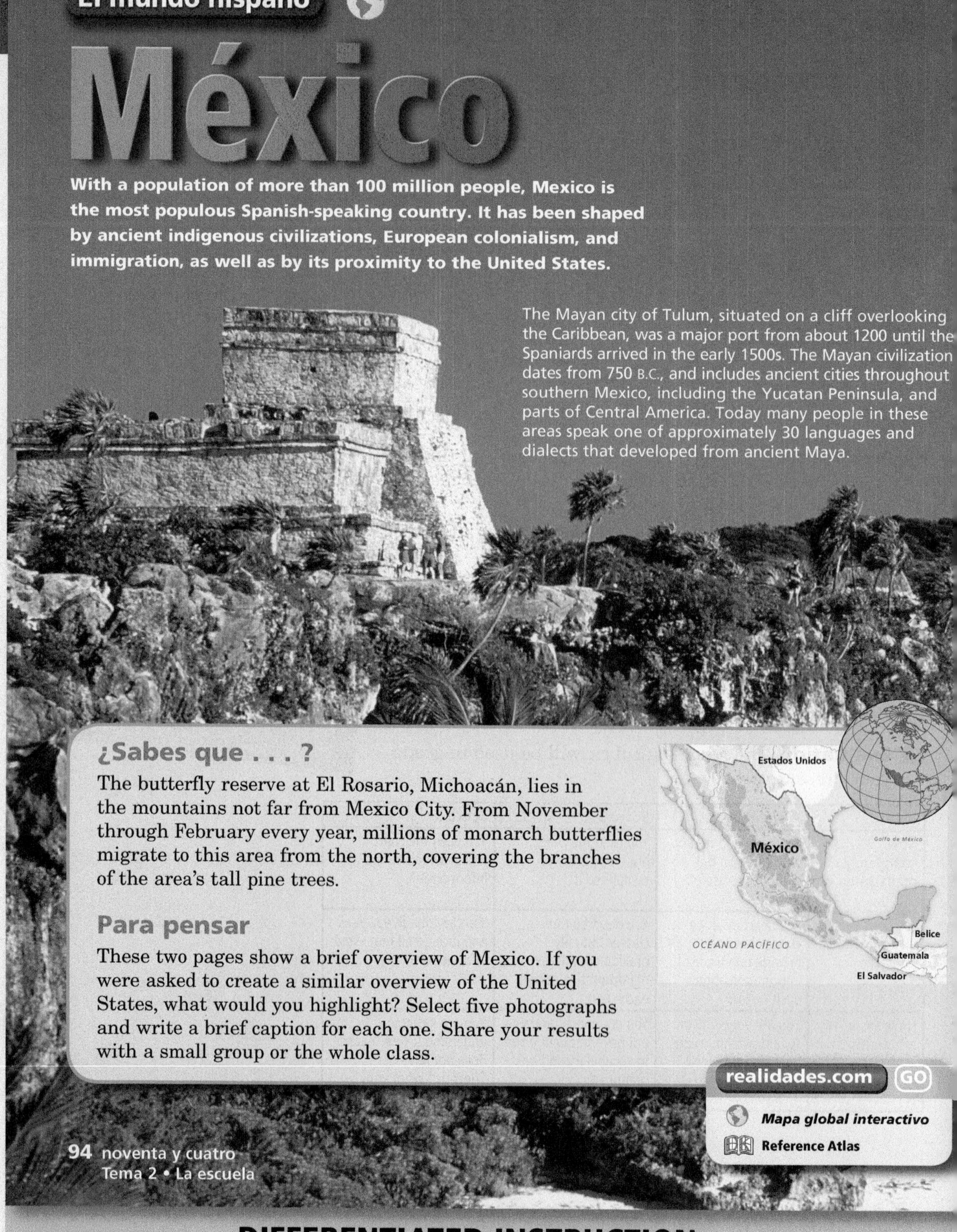

El mundo hispano

México

With a population of more than 100 million people, Mexico is the most populous Spanish-speaking country. It has been shaped by ancient indigenous civilizations, European colonialism, and immigration, as well as by its proximity to the United States.

The Mayan city of Tulum, situated on a cliff overlooking the Caribbean, was a major port from about 1200 until the Spaniards arrived in the early 1500s. The Mayan civilization dates from 750 B.C., and includes ancient cities throughout southern Mexico, including the Yucatan Peninsula, and parts of Central America. Today many people in these areas speak one of approximately 30 languages and dialects that developed from ancient Maya.

¿Sabes que . . . ?

The butterfly reserve at El Rosario, Michoacán, lies in the mountains not far from Mexico City. From November through February every year, millions of monarch butterflies migrate to this area from the north, covering the branches of the area's tall pine trees.

Para pensar

These two pages show a brief overview of Mexico. If you were asked to create a similar overview of the United States, what would you highlight? Select five photographs and write a brief caption for each one. Share your results with a small group or the whole class.

realidades.com GO

Mapa global interactivo

Reference Atlas

94 noventa y cuatro
Tema 2 • La escuela

DIFFERENTIATED INSTRUCTION

Advanced Learners

Have students research and compare the Mayan and Aztec civilizations. Help them focus on when they existed, what they were like at their height, and some achievements and accomplishments of each.

Heritage Language Learners

Students whose heritage country is Mexico may enjoy researching the hometown of their ancestors. Perhaps they can find answers to such questions as: Who were the indigenous peoples of the area? What, if any, traces of those peoples still exist today?

Mexico's most famous dance company, el Ballet Folklórico de México, is a world-class troupe of more than 75 dancers and musicians. For more than five decades, this company has been touring the globe and performing traditional Mexican dances such as the *jarabe tapatío*, (better known in the United States as the Mexican hat dance), *la culebra*, and the *tilingo lingo*.

Mexico's capital is one of the largest cities in the world. It is also one of the oldest, dating back to 1500 B.C. It was here that the Aztecs built their capital, Tenochtitlán, in the 1300s. When the Spaniards arrived in 1519, Tenochtitlán had a population of more than 100,000—making it larger than most European cities.

▲ Many families in Mexico spend Sundays together. A popular spot for families in Mexico City is Xochimilco, where they can relax on colorful boats while enjoying a meal and music. The canals of Xochimilco are remnants of *chinampas*, the "floating gardens" that helped feed Tenochtitlán and other ancient cities in the valley of Mexico.

Focus on the boat in the middle picture. Note that many families spend Sundays relaxing together, a time that is very important to them. The photo reflects a modern-day use of a canal system built centuries ago.

Direct students to the *¿Sabes que...?* section. Ask who has seen a monarch butterfly. Elicit from students the importance of protecting the butterflies' habitat.

Some students may have difficulty computing the duration of the Mayan civilization. You may want to have a volunteer do the math on the board.

When discussing this time period, help students realize that there were no modern tools or machines. All work was done by manual labor and with pack animals, and many people were needed to build the great cities.

Have students make a timeline showing when each civilization was prominent in Mexico.

Direct attention to the *Para pensar* section and have students work in groups to discuss the question. Allow each group to present their ideas to the class.

Answers will vary.

Theme Project

Students can perform Step 3 at this point. (for more information, see p. 72-b.)

ENRICH YOUR TEACHING

Culture Note

In the summer, the monarch butterfly lives in Canada and the United States. In fall, however, all the monarchs fly to their winter home, a mountain in Angangueo, Mexico. Here so many butterflies gather that they weigh down the tree branches. When the sun hits them and they take flight, you can hear their wings flap. What is perhaps most amazing is the fact that the monarchs that migrate have never made the journey before. Each trip is made by a new generation that somehow knows how to find the way.

Review Activities

To talk about your school day: Have students bring in books from other classes. Randomly select a few and call on volunteers to tell what class each is from. For example, using the Spanish book, ask: *¿Es para la clase de ciencias naturales? (No. Es para la clase de español.)*

To talk about the order of things and ***things you need for school:*** Have students make a list of their classes for that day, numbering them in order. Have Student A point to a specific class on Student B's list and have Student B say what time it is and then describe it. For example, *En la tercera hora tengo la clase de matemáticas. Es divertida.* Be sure to have students include items they need from the list in *To talk about things you need for school.*

To describe your classes and ***Other useful words:*** Using the list created above, have students work in pairs to compare classes. For example, *La clase de tecnología es más difícil que la clase de inglés.* Be sure they use a variety of descriptions and comparisons.

Portfolio

Invite students to review the activities they completed in this chapter, including written reports, posters or other visuals, and resordings of oral presentations, or other projects. Have them select one or two items that they feel best demonstrate their achievements in Spanish to include in their portfolios. Have them include this with the Chapter Checklist and Self-Assessment Worksheet.

Additional Resources

Student Resources: Realidades para hispanohablantes, p. 68

Teacher Resources:

- Teacher's Resource Book: Situation Cards, p. 124, Clip Art, pp. 126–127
- Assessment Program: Chapter Checklist and Self-Assessment Worksheet, pp. T56–T57

▼ Objectives

- Review the vocabulary and grammar
- Demonstrate you can perform the tasks on p. 97

Repaso del capítulo

Vocabulario y gramática

to talk about your school day

el almuerzo	lunch
la clase	class
la clase de . . .	. . . class
arte	art
español	Spanish
ciencias naturales	science
ciencias sociales	social studies
educación física	physical education
inglés	English
matemáticas	mathematics
tecnología	technology/computers
el horario	schedule
en la . . . hora	in the . . . hour (class period)
la tarea	homework

to describe school activities

enseñar	to teach
estudiar	to study
hablar	to talk

to talk about the order of things

primero*, -a	first
segundo, -a	second
tercero*, -a	third
cuarto, -a	fourth
quinto, -a	fifth
sexto, -a	sixth
séptimo, -a	seventh
octavo, -a	eighth
noveno, -a	ninth
décimo, -a	tenth

*Changes to *primer, tercer* before a masculine singular noun.

For *Vocabulario adicional,* see pp. 472–473.

to talk about things you need for school

la calculadora	calculator
la carpeta de argollas	three-ring binder
el diccionario	dictionary
necesito	I need
necesitas	you need

to describe your classes

aburrido, -a	boring
difícil	difficult
divertido, -a	amusing, fun
fácil	easy
favorito, -a	favorite
interesante	interesting
más . . . que	more . . . than
práctico, -a	practical

other useful words

a ver . . .	Let's see
mucho	a lot
para	for
¿Quién?	Who?
(yo) tengo	I have
(tú) tienes	you have

subject pronouns

yo	I	**nosotros** **nosotras**	we *(masc., masc./fem.)* we *(fem.)*
tú **usted (Ud.)**	you *(fam.)* you *(form.)*	**vosotros** **vosotras** **ustedes (Uds.)**	you *(masc., masc./fem.)* you *(fem.)* you *(form.)*
él **ella**	he she	**ellos** **ellas**	they *(masc., masc./fem.)* they *(fem.)*

hablar *to talk*

hablo	**hablamos**
hablas	**habláis**
habla	**hablan**

DIFFERENTIATED INSTRUCTION

Students with Learning Difficulties

Have students review the *Repaso del capítulo* and create flashcards for any words that they do not know. Pair them with a student who is more confident with the vocabulary to practice. Before the test, provide students with a practice test, so they can become comfortable with the format.

Heritage Language Learners

Have students write a few paragraphs telling about their perfect school and class schedule: Where do they go to school? With whom do they attend classes? What classes do they take? What are their classes and teachers like? Encourage them to use as many vocabulary words from this chapter as they can.

Más repaso GO realidades.com | print

	realidades.com	print
Instant Check	✔	
Puzzles	✔	
Core WB pp. 38–39		✔
Comm. WB pp. 241, 242–244	✔	✔

Preparación para el examen

On the exam you will be asked to . . .	Here are practice tasks similar to those you will find on the exam . . .	For review go to your print or digital textbook . . .
Interpretive		
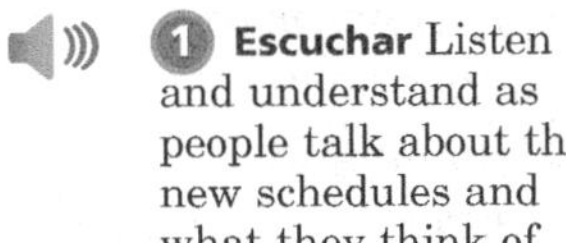 **1 Escuchar** Listen and understand as people talk about their new schedules and what they think of their classes	Listen to two students who have just attended some of the classes on their new schedules. a) Which class does each one like? Why? b) Which class does each one dislike? Why?	**pp. 74–77** *Vocabulario en contexto* **p. 75** Actividades 1–2 **p. 79** Actividad 7 **p. 80** Actividades 8–9
Interpersonal		
 **2 Hablar** Talk about activities you and your friends have in common	To get to know you, your homeroom advisor asks you to talk or write about what you and your friends have in common, such as school subjects that you all study and music or activities that you all like. For example, *cantamos.* You might also tell how you and your friends are different. For example, *Yo toco la guitarra y ellos practican deportes.*	**p. 80** Actividad 8 **p. 86** Actividad 16 **p. 87** Actividades 18–19 **p. 93** *Presentación oral*
Interpretive		
 **3 Leer** Read and understand someone's e-mail description of his or her classes	Read this e-mail that your friend received from his e-pal. What does the e-pal study in school? What does he think of his classes? Do you agree or disagree? Why? *¿Cómo son mis clases? A ver . . . Yo tengo ocho clases. Estudio ciencias naturales, inglés, español, educación física, geografía, matemáticas, tecnología y ciencias sociales. ¡Me gusta más la clase de inglés! Necesito hablar inglés aquí en Ecuador, pero es MUY difícil. Mi clase de geografía es muy aburrida y mi clase de educación física es muy divertida. Y, ¿cómo son tus clases?*	**pp. 74–77** *Vocabulario en contexto* **p. 78** Actividad 4 **pp. 90–91** *Lectura*
Presentational		
 **4 Escribir** Write your schedule including hour, class, and teacher's name, and give opinions about the classes	Write a note to a counselor listing reasons why you want to drop two of the classes on your schedule. What might be some reasons for wanting to change classes? You might say that your first hour class is boring and that your second hour class is difficult for you.	**p. 78** Actividad 5 **p. 79** Actividades 6–7 **p. 93** *Presentación oral*
Cultures • Comparisons		
 **5 Pensar** Demonstrate an understanding of cultural practices concerning sports	Think about the sports at your school that attract the most fans to their games or competitions. Are these the same sports that are most popular in Spanish-speaking countries? How do spectators show their enthusiasm? How is this similar to or different from the United States?	**p. 92** *La cultura en vivo*

DIFFERENTIATED ASSESSMENT

CORE ASSESSMENT
- **Assessment Program:** Examen del capítulo 2A, pp. 47–53
- **Audio Program DVD:** Cap. 2A, Track 16
- **ExamView:** Chapter Test, Test Banks A and B

ADVANCED/PRE-AP*
- **ExamView: Pre-AP* Test Bank**
- **Pre-AP* Resource Book,** pp. 66–69

STUDENTS NEEDING EXTRA HELP
- **Alternate Assessment Program:** Examen del capítulo 2A
- **Audio Program DVD:** Cap. 2A, Track 16

HERITAGE LEARNERS
- **Assessment Program: Realidades para hispanohablantes:** Examen del capítulo 2A
- **ExamView: Heritage Learner Test Bank**

Performance Tasks

Standards: 1.2, 1.3, 2.1, 4.2

Student Resource: Realidades para hispanohablantes, p. 69

Teacher Resources: Teacher's Resource Book: Audio Script, p. 117; Audio Program DVD: Cap. 2A, Track 15; Answer Keys: Student Edition, p. 29

1. Escuchar

Suggestions: Use the audio or read the script.

Script:

Boy: Me gusta mucho la clase de arte. Me gusta dibujar. Es una clase fantástica. Pero la clase de matemáticas... ¡Uf! Es mucho más difícil que mi clase de arte. A veces hay mucha tarea.

Girl: ¡La clase de matemáticas no es difícil! La tarea es muy fácil. Me gusta mucho el profesor. Él es muy divertido. Pero no me gusta la clase de educación física. No soy atlética.

Answers:

Boy: a) Art class, because he likes to draw. b) Math, because it's difficult and has lots of homework. Girl: a) Math: the homework is easy and she likes the teacher. b) Physical education: she's not athletic.

2. Hablar

Suggestions: Brainstorm possible vocabulary with students.

Answers will vary.

3. Leer

Suggestions: Remind students that almost all the vocabulary can be found on p. 96.

Answers:

He studies science, English, Spanish, physical education, geography, math, technology, and social studies. He likes English and thinks that geography is boring. Answers will vary.

4. Escribir

Suggestions: Brainstorm with students words to use for this activity.

Answers will vary.

5. Pensar

Suggestions: Suggest students use a Venn diagram to organize their writing.

Answers will vary.

2B Tu sala de clases

AT A GLANCE

Objectives

- **Listen to and read conversations and notes about school**
- **Talk and write about classes, classrooms, and where things are located**
- **Exchange information while describing someone's location**
- **Compare perspectives towards school and uniforms in the Spanish-speaking world and the United States**

Vocabulary

- Classroom items and furniture
- Computers
- Words to describe location

Grammar

- The verb ***estar***
- Plurals of nouns and articles

Culture

- Sor Juana Inés de la Cruz, p. 99
- School uniforms, p. 106
- Currency exchange rates, p. 109
- P.E. class in Spanish-speaking countries, p. 113
- Cultural perspectives on school, p. 116
- Facts about Central America, pp. 118–119

Recycle ♻

- Using the verb ***estar*** to ask how someone is
- Singular definite and indefinite articles

RESOURCES

	FOR THE STUDENT	ONLINE	DVD	PRINT	FOR THE TEACHER	ONLINE	PREEXP	DVD	PRINT
Plan					Interactive TE and Resources DVD	•		•	
					Teacher's Resource Book, pp. 144–175	•		•	•
					Pre-AP* Resource Book, pp. 66–69	•		•	•
					Lesson Plans	•			•
					Mapa global interactivo	•			
Introducción PP. **98–99**									
Present	Student Edition, pp. 98–99	•	•	•	Interactive TE and Resources DVD	•		•	
	DK Reference Atlas	•	•		Teacher's Resource Book, pp. 144–145	•		•	•
	Hispanohablantes WB, pp. 70–71			•	Galería de fotos		•		
					Fine Art Transparencies, 3	•	•	•	
					Map Transparencies, 12–18	•	•	•	
Vocabulario en contexto PP. **100–103**									
Present & Practice	Student Edition, pp. 100–103	•	•	•	Interactive TE and Resources DVD	•		•	
	Audio	•	•		Teacher's Resource Book, pp. 146–147, 150, 158–159	•		•	•
	Videohistoria	•	•		Vocabulary Clip Art	•	•	•	•
	Flashcards	•	•		Audio Program	•	•	•	
	Instant Check	•			Video Program: Videohistoria	•		•	
	Guided WB, pp. 69–76	•	•	•	Video Program Teacher's Guide: Cap. 2B	•		•	•
	Core WB, pp. 40–43	•	•	•	Vocabulary and Grammar Transparencies, 57–60	•	•	•	
	Comm. WB, pp. 39–41, 45	•	•	•	Answer Keys: Student Edition, 30–31	•	•	•	
	Hispanohablantes WB, pp. 72–73			•	TPR Stories, pp. 29–36	•		•	•
Assess and Remediate					Prueba 2B-1: Assessment Program, pp. 54–55	•		•	•
					Assessment Program para hispanohablantes, pp. 54–55	•		•	•

RESOURCES

	FOR THE STUDENT	ONLINE	DVD	PRINT	FOR THE TEACHER	ONLINE	PREEXP	DVD	PRINT
Vocabulario en uso PP. **104–106**									
Present & Practice	Student Edition, pp. 104–106	•	•	•	Interactive Whiteboard Vocabulary Activities	•		•	
	Instant Check	•			Interactive TE and Resources DVD	•		•	
	Comm. WB, p. 42	•	•	•	Teacher's Resource Book, pp. 148, 152–153, 157	•		•	•
	Hispanohablantes WB, pp. 74–75, 77			•	Communicative Pair Activities, pp. 152–153	•		•	•
	Communicative Pair Activities	•			Audio Program	•	•	•	
					Videomodelos	•		•	
					Answer Keys: Student Edition, pp. 31–32	•	•	•	•
Assess and Remediate					Prueba 2B–2 with Study Plan	•			
					Prueba 2B–2: Assessment Program, pp. 56–57	•		•	•
					Assessment Program para hispanohablantes, pp. 56–57	•		•	•
Gramática PP. **107–113**									
Present & Practice	Student Edition, pp. 107–113	•	•	•	Interactive Whiteboard Grammar Activities	•		•	
	Instant Check	•			Interactive TE and Resources DVD	•		•	
	Animated Verbs	•			Teacher's Resource Book, pp. 148–151, 154–155	•		•	•
	Tutorial Video: Grammar	•			Communicative Pair Activities, pp. 154–155	•		•	•
	Canción de hip hop	•			Audio Program	•	•	•	
	Guided WB, pp. 77–80	•	•	•	Videomodelos	•		•	
	Core WB, pp. 44–46	•	•	•	Video Program: GramActiva	•	•	•	
	Comm. WB, pp. 42–44, 46–47	•	•	•	Vocabulary and Grammar Transparencies, 61–62	•	•	•	
	Hispanohablantes WB, pp. 76–81			•	Answer Keys: Student Edition, pp. 32–34	•	•	•	
	Communicative Pair Activities	•							
Assess and Remediate					Pruebas 2B–3 and 2B–4 with Study Plans	•			
					Pruebas 2B–3, 2B–4: Assessment Program, pp. 58, 59	•		•	•
					Assessment Program para hispanohablantes, pp. 58, 59	•		•	•
¡Adelante! PP. **114–119**									
Application	Student Edition, pp. 114–119	•	•	•	Interactive TE and Resources DVD	•		•	
	Online Cultural Reading	•			Vocabulary and Grammar Transparencies, 64	•	•	•	
	Guided WB, pp. 81–82	•	•	•	Map Transparencies, 13	•	•	•	
	Comm. WB, pp. 48, 245–246	•	•	•	Answer Keys: Student Edition, p. 35	•	•	•	
	Hispanohablantes WB, pp. 82–87			•					
Repaso del capítulo PP. **120–121**									
Review	Student Edition, pp. 120–121	•	•	•	Interactive TE and Resources DVD	•		•	
	Online Puzzles and Games	•			Teacher's Resource Book, pp. 149, 156, 158–159	•		•	•
	Core WB, pp. 47–48	•	•	•	Audio Program	•	•	•	
	Comm. WB, pp. 247–250	•	•	•	Answer Keys: Student Edition, p. 35	•	•	•	
	Hispanohablantes WB, pp. 88–89			•					
	Instant Check	•							
Chapter Assessment									
Assess					Examen del capítulo 2B	•		•	•
					Assessment Program, pp. 60–66	•		•	•
					Alternate Assessment Program, pp. 19–24	•		•	•
					Assessment Program para hispanohablantes, pp. 60–66	•		•	•
					Audio Program, Cap. 2B Examen	•		•	
					ExamView: Test Banks A and B questions only online	•		•	
					Heritage Learner Test Bank	•		•	
					Pre-AP* Test Bank	•		•	

REGULAR SCHEDULE (50 MINUTES)

DAY	Warm-up / Assess	Preview / Present / Practice / Communicate	Wrap-up / Homework Options
1	**Warm-up (10 min.)** • Return Examen del capítulo 2A	**Chapter Opener (5 min.)** • Objectives • Arte y cultura **Vocabulario en contexto (30 min.)** • Presentation: Vocabulario en contexto • Actividades 1, 2	**Wrap-up and Homework Options (5 min.)** • Core Practice 2B-1, 2B-2
2	**Warm-up (5 min.)** • Homework check	**Vocabulario en contexto (40 min.)** • Presentation: Videohistoria *Un ratón en la clase* • View: Videohistoria • Video Activities 1, 2, 3, 4 • Actividad 3	**Wrap-up and Homework Options (5 min.)** • Core Practice 2B-3, 2B-4 • Prueba 2B-1: Vocabulary recognition
3	**Warm-up (10 min.)** • Actividades 4, 5 • Homework check ✔**Formative Assessment (10 min.)** • Prueba 2B-1: Vocabulary recognition	**Vocabulario en uso (25 min.)** • Interactive Whiteboard Vocabulary Activities • Actividades 6, 7, 8 • Audio Activities 5, 6 • Communicative Pair Activity	**Wrap-up and Homework Options (5 min.)** • Writing Activity 10 • Prueba 2B-2 with Study Plan: Vocabulary production
4	**Warm-up (5 min.)** • Fondo cultural • Homework check ✔**Formative Assessment (10 min.)** • Prueba 2B-2 with Study Plan: Vocabulary production	**Gramática y vocabulario en uso (30 min.)** • Exploración del lenguaje • Presentation: The verb *estar* • View: GramActiva video • Interactive Whiteboard Grammar Activities • Actividades 9, 10, 11	**Wrap-up and Homework Options (5 min.)** • Core Practice 2B-5
5	**Warm-up (10 min.)** • Writing Activity 11 • Homework check	**Gramática y vocabulario en uso (35 min.)** • View: GramActiva video • Actividades 12, 13, 14 • Audio Activity 7 • Communicative Pair Activity	**Wrap-up and Homework Options (5 min.)** • Prueba 2B-3 with Study Plan: The verb ***estar*** • El mundo hispano
6	**Warm-up (5 min.)** • Homework check ✔**Formative Assessment (10 min.)** • Prueba 2B-3 with Study Plan: The verb *estar*	**Gramática y vocabulario en uso (30 min.)** • Presentation: The plurals of nouns and articles • View: GramActiva video • Interactive Whiteboard Grammar Activities • Actividades 15, 16, 17, 18 • El español en el mundo del trabajo	**Wrap-up and Homework Options (5 min.)** • Core Practice 2B-6
7	**Warm-up (10 min.)** • Writing Activity 12 • Homework check	**Gramática y vocabulario en uso (35 min.)** • View: GramActiva video • Audio Activities 8, 9 • Actividades 19, 20 • Pronunciación • Fondo cultural	**Wrap-up and Homework Options (5 min.)** • Core Practice 2B-7 • Prueba 2B-4 with Study Plan: The plurals of nouns and articles
8	**Warm-up (10 min.)** • Writing Activity 13 • Homework check ✔**Formative Assessment (10 min.)** • Prueba 2B-4 with Study Plan: The plurals of nouns and articles	**¡Adelante! (25 min.)** • Lectura • ¿Comprendes? • Presentación escrita: Steps 1, 5 • Perspectivas del mundo hispano	**Wrap-up and Homework Options (5 min.)** • Presentación escrita: Step 2 • Preparación para el examen 3, 4, 5
9	**Warm-up (5 min.)** • Homework check	**¡Adelante! (20 min.)** • Presentación escrita: Step 3 **Repaso del capítulo (20 min.)** • Vocabulario y gramática • Preparación para el examen 1, 2	**Wrap-up and Homework Options (5 min.)** • Presentación escrita: Step 4 • Core Practice 2B-8, 2B-9 • Instant Check • Examen del capítulo 2B
10	**Warm-up (10 min.)** • Homework check ✔**Summative Assessment (40 min.)** • Examen del capítulo 2B		

BLOCK SCHEDULE (90 MINUTES)

DAY	Warm-up / Assess	Preview / Present / Practice / Communicate	Wrap-up / Homework Options
1	**Warm-up (10 min.)** • Return Examen del capítulo 2A	**Chapter Opener (5 min.)** • Objectives • Arte y cultura **Vocabulario en contexto (60 min.)** • Presentation: Vocabulario en contexto • Actividades 1, 2 • Presentation: Videohistoria *Un ratón en la clase* • View: Videohistoria • Video Activities 1, 2, 3, 4 • Actividad 3 **Vocabulario en uso (10 min.)** • Interactive board Vocabulary Activities • Actividades 4, 5	**Wrap-up and Homework Options (5 min.)** • Core Practice 2B-1, 2B-2, 2B-3, 2B-4 • Prueba 2B-1: Vocabulary recognition
2	**Warm-up (10 min.)** • Homework check **✓Formative Assessment (10 min.)** • Prueba 2B-1: Vocabulary recognition	**Gramática y vocabulario en uso (65 min.)** • Actividades 6, 7, 8 • Audio Activities 5, 6 • Communicative Pair Activity • Exploración del lenguaje • Fondo cultural • Presentation: The verb ***estar*** • View: GramActiva video • Interactive Whiteboard Grammar Activities • Actividades 9, 10, 11	**Wrap-up and Homework Options (5 min.)** • Core Practice 2B-5 • Writing Activity 10 • Prueba 2B-2 with Study Plan: Vocabulary production
3	**Warm-up (10 min.)** • Homework check • Writing Activity 11 **✓Formative Assessment (10 min.)** • Prueba 2B-2 with Study Plan: Vocabulary production	**Gramática y vocabulario en uso (65 min.)** • Actividades 12, 13, 14 • Audio Activity 7 • Communicative Pair Activity • Presentation: The plurals of nouns and articles • View: GramActiva video • Interactive Whiteboard Grammar Activities • Actividades 15, 16, 17, 18 • El español en el mundo del trabajo • Pronunciación	**Wrap-up and Homework Options (5 min.)** • Core Practice 2B-6, 2B-7 • Pruebas 2B-3, 2B-4 with Study Plans: The verb ***estar,*** The plurals of nouns and articles
4	**Warm-up (10 min.)** • Homework check • Writing Activity 13 **✓Formative Assessment (15 min.)** • Pruebas 2B-3, 2B-4 with Study Plans: The verb ***estar,*** The plurals of nouns and articles	**Gramática y vocabulario en uso (30 min.)** • Audio Activities 8, 9 • Actividades 19, 20 • Fondo cultural • Writing Activity 13 **¡Adelante! (30 min.)** • Lectura • ¿Comprendes? • Presentación escrita: Steps 1, 5	**Wrap-up and Homework Options (5 min.)** • Presentación escrita: Step 2 • Lectura
5	**Warm-up (5 min.)** • Homework check	**¡Adelante! (50 min.)** • Perspectivas del mundo hispano • El mundo hispano • Presentación escrita: Step 3 **Repaso del capítulo (30 min.)** • Vocabulario y gramática • Situation Cards • Communicative Pair Activities • Preparación para el examen 1, 2, 3, 4, 5	**Wrap-up and Homework Options (5 min.)** • Presentación escrita: Step 4 • Core Practice 2B-8, 2B-9 • Instant Check • Examen del capítulo 2B
6	**Warm-up (15 min.)** • Homework check • Answer questions **Repaso del capítulo (25 min.)** **✓Summative Assessment (45 min.)** • Examen del capítulo 2B		**Wrap-up and Homework Options (5 min.)** • El mundo hispano

Standards for *Capítulo* 2B

- To achieve the goals of the Standards, students will:

Communication

1.1 Interpersonal

- Talk about personal and classroom items and furniture
- Talk about the locations of: objects in a classroom setting; people in a photo

1.2 Interpretive

- Listen to information about: classroom items and furniture; the use of location words
- Read: a picture-based story; information about classroom items and furniture; a dialogue requiring understanding of the irregular verb ***estar***; a dialogue requiring understanding of articles; a journalistic article about UNICEF; a note about a students request for information
- Listen to and watch a video about a classroom prank
- Compare a photo to oral descriptions of a Spanish club

1.3 Presentational

- Present information about classroom items and furniture
- Retell portions of a story they have heard
- Present a dialogue requiring understanding of articles
- Compose: a paragraph about their classroom; a letter to a pen pal
- Write a fictional e-mail to a friend about classes

Culture

2.1 Practices and Perspectives

- Discuss women's access to education in seventeenth century Mexico; the widespread use of school uniforms; how physical education classes and team sports are conducted
- Explain that school demands a high percentage of students' time; Costa Rican efforts to protect endangered species; the communicative functions of the ***huipil***

2.2 Products and Perspectives

- Explain the structure educational systems
- Talk about the ***huipil***

Connections

3.1 Cross-curricular

- Discuss the seventeenth-century Mexican intellectual, Sor Juana Inés de la Cruz; currency of Spanish-speaking countries
- Read a journalistic article about UNICEF

Comparisons

4.1 Language

- Talk about vocabulary through the recognition of cognates; the verbal and nonverbal expression, ***¡Ojo!***; about the irregular verb ***estar***; the pronunciation of the letter ***g***
- Explain number agreement with nouns and articles

4.2 Culture

- Compare: the use of school uniforms; influence of women writers on perspectives; the design of physical education class; commitments to and behavior in school
- Consider the hypothetical result of United States expansion south to Panama in the nineteenth century

Communities

5.1 Beyond the School

- Consider the need for Spanish speakers in different types of jobs in the educational field

Capítulo

2B Tu sala de clases

▾ Chapter Objectives

Communication

By the end of this chapter you will be able to:

- Listen to and read conversations and notes about school
- Talk and write about classes, classrooms, and where things are located
- Exchange information while describing someone's location

Culture

You will also be able to:

- Compare perspectives towards school and uniforms in the Spanish-speaking world and the United States

You will demonstrate what you know and can do:

- Presentación escrita, p. 117
- Preparación para el examen, p. 121

You will use:

Vocabulary

- Classroom items and furniture
- Computers
- Words to describe location

Grammar

- The verb *estar*
- Plurals of nouns and articles

Exploración del mundo hispano

Country Connection
Classrooms and School Supplies

realidades.com GO

Reference Atlas

Videocultura y actividad

Mapa global interactivo

Estudiantes mexicanos

ENRICH YOUR TEACHING

Using Backward Design

Have students preview the sample performance tasks on *Preparación para el examen*, p. 121, and connect them to the Chapter Objectives. Explain to students that by completing the sample tasks they can self-assess their learning progress.

Mapa global interactivo

Download the *Mapa global interactivo* files for Chapter 2B and preview the activities. In Activity 1, you look at the countries that comprise Central America. In Activity 2, you explore the geography of Nicaragua.

Arte y cultura | México

Sor Juana Inés de la Cruz (1648–1695), born near Mexico City, was one of the greatest intellectuals of her time. She wrote poetry, essays, music, and plays. Sor Juana also defended a woman's right to an education at a time when few women had access to it. She entered a convent at the age of 19 and over the years built a library of several thousand books. Sor Juana's living quarters in the convent became a meeting place for other writers and intellectuals, who were drawn to her because of her intelligence and knowledge.

- How are various aspects of Sor Juana's life represented in this painting? If you were to pose for a portrait, what objects would you include that represent you and your interests?

Retrato de Sor Juana Inés de la Cruz, siglo XVII ▶
Foto: Archivo Agencia EL UNIVERSAL.

PresentationExpress™
See pp. 98a–98b

Chapter Opener

Core Instruction

Resources: Map Transparencies 12–18

Suggestions: Review the objectives. Explain to students that they will be learning to talk about classroom objects and locations. The video story is about what happens when a hamster escapes in a classroom. The *GramActiva* Video will help students learn the present tense of ***estar*** and the plurals of nouns and articles. Show the transparencies to help students locate the places featured in the chapter.

Videocultura View *Los uniformes escolares* with the class to learn more about different types of uniforms.

Arte y cultura

Standards: 2.1, 2.2, 4.2

Resources: Fine Art Transparencies, p. 3

Suggestions: Point out the dates of Sor Juana's birth and death and ask students what they know about that era (science, arts, and historical events). What opportunities did women have in the seventeenth century to be independent professionals, artists, and scientists?

Answers will vary.

TEACHING WITH ART

Resources: Fine Art Transparencies, p. 3

Culture Note

Direct attention to the photo and point to the insignia that the students have on their sweaters and vests. In addition to uniforms (see *Fondo cultural,* p.106) some schools require their students to wear the official school seal. Others may require school-specific uniform colors.

DIFFERENTIATED INSTRUCTION

Digital resources such as the ***Interactive Whiteboard*** activity banks, ***Videomodelos***, additional ***Online Activities, Study Plans***, automatically graded ***Leveled Workbook***, animated ***Grammar Tutorials, Flashcards***, and ***Vocabulary and Grammar Videos*** will help you reach students of different ability levels and learning styles.

STUDENTS NEEDING EXTRA HELP

Guided Practice Activities
- Flashcards, pp. 69–72
- Vocabulary Check, pp. 73–76
- Grammar Support, pp. 77–80

HERITAGE LEARNERS

Realidades para hispanohablantes
- Chapter Opener, pp. 70–71
- A primera vista, p. 72
- Videohistoria, p. 73
- Manos a la obra, pp. 74–81
- ¡Adelante!, pp. 82–87
- Repaso del capítulo, pp. 88–89

ADVANCED/PRE-AP*

Pre-AP* Resource Book,
- pp. 66–69

Communications Workbook
- Integrated Performance Assessment, p. 247

Vocabulario en contexto

Core Instruction

Standards: 1.2

Resources: Teacher's Resource Book: Input Script, p. 146, Clip Art, pp. 158–159, Audio Script, p. 147; Voc. and Gram. Transparencies 57–58; TPR Stories, pp. 29–36; Audio Program DVD: Cap. 2B, Tracks 1–2

Focus: Presenting vocabulary for classroom items, furniture, and location; introducing lexical use of ***estar,*** gender and number of nouns, plural articles

Suggestions: Use the Input Script from the *Teacher's Resource Book* or use the *TPR Stories Book* to introduce the new vocabulary. Show the transparencies. Have students look at the picture of the classroom in their books and touch the pictures as you describe the scene. Use the new vocabulary to name items in your classroom and have volunteers move around the room to touch the objects you name. If possible, use your classroom computer to identify its parts.

Teacher-to-Teacher

Draw a desktop with five items on a transparency. (See p. 101.) Start with a computer in the middle. Then, describe the location of each item to students using the prepositions of location. Students draw the scene. Finally, show students your master drawing on the overhead. Have students correct their drawings. As an extension, have students work in pairs to create their own drawings and describe them to another pair.

Block Schedule

Have students put their heads down on their desks while one student moves an object in the classroom. When done, everyone raises their heads, and the student who moved the object asks: *¿Dónde está (la papelera)?* The first student to spot it must accurately describe its location and then becomes "It."

Read, listen to, and understand information about
- the classroom
- where objects are located

Vocabulario en contexto

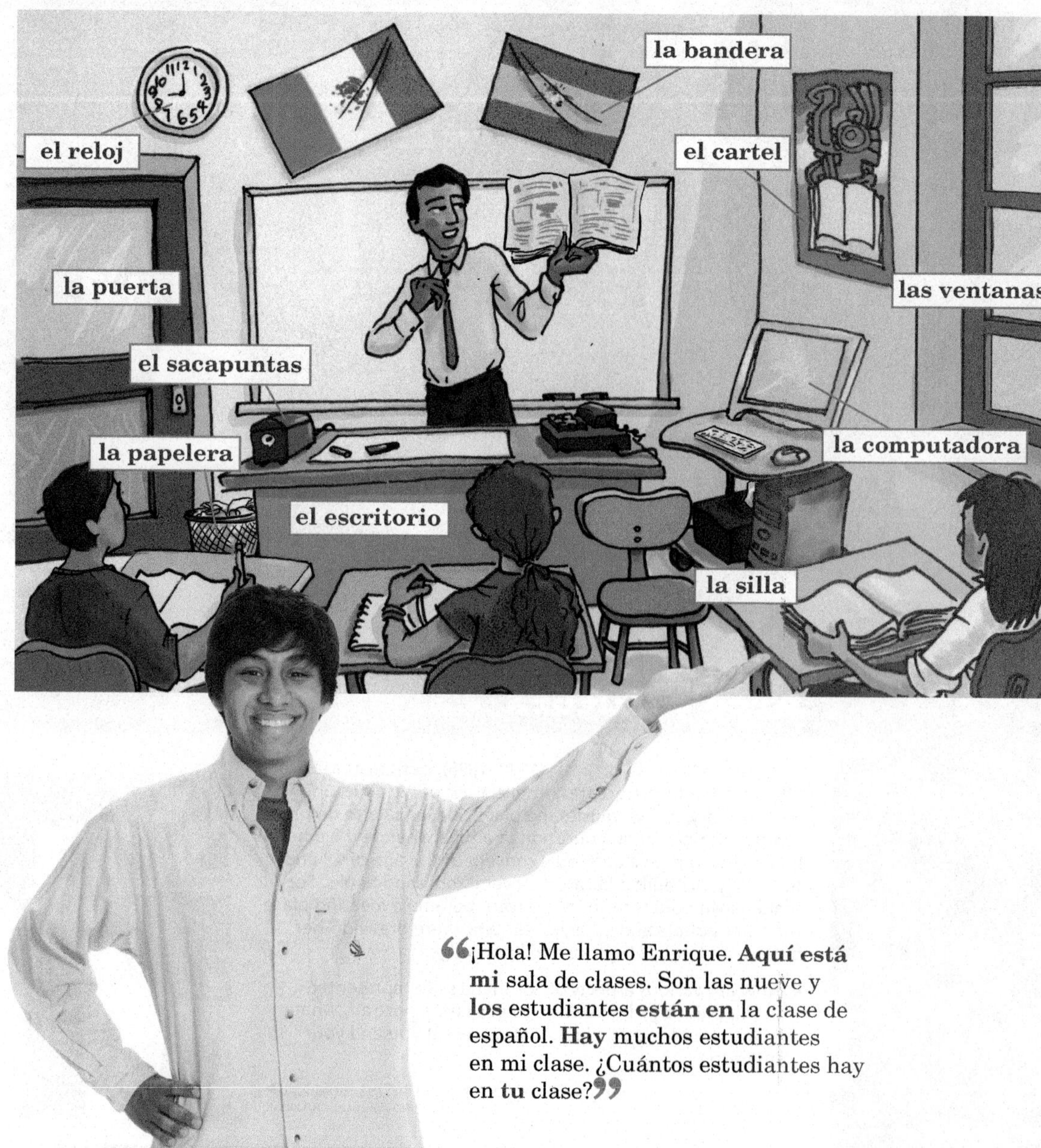

"¡Hola! Me llamo Enrique. **Aquí está mi** sala de clases. Son las nueve y **los estudiantes están en** la clase de español. **Hay** muchos estudiantes en mi clase. ¿Cuántos estudiantes hay en **tu** clase?"

DIFFERENTIATED INSTRUCTION

Heritage Language Learners

Have students make their own vocabulary lists of classroom objects, adding other words they know. If necessary, help them with spelling.

Multiple Intelligences

Logical/Mathematical: Have students count objects in their classroom for which they've learned words. Have them write sentences: *Hay tres computadoras en la sala de clases. Hay treinta pupitres,* etc. The class can listen to the sentences and tell whether they are accurate.

Para decir más . . .

el disco compacto	compact disc
el DVD	DVD (disc)

—Elena, ¿es tu cuaderno?
—No, es el cuaderno **de** David.

La hoja de papel está **debajo del** bolígrafo.
El bolígrafo está **encima de la** hoja de papel.
El ratón está **al lado del** teclado.
La bandera está **detrás de la** computadora.
La silla está **delante de la** mesa.

1 ¿Qué hay en la sala de clases?

Escuchar

Look at Enrique's classroom. You will be asked if certain things are there. If you see the item mentioned, raise your hand and give a "thumbs-up" sign. If you don't see it, give a "thumbs-down" sign.

2 En la sala de clases

Escuchar

Look at the picture of Enrique's classroom again. Listen to where various items are located. If the description is correct, raise one hand, but if the description is not correct, raise both hands.

Más práctica GO

realidades.com		print
Instant Check	✔	
Guided WB pp. 69–72	✔	✔
Core WB pp. 40–41	✔	✔
Comm. WB p. 45	✔	✔
***Hispanohablantes* WB** p. 72		✔

1 Standards: 1.2

Resources: Teacher's Resource Book: Audio Script, p. 147; Audio Program DVD: Cap. 2B, Track 3; Answer Keys: Student Edition, p. 30

Focus: Listening to and recognizing vocabulary for classroom objects and locations

Suggestions: Explain to students that they will be listening for the name of the objects, and that it might appear in either of the large pictures. Allow students to listen more than once.

Script and Answers:

1. ¿Hay una computadora en la sala de clases? (up)
2. ¿Hay un teclado? (up)
3. ¿Hay una tele? (down)
4. ¿Hay un sacapuntas? (up)
5. ¿Hay una mochila? (down)
6. ¿Hay una ventana? (up)
7. ¿Hay un cartel? (up)
8. ¿Hay una puerta? (up)
9. ¿Hay una guitarra? (down)
10. ¿Hay un reloj? (up)

2 Standards: 1.2

Resources: Teacher's Resource Book: Audio Script, p. 147; Audio Program DVD: Cap. 2B, Track 4; Answer Keys: Student Edition, p. 30

Focus: Listening to and recognizing vocabulary for classroom objects and locations

Suggestions: Tell students that most of the objects referred to in this exercise are pictured on p.100.

Script and Answers:

1. La computadora está al lado del profesor. *(computer)*
2. La silla está delante del escritorio. *(chair)*
3. La bandera está detrás de la computadora. *(flag)*
4. La papelera está al lado del escritorio del profesor. *(wastepaper basket)*
5. El cartel está en la pared. *(poster)*
6. El reloj está al lado del sacapuntas. *(clock)*

BELLRINGER REVIEW

Show Voc. and Gram. Trans. 48. to review school subjects. Ask students to name another subject they take and describe an object in that classroom.

ENRICH YOUR TEACHING

Teacher-to-Teacher

Have students make decorative labels for objects in the classroom. Have them place the labels as they tell where the object is located: *El sacapuntas está al lado del diccionario.*

21st Century Skills

Critical Thinking and Problem Solving After students have worked with the digital tools for this section of the chapter (eBook with embedded audio, flashcards, and audio activities), have them work with a partner to compare their current classroom to the one pictured on page 100. They should use a graphic organizer, such as a Venn diagram, to summarize the similarities and differences.

Teacher-to-Teacher

Have students create Spanish labels for items in one of their other classrooms. Ask the teachers' permission to post the labels.

Videohistoria

Core Instruction

Standards: 1.2, 4.1

Resources: Voc. and Gram. Transparencies 59–60; Audio Program DVD: Cap. 2B, Track 5

Focus: Presenting additional vocabulary about classroom objects and location

Suggestions:

Pre-reading: Direct students' attention to the *Strategy*. Remind them that pictures can often help in predicting what will happen in a story. Have students close their books. Using the transparencies with the dialogues covered up, go panel by panel and ask students to predict the outcome of the story. Why did Manolo pull a prank? *(Manolo no tiene la tarea.)*

Reading: Using the transparencies and pantomime, help students understand the new words in blue type. Discuss how the word ***ratón*** has multiple meanings, both in English and Spanish. Be sure students understand that the animal in the story is actually a hamster, and that Manolo is exaggerating by calling it ***un ratón.***

Post-reading: Complete *Actividad* 3 to check comprehension.

Video

Core Instruction

Standards: 1.2, 4.1, 4.2

Resources: Teacher's Resource Book: Video Script, p. 150; Video Program: Cap. 2B; Video Program Teacher's Guide: Cap. 2B

Focus: Listening to contextualized vocabulary

Suggestions:

Viewing: Show the video without pausing. Then go back and show it again, stopping along the way to check comprehension. Ask students which parts of the video were easier to understand than others. Why? Which words did they recognize as being similar to English words?

Post-viewing: Complete the Video Activities in the *Communication Workbook*.

Un ratón en la clase

¿Qué pasa en la clase de ciencias sociales?
Lee la historia.

México

Strategy

Predicting the outcome
Look at the pictures before you read to help you predict what will happen.

- Will Manolo get away with his prank?

Claudia: ¿**Qué es esto?**
Teresa: Es mi hámster. Es para la clase de ciencias naturales.
Claudia: ¿Cómo se llama?
Teresa: Paquito.

5

Claudia: ¡Está **allí,** delante de la mesa!
Teresa: ¡Ay, mi Paquito!
Manolo: Pues, ahora está detrás de la computadora.
Teresa: ¡Manolo! Es el ratón de la computadora. No es mi Paquito.

6

El director de la escuela, el Sr. Treviño, entra en la clase.
Carlos: ¡Ay! ¡Aquí está! Está en mi **mochila.**
Sr. Treviño: ¡Silencio, por favor!

Sr. Treviño Teresa, hablamos en mi oficina.
Teresa: Sí, señor.

DIFFERENTIATED INSTRUCTION

Heritage Language Learners

Have students extend the story by writing Manolo's excuse to the ***Profesora.*** Check students' work and provide feedback as necessary.

Manolo: ¡Carlos! No tengo mi tarea.

Carlos: ¿Qué?

Manolo: Tengo una idea . . .

Carlos: ¡Un ratón! Profesora, ¡hay un ratón debajo de la silla!

Profesora: ¿Un ratón en la clase de ciencias sociales? **¿Dónde** está? ¿Dónde?

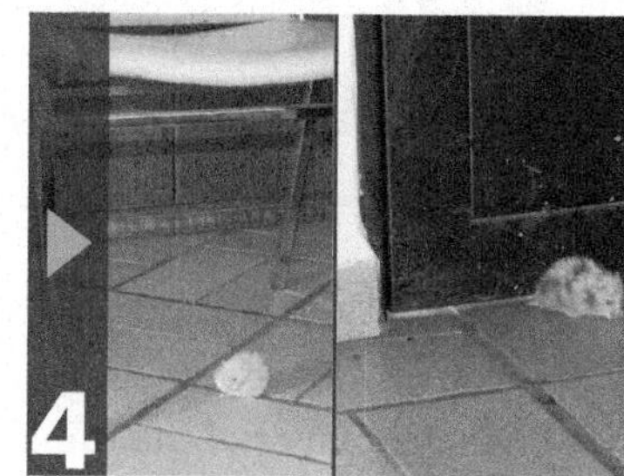

Estudiante: Ahora está debajo de la silla.

Manolo: Y ahora está al lado de la puerta. **Es un** ratón muy impaciente.

Teresa: ¡No es un ratón! Es mi hámster, y se llama Paquito.

Profesora: Y ahora, Manolo, ¿tu tarea?

Manolo: Pues, profesora . . .

3 ¿Comprendes?

Leer

Answer *cierto* or *falso* to the following statements.

1. El hámster es para la clase de inglés.
2. Manolo no tiene la tarea.
3. Paquito está al lado de la puerta.
4. Paquito está detrás de la computadora.
5. Paquito está detrás de la mochila.
6. El director está muy serio.

Más práctica GO

	realidades.com	print
Instant Check	✔	
Guided WB pp. 73–76	✔	✔
Core WB pp. 42–43	✔	✔
Comm. WB pp. 39–40, 41	✔	✔
***Hispanohablantes* WB** p. 73		✔

3 Standards: 1.2, 1.3

Resources: Answer Keys: Student Edition, p. 31

Focus: Reading to check comprehension of the *Videohistoria*

Suggestions: Have students read each sentence and figure out the vocabulary. Then ask volunteers to read a sentence and answer ***cierto*** or ***falso.***

Answers:

1. falso
2. cierto
3. cierto
4. falso
5. falso
6. cierto

Extension: Ask volunteers to role-play the *Videohistoria*. Let students choose their parts. Do not correct pronunciation if it would be comprehensible to a heritage speaker.

Pre-AP* Support

- **Learning Objective:** Interpretive: Audio
- **Activity:** Before listening to the audio, have students copy this paragraph from the board/ overhead:

  ¡Profesora! ¡Hay un ratón _____ de la silla! Y ahora está al _____ de la puerta. ¡Oh, no! Ahora está _____ de la computadora.

  Have students complete the paragraph as they listen to the audio.
- ***Pre-AP* Resource Book:*** Comprehensive guide to Pre-AP* vocabulary skill development, pp. 51–57

Additional Resources

- Communication Wbk.: Audio Act. 5, p. 41
- Teacher's Resource Book: Audio Script, p. 147
- Audio Program DVD: Cap. 2B, Track 8

ENRICH YOUR TEACHING

Teacher-to-Teacher

Have students draw classroom objects on note cards. On the back of each card, students should write the Spanish word. Have students work in pairs and arrange the note cards next to, underneath, in front of, or behind another card on their desktops. Students then take turns asking the location of the objects. Example: *¿Dónde está la bandera? La bandera está al lado de la ventana.*

ASSESSMENT

Quiz: Vocabulary Recognition

- Prueba 2B-1: pp. 54–55

INTERACTIVE WHITEBOARD
Vocabulary Activities 2B

4 Standards: 1.3

Resources: Answer Keys: Student Edition, p. 31

Focus: Writing to identify classroom objects

Suggestions: Remind students that ***hay*** means "there is" or "there are," and that no other verb is required.

Answers:

1. **Hay un sacapuntas.**
2. **...un reloj.**
3. **...una silla.**
4. **...una mochila.**
5. **...un cartel.**
6. **...una papelera.**
7. **...unas ventanas.**
8. **...una mesa.**

Extension: Have students tell what items they have in their backpacks.

BELLRINGER REVIEW

Use the objects pictured in *Actividad* 4 to quickly review indefinite articles.

5 Standards: 1.2

Resources: Answer Keys: Student Edition, p. 31

Focus: Comprehending vocabulary words

Recycle: Classroom vocabulary

Suggestions: Remind students that they need to decide if the sentence is logical or not. They should not base their responses on the photo.

Answers:

1. **Una mochila—¡No! Un pupitre—¡Sí!**
2. **La sala de clase—¡No! Debajo de—¡Sí!**
3. **Un diccionario... Un sacapuntas...**
4. **Bailar... Enseñar...**
5. **Necesitan... Necesita, sí.**
6. **La chica... El chico...**

Extension: Have students create their own sets of items like those in the activity.

Objectives

- Write and talk about objects in a classroom
- Describe a bedroom and a classroom
- Exchange information about school supplies and their location

Vocabulario en uso

4 ¿Qué hay?

Escribir

Write the names of the things you see.

Modelo
Hay una bandera.

1. 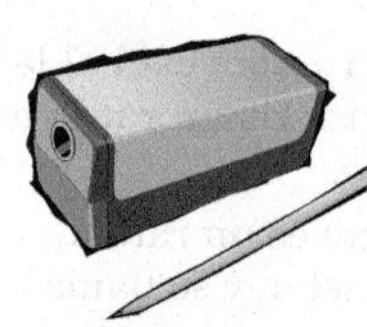
2. 

3. 
4. 
5. 

6. 
7. 
8. 

5 ¿Es lógico o no?

Pensar • Escribir

Write the word that doesn't belong in each group. Then supply a word that logically belongs.

Modelo
el ratón el teclado la pantalla la ventana
La ventana: ¡No! La computadora: ¡Sí!

1. una mesa una silla una mochila un escritorio
2. la sala de clases al lado de detrás de encima de
3. un diccionario una calculadora un reloj una computadora
4. leer estudiar escribir bailar
5. está habla necesitan trabaja
6. el profesor la chica el estudiante el señor

Los estudiantes y la tarea

DIFFERENTIATED INSTRUCTION

Students with Learning Difficulties

Students with language processing difficulties may need extra help with *Actividad* 5. Go item by item and ask them to tell you the characteristics of each. Guide them to see what the categories are that link the items. *Actividad* 7, and others like it, are perfect for cooperative learning; however, it is very important that students with learning difficulties are matched up with the appropriate partners.

6 ¿Dónde está? | 

Hablar

Take turns with a partner to ask and tell where various items in Beto's bedroom are located.

Modelo

A —*¿Dónde está el escritorio?*
B —*Está debajo de la ventana.*

Nota

When the preposition *de* is followed by the masculine definite article *el*, the contraction *del* must be used.

- La papelera está al lado del escritorio.

Estudiante A

¿Dónde está . . . ?

Estudiante B

al lado de
delante de
debajo de
detrás de
encima de

7 Juego |  | 

Hablar • Escuchar

1. Work with a partner. Your partner will face away from you and have a blank piece of paper and a pen or a pencil.
2. Choose four classroom items and arrange them on your desk, putting objects on top of others, next to each other, and so forth.
3. Your partner will ask you questions about what is on your desk and how the items are positioned. Based on your answers, he or she will try to draw the arrangement on your desk.
4. When your teacher tells you to stop, see how closely the picture matches the actual arrangement. Then switch roles.

Modelo

A —*¿Tienes un sacapuntas?*
B —*No, no tengo un sacapuntas.*
A —*¿Tienes una calculadora?*
B —*Sí, tengo una calculadora.*
A —*¿Dónde está?*
B —*Está encima de la carpeta.*

Para decir más . . .

a la izquierda de	to the left of
a la derecha de	to the right of

6 Standards: 1.1

Focus: Talking with a partner about locations of items in a bedroom

Suggestions: Help Student A see that there are multiple items to choose from, and that they can be chosen in any order. This can also be turned into a whole-class guessing game.

Answers will vary. Items will include: **la ventana, la computadora, el escritorio, la mochila, la silla, la papelera, la mesa, el reloj, el cartel.**

7 Standards: 1.1, 1.2

Resources: Teacher's Resource Book: GramActiva BLM, p. 157

Focus: Describing and listening for locations of objects

Recycle: Classroom vocabulary

Suggestions: Remind students that vocabulary in the *Para decir más...* will be helpful to them in completing an activity, but that it is not tested. Demonstrate how to play the game. Walk around the room, prompting students if necessary and monitoring their accuracy.

Answers will vary.

Pre-AP* Support

- **Learning Objective:** Presentational Speaking
- **Activity:** Ask students to bring a sketch of their room, or a picture of a classroom downloaded from the Internet, showing the position of various items. Have students briefly describe their sketch or picture in front of the class using the vocabulary from this chapter.
- ***Pre-AP* Resource Book:*** Comprehensive guide to Pre-AP* speaking skill development, pp. 39–50

ENRICH YOUR TEACHING

Culture Note

Since many Spanish-speaking countries have an evening class schedule (in addition to a day schedule), most evening school students will do their homework in the morning. Ask students to imagine doing their homework at 8:00 A.M., instead of later in the day. What advantages and disadvantages are there?

Teacher-to-Teacher

Provide pairs of students two very similar pictures of a classroom but with five or six differences. Without looking at each other's pictures, have the students ask one another questions about the objects and their locations until they have identified all the differences.

Teacher-to-Teacher

Give the following classroom instructions for students to follow: *Pongan la mochila encima de la silla, pongan la papelera debajo de la ventana, pongan el bolígrafo encima del escritorio del profesor/de la profesora,* etc. Have students work in small groups to write additional instructions to give to other groups to follow.

Exploración del lenguaje

Core Instruction

Standards: 4.1

Suggestions: Demonstrate the *¡Ojo!* gesture. Have students discuss what kinds of gestures they use to communicate or are familiar with. Do different age groups have different types of body language? Are there different types of body language to indicate different relationships between people?

Fondo cultural

Standards: 2.1, 4.2

Suggestions: Have students look at the picture. Ask them to discuss the advantages and disadvantages of uniforms. Remind them about the insignias on the chapter opener photo.

Answers will vary.

8

Standards: 1.2

Resources: Answer Keys: Student Edition, p. 32

Focus: Writing and talking about the classroom

Suggestions: Have students write their answers at the beginning of the class period while you take attendance.

Answers will vary but will include:

1. **La puerta está...**
2. **Hay un/una...al lado de la puerta.**
3. ***Sí / No* hay ventanas en la clase. Hay...ventana(s).**
4. ***Sí / No* hay un reloj en la clase. El reloj está...**
5. **Hay...escritorios y...sillas.**
6. **Hay...**

Additional Resources

- Communication Wbk.: Audio Act. 6, p. 42
- Teacher's Resource Book: Audio Script, p. 148, Communicative Pair Activity BLM, pp. 152–153
- Audio Program DVD: Cap. 2B, Track 8

ASSESSMENT

Prueba 2B-2 with Study Plan (online only)

Quiz: Vocabulary Production

- Prueba 2B-2: pp. 56–57

Exploración del lenguaje

Language through gestures

In Spanish, just as in English, nonverbal body language in the form of gestures, or *gestos,* is very important to communication.

You saw the expression *¡Ojo!* in the video *Un ratón en la clase*. The word literally means "eye," but it is used to mean "be careful" or "pay attention." It is usually accompanied by a gesture, and often people use the *¡Ojo!* gesture without saying the word.

Fondo Cultural | El mundo hispano

School uniforms Many schools in Spanish-speaking countries require their students to wear uniforms. Often students wear a full uniform, like the ones you see in the photo. Sometimes the uniform consists of something more like a smock that is worn over a student's regular clothes and helps protect them from becoming dirty or torn during the school day.

- How are these uniforms similar to or different from those worn by high school students in the United States?

Estudiantes durante el descanso (*break*), Santa Clara, Cuba

8 Y tú, ¿qué dices? 

Escribir • Hablar

Describe your classroom.

1. ¿Dónde está la puerta?
2. ¿Qué hay al lado de la puerta?
3. ¿Hay ventanas en la clase? ¿Cuántas?
4. ¿Hay un reloj en la clase? ¿Dónde está?
5. ¿Cuántos escritorios y sillas hay?
6. ¿Qué más *(What else)* hay?

DIFFERENTIATED INSTRUCTION

Students with Learning Difficulties

From time to time, allow students to refer to the vocabulary section of their notebooks when doing activities that require memorization. For *Gramática,* have them write all forms of ***estar*** into their grammar notebook section. Understanding and mastering verb forms can prove difficult and may require numerous reinforcement exercises.

Heritage Language Learners

Have students make a list of appropriate gestures used in Spanish-speaking communities. Then have them compare these with body language used by people in the United States.

Gramática

▼ Objectives

- Write about and discuss the location of people and things
- Listen to a description of the position of people in a photo
- Compare prices for backpacks in Spanish-speaking countries

The verb *estar*

The *-ar* verbs you have used until now are called **regular verbs** because they follow a regular pattern. Verbs that do not follow a regular pattern are called **irregular verbs.**

Estar is irregular because the *yo* form doesn't follow a regular pattern and because the forms *estás, está,* and *están* require accent marks.

Use *estar* to tell how someone feels or where someone or something is located.

(yo) **estoy**	(nosotros) (nosotras) **estamos**
(tú) **estás**	(vosotros) (vosotras) **estáis**
Ud. (él) (ella) **está**	Uds. (ellos) (ellas) **están**

¿Recuerdas?

You have used the verb *estar* to ask how someone is.

- ¿Cómo **estás**?
- ¿Cómo **está** Ud.?

Más ayuda realidades.com

- ***GramActiva* Video**
- **Tutorial:** *Estar*
- **Animated Verbs**
- ***GramActiva* Activity**

9 ¡Hola! ¿Cómo estás?

Escribir

Write the correct forms of *estar* on a separate sheet of paper.

Marcos:	¡Buenos días! ¿Cómo __1.__ Uds.?
Paula y Roberta:	¡Hola, Marcos! Nosotras __2.__ bien, gracias. ¿Y tú?
Marcos:	__3.__ muy bien. ¿Dónde __4.__ Pedro y Juana?
Roberta:	Pedro __5.__ en la sala de clases. Juana __6.__ en la oficina.

10 ¿En qué clase están?  

Hablar

Take turns with a partner to give the correct forms of *estar* as you tell what class each person is in.

Modelo

ella  

Ella está en la clase de tecnología.

1. yo 

2. los profesores 
3. la profesora 

4. nosotros 

5. ella 
6. tú 

ENRICH YOUR TEACHING

Advanced Learners/Pre-AP*

Demonstrate how important body language can be by telling students a story using only Spanish. Even though students don't have the vocabulary or grammar to understand the entire story, use gestures to help them. For example: *¡Vamos! Ya es tarde* (point to your watch impatiently) *y tengo hambre* (rub your stomach). *Tengo ganas de comer* (place your fingertips together and bring your hand up close to your mouth. Repeat the motion several times). See p. 442 for more gestures.

Gramática

Core Instruction

Standards: 4.1

Resources: Voc. and Gram. Transparency 61; Teacher's Resource Book: Video Script, p. 150; Video Program: Cap. 2B

INTERACTIVE WHITEBOARD
Grammar Activities 2B

Suggestions: Direct attention to the *¿Recuerdas?* Point out additional examples of ***estar*** that students have encountered. Show the *GramActiva* Video to reinforce the presentation. Ask questions for each verb form: *¿Cómo estás? Yo estoy muy bien. ¿Cómo está(n) usted(es)?* Be sure students notice the accents, and that they understand the importance of including them when writing.

9 Standards: 1.2

Resources: Answer Keys: Student Edition, p. 32

Focus: Completing a dialogue using forms of ***estar***

Suggestions: Have students read the exercise before answering and identify the subject of each statement. Have volunteers perform the dialogue.

Answers:

1. están
2. estamos
3. Estoy
4. están
5. está
6. está

10 Standards: 1.1

Resources: Answer Keys: Student Edition, p. 32

Focus: Using correct forms of ***estar*** in a school context

Recycle: Names of classes

Suggestions: Review the school subjects before students begin the activity.

Answers:

1. (Yo) estoy en la clase de español.
2. Los profesores están en la clase de ciencias naturales.
3. La profesora está en la clase de matemáticas.
4. Nosotros estamos en la clase de inglés.
5. Ella está en la clase de arte.
6. Tú estás en la clase de educación física.

Extension: Use names of students in some of the sentences to practice matching subject pronouns and names.

BELLRINGER REVIEW

Go around the room and have students state where they are in relation to another student or a classroom object. Example: *Yo estoy al lado de la ventana.*

11 Standards: 1.2

Resources: Teacher's Resource Book: Audio Script, p. 148; Audio Program DVD: Cap. 2B, Track 8; Answer Keys: Student Edition, p. 33

Focus: Listening to and responding to information about a photo

Suggestions: Have students examine the photograph, saying the names of the people, indicating what they are doing, and identifying objects that appear. Allow students to listen more than once.

Script and Answers:

1. **Yo estoy detrás de Sara. *(cierto)***
2. **El señor Salas está debajo del escritorio. *(falso)***
3. **Julián y Mateo están delante de Rosa. *(falso)***
4. **Sara y yo estamos al lado del escritorio. *(cierto)***
5. **José y Lucita están encima del escritorio. *(cierto)***
6. **Benito está delante del señor Salas. *(cierto)***

12 Standards: 1.1

Resources: Answer Keys: Student Edition, p. 33

Focus: Speaking about the locations of people in a photo

Suggestions: Be sure students understand that they are describing locations from Javier's perspective.

Answers will vary but may include:

1. **Julián y Mateo están detrás de Rosa.**
2. **Rosa está al lado del escritorio.**
3. **Sara está delante de mí.**
4. **Yo estoy detrás de Sara.**
5. **El Sr. Salas está delante del escritorio.**
6. **Lucita y José están encima del escritorio.**
7. **Benito está delante del escritorio.**
8. **Sara y yo estamos a la izquierda del escritorio.**

Block Schedule

Have students stand in two facing lines. The first student in Group A will name a person or people, such as ***Carmen y Mateo.*** The first student in Group B will answer with ***Ellos están.*** Tally points on the board.

11 ¿Cierto o falso?

Escuchar

Write the numbers 1–6 on a sheet of paper. Listen to the statements about Javier's Spanish club photo and write *cierto* or *falso* based on the information provided as you view the photograph from *your* perspective.

12 ¿Y dónde están todos?

Hablar

Work with a partner. Using the club picture above, find out where the various students are located from *Javier's* perspective. Follow the model.

Modelo

A —*¿Y dónde está Lucita?*
B —*Lucita está encima del escritorio.*

1. Julián y Mateo
2. Rosa
3. Sara
4. yo
5. el Sr. Salas
6. Lucita y José
7. Benito
8. Sara y yo

En la clase de ciencias naturales

DIFFERENTIATED INSTRUCTION

Heritage Language Learners

Have students bring in photographs. Ask them to break into small groups to describe the location of people and things in the photos. Encourage students to indicate location by using ***estar*** and vocabulary they have learned.

Students with Special Needs

Some students may have difficulty visualizing spatial relationships from a photo. Bring in small dolls, name them, and place them in order in front of the student. This will make the relationships more concrete.

13 Juego 

Escribir • Hablar

Work with a partner. Write down the name of someone in the classroom. Your partner can ask only *sí / no* questions to find out the name. When your partner has guessed the mystery student's identity, change roles.

Modelo

A —*¿Es una estudiante?*
B —*Sí.*
A —*¿Está al lado de Tomás?*
B —*No.*
A —*¿Está detrás de mí?*
B —*Sí.*
A —*¿Es Patricia?*
B —*Sí.*

Para decir más . . .

detrás de mí	behind me
detrás de ti	behind you

14 Leer • Pensar

Conexiones | Las matemáticas

Los precios de mochilas en el mundo hispano

Most countries have their own currencies. In Mexico, people pay for their purchases in *pesos,* in Peru they use *nuevos soles,* and so on. The value of each currency can go up or down daily in relation to other countries' currencies. For example, a dollar might be worth 10 Mexican *pesos* one day and 11 *pesos* the following day. Read the prices for *una mochila* in six different countries.

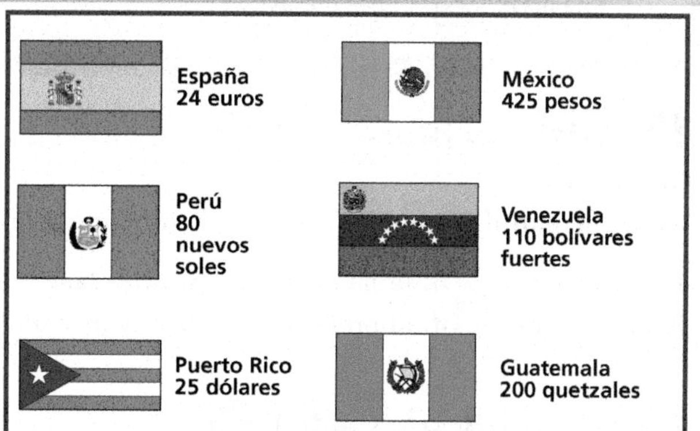

1. How much does a typical *mochila* cost in your community?
2. Convert the prices for *una mochila* into dollars. You can find a currency converter on the Internet.
3. How do these prices compare to those in your community? Why might the same item have different values in different countries?

Más práctica GO

	realidades.com	print
Instant Check	✔	
Guided WB pp. 77–78	✔	✔
Core WB p. 44	✔	✔
Comm. WB pp. 42, 46	✔	✔
***Hispanohablantes* WB** pp. 74–77		✔

Practice and Communicate 2B

BELLRINGER REVIEW

Use Transparency 63 to quickly review location of classroom objects. Instead of having students write sentences, you may want to have them say where the object is.

13 Standards: 1.1

Focus: Asking questions to determine the identity of a classmate

Suggestions: Point out the *Para decir más...* and demonstrate the words. Model the questions before students begin.

Answers will vary but may include:
al lado de, delante de, detrás de.

14 Standards: 3.1

Focus: Reading and calculating international currencies; making a cross-curricular connection

Suggestions: Bring in prices of other school supplies that you've found on the Internet (or have students do a search themselves) to reinforce the concept that items not only have different prices but different values in various countries.

Answers will vary.

Additional Resources

- Communication Wbk.: Audio Act. 7, p. 42
- Teacher's Resource Book: Audio Script, p. 148
- Audio Program DVD: Cap. 2B, Track 9

ENRICH YOUR TEACHING

Culture Note

The official currency of Venezuela, the ***bolívar,*** is named after Simón Bolívar, the "Great Liberator." The ***quetzal,*** the official unit of money in Guatemala, is named after a rare, exotic bird found only in Central American rain forests. Have students research these and other currencies to see what they look like. •

21st Century Skills

Media Literacy If students do research on the Internet for Activity 14, remind them that the Web sites they use should be compared and evaluated to find those that have the best and most accurate information, and the best, most accessible design.

ASSESSMENT

Prueba 2B-3 with Study Plan (online only)

Quiz: The verb *estar*

- Prueba 2B-3: p. 58

Gramática

Core Instruction

Standards: 4.1

Resources: Voc. and Gram. Transparency 62; Teacher's Resource Book: Video Script, p. 151; Video Program: Cap. 2B

INTERACTIVE WHITEBOARD

Grammar Activities 2B

Suggestions: Direct attention to the *¿Recuerdas?* Show the *GramActiva* Video to reinforce the presentation. ***Unos / unas*** is difficult for many English speakers to grasp, so you will want to give additional examples. Use the transparency for additional practice.

15 Standards: 1.2

Resources: Answer Keys: Student Edition, p. 34

Focus: Writing plural forms of nouns and articles

Recycle: School vocabulary

Suggestions: Encourage students to try chanting the singular and then the plural with a rap-like cadence to make the pattern second-nature: ***el cuaderno, los cuadernos, la bandera, las banderas,*** etc. Then have them go back and forth between definite and indefinite articles.

Answers:

1. los cuadernos
2. las banderas
3. las papeleras
4. los profesores
5. unas clases
6. unas mochilas
7. unos escritorios
8. unos pupitres

16 Standards: 1.2, 1.3

Resources: Answer Keys: Student Edition, p. 34

Focus: Definite article agreement

Recycle: School supplies

Suggestions: Encourage students to work together to select the appropriate articles before they carry on the conversation. Be sure they use the definite article in all cases.

Answers:

1. los
2. la
3. los
4. los
5. la
6. las
7. los
8. las
9. la
10. las

Extension: Have students create their own dialogues based on real objects.

Gramática

Objectives

- Identify and describe the location of objects around school
- Exchange information about the location of things in a classroom

The plurals of nouns and articles

To make nouns plural you usually add *-s* to words ending in a vowel and *-es* to words ending in a consonant.

silla → sillas   teclado → teclados   cartel → carteles

Singular nouns that end in *z* change the *z* to *c* in the plural.

el lápiz → los lápices

The plural definite articles are *los* and *las*. Like *el* and *la*, they both mean "the."

las sillas → *the chairs*

The plural indefinite articles are *unos* and *unas*. They both mean "some" or "a few."

unos carteles → *some posters*

Singular	Plural
el reloj la ventana	los relojes las ventanas
un cuaderno una mesa	unos cuadernos unas mesas

¿Recuerdas?

You have used definite and indefinite articles in the singular:

- **el, la** = the
- **un, una** = a, an

Más ayuda realidades.com

- ***GramActiva* Video Tutorials:** Noun-adjective agreement, Singular plural formation
- ***Canción de hip hop:*** *¿Qué hay?*
- ***GramActiva* Activity**

15 Palabras plurales

Escribir

Write the plural forms of the articles and nouns below.

1. el cuaderno
2. la bandera
3. la papelera
4. el profesor
5. una clase
6. una mochila
7. un escritorio
8. un pupitre

16 ¡A estudiar!

Hablar • Leer

Marta and Berta are getting ready for school. Read the dialogue with a partner and fill in the blanks with the correct definite articles.

Marta: ¿Dónde están __1.__ lápices?

Berta: Aquí están, en __2.__ mochila.

Marta: ¿Y tienes __3.__ bolígrafos y __4.__ libros?

Berta: No. Están allí, encima de __5.__ mesa, debajo de __6.__ ventanas.

Marta: Ah, sí. ¿Y __7.__ cuadernos y __8.__ carpetas? ¿Dónde están?

Berta: Están encima de __9.__ mesa, detrás de __10.__ computadoras.

DIFFERENTIATED INSTRUCTION

Students with Learning Difficulties

Provide students with a two-column graphic organizer. Have them write examples of singular nouns in one column and the corresponding plural forms in the next. Have them record this information in their grammar notebook section. Provide numerous examples of situations in which ***el, la, los,*** and ***las*** are used.

Multiple Intelligences

Interpersonal/Social: Have students work in groups to write a short dialogue in which they ask a parent to help them find their things before they leave for school. They can record their dialogues for their portfolios.

17 Más palabras plurales

Escuchar • Hablar

You will hear eight words. Say the plural form of each word as you hear it.

Modelo

You will hear: *el libro*
You will say: *los libros*

18 Es el cuaderno de . . .

Hablar

Work in groups of four. Each of you should choose a classroom object you have brought to class. Show your group what you have chosen. Your teacher will collect all the items, then place them in view in different parts of the classroom. Ask your group where your object is. Take turns until all members of your group have asked their question.

Modelo

A —*¿Dónde está mi calculadora?*
B —*Tu calculadora está debajo de la silla de Margarita.*

> **Nota**
>
> In Spanish, you express possession by using *de* and the name of the owner of the item.
>
> - el escritorio **de** la profesora
>   *the teacher's desk*

El español en el mundo del trabajo

School districts in the United States have many positions in which employees need to speak Spanish. For example, school counselors work with new students and parents from Spanish-speaking countries. Counselors help them set up schedules, talk about school policies, and answer questions. Both the parents and the new students feel much more comfortable when the counselor can communicate with them in Spanish.

- Does your district need employees who speak Spanish? In what other jobs within a school system would speaking Spanish be helpful?

ENRICH YOUR TEACHING

Teacher-to-Teacher

Use the Clip Art from the *Teacher's Resource Book* to create flashcards to practice articles and plurals. Some should show single objects. Others should show multiple copies of one object.

21st Century Skills

Initiative and Self-Direction As a follow-up to the *Comunidad* questions, have students work in pairs to find out about jobs requiring Spanish in their community. Have the students develop a basic plan of study that would give them the qualifications they would need to be eligible for such jobs.

Practice and Communicate 2B

17 Standards: 1.2

Resources: Teacher's Resource Book: Audio Script, p. 148; Audio Program DVD: Cap. 2B, Track 10; Answer Keys: Student Edition, p. 34

Focus: Listening and speaking using plural nouns and articles

Suggestions: Play the audio or read the script and have the class respond with the appropriate plural.

Script and Answers:

1. la mesa *(las mesas)*
2. la ventana *(las ventanas)*
3. el escritorio *(los escritorios)*
4. la mochila *(las mochilas)*
5. el teclado *(los teclados)*
6. el reloj *(los relojes)*
7. la bandera *(las banderas)*
8. el estudiante *(los estudiantes)*

18 Standards: 1.1, 1.2

Focus: Speaking about the locations of classroom objects; ***mi; tu;*** possessive with ***de***

Suggestions: Be sure students don't volunteer anything of any value. Return all items to students before the end of the class period. Remind them of the *Nota* on p. 111.

Answers will vary.

El español en el mundo del trabajo

Core Instruction

Standards: 5.1

Focus: Professions in schools

Suggestions: Have school employees who speak Spanish in their jobs tell students about what they do and why Spanish is important.

Answers will vary but may include: **secretary, principal, teacher, nurse, social worker.**

Theme Project

Students can perform Step 4 at this point. Be sure they understand your corrections and suggestions. (For more information, see p. 72-b.)

2B Practice and Communicate

19 Standards: 1.1, 1.2

Focus: Asking and answering questions in authentic context

Suggestions: Be sure students understand that they can choose among the options to create their questions.

Answers will vary.

Suggestions: Have students compare their classroom to the one in the picture. Or, bring in other photos of classrooms to have students describe.

20 Standards: 1.3

Focus: Writing a paragraph about the classroom

Suggestions: Assign this as homework. Students should list or outline what they want to talk about and some of the words they want to use.

Answers will vary.

Pre-AP* Support

- **Learning Objective:** Interpersonal Writing
- **Activity 19:** Have students expand on their questions and answers to the activity by writing an email to one of the students in the picture asking for more details about their classroom, and about the class they are taking.
- ***Pre-AP* Resource Book:*** Comprehensive guide to Pre-AP* writing skill development, pp. 27–38

Additional Resources

- Communication Wbk.: Audio Act. 8–9, pp. 43–44
- Teacher's Resource Book: Audio Script, pp. 148–149, Communicative Pair Activity BLM, pp. 154–155
- Audio Program DVD: Cap. 2B, Tracks 11–12

ASSESSMENT

Prueba 2B-4 with Study Plan (online only)

Quiz: The plural of nouns and articles

- Prueba 2B-4: p. 59

19 Una clase de inglés

Hablar • Escribir

Look at this picture of a high school class in Cuba.

1. Study the photograph and make a list in Spanish of items you can name.
2. Write two questions about the photograph, then ask your partner the questions. Use the models below.

Modelo

A —*¿Cuántos estudiantes hay en la clase?*
B —*Hay seis estudiantes.*
A —*¿Hay banderas en la clase?*
B —*No, no hay banderas.*

¿Qué es esto?	¿Quién está . . . ?
¿Cuántos(as) . . . hay?	¿Hay . . . ?
¿Dónde está(n) . . . ?	¿Qué hay?

20 Y tú, ¿qué dices?

Escribir

Look around your classroom and write five sentences about it.

Modelo

En mi clase de español hay 33 estudiantes. Hay 35 pupitres y un escritorio. El escritorio está delante de los pupitres. La computadora está encima del escritorio. No hay bandera en mi clase.

Más práctica GO

realidades.com | print

	realidades.com	print
Instant Check	✔	
Guided WB pp. 79–80	✔	✔
Core WB pp. 45–46	✔	✔
Comm. WB pp. 43–44, 47	✔	✔
***Hispanohablantes* WB** pp. 79–81		✔

DIFFERENTIATED INSTRUCTION

Students with Learning Difficulties

Students might need to use their vocabulary notebook section to do *Actividad* 19. You might need to modify *Actividad* 20, having students write three sentences, instead of five. For *Pronunciación,* have students put the rule for ***g*** in their grammar notebook section.

Advanced Learners

Have students choose a Spanish-speaking country and research the educational system. They should include information about requirements for attendance, whether schools are primarily private or public, how schools are divided based on ages, and the country's literacy rate.

Pronunciación

The letter *g*

In Spanish, the letter *g* sounds like *g* in "go" when it is followed by *a*, *o*, or *u*, although it often has a slightly softer sound than in English. Listen to and say the following words and sentences:

Gustavo	domin**go**	ten**go**
a**go**sto	pre**gu**nta	lue**go**
ami**go**	ar**go**llas	**ga**to

In Spanish, the letter *g* sounds like the letter *h* in "hot" when it is followed by *e* or *i*. Listen to and say the following words. Some of these words you have not yet heard or seen. Can you guess the meanings of the cognates?

intelig**e**nte	**ge**neroso	**ge**neral
gimnasio	tecnolo**gía**	biolo**gía**

Try it out! See if you can guess how to pronounce the following Spanish first names. Keep in mind the pronunciation rules for the *g* sound.

Gabriela	Ángela	Gerardo
Gilberto	Gustavo	Rodrigo
Olga	Rogelio	Gregorio

Estudiantes en un gimnasio

Fondo Cultural | El mundo hispano

School gyms are rare in Spanish-speaking countries. Students usually have physical education classes in the school's *patio*. High school students usually have P.E. one or two times a week, sometimes before or after regular school hours. School sports teams are also less common than in the United States.

- What are some reasons that schools in Spanish-speaking countries might place less emphasis on physical education, sports, and gymnasiums?

Una clase de educación física de una escuela primaria, México

Practice and Communicate 2B

Pronunciación
Core Instruction

Standards: 4.1

Resources: Teacher's Resource Book: Audio Script, p. 149; Audio Program DVD: Cap. 2B, Track 13

Suggestions: Have students practice the syllables ***ga-, go-,*** and ***gu-,*** perhaps singing them on a tone. Then have them practice ***gi-*** and ***ge-,*** alternating between them with each breath, emphasizing the exhaling.

Have students work in pairs to create tongue twisters using words with both hard and soft ***g*** and present them to the class. Give them additional words to include. Example: *Gustavo es inteligente y su amiga, Olga, es graciosa.*

Fondo cultural

Standards: 2.1, 4.2

Suggestions: Have students consider the value that their local culture places on sports and physical activity as part of an education.

Answers will vary, but may include: **lack of space, more emphasis on academics.**

Theme Project

Students can perform Step 5 at this point. (For more information, See p. 72-b.)

ENRICH YOUR TEACHING

Culture Note

The school's ***patio*** is used for many other activities, not just for sports. For example, in some schools during the morning, students line up and pledge allegiance to the flag. During special occasions, the ***patio*** is used for student performances. In a sense, it can almost be considered an outdoor auditorium.

Teacher-to-Teacher

For writing activities, such as *Actividad* 20, use samples produced by students to write a longer composition on the board. This should include their best ideas. Use the exercise to model correct spelling and punctuation.

Common Core: Reading

Lectura

Core Instruction

Standards: 1.2, 3.1

Focus: Reading a narrative about UNICEF

Suggestions:

Pre-reading: Direct students' attention to the *Strategy*. Have students scan the reading for cognates and to tell what the main ideas are in this text. Ask students to take a good look at the illustrations and predict how they might relate to the reading.

Reading: Have students read the article, stopping to make note of the important information in each paragraph. Tell students to refer to their list of predictions as they read and make a checkmark next to each one that is mentioned in the article.

Post-reading: Invite students to share which of their predictions were mentioned in the article. Then have them complete the *¿Comprendes?* questions in class or as homework.

BELLRINGER REVIEW

Write these cognates on the board and ask students to tell what the English equivalent is:

dignidad protección dieta familia

(**Answers:** dignity, protection, diet, family)

Block Schedule

Have students discuss the list of items that children in every nation should have. Do they feel these are privileges or necessities? Do they feel that these goals are being met where they live?

Objectives

- Read about a United Nations program for children
- Make predictions about what you will read

Lectura

Lee este artículo sobre el UNICEF.

Strategy

Predicting outcomes
Think about what you would consider to be basic rights for children around the world. Jot down four of them on a piece of paper. As you read the article, see if your ideas are included.

El UNICEF y una convención para los niños[1]

¿Sabes que es un privilegio estar en una escuela, tener una mochila con libros, unos lápices, una calculadora, unas hojas de papel y un profesor bueno? En ciertas[2] naciones, ir a la escuela es difícil o no es posible.

El UNICEF es la organización internacional de las Naciones Unidas que trabaja para los niños. UNICEF es una sigla[3] inglesa que significa "Fondo Internacional de Emergencia de las Naciones Unidas para los Niños". Tiene siete oficinas regionales en diversas naciones y un Centro de Investigaciones en Italia.

El 20 de noviembre de 1989, la Organización de las Naciones Unidas escribió[4] "una convención para los niños" en inglés, árabe, chino, ruso y francés.

[1]children [2]certain [3]acronym [4]wrote

Esta convención dice que[5] los niños de todas[6] las naciones necesitan:

- dignidad
- una casa
- protección
- una buena dieta
- la práctica de deportes
- atención especial para los niños con problemas físicos
- amor y la comprensión de la familia
- expresar sus opiniones
- una comunidad sin[7] violencia
- ir a la escuela para ser inteligentes y sociables

[5]says that [6]all [7]without

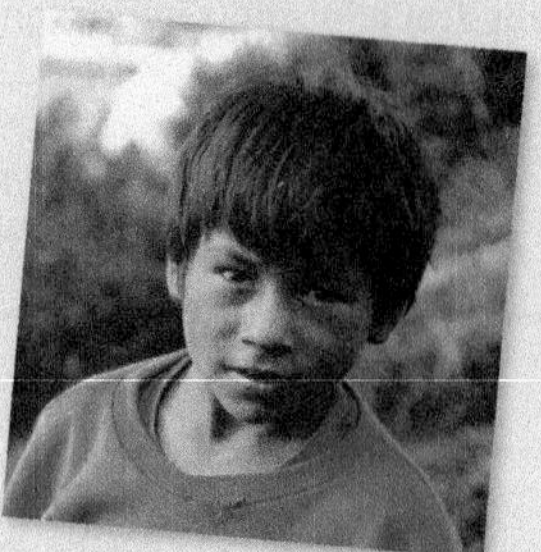

114

DIFFERENTIATED INSTRUCTION

Students with Learning Difficulties

Point out the *Strategy* and provide examples of the concept of "basic rights." Before reading, go through *¿Comprendes?* highlighting key words and phrases. Students might need to read through passage a number of times to comprehend information. Doing guided reading with students may be useful.

Advanced Learners

Have students research other organizations that provide aid to children. Can they find Spanish-language information about the organizations? Have them bring in examples to share with the class.

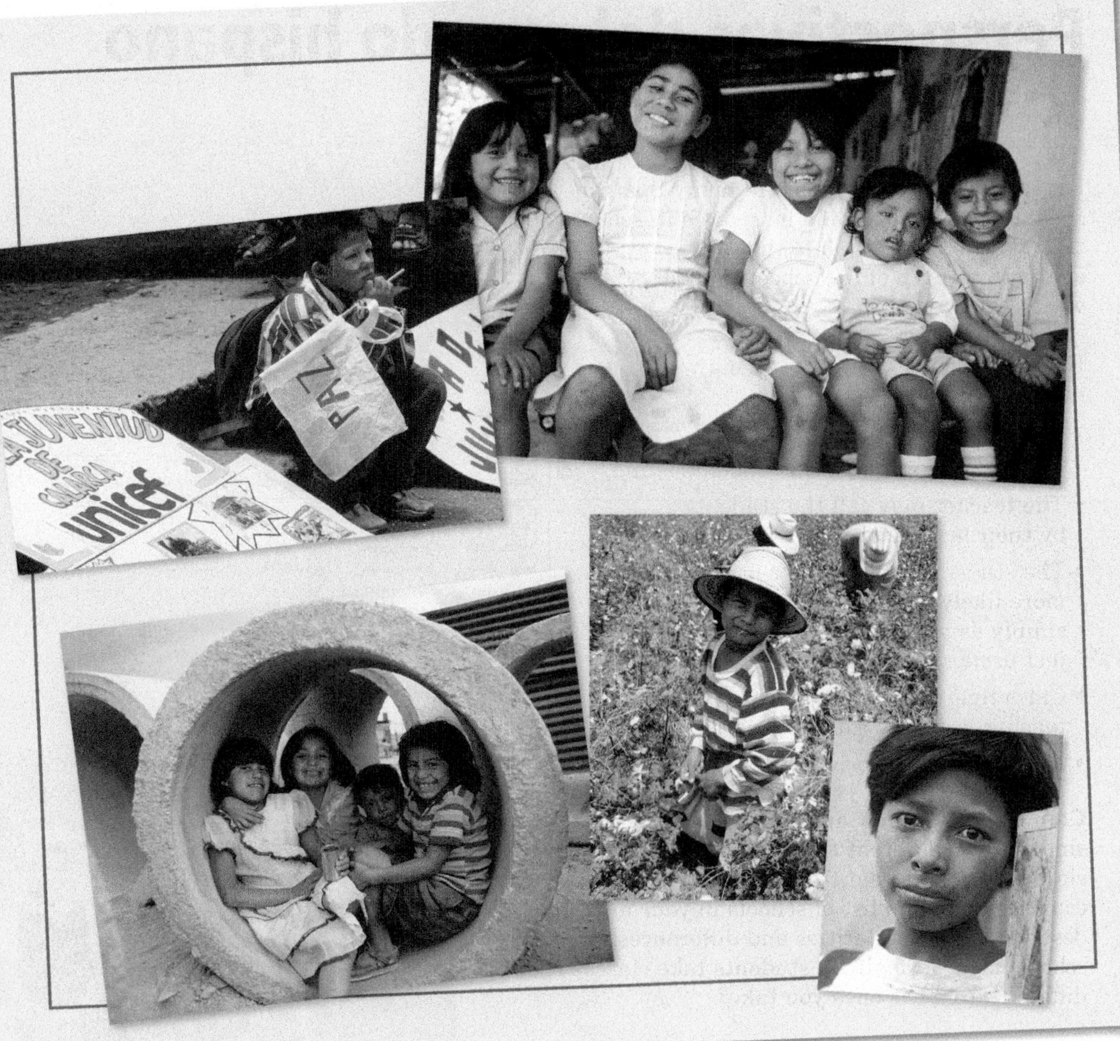

¿Comprendes?

1. Para los estudiantes de todas las naciones es fácil estar en una escuela y tener una mochila. ¿Cierto o falso?
2. ¿Cuántas oficinas regionales tiene UNICEF?
3. ¿Qué significa la sigla UNICEF?
4. ¿Dónde está el Centro de Investigaciones?
5. La convención es para los niños de todas las naciones. ¿Cierto o falso?
6. Según la convención para los niños, ¿cuáles (*what*) son cuatro cosas que necesitan los niños?

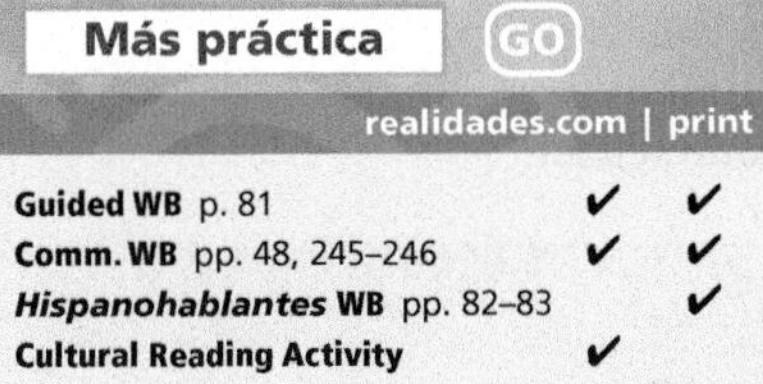

Más práctica GO

	realidades.com	print
Guided WB p. 81	✔	✔
Comm. WB pp. 48, 245–246	✔	✔
***Hispanohablantes* WB** pp. 82–83		✔
Cultural Reading Activity	✔	

¿Comprendes? Standards: 1.2, 1.3

Resources: Answer Keys: Student Edition, p. 35

Focus: Demonstrating reading comprehension

Suggestions: Help students understand the questions that contain cognates and decodable words. Have students discuss the questions and answers in small groups.

Answers:

1. **falso**
2. **siete**
3. **Fondo Internacional de Emergencia de las Naciones Unidas para los Niños (United Nations International Children's Emergency Fund).**
4. **El Centro de Investigaciones está en Italia.**
5. **cierto**
6. **Answers will vary but will include any of the items in the list on p. 114.**

Pre-AP* Support

- **Learning Objective:** Interpretive: Print
- **Activity:** Have students read each paragraph of the *Lectura* text silently. Pause after each paragraph to read teacher-made true/false statements.
- ***Pre-AP* Resource Book:*** Comprehensive guide to Pre-AP* reading skill development, pp. 19–26

For Further Reading

Student Resource: Realidades para hispanohablantes: Lectura 2, pp. 84–85

ENRICH YOUR TEACHING

Culture Note

UNICEF is a private, nonprofit organization supported by volunteers who help raise funds selling the well-known UNICEF greeting cards and conducting the "Trick or Treat for UNICEF" program. The agency seeks to generate understanding of the rights and needs of children everywhere. UNICEF helps children get the care they need as infants and encourages families to educate girls as well as boys. Funds are used to reduce infant deaths and illnesses and to protect children from war or natural disasters.

Perspectivas del mundo hispano

Core Instruction

Standards: 2.1, 2.2, 4.2

Focus: Reading about school in Spanish-speaking countries

Presentation: Have students vote about whether they spend too much time, too little time, or just the right amount of time in school. Tally the results on the board. Tell them that the school year in Spanish-speaking countries is usually longer than in the United States. Call attention to the graph. Point out the variations. Tell students that the way classes are run is different, too. Have volunteers read the bulleted items. Are there any that students find preferable to what they experience? Have students complete the *Check it out!*

Suggestions: Most students will not like the idea of spending more time in school, but have them enumerate possible benefits to a longer school year. How would they like the added time spent? Ask how the rules might affect students and classes. Find out if students like the idea of wearing a uniform or having class lectures instead of class discussion, and why.

Direct attention to the *Think about it!* section and have students discuss the questions.

Answers will vary.

Culture Note

In the United States it is common to use a letter grading system, where generally A = 90–100%, B = 80–90%, and so on. In the majority of Spanish-speaking countries, however, the grading system is generally based on the numbers 1–10, rather than on letter grades.

Teacher-to-Teacher

e-amigos: Have students e-mail descriptions of their Spanish classes to their *e-amigos*. Have them print out or e-mail you their messages.

Additional Resources

Student Resource: Realidades para hispanohablantes, p. 86

Perspectivas del mundo hispano

¿Cómo es la escuela?

Did you know that students in many Spanish-speaking countries spend more time in school than you do? The graph to the right shows the length of the school year in various countries.

País	Días de escuela
Chile	235
Colombia	210
México	205
España	200
Argentina	185
Est Un	1

Here are some other facts you may not know:

- In many schools, when a teacher enters the classroom, the students stand.
- The teacher may call the students by their last name.
- The students, on the other hand, are more likely to address their teacher simply as *maestro(a), profesor(a),* or just *profe,* without a last name.
- Class time is generally spent with the teacher lecturing rather than with class discussion.
- Many public and private schools require uniforms.

Check it out! How are other schools in your area similar to or different from yours? How are they similar to or different from those in Spanish-speaking countries? Make a list of schools in your area and describe these similarities and differences. Are some schools more formal? Do students take classes that are different from the ones you take?

Think about it! Based on the information above, what might you assume are the attitudes toward school in Spanish-speaking cultures? How are these the same as or different from attitudes in your community? List five suggestions that might help an exchange student from Mexico City adjust to your school.

DIFFERENTIATED INSTRUCTION

Multiple Intelligences

Logical/Mathematical: Have students find out about the length of the school day and year in a Spanish-speaking country not included in the graph. Ask them to compare their own curriculum with that of students of the same age in the country of their choice. Have them present this information to the class in the form of a graph.

Heritage Language Learners

Some students may have gone to school in their heritage country. If so, ask them to tell what adjustments they found difficult when they came to school in the United States. Ask them to share what they prefer about each system.

- Write a description of your classroom
- Make a sketch to remember ideas

Presentación escrita

Tu sala de clases

Task
Your pen pal from Mexico is coming to visit your school. Write him or her a note describing your Spanish classroom.

1 Prewrite Sketch your classroom, showing and labeling the items you intend to describe.

2 Draft Write the first draft of your note. Use your sketch to remember which items you want to describe and where they are. Use the model to organize your draft.

Modelo

En mi sala de clases hay cuatro ventanas. Mi pupitre está delante del escritorio de la profesora. La bandera está al lado de la puerta. Las computadoras están encima de la mesa.

3 Revise Check your note for correct spelling, as well as for the categories under Evaluation. Share your note with a partner, who will check for the following:

- Is your note easy to understand?
- Could you add other information?
- Are there any errors?

Rewrite your note making any necessary changes.

4 Publish Make a final copy of your note for display in the classroom or for your portfolio.

5 Evaluation The following rubric will be used to grade your note.

Rubric	Score 1	Score 3	Score 5
Use of newly acquired vocabulary	You use very little variation of vocabulary with frequent usage errors.	You use limited vocabulary with some usage errors.	You use an extended variety of vocabulary with very few usage errors.
Correct use of the verb *estar*	You use many repetitions of incorrect verb forms.	You use frequent repetitions of incorrect verb forms.	You use very few incorrect verb forms.
Amount of information	You provide information about two or fewer items in the classroom.	You provide information about three or fewer items in the classroom.	You provide information about four or more items in the classroom.

Strategy

Creating visuals
Creating a sketch or a drawing can help you remember the things you want to write about in a description.

Writing 2B

Common Core: Writing

Presentación escrita

Expository

Standards: 1.3

Resources: Voc. and Gram. Transparency 64

Focus: Writing to a Mexican pen pal about the American student's classroom

Suggestions: Introduce the task to the class and then have them work through each step of the process. You may want to provide a model of a top-scoring note.

Portfolio

Have students include their notes in their portfolios.

Pre-AP* Support

- **Learning Objective:** Interpersonal Writing
- **Activity:** Have students convert their notes into e-mails to their pen pals in Mexico. Expand the task by asking students to include at least one question for the recipient of the communication.
- ***Pre-AP* Resource Book:*** Comprehensive guide to Pre-AP* writing skill development, pp. 27–38

Teacher-to-Teacher

Pen pal Web sites serve to connect pen pals from different countries; some are geared for classrooms and students. Find out about setting students up with pen pals through school or home computers. You may contact a school in a Spanish-speaking city and set up a "sister" class for exchanging letters through regular mail service.

Additional Resources

Student Resources: Realidades para hispanohablantes, p. 87; Guided Practice: Presentación escrita, p. 82

ENRICH YOUR TEACHING

Teacher-to-Teacher

Careers: *Tema* 2 has focused on school and classes. Have students work in small groups to talk about a career as a Spanish teacher. Have them list words and expressions they have learned that would be helpful and share them.

21st Century Skills

Technology Literacy Help students conduct an Internet search to find photos and graphics to illustrate the items they describe in their notes. They can scan their sketches and devise ways to link visuals to them.

ASSESSMENT

Presentación escrita

- Assessment Program: Rubrics, p. T29

Review the rubric with students. Go over the descriptions of the different levels of performance. After assessing students, help individuals understand how their performance could be improved. (See Teacher's Resource Book for suggestions on using rubrics in assessment.)

El mundo hispano

Core Instruction

Standards: 2.1, 2.2, 4.2

Resources: Map Transparency 13

Mapa global interactivo, Actividad 1 Look at the countries that comprise Central America.

Focus: Reading about the countries of Central America

Suggestions: After students have read the text, show a map of Central America and identify the seven countries. Have students locate Belize and explain why Spanish is not the language of that country. Point out the narrowness of this stretch of land and the Caribbean Sea and the Pacific Ocean on either side. Only Belize and El Salvador do not have access to both bodies of water. How might this affect trade and other aspects of life in those countries?

Direct attention to the photo in the middle of p. 118. Discuss sea turtles and the efforts of Costa Rica to protect the environment. Since there are rain forests in this part of the world, ask what we can tell about the climate.

Note the photo of the women and discuss the indigenous Mayan population of Guatemala. This picture shows how certain traditions have survived the centuries. Discuss the messages in the clothing these women are wearing. How might this have been useful?

The top photo focuses on the modern city of Granada, Nicaragua; an important trading center. What may have helped this city become so important? Discuss whether Nicaragua would have been a good alternative site for the canal. Which do students think would have been the better choice? Why?

Direct attention to the bottom picture. Have students explain why forts to protect the ships and their cargo were built along this coast. Ask why they think the silver and gold from Peru was carried overland to the coast. Was this really the best route?

Direct students to the *¿Sabes que...?* section. Discuss possible reasons for Spain to have had an interest in a canal. How many years passed before it was built?

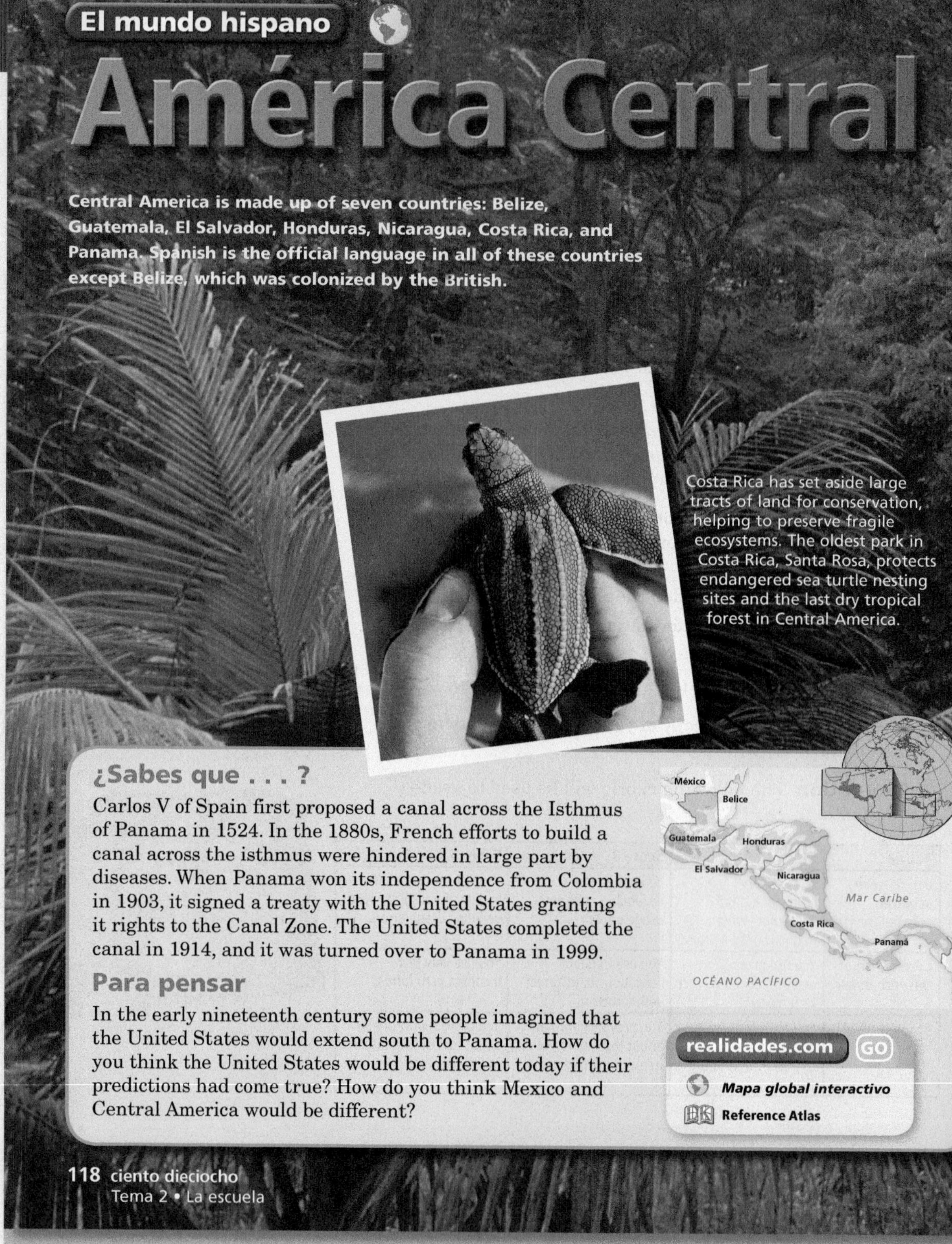

América Central

Central America is made up of seven countries: Belize, Guatemala, El Salvador, Honduras, Nicaragua, Costa Rica, and Panama. Spanish is the official language in all of these countries except Belize, which was colonized by the British.

Costa Rica has set aside large tracts of land for conservation, helping to preserve fragile ecosystems. The oldest park in Costa Rica, Santa Rosa, protects endangered sea turtle nesting sites and the last dry tropical forest in Central America.

¿Sabes que . . . ?

Carlos V of Spain first proposed a canal across the Isthmus of Panama in 1524. In the 1880s, French efforts to build a canal across the isthmus were hindered in large part by diseases. When Panama won its independence from Colombia in 1903, it signed a treaty with the United States granting it rights to the Canal Zone. The United States completed the canal in 1914, and it was turned over to Panama in 1999.

Para pensar

In the early nineteenth century some people imagined that the United States would extend south to Panama. How do you think the United States would be different today if their predictions had come true? How do you think Mexico and Central America would be different?

DIFFERENTIATED INSTRUCTION

Multiple Intelligences

Visual/Spatial: Have students create a map of Central America, including major cities, rain forests, indigenous wildlife, and other facts or phenomena they find interesting or important.

Heritage Language Learners

Have students find out about the indigenous people of their heritage country or of another Spanish-speaking country of their choice. Does the Spanish spoken there today have words that came from the indigenous language(s)?

Founded by the Spanish in 1524, the Nicaraguan city of Granada became an important trading center. The town enjoys easy access to the Caribbean, yet is located less than 100 miles from the Pacific. In the nineteenth and twentieth centuries Nicaragua was proposed as an alternate site for a canal linking the Atlantic and Pacific oceans.

Guatemala has a large indigenous population, many descended from the Maya. These women are wearing the traditional hand-woven *huipil*, which is a very "communicative" part of their clothing. The *huipil* identifies the wearer's village, her marital status, her religious beliefs, wealth, and personality. A well-woven *huipil* may last 20 to 30 years.

From the 1500s to the end of the 1700s, the coasts of Spanish America were plagued by pirates. Panamanian ports were perfect targets, since the silver and gold mined in Peru were loaded on Panama's Pacific coast and carried overland to the Atlantic, where they were put on ships bound for Spain. Fuerte San Lorenzo, on Panama's Atlantic coast, was part of a network of forts that were meant to protect ships and their precious cargo.

Culture 2B

Suggestions: Help students see the value of a canal connecting the Caribbean and the Pacific Ocean—and of canals in general. Some students may not understand how it is possible that Belize was colonized by the British, yet is surrounded by countries colonized by the Spanish. Discuss how the English, the Spanish, and the French colonized most of the Americas.

Direct attention to the *Para pensar* section and have students discuss the questions.

Answers will vary.

Mapa global interactivo, Actividad 2
Explore the geography of Nicaragua.

ENRICH YOUR TEACHING

Teacher-to-Teacher

Have students research the Panama Canal. They should find out when it was finally built, who built it and under what circumstances, and the status of the Canal today.

21st Century Skills

Information Literacy Have students research one of the following: conservation efforts in Costa Rica, Mayan population in Guatemala, Nicaragua as alternate site for the canal. Encourage students to focus on the most current aspects of these topics, such as the current status of the endangered sea turtles. Have students summarize their findings for the class.

Review Activities

To talk about classroom items: Point to classroom items and have students identify them by name. Call on volunteers to tell what vocabulary items are not in their classroom. For example: *En la sala de clase hay una mesa pero no hay un sacapuntas.*

To talk about classroom furniture: Have students make a list of the furniture that can be in a classroom. Have Student A point to a specific piece of furniture and have Student B say what it is. For example, *¿Es una mesa? No. Es una silla.*

To talk about parts of a classroom and ***to indicate location:*** Using the list created above, have students work in pairs, asking and telling where different items are located relative to the parts of the classroom. For example: *¿Dónde está el escritorio? Está al lado (debajo de) la ventana.*

To indicate possession, to identify (description, quantity) and ***to identify gender and quantity of nouns:*** Have students work in groups. Tell them to put several classroom objects in front of them. Have Student A point to an item and ask what it is and Student B will name the item and say whose it is. For example, *¿Qué es esto? Es una calculadora; es tu calculadora.*

Estar: Ask volunteers to give the forms of ***estar*** by briefly reviewing the stem and verb endings. You may want them to create sentences for each form.

Portfolio

Invite students to review the activities they completed in this chapter, including written reports, posters or other visuals, and recordings of oral presentations, or other projects. Have them select one or two items that they feel best demonstrate their achievements in Spanish to include in their portfolios. Have them include this with the Chapter Checklist and Self-Assessment Worksheet.

Additional Resources

Student Resources: Realidades para hispanohablantes, p. 88

Teacher Resources:

- Teacher's Resource Book: Situation Cards, p. 156, Clip Art, pp. 158–159
- Assessment Program: Chapter Checklist and Self-Assessment Worksheet, pp. T56–T57

Repaso

Objectives

- Review the vocabulary and grammar
- Demonstrate you can perform the tasks on p. 121

Repaso del capítulo

Vocabulario y gramática

to talk about classroom items

la bandera	flag
el cartel	poster
la computadora	computer
la mochila	bookbag, backpack
la pantalla	(computer) screen
la papelera	wastepaper basket
el ratón	(computer) mouse
el reloj	clock
el sacapuntas	pencil sharpener
el teclado	(computer) keyboard

to talk about classroom furniture

el escritorio	desk
la mesa	table
la silla	chair

to talk about parts of a classroom

la puerta	door
la ventana	window

to indicate location

al lado de la / del	next to, beside
allí	there
aquí	here
debajo de la / del	underneath
delante de la / del	in front of
detrás de la / del	behind
¿Dónde?	Where?
en	in, on
encima de la / del	on top of

For *Vocabulario adicional*, see pp. 472–473.

to indicate possession

de	of
mi	my
tu	your

to identify (description, quantity)

Es un(a) . . .	It's a . . .
Hay	There is, There are
¿Qué es esto?	What is this?

estar *to be*

estoy	**estamos**
estás	**estáis**
está	**están**

to identify gender and quantity of nouns

los, las	the
unos, unas	some

DIFFERENTIATED INSTRUCTION

Students with Learning Difficulties

Have students review the *Repaso del capítulo* and create flashcards for any words that they do not know. Pair them with a student who is more confident with the vocabulary to practice. Before the test, provide students with a practice test, so they can become comfortable with the format.

Heritage Language Learners

Have students write a few paragraphs telling about the classroom of their favorite class: What things are in the classroom? Where is their desk? Where is the teacher's desk? Where are the computers, posters, etc.? Encourage them to use as many vocabulary words from this chapter as they can.

Más repaso GO realidades.com | print

Instant Check	✓	
Puzzles	✓	
Core WB pp. 47–48		✓
Comm. WB pp. 247, 248–250	✓	✓

Preparación para el examen

On the exam you will be asked to . . .	Here are practice tasks similar to those you will find on the exam . . .	For review go to your print or digital textbook . . .
Interpretive		
 **1 Escuchar** Listen to and identify classrooms and locations	Listen as a student frantically asks some of his friends where he left his homework. Can you identify all of the classrooms and places they suggest that he look?	**pp. 100–103** *Vocabulario en contexto* **p. 105** Actividades 6–7 **p. 111** Actividad 18
Interpersonal		
 **2 Hablar • Escribir** Talk or write about where someone is located by describing where that person is in relation to objects in the classroom	You are trying to find out the name of someone in your class. You ask the person next to you, but he doesn't understand whom you are talking about. Give at least three statements that would help him identify the person. You might include where he or she is in relation to the teacher's desk, the window, someone else's desk, and so on.	**pp. 100–103** *Vocabulario en contexto* **p. 105** Actividades 6–7 **p. 108** Actividades 11–12 **p. 109** Actividad 13 **p. 111** Actividad 18
Interpretive		
 **3 Leer** Read and understand a letter that contains questions and concerns about school issues	The school counselor has asked you to help him read a note written by a new Spanish-speaking student at school. After reading it, tell the counselor what the problem is and the kinds of questions the student asks. Necesito una clase para la primera hora. ¿Cómo es la clase de tecnología, fácil o difícil? ¿Qué necesito para la clase? ¿Cuántos estudiantes hay en la clase? ¿Hay mucha tarea?	**pp. 100–103** *Vocabulario en contexto* **p. 112** Actividad 19 **p. 114** *Lectura*
Presentational		
 **4 Escribir** Write an email to a friend about one of her classes	You have just moved to a new town and are sending an e-mail to a friend from your old school. You have lots of questions about her classes. Write at least three questions about one of her classes: whether she likes it, how many students are in it, where her desk is in the room, what else is in the room, etc.	**pp. 100–103** *Vocabulario en contexto* **p. 112** Actividad 19
Cultures • Comparisons		
5 Pensar Demonstrate an understanding of cultural differences in schools	Think about how students and teachers interact within a typical classroom in a Spanish-speaking country. What are at least four things you might find different from most schools in the United States?	**p. 106** *Fondo cultural* **p. 113** *Fondo cultural* **p. 116** *Perspectivas del mundo hispano*

Review 2B

Performance Tasks

Standards: 1.1, 1.2, 1.3, 4.2

Student Resource: Realidades para hispanohablantes, p. 89

Teacher Resources: Teacher's Resource Book: Audio Script, p. 149; Audio Program DVD: Cap. 2B, Track 15; Answer Keys: Student Edition, p. 35

1. Escuchar

Suggestions: Play the audio or read the script.

Script:

Juan: ¡Ay! Mi tarea...¿Dónde está? Necesito mi tarea para la clase de matemáticas. Ana, ¿dónde está mi tarea?
Ana: ¿Tu tarea? Está en la clase de ciencias sociales, en el escritorio del profesor.
Juan: Gracias, Ana. ¡Ay! No está aquí. Daniel, ¿dónde está mi tarea de matemáticas?
Daniel: Está en la clase de tecnología...al lado de la computadora.
Juan: Gracias.

Answers:

Clase de matemáticas, clase de ciencias sociales—en el escritorio del profesor, clase de tecnología—al lado de la computadora

2. Hablar

Suggestions: Pair students for this activity. Give them time to prepare before they speak.

Answers will vary.

3. Leer

Suggestions: If students have difficulty reading and understanding this note, refer them to the vocabulary list to study words they do not recognize.

4. Escribir

Suggestions: Have students try this activity without consulting the vocabulary list, notes, or completed activities.

5. Pensar

Suggestion: Encourage students to read the *Perspectivas del mundo hispano* and *Fondos culturales* to prepare for this task.

DIFFERENTIATED ASSESSMENT

CORE ASSESSMENT
- **Assessment Program:** Examen del capítulo 2B, pp. 60–66
- **Audio Program DVD:** Cap. 2B, Track 16
- **ExamView:** Chapter Test, Test Banks A and B

ADVANCED/PRE-AP*
- **ExamView: Pre-AP* Test Bank**
- **Pre-AP* Resource Book,** pp. 66–69

STUDENTS NEEDING EXTRA HELP
- **Alternate Assessment Program:** Examen del capítulo 2B
- **Audio Program DVD:** Cap. 2B, Track 16

HERITAGE LEARNERS
- **Assessment Program: Realidades para hispanohablantes:** Examen del capítulo 2B
- **ExamView: Heritage Learner Test Bank**

Tema

3 La comida

3A ¿Desayuno o almuerzo?

- **Foods and beverages for breakfast and lunch**

Vocabulary: foods; beverages; adverbs of frequency; expressions to show surprise

Grammar: present tense of ***-er*** and ***-ir*** verbs; ***me gusta(n), me encanta(n)***

Cultural Perspectives: meals in the Spanish-speaking world

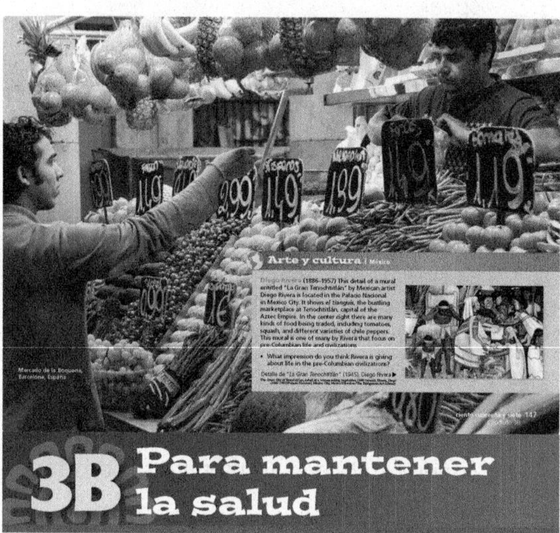

3B Para mantener la salud

- **Foods and beverages for dinner; food, health, and exercise choices**

Vocabulary: food; beverages; expressions to discuss health and indicate preference, agreement, disagreement, and quantity; adjectives to describe food

Grammar: the plural of adjectives; the verb ***ser***

Cultural Perspectives: opinions regarding diet and health

THEME SUPPORT

Bulletin Boards

Theme: *La comida*

Ask students to cut out, copy, or download photos of foods and beverages from around the world, people engaged in various forms of exercise, and recipes in Spanish. Cluster photos according to the following themes: healthy foods and beverages, unhealthy foods and beverages, exercise, and recipes.

Hands-on Culture

Recipe: *Tortilla española*

This popular dish from Spain can be eaten at breakfast, as an appetizer, or as a light supper.

Ingredients:

4 eggs	½ c. olive oil
3 potatoes	⅜ T. salt
1 small onion	

1. Scrub the potatoes and peel the onion. Slice the potatoes and onion.
2. In a frying pan, sauté the potatoes and onion in the olive oil until they are lightly browned. Add salt.
3. Beat the eggs thoroughly. Pour them over the potatoes and onion.
4. Cook the mixture over low heat for three to four minutes, until the eggs set.
5. Place a plate over the frying pan, and flip the ***tortilla*** onto the plate. Slide the ***tortilla*** back into the pan, the uncooked side down. Continue cooking over low heat for three to four minutes.
6. Place the ***tortilla*** on a serving plate and let it cool before serving.

Game

Categorías

This game is a timed relay race. Play it to review vocabulary before the Vocabulary production quiz.

Players: the entire class

Materials: paper, pens

Rules:

1. Arrange students' desks in five rows. Ask students to clear their desks. Give the first student in each row a sheet of paper and a pen.
2. Call out one of the following categories: ***desayuno, almuerzo, cena, bebidas,*** or ***salud.*** Tell students they have one minute to write as many words from the category as they can on their row's sheet of paper.
3. After you say ***"empiecen,"*** the first student in each row writes a word, then passes the paper and pen to the next student. That student writes another word, then passes it to the third student, and so on until the paper reaches the end of the row. The last student brings the paper to the first student and the relay begins again until you call time.
4. Rows exchange papers for correction. The team with the most words spelled correctly wins a point.
5. Continue play until all the categories have been completed. If there is a tie at the end of play, have students define each word on their row's list. The winner is the row that defines all words correctly first.

Variation: Have a relay spelling bee. Call out a vocabulary word or expression, and have each student in a row write one letter of the word.

THEME PROJECT

Para la salud: Vacaciones

Overview: Students create a brochure for electronic or print delivery, describing a day at a health resort. The brochure includes a schedule of the day's activities and descriptions of breakfast, lunch, and dinner with photos or drawings of each meal and one of the activities. Students present the brochures to the class as if they were sales representatives from the resort.

Resources: page layout and editing software, construction paper, magazines, scissors, glue, colored pencils and markers

Sequence: (suggestions for when to do each step are found throughout the chapters)

STEP 1. Review instructions so students know what is expected of them. Hand out the "Theme 3 Project Instructions and Rubric" from the *Teacher's Resource Book.*

STEP 2. Students submit a rough sketch of their brochure. Return the sketches with your suggestions. For vocabulary and grammar practice, ask students to partner and present their sketches to each other.

STEP 3. Students do layouts on construction paper. Encourage students to work in pencil first and to try different arrangements before drawing pictures or gluing magazine clippings and writing the content of the brochure.

3B

STEP 4. Students submit a draft of their meal descriptions and schedule. Note your corrections and suggestions, then return the drafts to students.

STEP 5. Students complete and present their brochure to the class, trying to "sell" their health package to classmates.

Options:

1. Students design a one-week lunch plan for the school cafeteria using the MyPlate Food Guide.
2. Students create a diet and exercise guide for someone wanting to get in shape.

Assessment:

Here is a detailed rubric for assessing this project:

Theme 3 Project: *Para la salud: Vacaciones*

RUBRIC	Score 1	Score 3	Score 5
Evidence of Planning	You provided no written draft or page layout.	Your draft was written and layout created, but not corrected.	You corrected your draft and layout.
Your use of illustrations	You included no photos / visuals.	You included photos / visuals, but your layout was unorganized.	Your brochure was easy to read, complete, and accurate.
Your presentation	You included little of the required information for the brochure and made no attempt to "sell" the product.	You included most of the required information for the brochure and made some attempt to "sell" the product.	You included all of the required information for the brochure and tried to "sell" the product.

21st Century Skills

Look for tips throughout *Tema* 3 to enrich your teaching by integrating 21st Century Skills. Suggestions for the Theme Project and Theme Support follow below.

Theme Project

Modify the Theme Project with one or more of these suggestions:

Promote Media Literacy
Beforehand, students should select several Web sites that provide accurate information about their resort. Knowing about climate, geography, and locally-grown foods will help them craft their brochure.

Encourage Flexibility and Adaptability
Have students think about their audience. Is the brochure aimed at a specific age group, or at people in a challenging situation? How will factors such as age affect the material included and the language used? The handout "Solve Problems" will help them make decisions.

Support Creativity and Innovation
Encourage students to think outside the box when planning their brochures. They can, for example, create an electronic brochure that combines different kinds of media: text, photos, video. The more creative the presentation of the material, the more appealing it will be to different audiences.

Theme Culture

Foster Social and Cross-Cultural Skills
Have students review the *Fondo cultural* on page 134 and then plan a public service announcement about the importance of breakfast. Have them devise a slogan and include food examples from traditional breakfasts in the United States and from the Spanish-speaking world.

Videocultura View *El maíz: comida esencial* with the class to find out how corn is prepared in Spanish-speaking countries.

3A ¿Desayuno o almuerzo?

AT A GLANCE

Objectives
- **Listen to and read descriptions of meals and menus**
- **Talk and write about foods you and others like and dislike**
- **Exchange information about food preferences**
- **Prepare a snack from the Spanish-speaking world and compare it to snacks you enjoy**
- **Trace the history of some foods originally native to the Americas and Europe**

Vocabulary
- Foods and beverages for breakfast and lunch
- Expressions of frequency

Grammar
- Present tense of ***-er*** and ***-ir*** verbs
- ***Me gustan, me encantan***

Culture
- Bartolomé Murillo, p. 123
- Fruits and vegetables from the Americas, p. 131
- Typical breakfasts in Spanish-speaking countries, p. 134
- Fruits imported from Chile, p. 139
- Popular snacks in Spanish-speaking countries, p. 140

Recycle ♻
- Present tense of *-ar* verbs
- Expressions of agreement and disagreement

RESOURCES

	FOR THE STUDENT	ONLINE	DVD	PRINT	FOR THE TEACHER	ONLINE	PREEXP	DVD	PRINT
Plan					Interactive TE and Resources DVD	•		•	
					Teacher's Resource Book, pp. 178–213	•		•	•
					Pre-AP* Resource Book, pp. 70–73	•		•	•
					Lesson Plans	•			•
					Mapa global interactivo	•			
Introducción pp. 122–123									
Present	Student Edition, pp. 122–123	•	•	•	Interactive TE and Resources DVD	•		•	
	DK Reference Atlas	•	•		Teacher's Resource Book, pp. 178–181	•		•	•
	Videocultura	•	•		Galería de fotos		•		
	Hispanohablantes WB, pp. 90–91			•	Fine Art Transparencies, 41	•	•	•	
					Map Transparencies, 13, 15–18	•	•	•	
Vocabulario en contexto pp. 124–127									
Present & Practice	Student Edition, pp. 124–127	•	•	•	Interactive TE and Resources DVD	•		•	
	Audio	•	•		Teacher's Resource Book, pp. 182–183, 186, 194–196	•		•	•
	Videohistoria	•	•		Vocabulary Clip Art	•	•	•	•
	Flashcards	•	•		Audio Program	•	•	•	
	Instant Check	•			Video Program: Videohistoria	•		•	
	Guided WB, pp. 83–92	•	•	•	Video Program Teacher's Guide: Cap. 3A	•		•	•
	Core WB, pp. 49–52	•	•	•	Vocabulary and Grammar Transparencies, 65–68	•	•	•	
	Comm. WB, pp. 49–50, 51, 56	•	•	•	Answer Keys: Student Edition, p. 36	•	•	•	
	Hispanohablantes WB, pp. 92–93			•	TPR Stories, pp. 37–48	•		•	•
Assess and Remediate					Prueba 3A–1: Assessment Program, pp. 67–68	•		•	•
					Assessment Program para hispanohablantes, pp. 67–68	•		•	•

RESOURCES

	FOR THE STUDENT	ONLINE	DVD	PRINT	FOR THE TEACHER	ONLINE	PREEXP	DVD	PRINT
Vocabulario en uso pp. 128–131									
Present & Practice	Student Edition, pp. 128–131	•	•	•	Interactive Whiteboard Vocabulary Activities	•		•	
	Instant Check	•			Interactive TE and Resources DVD	•		•	
	Comm. WB, p. 52	•	•	•	Teacher's Resource Book, pp. 184, 188–189	•		•	•
	Hispanohablantes WB, pp. 94–95			•	Communicative Pair Activities, pp. 188–189	•		•	•
	Communicative Pair Activities	•			Audio Program	•	•	•	
					Vocabulary and Grammar Transparencies, 2	•	•	•	
					Videomodelos	•		•	
					Answer Keys: Student Edition, p. 37–39	•	•	•	•
Assess and Remediate					Prueba 3A–2 with Study Plan	•			
					Prueba 3A–2: Assessment Program, pp. 69–70	•		•	•
					Assessment Program para hispanohablantes, pp. 69–70	•		•	•
Gramática pp. 132–137									
Present & Practice	Student Edition, pp. 132–137	•	•	•	Interactive Whiteboard Grammar Activities	•		•	
	Instant Check	•			Interactive TE and Resources DVD	•		•	
	Animated Verbs	•			Teacher's Resource Book, pp. 184–187, 190–191, 193	•		•	•
	Tutorial Video: Grammar	•			Communicative Pair Activities, pp. 190–191	•		•	•
	Canción de hip hop	•			Audio Program	•	•	•	
	Guided WB, pp. 93–96	•	•	•	Videomodelos	•		•	
	Core WB, pp. 53–55	•	•	•	Video Program: GramActiva	•	•	•	
	Comm. WB, pp. 53–55, 57-58, 251	•	•	•	Vocabulary and Grammar Transparencies, 65–66, 69, 71–72	•	•	•	
	Hispanohablantes WB, pp. 96–101			•	Answer Keys: Student Edition, pp. 39–41	•	•	•	
	Communicative Pair Activities	•							
Assess and Remediate					Pruebas 3A–3 and 3A–4 with Study Plans	•			
					Pruebas 3A–3, 3A–4: Assessment Program, pp. 71, 72	•		•	•
					Assessment Program para hispanohablantes, pp. 71, 72	•		•	•
¡Adelante! pp. 138–143									
Application	Student Edition, pp.138–143	•	•	•	Interactive TE and Resources DVD	•		•	
	Online Cultural Reading	•			Map Transparencies: 15	•	•	•	
	Guided WB, pp. 97–98	•	•	•	Answer Keys: Student Edition, p. 42	•	•	•	
	Comm. WB, pp. 59, 252	•	•	•					
	Hispanohablantes WB, pp. 102–107			•					
Repaso del capítulo pp. 144–145									
Review	Student Edition, pp. 144–145	•	•	•	Interactive TE and Resources DVD	•		•	
	Online Puzzles and Games	•			Teacher's Resource Book, pp. 185, 192, 194–196	•		•	•
	Core WB, pp. 56–57	•	•	•	Audio Program	•	•	•	
	Comm. WB, pp. 253–256	•	•	•	Answer Keys: Student Edition, p. 42	•	•	•	
	Hispanohablantes WB, pp. 108–109			•					
	Instant Check	•							
Chapter Assessment									
Assess					Examen del capítulo 3A	•		•	•
					Assessment Program, pp. 73–79	•		•	•
					Alternate Assessment Program, pp. 25–29	•		•	•
					Assessment Program para hispanohablantes, pp. 73–79	•		•	•
					Audio Program, Cap. 3A, Examen	•		•	
					ExamView: Test Banks A and B questions only online	•		•	
					Heritage Learner Test Bank	•		•	
					Pre-AP* Test Bank	•		•	

3A Lesson Plans

REGULAR SCHEDULE (50 MINUTES)

DAY	Warm-up / Assess	Preview / Present / Practice / Communicate	Wrap-up / Homework Options
1	**Warm-up** (10 min.) • Return Examen del capítulo 2B	**Chapter Opener** (5 min.) • Objectives • Arte y cultura **Vocabulario en contexto** (30 min.) • Presentation: Vocabulario en contexto • Actividades 1, 2	**Wrap-up and Homework Options** (5 min.) • Core Practice 3A-1, 3A-2
2	**Warm-up** (5 min.) • Homework check	**Vocabulario en contexto** (40 min.) • Presentation: Videohistoria *El desayuno* • View: Videohistoria • Video Activities 1, 2, 3, 4 • Actividad 3	**Wrap-up and Homework Options** (5 min.) • Core Practice 6, 9, 10, 11 • Prueba 3A-1: Vocabulary recognition
3	**Warm-up** (10 min.) • Actividad 4 • Homework check ✓**Formative Assessment** (10 min.) • Prueba 3A-1: Vocabulary recognition	**Vocabulario en uso** (25 min.) • Interactive Whiteboard Vocabulary Activities • Actividades 5, 7, 8 • Exploración del lenguaje • Audio Activities 5, 6	**Wrap-up and Homework Options** (5 min.) • Actividades 6, 9, 10, 11 • Prueba 3A-2 with Study Plan: Vocabulary production
4	**Warm-up** (15 min.) • Writing Activity 10 • Communicative Pair Activity • Homework check ✓**Formative Assessment** (10 min.) • Prueba 3A-2 with Study Plan: Vocabulary production	**Gramática y vocabulario en uso** (20 min.) • Presentation: Present tense of ***-er*** and ***-ir*** verbs • View: GramActiva video • Interactive Whiteboard Grammar Activities • Actividades 12, 13 • Audio Activity 7	**Wrap-up and Homework Options** (5 min.) • Core Practice 3A-5
5	**Warm-up** (10 min.) • Writing Activity 11 • Homework check	**Gramática y vocabulario en uso** (35 min.) • Actividades 14, 15, 16 • Fondo cultural • Communicative Pair Activity	**Wrap-up and Homework Options** (5 min.) • Prueba 3A-3 with Study Plan: Present tense of ***-er*** and ***-ir*** verbs
6	**Warm-up** (5 min.) • Review of ***-er*** and ***-ir*** verbs ✓**Formative Assessment** (10 min.) • Prueba 3A-3 with Study Plan: Present tense of ***-er*** and ***-ir*** verbs	**Gramática y vocabulario en uso** (30 min.) • Presentation: Me gustan, me encantan • View: GramActiva video • Interactive Whiteboard Grammar Activities • Actividades 17, 18, 19 • Audio Activities 8, 9	**Wrap-up and Homework Options** (5 min.) • Core Practice 3A-6, 3A-7 • Actividad 20 • Prueba 3A-4 with Study Plan: Me gustan, me encantan
7	**Warm-up** (15 min.) • Writing Activities 12, 13 • Homework check ✓**Formative Assessment** (10 min.) • Prueba 3A-4 with Study Plan: Me gustan, me encantan	**Gramática y vocabulario en uso** (10 min.) • Pronunciación • El español en la comunidad **¡Adelante!** (10 min.) • Lectura • ¿Comprendes?	**Wrap-up and Homework Options** (5 min.) • La cultura en vivo: Make recipe • Lectura
8	**Warm-up** (5 min.) • Fondo cultural	**¡Adelante!** (40 min.) • La cultura en vivo: Finish • El mundo hispano • Presentación oral: Step 1 • Situation Cards • Communicative Pair Activities	**Wrap-up and Homework Options** (5 min.) • Presentación oral: Step 2 • Preparación para el examen 3, 4, 5
9	**Warm-up** (5 min.) • Homework check	**¡Adelante!** (30 min.) • Presentación oral: Step 3 **Repaso del capítulo** (10 min.) • Vocabulario y gramática • Preparación para el examen 1, 2	**Wrap-up and Homework Options** (5 min.) • Core Practice 3A-8, 3A-9 • Instant Check • El mundo hispano • Examen del capítulo 3A
10	**Warm-up** (10 min.) • Homework check • Answer questions ✓**Summative Assessment** (40 min.) • Examen del capítulo 3A		

BLOCK SCHEDULE (90 MINUTES)

DAY	Warm-up / Assess	Preview / Present / Practice / Communicate	Wrap-up / Homework Options
1	**Warm-up** (10 min.) • Return Examen del capítulo 2B	**Chapter Opener** (5 min.) • Objectives • Arte y cultura **Vocabulario en contexto** (55 min.) • Presentation: Vocabulario en contexto • Actividades 1, 2 • Presentation: Videohistoria *El desayuno* • View: Videohistoria • Video Activities 1, 2, 3 • Actividad 3 **Vocabulario en uso** (15 min.) • Interactive Whiteboard Vocabulary Activities • Actividades 5, 6, 7	**Wrap-up and Homework Options** (5 min.) • Core Practice 3A-1, 3A-2, 3A-3, 3A-4 • Prueba 3A-1: Vocabulary recognition
2	**Warm-up** (10 min.) • Actividad 4 • Homework check ✔**Formative Assessment** (10 min.) • Prueba 3A-1: Vocabulary recognition	**Gramática y vocabulario en uso** (65 min.) • Actividades 8, 9, 11 • Exploración del lenguaje • Audio Activities 5, 6 • Writing Activity 10 • Communicative Pair Activity • Presentation: Present tense of ***-er*** and ***-ir*** verbs • View: GramActiva video • Interactive Whiteboard Grammar Activities • Actividades 12, 13 • Audio Activity 7	**Wrap-up and Homework Options** (5 min.) • Actividad 10 • Core Practice 3A-5 • Prueba 3A-2 with Study Plan: Vocabulary production
3	**Warm-up** (5 min.) • Homework check ✔**Formative Assessment** (10 min.) • Prueba 3A-2 with Study Plan: Vocabulary production	**Gramática y vocabulario en uso** (70 min.) • Actividades 14, 15, 16 • Fondo cultural • Communicative Pair Activity • Writing Activity 11 • Presentation: Me gustan, me encantan • View: GramActiva video • Interactive Whiteboard Grammar Activities • Actividades 17, 18, 19 • Writing Activities 12, 13	**Wrap-up and Homework Options** (5 min.) • Core Practice 3A-6, 3A-7 • Actividad 20 • Pruebas 3A-3, 3A-4 with Study Plans: Present tense of ***-er*** and ***-ir*** verbs, Me gustan, me encantan
4	**Warm-up** (10 min.) • Homework check ✔**Formative Assessment** (15 min.) Pruebas 3A-3, 3A-4 with Study Plans: Present tense of ***-er*** and ***-ir*** verbs, Me gustan, me encantan	**Gramática y vocabulario en uso** (20 min.) • Pronunciación • El español en la comunidad • Audio Activities 8, 9 • La cultura en vivo: churros y chocolate • Presentación oral: Step 1 **¡Adelante!** (40 min.) • Lectura • ¿Comprendes? • Fondo cultural	**Wrap-up and Homework Options** (5 min.) • Presentación oral: Step 2 • La cultura en vivo: Make recipe • Lectura
5	**Warm-up** (5 min.) • Homework check	**¡Adelante!** (50 min.) • El mundo hispano • Presentación oral: Step 3 **Repaso del capítulo** (30 min.) • Vocabulario y gramática • Preparación para el examen 1, 2, 3, 4, 5	**Wrap-up and Homework Options** (5 min.) • Core Practice 3A-8, 3A-9 • Instant Check • Examen del capítulo 3A
6	**Warm-up** (15 min.) • Homework check • Answer questions **Repaso del capítulo** (25 min.) • Situation Cards • Communicative Pair Activities ✔**Summative Assessment** (45 min.) • Examen del capítulo 3A		**Wrap-up and Homework Options** (5 min.) • El mundo hispano

Standards for *Capítulo* 3A

- To achieve the goals of the Standards, students will:

Communication

1.1 Interpersonal
- Talk about: preferences concerning foods and beverages; eating habits during different meals; favorite activities; ***churros y chocolate***

1.2 Interpretive
- Listen to and understand information about food items
- Listen to information about breakfast and lunch
- Read: a picture-based story; recipes for meals and beverages in Spanish; information about eating habits during different meals; a restaurant menu; about fruits and vegetables of Spanish-speaking countries
- Listen to and watch a video about breakfast foods
- Read and be able to respond to a magazine food quiz

1.3 Presentational
- Present information about: foods and beverages; eating habits during meals; the origins of food items; a restaurant menu; food and drink preferences

Culture

2.1 Practices and Perspectives
- Interpret the value of fresh fruit from a historical, socioeconomic perspective
- Explain breakfast habits in Spanish-speaking countries
- Talk about the ingredients of ***enchiladas***

2.2 Products and Perspectives
- Discuss Bartolomé Murillo and his painting; ***churros y chocolate***
- Interpret that many Latin American meals result from the Columbian Exchange of produce items; the connection between produce exports and economics in Latin American countries

Connections

3.1 Cross-curricular
- Discuss Bartolomé Murillo; the ingredients of ***enchiladas***; the nutritional values of tropical fruits; geological features of South America; Machu Picchu; the Galápagos Islands and tortoise
- Make ***churros y chocolate***

Comparisons

4.1 Language
- Talk about new vocabulary through the recognition of cognates; the usage of ***me gustan*** and ***me encantan***
- Explain that nouns can modify other nouns
- Explain the present tense of ***-er*** and ***-ir*** verbs
- Explain the pronunciation of the letters ***h*** and ***j***

4.2 Culture
- Explain the Columbian Exchange of produce items
- Compare: typical breakfast habits; ***churros y chocolate*** to popular food and drink combinations in the United States; the creation of environmentally protected areas

Communities

5.1 Beyond the School
- Discover the local availability of foods from Spanish-speaking countries

5.2 Lifelong Learner
- Realize the value of being able to read a restaurant menu

Capítulo

3A ¿Desayuno o almuerzo?

Chapter Objectives

Communication
By the end of this chapter you will be able to:
- Listen to and read descriptions of meals and menus
- Talk and write about foods you and others like and dislike
- Exchange information about food preferences

Culture
You will also be able to:
- Prepare a snack from the Spanish-speaking world and compare it to snacks you enjoy
- Trace the history of some foods originally native to the Americas and Europe

You will demonstrate what you know and can do:
- Presentación oral, p. 141
- Preparación para el examen, p. 145

You will use:

Vocabulary
- Foods and beverages for breakfast and lunch
- Expressions of frequency

Grammar
- Present tense of *-er* and *-ir* verbs
- *Me gustan, me encantan*

Exploración del mundo hispano

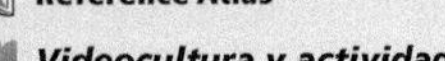

Reference Atlas

Videocultura y actividad

Mapa global interactivo

ENRICH YOUR TEACHING

Using Backward Design
Have students preview the sample performance tasks on *Preparación para el examen*, p. 145, and connect them to the Chapter Objectives. Explain to students that by completing the sample tasks they can self-assess their learning progress.

Mapa global interactivo
Download the *Mapa global interactivo* files for Chapter 3A and preview the activities. Use Activity 1 to travel to Sevilla, Spain. Activity 2 takes you to Chile. In Activity 3, you visit Lake Titicaca on the borders of Bolivia and Peru.

Un almuerzo con toda la familia

Arte y cultura | España

Bartolomé Murillo (1617–1682) was the first Spanish painter to become famous throughout Europe. Several of his early paintings featured children from his native Sevilla. Murillo used color, light, and a natural portrayal of his subjects to create memorable masterpieces.

- Study the painting and come up with three adjectives that describe it. Would you say the impression Murillo gives of the boys is positive or negative? Why?

"Niños comiendo fruta" (ca. 1650), Bartolomé Murillo ▶

DIFFERENTIATED INSTRUCTION

Digital resources such as the ***Interactive Whiteboard*** activity banks, ***Videomodelos***, additional ***Online Activities, Study Plans***, automatically graded ***Leveled Workbook***, animated ***Grammar Tutorials, Flashcards***, and ***Vocabulary and Grammar Videos*** will help you reach students of different ability levels and learning styles.

STUDENTS NEEDING EXTRA HELP

Guided Practice Activities
- Flashcards, pp. 83–88
- Vocabulary Check, pp. 89–92
- Reading Support, p. 97

HERITAGE LEARNERS

Realidades para hispanohablantes
- Chapter Opener, pp. 90–91
- A primera vista, p. 92
- Videohistoria, p. 93
- Manos a la obra, pp. 94–101
- ¡Adelante!, pp. 102–107
- Repaso del capítulo, pp. 108–109

ADVANCED/PRE-AP*

Pre-AP* Resource Book,
- pp. 70–73

Communication Workbook
- Integrated Performance Assessment, p. 253

PresentationExpress™
See pp. 122c–122d

Chapter Opener

Core Instruction

Resources: Map Transparencies 13, 15–18

Suggestions: Point out the chapter title. Students already know the word ***almuerzo.*** Can they guess the meaning of ***desayuno?*** As students read through the Objectives, tell them that they will be learning vocabulary for different foods and beverages and how to say what they like and don't like for breakfast and lunch. In the *Videohistoria,* students will see a comical episode about cultural misunderstandings about what people eat. Explain that different cultures have different practices associated with meals, and students will explore these in this chapter.

Videocultura View *El maíz: comida esencial* with the class to find out how corn is prepared in Spanish-speaking countries.

Arte y cultura

Standards: 2.1, 2.2, 3.1

Resources: Fine Art Transparencies, p. 41

Suggestions: To help students answer the question, remind them of the techniques and themes mentioned in the reading.

Answers will vary but may include adjectives such as *touching, simple,* or *realistic.* Students may suggest that Murillo's painting is positive, as the boys appear content, despite their possible hardships.

Mapa global interactivo, Actividad 1
Discover Sevilla, Spain and the seventeenth-century artist Bartolomé Murillo.

TEACHING WITH ART

Resources: Fine Art Transparencies, p. 41

Ask students: How old do you think the boys are? What do you think their relationship is to one another? What is the feeling that they give off in the painting? How is that feeling portrayed?

Vocabulario en contexto

Core Instruction

Standards: 1.2

Resources: Teacher's Resource Book: Input Script, p. 182, Clip Art, pp. 194–196, Audio Script, p. 183; Voc. and Gram. Transp. 65–66; TPR Stories, pp. 37–48; Audio Program DVD: Cap. 3A, Tracks 1–2

Focus: Presenting new vocabulary for foods and beverages eaten for breakfast and lunch

Suggestions: Use the Input Script for *Capítulo* 3A. Tell students what you like and don't like to eat for breakfast, using p. 124 as a framework. Have students point to the items in their books as they hear them. You can use Transparency 65 to confirm students' understanding. Then ask a volunteer to read the narrative. Make a list on the board or overhead of words that cannot be identified through visuals. Have the class work together to understand their meanings. Point out the footnote about the word ***agua.***

Extension: Tell students they have $8.00 to buy lunch at *El Restaurante de la Plaza.* Ask them to say what they would order.

BELLRINGER REVIEW

To review numbers, put these number sequences on the board and ask that students complete the sequences:

1. 1, ___, 5, ___, 9
2. 13, ___, 19, 22
3. 30, ___, 40, 45, ___, 55

Block Schedule

Have students write the new vocabulary for food and beverage items in Spanish on individual index cards. Collect the cards and put them into a box. Then assign each student either breakfast or lunch. Students should choose three cards and tell you if the food is logical for the meal you assigned them.

Read, listen to, and understand information about

- foods and beverages for breakfast and lunch

Vocabulario en contexto

*Note that *agua* is a feminine noun. However, you use the masculine article *el* to make it easier to say.

"**El desayuno** es mi **comida** favorita. **En el desayuno,** yo **como** cereal **con** leche, tocino y **pan tostado. Todos los días bebo** jugo de naranja. **Nunca** bebo té **sin** leche. Y tú, ¿qué **comes** en el desayuno?"

DIFFERENTIATED INSTRUCTION

Students with Learning Difficulties

You may wish to provide students with a two-column chart to help them organize vocabulary. Charts can be found in the *Voc. and Gram. Transparencies*. Have students label the columns ***Para beber*** and ***Para comer,*** and the rows ***El desayuno*** and ***El almuerzo.***

Multiple Intelligences

Interpersonal/Social: Have students write grocery lists with four or five items that they see in the advertisement. Then, have students work in pairs. Tell students to take turns reading prices from the advertisement while their partner checks items off of the list. This activity will recycle numbers and reinforce vocabulary.

El Restaurante de la Plaza

¡Para un almuerzo rápido!

la ensalada de frutas $3.25	
el sándwich de jamón y queso $3.50	la pizza $1.75
la hamburguesa $3.75	el café $1.00
el perrito caliente $1.50	los refrescos $1.00
las papas fritas $1.25	los jugos $1.35
la sopa de verduras $1.80	el té helado $1.00

“**Me encanta** el Restaurante de la Plaza. La comida es muy buena. **En el almuerzo,** como una ensalada de frutas o un sándwich de jamón y queso. **Siempre** bebo agua. Es importante **beber** mucha agua, **¿verdad?**”

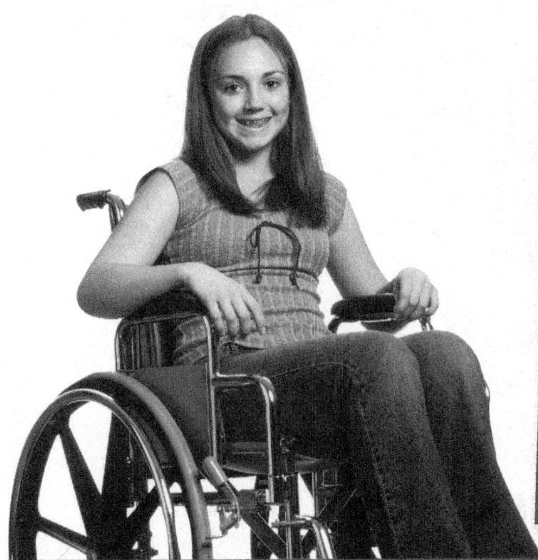

1 ¿Beber o comer?

Escuchar

Listen to the names of ten foods and beverages. If an item is a food, pantomime eating. If it's a beverage, pantomime drinking.

2 ¿El desayuno o el almuerzo?

Escuchar

Listen as different people tell what they are eating. Hold up one hand if the meal is *el desayuno* and hold up both hands if it is *el almuerzo.*

Más práctica GO

	realidades.com	print
Instant Check	✔	
Guided WB pp. 83–88	✔	✔
Core WB pp. 49–50	✔	✔
Comm. WB p. 56	✔	✔
***Hispanohablantes* WB** p. 92		✔

1 Standards: 1.2

Resources: Teacher's Resource Book: Audio Script, p. 183; Audio Program DVD: Cap. 3A, Track 3; Answer Keys: Student Edition, p. 36

Focus: Listening to food and beverage vocabulary

Suggestions: Use the audio or read the script. You may want to decide on standard gestures for eating and drinking, then model them for the class.

Script and Answers:

1. **la pizza *(eating)***
2. **el perrito caliente *(eating)***
3. **el agua *(drinking)***
4. **el jamón *(eating)***
5. **el té *(drinking)***
6. **el pan *(eating)***
7. **el queso *(eating)***
8. **la limonada *(drinking)***
9. **la leche *(drinking)***
10. **el cereal *(eating)***

2 Standards: 1.2

Resources: Teacher's Resource Book: Audio Script, p. 183; Audio Program DVD: Cap. 3A, Track 4; Answer Keys: Student Edition, p. 36

Focus: Listening to food vocabulary and distinguishing between breakfast and lunch

Suggestions: Use the audio or read the script aloud. Pause to check students' progress after each item. Remind students that they should focus on the vocabulary for food and beverages, and that they should not worry about understanding every word.

Script and Answers:

1. **Como un sándwich de jamón y queso. *(both hands)***
2. **Yo como el pan tostado y jugo de naranja. *(one hand)***
3. **Y yo como los huevos con tocino. ¡Mmmm! *(one hand)***
4. **Me gusta comer las hamburguesas. *(both hands)***
5. **Yo como la ensalada de frutas y pan. *(both hands)***
6. **Y yo siempre como el cereal con leche y salchichas. *(one hand)***

ENRICH YOUR TEACHING

Culture Note

Often, soft drinks from Spanish-speaking cultures tend to be fruitier and sweeter than drinks produced in the United States. Drinks with natural ingredients are very popular. For example, ***horchata*** is a well-known drink in Spain and Mexico. Throughout Mexico, it is possible to find ***horchata*** made with water or milk, rice, almonds, cinnamon, and sugar; while in Valencia, Spain, ***horchata*** is made with ***chufa*** (also known as *tiger nut*), water, a touch of cinnamon, and sugar.

Videohistoria

Core Instruction

Standards: 1.2

Resources: Voc. and Gram. Transparencies 67–68; Audio Program DVD: Cap. 3A, Track 5

Focus: Presenting additional contextualized vocabulary and grammar; recognizing similarities and differences between breakfast and lunch in Costa Rica and the United States; previewing the video

Suggestions:

Pre-reading: Discuss the questions in the *Strategy.* Making sure that students' books are closed, use the transparencies to ask them to determine what attitudes Tomás and the others have about breakfast. Also, have them predict what is going to happen following the end of the story.

Reading: Model the dialogue for the first panel with a volunteer. Begin the reading again with volunteers playing the roles of the characters. Using the transparencies, help students understand the new words in blue type.

Post-reading: Complete *Actividad* 3 to check comprehension.

Video

Core Instruction

Standards: 1.2

Resources: Teacher's Resource Book: Video Script, p. 186; Video Program: Cap. 3A; Video Program Teacher's Guide: Cap. 3A

Focus: Listening to new vocabulary presented in story form; using visuals to understand new vocabulary

Suggestions:

Pre-viewing: Tell students that this video is called *El desayuno*. Ask them to list words that they think they will hear in the video.

Pre-AP* Support

- **Learning Objective:** Interpersonal Speaking
- **Activity:** Have students create a short conversation based on Scenes 4 or 8 of this video. Students can play the roles of the mother and Tomás as they discuss breakfast or lunch options, replacing the items mentioned with others they would prefer to eat.
- ***Pre-AP* Resource Book:*** Comprehensive guide to Pre-AP* vocabulary skill development, pp. 51–57

El desayuno

Tomás es de los Estados Unidos. Está en Costa Rica para estudiar. ¿Qué come el primer día? Lee la historia.

Strategy

Using prior experience
Think about breakfast. Do you like a big breakfast? A small one? No breakfast at all? Look at the pictures and see if you can figure out how Tomás feels about breakfast.

1

Mamá: A ver . . . tocino, salchichas, huevos . . .
Papá: ¡Uy! Es mucha comida. No **comprendo.** Tú nunca comes el desayuno.
Mamá: No es mi desayuno. Es para Tomás, **por supuesto.** Los americanos comen mucho en el desayuno.

5

Tomás: Comparto los huevos, el tocino y las salchichas.
Raúl: ¿Compartes tu desayuno? Muchas gracias, Tomás.

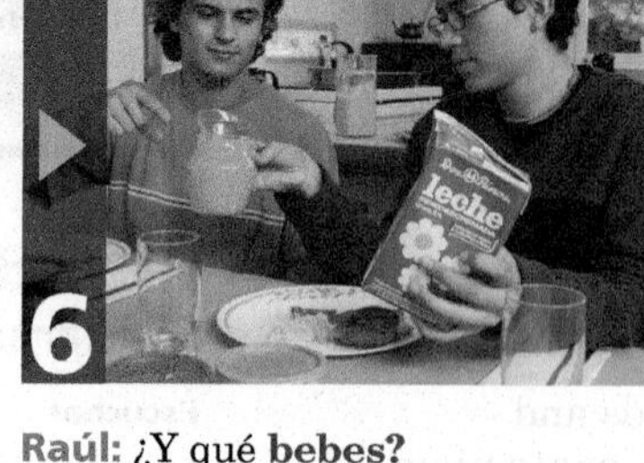

6

Raúl: ¿Y qué **bebes?**
Tomás: Jugo de naranja, por favor.
Raúl: Te gusta la leche, ¿no?
Tomás: Más o menos.

7

Raúl: Papá, ¿unos huevos?
Papá: No, gracias. ¡La comida es para Uds.!

DIFFERENTIATED INSTRUCTION

Students with Special Needs

You may wish to provide hearing-impaired students with a copy of the script so that they may follow along and engage in post-viewing activities.

Multiple Intelligences

Bodily/Kinesthetic: Have students prepare a short dialogue based on the *Videohistoria* in which they change the foods that are discussed. Encourage them to be comical in their selections. Then have students present their dialogues to the class.

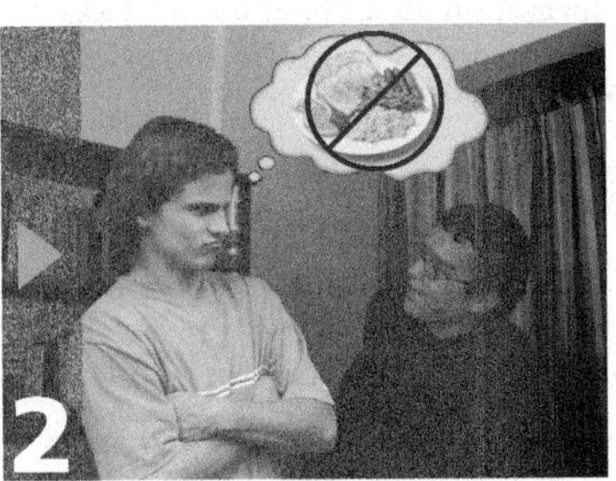

Raúl: No comes mucho en el desayuno, ¿verdad?

Tomás: ¡No! **¡Qué asco!**

Tomás: No me gusta nada el desayuno. A veces bebo jugo de naranja y como pan tostado.

Raúl: Yo tampoco como mucho.

Mamá: Buenos días, Tomás. Aquí tienes tu desayuno. Huevos, tocino, salchichas, pan tostado, cereal con leche . . .

Tomás: Gracias. Es un desayuno muy bueno. **Me encantan** los huevos y el tocino.

Mamá: **¿Cuál** es tu almuerzo favorito, Tomás?

Tomás: Me gustan las hamburguesas, la pizza, **la ensalada . . .**

Mamá: Bueno . . . ¡pizza, hamburguesas y ensalada para el almuerzo!

3 ¿Comprendes?

Escribir

Lee las frases. Escribe los números del 1 al 6 en una hoja de papel y escribe *C (cierto)* si la frase es correcta y *F (falso)* si es incorrecta.

1. Tomás está en Costa Rica.
2. La mamá de Raúl siempre come mucho en el desayuno.
3. A Tomás le gusta comer mucho en el desayuno.
4. Hoy Tomás no come mucho en el desayuno.
5. Tomás comparte el desayuno con Raúl.
6. A Tomás le gustan las hamburguesas y la pizza.

Más práctica GO

realidades.com | print

Instant Check	✔	
Guided WB pp. 89–92	✔	✔
Core WB pp. 51–52	✔	✔
Comm. WB pp. 49–50, 51, 52	✔	✔
***Hispanohablantes* WB** p. 93		✔

Viewing: Show the video once without pausing. Show it again, stopping to ask questions and check comprehension. Remind students that they may not understand every word in the video, but that they should listen and watch for overall understanding. Show the segment a final time without pausing. See the *Teacher's Resource Book* for more ways to teach with video.

Post-viewing: Complete the Video Activities in the *Communication Workbook*.

BELLRINGER REVIEW

Show the third scene of Voc. and Gram. Transparency 68. Ask students to tell what food items they see on the table.

3

Standards: 1.2, 1.3

Resources: Answer Keys: Student Edition, p. 37

Focus: Reading for comprehension

Suggestions: You may wish to do this as a listening activity, reading the sentences to the students and having them call out the words ***cierto*** or ***falso.*** When students answer ***falso,*** have them supply the correct information and identify the panel number in which it is found.

Answers: **1. C; 2. F; 3. F; 4. F; 5. C; 6. C**

Teacher-to-Teacher

Have students use the Clip Art from the *Teacher's Resource Book* to create their own supermarket advertisement based on the example on p. 124. Suggest that they give their supermarket a name and provide a price for each item.

Additional Resources

- Communication Wbk.: Audio Act. 5, p. 51
- Teacher's Resource Book: Audio Script, p. 183
- Audio Program DVD: Cap. 3A, Track 8

ENRICH YOUR TEACHING

Culture Note

Meals in Spanish-speaking countries vary by country and region. In some cities, it is common to have a light breakfast and to have lunch as the main meal. In rural areas, however, families tend to eat what they produce for themselves. Breakfast might include steak, corn, milk, eggs, or beans. In Costa Rica, breakfast usually includes ***gallo pinto*** (a mix of rice and black beans), eggs, toast, and tropical fruit juice. Have students compare their breakfast with a Costa Rican breakfast, and talk about why such differences might exist.

ASSESSMENT

Quiz: Vocabulary Recognition

- Prueba 3A-1: pp. 67–68

INTERACTIVE WHITEBOARD
Vocabulary Activities 3A

4 Standards: 1.3

Resources: Voc. and Gram. Transparency 2

Focus: Writing names of breakfast and lunch foods; using a Venn diagram to organize ideas

Suggestions: Ask questions such as *¿Comes una hamburguesa en el desayuno? ¿Comes yogur en el almuerzo?* By answering these questions, students will begin to classify the foods. Once they have two or three examples, they can fill in the rest of the vocabulary.

Answers will vary but should include:

el desayuno: los huevos, las salchichas, el tocino, el cereal, el pan tostado

el almuerzo: la hamburguesa, las papas fritas, el perrito caliente, el sándwich de jamón y queso, la sopa de verduras, los refrescos, el té helado, la limonada, las galletas

Both: el yogur de fresa, el jamón, los plátanos, el café, los jugos, el té, el agua, la leche, el queso, el pan

BELLRINGER REVIEW

To review prepositions, provide a word bank of prepositions on the board. Placing a food prop on, in front of, behind a desk, ask: *¿Dónde está...?*

5 Standards: 1.2

Resources: Teacher's Resource Book: Audio Script, p. 184; Audio Program DVD: Cap. 3A, Track 6; Answer Keys: Student Edition, p. 37

Focus: Listening to descriptions of foods

Recycle: Prepositions of location

Suggestions: Use the audio or read the script aloud. Explain that items near the bottom of the page are in the front, and those near the top are in the back.

Script and Answers:

1. **Los huevos están al lado de la ensalada. *(F)***
2. **El queso está al lado del jamón. *(F)***
3. **La hamburguesa está al lado de las papas fritas. *(C)***
4. **Las manzanas están detrás de los plátanos. *(F)***
5. **El sándwich está detrás del perrito caliente. *(C)***
6. **Las salchichas y el tocino están debajo de los huevos y la ensalada. *(C)***
7. **El pan tostado está delante del cereal. *(F)***
8. **El yogur está al lado del jamón. *(C)***

Manos a la obra

Vocabulario en uso

Objectives

- Listen to a description of breakfast and lunch foods
- Write about and discuss what you and others eat and drink for breakfast and lunch
- Exchange information about likes and dislikes
- Read about the American and European origins of foods to analyze a recipe

4 ¿El desayuno o el almuerzo?

Pensar • Escribir

Think about what people usually eat for breakfast and lunch. Copy the Venn diagram on a sheet of paper. Which foods pictured below would usually be eaten for breakfast, and which for lunch? Write the Spanish words in the appropriate oval for *el desayuno* or *el almuerzo.* Which items could be eaten for either breakfast or lunch? Write them in the overlapping area.

Modelo

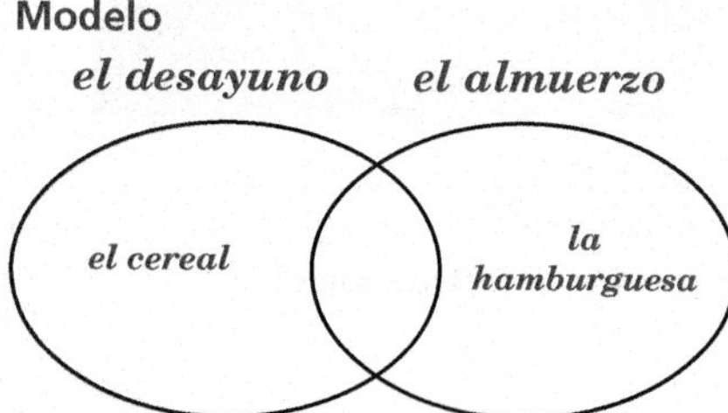

5 ¿Dónde están?

Escuchar • Escribir

Vas a escuchar ocho descripciones sobre el dibujo de esta página. Escribe los números del 1 al 8 en una hoja de papel y escribe *C* si la descripción es cierta y *F* si es falsa.

DIFFERENTIATED INSTRUCTION

Advanced Learners/Pre-AP*

Ask students to think of three brand names of food or drink items. Have them say only the brand name, and call on a volunteer to explain what it is. The student who responds should continue the game by saying another brand name and calling on another volunteer to describe it.

Students with Special Needs

For *Actividad* 4, pair visually-impaired students with other students who will say the Spanish names of the items pictured. Then have the visually impaired students say whether or not the item is appropriate for ***desayuno, almuerzo,*** or ***los dos.***

6 ¿Qué bebes?

Escribir

1. On a sheet of paper, make three columns with these headings: *Todos los días, A veces, Nunca.* Write the names of these beverages under the appropriate heading based on how often you drink them.

2. Write complete sentences telling how often you drink these beverages.

Modelo

Bebo limonada todos los días.
Bebo leche a veces.
Nunca bebo café.

También se dice . . .

beber = tomar *(México)*
el jugo = el zumo *(España)*
la naranja = la china *(Puerto Rico)*
las papas = las patatas *(España)*
el plátano = la banana, el guineo *(Puerto Rico)*
el sándwich = el bocadillo *(España)*, la torta *(México)*

7 ¿Qué comes?

Hablar

Trabaja con otro(a) estudiante y habla de lo que comes.

Modelo

A —*¿Comes cereal?*
B —*Sí, como cereal todos los días.*
o: *No, nunca como cereal.*

Estudiante A

Estudiante B

Sí, todos los días.
Sí, a veces.
Sí, siempre.
No, nunca.
No, ¡qué asco!

Practice and Communicate 3A

6 Standards: 1.3

Focus: Writing about food in a personalized context

Suggestions: Review the meanings of ***todos los días, a veces,*** and ***nunca.*** When students have finished Step 1, ask a volunteer to read the *Modelo* for Step 2. Direct students to the *También se dice*... and encourage them to be creative in using these regional variations as you do the activity in class.

Answers will vary.

7 Standards: 1.1

Resources: Answer Keys: Student Edition, p. 38

Focus: Asking and answering questions about eating habits

Suggestions: Have volunteers read the model on the page. Then have them use a vocabulary word not given in the activity to personalize the roles of Student A and Student B. They can also add ***en el desayuno*** or ***en el almuerzo*** to their questions and answers: *¿Comes cereal en el desayuno? Sí, a veces como cereal en el desayuno.*

Answers:

Student A
¿Comes pan?
¿Comes sopa?
¿Comes frutas?
¿Comes yogur?
¿Comes pan tostado?
¿Comes tocino?
¿Comes sándwiches?

Student B
Answers will vary.

ENRICH YOUR TEACHING

Culture Note

Sandwiches in Spain and Mexico differ in more than just name. In Spain, ***un bocadillo*** may be composed of a hard roll with a piece of cheese, cured beef, or ***tortilla española***—a Spanish omelette. In Mexico, ***una torta*** almost always contains refried beans, chilies, lettuce, tomato, and ham, chicken, or cheese.

21st Century Skills

Critical Thinking and Problem Solving Have students work in small groups to discuss the merits of the different types of meals presented in this section: light breakfast vs. heavier type breakfast; light lunch vs. heavier lunch. Ask them to think about why such choices are made, and how the type of meals one eats regularly affects one's overall health.

8 Standards: 1.1

Resources: Answer Keys: Student Edition, p. 38

Focus: Talking about food likes and dislikes

Suggestions: Ask pairs of volunteers to read the *Modelo* once as it is in the book. Then have Student A ask the question and select any student to respond. Remind Student B that he or she can select any response from the *Estudiante B* balloon, but that it should reflect his or her own opinion.

Answers for Student B will vary. Student A answers:

1. **Te gustan los huevos, ¿verdad?**
2. **Te gustan las galletas, ¿verdad?**
3. **Te gustan los refrescos, ¿verdad?**
4. **Te gustan las papas fritas, ¿verdad?**
5. **Te gustan las hamburguesas, ¿verdad?**
6. **Te gustan las salchichas, ¿verdad?**
7. **Te gustan los perritos calientes, ¿verdad?**

Extension: Have students repeat the activity using drinks, which are sometimes singular. They should say ***me gusta*** and ***me encanta,*** when appropriate. You may want to provide the vocabulary transparency to remind students of vocabulary options.

Exploración del lenguaje
Core Instruction

Standards: 4.1

Resources: Answer Keys: Student Edition, p. 39

Suggestions: Provide an example of a noun modifying another noun in English, such as *peanut butter sandwich*. Have students come up with additional examples in English in order to internalize the concept. Refer students to the vocabulary presented on pp. 124–125 to complete the *Try it out!* Ask volunteers to share their answers.

You may want to point out that ***la ensalada de frutas*** and ***la sopa de verduras*** have plural modifiers because they are made from a combination of ingredients, while ***la sopa de tomate*** uses the singular because there is only one main ingredient.

Answers will vary but should include:

el yogur de fresa; el jugo de naranja; el jugo de manzana; la ensalada de frutas; el sándwich de jamón y queso; la sopa de verduras

la sopa de tomate	**la ensalada de lechuga**
el jugo de piña	**el sándwich de pollo**

8 Mis comidas favoritas

Hablar

Trabaja con otro(a) estudiante y habla de las comidas que te gustan y que no te gustan.

Modelo

A —*Te gustan los plátanos, ¿verdad?*
B —*Sí, ¡por supuesto! Me encantan.*

Estudiante A

Estudiante B

Sí, ¡por supuesto! Me encantan.
Sí, más o menos.
No, no me gustan.
No, ¡qué asco!

Exploración del lenguaje

Using a noun to modify another noun

In English, one noun is often used to describe another noun: *vegetable soup, strawberry yogurt.* Notice that the noun that is being described comes second.

In Spanish, however, the noun that is being described comes first and is followed by *de* + the describing noun: *la sopa* ***de*** *verduras, el yogur* ***de*** *fresa.* Notice that you don't use a definite article in front of the second noun.

The form of the noun following *de* does not change even when the first noun becomes plural.

el sándwich de **jamón**
los sándwiches de **jamón**

Try it out! Name five examples of foods or beverages from this chapter that follow this pattern.

Now that you know the pattern, say what these foods and beverages are called in Spanish:

DIFFERENTIATED INSTRUCTION

Multiple Intelligences

Visual/Spatial: Have students illustrate some of the word combinations in the *Exploración del lenguaje* by cutting images from a magazine and pasting them on a poster board. For example, students could illustrate ***un sándwich de queso*** by using a photo of a sandwich, the word ***de,*** and a photo of cheese.

Advanced Learners

Have students use the *Conexiones: La historia* reading in *Actividad* 9 to begin a research project about the development of the Spanish colonies in Central and South America after the arrival of Columbus. Have students focus on the trade that occurred between Spain and the New World.

9 El intercambio entre dos mundos

Leer

Conexiones | La historia

Think about how your meals would be different without corn, beans, squash, tomatoes, avocados, chiles, peanuts, cashews, turkey, pineapples, potatoes, vanilla, and chocolate. What do these foods have in common? They all had their origin in the Americas and were unknown in Europe until Columbus brought them there from his voyages in the fifteenth century. Today these foods are found in dishes in many countries.

The product exchange benefited both sides of the Atlantic Ocean. The Europeans brought to the Americas a wide range of foods including chicken, pork, beef, milk, cheese, sugar, grapes, and grains such as wheat and barley.

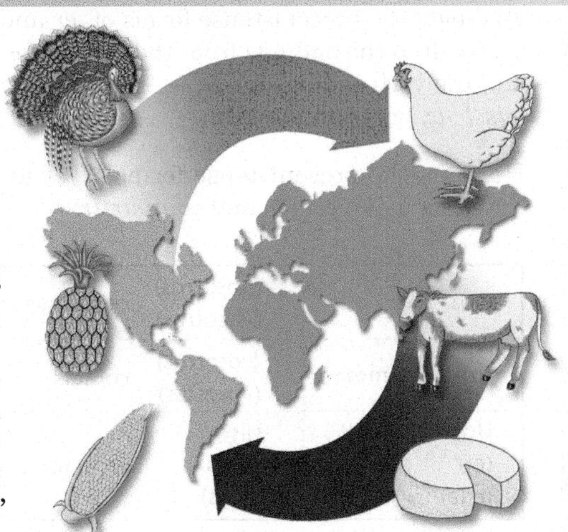

10 Las enchiladas

Leer • Escribir

Read the list of ingredients for a traditional Mexican dish of *enchiladas.* Based upon the information you just read and saw on the map, write which ingredients had their origins in the Americas and which came from Europe.

Enchiladas de pollo[1] con salsa de tomate

Ingredientes:

12 tortillas de maíz[2]
1 taza[3] de pollo
1 taza de queso fresco[4]
6 tomates grandes[5]
2 cebollas[6] no muy grandes
crema
aceite[7] de maíz

[1]chicken [2]corn [3]cup [4]fresh [5]large [6]onions [7]oil

11 Y tú, ¿qué dices?

Escribir • Hablar

1. ¿Cuál es tu comida favorita, el desayuno o el almuerzo?
2. ¿Cuál es tu almuerzo favorito? ¿Y tu desayuno favorito?
3. ¿Qué frutas te gustan más?

Practice and Communicate 3A

9 Standards: 2.2, 4.2

Focus: Making a cross-curricular connection to social studies / history, focusing on the Columbian Exchange

Suggestions: Make a list of some of the foods mentioned, and ask students if they have any insights into their origins. Check to see if students were correct in their predictions. Ask students to tell who they think benefited more from the exchange, the Europeans or the Americans.

10 Standards: 1.2, 1.3, 2.2, 3.1

Resources: Answer Keys: Student Edition, p. 39

Focus: Reading a Mexican recipe; writing about intercultural ingredients

Suggestions: Tell students you're going to be making ***enchiladas de pollo*** for dinner tonight. Have volunteers tell you what to put on your shopping list as you write it on the board.

Answers:
- **Americas: tortillas de maíz, tomates, aceite de maíz**
- **Europe: pollo, queso, cebollas, crema**

11 Standards: 1.1, 1.3

Focus: Writing and speaking about meals

Suggestions: When students have completed the activity, have volunteers ask the questions and call on other classmates.

Answers will vary.

Additional Resources

- Communication Wbk.: Audio Act. 6, p. 52
- Teacher's Resource Book: Audio Script, p. 184, Communicative Pair Activity BLM, pp. 188–189
- Audio Program DVD: Cap. 3A, Track 8

ENRICH YOUR TEACHING

Culture Note

Corn, tomatoes, and chilies are staples of the Mexican kitchen. Tortillas are present at every meal and are even made into a delicious soup. Chilies, tomatoes, and onions are used in many different ways, both raw and cooked, to make a variety of ***salsas*** that may be included in any meal—even breakfast.

Teacher-to-Teacher

Have each student find a recipe for a traditional dish from a Spanish-speaking culture. Have them write the recipe in English, tell the country it is from, and illustrate the page. Then compile all of the recipes, and ask a volunteer to design a cover. Make copies, bind the recipes, and distribute them to students in the class.

ASSESSMENT

Prueba 3A-2 with Study Plan (online only)

Quiz: Vocabulary Production
- Prueba 3A-2: pp. 69–70

▼ Objectives

- Read, write, and talk about what you and others eat for breakfast and lunch, and about everyday activities
- Exchange information with classmates about favorite foods and drinks

Gramática

BELLRINGER REVIEW

Write an **-ar** verb on an overhead or on the board, and ask a volunteer to review the conjugation process.

Gramática

Core Instruction

Standards: 4.1

Resources: Voc. and Gram. Transparency 69; Teacher's Resource Book: Video Script, pp. 186–187; Video Program: Cap. 3A

INTERACTIVE WHITEBOARD
Grammar Activities 3A

Suggestions: Direct students' attention to *¿Recuerdas?* Use the transparencies to reinforce the verb forms. Use the lists of familiar infinitives to have students practice creating the forms of the verbs. Use the *GramActiva* Video to introduce the grammar or reinforce your explanation.

12 Standards: 1.2, 1.3

Resources: Answer Keys: Student Edition, p. 39

Focus: Writing complete sentences with forms of an **-ir** verb

Suggestions: Point out that each sentence will use a form of the verb ***compartir.*** Students may need to be reminded that ***tú + yo*** requires the ***nosotros(as)*** form of the verb.

Answers:

1. **Tomás comparte una pizza con María.**
2. **Tú compartes unos sándwiches con Ramón.**
3. **Nosotros compartimos unas papas fritas con los estudiantes.**
4. **Uds. comparten unas galletas con el profesor.**
5. **Ellas comparten unos perritos calientes con nosotros.**
6. **Tú y yo compartimos unos plátanos con Luis y Roberta.**
7. **Yo comparto *(student's choice)* con mi amigo.**

Pre-AP* Support

- **Learning Objective:** Interpersonal Writing
- **Activity:** As a warm-up activity for five days, have students list what they have eaten for breakfast or lunch. At the end of the week, have them write a short email to a nutritionist asking for tips to improve their eating habits–or indicating how well they follow healthy eating guidelines.
- ***Pre-AP* Resource Book:*** Comprehensive guide to Pre-AP* writing skill development, pp. 27–38

Present tense of *-er* and *-ir* verbs

To create the present-tense forms of *-er* and *-ir* verbs, drop the endings from the infinitives, then add the verb endings *-o, -es, -e, -emos* / *-imos, -éis* / *-ís,* or *-en* to the stem.

Here are the present-tense forms of *-er* and *-ir* verbs using *comer* and *compartir:*

(yo)	como	(nosotros) (nosotras)	com**emos**
(tú)	com**es**	(vosotros) (vosotras)	com**éis**
Ud. (él) (ella)	com**e**	Uds. (ellos) (ellas)	com**en**

(yo)	compart**o**	(nosotros) (nosotras)	compart**imos**
(tú)	compart**es**	(vosotros) (vosotras)	compart**ís**
Ud. (él) (ella)	compart**e**	Uds. (ellos) (ellas)	compart**en**

¿Recuerdas?

The pattern of present-tense *-ar* verbs is:

toco	tocamos
tocas	tocáis
toca	tocan

- Regular *-er* verbs that you know are *beber, comer, comprender, correr,* and *leer.*
- Regular *-ir* verbs that you know are *compartir* and *escribir.*
- You also know the verb *ver.* It is regular except in the *yo* form, which is *veo.*

Más ayuda 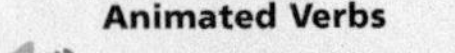

realidades.com

***GramActiva* Video**
Tutorial: -er verbs, -ir verbs, Regular verbs, Stem-endings
Animated Verbs

Canción de hip hop: *¿Qué comes?*

***GramActiva* Activity**

▼12 ¿Quiénes comparten el almuerzo?

Escribir

On a sheet of paper, write complete sentences saying what each person is sharing and with whom. Follow the model.

Modelo

Elena / una manzana / Raúl
Elena comparte una manzana con Raúl.

1. Tomás / una pizza / María
2. tú / unos sándwiches / Ramón
3. nosotros / unas papas fritas / los estudiantes
4. Uds. / unas galletas / el profesor
5. ellas / unos perritos calientes / nosotros
6. tú y yo / unos plátanos / Luis y Roberta
7. yo / ¿-? / mi amigo

Unos amigos comparten el almuerzo, Ciudad de México.

DIFFERENTIATED INSTRUCTION

Students with Learning Difficulties

When presenting the *Gramática*, point out the infinitives and demonstrate how the **-er** and **-ir** are removed and new endings added. Ask students to recall the process of changing verb forms with **-ar** verbs. Some students may benefit from repeating the conjugations with new endings until they have internalized the process.

Multiple Intelligences

Visual/Spatial: Have students draw pictures to illustrate the **-er** and **-ir** verbs they know. Ask them to write a subject pronoun for each illustration. Have pairs exchange papers and say what the people are doing in the drawings.

13 ¿Qué beben y qué comen? 

Hablar

Work with a partner. Use the verbs *comer* and *beber* to ask questions.

Juan / desayuno 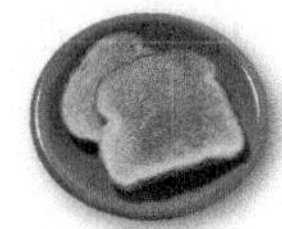

Modelo

A —*¿Qué come Juan en el desayuno?*
B —*Juan come pan tostado.*

Miguel y Carlos / almuerzo 

Modelo

A —*¿Qué beben Miguel y Carlos en el almuerzo?*
B —*Miguel y Carlos beben limonada.*

1. Raúl y Gloria / desayuno 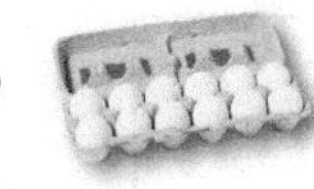
2. tú / almuerzo 
3. Graciela y Carlos / desayuno 

4. Carolina / almuerzo 
5. tu familia y tú / desayuno 
6. tú / almuerzo **¡Respuesta personal!**

14 Una tarjeta postal

Leer • Escribir

Lee la tarjeta postal *(post card)* de una amiga de Venezuela. En una hoja de papel, escribe la forma correcta del verbo apropiado que está entre paréntesis.

Querida Amalia:

Elena y yo estamos en Caracas. Nosotros 1. (comprender / correr) todos los días y 2. (comer / ver) muy bien.

Los estudiantes aquí 3. (comer / leer) mucha pizza y 4. (ver / beber) mucho café. Ellos 5. (leer / beber) muchos libros y 6. (escribir / ver) mucho también para las clases. Las clases son difíciles pero me encantan.

En la clase de español nosotros 7. (correr / leer) revistas y cuentos en español. Elena 8. (comprender / beber) muy bien pero para mí es un poco difícil.

Tengo que estudiar. ¡Hasta luego!
Tu amiga,
Carolina

Más práctica 

realidades.com | print

Instant Check	✔	
Guided WB pp. 93–94	✔	✔
Core WB p. 53	✔	✔
Comm. WB pp. 53, 57	✔	✔
***Hispanohablantes* WB** pp. 94–97		✔

Practice and Communicate 3A

BELLRINGER REVIEW

Use Transparency 70 to quickly review food vocabulary.

13 Standards: 1.1, 1.2

Resources: Answer Keys: Student Edition, p. 40

Focus: Asking questions using ***comer*** and ***beber***

Suggestions: Ask volunteers to demonstrate the models. Point out that no article is necessary in front of the names of the foods and drinks.

Answers:

1. **¿Qué comen Raúl y Gloria en el desayuno? Raúl y Gloria comen huevos.**
2. **¿Qué comes tú en el almuerzo? Yo como hamburguesas.**
3. **¿Qué comen Graciela y Carlos en el desayuno? Graciela y Carlos comen cereal.**
4. **¿Qué come Carolina en el almuerzo? Carolina come yogur.**
5. **¿Qué beben tu familia y tú en el desayuno? Nosotros bebemos jugo de naranja.**
6. **¿Qué comes tú en el almuerzo? Yo como *(answers will vary).***

14 Standards: 1.2, 1.3

Resources: Answer Keys: Student Edition, p. 40

Focus: Reading a letter and writing correct verb forms

Suggestions: Encourage students to scan the paragraph before writing the verb forms.

Answers:

1. **corremos**
2. **comemos**
3. **comen**
4. **beben**
5. **leen**
6. **escriben**
7. **leemos**
8. **comprende**

Additional Resources

- Communication Wbk.: Audio Act. 7, p. 53
- Teacher's Resource Book: Audio Script, p. 184
- Audio Program DVD: Cap. 3A, Track 9

ASSESSMENT

Prueba 3A-3 with Study Plan (online only)

Quiz: Present tense of *-er* and *-ir* verbs

- Prueba 3A-3: p. 71

ENRICH YOUR TEACHING

Culture Note

In Latin America, to say what they eat for breakfast, people often use the verb ***desayunar,*** e.g., *Desayunamos huevos con tocino.* ***Comer*** can be used for any meal, but it's generally used when referring to lunch, and ***cenar*** is used to refer to the evening meal. ***Almuerzo*** is another word used throughout Latin America to describe lunch.

21st Century Skills

Technology Literacy Have students access the digital technology available in **realidades.com** for this section (like the *GramActiva* Video, and the *Canción de hip hop*). After reviewing, ask them to work in small groups to compose the reply postcard from Amalia to her friend Carolina in Activity 14.

3A Practice and Communicate

BELLRINGER REVIEW

Use Transparencies 65–66 to review vocabulary for food and drinks. Give students sentences such as *Yo como hamburguesas en el desayuno*, and have students tell you if each sentence is ***lógica*** or ***ilógica.***

15 Standards: 1.1, 1.3

Resources: Teacher's Resource Book: GramActiva BLM, p. 193

Focus: Writing and talking about foods in a personalized context

Suggestions: Give each student a copy of the chart or have them create their own. Direct attention to the *Para decir más...* for additional words. You might also provide a list of other words that students want to use. Tell students to keep their charts for *Actividad* 16.

Answers will vary.

16 Standards: 1.3

Focus: Writing and reading sentences based on chart information

Suggestions: Remind students to use the chart from *Actividad* 15 to complete this activity. Be sure that sentences include correct verb forms. Write a sample sentence on the board to get students started. Ask volunteers to say their completed sentences for the class.

Answers will vary.

Fondo cultural

Standards: 1.2, 2.1, 4.2

Suggestions: Have students discuss what they typically eat for breakfast, and tell what their idea of an American breakfast is.

Answers will vary but may include cereal, bacon, eggs, sausages, waffles, and pancakes.

Theme Project

Give students copies of the Theme Project outline and rubric from the *Teacher's Resource Book*. Explain the task to them, and have them perform Step 1. (For more information, see p. 122-b.)

15 Los sábados y la comida

Escribir • Hablar

What do you and your classmates eat and drink for breakfast and lunch on Saturdays? Make a chart like the one below on a sheet of paper and complete each box with information about yourself. Then survey two classmates to find out what their habits are. Record the information in the chart.

	¿Qué comes?	¿Qué bebes?
el desayuno	yo: *huevos, pan tostado, tocino* Sandra: *cereal, plátanos, pan tostado*	
el almuerzo		

Modelo

Los sábados, ¿qué comes en el desayuno? ¿Qué bebes?
¿Qué comes en el almuerzo? ¿Qué bebes?

Para decir más . . .

la crema de cacahuates	peanut butter
el pan dulce	breakfast pastry
el panqueque	pancake
el pollo	chicken

16 Los hábitos de la clase

Escribir • Hablar

Use your completed chart from Actividad 15 to write summary statements based on your survey. Be prepared to read your sentences to the class.

Modelo

Sandra y yo comemos huevos y cereal en el desayuno.
Gregorio no bebe jugo de naranja en el desayuno y le gusta mucho la leche.
Sofía come cereal y bebe leche en el desayuno.

Fondo Cultural | El mundo hispano

El desayuno From the popular *churros* and hot chocolate in Spain to the *pan dulce* served in many countries, a wide variety of foods can be found on the breakfast table in the Spanish-speaking world. Most often, people prefer a light breakfast of bread or a roll, coffee or tea, and possibly juice. Items such as cereal, eggs, ham, or sausage are less common.

- In Spain you can ask for a *desayuno americano.* What do you think you would be served?

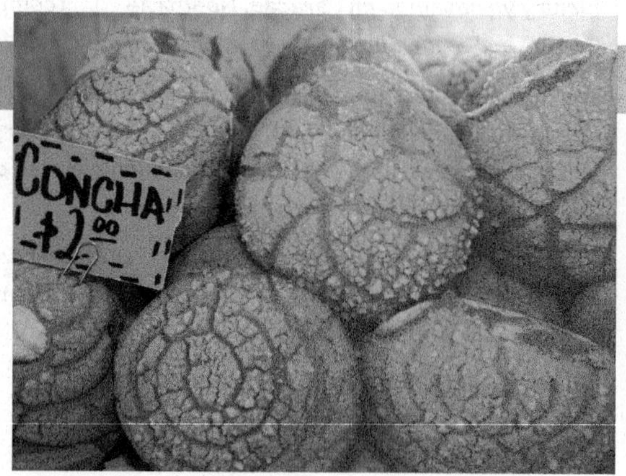

El pan dulce es un desayuno popular en México.

DIFFERENTIATED INSTRUCTION

Students with Learning Difficulties

For *Actividad* 15, provide students with colored pencils. Make sure that students fill in their charts with their own information first. For each classmate that they include, have them write with a different color. This will help them to keep their information more organized.

Students with Special Needs

For *Actividad* 17, some students may have difficulty manipulating three pieces of paper. You may want to provide students with four different index cards, labeled ***me gusta, me gustan, no me gusta,*** and ***no me gustan.***

Objectives

- Indicate and write about what you like and don't like to eat
- Read and answer questions about a food survey and a menu
- Exchange information about food preferences

Gramática

Me gustan, me encantan

Use *me gusta* and *me encanta* to talk about a singular noun.

Me gusta **el** té pero me encanta **el** té helado.

Use *me gustan* and *me encantan* to talk about plural nouns.

Me encantan **las** fresas pero no me gustan mucho **los** plátanos.

When you use *me gusta(n)* and *me encanta(n)* to talk about a noun, include *el, la, los,* or *las*.

Me encanta **el** jugo de naranja pero no me gusta **la** leche.

¿Qué te gustan más, **las** hamburguesas o **los** perritos calientes?

Más ayuda realidades.com

- **GramActiva Video Tutorial:** *-ar* verbs
- **GramActiva Activity**

17 ¿Gusta o gustan?

Escuchar • GramActiva

1. Tear a sheet of paper in thirds. On the first piece, write *No.* On the second piece write *me gusta.* On the third piece, write *n.*

2. You will hear eight food items. Indicate whether you like each item by holding up one, two, or all three pieces of paper. Remember to use *me gustan* when the item you hear is plural!

18 ¿Qué te gusta?

Escribir

Indicate how much you *do* or *do not* like the foods pictured below.

Modelo

Me gustan las manzanas.
o: *No me gustan nada las manzanas.*
o: *Me encantan las manzanas.*

1. 
2. 
3. 
4. 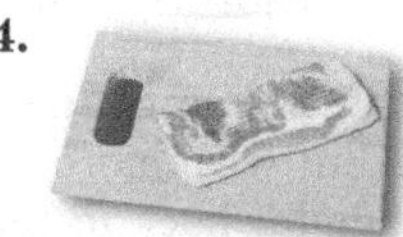
5. 
6. 

ENRICH YOUR TEACHING

Teacher-to-Teacher

For more practice with the concepts of ***me gustan*** and ***me encantan,*** write a list of specific people, places, and things that students can identify, such as sports teams, individual athletes, singers, musical groups, or celebrities. Have students work in pairs to ask and say whether or not they like the items on the list.

21st Century Skills

Collaboration Have students work in groups of four to develop a role-playing activity. Two members of the group will represent children about 12 years of age; two will be camp counselors. After hearing what the children like to eat, the counselors will offer eating suggestions, addressing both what the "children" like to eat, and what would be healthier choices.

Gramática

Core Instruction

Standards: 4.1

Resources: Teacher's Resource Book: Video Script, p. 187; Video Program: Cap. 3A

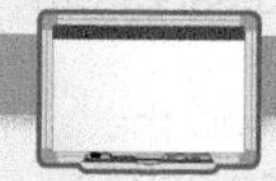

INTERACTIVE WHITEBOARD
Grammar Activities 3A

Suggestions: Use the *GramActiva* Video either as an initial introduction or as a follow-up to your explanation. Have students brainstorm foods and drinks and write them in the plural on the board. Ask volunteers to tell their likes and dislikes using ***me gusta(n), no me gusta(n),*** or ***me encanta(n)*** and the words listed on the board. Then provide some singular nouns to show the contrast.

17 Standards: 1.2

Resources: Teacher's Resource Book: Audio Script, p. 184; Audio Program DVD: Cap. 3A, Track 10; Answer Keys: Student Edition, p. 41

Focus: Listening to food vocabulary and indicating likes and dislikes

Suggestions: Use the audio or read the script aloud. Pause after each item to check the responses.

Script

1. la sopa
2. las hamburguesas
3. el tocino
4. las fresas
5. el pan
6. el yogur
7. las galletas
8. los huevos

Answers will vary but should include:

1. gusta
2. gustan
3. gusta
4. gustan
5. gusta
6. gusta
7. gustan
8. gustan

18 Standards: 1.3

Resources: Answer Keys: Student Edition, p. 41

Focus: Writing personalized sentences about food preferences

Suggestions: When students have finished the sentences, ask volunteers to express their opinions to the class. For each statement, ask a follow-up question to another student, such as *¿Y a ti? ¿Te gustan también...?*

Answers will vary but should include:

Me gusta(n)... **Me encantan...**
No me gusta(n) nada...

19 Standards: 1.1, 1.2, 1.3

Resources: Voc. and Gram. Transparency 71

Focus: Answering survey questions about likes and dislikes

Recycle: Definite articles; ***ni...ni, a mí también, a mí tampoco;*** vocabulary from previous chapters

Suggestions: Have students read the entire survey for comprehension before writing their answers. You may wish to provide your own preferences as a model for the students.

Answers will vary.

Extension: Using the survey as a model, have students create their own survey, consisting of five to seven questions. They should include items that have to do with food, school, and leisure time activities.

Pronunciación
Core Instruction

Standards: 4.1

Resources: Teacher's Resource Book: Audio Script, p. 185; Audio Program DVD: Cap. 3A, Track 13

Suggestions: Use an exaggerated tone to emphasize the pronunciation distinctions as you read through the list. If you choose to use the audio, pause it after each word and repeat the word. Have students say it with you a third time.

Try it out! Have the class refer to pp. 124–125 for food vocabulary. Ask volunteers to say examples of ***h*** and ***j*** words.

Try it out! Read through the ***trabalenguas*** slowly with class. Use the picture to help students grasp the meaning. You may want to explain that ***había*** means "there was." Then have them read it together a few times. Finally, ask volunteers to say the ***trabalenguas*** for the class.

Theme Project

Students can perform Step 2 at this point. Be sure students understand your suggestions. (For more information, see p. 122-b.)

19 ¿Qué te gusta más?

Escribir • Hablar

1. A popular magazine has provided this survey to see how much you and a friend have in common. On a sheet of paper, write the numbers 1–7 and then write your preferences.
2. Take turns asking your partner about the survey items. Keep track of your similarities and differences. See how the magazine rates you.

Modelo

¿La comida mexicana o la comida italiana?

A —*¿Qué te gusta más, la comida mexicana o la comida italiana?*

B —*Me gusta más la comida italiana.*

o:—*No me gusta ni la comida mexicana ni la comida italiana.*

A —*A mí también.*

o:—*A mí me gusta la comida mexicana.*

o:—*A mí tampoco.*

¿Qué te gusta más?

¿Tu amigo(a) y tú son muy similares o muy diferentes? Completa este *quiz* y compara tus respuestas con las de un(a) amigo(a).

1	la comida mexicana	*o*	la comida italiana
2	el desayuno	*o*	el almuerzo
3	el cereal con fruta	*o*	el cereal sin fruta
4	las revistas	*o*	los libros
5	la música rock	*o*	la música rap
6	los amigos graciosos	*o*	los amigos serios
7	las hamburguesas con queso	*o*	las hamburguesas sin queso

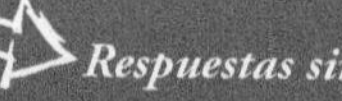

Respuestas similares:

7–6 ¡Uds. son gemelos![1]
5–4 Tienen mucho en común, ¿verdad?
3–2 ¡Un poco similares / un poco diferentes!
1–0 ¿Los opuestos[2] se atraen?[3] ¡Por supuesto!

[1]twins [2]opposites [3]attract

Pronunciación

The letters *h* and *j*

In Spanish, the letter *h* is never pronounced. Listen to and say these words:

hora	hablar	hasta	hola
hoy	hace	hacer	hotel

The letter *j* is pronounced like the letter *h* in "hat" but with more of a breathy sound. It is made far back in the mouth—almost in the throat. Listen to and say these words:

trabajar	dibujar	jugar	videojuegos
hoja	jueves	junio	julio

Try it out! Find and say five examples of foods or beverages from this chapter that have *h* or *j* in their spelling.

Try it out! Say this *trabalenguas* three times as fast as you can:

Debajo del puente de Guadalajara había un conejo debajo del agua.

DIFFERENTIATED INSTRUCTION

Students with Learning Difficulties

To reinforce the vocabulary in *Act.* 19, suggest specific examples that students might know, rather than just giving them the word in English. Take extra time with the model, as it may be confusing to students. For *Act.* 20, have students read the *¿Comprendes?* questions first, then refer to the visuals before reading the menu.

Heritage Language Learners

Be careful to emphasize the distinction between ***h*** and ***j*** to students, especially in writing. It is not uncommon to see the silent ***h*** left out in writing, so monitor this carefully when checking student work.

20 ¿Qué comida hay en el Ciberc@fé @rrob@?

Leer • Escribir • Hablar

Lee el menú y contesta las preguntas.

Menú del Ciberc@fé @rrob@

Desayunos

No. 1 Huevos: *(jamón, tocino, chorizo*[1]*)*. $27.00
Con cóctel de fruta $30.00

No. 2 Sincronizadas: *(tortilla de harina,*[2] *queso amarillo, jamón)* $33.00
Con cóctel de fruta $36.00

No. 3 Cuernitos: *(jamón, queso, tomate y lechuga)* $30.00
Con cóctel de fruta $33.00

No. 4 Chilaquiles: *verdes o rojos* $21.00
Con cóctel de fruta $24.00

No. 5 Omelet: *(con pollo, jamón, tomate, cebolla, champiñones*[3] *o queso)* $27.00

No. 6 Crepas *(champiñones, jamón, pollo)* $19.00

Refrescos $7.50 Café $6.00 Jugos $11.50 Té o té helado $6.00

Tel.: 212 03 95

16 de septiembre #65
Col. Centro

[1]spicy sausage [2]flour [3]mushrooms

> **Strategy**
>
> **Skimming**
> Look quickly through the menu. What meal is it for? Find three dishes you recognize and two that are new to you.

Crepas de cuitlacoche

Chilaquiles

¿Comprendes?

1. Comes el desayuno No. 1, con un jugo de naranja. ¿Cuál es el precio *(price)* del desayuno?
2. Comes un omelet con un café. ¿Cuál es el precio?
3. No te gustan nada los huevos. ¿Qué comes del menú?
4. No te gusta ni el café ni el té helado. ¿Qué bebes?

Más práctica GO

	realidades.com	print
Instant Check	✔	
Guided WB pp. 95–96	✔	✔
Core WB pp. 54–55	✔	✔
Comm. WB pp. 53–55, 58, 251	✔	✔
***Hispanohablantes* WB** pp. 98–101		✔

El español en la comunidad

Foods from different Spanish-speaking countries have become very popular in the United States. Visit a local grocery store and make a list of different types of foods that come from Spanish-speaking countries. Which of these foods have you tried?

Practice and Communicate 3A

20

Standards: 1.2, 1.3, 4.1, 5.2

Resources: Voc. and Gram. Transparency 72; Answer Keys: Student Edition, p. 41

Focus: Reading a menu

Suggestions: Direct students' attention to the *Strategy*. Have the class list familiar foods and identify new ones using the footnotes at the bottom of the menu.

Answers:

1. **$38.50 (treinta y ocho dólares y cincuenta centavos)**
2. **$33.00 (treinta y tres dólares)**
3. **Como sincronizadas, chilaquiles o cuernitos.**
4. **Bebo jugos.**

Pre-AP* Support

- **Learning Objective:** Interpretive: Print
- **Activity 20:** Students use reading comprehension skills to answer questions about a menu.

El español en la comunidad

Core Instruction

Standards: 5.1

Focus: Enhancing Spanish language and cultural knowledge through community experiences

Suggestions: Have students talk about items they have eaten that are typical of Spanish-speaking cultures. Ask them to brainstorm a list of items that might not be well-known in the United States. Compile students' findings into one list, type it, and distribute copies to each student as a shopping list of new items to try.

Additional Resources

- Communication Wbk.: Audio Act. 8–9, pp. 53–55
- Teacher's Resource Book: Audio Script, pp. 184–185, Communicative Pair Activity BLM, pp. 190–191
- Audio Program DVD: Cap. 3A, Tracks 11–12

ASSESSMENT

Prueba 3A-4 with Study Plan (online only)

Quiz: *Me gustan, me encantan*

- Prueba 3A-4: p. 72

ENRICH YOUR TEACHING

Culture Note

There are several Mexican dishes made from leftover tortillas, including one called ***chilaquiles.*** The tortillas are cut into strips, dried, fried, and then cooked in a sauce made from tomato, onion, and chile. They are then covered with cheese and heavy cream. This is a popular breakfast favorite. ***Cuernitos*** are croissants and are often served as a sandwich with ham, cheese, and tomato. ***Sincronizadas*** are two flour tortillas with ham and cheese in the middle. They are first grilled on both sides, then cut into four even pieces.

 Common Core: Reading

Lectura

Core Instruction

Standards: 1.2, 1.3, 3.1, 4.1

Focus: Reading about fruits and vegetables native to the Americas; reading a recipe for a ***licuado***

Suggestions:

Pre-reading: Direct students' attention to the *Strategy.* Have students look at the photos and ask if they recognize the fruits and vegetables. Have them look at the recipe on p. 139 and identify which part lists ingredients and which part is the instructions.

Reading: Remind students that it is not important to understand every word, but rather the passage as a whole. Have students discuss the question about which of these fruits they enjoy eating, or if they've not tried them, which ones look interesting. Have students predict what the recipe is for. As they read, ask them to write down unknown words on a separate sheet of paper. Then have them go back and attempt to find the meaning of these words based on their background knowledge and visual cues.

Post-reading: Have students write their answers to the *¿Comprendes?* questions as homework and then share them in class the next day.

BELLRINGER REVIEW

Show large flashcards (from Clip Art) for several fruits, vegetables, and dairy products. Have students name each item aloud in unison.

Pre-AP* Support

- **Learning Objective:** Interpretive: Print
- **Activity:** Read to the class the first paragraph followed by several true/false statements. Then, read each fruit description aloud to model the pronunciation. Have volunteers repeat each description.
- ***Pre-AP* Resource Book:*** Comprehensive guide to Pre-AP* reading skill development, pp. 19–26

Lectura

Objectives

- Read about fruits native to the Americas
- Use cognates and context to understand unknown words
- Learn about produce imported from Chile

Frutas y verduras de las Américas

Hay muchas frutas y verduras que son originalmente de las Américas que hoy se comen en todos los países. Las verduras más populares son la papa, el maíz, los frijoles y muchas variedades de chiles. También hay una gran variedad de frutas como la papaya, la piña y el aguacate. Estas frutas y verduras son muy nutritivas, se pueden preparar fácilmente y son muy sabrosas. La papaya y la piña son frutas que se comen en el desayuno o de postre. ¿Cuáles de estas frutas comes?

Strategy

Making guesses

When you find an unknown word, try to guess the meaning. Is it a cognate? What might it mean within the context of the reading and other words around it? Keep reading and the meaning may become clear.

la papaya

Es una fruta con mucha agua. Es perfecta para el verano. Tiene más vitamina C que la naranja.

el aguacate

La pulpa del aguacate es una fuente de energía, proteínas, vitaminas y minerales. Tiene vitaminas A y B.

el mango

Aunque[1] el mango es originalmente del Asia, se cultiva en las regiones tropicales de muchos países de las Américas. Tiene calcio y vitaminas A y C, como la naranja.

[1]Although

DIFFERENTIATED INSTRUCTION

Students with Learning Difficulties

When students are given longer reading passages, it may be beneficial to pair students with learning difficulties with a more skillful reader, who can help them apply the reading strategies that they have learned. These strategies might include using prior knowledge, visual cues, or cognates to deduce meaning.

Multiple Intelligences

Visual/Spatial: Have students research fruits from Latin America and prepare a poster showing pictures and informative captions in Spanish.

¿Comprendes?

1. ¿Qué vitaminas tienen las frutas en la página anterior?
2. De las frutas y verduras del artículo, ¿cuáles *(which ones)* te gustan? ¿Cuáles no te gustan?
3. ¿Qué otras frutas te gustan? ¿Comes estas frutas en el desayuno o en el almuerzo?
4. ¿Qué fruta no es originalmente de las Américas?

Más práctica GO

realidades.com | print

Guided WB p. 97	✔	✔
Comm. WB pp. 59, 252	✔	✔
***Hispanohablantes* WB** pp. 102–103		✔
Cultural Reading Activity	✔	

Fondo Cultural | Chile

Frutas y verduras During winter, the United States imports a wide range of fruits from Chile such as cherries, peaches, and grapes. When you purchase grapes from a supermarket in January, look to see if they have a label that says *Producto de Chile* or *Importado de Chile*.

- What are some other fruits and vegetables in your local market that are products of other countries?

Uvas de Chile

Licuado de plátano

Suggestions: If possible, have volunteers bring in the ingredients and supplies to make the recipe in class. Be absolutely certain that students do not have food allergies before doing this. Have students read the recipe and point to each item. Ask the class to read the recipe and tell you what to do. Provide them with the phrase ***Ud. necesita...*** so that they are able to give you instructions.

¿Comprendes? Standards: 1.2, 1.3

Resources: Answer Keys: Student Edition, p. 42

Focus: Writing and talking about the information in the reading

Suggestions: Have students read each question and then re-read the text, looking for key words to answer the questions. When students have completed the activity, have one student ask the questions and volunteers give their answers.

Answers:

1. **Las frutas tienen vitaminas A, B y C.**
2. **Answers will vary.**
3. **Answers will vary.**
4. **el mango**

Fondo cultural

Standards: 2.2, 5.1

Suggestions: After reading the passage, you may wish to ask students to begin a sticker collection. Reward them with a point or other compensation for every sticker that they bring in from fruits imported from a Spanish-speaking country. Title a blank piece of poster board ***Las frutas importadas,*** have students add the stickers, and display it in class.

Answers will vary but may include citrus fruits, pears, avocados, papayas, and guava fruit.

Mapa global interactivo, Actividad 2
Explore the geography and topography of Chile.

ENRICH YOUR TEACHING

Culture Note

In Latin America there are many little shops that sell ***licuados*** made from different fruits. A ***licuado*** can serve as a quick meal any time during the day.

Teacher-to-Teacher

If you plan to prepare a variety of foods and beverages for your students, you may want to submit your class lists to the school nurse first. Ask him or her to check for any allergies that are on record for your students. That way, you'll know who needs to avoid anything you are preparing.

For Further Reading

Student Resource: Realidades para hispanohablantes, Lectura 2, pp. 104–105

La cultura en vivo

Core Instruction

Standards: 2.2, 3.1, 4.2

Focus: Reading about making ***churros*** and ***chocolate***

Suggestions: Begin a class discussion about snack foods. Talk about foods sold by sidewalk vendors in the United States, such as soft pretzels and hot dogs. Encourage students to talk about what snacks they like, where and when they tend to eat them, and whether alone or in a group. Introduce the idea of ***churros*** and chocolate. Have students read the first paragraph. If students have personal experience with ***churros,*** let them share with the class.

Continue the discussion and remind students that people in Spanish-speaking countries often sit and socialize with friends and enjoy a snack. ***Churros*** are not as sweet as doughnuts and are often dipped in hot chocolate. The chocolate mentioned here is thicker and richer than that usually served in the United States. Point out the recipe. Tell students they might like to try making this at home with an adult.

Direct attention to the *Think about it!* section and have students discuss the questions.

Answers will vary.

Preparing hot foods in the classroom may not be an option. However, you may be able to get some ***churros*** for the students to taste. Another option is to prepare ***churros*** and chocolate for a food festival. Some parents may be willing to participate and help prepare the food.

Point out that ***churros*** are brought in a ***churrería,*** not a grocery store. Compare ***churrerías*** to doughnut shops. Ask why people might prefer to get doughnuts from a doughnut shop rather than an all-purpose grocery store. (Answers will vary but may include more variety: it's their specialty and so it is apt to be better; freshness; a place to sit and chat.)

Additional Resources

Student Resource: Realidades para hispanohablantes, p. 106

¡Adelante!

La cultura en vivo

Churros y chocolate

In many Spanish-speaking countries, a popular snack is the combination of *churros y chocolate.* Churros are long, slender doughnut-like pastries fried in hot oil. Small restaurants called *churrerías* specialize in churros and cups of delicious hot chocolate. You can also find churros being sold in stands on the street.

Chocolate y churros

Try it out! Here's the recipe to try. Churros are high in fat and calories, so you won't want to sample too many of them!

Churros

1 cup water

$\frac{1}{4}$ teaspoon salt

4 large eggs

1 cup sugar

$\frac{1}{2}$ cup unsalted butter *(= 1 stick)*

1 cup all-purpose flour

oil for deep frying

In a heavy saucepan, bring water, butter, and salt to a full boil. Remove from heat. Add the flour all at once, stirring briskly. Stir until the mixture pulls away from the side of the pan and forms a ball. Put the mixture in a bowl. With an electric mixer on medium speed, add one egg at a time. After adding the last egg, beat the mixture for one more minute.

With adult supervision, heat 2–3 inches of oil to 375° F in a deep, heavy pan. Fit a pastry bag or cookie press with a $\frac{1}{2}$ inch star tip. Pipe out 6 inch-long tubes of dough into the oil. ***Be extremely cautious adding dough to the oil, because the oil may spatter and burn you!*** Fry, turning a few times, for 3–5 minutes or until golden brown. Place the sugar on a plate. Drain the churros well on paper towels and then roll them in the sugar.

Chocolate caliente

To make hot chocolate in Mexico, cacao beans are ground to a powder. Cinnamon, powdered almonds, and sugar are then added, and hot milk is poured in. The mixture is whipped with a wooden whisk called *un molinillo* or *un batidor.* You can find Mexican-style chocolate for making *chocolate caliente* in many supermarkets.

Un molinillo

Think about it! What kinds of food and drink do you and your friends like? Is chocolate among the popular choices? Can you think of combinations of food and drink that are popular with many people in the United States? Are these combinations popular elsewhere?

DIFFERENTIATED INSTRUCTION

Heritage Language Learners

Students may be familiar with other snacks from Spanish-speaking countries. If so, allow them to describe the snack and tell whether there is a special way to eat it. If not, they might enjoy researching such a food from their heritage country.

Presentación oral 

¿Y qué te gusta comer?

- Role-play an interview about classes, favorite activities, and favorite foods
- Use a list of questions to get the information you want

Task
You and a partner will role-play a telephone conversation between an exchange student from the United States and a member of his or her host family in Uruguay.

1 Prepare Be sure to prepare for both roles. Here's how:

Host student: List at least four questions for the exchange student. Find out what he or she likes to study, eat and drink for breakfast and lunch, and his or her favorite activities.

Exchange student: Write some possible answers to questions from the host student and be prepared to give information about yourself.

2 Practice Work with a partner to practice different questions and different responses. Here's how you might start your conversation:

HOST STUDENT: ¡Hola, Pablo! Soy Rosa.

EXCHANGE STUDENT: ¡Hola, Rosa! ¿Cómo estás?

HOST STUDENT: Bien, gracias. Pues Pablo, ¿te gusta . . . ?

Continue the conversation. Use your notes in practice, but not to present.

3 Present You will be paired with another student, and your teacher will assign roles. The host student begins the conversation. Listen to your partner's questions and responses and keep the conversation going.

4 Evaluation The following rubric will be used to grade your presentation.

Rubric	Score 1	Score 3	Score 5
Completion of task	You ask or answer two questions during the conversation.	You ask or answer three questions during the conversations.	You ask or answer four or more questions during the conversation.
How easily you are understood	You are extremely difficult to understand. Your teacher could only recognize isolated words and phrases.	You are understandable, but have frequent errors in vocabulary and/or grammar that hinder your comprehensibility.	You are easily understood. You teacher does not have to "decode" what you are trying to say.
Your ability to keep the conversation going	You provide no conversational response or follow-up to what your partner says.	You provide frequent response or follow-up to what your partner says.	You always provide a response to your partner, listen and ask follow-up questions or volunteer additional information.

Strategy

Making lists
Making lists of questions can help you in conversations where you need to find out specific information.

ENRICH YOUR TEACHING

21st Century Skills

Communication Have two students prepare a script for an interview for a "foodie" radio program. One student is the interviewer and conducts a phone interview with a celebrity. The questions and answers deal with what the celebrity does to keep fit and to maintain a high energy level.

Speaking 3A

 Common Core: Speaking

Presentación oral

Core Instruction

Standards: 1.1, 1.3

Focus: Role-playing a telephone conversation between an American exchange student and a host student in Uruguay

Suggestions: Point out the *Strategy*. Read through the assignment and the 4-step approach with students.

1. Prepare Provide time for students to complete this step individually. Students may need to refer to *Capítulos* 1A and 1B to guide them while writing their questions and answers. Students may want to keep their written questions and answers to add to their portfolio.

2. Practice Pair up students and have them work with another pair of students.

3. Present Students should not use their notes for this step. Remind them to listen carefully to the questions and answers so they can answer accurately.

4. Evaluation Your students may want to place a copy of your comments and their grade, along with the questions they prepared in advance, in their portfolios.

Pre-AP* Support

Pre-AP* Resource Book: Comprehensive guide to Pre-AP* speaking skill development, pp. 39–50

Portfolio

Make video or audio recordings of student presentations in class, or assign the RealTalk activity so they can record their presentations online. Include the recording in their portfolios.

Additional Resources

Student Resources: Realidades para hispanohablantes, p. 107; Guided Practice: Presentación oral, p. 98

ASSESSMENT

Presentación oral

- Assessment Program: Rubrics, p. T29

Review the rubric with students. Go over the descriptions of the different levels of performance. After assessing students, help individuals understand how their performance could be improved. (See Teacher's Resource Book for suggestions on using rubrics in assessment.)

El mundo hispano

Core Instruction

Standards: 2.2, 3.1, 4.2

Resources: Voc. and Gram. Transparencies, 15

Mapa global interactivo, Actividad 3 Discover Lake Titicaca on the borders of Bolivia and Peru.

Focus: Reading about the countries in northern South America

Suggestions: After students read the text, display a map of South America. Focus on the northern part of the continent, and draw attention to the five countries featured here. Point out that this is a region of contrasts. Focus on the topography. Draw attention to the mountains and valleys, the rainforests and deserts. Note that the steep, rugged mountains make farming difficult. Point out the background photo of the terraced fields. Help students understand that terracing, an ancient system of agriculture, was necessary for successful farming. Terracing created shelves that slowed the course of the water, allowing it to soak into the ground, and thus making it possible to cultivate crops. Scientists have discovered that these ancient systems work better than some modern techniques.

Point out that these mountains are at a very high altitude, and that South America has the highest navigable body of water in the world. (Show Lake Titicaca on the map.) Guide students to understand that in comparison, very little takes place in the United States at 12,500 ft. Note that Bolivia is one of two landlocked countries in South America.

Direct attention to the top photo on p.143. Have students hypothesize about how the Inca managed to precisely carve huge stone blocks and move them into place. Help them understand what an achievement this was. Use the map to show the extent of the Inca civilization.

Direct attention to the middle photo on p.143. Venezuela is rich in oil. It contributes 13% to 18% of the oil used in the United States. Have students discuss how the discovery of oil in Venezuela has affected its economy.

El mundo hispano

América del Sur

Parte norte

Venezuela, Colombia, Ecuador, Peru, and Bolivia form a region of contrasts, with mountains and lowlands, rain forests and deserts, immense wealth and extreme poverty, remote villages and modern cities. A rugged geography, ancient indigenous civilizations, and abundant natural resources have made this one of the most culturally diverse regions in the world.

Constructed more than 500 years ago, the terraced fields in the highlands of Bolivia were a sophisticated system for conserving soil and water, and some remain in use today. In the 1980s archaeologists reconstructing ancient agricultural systems on the shore of Lake Titicaca (at 12,500 feet the highest navigable body of water in the world) found that these ancient systems worked better in this difficult environment than many modern agricultural techniques.

¿Sabes que . . . ?

The term *America* first appeared on a German map in 1507. The Americas are named for the Italian navigator Amerigo Vespucci, who produced the first European charts of mainland South America in 1497.

Para pensar

The countries of northern South America are lands of varied geography. Think about the North American continent. It is also a land of geographical contrasts. In what ways are both regions rich in natural resources, environmentally protected areas, and ancient civilizations?

realidades.com GO

Mapa global interactivo

Reference Atlas

DIFFERENTIATED INSTRUCTION

Advanced Learners

Have students research the Inca empire. Allow them to focus on a specific topic of their choice, such as the rediscovered city of Machu Picchu. Encourage them to present their findings to the class, or to create a display.

Heritage Language Learners

The heritage country of some students may have been presented here. If so, have them research the natural resources of that country, and make a brief presentation of their findings.

"Rediscovered" in 1911, the mountaintop city of Machu Picchu in Peru was part of the Incan empire, which in the sixteenth century extended from present-day Ecuador to Chile. Machu Picchu's buildings were made of huge, precisely carved stone blocks that were hauled into place without wheels or heavy draft animals.

Venezuela is one of the most important sources of oil consumed in the United States. Other important Latin American oil producers include Mexico, Colombia, and Ecuador, with new deposits being found every year. Latin America and Canada account for approximately 46 percent of oil imports to the United States. In contrast, the Middle East accounts for approximately 23 percent.

The Galapagos Islands, also called *las islas encantadas* (the enchanted islands), lie 600 miles off the coast of Ecuador. It is believed that the Incas may have traveled to the islands in large ocean-going rafts. In 1835, the naturalist Charles Darwin spent weeks there studying the islands' unique animal life. *Galápagos* are giant tortoises that are native to these islands, which are now a national park and wildlife sanctuary.

Culture 3A

Point out the bottom photo on p.143. Have students locate the Galapagos Islands on a map. Explain that these islands have animals that are not known to exist anywhere else in the world. As a result, the islands are now a wildlife sanctuary and national park.

Direct attention to the *¿Sabes que...?* section. Discuss Vespucci with students. Have them compare the dates of his travels and those of Columbus. Let them give an opinion about the naming of the continents.

Point out that this section only talks about the northern part of the continent. The southern part will be discussed later. Make sure students understand that much of South America is rural and that many descendants of the original indigenous people still live there and speak their own language rather than Spanish. The big cities, however, are very much like cities elsewhere.

Direct attention to the *Para pensar* section and have students discuss the question.

Answers will vary.

Theme Project

Students can perform Step 3 at this point. (For more information, see p. 122-b.)

ENRICH YOUR TEACHING

Teacher-to-Teacher

As an ongoing project, have students create a bulletin board on South America. They may wish to begin by making a large map of the continent. As they learn about a country, they can label it and research principal products, major cities, and historical information.

21st Century Skills

Information Literacy Ask students to conduct some research about one of the ancient sites mentioned or one of the other topics in the spread (oil production in South America, the Galápagos Islands). For their research, they should find three Web sites, and choose one of them as the source of a presentation they will make to the class. As part of their presentation, they should include comments about why they chose the Web site.

Review Activities

To talk about breakfast and lunch, to talk about beverages: Have students work in pairs to quiz each other on the vocabulary. They may find it useful to create flashcards with pictures on them.

To talk about eating and drinking: Have students ask others what they like to eat and drink.

To indicate how often: Have students make a list of their favorite foods and beverages and talk about how often they eat them.

To show surprise, to say that you like / love something: Have students brainstorm a list of foods and beverages that they like and dislike. Ask them to read their lists to a partner and react using one of these phrases.

Portfolio

Invite students to review the activities they have completed in this chapter, including written reports, posters or other visuals, recordings of oral presentations, or other projects. Have them select one or two items that they feel best demonstrate their achievements in Spanish. These products should be included in students' portfolios. Have them include this with the Chapter Checklist and Self-Assessment Worksheet.

Additional Resources

Student Resources: Realidades para hispanohablantes, p. 108

Teacher Resources:

- Teacher's Resource Book: Situation Cards, p. 192, Clip Art, pp. 194–196
- Assessment Program: Chapter Checklist and Self-Assessment Worksheet, pp. T56–T57

Objectives

- Review the vocabulary and grammar
- Demonstrate you can perform the tasks on p. 145

Repaso del capítulo

Vocabulario y gramática

to talk about breakfast

en el desayuno	for breakfast
el cereal	cereal
el desayuno	breakfast
los huevos	eggs
el pan	bread
el pan tostado	toast
el plátano	banana
la salchicha	sausage
el tocino	bacon
el yogur	yogurt

to talk about lunch

en el almuerzo	for lunch
la ensalada	salad
la ensalada de frutas	fruit salad
las fresas	strawberries
la galleta	cookie
la hamburguesa	hamburger
el jamón	ham
la manzana	apple
la naranja	orange
las papas fritas	French fries
el perrito caliente	hot dog
la pizza	pizza
el queso	cheese
el sándwich de jamón y queso	ham and cheese sandwich
la sopa de verduras	vegetable soup

to talk about beverages

el agua *f.*	water
el café	coffee
el jugo de manzana	apple juice
el jugo de naranja	orange juice
la leche	milk
la limonada	lemonade
el refresco	soft drink
el té	tea
el té helado	iced tea

to talk about eating and drinking

beber	to drink
comer	to eat
la comida	food, meal
compartir	to share

to indicate how often

nunca	never
siempre	always
todos los días	every day

to say that you like / love something

Me / te encanta(n) ___.	I / you love (___).
Me / te gusta(n) ___.	I / you like (___).

other useful words

comprender	to understand
con	with
¿Cuál?	Which? What?
más o menos	more or less
por supuesto	of course
¡Qué asco!	How awful!
sin	without
¿Verdad?	Right?

present tense of *-er* verbs

como	**comemos**
comes	**coméis**
come	**comen**

present tense of *-ir* verbs

comparto	**compartimos**
compartes	**compartís**
comparte	**comparten**

For *Vocabulario adicional,* see pp. 472–473.

DIFFERENTIATED INSTRUCTION

Students with Learning Difficulties

Have students review the *Repaso del capítulo* and create flashcards for any words that they do not know. Pair them with a student who is more confident with the vocabulary to practice. Before the test, provide students with a practice test, so they can become comfortable with the format.

Heritage Language Learners

Have students write a few paragraphs telling about their perfect lunch: Where are they going to eat? Whom are they going to invite to eat with them? What food are they going to eat? What will they have to drink? Encourage them to use as many vocabulary words from this chapter as they can.

Más repaso GO realidades.com | print

Instant Check	✔	
Puzzles	✔	
Core WB pp. 56–57		✔
Comm. WB pp. 253, 254–256	✔	✔

Preparación para el examen

On the exam you will be asked to . . .	Here are practice tasks similar to those you will find on the exam . . .	For review go to your print or digital textbook . . .
Interpretive		
 **1 Escuchar** Listen and understand as people describe what they eat and drink for lunch	Listen as three students describe what they typically eat and drink for lunch. Which is most like the kind of lunch you eat? Did they mention anything you could not buy in your school cafeteria?	**pp. 124–127** *Vocabulario en contexto* **p. 125** Actividades 1–2 **p. 128** Actividad 5
Interpersonal		
 **2 Hablar** Tell someone what you typically eat for breakfast and ask the same of others	Your Spanish club is meeting for breakfast before school next week. Find out what other people in your class typically eat for breakfast. After you tell at least two people what you eat for breakfast, ask what they like to eat. Does everyone eat the same kind of breakfast or do you all like to eat different things?	**p. 129** Actividad 7 **p. 130** Actividad 8 **p. 131** Actividad 11 **p. 133** Actividad 13 **p. 134** Actividades 15–16 **p. 141** *Presentación oral*
Interpretive		
 **3 Leer** Read and understand words that are typically found on menus	You are trying to help a child order from the lunch menu below, but he is very difficult to please. He doesn't like anything white. And he refuses to eat anything that grows on trees. Which items from the menu do you think he would refuse to eat or drink? ALMUERZO hamburguesa — plátanos pizza — manzana ensalada — leche	**pp. 124–127** *Vocabulario en contexto* **p. 131** Actividad 10 **p. 137** Actividad 20 **pp. 138–139** *Lectura*
Presentational		
 **4 Escribir** Write a list of foods that you like and others that you dislike	Your Spanish club is sponsoring a "Super Spanish Saturday." Your teacher wants to know what foods the class likes and dislikes so that the club can buy what most people like. Write the headings *Me gusta(n)* and *No me gusta(n)* in two columns. List at least four items that you like to eat and drink for breakfast and four items for lunch. Then list what you don't like to eat and drink for these same meals.	**p. 128** Actividad 4 **p. 129** Actividad 6 **p. 131** Actividad 11 **p. 134** Actividad 16 **p. 135** Actividad 18 **p. 137** Actividad 20
Comparisons		
5 Pensar Demonstrate an understanding of cultural differences regarding snacks	Think about popular food combinations in the United States, such as a cup of coffee and a doughnut. What is a similar combination that is popular in many Spanish-speaking countries, and where are you able to buy it?	**p. 140** *La cultura en vivo*

DIFFERENTIATED ASSESSMENT

CORE ASSESSMENT
- **Assessment Program:** Examen del capítulo 3A, pp. 73–79
- **Audio Program DVD:** Cap. 3A, Track 16
- **ExamView:** Chapter Test, Test Banks A and B

ADVANCED/PRE-AP*
- **ExamView: Pre-AP* Test Bank**
- **Pre-AP* Resource Book,** pp. 70–73

STUDENTS NEEDING EXTRA HELP
- **Alternate Assessment Program:** Examen del capítulo 3A
- **Audio Program DVD:** Cap. 3A, Track 16

HERITAGE LEARNERS
- **Assessment Program: Realidades para hispanohablantes:** Examen del capítulo 3A
- **ExamView: Heritage Learner Test Bank**

Performance Tasks

Standards: 1.1, 1.2, 1.3, 4.2

Student Resource: Realidades para hispanohablantes, p. 109

Teacher Resources: Teacher's Resource Book: Audio Script, p. 185; Audio Program DVD: Cap. 3A, Track 15; Answer Keys: Student Edition, p. 42

1. Escuchar

Suggestions: Play the audio or read the script.

Script

Marco: Siempre como una hamburguesa y papas fritas en el almuerzo. Por supuesto, necesito comer frutas y verduras, pero no me gustan.
Elena: ¡Qué asco! ¡Una hamburguesa y papas fritas! Nunca como papas fritas. Todos los días como una ensalada de frutas o sopa de verduras, ¡con una galleta, claro!
Tomás: ¿Cuál es mi comida favorita? Pues, no como mucho en el almuerzo. Como pizza o un perrito caliente y bebo un refresco.

Answers will vary.

2. Hablar

Suggestions: Allow time for students to work on this task in class. If students have difficulty with spontaneous conversation, have them write their messages first.

Answers will vary.

3. Leer

Suggestions: Have students read their answers to the class. Ask which items the boy would eat or drink.

Answers:
Eat: ensalada, hamburguesa y pizza
Not eat: plátanos, manzana y leche

Extension: Have students list items from p. 144 that the boy would eat or drink.

4. Escribir

Suggestions: Have students try this activity without the vocabulary list or notes.

5. Pensar

Suggestions: Remind students that in the United States we often snack on packaged foods. How does this differ from Spanish-speaking cultures?

Answers: ***Churros* and *chocolate* can be purchased in *churrerías* or at street stands.**

3B Para mantener la salud

AT A GLANCE

Objectives

- **Listen to and read descriptions of healthy and unhealthy lifestyles**
- **Talk and write about food, health, and exercise choices**
- **Exchange information while expressing your opinions about food choices and health**
- **Understand cultural perspectives on medicines and health care**
- **Compare traditional foods, markets, and festivals in the Spanish-speaking world with those in the United States**

Vocabulary

- Food groups
- Healthy activities
- Ways to describe foods

Grammar

- Plurals of adjectives
- The verb ***ser***

Culture

- Diego Rivera's mural of ***el tianguis,*** p. 147
- ***el mate,*** p. 152
- ***la Tomatina,*** p. 156
- ***los mercados,*** p. 160
- Soccer and the World Cup, p. 163
- Herbal remedies, p. 164

Recycle ♻

- Gender agreement of adjectives and nouns
- Using ***ser*** to talk about what a person is like
- Present tense of ***-ar*** verbs
- ***me gusta(n)***

RESOURCES

	FOR THE STUDENT	ONLINE	DVD	PRINT	FOR THE TEACHER	ONLINE	PREEXP	DVD	PRINT
Plan					Interactive TE and Resources DVD	•		•	
					Teacher's Resource Book, pp. 214–246	•		•	•
					Pre-AP* Resource Book, 70–73	•		•	•
					Lesson Plans	•			•
					Mapa global interactivo	•			
Introducción PP. 146–147									
Present	Student Edition, pp. 146–147	•	•	•	Interactive TE and Resources DVD	•		•	
	DK Reference Atlas	•	•		Teacher's Resource Book, pp. 214–215	•		•	•
	Hispanohablantes WB, pp. 110–111			•	Galería de fotos		•		
					Fine Art Transparencies, 52	•	•	•	
					Map Transparencies, 12, 13, 15–18	•	•	•	
Vocabulario en contexto PP. 148–151									
Present & Practice	Student Edition, pp. 148–151	•	•	•	Interactive TE and Resources DVD	•		•	
	Audio	•	•		Teacher's Resource Book, pp. 216–218, 220, 228–230	•		•	•
	Videohistoria	•	•		Vocabulary Clip Art	•	•	•	•
	Flashcards	•	•		Audio Program	•	•	•	
	Instant Check	•			Video Program: Videohistoria	•		•	
	Guided WB, pp. 99–108	•	•	•	Video Program Teacher's Guide: Cap. 3B	•		•	•
	Core WB, pp. 58–61	•	•	•	Vocabulary and Grammar Transparencies, 73–76	•	•	•	
	Comm. WB, pp. 60–63, 66	•	•	•	Answer Keys: Student Edition, pp. 43–44	•	•	•	
	Hispanohablantes WB, pp. 112–113			•	TPR Stories, pp. 37–48	•		•	•
Assess and Remediate					Prueba 3B–1: Assessment Program, pp. 80–81	•		•	•
					Assessment Program para hispanohablantes, pp. 80–81	•		•	•

RESOURCES

	FOR THE STUDENT	ONLINE	DVD	PRINT	FOR THE TEACHER	ONLINE	PREEXP	DVD	PRINT
Vocabulario en uso PP. **152–155**									
Present & Practice	Student Edition, pp. 152–155	•	•	•	Interactive Whiteboard Vocabulary Activities	•		•	
	Instant Check	•			Interactive TE and Resources DVD	•		•	
	Comm. WB, p. 64	•	•	•	Teacher's Resource Book, pp. 218, 222–223	•		•	•
	Hispanohablantes WB, pp. 114–115			•	Communicative Pair Activities, pp. 222–223	•		•	•
	Communicative Pair Activities	•			Audio Program	•	•	•	
					Videomodelos	•		•	
					Vocabulary and Grammar Transparencies, 78	•	•		•
					Answer Keys: Student Edition, pp. 44–46	•	•	•	•
Assess and Remediate					Prueba 3B–2 with Study Plan	•			
					Prueba 3B–2: Assessment Program, pp. 82–83	•		•	•
					Assessment Program para hispanohablantes, pp. 82–83	•		•	•
Gramática PP. **156–161**									
Present & Practice	Student Edition, pp. 156–161	•	•	•	Interactive Whiteboard Grammar Activities	•		•	
	Instant Check	•			Interactive TE and Resources DVD	•		•	
	Animated Verbs	•			Teacher's Resource Book, pp. 218–221, 224–225, 227	•		•	•
	Tutorial Video: Grammar	•			Communicative Pair Activities, pp. 224–225	•		•	•
	Canción de hip hop	•			Audio Program	•	•	•	
	Guided WB, pp. 109–112	•	•	•	Videomodelos	•		•	
	Core WB, pp. 62–64	•	•	•	Video Program: GramActiva	•	•	•	
	Comm. WB, pp. 64–65, 67–68, 257	•	•	•	Vocabulary and Grammar Transparencies, 77, 79	•	•	•	
	Hispanohablantes WB, pp. 116–121			•	Answer Keys: Student Edition, pp. 47–48	•	•	•	
	Communicative Pair Activities	•							
Assess and Remediate					Pruebas 3B–3 and 3B–4 with Study Plans	•			
					Pruebas 3B–3, 3B–4: Assessment Program, pp. 84, 85	•		•	•
					Assessment Program para hispanohablantes, pp. 84, 85	•		•	•
¡Adelante! PP. **162–167**									
Application	Student Edition, pp.162–167	•	•	•	Interactive TE and Resources DVD	•		•	
	Online Cultural Reading	•			Vocabulary and Grammar Transparencies, 80	•	•		•
	Guided WB, pp. 113–114	•	•	•	Map Transparencies, 16	•	•	•	
	Comm. WB, pp. 69, 258	•	•	•	Answer Keys: Student Edition, p. 49	•	•	•	
	Hispanohablantes WB, pp. 122–127			•					
Repaso del capítulo PP. **168–169**									
Review	Student Edition, pp. 168–169	•	•	•	Interactive TE and Resources DVD	•		•	
	Online Games and Puzzles	•			Teacher's Resource Book, pp. 219, 226, 228–230	•		•	•
	Core WB, pp. 65–66	•	•	•	Audio Program	•	•	•	
	Comm. WB, pp. 259–262	•	•	•	Answer Keys: Student Edition, p. 49	•	•	•	
	Hispanohablantes WB, pp. 128–129			•					
	Instant Check	•							
Chapter Assessment									
Assess					Examen del capítulo 3B	•		•	•
					Assessment Program, pp. 86–92	•		•	•
					Alternate Assessment Program, pp. 30–34	•		•	•
					Assessment Program para hispanohablantes, pp. 86–92	•		•	•
					Audio Program, Cap. 3B, Examen	•		•	
					ExamView: Test Banks A and B questions only online	•		•	
					Heritage Learner Test Bank	•		•	
					Pre-AP* Test Bank	•		•	

REGULAR SCHEDULE (50 MINUTES)

DAY	Warm-up / Assess	Preview / Present / Practice / Communicate	Wrap-up / Homework Options
1	**Warm-up** (10 min.) • Return Examen del capítulo 3A	**Chapter Opener** (5 min.) • Objectives • Arte y cultura **Vocabulario en contexto** (30 min.) • Presentation: Vocabulario en contexto • Actividades 1, 2	**Wrap-up and Homework Options** (5 min.) • Core Practice 3B-1, 3B-2
2	**Warm-up** (5 min.) • Homework check	**Vocabulario en contexto** (40 min.) • Presentation: Videohistoria *Para mantener la salud* • View: Videohistoria • Video Activities 1, 2, 3, 4 • Actividad 3	**Wrap-up and Homework Options** (5 min.) • Core Practice 3B-3, 3B-4 • Prueba 3B-1: Vocabulary recognition
3	**Warm-up** (10 min.) • Actividades 4, 5 • Homework check ✔**Formative Assessment** (10 min.) • Prueba 3B-1: Vocabulary recognition	**Vocabulario en uso** (25 min.) • Fondo cultural • Interactive Whiteboard Vocabulary Activities • Actividades 6, 7, 8, 10 • Audio Activities 5, 6	**Wrap-up and Homework Options** (5 min.) • Writing Activity 10 • Prueba 3B-2 with Study Plan: Vocabulary production
4	**Warm-up** (5 min.) • Actividad 9 • Homework check ✔**Formative Assessment** (10 min.) • Prueba 3B-2 with Study Plan: Vocabulary production	**Gramática y vocabulario en uso** (30 min.) • Actividad 11 • Presentation: The plurals of adjectives • View: GramActiva video • Interactive Whiteboard Grammar Activities • Actividades 12, 13, 14 • Fondo cultural	**Wrap-up and Homework Options** (5 min.) • Core Practice 3B-5 • Prueba 3B-3 with Study Plan: The plurals of adjectives
5	**Warm-up** (15 min.) • Writing Activity 11 • Audio Activity 7 • Homework check ✔**Formative Assessment** (10 min.) • Prueba 3B-3 with Study Plan: The plurals of adjectives	**Gramática y vocabulario en uso** (20 min.) • Communicative Pair Activity • Pronunciación • Presentation: The verb ***ser*** • View: GramActiva video • Interactive Whiteboard Grammar Activities • Actividad 16	**Wrap-up and Homework Options** (5 min.) • Writing Activities 12, 13
6	**Warm-up** (5 min.) • Homework check	**Gramática y vocabulario en uso** (40 min.) • View: GramActiva video • Actividades 15, 17, 18 • Audio Activities 8, 9 • Communicative Pair Activity • El español en el mundo del trabajo	**Wrap-up and Homework Options** (5 min.) • Core Practice 3B-6, 3B-7 • Prueba 3B-4 with Study Plan: The verb ***ser***
7	**Warm-up** (10 min.) • Fondo cultural • Homework check ✔**Formative Assessment** (10 min.) • Prueba 3B-4 with Study Plan: The verb ***ser***	**Gramática y vocabulario en uso** (25 min.) • Exploración del lenguaje • Actividades 19, 20	**Wrap-up and Homework Options** (5 min.) • Perspectivas del mundo hispano
8	**Warm-up** (5 min.) • Homework check	**¡Adelante!** (40 min.) • Lectura • ¿Comprendes? • Fondo cultural • Presentación escrita: Steps 1, 5 • El mundo hispano	**Wrap-up and Homework Options** (5 min.) • Presentación escrita: Step 2 • Preparación para el examen 3, 4, 5 • Lectura • El mundo hispano
9	**Warm-up** (5 min.) • Homework check	**¡Adelante!** (20 min.) • Presentación escrita: Step 3 **Repaso del capítulo** (20 min.) • Vocabulario y gramática • Preparación para el examen 1, 2	**Wrap-up and Homework Options** (5 min.) • Presentación escrita: Step 4 • Core Practice 3B-8, 3B-9 • Instant Check • Examen del capítulo 3B
10	**Warm-up** (10 min.) • Homework check ✔**Summative Assessment** (40 min.) • Examen del capítulo 3B		

BLOCK SCHEDULE (90 MINUTES)

DAY	Warm-up / Assess	Preview / Present / Practice / Communicate	Wrap-up / Homework Options
1	**Warm-up** (10 min.) • Return Examen del capítulo 3A	**Chapter Opener** (5 min.) • Objectives • Arte y cultura **Vocabulario en contexto** (60 min.) • Presentation: Vocabulario en contexto • Actividades 1, 2 • Presentation: Videohistoria *Para mantener la salud* • View: Videohistoria • Video Activities 1, 2, 3, 4 • Actividad 3 **Vocabulario en uso** (10 min.) • Actividades 6, 7	**Wrap-up and Homework Options** (5 min.) • Core Practice 3B-1, 3B-2, 3B-3, 3B-4 • Prueba 3B-1: Vocabulary recognition
2	**Warm-up** (10 min.) • Actividades 4, 5 • Homework check ✔**Formative Assessment** (10 min.) • Prueba 3B-1: Vocabulary recognition	**Vocabulario en uso** (65 min.) • Fondo cultural • Interactive Whiteboard Vocabulary Activities • Actividades 8, 9, 10, 11 • Audio Activities 5, 6 • Pronunciación • Communicative Pair Activity	**Wrap-up and Homework Options** (5 min.) • Writing Activity 10 • Prueba 3B-2 with Study Plan: Vocabulary production
3	**Warm-up** (5 min.) • Homework check ✔**Formative Assessment** (10 min.) • Prueba 3B-2 with Study Plan: Vocabulary production	**Gramática y vocabulario en uso** (70 min.) • Presentation: The plurals of adjectives • View: GramActiva video • Actividades 12, 13, 14 • Fondo cultural • Audio Activity 7 • Writing Activity 11 • Presentation: The verb ***ser*** • View: GramActiva video • Interactive Whiteboard Grammar Activities • Actividades 15, 16, 17, 18 • Audio Activities 8, 9 • Communicative Pair Activity	**Wrap-up and Homework Options** (5 min.) • Core Practice 3B-5, 3B-6, 3B-7 • Writing Activities 12, 13 • Pruebas 3B-3, 3B-4 with Study Plans: The plurals of adjectives, The verb ***ser***
4	**Warm-up** (15 min.) • Homework check ✔**Formative Assessment** (15 min.) • Pruebas 3B-3, 3B-4 with Study Plans: The plurals of adjectives, The verb ***ser***	**Gramática y vocabulario en uso** (20 min.) • Fondo cultural • El español en el mundo del trabajo • Exploración del lenguaje • Actividades 19, 20 **¡Adelante!** (35 min.) • Lectura • ¿Comprendes? • Fondo cultural • Presentación escrita: Steps 1, 5	**Wrap-up and Homework Options** (5 min.) • Presentación escrita: Step 2 • Lectura
5	**Warm-up** (5 min.) • Homework check	**¡Adelante!** (50 min.) • Presentación escrita: Step 3 • Perspectivas del mundo hispano • El mundo hispano **Repaso del capítulo** (30 min.) • Vocabulario y gramática • Preparación para el examen 1, 2, 3, 4, 5	**Wrap-up and Homework Options** (5 min.) • Presentación escrita: Step 4 • Core Practice 3B-8, 3B-9 • Instant Check • Examen del capítulo 3B
6	**Warm-up** (15 min.) • Homework check • Answer questions **Repaso del capítulo** (25 min.) • Situation Cards • Communicative Pair Activities ✔**Summative Assessment** (45 min.) • Examen del capítulo 3B		**Wrap-up and Homework Options** (5 min.) • El mundo hispano

Standards for *Capítulo* 3B

- To achieve the goals of the Standards, students will:

Communication

1.1 Interpersonal
- Talk about food groups and healthy diet
- Talk about food preferences and meals
- Talk about healthy lifestyle choices
- Talk about the personality traits of various people

1.2 Interpretive
- Read and listen to information about food groups
- Read and listen to information about health habits
- Listen to ways to describe food
- Read a picture-based story
- Listen to and watch a video about healthy diet

1.3 Presentational
- Present information about foods and beverages
- Present information about healthy lifestyle choices
- Present information about personality traits of people

Culture

2.1 Practices and Perspectives
- Explain past and present open-air markets
- Talk about the communal nature of ***mate***
- Talk about ***La Tomatina*** festival

2.2 Products and Perspectives
- Talk about Diego Rivera and his painting
- Talk about ***mate***

Connections

3.1 Cross-curricular
- Discuss Diego Rivera
- Discuss nutrition
- Reinforce math and graphing abilities skills

3.2 Target Culture
- Watch and listen to a video

Comparisons

4.1 Language
- Talk about new vocabulary through the recognition of cognates
- Explain gender agreement in use of adjectives
- Explain the pronunciation of the letters ***l*** and ***ll***
- Explain number agreement in use of adjectives
- Explain the present tense of the irregular verb ***ser***

4.2 Culture
- Compare ***mate*** to its counterpart in the United States
- Compare ***La Tomatina*** to festivals in the United States
- Compare places people shop for produce

Communities

5.1 Beyond the School
- Understand the value of Spanish-speaking ability in a career such as culinary arts

Capítulo 3B Para mantener la salud

Chapter Objectives

Communication

By the end of this chapter you will be able to:
- Listen to and read descriptions of healthy and unhealthy lifestyles
- Talk and write about food, health, and exercise choices
- Exchange information while expressing your opinions about food choices and health

Culture

You will also be able to:
- Understand cultural perspectives on medicines and health care
- Compare traditional foods, markets, and festivals in the Spanish-speaking world with those in the United States

You will demonstrate what you know and can do:
- Presentación escrita, p. 165
- Preparación para el examen, p. 169

You will use:

Vocabulary
- Food groups
- Healthy activities
- Ways to describe foods

Grammar
- Plurals of adjectives
- The verb *ser*

Exploración del mundo hispano

Country Connection
Healthy Foods and Activities

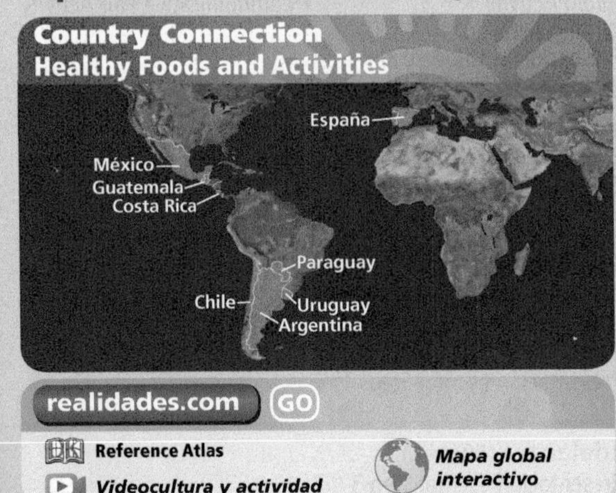

realidades.com GO

Reference Atlas

Videocultura y actividad

Mapa global interactivo

Mercado de la Boquería, Barcelona, España

ENRICH YOUR TEACHING

Using Backward Design

Have students preview the sample performance tasks on *Preparación para el examen,* p. 169, and connect them to the Chapter Objectives. Explain to students that by completing the sample tasks they can self-assess their learning progress.

Mapa global interactivo

Download the *Mapa global interactivo* files for Chapter 3B and preview the activities. Activity 1 takes you to the Zócalo and the Palacio Nacional in Ciudad de México. Activity 2 visits Spain, winner of the 2010 World Cup. In Activity 3, you locate Iguazú Falls and identify surrounding countries.

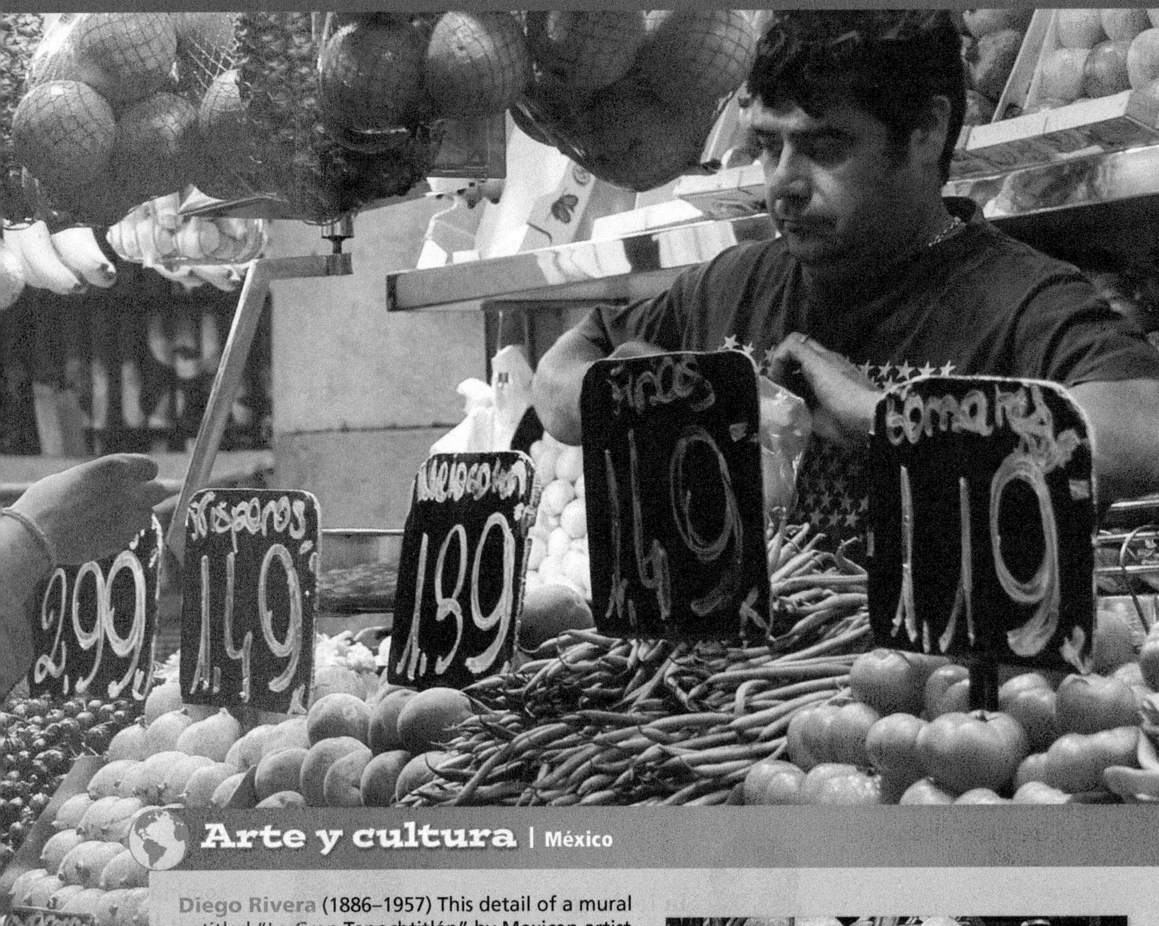

Arte y cultura | México

Diego Rivera (1886–1957) This detail of a mural entitled "La Gran Tenochtitlán" by Mexican artist Diego Rivera is located in the Palacio Nacional in Mexico City. It shows *el tianguis*, the bustling marketplace at Tenochtitlán, capital of the Aztec Empire. In the center right there are many kinds of food being traded, including tomatoes, squash, and different varieties of chile peppers. This mural is one of many by Rivera that focus on pre-Columbian life and civilizations.

- What impression do you think Rivera is giving about life in the pre-Columbian civilizations?

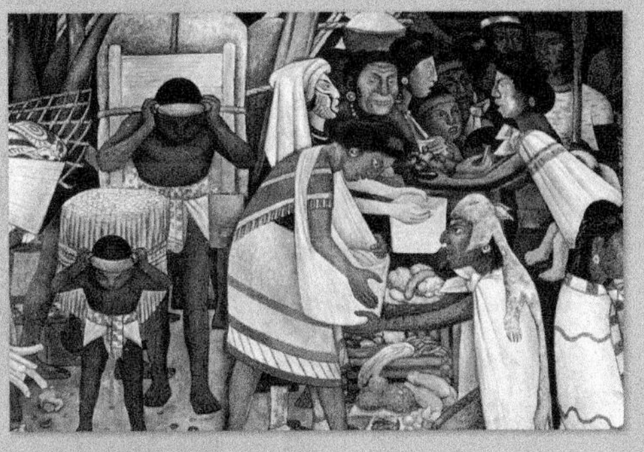

Detalle de *"La Gran Tenochtitlán"* (1945), Diego Rivera ▶

PresentationExpress™
See pp. 146a–146b

Chapter Opener

Core Instruction

Resources: Map Transparencies 12, 13, and 15–18

Suggestions: Introduce students to the chapter theme and review the objectives. Tell them they will be learning to talk about healthy eating and health habits. Brainstorm a list of healthy foods and "junk" food that students eat, and discuss some of their eating habits. The *A primera vista* video is about the diet and exercise habits of three teens.

Videocultura View *El maíz: comida esencial* with the class to find out how corn is prepared in Spanish-speaking countries.

Arte y cultura

Standards: 2.1, 2.2, 3.1

Resources: Fine Art Transparencies, p. 52

Suggestions: Explain that ***el tianguis*** was a central marketplace for the Aztecs. In modern Mexico these markets have the same name and many of the same goods are traded. Have students provide examples of markets in the United States. Do any traditional markets exist near you? What goods are sold?

Answers will vary.

Mapa global interactivo, Actividad 1 Find the Zócalo and the Palacio Nacional in Ciudad de México.

TEACHING WITH ART

Resources: Fine Art Transparencies, p. 52

Share with students that Tenochtitlán was located in what is now Mexico City. It was the capital of the Aztec civilization until 1521, when the Spanish defeated the Aztecs. After the Mexican Revolution (1910–1940), Diego Rivera and other artists were asked to paint large murals in Mexico City to convey a sense of pride in Mexico's past and hope for her future.

DIFFERENTIATED INSTRUCTION

Digital resources such as the ***Interactive Whiteboard*** activity banks, ***Videomodelos***, additional ***Online Activities, Study Plans***, automatically graded ***Leveled Workbook***, animated ***Grammar Tutorials, Flashcards***, and ***Vocabulary and Grammar Videos*** will help you reach students of different ability levels and learning styles.

STUDENTS NEEDING EXTRA HELP

Guided Practice Activities
- Flashcards, pp. 99–104
- Vocabulary Check, pp. 105–108
- Grammar Support, pp. 109–112

HERITAGE LEARNERS

Realidades para hispanohablantes
- Chapter Opener, pp. 110–111
- A primera vista, p. 112
- Videohistoria, p. 113
- Manos a la obra, pp. 114–121
- ¡Adelante!, pp. 122–127
- Repaso del capítulo, pp. 128–129

ADVANCED/PRE-AP*

Pre-AP* Resource Book,
- pp. 70–73

Communication Workbook
- Integrated Performance Assessment, p. 259

Vocabulario en contexto

Core Instruction

Standards: 1.2, 3.1

Resources: Teacher's Resource Book: Input Script, p. 216, Clip Art, pp. 228–230, Audio Script, p. 217; Voc. and Gram. Transparencies 73–74; TPR Stories Book, pp. 37–48; Audio Program DVD: Cap. 3B, Tracks 1–2

Focus: Presenting vocabulary and information about food groups

Suggestions: Use the story in the *TPR Stories Book* to present the new vocabulary and grammar, or use the Input Script from the *Teacher's Resource Book.* Bring plastic foods to class like those you would find in a child's toy kitchen. Present the vocabulary in three sets: fruits and vegetables, proteins and grains, and words to discuss health. Have students look at the pictures and guess what the words mean. Ask students to explain the connection between the colors in the chart and the circles around the foods. Ask them to guess the meanings of *granos* (grains); *productos lácteos* (dairy products), and *proteína* (protein), based on the foods and related colors.

Ask questions that require a limited verbal response: *¿Te gustan las verduras? ¿Comes muchas uvas? ¿Los pasteles son buenos para la salud?* Have students "shop" for the plastic food items. Be sure they take foods from each of the food groups. Have them organize the items as you call out food groups.

Hand out copies of the Vocabulary Clip Art. Have students tear the images into individual food items. Describe different meals to students and have them group the foods as they would on a cafeteria tray. (If your class is small, you might be able to borrow real trays from the cafeteria.) Then ask if the meal you described is good or bad for one's health.

Block Schedule

Have students create posters illustrating the MyPlate food groups. They can cut out pictures from magazines or grocery store ads. Encourage them to find additional foods and place them in the appropriate categories. They should label their posters and explain them to the class.

Objectives

Read, listen to, and understand information about
- food groups
- healthy activities
- ways to describe food

Vocabulario en contexto

El plato nutritivo es la forma más práctica de indicar la comida que **debes** comer **cada día. Para mantener la salud,** es importante comer de **todos** los grupos.

DIFFERENTIATED INSTRUCTION

Students with Learning Difficulties

Have students write the new vocabulary in the vocabulary section of their notebook, accompanied by pictures and English translations, if needed. For *Actividad* 1, you might prepare students by naming individual items and having the students touch them before they hear them in context.

Heritage Language Learners

Have students make two lists: one of their favorite foods and the other of foods they think they should be eating. Using their lists, have students discuss what they know about diet and activities to maintain good health. Check the lists for spelling.

caminar

levantar pesas

—¿Qué **haces** para mantener la salud?

—Pues, cada día **hago ejercicio.** Camino, monto en bicicleta y practico deportes.

—¡Uf! **Tengo hambre.** ¿**Por qué** no comemos **algo** en el restaurante "A tu salud"? Los sándwiches son muy **sabrosos.**

—¡Por supuesto!

1 ¿Qué debes comer?

Escuchar

Your teacher is giving a lecture on foods that you should eat from the Food Guide Pyramid. Touch each item as it is mentioned. Listen carefully for the names of the foods.

Más práctica GO

realidades.com | print

	realidades.com	print
Instant Check	✔	
Guided WB pp. 99–104	✔	✔
Core WB pp. 58–59	✔	✔
Comm. WB p. 66	✔	✔
***Hispanohablantes* WB** p. 112		✔

2 Para mantener la salud

Escuchar

Listen to students talk about things they do. Give a "thumbs-up" sign if they are describing things that are healthy and a "thumbs-down" sign if the things are unhealthy.

Language Input 3B

1 Standards: 1.2, 3.1

Resources: Teacher's Resource Book: Audio Script, p. 217; Audio Program DVD: Cap. 3B, Track 3; Answer Keys: Student Edition, p. 43

Focus: Listening to identify food and beverage vocabulary

Suggestions: Play the audio or use the script to read the activity aloud. Tell students that some of the sentences contain more than one food item.

Script and Answers:

1. **Necesitas beber leche o comer queso. *(milk)***
2. **El pescado y el pollo son buenos para la salud. *(fish, chicken)***
3. **Las judías verdes y las zanahorias son verduras importantes. *(green beans, carrots)***
4. **No debes comer mucho helado. *(ice cream)***
5. **Las papas son buenas para la salud. *(potatoes)***
6. **El arroz es bueno para la salud. *(rice)***
7. **No es bueno comer muchos pasteles. *(pastries)***
8. **Debes comer las uvas u otra fruta cada día. *(grapes)***

2 Standards: 1.2, 3.1, 4.1

Resources: Teacher's Resource Book: Audio Script, p. 217; Audio Program DVD: Cap. 3B, Track 4; Answer Keys: Student Edition, p. 43

Focus: Listening to food and health vocabulary in context

Suggestions: Play the audio or read the script. Repeat the activity until students indicate understanding.

Script and Answers:

1. **Me gusta mucho correr. *(up)***
2. **Nunca hago ejercicio. *(down)***
3. **Practico deportes. *(up)***
4. **Como pasteles cada día. *(down)***
5. **Mis amigos y yo levantamos pesas. *(up)***
6. **Bebo agua cada día. *(up)***
7. **Nunca como verduras. ¡Son horribles! *(down)***
8. **Me gustan los espaguetis con tomate. *(up)***

ENRICH YOUR TEACHING

Culture Note

Food items may have many different names across cultures. Green beans, for example, may be called ***judías verdes, ejotes, habas, alubias,*** and ***habichuelas.*** Some may assume the term ***judías verdes*** is a reference to Jewish people. It is in fact from the Arabic *yudiyaa,* the word for "bean."

21st Century Skills

Flexibility and Adaptability Work with a partner in a role-play as nutritional counselor and elderly client. The counselor creates a plan for the client that includes both nutrition and exercise. Have students think about how the regimens would differ if the client were a teenager.

Teacher-to-Teacher

Make a Food Plate chart and display it in the classroom. While studying this chapter, have students add labels of foods they eat to the different parts of the *MiPlato* diagram.

Videohistoria

Core Instruction

Standards: 1.2

Resources: Voc. and Gram. Transparencies 75–76; Audio Progra[...]

Focus: Pre[...] vocabular[...] video

Tues 11/29
Videohistoria
strategy –
walk thru w/ photos
– Read in groups of 3, watch video

Suggesti[...]

Pre-readi[...] *Strategy*[...] panel by[...] Do stude[...] panel 8? Do they remember th[...] as planning this meal in the last chapter?

Reading: Read the captions or play the audio. Using the transparencies and non-verbal clues, help students understand the new words in blue type.

Post-reading: Have students complete *Actividad* 3 to check comprehension.

Video

Core Instruction

Standards: 1.2

Resources: Teacher's Resource Book: Video Script, p. 220; Video Program: Cap. 3B; Video Program Teacher's Guide: Cap. 3B

Focus: Comprehending contextualized language about healthy eating habits

Suggestions:

Pre-viewing: Review the *Videohistoria* reading, and have students list the key ideas. Play a video excerpt with the sound muted, and ask students which panel of the *Videohistoria* it corresponds to.

Viewing: Show the video without pausing. Then show it again, stopping along the way to check new vocabulary. Ask students to identify unfamiliar words or behavior. Were any parts of the video easier to understand? Why? Which words were similar to English words?

Post-viewing: Complete the Video Activities in the *Communication Workbook*.

Para mantener la salud

¿Qué hacen Raúl, Tomás y Gloria para mantener la salud? Lee la historia.

Strategy

Using visuals to make predictions
Before you read the story, use the pictures to predict what will happen. This will help you understand the story better as you read.

- How did your predictions compare with what you read?

Tomás: **Tengo sed . . .**
Raúl: ¿Qué **prefieres?** ¿Te gusta el café? El café de Costa Rica es muy bueno.
Tomás: ¡Pero el café es **malo** para la salud! **Prefiero una bebida** como . . . un jugo de fruta.

5

Tomás: ¡Me gusta hacer algo cada día! Hago ejercicio, levanto pesas o camino todos los días.

6

Tomás: Tengo hambre.
Raúl: ¿Por qué no comemos en la soda?*

Tomás: La comida aquí es muy buena. Ahora no tengo hambre. ¿Y tú?
Raúl: **¡Creo que no!**
Gloria: Pues, **creo que** debemos ir a casa.

* *La soda* is the word for a casual restaurant in Costa Rica.

DIFFERENTIATED INSTRUCTION

Students with Special Needs

Some students may have difficulty matching the characters' speech in the *Videohistoria* dialogues with the people in the photos. As students read, use the transparencies and point to the characters. Have students do the same in their books.

Multiple Intelligences

Visual/Spatial: Ask students to create a poster with foods they eat and exercises they do to stay healthy. Have them include activities from *Capítulo* 1A. The poster should include information about why the foods and exercises are healthy. Display the posters in class.

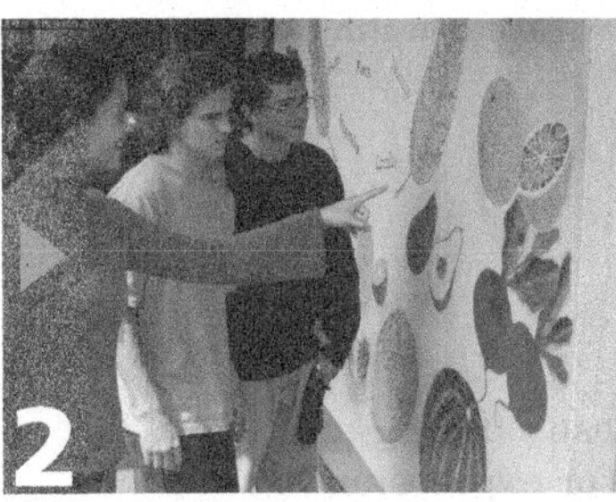

Raúl: ¡Ah! **Estoy de acuerdo,** un refresco.

Tomás: Raúl, ¿por qué hablas de *refrescos?* A mí me gustan los jugos de fruta.

Gloria: **Porque,** Tomás, ¡un *refresco* en Costa Rica *es* un jugo de fruta!

Raúl: Dos refrescos de mango con leche.

Gloria: Y un refresco de mango con agua, por favor.

Tomás: ¡Es *muuuy* sabroso!

Gloria y Raúl: Sí, sí . . . ¡y todos los refrescos aquí son buenos para la salud!

Gloria: Tomás, ¿qué haces para mantener la salud?

Mamá: ¡A comer **la cena!**

Los jóvenes: *¡Uf!*

3 ¿Comprendes?

Escribir • Hablar

1. ¿Por qué no bebe café Tomás?
2. En Costa Rica, ¿qué es *un refresco?*
3. ¿Los refrescos en Costa Rica son buenos o malos para la salud?
4. Según Tomás, ¿cómo es la comida en la soda?
5. En casa, ¿qué está en la mesa?

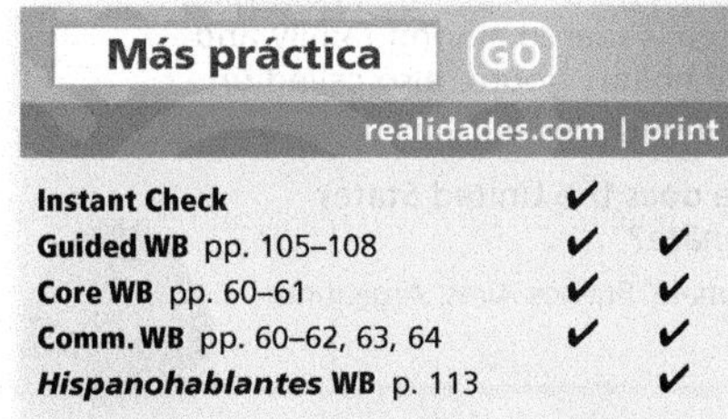

Más práctica GO

realidades.com | print

	realidades.com	print
Instant Check	✔	
Guided WB pp. 105–108	✔	✔
Core WB pp. 60–61	✔	✔
Comm. WB pp. 60–62, 63, 64	✔	✔
***Hispanohablantes* WB** p. 113		✔

3 Standards: 1.1, 1.3

Resources: Answer Keys: Student Edition, p. 44

Focus: Reading comprehension

Suggestions: Have students scan for key words that will help them answer the questions. When reviewing, ask that students point out where they found the information for the answer. Point out that the question ***¿Por qué?*** is two words with an accent mark on ***qué.*** The answer, ***Porque...,*** is one word with no accent.

Answers:

1. **Porque el café es malo para la salud.**
2. **Un refresco en Costa Rica es un jugo de frutas.**
3. **Los refrescos en Costa Rica son buenos para la salud.**
4. **La comida es muy buena.**
5. **La cena está en la mesa: hamburguesas, pizza, ensalada, jugo de manzana.**

Pre-AP* Support

- **Learning Objective:** Interpretive: Audio
- **Activity:** Have students write a paragraph describing what they eat for a particular meal and whether or not it is healthy. Then, have students record their presentations. Ask them to create two multiple-choice questions to accompany what they have recorded. Redistribute the presentations to other students. Have them listen to them and answer the questions.
- ***Pre-AP* Resource Book:*** Comprehensive guide to Pre-AP* vocabulary skill development, pp. 51–57

Teacher-to-Teacher

Have students work in pairs and give instructions to a classmate about the foods he/she should or should not eat to maintain good health, selecting the foods from pictures or props. You should model what they need to say: *Para mantener la salud, debes comer zanahorias y judías verdes. No debes comer pasteles.* Remind them to include foods from *Capítulo* 3A.

Additional Resources

- Communication Wbk.: Audio Act. 5, p. 63
- Teacher's Resource Book: Audio Script, pp. 217–218
- Audio Program DVD: Cap. 3B, Track 6

ASSESSMENT

Quiz: Vocabulary Recognition

- Prueba 3B-1: pp. 80–81

ENRICH YOUR TEACHING

Culture Note

In Costa Rica, ***gallo pinto,*** the national dish of fried rice and black beans, is served as a breakfast food. Many meals are derivatives of ***gallo pinto,*** including ***arroz con pollo*** or ***arroz con atún.*** At lunch, ***gallo pinto*** becomes ***casado:*** rice and beans accompanied by cabbage and tomato salad, fried plantains, and meat.

Teacher-to-Teacher

Review foods introduced in *Capítulo* 3A. Have students work in small groups to create menus for three meals in a health-food restaurant. Have students think of a creative name for their restaurant, write their menus, and decorate them with drawings or pictures. Display the menus.

INTERACTIVE WHITEBOARD
Vocabulary Activities 3B

4 Standards: 1.3

Resources: Answer Keys: Student Edition, p. 44

Focus ... food vocab...

Sugg... their ... colu... volu... Acce... repl...

Ans... may vary.

1. **el arroz...el bistec**
2. **los pasteles...la lechuga**
3. **ver la televisión...levantar pesas**
4. **sabroso...¡Qué asco!**
5. **comer mucho...mantener la salud**
6. **los tomates...el arroz**
7. **un día...siempre**
8. **las papas...el pescado**
9. **el pescado...el pastel**

5 Standards: 1.3

Resources: Answer Keys: Student Edition, p. 45

Focus: Thinking about and writing food vocabulary

Recycle: Foods and beverages

Suggestions: Tell students to use words from both *Capítulo* 3A and *Actividad* 4.

Answers will vary but may include:

En el refrigerador:
pescado, pollo, bistec, helado, pan, leche, jugo, salchichas, tocino, jamón, queso, yogur, ensalada, lechuga, refrescos, limonada, té helado, mantequilla

No necesitan refrigerador:
cereal, té, agua, café, cebollas, guisantes, papas, uvas, espaguetis, arroz, judías verdes, tomates, zanahorias, pasteles

Fondo cultural

Standards: 2.1, 2.2, 4.2

Suggestions: Explain that leaves from the ***yerba mate*** tree are used to make the herbal tea. The ***bombilla*** is a filtered metal straw to strain leaf fragments. The gourd is passed from person to person. Ask: What qualifies a beverage or food as "national"?

Answers will vary, but may include coffee, iced tea, or soft drinks.

Objectives

- Identify foods from the different groups
- Discuss food preferences and healthy food choices
- Exchange information while giving advice about staying healthy
- Read and write about healthy activities

Vocabulario en uso

4 ¡Claro que no!

Leer • Escribir

For each group of words, choose the word or expression that doesn't belong and write it down on a sheet of paper. Then think of one more word or expression that does fit with the group and write it down beside the first word you wrote.

Modelo

la cebolla	la lechuga	la uva

la uva ... *la zanahoria*

1.	el pollo	el pescado	el arroz
2.	las zanahorias	los pasteles	las judías verdes
3.	caminar	correr	ver la televisión
4.	malo	horrible	sabroso
5.	comer mucho	levantar pesas	hacer ejercicio
6.	los tomates	el pan	los espaguetis
7.	cada día	un día	todos los días
8.	el bistec	las papas	el pollo
9.	la mantequilla	el helado	el pescado

5 ¿En el refrigerador o no?

Pensar • Escribir

Escribe dos listas. En la primera lista, escribe las comidas y bebidas que deben estar en el refrigerador. En la segunda lista, escribe las comidas y bebidas que no necesitan estar en el refrigerador.

Fondo Cultural | Argentina | Paraguay | Uruguay

El mate is the national beverage of Argentina, Paraguay, and Uruguay. This herbal tea is shared among family and friends. It is served hot in a hollow gourd, also called *un mate,* with a straw called *una bombilla.*

- What national beverage does the United States have that compares to *mate?*

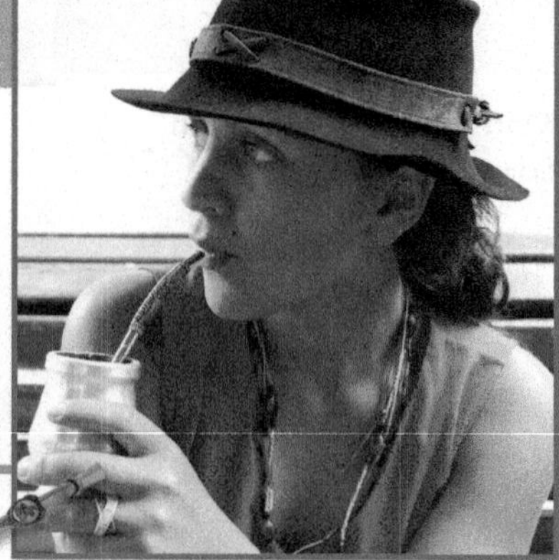

Una mujer toma mate, Buenos Aires, Argentina.

DIFFERENTIATED INSTRUCTION

Heritage Language Learners

Have students ask family members or research herbs or spices that are important ingredients in heritage cooking (e.g., ***chipotle, cilantro, comino, coco***). Have students find out if these ingredients are readily available in your area. What dishes are prepared with these ingredients? Have students prepare their research in written form. Be sure to correct spelling.

Students with Learning Difficulties

For *Actividad* 4, have students describe the characteristics of each item to help them see the categories. For *Actividad* 5, provide a sheet with a simple drawing of a refrigerator and have students write the words that belong in the refrigerator inside the picture, with the others outside.

Practice and Communicate 3B

6 ¿Qué prefieres? | 

Hablar

Ask your partner which of two foods he or she prefers. Your partner will answer and ask you which one you prefer.

Modelo

A —*¿Qué prefieres, carne o pescado?*
B —*Prefiero carne. Y tú, ¿qué prefieres?*
o:—*No como ni carne ni pescado. Y tú, ¿qué prefieres?*
B —*Prefiero pescado.*

Estudiante A

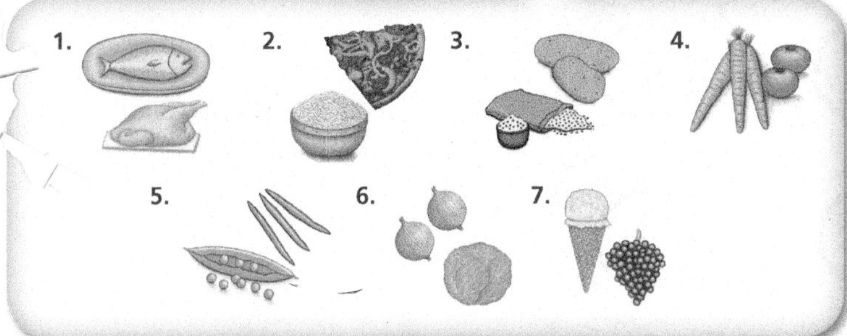

Estudiante B

¡Respuesta personal!

7 ¿Sí o no? |

Hablar • Pensar

Habla de lo que debes comer y beber para mantener la salud.

Modelo

A —*¿Debo beber leche cada día para mantener la salud?*
B —*Creo que sí.*
o:—*Creo que no.*

Estudiante A

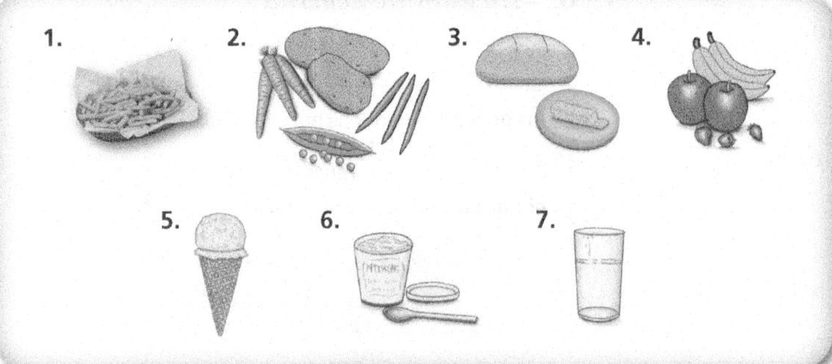

Estudiante B

Creo que . . .

6 Standards: 1.1

Resources: Answer Keys: Student Edition, p. 45

Focus: Talking about food preferences

Suggestions: Discuss the options in the *Modelo* with students. Be sure they understand that they are to answer truthfully.

Answers will vary but will include:

1. **¿Qué prefieres, pescado o pollo?**
2. **¿...pizza o espaguetis?**
3. **¿...papas o arroz?**
4. **¿...zanahorias o tomates?**
5. **¿...guisantes o judías verdes?**
6. **¿...cebollas o lechuga?**
7. **¿...helado o uvas?**

7 Standards: 1.1, 3.1

Resources: Answer Keys: Student Edition, p. 46

Focus: Talking about maintaining good health

Suggestions: Discuss what kinds of foods should be eaten daily and which should not be eaten in excess. Ask volunteers to perform their conversations.

Answers:

1. **—¿Debo comer papas fritas cada día para mantener la salud?**
   —Creo que no.
2. **¿...verduras...? Creo que sí.**
3. **¿...pan y mantequilla...? Creo que no.**
4. **¿...frutas...? Creo que sí.**
5. **¿...helado...? Creo que no.**
6. **¿...yogur...? Creo que sí.**
7. **¿...beber agua...? Creo que sí.**

Extension: Have students reverse roles and use ***necesito*** instead of ***debo.***

Pre-AP* Support

- **Learning Objective:** Presentational Writing
- **Activity:** Have students turn the lists of foods they created for Activity 5 into a persuasive paragraph explaining why the foods on each list should or should not be in the refrigerator. Student may cite health, taste, or other reasons in their arguments.
- ***Pre-AP* Resource Book:*** Comprehensive guide to Pre-AP* writing skill development, pp. 27–38

ENRICH YOUR TEACHING

Culture Note

The names of many foods in Mexico come from ***náhuatl,*** the ancient language of the Aztecs that is still spoken today in various dialects. Words from ***náhuatl*** often end in ***-te*** (formerly ***-tl***). Examples include: ***chocolate, cacahuate*** (peanut), ***ejote*** (green bean), ***elote*** (corn), and ***tomate.***

Advanced Learners/Pre-AP*

Create a "refrigerator" out of a cardboard box with a flap for the door. Bring real food items, or empty packaging that suggests these items, to class. Place several of the items in the refrigerator, then open the door for students to see for three seconds. Close the door and have them list as many items as they can remember.

3B Practice and Communicate

Thurs 11/29

8 Standards: 1.1

Resources: Answer Keys: Student Edition, p. 46

Focus: Talking about foods and beverages appropriate for certain times of day

Recycle: Telling time

Suggestions: Point out the *Para decir más....* Students are not held responsible for these words, but should use them in their answers. Show the transparencies with food vocabulary while students practice the conversation. Point out that Student B should give a personal response.

Answers will vary but will include:

1. **Son las doce (es mediodía)...**
2. **Son las diez de la noche...**
3. **Son las nueve de la mañana...**
4. **Son las siete de la mañana...**
5. **Son las seis de la tarde (*or* de la mañana)...**
6. **Son las tres de la tarde...**

9 Standards: 1.2, 1.3

Focus: Reading for comprehension and writing with new vocabulary

Suggestions: While students are working, walk around the room to support students who need assistance. Remind students to keep their work for *Actividad* 10.

Answers will vary.

10 Standards: 1.1

Focus: Talking about maintaining good health

Suggestions: When students have discussed all seven items, have them reverse roles and practice again.

Answers will vary.

8 ¿Hay algo para comer? |  | 

Hablar

Habla de lo que debes comer y beber a las horas indicadas.

Para decir más . . .

de la mañana	in the morning
de la tarde	in the afternoon
de la noche	in the evening

Modelo

A —*Son las ocho de la mañana y tengo hambre y sed. ¿Qué debo comer y beber?*
B —*Debes comer cereal y pan tostado, y debes beber jugo de manzana.*

Estudiante A

Estudiante B

¡Respuesta personal!

9 Los buenos consejos

Leer • Escribir

Da consejos *(Give advice)* sobre lo que es bueno o malo para la salud. Copia y completa las frases. Necesitas tus frases para la Actividad 10.

1. Para mantener la salud, debes ___ todos los días.
2. Necesitas beber ___ cada día.
3. Debes comer ___ en la cena.
4. ___ es malo para la salud.
5. El jugo de zanahoria es ___.
6. Debes comer ___ todos los días.
7. Nunca debes comer ___.

10 ¿Estás de acuerdo? |

Hablar

Lee tus consejos de la Actividad 9 a otro(a) estudiante. ¿Está de acuerdo con tus consejos?

Modelo

A —*Para mantener la salud, debes practicar deportes todos los días.*
B —*Estoy de acuerdo.*
o: —*No estoy de acuerdo.*

También se dice . . .

los guisantes = los chícharos *(México)*, las arvejas *(Argentina, Bolivia)*

el tomate = el jitomate *(México)*

DIFFERENTIATED INSTRUCTION

Students with Special Needs

Some students may be unable to read the clock faces in *Actividad* 8, so you may want to give them pictures of digital clocks instead. Others may need help filling in the blanks in *Actividad* 9. Offer a list of three choices for each blank and allow students to choose the one they prefer.

Multiple Intelligences

Verbal/Linguistic: Have students research fast-food restaurants in Spanish-speaking countries. How many are there? Are they popular? Where do most people prefer to eat? What are some of the slogans used to sell the food? Students can present their findings in the form of a poster, a report, or an oral presentation.

Practice and Communicate 3B

11 ¿Qué haces . . .?

Leer • Escribir • Hablar

Take this test on healthy activities to see how you rate.

1. Write your answers in complete sentences on a sheet of paper.
2. Ask a partner each question. Tally your partner's *sí* and *no* answers.
3. Write three recommendations so your partner can have a healthier lifestyle.

Modelo

Debes caminar o correr todos los días.

¿Qué haces para mantener la salud?

Contesta las preguntas según las actividades que haces cada día. Cada "sí" = 1 punto.

sí	no	
○	○	**1.** ¿Haces ejercicio?
○	○	**2.** ¿Practicas deportes?
○	○	**3.** ¿Comes verduras?
○	○	**4.** ¿Comes frutas?
○	○	**5.** ¿Caminas o corres?
○	○	**6.** ¿Comes un buen desayuno?
○	○	**7.** ¿Comes comida que es buena para la salud?
○	○	**8.** ¿Bebes cinco vasos* de agua?
○	○	**9.** ¿Pasas tiempo con amigos?
○	○	**10.** ¿Ves tres horas o menos de televisión?

9–10 puntos *¡Felicidades! ¡Haces mucho para mantener la salud!*

6–8 puntos *Bueno, pero debes hacer más para mantener la salud.*

0–5 puntos *¡Ay, ay, ay! Necesitas hacer algo para mantener la salud.*

*glasses

Pronunciación

The letters *l* and *ll*

In Spanish, the letter *l* is pronounced much like the letter *l* in the English word "leaf." Listen to and say these words:

lechuga	lunes	pasteles	helado
almuerzo	sol	abril	difícil

For most Spanish speakers, the letter combination *ll* is similar to the sound of the letter *y* in "yes." Listen to and say these words:

llamo	silla	allí	llueve
cebolla	pollo	ella	mantequilla

Try it out! Listen to this song and then sing it.

Canta el gallo, canta el gallo
con el kiri, kiri, kiri, kiri, kiri;
La gallina, la gallina
con el cara, cara, cara, cara, cara;
Los polluelos, los polluelos
con el pío, pío, pío, pío, pío, pío, pí.

Extra Time Activity?

...rency 78 ... giving ... health ... n the ... culties with th... ansparency to do the reading as a class.

Answers will vary.

Extension: Have students interview family members and report to the class.

Pronunciación

Core Instruction

Standards: 4.1

Resources: Teacher's Resource Book: Audio Script, p. 218, Audio Program DVD: Cap. 3B, Tracks 8–9

Focus: Pronouncing the letters ***l*** and ***ll***

Suggestions: Demonstrate the difference between the pronunciation of ***l*** and ***ll.*** Have students repeat the words. Play the song from the audio.

Try it out! Before listening to the song, have students look at the picture and match ***gallo, gallina,*** and ***polluelos*** with the correct images.

Additional Resources

- Communication Wbk.: Audio Act. 6, p. 64
- Teacher's Resource Book: Audio Script, p. 218, Communicative Pair Activity BLM, pp. 222–223
- Audio Program DVD: Cap. 3B, Track 7

ENRICH YOUR TEACHING

Teacher-to-Teacher

Tell students that the song uses onomatopoeia (***onomatopeya***), words formed by imitating sounds. Students may enjoy learning how Spanish represents the sounds made by other animals. These provide very good pronunciation practice.

21st Century Skills

Collaboration Working in small groups, have students compare their responses to the survey in Activity 11 and draw conclusions about the group's habits. Do their classmates eat well? Do they eat the right foods at the right time of day? Do they exercise regularly? After comparing the results for the whole class, students should come up with a plan for overall improvement of health habits, if necessary.

ASSESSMENT

Prueba 3B-2 with Study Plan (online only)

Quiz: Vocabulary Production

- Prueba 3B-2: pp. 82–83

Gramática

Core Instruction

Standards: 4.1

Resources: Teacher's Resource Book: Video Script, p. 220; Video Program: Cap. 3B

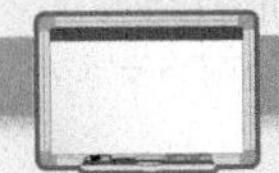

INTERACTIVE WHITEBOARD
Grammar Activities 3B

Suggestions: Remind students that adjectives agree in gender with nouns and point out the *¿Recuerdas?* Explain that adjectives also agree in number with the noun they modify. Remind students that a mixed-gender group of people also takes the masculine form. Reinforce the use of the plurals of adjectives by showing the *GramActiva* Video.

12 Standards: 4.1

Resources: Teacher's Resource Book: GramActiva BLM, p. 227

Focus: Reading adjectives and adding the correct gender and plural ending

Suggestions: Give students copies of the *GramActiva BLM* to use for their cards. Use the transparencies or the *Clip Art* to provide the cues. Allow adequate time for them to select the correct cards.

Answers will vary.

Fondo cultural

Standards: 2.1, 4.2

Suggestions: Ask: Would you participate in a festival like this? Why or why not? How might a celebration like *La Tomatina* be good or bad for a community?

Answers will vary.

Objectives

- Express opinions about food and describe people
- Discuss and compare food and beverage preferences with classmates

Gramática

The plurals of adjectives

Just as adjectives agree with a noun depending on whether it's masculine or feminine, they also agree according to whether the noun is singular or plural. To make adjectives plural, just add an *-s* after the vowel at the end of the adjective. If the adjective ends in a consonant, add *-es.*

La hamburguesa es sabrosa. Las hamburguesas son sabrosas.

El pastel es muy popular. Los pasteles son muy populares.

When an adjective describes a group including both masculine and feminine nouns, use the masculine plural form.

La lechuga, las zanahorias y los tomates son buenos para la salud.

Don't forget that the singular form of *mucho* means "much" or "a lot of," but that the plural form, *muchos(as),* means "many."

No como mucha carne, pero como muchas verduras.

¿Recuerdas?

Adjectives agree in gender with the masculine or feminine nouns they describe.

- **El bistec** es sabroso.
- **La ensalada** es sabrosa.

Más ayuda realidades.com

 *GramActiva* **Video**

 ***Canción de hip hop:*** *¿Sabroso o malo?*

GramActiva **Activity**

12 ¿Sabroso o sabrosa?

Pensar • Leer • GramActiva

Your teacher will give you a GramActiva worksheet. Tear or cut apart the different adjective stems and endings that are printed on the sheet. Then your teacher will show you pictures of several foods. Show how you feel about each food item by holding up the appropriate adjective stem and the appropriate ending.

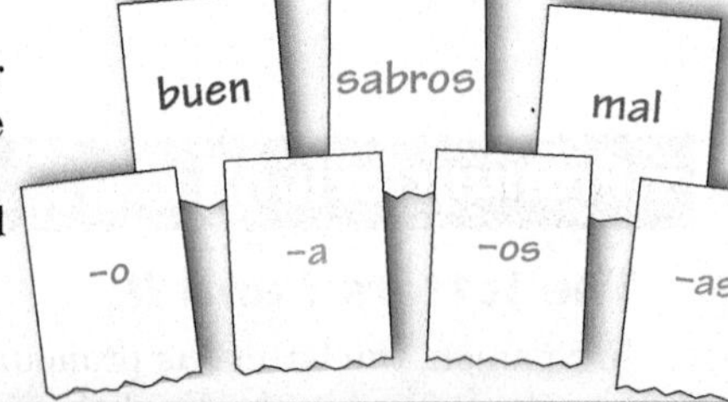

Fondo Cultural | España

La Tomatina How would you like to attend a festival where a gigantic food fight with tomatoes is the highlight of the day? That's what happens at the annual *Fiesta de la Tomatina* in Buñol, Spain. After the town council distributes more than 130 tons of ripe tomatoes to participants, the hour-long tomato-throwing festival begins.

- Describe any food festivals unique to your community or your state. How do they compare to *La Tomatina?*

La Tomatina, en Buñol, España

DIFFERENTIATED INSTRUCTION

Heritage Language Learners

Have students write ten adjectives used to describe foods. They should think of taste, color, and texture. Have them write sentences using the adjectives and hand them in for correction.

Students with Learning Difficulties

Have students refer to pp. 70 and 96 for a list of adjectives to add to the following nouns. Students should select adjectives appropriate for the noun and make sure that the endings are correct in number and gender. (Nouns: ***las señoritas; los profesores; las calculadoras; las clases***)

13 ¿Cómo son? |  |

Escribir • Hablar

1. For each of these adjectives, name two famous people, cartoon characters, or people in your school whom the adjective fits. Then write a sentence that describes both of them.

Modelo

A —*Creo que Cameron Diaz y Antonio Banderas son talentosos.*

1. artístico, -a	3. atrevido, -a	5. serio, -a	7. divertido, -a
2. deportista	4. gracioso, -a	6. talentoso, -a	8. trabajador, -a

2. Now read your sentences to a partner. Does your partner agree? Who fits the adjectives in your partner's opinion?

 **Modelo**

B —*Estoy de acuerdo. Julia Roberts y Tom Cruise son talentosos también.*

o: —*Sí, pero Julia Roberts y Tom Cruise son más talentosos que Cameron Diaz y Antonio Banderas.*

Más práctica GO

realidades.com | print

	realidades.com	print
Instant Check	✔	
Guided WB pp. 109–110	✔	✔
Core WB p. 62	✔	✔
Comm. WB pp. 64, 67, 257	✔	✔
Hispanohablantes WB pp. 114–117		✔

14 ¿Qué prefieres? |  |

Escribir • Hablar

Your class will be divided into groups of five to see what your favorite foods and beverages are.

Conexiones | Las matemáticas

1. Ask your group members what their favorites are from each of the following groups: *frutas, verduras, carnes,* and *bebidas.* Write the answers on a sheet of paper.

Modelo

A —*¿Qué verduras prefieres?*

B —*Prefiero las zanahorias.*

2. Tally the results to see which foods and beverages are the most popular in each group. Indicate these favorites on a bar graph as shown. As a group, write four sentences that summarize your results. Compare your group's preferences to those of the other groups.

Prefieren . . .

frutas — manzanas

verduras — papas

carnes — bistec

bebidas — refrescos

1 2 3 4 5

Número de estudiantes

Modelo

Del grupo de las verduras, cuatro estudiantes prefieren las papas.

Practice and Communicate 3B

13 Standards: 1.1, 1.3

Focus: Writing and discussing sentences using adjectives

Recycle: Adjectives to describe people

Suggestions: Brainstorm a list of people for Step 1. After Step 2, have several pairs of students share their opinions with the class.

Answers will vary.

Common Errors: Some students will try to assign gender to adjectives that are neutral, such as ***deportista.***

BELLRINGER REVIEW

Show large flashcards from *Capitulo* 1B representing personality traits. Have volunteers name two class members who exhibit each trait.

14 Standards: 1.1, 1.3

Focus: Talking about and charting favorite foods; cross-curricular study

Recycle: Food and beverage vocabulary

Suggestions: Students can refer to the *Repaso* in *Capítulos* 3A and 3B to review names of foods and beverages.

Answers will vary.

Extension: Divide the class into four groups: ***frutas, verduras, proteínas, bebidas.*** Have each group make a poster classifying foods from *Capítulos* 3A and 3B.

Theme Project

Students can perform Step 4 at this point. Be sure they understand your corrections and suggestions. (See p. 122-b.)

Additional Resources

- Communication Wbk.: Audio Act. 7, p. 64
- Teacher's Resource Book: Audio Script, p. 218
- Audio Program DVD: Cap. 3B, Track 10

ENRICH YOUR TEACHING

Culture Note

The tomato has been cultivated in the Andes since prehistoric times. Tomato growing spread from South America to Mexico more than 3,000 years ago. Tomatoes were then brought to Europe. By 1550, tomatoes were being grown in Italy.

Teacher-to-Teacher

Some students might enjoy creating a slideshow using presentation software with pictures of people well known to the class. They can have graphics appear that include plural forms of adjectives. Place strict limits: No unkind characterizations are allowed, except for fictional characters.

ASSESSMENT

Prueba 3B-3 with Study Plan (online only)

Quiz: The plurals of adjectives

- Prueba 3B-3: p. 84

Gramática

Core Instruction

Standards: 4.1

Resources: Voc. and Gram. Transparency 77; Teacher's Resource Book: Video Script, pp. 220–221; Video Program: Cap. 3B

INTERACTIVE WHITEBOARD
Grammar Activities 3B

Suggestions: Direct attention to the *¿Recuerdas?* Have students practice ***ser*** by first saying their own names *(Soy...)*. Then point to or group other students to demonstrate the other forms.

15 Standards: 1.2, 1.3

Resources: Answer Keys: Student Edition, p. 47

Focus: Reading comprehension and writing appropriate forms of the verb ***ser***

Suggestions: Have students scan the paragraph and identify the subjects before writing their answers.

Answers:

1. eres	4. somos	7. somos
2. soy	5. son	8. es
3. son	6. es	9. somos

16 Standards: 1.2

Resources: Teacher's Resource Book: Audio Script, p. 219; Audio Program DVD: Cap. 3B, Track 11; Answer Keys: Student Edition, p. 47

Focus: Listening comprehension about food sold in a market

Suggestions: Play the audio or read the script two or three times to allow students to focus on the comments before they write.

Script and Answers:

1. Las zanahorias son muy buenas.
2. La papa es sabrosa.
3. Las cebollas son malas.
4. Señor, los guisantes son horribles.
5. El pescado no es bueno.

Gramática

Objectives

- Listen to descriptions of food in a market
- Describe people, places, and foods
- Compare opinions about food with a classmate
- Read and write about pizza

The verb *ser*

Ser, which means "to be," is an irregular verb. Use *ser* to describe what a person or thing is like. Here are the present-tense forms:

(yo)	soy	(nosotros) (nosotras)	somos
(tú)	eres	(vosotros) (vosotras)	sois
Ud. (él) (ella)	es	Uds. (ellos) (ellas)	son

¿Recuerdas?

In previous chapters, you learned how to talk about what a person is like.

—Tú **eres** muy deportista, ¿no?

—Sí, **soy** deportista.

—Mi amigo Pablo **es** deportista también.

Más ayuda realidades.com

***GramActiva* Video**
Tutorial: *ser*
Animated Verbs

***GramActiva* Activity**

15 Línea romántica

Leer • Escribir

Rafa has to tell his father why the cell phone bill was so high. Complete his explanations by using the correct form of the verb *ser*.

¡Ay, Papá, tú __1.__ muy estricto! ¡Yo __2.__ un chico *muuuy* sociable! Hablo con mis amigas porque todas __3.__ muy simpáticas. Hablo con Lidia porque nosotros __4.__ muy deportistas. Mis conversaciones con ella siempre __5.__ muy interesantes. Fátima __6.__ muy estudiosa. Hablamos mucho porque ella y yo __7.__ inteligentes y hablamos de las clases. Y hablo con Lorena porque __8.__ muy graciosa y nosotros __9.__ muy buenos amigos.

16 Escucha y escribe

Escuchar • Escribir

You will hear comments from five customers about the food being sold in a market. On a sheet of paper, write the numbers 1–5. As you listen, write the comments next to the numbers.

DIFFERENTIATED INSTRUCTION

Students with Learning Difficulties

For *Actividad* 17, provide a limited list of possible adjectives for each person or item. As a first step, so students can focus on the verb form, give them adjectives that already agree. Then have them choose another adjective from the list and make the agreement themselves.

Advanced Learners

Some students may notice that *¿Cómo estás?* and *¿Cómo está Ud.?* use a different verb for "to be" from the one shown above. If so, it is appropriate to go ahead and give them a limited explanation of the difference between ***ser*** and ***estar***. The formal explanation is in *Capítulo* 5B, p. 258.

17 En tu escuela

Hablar • Escribir

Describe the people and places in your school.

Modelo

el / la profesor(a) de tu clase de español
La profesora de mi clase de español es muy simpática.

1. tu clase de español
2. las chicas en tu clase de español
3. los chicos en tu clase de español
4. el / la director(a) de tu escuela
5. la comida de la cafetería
6. tú y tus a

P. 157 Review adj.
Act. 13 part 1
SER review
SER PPT — 10
#14 15

#17 homework

Thurs PPT — Friday
early finish — wksht ~~review~~

18 ¿Sabroso o malo?

Hablar

En tu opinión, ¿cómo son las comidas y las bebidas? Habla co
Usa los verbos *comer* o *beber.*

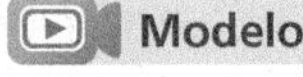

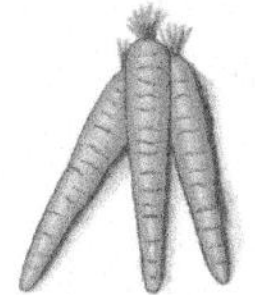

A —*¿Comes zanahorias en la cena?*
B —*No, no como zanahorias en la cena porque*
o: —*Sí, como zanahorias en la cena porque son*
para la salud.

Estudiante A

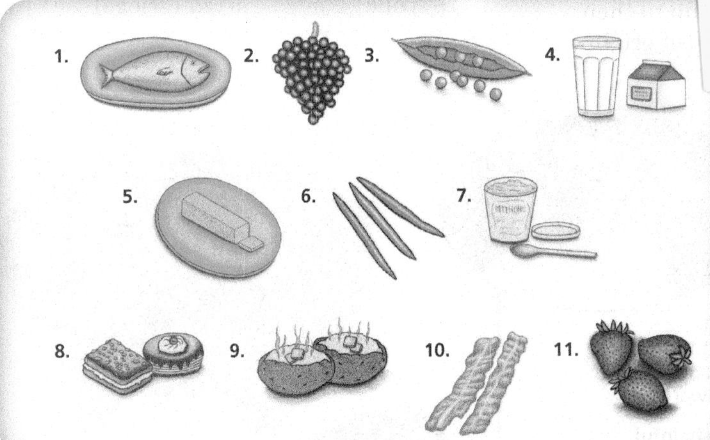

horrible
¡Respuesta personal!

Más práctica GO
realidades.com | print

Instant Check	✔	
Guided WB pp. 111–112	✔	✔
Core WB pp. 63–64	✔	✔
Comm. WB pp. 65, 68	✔	✔
Hispanohablantes WB pp. 118–121		✔

Practice and Communicate 3B

17 Standards: 1.2, 1.3

Resources: Answer Keys: Student Edition, p. 47

Focus: Speaking and writing about people and places

Recycle: Adjectives

Suggestions: Remind students that ***tu*** **ase** becomes ***mi clase*** and ***tú y tus*** **igos** becomes ***mis amigos y yo.*** mind them to write full sentences d to watch for agreement.

swers:

1. Mi clase de español es...
2. ...son...
3. ...son...
4. ...es...
5. ...es...
6. ...somos...

mmon Errors: Students may forget to e subject-verb and noun-adjective ements. Model the correct forms.

RINGER REVIEW

students call out the names of the in *Actividad* 18 as you call out the numbers in random order.

18 Standards: 1.1

Resources: Answer Keys: Student Edition, p. 48

Focus: Giving opinions about foods

Recycle: Foods and beverages

Suggestions: Model the options in the answers.

Answers will include:

1. ¿Comes pescado en la cena?
2. ¿...uvas...?
3. ¿...guisantes...?
4. ¿Bebes leche...?
5. ¿Comes mantequilla...?
6. ¿...judías verdes...?
7. ¿...yogur...?
8. ¿...pasteles...?
9. ¿...papas...?
10. ¿...tocino...?
11. ¿...fresas...?

Additional Resources

- Communication Wbk.: Audio Act. 8-9, p. 65
- Teacher's Resource Book: Audio Script, p. 219, Communicative Pair Activity BLM, pp. 224–225
- Audio Program DVD: Cap. 3B, Tracks 12–13

ENRICH YOUR TEACHING

Culture Note

The variety of fresh fruits and vegetables sold in open-air and interior markets in Spanish-speaking countries is amazingly assorted. A number of markets also serve hot meals at reasonable prices. Many people like to visit the markets during lunchtime.

21st Century Skills

Communication Have students imagine they are visiting the open-air market pictured in Activity 16. Have them compose a postcard to a Spanish-speaking friend describing what they see and hear around them.

ASSESSMENT

Prueba 3B-4 with Study Plan (online only)

Quiz: The verb *ser*

- Prueba 3B-4: p. 85

Fondo cultural

Standards: 2.1, 4.2

Suggestions: Ask students what they find interesting about the picture. Discuss the differences between open-air markets and supermarkets. Ask if there are open-air markets in your community.

Answers will vary.

Exploración del lenguaje

Core Instruction

Standards: 4.1

Resources: Answer Keys: Student Edition, p. 48

Suggestions: You may want to discuss word origins in English with the class before reading the *Exploración del lenguaje*. Have students match the obvious words first, and discuss the similarities between the words.

Answers:

1. agua...*aqua*
2. arroz...*óryza*
3. pan...*pane*
4. bistec...*beefsteak*
5. salchichas...*salciccia*
6. pescado...*piscatu*
7. café...*kahvé*
8. pollo...*pullu*

El español en el mundo del trabajo

Core Instruction

Standards: 5.1

Suggestions: Have students research the names of restaurants in your area that serve food from Spanish-speaking cultures.

Answers will vary.

Theme Project

Students can perform Step 5 at this point. (For more information, see p. 122-b.)

Block Schedule

Have students look at a newspaper's food section to get ideas for their own food article or advertisement. They can write a recipe, draw a food comic strip, or create supermarket ads.

Fondo cultural | El mundo hispano

Los mercados, or open-air markets, are common throughout Latin America. Many towns have a central market, held on a given day of the week, where people come from all around to buy and sell food, as well as flowers, crafts, and clothing.

- How does this market compare with the ways in which fruits and vegetables are bought and sold in your community?

Un mercado guatemalteco

Exploración del lenguaje

Where did it come from?

The names of many foods in Spanish come from Latin as well as from other languages as diverse as Arabic, Italian, Greek, Turkish, and English. While it's clear that the word *espaguetis* comes from the Italian word *spaghetti,* it's not obvious that the word *zanahoria* comes from the Arabic word *safunariya.*

Try it out! Read the Spanish words in the first column and match them up to their counterparts in their language of origin.

agua	*piscatu* (latín)
arroz	*aqua* (latín)
pan	*beefsteak* (inglés)
bistec	*panis* (latín)
salchichas	*pullu* (latín)
pescado	*kahvé* (turco)
café	*salciccia* (italiano)
pollo	*óryza* (griego)

El español en el mundo del trabajo

Rick Bayless's career as a world-class Mexican chef began at the age of 14, when he visited Mexico and decided to study Spanish. Since 1987, Rick has opened gourmet Mexican restaurants, created and starred in cooking shows, written cookbooks, and won many awards.

- How would Rick's Spanish skills be helpful in his career?

Un molcajete *(mortar and pestle)* de México

DIFFERENTIATED INSTRUCTION

Multiple Intelligences

Verbal/Linguistic: Ask students why food items often have names borrowed from other cultures. Have them research the origins of some of their favorite food items and the etymology of the names. Have them present their findings to the class.

Heritage Language Learners

Have students choose four food items and explore the different names they have in different Spanish-speaking countries. How did these differences arise? Where did the names come from? If the name is borrowed from another language, what is the historical connection?

19 Una pizza para la buena salud

Leer • Escribir

Lee este anuncio *(ad)* de una pizzería y contesta las preguntas.

> **Strategy**
> **Using cognates**
> Be sure to look for cognates to help you read this ad.

Pizzería Lilia
¡Pizzas saludables!

A veces la pizza tiene muchas calorías y grasas que no son buenas para la salud.

La Pizzería Lilia tiene una variedad de pizzas con ingredientes que son buenos y saludables.

- Menos queso
- Usamos ingredientes nutritivos
  - Más verduras (tienen pocas calorías y son muy nutritivas)
- Evita[1] la combinación de carnes
  - Las carnes tienen mucho sodio y grasas
  - El pollo o el jamón son mejores[2] que las salchichas

¡Llámanos!
¡Estamos aquí para servirte!
372 42 89
Calle Independencia 28

[1]Avoid [2]better

1. Find and list three cognates in this ad.
2. Write three recommendations in Spanish for a healthier pizza.

20 Y tú, ¿qué dices?

Escribir • Hablar

1. Describe tu pizza favorita.
2. ¿Crees que la pizza es buena o mala para la salud? ¿Por qué?
3. ¿Qué verduras prefieres? ¿Qué verduras no te gustan?
4. ¿Qué ejercicio haces con los brazos? ¿Qué ejercicio haces con las piernas?

19 Standards: 1.2

Resources: Voc. and Gram. Transparency 79; Answer Keys: Student Edition, p. 48

Focus: Reading and writing with contextualized vocabulary

Suggestions: Point out the *Strategy* and have students scan the text for cognates. Have students read the ad and list the health benefits of each ingredient. Can students guess the meaning of ***saludable?***

Answers will vary but may include:
1. **pizza, ingredientes, calorías, variedad, usamos, nutritivos, combinación, sodio**
2. **It should have less cheese.**
   It should have lots of vegetables.
   It should have chicken or ham.

Extension: Have students write their own ads for a vegetarian restaurant, a juice bar, or a gourmet sandwich shop. Have students list words related to health and food, and then work in pairs to draft the ad. Ads should include a name for the business, address, and telephone number.

Pre-AP* Support

- **Learning Objective:** Interpretive: Print
- **Activity 19:** Students practice reading comprehension skills as they answer questions about an ad.
- ***Pre-AP* Resource Book:*** Comprehensive guide to Pre-AP* reading skill development, pp. 19–26

BELLRINGER REVIEW

Use Voc. and Gram. Transparency 5 (Word Web/graphic organizer). Have the class brainstorm foods that belong to each category. Categories: *carnes, frutas, bebidas, verduras* with *comida* in the center.

20 Standards: 1.1, 1.2

Focus: Reading and speaking about food, likes and dislikes

Suggestions: Students may like ingredients not listed in the vocabulary from *Capítulos* 3A or 3B. Encourage them to use a dictionary to find words such as ***jalapeño, pimiento, piña, aceituna, oliva,*** and ***hongo.***

Answers will vary.

ENRICH YOUR TEACHING

Culture Note

The mortar and pestle has different names in different countries. The ***molcajete*** pictured on p. 160 is used in Mexico to grind chiles, spices, and grain, and to make guacamole, among other things. In other countries, it may be called a ***mortero y mano de moler*** or ***pilón y maceta.***

Teacher-to-Teacher

Have students think about milk or orange juice ads they have seen. Have them create an ad that endorses a vegetable or fruit from this chapter. Display their posters in the room.

3B Reading

Common Core: Reading

Lectura

Core Instruction

Standards: 1.2, 1.3

Resources: Voc. and Gram. Transparency 80

Focus: Reading an article about athletes' diets

Suggestions:

Pre-reading: Point out the *Strategy* and be sure students understand skimming. Remind them that using prior knowledge and prediction will help them understand new texts. Use the transparency to make this a whole-class activity. Have students also find cognates.

Reading: Have students read the pie chart. As they read, have them tell you in which segment the various food items fall.

Post-reading: Have students review their skimming predictions and see how accurate they were. Have them identify cognates they noticed in the reading.

BELLRINGER REVIEW

Show Voc. and Gram. Transparency 80. Have students name the foods pictured and tell whether or not they are good for your health. (Cover the text.)

Teacher-to-Teacher

Have students keep a weekly list of what they eat to track carbohydrate, protein, and fat intake. At the end of the week, ask them to draw a pie chart to display the information.

Pre-AP* Support

- **Learning Objective:** Interpretive: Audio
- **Activity:** Have students carefully read the captions under each of the pictures as a homework assignment. In class the next day, have students work in groups of three and alternate reading one of the captions to the other two members as a dictation activity, writing what they hear. After they finish writing, have the groups confirm their work.
- ***Pre-AP* Resource Book:*** Comprehensive guide to Pre-AP* reading skill development, pp. 19–26

Objectives

- Read about a sports diet and learn about an athlete
- Skim what you read to find specific information
- Learn about soccer in Spanish-speaking countries and compare attitudes towards soccer with those in the United States

Lectura
La comida de los atletas

Lee este artículo *(article)* de una revista deportiva. ¿Qué comen y qué beben los atletas profesionales para mantener la salud y estar en buena forma?

Strategy

Skimming

List three things that you would expect to find in an article about athletes' eating habits. Skim the article to find the information.

¿Qué come un jugador de fútbol?

Los jugadores[1] de fútbol comen comidas equilibradas con muchos carbohidratos, minerales y vitaminas. Ellos consumen cerca de 5.000 calorías en total todos los días.

17% Proteínas
13% Grasas
70% Carbohidratos

Para el desayuno el día de un partido[2], un jugador típico come mucho pan con mantequilla y jalea[3], yogur y té.

Para el almuerzo antes del[4] partido, come pan, pasta, pollo sin grasa, verduras, frutas y una ensalada.

Para la cena después del[5] partido, el atleta come papas, carne sin grasa y más verduras y frutas.

También es muy importante beber muchos líquidos. La noche antes del partido, el jugador bebe un litro de jugo de naranja y durante el partido bebe hasta[6] dos litros de agua y bebidas deportivas.

 [1]players [2]game [3]jam [4]before the [5]after the [6]up to

DIFFERENTIATED INSTRUCTION

Heritage Language Learners

Remind students to pay close attention to the correct spelling of words that that are frequently spelled incorrectly: ***mantequilla*** (not *mantequiya*), ***pollo*** (not *poyo*), ***jalea*** (not *jallea*), and ***atleta*** (not *athleta*). Keep track of words that give them spelling difficulties and do a dictation periodically to check them.

Students with Learning Difficulties

Many students have problems skimming. Suggest that they move their fingers along the lines to find any information they understand. The strategy of using expectations to aid in reading can be very helpful. Stress that they will not understand every word, nor will they need to.

[7]team

¿Comprendes?

1. ¿Qué debe comer Carlos Tévez antes de un partido de fútbol?
2. ¿Qué debe beber?
3. ¿Qué comida no debe comer Carlos?
4. ¿Es tu dieta diferente de la dieta de un jugador de fútbol profesional? ¿Cómo?
5. ¿Cuál es la fecha de nacimiento *(birth date)* de Carlos? Escribe tu fecha de nacimiento como lo hacen en los países hispanohablantes.

Más práctica GO

	realidades.com	print
Guided WB p. 113	✔	✔
Comm. WB pp. 69, 258	✔	✔
***Hispanohablantes* WB** pp. 122–123		✔
Culture Reading Activity	✔	

Fondo Cultural | El mundo hispano

¡Gooooooooooool! Scoring the winning *gol* in soccer is the most exciting moment of the game. *El fútbol* is the most popular sport in the world, and it has many *fanáticos* (fans) in every Spanish-speaking country. Every four years, teams throughout the world compete regionally in order to become one of the 32 teams to advance to the World Cup *(la Copa Mundial)* competition. Many Spanish-speaking countries compete in what has become the most widely watched sporting event in the world. Since the competition began in 1930, three Spanish-speaking countries have won the World Cup competition: Uruguay in 1930 and 1950, Argentina in 1978 and 1986, and Spain in 2010.

- How does the enthusiasm for soccer in the United States compare with the rest of the world's view of this sport? Why do you think this is so?

España gana la Copa Mundial, 2010.

Reading 3B

¿Comprendes? Standards: 1.2, 1.3

Resources: Answer Keys: Student Edition, p. 49

Focus: Demonstrating reading comprehension; learning to write dates using Spanish language conventions

Suggestions: Review the verb ***deber*** with students. Have students refer back to the reading as they write their answers.

Answers:

1. **pan y mantequilla y jalea, yogur, pasta, pollo, verduras, frutas y una ensalada**
2. **Debe beber un litro de jugo de naranja y hasta dos litros de agua y bebidas deportivas.**
3. **Answers will vary.**
4. **Answers will vary.**
5. **El 2 de mayo. Answers will vary.**

Fondo cultural

Standards: 2.2, 3.1, 4.2

Suggestions: Ask if students have seen a World Cup soccer match. Discuss how soccer has become popular in the United States. Find out who plays soccer in your class and invite them to talk about the sport.

Answers will vary.

Mapa global interactivo, Actividad 2 Explore Spain, home of the winners of the 2010 World Cup in soccer.

Teacher-to-Teacher

Careers: *Tema* 3 has focused on food that is good and bad for health. Have students work in small groups to talk about a career in the field of nutrition. Have them write a list of foods in Spanish that a 5-year-old child might eat and categorize them as healthful and unhealthful. Ask groups to share their lists.

For Further Reading

Student Resource: Realidades para hispanohablantes: Lectura 2, pp. 124–125

ENRICH YOUR TEACHING

Culture Note

Soccer is quickly gaining a strong following in the United States, and many youth soccer clubs have developed across the country. Soccer historians give the credit to Pelé, the star soccer player from Brazil who, in the 1970s, fascinated sports fans in the United States with his finesse and agility.

Teacher-to-Teacher

It might be fun to have students make a poster showing a soccer field with the players' positions labeled. Have students search the Internet for the Spanish names of the positions, such as: ***delantero*** ("forward"), ***centrocampista*** ("center"), and ***portero*** or ***arquero*** ("goalie" or "goalkeeper"). This may be a project for soccer enthusiasts in the class.

Perspectivas del mundo hispano

Core Instruction

Standards: 2.1, 3.1, 4.2

Focus: Reading about traditional remedies as medical treatments

Suggestions: Point out that finding ways to stay healthy is a perennially popular topic. Natural remedies and herbs are among those often mentioned. Neither of them is really new and many, such as eating chicken soup for a cold, have passed down from generation to generation. Have students read the text. Discuss what they may know about the remedies mentioned. Also discuss researching herbal remedies as modern-day solutions. Assign the *Check it out!* section for homework. Discuss their responses at a later time.

Locate the Amazon rainforest on a map. Point out that a great deal of research into the benefits of herbal remedies takes place there. Discuss how scientists feel the rainforest has so much to offer because of its abundance of plants and animals, many of which are still not generally known elsewhere.

Direct attention to the *Think about it!* section and have students discuss the questions.

Answers will vary.

Additional Resources

Student Resource: Realidades para hispanohablantes, p. 126

Pre-AP* Support

- **Learning Objective:** Presentational Speaking (Cultural Comparison)
- **Background:** This task prepares students for the Spoken Presentational Communication tasks that focus on cultural comparisons.
- **Activity:** Have students prepare a two-minute (maximum) presentation on the following topic: Use of herbal remedies to supplement traditional medicine across cultures. Think of the use of *yerbabuena* in Mexico. Compare this to home remedies people in your family or community use to treat different ailments. Give your opinion on the use of herbs to treat illnesses.
- ***Pre-AP* Resource Book:*** Comprehensive guide to Pre-AP* speaking skill development, pp. 39–50

Perspectivas del mundo hispano

¿Qué haces para mantener la salud?

Have you ever eaten chicken soup when you have a cold? How about putting aloe on a sunburn? In many countries, including those in the Spanish-speaking world, traditional remedies consisting of medicinal herbs have been used for centuries to treat common medical problems. In Mexico, a mint known as *yerbabuena* may be made into tea and given to someone with a stomachache. Remedies such as these may not be prescribed by licensed physicians, but people have confidence in them because they have been passed down through the generations. Many of those herbs are very safe, though some may have harmful side effects.

Estos hombres estudian plantas medicinales en la selva *(jungle)* amazónica.

Researchers are studying traditional herbal remedies to find modern-day medical solutions. In the Amazon rainforest in South America, an amazing abundance of plant life may hold the key to treating a wide variety of common ailments and diseases. Drug companies are looking for cures found in these plants and herbs that could be reproduced in today's modern drugs.

Increasingly, medicinal herbs are accepted not only as the basis for pharmaceutical drugs, but also for their own inherent healing qualities. In many countries, including the United States, herbal remedies are sometimes used in combination with conventional health care.

Check it out! What alternatives to conventional medical care are available in your community? Make a list of all the health care services you can think of that are not provided by traditional physicians. Are there health stores that sell herbal medicines? What types of herbal medicines are being sold and what remedies are attributed to these medicines?

Think about it! In many Spanish-speaking cultures, herbal remedies have been accepted for centuries. Do you think that medicinal herbs can provide relief and cures? Why or why not?

En un mercado de Guanajuato, México

DIFFERENTIATED INSTRUCTION

Advanced Learners

Have students learn about the Amazon rainforest, where it is located, and why scientists are interested in the plants and animals that live there. Ask students to give a short explanation about possible medicines and cures that might come from the region.

Heritage Language Learners

Students may be familiar with traditional remedies. Are there any that have been passed down in their family or in families they know? Encourage them to share their stories with the class.

Presentación escrita

Para mantener la salud

- Create a poster promoting healthy choices
- Gather information from a number of sources

Task
You are researching good eating and exercise habits for your health class. Make a poster in Spanish with five health suggestions.

1 Prewrite Ask people at school and home about good eating and exercise habits for teens. List their ideas under these headings to organize your information.

- *Debes comer . . .*
- *No debes beber mucho(a) . . .*
- *Debes beber . . .*
- *No debes comer mucho(a) . . .*
- *Debes . . . para mantener la salud*

2 Draft Decide how to present the information logically as you write your first draft. Use visuals for clarity and give your poster a title.

3 Revise Share your draft with a partner. Your partner should check the following:

- Have you communicated five suggestions well?
- Do the visuals convey meaning? Is the poster attractive?
- Are the vocabulary and grammar correct?

Rewrite your poster making any necessary changes.

4 Publish Make a final copy for posting in the nurse's office, a community center, your classroom, or your portfolio.

5 Evaluation The following rubric will be used to grade your presentation.

Rubric	Score 1	Score 3	Score 5
Completion of task	You included at least three suggestions for a healthy lifestyle.	You included at least four suggestions for a healthy lifestyle.	You included five or more suggestions for a healthy lifestyle.
Accuracy of vocabulary and grammar	You had very little variation of vocabulary use with many grammar errors.	You had limited usage of vocabulary and some grammar errors.	You had extended use of a variety of vocabulary with very few grammar errors.
Effective use of visuals	You included only three visuals that clearly connect to information.	You included only four visuals that clearly connect to information.	You included five visuals that clearly connect to information.

Strategy

Gathering information
Use information from a variety of sources to help you create a more complete presentation on a topic.

Writing 3B

Common Core: Writing

Presentación escrita

Core Instruction

Standards: 1.3

Focus: Writing about good eating habits and exercise; adding illustrations or designs to enhance a presentation

Suggestions: Review the task, steps, and rubric with students. Point out that students should use reliable sources that know about health. Encourage students to make their posters visually appealing as well as persuasive. Review the rubric with the class to explain how you will grade the posters. Make and display a poster of your own as a model. Use a sample poster and show how it would be graded.

Have students present their posters to the class. Ask them how they might change their habits after completing this project.

Pre-AP* Support

- **Learning Objective:** Presentational Writing
- **Activity:** You've created your healthy-living suggestions poster. Now, write a brief, persuasive paragraph to explain your recommendations. Why should people follow these suggestions? How would their health benefit from doing so?
- ***Pre-AP* Resource Book:*** Comprehensive guide to Pre-AP* writing skill development, pp. 27–38

Portfolio

Have students include their posters in their portfolios.

Additional Resources

Student Resource: Realidades para hispanohablantes, p. 127; Guided Practice: Presentación escrita, p. 114

ENRICH YOUR TEACHING

Teacher-to-Teacher

e-amigos: Have students write their *e-amigos* with suggestions for ways students at their school could improve their health. Have students print out or e-mail you the exchanges.

21st Century Skills

Critical Thinking and Problem Solving Have students create a "Biggest Winner" program for the school—a contest to find the student able to establish and follow the healthiest nutrition and fitness regimen, developing rules, an eating plan, and an exercise plan for contestants to follow.

ASSESSMENT

Presentación escrita

- Assessment Program: Rubrics, p. T30

Go over the descriptions of the different levels of performance. After assessing students, help individuals understand how their performance could be improved. (See Teacher's Resource Book for suggestions on using rubrics in assessment.)

El mundo hispano

Core Instruction

Standards: 2.1, 2.2, 3.2, 4.2

Resources: Map Transparencies 16

Mapa global interactivo, Actividad 3 Find the location of the Iguazú Falls and identify the surrounding countries.

Focus: Reading about the countries in southern South America

Suggestions: After students read the selection, display a map of South America. Point out the four countries highlighted in this section. Note characteristics such as coastal access or mountainous areas. Point out that, unlike the South American countries discussed earlier, the populations of these countries, with the exception of Paraguay, live mainly in large cities. Note that these cities, like those of the United States, were shaped largely by mass immigration from southern and eastern Europe. Ask if students would expect to see a large indigenous population.

Direct attention to the photo at the top of p. 167. Ask students to hypothesize where in Chile they imagine these people might live.

Point out that when the Spanish arrived, they brought with them not only their language and culture, but their animals as well. Ask students to describe how these animals may have affected the land and the environment, as well as the present-day culture. Entertain the idea that perhaps some indigenous animals of the time when the Spanish arrived no longer exist because of the animals brought from Europe.

Focus on the photo at the bottom of p.167. Point out that Buenos Aires is one of the most cosmopolitan cities in the world. Locate it on a map. Guide students to understand that prior to mass transportation and air travel, coastal cities had more immigrants than interior cities. People arrived by boat at a port city and many of them stayed. Have students think about why the citizens of Buenos Aires are known as ***porteños.***

DIFFERENTIATED INSTRUCTION

Heritage Language Learners

Have students choose a South American country and research foods and regional dishes. If possible, students should relate them to the geography of the region.

The Spanish were able to topple large, centralized empires such as those of the Aztecs and Incas quickly, but they were never able to conquer the smaller indigenous groups in the more remote regions. Chile's Pehuenche suffered defeats in the nineteenth century, but they still struggle to maintain their lands and culture. ▶

◀ Spain introduced horses, cows, sheep, and pigs to the Americas in the sixteenth century, transforming the ecology, culture, and economy of the region. In the nineteenth century, the growth of cities, the expansion of railways, and improvements in shipping created a worldwide market for South American meat and hides—and helped spur the development of the cowboy culture throughout the Americas. As on ranches in the western United States and northern Mexico, the main house of an Argentine or Uruguayan *estancia* served as a residence, office, and military stronghold.

With its wide boulevards, parks, museums, and diverse cultural life, Buenos Aires is considered one of the most cosmopolitan cities in the world. Argentina has produced world-class writers such as Jorge Luis Borges, Julio Cortázar, and José Hernández, who wrote a classic about the life of the *gauchos*. The tango, the first dance from Latin America to gain international popularity, is a favorite of the *porteños*—the residents of Buenos Aires.

Culture 3B

Locate Paraguay on the map. Unlike the other countries in southern South America, it is mostly rural. Most people do not live in large cities. Have students hypothesize as to why this might be. If necessary, point to the fact that it is landlocked. Can students recall the other landlocked South American country? *(Bolivia)*

Direct attention to the background photo. Based on their reading, have students identify it. Emphasize that South America has a great deal of natural beauty and an abundance of remarkable wildlife.

Have students focus on the *¿Sabes que…?* Use the map to show the path of the Andes. Point out the extreme differences in the two points mentioned in the text. Have students calculate the height of Chile's Torre del Paine. Note that this is still at a very high altitude.

Discuss the concerns of the environmentalist groups at Iguazú Falls. The number of tourists who visit is large, and the balance of nature is delicate. Sometimes just the presence of people is enough to destroy some aspect of a natural site. Once gone, it is often gone for good. Discuss how construction and population growth cause changes in nature. Can students relate this to any environmental issues in their community, state, or region?

Direct attention to the *Para pensar* section and have students discuss the questions. **Answers** will vary.

ENRICH YOUR TEACHING

Teacher-to-Teacher

Have students add to the bulletin board display on South America. (See notes for p. 143.) They can fill in facts about ***gauchos*** and the Iguazú Falls. Encourage them to include information on artistic contributions of all the countries.

21st Century Skills

Communication Have students choose one of the locations shown on these pages (like the *cataratas de Iguazú*, or the city of Buenos Aires, in Argentina) and create a brochure or travel guide for that location, deciding on a particular audience and gearing the language and choices of places of interest based on that.

3B Review

Review Activities

To talk about food and beverages: Have students work in pairs to quiz each other on the vocabulary. They may use flashcards or use the MyPlate information. Use classroom posters, plastic foods, or magazines to help students review the vocabulary. Have them include *Tengo hambre* and *Tengo sed* in practicing the foods and beverages.

To discuss health: Have students work in pairs and give each other recommendations using *Para mantener la salud* ____. Have them agree or disagree, saying what is good or bad.

To indicate preference or agreement / disagreement: Give students choices of two items and ask their preference. Then have them agree or disagree with statements you make about whether something is good or bad for health.

To describe something: Give names of activities or foods and have students describe them.

Portfolio

Invite students to review the activities they completed in this chapter, including written reports, posters or other visuals, and recordings of oral presentations or other projects. Have them select one to two items that they feel best demonstrate their achievements in Spanish to include in their portfolios. Have them include this with the Chapter Checklist and Self-Assessment Worksheet.

Additional Resources

Student Resources: Realidades para hispanohablantes, p. 128

Teacher Resources:

- Teacher's Resource Book: Situation Cards, p. 226, Clip Art, pp. 228–230
- Assessment Program: Chapter Checklist and Self-Assessment Worksheet, pp. T56–T57

Repaso | | |

Repaso del capítulo

Vocabulario y gramática

Objectives

- Review the vocabulary and grammar
- Demonstrate you can perform the tasks on p. 169

to talk about food and beverages

la cena	dinner
el bistec	beefsteak
la carne	meat
el pescado	fish
el pollo	chicken
la cebolla	onion
los guisantes	peas
las judías verdes	green beans
la lechuga	lettuce
las papas	potatoes
los tomates	tomatoes
las uvas	grapes
las zanahorias	carrots
el arroz	rice
los cereales	grains
los espaguetis	spaghetti
las grasas	fats
la mantequilla	butter
el helado	ice cream
los pasteles	pastries
las bebidas	beverages

to talk about being hungry and thirsty

Tengo hambre.	I'm hungry.
Tengo sed.	I'm thirsty.

to discuss health

caminar	to walk
hacer ejercicio	to exercise
(yo) hago	I do
(tú) haces	you do
levantar pesas	to lift weights
para la salud	for one's health
para mantener la salud	to maintain one's health

to indicate a preference

(yo) prefiero	I prefer
(tú) prefieres	you prefer
deber	should, must

to indicate agreement or disagreement

creer	to think
Creo que . . .	I think . . .
Creo que sí / no.	I (don't) think so.
(No) estoy de acuerdo.	I (don't) agree.

to ask a question or give an answer

¿Por qué?	Why?
porque	because

to express quantity

algo	something
muchos, -as	many
todos, -as	all

to describe something

horrible	horrible
malo, -a	bad
sabroso, -a	tasty, flavorful

other useful words

cada día	every day

plurals of adjectives

MASCULINE	FEMININE
SINGULAR / PLURAL	SINGULAR / PLURAL
sabroso / sabrosos	sabrosa / sabrosas
popular / populares	popular / populares

ser *to be*

soy	somos
eres	sois
es	son

For *Vocabulario adicional,* see pp. 472–473.

DIFFERENTIATED INSTRUCTION

Students with Learning Difficulties

Have students review the *Repaso del capítulo* and create flashcards for any words that they do not know. Pair them with a student who is more confident with the vocabulary to practice. Before the test, provide students with a practice test, so they can become comfortable with the format.

Heritage Language Learners

Have students write a few paragraphs telling about their perfect dinner celebration: Where are they going to have it? Whom are they going to invite? What food are they going to eat? Encourage them to use as many vocabulary words from this chapter as they can.

Más repaso GO realidades.com | print

Instant Check	✔	
Puzzles	✔	
Core WB pp. 65–66		✔
Comm. WB pp. 259, 260–262	✔	✔

Preparación para el examen

On the exam you will be asked to . . .	Here are practice tasks similar to those you will find on the exam . . .	For review go to your print or digital textbook . . .
Interpretive		
 **1 Escuchar** Listen and understand as people describe a healthy or unhealthy lifestyle	Listen as two people are interviewed about their habits. See if you can tell which one is an Olympic skier and which one is a drummer. Be prepared to explain your "educated guesses."	**pp. 148–151** *Vocabulario en contexto* **p. 149** Actividad 2
Interpersonal		
 **2 Hablar** Express your opinion about food preferences	During a telephone survey, you are asked some questions in Spanish about your food preferences. Say whether you think each food choice is good or bad for your health.	**p. 153** Actividades 6–7 **p. 154** Actividades 8, 10 **p. 157** Actividad 14 **p. 159** Actividad 18
Interpretive		
 **3 Leer** Read and compare what people do and eat in order to determine whether they lead a healthy or unhealthy lifestyle	Read the online conversation that you have just joined in a chat room. Decide whether each person has a healthy or unhealthy lifestyle, based on what they tell each other. Chato: *¿Qué hago yo? Cuando hace buen tiempo, corro por treinta minutos. Cuando llueve, levanto pesas.* Chispa: *No me gusta hacer ejercicio. Prefiero comer papas fritas. Son muy sabrosas.* Andrés: *¿Papas fritas? Son horribles para la salud. Para mantener la salud, nunca debes comer papas fritas.*	**pp. 148–151** *Vocabulario en contexto* **p. 154** Actividad 9 **p. 155** Actividad 11 **p. 161** Actividad 19 **pp. 162–163** *Lectura*
Presentational		
 **4 Escribir** Write a list of things a person should do to maintain a healthy lifestyle	Many people think that teens don't know anything about a healthy lifestyle. You and your friends are compiling a top-ten list of ways to improve teens' health. Write at least three suggestions for the list.	**p. 154** Actividad 9 **p. 155** Actividad 11 **p. 161** Actividad 19 **p. 165** *Presentación escrita*
Cultures • Comparisons		
 **5 Pensar** Demonstrate an understanding of cultural perspectives regarding health care	Give an example of an herbal remedy that is accepted in a Spanish-speaking country as a remedy for a common ailment. Compare this with a similar herbal/natural remedy believed by many in the United States to be a cure for a common ailment.	**p. 164** *Perspectivas del mundo hispano*

DIFFERENTIATED ASSESSMENT

CORE ASSESSMENT
- **Assessment Program:** Examen del capítulo 3B, pp. 86–92
- **Audio Program DVD:** Cap. 3B, Track 16
- **ExamView:** Chapter Test, Test Banks A and B

ADVANCED/PRE-AP*
- **ExamView: Pre-AP* Test Bank**
- **Pre-AP* Resource Book,** pp. 70–73

STUDENTS NEEDING EXTRA HELP
- **Alternate Assessment Program:** Examen del capítulo 3B
- **Audio Program DVD:** Cap. 3B, Track 16

HERITAGE LEARNERS
- **Assessment Program: Realidades para hispanohablantes:** Examen del Capítulo 3B
- **ExamView: Heritage Learner Test Bank**

Performance Tasks

Standards: 1.2, 1.3, 2.1, 4.2

Student Resource: Realidades para hispanohablantes, p. 129

Teacher Resources: Teacher's Resource Book: Audio Script, p. 219; Audio Program DVD: Cap. 3B, Track 15; Answer Keys: Student Edition, p. 49

1. Escuchar

Suggestions: Play the audio or read the script.

Script and Answers:

1. **Cada día, a las cinco y media de la mañana, levanto pesas por treinta minutos y camino por una hora. Nunca como pasteles ni papas fritas porque son malos para la salud. *(Olympic skier)***
2. **Nunca como el desayuno porque no tengo tiempo para comer. Para el almuerzo prefiero la comida rápida: una hamburguesa con un refresco. *(drummer)***

2. Hablar

Suggestions: Remind students that adjectives must agree with nouns in gender and number.

Answers will vary.

3. Leer

Suggestions: Have students list the clues to the answers as they read.

Answers:

Chato and Andrés lead a healthy lifestyle. Chispa leads an unhealthy lifestyle.

4. Escribir

Suggestions: Have students write their suggestions, then exhange their answers with a partner and correct any mistakes.

Answers will vary.

5. Pensar

Suggestions: Have students re-read the *Perspectivas del mundo hispano* information as homework.

Los pasatiempos

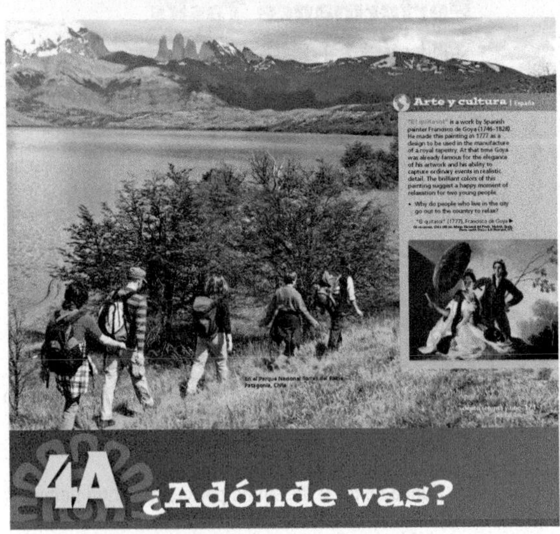

4A ¿Adónde vas?

- **Leisure activities and locations in your community**

Vocabulary: leisure activities; places; expressions to tell where and with whom you go; expressions to talk about when things are done

Grammar: the verb *ir;* interrogative words

Cultural Perspectives: leisure activities in the Spanish-speaking world

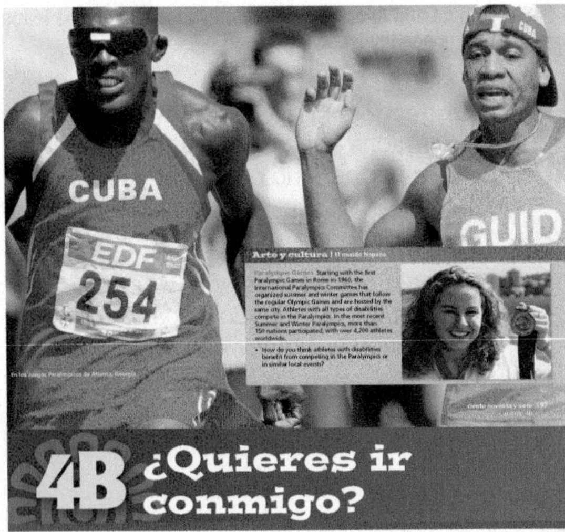

4B ¿Quieres ir conmigo?

- **Activities outside of school and invitations**

Vocabulary: leisure activities; feelings; expressions for extending, accepting, and declining invitations; expressions to tell when something happens

Grammar: ***ir*** + ***a*** + ***infinitive***; the verb ***jugar***

Cultural Perspectives: opinions on after-school activities

THEME SUPPORT

Bulletin Boards

Theme: *Tiempo libre*

Ask students to cut out, copy, or download photos of buildings and outdoor locations in Spanish-speaking countries and people engaged in leisure activities. Cluster photos of activities around photos of places where the activities might take place.

Hands-on Culture

Craft: *Migajón*

Migajón is the soft part of bread. It is used throughout Latin America as the base for a modeling material to create decorations and miniature toys.

Materials:

2 slices of white bread per student
2 tablespoons of white glue per student
acrylic paints
paint brushes

Steps:

1. Trim the crust from the bread and tear it into pieces.
2. Knead the glue into the bread. Continue to work the bread until the stickiness disappears and it becomes clay-like.
3. Shape the ***migajón*** into a small figure, such as an animal, car, or flower.
4. Set the figure aside for two to three days to let it air dry and become hard.
5. Decorate the figure with paint.

Game

Pregúntame

Play this game after you present *Gramática: Asking questions* in *Capítulo* 4A.

Players: the entire class

Materials: paper, pens, 2 paper bags

Steps:

1. Write all the question words and phrases from the *Gramática* on the chalkboard.
2. Divide the class into two teams. Teams write 11 sentences that would answer questions using the words and phrases from the board. Teams write one sentence for each question word or phrase.
   Question word: ¿Adónde?
   Team writes: Voy a la biblioteca.
   Question phrase: ¿Con quién?
   Team writes: Ella va con Roberto.
3. Collect the strips of paper and place them in two paper bags, one for each team.
4. Toss a coin to determine which team begins the game.
5. Draw a sentence from the Team 1 bag and read it aloud. Students from Team 2 have ten seconds to confer, then ask a question the sentence would answer. If the question is correct, Team 2 earns a point. If more than one question is possible, Team 2 may ask a second question to earn another point.
   Sentence: Él va a la playa a las diez.
   First question: ¿Adónde va?
   Second question: ¿Cuándo va a la playa?
6. Repeat Step 5 for the other team.
7. The winner is the team with the most points after both bags have been emptied.

Variation: You write the sentences, making some of them simple and others more complex. Begin play with the simple sentences and progress to the more complex ones.

THEME PROJECT

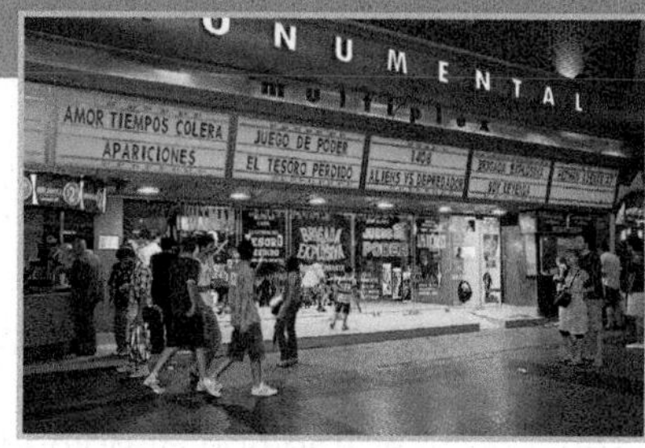

Guía para el tiempo libre

Overview: Students create a weekend entertainment guide for electronic or print delivery, featuring the times and locations of six different events and an illustration of each event. They then present their guide to the class.

Resources: online or print samples of weekend entertainment guides; image editing and page layout software and/or construction paper, magazines, scissors, glue, colored markers

Sequence: (suggestions for when to do each step appear throughout the chapters)

4A **STEP 1.** Review instructions so students know what is expected of them. Hand out the "Theme 4 Project Instructions and Rubric" from the *Teacher's Resource Book.*

STEP 2. Students look at examples of entertainment guides on the Internet or in their local newspaper. They then brainstorm what to include in their guide.

STEP 3. Students submit a rough sketch of their guide. Return the sketches with your suggestions.

4B **STEP 4.** Students create layouts. Encourage students to think through the details of their designs before implementing them and before writing the content of the guide.

STEP 5. Students submit a draft of the information in their guide. Note your corrections and suggestions, then return the drafts to students. For additional oral practice, students use their guides to invite a partner to one of the events.

STEP 6. Students complete and present their guide to the class, describing each of the events featured.

Options:

1. Students write and act out a script for a T.V. entertainment show describing upcoming events.
2. Students make a collage or slide show of their favorite leisure activities and write a paragraph about when and where they do them.

Assessment:

Here is a detailed rubric for assessing this project:

Theme 4 Project: *Guía para el tiempo libre*

RUBRIC	Score 1	Score 3	Score 5
Evidence of planning	You provided no written draft or page layout.	Your draft was written and layout created, but not corrected.	You corrected your draft and layout.
Your use of illustrations	You included no photos or illustrations.	You included photos or illustrations, but your layout was unorganized.	Your guide was easy to read, complete, and accurate.
Your presentation	Your guide and presentation included little of the required information.	Your guide and presentation included most of the required information.	Your guide and presentation included all of the required information.

21st Century Skills

Look for tips throughout *Tema* 4 to enrich your teaching by integrating 21st Century Skills. Suggestions for the Theme Project and Theme Support follow below.

Theme Project

Modify the Theme Project with one or more of these suggestions:

Encourage Creativity and Innovation
Invite students to design a novel weekend entertainment guide using electronic, print, and other media. The handout "Innovate" will help them develop, plan, and implement their groundbreaking guide.

Support Critical Thinking and Problem Solving
Have students think about their audience. Would they rather attract a small and specific group of people, or a more general group? How would the target audience affect their plans for the guide? The handout "Make Decisions" can help them analyze their options.

Develop Media Literacy
Have students consider advertising for their guide. Mention elements of an ad campaign, such as street signs, newspaper ads, radio, television, and Internet. Which advertising elements would work best to reach the audience they chose, and why?

Theme Culture

Develop Flexibility and Adaptability
Have students review *Fondo cultural* on pages 177 and 181 and compare what they do in their free time to what teens in Spanish-speaking countries do. Have them write a paragraph about how to adapt their free time activities to living or visiting in another country.

Videocultura View *Los pasatiempos* online with the class to learn more about leisure time in Spanish-speaking countries.

4A ¿Adónde vas?

AT A GLANCE

Objectives

- **Listen and read about leisure activities and schedules**
- **Talk and write about places to go and activities to do during free time**
- **Exchange information about weekend plans**
- **Understand the meaning and role of children's rhymes from the Spanish-speaking world**
- **Compare leisure activities in the Spanish-speaking world and the United States**

Vocabulary

- Leisure activities
- Places in the community
- When things are done

Grammar

- The verb ***ir***
- Asking questions

Culture

- Francisco de Goya, p. 171
- Pedro Lázaro, p. 177
- ***la plaza,*** p. 177
- Popularity of sports clubs and gyms, p. 181
- Tradition of going to the movies, p. 185
- Old San Juan, pp. 186, 187
- Andean music, p. 189
- Chants and songs, p. 190

Recycle

- The verb ***ir***
- The present tense of ***-ar*** verbs
- The present tense of ***-er*** and ***-ir*** verbs
- Infinitives

RESOURCES

	FOR THE STUDENT	ONLINE	DVD	PRINT	FOR THE TEACHER	ONLINE	PREEXP	DVD	PRINT
Plan					Interactive TE and Resources DVD	•		•	
					Teacher's Resource Book, pp. 248–283	•		•	•
					Pre-AP* Resource Book, pp. 74–77	•		•	•
					Lesson Plans	•			•
					Mapa global interactivo	•			
Introducción PP. **170–171**									
Present	Student Edition, pp. 170–171	•	•	•	Interactive TE and Resources DVD	•		•	
	DK Reference Atlas	•	•		Teacher's Resource Book, pp. 248–283	•		•	•
	Videocultura	•	•		Galería de fotos		•		
	Hispanohablantes WB, pp. 130–131			•	Fine Art Transparencies, 27	•	•	•	
					Map Transparencies, 12–18, 20	•	•	•	
Vocabulario en contexto PP. **172–175**									
Present & Practice	Student Edition, pp. 172–175	•	•	•	Interactive TE and Resources DVD	•		•	
	Audio	•	•		Teacher's Resource Book, pp. 252–254, 256, 264–265	•		•	•
	Videohistoria	•	•		Vocabulary Clip Art	•	•	•	•
	Flashcards	•	•		Audio Program	•	•	•	
	Instant Check	•			Video Program: Videohistoria	•		•	
	Guided WB, pp. 115–124	•	•	•	Video Program Teacher's Guide: Cap. 4A	•		•	•
	Core WB, pp. 67–70	•	•	•	Vocabulary and Grammar Transparencies, 81–84	•	•	•	
	Comm. WB, pp. 70–72, 75	•	•	•	Answer Keys: Student Edition, pp. 50–51	•	•	•	
	Hispanohablantes WB, pp. 132–133			•	TPR Stories, pp. 49–61	•		•	•
Assess and Remediate					Prueba 4A–1: Assessment Program, pp. 93–94	•		•	•
					Assessment Program para hispanohablantes, pp. 93–94	•		•	•

RESOURCES

	FOR THE STUDENT	ONLINE	DVD	PRINT	FOR THE TEACHER	ONLINE	PREEXP	DVD	PRINT
Vocabulario en uso PP. **176–179**									
Present & Practice	Student Edition, pp. 176–179	•	•	•	Interactive Whiteboard Vocabulary Activities	•		•	
	Instant Check	•			Interactive TE and Resources DVD	•		•	
	Comm. WB, p. 73	•	•	•	Teacher's Resource Book, pp. 253–254, 258–259, 263	•		•	•
	Hispanohablantes WB, pp. 134–135			•	Communicative Pair Activities, pp. 258–259	•		•	•
	Communicative Pair Activities	•			Audio Program	•	•	•	
					Videomodelos	•		•	
					Vocabulary and Grammar Transparencies, 11	•	•	•	
					Answer Keys: Student Edition, pp. 51–52	•	•	•	•
Assess and Remediate					Prueba 4A–2 with Study Plan	•			
					Prueba 4A–2: Assessment Program, pp. 95–96	•		•	•
					Assessment Program para hispanohablantes, pp. 95–96	•		•	•
Gramática PP. **180–187**									
Present & Practice	Student Edition, pp. 180–187	•	•	•	Interactive Whiteboard Grammar Activities	•		•	
	Instant Check	•			Interactive TE and Resources DVD	•		•	
	Animated Verbs	•			Teacher's Resource Book, pp. 256–257, 254–255, 260–261	•		•	•
	Tutorial Video: Grammar	•			Communicative Pair Activities, pp. 260–261	•		•	•
	Canción de hip hop	•			Audio Program	•	•	•	
	Guided WB, pp. 125–129	•	•	•	Videomodelos	•		•	
	Core WB, pp. 71–73	•	•	•	Video Program: GramActiva	•	•	•	
	Comm. WB, pp. 73–74, 76–77, 263	•	•	•	Vocabulary and Grammar Transparencies, 85–87	•	•	•	
	Hispanohablantes WB, pp. 136–141			•	Map Transparencies, 14	•	•	•	
	Communicative Pair Activities	•			Answer Keys: Student Edition, pp. 52–54	•	•	•	
Assess and Remediate					Pruebas 4A–3 and 4A–4 with Study Plans	•			
					Pruebas 4A–3, 4A–4: Assessment Program, pp. 97, 98	•		•	•
					Assessment Program para hispanohablantes, pp. 97, 98	•		•	•
¡Adelante! PP. **188–193**									
Application	Student Edition, pp. 188–193	•	•	•	Interactive TE and Resources DVD	•		•	
	Online Cultural Reading	•			Map Transparencies, 15–17, 20	•	•	•	
	Guided WB, pp. 130–132	•	•	•	Answer Keys: Student Edition, p. 55	•	•	•	
	Comm. WB, pp. 77–78, 264	•	•	•					
	Hispanohablantes WB, pp. 142–147			•					
Repaso del capítulo PP. **194–195**									
Review	Student Edition, pp. 194–195	•	•	•	Interactive TE and Resources DVD	•		•	
	Online Puzzles and Games	•			Teacher's Resource Book, pp. 255, 262, 264–265	•		•	•
	Core WB, pp. 74–75	•	•	•	Audio Program	•	•	•	
	Comm. WB, pp. 265–268	•	•	•	Answer Keys: Student Edition, p. 55	•	•	•	
	Hispanohablantes WB, pp. 148–149			•					
	Instant Check	•							
Chapter Assessment									
Assess					Examen del capítulo 4A	•		•	•
					Assessment Program, pp. 99–104	•		•	•
					Alternate Assessment Program, pp. 35–39	•		•	•
					Assessment Program para hispanohablantes, pp. 99–104	•		•	•
					Audio Program, Cap. 4A, Examen	•		•	
					ExamView: Test Banks A and B questions only online	•		•	
					Heritage Learner Test Bank	•		•	
					Pre-AP* Test Bank	•		•	

REGULAR SCHEDULE (50 MINUTES)

DAY	Warm-up / Assess	Preview / Present / Practice / Communicate	Wrap-up / Homework Options
1	**Warm-up** (10 min.) • Return Examen del capítulo 3B	**Chapter Opener** (5 min.) • Objectives • Arte y cultura **Vocabulario en contexto** (30 min.) • Presentation: Vocabulario en contexto • Actividades 1, 2	**Wrap-up and Homework Options** (5 min.) • Core Practice 4A-1, 4A-2
2	**Warm-up** (5 min.) • Homework check	**Vocabulario en contexto** (40 min.) • Presentation: Videohistoria *Un chico reservado* • View: Videohistoria • Video Activities 1, 2, 3, 4 • Actividad 3	**Wrap-up and Homework Options** (5 min.) • Core Practice 4A-3, 4A-4 • Prueba 4A-1: Vocabulary recognition
3	**Warm-up** (10 min.) • Actividad 5 • Homework check ✔**Formative Assessment** (10 min.) • Prueba 4A-1: Vocabulary recognition	**Vocabulario en uso** (25 min.) • Actividades 4, 6, 7 • Fondo cultural • Interactive Whiteboard Vocabulary Activities • Exploración del lenguaje • Audio Activities 5, 6	**Wrap-up and Homework Options** (5 min.) • Writing Activity 10 • Prueba 4A-2 with Study Plan: Vocabulary production
4	**Warm-up** (10 min.) • Actividad 9 • Homework check ✔**Formative Assessment** (10 min.) • Prueba 4A-2 with Study Plan: Vocabulary production	**Gramática y vocabulario en uso** (25 min.) • Actividad 8 • Communicative Pair Activity • Presentation: The verb ***ir*** • View: GramActiva video • Interactive Whiteboard Grammar Activities • Actividades 11, 12	**Wrap-up and Homework Options** (5 min.) • Writing Activity 11
5	**Warm-up** (10 min.) • Actividad 10 • Homework check	**Gramática y vocabulario en uso** (35 min.) • Actividades 13, 14 • Audio Activity 7 • Fondo cultural • El español en la comunidad • Pronunciación	**Wrap-up and Homework Options** (5 min.) • Core Practice 4A-5 • Prueba 4A-3 with Study Plan: The verb ***ir***
6	**Warm-up** (5 min.) • Homework check ✔**Formative Assessment** (10 min.) • Prueba 4A-3 with Study Plan: The verb ***ir***	**Gramática y vocabulario en uso** (30 min.) • Presentation: Asking questions • View: GramActiva video • Interactive Whiteboard Grammar Activities • Actividades 15, 17, 18 • Audio Activities 8, 9	**Wrap-up and Homework Options** (5 min.) • Core Practice 4A-6, 4A-7 • Actividad 16 • Prueba 4A-4 with Study Plan: Asking questions
7	**Warm-up** (15 min.) • Writing Activities 12, 13 • Homework check ✔**Formative Assessment** (10 min.) • Prueba 4A-4 with Study Plan: Asking questions	**Gramática y vocabulario en uso** (20 min.) • Communicative Pair Activity • Fondos culturales • Actividad 19	**Wrap-up and Homework Options** (5 min.) • El mundo hispano
8	**Warm-up** (5 min.) • Homework check	**¡Adelante!** (40 min.) • Lectura • ¿Comprendes? • Fondo cultural • La cultura en vivo • Presentación oral: Step 1	**Wrap-up and Homework Options** (5 min.) • Presentación oral: Step 2 • Preparación para el examen 3, 4, 5 • Lectura
9	**Warm-up** (5 min.) • Homework check	**¡Adelante!** (30 min.) • Presentación oral: Step 3 **Repaso del capítulo** (10 min.) • Vocabulario y gramática • Preparación para el examen 1, 2	**Wrap-up and Homework Options** (5 min.) • Core Practice 4A-8, 4A-9 • Instant Check • Examen del capítulo 4A
10	**Warm-up** (10 min.) • Homework check • Answer questions ✔**Summative Assessment** (40 min.) • Examen del capítulo 4A		

BLOCK SCHEDULE (90 MINUTES)

DAY	Warm-up / Assess	Preview / Present / Practice / Communicate	Wrap-up / Homework Options
1	**Warm-up** (10 min.) • Return Examen del capítulo 3B	**Chapter Opener** (5 min.) • Objectives • Arte y cultura **Vocabulario en contexto** (50 min.) • Presentation: Vocabulario en contexto • Actividades 1, 2 • Presentation: Videohistoria *Un chico reservado* • View: Videohistoria • Video Activities 1, 2, 3, 4 • Actividad 3 **Vocabulario en uso** (20 min.) • Interactive Whiteboard Vocabulary Activities • Actividades 4, 5, 6, 7 • Fondo cultural	**Wrap-up and Homework Options** (5 min.) • Core Practice 4A-1, 4A-2, 4A-3, 4A-4 • Prueba 4A-1: Vocabulary recognition
2	**Warm-up** (10 min.) • Actividad 10 • Homework check ✓**Formative Assessment** (10 min.) • Prueba 4A-1: Vocabulary recognition	**Gramática y vocabulario en uso** (65 min.) • Exploración del lenguaje • Audio Activities 5, 6 • Actividades 8, 9 • Communicative Pair Activity • Presentation: The verb *ir* • View: GramActiva video • Interactive Whiteboard Grammar Activities • Actividades 11, 12, 13 • Audio Activity 7	**Wrap-up and Homework Options** (5 min.) • Writing Activity 10 • Core Practice 4A-5 • Prueba 4A-2 with Study Plan: Vocabulary production
3	**Warm-up** (5 min.) • Homework check ✓**Formative Assessment** (10 min.) • Prueba 4A-2 with Study Plan: Vocabulary production	**Gramática y vocabulario en uso** (70 min.) • Fondo cultural • Actividad 14 • El español en la comunidad • Pronunciación • Presentation: Asking questions • View: GramActiva video • Interactive Whiteboard Grammar Activities • Actividades 15, 17, 18 • Audio Activities 8, 9 • Writing Activities 12, 13	**Wrap-up and Homework Options** (5 min.) • Writing Activity 11 • Core Practice 4A-6, 4A-7 • Pruebas 4A-3, 4A-4 with Study Plans: The verb *ir*, Asking questions
4	**Warm-up** (10 min.) • Actividad 16 • Homework check ✓**Formative Assessment** (15 min.) • Pruebas 4A-3, 4A-4 with Study Plans: The verb *ir*, Asking questions	**Gramática y vocabulario en uso** (25 min.) • Fondos culturales • Communicative Pair Activity • Actividad 19 **¡Adelante!** (35 min.) • Lectura • ¿Comprendes? • Fondo cultural • Presentación oral: Step 1	**Wrap-up and Homework Options** (5 min.) • El mundo hispano • Presentación oral: Step 2
5	**Warm-up** (5 min.) • Homework check	**¡Adelante!** (50 min.) • La cultura en vivo • Presentación oral: Step 3 **Repaso del capítulo** (30 min.) • Vocabulario y gramática • Preparación para el examen 1, 2, 3, 4, 5	**Wrap-up and Homework Options** (5 min.) • Core Practice 4A-8, 4A-9 • Instant Check • Examen del capítulo 4A
6	**Warm-up** (15 min.) • Homework check • Answer questions **Repaso del capítulo** (25 min.) • Situation Cards • Communicative Pair Activities ✓**Summative Assessment** (45 min.) • Examen del capítulo 4A		**Wrap-up and Homework Options** (5 min.) • Lectura

Standards for *Capítulo* 4A

- To achieve the goals of the Standards, students will:

Communication

1.1 Interpersonal

- Talk about leisure activities and locations
- Talk about where they go on different days of the week

1.2 Interpretive

- Read and listen to information about leisure activities
- Read a picture-based story; a letter telling how an exchange student spends her time; an advertisement for a cinema; about Old San Juan, Puerto Rico; a mall advertisement about scheduled activities
- Listen to and watch a video about leisure activities
- Listen to information about a plaza

1.3 Presentational

- Present information about: leisure activities and locations; about Tegucigalpa; a cinema; the history of Puerto Rico
- Reply to an e-mail message
- Perform a short skit about a student's first day of school

Culture

2.1 Practices and Perspectives

- Explain leisure enjoyment in the eighteenth-century Spanish aristocracy
- Talk about: the use of the town square in Spanish-speaking cultures; school-based exercise; movie-going habits; restoration of historic districts in Puerto Rico

2.2 Products and Perspectives

- Discuss Francisco de Goya and his painting; Pedro Lázaro and his painting; Andean music and instruments; about Spanish architecture in the United States

Connections

3.1 Cross-curricular

- Discuss Francisco de Goya; the history of Puerto Rico; the influence of Spain's colonial history on the United States
- Reinforce math and graphing abilities skills

3.2 Target Culture

- Recite the Mexican folk song, "La Bamba"
- Practice songs to games played by children

Comparisons

4.1 Language

- Talk about new vocabulary through the recognition of cognates; the correct placement of stress and accents; origins of the Spanish days of the week
- Explain the verb ***ir***, the use of interrogatives

4.2 Culture

- Compare: social gathering places to plazas; school-based sports and exercise activities; movie going habits of teens; restoration of historic districts; the influence of musical intruments; songs sung during children's games

Communities

5.1 Beyond the School

- Identify opportunities to explore local Spanish-speaking communities

Capítulo

4A ¿Adónde vas?

Chapter Objectives

Communication

By the end of this chapter you will be able to:

- Listen and read about leisure activities and schedules
- Talk and write about places to go and activities to do during free time
- Exchange information about weekend plans

Culture

You will also be able to:

- Understand the meaning and role of children's rhymes from the Spanish-speaking world
- Compare leisure activities in the Spanish-speaking world and the United States

You will demonstrate what you know and can do:

- Presentación oral, p. 191
- Preparación para el examen, p. 195

You will use:

Vocabulary
- Leisure activities
- Places in the community

Grammar
- The verb *ir*
- Asking questions

Exploración del mundo hispano

Country Connection
Pastimes and Places to Go

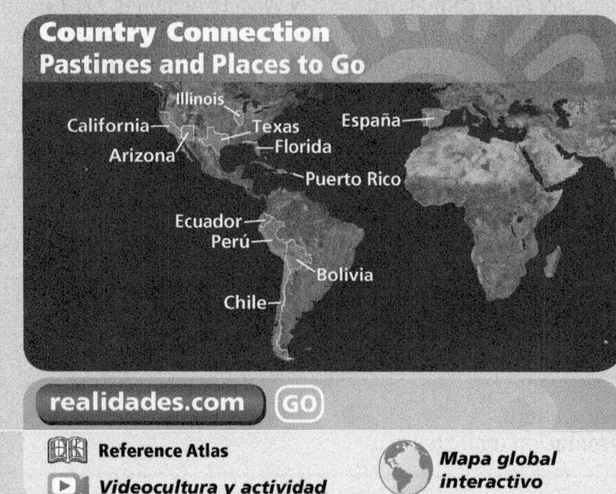

realidades.com GO

Reference Atlas

Videocultura y actividad

Mapa global interactivo

ENRICH YOUR TEACHING

Using Backward Design

Have students preview the sample performance tasks on *Preparación para el examen,* p. 195, and connect them to the Chapter Objectives. Explain to students that by completing the sample tasks they can self-assess their learning progress.

Mapa global interactivo

Download the *Mapa global interactivo* files for Chapter 4A and preview the activities. Use Activity 1 to travel to Madrid, Spain. Activity 2 takes you to Chicago's Pilsen neighborhood. In Activities 3 and 4, you visit historic San Juan, Puerto Rico and Saint Augustine, Florida.

Arte y cultura | España

"El quitasol" is a work by Spanish painter Francisco de Goya (1746–1828). He made this painting in 1777 as a design to be used in the manufacture of a royal tapestry. At that time Goya was already famous for the elegance of his artwork and his ability to capture ordinary events in realistic detail. The brilliant colors of this painting suggest a happy moment of relaxation for two young people.

- Why do people who live in the city go out to the country to relax?

"El quitasol" (1777), Francisco de Goya ▶
Oil on canvas, 104 x 152 cm. Museo Nacional del Prado, Madrid, Spain. Photo credit: Scala / Art Resource, NY.

En el Parque Nacional Torres del Paine, Patagonia, Chile

DIFFERENTIATED INSTRUCTION

Digital resources such as the ***Interactive Whiteboard*** activity banks, ***Videomodelos***, additional ***Online Activities, Study Plans***, automatically graded ***Leveled Workbook***, animated ***Grammar Tutorials, Flashcards***, and ***Vocabulary and Grammar Videos*** will help you reach students of different ability levels and learning styles.

STUDENTS NEEDING EXTRA HELP

Guided Practice Activities
- Flashcards, pp. 115–120
- Vocabulary Check, pp. 121–124
- Reading Support, pp. 130–131

HERITAGE LEARNERS

Realidades para hispanohablantes
- Chapter Opener, pp. 130–131
- A primera vista, p. 132
- Videohistoria, p. 133
- Manos a la obra, pp. 134–141
- ¡Adelante!, pp. 142–147
- Repaso del capítulo, pp. 148–149

ADVANCED/PRE-AP*

Pre-AP* Resource Book,
- pp. 74–77

Communications Workbook
- Integrated Performance Assessment, p. 265

PresentationExpress™
See pp. 170c–170d

Chapter Opener

Core Instruction

Resources: Map Transparencies 12–18, 20

Suggestions: Have students list the places in your community where they go for leisure activities. Explain that in this chapter they will be learning to talk about the places they go for fun. They will also learn to ask questions of others. The *A primera vista* video focuses on a group of Spanish teens introducing themselves to a new student and talking about their preferred activities.

Videocultura View *Los pasatiempos* online with the class to learn more about leisure time in Spanish-speaking countries.

Arte y cultura

Standards: 2.1, 2.2, 3.1

Resources: Fine Art Transparencies, p. 27

Suggestions: Explain that Goya is one of the great Spanish painters. Bring in additional examples of his work to share with students.

Answers will vary but may include that people enjoy being in a quieter, less polluted environment, surrounded by nature.

Mapa global interactivo, Actividad 1 Discover places of interest in Madrid, Spain.

Culture Note

The *Parque Nacional Torres del Paine* was established in 1959. It lies in the Patagonian region of southern Chile. Within the park borders, visitors can view glaciers and mountains, and hike alongside rivers and lakes. The park was designated a World Biosphere Reserve by UNESCO in 1978.

4A Language Input

Vocabulario en contexto

Core Instruction

Standards: 1.2, 4.1

Resources: Teacher's Resource Book: Input Script, p. 252, Clip Art, pp. 264–265, Audio Script, p. 253; Voc. and Gram. Transparencies 81–82; TPR Stories Book, pp. 49–61; Audio Program DVD: Cap. 4A, Tracks 1–2

Focus: Presenting new vocabulary about places to go

Suggestions: Use the story in the *TPR Stories Book* to present the new vocabulary and grammar, or use the Input Script from the *Teacher's Resource Book*. Present the vocabulary in two sets: places to go during the week and places to go on weekends. Use the transparencies to reinforce meaning as you describe places to go. Draw a map of your town on the board or overhead and locate the various locales as you describe them. Have students raise their hands if you mention a place that they go. Remind students that they will be held responsible for the words in the *Más vocabulario*.

Pre-AP* Support

- **Learning Objective:** Interpretive: Audio
- **Activity:** Have students copy from the board the following chart:

Nombre del estudiante	Actividad

Have four pairs of students volunteer to re-create and read aloud to the class one of the dialogs presented on pp. 172–173. Then, the rest of the class completes the chart from what they hear.

- ***Pre-AP* Resource Book:*** Comprehensive guide to Pre-AP* vocabulary skill development, pp. 51–57

Block Schedule

Divide students into groups of five or six. Allow each group to have one open book. Students take turns secretly writing down one of the places shown. The others ask, ***¿Vas a(l)...?*** until they guess the destination. When it is guessed, the first student confirms the answer: ***Sí, voy a(l)....*** Continue until all have had a turn.

Vocabulario en contexto

Objectives

Read, listen to, and understand information about
- places to go when you're not in school
- plans for leisure time

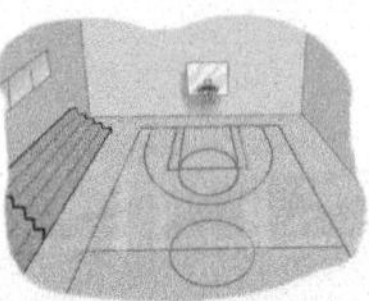
el gimnasio

el parque

el centro comercial

ir de compras

el trabajo

la lección de piano

el cine

ver una película

la biblioteca

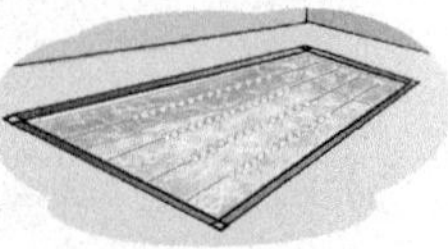
la piscina

—En tu **tiempo libre después de** las clases, ¿qué haces?

—**Voy** al gimnasio **para** levantar pesas y al parque para correr. ¿Y tú?

—Hoy voy a mi trabajo. No voy a mi lección de piano.

—¿**Con quién** vas al centro comercial?

—Voy con Guillermo, y **después vamos** al cine. ¿Y tú?

—Voy a la biblioteca para estudiar. Después voy al **Café** del Mundo con Lucila.

DIFFERENTIATED INSTRUCTION

Students with Learning Difficulties

To help students acquire the structure ***a + el = al,*** use the Clip Art from the *Teacher's Resource Book* and provide each student with copies of the various pictures. Help them label the pictures with the appropriate prepositions: ***al, a la,*** and ***a las.*** They can use these as flashcards for drill. Be sure to point out the *Nota* on p. 177.

Advanced Learners

Have students create a calendar for the coming month on which they label where they are going and at what times. They can quiz one another: *¿Qué haces los (domingos)? ¿Qué haces el (18)?*

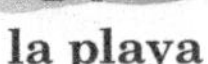
la playa

el restaurante

el campo

las montañas

Más vocabulario

la iglesia	church
la mezquita	mosque
la sinagoga	synagogue
el templo	temple; Protestant church

—¿Qué haces **los domingos**?

—Voy **con mis amigos** a la playa. Allí comemos el almuerzo. Hay un restaurante muy bueno. ¿Y tú?

—**Generalmente** voy al campo o a las montañas.

1 ¿Estás de acuerdo?

Escuchar

You will hear Elena describe where she does seven activities. If a statement is logical, give a "thumbs-up" sign. If it is not logical, make a "thumbs-down" sign.

2 ¡Muchas actividades!

Escuchar

Listen to Antonio describe his weekly list of after-school activities. As he names his activities, touch the corresponding picture(s).

Más práctica GO

realidades.com | print

	realidades.com	print
Instant Check	✔	
Guided WB pp. 115–120	✔	✔
Core WB pp. 67–68	✔	✔
Comm. WB p. 75	✔	✔
Hispanohablantes WB p. 132		✔

Language Input 4A

1 Standards: 1.2

Resources: Teacher's Resource Book: Audio Script, p. 253; Audio Program DVD: Cap. 4A, Track 3; Answer Keys: Student Edition, p. 50

Focus: Listening comprehension about locations for activities

Suggestions: Play the audio or read the script. Repeat the activity. Then ask the class to name the seven activities that Elena describes.

Script and Answers:

1. **Me gusta esquiar en la piscina. *(down)***
2. **Voy a la biblioteca para leer. *(up)***
3. **Bailamos en casa. *(up)***
4. **Practico deportes en el gimnasio. *(up)***
5. **Veo una película en el parque. *(down)***
6. **Nado en el cine. *(down)***
7. **Bebo café en el restaurante. *(up)***

2 Standards: 1.2

Resources: Teacher's Resource Book: Audio Script, p. 253; Audio Program DVD: Cap. 4A, Track 4; Answer Keys: Student Edition, p. 50

Focus: Listening comprehension and identification of place

Suggestions: Play the audio or read the script. As students listen and point, walk around the classroom and note whether or not they point to the correct picture. Explain that some sentences contain two activities or places. Confirm answers using the transparencies.

Script and Answers:

1. **Voy a la biblioteca para estudiar. *(library)***
2. **Me gusta correr en el parque. *(park)***
3. **Voy de compras al centro comercial. *(shopping/mall)***
4. **El viernes voy al cine con Paco. *(movie theater)***
5. **El sábado voy a mi trabajo en el restaurante. *(work/restaurant)***
6. **El domingo voy a la playa. *(beach)***

ENRICH YOUR TEACHING

Culture Note

On Sundays in many Spanish-speaking countries, it is common for entire families to go out together. Often, they will attend a religious service, then have something to eat at a restaurant, and then spend time in a park or at the movies. They may also gather at the home of a family member or friend.

Teacher-to-Teacher

Prepare a map handout with various places in your community pictured on it. Include places where your students work. As you describe an imaginary itinerary for one of your students, have students trace the route on the map. Put up a transparency with a completed map so that they can check their work.

Videohistoria

Core Instruction

Standards: 1.2

Resources: Voc. and Gram. Transparencies 83–84; Audio Program DVD: Cap. 4A, Track 5

Focus: Presenting additional contextualized vocabulary and grammar; previewing the video

Suggestions:

Pre-reading: Direct attention to the *Strategy*. Point out that scanning the text before reading in a detailed way can help in understanding the whole story. Use the transparencies to go panel by panel. Cover the dialogue and ask students to predict what activities are being talked about. Uncover the dialogue and have students scan to find the phrases that support their predictions. Show students where Madrid and Salamanca are located, using the map on Transparency 18.

Reading: Use the audio or have volunteers read the parts aloud. Stop periodically to check comprehension. Give students verbal and nonverbal clues to help them understand the new words in blue.

Post-reading: Complete *Actividad* 3 to check comprehension.

Video

Core Instruction

Standards: 1.2

Resources: Teacher's Resource Book: Video Script, p. 256; Video Program: Cap. 4A; Video Program Teacher's Guide: Cap. 4A

Focus: Comprehending a story about a new student meeting classmates; talking about leisure activities

Suggestions:

Pre-viewing: Ask students if they've experienced being in a new location, or if they've befriended new students. Explain that the video deals with this situation. Remind them that they will not understand every word, and that they will be hearing the ***vosotros*** form of certain verbs.

Viewing: Show the video once without pausing. Then go back and show it again, using the graphics-supported version. Stop along the way to check comprehension. Show the segment a final time without pausing.

Post-viewing: Complete the video activities in the *Communication Workbook.*

Un chico reservado

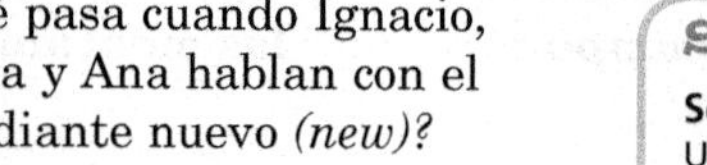

¿Qué pasa cuando Ignacio, Elena y Ana hablan con el estudiante nuevo *(new)*? Lee la historia.

Strategy

Scanning
Use the visuals to predict what different activities Ana, Elena, Ignacio, and Javier are talking about. Then look in the dialogues to find the corresponding word or phrase that describes each activity.

Ignacio: Mira, el estudiante nuevo es un poco reservado, ¿verdad?

Elena: Ah, sí . . . Está allí **solo.** ¿Por qué no hablamos con él?

Ignacio: Sí, ¡vamos!

5

Ana: Los lunes voy a mi lección de piano y los martes, miércoles y jueves voy a la biblioteca para estudiar. Y Javier, ¿qué haces **los fines de semana?**

6

Javier: ¿Los fines de semana? **Me quedo en casa.** No tengo muchos amigos aquí.

Ignacio: ¿Qué te gusta hacer?

Javier: ¡Me gusta el fútbol!

Ana: **¡No me digas!** Pues, nosotros vamos al parque para practicar fútbol.

Javier: **¿Cuándo?**

Ana: El sábado.

Javier: Está bien.

DIFFERENTIATED INSTRUCTION

Advanced Learners

Have students rewrite the dialogue for the various characters, substituting other activities or places that they've learned. They could also personalize it using names of classmates. Have them perform their dialogues for the class. Encourage creativity.

Heritage Language Learners

Have students write a short paragraph telling what they usually do each day of the week. Allow them to use vocabulary that has not yet been taught, if they desire. Verify their spelling and have them make necessary corrections before placing the paragraphs in their portfolios.

Elena: Hola. Me llamo Elena. Él es Ignacio, y ella es Ana.
Javier: Mucho gusto. Me llamo Javier.
Elena: Encantada . . . **¿De dónde eres?**
Javier: Soy **de** Salamanca.

Ana: Pues, Javier, ¿vas después de las clases **con tus amigos?**
Javier: No, voy **a casa.**

Javier: **¿Adónde** vais* vosotros después de las clases?
Elena: Los lunes, miércoles y viernes voy a mi trabajo en el centro comercial.
Ignacio: Generalmente voy al gimnasio. Me gusta levantar pesas.

8

Elena: Pero Ana, ¿fútbol?
Ana: ¿Por qué no? ¡No tiene muchos amigos y le gusta el fútbol!

3 ¿Comprendes?

Leer • Escribir • Hablar

En una hoja de papel completa las frases según la *Videohistoria.*

1. Javier es de . . .
2. Después de las clases Javier va . . .
3. Después de las clases Ignacio va al . . .
4. El jueves Ana va a la . . .
5. A Javier le gusta practicar . . .
6. Todos van al parque el . . .

Más práctica GO

realidades.com | print

	realidades.com	print
Instant Check	✔	
Guided WB pp. 121–124	✔	✔
Core WB pp. 69–70	✔	✔
Comm. WB pp. 70–71, 72, 73	✔	✔
***Hispanohablantes* WB** p. 133		✔

*Remember that in Spain, the *vosotros(as)* form of verbs is used when speaking to a group of people you would address individually with *tú*.

3 Standards: 1.2, 1.3

Resources: Answer Keys: Student Edition, p. 51

Focus: Demonstrating comprehension of the *Videohistoria*

Suggestions: Tell students that they can refer to the *Videohistoria* captions when they answer the questions. Have them tell in what panel they found the information to complete the sentences.

Answers:
1. **... Salamanca.** ***(panel 2)***
2. **... a casa.** ***(panel 3)***
3. **... gimnasio.** ***(panel 4)***
4. **... biblioteca.** ***(panel 5)***
5. **... el fútbol (deportes).** ***(panel 6)***
6. **... sábado.** ***(panel 7)***

Extension: Have students use the captions to create their own open-ended sentences. If you prefer, they can write true or false statements. Have students give their papers to classmates to complete the statements. Have several volunteers write sentences on the board for the class to review.

Additional Resources

- Communication Wbk.: Audio Act. 5, p. 72
- Teacher's Resource Book: Audio Script, pp. 253–254
- Audio Program DVD: Cap. 4A, Track 7

ENRICH YOUR TEACHING

Culture Note

Salamanca, located northwest of Madrid, is one of the oldest university cities in Europe. The university was founded in 1218. Salamanca was originally a Roman military camp called Salmantica. It is located on the Tormes River and is the setting for one of the classics of Spanish literature, *Lazarillo de Tormes.*

21st Century Skills

Social and Cross-Cultural Skills Remind students of the tools available in **realidades.com**, such as the eText with embedded audio files, that can help them develop their fluency and cross-cultural social skills, as they listen to and become familiar with the regional accents of the native speakers of the videos.

Quiz: Vocabulary Recognition
- Prueba 4A-1: pp. 93–94

INTERACTIVE WHITEBOARD
Vocabulary Activities 4A

4 Standards: 1.2, 1.3

Resources: Answer Keys: Student Edition, p. 51

Focus: Reading and completing sentences about where certain activities take place

Suggestions: Review the places pictured before students begin. Brainstorm logical responses for the *¡Respuesta personal!*

Answers:

1. **... el gimnasio (el parque).**
2. **... la piscina (la playa).**
3. **... el cine.**
4. **... la biblioteca (casa, la escuela).**
5. **... el centro comercial.**
6. **... las montañas.**
7. **... el restaurante (casa, el café).**

Extension: Have students create illogical sentences, e.g., *Nado en la biblioteca.* Ask volunteers to write theirs on the board and have the class correct them.

BELLRINGER REVIEW

Show Voc. and Gram. Transparency 81. Ask students to look at the transparency for 10 seconds, then turn off the light and cover one of the pictures with a coin. When you turn the light back on, ask for individuals to tell you which image has been covered. Continue with several images.

5 Standards: 1.3

Resources: Teacher's Resource Book: Video Program: GramActiva, p. 263

Focus: Writing about frequency of going certain places

Recycle: Expressions of frequency

Suggestions: Have students identify each picture before they begin. As students work, walk around the room, checking that they understand what to do.

Answers will vary.

Extension: Draw the line diagram on the board and have volunteers write places they go under the correct time expression.

Vocabulario en uso

Objectives

- Write and talk about places you go in your free time
- Listen to a description of a plaza
- Discuss and compare where you go and how often

4 ¿Qué haces en . . . ?

Escribir • Hablar

Completa las frases lógicamente.

1. Hago ejercicio en . . .
2. Nado en . . .
3. Veo películas en . . .
4. Leo libros y revistas en . . .
5. Voy de compras en . . .
6. Esquío en . . .
7. Como el desayuno en . . .

5 ¿Vas mucho a . . . ?

Escribir

On a sheet of paper, copy the diagram below and write the names of the places you go under the appropriate expression of frequency.

todos los días — mucho — a veces — nunca

la playa

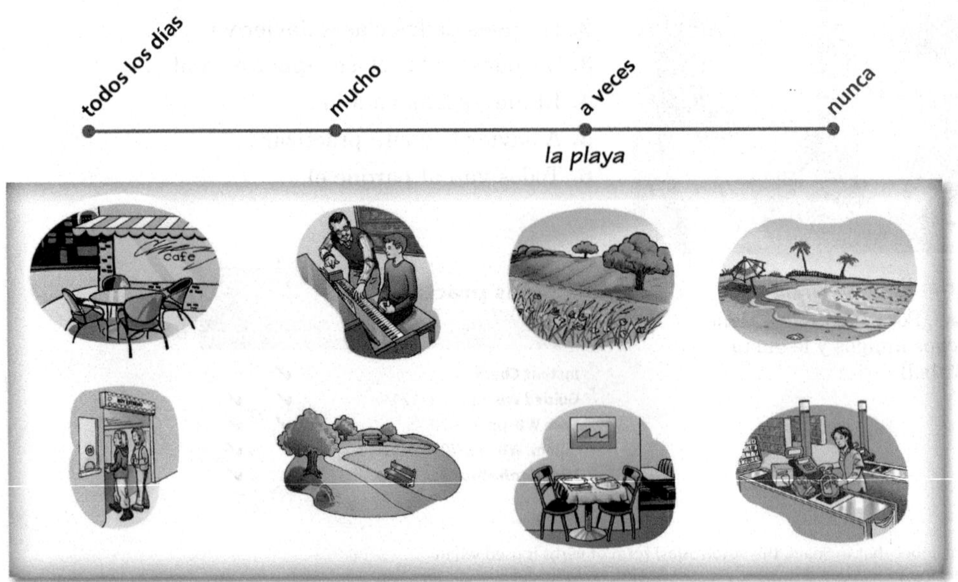

DIFFERENTIATED INSTRUCTION

Students with Special Needs

Students who have difficulty writing can be given copies of the pictures from the Clip Art in the *Teacher's Resource Book.* Prepare a large version of the diagram and have them place the pictures under the appropriate expressions.

Advanced Learners/Pre-AP*

Have students write an original sentence using each one of the places mentioned in *Actividad* 5. Ask students to read their sentences to the class.

6 ¡No me digas!

Hablar

Work with a partner. Using what you wrote for Actividad 5, take turns saying where you go and how often. React to your partner's statements. Follow the model.

Modelo

A —*Voy a la playa a veces.*
B —*¡No me digas! Yo voy a la playa a veces también.*
o:—*¡No me digas! Yo nunca voy a la playa.*
o:—*Pues, yo voy a la playa todos los días.*

Nota

When *a* is used before *el*, the two words form the contraction *al (to the)*:

a + el = al

- Voy **al** centro comercial a veces, pero voy **a la** piscina mucho.

También se dice . . .

la piscina = la alberca *(México)*; la pileta *(América del Sur)*

el restaurante = el restaurán *(América del Sur)*

7 Escucha y escribe

Escuchar • Escribir

Look at the painting of the plaza below. On a sheet of paper, write the numbers 1–6. You will hear six statements about the painting. Write what you hear.

Fondo Cultural | El mundo hispano

Strolling through the main square (*la plaza mayor*) of most towns and cities in Spanish-speaking countries is a popular activity for young and old alike. The *plaza mayor* is typically ringed by stores, cafés, churches, and government buildings. Here people go to eat, shop, worship, and conduct business, and gather for festivals and celebrations. This painting by Pedro Lázaro (1956–) celebrates the beauty and importance of the *plaza* in Hispanic culture.

- What social gathering place in your community is similar to *la plaza*?

"La plaza" (1981), Pedro Lázaro ▶

Practice and Communicate 4A

6 Standards: 1.1

Focus: Talking about places people go and how often in a personalized context

Recycle: Expressions of frequency

Suggestions: Point out the *Nota* if you have not already explained this concept. Remind students of the examples they saw earlier. Show the transparencies and have students tell you the preposition for each place or activity. Be sure Student B understands the options in the *Modelo*.

Answers will vary.

7 Standards: 1.2, 1.3

Resources: Teacher's Resource Book: Audio Script, p. 253; Audio Program DVD: Cap. 4A, Track 6; Answer Keys: Student Edition, p. 52

Focus: Listening and writing information about a painting

Suggestions: Play the audio or read the script. Allow students to listen several times. Use the *Fine Art Transparencies* to guide students' attention as they listen.

Script and Answers:

1. **Hay muchas personas en la plaza.**
2. **Hace buen tiempo hoy.**
3. **¿Ves la casa amarilla?**
4. **Muchas personas hablan en la plaza.**
5. **Voy a la plaza con mis amigos.**
6. **Me encanta la iglesia.**

Fondo cultural

Standards: 2.1, 4.2

Suggestions: Point out that the main ***plaza*** is the hub of most towns or cities, and that people often arrange to meet at the ***plaza,*** both for business and pleasure.

Answers will vary but may include such places as malls, post offices, etc.

ENRICH YOUR TEACHING

Culture Note

Lázaro's painting captures an essential feature of Hispanic towns: they are often built around the central focal point of the *plaza mayor*. Point out to students that the themes of *plaza* and community have been depicted by numerous artists in the Spanish-speaking world. You might show students paintings such as "Plaza Morazán en Tecucigalpa" by José Antonio Velásquez, sections of the "El Tianguis" mural by Diego Rivera, or contemporary works by Ernest Descals and Carmen Lomas Garza representing plazas and gatherings. Why do students think that this theme is important in Hispanic painting?

Teaching with Art

Artist Pedro Lázaro has depicted village life in a way that is representational without being photographic. His art is similar in style to American Primitive artists such as Grandma Moses. Bring in examples for students to compare.

4A Practice and Communicate

Exploración del lenguaje
Core Instruction

Standards: 4.1

Resources: Answer Keys: Student Edition, p.52

Suggestions: Remind students that what is now Spain was a Roman province for centuries. Have students research the origins of the English days of the week and make comparisons with the Latin / Spanish versions.

Answers:

1. c	5. b
2. e	6. f
3. a	7. d
4. g	

The Latin word for day is *dies*.

8 Standards: 1.1

Focus: Asking and telling about where you go on specific days

Recycle: Vocabulary for leisure activities

Suggestions: Direct attention to the *Nota*. Point out that the article is required, unlike in English. Go through possible answers that Student B might give before students begin.

Answers will vary.

Common Errors: Students often try to use ***en*** before days of the week. To reinforce the correct structure, have Student B include the article and day of the week in the answers.

Extension: Have the class brainstorm places and activities they have learned and write them on the board. Then write, ***¿Cuándo vas...?*** and give a possible answer (***los jueves, los sábados,*** etc.). Then have volunteers ask and answer the question.

Exploración del lenguaje

Origins of the Spanish days of the week

The word *sábado,* like many Spanish words, is based on Latin. The Spanish days of the week come from the Latin names for the gods, planets, sun, and moon, all of which were important in Roman daily life.

Try it out! Match the Spanish days of the week with their Latin origins.

1. lunes	a. *dies Mercurii:* named after Mercury, the god of commerce and travelers
2. martes	b. *dies Veneris:* named after Venus, the goddess of beauty and love
3. miércoles	c. *dies lunae:* the day dedicated to the moon *(luna)*
4. jueves	d. *dies solis:* named after the sun *(sol),* but later changed to *dies Dominicus,* which means "the Lord's day"
5. viernes	e. *dies Martis:* dedicated to Mars, the god of war
6. sábado	f. *dies Saturni:* named after Saturn; also called *dies Sabbati,* based on the Hebrew word *shabbath,* or "day of rest"
7. domingo	g. *dies Jovis:* named after Jove, or Jupiter, the ruler of the gods

• Since you know *día* means "day" in Spanish, what is the word for "day" in Latin?

8 ¿Adónde vas?  

Hablar

Habla con otro(a) estudiante sobre los lugares *(about the places)* adónde vas y cuándo vas allí.

Nota

To say that something usually happens on a certain day every week, use *los* with the day of the week:

• Generalmente ellos van al campo **los viernes** o **los sábados.**

Modelo

los lunes

A —*¿Adónde vas los lunes?*

B —*Generalmente voy a mi lección de piano.*

o: —*Generalmente me quedo en casa.*

Estudiante A

1. los miércoles
2. los viernes
3. los sábados
4. los domingos
5. los fines de semana
6. después de las clases

Estudiante B

¡Respuesta personal!

DIFFERENTIATED INSTRUCTION

Students with Learning Difficulties

If students have trouble with mathematics skills in *Actividad* 9, give them the formula for converting percentages: the number of students who gave a particular answer is divided by the total number of students in the class. Allow students to use calculators as necessary.

Advanced Learners

Have students research the origins of the Spanish names of the months. Have them prepare a poster or handout with a two-column chart like the one in the *Exploración del lenguaje*. They could also create a matching exercise like the one there.

9 Cuando no estamos en la escuela . . . | 

Hablar • Pensar • Escribir

¿Cómo pasan el tiempo tus compañeros de clase cuando no están en la escuela? Sigue *(follow)* los pasos.

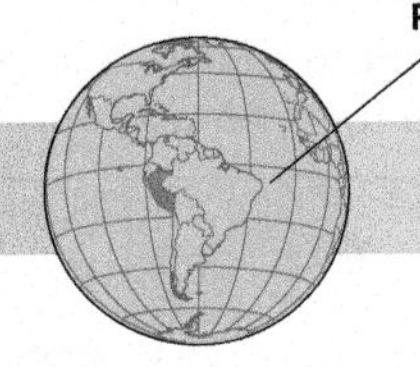

Conexiones | Las matemáticas

Un grupo de amigas en el Parque Central, Lima, Perú

1. Working in groups of four, take turns asking each person how often he or she does the activities listed below. Answer using *mucho*, *a veces*, or *nunca*. Keep a group tally of the responses.

ver películas	usar la computadora	ir a un trabajo
correr	ir de compras	ir a la biblioteca

 **Modelo**

A —*¿Con qué frecuencia* (How often) *usas la computadora?*
B —*Uso la computadora mucho.*

2. Get together with another group of four and combine the results of your tally sheets. Prepare summary statements to report to the class.
3. Report your summary statements to the class and make a class total. Convert each total to a percentage.
4. Create a bar graph like the one below for each activity that shows the class's frequency of participation.

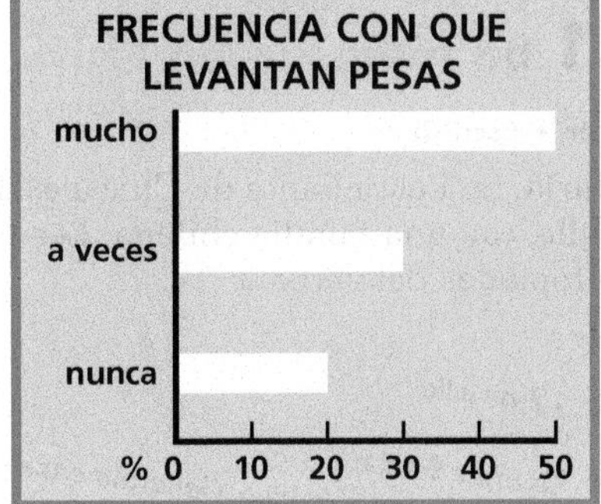

10 Y tú, ¿qué dices? |

Escribir • Hablar

1. ¿Dónde ves más películas, en casa o en el cine?
2. Cuando vas de compras, ¿adónde vas?
3. ¿Adónde vas los fines de semana? ¿Vas solo(a) o con tus amigos?

Practice and Communicate 4A

9 Standards: 1.1, 1.2, 1.3, 3.1

Resources: Voc. and Gram. Transparency 11
Focus: Talking about activities and how often people do them; making a cross-curricular connection with mathematics
Recycle: Leisure activities
Suggestions: Give students the directions for each step just before it is done. Encourage speed in gathering the information in Step 1. You might give students a prepared checklist for tracking the answers. Help students with the mathematical operation, if necessary, or have students explain it to others. Use the graphic organizer from the transparencies for creating the bar graph in Step 4.
Answers will vary.

10 Standards: 1.1, 1.2

Focus: Writing and speaking in a personalized context
Suggestions: Have students deduce the meaning of ***solo(a)*** in item 3 using cognate recognition or context clues (it's the opposite of ***con tus amigos***).
Answers will vary but will include:
ves, veo, corres, corro, usas, uso, vas, voy.

Additional Resources

- Communication Wbk.: Audio Act. 6, p. 73
- Teacher's Resource Book: Audio Script, p. 254, Communicative Pair Activity BLM, pp. 258–259
- Audio Program DVD: Cap. 4A, Track 8

ASSESSMENT

Prueba 4A-2 with Study Plan (online only)

Quiz: Vocabulary Production
- Prueba 4A-2: pp. 95–96

ENRICH YOUR TEACHING

Teacher-to-Teacher

Some students might enjoy doing a more extensive survey of their classmates' leisure preferences. Help them create lists of activities or places that are popular in your community. They can include some humorous choices. Ask them to use their lists to create a written survey with questions for everyone to answer. Have them compile the information and give a presentation of their findings to the class, complete with bar charts produced using presentation software.

Gramática

Core Instruction

Standards: 4.1

Resources: Voc. and Gram. Transparency 85; Teacher's Resource Book: Video Script, p. 256; Video Program: Cap. 4A

INTERACTIVE WHITEBOARD
Grammar Activities 4A

Suggestions: Direct attention to the *¿Recuerdas?* Use the transparency to reinforce the verb forms or write them on the board. Ask the question *¿Adónde vas?* of several students. Then point to another student and ask, *¿Adónde va?* Continue through the verb forms. For additional reinforcement, play the *GramActiva* Video.

11 Standards: 1.2, 3.1

Resources: Answer Keys: Student Edition, p. 52

Focus: Reading and writing forms of the verb ***ir*** in context

Suggestions: Have students number their papers 1–6 and complete the assignment. Walk around the room as they work, assisting with comprehension. When students have finished, ask volunteers to read a sentence using the correct form of the verb.

Answers:

1. voy
2. va
3. van
4. van
5. vamos
6. vas

Block Schedule

Have students write a list of five places they go. Divide the class into groups of five. Name a leader in each group. The leader asks the person to the right, *¿Vas a (la biblioteca)?* The person responds with ***Sí, voy...*** or ***No, no voy...*** according to his or her list. The leader continues asking questions twice around the circle, and then must try to restate where everyone is going without making any errors. Play continues around the circle.

Manos a la obra

Gramática

Objectives

- Talk, read, and write about where you and others go
- Exchange information about where to go to do leisure activities

The verb *ir*

To say where someone is going, use the verb *ir*. Here are its present-tense forms:

(yo)	voy	(nosotros) (nosotras)	vamos
(tú)	vas	(vosotros) (vosotras)	vais
Ud. (él) (ella)	va	Uds. (ellos) (ellas)	van

The verb *ir* is almost always followed by *a*. To ask where someone is going, use *¿Adónde?*

¿Adónde vas? Where are you going (to)?

- You will often hear people say *¡Vamos!* This means, "Let's go!"

¿Recuerdas?

You have used the infinitive *ir* to talk about going to school.

- Me gusta **ir** a la escuela.

Más ayuda realidades.com

***GramActiva* Video**
Animated Verbs

Canción de hip hop:
¿Adónde vas?

***GramActiva* Activity**

11 Un invierno en Chile

Leer • Escribir

María, una estudiante de Chicago, Illinois, pasa un año en Santiago, Chile, con una familia chilena. Lee la carta *(letter)* y escribe las formas apropiadas del verbo *ir*.

17 de julio

Querida Sonia:
¿Cómo estás? Yo, bien. Generalmente paso tiempo en casa los fines de semana, pero a veces yo __1.__ a Portillo con la familia para esquiar. Hace mucho frío allí y por eso mi "mamá" chilena no __2.__ siempre con nosotros. En Portillo hay una escuela para los esquiadores y muchos chicos simpáticos __3.__ a las lecciones. También hay un cibercafé con computadoras. Muchas personas __4.__ allí para pasar tiempo con los amigos. Nosotros __5.__ el domingo. Y tú, ¿ __6.__ a la playa todos los días con tus amigos?

Hasta luego,
María

Portillo, Chile

DIFFERENTIATED INSTRUCTION

Students with Learning Difficulties

In *Actividad* 13, some students may have difficulty with the compound subjects and with going from ***tú*** to the first person. They may also confuse ***tus*** with ***tú.*** You may want to provide them with a chart showing the transformations necessary for completing the sentences.

Multiple Intelligences

Verbal/Linguistic: Have students research places to go in Chile and present their information as a postcard telling where they are going with their Chilean friends. Students can use pictures from magazines or the Internet to make the postcard look authentic.

12 La carta

Leer • Hablar

Lee la carta de María en la Actividad 11 y contesta las preguntas.

1. ¿Quién no va a veces con la familia a Portillo?
2. ¿Por qué a María le gusta ir a las lecciones de esquí?
3. ¿Adónde van para usar las computadoras?
4. ¿Cuándo van al cibercafé?
5. ¿Adónde van muchas personas para pasar tiempo con los amigos?

13 ¿Adónde van todos? |

Leer • Hablar • Escribir

1. Read the sentence and determine who does the activity. Using the correct form of *ir*, ask where they go to do the activity. Your partner will answer with the most logical place.

Modelo

A —Te gusta esquiar. *(tú) ¿Adónde vas?*
B —*Voy a las montañas para esquiar.*

1. Te gusta levantar pesas.
2. Tú y tu amigo corren mucho.
3. Tus amigos y tú ven muchas películas.
4. A tu amigo le gusta comer bistec.
5. Tus amigas nadan muy bien.
6. Tus amigos hacen ejercicio todos los días.

2. Now write four sentences about yourself and your friends, saying where you go and for what purpose.

Modelo

Vamos a . . . para . . .

Fondo Cultural | El mundo hispano

Sports clubs and gyms are very popular in Spanish-speaking countries. Since there are few school-based sports teams, many young people join private gyms for individual exercise or play for privately sponsored teams in order to compete in their favorite sports.

- What do you think students would do if your school did not offer opportunities for playing and competing in sports?

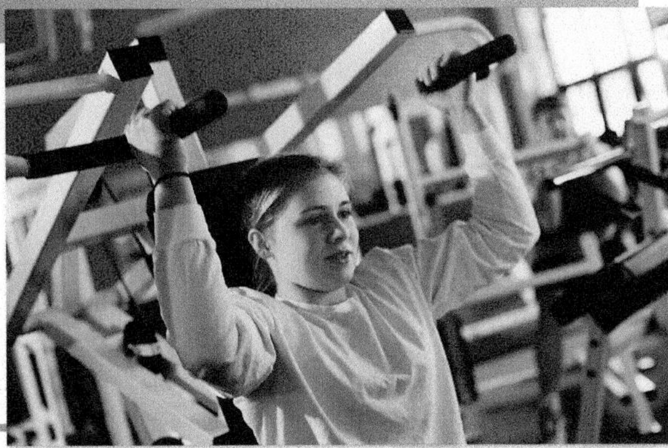

Estudiantes en el gimnasio

12 Standards: 1.2, 1.3

Resources: Answer Keys: Student Edition, p. 53

Focus: Reading a letter and orally answering questions about it

Suggestions: Have students take turns reading the letter in *Actividad* 11 aloud. Then ask the class the questions.

Answers:

1. **La "mamá" chilena no va a veces con la familia.**
2. **Porque muchos chicos simpáticos van a las lecciones.**
3. **Van a un cibercafé.**
4. **Van el domingo.**
5. **Van a la playa.**

BELLRINGER REVIEW

Name a place and ask students what one does there: *Vas a (la biblioteca). ¿Qué haces allí?* Students answer: *Leo libros y revistas. Estudio.* Continue asking about other places.

13 Standards: 1.1, 1.2, 1.3

Resources: Answer Keys: Student Edition, p. 53

Focus: Reading, speaking, and writing about activities and places

Suggestions: For Step 1, you may want to state the item and ask the ***¿Adónde...?*** question for each item so that students hear what they should respond to. For Step 2, be sure students know that they can use any of the items in their responses or can create new ones.

Answers:

1. **¿Adónde vas? Voy al gimnasio para levantar pesas.**
2. **¿Adónde van Uds.? Vamos al parque para correr.**
3. **¿Adónde van Uds.? Vamos al cine para ver películas.**
4. **¿Adónde va? Va al restaurante.**
5. **¿Adónde van? Van a la piscina.**
6. **¿Adónde van? Van al gimnasio.**

Extension: Repeat Step 1 of the activity, but have students work in pairs.

Fondo cultural

Standards: 2.1, 4.2

Suggestions: Students may have difficulty imagining the situation posed in the question. Point out that students in other countries find outlets for exercise and sports despite the lack of school-sponsored competitions.

Answers will vary.

ENRICH YOUR TEACHING

Culture Note

Portillo is recognized as one of the finest resorts in South America, but it offers much more than just skiing and snowboarding. You can relax in one of the two lodges, take a yoga class, go to the movie theater, visit the game room, or use the gym. Portillo provides a relaxing vacation atmosphere for skiers and non-skiers alike.

21st Century Skills

Technology Literacy Have students use the technology tools available in **realidades.com**, such as the animated verbs and the *Canción de hip hop*, to review the verb *ir* and its conjugations through fun and exciting digital formats.

14 Standards: 1.1, 1.2, 1.3

Focus: Writing and talking about what people like to do and where they do it

Suggestions: Point out to students that they need to write ten sentences, five stating what they like to do and five telling where they do each activity. Stress that they should not let other teams see their sentences. As students work in groups of four, walk around the room to monitor understanding, and correct sentence formation, speaking, and pronunciation.

Answers will vary.

El español en la comunidad

Core Instruction

Standards: 5.1

Suggestions: Ask a student to read *El español en la comunidad.* When students discuss the questions, ask: If you have not visited a neighborhood with a Spanish-speaking community, what would you expect to find in one? Correct any misconceptions.

Answers will vary.

Mapa global interactivo, Actividad 2 Explore Chicago's Pilsen neighborhood.

Pre-AP* Support

- **Learning Objective:** Interpersonal Writing
- **Activity:** Have students bring to class three personal photos (or pictures from a magazine) of places they might go to after school or on weekends. Have them "send" an email to a classmate, with the photos as attachments. The subject of the email is 'mis actividades favoritas'. Have student recipients draft replies, asking a different question about each photo.
- ***Pre-AP* Resource Book:*** Comprehensive guide to Pre-AP* communication skill development, pp. 10–57

14 Juego |  | 

Escribir • Hablar

Play this game in teams of two.

1. With a partner, write five sentences saying what the two of you like to do in your free time and when. Also write sentences saying where you go for these activities.

   Modelo

   Nosotros corremos después de las clases. (Vamos al gimnasio.)

2. Read one of your statements about activities to another team of classmates, but don't read the part that tells where you go. Then have one person try to guess where you go to do this activity. If the student answers correctly, his or her team wins a point. The team that earns the most points wins.

   Modelo

   A —*Nosotros corremos después de las clases.*
   B —*Uds. van al gimnasio, ¿verdad?*
   A —*Sí, vamos al gimnasio para correr.*
   o: —*No, no vamos al gimnasio para correr. Vamos al parque.*

El español en la comunidad

In many businesses and neighborhoods in the United States, you can hear Spanish being spoken. For example, the Pilsen neighborhood in Chicago, Illinois, is home to one of the nation's largest Mexican communities. The colorful murals, thriving businesses, and popular restaurants give Pilsen its own character.

- Are there areas near you where you can see expressions of community for Spanish speakers? What are they?

En la comunidad de Pilsen, en Chicago

DIFFERENTIATED INSTRUCTION

Student with Special Needs

Students with hearing impairments may benefit from seeing hand signals to indicate where syllabic stress falls. You might use an open hand to indicate a stressed syllable and a closed one to indicate an unstressed one.

Heritage Language Learners

Students may have trouble remembering to use written accents on words. Dictate a mixture of words that require accent marks and those that do not. Ask students to write the words, inserting necessary accent marks based on the rules they've learned.

▼ Pronunciación

Stress and accents

How can you tell which syllable to stress, or emphasize, when you see words written in Spanish? Here are some general rules.

1. When words end in a vowel, *n*, or *s*, place the stress on the next-to-last syllable. Copy each of these words and draw a line under the next-to-last syllable. Then listen to and say these words, making sure you stress the underlined syllable:

centro	pasteles	piscina
computadora	trabajo	parque
mantequilla	escriben	generalmente

2. When words end in a consonant (except *n* or *s*), place the stress on the last syllable. Listen to and say these words, making sure you stress the last syllable:

señor	nariz	escribir
profesor	reloj	arroz
trabajador	comer	español

3. When a word has a written accent, place the stress on the accented syllable. One reason for written accents is to indicate exceptions to the first two rules. Listen to and say these words. Be sure to emphasize the accented syllable.

café	número	teléfono
difícil	película	lápiz
fácil	plátano	artístico

Try it out! Listen to the first verse of the song "La Bamba" and say each word with the stress on the correct syllable. Then listen to the recording again and see if you can sing along with the first verse.

Para bailar la bamba, para bailar la bamba
se necesita una poca de gracia,
una poca de gracia y otra cosita
y arriba y arriba,
y arriba y arriba y arriba iré.
Yo no soy marinero, yo no soy marinero,
por ti seré, por ti seré, por ti seré.

Más práctica GO realidades.com | print

Instant Check	✔	
Guided WB pp. 125–126	✔	✔
Core WB p. 71	✔	✔
Comm. WB pp. 73, 74, 76	✔	✔
***Hispanohablantes* WB** pp. 134–137		✔

Pronunciación

Core Instruction

Standards: 3.2, 4.1

Resources: Teacher's Resource Book: Audio Script, pp. 254–255; Audio Program DVD: Cap. 4A, Tracks 10–11

Suggestions: Take each of the rules separately. Spend time drilling each stress pattern and its rules before moving on to the next step. Play the audio as many times as necessary.

Try it out! After students have completed the activity, ask two students to read one line at a time together. Correct pronunciation errors. Play the song and encourage students to sing.

Have students write the words to the song *"La Bamba"* and highlight accent and stress points mentioned in Steps 1, 2, and 3.

Teaching with Music

Songs are an excellent means of teaching rhythm and stress as students acquire a second language. Bring in other music from your collection or from libraries. Choose songs that have easy, singable lyrics.

Theme Project

Give students copies of the Theme Project outline and rubric from the *Teacher's Resource Book*. Explain the task to them, and have them perform Step 1. (For more information, see p. 170-b.)

Additional Resources

- Communication Wbk.: Audio Act. 7, p. 73
- Teacher's Resource Book: Audio Script, pp. 254–255
- Audio Program DVD: Cap. 4A, Track 9

ENRICH YOUR TEACHING

Culture Note

"La Bamba" is a folk song popularized by Ritchie Valens (1941–1959), a young singer from a Mexican American family in California. His last name was Valenzuela, but he changed it when he became a performer. Valens died in a small-plane crash with Buddy Holly, shortly before his eighteenth birthday.

21st Century Skills

Communication Encourage students to investigate a local business where Spanish is spoken, and to gather information about the products it offers and the Spanish-speaking communities they serve. Alternatively, have students look at newspaper inserts or flyers for local stores in the target language, and report on the kinds of products on offer.

ASSESSMENT

Prueba 4A-3 with Study Plan (online only)

Quiz: The verb *-ir*

- Prueba 4A-3: p. 97

4A Practice and Communicate

Gramática

Core Instruction

Standards: 4.1

Resources: Voc. and Gram. Transparency: 86; Teacher's Resource Book: Video Script, p. 257; Video Program: Cap. 4A

INTERACTIVE WHITEBOARD
Grammar Activities 4A

Suggestions: Be sure that students understand how questions are formed in English, and the relationship between the kind of information you are seeking and the way a question is asked. Go through the list of questions. Point out the use of the double question marks. Then point out the written accent marks on question words and explain that they are extra clues to the fact a question is being asked. Use the transparency and cover the English to check comprehension. When students seem to be grasping the concept, give them a statement and see if they can tell you what question they would ask to get that answer. Show the *GramActiva* Video to reinforce the concept.

15 Standards: 1.2, 1.3

Resources: Answer Keys: Student Edition, p. 54

Focus: Identifying interrogatives and word order

Suggestions: Write the words on strips of paper and show students how to resequence them. Tell them to be sure to capitalize appropriate words. Be sure they understand that they are to answer the questions truthfully.

Answers:

1. ¿De dónde eres tú?
2. ¿Adónde van Uds. los fines de semana?
3. ¿Cuándo van Uds. al centro comercial?
4. ¿Cuántas clases tienes?
5. ¿Qué haces tú después de las clases?
6. ¿Con quién vas tú al centro comercial?

Answers to the questions will vary.

Gramática

Objectives

- Write and answer questions about leisure activities
- Exchange information about where you and others go in your free time
- Read and write about places in San Juan, Puerto Rico

Asking questions

You use interrogative words *(who, what, where,* and so on) to ask questions.

¿Qué?	*What?*	¿Adónde?	*(To) Where?*
¿Cómo?	*How?, What?*	¿De dónde?	*From where?*
¿Quién?	*Who?*	¿Cuál?	*Which?, What?*
¿Con quién?	*With whom?*	¿Por qué?	*Why?*
¿Dónde?	*Where?*	¿Cuándo?	*When?*
¿Cuántos, -as?	*How many?*		

In Spanish, when you ask a question with an interrogative word you put the verb before the subject.

¿Qué come Elena en el restaurante?	*What does Elena eat at the restaurant?*
¿Adónde van Uds. después de las clases?	*Where do you go after classes?*
¿Por qué va Ignacio a la playa todos los días?	*Why does Ignacio go to the beach every day?*

You have already used several interrogative words. Notice that all interrogative words have a written accent mark.

For simple questions that can be answered by *sí* or *no,* you can indicate with your voice that you're asking a question:

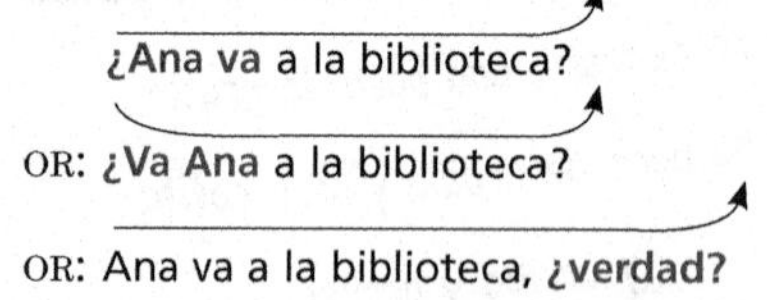

¿Ana va a la biblioteca?

OR: ¿Va Ana a la biblioteca?

OR: Ana va a la biblioteca, ¿verdad?

Más ayuda realidades.com

GramActiva **Video**
Tutorials: Questions with Interrogative Words, Question-word Questions, Formation of yes-no questions

GramActiva **Activity**

15 Preguntas revueltas

Pensar • Escribir

Your new pen pal from Bolivia has sent you an e-mail, but all his questions are scrambled. Unscramble them and write them in the correct order. Then answer his questions.

1. ¿ / eres / de dónde / tú / ?
2. ¿ / Uds. / adónde / van / los fines de semana / ?
3. ¿ / al centro comercial / cuándo / van / Uds. / ?
4. ¿ / clases / tienes / cuántas / ?
5. ¿ / tú / qué / después de las clases / haces / ?
6. ¿ / vas / tú / con quién / al centro comercial / ?

DIFFERENTIATED INSTRUCTION

Heritage Language Learners

Using the interrogative words taught on this page, have students prepare a list of questions that they would like to ask their favorite singer, actor, athlete, or other person. Have students exchange lists and answer the questions as if they were the well-known individuals.

Students with Special Needs

Write the words in *Actividad* 15 on individual cards and help students sort them into proper order. Use a different color card for the interrogative words so that they stand out. Emphasize the accent marks so students notice them.

16 ¿Cómo es el cine?

Leer • Pensar • Escribir

Lee este anuncio del cine.

Según el anuncio del Cine Parque Arauco, escribe la palabra apropiada para cada pregunta.

1. ¿___ es la calidad de la proyección en el cine? *Excelente.*
2. ¿___ comen muchas personas allí? *Palomitas.*
3. ¿___ es el nombre del cine? *Cine Parque Arauco.*
4. ¿___ van las personas a ver películas muy tarde *(late)* por la noche? *Los miércoles, viernes y sábados.*
5. ¿___ está el cine? *Delante del Centro Comercial Gigante.*

Cuándo	Por qué
Cómo	Cuál
Dónde	Qué

Fondo Cultural | El mundo hispano

Movies are a popular form of entertainment for teenagers in Spanish-speaking countries. Spain, Mexico, Argentina, Colombia, and Venezuela have important film industries, but movies from the United States are also popular. Spanish-speaking teens tend to go to the movies in groups.

- How do your movie-going habits compare with those of teens in Spanish-speaking countries?
- Are movies from Spanish-speaking countries popular in your community? Why or why not?

Los actores españoles Penélope Cruz y Javier Bardem

16 Standards: 1.2, 1.3

Resources: Voc. and Gram. Transparency 87; Answer Keys: Student Edition, p. 54

Focus: Reading a theater ad and completing questions about it using appropriate interrogatives

Suggestions: Read through the ad with the class, activating prior knowledge, using cognates, and using context to help with meaning. Remind students that they do not have to know the meaning of every word to understand the general message. Point out the interrogatives in the word bank. Help students see how the words in italics are key to knowing which interrogative to choose.

Answers:

1. **Cómo**
2. **Qué**
3. **Cuál**
4. **Cuándo**
5. **Dónde**

Common errors: Students often forget to write accent marks on question words. Demonstrate that omitting them can often change meaning.

Fondo cultural

Standards: 2.1, 4.2

Suggestions: Ask students to describe their movie-going habits. Have any students seen foreign films? Which ones? Were they dubbed or subtitled?

Answers will vary.

ENRICH YOUR TEACHING

Teacher-to-Teacher

Tell students that they are going to match up perfect friends in the class. To do so, they must create a survey questionnaire with questions that reveal people's personalities and interests, where they like to go, etc. Have them work in small groups to come up with six questions in each group. When they're done, have the groups report their questions as you write them on the board or overhead. Have the class vote on the ten best questions. Create a survey form that students can answer for homework. Have volunteers tally the results and match up the people who have the most similar answers.

4A Practice and Communicate

▾17 Standards: 1.1, 1.3

Focus: Writing and speaking about weekend activities; reviewing forms of ***ir***

Suggestions: Allow students to choose the three classmates for Step 1, but pair students for Step 2. Give them copies of the chart to fill out to save time. If they are drawing their own charts, be sure that they understand to omit the information shown in the example.

Answers will vary.

BELLRINGER REVIEW

Call out simple questions and have students give possible answers.

▾18 Standards: 1.1

Focus: Writing and talking about a photo

Suggestions: Have the class study the photo and discuss its important features. Then have students work individually on Step 1. While students are conversing in pairs for Step 2, walk around the room to monitor correct word usage, syntax, and pronunciation. Then have volunteers ask their questions in front of the class while others answer.

Answers will vary.

Pre-AP* Support

- **Learning Objective:** Interpersonal Speaking
- **Activity 18:** Students practice informal conversation skills as they ask and answer questions about a photo.
- ***Pre-AP* Resource Book:*** Comprehensive guide to Pre-AP* speaking skill development, pp. 39–50

Fondo cultural

Standards: 4.2

Suggestions: If yours is a relatively new community, suggest that students think of places they have seen on vacations or other trips.

Answers will vary.

▾17 Los fines de semana | 

Escribir • Hablar

1. Copy a chart like this one on a separate sheet of paper and fill in information about one activity you do on the weekends. Then find out the same information from three classmates.

Modelo

A —*¿Adónde vas los fines de semana?*
B —*Voy al centro comercial.*
A —*¿Con quién vas?*
B —*Voy con Selena.*
o: —*Voy solo(a).*

Nombre	¿Adónde vas?	¿Con quién?
yo	a mi lección de guitarra	solo(a)
Laura	al centro comercial	con Selena

2. Tell the class or a classmate where you and each of the three people you interviewed are going and with whom.

Modelo

Yo voy a mi lección de guitarra solo(a).
Laura va al centro comercial con Selena.

▾18 Y tú, ¿qué preguntas? | 

Escribir • Hablar

Habla con otro(a) estudiante sobre *(about)* la foto.

1. Mira la foto y escribe cuatro preguntas sobre el parque, las personas y las actividades.
2. Haz tus preguntas *(ask your questions)* a otro(a) estudiante.

Más práctica GO

realidades.com | print

	realidades.com	print
Instant Check	✔	
Guided WB pp. 127–129	✔	✔
Core WB pp. 72–73	✔	✔
Comm. WB p. 77	✔	✔
Hispanohablantes WB pp. 138–141		✔

▾Fondo Cultural | Puerto Rico

Old San Juan is a popular and lively part of Puerto Rico's capital, San Juan. Puerto Rican authorities are making great efforts to preserve colonial houses and other buildings and restore them to their original beauty.

- Are there historic areas near your community that have been or that are being restored? How do they compare with those in Old San Juan?

El Viejo San Juan, Puerto Rico

DIFFERENTIATED INSTRUCTION

Students with Learning Difficulties

If students have trouble deciding what to ask about the photo in *Actividad* 18, you might give them a list of statements from which they can derive questions. If this is still difficult, help them identify the appropriate interrogative words and have them create the questions from those.

Multiple Intelligences

Intrapersonal/Introspective: Some students might enjoy a personalized version of *Actividad* 18. Invite students to bring in a few vacation photos to share. Pair students and have them ask and answer questions about their photos.

19 ¡Vamos al Viejo San Juan!

Leer • Escribir

Puerto Rico has been a commonwealth of the United States since 1952. It is an island with a fascinating past. Look at the photos and read about a historic section of Puerto Rico's capital. Then answer the questions below.

Conexiones | La historia

El Viejo[1] San Juan es una zona histórica, pintoresca, colonial y muy popular en la capital de Puerto Rico. Los jóvenes[2] pasan el tiempo con sus amigos en los parques, cafés y plazas. Allí cantan, bailan y comen en los restaurantes típicos.

El Morro Construido en el siglo[5] XVI para combatir los ataques de los piratas ingleses y franceses[6]

Datos importantes:

- Cristóbal Colón llega[3] aquí durante su segunda visita a las Américas en 1493
- El Viejo San Juan llega a ser[4] la capital de Puerto Rico en 1521

La Catedral de San Juan tiene muchas obras de arte[7]. Allí descansan[8] los restos[9] de Juan Ponce de León, famoso explorador de la Florida.

[1]Old [2]young people [3]arrives [4]becomes [5]century [6]French [7]works of art [8]lie [9]remains

1. For how many years has San Juan been the capital of Puerto Rico?
2. On which of his voyages did Christopher Columbus land on Puerto Rico?
3. Why did the Spaniards build El Morro?
4. What are two things you'll see when you visit the cathedral?

ENRICH YOUR TEACHING

Culture Note

Puerto Ricans are American citizens. However, they do not have the right to vote for president or for full representation in Congress. Puerto Rico does send an observer to the U.S. House of Representatives. This individual cannot vote on laws but does vote in Congressional committees. The question of Puerto Rico becoming the 51st state has been debated for some time, and Puerto Ricans remain divided on the issue.

Teacher-to-Teacher

Have students plan a trip to Puerto Rico using guidebooks, encyclopedias, and the Internet. Students can work in small groups to write sentences saying where they plan to go while they are there.

Practice and Communicate 4A

19 Standards: 1.2, 1.3, 3.1

Resources: Voc. and Gram. Transparency 14; Answer Keys: Student Edition, p. 54

Focus: Reading about Old San Juan; making a cross-curricular connection

Suggestions: Show Transparency 14 or refer to the map on p. xxi for another view of Puerto Rico. Have students read the questions in English before they begin to read. Be sure they know that they are to answer in English.

Answers:

1. **San Juan has been the capital of Puerto Rico since 1521.**
2. **Christopher Columbus landed on Puerto Rico during his second voyage to the Americas.**
3. **Spaniards built El Morro to combat the attacks of English and French pirates.**
4. **Two things that one can see in the cathedral are the remains of Juan Ponce de León and many works of art.**

Mapa global interactivo, Actividad 3 Visit San Juan, Puerto Rico, and locate the historic fort Castillo del Morro.

Theme Project

Students can perform Step 2 at this point. Be sure students understand the task. (For more information, see p. 170-b.)

Additional Resources

- Communication Wbk.: Audio Act. 8–9, p. 74
- Teacher's Resource Book: Audio Script, p. 255, Communicative Pair Activity BLM, pp. 260–261
- Audio Program DVD: Cap. 4A, Tracks 12–13

ASSESSMENT

Prueba 4A-4 with Study Plan (online only)

Quiz: Asking Questions

- Prueba 4A-4: p. 98

Common Core: Reading

Lectura

Core Instruction

Standards: 1.2, 1.3, 4.1

Resources: Voc. and Gram. Transparency 88

Focus: Reading a mall advertisement about available activities

Suggestions:

Pre-reading: Direct students' attention to the *Strategy*. Point out the words in the glosses. To activate students' prior knowledge, bring in brochures from a local mall with similar information and have students identify the events. Have them scan the *Lectura* to see if any of the events are similar. Have them identify the calendar organization of the brochure.

Reading: Have students take turns reading sections of the brochure. Remind them that context and cognates can help them understand what they read. Help them decode unfamiliar words.

Post-reading: Have students answer the *¿Comprendes?* questions to check comprehension. When they have finished, discuss the questions and answers in class.

BELLRINGER REVIEW

Show Voc. and Gram. Transparency 30 to review days of the week and months.

Pre-AP* Support

- **Learning Objective:** Presentational Writing
- **Activity:** Have students research a cultural calendar for their community or city on the Internet. Have them write a brief, persuasive paragraph about one of the upcoming events attempting to convince a friend or relative to attend this event.
- ***Pre-AP* Resource Book:*** Comprehensive guide to Pre-AP* writing skill development, pp. 27–38

Objectives

- Read about after-school and weekend activities at a mall
- Use prior knowledge to better understand what you read
- Compare the instruments used in Andean music to those used in music you enjoy

Lectura

Al centro comercial

Lee las actividades diferentes que puedes hacer en la semana del 11 al 17 de enero durante tu tiempo libre.

Strategy

Using prior knowledge
Think about what you know about special-event weeks at shopping centers. List events that you think might be offered at a mall.

¡Vamos a la Plaza del Sol!

Aquí en la Plaza del Sol, ¡siempre hay algo que hacer!

Actividades para el 11 al 17 de enero

Día	Hora	Actividad
11 *lunes*	7.00 p.m.	Música andina
12 *martes*	7.00 P.M.	Clase de yoga
13 *miércoles*	8.00 P.M.	Noche de jazz
14 *jueves*	7.00 P.M.	Clase de repostería[1]
15 *viernes*	8.00 P.M.	Música andina
16 *sábado*	1.30 P.M.	Exposición de fotografía
	2.00 P.M.	Show infantil
	4.00 P.M.	Exhibición de yoga
	8.00 P.M.	Sábado flamenco
17 *domingo*	1.30 P.M.	Exposición de fotografía
	2.00 P.M.	Show infantil
	4.00 P.M.	Exhibición de yoga
	8.00 P.M.	Noche de tango

Música andina
El grupo Sol Andino toca música andina fusionada con bossa nova y jazz el lunes a las 8.00 P.M. Abierto[2] al público.

Clase de yoga
La práctica de yoga es todos los martes desde las 7.00 hasta las 9.00 P.M. La instructora Lucía Gómez Paloma enseña los secretos de esta disciplina. Inscríbase[3] al teléfono 224-24-16. Vacantes limitadas.

[1]pastry making [2]Open [3]Register

DIFFERENTIATED INSTRUCTION

Students with Learning Difficulties

Some students may have difficulty sorting out information when it is presented in an advertisement like this. Help them identify that it's a calendar by pointing out the days and dates. Help them see that the four featured events are among those mentioned in the calendar portion.

Advanced Learners

Have students go on the Internet to find shopping malls or cultural centers in Spanish-speaking countries that feature activities similar to those in the reading. Have them print out the schedules and identify in English the basic information.

Sábado flamenco

El Sábado flamenco es el programa más popular de la semana. María del Carmen Ramachi baila acompañada por el guitarrista Ernesto Hermoza el sábado a las 8.00 P.M. Es una noche emocionante y sensacional de música y danza. Abierto al público.

Clase de repostería

Inscríbase gratis[4] en la clase de repostería programada para el jueves a las 7.00 P.M. Preparamos unos pasteles deliciosos gracias a la Repostería Ideal y al maestro Rudolfo Torres. Inscríbase al teléfono 224-24-16. Vacantes limitadas.

[4]free

¿Comprendes?

1. You will be in town from January 9 through February 2. Will you be able to take part in these activities? In which ones?
2. Which events require you to sign up in advance? Which do not?
3. You have to baby-sit your six-year-old sister. Which day(s) would be best to go with her?
4. Según los intereses de estos chicos, ¿a qué eventos van ellos?

Raquel:	Me gusta mucho hacer ejercicio.
Roberto:	Me encantan los pasteles.
Teresa:	Estudio baile. Tomo lecciones todos los jueves.
Alejandro:	Me gusta escuchar música; toda clase de música.

5. ¿Qué actividad es más interesante para ti?

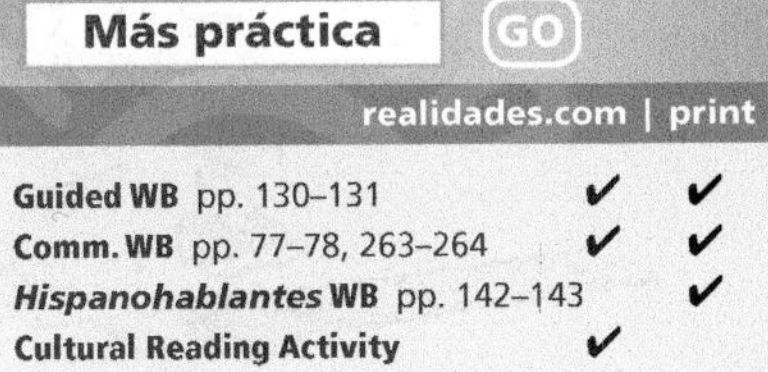

Más práctica GO

realidades.com | print

	realidades.com	print
Guided WB pp. 130–131	✔	✔
Comm. WB pp. 77–78, 263–264	✔	✔
***Hispanohablantes* WB** pp. 142–143		✔
Cultural Reading Activity	✔	

Fondo cultural | Bolivia • Chile Ecuador • Perú

Andean music has become popular worldwide. This haunting style of music originated in the Andes mountains of Peru, Ecuador, Bolivia, and Chile. Performers sometimes wear typical Andean attire. Instruments commonly used in Andean music include the *quena* flute, *siku* panpipes, and a small guitar called a *charango*.

- The Andean sound is created using a particular set of instruments. What instruments define the music you enjoy?

Músicos en la Plaza de Armas, Cuzco, Perú

¿Comprendes? Standards: 1.3

Resources: Answer Keys: Student Edition, p. 55

Answers:

1. **Yes, in all of them.**
2. **Yoga and the pastry class have limited spaces available; the Andean music and flamenco are open to the public.**
3. **Saturday the 16th and Sunday the 17th, because there's a children's show.**
4. **Raquel: yoga; Roberto: pastry making class; Teresa: flamenco and tango; Alejandro: Andean music and jazz**
5. **Answers will vary.**

Fondo cultural

Standards: 2.2, 4.2

Resources: Voc. and Gram. Transparencies 15–17

Suggestions: Use the transparencies to point out the Andean region. Bring in examples of Andean music for students to enjoy. Explain that flutes like the ***quena*** and ***siku*** are very ancient, and that similar instruments exist in many parts of the world.

Answers will vary.

Teaching with Music

Play some Andean music for the class and point out the instruments mentioned in the *Fondo cultural.*

Theme Project

Students can perform Step 3 at this point. Be sure that students understand your suggestions. (For more information, see p. 170-b.)

For Further Reading

Student Resource: Realidades para hispanohablantes: Lectura 2, pp. 144–145

ENRICH YOUR TEACHING

Culture Note

Shopping malls are common in many parts of the Spanish-speaking world. You will find very elegant ones, for example, in cities like Mexico City. Many of the stores would be familiar to students, either because they are American chain stores or because they are similar in style.

21st Century Skills

Initiative and Self-Direction Remind students of the tools available for extra reading support in **realidades.com**. Computer-corrected activities use different strategies to help students comprehend the new vocabulary, monitor their learning needs, and progress at their own pace through the reading.

La cultura en vivo

Core Instruction

Standards: 3.2, 4.2

Resources: Audio Program DVD: Cap. 4A, Track 14

Focus: Reading about and learning children's rhymes

Suggestions: Begin class by reciting a few words from an English nursery rhyme that students would likely know. Ask them to identify it. Ask if they remember any jump-rope rhymes. If students are unfamiliar with these, elicit something they do know and use it. Direct attention to the top photo of children jumping rope. Point out that it is easier to jump rope to a chant, as it helps you keep the beat and jump at the right time. Have students read the first two paragraphs. Practice the rhyme and the chant with the class.

If you can, go outdoors for this activity. A real jump rope works best. In the classroom, use a short piece of rope or string with a paper clip in the middle and a volunteer to demonstrate how a song helps to keep the beat while jumping rope. Students will hear the rope or paper clip hit the desk or floor.

Have students work in three groups. For the first chant, one student can say it, indicating another group member with each word, and the last person is "It." That person takes the role of saying the rhyme and the first one moves on to group 2. Students in group 2 jump rope to the chant, moving on to group 3 when their turn is over. Students in group 3 play the game described while singing the song. Each moves on to group 1 when the turn is over. Students continue until all have had a turn.

Direct attention to the *Think about it!* section and have students discuss the questions.

Answers will vary.

Additional Resources

Student Resource: Realidades para hispanohablantes, p. 146

La cultura en vivo

Rimas infantiles

Can you remember the chants and songs you learned as a child? Or do you remember the rhymes you or your friends recited while jumping rope?

Here are some chants and songs that children in the Spanish-speaking world use when they play. The first one is a Spanish-language equivalent to "Eenie, meenie, minie, moe . . ." It is a nonsense rhyme used to select the person who will be "It" in various games.

Tin Marín de dopingüé
cucaramanga titirifuera
yo no fui,
fue Teté.
pégale, pégale,
que ella fue.

Niña saltando a la cuerda

Here's a chant for jumping rope:

Salta, salta la perdiz	**The partridge jumps and jumps**
por los campos de maíz.	**Through the cornfields.**
¡Ten cuidado, por favor,	**Be careful, please!**
porque viene el cazador!	**Here comes the hunter!**
	(The jump rope then turns faster.)

Try it out! Here's a traditional game that combines Spanish, math, and hopping over a board. Place a long, narrow board on the floor. Take turns hopping with both feet from one side of the board to the other. Go forward as you hop. When you get to the end of the board, jump and turn in the air, facing the direction you came from. Continue hopping from side to side back to the other end. Be very careful! Try this in an area where you won't hurt yourself. As you are hopping, sing this song:

Brinca la tablita	**Jump over the board**
que yo la brinqué.	**That I already jumped.**
Bríncala tú ahora	**Now you jump**
que yo me cansé.	**Since I'm tired.**
Dos y dos son cuatro,	**Two and two are four,**
cuatro y dos son seis.	**Four and two are six.**
Seis y dos son ocho,	**Six and two are eight,**
y ocho dieciséis,	**And eight are sixteen,**
y ocho veinticuatro,	**And eight are twenty-four,**
y ocho treinta y dos.	**And eight are thirty-two.**
Y diez que le sumo	**And ten that I add**
son cuarenta y dos.	**Equals forty-two.**

Think about it! What rhymes and songs do you know? What purpose do they serve in play?

DIFFERENTIATED INSTRUCTION

Multiple Intelligences

Musical/Rhythmic: Have students learn other songs or rhymes from a Spanish-speaking country. Have them research this topic, learn one rhyme or song, and present it to the class, telling where it came from and when children use it.

Heritage Language Learners

Students may be familiar with these or other children's songs and rhymes. If so, allow them to present them to the class with an explanation of when and how the song or rhyme is used.

Presentación oral 

Un estudiante nuevo

- Role-play a conversation with another student about how you spend your free time
- Use models to prepare for your performance

Task
You and a partner will play the roles of a new student and a student who has been at the school for a while. Find out information about the new student.

1 Prepare You will need to prepare for both roles.

Current student: List at least four questions. Greet the student and introduce yourself. Find out where the new student is from, what activities he or she likes to do and on what days, and where he or she goes and with whom.

New student: Look at the questions the current student will ask you and note your answers.

2 Practice Work with a partner to practice different questions and responses. Be sure you are comfortable in both roles as you go through your presentation. Use your notes in practice, but not to present. Try to:

- get and give information
- keep the conversation going
- speak clearly

3 Present You will be paired with another student and your teacher will assign roles. The current student begins by greeting the new student. Listen to your partner's questions and responses and keep the conversation going.

4 Evaluation The following rubric will be used to grade your presentation.

Rubric	Score 1	Score 3	Score 5
Completion of task	You ask or answer two questions.	You ask or answer three questions.	You ask or answer four or more questions.
Your ability to keep the conversation going	You have no response or follow-up to what your partner says.	You have frequent response or follow-up to what your partner says.	You always respond to your partner and ask follow-up questions.
How easily you are understood	You are very difficult to understand. The teacher could only recognize isolated words and phrases.	You are understandable, but have frequent errors in vocabulary and/or grammar that hinder understanding.	You are easily understood. Your teacher does not have to "decode" what you are trying to say.

Strategy

Using models
It helps to go back and review models that prepare you for a task like this role play. Reread *A primera vista* (pp. 172–175). Pay attention to the different questions and answers that will help you with this task.

Speaking 4A

 Common Core: Speaking

Presentación oral

Core Instruction

Standards: 1.1, 1.3

Focus: Talking about a new student's first day of class

Suggestions: Go over the task, the 4-Step, and the rubric with students. Point out the *Strategy*. Give students time to do the review suggested. Help them identify the questions that will be most important for them. Review the rubric with the class to explain how you will grade the performance task. Do a presentation of your own to model a top-scoring presentation.

Step 1: Pair the students. The experienced student may need to review *A primera vista,* pp.172–173 and *Videohistoria,* pp.174–175, to complete his or her role.

Step 2: Allow students time to practice both roles. Monitor their progress.

Step 3: Students should not use their notes for this part. Remind the new student to listen carefully in order to answer accurately.

Step 4: Students can add the written questions and answers to their portfolio.

Pre-AP* Support

- ***Pre-AP* Resource Book:*** Comprehensive guide to Pre-AP* speaking skill development, pp. 39–50

Portfolio

Make video or audio recordings of student presentations in class, or assign the RealTalk activity so they can record their presentations online. Include the recording in their portfolios.

Additional Resources

Student Resources: Realidades para hispanohablantes, p. 147; Guided WB: Presentación oral, p. 132

ENRICH YOUR TEACHING

21st Century Skills

Leadership and Responsibility Have students use what they have learned while preparing for their *Presentación oral* about meeting new people to introduce themselves to one Spanish-speaking student at their school whom they don't know well. Students should use the questions they prepared for this task to initiate the conversation.

ASSESSMENT

Presentación oral

- Assessment Program: Rubrics, p. T30

Go over the descriptions of the different levels of performance. After assessing students, help individuals understand how their performance could be improved.

El mundo hispano

Core Instruction

Standards: 2.2, 3.1

Resources: Voc. and Gram. Transparency 20

Mapa global interactivo, Actividad 4 Locate Saint Augustine, Florida and the historic fort Castillo de San Marcos.

Focus: Reading about historical Spanish influences in the United States

Suggestions: Display a map of the United States. Locate St. Augustine, Florida, and Plymouth, Massachusetts, as you discuss the first colonists. Using a world map, point out the origins of the colonists in Spain and England. As you discuss the lands held by Spain, locate them on a world map so that students can see the vastness of the Spanish holdings.

Direct attention to the top left photo on p. 193. Tell students that the English and Spanish were joined by the French in colonizing North America. Can students name a French-speaking region in North America? (Quebec) Discuss the French Quarter in New Orleans. Even today, the French influence can be seen in the city and in the names of other places in Louisiana. Point out that although the French left their mark, the Spanish rebuilt the city and their influence is found in the architecture. For example, many homes there are built around courtyards and feature wrought-iron grilles and balconies, both very indicative of Spanish influence.

Focus attention on the picture of the Castillo, a national monument since 1924. Discuss its original purpose, and have students give their ideas as to why ships returning to Spain needed protection. Help them understand that the ships were carrying riches from America to Spain.

Teacher-to-Teacher

Have groups of students choose one of the cities or buildings featured here to research. Have them prepare posters and reports complete with photographs and drawings. When students have finished, make these available in a resource center in your classroom so that others can learn from and enjoy them.

El mundo hispano 

Estados Unidos

Histórico

The oldest permanent European settlement in the United States, St. Augustine, Florida, was established by Spain in 1565—55 years before the Pilgrims landed at Plymouth Rock. For more than two centuries after that, the Spanish controlled a large territory in North America that included what is now Mexico, parts of the southern United States, the states of Texas, New Mexico, Arizona, California, Nevada, and parts of Colorado and Utah.

Constructed as a mission in 1718, the Alamo (in San Antonio, Texas) today is best known as a key battleground in the secession of Texas from Mexico in 1836. The defeat of the Texans at the Alamo became a rallying cry for Texas independence, and Texas gained its freedom from Mexico two months later.

¿Sabes que . . . ?

The language of the Nahua peoples of central Mexico, which included the Aztecs, is related to the languages of the Shoshone, Comanche, and Hopi tribes in the United States. When Spaniards pushed north from the newly conquered central Mexico, they often followed ancient Native American trade routes and used Nahua people as guides.

Para pensar

You can find many Spanish names of cities, counties, and states in the United States. Work with a partner and write a list of at least ten places with Spanish names and then try to guess what they mean in English.

realidades.com GO

Mapa global interactivo

Reference Atlas

DIFFERENTIATED INSTRUCTION

Advanced Learners

Have students research Fray Junípero Serra on the Internet and report back to the class. Who was he? When did he live? What is his importance in the history of California?

Heritage Language Learners

Have students research the architecture in one of the following states: Texas, New Mexico, Arizona, or California. Have them look for architecture that shows a Spanish influence and write a report about it to present the class.

The French Quarter in New Orleans was named after the French who first settled here. In spite of its name, most of the buildings date to when Spain ruled Louisiana (1763–1803). Fires ravaged the area in 1788 and 1794, so when the rebuilding was done, the architectural style was Spanish. This can be seen in the landscaped patios and iron grillwork on balconies. Despite the destruction caused by Hurricane Katrina, the French Quarter remains.

A network of Spanish Catholic missions once extended throughout the Americas. Many cities in the southwestern United States, including San Francisco, San Diego, and Santa Fe, were originally built around Catholic missions, which in turn were often located at Native American villages or religious sites. The Mission San Xavier del Bac, in Arizona, combines the name of a Catholic saint (San Xavier) with the name of the Papago village where it was built (Bac, which means "where the water emerges"). Constructed in the early 1700s, the mission is still used by the Papago people and is considered one of the world's architectural treasures. ▼

Spain built the Castillo de San Marcos to protect both St. Augustine (Florida) and the sea routes for ships returning to Spain from enemy attacks. This fort was started in 1672 and took 23 years to build. When Spain sold Florida to the United States in 1821, the fort was renamed Fort Marion. The Castillo has been a National Monument since 1924.

Point out the picture of the Alamo on p. 192. Most students will have heard of it, but many may not know that it was built as a mission. Then note the photo of the mission on p. 193, and have students reread the paragraph. At one time a network of missions extended throughout the Americas. Cities often grew up around the missions (San Diego, Los Angeles, San Francisco). Some missions still exist and are open to visitors.

Have students read the *¿Sabes que...?* section. Discuss possible explanations about how these languages could be related.

Discuss the battle of the Alamo, in San Antonio. Point out its location on the map. Point out its proximity to Mexico and remind students that Texas was at that time part of Mexico. Mexico won the battle for the Alamo, but Texas won its independence soon thereafter.

Discuss the missions that extended throughout the Americas. Point out that the missionaries' goal was to convert the indigenous people to Christianity.

Direct attention to the *Para pensar* section and have students discuss the questions. **Answers** will vary.

ENRICH YOUR TEACHING

Teacher-to-Teacher

Have students work in groups to find the locations of the missions in California. Have them note the locations on a map and estimate the number of miles from one to the next. This mileage is the distance a rider on horseback could cover in a day.

21st Century Skills

Critical Thinking and Problem-Solving Have teams of students research the history of the Spanish missions in New Mexico, or other parts of the southwestern United States, focusing on the relations between the Native American population and the Spaniards. Have them consider questions such as: What were the goals of the missions? What changes did they bring into the region? Did any conflicts arise during the process? Why?

Review Activities

To talk about leisure activities and places: Have students work in pairs to quiz each other on the vocabulary. They can create flashcards, writing the Spanish word on one side of an index card and the English meaning on the other. Provide copies of the Clip Art for this purpose.

To ask and tell where, with whom, and when you go: Have students work in pairs to practice asking and answering questions about their leisure activities.

Portfolio

Invite students to review the activities they completed in this chapter, including written reports, posters or other visuals, recordings of oral presentations, or other projects. Have them select one or two items that they feel best demonstrate their achievements in Spanish to include in their portfolios. Have them include this with the Chapter Checklist and Self-Assessment Worksheet.

Additional Resources

Student Resources: Realidades para hispanohablantes, p. 148

Teacher Resources:

- Teacher's Resource Book: Situation Cards, p. 262, Clip Art, pp. 264–265
- Assessment Program: Chapter Checklist and Self-Assessment Worksheet, pp. T56–T57

Objectives

- Review the vocabulary and grammar
- Demonstrate you can perform the tasks on p. 195

Repaso del capítulo

Vocabulario y gramática

to talk about leisure activities

ir de compras	to go shopping
ver una película	to see a movie
la lección de piano	piano lesson (class)
Me quedo en casa.	I stay at home.

to talk about places

la biblioteca	library
el café	café
el campo	countryside
la casa	home, house
en casa	at home
el centro comercial	mall
el cine	movie theater
el gimnasio	gym
la iglesia	church
la mezquita	mosque
las montañas	mountains
el parque	park
la piscina	swimming pool
la playa	beach
el restaurante	restaurant
la sinagoga	synagogue
el templo	temple, Protestant church
el trabajo	work, job

to tell where you go

a	to *(prep.)*
a la, al *(a + el)*	to the
¿Adónde?	(To) Where?
a casa	(to) home

to tell with whom you go

¿Con quién?	With whom?
con mis / tus amigos	with my / your friends
solo, -a	alone

to talk about when things are done

¿Cuándo?	When?
después	afterwards
después (de)	after
los fines de semana	on weekends
los lunes, los martes . . .	on Mondays, on Tuesdays . . .
tiempo libre	free time

to talk about where someone is from

¿De dónde eres?	Where are you from?
de	from, of

to indicate how often

generalmente	generally

other useful words and expressions

¡No me digas!	You don't say!
para + *infinitive*	in order to + *infinitive*

ir *to go*

voy	**vamos**
vas	**vais**
va	**van**

For *Vocabulario adicional,* see pp. 472–473.

DIFFERENTIATED INSTRUCTION

Students with Learning Difficulties

Have students review the *Repaso del capítulo* and create flashcards for any words that they do not know. Pair them with a student who is more confident with the vocabulary to practice. Before the test, provide students with a practice test, so they can become comfortable with the format.

Heritage Language Learners

Have students write a few paragraphs telling about their perfect weekend: Where are they going to go? Whom are they going to invite to go with them? What are they going to do? Encourage them to use as many vocabulary words from this chapter as they can.

Más repaso GO realidades.com | print

	realidades.com	print
Instant Check	✔	
Puzzles	✔	
Core WB pp. 74–75		✔
Comm. WB pp. 265, 266–268	✔	✔

Preparación para el examen

On the exam you will be asked to . . .	Here are practice tasks similar to those you will find on the exam . . .	For review go to your print or digital textbook . . .
Interpretive		
 **1 Escuchar** Listen and understand as people ask questions about weekend events	Two friends are trying to make plans for the weekend. Based on their dialogue, what do they finally agree on? a) Who is going? b) Where are they going? c) When are they going?	**pp. 172–175** *Vocabulario en contexto* **p. 186** Actividad 17
Interpersonal		
 **2 Hablar** Talk about places to go and things to do on the weekend	Your parents want to know what you're doing this weekend. Mention at least three places you plan to go or things you plan to do. For example, you might say *Voy de compras con mis amigos.*	**pp. 172–175** *Vocabulario en contexto* **p. 177** Actividad 6 **p. 178** Actividad 8 **p. 181** Actividad 13 **p. 182** Actividad 14 **p. 186** Actividad 17
Interpretive		
 **3 Leer** Read about what a person does on particular days of the week	Someone has left his or her planner at your house. Read the schedule for two days to try to figure out what type of person owns it. Indicate whether you agree or disagree with the statements about the person. MARTES: 6:00 Desayuno 4:00 Lección de piano 5:00 Trabajo 8:30 Clase aeróbica JUEVES: 3:30 Gimnasio 4:30 Piscina 6:00 Trabajo 8:00 Biblioteca *¿Estás de acuerdo o no? a) Es muy perezoso(a); b) Es atlético(a); c) Le gusta ir de compras.*	**pp. 172–175** *Vocabulario en contexto* **p. 176** Actividad 4 **p. 180** Actividad 11 **pp. 188–189** *Lectura*
Presentational		
 **4 Escribir** Write a short note to a friend to let him or her know where you are going after school	Your friend is taking a make-up test after school, so you need to write her a short note to tell her what you are doing after school today. In the note, tell her where you are going and then at what time you are going home.	**p. 176** Actividad 4 **p. 179** Actividad 10 **p. 181** Actividad 13 **p. 182** Actividad 14 **p. 186** Actividad 18
Cultures • Comparisons		
5 Pensar Demonstrate an understanding of rhymes, songs, and games from Spanish-speaking cultures	Think about your favorite childhood game. How does it compare to the children's games you learned about in this chapter? Describe a traditional game from a Spanish-speaking country.	**p. 190** *La cultura en vivo*

DIFFERENTIATED ASSESSMENT

CORE ASSESSMENT
- **Assessment Program:** Examen del capítulo 4A, pp. 99–104
- **Audio Program DVD:** Cap. 4A, Track 17
- **ExamView:** Chapter Test, Test Banks A and B

ADVANCED/PRE-AP*
- **ExamView: Pre-AP* Test Bank**
- **Pre-AP* Resource Book,** pp. 74–77

STUDENTS NEEDING EXTRA HELP
- **Alternate Assessment Program:** Examen del capítulo 4A
- **Audio Program DVD:** Cap. 4A, Track 17

HERITAGE LEARNERS
- **Assessment Program: Realidades para hispanohablantes:** Examen del capítulo 4A
- **ExamView: Heritage Learner Test Bank**

Performance Tasks

Standards: 1.1, 1.2, 1.3, 4.2

Student Resource: Realidades para hispanohablantes, p. 149

Teacher Resources: Teacher's Resource Book: Audio Script, p. 255; Audio Program DVD: Cap. 4A, Track 16; Answer Keys: Student Edition, p. 55

1. Escuchar

Suggestions: Play the audio or read from the script until all students know the answers. Ask students to suggest answers to the questions.

Script:

—¿Adónde vas el fin de semana?
—El sábado me quedo en casa, pero el domingo voy al cine.
—¿A qué hora vas?
—A las nueve y media. Y tú, ¿qué haces el fin de semana?
—Yo también voy al cine el domingo.
—¿Por qué no vamos a las nueve y media?
—Yo prefiero ir a las siete.
—Bien… estoy de acuerdo. ¡A las siete!

Answers:
a) two boys b) to the movies c) Sunday at 7:00

2. Hablar

Suggestions: Allow individual study time in class. If students have difficulty with spontaneous conversation, have them write what they're going to say and practice until they can say it without consulting their notes.

Answers will vary.

3. Leer

Suggestions: Some students will understand this better if they transcribe it in planner form.

Answers: a) no b) sí c) no

4. Escribir

Suggestions: Have students try this activity without consulting the vocabulary list, notes, or completed activities.

Answers will vary.

5. Pensar

Suggestions: Have students reread *La cultura en vivo* if they need to.

Answers will vary.

4B ¿Quieres ir conmigo?

AT A GLANCE

Objectives
- **Listen to and read invitations and responses**
- **Discuss and write an invitation and an activity plan**
- **Exchange information while responding to an invitation**
- **Understand cultural differences regarding extracurricular activities**
- **Compare and contrast the careers of two athletes**

Vocabulary
- Sports and activities outside of school
- Telling time
- Extending, accepting, and declining invitations

Grammar
- ***Ir + a*** + infinitive
- The verb ***jugar***

Culture
- The Paralympics, p. 197
- ***fiestas,*** p. 205
- Sergio García and Paola Espinosa, pp. 212, 213
- Rebecca Lobo, p. 213
- Leisure activities, p. 214

Recycle ♻
- Telling time
- The verb ***estar***
- The verb ***ir***
- Infinitives

RESOURCES

	FOR THE STUDENT	ONLINE	DVD	PRINT	FOR THE TEACHER	ONLINE	PREEXP	DVD	PRINT
Plan					Interactive TE and Resources DVD	•		•	
					Teacher's Resource Book, pp. 284–314	•		•	•
					Pre-AP* Resource Book, 74–77	•		•	•
					Lesson Plans	•			•
					Mapa global interactivo	•			
Introducción PP. **196–197**									
Present	Student Edition, pp. 196–197	•	•	•	Interactive TE and Resources DVD	•		•	
	DK Reference Atlas	•	•		Teacher's Resource Book, pp. 284–285	•		•	•
	Hispanohablantes WB, pp. 150–151			•	Galería de fotos		•		
					Map Transparencies, 16–18, 20	•	•	•	
Vocabulario en contexto PP. **198–201**									
Present & Practice	Student Edition, pp. 198–201	•	•	•	Interactive TE and Resources DVD	•		•	
	Audio	•	•		Teacher's Resource Book, pp. 286–288, 290, 298–299	•		•	•
	Videohistoria	•	•		Vocabulary Clip Art	•	•	•	•
	Flashcards	•	•		Audio Program	•	•	•	
	Instant Check	•			Video Program: Videohistoria	•		•	
	Guided WB, pp. 133–142	•	•	•	Video Program Teacher's Guide: Cap. 4B	•		•	•
	Core WB, pp. 76–79	•	•	•	Vocabulary and Grammar Transparencies, 89–92	•	•	•	
	Comm. WB, pp. 79–81, 84	•	•	•	Answer Keys: Student Edition, p. 56	•	•	•	
	Hispanohablantes WB, pp. 152–153			•	TPR Stories, pp. 49–61	•		•	•
Assess and Remediate					Prueba 4B–1: Assessment Program, pp. 105–106	•		•	•
					Assessment Program para hispanohablantes, pp. 105–106	•		•	•

RESOURCES

	FOR THE STUDENT	ONLINE	DVD	PRINT	FOR THE TEACHER	ONLINE	PREEXP	DVD	PRINT
Vocabulario en uso PP. **202–205**									
Present & Practice	Student Edition, pp. 202–205	•	•	•	Interactive Whiteboard Vocabulary Activities	•		•	
	Instant Check	•			Interactive TE and Resources DVD	•		•	
	Comm. WB, p. 81	•	•	•	Teacher's Resource Book, pp. 287–288, 292–293	•		•	•
	Hispanohablantes WB, pp. 154–155			•	Communicative Pair Activities, pp. 292–293	•		•	•
	Communicative Pair Activities	•			Audio Program	•	•	•	
					Videomodelos	•		•	
					Map Transparencies, 12	•	•	•	
					Answer Keys: Student Edition, pp. 57–59	•	•	•	•
Assess and Remediate					Prueba 4B–2 with Study Plan	•			
					Prueba 4B–2: Assessment Program, pp. 107–108	•		•	•
					Assessment Program para hispanohablantes, pp. 107–108	•		•	•
Gramática PP. **206–211**									
Present & Practice	Student Edition, pp. 206–211	•	•	•	Interactive Whiteboard Grammar Activities	•		•	
	Instant Check	•			Interactive TE and Resources DVD	•		•	
	Animated Verbs	•			Teacher's Resource Book, pp. 288–291, 294–295, 297	•		•	•
	Tutorial Video: Grammar	•			Communicative Pair Activities, pp. 294–295	•		•	•
	Canción de hip hop	•			Audio Program	•	•	•	
	Guided WB, pp. 143–146	•	•	•	Videomodelos	•		•	
	Core WB, pp. 80–82	•	•	•	Video Program: GramActiva	•	•	•	
	Comm. WB, pp. 82–83, 85–86, 269	•	•	•	Vocabulary and Grammar Transparencies, 93–95	•	•	•	
	Hispanohablantes WB, pp. 156–161			•	Map Transparencies, 18	•	•	•	
	Communicative Pair Activities	•			Answer Keys: Student Edition, pp. 59–62	•	•	•	
Assess and Remediate					Pruebas 4B–3 and 4B–4 with Study Plans	•			
					Pruebas 4B–3, 4B–4: Assessment Program, pp. 109, 110	•		•	•
					Assessment Program para hispanohablantes, pp. 109, 110	•		•	•
¡Adelante! PP. **212–217**									
Application	Student Edition, pp. 212–217	•	•	•	Interactive TE and Resources DVD	•		•	
	Online Cultural Reading	•			Vocabulary and Grammar Transparencies, 2	•	•	•	
	Guided WB, pp. 147–148	•	•	•	Map Transparencies, 20	•	•	•	
	Comm. WB, pp. 87, 270	•	•	•	Answer Keys: Student Edition, p. 62	•	•	•	
	Hispanohablantes WB, pp. 162–167			•					
Repaso del capítulo PP. **218–219**									
Review	Student Edition, pp. 218–219	•	•	•	Interactive TE and Resources DVD	•		•	
	Online Puzzles and Games	•			Teacher's Resource Book, pp. 289, 296, 298–299	•		•	•
	Core WB, pp. 83–84	•	•	•	Audio Program	•	•	•	
	Comm. WB, pp. 271–274	•	•	•	Answer Keys: Student Edition, p. 62	•	•	•	
	Hispanohablantes WB, pp. 168–169			•					
	Instant Check	•							
Chapter Assessment									
Assess					Examen del capítulo 4B	•		•	•
					Assessment Program, pp. 111–117	•		•	•
					Alternate Assessment Program, pp. 40–45	•		•	•
					Assessment Program para hispanohablantes, pp. 111–117	•		•	•
					Audio Program, Cap. 4B, Examen	•		•	
					ExamView: Test Banks A and B questions only online	•		•	
					Heritage Learner Test Bank	•		•	
					Pre-AP* Test Bank	•		•	

REGULAR SCHEDULE (50 MINUTES)

DAY	Warm-up / Assess	Preview / Present / Practice / Communicate	Wrap-up / Homework Options
1	**Warm-up (10 min.)** • Return Examen del capítulo 4A	**Chapter Opener (5 min.)** • Objectives • Arte y cultura **Vocabulario en contexto (30 min.)** • Presentation: Vocabulario y gramática en contexto • Actividades 1, 2	**Wrap-up and Homework Options (5 min.)** • Practice Workbook 4B-1, 4B-2
2	**Warm-up (5 min.)** • Homework check	**Vocabulario en contexto (40 min.)** • Presentation: Videohistoria *¡A jugar!* • View: Videohistoria • Video Activities 1, 2, 3, 4 • Actividad 3	**Wrap-up and Homework Options (5 min.)** • Practice Workbook 4B-3, 4B-4 • Prueba 4B-1: Vocabulary recognition
3	**Warm-up (10 min.)** • Actividad 7 • Homework check ✔**Formative Assessment (10 min.)** • Prueba 4B-1: Vocabulary recognition	**Vocabulario en uso (25 min.)** • Interactive Whiteboard Vocabulary Activities • Actividades 4, 5, 6, 8, 9 • Audio Activities 5, 6	**Wrap-up and Homework Options (5 min.)** • Writing Activity 10 • Heritage Learner Workbook 4B-1, 4B-2
4	**Warm-up (10 min.)** • Actividad 12 • Homework check	**Gramática y vocabulario en uso (35 min.)** • Actividades 10, 11 • Exploración del lenguaje • Fondo cultural • Presentation: *ir* + *a* + infinitive • View: GramActiva video • Interactive Whiteboard Grammar Activities • Actividades 13, 14, 15	**Wrap-up and Homework Options (5 min.)** • Practice Workbook 4B-5, 4B-6 • Prueba 4B-2 with Study Plan: Vocabulary production
5	**Warm-up (10 min.)** • Communicative Pair Activity • Homework check ✔**Formative Assessment (10 min.)** • Prueba 4B-2 with Study Plan: Vocabulary production	**Gramática y vocabulario en uso (25 min.)** • Actividad 17 • Audio Activity 7 • Presentation: The verb *jugar* • View: GramActiva video • Interactive Whiteboard Grammar Activities • Actividades 18, 20	**Wrap-up and Homework Options (5 min.)** • Writing Activities 11, 12, 13 • Prueba 4B-3 with Study Plan: *ir* + *a* + infinitive
6	**Warm-up (10 min.)** • Actividad 16 • Homework check ✔**Formative Assessment (10 min.)** • Prueba 4B-3 with Study Plan: *ir* + *a* + infinitive	**Gramática y vocabulario en uso (25 min.)** • Actividad 19 • Audio Activities 8, 9 • Communicative Pair Activity • Pronunciación • El español en el mundo del trabajo	**Wrap-up and Homework Options (5 min.)** • Practice Workbook 4B-7 • Heritage Learner Workbook 4B-4, 4B-5 • Prueba 4B-4 with Study Plan: The verb *jugar*
7	**Warm-up (10 min.)** • Actividad 21 • Homework check ✔**Formative Assessment (10 min.)** • Prueba 4B-4 with Study Plan: The verb *jugar*	**Gramática y vocabulario en uso (5 min.)** • Actividad 22 **¡Adelante! (20 min.)** • Lectura • Fondo cultural	**Wrap-up and Homework Options (5 min.)** • ¿Comprendes?
8	**Warm-up (5 min.)** • Homework check	**¡Adelante! (30 min.)** • Perspectivas del mundo hispano • El mundo hispano • Presentación escrita: Steps 1, 5 **Repaso del capítulo (10 min.)** • Vocabulario y gramática	**Wrap-up and Homework Options (5 min.)** • Presentación escrita: Step 2 • Preparación para el examen 3, 4, 5
9	**Warm-up (5 min.)** • Homework check	**¡Adelante! (20 min.)** • Presentación escrita: Step 3 **Repaso del capítulo (20 min.)** • Preparación para el examen 1, 2	**Wrap-up and Homework Options (5 min.)** • Presentación escrita: Step 4 • Practice Workbook 4B-8, 4B-9 • Instant Check • Examen del capítulo 4B
10	**Warm-up (10 min.)** • Homework check ✔**Summative Assessment (40 min.)** • Examen del capítulo 4B		

BLOCK SCHEDULE (90 MINUTES)

DAY	Warm-up / Assess	Preview / Present / Practice / Communicate	Wrap-up / Homework Options
1	**Warm-up (10 min.)** • Return Examen del capítulo 4A	**Chapter Opener (5 min.)** • Objectives • Arte y cultura **Vocabulario en contexto (60 min.)** • Presentation: Vocabulario y gramática en contexto • Actividades 1, 2 • Presentation: Videohistoria *¡A jugar!* • View: Videohistoria • Video Activities 1, 2, 3, 4 • Actividad 3 **Vocabulario en uso (10 min.)** • Actividades 4, 5, 6	**Wrap-up and Homework Options (5 min.)** • Practice Workbook 4B-1, 4B-2, 4B-3, 4B-4 • Heritage Learner Workbook 4B-1, 4B-2 • Prueba 4B-1: Vocabulary recognition
2	**Warm-up (10 min.)** • Homework check **✓Formative Assessment (10 min.)** • Prueba 4B-1: Vocabulary recognition	**Vocabulario en uso (65 min.)** • Actividades 7, 8, 9, 10, 11, 12 • Fondo cultural • Audio Activities 5, 6 • Exploración del lenguaje • Communicative Pair Activity • Interactive Whiteboard Vocabulary Activities	**Wrap-up and Homework Options (5 min.)** • Writing Activity 10 • Prueba 4B-2 with Study Plan: Vocabulary production
3	**Warm-up (5 min.)** • Homework check **✓Formative Assessment (10 min.)** • Prueba 4B-2 with Study Plan: Vocabulary production	**Gramática y vocabulario en uso (70 min.)** • Presentation: *ir* + *a* + infinitive • View: GramActiva video • Actividades 13, 14, 15, 17 • Audio Activity 7 • Writing Activity 11 • Communicative Pair Activity • Presentation: The verb *jugar* • View: GramActiva video • Actividades 18, 19 • Audio Activities 8, 9 • Interactive Whiteboard Grammar Activities	**Wrap-up and Homework Options (5 min.)** • Practice Workbook 4B-5, 4B-6, 4B-7 • Heritage Learner Workbook 4B-4, 4B-5 • Writing Activities 12, 13 • Pruebas 4B-3, 4B-4 with Study Plans: *ir* + *a* + infinitive, The verb *jugar*
4	**Warm-up (15 min.)** • Actividades 16, 20 • Homework check **✓Formative Assessment (15 min.)** • Pruebas 4B-3, 4B-4 with Study Plans: *ir* + *a* + infinitive, The verb *jugar*	**Gramática y vocabulario en uso (20 min.)** • Pronunciación • El español en el mundo del trabajo • Actividades 21, 22 • Fondo cultural • Presentación escrita: Steps 1, 5 • Interactive Whiteboard Grammar Activities **¡Adelante! (35 min.)** • Lectura • ¿Comprendes?	**Wrap-up and Homework Options (5 min.)** • Presentación escrita: Step 2 • Lectura
5	**Warm-up (5 min.)** • Homework check	**¡Adelante! (45 min.)** • Presentación escrita: Step 3 • Perspectivas del mundo hispano • El mundo hispano **Repaso del capítulo (35 min.)** • Vocabulario y gramática • Preparación para el examen 1, 2, 3, 4, 5	**Wrap-up and Homework Options (5 min.)** • Presentación escrita: Step 4 • Practice Workbook 4B-8, 4B-9 • Instant Check • Examen del capítulo 4B
6	**Warm-up (15 min.)** • Homework check • Answer questions **Repaso del capítulo (25 min.)** • Situation Cards • Communicative Pair Activities **✓Summative Assessment (45 min.)** • Examen del capítulo 4B		**Wrap-up and Homework Options (5 min.)** • El mundo hispano

Standards for *Capítulo* 4B

- To achieve the goals of the Standards, students will:

Communication

1.1 Interpersonal
- Talk about: sports and pastimes; emotions and states of being; when certain events and activities occur; cellular phone usage; experiences of family immigration
- Extend, accept, or decline invitations

1.2 Interpretive
- Read and listen to information about sports and pastimes
- Listen to information about how people are feeling
- Read: a picture-based story; about emotions and states of being; an advertisement for a sports training school; an advertisement for a campground; about athletes Sergio García and Paola Espinosa
- Listen to and watch a video about sports and pastimes

1.3 Presentational
- Present information about: sports and pastimes; emotions and states of being; when certain activities occur; a sports training school; Sergio García and Paola Espinosa
- Write about cellular phone usage
- Present an account of an interview about immigration

Culture

2.1 Practices and Perspectives
- Talk about the festival, ***La Noche de los rábanos;*** how students traditionally engage in activities outside of school

2.2 Products and Perspectives
- Talk about the elaborate radish-sculpting of ***La Noche de los rábanos***

Connections

3.1 Cross-curricular
- Reinforce math and metric conversion skills
- Apply knowledge of geography and current events

3.2 Target Culture
- Read an advertisement for a sports training school

Comparisons

4.1 Language
- Talk about new vocabulary through the recognition of cognates; the use of ***ir*** in conjunction with ***a*** and an infinitive; the pronunciation of the letter ***d***
- Explain that words are borrowed across languages
- Compare the use of ***jugar*** idioms with English

4.2 Culture
- Compare: specialized, regional crafts and products; how students engage in activities outside of school

Communities

5.1 Beyond the School
- Consider local opportunities for Spanish-speakers in the health care professions
- Interview a Spanish-speaker about the immigrant experience

5.2 Lifelong Learner
- Read about athletes Sergio García and Paola Espinosa
- Explain the current influence of Spanish-speakers in areas like politics, music, poetry, and science

Capítulo

4B ¿Quieres ir conmigo?

Chapter Objectives

Communication

By the end of this chapter you will be able to:
- **Listen to and read invitations and responses**
- **Discuss and write an invitation and an activity plan**
- **Exchange information while responding to an invitation**

Culture

You will also be able to:
- **Understand cultural differences regarding extracurricular activities**
- **Compare and contrast the careers of two athletes**

You will demonstrate what you know and can do:
- **Presentación escrita, p. 215**
- **Preparación para el examen, p. 219**

You will use:

Vocabulary
- **Sports and activities outside of school**
- **Telling time**
- **Extending, accepting, and declining invitations**

Grammar
- ***Ir + a +* infinitive**
- **The verb *jugar***

Exploración del mundo hispano

Country Connection
After-school Activities

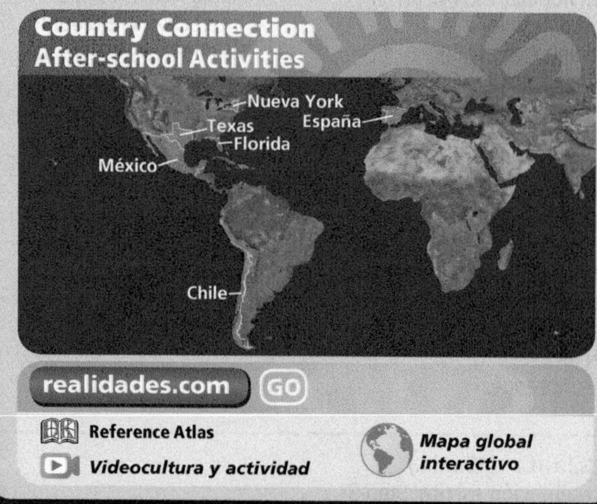

realidades.com GO

Reference Atlas
Videocultura y actividad
Mapa global interactivo

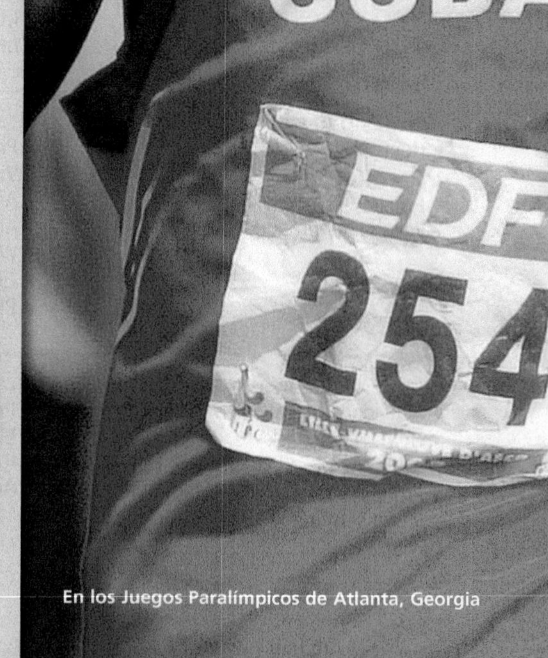

En los Juegos Paralímpicos de Atlanta, Georgia

196 ciento noventa y seis
Tema 4 • Los pasatiempos

ENRICH YOUR TEACHING

Using Backward Design

Have students preview the sample performance tasks on *Preparación para el examen,* p. 219, and connect them to the Chapter Objectives. Explain to students that by completing the sample tasks they can self-assess their learning progress.

Mapa global interactivo

Download the *Mapa global interactivo* files for Chapter 4B and preview the activities. Activity 1 takes you to Oaxaca, México. Activity 2 visits the coastal areas of Spain. In Activity 3, you visit Miami's Calle Ocho.

Arte y cultura | El mundo hispano

Paralympic Games Starting with the first Paralympic Games in Rome in 1960, the International Paralympics Committee has organized summer and winter games that follow the regular Olympic Games and are hosted by the same city. Athletes with all types of disabilities compete in the Paralympics. In the most recent Summer and Winter Paralympics, more than 150 nations participated, with over 4,200 athletes worldwide.

- How do you think athletes with disabilities benefit from competing in the Paralympics or in similar local events?

PresentationExpress™
See pp. 196a–196b

Chapter Opener

Core Instruction

Resources: Map Transparencies 12, 16–18, 20

Suggestions: As you go over the objectives of the chapter, point out that the video segments will introduce more leisure-time vocabulary. Introduce the theme of the chapter by asking students what they like to do in their free time. How many enjoy concerts? How many participate in sports or other outdoor activities? Brainstorm a list of activities.

Help students locate the cities, states, and countries featured in the chapter by using the map transparencies.

Videocultura View *Los pasatiempos* with the class to learn more about leisure time in Spanish-speaking countries.

Arte y cultura

Standards: 3.1

Suggestions: Emphasize that the Paralympic Games promote international competition and fellowship among athletes with disabilities. Ask students to name similar local competitions and the events in which those athletes compete.

Answers will vary.

DIFFERENTIATED INSTRUCTION

Digital resources such as the ***Interactive Whiteboard*** activity banks, ***Videomodelos***, additional ***Online Activities, Study Plans***, automatically graded ***Leveled Workbook***, animated ***Grammar Tutorials, Flashcards***, and ***Vocabulary and Grammar Videos*** will help you reach students of different ability levels and learning styles.

STUDENTS NEEDING EXTRA HELP

Guided Practice Activities
- Flashcards, pp. 133–138
- Vocabulary Check, pp. 139–142
- Reading Support, p. 147

HERITAGE LEARNERS

Realidades para hispanohablantes
- Chapter Opener, pp. 150–151
- A primera vista, p. 152
- Videohistoria, p. 153
- Manos a la obra, pp. 154–161
- ¡Adelante!, pp. 162–167
- Repaso del capítulo, pp. 168–169

ADVANCED/PRE-AP*

Pre-AP* Resource Book,
- pp. 74–77

Communications Workbook
- Integrated Performance Assessment, p. 271

Vocabulario en contexto

Core Instruction

Standards: 1.2, 4.1

Resources: Teacher's Resource Book: Input Script, p. 286, Clip Art, pp. 298–299, Audio Script, p. 287; Voc. and Gram. Transparencies 89–90; TPR Stories Book, pp. 49–61; Audio Program DVD: Cap. 4B, Tracks 1–2

Focus: Presenting vocabulary about non-school activities

Suggestions: Use the Input Script from the *Teacher's Resource Book* or the story in the *TPR Stories Book* to help present the new vocabulary and grammar. Or you can use the transparencies to present the new vocabulary and to talk about what activities you like to do. Ask such questions as: *¿Qué te gusta practicar más, el béisbol o el fútbol americano?* Continue the questions until students seem comfortable with the vocabulary. Have students look at the schedule, and point out that it uses the 24-hour clock, which is common in Spanish-speaking cultures. Ask students to recall this concept, and have them tell you what time 13:00 and 16:00 are.

Have students predict what is happening in the pictures on p.199. Ask volunteers to read the parts of Rosa and her friends. Then have students list words they recognize in the conversation.

BELLRINGER REVIEW

Review the 24-hour clock by writing these times on the board and asking students to tell you the times using the 12-hour clock: *14:45 16:30 18:15 23:10.*

Block Schedule

Have students create advertisements for a sports club or outdoor recreation facility. They should include a variety of activities, hours of operation, and contact information. Suggest that they illustrate the advertisements, then post them in the room to be used to guide further conversations.

Objectives

Read, listen to, and understand information about
- sports and activities outside of school
- extending and responding to invitations

Vocabulario en contexto

Parque de la Independencia

¿Te gustan los deportes? ¡Puedes practicar con uno de nuestros expertos! ¿Juegas bien o juegas mal? ¡No importa! Hay un deporte para ti.

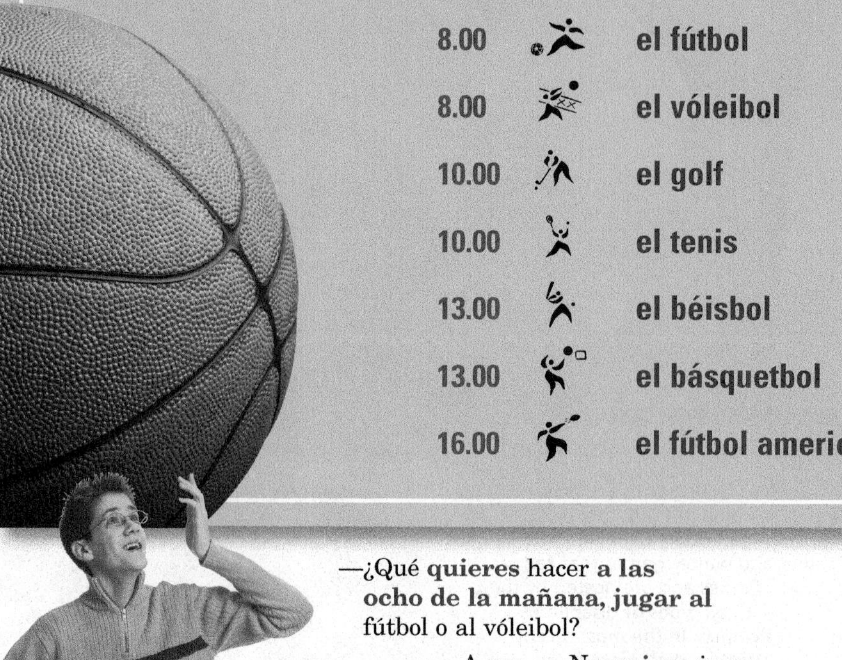

8.00	el fútbol
8.00	el vóleibol
10.00	el golf
10.00	el tenis
13.00	el béisbol
13.00	el básquetbol
16.00	el fútbol americano

—¿Qué **quieres** hacer a las **ocho de la mañana, jugar al** fútbol o al vóleibol?

—A ver . . . No **quiero** jugar al fútbol. **Juego** muy **mal.** Prefiero jugar al vóleibol. Necesito practicar más. ¿Y qué **te gustaría** hacer a las cuatro **esta tarde?**

—**Me gustaría** jugar al fútbol americano.

DIFFERENTIATED INSTRUCTION

Students with Special Needs

If students are unable to act out the vocabulary for *Actividad* 2 on p. 199, ask them to write each adjective on a sheet of paper or say it aloud.

Students with Learning Difficulties

Have students add new words to their vocabulary notebook section and accompany these words with pictures and English translations if needed. For *Actividad* 2, provide students with a few examples of what is expected of them.

el concierto

la fiesta

el baile

el partido

—¡Hola! ¡Soy Rosa! ¿Quieres hacer algo **conmigo este fin de semana?** Hay un concierto en el parque.

—**Lo siento,** pero no **puedo.** Estoy **demasiado ocupado** y tengo mucha tarea.

—No puedo porque **tengo que** trabajar. Trabajo **esta noche** a las siete y mañana trabajo **a la una de la tarde. Voy a estar** un poco **cansada. ¡Ay! ¡Qué pena!**

—¡Qué **triste!** No, no puedo ir **contigo.** Estoy **un poco enferma.**

ir de cámping

ir de pesca

—**¡Qué buena idea!** Pero no me gustan los conciertos. Prefiero ir de cámping. Siempre estoy muy **contenta** cuando voy de cámping. . . . **¿A qué hora?** ¿Mañana a las cinco de la tarde? **Entonces,** nos vemos.

1 ¡Deportemanía! 

Escuchar

Marcela is a sports fanatic! As she lists the days on which she will play the various sports, touch the picture of each sport.

2 ¿Cómo estás? 

Escuchar

You will hear how five people are feeling. Act out the adjectives that you hear.

Más práctica GO

	realidades.com	print
Instant Check	✔	
Guided WB pp. 133–138	✔	✔
Core WB pp. 76–77	✔	✔
Comm. WB p. 84	✔	✔
***Hispanohablantes* WB** p. 152		✔

Language Input 4B

1 Standards: 1.2

Resources: Teacher's Resource Book: Audio Script, p. 287; Audio Program DVD: Cap. 4B, Track 3; Answer Keys: Student Edition, p. 56

Focus: Listening for comprehension

Suggestions: Play the audio or read the script. Monitor to verify that students are correctly identifying the sports.

Script and Answers:

1. **El lunes tengo que practicar el golf. *(golf)***
2. **El martes hay un partido de básquetbol. *(basketball)***
3. **El miércoles juego al tenis con Lorenzo. *(tennis)***
4. **El jueves tengo que jugar al béisbol. *(baseball)***
5. **El viernes hay un partido de vóleibol. *(volleyball)***
6. **El sábado tengo que jugar al fútbol. *(soccer)***

2 Standards: 1.2

Resources: Teacher's Resource Book: Audio Script, p. 287; Audio Program DVD: Cap. 4B, Track 4; Answer Keys: Student Edition, p. 56

Focus: Listening for comprehension

Suggestions: First agree on the body language to represent the different feelings. In a large class, you may wish to have volunteers act out the words, and ask the rest of the class whether or not they agree with what they see.

Script and Answers:

1. **¡Uf! Estoy muy cansada. *(tired)***
2. **Lo siento pero estoy muy mal, muy enfermo. *(sick)***
3. **No tengo tarea esta noche. Estoy muy contenta. *(happy)***
4. **¿La señora Sánchez no enseña la clase de español? Estoy triste. *(sad)***
5. **Tengo mucho que hacer. Estoy ocupado. *(busy)***

Extension: Give students three situations using known vocabulary, such as *Tengo que estudiar* or *No hay clases.* Ask them to give you at least one adjective to describe how they might feel in each situation.

ENRICH YOUR TEACHING

Culture Note

The musical sounds of Latin America have a variety of origins, most linked to regional history. Instruments include panpipes, steel drum, marimba, maracas, and ***guitarrón.*** Ask students to list some singers who have a distinct Latin American sound.

21st Century Skills

Technology Literacy Have students create a monthly calendar for the class Web site showing all activities that class members might be interested in. Have them use the calendar to promote a class discussion of any activities in which the class might want to participate.

Videohistoria

Core Instruction

Standards: 1.2

Resources: Voc. and Gram. Transparencies 91–92; Audio Program DVD: Cap. 4B, Track 5

Focus: Extending the presentation of contextualized vocabulary and grammar; previewing the language video

Suggestions:

Pre-reading: Direct students' attention to the *Strategy.* Have students identify the questions they think are invitations. Then have students close their books. Using the transparencies, go panel by panel and ask students who seems to be doing the inviting, who is accepting, and what they think will happen next.

Reading: Read the captions with students, using the transparencies and pantomime to help them understand the new words in blue type. Have students repeat some of the expressions, such as ***¡Oye! ¡Genial!*** and ***¡Por supuesto!*** Ask students to try to determine the meanings of the expressions, based on context clues.

Post-reading: Complete *Actividad* 3 to check comprehension.

Video

Core Instruction

Standards: 1.2

Resources: Teacher's Resource Book: Video Script, p. 290; Video Program: Cap. 4B; Video Program Teacher's Guide: Cap. 4B

Focus: Viewing and understanding the language input video

Suggestions:

Pre-viewing: Remind students that they do not need to get every word in order to understand what is happening. Remind them that body language and gestures can aid in comprehension. Show them a short clip of the video with the volume muted. Discuss how the characters' body language helps express their feelings.

Viewing: Show the video without pausing. Show it again, stopping along the way to verify new vocabulary and to check general understanding.

Post-viewing: Complete the video activities in the *Communication Workbook.*

¡A jugar!

Ignacio, Javier, Ana y Elena están en el Parque del Retiro en Madrid. ¿Qué van a jugar y hacer? ¿De qué hablan? Lee la historia.

Strategy

Looking to find key questions
Before you read the story, skim to find where the characters are asking questions. The answers may point to important information in the story.

- Look at the questions. Which characters are offering invitations? What do you think they will do?

Hoy es sábado y hace buen tiempo. Ignacio, Javier, Ana y Elena están en el parque para jugar al fútbol.

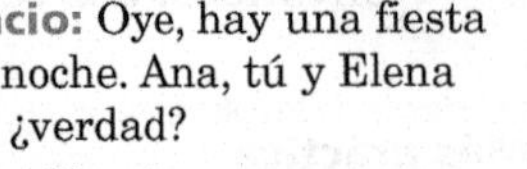

Ignacio: Oye, hay una fiesta esta noche. Ana, tú y Elena vais, ¿verdad?
Ana: ¡Claro!
Ignacio: Javier, ¿quieres ir con nosotros a la fiesta?
Elena: ¡Qué buena idea!

Javier: ¿A qué hora es la fiesta?
Ana: A las nueve **de la noche.** En la escuela.

Javier: ¿Tengo que bailar?
Ana: Pues, sí. Puedes bailar conmigo y con Elena.
Javier: No **sé** bailar muy bien.
Ana: ¡Vamos, Javier!
Javier: Bien, voy.

DIFFERENTIATED INSTRUCTION

Heritage Language Learners

Have students write three sentences about their favorite sport, including teams and athletes that they follow. Collect the first draft of their sentences, and correct any spelling and grammar mistakes.

Multiple Intelligences

Verbal/Linguistic: Ask students to write a few short lines of dialogue to change the ending of the *Videohistoria*. In the new ending, Javier should not accept the invitation to the party, and he should give two or three reasons why he will not go.

Language Input 4B

Ignacio: ¡Oye, Javier! ¡Sabes jugar muy bien al fútbol!

Javier: Y tú también . . . Pero necesito practicar más. Ana, ¿quieres jugar?

Ana: ¡Por supuesto! Vamos a jugar.

Elena: Estoy demasiado cansada y tengo sed. ¿Por qué no tomamos un refresco?

Ignacio: ¡Genial! Yo también estoy un poco cansado.

Ana: ¿Juegas al vóleibol esta tarde?

Elena: Sí, a las seis.

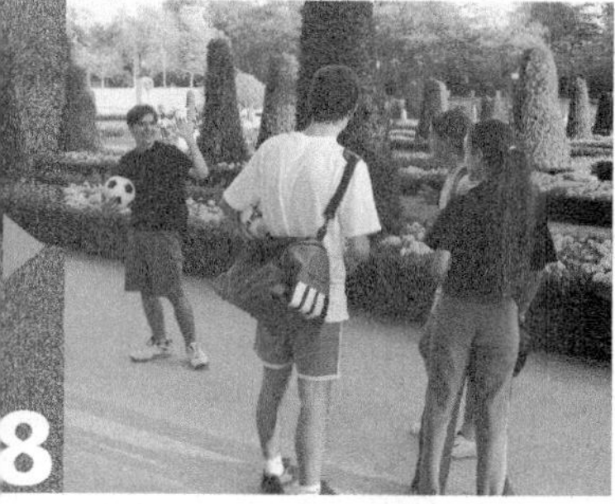

Javier: Hasta las nueve, entonces.

Ignacio: ¡Genial! Hasta más tarde.

3 ¿Comprendes?

Escribir • Hablar

¿Quién habla: Ana, Elena, Ignacio o Javier?

1. No sé bailar bien.
2. Necesito practicar más.
3. Necesito beber algo después de jugar al fútbol.
4. Juego al vóleibol a las seis.
5. Voy a la fiesta a las nueve.
6. Estoy cansado.

Más práctica GO

realidades.com | print

	realidades.com	print
Instant Check	✔	
Guided WB pp. 139–142	✔	✔
Core WB pp. 78–79	✔	✔
Comm. WB pp. 79–80, 81	✔	✔
Hispanohablantes WB p. 153		✔

3 Standards: 1.2, 1.3

Resources: Answer Keys: Student Edition, p. 56

Focus: Reading for comprehension

Suggestions: When reviewing the answers, have students give the number of the panel and read the sentence that supports each one. Have students read the answers as if they were the person. For example, *No sé bailar bien. Soy Javier.*

Answers:

1. Javier
2. Javier
3. Elena
4. Elena
5. Ana
6. Ignacio

Pre-AP* Support

- **Learning Objective:** Presentational Writing and Speaking
- **Activity:** As a post-viewing activity, have groups of students rewrite the fifth and sixth frames of the story, replacing the invitation to the party with another activity, along with its place and time. Then, have volunteers act out their new version of the scene. You may want to record the new scene to share with other classes.
- ***Pre-AP* Resource Book:*** Comprehensive guide to Pre-AP* vocabulary skill development, pp. 51–57

Teacher-to-Teacher

Call attention to the word ***vais*** on panel 5 of the video. Remind students that ***vais*** is the informal way to say "you go" or "you are going" when referring to more than one person. This plural informal verb form is used much more often in Spain than in other Spanish-speaking countries, where ***ustedes van*** would most likely be used instead. Since the video story takes place in Madrid, it is natural for the characters to use ***vais***.

Additional Resources

- Communication Wbk.: Audio Act. 5, p. 81
- Teacher's Resource Book: Audio Script, p. 288
- Audio Program DVD: Cap. 4B, Track 7

ENRICH YOUR TEACHING

Culture Note

In the United States, when young people get together, they frequently go to a friend's house to watch TV or play video games. In Spanish-speaking countries, however, young people usually gather in a ***plaza, café,*** or a park. They talk, listen to music, have a snack, or enjoy an informal game of soccer.

21st Century Skills

Social and Cross Cultural Skills After viewing the video, have students make a list of all the activities mentioned by the young people. Working in small groups, have students discuss any differences and similarities between their own after-school activities and those represented in the *Videohistoria*. Which ones would they participate in and enjoy? Which they would definitely not want to do? Why?

ASSESSMENT

Quiz: Vocabulary Recognition

- Prueba 4B-1: pp. 105–106

INTERACTIVE WHITEBOARD
Vocabulary Activities 4B

4 Standards: 1.1

Resources: Answer Keys: Student Edition, p. 57

Focus: Expressing what you would and wouldn't like to do

Suggestions: Emphasize that students will be using ***Me gustaría*** ("I *would* like") as opposed to ***Me gusta*** ("I like").

Answers will vary but should include:

(No) me gustaría ...
1. **ir a un concierto.**
2. **ir al baile.**
3. **ir al partido.**
4. **ir de cámping.**
5. **ir de pesca.**

5 Standards: 1.1, 1.2

Resources: Answer Keys: Student Edition, p. 57

Focus: Communicating about sports

Suggestions: Tell students that they will need this information for *Actividad* 6.

Answers will vary but should include:

Sé / No sé jugar al...
1. **básquetbol.**
2. **fútbol americano.**
3. **vóleibol.**
4. **tenis.**
5. **golf.**
6. **fútbol**

6 Standards: 1.1

Focus: Using new vocabulary in personal contexts and conversations

Suggestions: Have students move around the room and interact with several different classmates.

Answers will vary.

Block Schedule

Have students in small groups dramatize going to a sports event. They should decide what event they will go to, who will go with them, and when they will go.

Vocabulario en uso

Objectives
- Write and talk about activities you would like to do, and sports you know how to play
- Listen to invitations and responses
- Discuss what activities you and others will do and at what time
- Exchange information while extending, accepting, and declining invitations

4 Me gustaría ir . . .

Hablar

Say whether or not you would like to do these things this weekend.

Modelo
Me gustaría ir a una fiesta este fin de semana.
o: *No me gustaría ir a una fiesta este fin de semana.*

1. 
2. 
3.
4. 
5. 

5 No sé jugar . . .

Escribir • Hablar

Indica si sabes o no sabes jugar estos deportes.

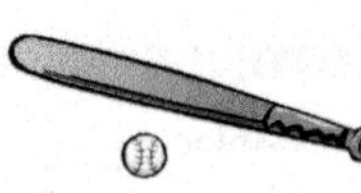

Modelo
Sé jugar al béisbol muy bien.
o: *No sé jugar al béisbol.*

1.
2. 
3.
4.
5.
6. 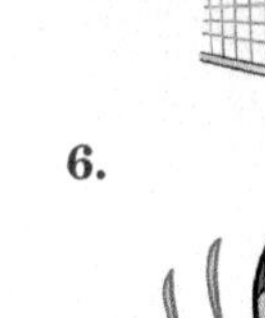

6 ¿Qué deportes practicas?

Hablar

Using the information from Actividad 5, ask and tell about which sports you know, or don't know, how to play.

Modelo
A —*¿Sabes jugar al béisbol?*
B —*¡Por supuesto! Sé jugar al béisbol muy bien.*
o:—*No, no sé jugar al béisbol.*

DIFFERENTIATED INSTRUCTION

Advanced Learners

Ask students to use the Internet to research a well-known athlete of Spanish-speaking origin. Have them present a short profile of the athlete, including which sports he or she plays, his or her statistics, and what team he or she plays for, if appropriate.

Students with Learning Difficulties

Actividad 9 requires students to listen, process, and write at the same time, which can be challenging. You may want to divide this into two separate tasks: first listening for the event, then listening for the response.

7 ¿Cómo estás?

Leer • Escribir

You've asked your friends how they are. Now read each friend's reply and write the correct form of the missing word from the list.

cansado, -a	contento, -a
enfermo, -a	mal
ocupado, -a	triste

Tú: ¿Cómo estás?

Felipe: Muy __1.__. Voy a un concierto esta noche con mis amigos.

Miguel: ¡ __2.__! Mi clase de ciencias es muy aburrida y no me gusta nada el profesor.

Marta: Estoy __3.__. Me duele la cabeza. Hoy no puedo jugar al tenis ni patinar.

Carlos: Estoy __4.__. Todos mis amigos van a la playa el sábado pero tengo que trabajar.

Gabriela: Un poco __5.__. Todas las noches trabajo en el centro comercial.

Dolores: Demasiado __6.__. Juego al básquetbol después de las clases, tomo lecciones de piano y practico cada día y tengo un trabajo también.

8 Lo siento

Hablar

Ask your partner if he or she wants to do these activities with you. Your partner can't go, and will offer excuses to explain why.

Modelo

A —*¡Oye! ¿Quieres patinar conmigo esta tarde?*
B —*Lo siento. Hoy no puedo. Estoy demasiado enfermo(a).*

Estudiante A

Estudiante B

muy	ocupado, -a
demasiado	enfermo, -a
un poco	cansado, -a
	triste
	mal

¡Respuesta personal!

9 Escucha y escribe

Escuchar • Escribir

You will hear three invitations to events and the responses given. On a sheet of paper, write the numbers 1–3. As you listen, write down what each invitation is for and whether the person accepted it (write *sí*) or turned it down (write *no*).

Practice and Communicate 4B

7 Standards: 1.2, 1.3

Resources: Answer Keys: Student Edition, p. 57

Focus: Reading for comprehension; using contextualized vocabulary

Suggestions: Have students read the entire dialogue before answering.

Answers:

1. contento
2. mal
3. enferma
4. triste
5. cansada
6. ocupada

8 Standards: 1.1

Resources: Answer Keys: Student Edition, p. 57

Focus: Using personalized vocabulary to extend and decline invitations

Recycle: The body; school subjects

Suggestions: Be sure students can think of an excuse for why they can't do each activity.

Answers will vary but should include:

1. ir de pesca
2. jugar al básquetbol
3. ir de compras
4. montar en bicicleta
5. jugar al fútbol

9 Standards: 1.2

Resources: Teacher's Resource Book: Audio Script, p. 287; Audio Program DVD: Cap. 4B, Track 6; Answer Keys: Student Edition, p. 58

Focus: Listening for comprehension

Suggestions: Before the activity, remind students to listen for intonations that indicate a positive or negative reaction.

Script and Answers:

1. —¿Puedes ir conmigo al baile esta noche? *(ir al baile)*
   —¡Qué pena! Tengo que trabajar. *(no)*
2. —¿Te gustaría ir conmigo al partido esta tarde? *(ir al partido)*
   —¡Qué buena idea! Me gustaría mucho. *(sí)*
3. —Voy a jugar al golf el domingo. ¿Quieres jugar? *(jugar al golf)*
   —¿Contigo? ¡Genial! *(sí)*

ENRICH YOUR TEACHING

Culture Note

If you are invited to a party, a dinner, or other event in a Spanish-speaking country and you cannot accept the invitation, it is usually best to offer an explanation. Just saying *Lo siento. Ya tengo planes.* ("I'm sorry. I already have plans."), may be seen as rude. It is also customary to bring the host or hostess a gift.

Teacher-to-Teacher

Using transparencies or photos of activities, have students write three sentences saying why they cannot do certain things. Tell them to make their excuses logical or illogical. For example, students may say *No puedo montar en monopatín. Estoy demasiado contenta.* Then have the class decide whether or not the excuse makes sense.

10 Standards: 1.1

Resources: Answer Keys: Student Edition, p. 58
Focus: Expressing the time of an event
Recycle: Telling time
Suggestions: Review the vocabulary. Go over the *Nota*, reminding students to refer to it as they do the activity. Review the *Modelo* to reinforce the structure.
Answers:

1. —¿A qué hora es el concierto?
   —A las nueve de la noche.
2. —¿A qué hora es la fiesta?
   —A las dos y media de la tarde.
3. —¿A qué hora es el partido?
   —A la una y media de la tarde.
4. —¿A qué hora es el baile?
   —A las ocho y media de la noche.
5. —¿A qué hora es la cena?
   —A las siete y media de la noche.
6. —¿A qué hora es el desayuno?
   —A las siete de la mañana.

Common Errors: Students may say *¿Qué hora?* instead of *¿A qué hora?* and **en la mañana** instead of **de la mañana.**

11 Standards: 1.1

Resources: Answer Keys: Student Edition, p. 59
Focus: Using contextualized vocabulary in conversation
Recycle: *ir;* place names
Suggestions: Review the responses, making sure students know how to accept and decline an invitation.
Answers:

1. ir al baile; A las siete y media de la noche.
2. ir a la fiesta; A las ocho y media de la noche.
3. ir al cine; A las cinco y media de la tarde.
4. ir a la piscina; A la una de la tarde.
5. ir al partido de fútbol; A las cuatro y cuarto de la tarde.
6. ir de compras (ir al centro comercial); A las once de la mañana.

Theme Project

Students can perform Step 4 at this point. (For more information, see p. 170-b.)

Pre-AP* Support

- **Learning Objective:** Interpersonal Writing
- **Activity 10:** Have pairs of students select one of the activities pictured, and draft an enthusiastic e-mail inviting their partner to attend. The partner will reply, apologizing for not being able to go.
- ***Pre-AP* Resource Book:*** Comprehensive guide to Pre-AP* communication skill development, pp. 10–57

10 ¿A qué hora? 

Hablar

Take turns asking and telling what time the following activities take place.

8:00

Modelo
A —*¿A qué hora es la película?*
B —*A las ocho de la noche.*

1. 9:00
2. 2:30
3.  1:30
4. 8:30
5. 7:30
6. 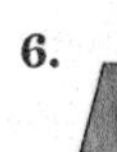   7:00

11 Una invitación para el sábado

Hablar

Invite your partner to these places, and tell at what time you will go. Your partner will accept or decline. Follow the model.

Modelo
A —*¿Te gustaría ir al concierto el sábado?*
B —*¿A qué hora?*
A —*A la una y media de la tarde.*
B —*¡Genial! ¡Nos vemos el sábado!*

1:30

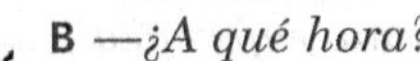

Nota

To ask and tell what time something happens, you say:
- **¿A qué hora** vas?
- Voy **a la** una.
- Voy **a las** tres y media.

To specify what part of the day, add:
de la mañana* *in the morning (A.M.)*
de la tarde *in the afternoon (P.M.)*
de la noche *in the evening, at night (P.M.)*

**Mañana* means "tomorrow"; *la mañana* means "morning."

Estudiante A

1. 7:30
2. 8:30
3. 5:30
4. 1:00
5. 4:15
6. 11:00

Estudiante B

¡Por supuesto! Me gustaría mucho.
Lo siento, pero no puedo.
¡Ay! ¡Qué pena! Tengo que trabajar.
¡Genial! Nos vemos el sábado.
¡Qué buena idea! ¡Gracias!
¡Respuesta personal!

DIFFERENTIATED INSTRUCTION

Multiple Intelligences

Visual/Spatial: Have students draw a three-panel cartoon. In their cartoon, they should write a dialogue in which one character invites the other(s) to do something. There should be a response, and then a comment or conclusion. Ask students to post their cartoons or to present them to the class.

Heritage Language Learners

Refer students to the *Exploración del lenguaje* at the top of p. 205. Ask students to identify additional Spanish words and expressions that are borrowed from English.

Exploración del lenguaje

Spanish words borrowed from English

Languages often borrow words from one another. For example, "rodeo" and "patio" are Spanish words that have found their way into English. There are also many examples of English words that have entered Spanish. By recognizing these familiar words, you can increase your vocabulary in Spanish.

Try it out! Read the sentences and identify the "borrowed words." Don't forget to pronounce the words correctly in Spanish.

Quiero hacer videos.
¿Quieres jugar al básquetbol conmigo?
Practico el rugby y el ráquetbol.
Juego al fútbol en el cámping.
¡Me encantan los sándwiches!

12 Y tú, ¿qué dices? | 

Escribir • Hablar

1. ¿A qué hora te gusta ir al cine?
2. ¿Estás más contento(a) cuando practicas un deporte o cuando ves la televisión?
3. ¿Qué deportes te gustan más?
4. ¿Este fin de semana tienes que trabajar o puedes pasar tiempo con amigos?

Fondo Cultural | México

La Noche de los Rábanos is just one of the many kinds of *fiestas* in the Spanish-speaking world. On the evening of December 23, people set up booths around the *zócalo* (town square) of Oaxaca, Mexico, to display and sell radishes *(los rábanos)* sculpted into a fantastic array of shapes. *Oaxaqueños* and visitors alike crowd the square to view the amazing creations.

- Do you know communities or regions in the United States that are known for particular crafts or products?

Rábanos esculpidos *(sculpted)*, Oaxaca, México

ENRICH YOUR TEACHING

Culture Note

A wide range of handicrafts is produced in Oaxaca, including black pottery, glass pottery, weavings, and brightly colored woodcarvings of small animals (***alebrijes***). Artisans bring their wares to the ***zócalos*** to sell. Artisans pass their knowledge from one generation to another.

21st Century Skills

Creativity and Innovation Have students work in small groups, divided into teams. Each team has to come up with five words in English borrowed from Spanish. Taking turns, a volunteer will go over to the opposite team, look at one of the words in their list, and mime it for his or her other team members to guess. Set a time limit for guessing, and assist students by verifying their loanword choices.

Practice and Communicate 4B

Exploración del lenguaje
Core Instruction

Standards: 4.1

Focus: Identifying examples of borrowed words

Suggestions: Review *Try it out!* with students. For further practice, have them work with a partner to scan the glossary for additional borrowed words.

12 Standards: 1.1, 1.3

Focus: Using vocabulary in a personalized context

Suggestions: Encourage students to be as detailed as possible in their answers.

Answers will vary.

Extension: Have students create one additional question to ask their classmates. Then, as a class, ask volunteers to read their questions and select students to answer them.

Fondo cultural

Standards: 2.1, 2.2, 4.2

Resources: Map Transparency 12

Suggestions: Locate Oaxaca on the map transparency. Ask students if they have seen foods carved into shapes. When is this done, and why? How does this practice in the United States differ from what is done with the ***rábanos*** in Oaxaca?

Mapa global interactivo, Actividad 1 Explore the geography of Oaxaca, México.

Additional Resources

- Communication Wbk.: Audio Act. 6, p. 81
- Teacher's Resource Book: Audio Script, p. 288, Communicative Pair Activity BLM, pp. 292–293
- Audio Program DVD: Cap. 4B, Track 8

ASSESSMENT

Pueba 4B-2 with Study Plan (online only)

Quiz: Vocabulary Production
- Prueba 4B-2: pp. 107–108

Gramática

Core Instruction

Standards: 4.1

Resources: Voc. and Gram. Transparency 95; Teacher's Resource Book: Video Script, p. 290; Video Program: Cap. 4B

INTERACTIVE WHITEBOARD
Grammar Activities 4B

Suggestions: Emphasize that the second verb is always in the infinitive and that only the forms of *ir* change. Play the *GramActiva* Video and/or use the transparency as an introduction or to reinforce your own presentation.

13 Standards: 1.2, 1.3

Resources: Teacher's Resource Book: Audio Script, p. 288; Audio Program DVD: Cap. 4B, Track 9; Answer Keys: Student Edition, p. 59

Focus: Listening for comprehension

Suggestions: Use the audio or read the script aloud. Have students first listen to the messages without taking notes.

Script and Answers:

¡Hola! Soy Rosario. ¿Qué pasa? Tomás y yo vamos a patinar esta tarde. ¿Te gustaría ir con nosotros? Vamos a estar en el parque a las cuatro. Hasta luego. *(Rosario: 1. al parque; 2. patinar; 3. a las cuatro)*

¡Oye! ¿Cómo estás? Soy Pablo. ¿Puedes ir al gimnasio conmigo? No tengo que trabajar hoy. Muchos estudiantes van a jugar al vóleibol a las siete. Háblame por teléfono si puedes ir. *(Pablo: 1. al gimnasio; 2. jugar al vóleibol; 3. a las siete)*

14 Standards: 1.3

Resources: Answer Keys: Student Edition, p. 60

Focus: Writing and saying what people are going to do

Recycle: Telling time

Answers:

1. **Angélica va a trabajar a las tres y media de la tarde.**
2. **Yo voy a jugar al vóleibol a las cuatro de la tarde.**
3. **Esteban y un amigo van a jugar al fútbol a las diez de la mañana.**
4. **Angélica y el Sr. Ríos van a ir de pesca a las siete de la mañana.**
5. **Los señores Ríos van a ir de compras a las siete y media de la noche.**
6. **Angélica, Esteban y yo vamos a ir al cine a las ocho de la noche.**

Gramática

Objectives

- Listen to phone messages about invitations
- Write about and discuss plans
- Read an ad and extend an invitation by phone

Ir + *a* + infinitive

Just as you use "going" + an infinitive in English to say what you are going to do, in Spanish you use a form of the verb ***ir* + *a* + an infinitive** to express the same thing:

Voy a jugar al tenis hoy.
I'm going to play tennis today.

¿Tú vas a jugar al golf esta tarde?
Are you going to play golf this afternoon?

Mis amigas van a ir de cámping mañana.
My friends are going camping tomorrow.

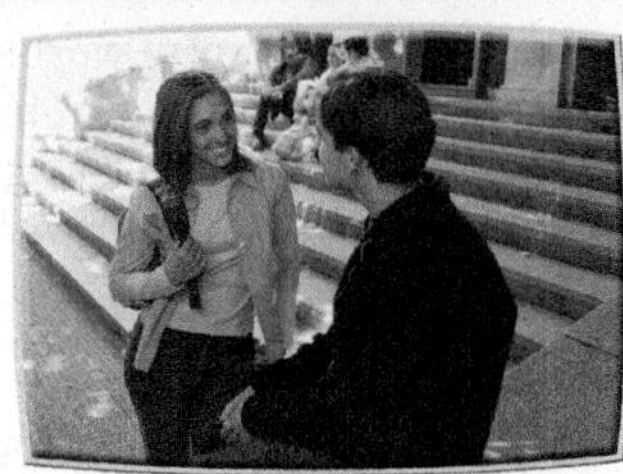

Javier: ¿**Van a jugar** conmigo, o no?
Ana: Sí, **vamos a jugar** contigo.

Más ayuda realidades.com

GramActiva Video Tutorials: Future with *ir* + *a* + infinitive, *Vamos a* + infinitive

Canción de hip hop: *¿Qué vas a hacer?*

***GramActiva* Activity**

13 Escucha y escribe

Escuchar • Escribir

Rosario and Pablo have left messages on your answering machine telling you what they are going to do and inviting you to join them. On a sheet of paper, write their names and, under each one, the numbers 1–3. As you listen to each message, write down information to answer these three questions:

1. ¿Adónde quiere ir? **2.** ¿Qué va a hacer? **3.** ¿A qué hora va a ir?

14 Este fin de semana vamos a . . .

Escribir • Hablar

¿Qué va a hacer la familia Ríos este fin de semana?

Modelo

Esteban /  / **8:00** *Esteban va a estudiar a las ocho de la noche.*

1. Angélica / 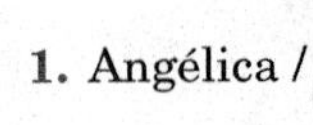 / **3:30** 

2. Yo /  / **4:00**

3. Esteban y un amigo /  / **10:00** 

4. Angélica y el Sr. Ríos /  / **7:00**

5. Los señores Ríos /  / **7:30**

6. Angélica, Esteban y yo /  / **8:00**

DIFFERENTIATED INSTRUCTION

Advanced Learners/Pre-AP*

Have students create a mini-journal in which they tell what they are going to do each day of the week after school. Have them include the phrases ***de la mañana, de la tarde,*** and ***de la noche.*** Suggest that they include details such as with whom they will do the activities, where they will go, and why they plan to do them.

Students with Learning Difficulties

You may want to provide a chart similar to the one in *Actividad* 15 to help students organize information for *Actividad* 13. Across the top, use the headings *Rosario* and *Pablo*. Down the side use the headings ***¿Adónde?, ¿Qué?,*** and ***¿A qué hora?***

15 ¿Qué vas a hacer? |  |

Escribir • Hablar

1. Make a chart like this one to describe five things you're going to do, when you're going to do them, and with whom. Use the following words to say when you're going to do these things: *esta tarde, esta noche, mañana, el jueves, el fin de semana.*

Modelo

¿Qué?	¿Cuándo?	¿Con quién?
tocar la guitarra	esta tarde	mis amigos

2. Ask your partner what his or her plans are.

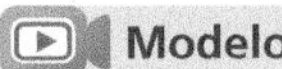

Modelo

A —*¿Qué vas a hacer esta tarde?*
B —*Esta tarde mis amigos y yo vamos a tocar la guitarra.*

Mañana voy a tocar la guitarra.

16 El teléfono celular |

Leer • Escribir • Hablar

Lee el anuncio para el teléfono celular y contesta las preguntas.

1. ¿Por qué es bueno tener un teléfono celular?
2. ¿Te gusta hablar por teléfono celular? ¿Con quién?
3. ¿Crees que es bueno o malo usar un teléfono celular en un restaurante? ¿Por qué?

17 ¿Quieres ir conmigo? |  |

Hablar

Pretending to use a cell phone, greet a partner and invite him or her to do something with you. Your partner can't go and should tell you why.

Modelo

A —*Hola, Sara. Soy Rosa. ¿Quieres jugar al tenis conmigo esta tarde?*
B —*Lo siento, hoy no puedo. Voy a estudiar para la clase de inglés.*
A —*¡Ay! ¡Qué pena!*

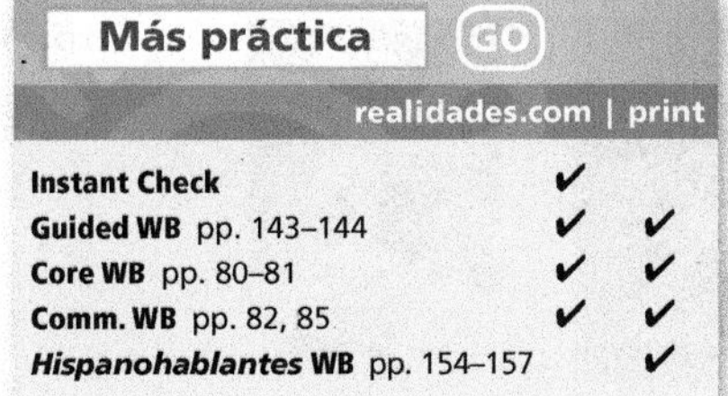

Más práctica GO

realidades.com | print		
Instant Check	✔	
Guided WB pp. 143–144	✔	✔
Core WB pp. 80–81	✔	✔
Comm. WB pp. 82, 85	✔	✔
***Hispanohablantes* WB** pp. 154–157		✔

Practice and Communicate 4B

15 Standards: 1.1, 1.3

Resources: Teacher's Resource Book: GramActiva BLM, p. 297

Focus: Using new vocabulary

Suggestions: Brainstorm a few activities to aid student recall.

Answers will vary.

16 Standards: 1.1, 1.2, 1.3

Resources: Voc. and Gram. Transparency 95; Answer Keys: Student Edition, p. 60

Focus: Reading for comprehension and writing with accuracy

Suggestions: Form groups of students with varying abilities to interpret the ad. Discuss the questions as a class.

Answers:

1. **¡Con un teléfono celular puedes hacer planes para hacerlo todo!**
2. **Answers will vary.**
3. **Answers will vary.**

17 Standards: 1.1

Focus: Having a telephone conversation

Suggestions: You may want students to prepare two conversations, so that they get a chance both to extend and decline an invitation. Each pair can choose one conversation to present aloud to the class. Encourage them to present it without a script.

Answers will vary.

Additional Resources

- Communication Wbk.: Audio Act. 7, p. 82
- Teacher's Resource Book: Audio Script, p. 288
- Audio Program DVD: Cap. 4B, Track 10

ENRICH YOUR TEACHING

Teacher-to-Teacher

Have small groups choose a Latin American country to research. They should find out about the foods, music, and customs associated with a particular ***fiesta*** in that country, then write an invitation to the ***fiesta.*** They should include what time, where, and what country they will be representing. You might want to write a model invitation, either on the board or as a handout. If possible, plan a day for your ***fiestas,*** complete with ***comida, música, bailes ¡y más!***

ASSESSMENT

Prueba 4B-3 with Study Plan (online only)

Quiz: *Ir + a +* infinitive

- Prueba 4B-3: p. 109

4B Practice and Communicate

Gramática

Core Instruction

Standards: 4.1

Resources: Voc. and Gram. Transparencies 93–94; Teacher's Resource Book: Video Script, pp. 290–291; Video Program: Cap. 4B

INTERACTIVE WHITEBOARD
Grammar Activities 4B

Suggestions: Highlight the difference between a stem-changing verb, such as ***jugar,*** and a regular ***-ar*** verb, such as ***hablar,*** by using a different color chalk or pen for the stem-changes. Play the *GramActiva* Video as an introduction or to reinforce your own presentation of the verb ***jugar.***

BELLRINGER REVIEW

Use Transparency 94 to quickly review sports activities. You may want to have students say the answers aloud instead of having to write sentences.

18 Standards: 1.3

Resources: Answer Keys: Student Edition, p. 61

Focus: Saying what sports people play

Suggestions: Ask students if they recognize any of the athletes in the pictures. Point out the *También se dice...* to give students additional vocabulary.

Answers:

1. **Sergio García juega al golf.**
2. **Rebecca Lobo y Eduardo Nájera juegan al básquetbol.**
3. **David Villa juega al fútbol.**
4. **Hanley Ramirez y Jaime García juegan al béisbol.**
5. **Answers will vary.**

Common Errors: With stem-changing verbs, students may overgeneralize and change all forms.

Extension: For homework, have students choose five sports. For each sport, ask them to write a sentence about one or more athletes who play it.

Theme Project

Students can perform Step 5 at this point. Be sure they understand your corrections and suggestions. (For more information, see p. 170-b.)

Gramática

Objectives

- Read, write, and talk about sports and athletes
- Exchange information about sports while playing a game
- Read and write about camping in Spain

The verb *jugar*

Use the verb *jugar* to talk about playing a sport or a game. Even though *jugar* uses the same endings as the other *-ar* verbs, it has a different stem in some forms. For those forms, the *-u-* becomes *-ue-*. This kind of verb is called a "stem-changing verb." Here are the present-tense forms:

(yo)	juego	(nosotros) (nosotras)	jugamos
(tú)	juegas	(vosotros) (vosotras)	jugáis
Ud. (él) (ella)	juega	Uds. (ellos) (ellas)	juegan

Nota

Many Spanish speakers always use *jugar a* and the name of the sport or game:
- ¿Juegas al vóleibol?

Others do not use the *a:*
- ¿Juegas vóleibol?

Más ayuda realidades.com

GramActiva **Video Animated Verbs**

GramActiva **Activity**

18 ¿A qué juegan?

Escribir

Escribe frases para decir qué deportes practican estas personas.

Albert Pujols

Modelo

Albert Pujols juega al béisbol.

1. Sergio García

2. 
Rebecca Lobo y 
Eduardo Nájera

3. 

David Villa

4. Hanley Ramírez y Jaime García

5. Y tus amigos y tú, ¿a qué juegan Uds.?

También se dice . . .

el básquetbol = el baloncesto *(muchos países)*
el fútbol = el balompié *(muchos países)*
el vóleibol = el balonvolea *(España)*

DIFFERENTIATED INSTRUCTION

Heritage Language Learners

Have students prepare an oral presentation on their favorite sport or athlete. Students presenting a sport not covered in this chapter should provide a poster to support their presentation.

Students with Learning Difficulties

The advertisement in *Actividad* 20 might intimidate students because of all the unknown vocabulary. Help them review the ad for vocabulary they already know. Then read the ad with them, emphasizing key words and phrases that will help students understand the meaning.

19 Juego | 

Dibujar • Escribir • Hablar • GramActiva

1. On each of two index cards, draw a picture that represents a sport or game and write *muy bien, bien,* or *mal* to show how well you play that sport or game. Don't let your classmates see your cards.

2. Get together with five other students. Put all the cards face down in the center of your group. Choose a card and try to identify who drew it by asking the others how well they play what is pictured. Keep track of what you learn about your classmates.

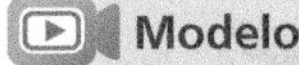

Modelo

A —*Enrique, ¿juegas bien al tenis?*
B —*No, juego muy mal al tenis.*

3. Write six sentences about the sports and games the students in your group play.

Modelo

Óscar y Nacho juegan muy bien al fútbol. Teresa y yo jugamos bien al golf.

20 La ciudad deportiva

Leer • Escribir • Hablar

Lee sobre el sueño *(dream)* de Iván Zamorano y contesta las preguntas.

Mi sueño[1]

Quiero una ciudad[2] dedicada al deporte, a la familia y los niños.[3] Quiero servicios de calidad internacional, con profesores de excelencia. En mi sueño, los niños y jóvenes juegan y practican deportes para ser mejores.[4] Este sueño ya es realidad y quiero compartirlo contigo. El lugar[5] para hacer deporte en familia.

Escuelas de Fútbol, Tenis, Hockey

Inicio de inscripción[6]: 23 de marzo, a las 8
Inicio de actividades: 1 de abril, a las 14 horas

Avenida Pedro Hurtado 2650, Las Condes, Santiago, Chile
Teléfono: 212 2711

[1]dream [2]city [3]children [4]better [5]place [6]registration

1. ¿Cuál es el sueño de Iván Zamorano?
2. ¿Qué deportes juegan en la Ciudad Deportiva de Iván?
3. ¿Qué día empieza *(begins)* la inscripción para las escuelas? ¿A qué hora?
4. ¿A qué hora empiezan las actividades?
5. ¿Te gustaría ir a la Ciudad Deportiva de Iván Zamorano? ¿Por qué?

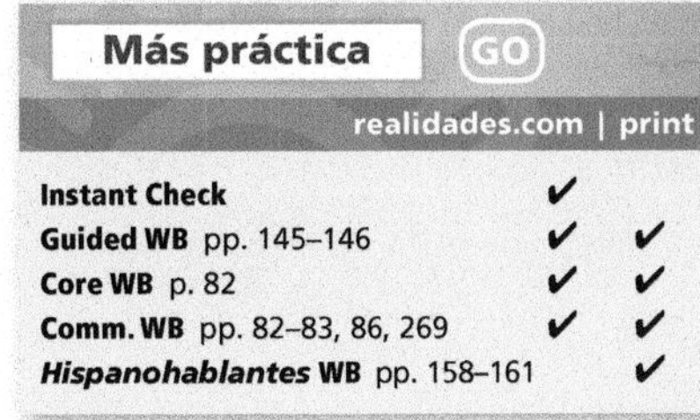

Más práctica GO

realidades.com | print

	realidades.com	print
Instant Check	✔	
Guided WB pp. 145–146	✔	✔
Core WB p. 82	✔	✔
Comm. WB pp. 82–83, 86, 269	✔	✔
***Hispanohablantes* WB** pp. 158–161		✔

19 Standards: 1.1, 1.3

Focus: Writing and speaking in personalized contexts; using the verb ***jugar***

Suggestions: Note the placement of ***bien*** and ***muy mal.*** To keep track of who plays what, have students take notes as each person speaks: ***Ana: tenis/bien.*** For part 3, encourage students to vary the subjects, as in the model, talking about what they play ***(yo)***, what another classmate plays ***(él/ella)***, what other students play ***(ellas/ellos)***, and what they *and* others play ***(nosotros)***.

Answers: will vary.

20 Standards: 1.2, 1.3, 3.2

Resources: Answer Keys: Student Edition, p. 61

Focus: Reading for comprehension

Suggestions: Have students scan the ad for cognates. Read the ad aloud, and then ask a volunteer to reread it.

Answers:

1. **Quiere una ciudad dedicada al deporte, a la familia y a los niños. Quiere servicios de calidad internacional, con profesores de excelencia.**
2. **fútbol, tenis y hockey**
3. **el 23 de marzo, a las ocho**
4. **a las dos de la tarde**
5. **Answers will vary.**

Pre-AP* Support

- **Learning Objective:** Interpretive: Print
- **Activity 20:** This activity helps students practice key interpretive skills. Remind students to practice strategies for effectively synthesizing information from authentic sources.

Additional Resources

- Communication Wbk.: Audio Act. 8–9, pp. 82–83
- Teacher's Resource Book: Audio Script, pp. 288–289, Communicative Pair Activity BLM, pp. 294–295
- Audio Program DVD: Cap. 4B, Tracks 11–12

ENRICH YOUR TEACHING

Culture Note

Baseball was first introduced to Cuba over 100 years ago and its popularity spread to other Spanish-speaking countries of the Caribbean. The Dominican Republic has produced many baseball superstars. The government finances stadiums and local fields and pays the coaches' salaries.

21st Century Skills

Creativity and Innovation Have students create a proposal for their dream sports complex. They should describe the facilities available, the location of the complex, and which special training and activities are offered. Their complex can be devoted to one single sport or to several, to more traditional sports (like baseball), or less traditional ones (like underwater hockey).

ASSESSMENT

Prueba 4B-4 with Study Plan (online only)

Quiz: The verb *jugar*

- Prueba 4B-4: p. 110

Pronunciación

Core Instruction

Standards: 4.1

Resources: Teacher's Resource Book: Audio Script, p. 289; Audio Program DVD: Cap. 4B, Track 13

Suggestions: Read the *Pronunciación* with students or use the audio. Model the two sounds of the letter *d:* exaggerating the *d* sound in ***doce*** and the *th* sound in ***cansado.*** Then have the class repeat. If possible, record the tongue twister as students say it. See if students can hear the difference between the two sounds.

El español en el mundo del trabajo

Core Instruction

Standards: 5.1

Suggestions: Have students determine the meaning of the quotation in the reading and use it as a model to say how they feel about volunteer work. To help students answer the questions, brainstorm different volunteer opportunities on the board.

Answers will vary.

Extension: If possible, invite a health care worker to your class to talk about ways in which knowledge of Spanish is helpful in his or her job.

Block Schedule

Have students create a brochure for a favorite vacation spot. They should include artwork and text that describes the kinds of activities available for guests. You may wish to provide a model, or refer them to the brochure on p. 211.

Pronunciación

The letter *d*

In Spanish, the pronunciation of the letter *d* is determined by its location in a word. When *d* is at the beginning of a word, or when it comes after *l* or *n,* it sounds similar to the *d* in "dog." Listen, then say these words:

diccionario	doce	donde
domingo	desayuno	día
deportes	calendario	bandera

When *d* comes between vowels and after any consonant except *l* or *n,* it sounds similar to the *th* of "the." Listen, then say these words:

cansado	ocupado	puedes
idea	sábado	partido
tarde	ensalada	atrevido

Try it out! Here is a tongue twister to give you practice in pronouncing the *d,* but also to give you something to think about!

Porque puedo, puedes,
porque puedes, puedo;
Pero si no puedes,
yo tampoco puedo.

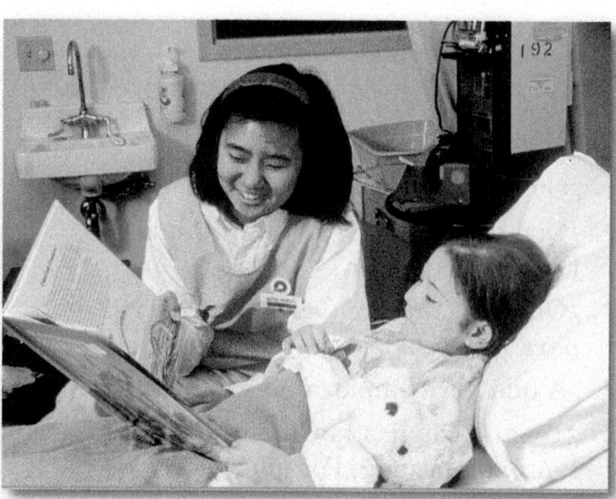

Una voluntaria en un hospital

El español en el mundo del trabajo

There are many opportunities to use Spanish in the healthcare field—in hospitals, emergency rooms, and neighborhood clinics. This young woman volunteers in a California hospital. Since many of the patients come from Spanish-speaking homes, she is able to speak with them and their families in Spanish. *"Para mí, trabajar como voluntaria es una de mis actividades favoritas. Creo que mi trabajo es importante."*

- What opportunities are there in your community to do volunteer work where speaking Spanish is helpful?

DIFFERENTIATED INSTRUCTION

Heritage Language Learners

Have students create a poster for a community organization that is looking for volunteers who speak Spanish.

Students with Special Needs

Students may have difficulty hearing the difference between the two sounds of the letter *d* if they are looking at the words. Have them close their eyes as they listen. Some may have particular difficulty with the *th* sound. Consider writing a small *th* over the letter *d* in the relevant words on the board to help students get used to the sound.

21 ¡Vamos de cámping!

Leer • Pensar • Escribir

Tourism is an important industry in Spain. Many tourists prefer to go camping rather than stay in hotels. Read the following brochure about a campground and then answer the questions.

Conexiones | Las matemáticas

Camping Las Palmas

Miramar
Teléfono: 962 41 42 73 Fax: 962 01 55 05

85 kilómetros al sur de Valencia
110 kilómetros al norte de Alicante

- Un camping ideal
- Muchas actividades para todos
- Una buena opción para sus vacaciones

Con bellas palmas que dan[1] mucha sombra,[2] directamente sobre una bella playa. Ideal para toda la familia. Un sitio excelente para pescar.

[1]give [2]shade

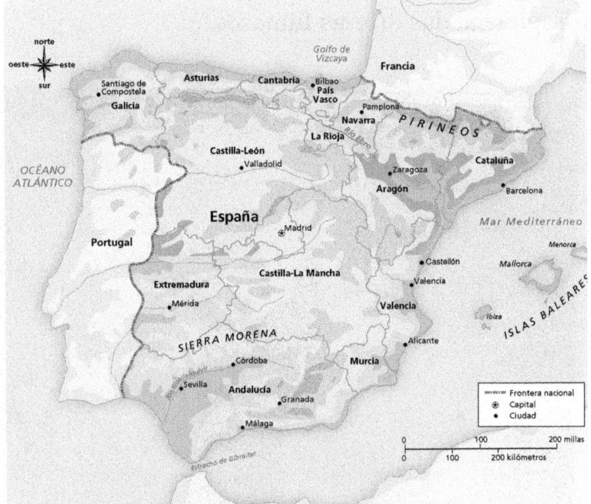

1. ¿Qué distancia en millas[3] hay entre[4] Valencia y el Camping Las Palmas?
2. ¿Qué distancia hay entre Alicante y el Camping Las Palmas?

Para convertir kilómetros en millas, es necesario dividir el número de kilómetros por 1.6.

[3]miles [4]between

Para decir más . . .
200 = doscientos

22 Y tú, ¿qué dices? | Talk!

Escribir • Hablar

1. ¿Con quién te gustaría ir a una fiesta? ¿Por qué?
2. ¿Qué prefieres, ir de pesca o ir a un baile?
3. ¿Qué vas a hacer mañana a las ocho de la noche?
4. ¿Qué vas a hacer este fin de semana?
5. ¿Te gustaría ver un partido de fútbol o ir a un concierto?

Practice and Communicate 4B

21 Standards: 1.2, 3.1

Resources: Map Transparency 18; Answer Keys: Student Edition, p. 62

Focus: Reading comprehension

Suggestions: Before beginning, have students talk about the title and the photograph. Ask them to compare what they see to vacations and camping trips that they have been on or know about. Remind students that they will not know every word. Have them identify some cognates, such as ***palmas*** and ***ideal.***

Answers:

1. **Entre Valencia y el Camping Las Palmas hay 53.13 millas.**
2. **Entre Alicante y el Camping Las Palmas hay 68.75 millas.**

Mapa global interactivo, Actividad 2
Compare the coastal areas of Spain

22 Standards: 1.1, 1.3

Focus: Answering questions about sports

Suggestions: After students have written their answers, have them work with a partner to ask and answer the questions.

Answers: will vary.

Extension: Have students create additional open-ended questions based on those in *Actividad* 22. For example, they can change ***ir a una fiesta*** to ***jugar al tenis.*** Encourage them to create original questions as well.

Theme Project

Students can perform Step 6 at this point. Record their presentations for inclusion in their portfolios. (For more information, see p. 170-b.)

ENRICH YOUR TEACHING

Culture Note

Because Spain has a variety of landscapes, there are many different kinds of sporting activities available—from fishing, swimming, and parasailing to hiking, mountain climbing, cave exploring, and canoeing. In addition to all the activities, tourists enjoy the wonderful food, museums, architecture, and climate.

Teacher-to-Teacher

Choose a question from *Y tú, ¿qué dices?*, or create a similar one to ask students as they prepare to start class. If you present them with a question upon entering, communication can begin immediately.

Teacher-to-Teacher

e-amigos: Have students write their *e-amigos* to ask three questions about leisure activities. Have them print out or e-mail you their questions and responses.

Common Core: Reading

Lectura

Core Instruction

Standards: 1.2, 1.3, 5.2, 4.1

Focus: Developing reading strategies and interpretive skills; comparing the lives of two people

Suggestions:

Pre-reading: Direct attention to the *Strategy*. Have students skim the two articles and write a list of cognates. Have them share their lists with the class and write them on the board. Encourage students to use other context clues, such as dates and numbers.

Reading: Have students read the article about Sergio García first. Ask them to make a list of words they do not understand. Then have them read the piece about Paola Espinosa. Did they find similar words, or were there additional unfamiliar words?

Post-reading: Ask students what they learned about Sergio García. What did they learn about Paola Espinosa? Discuss how these two athletes are alike. Then have students think about what makes each one unique.

BELLRINGER REVIEW

Have students identify these cognates in English:

objetivo profesional evidente universidad

(**Answers:** objective, professional, evident, university)

Pre-AP* Support

- **Learning Objective:** Presentational Writing
- **Activity:** Have students write a brief persuasive paragraph describing their own favorite athlete. Remind them to supply supporting details that encourage their readers to view the athlete positively.
- ***Pre-AP* Resource Book:*** Comprehensive guide to Pre-AP* writing development, pp. 27–38

Objectives

- Read about and compare the lives of two famous athletes
- Use cognates to understand new words
- Learn more about an Hispanic athlete and role model

Lectura

Sergio y Paola: Dos deportistas dotados[1]

Lee dos artículos de una revista deportiva. Vas a conocer a[2] Sergio García y a Paola Espinosa, dos atletas famosos.

Strategy

Cognates

Use the cognates in the following article to help you understand what is being said about the athletes.

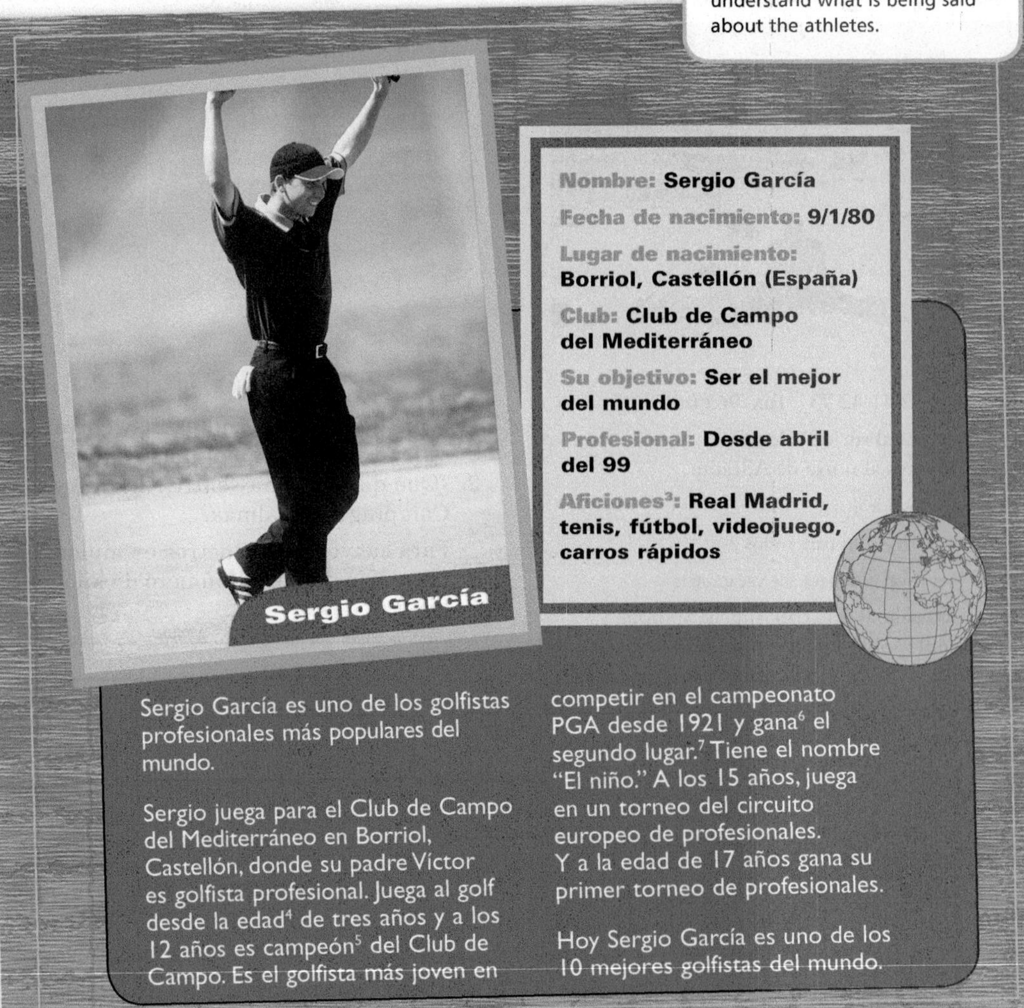

Nombre: Sergio García

Fecha de nacimiento: 9/1/80

Lugar de nacimiento: Borriol, Castellón (España)

Club: Club de Campo del Mediterráneo

Su objetivo: Ser el mejor del mundo

Profesional: Desde abril del 99

Aficiones[3]: Real Madrid, tenis, fútbol, videojuego, carros rápidos

Sergio García es uno de los golfistas profesionales más populares del mundo.

Sergio juega para el Club de Campo del Mediterráneo en Borriol, Castellón, donde su padre Víctor es golfista profesional. Juega al golf desde la edad[4] de tres años y a los 12 años es campeón[5] del Club de Campo. Es el golfista más joven en competir en el campeonato PGA desde 1921 y gana[6] el segundo lugar.[7] Tiene el nombre "El niño." A los 15 años, juega en un torneo del circuito europeo de profesionales. Y a la edad de 17 años gana su primer torneo de profesionales.

Hoy Sergio García es uno de los 10 mejores golfistas del mundo.

[1]gifted [2]You will meet [3]Interests [4]age [5]champion [6]he wins [7]second place

DIFFERENTIATED INSTRUCTION

Advanced Learners

Have students choose an athlete in the school to interview. Suggest that they find out information similar to what they have read about Sergio and Paola. Tell them that they can conduct the interview in English, if the athlete is not a Spanish-speaking student, but that they should write a summary in Spanish to share with the class.

Heritage Language Learners

Ask students to discuss athletes they are familiar with from a variety of sports. As they are talking, guide their discussion by asking: How old is this person? Where was he or she born? What are some of his or her biggest accomplishments or statistics? Do you think that he or she is a good role model? Why or why not?

Nombre: Paola Milagros Espinosa Sánchez

Fecha de nacimiento: 31/7/86

Su objetivo: Ser la clavadista[8] número uno del mundo

Lugar de nacimiento: La Paz, Baja California (México)

Aficiones: Nadar, practicar gimnasia, viajar, pasar tiempo con su familia

Paola Espinosa es la mejor[9] clavadista de saltos[10] en plataforma y en saltos sincronizados de México. Tiene el nombre de "la princesa mexicana del clavado" y es una heroína nacional.

De niña, le gusta nadar y hacer gimnasia. Compite[11] como clavadista desde la edad de 10 años. A los 18 años, participa en sus primeros Juegos Olímpicos. ¡Y a los 22 años gana la medalla de bronce en los Juegos Olímpicos de Beijing!

Paola dice que es necesario practicar todos los días. Su meta[12] es ganar la medalla de oro en los próximos Juegos Olímpicos.

[8]diver [9]best [10]dives [11]competes [12]goal

¿Comprendes?

Copy this Venn diagram on a sheet of paper. Make a list in English of at least eight facts that you learned about Sergio and Paola. Write the facts on your Venn diagram. Include information about Sergio in the left oval, information about Paola in the right oval, and any fact that applies to both of them in the overlapping oval.

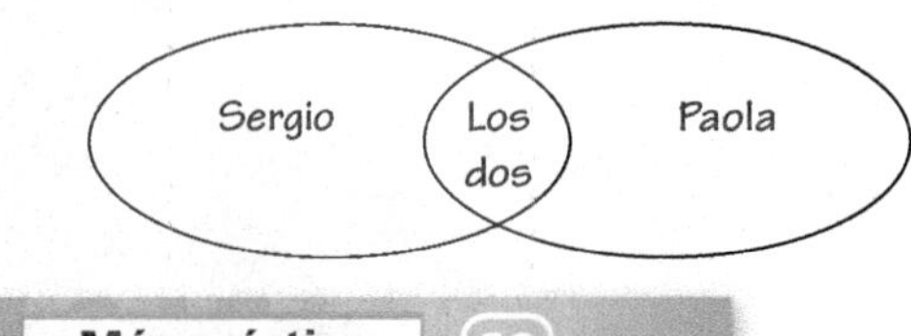

Más práctica GO

realidades.com | print

	realidades.com	print
Guided WB p. 147	✔	✔
Comm. WB pp. 87, 270	✔	✔
***Hispanohablantes* WB** pp. 162–163		✔
Cultural Reading Activity	✔	

Fondo Cultural | Estados Unidos

Una jugadora profesional Rebecca Lobo, former professional basketball player, won a gold medal in the 1996 Olympics. She became one of the WNBA's original players. Rebecca wrote a book called *The Home Team,* which tells about her life and her mother's struggle against breast cancer. In 2001, she established a college scholarship fund for minority students who plan to enter the healthcare field. Today, Rebecca is an announcer for the WNBA.

- Rebecca Lobo is a popular motivational speaker. What message do you think she gives to her audiences?

¿Comprendes? Standards: 1.2

Resources: Voc. and Gram. Transparency 2; Answer Keys: Student Edition, p. 62

Focus: Comparing Sergio García and Paola Espinosa

Suggestions: Use the transparency for a blank Venn diagram. Remind students to look at both the profiles and the paragraphs to find facts about the two athletes. When reviewing answers, ask students questions such as: *¿Quién juega en el Club de Campo del Mediterráneo?*

Answers: will vary but may include:

Sergio García:
from Spain
began playing golf when three years old
his father is a golfer
Los dos:
they both want to be the best
they both achieved success young
Paola Espinosa:
from Mexico
is called the "princess of the diving board"
likes to travel

Fondo cultural

Standards: 4.2

Suggestions: After reading the text, discuss the question with students. Encourage them to think about how Rebecca Lobo's struggles and accomplishments may affect her message. Ask students to name other celebrities or athletes who have overcome struggles. How do they compare with Rebecca Lobo?

Answers will vary.

Teacher-to-Teacher

Have students write a short autobiographical "snapshot." They can follow the format used in the boxes to the right of the photos. Encourage them to use vocabulary from this chapter.

For Further Reading

Student Resource: Realidades para hispanohablantes: Lectura 2, pp. 164–165

ENRICH YOUR TEACHING

Culture Note

In the 1950s, the *"Ticas"* of Costa Rica formed the first women's soccer team in Latin America. However, it wasn't until 1982 that the Federation of International Football Associates decided to make women's soccer official. By 1985, only one South American country had a team—Brazil. Today almost all South American countries have women's soccer teams. Despite a long struggle for acceptance, women's professional sports teams are gaining popularity.

Perspectivas del mundo hispano

Core Instruction

Standards: 2.1, 4.2

Focus: Reading about leisure activities of students in Spanish-speaking countries

Suggestions: Ask students what they do in their spare time. Tell them that in many Spanish-speaking countries, spare time is not necessarily free time. Many students use it to learn a foreign language or practice a sport in an athletic club. Have students read the text and point out similarities and differences between their experience and that of the students described. Direct attention to the photos. Of course many students in the United States also participate in these and similar activities. Mention that in general, high-school students in Spanish-speaking countries do not have jobs.

Have students think about how a schedule like the one described would affect their lives. What would change? Would they have to stop doing something? Ask if this schedule sounds enjoyable. Remember that many students today hold jobs out of necessity, and that many have very full schedules, much like the one described here.

Direct attention to the *Think about it!* section and have students discuss the question.

Answers will vary.

Teacher-to-Teacher

Careers: *Tema* 4 has focused on leisure activities. Have students work in small groups to talk about a career in the field of recreation. Have them write a list of activities that they might implement as director of an after-school recreation center for middle school students. Ask groups to share their lists.

Additional Resources

Student Resource: Realidades para hispanohablantes, p. 166

Perspectivas del mundo hispano

¿Qué haces en tu tiempo libre?

In many Spanish-speaking countries, extracurricular activities traditionally play a much smaller role in school life than in the United States. Students usually participate in activities such as music and athletics at clubs and institutions outside of school.

¿Te gusta jugar al ajedrez?

Although some schools have teams, many students who are interested in sports attend clubs such as el Club Deportivo General San Martín. At these clubs teens practice and compete on teams. They also participate in individual sports such as tennis. The competition between clubs is sometimes more intense than the competition between schools.

Students with artistic talents often go to a private institute to take music, dance, or art lessons. They might attend el Instituto de Música Clásica or el Instituto de Danza Julio Bocca.

Many students spend their time outside of classes studying a foreign language. They might learn English at la Cultura Inglesa or French at la Alianza Francesa.

In general, students do not hold jobs. They spend their time studying, being with family and friends, and participating in different activities.

Trabajando después de las cla

Check it out! Take a survey of your friends to find out what they do after school. Do they work a part-time job? Do they participate in a sport with a school team or in extracurricular activities at school? Do they belong to a club or organization outside of school?

Think about it! How do the practices in your community compare with what you have learned about young people's after-school activities in Spanish-speaking countries?

DIFFERENTIATED INSTRUCTION

Advanced Learners

Have students research schools in the United States where students can go if they have artistic talents; for example, the Juilliard School, music conservatories, etc. Have them find out more about the schools listed in the text. Ask them to compare the schools and make a short presentation to the class.

Students with Special Needs

Students may participate in special activities or groups. If they wish, invite them to share their experiences with the class.

- Write an invitation to a special event
- Organize information by using an invitation format

Presentación escrita

Una invitación

Task

Invite a friend to go to a special event with you.

1. **Prewrite** Think of an event to invite a friend to, such as a concert, game, or party. Write an invitation that includes:
   - the name of the event
   - the day, time, and location
   - who is going
2. **Draft** Use the information from Step 1 to write a first draft. Begin your invitation with *¡Hola . . . !* and close with *Tu amigo(a)* and your name.
3. **Revise** Check your note for spelling and grammar, then share with a partner. Your partner should check the following:
   - Did you give all the necessary information?
   - Is there anything to add or change?
   - Are there any errors?
4. **Publish** Write a final copy of your invitation. You might give it to your friend or include it in your portfolio.
5. **Evaluation** The following rubric will be used to grade your invitation.

Rubric	Score 1	Score 3	Score 5
Amount of information	You give very few or no details or examples about locations and activities.	You give only a few details or examples about locations and activities.	You consistently give many details and examples about locations, times, and activities.
Use of vocabulary expressions	You have very little variation of vocabulary usage with frequent incorrect usage.	You have limited usage of vocabulary; some usage errors.	You have extended use of a variety of vocabulary; few usage errors.
Accuracy of sentence structures	You have at least three sentences; many grammar errors.	You have at least three sentences; some grammar errors.	You have at least three sentences; very few grammar errors.

Strategy

Organizing information
Thinking about the correct format and necessary information beforehand will help you create a better invitation.

Writing 4B

Common Core: Writing

Presentación escrita

Expository

Standards: 1.3

Focus: Writing an invitation

Suggestions: Review the assignment, the 5-step approach, and the rubric with the class. Make an invitation of your own as a model for students to use. Refer them to the *Strategy,* and have them write the information to be included in their invitations before beginning. You may wish to have them give you rough drafts.

In Spanish, review the 5-Ws: *Who, What, Where, When, Why,* and have volunteers suggest how these could be included in an invitation.

Encourage students to make their invitations appealing with artwork or calligraphy.

Pre-AP* Support

- ***Pre-AP* Resource Book:*** Comprehensive guide to Pre-AP* writing skill development, pp. 27–38

Teacher-to-Teacher

Have students work in groups to create a singing telegram inviting a special friend to an event. The class can evaluate the telegrams in categories, such as most original, best singing, most humorous.

Portfolio

Attach a copy of the grading rubric to the final copy of the invitation, and include both in students' portfolios.

Additional Resources

Student Resources: Realidades para hispanohablantes, p. 167; Guided WB: Presentación escrita, p. 148

ENRICH YOUR TEACHING

21st Century Skills

Collaboration Have students review the proposed activities and decide as a group which one would be most appropriate to share with a real or imaginary exchange student from a Spanish-speaking country. Have them adjust the invitation for that person, including why it would be an interesting cultural event. Each person in the group should have a specific assignment in creating the new invitation.

ASSESSMENT

Presentación escrita

- Assessment Program: Rubrics, p. T30

  Go over the descriptions of the different levels of performance. After assessing students, help individuals understand how their performance could be improved. (See Teacher's Resource Book for suggestions on using rubrics in assessment.)

El mundo hispano

Core Instruction

Standards: 1.1, 1.3, 2.1, 5.1, 5.2

Resources: Voc. and Gram. Transparency 20

Mapa global interactivo, Actividad 3 Visit Miami's Calle Ocho.

Focus: Reading about the current influence of Spanish speakers in the United States

Suggestions: Have students read the selection. Locate Mexico, Cuba, and Puerto Rico on the maps. Discuss the latest census results in the United States and how most Spanish speakers in this country say they are from one of these locations. Have students think about the reasons people from Spanish-speaking countries now immigrate to the United States.

Have students read about the astronauts featured and discuss their achievements. Direct attention to the photo at the top of p. 217. Discuss the contribution of Spanish speakers to the arts. New York City has a large concentration of Puerto Ricans. Locate Puerto Rico and New York City on the maps. Ask students to hypothesize as to why so many Puerto Ricans went to New York City when other parts of the country are much closer. Have students consider the idea that people go where they have family. Moving to a new country is difficult; being with family greatly eases the transition. Remind students that Puerto Rico is a territory of the United States, which means that Puerto Ricans have an automatic right to immigrate.

Have students read the middle paragraph on p. 217. Discuss Miami and Calle Ocho. This street has become famous for its Cuban atmosphere and festivals. Help students see the proximity of Cuba and Miami on the map. Mention that because of the political situation in Cuba, many Cubans left their country and arrived on the shores of Florida. The Cuban influence is evident throughout Miami.

El mundo hispano 

Estados Unidos

Contemporáneo

According to the 2010 census, 50,477,594 people (about 16 percent of the total population of the United States) classified themselves as being of Spanish or Hispanic descent. Out of that number, 39,412,310 indicated that they were of either Mexican, Puerto Rican, Cuban, or Dominican descent. The remaining 11,065,384 people checked "Other Hispanic/Latino" on their census questionnaires. This broad category included people who came from or who had ancestral ties to other Spanish-speaking countries in the Caribbean, Central and South America, or Spain.

Born in Costa Rica, Dr. Franklin Chang-Díaz (left) was the first Hispanic astronaut to fly in space. He was selected by NASA in 1980 and is a veteran of seven space flights. In 1990, Californian Dr. Ellen Ochoa (right) became the first Hispanic female astronaut. Since then she has logged more than 978 hours in space. Her dream is to help build a space station, which she considers "critical . . . to human exploration in space." Both Dr. Ochoa and Dr. Chang-Díaz are the recipients of many honors for their technical contributions and their scholarship. ▶

¿Sabes que . . . ?

The influence of Spanish-speaking cultures is evident throughout the United States. Musical artists such as Enrique Iglesias, Shakira, and Marc Anthony sell millions of CDs. Actors such as Salma Hayek, Jennifer López, Cameron Díaz, and Martin Sheen earn great acclaim for their work. And in politics, Spanish-speaking Americans serve in Congress and top-level Cabinet posts.

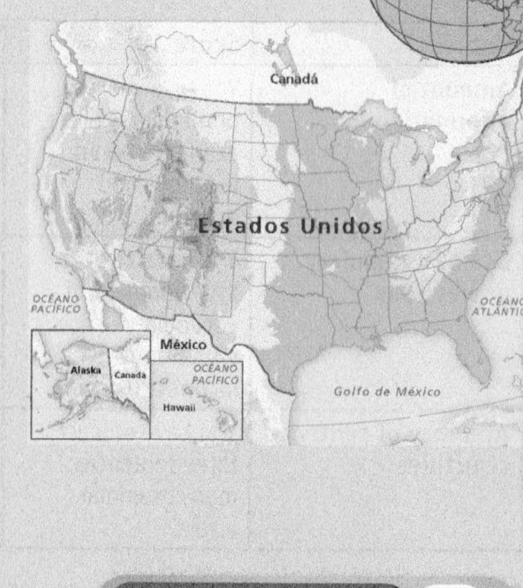

Para pensar

Work with a partner and interview a classmate, friend, or acquaintance who is Spanish-speaking or who has ties to a Spanish-speaking country. What is the person's name? Where did the family come from, and when? Why did the family move to your community? If this person had one thing to say to you and your classmates about the immigrant experience and cultural differences, what might that be? Write a short account of the interview and present it to your class or to a small group.

realidades.com GO

Mapa global interactivo

Reference Atlas

DIFFERENTIATED INSTRUCTION

Advanced Learners

Have students choose a major city or region in the United States with a large Spanish-speaking population, research celebrations and businesses that reflect the Spanish-speaking culture, and prepare a short report indicating their findings.

Heritage Language Learners

Have students find out if there is a city or region in the United States that has a large concentration of people from their heritage country. Have them identify the place and find out why people from their heritage country concentrated there.

The music and poetry of New York City's Puerto Rican community are a creative blend of English and Spanish. *Nuyoricans* of the *Loisaida* (Lower East Side) rub shoulders with people of diverse ethnic backgrounds creating sounds and rhythms unlike any other in the world. The Nuyorican Poets Café has become an institution on the *Loisaida*, where poets, writers, performance artists, musicians, and visual artists of all nationalities can find an outlet for their work.

More than half of Miami's population is of Spanish-speaking descent. Calle Ocho is the heart of Little Havana, the largest Cuban American community in the United States. The Calle Ocho Festival, which takes place at the end of Carnaval Miami, is a great time to sample Cuban food and dance to some of the world's greatest salsa artists.

More Mexicans visit the border town of Laredo, Texas, than any other city in the United States; and more United States citizens visit the Mexican border town of Tijuana than any other foreign city. Most of the visitors come from nearby areas and stay for only a few hours to visit or shop.

Culture 4B

Have students focus on the information under the photo of the road signs. Discuss how people who live near the Mexico-United States border often go to the other country for brief visits.

Direct students to the *¿Sabes que...?* section. Discuss the people mentioned and highlight their achievements.

Emphasize that people emigrate for a variety of reasons. Some students may not understand that many people emigrate for political reasons. Explain, if necessary, that not all countries offer the same opportunities and freedoms.

Direct attention to the *Para pensar* section. Have students complete it and present it to the class another day.

Answers will vary.

ENRICH YOUR TEACHING

Teacher-to-Teacher

Latin American foods are very popular in the United States. Have students research one or two major cities across the nation for restaurants that offer cuisine from Spanish-speaking countries. Have them sort the restaurants according to the country of origin and make a bar graph indicating the countries represented. Which country has the most widespread representation?

Review Activities

Talking about leisure activities and describing how someone feels: Have students work in pairs to quiz each other. They should take turns being Student A and Student B. Student A can pantomime an activity as Student B says the word in Spanish.

Extending, accepting, and declining invitations; telling what time something happens: Student A will invite Student B to an activity and state what time it will take place. Student B will give an excuse why he or she cannot go based on how he or she feels.

Jugar: Have students write the six pronouns on separate note cards, shuffle the cards, and hold them up one at a time. Student pairs will take turns saying the appropriate form of ***jugar.*** To reinforce vocabulary, ask them to add a sport to create sentences, for example, *Ellos juegan al tenis.*

Portfolio

Invite students to review the activities they completed in this chapter, including written reports, posters or other visuals, recordings of oral presentations, or other projects. Have them select one or two items they feel best demonstrate their achievements in Spanish. Include these items in students' portfolios. Have them include this with the Chapter Checklist and Self-Assessment Worksheet.

Additional Resources

Student Resources: Realidades para hispanohablantes, p. 168

Teacher Resources:

- Teacher's Resource Book: Situation Cards, p. 296, Clip Art, pp. 298–299
- Assessment Program: Chapter Checklist and Self-Assessment Worksheet, pp. T56–T57

Objectives

- Review the vocabulary and grammar
- Demonstrate you can perform the tasks on p. 219

Repaso del capítulo

Vocabulario y gramática

to talk about leisure activities

el baile	dance
el concierto	concert
la fiesta	party
ir + a + *infinitive*	to be going to + *verb*
ir de cámping	to go camping
ir de pesca	to go fishing
jugar al básquetbol	to play basketball
jugar al béisbol	to play baseball
jugar al fútbol	to play soccer
jugar al fútbol americano	to play football
jugar al golf	to play golf
jugar al tenis	to play tennis
jugar al vóleibol	to play volleyball
el partido	game, match
(yo) sé	I know (how)
(tú) sabes	you know (how)

to describe how someone feels

cansado, -a	tired
contento, -a	happy
enfermo, -a	sick
mal	bad, badly
ocupado, -a	busy
triste	sad

to tell what time something happens

¿A qué hora?	(At) what time?
a la una	at one (o'clock)
a las ocho	at eight (o'clock)
de la mañana	in the morning
de la noche	in the evening, at night
de la tarde	in the afternoon
esta noche	this evening
esta tarde	this afternoon
este fin de semana	this weekend

to extend, accept, or decline invitations

conmigo	with me
contigo	with you
(yo) puedo	I can
(tú) puedes	you can
¡Ay! ¡Qué pena!	Oh! What a shame!
¡Genial!	Great!
lo siento	I'm sorry
¡Oye!	Hey!
¡Qué buena idea!	What a good / nice idea!
(yo) quiero	I want
(tú) quieres	you want
¿Te gustaría?	Would you like?
Me gustaría	I would like
Tengo que ___.	I have to ___.

other useful words and expressions

demasiado	too
entonces	then
un poco (de)	a little

jugar (a) ***to play (games, sports)***

juego	**jugamos**
juegas	**jugáis**
juega	**juegan**

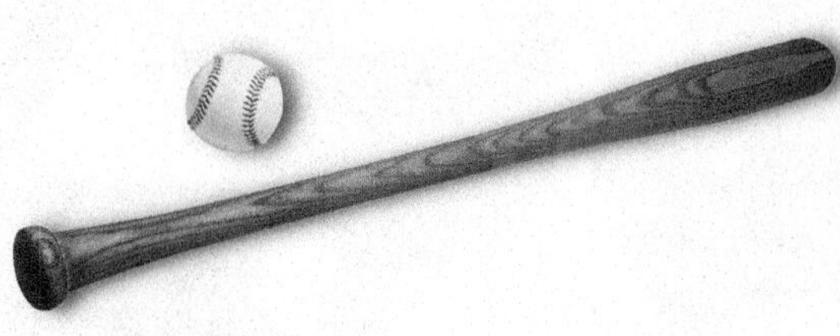

For *Vocabulario adicional,* see pp. 472–473.

ENRICH YOUR TEACHING

Students with Learning Difficulties

Have students review the *Repaso del capítulo* and create flashcards for any words that they do not know. Pair them with a student who is more confident with the vocabulary to practice. Before the test, provide students with a practice test, so they can become comfortable with the format.

Heritage Language Learners

Have students write a few paragraphs telling about their perfect game or other sports event: Where is it going to be? Whom are they going to invite to play (or see the event) with them? What sport will they play or see? Encourage them to use as many vocabulary words from this chapter as they can.

Más repaso GO realidades.com | print

	realidades.com	print
Instant Check	✔	
Puzzles	✔	
Core WB pp. 83–84		✔
Comm. WB pp. 271, 272–274	✔	✔

Preparación para el examen

On the exam you will be asked to . . .	Here are practice tasks similar to those you will find on the exam . . .	For review go to your print or digital textbook . . .
Interpretive		
 **1 Escuchar** Listen to and understand messages that give information about when and where to meet someone	On your answering machine, you hear your friend asking if you can go somewhere with her this weekend. Based on her message, try to tell: a) where she is going; b) what she is going to do; and c) what time she wants to go.	**pp. 198–201** *Vocabulario en contexto* **p. 203** Actividad 9 **p. 206** Actividad 13
Interpersonal		
 **2 Hablar** Make excuses for not accepting an invitation	You and a friend have planned a camping trip this weekend, but another friend now wants you to do something with him. With a partner, take turns rehearsing excuses for declining his invitation.	**p. 202** Actividad 4 **p. 203** Actividad 8 **p. 204** Actividad 11 **p. 207** Actividad 17
Interpretive		
 **3 Leer** Read and understand short messages about accepting or declining invitations	You find notes under your desk that were written to the person who was sitting there before you. Read them to see why people declined an invitation to a party:	**pp. 198–201** *Vocabulario en contexto* **p. 203** Actividad 7 **pp. 212–213** *Lectura*

a) Me gustaría, pero no puedo. Tengo que estudiar para un examen.

b) ¡Genial! ¡Una fiesta! Ay, pero no puedo. Voy de cámping.

c) ¿A las siete? No puedo. Juego un partido de vóleibol a las siete y media. Lo siento.

Presentational		
 **4 Escribir** Write a short note telling what you are going to do during the week	As a counselor for an after-school program for children, you must write a note to the parents telling them at least three things their children are going to do during the week. (Hint: Start your note with *¡Hola! Esta semana . . .*)	**pp. 198–201** *Vocabulario en contexto* **p. 206** *ir* + *a* + infinitive; Actividad 14 **p. 207** Actividad 15 **p. 215** *Presentación escrita*
Cultures • Comparisons		
 **5 Pensar** Demonstrate an understanding of cultural differences regarding extra-curricular activities	Think about what you and your friends typically do after school. Are your activities usually school-related? How would you compare what you do to what some Hispanic teens do in their after-school time?	**p. 214** *Perspectivas del mundo hispano*

DIFFERENTIATED ASSESSMENT

CORE ASSESSMENT
- **Assessment Program:** Examen del capítulo 4B, pp. 111–117
- **Audio Program DVD:** Cap. 4B, Track 16
- **ExamView:** Chapter Test, Test Banks A and B

ADVANCED/PRE-AP*
- **ExamView: Pre-AP* Test Bank**
- **Pre-AP* Resource Book,** pp. 74–77

STUDENTS NEEDING EXTRA HELP
- **Alternate Assessment Program:** Examen del capítulo 4B
- **Audio Program DVD:** Cap. 4B, Track 16

HERITAGE LEARNERS
- **Assessment Program: Realidades para hispanohablantes:** Examen del capítulo 4B
- **ExamView: Heritage Learner Test Bank**

Performance Tasks

Standards: 1.1, 1.2, 1.3, 4.2

Student Resource: Realidades para hispanohablantes, p. 169

Teacher Resources: Teacher's Resource Book: Audio Script, p. 289; Audio Program DVD: Cap. 4B, Track 15; Answer Keys: Student Edition, p. 62

1. Escuchar

Suggestions: Use the audio or read the script.

Answers and Script:

Hola, Toni, soy Susi. Yo voy al centro comercial después de las clases, a las cuatro de la tarde. ¿Te gustaría ir conmigo? Voy a comprar algo para un amigo.

a. **Susi is going to the mall.**
b. **Susi is going to buy something for her friend.**
c. **Susi is going at 4:00 in the afternoon.**

2. Hablar

Suggestions: Remind students that their excuses should sound legitimate. Ask them to tell how they feel, and to mention another activity that is preventing them from attending.

Answers will vary.

3. Leer

Suggestions: Tell students to scan the readings for the key word that says why the person cannot go, and then have them read the entire passage.

Answers:

a. **The person has to study for a test.**
b. **The person is going camping.**
c. **The person is going to a volleyball game.**

4. Escribir

Suggestions: Remind students that verbs will be in the third person since they are describing what students will do.

Answers will vary.

5. Pensar

Suggestions: Have students refer to *Perspectivas del mundo hispano* on p. 214.

Answers will vary.

5A Una fiesta de cumpleaños

- **Family relationships and celebrations**

Vocabulary: family and parties

Grammar: the verb ***tener;*** possessive adjectives

Cultural Perspectives: the importance of family; the ***quinceañera*** tradition

5B ¡Vamos a un restaurante!

- **Personal descriptions and eating out**

Vocabulary: describing people and ordering a meal

Grammar: the verb ***venir;*** the verbs ***ser*** and ***estar***

Cultural Perspectives: family celebrations; dining in restaurants; family mealtimes

THEME SUPPORT

Bulletin Boards

Theme: *Fiestas de familia*

Ask students to cut out, copy, or download photos of family celebrations and meals from many cultures. Cluster photos into categories of celebrations—weddings, baptisms, birthdays, bar and bas mitzvahs, graduations, and so on—so that similarities and differences are evident.

Hands-on Culture

Recipe: *Pastel de tres leches*

This dish is popular throughout the Spanish-speaking world for family celebrations.

Ingredients:

4 eggs
2 c. flour
¾ c. oil
1 T. baking powder
1 c. milk
1 c. sugar

1. Mix all the ingredients together well.
2. Grease and flour a 9″ × 11″ cake pan. Pour the batter into the pan.
3. Bake at 400 degrees Fahrenheit for about 30 minutes.
4. Immediately after taking the cake out of the oven, prick it all over with a fork. Next, pour the following mixture evenly over the top of the cake:

   1 can sweetened condensed milk
   1 can evaporated milk
   1 small carton half and half
5. After the cake cools, ice it with whipped cream.

Game

¿Han visto a mi amigo?

Play this game in *Capítulo* 5B, after students have learned vocabulary for physical descriptions.

Players: 15 to 20

Materials: scarf for blindfold

Rules:

1. Players stand in line. The first player in line is designated the Leader. The Leader wears a blindfold. The following exchange takes place:
   Leader: *¿Han visto a mi amigo?*
   Others: *No, señor/señorita.*
   Leader: *¿Saben dónde está mi amigo?*
   Others: *Sí, señor/señorita.*
2. The Leader then takes eight slow steps forward. While he or she is doing this, the others switch places quickly. The player who ends up directly behind the Leader must remain quiet.
   Others: *¿Quién está detrás de ti?*
3. The Leader guesses who is standing directly behind him or her. The Leader is allowed to ask three questions before guessing a name. For example:
   Leader: *¿Es chico o chica?*
   Others: *Es chica.*
   Leader: *¿Es alta?*
   Others: *No, es baja.*
   Leader: *¿Tiene el pelo negro?*
   Others: *No, tiene el pelo rubio.*
   Leader: *¿Es Emily?*
4. If the Leader guesses correctly, he or she gets another turn. If not, another player becomes the Leader and the game begins again.

Variation: Each of the other players holds an object that the Leader asks questions about and then guesses.

THEME PROJECT

Árbol genealógico con fotos y descripciones

Overview: Students create three-generation family trees on posters, featuring photos of family members and brief descriptions under each photo. Then they present the posters to the class, explaining the relationships on the tree and describing selected family members.

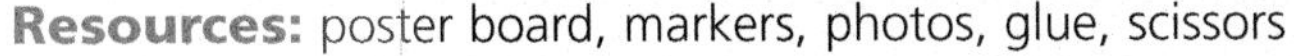

Resources: poster board, markers, photos, glue, scissors

Sequence: (suggestions for when to do each step appear throughout the chapters)

STEP 1. Review instructions so students know what's expected of them. Hand out the "Theme 5 Project Instructions and Rubric" from the *Teacher's Resource Book.*

STEP 2. Students submit a rough sketch of their tree. Return the drafts with your suggestions. For grammar and vocabulary practice, ask students to partner and present their drafts to each other.

STEP 3. Students create layout on poster board, leaving room for photos and descriptions. Encourage them to work in pencil first and to try different arrangements before gluing photos or decorations.

STEP 4. Students submit a draft of the personal descriptions. Note your corrections and suggestions, then return drafts to students.

STEP 5. Students present their posters to the class, explaining the relationships and giving descriptions of family members.

Options:

1. Students diagram a fictitious or famous family.
2. Students limit their tree to one set of grandparents.

Assessment:

Here is a detailed rubric for assessing this project:

Theme 5 Project: *Árbol genealógico con fotos y descripciones*

RUBRIC	Score 1	Score 3	Score 5
Evidence of planning	You submitted no draft, created no layout.	You submitted the drafts and created the layout, but didn't correct them.	You submitted and corrected the draft, created the layout.
Use of illustrations	You included no photos or visuals.	You included very few photos or visuals.	You included several photos or visuals.
Presentation	You included some details and dialogue for characters.	You described yourself and at least two family members.	You described yourself and three or more family members.

21st Century Skills

Look for tips throughout *Tema 5* to enrich your teaching by integrating 21st Century Skills. Suggestions for the Theme Project and Theme Culture follow below.

Theme Project

Modify the Theme Project with one or more of these suggestions:

Develop Technology Literacy

Have students combine different types of media, both print and electronic, to make their family tree presentations more appealing. To improve their use of the language and make sure they are prepared to do well on the project, encourage them to use the online resources available for review, such as the GramActiva and the tutorial videos.

Encourage Creativity and Innovation

Students can make their presentations more interesting by adding an unusual biographical fact about each person. Encourage students to keep it simple and to interview the family members first to get the information.

Support Collaboration

Once students have their family trees, have them work in a group and "mix and match" their families to create a new, fictitious family. Suggest that students put family members together who have the most in common.

Theme Culture

Develop Social and Cross-Cultural Skills

Using the information in the Fondo cultural, p. 239, and their own family names, have students give some of their relatives a name based on the Spanish naming system.

Videocultura View *La quinceañera* with the class to find out how teens in Spanish-speaking countries prepare for this rite of passage.

5A Una fiesta de cumpleaños

AT A GLANCE

Objectives

- **Listen to and read descriptions of family members and family relationships**
- **Talk and write about family, friends, and celebrations**
- **Exchange information while describing your family**
- **Understand cultural perspectives on family celebrations in the Spanish-speaking world**
- **Learn to make *papel picado* and explain how this craft is used in celebrations**

Vocabulary

- Family members and pets
- Telling ages
- Party decorations and celebration activities

Grammar

- The verb ***tener***
- Possessive adjectives

Culture

- Carmen Lomas Garza, p. 221
- ***papel picado,*** pp. 226, 240
- Spanish royal family, p. 230
- Francisco de Goya, p. 231
- Diego Rivera, p. 236
- ***quinceañera*** traditions, p. 238
- Last names in the Spanish-speaking world, p. 239

Recycle ♻

- ***tengo, tienes***
- ***tener que*** + infinitive
- ***de*** to show possession or relationship
- Classroom supplies
- ***gustar, encantar***
- ***-ar*** and ***-er*** verbs
- ***estar***
- Personal descriptions
- Prepositions of location

RESOURCES

	FOR THE STUDENT	ONLINE	DVD	PRINT	FOR THE TEACHER	ONLINE	PREEXP	DVD	PRINT
Plan					Interactive TE and Resources DVD	•		•	
					Teacher's Resource Book, pp. 2–37	•		•	•
					Pre-AP* Resource Book, pp. 78–81	•		•	•
					Lesson Plans	•			•
					Mapa global interactivo	•			
Introducción PP. **220–221**									
Present	Student Edition, pp. 220–221	•	•	•	Interactive TE and Resources DVD	•		•	
	DK Reference Atlas	•	•		Teacher's Resource Book, pp. 2–5	•		•	•
	Videocultura	•	•		Galería de fotos		•		
	Hispanohablantes WB, pp. 170–171			•	Fine Art Transparencies, 34	•	•	•	
					Map Transparencies, 12, 14, 16–18, 20	•	•	•	
Vocabulario en contexto PP. **222–225**									
Present & Practice	Student Edition, pp. 222–225	•	•	•	Interactive TE and Resources DVD	•		•	
	Audio	•	•		Teacher's Resource Book, pp. 6–8, 10, 18–21	•		•	•
	Videohistoria	•	•		Vocabulary Clip Art	•	•	•	•
	Flashcards	•	•		Audio Program	•	•	•	
	Instant Check	•			Video Program: Videohistoria	•		•	
	Guided WB, pp. 149–158	•	•	•	Video Program Teacher's Guide: Cap. 5A	•		•	•
	Core WB, pp. 85–88	•	•	•	Vocabulary and Grammar Transparencies, 96–99	•	•	•	
	Comm. WB, pp. 89–91, 95	•	•	•	Answer Keys: Student Edition, pp. 63–64	•	•	•	
	Hispanohablantes WB, pp. 172–173			•	TPR Stories, pp. 62–76	•		•	•
Assess and Remediate					Prueba 5A–1: Assessment Program, pp. 119–120	•		•	•
					Assessment Program para hispanohablantes, pp. 119–120	•		•	•

RESOURCES

	FOR THE STUDENT	ONLINE	DVD	PRINT	FOR THE TEACHER	ONLINE	PREEXP	DVD	PRINT
Vocabulario en uso PP. **226–227**									
Present & Practice	Student Edition, pp. 226–227	•	•	•	Interactive Whiteboard Vocabulary Activities	•		•	
	Instant Check	•			Interactive TE and Resources DVD	•		•	
	Comm. WB, p. 92	•	•	•	Teacher's Resource Book, pp. 8, 12–13	•		•	•
	Hispanohablantes WB, pp. 174–175			•	Communicative Pair Activities, pp. 12–13	•		•	•
	Communicative Pair Activities	•			Audio Program	•	•	•	
					Videomodelos	•		•	
					Fine Art Transparencies, 35	•	•	•	
					Answer Keys: Student Edition, pp. 64–65	•	•	•	•
Assess and Remediate					Prueba 5A–2 with Study Plan	•			
					Prueba 5A–2: Assessment Program, pp. 121–122	•		•	•
					Assessment Program para hispanohablantes, pp. 121–122	•		•	•
Gramática PP. **228–237**									
Present & Practice	Student Edition, pp. 228–237	•	•	•	Interactive Whiteboard Grammar Activities	•		•	
	Instant Check	•			Interactive TE and Resources DVD	•		•	
	Animated Verbs	•			Teacher's Resource Book, pp. 8–9, 10–11, 14–15	•		•	•
	Tutorial Video: Grammar	•			Communicative Pair Activities, pp. 14–15	•		•	•
	Canción de hip hop	•			Audio Program	•	•	•	
	Guided WB, pp. 159–162	•	•	•	Videomodelos	•		•	
	Core WB, pp. 89–91	•	•	•	Video Program: GramActiva	•	•	•	
	Comm. WB, pp. 92–94, 96–97, 275	•	•	•	Fine Art Transparencies, pp. 25, 26, 51	•	•	•	
	Hispanohablantes WB, pp. 176–181			•	Vocabulary and Grammar Transparencies, 100–103	•	•	•	
	Communicative Pair Activities	•			Answer Keys: Student Edition, pp. 65–68	•	•	•	
Assess and Remediate					Pruebas 5A–3 and 5A–4 with Study Plans	•			
					Pruebas 5A–3, 5A–4: Assessment Program, pp. 123, 124	•		•	•
					Assessment Program para hispanohablantes, pp. 123, 124	•		•	•
¡Adelante! PP. **238–243**									
Application	Student Edition, pp. 238–243	•	•	•	Interactive TE and Resources DVD	•		•	
	Online Cultural Reading	•			Teacher's Resource Book, p. 11	•		•	•
	Guided WB, pp. 163–164	•	•	•	Video Program: Videomisterio ¿Eres tú, María?	•		•	
	Comm. WB, pp. 98, 276	•	•	•	Video Program Teacher's Guide: Cap. 5A	•		•	
	Hispanohablantes WB, pp. 182–187			•	Videomisterio Quiz		•		
	¿Eres tú, María? Video WB, pp. 1–9	•	•	•	Answer Keys: Student Edition, p. 69	•	•	•	
Repaso del capítulo PP. **244–245**									
Review	Student Edition, pp. 244–245	•	•	•	Interactive TE and Resources DVD	•		•	
	Online Puzzles and Games	•			Teacher's Resource Book, pp. 9, 16, 18–21	•		•	•
	Core WB, pp. 92–93	•	•	•	Audio Program	•	•	•	
	Comm. WB, pp. 277–281	•	•	•	Answer Keys: Student Edition, p. 70	•	•	•	
	Hispanohablantes WB, pp. 188–189			•					
	Instant Check	•							
Chapter Assessment									
Assess					Examen del capítulo 5A	•		•	•
					Assessment Program, pp. 125–132	•		•	•
					Alternate Assessment Program, pp. 47–51	•		•	•
					Assessment Program para hispanohablantes, pp. 125–132	•		•	•
					Audio Program, Cap. 5A, Examen	•		•	
					ExamView: Test Banks A and B questions only online	•		•	
					Heritage Learner Test Bank	•		•	
					Pre-AP* Test Bank	•		•	

5A Lesson Plans

REGULAR SCHEDULE (50 MINUTES)

DAY	Warm-up / Assess	Preview / Present / Practice / Communicate	Wrap-up / Homework Options
1	**Warm-up** (10 min.) • Return Examen del capítulo 4B	**Chapter Opener** (5 min.) • Objectives • Arte y cultura **Vocabulario en contexto** (30 min.) • Presentation: Vocabulario en contexto • Actividades 1, 2	**Wrap-up and Homework Options** (5 min.) • Core Practice 5A-1, 5A-2
2	**Warm-up** (5 min.) • Homework check	**Vocabulario en contexto** (40 min.) • Presentation: Videohistoria *¡Feliz cumpleaños!* • View: Videohistoria • Video Activities 1, 2, 3, 4 • Actividad 3	**Wrap-up and Homework Options** (5 min.) • Core Practice 5A-3, 5A-4 • Prueba 5A-1: Vocabulary recognition
3	**Warm-up** (10 min.) • Actividades 4, 5 • Homework check **Formative Assessment** (10 min.) • Prueba 5A-1: Vocabulary recognition	**Vocabulario en uso** (25 min.) • Interactive Whiteboard Vocabulary Activities • Actividades 6, 7 • Fondo cultural • Audio Activities 5, 6 • Communicative Pair Activity	**Wrap-up and Homework Options** (5 min.) • Writing Activity 10 • Prueba 5A-2 with Study Plan: Vocabulary production
4	**Warm-up** (10 min.) • Actividad 8 • Homework check ✓**Formative Assessment** (10 min.) • Prueba 5A-2 with Study Plan: Vocabulary production	**Gramática y vocabulario en uso** (25 min.) • Presentation: The verb ***tener*** • View: GramActiva video • Interactive Whiteboard Grammar Activities • Actividades 9, 10, 11, 12	**Wrap-up and Homework Options** (5 min.) • Writing Activity 11
5	**Warm-up** (10 min.) • Actividad 13 • Homework check	**Gramática y vocabulario en uso** (35 min.) • Actividades 14, 15 • Fondo cultural • Actividades 16, 17 • Fondo cultural • Audio Activity 7 • Presentation: Possessive adjectives • Actividad 19	**Wrap-up and Homework Options** (5 min.) • Core Practice 5A-5 • Actividad 18 • Prueba 5A-3 with Study Plan: The verb ***tener***
6	**Warm-up** (5 min.) • Homework check ✓**Formative Assessment** (10 min.) • Prueba 5A-3 with Study Plan: The verb ***tener***	**Gramática y vocabulario en uso** (30 min.) • View: GramActiva video • Interactive Whiteboard Grammar Activities • Actividades 21, 22 • Audio Activities 8, 9 • Exploración del lenguaje • Actividades 23, 24	**Wrap-up and Homework Options** (5 min.) • Core Practice 5A-6, 5A-7 • Actividad 20 • Prueba 5A-4 with Study Plan: Possessive adjectives
7	**Warm-up** (15 min.) • Writing Activities 12, 13 • Homework check ✓**Formative Assessment** (10 min.) • Prueba 5A-4 with Study Plan: Possessive adjectives	**Gramática y vocabulario en uso** (20 min.) • Communicative Pair Activity • Pronunciación • Fondo cultural • El español en la comunidad • Actividades 25, 26	**Wrap-up and Homework Options** (5 min.) • La cultura en vivo
8	**Warm-up** (5 min.) • Homework check	**¡Adelante!** (30 min.) • Lectura • ¿Comprendes?; Vamos a comparar • Fondo cultural • Presentación oral: Step 1 **Repaso del capítulo** (10 min.) • Vocabulario y gramática • Preparación para el examen 1, 2	**Wrap-up and Homework Options** (5 min.) • Presentación oral: Step 2 • Preparación para el examen 3, 4, 5 • Lectura
9	**Warm-up** (2 min.) • Homework check	**¡Adelante!** (46 min.) • Presentación oral: Step 3 • Videomisterio: *¿Eres tú, María?*, Episodio 1	**Wrap-up and Homework Options** (2 min.) • Core Practice 5A-8, 5A-9 • Instant Check • Examen del capítulo 5A
10	**Warm-up** (10 min.) • Homework check • Answer questions ✓**Summative Assessment** (40 min.) • Examen del capítulo 5A		

BLOCK SCHEDULE (90 MINUTES)

DAY	Warm-up / Assess	Preview / Present / Practice / Communicate	Wrap-up / Homework Options
1	**Warm-up** (10 min.) • Return Examen del capítulo 4B	**Chapter Opener** (5 min.) • Objectives • Arte y cultura **Vocabulario en contexto** (50 min.) • Presentation: Vocabulario en contexto • Actividades 1, 2 • Presentation: Videohistoria *¡Feliz cumpleaños!* • View: Videohistoria • Video Activities 1, 2, 3, 4 • Actividad 3 **Vocabulario en uso** (20 min.) • Interactive Whiteboard Vocabulary Activities • Actividades 4, 5, 6, 7 • Fondo cultural	**Wrap-up and Homework Options** (5 min.) • Core Practice 5A-1, 5A-2, 5A-3, 5A-4 • Prueba 5A-1: Vocabulary recognition
2	**Warm-up** (10 min.) • Actividad 8 • Homework check ✔**Formative Assessment** (10 min.) • Prueba 5A-1: Vocabulary recognition	**Gramática y vocabulario en uso** (65 min.) • Audio Activities 5, 6 • Writing Activity 10 • Communicative Pair Activity • Presentation: The verb ***tener*** • View: GramActiva video • Interactive Whiteboard Grammar Activities • Actividades 9, 10, 11, 12, 13 • Audio Activity 7	**Wrap-up and Homework Options** (5 min.) • Core Practice 5A-5 • Prueba 5A-2 with Study Plan: Vocabulary production
3	**Warm-up** (5 min.) • Homework check ✔**Formative Assessment** (10 min.) • Prueba 5A-2 with Study Plan: Vocabulary production	**Gramática y vocabulario en uso** (70 min.) • Actividades 14, 15 • Fondo cultural • Actividades 16, 17 • Fondo cultural • Writing Activity 11 • Presentation: Possessive adjectives • View: GramActiva video • Interactive Whiteboard Grammar Activities • Actividades 18, 19 • Writing Activities 12, 13	**Wrap-up and Homework Options** (5 min.) • Core Practice 5A-6, 5A-7 • Pruebas 5A-3, 5A-4 with Study Plans: The verb ***tener,*** Possessive adjectives
4	**Warm-up** (10 min.) • Actividad 20 • Homework check ✔**Formative Assessment** (15 min.) • Pruebas 5A-3, 5A-4 with Study Plans: The verb ***tener,*** Possessive adjectives	**Gramática y vocabulario en uso** (55 min.) • Actividades 21, 22 • Audio Activities 8, 9 • Communicative Pair Activity • Exploración del lenguaje • Actividades 23, 24 • Pronunciación • Fondo cultural • El español en la comunidad • Actividades 25, 26 **¡Adelante!** (5 min.) • Presentación oral: Step 1	**Wrap-up and Homework Options** (5 min.) • Presentación oral: Step 2 • La cultura en vivo
5	**Warm-up** (5 min.) • Presentación oral: Step 2	**¡Adelante!** (50 min.) • Presentación oral: Step 3 • Lectura • ¿Comprendes?; Vamos a comparar • Fondo cultural **Repaso del capítulo** (30 min.) • Vocabulario y gramática • Preparación para el examen 1, 2, 3, 4, 5	**Wrap-up and Homework Options** (5 min.) • Core Practice 5A-8, 5A-9 • Instant Check • Lectura • Examen del capítulo 5A
6	**Warm-up** (15 min.) • Homework check • Situation Cards **Repaso del capítulo** (10 min.) • Communicative Pair Activities ✔**Summative Assessment** (40 min.) • Examen del capítulo 5A	**¡Adelante!** (20 min.) • Videomisterio: *¿Eres tú, María?*, Episodio 1	**Wrap-up and Homework Options** (5 min.) • Videomisterio

Standards for *Capítulo* 5A

- To achieve the goals of the Standards, students will:

Communication

1.1 Interpersonal
- Talk about families and celebrations
- Talk about classes and school materials
- Talk about favorite activities and preferences
- Talk about the royal family of Spain
- Talk about personal heroes

1.2 Interpretive
- Read and listen to information about family celebrations
- Read a picture-based story
- Listen to and watch a video about a birthday party
- Read about the royal families of Carlos IV, Juan Carlos I
- Read about the family of Carlos IV
- Read a child's birthday card
- Read about a ***quinceañera***
- Watch and listen to a video mystery
- Read a public service announcement

1.3 Presentational
- Present information about families and celebrations
- Write about how family members are related

Culture

2.1 Practices and Perspectives
- Explain Hispanic names and naming conventions
- Describe celebration traditions like the ***piñata***

2.2 Products and Perspectives
- Discuss Carmen Lomas Garza and her painting
- Discuss ***papel picado***
- Discuss the royal family of Spain
- Discuss Francisco de Goya and his painting
- Discuss the family of Carlos IV
- Discuss Diego Rivera and his portrayal of indigenous people through painting

Connections

3.1 Cross-curricular
- Discuss important artists and their work: Lomas Garza, Goya
- Discuss the royal family of Spain

3.2 Target Culture
- Read a version of the fairy tale "La Cenicienta"

Comparisons

4.1 Language
- Talk about new vocabulary through the recognition of cognates
- Compare the uses of ***tener*** idioms with English
- Compare the use of possessive adjectives
- Explain the use of diminutives in Spanish

4.2 Culture
- Compare family celebrations
- Compare crafts
- Compare the role of families
- Compare pictorial representations of families

Communities

5.1 Beyond the School
- Identify Hispanic surnames in a local phonebook

5.2 Lifelong Learner
- View a video mystery series

Capítulo 5A Una fiesta de cumpleaños

Chapter Objectives

Communication

By the end of this chapter you will be able to:
- Listen to and read descriptions of family members and family relationships
- Talk and write about family, friends, and celebrations
- Exchange information while describing your family

Culture

You will also be able to:
- Understand cultural perspectives on family celebrations in the Spanish-speaking world
- Learn to make *papel picado* and explain how this craft is used in celebrations

You will demonstrate what you know and can do:
- Presentación oral, p. 241
- Preparación para el examen, p. 245

You will use:

Vocabulary
- Family members and pets
- Telling ages
- Party decorations and celebration activities

Grammar
- The verb *tener*
- Possessive adjectives

Exploración del mundo hispano

Country Connection
Family Celebrations

realidades.com 

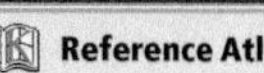 Reference Atlas

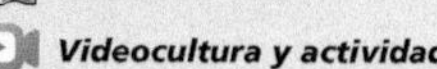 *Videocultura y actividad*

 *Mapa global interactivo*

ENRICH YOUR TEACHING

Using Backward Design

Have students preview the sample performance tasks on *Preparación para el examen,* p. 245, and connect them to the Chapter Objectives. Explain to students that by completing the sample tasks they can self-assess their learning progress.

Mapa global interactivo

Download the *Mapa global interactivo* files for Chapter 5A and preview the activities. Use Activity 1 to explore the Palacio Real and its surroundings in Madrid, Spain. Activity 2 looks at Mexico and the countries of Central America, the region known as Mesoamerica.

Una familia mexicanoamericana celebrando un cumpleaños

Arte y cultura | Estados Unidos

Carmen Lomas Garza (1948–) is best known for her paintings that show Mexican American family life in her native South Texas in the 1950s.

- What do you see in the painting that would make this family celebration similar to or different from family parties that you're familiar with?

▼ "Barbacoa para cumpleaños / Birthday Party Barbecue" (1993), Carmen Lomas Garza

Alkyds on canvas, 36 x 48 inches. © 1993 Carmen Lomas Garza (reg. 1994). Photo credit: M. Lee Fatherree. Collection of Federal Reserve Bank of Dallas

PresentationExpress™
See pp. 220c–220d

Chapter Opener

Core Instruction

Resources: Map Transparencies 12, 14, 16–18, 20

Suggestions: Explain that strong family ties are central to the social structures of many Spanish-speaking countries. Remember that for some students, the family is a sensitive subject. When possible, offer an alternative to focusing on a student's own family by using a fictional family or that of a famous person.

Videocultura View *La quinceañera* with the class to find out how teens in Spanish-speaking countries prepare for this rite of passage.

Arte y cultura

Standards: 2.2, 3.1, 4.2

Resources: Fine Art Transparencies, p. 34

Suggestions: Emphasize that Lomas Garza based this painting on childhood memories and experiences in a close-knit Mexican American community. Discuss the childlike style of the painting. Point out that this style imitates a traditional Mexican art style.

Answers will vary but may include decorations, games, or the people present.

TEACHING WITH ART

Resources: Fine Art Transparencies, p. 34

Suggestions: To guide discussion of the painting, ask: Who is present in the painting? What are the decorations like? What story does the picture tell? What feelings does the artist convey, and how?

DIFFERENTIATED INSTRUCTION

Digital resources such as the ***Interactive Whiteboard*** activity banks, ***Videomodelos***, additional ***Online Activities***, ***Study Plans***, automatically graded ***Leveled Workbook***, animated ***Grammar Tutorials***, ***Flashcards***, and ***Vocabulary and Grammar Videos*** will help you reach students of different ability levels and learning styles.

STUDENTS NEEDING EXTRA HELP

Guided Practice Activities
- Flashcards, pp. 149–154
- Vocabulary Check, pp. 155–158
- Grammar Support, pp. 159–162

HERITAGE LEARNERS

Realidades para hispanohablantes
- Chapter Opener, pp. 170–171
- A primera vista, p. 172
- Videohistoria, p. 173
- Manos a la obra, pp. 174–181
- ¡Adelante!, pp. 182–187
- Repaso del capítulo, pp. 188–189

ADVANCED/PRE-AP*

Pre-AP* Resource Book,
- pp. 78–81

Communications Workbook
- Integrated Performance Assessment, p. 277

5A Language Input

Vocabulario en contexto

Core Instruction

Standards: 1.2

Resources: Teacher's Resource Book: Input Script, p. 6, Clip Art, pp. 18–21, Audio Script, p. 7; Voc. and Gram. Transparencies 96–97; TPR Stories Book, pp. 62–76; Audio Program DVD: Cap. 5A, Tracks 1–2

Focus: Presenting visualized vocabulary for family members, celebrations, and parties

Suggestions: Use the transparencies to present the vocabulary in three sections: the family tree, Cristina's introduction to her family, and the party.

Ask questions that require limited verbal response, such as: *¿Es Esteban el padre de Cristina? ¿Te gusta comer dulces?*

If students are unfamiliar with the structure of a family tree, emphasize that the youngest members are at the bottom, then parents in the middle, and grandparents at the top. Explain the structure of the tree: for example, people who are connected with a horizontal blue line are brothers and sisters.

For sample presentation scripts, use the Input Script from the *Teacher's Resource Book*, or use the *TPR Stories Book*.

BELLRINGER REVIEW

Have students write two sentences telling how old four of their family members or friends are. (Ex. *Mi primo James tiene quince años.*)

Block Schedule

Have students make family tree posters or collages. They can either use real photos or make fictional collages using pictures from magazines, downloaded pictures, or illustrations. Have them label each family member: for example, ***Susana, mi tía.*** They can also include a few sentences on the poster: *Mi padre es simpático.* Point out that each person has to identify in relation to the student. Provide students with additional vocabulary words, based on their individual family structures.

Objectives

Read, listen to, and understand information about
- families
- parties and celebrations

Vocabulario en contexto

mis abuelos

Ricardo
mi abuelo, 68

Ana María
mi abuela, 61

Más vocabulario

el padrastro stepfather
la madrastra stepmother
el hermanastro stepbrother
la hermanastra stepsister

mis padres

María
mi madre, 39

José Antonio
mi padre, 42

Josefina
mi tía, 38

Andrés
mi tío, 42

mis tíos

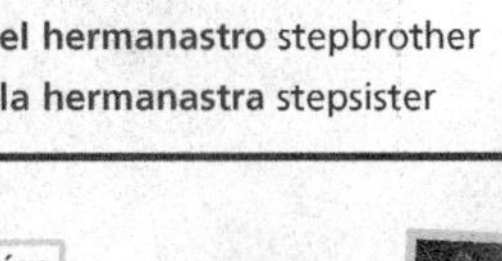

Capitán
mi perro

Michi
mi gato

mis hermanos

Angélica
mi hermana, 16

Esteban
mi hermano, 15

Cristina
yo, 13

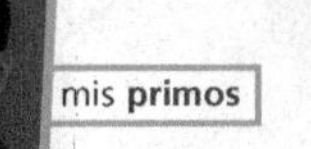

Carolina
mi prima, 17

Gabriel
mi primo, 13

mis primos

“¡Hola! Me llamo Cristina. Hoy es mi **cumpleaños.** Toda mi familia va a **preparar** una fiesta para **celebrar.** ¡Va a ser muy divertido!”

“Aquí está mi familia. Tengo dos hermanos: mi hermana **mayor,** Angélica, **que tiene 16 años,** y mi hermano, Esteban, que tiene 15 años. Y aquí están mis primos: Carolina tiene 17 años. **Su** hermano **menor,** Gabriel, tiene **sólo** 13 años”.

“Mira a **las personas** de **las fotos.** Es la familia de mi tía Josefina. Mi tío Andrés es **el esposo** de Josefina. Ellos tienen dos **hijos: su hijo** Gabriel y su **hija** Carolina” .

DIFFERENTIATED INSTRUCTION

Heritage Language Learners

Ask students who are familiar with other cultures to describe typical families from their heritage culture. Does active family life include extended family members? Do family members live nearby?

Students with Learning Difficulties

If students are struggling with vocabulary words and their meanings because of the organization of the family tree, suggest that they look at the vocabulary list on p. 244 for another list. Review the family tree prior to starting *Actividad* 1.

el regalo

la cámara

“Hoy es el cumpleaños de Cristina. Tengo un regalo para ella. Es una cámara. A Cristina **le encanta sacar fotos**”.

1 La familia de Cristina

Escuchar

Listen as Cristina describes her family. If her statement is true, give a "thumbs-up" sign. If it is false, give a "thumbs-down" sign.

2 Preparamos la fiesta

Escuchar

Now listen as Cristina and her mother prepare for the birthday party. Look at the items in the party shop ad on this page and touch each item they mention.

Más práctica GO
realidades.com | print

Instant Check	✔	
Guided WB pp. 149–154	✔	✔
Core WB pp. 85–86	✔	✔
Comm. WB p. 95	✔	✔
Hispanohablantes WB p. 172		✔

Language Input 5A

1 Standards: 1.2

Resources: Teacher's Resource Book: Audio Script, p. 7; Audio Program DVD: Cap. 5A, Track 3; Answer Keys: Student Edition, p. 63

Focus: Listening comprehension about family members' ages and names

Suggestions: Review the words ***menor*** and ***mayor.*** Then play the audio or read the script. You may wish to allow students to hear the entire script once before asking them to respond.

Script and Answers:

1. **Mi hermano se llama Esteban. *(up)***
2. **Mi tío tiene cuarenta y dos años. *(up)***
3. **Mi hermana menor se llama Ana Isabel. *(down)***
4. **Mi madre tiene treinta y ocho años. *(down)***
5. **Mi perro se llama Michi. *(down)***
6. **Mi primo se llama Esteban. *(down)***
7. **Mi abuela es mayor que mi abuelo. *(down)***
8. **Mi perro se llama Capitán. *(up)***

Common Errors: Students confuse similar words that differentiate gender, such as ***primo*** and ***prima.*** Remind them that words ending in *a* are usually feminine and words ending in *o* are usually masculine.

2 Standards: 1.2

Resources: Teacher's Resource Book: Audio Script, p. 7; Audio Program DVD: Cap. 5A, Track 4; Answer Keys: Student Edition, p. 63

Focus: Listening comprehension about preparing for a party

Suggestions: Play the audio or read the script. Pause between each statement to monitor students. Have them listen to the script again as you review the answers.

Script and Answers:

1. **Necesitamos muchos globos, ¿no? *(balloons)***
2. **A Angélica le encantan las flores. *(flowers)***
3. **A los chicos les encanta la piñata, ¿no? *(piñata)***
4. **Hay globos y luces en la fiesta de cumpleaños, ¿no? *(balloons, lights)***
5. **Ya tenemos dulces, ¿verdad? *(candies)***
6. **No me gusta el papel picado de plástico. *(cut-paper decorations)***
7. **Y en el pastel vamos a escribir "¡Feliz cumpleaños!". *(cake)***

ENRICH YOUR TEACHING

Culture Note

Paper flowers are popular party decorations in Mexico. The flowers are made from tissue paper (***papel de china***) that is folded and bound together with wire. While some paper flowers require a great deal of skill to fold, cut, and shape, there are more simple techniques that children can use to create these decorations.

Teacher-to-Teacher

Have students plan a party where every guest has to bring things to the party. Show students how to make a simple invitation with entries as follows: ***La fecha:*** _____, ***La hora:*** _____; ***El lugar:*** _____ (for example, ***en la casa de Martina***). Then have students request that people bring food or decorations next to the entry: ***Por favor, necesitamos:*** _____ ***y*** _____.

Videohistoria

Core Instruction

Standards: 1.2, 2.1

Resources: Voc. and Gram. Transparencies 98–99; Audio Program DVD: Cap. 5A, Track 5

Focus: Presenting contextualized vocabulary; previewing the video

Suggestions:

Pre-reading: Have students read the *Strategy*, look at the pictures, then point out details that will help them with the story line. Using the transparencies, ask students to predict what will happen panel by panel.

Reading: Have students play the roles of the characters or use the audio. Using transparencies, and non-verbal clues, help students understand the new words in blue type. Ask comprehension questions.

Post-reading: Complete *Actividad* 3.

Video

Core Instruction

Standards: 1.2, 2.1

Resources: Teacher's Resource Book: Video Script, p. 10; Video Program: Cap. 5A; Video Program Teacher's Guide: Cap. 5A

Focus: Hearing and seeing contextualized vocabulary; listening comprehension

Suggestions:

Pre-viewing: Remind students to use prior experience to help them understand the video. Have them think of birthday parties they have attended and how people react when they are recorded on video. Tell them that when they see the images for the new vocabulary words in the video, they should try to listen for these words in the conversation.

Viewing: Show the video once without pausing, and then show it again, stopping to check for comprehension. Write difficult words on the board. Show the segment a final time without pausing.

Post-viewing: Complete the Video Activities in the *Communication Workbook*.

¡Feliz cumpleaños!

¿Qué pasa en la fiesta de Cristina? Lee la historia.

Strategy

Using visuals
Look at the pictures as you read to help you get the details of the story.

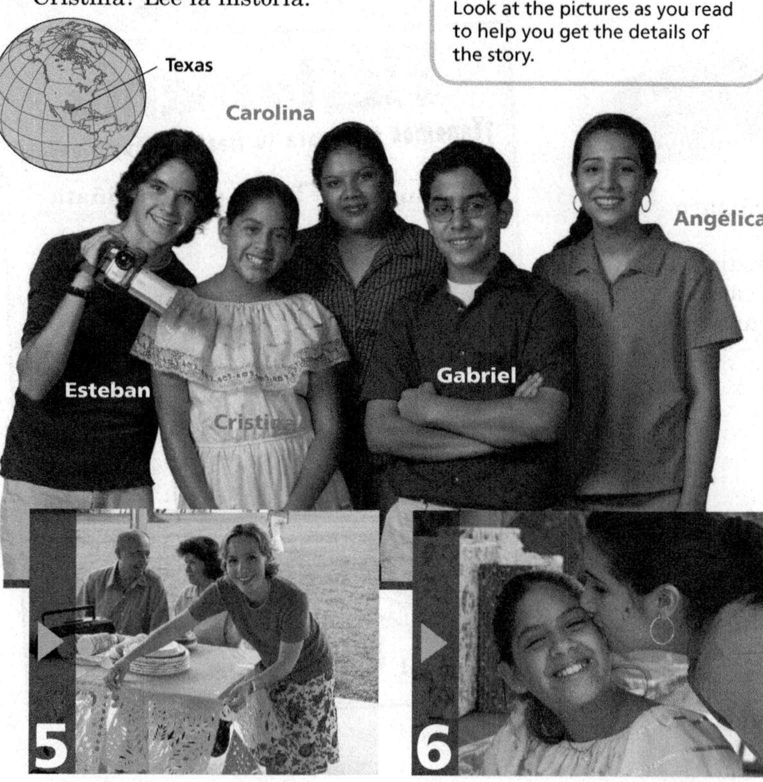

Esteban: Vamos a **hacer un video.** Uno . . . dos . . . tres . . . ¡Acción!

Angélica: Hola, me llamo Angélica. Hoy es el cumpleaños de **nuestra** hermana, Cristina. Todos están aquí para celebrar.

Angélica: Aquí está mi madre. A **mamá** le gustan **las decoraciones.**

Madre: Sí. A mí me encanta **decorar** con papel picado.

Angélica: Y aquí está Cristina. Hoy es su cumpleaños. **¡Feliz cumpleaños!**

Cristina: ¿Cuándo puedo **abrir** mis regalos?

Angélica: Ahora no. Primero, la piñata.

Padre: ¡Vamos, Gabriel! ¿Puedes **romper** la piñata?

Gabriel: ¡Por supuesto!

Todos: *Dale, dale, dale, no pierdas el tino, porque si lo pierdes, pierdes el camino.*

(¡Crac! *Gabriel rompe la piñata y . . .*)

DIFFERENTIATED INSTRUCTION

Multiple Intelligences

Musical/Rhythmic: Have students use the Internet or library resources to look for Spanish folk songs like the ***piñata*** song. Have them bring in the lyrics, and if you are familiar with the tune, have students sing along. Suggest that students find out on which occasions the song is sung.

Students with Learning Difficulties

Preview the questions for *Actividad* 3 by reading them with students. Have students look carefully at the pictures from the *Videohistoria* to see if they can predict any answers to the questions. Preview the new vocabulary words.

Angélica: Aquí están mis abuelos. ¿Y **cuántos años tienen Uds.?**

Abuelo: Pues, yo tengo sesenta y ocho años y tu abuela . . .

Abuela: Por favor, Ricardo. Angélica, ¡qué pregunta!

Angélica: Aquí está Gabriel, mi primo menor. Le gusta mucho el fútbol. Y aquí está mi prima. ¿Cómo te llamas?

Carolina: Pero, Angélica, tú sabes mi nombre.

Angélica: Sí, pero es para el video. Por favor . . .

Angélica: Él es **nuestro** padre. ¿Qué haces, **papá?**

Padre: Voy a preparar unas hamburguesas y después voy a sacar fotos de la fiesta.

Madre: ¡Gabriel! ¡La piñata! ¡El pastel! ¡Ay, no!

3 ¿Comprendes?

Escribir • Hablar

1. ¿Quién va a hacer el video, Gabriel o Esteban?
2. ¿Quién tiene sesenta y ocho años, el abuelo o la abuela?
3. ¿A quién le gusta jugar al fútbol, a Esteban o a Gabriel?
4. ¿Qué va a hacer el padre, decorar o preparar hamburguesas?
5. ¿Con qué decora la madre, con globos o con papel picado?
6. ¿Quién rompe la piñata, Cristina o Gabriel?

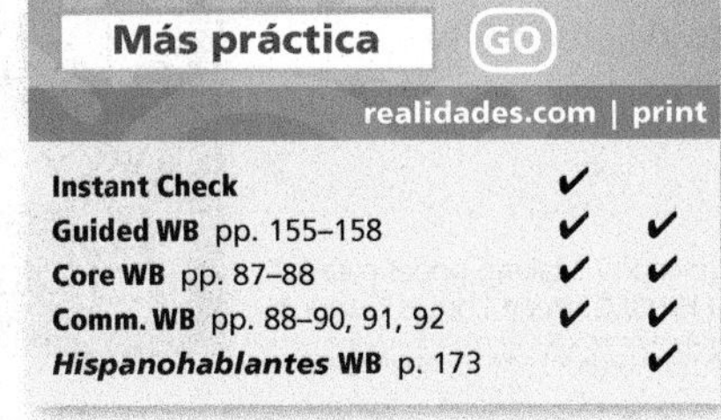

Más práctica GO

	realidades.com	print
Instant Check	✔	
Guided WB pp. 155–158	✔	✔
Core WB pp. 87–88	✔	✔
Comm. WB pp. 88–90, 91, 92	✔	✔
***Hispanohablantes* WB** p. 173		✔

3 Standards: 1.1, 1.3

Resources: Answer Keys: Student Edition, p. 64

Focus: Reading for understanding

Suggestions: Point out to students that each question is asking them to identify one of two possible responses. When reviewing the responses, have students say in which panel they found the information.

Answers:

1. **Esteban va a hacer el video.**
2. **El abuelo (de Cristina) tiene sesenta y ocho años.**
3. **A Gabriel le gusta el fútbol.**
4. **El padre va a preparar hamburguesas.**
5. **La madre decora con papel picado.**
6. **Gabriel rompe la piñata.**

Pre-AP* Support

- **Learning Objective:** Presentational Writing and Speaking
- **Activity:** As a post-viewing activity, have groups of students rewrite the first three frames of the video, changing the names, the family members, and other details of the scene. Then have students act their new versions of the scene in front of the class.
- ***Pre-AP* Resource Book:*** Comprehensive guide to Pre-AP* vocabulary skill development, pp. 51–57

Additional Resources

- Communication Wbk.: Audio Act. 5, p. 91
- Teacher's Resource Book: Audio Script, pp. 7–8
- Audio Program DVD: Cap. 5A, Track 6

ENRICH YOUR TEACHING

Culture Note

Piñatas are crafts that serve as both party decorations and entertainment. Although other materials are now common, traditional ***piñatas*** are made from a clay pot, or ***olla de barro,*** with papier-mâché attached to complete the desired shape. Curled strips and streamers of tissue paper are then glued on the outside. The breaking of the ***piñata*** is a ritual, with a song urging the blindfolded child to hit the ***piñata*** and bring down the shower of candies, fruit, or small toys that it contains.

Search online with the keyword ***piñata*** to read more about the tradition, learn how to create a piñata, and view different designs.

ASSESSMENT

Quiz: Vocabulary Recognition

- Prueba 5A-1: pp. 119–120

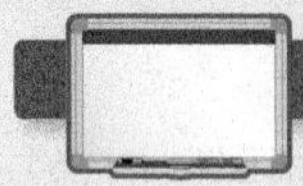

INTERACTIVE WHITEBOARD
Vocabulary Activities 5A

4 Standards: 1.2, 1.3
Resources: Answer Keys: Student Edition, p. 64
Focus: Using new vocabulary orally and in writing
Suggestions: If students are having difficulties determining the relationship, refer them to the family tree on p. 222.
Answers:

1. tía
2. abuelo
3. hermanastro
4. primos
5. tío
6. abuelos
7. hermanastra
8. primo

BELLRINGER REVIEW

Distribute Clip Art (TRB 1A). Working in pairs, have students show their partners two of the activities that five family members or friends like to do. (Ex. *A mi hermano le gusta patinar.*)

5 Standards: 1.2, 1.3
Resources: Answer Keys: Student Edition, p. 64
Focus: Choosing vocabulary words based on contextual clues
Suggestions: Ask students to read through the *Actividad* before beginning. Remind them to focus on meaning when they see verbs, since both choices are in the same person.
Answers:

1. celebramos
2. tiene
3. le
4. decoran
5. luces
6. flores
7. nuestro
8. video
9. sacar
10. rompemos
11. dulces
12. abrir

Fondo cultural

Standards: 2.1, 2.2, 4.2
Resources: Fine Art Transparencies, p. 35
Suggestions: Refer students again to the ***papel picado*** in Lomas Garza's painting on p. 220 and in the *Videohistoria* on p. 224. Point out that some cutouts are very intricate, while others are more simple. Like the paper flowers, ***papel de china*** is often used for ***papel picado.***
Answers will vary but may include paper dolls and snowflakes.

Objectives

- Write and talk about family members and celebrations
- Exchange information while discussing your family and family activities with a classmate

Vocabulario en uso

4 ¿Quién es?

Leer • Escribir • Hablar

Completa cada frase con la palabra apropiada.

Modelo
La madre de mi madre es mi abuela.

1. La esposa de mi tío es mi ___.
2. El padre de mi padre es mi ___.
3. El hijo de mi madrastra es mi ___.
4. Paco y Ana son mis tíos. Sus hijos son mis ___.
5. El hermano de mi madre es mi ___.
6. Los padres de mi padre son mis ___.
7. La hija de mi padrastro es mi ___.
8. El hermano de mi prima es mi ___.

5 En la fiesta de cumpleaños

Leer • Escribir • Hablar

Escribe la palabra apropiada para completar cada frase.

Hoy 1. *(celebramos / sacamos)* la fiesta de cumpleaños de mi hermana menor, Cristina. ¿Cuántos años 2. *(es / tiene)* ella? Trece.

A nuestra madre 3. *(le / me)* encantan las fiestas. Mamá y mi hermana 4. *(decoran / rompen)* el patio con 5. *(luces / pasteles)* y 6. *(fiestas / flores)*.

A 7. *(nuestro / nuestra)* hermano le gusta hacer un 8. *(regalo / video)* o 9. *(abrir / sacar)* fotos de la fiesta. Siempre hay una piñata que nosotros 10. *(abrimos / rompemos)*. En la piñata hay 11. *(dulces / flores)* sabrosos. Ahora Cristina va a 12. *(romper / abrir)* sus regalos.

Fondo Cultural | México

El papel picado Mexican families frequently decorate for celebrations by using *papel picado* (cut paper). It is made by folding and cutting layers of colored tissue paper to create designs or scenes that are then hung as decorations.

- What crafts do you know that use similar techniques?

"Haciendo papel picado / Making papel picado" (1998),Carmen Lomas Garza

DIFFERENTIATED INSTRUCTION

Multiple Intelligences

Visual/Spatial: Have students bring in a photo of a recent family celebration or a magazine cutout of people at a party. Then have them brainstorm what they could say to describe the scene. In small groups, have them ask and answer questions such as: *¿Qué celebran? ¿Quién está en la fiesta? ¿Qué hacen?*

Students with Learning Difficulties

Preview *Actividad* 4 by helping students to provide the English for the item stems (*La esposa de mi padre* is "my father's wife.") For *Actividad* 5, have students read each phrase aloud twice, using a different answer choice each time. This will facilitate the meaning.

6 Mi familia | 

Hablar

Habla de los miembros de tu familia o de otra familia.

Dos hermanos de la República Dominicana

Modelo

hermanos

A —*¿Tienes hermanos?*
B —*Sí, tengo un hermano y una hermana.*
o: *No, no tengo hermanos.*
A —*¿Cómo se llaman?*
B —*Mi hermano se llama David y mi hermana se llama Abby.*

Para decir más . . .
el (la) hijo(a) único(a) — only child

Estudiante A

1. tíos
2. primos
3. un abuelo
4. una hermana mayor
5. hermanos menores
6. una tía favorita
7. una abuela
8. un gato o un perro

Estudiante B

¡Respuesta personal!

7 A mi familia le gusta . . . |  | 

Hablar

Habla de las actividades favoritas de los miembros de tu familia o de otra familia.

Modelo

primo

A —*¿Qué le gusta hacer a tu primo?*
B —*Le gusta sacar fotos.*

Estudiante A

1. padre
2. madre
3. abuelo
4. hermana
5. prima o primo favorito(a)
6. tía o tío favorito(a)
7. perro o gato

Estudiante B

¡Respuesta personal!

8 Y tú, ¿qué dices? |  |

Escribir • Hablar

1. Describe a una persona de tu familia o de otra familia. ¿Cómo se llama? ¿Cuántos años tiene? ¿Cómo es? ¿Qué le gusta hacer?
2. ¿Tienes un perro o un gato? ¿Cómo se llama? ¿Cuántos años tiene?
3. ¿Qué te gusta hacer durante *(during)* una fiesta de cumpleaños?

6 Standards: 1.1

Resources: Answer Keys: Student Edition, p. 65

Focus: Asking and telling about family

Suggestions: Students can talk about their families or fictional ones.

Answers will vary for Student B, but Student A will say:

—¿Tienes (1. tíos; 2. primos; 3. un abuelo; 4. una hermana mayor; 5. hermanos menores; 6. una tía favorita; 7. una abuela; 8. un gato o un perro)?
—¿Cómo (1. se llaman; 2. se llaman; 3. se llama; 4. se llama; 5. se llaman; 6. se llama; 7. se llama; 8. se llama)?

7 Standards: 1.1

Resources: Answer Keys: Student Edition, p. 65

Focus: Using family vocabulary

Recycle: Leisure activities

Suggestions: Brainstorm leisure activities with students for *¡Respuesta personal!*

Answers will vary for Student B, but Student A will say:

—¿Qué le gusta hacer (1. a tu padre; 2. a tu madre; 3. a tu abuelo; 4. a tu hermana; 5. a tu prima o primo favorito; 6. a tu tía o tío favorito; 7. a tu perro o gato)?

B17
p. 226 – Act 5
6 – 7
partner – ask for volunteers / sticks
#8
#8 – #1 Homework / Friday

ENRICH YOUR TEACHING

Culture Note

Papel picado designs often depict humans, animals, and flowers, and contain lattice-work and lettering. The color schemes implemented are usually representative of the celebration the art was created for, such as red, white, and green—the colors of the Mexican flag—for Mexico's Independence Day.

21st Century Skills

Creativity and Innovation Have students recycle vocabulary and grammar concepts by using a combination of print and visuals to create a chart on which they match each family member or friend with a color that represents a personality trait.

ASSESSMENT

Prueba 5A-2 with Study Plan (online only)

Quiz: Vocabulary Production
- Prueba 5A-2: pp. 121–122

Gramática

Core Instruction

Standards: 4.1

Resources: Voc. and Gram. Transparency 100; Teacher's Resource Book: Video Script, pp. 10–11; Video Program: Cap. 5A

INTERACTIVE WHITEBOARD

Grammar Activities 5A

Focus: Learning the verb ***tener***

Suggestions: Direct students' attention to the *¿Recuerdas?* Use the transparency to reinforce the forms of ***tener.*** Emphasize that ***tenemos*** and ***tenéis*** are the only forms that don't have the ***e → ie*** stem change. Use the *GramActiva* Video as a follow-up after your own grammar explanation.

9 Standards: 1.2, 1.3

Resources: Answer Keys: Student Edition, p. 65

Focus: Using forms of the verb ***tener***

Suggestions: Point out that a *Rompecabezas* is a puzzle or brain teaser.

Answers:

1. tiene
2. tenemos
3. tienen
4. tiene

Enrique tiene 23 años.
(19+17+17+12+12 = 77; 100-77=23)

10 Standards: 1.1

Resources: Answer Keys: Student Edition, p. 66

Focus: Using ***tener*** and new vocabulary

Suggestions: Have student volunteers act out the model.

Answers:

1. —¿Qué tiene David para la fiesta?
—David tiene los dulces.
2. —¿Qué tiene Yolanda para la fiesta?
—Yolanda tiene el pastel.
3. —¿Qué tiene tu abuela para la fiesta?
—Mi abuela tiene las luces.
4. —¿Qué tienes tú para la fiesta?
—Tengo los regalos.
5. —¿Qué tienen Uds. para la fiesta?
—Tenemos los globos.
6. —¿Qué tienen Juan y Marcos para la fiesta?
—Tienen las flores.

Manos a la obra

Gramática

Objectives

- Talk about what people have and have to do
- Interview a classmate and write a description of a classmate's family and their ages
- Read about, identify, and describe the ages of members of the Spanish royal family

The verb *tener*

The verb *tener* is used to show relationship or possession.

Tengo un hermano mayor.	*I have an older brother.*
Tenemos un regalo para Tere.	*We have a gift for Tere.*

Some expressions in Spanish use *tener* where English uses "to be."

Mi primo tiene dieciséis años.	*My cousin is sixteen years old.*
Tengo hambre y sed.	*I am hungry and thirsty.*

Here are all the present-tense forms of *tener:*

(yo)	tengo	(nosotros) (nosotras)	tenemos
(tú)	tienes	(vosotros) (vosotras)	tenéis
Ud. (él) (ella)	tiene	Uds. (ellos) (ellas)	tienen

¿Recuerdas?

You have been using the verb *tener* for several chapters.

- **¿Tienes** una bicicleta?
- **Tengo** que hacer ejercicio.

Más ayuda realidades.com

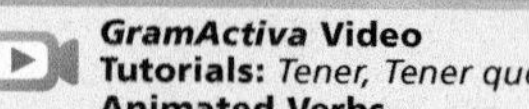
GramActiva Video Tutorials: *Tener, Tener que*
Animated Verbs

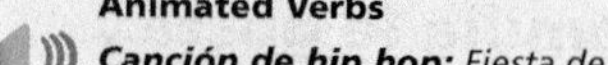
Canción de hip hop: *Fiesta de cumpleaños*

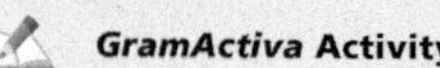
GramActiva Activity

9 Rompecabezas

Leer • Escribir • Pensar

Escribe la forma apropiada del verbo *tener* para cada frase. Luego *(Then)* resuelve el problema.

El total de las edades *(ages)* de los hijos de nuestra familia es cien. Marta __1.__ 19 años. Paco y yo __2.__ dos años menos que Marta. Laura y Eva __3.__ cinco años menos que Paco y yo. ¿Cuántos años __4.__ nuestro hermano mayor, Enrique?

10 ¿Qué hay para la fiesta?

Hablar

Pregunta a otro(a) estudiante qué tienen estas personas para la fiesta.

Ana

Modelo

A — *¿Qué tiene Ana?*
B — *Ana tiene la piñata.*

1. David

2. Yolanda
3. tu abuela
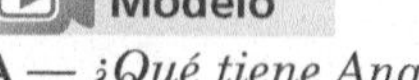
4. tú

5. Uds.

6. Juan y Marcos

DIFFERENTIATED INSTRUCTION

Multiple Intelligences

Visual/Spatial: Assign a Spanish-speaking country to the class. Have students make a decorative poster-size chart for a festival or celebration particular to that country. Each poster should include the country, the celebration, the time of year it takes place and a visual representation of its cultural or historical significance.

Students with Learning Difficulties

Make photocopies of *Actividad* 9. Have students underline the digits and the words for numbers. By highlighting the numbers, they may have an easier time solving the puzzle as they read it. For *Actividad* 11, work with students to create a format for taking notes. Let them know they do not need to write out a long sentence or copy their partner's response down word for word.

11 Entrevista |  | 

Hablar • Escribir

Interview a partner. Find out the answers to the following questions. Your partner may answer based on his or her own family or on a TV family. Write your partner's answers so that you can report your interview to the class.

1. ¿Cómo te llamas y cuántos años tienes? ¿Qué te gusta hacer?
2. ¿Cuántos hermanos mayores o menores tienes?
3. ¿Cómo se llaman tus hermanos(as) y cuántos años tienen?
4. ¿Cómo son tus hermanos(as)?
5. ¿Qué le gusta hacer a uno(a) de tus hermanos(as)?
6. ¿Tienes perros o gatos? ¿Cómo se llama(n)?

Nota

To say that a person likes or loves something, you use *le gusta(n)* or *le encanta(n)*. When you include the name of the person or the pronoun, be sure to add *a:*

- **A Pedro le** gustan los dulces.
- **A ella le** encanta sacar fotos.

12 ¡Reportaje!

Escribir • Hablar

Based on your notes from Actividad 11, write a report of your interview. Your teacher may ask you to read your report to the class.

Modelo

Anita tiene 13 años y le encanta escuchar música. Anita tiene tres hermanos: un hermano mayor y dos hermanos menores. Su hermano mayor, Peter, tiene 16 años. Sus hermanos menores se llaman Lisa y Kevin. Ellos tienen sólo once y ocho años. Son simpáticos y deportistas. A Kevin le gusta jugar al básquetbol. Anita no tiene ni perros ni gatos.

13 Preparar una fiesta de cumpleaños

Escribir • Hablar

Contesta las preguntas.

Cuando tu familia celebra un cumpleaños, ¿quién tiene que . . .

1. . . . decorar la casa? ¿Con qué?
2. . . . preparar la comida y las bebidas?
3. . . . comprar los regalos?
4. . . . hacer el pastel?
5. . . . hacer el video o sacar fotos?

¿Recuerdas?

Remember that *tener que* + infinitive means "to have to" (do something).

- Sofía **tiene que** decorar el pastel.

Celebrando un cumpleaños con una piñata

Practice and Communicate 5A

11 Standards: 1.1, 1.2, 1.3

Focus: Using family vocabulary and grammar in a personalized context

Recycle: Saying names; expressing likes; talking about activities

Suggestions: Explain that students will need this information to complete *Actividad* 12. Point out question 4, and explain to students that the question *¿Cómo son?* should be answered with a description of the person's physical and personality characteristics.

Answers will vary.

12 Standards: 1.3

Focus: Writing a paragraph based on an interview; ***tener;*** family vocabulary

Suggestions: Students can trade papers and check each other's work for content accuracy, as well as grammar and spelling. Then have students prepare a final copy, which can be read to the class.

Answers will vary.

13 Standards: 1.1, 1.3

Focus: Using vocabulary and grammar

Suggestions: Direct students' attention to the *¿Recuerdas?*, and practice answering using ***tener que* + infinitive.** Encourage students to speak about more than one person doing something: for example, *Mi padre y mi tio tienen que preparar las bebidas.*

Answers will vary.

ENRICH YOUR TEACHING

Culture Note

In many Spanish-speaking countries, people would almost never consider missing an important family event such as a baptism, wedding, or birthday. Parties for such events span several generations, with everyone from babies to grandparents celebrating together. Good friends are also included in family events.

Teacher-to-Teacher

Cooperative learning is an excellent tool, but students must be monitored to stay on task. *Actividades* 11 and 12 provide an opportunity for you to hold students accountable for their cooperative activity by asking them to produce an oral or written response after working with their group.

Teaching with Photos

In small groups, have students describe the scene using their vocabulary. Start them off with *En la fiesta, hay...* and have them create two or three original sentences to be shared with the class. Once the responses have been discussed, ask students to compare the people and activities pictured with what might go on at their own birthday party.

5A Practice and Communicate

14 Standards: 1.2

Resources: Voc. and Gram. Transparency 102; Answer Keys: Student Edition, p. 66

Focus: Reading comprehension; ***tener***

Suggestions: Upon completion, brainstorm unfamiliar words, write them on the board, and have students guess their meanings using contextual cues.

Answers:

1. tenemos	4. tengo	7. tiene
2. Tengo	5. tiene	8. tienen
3. tiene	6. tiene	9. Tienes

Extension: Have students use the transparency to create an imaginary family tree as preparation for the Theme Project.

15 Standards: 1.1, 1.2

Resources: Answer Keys: Student Edition, p. 67

Focus: Speaking using family vocabulary

Suggestions: Point out the relationship of the silhouette figures to the photo.

Answers to silhouette numbers:

1. el rey Juan Carlos I	6. el príncipe Felipe
2. Jaime	7. Leonor
3. Elena	8. la reina Sofía
4. la princesa Letizia	9. la infanta Cristina
5. Sofía de Borbón y Ortiz	10. Iñaki
	11. Irene

Fondo cultural

Standards: 3.1

Suggestions: Remind students that monarchies are governments with kings and/or queens.

Answers will vary but may include England, Jordan, the Netherlands, etc.

Additional Resources

- Communication Wbk.: Audio Act. 7, p. 92
- Teacher's Resource Book: Audio Script, p. 8
- Audio Program DVD: Cap. 5A, Track 8

ASSESSMENT

Prueba 5A-3 with Study Plan (online only)

Quiz: The verb *tener*

- Prueba 5A-3: p. 123

14 La familia de Sofía

Leer • Escribir

Look carefully at the photograph of Sofía's family, the royal family of Spain, as they celebrate her special day. As Sofía describes this family photo, complete the story with the appropriate forms of the verb *tener*.

Me llamo Sofía de Borbón y Ortiz. Mi cumpleaños es el 29 de abril. Nosotros __1.__ muchas fiestas en mi familia. En la foto celebramos un día muy especial para mí. Es el día de mi bautizo. (Yo) __2.__ una hermana mayor que se llama Leonor. Ella __3.__ dos años. También (yo) __4.__ seis primos; dos chicas y cuatro chicos: Victoria Federica que __5.__ siete años y su hermano Felipe. Felipe __6.__ nueve años. Victoria y Felipe son los hijos de mis tíos, la infanta[1] Elena y su esposo, Jaime. Ellos están a la izquierda, en el fondo[2] de la foto. A la derecha, en el fondo, están mis tíos Cristina e Iñaki con su hija Irene que __7.__ sólo cuatro meses más que mi hermana. Yo estoy en los brazos de mi mamá, la princesa Letizia. Mi padre, el príncipe Felipe, está al lado de ella con mi hermana. Mis abuelos, el rey Juan Carlos I y la reina Sofía, __8.__ 69 años. Ellos están a los dos lados de mis padres. Ellos son los reyes[3] de España. ¿ __9.__ tú tíos y primos? Me encanta tener una familia grande.

[1] In the Spanish royal family, *una infanta* is a princess *(una princesa)* who is not heir to the throne.
[2] background
[3] Note that *el rey + la reina = los reyes*

La familia de Juan Carlos I, rey de España

Fondo cultural | España

La Familia Real *(royal)* de España Juan Carlos I and Sofía have been king and queen of Spain since 1975.

- What other countries can you name that have monarchies?

Más práctica GO realidades.com | print

	realidades.com	print
Instant Check	✔	
Guided WB pp. 159–160	✔	✔
Core WB p. 89	✔	✔
Comm. WB pp. 92, 96	✔	✔
***Hispanohablantes* WB** pp. 174–177, 181		✔

15 ¿Quiénes son los miembros de la Familia Real?

Leer • Hablar • Pensar

Work with a partner to identify the members of the royal family. Use the photograph and answers from Actividad 14 to help.

Modelo

A —*Creo que el número uno es el abuelo de Sofía. Se llama Juan Carlos I.*
B —*Estoy de acuerdo.*
o: —*No estoy de acuerdo.*

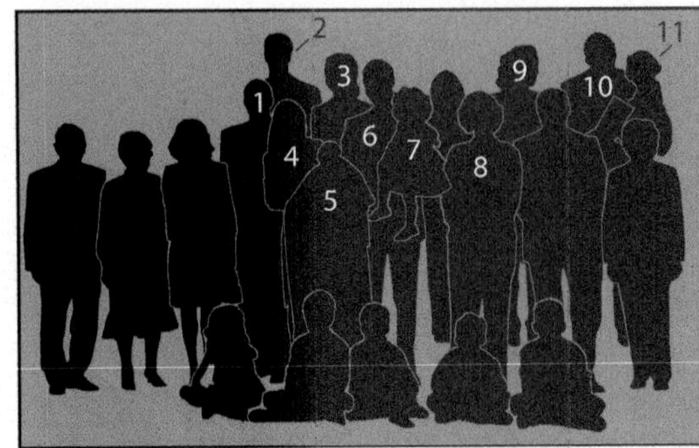

DIFFERENTIATED INSTRUCTION

Multiple Intelligences

Visual/Linguistic: Have students create and describe a fictional "royal family" and a fictional country for the family to rule. Have them present their family to a small group.

Students with Special Needs

Matching the silhouette to the photograph may be especially difficult for students with visual problems. Pair students who have strong spatial skills with those who don't.

Practice and Communicate 5A

16 La familia de Carlos IV

Leer

Before the age of photography, painted portraits were used to capture the images of people. Look carefully at the painting "La familia de Carlos IV" by Francisco de Goya and then read about the family.

Conexiones | El arte

La familia real tiene mucha importancia en la historia de España. Es el año 1800: Carlos IV *(Cuarto)* no es un rey popular y muchas personas creen que es demasiado indeciso[1]. En este cuadro[2] del pintor Francisco de Goya, puedes ver a la familia del rey Carlos IV. Carlos IV reinó[3] de 1788 a 1808.

- El pintor también está en el cuadro. ¿Puedes ver a Goya? ¿Dónde está?

"La familia de Carlos IV" (1800), Francisco de Goya ▶
Oil on canvas, 110 1/4" x 132 1/4" (280 x 336 cm). Museo Nacional del Prado, Madrid. Photo credit: Scala / Art Resource, NY.

[1]indecisive [2]painting [3]reigned

17 Carlos IV y su familia

Pensar • Hablar

Work with a partner. Point to different people in Goya's painting of the royal family and ask your partner who he or she thinks they are.

Modelo

A —*¿Quién es?*
B —*Creo que es el hijo menor.*

"Autorretrato" (*ca.* 1815)
Oil on canvas. Academia de San Fernando, Madrid, Spain. Courtesy The Bridgeman Art Library International Ltd.

Francisco de Goya (1746–1828) was one of the greatest Spanish painters and is considered by many to be the "Father of Modern Art." He was known for a wide range of art themes, including portraits of the royal family and other members of the nobility.

Fondo Cultural | España

Dos familias reales The family photo of the Spanish royal family on the preceding page was taken over 200 years after Goya painted the portrait of Juan Carlos I's ancestor and his family. Study the two pictures as you answer these questions.

- In what ways are the two pictures similar?
- How are they different?
- How would you compare them to your own family portraits?

16 Standards: 1.2, 2.2, 3.1

Resources: Answer Keys: Student Edition, p. 67
Fine Art Transparencies, p. 26

Focus: Reading comprehension; looking at art

Suggestions: As students read the passage, have them identify the cognates. Upon completion, ask a volunteer to summarize the main idea of the reading.

Answer: **Goya está a la izquierda.**

Extension: Have students work in groups to research Goya's work. Use the Internet to find three or four other paintings by Goya, and assign each one to a different group. Have that group research the painting, and provide a print to show the class as they discuss its meaning.

17 Standards: 1.1

Focus: Using family vocabulary; analyzing art

Suggestions: Remind students that they do not have to name the people but just practice the family vocabulary and make good guesses as to relationships.

You can have Student A respond to Student B's statement by saying *Estoy de acuerdo* or *No estoy de acuerdo.*

Answers will vary.

Fondo cultural

Standards: 3.1, 4.2

Resources: Fine Art Transparencies, p. 25

Mapa global interactivo, Actividad 1
Explore the Palacio Real and its surroundings in Madrid, Spain.

Suggestions: To find differences and similarities, have students compare the number, age, clothing, and poses of the people in the paintings.

Answers will vary.

Theme Project

Give students copies of the Theme Project outline and rubric from the *Teacher's Resource Book.* Explain the task to them, and have them perform Step 1. (For more information, see p. 220-b.)

ENRICH YOUR TEACHING

Culture Note

In 1975, upon the death of General Francisco Franco, King Juan Carlos I acceded to the throne of Spain as a constitutional monarch. While the king technically is the head of government, decisions and laws are made by a representative body, the ***Cortes.*** King Juan Carlos I will be succeeded by his son, Felipe, Prince of Asturias.

21st Century Skills

Critical Thinking and Problem Solving When students compare the two versions of the royal family, have them use a Venn diagram to show what is unique about each version (of the family) and what might be common to both.

Gramática

Core Instruction

Standards: 4.1

Resources: Voc. and Gram. Transparency 101; Teacher's Resource Book: Video Script, p. 11; Video Program: Cap. 5A

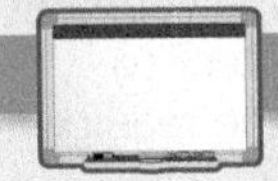

INTERACTIVE WHITEBOARD

Grammar Activities 5A

Focus: Possessive adjectives

Suggestions: Direct students' attention to the *¿Recuerdas?* Point out that they have already been using some of the possessive adjectives presented and ask volunteers for some examples.
(***mi hermano***, ***tu cumpleaños***)

Use the textbook and transparencies to present possessive adjectives. Use the *GramActiva* Video to reinforce your grammar explanation.

Point out that possessive adjectives must match the noun in number and gender and provide a few examples on the board. Underline the endings of the adjectives and nouns to emphasize agreement.

BELLRINGER REVIEW

Have students refer to page 222 and share with the class the relationship between any two people pictured.
(Ex. *José Antonio es el padre de Esteban.*)

18 Standards: 1.2, 3.2

Resources: Answer Keys: Student Edition, p. 67

Focus: Reading comprehension; using possessive adjectives

Suggestions: Have students read the entire story silently before filling in the correct forms of the adjectives. Ask students to guess which fairy tale this is.

Have them use the diagram above to check adjective agreement for gender and plural endings.

Answers:

1. Sus
2. Su
3. sus
4. nuestra
5. mi
6. tus
7. de
8. Nuestra

Gramática

Objectives

- Identify to whom something belongs
- Read and write about family relationships
- Read and listen to a description of a birthday card
- Survey and interview classmates to write about birthday celebrations

Possessive adjectives

You use possessive adjectives to tell what belongs to someone or to show relationships. In English, the possessive adjectives are *my, your, his, her, its, our,* and *their.*

Here are the possessive adjectives in Spanish:

mi(s)	nuestro(s) nuestra(s)
tu(s)	vuestro(s) vuestra(s)
su(s)	su(s)

¿Recuerdas?

You know that *de* shows possession or relationship and is the equivalent of *-'s* and *-s'*:

- el regalo **de** Ana
- los primos **de** mis amigos

Javier y yo con **nuestra** abuela

Mis padres con **su** regalo

Like other adjectives, possessive adjectives agree in number with the nouns that follow them. Only *nuestro* and *vuestro* have different masculine and feminine endings.

mi cámara	mis cámaras
nuestro abuelo	nuestros abuelos
nuestra hija	nuestras hijas

Su and *sus* can have many different meanings: *his, her, its, your,* or *their.* To be more specific, you can use *de* + noun or pronoun.

sus flores = las flores de ella

sus regalos = los regalos de Javier y Carlos

Más ayuda realidades.com

***GramActiva* Video**
Tutorials: Possessive Adjectives, Possessive Adjectives (Long Form), Possessive with *de* + pronoun

***GramActiva* Activity**

18 La Cenicienta y su familia

Leer • Escribir

Escribe la palabra o los adjetivos posesivos apropiados para completar la historia de la Cenicienta.
La Cenicienta es un personaje de un cuento muy famoso. ¿Quién es?

Cenicienta tiene una madrastra y dos hermanastras muy perezosas. __1.__ *(Sus / Tus)* hermanastras se llaman Griselda y Anastasia. __2.__ *(Nuestra / Su)* madrastra y __3.__ *(su / sus)* hermanastras siempre dicen: "¡Cenicienta! Tenemos hambre. ¿Dónde está __4.__ *(mi / nuestra)* comida?" Cada mañana Griselda le dice: "Quiero __5.__ *(mi / su)* desayuno. ¿Dónde está?" Una noche Cenicienta va al baile del príncipe. Él le pregunta a Cenicienta: "¿Cómo te llamas? ¿Quiénes son __6.__ *(tu / tus)* padres?" Las hermanastras __7.__ *(de / su)* Cenicienta ven al príncipe cuando baila con Cenicienta. Ellas dicen: "¡ __8.__ *(Nuestra / Su)* hermanastra baila con el príncipe! ¡Qué ridículo!".

DIFFERENTIATED INSTRUCTION

Heritage Language Learners

Be sure to closely monitor the agreement of adjectives and verbs in written exercises. It is not uncommon for students who have not had extensive formal writing practice in Spanish to spell phonetically. If they commonly drop certain sounds when speaking, they may tend to drop those letters in their writing.

Advanced Learners/Pre-AP*

Ask students to make a small poster presenting their hero, including a photo. They can choose a family member, a public figure, an athlete, and so on. Have them tell the person's name and age, and then list several characteristics that explain why he or she is a hero.

19 ¿Quién es tu héroe o heroína? 

Leer • Escribir • Hablar

Lee el anuncio y contesta las preguntas.

1. En este anuncio, ¿quién es el héroe? ¿De quiénes es el héroe?
2. Trabaja con otro(a) estudiante. Pregunta quién es su héroe o heroína.

Modelo

A —*¿Quién es tu héroe o heroína? ¿Cómo es?*
B —*Mi heroína es mi madre. Es muy inteligente.*

20 ¿Dónde está o dónde están?

Leer • Pensar

Un grupo de estudiantes busca *(is looking for)* sus decoraciones para una fiesta en la escuela. Empareja *(Match)* cada pregunta con la respuesta más apropiada.

1. ¿Dónde están tus flores?
2. ¿Dónde está el papel picado de Clara?
3. ¿Dónde está mi papel picado?
4. ¿Dónde están los globos de Marta y Tere?
5. ¿Dónde están las flores de Teodoro?
6. ¿Dónde están mis globos?

a. Tu papel picado está allí.
b. Sus flores están allí.
c. Mis globos están allí.
d. Mis flores están detrás del escritorio.
e. Tus globos están debajo de la mesa.
f. Su papel picado está debajo de la carpeta.
g. Sus globos están al lado de la computadora.

Practice and Communicate 5A

19 Standards: 1.1, 1.2, 1.3

Resources: Answer Keys: Student Edition, p. 67

Focus: Reading comprehension; using possessive adjectives

Suggestions: Ask students to give examples of people that they consider heroes before beginning.

Answers will vary but may include:

1. **El padre es el héroe de su hijo.**
2. **¿Quién es tu héroe o heroína? Mi héroe es... / Mi heroína es...**

BELLRINGER REVIEW

Put the words ***mi, tu, nuestro,*** and ***su*** on the board, and show students pictures of the vocabulary from this chapter. As you hold up a picture, point to a possessive adjective, and have students say the correct form of the possessive adjective before the noun.

20 Standards: 1.2

Resources: Answer Keys: Student Edition, p. 68

Focus: Using possessive adjectives

Suggestions: Remind students that they are not matching the possessive adjectives from the first column to the second but are answering the question logically. Point out that there are seven possible answers and only six questions.

Answers:

1. d	4. g
2. f	5. b
3. a	6. e

Extension: Have students write three sentences about their friends or family members using possessive adjectives: *Mi amiga Paula tiene dos hermanos. Sus hermanos son muy deportistas.*

Pre-AP* Support

- **Learning Objective:** Interpersonal Writing
- **Activity:** Have students bring to class pictures of four family members, including themselves (or an imaginary family with pictures from a magazine). Then ask them to draft an e-mail to a partner about family relationships using possessive adjectives. *(Es mi madre, Emily. Su esposo se llama Carl. Son mis hermanos, Sheridan y Taylor. Su perro se llama Amber.)*
- ***Pre-AP* Resource Book:*** Comprehensive guide to Pre-AP* communication skill development, pp. 10–57

ENRICH YOUR TEACHING

Teacher-to-Teacher

Have students bring in a photo of their family, a school function (sports event, club photo), or a photo of themselves on vacation. Working with partners, have students describe the photos. You may want to provide a list of possessive adjectives that you feel students need to practice, and have them include those words in their descriptions. After correcting spelling and grammar errors, have students write their descriptions on construction paper and attach the photos. Display them in the classroom.

21 Standards: 1.1, 1.3

Resources: Teacher's Resource Book: GramActiva BLM, p. 17

Focus: Playing a game using possessive adjectives and ***tener***

Recycle: Classroom objects

Suggestions: Have students write on the template before making it into a cube. Remind students that they must focus on both the forms of ***tener*** and the possessive adjective for the subject pronoun they roll.

Answers will vary.

22 Standards: 1.1

Focus: Using possessive adjectives, classroom vocabulary, and ***tener***

Recycle: Classroom vocabulary

Suggestions: For part 1, suggest that students make a two-column chart in their notebooks. In part 2, students can expand the chart to include their classmate. For part 3, encourage students to vary the subjects of their sentences to include the first person singular and plural, and the third person singular.

Answers will vary.

Block Schedule

Brainstorm names of families from television shows or movies. Have students write a paragraph about one of the families, including the names of the members, their relationships, their physical and personality traits, and so on.

Additional Resources

- Communication Wbk.: Audio Act. 8–9, pp. 93–94
- Teacher's Resource Book: Audio Script, pp. 8–9, Communicative Pair Activity BLM, pp. 14–15
- Audio Program DVD: Cap. 5A, Tracks 10–11

ASSESSMENT

Prueba 5A-4 with Study Plan (online only)

Quiz: Possessive Adjectives

- Prueba 5A-4: p. 124

21 Juego

Hablar • GramActiva

Modelo

Uds. tienen su calculadora.

1. Working with a partner, make a set of two cubes using the template your teacher will give you.
   - **Cube 1** Write a different subject pronoun on each side.
   - **Cube 2** Write a different classroom object on each side. Make three of them singular and three of them plural.
   - **Both cubes** Write a different point value from 1 to 6 on each side.
2. You and your partner will play against another pair of students. Team 1 rolls both of your cubes and says a sentence using the correct form of the verb *tener,* the appropriate possessive adjective, and the classroom object. If the sentence is correct, Team 1 receives the total points shown on the cubes. Team 2 then rolls the other cubes. Continue until a team reaches 100 points or time is called.

22 ¿Qué tienen y para qué clase?  

Hablar

¿Qué tienen tus compañeros hoy?

1. Escribe cinco cosas *(things)* que usas en la escuela y para qué clases son.
2. Pide *(Ask for)* las respuestas a tres compañeros y escríbelas en una hoja de papel.

   Modelo

   A —*¿Qué tienes para tus clases hoy?*
   B —*Tengo mi calculadora para la clase de matemáticas y mi carpeta para la clase de inglés.*
3. Escribe cinco frases para describir las cosas que tienen los estudiantes para las clases de hoy.

   Modelo

   Ana tiene su carpeta para la clase de inglés.
   Paco y yo tenemos nuestros lápices para la clase de arte.

¿Recuerdas?

You have been using vocabulary for classroom supplies for several chapters.

Más práctica GO

realidades.com | print

Instant Check	✔	
Guided WB pp. 161–162	✔	✔
Core WB pp. 90–91	✔	✔
Comm. WB pp. 93–94, 97, 275	✔	✔
Hispanohablantes WB pp. 178–181		✔

DIFFERENTIATED INSTRUCTION

Heritage Language Learners

When presenting the *Exploración del lenguaje* on p. 235, ask students to list additional examples of diminutives. Do they or their family members commonly use diminutives? Whom would they most often address or describe using diminutives?

Students with Special Needs

Prepare an extra set of dice for any students who have difficulties with fine motor skills.

Exploración del lenguaje

Diminutives

In Spanish you can add the suffix *-ito(a)* to a word to give it the meaning of "small" or "little." It can also be used to show affection. Words with this suffix are called diminutives *(diminutivos)*.

abuelo → abuel**ito**

perros → perr**itos**

hermana → herman**ita**

Now that you know what the suffix *-ito(a)* means, can you figure out the meanings of these words?

abuelita gatito Miguelito hijita

Some very popular names are diminutives. What do you think the diminutives of these names are?

Ana Juana Eva Lola

23 ¡Feliz cumpleaños!

Leer • Pensar

Read the birthday card. Who is it for? Find the diminutives. What words in the poem do you understand? How many objects in the picture can you name in Spanish?

24 La fiesta de cumpleaños

Escuchar

En una hoja de papel, escribe los números del 1 al 6. Mira la tarjeta *(card)* de cumpleaños y escucha las frases. Si la frase es cierta, escribe *C*. Si es falsa, escribe *F*.

ENRICH YOUR TEACHING

Culture Note

In Mexico, the use of the diminutive is so common that *not* to use it when talking of one's grandparents, for example, would seem to show a lack of affection. Friends often refer to each other using the diminutive form even as adults, and older siblings refer to their ***hermanitos*** using the diminutive, such as Carmelita, Teresita, Elenita, etc.

Teacher-to-Teacher

Have students create a birthday card in Spanish. You can help by providing Spanish-language cards for wording. Collect them and keep them in a folder. Then, whenever another student or staff member has a birthday, you can give him or her one of the student-made cards to celebrate.

Exploración del lenguaje

Core Instruction

Standards: 4.1

Resources: Answer Keys: Student Edition, p. 68

Suggestions: Point out that in English diminutives are formed by adding *-y* or *-ie* to words: Bobby, doggie. Note that the diminutives of some names are first turned into nicknames: ***Manuel*** becomes ***Manolo,*** then ***Manolito; Dolores*** becomes ***Lola,*** then ***Lolita,*** etc.

Answers:

little grandma, kitty, little Miguel, little daughter; Anita, Juanita, Evita, Lolita

23 Standards: 1.2

Resources: Voc. and Gram. Transparency 103; Answer Keys: Student Edition, p. 68

Focus: Reading for understanding

Suggestions: Remind students that they do not need to understand every word to understand the message.

Answers:

The birthday card is for a child. Diminutives: *globitos, pastelito, regalitos, perritos, contentitos, añitos.*
Objects: *luces, flores, globos, pastel, perro, piñata, regalos, papel picado*

24 Standards: 1.2

Resources: Teacher's Resource Book: Audio Script, p. 8; Audio Program DVD: Cap. 5A, Track 9; Answer Keys: Student Edition, p. 68

Focus: Listening for understanding

Suggestions: Play the audio or read the script. Allow students to listen a second time, and give time between each statement for them to determine the answer. Finally, allow them to listen to check their work.

Script and Answers:

1. **La fiesta es en un restaurante. *(F)***
2. **Usan globos para decorar. *(C)***
3. **Hay muchos perritos en la fiesta. *(C)***
4. **Van a comer pastel en la fiesta de cumpleaños. *(C)***
5. **Van a abrir regalos en la fiesta. *(C)***
6. **Hay un gato en la fiesta. *(F)***

Pronunciación
Core Instruction

Standards: 4.1

Resources: Teacher's Resource Book: Audio Script, p. 9; Audio Program DVD: Cap. 5A, Tracks 12–13

Suggestions: When you model the English consonants, exaggerate the puff of air. Distribute tissues so students can see them move when they say the English words. Then have students say the Spanish words with you. Remind them that you can check their pronunciation by watching the tissue.

Allow students to listen to the nursery rhyme a few times before repeating it. Use the tissues again to check the pronunciation.

Fondo cultural

Standards: 2.1, 2.2, 3.1

Resources: Fine Art Transparencies, p. 51

Mapa global interactivo, Actividad 2

Look at Mexico and the countries of Central America, the region known as Mesoamerica.

Suggestions: To help students answer the question, point out that the woman seems to be working laboriously on preparing the tortilla. Ask students how they feel when they are putting a lot of physical effort into a task.

Answers will vary but may include empathetic, admiring, or intrigued.

El español en la comunidad
Core Instruction

Standards: 4.2, 5.1

Suggestions: Have students read their lists to the class. Keep a tally on the board of which names appear in the telephone book and how often they appear. Have students rank them and create a bar graph to compare them.

Pronunciación | 

The letters *p, t,* and *q*

In English the consonants *p, t, q,* and the hard *c* sound are pronounced with a little puff of air.

Hold a tissue loosely in front of your mouth as you say these English words. You will notice that the tissue moves.

pan	papa	too	tea
comb	case	park	take

Now say these Spanish words with the tissue in front of your mouth. Try to say the consonants so that there is no puff of air and the tissue does not move.

pan	papá	tú	tía
cómo	queso	parque	taco

Try it out! Listen to this nursery rhyme. Listen particularly for the *p, t,* and *q* sounds. Then repeat the rhyme.

Tortillitas para mamá,
tortillitas para papá.
Las quemaditas,[1] para mamá,
las bonitas,[2] para papá.

[1] The burned ones [2] The pretty ones

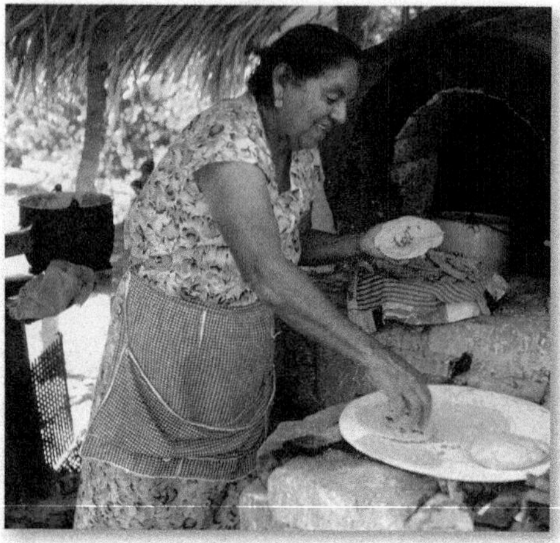

Haciendo tortillas en Chiapas, México

Fondo Cultural | México

Diego Rivera (1886–1957) This painting by Mexican muralist Diego Rivera shows a woman grinding maize on a *metate,* a utensil used for grinding grain. This is one of many paintings in which Rivera portrays the daily life of the indigenous peoples of Mexico.

- Through paintings, an artist conveys feelings to the viewer. What do you think Rivera wants you to feel about this woman and her task?

"La molendera" (1926), Diego Rivera

Oil on canvas, 35 7/16 X 46 1/16 inches. Museo Nacional de Arte Moderno, Instituto Nacional de Bellas Artes, Mexico City, D.F., Mexico. © 2009 Banco de México Diego Rivera & Frida Kahlo Museums Trust, México, D.F. / Artists Rights Society (ARS), New York.

El español en la comunidad

The five most common last names in the United States, in order, are Smith, Johnson, Williams, Brown, and Jones. The five most common last names in the United States for people of Spanish-speaking heritage, in order, are García, Martínez, Rodríguez, López, and Hernández.

- Look up these names in your school directory or local phone listings. Count the entries for each. Do the numbers in your community match the statistics above? Can you identify two other Hispanic last names common in your community or that you are familiar with?

DIFFERENTIATED INSTRUCTION

Heritage Language Learners

Have students name a food item that is a staple of the diet in their heritage country, as tortillas are in Mexico. If possible, have students bring in the recipe, and have a volunteer prepare the dish to share with the class.

Multiple Intelligences

Visual/Spatial: Explain that Diego Rivera made his art available to the public by painting murals. Using a long sheet of rolled paper, have students create a mural that depicts any of the cultural products, practices, or perspectives discussed in *Realidades.* Post the murals in the classroom and have other classmates try to identify their subjects and meanings.

25 Un cumpleaños divertido 

Hablar • Escribir

Find out from your classmates what they consider to be a great birthday. Make a chart like the one below on a sheet of paper and complete the first row about yourself. Then survey four classmates to find out what their preferences are and record the information in the chart.

Modelo

¿En qué mes es tu cumpleaños?
¿Cuál es tu actividad y lugar (place) *favorito?*
¿Cuáles son tus comidas favoritas?

	Mes del cumpleaños	Actividad y lugar favorito	Comidas favoritas
yo	julio	comer–un restaurante	pastel y helado
Miguel	enero	abrir regalos–en casa	pizza y ensalada
Anita	julio	bailar–un baile	hamburguesas y helado

26 ¿Quién es esta persona?

Escuchar • Hablar • Escribir • Leer

1. Use your completed chart from Actividad 25 and describe a classmate to the class. Do not give that person's name. The class will try to guess whom you are describing.

Modelo

Su cumpleaños es en enero. Para su cumpleaños le gusta abrir regalos en casa. Sus comidas favoritas en su cumpleaños son pizza y ensalada. ¿Quién es?

2. Write a paragraph describing the person you interviewed whose idea of a great birthday celebration is most like your own. Describe the similarities, but also mention differences.

Modelo

Nuestro cumpleaños es en julio. Nuestra comida favorita es el helado. El lugar favorito para mi cumpleaños es un restaurante porque me gusta comer. Su lugar favorito es un baile porque le gusta bailar. A ella le gustan las hamburguesas pero a mí me gusta el pastel. ¿Quién es la persona? Es Anita.

Un chico con su mejor amigo

25 Standards: 1.1, 1.3

Focus: Using party vocabulary in a personalized context

Recycle: Months; activities; places; food and drink vocabulary

Suggestions: As you read the directions, pause to discuss with students what it is that they like to do to celebrate their birthdays. How do these activities vary based on when the birthday is? You can either have students work in groups of 5 or give students time to go around the room and choose 4 students to interview. Remind students that they will need to use their charts for *Actividad* 26.

Answers will vary.

26 Standards: 1.2, 1.3

Focus: Using party vocabulary in a personalized context

Recycle: Months; activities; places; food and drink vocabulary

Suggestions: You might want to write the model on a transparency and highlight the parts that will be replaced. As students read their descriptions, encourage others to refer to their charts and guess which student is being described.

Answers will vary.

Pre-AP* Support

- **Learning Objective:** Interpersonal Speaking
- **Activity 25:** Students practice informal speaking skills as they ask and answer survey questions.

ENRICH YOUR TEACHING

Culture Note

Rivera's painting highlights the tortilla, a staple of the traditional Mexican diet. The tortilla can accompany any meal and is commonly made of corn meal (though in the north, tortillas are made of wheat flour). Formerly, tortillas were handmade every morning, but today families are more likely to purchase their tortillas from a ***tortillería.***

21st Century Skills

Collaboration Have students work in small groups to set up a chart similar to the one in Activity 25 for family members of the group. Determine through this chart what the family members have in common. (For example: three fathers like pizza, two mothers were born in May, etc.) Make sure all students in the group participate.

Theme Project

Students can perform Step 2 at this point. Be sure they understand your corrections and suggestions. (For more information, see p. 220-b.)

Common Core: Reading

Lectura

Core Instruction

Standards: 1.2, 2.1

Focus: Reading comprehension of a birthday invitation

Suggestions:

Pre-reading: Direct attention to the *Strategy*. Ask students what words they might look for that would indicate a day, date, or time. Then have them scan the invitation to find the answers.

Reading: Present the reading in three parts—the title and introductory paragraph, the invitation, and the quotations. Have students read each part silently before having a volunteer read them aloud. Pause every few sentences to check comprehension.

Post-reading: Ask a volunteer to summarize each section of the reading. Use the *¿Comprendes?* questions to check comprehension.

BELLRINGER REVIEW

Have students write three things they might expect to find at a formal dance or party.

Pre-AP* Support

- **Learning Objective:** Interpretive: Print and Audio
- **Activity:** Have students look at the invitation for thirty seconds and then close their books. Read teacher-made false statements about the invitation and ask volunteers to correct your statements.
- ***Pre-AP* Resource Book:*** Comprehensive guide to Pre-AP* reading skill development, pp. 19–26

Objectives

- Read about a *fiesta de quince años*
- Scan to find specific information more quickly
- Learn about and explain the Hispanic system of surnames

Lectura

Mis padres te invitan a mi fiesta de quince años

Para muchas jóvenes hispanas, el día de sus quince años es una ocasión muy especial. Toda la familia y muchos amigos van a misa en la iglesia y después celebran con una fiesta. Es una tradición especialmente importante en México, América Central y los países hispanos del Caribe. También es importante entre muchos hispanohablantes en los Estados Unidos.

Aquí está la invitación a la fiesta de quince años de María Teresa Rivera Treviño.

Strategy

Scanning
What information would you expect to find on an invitation? Read quickly through this invitation and find the names of María Teresa's parents and the date and times of the two events to which you are invited.

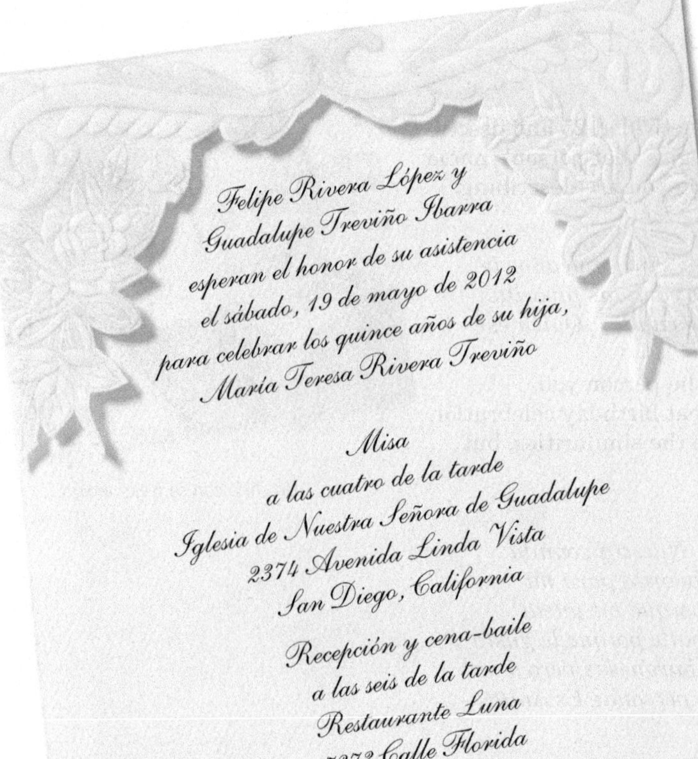
Felipe Rivera López y
Guadalupe Treviño Ibarra
esperan el honor de su asistencia
el sábado, 19 de mayo de 2012
para celebrar los quince años de su hija,
María Teresa Rivera Treviño

Misa
a las cuatro de la tarde
Iglesia de Nuestra Señora de Guadalupe
2374 Avenida Linda Vista
San Diego, California

Recepción y cena-baile
a las seis de la tarde
Restaurante Luna
7373 Calle Florida
San Diego, California

"Toda mi familia, mis amigos y yo vamos a la iglesia en la tarde. Después vamos a la recepción en un restaurante muy elegante donde comemos y bailamos. Bailo primero con mi padre y después con mis amigos".

DIFFERENTIATED INSTRUCTION

Students with Learning Difficulties

Provide photocopies of the invitation for students to use. Preview the *¿Comprendes?* questions with students, and have them highlight pertinent information on photocopies. When students write their ***nombre completo,*** they might draw a family tree with their parents' and grandparents' names to help them.

Heritage Language Learners

If students have been to a ***fiesta de quince años*** celebration, ask them to describe it. Who was there? What food was served? What did people do during the celebration? If they can, have them describe the gifts and decorations.

"Aquí estoy yo en el día de mis quince años. Es un día muy especial y toda la familia está conmigo para celebrar. Todo está perfecto para mi fiesta —la comida, las decoraciones, la música— ¡todo!"

¿Comprendes?

1. ¿Cuál es la fecha de los quince años de María Teresa?
2. Necesitas una hora para ir de tu casa a la Iglesia de Nuestra Señora de Guadalupe. ¿A qué hora tienes que salir *(leave)* de casa?
3. ¿Dónde y a qué hora es la recepción? Según la invitación, ¿qué van a hacer en la recepción?
4. ¿Qué actividad de la fiesta de quince años te gusta más?

¡Vamos a comparar!

The special celebration of a girl's fifteenth birthday is called *la quinceañera, los quince,* or *los quince años.* Think about an event in the lives of your friends that has the importance of a *quince años* celebration. How are the events similar or different?

Fondo Cultural | El mundo hispano

El nombre completo A person's full name *(nombre completo)* consists of a first name *(nombre),* which often consists of two names, plus two surnames—the father's family name *(apellido paterno),* followed by the mother's family name *(apellido materno).*

For example, look at the *nombres completos* of María Teresa's parents:

Felipe Rivera López y
Guadalupe Treviño Ibarra

- What is Felipe's *apellido paterno*?
- What is Guadalupe's *apellido materno*?
- Can you explain how María Teresa's name is formed?

María Teresa will most often use her first name and her father's family name. If she marries, she may add *de* and her husband's last name to her own name: María Teresa Rivera de García.

- Use the Spanish system to write your *nombre completo.* What advantages or disadvantages do you see to having a name formed this way?

Más práctica GO

	realidades.com	print
Guided WB p. 163	✔	✔
Comm. WB pp. 98, 276	✔	✔
***Hispanohablantes* WB** pp. 182–183		✔
Cultural Reading Activity	✔	

ENRICH YOUR TEACHING

Culture Note

La quinceañera, or ***los quince años,*** marks a young girl's coming of age. In recent years, ***los quince años*** have become very important in many Spanish-speaking communities in the United States. Some families host very elaborate ***fiestas,*** complete with formal wear for participants, catered receptions, a live band, and limousines. Others celebrate with smaller parties at home.

Teacher-to-Teacher

When discussing the *¡Vamos a comparar!* feature, many students will not have personal knowledge of such celebrations. Be sure they know they can discuss celebrations they might know about or have attended (for example, a Sweet Sixteen party, a bar or bat mitzvah, or a debutante ball).

¿Comprendes? Standards: 1.2, 1.3, 4.2

Resources: Answer Keys: Student Edition, p. 98
Focus: Reading comprehension
Suggestions: Have students read all the questions and then re-read the *Lectura* before answering the questions.
Answers:

1. **La fecha de los quince años de María Teresa es el 19 de mayo de 2012.**
2. **Tengo que salir a las tres de la tarde.**
3. **La recepción es en el Restaurante Luna a las seis de la tarde. En la fiesta, vamos (*or* ellos van) a cenar y bailar.**
4. **La actividad de la fiesta de quince años que me gusta más es (*answers will vary*).**

¡Vamos a comparar!

Focus: Reading comprehension
Suggestions: Have students brainstorm a list of events that are similar in importance to the *quinceañera* celebration. Ask them to describe each of the events on their lists.
Answers will vary.

Fondo cultural

Standards: 2.1, 4.2
Resources: Answer Keys: Student Edition, p. 69
Suggestions: Point out that in larger cities, most women simply use their own last names. They would be addressed only formally as *Sra. Treviño de López.* Discuss how last names can change for women in the United States. Ask students to state their opinions about changing last names. Have students work with partners to figure out what their last names would be using the Spanish-speaking system.
Answers:
Rivera; Ibarra; María Teresa Rivera (father's family name) Treviño (mother's family name)

For Further Reading

Student Resource: Realidades para hispanohablantes: Lectura 2, pp. 184–185

La cultura en vivo

Core Instruction

Standards: 2.1

Focus: Reading about and making ***papel picado***

Suggestions: Have students describe party decorations they are familiar with. Elicit that decorations are usually bright, lively, and evoke a celebratory feeling. They help set the mood. Explain that making ***papel picado*** is similar to making snowflakes, which students may have done in elementary school. Point to the picture at the bottom of the page, but note that not all ***papel picado*** looks alike.These are just examples.

Prepare the materials in advance. Pre-cut the paper to one size for all students. Use a variety of bright colors. Demonstrate the process by making a sample. Keep it simple, so the project moves quickly. Walk students through the steps. Remind them not to cut the hanging flap. Also they should not cut any folded edge completely. Some of it must remain intact to hold the paper together.

Paper punches come in a variety of sizes and shapes. They work well to make interior holes, stars, and other shapes.

To incorporate language use in this activity, you may want to give students words such as ***cortar, doblar, abrir, colgar***, or ***grapar.***

Additional Resources

Student Resource: Realidades para hispanohablantes, p. 186

La cultura en vivo

El papel picado

As you've seen in this chapter, *el papel picado* (cut paper) is a well-known Mexican craft. Colored tissue paper is cut into small patterns similar to making paper snowflakes. The cut paper is then hung on string to make a banner to use as decoration at many different celebrations. Here's how to make *papel picado* to decorate your classroom.

Una fiesta con música de mariachi

Materials

- colored tissue paper cut into 12" x 18" sheets
- scissors
- stapler
- string

1

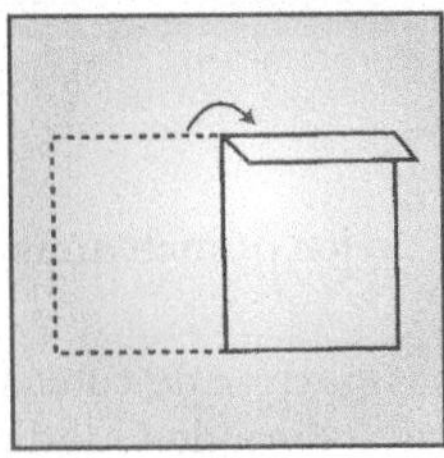

2

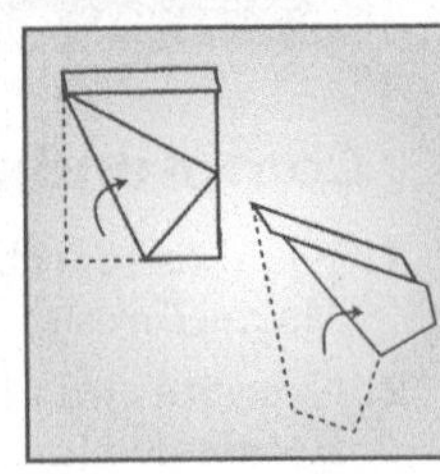

3

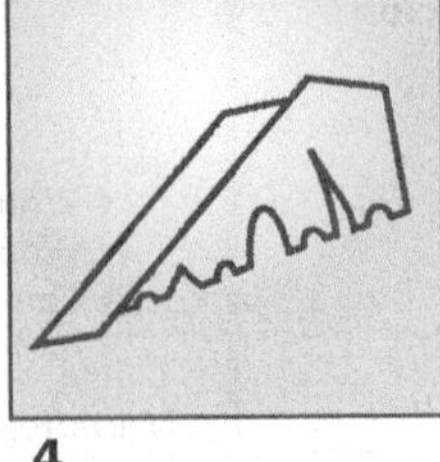

4

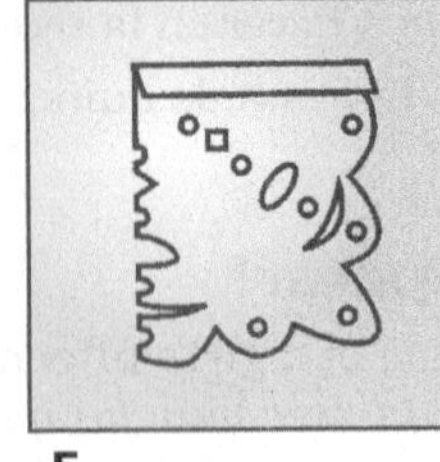

5

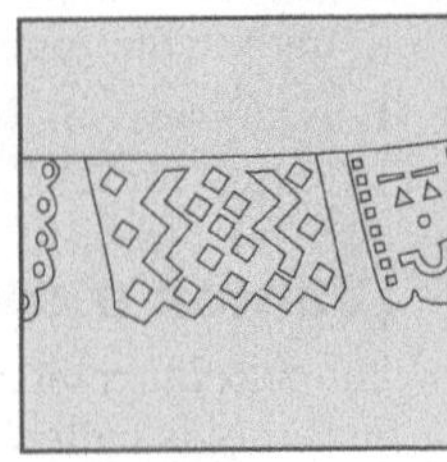

6

Directions

1. Spread the tissue paper flat. Fold down 1" on the 18" side for making a hanging flap.
2. Fold the paper in half on the 12" side and crease on the fold to make a sharp line.
3. Fold the paper twice, diagonally.
4. Cut out designs along the folded edge. Experiment with snowflake or other geometric designs.
5. Cut a scalloped design on the outside edge.
6. Open the cutout and staple to a string to hang across a room to decorate for a *fiesta*.

DIFFERENTIATED INSTRUCTION

Multiple Intelligences

Bodily/Kinesthetic: Some students may be able to produce intricate patterns. Encourage creativity. If they begin by cutting out a symmetrical shape and folding that, they may obtain interesting results. Remind them to include the hanging flap.

Students with Learning Difficulties

Some students may become frustrated with the level of detail necessary to make ***papel picado.*** Emphasize that the designs can be simple and do not need to be intricate to be festive. Provide assistance as necessary.

Objectives | Aplicación

Presentación oral 

- Describe your family members, their ages, and their likes and dislikes
- Use a chart to organize your ideas

Mi familia

Task
You are on an exchange program in Chile and your host family wants to know about your family back home. Show photographs and talk about three family members.

1 Prepare Bring in three family photos or "create" a family using magazine pictures. Use a chart to plan what to say about each person.

Nombre	Es mi ...	Edad	Actividad favorita
Isabel	hermana menor	9 años	le gusta cantar

2 Practice Go through your presentation several times. You can use notes to practice, but not to present. Try to:

- provide all the information for each family member
- use complete sentences
- speak clearly

Modelo
Se llama Isabel. Es mi hermana menor y tiene 9 años. A ella le gusta cantar. Es artística.

3 Present Show the photos and give information about each person.

4 Evaluation The following rubric will be used to grade your presentation.

Rubric	Score 1	Score 3	Score 5
How complete your preparation is	Your information is written down but without use of a chart.	You used the chart, but it is only partially completed.	You used the chart and provided all the information.
How much information you communicate	You bring in one photo and provide all the information.	You bring in two photos and provide all the information.	You bring in three photos and provide all the information.
How easily you are understood	You are extremely difficult to understand. Your teacher could only recognize isolated words and phrases.	You are understandable but have frequent errors in vocabulary and/or grammar that hinder your comprehensibility.	You are easily understood. Your teacher does not have to "decode" what you are trying to say.

Strategy
Using graphic organizers
Simple charts can help you organize your thoughts for a presentation.

ENRICH YOUR TEACHING

21st Century Skills

Communication After they give their presentations, have students come up with new categories to add to their charts, such as favorite color, favorite food, birthday month, and one thing each family member does *not* like to do. Ask students to integrate the new information into their charts.

Speaking 5A

Common Core: Speaking

Presentación oral

Core Instruction

Standards: 1.3

Focus: Speaking using vocabulary and grammar in a personal context

Suggestions: Review the task and the 4-step approach with students. Point out that their presentations must include the information listed in the chart; however, if they would like to add more information, they should not feel limited by the chart. For example, they may wish to add a column called *¿Cómo es?*

Review the rubric with the class before they begin. If possible, have students record the presentation. Hearing it two or three times may help you grade it more accurately.

Pre-AP* Support

- **Learning Objective:** Presentational Speaking
- **Activity:** Remind students to focus on the presentational speaking skills used in this task such as fluency, pronunciation, and comprehensibility.
- ***Pre-AP* Resource Book:*** Comprehensive guide to Pre-AP* speaking skill development, pp. 39–50

Portfolio

Make video or audio recordings of student presentations in class, or assign the RealTalk activity so they can record their presentations online. Include the recording in their portfolios.

Additional Resources

Student Resources: Realidades para hispanohablantes, p. 187; Guided Practice: Presentación oral, p. 164

ASSESSMENT

Presentación oral

- Assessment Program: Rubrics, p. T31

Go over the descriptions of the different levels of performance. After assessing students, help individuals understand how their performance could be improved.

Videomisterio

Core Instruction

Standards: 1.2, 1.3, 5.2

Resources: Teacher's Resource Book: Video Script, p. 11; Video Program: Cap. 5A; Video Program Teacher's Guide: Cap. 5A

Focus: Introducing the episode; scanning and reading the summary

Personajes importantes:

Lola Lago, detective
Doña Lupe, portera
Doña Gracia, vecina
María, sobrina de doña Gracia
Gabriel, empleado del kiosco (newspaper stand attendant)

Synopsis: As she is hurrying to leave her apartment at one in the morning, Lola Lago finds some keys and sees the letters *J. R. D.* with the number 8. She buys a copy of the newspaper for doña Gracia, a neighbor, and hands it to doña Lupe, the building supervisor *(**la portera**)*. But when doña Lupe brings it to doña Gracia, doña Lupe discovers doña Gracia unconscious. She calls an ambulance.

Suggestions:

Pre-viewing: Direct attention to the map, and explain that *Episodio* 1 takes place in Madrid, the capital of Spain. Review the *Nota cultural.* Discuss the *Palabras para comprender* and tell students these words are here only to help them understand the episode. They will not be responsible for these words on the test.

Visual scanning: Direct attention to the first photo and ask what ***Detectives privados*** might mean in English. Are these two words cognates? Before students read the *Resumen del episodio,* have them scan the text and find three other cognate words ***(capital, balcón, personas, importantes, entra)***.

Objective

- Understand the expanding plot of a mystery video set in Spain

¿Eres tú, María?

Madrid, España

Episodio 1

Antes de ver el video

Personajes importantes

Lola Lago, detective

Doña Lupe, portera

Nota cultural In many apartment buildings in Spain, you will find a *portero* or *portera*. In exchange for a small salary and free apartment (in Spain, an apartment is called *un piso),* this person watches over the building and its residents, doing small chores such as taking messages and receiving packages. Because the *portero* or *portera* knows everyone in the building, he or she is often a good source of information about the residents.

Resumen del episodio

Estamos en el piso de Lola Lago, una detective que trabaja en Madrid, la capital de España. Es la una de la mañana. Desde[1] su balcón, ella ve a dos personas hablando enfrente de un edificio[2]. ¿Qué pasa? Más tarde, Lola encuentra[3] algo muy importante en la calle[4]. Al día siguiente[5], doña Lupe, la portera del edificio, entra en el piso de doña Gracia y . . .

[1]From [2]building [3]finds [4]street [5]The next day

Palabras para comprender

investigar	to investigate
las llaves	keys
el periódico	newspaper
el piso	apartment; floor *(of a building)*

DIFFERENTIATED INSTRUCTION

Heritage Language Learners

Ask students to use the vocabulary from *Palabras para comprender* to write a summary of what happened in this episode. Encourage them to go back and use vocabulary from previous chapters and to focus on correct spelling and language accuracy.

Students with Learning Difficulties

Pause the video when necessary to have students make note of the clues. Have students make their list of clues to answer the *¿Comprendes?* questions and to predict the outcome of the *Episodio.*

"¿Qué es esto?
Mañana voy a investigar".

"A ver. Unas llaves . . ."

"¡Ay de mí! Necesito una ambulancia. Plaza del Alamillo. Número 8. Tercer piso. ¡Rápido!"

Después de ver el video

¿Comprendes?

Lee las frases y decide si son ciertas o falsas. Si una frase es falsa, escríbela con la información correcta.

1. Es la una de la tarde cuando Lola entra en su piso.
2. Ella está sola en su piso.
3. Lola ve a dos hombres hablando en la calle.
4. Las dos personas están muy contentas.
5. Lola encuentra un llavero con las iniciales "J.R.D.".
6. Lola compra *(buys)* una revista en la mañana.
7. Doña Lupe entra en el piso de Lola con el periódico.

Video 5A

Viewing: If there is time after viewing the full episode, select some key moments that you wish to highlight, such as the greeting exchange between Lola and Gabriel at the newspaper stand ***(kiosco)***. There are very few words written with the letter *k* in Spanish, and they are usually foreign words imported to Spanish.

Post-viewing: Have the class study the photos and ask who can tell what is happening in the episode at the time of each picture. Write the vocabulary presented in this episode on the board to help students create sentences for each picture. Dramatize the quotations below the photos.

¿Comprendes? Standards: 1.1, 1.2, 1.3

Resources: Answer Keys: Student Edition, p. 69

Focus: Verifying comprehension

Answers:

1. **falsa; Es la una de la mañana cuando Lola entra en su piso.**
2. **cierta**
3. **falsa; Lola ve a una mujer y a un hombre hablando en la calle.**
4. **falsa; Las dos personas no están muy contentas.**
5. **cierta**
6. **falsa; Lola compra un periódico en la mañana.**
7. **falsa**

Theme Project

Students can perform Step 3 at this point. (For more information, see p. 220-b.)

Additional Resources

- *¿Eres tú, María?* Video Workbook, Episode 1
- *¿Eres tú, María?* Teacher's Video Guide: Answer Key

ENRICH YOUR TEACHING

Teacher-to-Teacher

Have students search the Web for a virtual tour of Madrid. See if they can find a newspaper stand ***(kiosco)*** and buildings in Madrid. What do they notice about the sidewalks, doors, and windows? Point out that many buildings in Spanish cities have stores on the ground floor ***(piso bajo)*** and residential space above ***(primer piso,*** and ***segundo piso)***.

21st Century Skills

Technology Literacy Have students find Web sites to further explore Spain and Madrid. They should decide which topics interest them (sites to visit, data about Spain and/or Madrid) and find Web sites that supply that information. Have them work in small groups to evaluate and organize the information, then present it to the class.

Review Activities

To talk about family members and possessive adjectives: Have students draw fictional family trees and use the vocabulary to describe who each person is. Students can take turns asking how old each relative is and what they like: *Mi hermano menor tiene doce años y le gusta comer hamburguesas.*

To describe activities at parties: Have students work in pairs and plan a party. Have them create a chart and write what activities they are going to do, what food they are going to serve, and how they are going to decorate. Students will discuss their charts with another pair.

Tener: Have students write subject pronouns on note cards and shuffle them, face down. Student A picks a card and says the pronoun and Student B says or writes the appropriate form of ***tener.*** Students can roll their subject pronoun cubes for this as well.

To discuss and compare ages, talk about people, likes, and talk about animals: Have students work in groups of four or five and prepare a list with the name and age of each member of the group. Have students list two or three activities that each member likes to do and does not like and if they have an animal at home. *(Clara tiene X años. Le gusta comer en restaurantes y decorar las fiestas. Ella tiene/no tiene un gato.)*

Portfolio

Invite students to review the activities they completed in this chapter, including written reports, posters, or other visuals, and recordings of oral presentations or other projects. Have them select one or two items that they feel best demonstrate their achievements in Spanish to include in their portfolios.

Additional Resources

Student Resources: Realidades para hispanohablantes, p. 188

Teacher Resources:

- Teacher's Resource Book: Situation Cards, p. 16, Clip Art, pp. 18–21
- Assessment Program: Chapter Checklist and Self-Assessment Worksheet, pp. T56–T57

Repaso | | |

Objectives

- Review the vocabulary and grammar
- Demonstrate you can perform the tasks on p. 245

Repaso del capítulo

Vocabulario y gramática

to talk about family members

los abuelos	grandparents
el abuelo	grandfather
la abuela	grandmother
el esposo, la esposa	husband, wife
los hermanos	brothers; brother(s) and sister(s)
el hermano	brother
la hermana	sister
el hermanastro	stepbrother
la hermanastra	stepsister
los hijos	children; sons
el hijo	son
la hija	daughter
los padres (papás)	parents
el padre (papá)	father
la madre (mamá)	mother
el padrastro	stepfather
la madrastra	stepmother
los primos	cousins
el primo	(male) cousin
la prima	(female) cousin
los tíos	uncles; aunt(s) and uncle(s)
el tío	uncle
la tía	aunt

to discuss and compare ages

¿Cuántos años tiene(n) —?	How old is / are ___?
Tiene(n) ___ años.	He / She is / They are ___ (years old).
mayor *pl.* **mayores**	older
menor *pl.* **menores**	younger

to talk about people

la persona	person

to name animals

el gato	cat
el perro	dog

to discuss what someone likes

(a + *person***) le gusta(n) / le encanta(n)**	he / she likes / loves

For *Vocabulario adicional,* see pp. 472–473.

to describe activities at parties

abrir	to open
celebrar	to celebrate
decorar	to decorate
las decoraciones	decorations
hacer un video	to videotape
el video	video
preparar	to prepare
romper	to break
sacar fotos	to take photos
la foto	photo
la cámara	camera

to discuss celebrations

el cumpleaños	birthday
¡Feliz cumpleaños!	Happy birthday!
los dulces	candy
la flor *pl.* **las flores**	flower
el globo	balloon
la luz *pl.* **las luces**	light
el papel picado	cut-paper decorations
el pastel	cake
la piñata	piñata
el regalo	gift, present

other useful words

que	who, that
sólo	only

to indicate possession or relationship

tener *to have*

tengo	**tenemos**
tienes	**tenéis**
tiene	**tienen**

possessive adjectives

mi(s) my	**nuestro(s), -a(s)** our
tu(s) your	**vuestro(s), -a(s)** your *(pl.)*
su(s) your *(formal),* his, her, its	**su(s)** your *(pl.),* their

DIFFERENTIATED INSTRUCTION

Students with Learning Difficulties

Have students review the *Repaso del capítulo* and create flashcards for any words that they do not know. Pair them with a student who is more confident with the vocabulary to practice. Before the test, provide students with a practice test, so they can become comfortable with the format.

Heritage Language Learners

Have students write a few paragraphs telling about their perfect birthday celebration: Where are they going to have it? Whom are they going to invite? What food are they going to eat? What kind of music are they going to play? Encourage them to use as many vocabulary words from this chapter as they can.

Más repaso GO realidades.com | print

Instant Check	✔	
Puzzles	✔	
Core WB pp. 92–93		✔
Comm. WB pp. 277, 278–281	✔	✔

Preparación para el examen

On the exam you will be asked to . . .	Here are practice tasks similar to those you will find on the exam . . .	For review go to your print or digital textbook . . .
Interpretive		
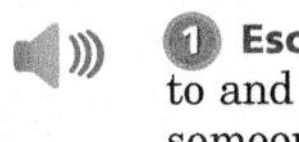 **1 Escuchar** Listen to and understand someone's description of a family member	At a friend's party, a woman is telling you stories about her brother, Jorge. a) How old is her brother? b) Who is older, the woman or her brother? c) What does her brother like to do?	**pp. 222–225** *Vocabulario en contexto* **p. 226** Actividad 4 **p. 227** Actividades 7–8 **p. 229** Actividad 11
Interpersonal		
 **2 Hablar** Describe some members of your family and what they like to do	At your first Spanish Club meeting, your teacher requests that all of you try to talk to each other in Spanish. Since you just learned how to talk about your family, you feel confident that you can talk about some of your family members. Tell about: a) how they are related to you; b) their ages; c) what they like to do; d) their personalities.	**pp. 222–225** *Vocabulario en contexto* **p. 226** Actividad 4 **p. 227** Actividad 7 **p. 229** Actividad 12 **p. 232** *Gramática: Possessive adjectives* **p. 237** Actividad 26
Interpretive		
 **3 Leer** Read and understand someone's description of a problem he or she is having with a family member	Read this letter to an advice columnist. Can you describe in English what Ana's problem is? Querida Dolores: Yo soy la hija menor de una familia de seis personas. Uno de mis hermanos mayores, Nacho, siempre habla de mí con mis padres. A él le encanta hablar de mis amigos y de mis actividades. Tenemos una familia muy simpática, pero ¡Nacho me vuelve loca! Ana	**pp. 222–225** *Vocabulario en contexto* **p. 226** Actividades 4–5 **p. 232** Actividad 18
Presentational		
 **4 Escribir** Write a brief note telling at least two facts about a friend or family member	The party planner at a local restaurant is helping you plan a birthday party for your cousin. Write a brief note telling her your cousin's name, age, two things he or she likes to do at a party, the kinds of decorations he or she likes, and one thing he or she loves to eat.	**p. 226** Actividad 5 **p. 227** Actividad 8 **p. 229** Actividad 12 **p. 237** Actividad 26
Cultures • Comparisons		
 **5 Pensar** Demonstrate an understanding of some ways that Spanish-speaking families celebrate special occasions	Think about what you would consider your most important birthday. Based on what you know about important family traditions, describe why a fifteenth birthday is important for a young Spanish-speaking girl and what you would expect to see at her celebration.	**pp. 222–225** *Vocabulario en contexto* **p. 226** *Fondo cultural* **pp. 238–239** *Lectura* **p. 240** *La cultura en vivo*

DIFFERENTIATED ASSESSMENT

CORE ASSESSMENT
- **Assessment Program:** Examen del capítulo 5A, pp. 124–132
- **Audio Program DVD:** Cap. 5A, Track 16
- **ExamView:** Chapter Test, Test Banks A and B

ADVANCED/PRE-AP*
- **ExamView: Pre-AP* Test Bank**
- **Pre-AP* Resource Book,** pp. 78–81

STUDENTS NEEDING EXTRA HELP
- **Alternate Assessment Program:** Examen del capítulo 5A
- **Audio Program DVD:** Cap. 5A, Track 16

HERITAGE LEARNERS
- **Assessment Program: Realidades Para Hispanohablantes:** Examen del capítulo 5A
- **ExamView: Heritage Learner Test Bank**

Performance Tasks

Standards: 1.1, 1.2, 1.3, 2.1, 2.2

Student Resource: Realidades para hispanohablantes, p. 189

Teacher Resources: Teacher's Resource Book: Audio Script, p. 9; Audio Program DVD: Cap. 5A, Track 15; Answer Keys: Student Edition, p. 70

1. *Escuchar*

Suggestions: Use the audio or read the script.

Script:

Pues, en mi familia, yo soy la hija reservada y trabajadora. Mi hermano mayor, Jorge, es muy sociable. Tiene treinta y ocho años. A él le gusta hacer videos. Es muy talentoso.

Answers:

a) He is 38 years old. **b) Her brother.**
c) He likes to make videos.

2. *Hablar*

Suggestions: Have students use a graphic organizer such as a family tree.

Answers will vary.

3. *Leer*

Suggestions: Have students use context and prior knowledge to determine Ana's problem. Help them comprehend the last line—*¡Nacho me vuelve loca!* (Nacho drives me crazy!)

Answers:

Ana's older brother Nacho always talks to their parents about Ana, her friends, and what they do.

4. *Escribir*

Suggestions: Refer students to *Actividad* 12 on p. 229 for a model.

Answers will vary.

5. *Pensar*

Suggestions: Have students re-read, *Vocabulario en contexto, Fondo cultural, Lectura,* and *La cultura en vivo* and look at the photos in order to write their description.

Answers will vary.

5B ¡Vamos a un restaurante!

AT A GLANCE

Objectives

- **Listen to, read, and write information about restaurant meals and service**
- **Write about plans for a celebration**
- **Exchange information while describing physical features of family members**
- **Understand cultural perspectives on meals and mealtimes in the Spanish-speaking world**
- **Explain aspects of the Hispanic history and culture of Santa Fe, New Mexico**

Vocabulary

- Describing people and things
- Food and table settings
- Eating out
- Expressing needs

Grammar

- The verb ***venir***
- The verbs ***ser*** and ***estar***

Culture

- Extended families, p. 247
- Getting a server's attention, p. 253
- ***arroz con leche,*** p. 259
- ***menú del día,*** p. 260
- Santa Fe, p. 263
- Cultural perspectives on mealtimes, p. 264

Recycle ♻

- Family members
- Adjective agreement
- The verb ***estar***
- The verb ***ser***
- The verb ***tener***
- Prepositions of location
- Foods

RESOURCES

	FOR THE STUDENT	ONLINE	DVD	PRINT	FOR THE TEACHER	ONLINE	PREEXP	DVD	PRINT
Plan					Interactive TE and Resources DVD	•		•	
					Teacher's Resource Book, pp. 38–71	•		•	•
					Pre-AP* Resource Book, pp. 78–81	•		•	•
					Lesson Plans	•			•
					Mapa global interactivo	•			
Introducción pp. **246–247**									
Present	Student Edition, pp. 246–247	•	•	•	Interactive TE and Resources DVD	•		•	
	DK Reference Atlas	•	•		Teacher's Resource Book, pp. 38–39	•		•	•
	Videocultura	•	•		Galería de fotos		•		
	Hispanohablantes WB, pp. 190–191			•	Fine Art Transparencies, 60	•	•	•	
					Map Transparencies, 12–13, 15–16, 18, 20	•	•	•	
Vocabulario en contexto pp. **248–251**									
Present & Practice	Student Edition, pp. 248–251	•	•	•	Interactive TE and Resources DVD	•		•	
	Audio	•	•		Teacher's Resource Book, pp. 40–41, 44, 52–54	•		•	•
	Videohistoria	•	•		Vocabulary Clip Art	•	•	•	•
	Flashcards	•	•		Audio Program	•	•	•	
	Instant Check	•			Video Program: Videohistoria	•		•	
	Guided WB, pp. 165–174	•	•	•	Video Program Teacher's Guide: Cap. 5B	•		•	•
	Core WB, pp. 94–97	•	•	•	Vocabulary and Grammar Transparencies, 104–107	•	•	•	
	Comm. WB, pp. 99–102, 105	•	•	•	Answer Keys: Student Edition, pp. 71–72	•	•	•	
	Hispanohablantes WB, pp. 192–193			•	TPR Stories, pp. 62–76	•		•	•
Assess and Remediate					Prueba 5B–1: Assessment Program, pp. 133–134	•		•	•
					Assessment Program para hispanohablantes, pp. 133–134	•		•	•

RESOURCES

	FOR THE STUDENT	ONLINE	DVD	PRINT	FOR THE TEACHER	ONLINE	PREEXP	DVD	PRINT
Vocabulario en uso PP. **252–255**									
Present & Practice	Student Edition, pp. 252–255	•	•	•	Interactive Whiteboard Vocabulary Activities	•		•	
	Instant Check	•			Interactive TE and Resources DVD	•		•	
	Comm. WB, pp. 102–103	•	•	•	Teacher's Resource Book, pp. 41–42, 46, 51	•		•	•
	Hispanohablantes WB, pp. 194–195			•	Communicative Pair Activities, p. 46	•		•	•
	Communicative Pair Activities	•			Audio Program	•	•	•	
					Videomodelos	•		•	
					Vocabulary and Grammar Transparencies, 83	•	•	•	
					Answer Keys: Student Edition, pp. 72–73	•	•	•	•
Assess and Remediate					Prueba 5B–2 with Study Plan	•			
					Prueba 5B–2: Assessment Program, pp. 135–136	•		•	•
					Assessment Program para hispanohablantes, pp. 135–136	•		•	•
Gramática PP. **256–261**									
Present & Practice	Student Edition, pp. 256–261	•	•	•	Interactive Whiteboard Grammar Activities	•		•	
	Instant Check	•			Interactive TE and Resources DVD	•		•	
	Animated Verbs	•			Teacher's Resource Book, pp. 42–45, 47, 49	•		•	•
	Tutorial Video: Grammar	•			Communicative Pair Activities, pp. 48–49	•		•	•
	Canción de hip hop	•			Audio Program	•	•	•	
	Guided WB, pp. 175–178	•	•	•	Videomodelos	•		•	
	Core WB, pp. 98–100	•	•	•	Video Program: GramActiva	•	•	•	
	Comm. WB, pp. 103–104, 106–107, 282	•	•	•	Vocabulary and Grammar Transparencies, 108–109, 111	•	•	•	
	Hispanohablantes WB, pp. 196–201			•	Answer Keys: Student Edition, pp. 73–75	•	•	•	
	Communicative Pair Activities	•							
Assess and Remediate					Pruebas 5B–3 and 5B–4 with Study Plans	•			
					Pruebas 5B–3, 5B–4: Assessment Program, pp. 137, 138	•		•	•
					Assessment Program para hispanohablantes, pp. 137, 138	•		•	•
¡Adelante! PP. **262–267**									
Application	Student Edition, pp. 262–267	•	•	•	Interactive TE and Resources DVD	•		•	
	Online Cultural Reading	•			Teacher's Resource Book, p. 45	•		•	•
	Guided WB, pp. 179–180	•	•	•	Video Program: Videomisterio ¿Eres tú, María?	•		•	
	Comm. WB, pp. 108, 283	•	•	•	Video Program Teacher's Guide: Cap. 5B	•		•	
	Hispanohablantes WB, pp. 202–207			•	Videomisterio Quiz		•		
	¿Eres tú, María? Video WB, pp. 10–19	•	•	•	Answer Keys: Student Edition, pp. 76–77	•	•	•	
Repaso del capítulo PP. **268–269**									
Review	Student Edition, pp. 268–269	•	•	•	Interactive TE and Resources DVD	•		•	
	Online Puzzles and Games	•			Teacher's Resource Book, pp. 43, 50, 52–54	•		•	•
	Core WB, pp. 101–102	•	•	•	Audio Program	•	•	•	
	Comm. WB, pp. 284–287	•	•	•	Answer Keys: Student Edition, p. 78	•	•	•	
	Hispanohablantes WB, pp. 208–209			•					
	Instant Check	•							
Chapter Assessment									
Assess					Examen del capítulo 5B	•		•	•
					Assessment Program, pp. 139–145	•		•	•
					Alternate Assessment Program, pp. 52–56	•		•	•
					Assessment Program para hispanohablantes, pp. 139–145	•		•	•
					Audio Program, Cap. 5B, Examen	•		•	
					ExamView: Test Banks A and B questions only online	•		•	
					Heritage Learner Test Bank	•		•	
					Pre-AP* Test Bank	•		•	

REGULAR SCHEDULE (50 MINUTES)

DAY	Warm-up / Assess	Preview / Present / Practice / Communicate	Wrap-up / Homework Options
1	**Warm-up** (10 min.) • Return Examen del capítulo 5A	**Chapter Opener** (5 min.) • Objectives • Arte y cultura **Vocabulario en contexto** (30 min.) • Presentation: Vocabulario en contexto • Actividades 1, 2	**Wrap-up and Homework Options** (5 min.) • Core Practice 5B-1, 5B-2
2	**Warm-up** (5 min.) • Homework check	**Vocabulario en contexto** (40 min.) • Presentation: Videohistoria *En el restaurante Casa Río* • View: Videohistoria • Video Activities 1, 2, 3, 4 • Actividad 3	**Wrap-up and Homework Options** (5 min.) • Core Practice 5B-3, 5B-4 • Prueba 5B-1: Vocabulary recognition
3	**Warm-up** (10 min.) • Actividad 6 • Homework check ✔**Formative Assessment** (10 min.) • Prueba 5B-1: Vocabulary recognition	**Vocabulario en uso** (25 min.) • Interactive Whiteboard Vocabulary Activities • Actividades 4, 5, 7 • Fondo cultural • Audio Activities 5, 6	**Wrap-up and Homework Options** (5 min.) • Writing Activity 10 • Actividad 10
4	**Warm-up** (5 min.) • Homework check	**Gramática y vocabulario en uso** (40 min.) • Actividades 8, 9 • Exploración del lenguaje • Presentation: The verb ***venir*** • View: GramActiva video • Interactive Whiteboard Grammar Activities • Actividades 12, 13, 14 • Pronunciación	**Wrap-up and Homework Options** (5 min.) • Core Practice 5B-5 • Actividad 11 • Prueba 5B-2 with Study Plan: Vocabulary production
5	**Warm-up** (10 min.) • Communicative Pair Activity • Homework check ✔**Formative Assessment** (10 min.) • Prueba 5B-2 with Study Plan: Vocabulary production	**Gramática y vocabulario en uso** (25 min.) • Audio Activity 7 • Presentation: The verbs ***ser*** and ***estar*** • View: GramActiva video • Interactive Whiteboard Grammar Activities • Actividades 15, 18, 19 • Fondo cultural	**Wrap-up and Homework Options** (5 min.) • Writing Activities 11, 12, 13 • Actividad 17 • Prueba 5B-3 with Study Plan: The verb ***venir***
6	**Warm-up** (10 min.) • Actividad 16 • Homework check ✔**Formative Assessment** (10 min.) • Prueba 5B-3 with Study Plan: The verb ***venir***	**Gramática y vocabulario en uso** (25 min.) • Actividades 20, 21 • Audio Activities 8, 9 • Communicative Pair Activity	**Wrap-up and Homework Options** (5 min.) • Core Practice 5B-6, 5B-7 • Prueba 5B-4 with Study Plan: The verbs ***ser*** and ***estar***
7	**Warm-up** (10 min.) • El español en el mundo del trabajo • Homework check ✔**Formative Assessment** (10 min.) • Prueba 5B-4 with Study Plan: The verbs ***ser*** and ***estar***	**¡Adelante!** (25 min.) • Lectura • ¿Comprendes? • Fondo cultural • Presentación escrita: Steps 1, 5	**Wrap-up and Homework Options** (5 min.) • Presentación escrita: Step 2
8	**Warm-up** (5 min.) • Homework check	**¡Adelante!** (40 min.) • Presentación escrita: Step 3 • Perspectivas del mundo hispano	**Wrap-up and Homework Options** (5 min.) • Presentación escrita: Step 4 • Instant Check
9	**Warm-up** (5 min.) • Homework check	**¡Adelante!** (20 min.) • Videomisterio: *¿Eres tú, María?,* Episodio 2 **Repaso del capítulo** (20 min.) • Vocabulario y gramática • Preparación para el examen 1, 2, 3, 4, 5	**Wrap-up and Homework Options** (5 min.) • Core Practice 5B-8, 5B-9 • Examen del capítulo 5B • Instant Check
10	**Warm-up** (10 min.) • Homework check ✔**Summative Assessment** (40 min.) • Examen del capítulo 5B		

DAY	BLOCK SCHEDULE (90 MINUTES)		
	Warm-up / Assess	**Preview / Present / Practice / Communicate**	**Wrap-up / Homework Options**
1	**Warm-up** (10 min.) • Return Examen del capítulo 5A	**Chapter Opener** (5 min.) • Objectives • Arte y cultura **Vocabulario en contexto** (60 min.) • Presentation: Vocabulario en contexto • Actividades 1, 2 • Presentation: Videohistoria *En el restaurante Casa Río* • View: Videohistoria • Video Activities 1, 2, 3, 4 • Actividad 3 **Vocabulario en uso** (10 min.) • Interactive Whiteboard Vocabulary Activities • Actividades 4, 5, 6	**Wrap-up and Homework Options** (5 min.) • Core Practice 5B-1, 5B-2, 5B-3, 5B-4 • Prueba 5B-1: Vocabulary recognition
2	**Warm-up** (10 min.) • Homework check ✔**Formative Assessment** (10 min.) • Prueba 5B-1: Vocabulary recognition	**Gramática y vocabulario en uso** (65 min.) • Actividades 7, 8, 9, 10 • Fondo cultural • Exploración del lenguaje • Audio Activities 5, 6 • Communicative Pair Activity • Presentation: The verb ***venir*** • View: GramActiva video • Interactive Whiteboard Grammar Activities • Actividad 12	**Wrap-up and Homework Options** (5 min.) • Writing Activity 10 • Actividad 11 • Prueba 5B-2 with Study Plan: Vocabulary production
3	**Warm-up** (5 min.) • Homework check ✔**Formative Assessment** (10 min.) • Prueba 5B-2 with Study Plan: Vocabulary production	**Gramática y vocabulario en uso** (70 min.) • View: GramActiva video • Actividades 13, 14 • Pronunciación • Audio Activity 7 • Communicative Pair Activity • Presentation: The verbs ***ser*** and ***estar*** • View: GramActiva video • Interactive Whiteboard Grammar Activities • Actividades 15, 18 • Audio Activities 8, 9	**Wrap-up and Homework Options** (5 min.) • Actividad 17 • Core Practice 5B-5, 5B-6, 5B-7 • Writing Activities 11, 12, 13 • Pruebas 5B-3, 5B-4 with Study Plans: The verb ***venir,*** The verbs ***ser*** and ***estar***
4	**Warm-up** (15 min.) • Actividad 16 • Homework check • El español en el mundo del trabajo ✔**Formative Assessment** (15 min.) • Pruebas 5B-3, 5B-4 with Study Plans: The verb ***venir,*** The verbs ***ser*** and ***estar***	**Gramática y vocabulario en uso** (25 min.) • Fondo cultural • Actividades 19, 20, 21 • Communicative Pair Activity **¡Adelante!** (30 min.) • Lectura • ¿Comprendes? • Fondo cultural • Presentación escrita: Steps 1, 5	**Wrap-up and Homework Options** (5 min.) • Presentación escrita: Step 2 • Lectura
5	**Warm-up** (5 min.) • Homework check	**¡Adelante!** (45 min.) • Presentación escrita: Step 3 • Perspectivas del mundo hispano **Repaso del capítulo** (35 min.) • Vocabulario y gramática • Preparación para el examen 1, 2, 3, 4, 5	**Wrap-up and Homework Options** (5 min.) • Presentación escrita: Step 4 • Core Practice 5B-8, 5B-9 • Instant Check • Examen del capítulo 5B
6	**Warm-up** (15 min.) • Homework check • Situation Cards **Repaso del capítulo** (10 min.) • Communicative Pair Activities ✔**Summative Assessment** (40 min.) • Examen del capítulo 5B	**¡Adelante!** (20 min.) • Videomisterio: *¿Eres tú, María?,* Episodio 2	**Wrap-up and Homework Options** (5 min.) • Videomisterio

Standards for *Capítulo* 5B

- To achieve the goals of the Standards, students will:

Communication

1.1 Interpersonal
- Talk about family members and others descriptively
- Talk about table settings, meal customs in Spanish-speaking cultures
- Talk about foods and beverages

1.2 Interpretive
- Read and listen to descriptions of family members
- Read and listen to information about restaurants, table settings, meal customs in Spanish-speaking cultures
- Read a picture-based story
- Listen to and watch a video about restaurant service
- Read a restaurant review
- Read a recipe for ***arroz con leche***
- Read a letter about a trip to Santa Fe

1.3 Presentational
- Present descriptions of people
- Write analogies to compare people and things
- Present information about food and beverages
- Present a skit between a server and customers
- Present information about Santa Fe

Culture

2.1 Practices and Perspectives
- Interpret that extended families tend to be close-knit in Spanish-speaking countries
- Interpret etiquette for summoning a server
- Interpret typical restaurant offerings in Spanish-speaking countries
- Describe the mealtime custom of ***sobremesa*** in Spanish-speaking countries
- Describe the communal function of ***plazas***

2.2 Products and Perspectives
- Discuss Xavier Nogués and his painting
- Discuss the communal function of ***plazas***

Connections

3.1 Cross-curricular
- Discuss important artists and their work: Nogués
- Follow a recipe for ***arroz con leche***
- Reinforce math and metric conversion skills
- Discuss historical facts about Santa Fe

Comparisons

4.1 Language
- Explain the use of adjectives ending in ***-ísimo***
- Talk about new vocabulary through the recognition of cognates
- Explain the use of the verb ***venir***
- Explain the pronunciation of the letters ***b*** and ***v***
- Explain the differences between the verbs ***ser*** and ***estar***

4.2 Culture
- Compare relationships with extended families
- Compare techniques for getting a server's attention
- Compare menu selections
- Compare local historical sites with those of Santa Fe

Communities

5.1 Beyond the School
- Discuss the need for Spanish-speaking employees at the U.S. Department of Agriculture

5.2 Lifelong Learner
- View a video mystery series

Capítulo 5B ¡Vamos a un restaurante!

Chapter Objectives

Communication

By the end of this chapter you will be able to:
- Listen to, read, and write information about restaurant meals and service
- Write about plans for a celebration
- Exchange information while describing physical features of family members

Culture

You will also be able to:
- Understand cultural perspectives on meals and mealtimes in the Spanish-speaking world
- Explain aspects of the Hispanic history and culture of Santa Fe, New Mexico

You will demonstrate what you know and can do:
- Presentación escrita, p. 265
- Preparación para el examen, p. 269

You will use:

Vocabulary
- Describing people and things
- Food and table settings
- Eating out
- Expressing needs

Grammar
- The verb *venir*
- The verbs *ser* and *estar*

Exploración del mundo hispano

Country Connection
Eating in a Restaurant with Your Family

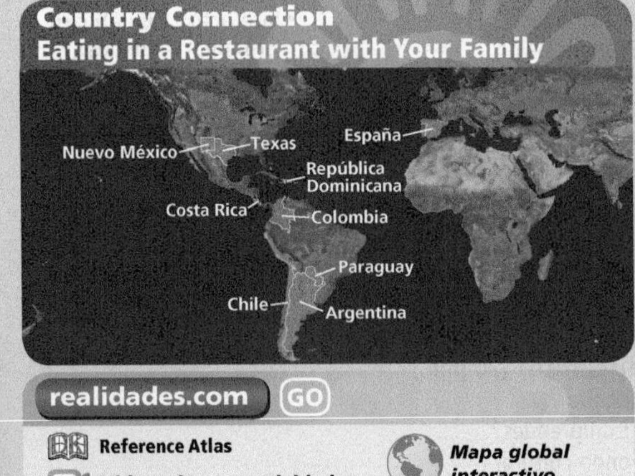

realidades.com GO

Reference Atlas
Videocultura y actividad
Mapa global interactivo

ENRICH YOUR TEACHING

Using Backward Design

Have students preview the sample performance tasks on *Preparación para el examen*, p. 269, and connect them to the Chapter Objectives. Explain to students that by completing the sample tasks they can self-assess their learning progress.

Mapa global interactivo

Download the *Mapa global interactivo* files for Chapter 5B and preview the activity. For this activity, you visit Santa Fe, New Mexico and travel the Camino Real.

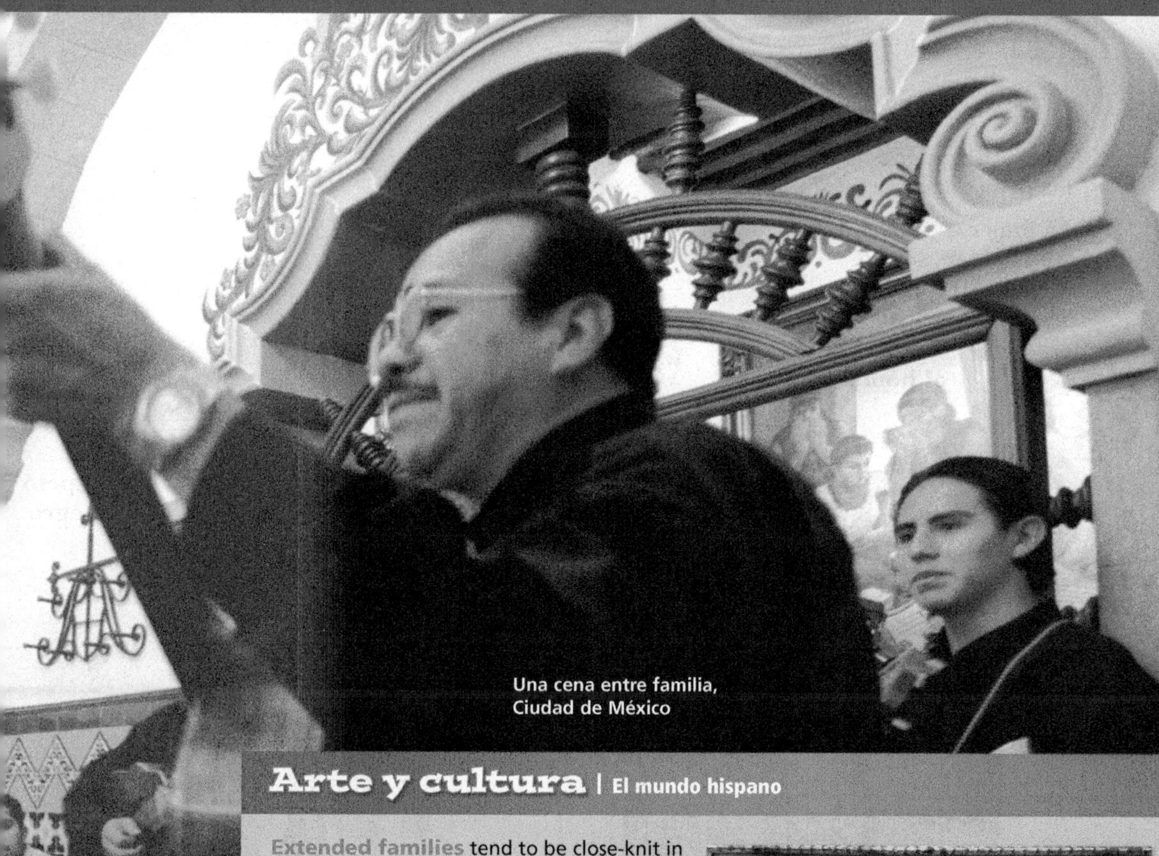

Una cena entre familia, Ciudad de México

Arte y cultura | El mundo hispano

Extended families tend to be close-knit in Spanish-speaking cultures. Parents, children, grandparents, aunts, uncles, and cousins get together often for meals, and not just on special occasions. It is not uncommon for three generations to live under one roof or in the same neighborhood.

- How do extended families in Spanish-speaking cultures compare with your family and those of your friends?
- How does the painting "Tarde de domingo" reflect the idea of extended families? Compare this to how you and your family spend weekends.

"Tarde de domingo" (1923), Xavier Nogués

Nogués, Xavier. Tarde de Domingo - Sunday afternoon, 1923. Canvas, 60 x 75 cm, Museo de Arte Moderno, Barcelona, Spain.

PresentationExpress™
See pp. 246a–246b

Chapter Opener

Core Instruction

Resources: Map Transparencies 12–13, 15–16, 18, 20

Suggestions: Explain that the students will learn to describe people and things and to talk about eating in a restaurant. They will also learn about cultural differences related to eating out. The *GramActiva* Videos will help students learn to use the verbs ***venir, ser,*** and ***estar.***

Videocultura View *La quinceañera* with the class to find out how teens in Spanish-speaking countries prepare for this rite of passage.

Arte y cultura

Standards: 2.1, 3.1, 4.2

Resources: Fine Art Transparencies, p. 60

Suggestions: Ask volunteers to talk about their extended families. Discuss how some family members in the United States may live hundreds of miles apart. Use Transparency 20 with the map of the United States and have students point out where members of their families live.

Answers will vary, but may mention the fact that in the painting, several generations seem to be involved in activities together.

TEACHING WITH ART

Resources: Fine Art Transparencies, p. 60

Suggestions: Explain to students that the cultural movement the painting belongs to emphasized both imagination and tradition in art. Have students describe aspects of the painting that appear to reflect those values.

Culture Note

Xavier Nogués was born in Barcelona, and was famous for his paintings, engravings, and cartoons. He was part of an early 20th century Catalonian cultural movement called (in Spanish) *Novecentismo,* or "1900-ism." *Novecentismo* was marked by a return to ideas of order and beauty in art, and was a reaction against the *Modernismo* of the time.

DIFFERENTIATED INSTRUCTION

Digital resources such as the ***Interactive Whiteboard*** activity banks, ***Videomodelos***, additional ***Online Activities, Study Plans***, automatically graded ***Leveled Workbook***, animated ***Grammar Tutorials, Flashcards***, and ***Vocabulary and Grammar Videos*** will help you reach students of different ability levels and learning styles.

STUDENTS NEEDING EXTRA HELP

Guided Practice Activities
- Flashcards, pp. 165–170
- Vocabulary Check, pp. 171–174
- Grammar Support, pp. 175–178

HERITAGE LEARNERS

Realidades para hispanohablantes
- Chapter Opener, pp. 190–191
- A primera vista, p. 192
- Videohistoria, p. 193
- Manos a la obra, pp. 194–201
- ¡Adelante!, pp. 202–207
- Repaso del capítulo, pp. 208–209

ADVANCED/PRE-AP*

Pre-AP* Resource Book,
- pp. 78–81

Communications Workbook
- Integrated Performance Assessment, p. 284

Vocabulario en contexto

Core Instruction

Standards: 1.2

Resources: Teacher's Resource Book: Input Script, p. 40, Clip Art, pp. 52–54, Audio Script, p. 41; Voc. and Gram. Transparencies 104–105; TPR Stories Book, pp. 62–76; Audio Program DVD: Cap. 5B, Tracks 1–2

Focus: Presenting new vocabulary about family; describing people

Suggestions: Use the story in the *TPR Stories Book* to present the new vocabulary and grammar, or use the Input Script from the *Teacher's Resource Book.*

Present the vocabulary in two sets: words to describe people and table settings: restaurant vocabulary. Say each word on the transparencies but wait to point to each picture until students point to the correct picture in the book. Describe people shown on the transparencies and have volunteers come up and point to the correct picture. For example: *la chica pelirroja, el hombre viejo con pelo canoso, el chico joven con pelo rubio.*

Bring in dishes, glasses, or plasticware. Place the objects on a desk and have students select the object after you say the vocabulary word.

BELLRINGER REVIEW

Show Fine Art Transparency 60. Have students write three descriptive sentences about the transparency to share with the class.

Objectives

Read, listen to, and understand information about

- descriptions of family members
- restaurant vocabulary
- table settings

Vocabulario en contexto

—Abuelito, ¿quiénes son las personas en la foto?

—La mujer es tu abuela y el hombre, soy yo. Y aquí está tu papá. Tiene sólo seis años.

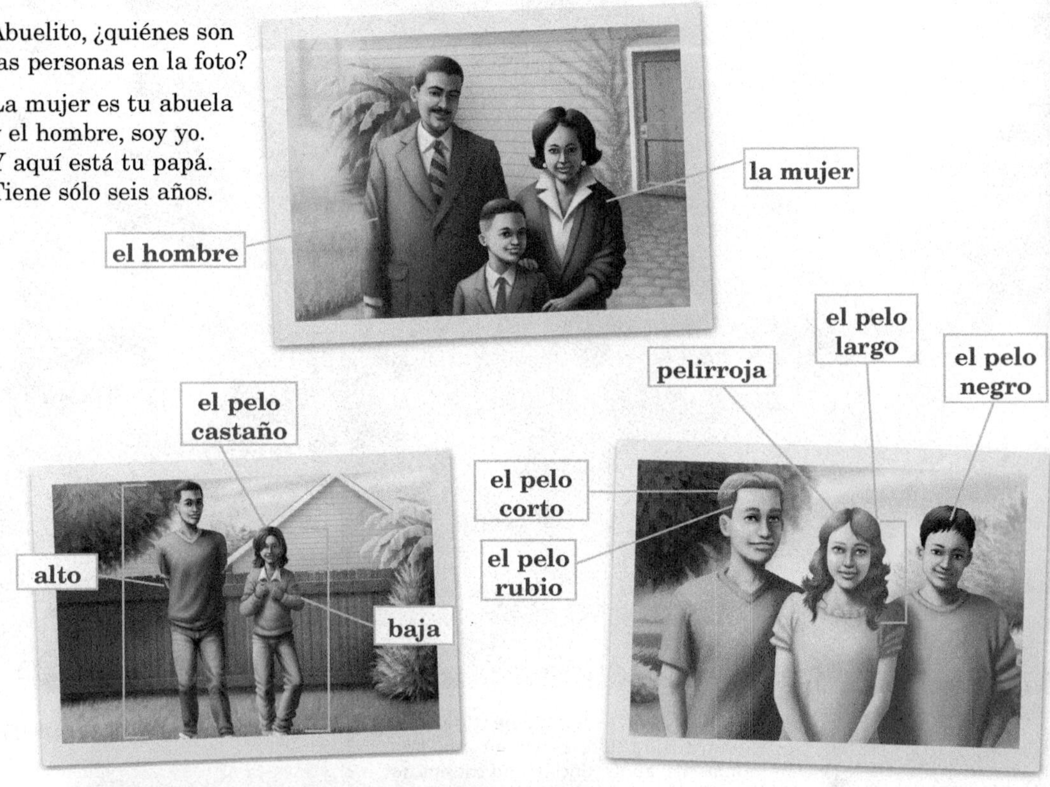

—¿Quién es **el joven** alto y **guapo?**

—Es tu primo Rafael.

—¿Y **la joven** baja al lado del primo Rafael?

—Es su amiga, Sara. Y estas **otras** personas son amigos también.

DIFFERENTIATED INSTRUCTION

Heritage Language Learners

Using the vocabulary on this page, have students talk about three members of their extended family, such as: *Mi abuela tiene el pelo canoso. Mi tía Rosa es muy joven.*

Students with Learning Difficulties

Encourage students to break their vocabulary list into small groups of related words. Students can then study categories such as: physical characteristics, hair colors, or table settings.

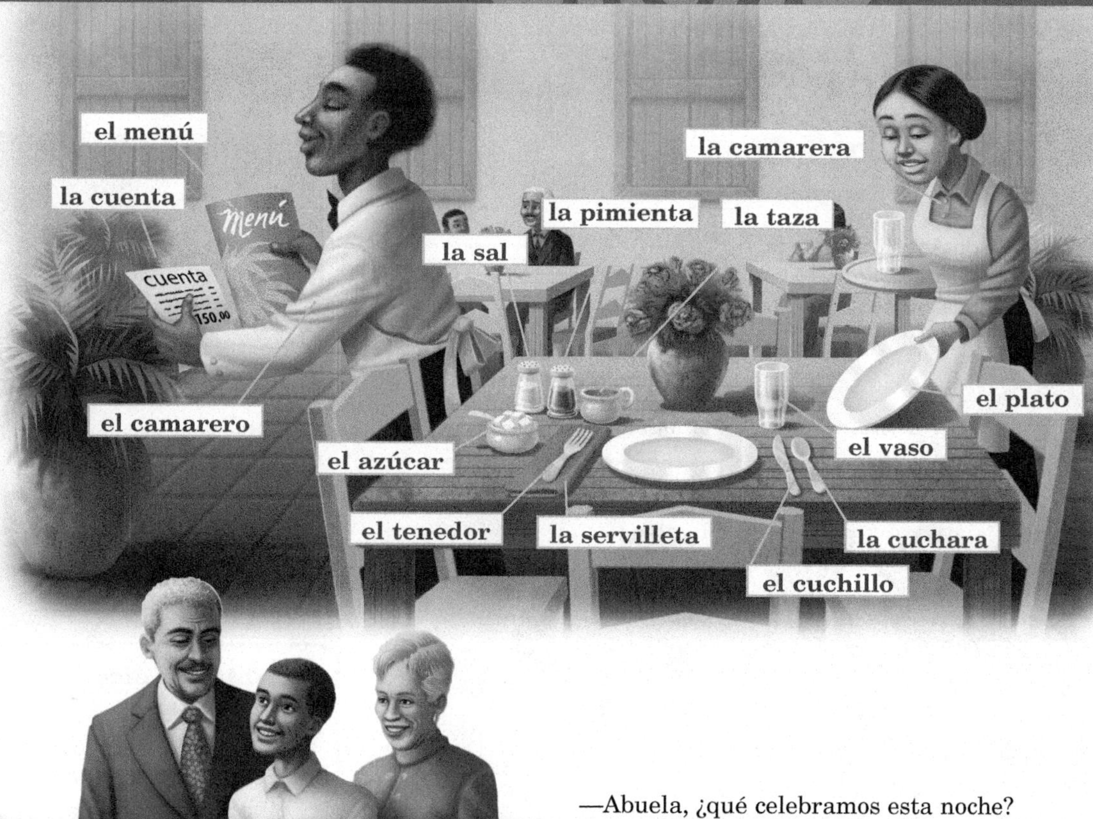

—Abuela, ¿qué celebramos esta noche?
—Es el cumpleaños de tu abuelo.
—¿Quiénes **vienen** a la fiesta?
—Toda la familia **viene.**

1 ¿Quiénes vienen?

Escuchar

Paquito is showing the family album to a friend. Point to the different pictures as he describes the people in the photographs.

Más práctica GO	realidades.com | print
Instant Check	✔
Guided WB pp. 165–170	✔ ✔
Core WB pp. 94–95	✔ ✔
Comm. WB p. 105	✔ ✔
***Hispanohablantes* WB** p. 192	✔

2 ¿Qué necesitas para . . . ?

Escuchar

You will hear seven statements about the table setting. If a statement is correct, indicate *cierto* by raising one hand. If a statement is incorrect, indicate *falso* by raising two hands.

Language Input 5B

1 Standards: 1.2

Resources: Teacher's Resource Book: Audio Script, p. 41; Audio Program DVD: Cap. 5B, Track 3; Answer Keys: Student Edition, p. 71

Focus: Listening comprehension of new vocabulary about family members

Suggestions: Before the activity, read the picture captions with students so they are familiar with the characters. All statements are from the perspective of the little boy.

Script and Answers:

1. **Mi padre está con mis abuelos. *(top)***
2. **Mi primo es alto. *(left)***
3. **En la foto, mi abuela tiene el pelo negro. *(top)***
4. **El chico con el pelo rubio es amigo de mi padre. *(right)***
5. **En la foto, mi padre es joven. Tiene seis años. *(top)***
6. **La chica baja se llama Sara. *(left)***
7. **El chico guapo es mi tío Rafael. *(left)***
8. **La chica pelirroja es amiga de mi padre. *(right)***

2 Standards: 1.2

Resources: Teacher's Resource Book: Audio Script, p. 41; Audio Program DVD: Cap. 5B, Track 4; Answer Keys: Student Edition, p. 71

Focus: Listening comprehension of vocabulary about table settings

Suggestions: Before playing the audio or reading the script to the class, introduce the artwork by calling out food items and asking the students to name the utensil they would use for that item.

Script and Answers:

1. **El plato está debajo del azúcar. *(falso)***
2. **El cuchillo está al lado del plato. *(cierto)***
3. **La sal está pero la pimienta no está. *(falso)***
4. **El tenedor está encima de la servilleta. *(cierto)***
5. **El vaso está encima de la taza. *(falso)***
6. **El menú no está en la mesa. *(cierto)***
7. **La cuchara está al lado del cuchillo. *(cierto)***

ENRICH YOUR TEACHING

Teacher-to-Teacher

Have students bring in pictures of families from magazines. Have them label the family members and the physical description of each person. Have them share their descriptions in small groups.

21st Century Skills

Communication Recommend that students use the eText with embedded audio files, the flashcards, and the online tutorials to further develop their fluency as they go through the chapter.

5B Language Input

Videohistoria

Core Instruction

Standards: 1.2

Resources: Voc. and Gram. Transparencies 106–107; Audio Program DVD: Cap. 5B, Track 5

Focus: Presenting additional contextualized vocabulary and grammar; previewing the video

Suggestions:

Pre-reading: Have students scan the *Videohistoria* for three expressions the waiter uses. Point out to the students that since the video takes place in Texas, where there are many people of Mexican descent, the video characters use the word ***mesero*** instead of ***camarero.***

Reading: Read the captions with the students or play the audio. Using the transparencies and non-verbal clues, help students understand the new words in blue type.

Post-reading: Complete *Actividad* 3 to check comprehension.

Video

Core Instruction

Standards: 1.2

Resources: Teacher's Resource Book: Video Script, p. 44; Video Program: Cap. 5B; Video Program Teacher's Guide: Cap 5B

Focus: Comprehending a story about ordering food in a restaurant

Suggestions:

Pre-viewing: Ask students if they have ever gone to a restaurant and had a server who was inexperienced.

Viewing: Show the video once without pausing. Show it again, stopping to check for comprehension. Ask students if Luis shows signs of nervousness.

Post-viewing: Complete the Video Activities in the *Communication Workbook.*

Block Schedule

Have students work in small groups and set a table, purposely leaving out some items. Have students take turns telling what they need: *Me falta(n)*___.

En el restaurante Casa Río

La familia de Angélica come la cena en este restaurante. Lee lo que pasa durante la comida.

> **Strategy**
>
> **Scanning**
> Think about what a waiter might say to you when you order in a restaurant. Look through the dialogue and find three expressions that the waiter uses.

Luis: Bienvenidos al restaurante Casa Río. Soy Luis, su mesero. Hoy es mi primer día de trabajo. Estoy un poco nervioso. El menú está en la mesa.

> **También se dice . . .**
>
> **el (la) camarero(a)** =
> el (la) mesero(a) *(México, Puerto Rico);* el (la) mozo(a) *(Argentina, Puerto Rico, Bolivia)*

5

Esteban: Señor, **me faltan** un cuchillo y un tenedor.

Luis: ¡Ah, sí! En un momento **le traigo** un cuchillo y un tenedor.

6

Luis: ¿Y para quién son las enchiladas?

Angélica: Creo que son para el señor de pelo castaño.

Luis: ¡Oh! ¡Gracias!

Angélica: **De nada.**

Luis: ¿Necesitan **algo más?** ¿Y cómo está la comida?

Mamá: La comida aquí es **deliciosa. ¡Qué rica!**

DIFFERENTIATED INSTRUCTION

Multiple Intelligences

Verbal/Linguistic: Have students write an original conversation using the vocabulary presented in the video. Help them focus on spelling and vocabulary. Students can work on this skit throughout the chapter.

Students with Learning Difficulties

Have students write the names of the family members on a piece of paper. As they read the *Videohistoria* or watch the video, they should write down what each person orders to eat or drink. They can refer to this list when they do *Actividad* 3.

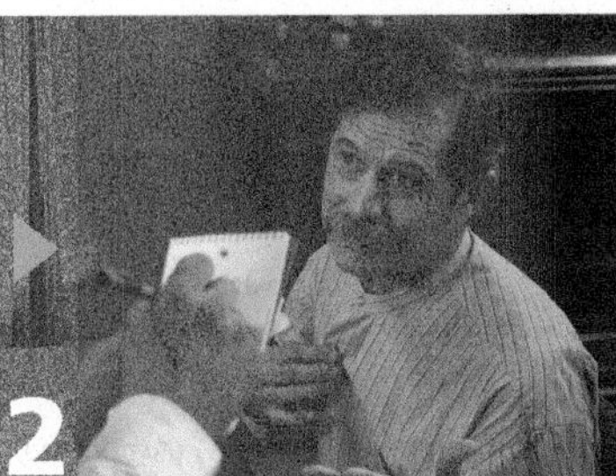

Luis: ¿Qué va a **pedir** Ud. de bebida?

Papá: ¡Uy! **Tengo calor.** Para mí, un té helado.

Mamá: Y yo **tengo frío.** Para mí, café.

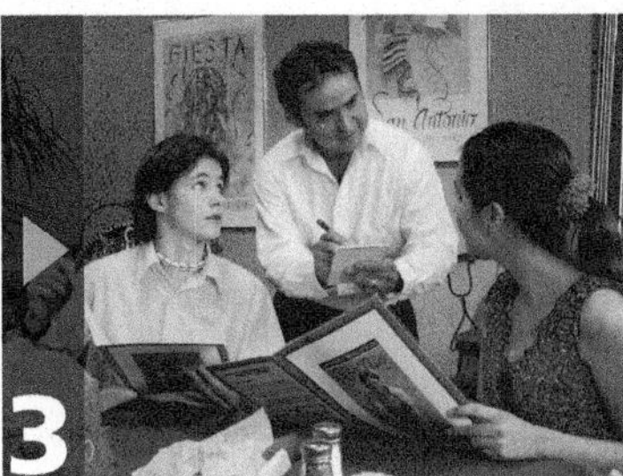

Luis: Y **ahora** . . . , ¿qué **desean** Uds. **de plato principal?**

Angélica: Quisiera el arroz con pollo.

Esteban: Para mí, una hamburguesa con papas fritas.

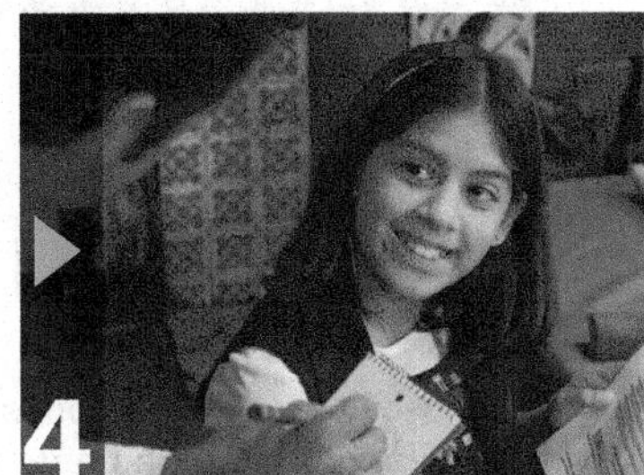

Luis: ¿Y qué desea Ud.?

Cristina: ¿Me trae las fajitas de pollo, por favor?

Luis: ¡Muy bien!

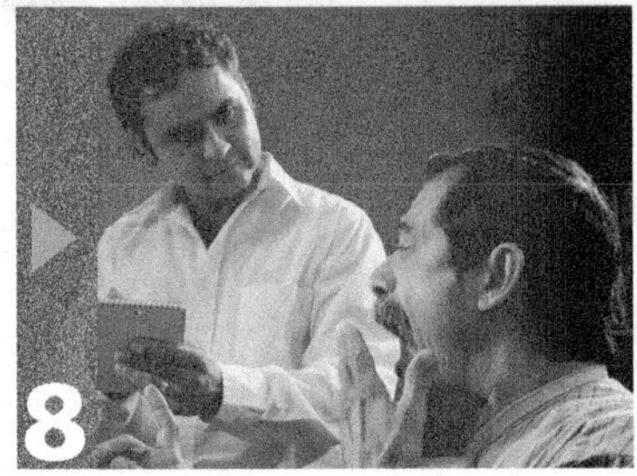

Luis: Ahora, ¿desean **postre?**

Mamá: Pues, sí. Y **otro** café, por favor.

Papá: Para mí, nada. Pero quisiera un café, yo también. Ahora **tengo sueño.**

3 ¿Comprendes?

Escribir • Hablar

1. ¿Cómo se llama el restaurante? ¿Cómo se llama el camarero?
2. ¿Por qué está nervioso Luis?
3. ¿Qué va a beber el padre? ¿Por qué?
4. ¿Quién come las fajitas? ¿La hamburguesa?
5. ¿Quién desea las enchiladas?
6. Según la mamá, ¿cómo es la comida?

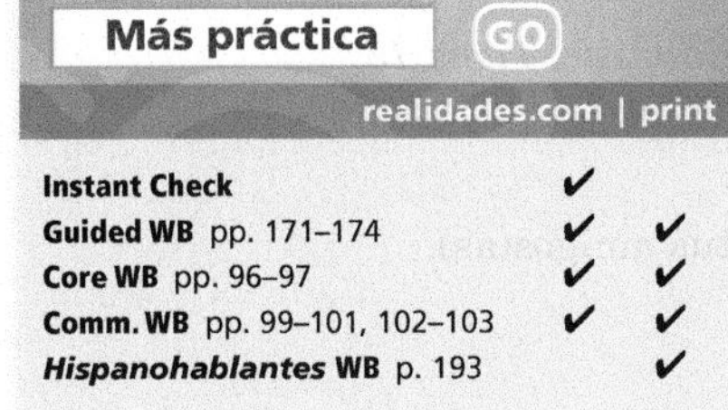

Más práctica GO

realidades.com | print

	realidades.com	print
Instant Check	✔	
Guided WB pp. 171–174	✔	✔
Core WB pp. 96–97	✔	✔
Comm. WB pp. 99–101, 102–103	✔	✔
***Hispanohablantes* WB** p. 193		✔

3 Standards: 1.1, 1.3

Resources: Answer Keys: Student Edition, p. 72

Focus: Reading for understanding

Suggestions: Before beginning the activity, brainstorm a list of question words. For each word, have students say what they need to look for to answer the question. For example, if the question begins with ***quién,*** they need to look for a person. To review, have students point out where they found the information for each answer.

Answers:

1. **Casa Río; Luis**
2. **porque es su primer día de trabajo**
3. **té helado, porque tiene calor**
4. **Cristina; Esteban**
5. **el señor de pelo castaño**
6. **La comida es deliciosa.**

Pre-AP* Support

- **Learning Objective:** Interpersonal Speaking
- **Activity:** Have students create a short dialogue based on Scenes 1 and 5 in the video. One student will assume the role of the waiter, who will greet the client, and take his or her order. The other student will be the client. In the new scene, the client is missing utensils other than a *cuchillo* and a *tenedor,* and is impatient about it.
- ***Pre-AP* Resource Book:*** Comprehensive guide to Pre-AP* vocabulary skill development, pp. 51–57

Teacher-to-Teacher

Have students create their own menus using the vocabulary from *Tema* 5. Using the *Videohistoria* as a model, have them write a dialogue between a server in a restaurant and a client. Brainstorm a list of words to describe food and drinks. Then have half of the class pretend to be happy with their meals and the other half of the class pretend to be disappointed.

ENRICH YOUR TEACHING

Culture Note

An ***enchilada*** is typically a corn tortilla wrapped around meat and cheese, covered in chili sauce, and topped with chopped onions, cheese, or sour cream. This is similar to ***papadzules,*** a traditional Mayan dish that is still strongly associated with the Yucatan. ***Papadzules*** are corn tortillas dipped in pumpkinseed sauce, rolled around chopped hard boiled egg, and smothered in tomato sauce. The ancient Maya reserved ***papadzules,*** or "food of the nobles," for special occasions and royalty.

Additional Resources

- Communication Wbk.: Audio Act. 5, p. 102
- Teacher's Resource Book: Audio Script, p. 41
- Audio Program DVD: Cap. 5B, Track 7

ASSESSMENT

Quiz: Vocabulary Recognition

- Prueba 5B-1: pp. 133–134

INTERACTIVE WHITEBOARD
Vocabulary Activities 5B

BELLRINGER REVIEW

Go around the room and describe different students. Have students respond with ***cierto*** or ***falso*** according to the information. For example: *Ella es rubia; ¿cierto o falso?*

4 Standards: 1.2

Resources: Teacher's Resource Book: Audio Script, p. 41; Audio Program DVD: Cap. 5B, Track 6; Answer Keys: Student Edition, p. 72

Focus: Understanding descriptions of people

Suggestions: Before students listen to the descriptions, have them look at the pictures concentrating on hair color, height, and age of each person. Play the audio or read the script aloud.

Script and Answers:

1. **Es muy guapo. Tiene el pelo negro. Le encanta hablar por teléfono. ¿Cuántos años tiene? Creo que tiene 20 años. Es joven. *(Alejandro)***
2. **Tiene el pelo canoso. Ni es alto ni bajo. Tiene 65 años pero le encanta montar en bicicleta. ¡Qué gracioso es! *(Jorge)***
3. **La joven es baja. Le gusta mucho esquiar. Sólo tiene 14 años. Es rubia y tiene el pelo largo. *(Rosalía)***
4. **¡Qué seria es ella! Tiene el pelo castaño y corto. Le encanta leer. Creo que tiene 60 años. *(María Elena)***
5. **Es pelirroja y muy guapa. Tiene 18 años. Le gusta mucho dibujar. *(Lucía)***

Extension: Bring in photos and ask students to describe the people.

5 Standards: 1.1, 1.2, 1.3

Focus: Describing people

Recycle: ***tener; gustar;*** leisure activities

Suggestions: Brainstorm a list of two feminine nouns and two masculine nouns. Have students suggest an adjective to describe each word on the list. Then write the plural of each word and have the students make the adjectives agree.

Answers will vary.

Common Errors: Remind students to make adjectives agree with nouns.

Extension: Have volunteers read their sentences, without saying who they are describing. Have students guess the name of the person who is being described.

Vocabulario en uso

Objectives

- Listen to and write descriptions of people
- Read and understand a conversation in a restaurant
- Explain what you like to order in a restaurant
- Play a guessing game about table settings
- Write recommendations based on a restaurant review

4 ¿Quiénces son?

Escuchar

Vas a escuchar descripciones de las personas en el dibujo. En una hoja de papel, escribe los números del 1 al 5. Al lado de cada número escribe el nombre de la persona que describen.

También se dice . . .

pelirrojo(a) = colorado(a) *(Argentina)*; colorín, colorina *(Chile)*
el pelo = el cabello *(muchos países)*
rubio(a) = güero(a) *(México)*

5 ¿Quién es?

Escribir • Hablar

1. Mira los dibujos de la Actividad 4 y escribe frases para describir a cada persona.

Modelo
El joven muy alto es Eduardo. Tiene 15 años. Tiene el pelo castaño. Le gusta jugar al tenis.

2. Describe a uno(a) de tus amigos(as).

¿Recuerdas?
Adjectives agree in number and gender with the nouns they describe.

DIFFERENTIATED INSTRUCTION

Advanced Learners

Have students find five pictures of people in your school. They can be members of the volleyball team, the Spanish club, or the football team or they may just be friends. Using the vocabulary introduced in this lesson, have students write captions for each picture.

Students with Learning Difficulties

Students may need help understanding that the adjective ***castaño*** in the model in *Actividad* 5 modifies the masculine noun ***pelo.*** Therefore the adjective will not change even if the subject changes from ***Eduardo*** to ***María Elena.*** *(María Elena tiene **el** pelo castañ**o.**)*

6 Las analogías

Leer • Pensar • Escribir

Many exams test your vocabulary by asking about the logical relationships, or analogies, between words. In analogies, the symbol ":" is used to mean "is to" *(es a)* and the symbol "::" is used to mean "as" *(como)*. For example:

la madre : la hija :: el padre : el hijo

You would read this as *"La madre es a la hija como el padre es al hijo."* Complete these analogies.

Modelo

trabajador : perezoso :: alto : bajo

1. aburrido : interesante :: largo : ______
2. comida : plato :: bebida : ______
3. escuela : profesora :: restaurante : ______
4. chico : joven :: abuelo : ______
5. bistec : plato principal :: pastel : ______
6. amigo : amiga :: hombre : ______
7. ensalada : tenedor :: sopa : ______

7 ¿Qué te gusta pedir?

Escribir

Escribe frases para decir lo que te gusta pedir cuando tienes . . .

Modelo

Cuando tengo hambre, me gusta pedir pizza en un restaurante.

1. 

2. 

3. 

4.  

5. 

Fondo Cultural | Costa Rica | Colombia

Getting a server's attention at a restaurant in a Spanish-speaking country sometimes differs from how it is done in other cultures. For example, in Costa Rica people often make a *pfft* sound to get a server's attention, while in Colombia people may raise or clap their hands. Be very careful in using this sort of attention-getting device—it may seem rude when done by someone from outside the culture!

- How do you get a server's attention in a restaurant here in the United States? Compare this to what is acceptable in some Spanish-speaking countries.

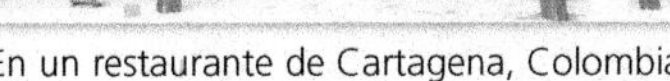

En un restaurante de Cartagena, Colombia

ENRICH YOUR TEACHING

Culture Note

Many restaurants in the Spanish-speaking world combine fine dining with a distinctive cultural performance. For example, in cities like Buenos Aires and Mendoza (both in Argentina), visitors and locals alike are given an opportunity to experience the ***tango*** first hand while enjoying typical cuisine. During the meal, ***tango*** music is performed while several dancers demonstrate Argentina's national dance.

Practice and Communicate 5B

6 Standards: 1.2, 1.3

Resources: Answer Keys: Student Edition, p. 72

Focus: Reading and writing about logical relationships; learning about analogies

Suggestions: Remind students that when looking for logical relationships between words, they should look beyond that of opposites. Another kind of relationship is a functional relationship (**a dish** is used to **serve food**).

Answers:

1. **corto**
2. **vaso**
3. **camarero**
4. **viejo**
5. **postre**
6. **mujer**
7. **cuchara**

BELLRINGER REVIEW

Show Voc. and Gram. Transparency 83, scene 1. Have students give names to the students pictured and write one true statement and one false statement using descriptive words found on p. 248. Ask a partner to respond with *"Es cierto"* or *"Es falso."*

7 Standards: 1.3

Focus: Asking for things orally and in writing

Recycle: ***tener hambre; tener sed***

Suggestions: Before beginning, review each picture by asking students: *¿Cómo está él (ella)?* Have them answer using the appropriate ***tener*** expression. Have students write their answers according to the model and then share their answers with the class.

Answers will vary.

Common Errors: Remind students to use ***tener*** rather than ***estar*** in these expressions.

Fondo cultural

Standards: 2.1, 4.2

Suggestions: Point out that it is always a good idea to use the ***Ud.*** form of the verb when talking to a server as well as to use polite expressions such as ***con permiso*** and ***por favor.***

Answers will vary but may include eye contact or polite expressions, such as "excuse me," to get someone's attention.

BELLRINGER REVIEW

Review the vocabulary for ordering in restaurants. You may also want to use Transparency 110 to review additional food and utensils vocabulary.

8 Standards: 1.1, 1.2

Resources: Answer Keys: Student Edition, p. 73

Focus: Reading and speaking using vocabulary for ordering in a restaurant

Suggestions: Have students number their papers 1–8 and write the letter of the correct response. Tell students they can refer to their papers so that they can practice the dialogue at a more natural pace. Ask for volunteers to read the dialogue.

Answers:

1. g 4. a 7. b
2. c 5. e 8. d
3. f 6. h

Extension: Have students come up with their own responses and read them to the class.

9 Standards: 1.1

Resources: Teacher's Resource Book: GramActiva BLM, p. 51

Focus: Using ***faltar*** to talk about missing items.

Suggestions: After having students review the *Nota,* arrange the pictures of table items on your desk, leaving out two items. Ask: *¿Qué me faltan?* After students answer correctly, place the missing items back on the desk. Then remove one item and ask: *¿Qué me falta?*

Answers will vary.

8 En el restaurante

Leer • Hablar

Con otro(a) estudiante, lee la conversación entre un camarero y dos jóvenes. Empareja *(Match)* lo que dice el camarero con lo que contestan *(answer)* los jóvenes para crear *(create)* la conversación.

Un restaurante en la Argentina

El camarero

1. Buenas noches. ¿Qué desean de bebida?
2. ¿Qué desea pedir de plato principal?
3. ¡Ay, señor! Le falta el cuchillo, ¿no?
4. ¿Le gusta la sopa?
5. Señorita, ¿qué desea Ud. de postre?
6. Señor, ¿le traigo otra bebida?
7. ¿Desean Uds. algo más?
8. Gracias por venir a nuestro restaurante.

Los jóvenes

a. Sí, está deliciosa. Umm. ¡Qué rica!
b. No, sólo la cuenta, por favor.
c. Quisiera el arroz con pollo, por favor.
d. De nada. Hasta luego.
e. Un helado, por favor.
f. Sí. ¿Me trae uno, por favor?
g. Para mí, un refresco y, para la señorita, un té helado.
h. Sí, por favor. Tengo mucha sed.

9 Juego

Hablar

1. Work in groups of three or four. Your teacher will give you copies of pictures of various table items. Cut or tear the pictures apart to make cards.
2. Arrange the pictures in a table setting on a desk. While the other players have their backs turned, hide one or more of the cards. Then ask: *¿Qué me falta?* The first player to say correctly *Te falta(n) . . .* and name the missing item(s) receives a point.
3. Put the hidden items back on the desk and continue playing until all players have had a chance to hide items. The player with the most points is the winner.

Nota

When one item is missing, use *me / te falta.* When more than one item is missing, use *me / te faltan.*

DIFFERENTIATED INSTRUCTION

Students with Special Needs

Have a pre-cut set of pictures available to students who would experience difficulties in the tasks of cutting or tearing. This is also a time-saving suggestion for setting up this activity.

Heritage Language Learners

Have students create a radio ad for a restaurant specializing in food from their heritage countries. The ad should include a description of the food, the hours of operation, and the location of the restaurant. Emphasize that they must speak clearly in the ad. You might want to have students record the ad and play it for the class.

Exploración del lenguaje

Adjectives ending in *-ísimo*

Muy + an adjective can be expressed in another way by adding the correct form of *-ísimo* to the adjective. The *-ísimo* ending conveys the idea of "extremely."

un chico muy guapo = un chico guapísimo
una clase muy difícil = una clase dificilísima

Adjectives that end in *-co* or *-ca* have a spelling change to *-qu-*. The *-o* or *-a* is dropped.

unos pasteles muy ricos = unos pasteles riquísimos

Try it out! Rework the following phrases using the correct *-ísimo* form.

un perro muy perezoso = ¿ ?
dos libros muy interesantes = ¿ ?
una clase muy aburrida = ¿ ?
unas chicas muy simpáticas = ¿ ?

10 El Café Buen Libro 

Leer • Pensar • Escribir • Hablar

Lee la crítica del café y lo que dicen estas *(these)* personas. ¿A quiénes recomiendas el café? ¿A quiénes no?

Café Buen Libro

Nuevo León, 28

✓✓ ++ $ ☺☺

Es un café tranquilo con un ambiente* intelectual donde puedes pasar el tiempo en la compañía de un buen amigo o un buen libro. Los precios son muy razonables. Puedes comer un sándwich, una ensalada, un postre riquísimo o simplemente beber un café. También tienen lo último en libros, videos y música. Un "plus" es la presentación de grupos musicales los fines de semana.

Ambiente
aburrido ✓
tranquilo ✓✓
fantástico ✓✓✓

Comida y bebida
regular +
buena ++
excelente +++

Precios
barato $
medio $$
caro $$$

Servicio
regular ☺
bueno ☺☺
superior ☺☺☺

* atmosphere

1. **Carmen:** "Quisiera comer un bistec sabroso".
2. **Marta:** "Me encanta escuchar música".
3. **Diego:** "Tengo muchísima hambre y poco tiempo".
4. **Lupe:** "Me gusta pasar tiempo con otras personas interesantes y graciosas".
5. **Ana:** "No tengo mucho dinero *(money)* ahora".
6. Y a ti, ¿te gustaría ir al Café Buen Libro? ¿Por qué?

Practice and Communicate 5B

Exploración del lenguaje

Core Instruction

Standards: 4.1

Resources: Answer Keys: Student Edition, p. 73

Suggestions: Remind students that since they are adding *-ísimo* to adjectives, the ending must agree in number and gender with the noun it is describing. Point out to students that *-ísimo* always has an accent mark.

Answers:

1. **perezosísimo**
2. **interesantísimos**
3. **aburridísima**
4. **simpatiquísimas**

10 Standards: 1.2, 1.3, 4.1

Resources: Answer Keys: Student Edition, p. 73

Focus: Reading, writing, and speaking about a place to eat

Recycle: Foods; likes

Suggestions: Have students look at the picture and give their opinions of what they think the restaurant is like. Review the symbols to the right of the text. How does the critic rate *Café Buen Libro?* Remind students to use cognates to help them understand the reading.

Answers:

1. **no**
2. **sí**
3. **no**
4. **sí**
5. **sí**
6. **Answers will vary.**

Extension: Have students choose a restaurant that they have been to and write a brief review. Encourage students to create their own rating system.

Additional Resources

- Communication Wbk.: Audio Act. 6, pp. 102–103
- Teacher's Resource Book: Audio Script, p. 42, Communicative Pair Activity BLM, p. 46
- Audio Program DVD: Cap. 5B, Track 8

ENRICH YOUR TEACHING

Culture Note

La Guía del Ocio is a guide to what's going on in major cities in Spain. It is available online and lists current films, plays, shows and musical events. It also includes a listing of most restaurants and cafes with brief descriptions for each. It is extremely useful for tourists looking to make the most of their stay.

21st Century Skills

Media Literacy Have students working in small groups research Web sites in specific Spanish-speaking cities to find restaurants they would like to visit. Have them evaluate each Web site for design, appeal, and accuracy. They should present their selected restaurants to the class and explain why they chose them, using the statements in Activity 10 as a model, if possible.

ASSESSMENT

Prueba 5B-2 with Study Plan (online only)

Quiz: Vocabulary Production

- Prueba 5B-2: pp. 135–136

Gramática

Core Instruction

Standards: 4.1

Resources: Voc. and Gram. Transparency 108; Teacher's Resource Book: Video Script, p. 44; Video Program: Cap. 5B

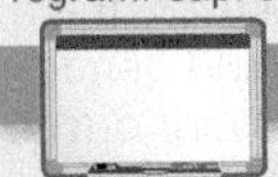

INTERACTIVE WHITEBOARD
Grammar Activities 5B

Suggestions: After presenting the forms of ***venir*** to the class, ask volunteers to put the forms of ***tener*** and ***venir*** on the board. Have students compare them side-by-side. Use the transparency to reinforce the verb. Use the *GramActiva* Video as a follow-up.

11 Standards: 1.2, 1.3

Resources: Answer Keys: Student Edition, p. 73

Focus: Reading and writing using ***venir***

Suggestions: Have students first read through the entire note for meaning, noting the various subjects. After completing the activity, have students check their work with a partner.

Answers:

1. vengo
2. venimos
3. viene
4. vienen
5. vienen
6. viene

12 Standards: 1.2, 1.3

Resources: Teacher's Resource Book: Audio Script, p. 42; Audio Program DVD: Cap. 5B, Track 9; Answer Keys: Student Edition, p. 74

Focus: Listening to and writing descriptions

Recycle: Describing people; family members

Suggestions: Play the audio or read the script several times. The first time, have students take brief notes. After listening again, have them write the full descriptions. Give students time to complete their drawings and have them listen a final time to check for accuracy.

Script and Answers:

1. Mi amigo Roberto viene. Él es altísimo y muy artístico.
2. La hermana de Roberto viene. Ella es muy alta, rubia y guapa.
3. Dos primos de Roberto vienen. Tienen el pelo corto. Uno es ordenado y el otro primo es desordenado.
4. El hermano de Roberto viene también. Él es bajo y tiene el pelo negro y largo.

Manos a la obra

Gramática

Objectives

- Read about and discuss celebrations and preparations
- Listen to a description of a family

The verb *venir*

You use *venir* to say that someone is coming to a place or an event.

¿A qué hora vienes a mi casa?
When are you coming to my house?

Siempre vengo a esta playa.
I always come to this beach.

Here are all the present-tense forms:

(yo)	vengo	(nosotros) (nosotras)	venimos
(tú)	vienes	(vosotros) (vosotras)	venís
Ud. (él) (ella)	viene	Uds. (ellos) (ellas)	vienen

Más ayuda realidades.com

- ***GramActiva* Video Tutorial:** Irregular verbs **Animated Verbs**
- ***GramActiva* Activity**

11 ¿Cómo vienen?

Leer • Escribir

Tu amigo Antonio invita a tu familia a su casa en el campo. Escribes una nota para explicar cómo y cuándo todos Uds. vienen. Completa la nota con las formas apropiadas del verbo *venir*.

Antonio:

¡Gracias por tu invitación! Yo **1.** en bicicleta con mi amiga, Marta. Nosotros **2.** a las dos porque Marta trabaja hasta la una. Mi abuela **3.** en tren[1] con mis padres. Ellos **4.** a las once para ayudar[2] con la cena. Mis hermanitos también **5.** en tren con mis padres. Mi hermana mayor, Cecilia, **6.** en monopatín. No sé a qué hora va a venir.

¡Nos vemos el sábado!

[1]train [2]to help

12 Escucha, escribe y dibuja

Escuchar • Escribir

Roberto, otro amigo de Antonio, también va a la fiesta con su familia. Vas a escuchar la descripción de su familia. Escribe las cuatro descripciones y después dibuja a la familia. Compara tu dibujo con el dibujo de otro(a) estudiante.

DIFFERENTIATED INSTRUCTION

Students with Learning Difficulties

Actividad 12 will be more manageable for students if they can focus on only a few words instead of the entire description. Provide students with a copy of the script. White out three or four adjectives and ask students to listen for them.

Advanced Learners/Pre-AP*

Have students write a letter to a friend describing a family party. Students should tell at what time different members of the family are coming and what each person is going to bring.

13 ¿Qué traen a tu casa?

Hablar

Estás en casa de un(a) amigo(a). Habla de lo que traen las personas a la casa.

Modelo

A —*Cuando tus tíos vienen a tu casa, ¿traen algo?*
B —*Sí, generalmente traen el postre.*
o: —*No, generalmente no traen nada.*

Nota

Traer, "to bring," follows the pattern of *-er* verbs except for the irregular *yo* form: *traigo.*

- Mañana **traigo** pasteles para todos.
- Y tú, ¿**traes** bebidas?

Estudiante A

1. tu(s) abuelo(s)
2. tu mejor amigo(a)
3. tus amigos
4. tus tíos
5. tus primos
6. los amigos de tus padres

Estudiante B

el plato principal
un regalo
nada
el postre
flores
¡Respuesta personal!

Pronunciación

The letters *b* and *v*

In Spanish, *b* and *v* are pronounced the same. At the beginning of a word or phrase, *b* and *v* sound like the *b* in "boy." Listen to and say these words:

voy bolígrafo vienen bien viejo video

In most other positions *b* and *v* have a softer "b" sound. The lips barely touch as the *b* or *v* sound is pronounced. Listen to and say these words:

abuelo divertido joven huevos globo Alberto

Try it out! Listen to and say this *trabalenguas:*

Cabral clava un clavo.
¿Qué clavo clava Cabral?

14 ¿Quiénes vienen?

Hablar

Estás en una fiesta en la escuela y hablas con los otros estudiantes.

1. ¿Quiénes vienen a la fiesta? ¿A qué hora vienen?
2. ¿Vienen todos los profesores a la fiesta? ¿Qué traen ellos?
3. ¿Traen los estudiantes pizza o sándwiches? ¿Frutas o pasteles?
4. ¿Quién trae las decoraciones? ¿Qué traes tú?

Más práctica GO

	realidades.com	print
Instant Check	✔	
Guided WB pp. 175–176	✔	✔
Core WB p. 98	✔	✔
Comm. WB pp. 103, 106	✔	✔
***Hispanohablantes* WB** pp. 194–197		✔

ENRICH YOUR TEACHING

Teacher-to-Teacher

On small pieces of paper, write the names of items that students might bring to a party. Be sure to have as many items as there are students. Pass around the papers and ask each student to choose one. The first student to start says: *Vengo a la fiesta y traigo refrescos. ¿Qué traes tú?* That student points to the next student, who replies: *Yo vengo a la fiesta y traigo pizza y él (ella) viene a la fiesta y trae refrescos. ¿Qué traes tú?* Have the class continue until someone forgets what a previous student is bringing. If someone breaks the chain, start again with the next person.

Practice and Communicate 5B

13 Standards: 1.1

Resources: Answer Keys: Student Edition, p. 74
Focus: Using the verb ***traer*** in conversation
Recycle: Foods; family members
Answers:

Student A
Answers will vary but correct verb forms are:
1. **tu abuelo viene / trae; tus abuelos vienen / traen**
2. **tu mejor amigo(a) viene / trae**
3. **tus amigos vienen / traen**
4. **tus tíos vienen / traen**
5. **tus primos vienen / traen**
6. **los amigos de tus padres vienen / traen**

Student B: Answers will vary.

Extension: Have students talk about what they bring to three different classes.

Pronunciación
Core Instruction

Standards: 4.1

Resources: Teacher's Resource Book: Audio Script, p. 43; Audio Program DVD: Cap. 5B, Track 11
Suggestions: Have students pronounce the consonants ***b*** and ***v*** and the example words. Say the tongue twister and ask volunteers to say it for the class.

14 Standards: 1.1, 1.3

Focus: Using ***venir*** and ***traer***
Recycle: Telling time; foods
Answers will vary.

Additional Resources

- Communication Wbk.: Audio Act. 7, p. 103
- Teacher's Resource Book: Audio Script, p. 43; Comm. Act. BLM, p. 47
- Audio Program DVD: Cap. 5B, Track 10

ASSESSMENT

Prueba 5B-3 with Study Plan (online only)

Quiz: The verb *venir*
- Prueba 5B-3: p. 123

Gramática

Core Instruction

Standards: 4.1

Resources: Voc. and Gram. Transparency 109; Teacher's Resource Book: Video Script, pp. 44–45; Video Program: Cap. 5B

INTERACTIVE WHITEBOARD

Grammar Activities 5B

Suggestions: Write several sample sentences on the board, leaving out ***ser*** or ***estar.*** Have students tell you which verb to use and the reason for their decision. Ask volunteers for sample sentences. Use the transparency to reinforce ***ser*** and ***estar.*** Use the *GramActiva* Video as a follow-up to your presentation.

15 Standards: 1.1

Resources: Answer Keys: Student Edition, p. 75

Focus: Using ***estar*** to talk about where people are and how they feel

Recycle: Places; adjectives

Suggestions: Remind students that adjectives agree in number and gender with the nouns they describe. Encourage Student B to come up with a personal reply to Student A's questions.

Answers:

Student A

1. —¿Dónde está Yolanda?
2. —¿Dónde están Miguel y Fernando?
3. —¿Dondé están Isabel y Raquel?
4. —¿Dónde está Ana María?
5. —¿Dónde está Federico?
6. —¿Dónde está Enrique?

Student B

Answers will vary.

Block Schedule

Have students bring in photos of their family members or friends and describe them using ***ser*** and ***estar.*** They should include information on where each person is from, what the person is like and where he or she is. Encourage volunteers to present their photos to the class. Ask students follow-up questions to their presentations. For example: *En esa foto, ¿está contenta tu prima?*

Gramática

Objectives

- Discuss and describe people and foods
- Read an interview and a recipe
- Exchange information while ordering and discussing food in a restaurant

The verbs *ser* and *estar*

You know that both *ser* and *estar* mean "to be." Their uses, however, are different.

(yo)	soy	(nosotros) (nosotras)	somos
(tú)	eres	(vosotros) (vosotras)	sois
Ud. (él) (ella)	es	Uds. (ellos) (ellas)	son

(yo)	estoy	(nosotros) (nosotras)	estamos
(tú)	estás	(vosotros) (vosotras)	estáis
Ud. (él) (ella)	está	Uds. (ellos) (ellas)	están

Use *ser* to talk about characteristics that generally do not change. *Ser* is used for descriptions that are not about conditions or location. For example:

- who a person is or what a person is like
- what something is or what something is like
- where a person or thing is from

Teresa es mi prima. Es muy graciosa.
Los tacos son mi comida favorita. Son riquísimos.
Mis tíos son de México. Son muy simpáticos.

Use *estar* to talk about conditions that tend to change. For example:

- how a person feels
- where a person or thing is

¿Dónde está Mariana? No está aquí.
No puede venir hoy porque está muy enferma.

Más ayuda realidades.com

- ***GramActiva*** **Video**
  Tutorial: *Ser and estar*
  Animated Verbs
- ***Canción de hip hop:*** *Camarero*
- ***GramActiva*** **Activity**

15 ¿Dónde están las otras personas?

Hablar

Estás en un café con un(a) amigo(a) y preguntas dónde están los otros amigos. Tu amigo(a) explica dónde están y cómo están.

Modelo

Marcos y Graciela A —*¿Dónde están Marcos y Graciela?*
B —*Están en la biblioteca. Están muy ocupados.*

Strategy

Using rhymes
To remember the uses of *estar,* memorize this rhyme:
For how you feel
And where you are,
Always use the verb *estar.*

Estudiante A

1. Yolanda
2. Miguel y Fernando
3. Isabel y Raquel
4. Ana María
5. Federico
6. Enrique

Estudiante B

la escuela	ocupado, -a
casa	enfermo, -a
el trabajo	cansado, -a
la lección de . . .	triste
la biblioteca	mal
	contento, -a

¡Respuesta personal!

DIFFERENTIATED INSTRUCTION

Multiple Intelligences

Musical/Rhythmic: Prior to *Actividad* 15, go over the Strategy box including the rhyme. Say it aloud with the students. Encourage them to create and share with the class any rhymes they make up that help them learn Spanish.

Practice and Communicate 5B

16 Entrevista con una chef

Leer • Escribir

Lee la entrevista con la chef Ortiz y completa la conversación con la forma apropiada del verbo *estar* o *ser*.

— Bienvenida, Chef Ortiz. ¿Cómo __1.__ Ud. hoy?
— __2.__ muy bien, gracias.
— Ud. trabaja aquí en Asunción ahora pero, ¿de dónde __3.__ Ud. originalmente?
— Mi familia y yo __4.__ del campo.
— ¿Y cuál __5.__ su trabajo aquí?
— Yo __6.__ directora de los chefs en el famoso restaurante La Capital.
— La Capital __7.__ un restaurante muy popular aquí. ¿Dónde __8.__ el restaurante?
— Al lado de la catedral.
— Los platos en su restaurante __9.__ muy típicos de Paraguay, ¿no?
— Sí, y según los clientes, la comida en nuestro restaurante __10.__ deliciosa.
— Y los postres __11.__ muy populares también, ¿no?
— Sí, tenemos pasteles ricos, helados simples con frutas exóticas, un poco de todo.
— ¡Muchas gracias, Chef Ortiz!
— De nada. Siempre __12.__ muy contenta de estar aquí con Uds.

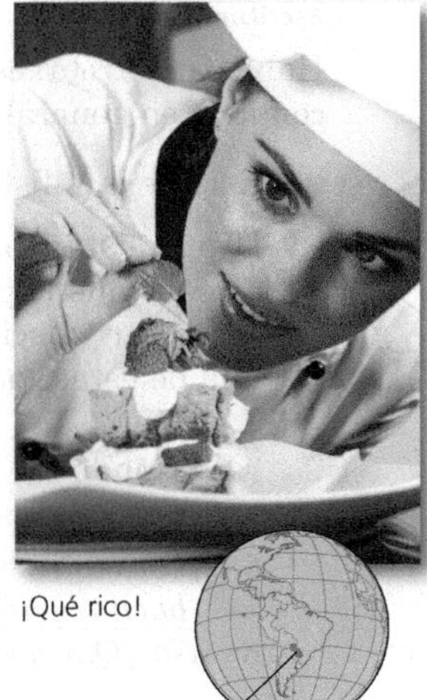

¡Qué rico!

Paraguay

17 Un postre delicioso

Leer • Pensar

Your grandmother has given you her recipe for *arroz con leche* and you want to try it out. But the ingredients are given in *gramos* and *litros* and you don't know what the customary measure equivalents are. Study the conversion chart, convert the measurements given in the recipe, and answer the question.

ARROZ CON LECHE

Para 8

- 300 gramos de arroz
- 3 litros de leche
- 400 gramos de azúcar
- un poco de vainilla
- canela[1]

Pon el arroz en remojo[2] con la leche una hora y media. Luego cocina a fuego lento[3] una hora más o menos. Añade[4] el azúcar y la vainilla y cocina unos 5 minutos más. Pon el arroz en el refrigerador y esparce[5] un poco de canela encima.

Conexiones | Las matemáticas

1 kilo (k) = 2,2 libras *(pounds)*
1 gramo (g) = 0,035 onzas *(ounces)*
1 litro (l) = 1,057 cuartos *(quarts)*

Multiplica los kilos, gramos o litros por su medida[6] correspondiente en el sistema que usas.

Calcula las onzas o los cuartos que hay en 300 gramos de arroz, tres litros de leche y 400 gramos de azúcar.

- ¿Cuántas libras hay en dos kilos de arroz?

[1]cinnamon [2]soak [3]cook slowly [4]Add [5]sprinkle [6]measure

BELLRINGER REVIEW

Read the rhyme in the *Strategy* on p. 258 and call on several volunteers to repeat it.

16 Standards: 1.2, 1.3

Resources: Answer Keys: Student Edition, p. 75

Focus: Reading about a chef and using present-tense forms of ***estar*** and ***ser***

Recycle: Locations; food vocabulary; adjectives

Suggestions: Remind students that after choosing the verb, they have to conjugate it correctly according to the subject. Review the answers with the class by having one volunteer play the role of the interviewer and another the role of Chef Ortiz.

Answers:

1. está	5. es	9. son
2. Estoy	6. soy	10. es
3. es	7. es	11. son
4. somos	8. está	12. estoy

17 Standards: 1.2, 3.1

Resources: Answer Keys: Student Edition, p. 75

Focus: Cross-curricular math activity

Suggestions: Before reading, brainstorm a list of measurements that might be used in a recipe. Ask students what metric measurements they are familiar with and which of those could be used to make a dessert. Explain to them that they are going to learn how to make ***arroz con leche,*** a typical dessert served in many Spanish-speaking countries. Point out the use of commas in place of decimal points when writing numbers in Spanish. You may want to allow students to use a calculator to make their conversions.

Answers:

300 gramos de arroz = 10,5 onzas
3 litros de leche = 3,1 cuartos
400 gramos de azúcar = 14 onzas
2 kilos de arroz = 4,4 libras

Theme Project

Students can perform Step 4 at this point. Be sure they understand your corrections and suggestions. (For more information, see p. 220-b.)

ENRICH YOUR TEACHING

Culture Note

In many restaurants in the capital city of Asunción, you can find ***sopa paraguaya,*** a traditional soup of Paraguay. It is said that a cook of the famous military leader Mariscal Francisco Solano López (1826–1870) invented the dish, made with balls of corn flour.

21st Century Skills

Creativity and Innovation After working with the *GramActiva* video, the *Canción de hip-hop*, and the *ser-estar* tutorial, have students work with a partner or small group to create a poem, a song, or a short story using *ser* and *estar*. Have students perform their piece for the class. The members of the class select the most creative piece as the winner.

18 Standards: 1.1, 1.3

Focus: Writing and speaking about food using ***ser***

Recycle: Foods and beverages

Suggestions: Brainstorm a list of foods and beverages by categories such as ***desayuno, almuerzo,*** or ***cena.*** Remind students that it is easier to recall vocabulary if they think of the category the word belongs to. Point out the *Nota* and explain that in this activity they will talk about food and drinks in general using ***ser.***

Answers will vary.

Common Errors: Remind students to make adjectives agree with nouns.

19 Standards: 1.1, 1.2, 4.1

Resources: Voc. and Gram. Transparency 111

Focus: Talking about items on a menu

Recycle: Food vocabulary

Suggestions: Have students read the menu and identify any new words. Ask them to guess the meaning of those words using context clues or cognates. Explain that ***estar*** is used when talking about how a food or beverage tastes.

Answers will vary.

Extension: Have students work in pairs to create their own ***menú del día,*** using the menu from Restaurante Hidalgo as a model.

Fondo cultural

Standards: 2.1, 4.2

Suggestions: Have students bring in a ***menú del día*** from a restaurant in their community that serves food from a Spanish-speaking country, or have them download one from the Internet.

Answers will vary but should include that pre-set menus don't give the widest selection but are often cheaper and faster.

Theme Project

Students can perform Step 5 at this point. Record their presentations for inclusion in their portfolio. (For more information, see p. 220-b.)

18 ¡Es buenísimo para la salud!

Escribir • Hablar

Habla con otro(a) estudiante sobre cómo son las comidas en general.

1. Escribe una lista de diez comidas y bebidas.
2. Usa tu lista y pregunta a un(a) compañero(a) si come lo que le preguntas. Tu compañero(a) va a contestar y decirte por qué come o no come cada una de estas comidas.

Modelo

A —*¿Comes muchas verduras?*
B —*¡Por supuesto! Las verduras son muy buenas para la salud.*
o:—*No. ¡Qué asco! Las verduras son horribles.*

Nota

To describe what a food item is like in general, use *ser*. To describe how a food item tastes at a particular time, use *estar*.

bueno (para la salud)	sabroso
malo (para la salud)	delicioso
rico	horrible
riquísimo	

19 ¡La sopa está riquísima!

Hablar

Estás en un restaurante y el (la) camarero(a) te pregunta cómo está todo. Mira el menú para contestar.

Modelo

A —*Señor(ita), ¿cómo está el arroz con pollo?*
B —*Está muy sabroso. Me encanta.*
o:—*Lo siento. Está malo. ¿Me trae otro plato principal?*

Fondo Cultural | El mundo hispano

El menú del día In many Spanish-speaking countries, restaurants and cafés often offer *un menú del día* or, as they are called in some parts of Mexico, *una comida corrida.* These daily menus usually offer one to three choices for each course at a reasonable fixed price.

- Do any restaurants that you know offer something similar to *el menú del día?* What would be the advantages and disadvantages of ordering from *un menú del día?*

Restaurante Hidalgo

Menú del día

$20,00

Sopas y Ensaladas
Ensalada de tomate y cebolla
Sopa de verduras
Sopa Hidalgo

Verduras
Papas fritas
Papas al horno
Guisantes con jamón

Platos principales
Bistec
Pescado
Arroz con pollo

Postres
Pastel de chocolate
Helado de mango o papaya
Frutas frescas

También se dice . . .

el menú = la carta *(México, España)*

DIFFERENTIATED INSTRUCTION

Multiple Intelligences

Visual/Spatial: Have students draw table settings with obvious errors such as a plate on top of a glass, a spoon under a plate, a tomato in a cup, and so on. Have them exchange their drawings with another student. Tell them to describe each error and explain how to fix the problem. For example: *El plato está encima del vaso. Debe estar al lado del plato.*

Heritage Language Learners

Ask students to choose a traditional dish from their heritage country and have them write a short paragraph describing the dish. Ask for volunteers to read their paragraphs to the class and have the class explain why they would or would not like the dish.

20 El menú del día |  | 

Escribir • Hablar

With a classmate, prepare to play the roles of a server and client *(cliente)* at the Restaurante Hidalgo. Write five questions that each one could ask. Use the menu in Actividad 19 to help you decide what to ask. Don't forget to use the formal *Ud.* form in your questions and answers.

Modelo

el (la) camarero(a)	el (la) cliente
¿Qué desea pedir de plato principal?	¿Cómo está el bistec?

21 En el restaurante | |

Hablar

Usa las preguntas y frases de la Actividad 20 para tener una conversación completa. En tu conversación habla de las sopas y ensaladas, verduras, platos principales y postres.

Modelo

A —*¿Qué desea pedir de plato principal?*
B —*No sé. ¿Cómo está el bistec?*
A —*Está muy sabroso.*
B —*¡Genial! Quisiera el bistec, por favor.*

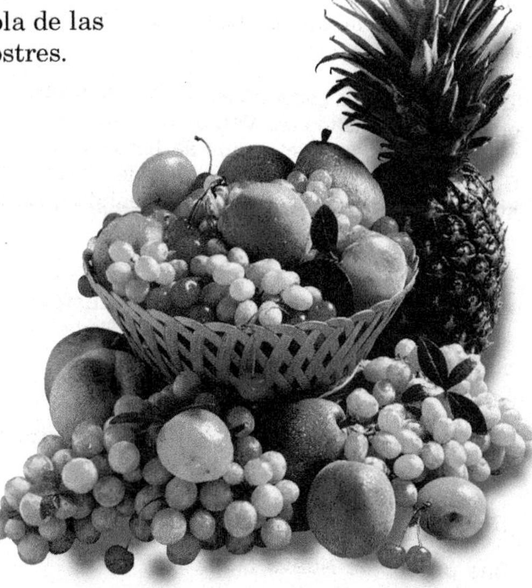

El español en el mundo del trabajo

How can you combine an interest in nutrition and health with skills in Spanish? Here's one example. As you know, the U.S. Department of Agriculture provides the public with a wide range of nutritional information through print materials and Web sites. Much of this information is available in Spanish. There is a need for federal employees who are knowledgeable to translate and work with the Spanish-speaking community on issues related to nutrition.

- What other opportunities can you think of that would combine communication skills with a knowledge of nutrition?

Más práctica GO

	realidades.com	print
Instant Check	✔	
Guided WB pp. 177–178	✔	✔
Core WB pp. 99–100	✔	✔
Comm. WB pp. 103–104, 107, 282	✔	✔
Hispanohablantes WB pp. 198–201		✔

Practice and Communicate 5B

20 Standards: 1.1, 1.3

Resources: Voc. and Gram. Transparency 111
Focus: Asking questions in a restaurant
Recycle: Food vocabulary; question words
Suggestions: Encourage students to ask about a variety of foods.
Answers will vary.

21 Standards: 1.1

Focus: Ordering in a restaurant
Recycle: Food vocabulary; questions
Suggestions: Have students refer to the charts they made in *Actividad* 20, but encourage them not to read them word for word. Ask for volunteers to repeat their dialogues for the class.
Answers will vary.

Pre-AP* Support

- **Learning Objective:** Interpersonal Speaking
- **Activities 20, 21:** Students practice informal speaking skills as they role play a server and client.

El español en el mundo del trabajo

Core Instruction

Standards: 5.1

Suggestions: Brainstorm a list of professions that require knowledge of nutrition. Ask students how Spanish would be useful.

Additional Resources

- Communication Wbk.: Audio Act. 8–9, pp. 103–104
- Teacher's Resource Book: Audio Script, p. 43, Communicative Pair Activity BLM, pp. 48–49
- Audio Program DVD: Cap. 5B, Tracks 12–13

ASSESSMENT

Prueba 5B-4 with Study Plan (online only)

Quiz: The verbs *ser* and *estar*
- Prueba 5B-4: p. 138

ENRICH YOUR TEACHING

Teacher-to-Teacher

Have students examine the *menú del día* on page 260, and use it as a model for creating their own menu of the day for a restaurant in their town or city. Have them write the menu in Spanish on a piece of poster board, and decorate it as they wish. Display the menus in the classroom.

21st Century Skills

Information Literacy Have students research Web sites from the United States and from some Spanish-speaking countries that deal with nutritional guidelines. Have them compare the information and identify similarities and differences.

Common Core: Reading

Lectura

Core Instruction

Standards: 1.2, 1.3, 3.1

Focus: Reading comprehension of a letter from relatives about a visit to Santa Fe

Mapa global interactivo, Actividad Visit Santa Fe, New Mexico and travel the Camino Real.

Suggestions:

Pre-reading: After students have completed the first activity in the *Strategy,* have them look at the menu, photos and captions that accompany the reading. Then ask them what kind of information they expected to find in the letter.

Reading: Have students read the letter without interruption. Remind them to use cognates to help them understand the reading and, when they come across words they don't know, to look for context clues. Point out the footnotes at the bottom of the page.

Post-reading: Have students make a list of the activities that Alicia and Pedro are planning for their friends. Ask students which activities they would like to participate in and which ones they would not enjoy.

Extension: Have students write a letter about a special place or a unique restaurant that would be interesting to visit in their community.

BELLRINGER REVIEW

Have students brainstorm what items they expect to find on the menu at a Mexican restaurant.

Pre-AP* Support

- **Learning Objective:** Presentational Speaking
- **Activity:** Pair students who have visited the same type of restaurant (Mexican, fast food, etc.) in their community. Ask them to compare their restaurants and share their experiences and recommendations with the class, using the letter from Alicia and Pedro as a model, if possible.
- ***Pre-AP* Resource Book:*** Comprehensive guide to Pre-AP* reading skill development, pp. 19–26

Teacher-to-Teacher

Have students create and display a Spanish version of the daily or weekly menu from the school cafeteria.

Objectives

- Read a letter about a visit to Santa Fe, New Mexico
- Skim to find specific information
- Compare the history of Santa Fe to that of your community

Lectura

Una visita a Santa Fe

Lee esta carta que escriben Alicia y Pedro. Ellos hablan de una visita que van a hacer sus primos a Santa Fe. ¿Qué cosas interesantes van a hacer? ¿Qué van a visitar?

Strategy

Skimming

Before you read this letter, make list of three pieces of information you might expect to find. Quickly skim the letter. What information did you find that was on your list

Queridos Rosario y Luis:

¡Esperamos[1] su visita en agosto! Aquí en Santa Fe vamos a hacer muchas cosas. ¿Saben que es una ciudad[2] con más de 400 años de historia y cultura? Vamos a visitar museos y tiendas, y vamos a comer comida típica. ¡Los cinco días van a pasar rápidamente![3].

Tenemos planes para pasar una noche muy especial en honor de su visita. Vamos a comer en un "restaurante" histórico que se llama Rancho de las Golondrinas[4]. Está a diez millas de nuestra casa, al sur de Santa Fe. El Rancho, en realidad, no es un restaurante; es una casa española.

Durante los días de su visita, el Rancho va a celebrar "un fandango", un baile histórico y típico, con una cena tradicional. Toda la comida es riquísima, pero nuestro plato favorito es el chile con carne y queso. Después de comer, vamos a bailar. ¡No sabemos bailar pero va a ser muy divertido! Mandamos[5] el menú con la carta.

¡Nos vemos en agosto!

Sus primos de Nuevo México,

Alicia y Pedro

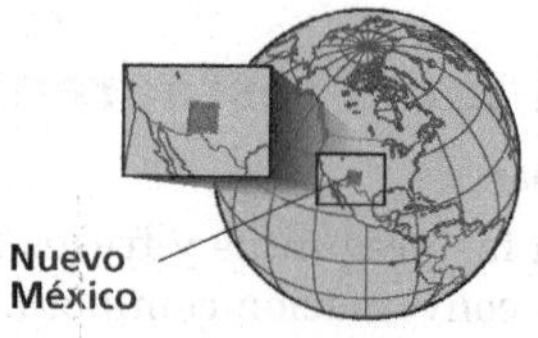

Un paraje[6] en El Camino Real[7] desde la Ciudad de México hasta Santa Fe, es del año 1710. Ahora es un museo.

[1]We're looking forward to [2]city [3]quickly [4]Swallows [5]We're sending [6]stopping place [7]the Royal Highway

DIFFERENTIATED INSTRUCTION

Advanced Learners

Have students write a letter inviting a relative or friend to visit them. Have them suggest activities, places to visit, and good restaurants. They can include photos or postcards with their letters.

Students with Learning Difficulties

Sometimes students can be intimidated by a large amount of text. Tell them to first scan through the letter to see how many cognates they can find. When they realize that they already know or can guess many of the words, they will feel more confident about the reading.

Menú del Fandango

Sopas
Sopa de arroz
Garbanzos con chile

Plato principal
Pollo relleno[8]
Chile con carne y queso

Postre
Bizcochitos[9]
Pudín de arroz con leche

Bebidas
Chocolate mexicano
Ponche
Café

[8] Stuffed chicken [9] Cookies

La Capilla de San Miguel, la iglesia más vieja de Santa Fe, del año 1626

El Palacio de los Gobernadores, construido en 1610, es el edificio *(building)* público más viejo de los Estados Unidos que todavía se usa. Ahora es un museo de historia.

¿Comprendes?

1. ¿Cuáles son cuatro actividades que los primos van a hacer durante la visita? ¿Cuál te gustaría hacer en Santa Fe?
2. ¿Por qué es importante Santa Fe?
3. ¿Por qué quieren ir Alicia y Pedro al Rancho de las Golondrinas?
4. Si no te gusta nada la comida picante *(spicy)*, ¿qué debes pedir del menú?
5. ¿Por qué es importante La Capilla de San Miguel?

Fondo Cultural | Los Estados Unidos

¡A pensar! Santa Fe was established thirteen years before Plymouth Colony was settled by the Mayflower Pilgrims. It has been a seat of government for Spain, Mexico, and the Confederacy.

- Find out when the oldest building in your community was built. How does it differ in age from the Palacio de los Gobernadores in Santa Fe?

Más práctica GO realidades.com | print

	realidades.com	print
Guided WB p. 179	✔	✔
Comm. WB pp. 108, 283	✔	✔
***Hispanohablantes* WB** pp. 202–203		✔
Cultural Reading Activity	✔	

Reading 5B

¿Comprendes? Standards: 1.2, 1.3

Resources: Answer Keys: Student Edition, p. 76

Focus: Demonstrate reading comprehension

Suggestions: Have students read the questions. For each one, ask whether the answer can be found in the letter, the menu, or in the captions. Then have them answer the questions.

Answers:

1. **visitar museos y tiendas; comer comida típica; comer en un "restaurante" histórico y bailar**
2. **porque tiene 400 años de historia**
3. **porque el Rancho va a celebrar "un fandango", y porque el Rancho es histórico y la comida es riquísima**
4. **Answers will vary but may include: sopa de arroz; pollo relleno; bizcochitos; pudín de arroz con leche**
5. **porque es la iglesia más vieja de Santa Fe**

Fondo cultural

Standards: 3.1, 4.2

Suggestions: Discuss the history of your school. Ask the students when it was built, if it was the first school to be built in the community, and if they consider it to be an old school or a new school. You might want to encourage students to research the history of their town outside of class and report their findings later.

Answers will vary.

Teaching with Photos

Have students study the photos of the buildings in Santa Fe. Ask them to guess which building is the oldest without reading the captions. Then ask volunteers to read the captions aloud and discuss them with the class.

Ask students to comment on the architecture of the three buildings. Then have them compare it to the architecture of older buildings in your area.

For Further Reading

Student Resource: Realidades para hispanohablantes: Lectura 2, pp. 204–205

ENRICH YOUR TEACHING

Culture Note

El Camino Real was once the name given to any major road in Spain or its colonies. In 1598, Don Juan de Oñate blazed the Camino Real de Tierra Adentro, which runs from Mexico City up to New Mexico. This road has existed for over 300 years. Efforts are being made to preserve this historic trail so that it will be in existence for years to come.

21st Century Skills

Collaboration Have students working in small groups research Santa Fe Web sites and gather information to write a travel guide for the city. Each person in the group should be responsible for a specific feature of the guide (restaurants, museums, special events, and so on). Have students report their findings to the class.

Perspectivas del mundo hispano

Core Instruction

Standards: 1.2, 2.1, 4.2

Focus: Reading about mealtime and the ***sobremesa***

Suggestions: Present the idea of spending a couple of hours every day conversing with family and friends. Call attention to the photos. Elicit from students that one photo shows friends and the other shows family spending time conversing after a meal. Explain that this is common in Spanish-speaking countries and that it is considered an important and valuable time. Have students read the text. Discuss how fast food and eating "on the go" conflict with the general attitude toward mealtime and the ***sobremesa.*** Emphasize that mealtime in Spanish-speaking cultures is a social time when the family relaxes and talks. Ask students to consider how their lives would be different if they were to do this. Ask where people get the time to spend two hours at lunch every day. Have students complete the *Check it out!* section and compare their answers in class. Direct attention to the *Think about it!* section and have students discuss the questions.

Answers will vary.

To incorporate language use, have students describe people in the photos, or have them imagine the conversations suggested by the photos.

Teacher-to-Teacher

Careers: *Tema* 5 has focused on family, food, celebrations, and restaurants. Have students work in small groups to talk about a career in restaurant management. Have them write a list of words and expressions they have learned that might be useful for managing a restaurant. Ask groups to share their lists.

Additional Resources

Student Resource: Realidades para hispanohablantes, p. 206

Perspectivas del mundo hispano

A la hora de comer

Imagine that you had two hours for lunch every day. Or imagine that every time you ate a meal, you sat down at a table with a friend or family member and had a lengthy conversation. Now imagine that you didn't jump up from dinner as soon as you finished eating. What do these situations have in common?

Una familia en la República Dominicana

In many Spanish-speaking cultures, even ordinary mealtimes are considered social events, a time to spend enjoying food and company. People often take time after a meal to relax, to sit around the table and enjoy a good conversation or just to have a laugh. This custom, called the *sobremesa,* is more important in many cultures than getting to the next appointment or saving time and money by buying a quick meal.

Una familia chilena come al aire libre, Renaca, Chile

Not surprisingly, most Spanish-speaking countries have very few drive-through restaurants. Since people rarely take food "to go," they might be surprised if you suggested grabbing a sandwich to eat in the car. In fact, many cars don't have cup-holders.

Check it out! Figure out how much time you and your family spend at breakfast, lunch, and dinner on days when you're not in school or at work. Compare your results with those of your classmates. Then complete the following statements about practices among families in your community.

Modelo

En mi comunidad, es común *(common)* comer el desayuno en quince minutos.

1. En mi comunidad, es común comer el desayuno en ________ .
2. En mi comunidad, es común comer el almuerzo en ________ .
3. En mi comunidad, es común comer la cena en ________ .

Think about it! What does your research say about the importance of relaxing and enjoying a leisurely meal with friends and family? How does it compare to what happens during meals in Spanish-speaking countries? Consider the two different attitudes towards mealtime. What benefits might each one have?

DIFFERENTIATED INSTRUCTION

Heritage Language Learners

Some students may practice a type of ***sobremesa*** in their families, or they may have experienced it. If so, allow them to share their experiences with the class. If not, have them ask family or friends about the tradition in their heritage country.

 Objectives | Aplicación

- Write a review of your favorite restaurant
- Use examples to persuade your reader

Presentación escrita

Un restaurante muy bueno

Task

Your school is creating a community guide for Spanish speakers. Your class is writing about restaurants. Write a review of your favorite restaurant.

Servicio — Platos principales — (Nombre del restaurante) — Otras comidas y bebidas — Postres — Descripción general

1. **Prewrite** Think about the restaurant you like best. Copy the word web. Write the name of the restaurant in the middle circle. Write words and expressions associated with each category inside the appropriate circles.

2. **Draft** Write your review of the restaurant using information from the word web. Include information that might persuade others to try the restaurant.

3. **Revise** Read through your review and check for agreement, verb forms, and spelling. Share your review with a partner. Your partner should check the following:
   - Did you provide information about all categories?
   - Did you use the correct forms of the verbs?
   - Do you have any errors in spelling or agreement?
   - Is the review persuasive?

4. **Publish** Write a final copy of your review, making any necessary changes or additions. You may want to add illustrations and include your review in a booklet with your classmates' reviews or in your portfolio.

5. **Evaluation** The following rubric will be used to grade your review.

Rubric	Score 1	Score 3	Score 5
Completion of task	You provide information in three categories from the word web.	You provide information in four categories from the word web.	You provide information in five categories from the word web.
Use of new and previously learned vocabulary	You use very limited and repetitive vocabulary.	You use only recently acquired vocabulary.	You use both recently acquired and previously learned vocabulary.
Accurate spelling/use of grammar	You have many patterns of misspelling and misuse of grammar.	You have frequent patterns of misspelling and misuse of grammar.	You have very few patterns of misspelling and misuse of grammar.
Correct use of verbs	You have many repetitions of incorrect verb forms.	You have frequent repetitions of incorrect verb forms.	You have very few incorrect verb forms.

Strategy

Persuasion
Give specific information and concrete examples to persuade your readers to try a restaurant.

ENRICH YOUR TEACHING

Teacher-to-Teacher

e-amigos: Have students send e-mails to their *e-amigos* to ask about their favorite restaurant. Encourage them to use the word webs they created in the *Presentación escrita*. Ask them to print out or e-mail you their exchanges.

21st Century Skills

Responsibility and Leadership As part of the effort to develop the community guide for the Spanish-speaking residents, have students interview members of the community about the kinds of foods they prefer. Make sure that as many preferences as possible are included in the guide, so that the entire community is represented.

Common Core: Writing

Presentación escrita

Core Instruction

Standards: 1.3

Focus: Writing about restaurants in a personalized context; using language for persuasion

Suggestions: Review the task and the 5-step approach with students. Point out the *Strategy* and the word web to the right of the directions. Remind students that their review should include service, main dishes, beverages, desserts, and atmosphere.

Have students use the review on p. 255 as a model.

Review the rubric with the class to explain how you will grade the reviews.

Pre-AP* Support

- **Learning Objective:** Presentational Writing
- **Activity:** Looking at the word web you created for this exercise, think about this restaurant's strong points. Then write a brief advertisement for this restaurant. Be sure to play up its strong points!
- ***Pre-AP* Resource Book:*** Comprehensive guide to Pre-AP* writing skill development, pp. 27–38

Portfolio

Have students include their written presentations in their portfolios.

Additional Resources

Student Resources: Realidades para hispanohablantes, p. 207; Guided Practice: Presentación escrita, p. 180

ASSESSMENT

Presentación escrita

- Assessment Program: Rubrics, p. T31

Go over the descriptions of the different levels of performance. After assessing students, help individuals understand how their performance could be improved.

Videomisterio

Core Instruction

Standards: 1.2, 1.3, 2.1, 5.2

Resources: Teacher's Resource Book: Video Script, p. 45; Video Program: Cap. 5B; Video Program Teacher's Guide: Cap. 5B

Focus: Preparing to view the video

Personajes importantes: Inspector Gil, inspector de policía; Inspector Peña, inspector de policía; Doña Gracia Salazar, la víctima del crimen; Lola Lago, detective; Doña Lupe Aguirre, portera

Synopsis: The ambulance arrives for the victim, doña Gracia. Everyone is wondering where doña Gracia's niece Maria is. Inspector Gil asks questions of Lola Lago, who saw two people hurriedly leave doña Gracia's apartment building the night before. He asks her to call if she has any more information.

Suggestions:

Pre-viewing: Review with students the events of the previous episode: Lola Lago, while watering her plants late at night, sees two people hurriedly leaving the building across the street. After they leave, she finds a keychain that one of them dropped. It is labeled with the letters *J.R.D.* and the number eight. The next morning, doña Lupe, the caretaker, enters doña Gracia Salazar's apartments, and discovers her unconscious on the floor.

Review the *Nota cultural* with the class. You may want to ask students if they have ever been in a square similar to the ***plazas*** in Spain. Point out the *Palabras para comprender,* giving examples in context and writing the sentences on the board. Remind students that these words are only used to help them understand the episode and that they are not responsible for this vocabulary.

Visual scanning: Point to the first two photos and ask who the people are (Inspector Gil and Inspector Peña) and what they might be doing in this episode. Then point to the third photo of doña Gracia, the victim. Where are they taking her? Before students read the *Resumen del episodio,* have them scan the text and find cognates. (***ambulancia, hospital, policía, incidente***) Ask them to read the *Resumen del episodio* carefully and ask questions about what will happen.

Videomisterio

▼ Objective

- Understand the expanding plot of a mystery video set in Spain

¿Eres tú, María?

Episodio 2

Antes de ver el video

Personajes importantes

Inspector Gil, inspector de policía

Inspector Peña, inspector de policía

Doña Gracia Salazar, la víctima del crimen

Resumen del episodio

En este episodio, la ambulancia llega[1] y lleva[2] a doña Gracia Salazar al hospital. También llegan dos inspectores de policía. Le hablan a doña Lupe, la portera, sobre el incidente en el piso de doña Gracia. Lola se presenta[3] a los dos hombres y les dice[4] lo que sabe del incidente.

[1] arrives [2] takes away [3] introduces herself [4] tells them

Nota cultural In the cities and towns of Spain and many Spanish-speaking countries, you will find *plazas,* open squares that are surrounded by buildings. The *plazas* are the social center of the community or neighborhood. They may contain benches, trees and flowers, statues, and fountains. In the evening, neighbors will spend time in the *plaza* sharing details about families, daily events, politics, and many other topics.

Palabras para comprender

vive *(vivir)*	she lives *(to live)*
la sobrina	niece
esperar	to wait
anoche	last night
vi *(ver)*	I saw *(to see)*
una barba	beard
¿Quién era?	Who was she?
ayudar	to help
saber	to know

DIFFERENTIATED INSTRUCTION

Heritage Language Learners

Ask students to use the vocabulary from *Palabras para comprender* to write a paragraph about what happened in this episode. Also, ask any student who has lived in or visited their heritage country to comment on the *Nota cultural.* What do ***plazas*** look like? What activities take place in ***plazas***? Encourage students to bring in photos to share with the class.

"Es doña Gracia Salazar. Vive en el tercer piso con su sobrina, María".

"Anoche a la una de la mañana, vi a un hombre y a una mujer".

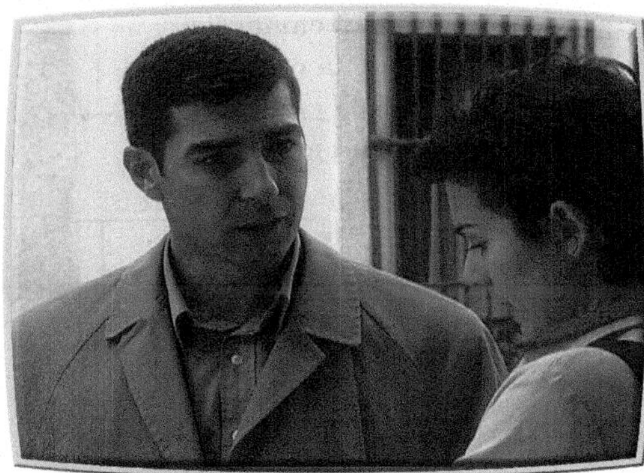

—¿Ud. es detective pero no tiene una descripción exacta ni del hombre ni de la mujer?

—A la una de la mañana es imposible ver mucho, ¿no?

Después de ver el video

¿Comprendes?

A. ¿Quién . . . ?

1. ¿Quién es la víctima?
2. ¿Quiénes viven en el tercer piso?
3. ¿Quién es la sobrina?
4. ¿Quién es doña Lupe?
5. ¿Quiénes llegan para investigar el crimen?
6. ¿Quién espera en la plaza?
7. ¿Quién dice que es imposible ver mucho a la una de la mañana?
8. ¿Quién quiere ayudar a los inspectores?

B. Escoge una de las fotos de esta página y escribe tres frases para describir la foto.

Más práctica GO

realidades.com | print

Actividades ✔

ENRICH YOUR TEACHING

Culture Note

There are many squares *(**plazas**)* in the city of Madrid, the capital of Spain. One of the most famous squares is *La Puerta del Sol,* in the center of the city. Have students research ***plazas*** in Spain. Ask students to look for pictures of ***plazas*** so that they can compare them to the description in the *Nota cultural.*

21st Century Skills

Initiative and Self-Direction Encourage students to develop their own process for understanding the video, depending on the kind of learner they are. As they work through the pre-viewing, viewing, and post-viewing tasks, they can identify and further develop the types of activities that are most effective for them.

Viewing: Play *Episodio 2* for the class. If there is time after viewing the full episode, select some key moments that you wish to highlight, such as when Inspector Gil questions Lola Lago.

Post-viewing: Have the class study the photos at the top of the page and ask volunteers to tell what is happening in the episode at the time of each picture. Write the vocabulary presented with this episode on the board to help students create sentences for each picture. Dramatize the quotations below the photos.

¿Comprendes? Standards: 1.1, 1.2, 1.3

Resources: Answer Keys: Student Edition, p. 77

Focus: Verifying comprehension

Suggestions: Have students work in pairs. Allow them to look at the video again for answers, but encourage them to answer the questions from memory.

Answers:

Parte A

1. **Doña Gracia Salazar es la víctima del crimen.**
2. **Doña Gracia Salazar y su sobrina María viven en el tercer piso.**
3. **María es la sobrina.**
4. **Doña Lupe Aguirre es la portera.**
5. **El Inspector Gil y el Inspector Peña llegan para investigar el crimen.**
6. **Lola Lago espera en la plaza.**
7. **Lola Lago.**
8. **Lola Lago quiere ayudar a los inspectores.**

Parte B

Answers will vary but may include:
Doña Gracia es la víctima del crimen. Ella vive en el tercer piso. Ella lee el periódico usualmente.

Teacher-to-Teacher

Have students rewrite the conversation that takes place between the Inspector and Lola Lago. Have them imagine that they saw the suspicious persons and are able to describe them using chapter vocabulary. Then, have students create a composite sketch of the man and woman Lola saw.

Additional Resources

- *¿Eres tú, María?* Video Workbook, Episode 2
- *¿Eres tú, María?* Teacher's Video Guide: Answer Key

Review Activities

To describe people: Have students bring in photos or pictures from a magazine. Student A will describe a person and Student B will identify the person being described. Have students reverse roles.

To describe how someone is feeling: Ask students to write three sentences to describe situations when someone would be warm, cold, or sleepy. Then have students get together in pairs and try to guess how their partner is feeling. For example, Student A says: *Son las diez de la noche y estudias en la biblioteca.* Student B says: *Tengo sueño.*

To describe table settings: Have students write a sentence describing what each item is used for without naming the object. Then have them work in pairs and guess the name of the object that is being described.

To talk about eating out: Have students work in pairs to practice a conversation between a waiter and a client in a restaurant.

Venir, ser, *and* estar: Have students play tic-tac-toe to practice conjugating the verbs. Students should set up a game board for each verb. Tell them to write a different subject pronoun in the corner of each box. They should then take turns filling in the boxes with the correct form of the verb, using the same strategy as tic-tac-toe. If the verb form is incorrect, the other person has a chance to take over the box by writing the correct conjugation.

Portfolio

Invite students to review the activities they completed in this chapter, including written reports, posters, or other visuals, and recordings of oral presentations, or other projects. Have them select one or two items that they feel best demonstrate their achievements in Spanish to include in their portfolios. Have them include this with the Chapter Checklist and Self-Assessment Worksheet.

Additional Resources

Student Resources: Realidades para hispanohablantes, p. 208

Teacher Resources:

- Teacher's Resource Book: Situation Cards, p. 50, Clip Art, pp. 52–54
- Assessment Program: Chapter Checklist and Self-Assessment Worksheet, pp. T56–T57

Repaso del capítulo

Vocabulario y gramática

Objectives

- Review the vocabulary and grammar
- Demonstrate you can perform the tasks on p. 269

to talk about people

el hombre	man
la mujer	woman
el joven	young man
la joven	young woman

to describe people and things

alto, -a	tall
bajo, -a	short *(stature)*
corto, -a	short *(length)*
guapo, -a	good-looking
joven	young
largo, -a	long
viejo, -a	old
el pelo	hair
canoso	gray
castaño	brown (chestnut)
negro	black
rubio	blond
pelirrojo, -a	red-haired

to describe how someone is feeling

tener calor	to be warm
tener frío	to be cold
tener sueño	to be sleepy

to talk about food

delicioso, -a	delicious
desear	to want
pedir *(e → i)*	to order
el plato principal	main dish
de plato principal	as a main dish
el postre	dessert
de postre	for dessert
rico, -a	rich, tasty

For *Vocabulario adicional,* see pp. 472–473.

to describe table settings

el azúcar	sugar
la cuchara	spoon
el cuchillo	knife
la pimienta	pepper
el plato	plate, dish
la sal	salt
la servilleta	napkin
la taza	cup
el tenedor	fork
el vaso	glass

to talk about eating out

el camarero, la camarera	waiter, waitress
la cuenta	bill
el menú	menu

to express needs

Me falta(n) . . .	I need . . .
Quisiera	I would like
traer	to bring
Le traigo . . .	I will bring you . . .
¿Me trae . . . ?	Will you bring me . . . ?
yo traigo	I bring

other useful words

ahora	now
¿Algo más?	Anything else?
De nada.	You're welcome.
otro, -a	other, another
¡Qué + *adjective!*	How . . . !

venir *to come*

vengo	**venimos**
vienes	**venís**
viene	**vienen**

DIFFERENTIATED INSTRUCTION

Students with Learning Difficulties

Have students review the *Repaso del capítulo* and create flashcards for any words that they do not know. Pair them with a student who is more confident with the vocabulary to practice. Before the test, provide students with a practice test, so they can become comfortable with the format.

Heritage Language Learners

Have students write a few paragraphs telling about their perfect birthday celebration: Where are they going to have it? Whom are they going to invite? What food are they going to eat? What kind of music are they going to play? Encourage them to use as many vocabulary words from this chapter as they can.

Más repaso GO realidades.com | print

Instant Check	✓	
Puzzles	✓	
Core WB pp. 101–102		✓
Comm. WB pp. 284, 285–287	✓	✓

Preparación para el examen

On the exam you will be asked to . . .	Here are practice tasks similar to those you will find on the exam . . .	For review go to your print or digital textbook . . .
Interpretive		
 **1 Escuchar** Listen and understand as people complain to room service that something is missing from their order	As you listen to complaints about room service, see if you can tell if there is: a) missing silverware; b) missing food; c) missing condiments; d) all of the above.	**pp. 248–251** *Vocabulario en contexto,* Actividad 2 **p. 254** Actividades 8–9 **p. 260** Actividades 18–19
Interpersonal		
 **2 Hablar** Describe physical characteristics of family members to another person	Your aunt and uncle are going to celebrate their anniversary with you in a restaurant, but they're late. You describe them to the waiter so that he can recognize them when they arrive. Mention at least two physical characteristics about each person, such as hair color, height, or age.	**pp. 248–251** *Vocabulario en contexto* **p. 252** Actividades 4–5 **p. 256** Actividad 12
Interpretive		
 **3 Leer** Read and understand a letter about an upcoming visit with a relative	As you read part of a letter about an upcoming trip to Santa Fe, can you determine what the writers are most looking forward to in the trip? What questions do they have about it? Queridos Alicia y Pedro: Nosotros también esperamos impacientemente nuestra visita a Santa Fe en el verano. Me encanta la idea de visitar una ciudad con mucha historia. Nuestra ciudad también es muy histórica. ¿Qué es una comida típica del Rancho de las Golondrinas?	**p. 255** Actividad 10 **p. 262** *Lectura*
Presentational		
 **4 Escribir** Write a short report telling whether people are coming to an event and what they are bringing with them	You and your classmates decide to bring either a main dish, dessert, eating utensils, glassware, plates, or condiments for the Spanish Club party. Write a note to the club president indicating who is coming and what they are bringing. For example: *Ryan viene y trae las servilletas.*	**p. 256** Actividad 11 **p. 257** Actividades 13–14 **p. 265** *Presentación escrita*
Comparisons		
5 Pensar Demonstrate an understanding of cultural perspectives regarding meals	Think about how you spend lunch or dinner time during the school week. What would be at least three things that would be different at mealtime if you were an exchange student in a Spanish-speaking country? What is a *sobremesa*?	**p. 253** *Fondo cultural* **p. 260** *Fondo cultural* **p. 264** *Perspectivas del mundo hispano*

DIFFERENTIATED ASSESSMENT

CORE ASSESSMENT
- **Assessment Program:** Examen del capítulo 5B, pp. 139–145
- **Audio Program DVD:** Cap. 5B, Track 16
- **ExamView:** Chapter Test, Test Banks A and B

ADVANCED/PRE-AP*
- **ExamView: Pre-AP* Test Bank**
- **Pre-AP* Resource Book,** pp. 78–81

STUDENTS NEEDING EXTRA HELP
- **Alternate Assessment Program:** Examen del capítulo 5B
- **Audio Program DVD:** Cap. 5B, Track 16

HERITAGE LEARNERS
- **Assessment Program: Realidades para hispanohablantes:** Examen del capítulo 5B
- **ExamView: Heritage Learner Test Bank**

Performance Tasks

Standards: 1.1, 1.2, 1.3, 2.1, 4.2

Student Resource: Realidades para hispanohablantes, p. 209

Teacher Resources: Teacher's Resource Book: Audio Script, p. 43; Audio Program DVD: Cap. 5B, Track 15; Answer Keys: Student Edition, p. 78

1. Escuchar

Suggestions: Play the audio or read the script.

Script:

Soy el señor Chávez. Me faltan sal y pimienta. Por favor, necesito sal para la hamburguesa y pimienta para las papas fritas.

Answers:

c. Missing condiments: Sr. Chávez is not missing silverware or food. He is missing salt and pepper.

2. Hablar

Suggestions: Remind students that adjectives must agree in number and gender with the person or thing they are describing.

Answers will vary.

3. Leer

Suggestions: Before beginning, have students skim the *Lectura* about Santa Fe on p. 262.

Answers:

They are looking forward to visiting the historical part of the city. They have questions about the meals served at the restaurant.

4. Escribir

Suggestions: Brainstorm a list of items that students would bring to a Spanish Club party. Review the forms of ***venir*** and ***traer.***

Answers will vary.

5. Pensar

Suggestions: Have students discuss what time they usually eat breakfast, lunch and dinner, where they eat these meals, and with whom. Refer students to p. 264 to review.

Answers will vary.

Tema 6 La casa

6A En mi dormitorio

- **A teen's bedroom**

Vocabulary: bedroom items; electronic equipment; colors; adjectives to describe things

Grammar: comparisons and superlatives; stem-changing verbs: ***poder*** and ***dormir***

Cultural Perspectives: typical teen's bedroom

6B ¿Cómo es tu casa?

- **Houses and household chores**

Vocabulary: rooms in a house and household chores

Grammar: affirmative ***tú*** commands; the present progressive tense

Cultural Perspectives: rooms in a house and chores

THEME SUPPORT

Bulletin Boards

Theme: *La casa*

Ask students to cut out, copy, or download photos of the exteriors of houses and apartment buildings from around the world and the interiors of the different rooms in a house. Cluster photos according to rooms; then place the photos of the exteriors of houses in a ring around the clusters.

Hands-on Culture

Craft: *Flores de papel*

Tissue paper flowers are a popular decoration in many Spanish-speaking homes.

Materials for one flower:

4 6″ × 12″ sheets of brightly colored tissue paper
1 green pipe cleaner
scissors

1. Stack the four sheets of tissue paper.
2. Starting at a long end of the sheets, fold the papers back and forth like a fan. When you finish, you should have a 12″-long closed fan, about 1″ wide.
3. Round the ends of the closed fan by cutting off the corners.
4. Place the middle of the pipe cleaner around the middle of the closed fan and twist it to squeeze the paper. Pull both ends of the pipe cleaner down to create a stem.
5. Fan out the paper on both sides of the pipe cleaner. Gently pull each sheet of paper up to create flower petals. Rearrange and straighten the petals to your liking.
6. Twist the two ends of the pipe cleaner together to create a sturdy stem.

Game

Casa de obstáculos

Play this game in *Capítulo* 6B, after students have learned affirmative ***tú*** commands. You may need to print out the irregular form of the affirmative ***tú*** command for the verb ***ir: ve.***

Players: the whole class

Materials: scarf for blindfold

Rules:

1. Designate different areas in the classroom as rooms in a house, and then rearrange desks, chairs, and tables to create an obstacle course.
2. Teach and write on the board the following words to help students give directions: ***párate*** (stop), and ***derecho*** (straight ahead).
3. Divide the class into two teams. Ask for a volunteer from each team to be the Searcher. Blindfold both volunteers and place them somewhere on the obstacle course.
4. Give each team a list of rooms and an activity to perform in each room.
5. On your cue, teams give their Searchers commands that will take them to the first room on the team's list. Once in the correct room, teams tell their Searchers what to do there. Searchers mime the activity they are told to do.
   Team members: *Ve derecho, párate, ve a la derecha, párate, ahora ve a la izquierda, párate. Estás en el comedor. Pon la mesa.*
6. The winner is the team whose Searcher first completes the obstacle course.

Variation: Team members take turns being the Searcher, switching out after the action is performed in a room.

THEME PROJECT

La casa de mis sueños

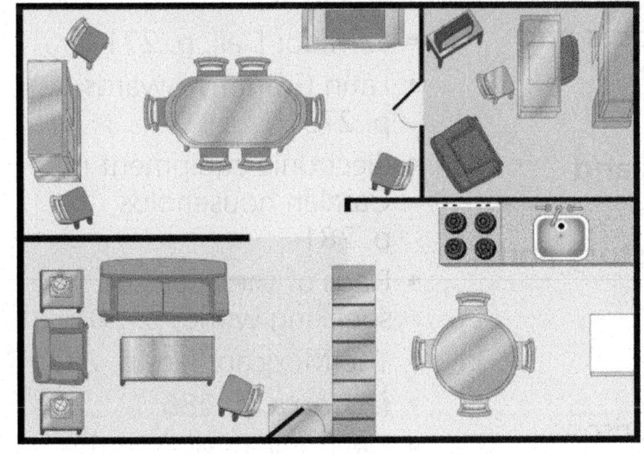

Overview: Students create a plan for their dream house on poster board or electronically, labeling each floor and room. They can use photos or drawings to furnish one bedroom. Then students write a short paragraph describing their dream house and bedroom and give an oral presentation, taking students on a tour of their house and bedroom.

Resources: poster board, magazines, markers, glue, crayons, colored pencils, scissors, or electronic layout tools and online images

Sequence: (suggestions for when to do each step appear throughout the chapters)

6A **STEP 1.** Review instructions so students know what is expected of them. Hand out the "Theme 6 Project Instructions and Rubric" from the *Teacher's Resource Book.*

STEP 2. Students submit a rough sketch of their house plan and bedroom layout. Return the drafts with your suggestions. For grammar and vocabulary practice, ask students to partner to compare sketches.

STEP 3. Students create their house plan on poster board and do the layout of their bedroom. Encourage them to try different arrangements in the bedroom before finalizing their plans.

6B **STEP 4.** Students submit a draft of the description of their house. Note your corrections and suggestions; then return drafts to students.

STEP 5. Students present their house plans to the class, taking the class on a room-by-room tour and then describing their bedroom in detail.

Options:

1. Students limit the plan to their ideal bedroom, label each item in it, and describe it in a paragraph.
2. Students create a house plan of their actual house or apartment.

Assessment:

Here is a detailed rubric for assessing this project:

Theme 6 Project: *La casa de mis sueños*

RUBRIC	Score 1	Score 3	Score 5
Evidence of planning	You didn't submit a sketch and draft.	You submitted the sketch and draft, but didn't correct them.	You submitted and corrected your sketch and draft.
Use of illustrations	You didn't include cutouts or drawings.	Your sketch is complete, but few labels and cutouts or drawings are included.	Several cutouts or drawings are included in your sketch.
Presentation	You list rooms in the house and items in the bedroom.	You describe the house and a few items in the bedroom.	You describe the house and most of the items in the bedroom in some detail.

21st Century Skills

Look for tips throughout *Tema* 6 to enrich your teaching by integrating 21st Century Skills. Suggestions for the Theme Project and Theme Culture follow below.

Theme Project

Modify the Theme Project with one or more of these suggestions:

Encourage Technology Literacy
As an alternative, have students make an electronic version of their dream house, combining audio, video, and online sources. Have the students set up an online contest on the class Web site, so that class members can vote for the best dream house.

Develop Collaboration
Have students research typical houses in Spanish-speaking countries and compare them to houses in the U.S., considering things such as outside color, materials, shape, and size. Have them compile, compare, and present the results to the class.

Support Critical Thinking and Problem Solving
Have students read the handout "Compare and Contrast," and then compare houses in different countries, discussing possible reasons for their findings and identifying any possible influences of one country on another.

Theme Culture

Promote Social and Cross-Cultural Skills
Have students work in small groups to interview native Spanish-speaking students, asking what posters, wall decorations, electronic equipment, and other favorite items they keep in their rooms. Students then compare the responses to their own.

Videocultura View *La casa* with the class to learn how people in various Spanish-speaking countries live.

6A En mi dormitorio

AT A GLANCE

Objectives

- **Listen to and read descriptions of bedrooms and colors**
- **Talk and write about your room**
- **Survey classmates about their bedrooms and compare theirs to your room**
- **Make a *luminaria* and understand the history and significance of this tradition**

Vocabulary

- Bedroom items
- Electronic equipment
- Colors
- Describing, comparing, and contrasting

Grammar

- Making comparisons
- The superlative
- Stem-changing verbs: ***poder*** and ***dormir***

Culture

- Salvador Dalí, p. 271
- Latin Grammy Awards, p. 279
- Electronic equipment in Catalan households, p. 281
- Flags of the Spanish-speaking world, p. 282
- The Mexican flag, p. 282
- ***la siesta,*** p. 286
- Electronic devices in the Spanish-speaking world, p. 289
- ***las luminarias,*** p. 290

Recycle

- ***estar*** to express location
- ***ser*** to describe physical characteristics
- ***más...que*** to compare things
- Classroom supplies
- ***puedes, puedo***
- Adjective agreement
- Possessive adjectives

RESOURCES

	FOR THE STUDENT	ONLINE	DVD	PRINT	FOR THE TEACHER	ONLINE	PREEXP	DVD	PRINT
Plan					Interactive TE and Resources DVD	•		•	
					Teacher's Resource Book, pp. 74–109	•		•	•
					Pre-AP* Resource Book, pp. 82–85	•		•	•
					Lesson Plans	•			•
					Mapa global interactivo	•			
Introducción PP. **270–271**									
Present	Student Edition, pp. 270–271	•	•	•	Interactive TE and Resources DVD	•		•	
	DK Reference Atlas	•	•		Teacher's Resource Book, pp. 74–77	•		•	•
	Videocultura	•	•		Galería de fotos		•		
	Hispanohablantes WB, pp. 210–211			•	Fine Art Transparencies, 14	•	•	•	
					Map Transparencies, 12, 15–18, 20	•	•	•	
Vocabulario en contexto PP. **272–275**									
Present & Practice	Student Edition, pp. 272–275	•	•	•	Interactive TE and Resources DVD	•		•	
	Audio	•	•		Teacher's Resource Book, pp. 78–80, 83, 92–93	•		•	•
	Videohistoria	•	•		Vocabulary Clip Art	•	•	•	•
	Flashcards	•	•		Audio Program	•	•	•	
	Instant Check	•			Video Program: Videohistoria	•		•	
	Guided WB, pp. 181–190	•	•	•	Video Program Teacher's Guide: Cap. 6A	•		•	•
	Core WB, pp. 102–106	•	•	•	Vocabulary and Grammar Transparencies, 112–115	•	•	•	
	Comm. WB, pp. 109–112, 116	•	•	•	Answer Keys: Student Edition, p. 79	•	•	•	
	Hispanohablantes WB, pp. 212–213			•	TPR Stories, pp. 77–91	•		•	•
Assess and Remediate					Prueba 6A–1: Assessment Program, pp. 147–148	•		•	•
					Assessment Program para hispanohablantes, pp. 147–148	•		•	•

RESOURCES

	FOR THE STUDENT	ONLINE	DVD	PRINT	FOR THE TEACHER	ONLINE	PREEXP	DVD	PRINT
Vocabulario en uso PP. **276–277**									
Present & Practice	Student Edition, pp. 276–277	•	•	•	Interactive Whiteboard Vocabulary Activities	•		•	
	Instant Check	•			Interactive TE and Resources DVD	•		•	
	Comm. WB, p. 113	•	•	•	Teacher's Resource Book, pp. 79–80, 86–87	•		•	•
	Hispanohablantes WB, pp. 214–215			•	Communicative Pair Activities, pp. 86–87	•		•	•
	Communicative Pair Activities	•			Audio Program	•	•	•	
					Videomodelos	•		•	
					Answer Keys: Student Edition, p. 80	•	•	•	•
Assess and Remediate					Prueba 6A–2 with Study Plan	•			
					Prueba 6A–2: Assessment Program, pp. 149–150	•		•	•
					Assessment Program para hispanohablantes, pp. 149–150	•		•	•
Gramática PP. **278–287**									
Present & Practice	Student Edition, pp. 278–287	•	•	•	Interactive Whiteboard Grammar Activities	•		•	
	Instant Check	•			Interactive TE and Resources DVD	•		•	
	Animated Verbs	•			Teacher's Resource Book, pp. 80–81, 83–84, 88–89	•		•	•
	Tutorial Video: Grammar	•			Communicative Pair Activities, pp. 88–89	•		•	•
	Canción de hip hop	•			Audio Program	•	•	•	
	Guided WB, pp. 191–194	•	•	•	Videomodelos	•		•	
	Core WB, pp. 107–109	•	•	•	Video Program: GramActiva	•	•	•	
	Comm. WB, pp. 113–115, 117–119, 288	•	•	•	Vocabulary and Grammar Transparencies, 116–118	•	•	•	
	Hispanohablantes WB, pp. 216–221			•	Answer Keys: Student Edition, pp. 81–84	•	•	•	
	Communicative Pair Activities	•							
Assess and Remediate					Pruebas 6A–3 to 6A–5 with Study Plans	•			
					Pruebas 6A–3 to 6A–5: Assessment Program, pp. 151–153	•		•	•
					Assessment Program para hispanohablantes, pp. 151–153	•		•	•
¡Adelante! PP. **288–293**									
Application	Student Edition, pp. 288–293	•	•	•	Interactive TE and Resources DVD	•		•	
	Online Cultural Reading	•			Teacher's Resource Book, pp. 84–85	•		•	•
	Guided WB, pp. 195–196	•	•	•	Video Program: Videomisterio ¿Eres tú, María?	•		•	
	Comm. WB, p. 289	•	•	•	Video Program Teacher's Guide: Cap. 6A	•		•	
	Hispanohablantes WB, pp. 222–227			•	Videomisterio Quiz		•		
	¿Eres tú, María? Video WB, pp. 20–26	•	•	•	Vocabulary and Grammar Transparencies, 119	•	•	•	
					Answer Keys: Student Edition, p. 84	•	•	•	
Repaso del capítulo PP. **294–295**									
Review	Student Edition, pp. 294–296	•	•	•	Interactive TE and Resources DVD	•		•	
	Online Puzzles and Games	•			Teacher's Resource Book, pp. 81, 90, 92–93	•		•	•
	Core WB, pp. 110–111	•	•	•	Audio Program	•	•	•	
	Comm. WB, pp. 290–293	•	•	•	Answer Keys: Student Edition, p. 84	•	•	•	
	Hispanohablantes WB, pp. 228–229			•					
	Instant Check	•							
Chapter Assessment									
Assess					Examen del capítulo 6A	•		•	•
					Assessment Program, pp. 154–161	•		•	•
					Alternate Assessment Program, pp. 57–62	•		•	•
					Assessment Program para hispanohablantes, pp. 154–161	•		•	•
					Audio Program, Cap. 6A, Examen	•		•	
					ExamView: Test Banks A and B questions only online	•		•	
					Heritage Learner Test Bank	•		•	
					Pre-AP* Test Bank	•		•	

6A Lesson Plans

REGULAR SCHEDULE (50 MINUTES)

DAY	Warm-up / Assess	Preview / Present / Practice / Communicate	Wrap-up / Homework Options
1	**Warm-up** (10 min.) • Return Examen del capítulo 5B	**Chapter Opener** (5 min.) • Objectives • Arte y cultura **Vocabulario en contexto** (30 min.) • Presentation: Vocabulario en contexto • Actividades 1, 2	**Wrap-up and Homework Options** (5 min.) • Core Practice 6A-1, 6A-2
2	**Warm-up** (5 min.) • Homework check	**Vocabulario en contexto** (35 min.) • Presentation: Videohistoria *El cuarto de Ignacio* • View: Videohistoria • Video Activities 1, 2, 3, 4 • Actividad 3 **Vocabulario en uso** (5 min.) • Actividad 5	**Wrap-up and Homework Options** (5 min.) • Core Practice 6A-3, 6A-4 • Actividad 6 • Prueba 6A-1: Vocabulary recognition
3	**Warm-up** (10 min.) • Actividad 4 • Homework check ✓**Formative Assessment** (10 min.) • Prueba 6A-1: Vocabulary recognition	**Vocabulario en uso** (25 min.) • Interactive Whiteboard Vocabulary Activities • Actividades 7, 8, 9 • Audio Activities 5, 6 • Communicative Pair Activity	**Wrap-up and Homework Options** (5 min.) • Writing Activity 10 • Prueba 6A-2 with Study Plan: Vocabulary production
4	**Warm-up** (5 min.) • Homework check ✓**Formative Assessment** (10 min.) • Prueba 6A-2 with Study Plan: Vocabulary production	**Gramática y vocabulario en uso** (30 min.) • Presentation: Making comparisons • View: GramActiva video • Interactive Whiteboard Grammar Activities • Actividades 10, 11, 12 • Fondo cultural • Audio Activity 7	**Wrap-up and Homework Options** (5 min.) • Core Practice 6A-5 • Writing Activity 11 • Prueba 6A-3 with Study Plan: Making comparisons
5	**Warm-up** (5 min.) • Homework check ✓**Formative Assessment** (10 min.) • Prueba 6A-3 with Study Plan: Making comparisons	**Gramática y vocabulario en uso** (30 min.) • Presentation: The superlative • View: GramActiva video • Interactive Whiteboard Grammar Activities • Actividades 13, 14, 15, 18 • Fondo cultural	**Wrap-up and Homework Options** (5 min.) • Core Practice 6A-6 • Actividades 16, 17, 19, 20, 21 • Writing Activity 12 • Prueba 6A-4 with Study Plan: The superlative
6	**Warm-up** (10 min.) • Audio Activity 8 • Homework check ✓**Formative Assessment** (10 min.) • Prueba 6A-4 with Study Plan: The superlative	**Gramática y vocabulario en uso** (25 min.) • Presentation: Stem-changing verbs: ***poder*** and ***dormir*** • View: GramActiva video • Interactive Whiteboard Grammar Activities • Actividades 23, 25, 27, 28 • Audio Activity 9	**Wrap-up and Homework Options** (5 min.) • Core Practice 6A-7 • Actividades 24, 26 • Writing Activity 13 • Prueba 6A-5 with Study Plan: Stem-changing verbs: ***poder*** and ***dormir***
7	**Warm-up** (10 min.) • Actividad 22 • Homework check ✓**Formative Assessment** (10 min.) • Prueba 6A-5 with Study Plan: Stem-changing verbs: ***poder*** and ***dormir***	**Gramática y vocabulario en uso** (20 min.) • Communicative Pair Activity • Pronunciación • Exploración del lenguaje • Fondo cultural • El español en la comunidad **¡Adelante!** (5 min.) • Presentación oral: Step 1	**Wrap-up and Homework Options** (5 min.) • Presentación oral: Step 2 • La cultura en vivo
8	**Warm-up** (5 min.) • Homework check	**¡Adelante!** (30 min.) • Presentación oral: Step 3 **Repaso del capítulo** (10 min.) • Vocabulario y gramática • Preparación para el examen 1, 2	**Wrap-up and Homework Options** (5 min.) • Preparación para el examen 3, 4, 5 • Instant Check
9	**Warm-up** (5 min.) • Homework check	**¡Adelante!** (40 min.) • Lectura • ¿Comprendes? • Fondo cultural • Videomisterio: *¿Eres tú, María?*, Episodio 3	**Wrap-up and Homework Options** (5 min.) • Core Practice 6A-8, 6A-9 • Examen del capítulo 6A • Lectura • Videomisterio
10	**Warm-up** (10 min.) • Homework check • Answer questions ✓**Summative Assessment** (40 min.) • Examen del capítulo 6A		

BLOCK SCHEDULE (90 MINUTES)

DAY	Warm-up / Assess	Preview / Present / Practice / Communicate	Wrap-up / Homework Options
1	**Warm-up** (10 min.) • Return Examen del capítulo 5B	**Chapter Opener** (5 min.) • Objectives • Arte y cultura **Vocabulario en contexto** (55 min.) • Presentation: Vocabulario en contexto • Actividades 1, 2 • Presentation: Videohistoria *El cuarto de Ignacio* • View: Videohistoria • Video Activities 1, 2, 3, 4 • Actividad 3 **Vocabulario en uso** (15 min.) • Interactive Whiteboard Vocabulary Activities • Actividades 4, 5	**Wrap-up and Homework Options** (5 min.) • Core Practice 6A-1, 6A-2, 6A-3, 6A-4 • Actividad 6 • Prueba 6A-1: Vocabulary recognition
2	**Warm-up** (10 min.) • Homework check ✔**Formative Assessment** (10 min.) • Prueba 6A-1: Vocabulary recognition	**Gramática y vocabulario en uso** (65 min.) • Actividades 7, 8, 9 • Audio Activities 5, 6 • Communicative Pair Activity • Presentation: Making comparisons • View: GramActiva video • Interactive Whiteboard Vocabulary Activities • Actividades 10, 11, 12 • Fondo cultural • Audio Activity 7	**Wrap-up and Homework Options** (5 min.) • Core Practice 6A-5 • Writing Activities 10, 11 • Pruebas 6A-2, 6A-3 with Study Plans: Vocabulary production, Making comparisons
3	**Warm-up** (10 min.) • Homework check ✔**Formative Assessment** (15 min.) • Pruebas 6A-2, 6A-3 with Study Plans: Vocabulary production, Making comparisons	**Gramática y vocabulario en uso** • Presentation: The superlative • View: GramActiva video • Interactive Whiteboard Grammar Activities • Actividades 13, 14, 15, 18 • Fondo cultural • Presentation: Stem-changing verbs: ***poder*** and ***dormir*** • View: GramActiva video • Interactive Whiteboard Grammar Activities • Actividades 23, 25, 27, 28	**Wrap-up and Homework Options** (5 min.) • Core Practice 6A-6, 6A-7 • Actividades 16, 17, 19, 20, 21 • Writing Activities 12, 13 • Pruebas 6A-4, 6A-5 with Study Plans: The superlative, Stem-changing verbs: ***poder*** and ***dormir***
4	**Warm-up** (15 min.) • Audio Activities 8, 9 • Homework check • Actividad 22 ✔**Formative Assessment** (15 min.) • Pruebas 6A-4, 6A-5 with Study Plans: The superlative; Stem-changing verbs: ***poder*** and ***dormir***	**Gramática y vocabulario en uso** (45 min.) • Actividades 24, 26 • Communicative Pair Activity • Pronunciación • Exploración del lenguaje • Fondo cultural • El español en la comunidad **¡Adelante!** (10 min.) • Presentación oral: Step 1	**Wrap-up and Homework Options** (5 min.) • Presentación oral: Step 2 • La cultura en vivo
5	**Warm-up** (5 min.) • Homework check	**¡Adelante!** (50 min.) • Presentación oral: Step 3 • Lectura • ¿Comprendes? • Fondo cultural **Repaso del capítulo** (30 min.) • Vocabulario y gramática • Preparación para el examen 1, 2, 3, 4, 5	**Wrap-up and Homework Options** (5 min.) • Core Practice 6A-8, 6A-9 • Examen del capítulo 6A • Instant Check • Lectura
6	**Warm-up** (15 min.) • Homework check • Situation Cards **Repaso del capítulo** (10 min.) • Communicative Pair Activities ✔**Summative Assessment** (40 min.) • Examen del capítulo 6A	**¡Adelante!** (20 min.) • Videomisterio: *¿Eres tú, María?*, Episodio 3	**Wrap-up and Homework Options** (5 min.) • Videomisterio

Standards for *Capítulo* 6A

- To achieve the goals of the Standards, students will:

Communication

1.1 Interpersonal

- Talk about: bedroom and home furnishings and arrangement; lifestyle and entertainment preferences; the distribution of home electronics; colors and color association; flag colors and symbolism; the importance of sleep

1.2 Interpretive

- Listen to: descriptions of bedrooms and bedroom furnishings; information about Spanish color words; information about students' personal preferences; the verbs ***poder*** and ***dormir*** in conversation
- Read a picture-based story
- Listen to and watch a video about bedroom neatness

1.3 Presentational

- Present information about: ways to describe things; entertainment preferences; items in the home
- Present a description of a bedroom using illustrations

Culture

2.1 Practices and Perspectives

- Discuss the Latin Grammy awards; ***la siesta***; the ***luminarias*** of Santa Fe

2.2 Products and Perspectives

- Discuss Salvador Dalí and his painting; the Latin Grammy awards; Spanish-style architecture
- Discuss a well-known riddle from Mexico; colors and symbols of Spanish-speaking countries' flags; a Spanish ***trabalenguas***

Connections

3.1 Cross-curricular

- Discuss Salvador Dalí
- Reinforce math skills
- Discuss interpretations of colors in psychology

Comparisons

4.1 Language

- Explain: comparisons in Spanish; superlatives in Spanish; the stem-changing verbs ***poder*** and ***dormir***; the pronunciation of the letters ***r*** and ***rr***
- Talk about new vocabulary through the recognition of cognates; building vocabulary through the use of root words

4.2 Culture

- Compare: distribution of home electronics; symbolism of Mexico's flag to United States' flags; the pros and cons of importing ***la siesta*** to the United States; the use of light to celebrate events
- Identify: the influence of Spanish architecture in the United States; pros and cons of the technological global community

Communities

5.2 Lifelong Learner

- Identify Latin recording artists whose music they enjoy
- View a video mystery series
- Visit the Web site of a prominent newspaper in Spain

Capítulo

6A En mi dormitorio

Chapter Objectives

Communication

By the end of this chapter you will be able to:

- Listen to and read descriptions of bedrooms and colors
- Talk and write about your room
- Survey classmates about their bedrooms and compare theirs to your room

Culture

You will also be able to:

- Make a *luminaria* and understand the history and significance of this tradition

You will demonstrate what you know and can do:

- Presentación oral, p. 291
- Preparación para el examen, p. 295

You will use:

Vocabulary

- Bedroom items
- Electronic equipment
- Colors
- Describing, comparing, and contrasting

Grammar

- Making comparisons
- The superlative
- Stem-changing verbs: *poder* and *dormir*

Exploración del mundo hispano

Country Connection
Homes and Traditions

realidades.com 

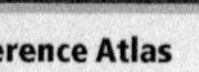 Reference Atlas

 *Videocultura y actividad*

 *Mapa global interactivo*

Dormitorio de una casa mexicana

ENRICH YOUR TEACHING

Using Backward Design

Have students preview the sample performance tasks on *Preparación para el examen,* p. 295, and connect them to the Chapter Objectives. Explain to students that by completing the sample tasks they can self-assess their learning progress.

Mapa global interactivo

Download the *Mapa global interactivo* files for Chapter 6A and preview the activities. In Activity 1, explore the region of Catalonia in northeast Spain. Activity 2 looks at the tradition of *luminarias* on both sides of the Rio Grande.

Arte y cultura | España

Salvador Dalí (1904–1989) was a painter born in Figueras, Spain. This is one of his most famous paintings, made when he was only 20. Here he has painted his sister, who appears only from the back.

- Why do you think that Dalí painted her looking out the window rather than facing the viewer?

"Muchacha en la ventana" (1925), Salvador Dalí ▶

PresentationExpress™
See pp. 270c–270d

Chapter Opener

Core Instruction

Resources: Map Transparencies 12, 15–18, 20

Suggestions: Explain that students will learn to talk about items in their bedrooms. Brainstorm a list of objects students may have in their rooms, including electronic equipment. Point out that students will learn to describe what is in their rooms using adjectives for color, size, and appearance. Tell students that the vocabulary will be reinforced as they watch the *Videohistoria,* in which Ignacio's mom rearranges the items in his room. Tell students that they will learn how to make comparisons of various items and will learn more stem-changing verbs.

Videocultura View *La casa* with the class to learn how people in various Spanish-speaking countries live.

Arte y cultura

Standards: 2.2, 3.1

Resources: Fine Art Transparencies, p.14

Suggestions: If possible, bring in reproductions of some of Dalí's later work to compare with *"Muchacha en la ventana."* Discuss the differences in style. Which are more realistic, and which are more abstract or surreal? If possible, show both a realistic and a surrealistic picture by Dalí, asking students if they can define the word "surreal" based on the painting. Which style do they prefer? Can they say why they prefer that style?

Answers will vary.

TEACHING WITH ART

Resources: Fine Art Transparencies, p. 14

DIFFERENTIATED INSTRUCTION

Digital resources such as the ***Interactive Whiteboard*** activity banks, ***Videomodelos***, additional ***Online Activities***, ***Study Plans***, automatically graded ***Leveled Workbook***, animated ***Grammar Tutorials***, ***Flashcards***, and ***Vocabulary and Grammar Videos*** will help you reach students of different ability levels and learning styles.

STUDENTS NEEDING EXTRA HELP

Guided Practice Activities
- Flashcards, pp. 181–186
- Vocabulary Check, pp. 187–190
- Grammar Support, pp. 191–194

HERITAGE LEARNERS

Realidades para hispanohablantes
- Chapter Opener, pp. 210–211
- A primera vista, p. 212
- Videohistoria, p. 213
- Manos a la obra, pp. 214–221
- ¡Adelante!, pp. 222–227
- Repaso del capítulo, pp. 228–229

ADVANCED/PRE-AP*

Pre-AP* Resource Book,
- pp. 82–85

Communications Workbook
- Integrated Performance Assessment, p. 290

Vocabulario en contexto

Core Instruction

Standards: 1.2

Resources: Teacher's Resource Book: Input Script, p. 60, Clip Art, pp.92–93, Audio Script, p. 78; Voc. and Gram. Transparencies 112–113; TPR Stories Book, pp. 77–91; Audio Program DVD: Cap. 6A, Tracks 1–2

Focus: Presenting new vocabulary for bedroom items, electronic equipment, and colors

Suggestions: Use the story in the *TPR Stories Book* to present the new vocabulary and grammar or use the Input Script from the *Teacher's Resource Book*. Present the vocabulary in four sets: parts of the house itself (wall, floor, window, closet), furniture, electronic equipment, and colors. Instead of using the transparencies, bring in old catalogs for students to look through, and ask them to point to the items as you say them. Ask questions about the vocabulary that require limited verbal response, such as: *¿Te gustaría tener/tienes* (item) *en tu dormitorio?* or *¿De qué color es* (item)?

BELLRINGER REVIEW

Show Voc. and Gram. Transparency 58. Have students write two sentences locating items that are on the table.

Block Schedule

Have pairs of students create dioramas of a bedroom using shoeboxes and construction paper. They should label the items they include. Have students exchange their dioramas with another pair, who will prepare three questions to ask about the room. Afterwards, have students discuss the rooms in groups of four, and present their discussions to the class.

Objectives

Read, listen to, and understand information about

- bedroom items
- electronic equipment
- colors
- comparisons

Vocabulario en contexto

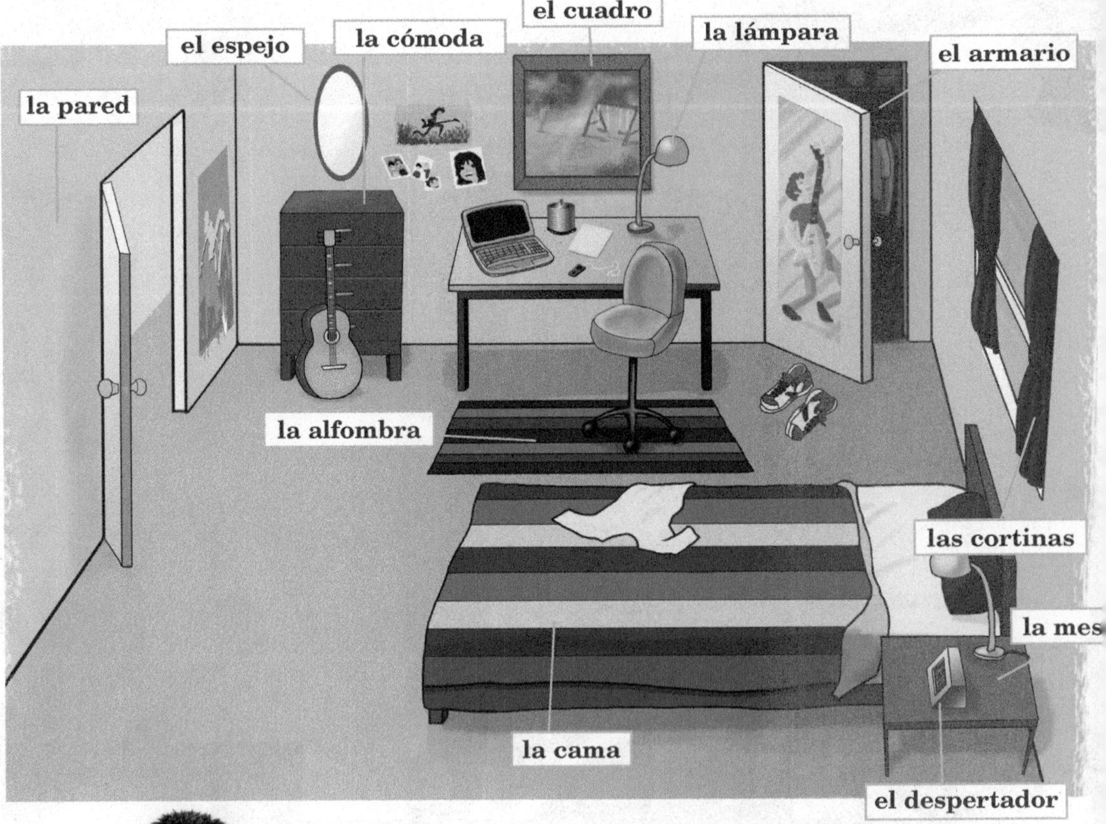

“Tengo **un dormitorio pequeño.** Las paredes son azules. Tengo carteles de mis grupos musicales favoritos en las paredes. Generalmente mi dormitorio está muy desordenado, pero hoy está ordenado. No comparto el dormitorio con otra persona—es mi **propio** dormitorio.

En mi dormitorio tengo todas mis **posesiones más importantes:** mi guitarra, mis discos compactos, mis fotos, mi computadora. ¿Por qué me gusta mucho mi dormitorio? ¡Está encima del garaje! ¡Es **el mejor** dormitorio para tocar y escuchar música!”.

DIFFERENTIATED INSTRUCTION

Students with Special Needs

As you go through the new words, have students add them to their vocabulary notebook section. Have them add pictures and/or English translations, if necessary.

Multiple Intelligences

Verbal/Linguistic: Using the text above as a model, ask students to create cloze passages to describe a bedroom and to provide a word bank with words that would fit logically in only one blank. Photocopy and distribute their passages and ask the rest of the class to fill in the blanks using the word bank.

— ¿Te gusta el disco compacto de Mano Negra?

— ¡Por supuesto! Me encanta su música. Pero es **menos** interesante **que** la música de Mecano.

— A mis padres les encanta **escuchar música**. Me **gustaría** tener mi **propio** equipo de sonido.

**El televisor* refers to the actual appliance. *La televisión* (*tele*) is the programming that is watched.

Para decir más . . .

el reproductor (de) mp3	mp3 player

los colores

amarillo, -a

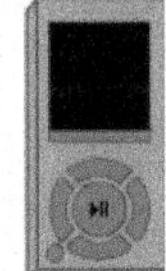
negro, -a

anaranjado, -a

azul

blanco, -a

gris

marrón

verde

rojo, -a

morado, -a

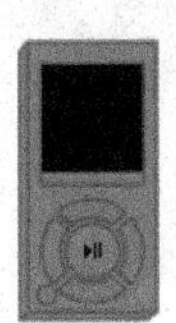
rosado, -a

1 Las posesiones

Escuchar

Escucha a Marcos describir su dormitorio. Mira el dibujo y toca cada cosa que menciona.

2 Los colores

Escuchar

Cuando escuches el nombre de un color, señala algo en estas páginas que es de ese color.

Más práctica GO

realidades.com | print

	realidades.com	print
Instant Check	✔	
Guided WB pp. 181–186	✔	✔
Core WB pp. 103–104	✔	✔
Comm. WB p. 116	✔	✔
Hispanohablantes WB p. 212		✔

1 Standards: 1.2

Resources: Teacher's Resource Book: Audio Script, p. 79; Audio Program DVD: Cap. 6A, Track 3; Answer Key: Student Edition, p. 79

Focus: Listening comprehension: bedroom items

Suggestions: Play the audio or read the script aloud. Let students listen more than once. Monitor the activity, making sure that students are pointing to the correct objects.

Script and Answers:

Mi cuarto es pequeño. Las paredes son de color azul. ***(the walls)***

La cama está al lado de la ventana. ***(the bed; the window)***

Tengo un cuadro grande y unos carteles en las paredes. ***(the painting; posters)***

El espejo está encima de la cómoda. ***(the mirror; the dresser)***

Y tengo una mesita con lámpara al lado de la cama. ***(the night stand, the lamp)***

Tengo una alfombra y unas cortinas. ***(the rug; the curtains)***

Y, claro, ¡tengo despertador! ***(the alarm clock)***

2 Standards: 1.2

Resources: Teacher's Resource Book: Audio Script, p. 79; Audio Program DVD: Cap. 6A, Track 4

Focus: Listening comprehension: colors

Suggestions: Play the audio or read the script aloud. You may want to have students also point to something in the classroom of the color mentioned.

Script and Answers:

Yo veo algo amarillo.
Yo veo algo anaranjado.
Yo veo algo azul.
Yo veo algo blanco.
Yo veo algo gris.
Yo veo algo marrón.
Yo veo algo morado.
Yo veo algo negro.
Yo veo algo rojo.
Yo veo algo rosado.
Yo veo algo verde.

Answers will vary.

ENRICH YOUR TEACHING

Culture Note

Compared with many Spanish-speaking countries, the colors on the outside of homes in the United States are conservative. It is not uncommon to see neighborhoods of brightly colored houses in both rural and urban areas of Central and South America.

Teacher-to-Teacher

Reinforce listening activities by personalizing them. After students role-play the people in the Audio activities, have them create their own listening activities to do with a partner or with the class. Record students' activities and reuse them throughout the lesson.

Videohistoria

Core Instruction

Standards: 1.2

Resources: Voc. and Gram. Transparencies 114–115; Audio Program DVD: Cap. 6A, Track 5

Focus: Presenting additional vocabulary and grammar in context

Suggestions:

Pre-reading: Direct attention to the *Antes de leer* questions. Ask students to share their feelings about others "organizing" their things. Have them look at the photos to predict how the mother and Ignacio feel in panel 4 and then in panel 8.

Reading: Ask students to role-play the characters of Ignacio and Mamá or play the audio. Using the transparencies and nonverbal clues, help students understand the new words in blue type.

Post-reading: Do *Actividad* 3 to check comprehension.

Video

Core Instruction

Standards: 1.2

Resources: Teacher's Resource Book: Video Script, p. 83; Video Program: Cap. 6A; Video Program Teacher's Guide: Cap. 6A

Focus: Listening comprehension of vocabulary in a story about a disorganized bedroom

Suggestions:

Pre-viewing: Review the *Strategy.* Tell students to listen for intonation to determine how Ignacio feels.

Viewing: Show the video without pausing. Show it again, pausing along the way to check comprehension. Write difficult words on the board. Show the segment a final time without pausing.

Post-viewing: Complete the Video Activities in the *Communication Workbook*.

El cuarto de Ignacio

¡El cuarto de Ignacio está muy desordenado!

España

Strategy

Using prior experience
Have you ever had someone go in and change things around in your room? How did you feel? Look at the photos and guess how Ignacio and his mother feel.

Mamá: Mira este cuarto . . . ¡qué **feo!** ¡Está muy desordenad[o!] Ignacio, ¿cómo puedes hacer est[o?]

También se dice . . .

el dormitorio = el *cuarto (España)*

Mamá: Tu cuarto está mucho más **bonito.** Los libros **grandes** están aquí, y **a la izquierda** están las revistas. Y los discos compactos están **a la derecha de** los libros. Es mejor, ¿no crees?

6

Ignacio: Mamá, no es el **mismo** cuarto. **Para ti,** está **mejor que** antes, pero **para mí,** está **peor.** Tengo todas mis posesiones más importantes aquí y ahora no sé dónde están.

Mamá: Pero Ignacio, ¿cómo puedes **dormir** con todas las cosas encima de la cama?

Ignacio: Mamá, siempre **duermo** bien.

Mamá: ¡Ay! Está bien. Nunca más voy a organizar tu cuarto.

DIFFERENTIATED INSTRUCTION

Heritage Language Learners

Have students write a short paragraph about what their bedrooms are like. Are they tidy or messy? Who cleans them? Who is allowed in? Students can refer to the *Videohistoria* for words to include in their paragraphs. When necessary, talk to students individually about spelling or grammatical errors they may have made.

Advanced Learners

Have students write a short paragraph describing their idea of a tidy bedroom. Tell them to begin their paragraph with an introductory sentence, such as: *Para mí, un dormitorio está ordenado cuando....* Remind them to use both new and old vocabulary, the verb ***estar,*** and prepositions of location.

Language Input 6A

Mamá: **¿De qué color** es esta camiseta? ¿Gris? ¿Blanca? Y esta camiseta de muchos colores, ¿qué es? ¡Ay, tengo que trabajar mucho en este cuarto!

Mamá: ¿Qué **podemos** hacer con este cuarto? El cuadro va en la pared y la lámpara va en la mesita. ¡Ay, ay, ay!

Ignacio: ¡Mamá! ¡Mi cuarto! ¡Mis **cosas**! ¿Dónde están?

Ignacio: ¡Eres la mejor mamá! Muchas gracias.
Mamá: De nada, Ignacio.

3 ¿Cierto o falso?

Leer • Escribir

Lee las frases y decide si son ciertas o falsas. Si una frase es falsa, escríbela con la información correcta.

1. El cuarto de Ignacio siempre está muy ordenado.
2. La madre de Ignacio no está contenta.
3. La madre de Ignacio trabaja en el cuarto de Ignacio.
4. Ignacio no puede dormir bien en su cama.
5. Ahora Ignacio sabe dónde están todas sus posesiones.
6. A Ignacio no le gusta el trabajo de su madre.
7. Mañana la madre de Ignacio va a organizar el cuarto de Ignacio.

Más práctica GO

realidades.com | print		
Instant Check	✔	
Guided WB pp. 187–190	✔	✔
Core WB pp. 105–106	✔	✔
Comm. WB pp. 109–111, 112	✔	✔
***Hispanohablantes* WB** p. 213		✔

3 Standards: 1.2, 1.3

Resources: Answer Key: Student Edition, p. 79

Focus: Reading for understanding

Suggestions: Remind students that the true / false statements should be considered in the order in which they occur in the story. For example, item 2 describes Mamá's attitude at the beginning of the story.

Answers:

1. **falsa: El cuarto de Ignacio está muy desordenado.**
2. **cierta**
3. **cierta**
4. **falsa: Ignacio siempre duerme bien.**
5. **falsa: Ignacio no sabe dónde están sus cosas.**
6. **cierta**
7. **falsa: Nunca más va a organizar su cuarto.**

Pre-AP* Support

- **Learning Objective:** Presentational Writing and Speaking
- **Activity:** As a post-viewing activity, have pairs of students write and act out a new scene for the video. Have them imagine a friend comes to visit Ignacio and is surprised by his newly organized room. Ignacio describes the changes to his room and expresses his satisfaction (or dissatisfaction) with the new order of things.
- ***Pre-AP* Resource Book:*** Comprehensive guide to Pre-AP* vocabulary skill development, pp. 51–57

Additional Resources

- Communication Wbk.: Audio Act. 5, p. 112
- Teacher's Resource Book: Audio Script, pp. 79–80
- Audio Program DVD: Cap. 6A, Track 7

ENRICH YOUR TEACHING

Teacher-to-Teacher

Bring in crayons and children's color-by-number books to use in a listening activity. Make copies of one image, distribute it to the class, and give students crayons. Describe each part of the image, for example: *Las flores son amarillas.* Have students check their work by comparing their final product to one that you completed.

21st Century Skills

Communication After students have reviewed the *Videohistoria* in **realidades.com** and role-played the video with a partner, have them create a similar but personalized skit explaining where things are in their room, what someone did to change the order, and how they reacted.

ASSESSMENT

Quiz: Vocabulary Recognition

- Prueba 6A-1: pp. 147–148

INTERACTIVE WHITEBOARD
Vocabulary Activities 6A

4 Standards: 1.3

Resources: Answer Key: Student Edition, p. 80

Focus: Learning vocabulary through word associations (opposites)

Recycle: Adjectives

Suggestions: Write a few words on the board and have students provide their opposites: ***mayor / menor, calor / frío, delicioso / horrible.***

Answers:

1. bonito, feo
2. grande, pequeño
3. derecha, izquierda
4. peor, mejor
5. alto, bajo
6. negro, blanco
7. ordenado, desordenado
8. joven, viejo

BELLRINGER REVIEW

Have the students match these items with their related activities:

Items:

la cama	*la lámpara*
la mesa	*el despertador*
el espejo	*el cuadro*

Activities:

ver	*decorar*
dormir	*estudiar*
mirar	*decir la hora*

5 Standards: 1.2, 1.3

Resources: Teacher's Resource Book: Audio Script, p. 79; Audio Program DVD: Cap. 6A, Track 6; Answer Key: Student Edition, p. 80

Focus: Listening comprehension

Recycle: Prepositions of location

Suggestions: Students are drawing and will need longer pauses, but tell them not to be too detailed. Let them listen again to check their answers.

Script and Answers:

1. Hay una mesita a la derecha de la cama.
2. Hay una lámpara encima de la mesita.
3. Hay una cómoda a la izquierda de la ventana.
4. Hay un espejo sobre la cómoda.
5. Mi escritorio está en la pared que está delante de la cama.
6. Hay una computadora encima del escritorio.
7. Hay una silla enfrente del escritorio.
8. Hay una alfombra grande entre el escritorio y la cama.

Vocabulario en uso

Objectives

- Listen to a description of a room and label a room diagram
- Draw and describe your own room
- Exchange information while describing rooms and playing a game

4 Las palabras opuestas

Escribir

Escribe las palabras de la lista y su opuesto *(opposite).*

Modelo

día *noche*

1. bonito	3. derecha	5. alto	7. ordenado
2. grande	4. peor	6. negro	8. joven

Strategy

Making word associations
Learning vocabulary as opposites helps you make quick associations to other words.

5 Escucha, dibuja y escribe

Escuchar • Escribir

Copia el dibujo en una hoja de papel. Vas a escuchar a Celia describir su dormitorio. Dibuja las cosas que ella menciona en los lugares *(places)* correctos y escribe las palabras en español para cada cosa.

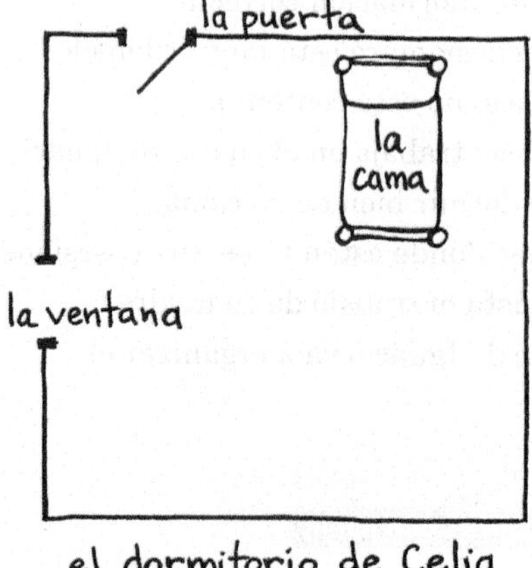

También se dice . . .

el dormitorio = la habitación, la alcoba *(España);* la pieza *(Argentina, Chile);* la recámara *(México)*

bonito = lindo, chulo *(México);* mono *(España)*

marrón = de color café, castaño, de color chocolate *(México, América del Sur)*

la cómoda = el gavetero, el buró *(México, muchos países)*

el armario = el guardarropa, el ropero *(México, muchos países)*

pequeño = chico *(México, otros países)*

DIFFERENTIATED INSTRUCTION

Students with Learning Difficulties
Prior to doing *Actividad* 4, do a number of examples with the students. Review with them how to use the textbook glossaries.

Heritage Language Learners
Have students share other words they may know to describe a bedroom or objects in a bedroom.

6 Tu propio dormitorio

Dibujar • Escribir

1. Dibuja tu propio dormitorio. Escribe el nombre de ocho cosas en el dibujo.
2. Escribe siete frases para describir o *(either)* tu dormitorio o el dormitorio de Celia de la Actividad 5.

Modelo

El espejo está al lado de la cama.
Las cortinas en el dormitorio son largas.

¿Recuerdas?

Use *estar* to tell the location of items.
Use *ser* to tell what items are like.

7 ¿Qué dormitorio es?  

Escuchar • Hablar

Trabaja con otro(a) estudiante. Muestra *(Show)* los dibujos de tu dormitorio y del dormitorio de Celia a tu compañero(a). Lee una de las frases que escribiste *(that you wrote)* en la Actividad 6. Tu compañero(a) tiene que identificar qué dormitorio describes.

Modelo

A —*El espejo está al lado de la cama.*
B —*Es tu propio dormitorio.*
o: —*Es el dormitorio de Celia.*

Strategy

Labeling
Put Spanish labels on the items in your bedroom so that you will see them every day. This will help you learn new words quickly.

8 Juego

Escuchar • Hablar

Trabajen en grupos de tres personas. Necesitan una moneda *(coin)* y uno de los dibujos de la Actividad 6. Una persona describe dónde está la moneda en el dormitorio. Los otros dos tratan de colocar *(try to place)* la moneda en el cuarto correctamente. La primera persona que coloca la moneda correctamente recibe un punto.

Modelo

La moneda está debajo de la cama.

9 ¿Quién soy yo?

Leer • Pensar • Hablar

Aquí tienes una adivinanza *(riddle)* popular en las escuelas primarias en México. Trabaja con otro(a) estudiante para resolver la adivinanza.

Cine no soy,
radio tampoco.
Tengo pantalla
y me creen poco.
¿Quién soy yo?

Practice and Communicate 6A

6 Standards: 1.3

Focus: Using vocabulary in a personalized context
Recycle: Prepositions of location; ***estar***
Suggestions: Call attention to the *¿Recuerdas?* Tell students that their drawings will be used for *Actividades* 7–8.
Answers will vary.

7 Standards: 1.1, 1.2

Focus: Practicing vocabulary and grammar
Recycle: Prepositions of location
Suggestions: Remind students to provide additional clues if their drawings have elements identical to those in Celia's room.
Answers will vary.

8 Standards: 1.1, 1.2

Focus: Using vocabulary in a game
Recycle: Prepositions of location
Suggestions: Students will need to listen to the sentence before placing the coins.
Answers will vary.

9 Standards: 1.1, 1.2, 2.2

Resources: Answer Key: Student Edition, p. 80
Focus: Reading comprehension
Suggestions: Tell students that word order is different in a poem.
Answers: **un televisor**

Additional Resources

- Communication Wbk.: Audio Act. 6, p. 113
- Teacher's Resource Book: Audio Script, p. 80, Communicative Pair Activity BLM, pp. 86–87
- Audio Program DVD: Cap. 6A, Track 8

ASSESSMENT

Prueba 6A-2 with Study Plan (online only)

Quiz: Vocabulary Production
- Prueba 6A-2: pp. 149–150

ENRICH YOUR TEACHING

Teacher-to-Teacher

Have students write the letters of the word ***grande*** vertically down the left margin of a page. Ask them to write a vocabulary word that begins with each of these letters. Have students share their lists with the class. Ask students to work with a partner to think of other examples of this same activity.

21st Century Skills

Creativity and Innovation Working with a partner, have students write a short riddle about their favorite object. Then have them work with other students to guess what the objects are. Have students set up a contest on the class Web site so that the class can choose the best riddle.

Gramática

Core Instruction

Standards: 4.1

Resources: Voc. and Gram. Transparency 116; Teacher's Resource Book: Video Script, p. 83; Video Program: Cap. 6A

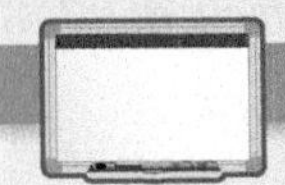

INTERACTIVE WHITEBOARD
Grammar Activities 6A

Suggestions: Direct attention to the *¿Recuerdas?* You may want to bring to class photos or objects for students to compare. Use the transparency to introduce the structure, giving model sentences for each of the four irregular comparatives. The *GramActiva* Video can serve as reinforcement of your explanation.

10 Standards: 1.2, 1.3

Resources: Teacher's Resource Book: Audio Script, p. 80; Audio Program DVD: Cap. 6A, Track 9; Answer Key: Student Edition, p. 81

Focus: Listening comprehension

Suggestions: Give students time to study the illustrations of the bedrooms before beginning the activity. Play the audio or read the script aloud. Allow students to listen more than once.

Script and Answers:

1. **Los dos cuartos están muy ordenados. *(F)***
2. **Al lado de la cama hay una mesita. *(C)***
3. **Encima de la mesita hay una lámpara pequeña. *(C)***
4. **En el centro del cuarto hay una alfombra grande. *(F)***
5. **A la izquierda de la alfombra está la cómoda. *(F)***
6. **Paco y Kiko tienen equipos de sonido. *(C)***

Extension: Have students use their drawings from *Actividad* 6 and compare their bedroom with that of a partner. Ask them to share their comparisons with the class and have the class indicate whether they agree or not.

Pre-AP* Support

- **Learning Objective:** Interpretive: Audio
- **Activity:** Have students write five comparative sentences about classmates or other well-known students or teachers in your school. (*Lauren es más deportista que Annie.*) Ask that they make some of their sentences false. Collect these sentences and randomly read several to the class as a *Cierta o Falsa* activity.
- ***Pre-AP* Resource Book:*** Comprehensive guide to Pre-AP* communication skill development, pp. 10–57

Manos a la obra

Gramática

Objectives

- Listen to a description of two different bedrooms
- Write about, discuss, and compare different music
- Exchange information while comparing opinions with a classmate

Making comparisons

Just as you can use *más . . . que* to compare two things, you can also use **menos . . . que** *(less . . . than).*

El disco compacto de Los Toros es **menos** popular **que** el disco compacto de Los Lobos.

The CD by Los Toros is less popular than the CD by Los Lobos.

¿Recuerdas?

You have learned to use *más . . . que* to compare two things.

- La clase de inglés es **más** interesante **que** la clase de matemáticas.

The adjectives *bueno(a), malo(a), viejo(a),* and *joven* and the adverbs *bien* and *mal* have their own comparative forms. *Más* and *menos* are not used with these comparative adjectives and adverbs.

Adjective	Adverb	Comparative	
bueno, -a	**bien**	**mejor (que)**	*better than*
malo, -a	**mal**	**peor (que)**	*worse than*
viejo, -a		**mayor (que)**	*older than*
joven		**menor (que)**	*younger than*

Mejor, peor, mayor, and *menor* have plural forms that end in *-es.*

Los videos de Shakira son **mejores que** los videos de Juanes.

Más ayuda realidades.com

***GramActiva* Video**
Tutorials: Comparing things that are equal, Comparing things that are not equal

***GramActiva* Activity**

10 Dos dormitorios

Escuchar • Escribir

En una hoja de papel, escribe los números del 1 al 6. Escucha las seis comparaciones de los dormitorios de Paco y de Kiko. Escribe *C* si la frase es cierta o *F* si es falsa.

El dormitorio de Paco

El dormitorio de Kiko

DIFFERENTIATED INSTRUCTION

Heritage Language Learners

Have students write sentences comparing their bedroom to that of a sibling or friend. Review their work for correct spelling and grammar.

11 ¡Viva la música! |  | 

Escribir • Hablar

1. Escribe cinco frases con comparaciones de los varios tipos de música que ves aquí. Usa estos *(these)* adjetivos en la forma correcta con *más . . . que* o *menos . . . que.*

aburrido, -a	interesante
bonito, -a	popular
divertido, -a	serio, -a
feo, -a	triste
importante	

Modelo

Para mí, la salsa es más divertida que la música rap.

2. Lee tus comparaciones a otro(a) estudiante para ver si Uds. están de acuerdo.

Modelo

A —*Para mí, la salsa es más divertida que la música rap.*

B —*Sí, estoy de acuerdo, pero la salsa es menos popular que la música rap.*

Para decir más . . .

los blues	la música rap
la música reggae	el jazz
la música clásica	la música rock
la música folklórica	la salsa
la música hip-hop	

12 ¿Cómo se comparan los dos?

Escribir • Hablar

Con otro(a) estudiante, escoge dos cosas o personas de cada categoría de la lista. En una hoja de papel, escribe una comparación de las dos. Después, túrnate *(take turns)* con tu compañero(a) para leer tus comparaciones y dar *(give)* tus opiniones.

Modelo

actividades

A —*Para mí, ir al cine es mejor que ver un video.*

B —*Estoy de acuerdo. Ver un video es menos divertido que ir al cine.*

1. actividades
2. deportes
3. comidas
4. clases
5. libros o revistas
6. personas famosas

Fondo Cultural | El mundo hispano

Latin Grammy awards recognize the talents of Spanish and Portuguese speaking artists from around the world every year. In recent years, Latin Grammy winners include Alejandro Sanz, Juan Luis Guerra, Nelly Furtado, Camila, Rubén Blades, Café Tacuba, Juanes, and Marc Anthony.

- Who are some Latin recording artists you enjoy and what is their music like?

El grupo mexicano Camila, con sus premios Grammy

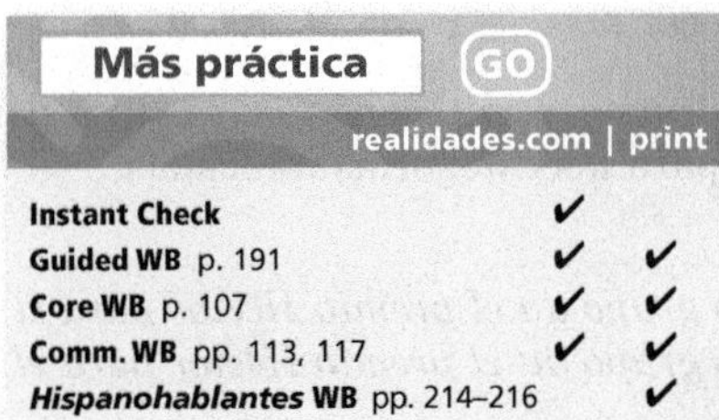

Más práctica GO

realidades.com | print

	realidades.com	print
Instant Check	✔	
Guided WB p. 191	✔	✔
Core WB p. 107	✔	✔
Comm. WB pp. 113, 117	✔	✔
Hispanohablantes WB pp. 214–216		✔

11 Standards: 1.1, 1.2, 1.3

Focus: Using comparatives to give personal opinions

Recycle: Adjectives to describe music

Suggestions: Have students give examples of different types of music. Remind them that adjectives agree with nouns. Point out that the definite articles show the gender of the words in *Para decir más....*

Answers will vary.

12 Standards: 1.1, 1.3

Focus: Using comparatives to express opinions

Recycle: Leisure activities and food

Suggestions: Explain that students will write about two people or things for each category and should complete their lists before writing their comparisons. Encourage them to use adjectives different from those at the top of the page.

Answers will vary.

Extension: Tape pictures that depict people, specific actions, or things to the board. Ask volunteers to select two pictures and place them side by side while saying a sentence such as: *Esquiar es más difícil que cocinar.*

Fondo cultural

Standards: 2.1, 2.2, 5.2

Suggestions: Ask students if they are familiar with Latin music groups and have them brainstorm some Latin recording artists. Play some selections from Grammy-winning artists in class.

Additional Resources

- Communication Wbk.: Audio Act. 7, p. 113
- Teacher's Resource Book: Audio Script, p. 80
- Audio Program DVD: Cap. 6A, Track 10

ASSESSMENT

Prueba 6A-3 with Study Plan (online only)

Quiz: Making Comparisons

- Prueba 6A-3: p. 151

ENRICH YOUR TEACHING

Culture Note

In recent years, Latin American music has extended its cross-over appeal and become popular throughout the world. The Latin Grammy Awards are broadcast every year in 140 countries, including the United States. These awards honor music recorded in Spanish or Portuguese in a great variety of genres. With talent from across the world, competition is high.

21st Century Skills

Initiative and Self-Direction Remind students that they have many tools to help them understand and practice the grammar concepts in this program. Direct them to the eText activities, to the GramActiva video, and the online tutorials, which make it possible for students to monitor their own progress and learning needs.

Gramática

Core Instruction

Standards: 4.1

Resources: Teacher's Resource Book: Video Script, pp. 83–84; Video Program: Cap. 6A

INTERACTIVE WHITEBOARD
Grammar Activities 6A

Suggestions: Before introducing the grammar point, give students a list of categories such as classes, musicians, or sports. Have students name the best or worst in their opinion. Use these opinions as a springboard to a discussion in Spanish. To follow up, provide students with two additional categories for which they have appropriate vocabulary to make comparisons in Spanish. Use the transparency to introduce superlatives. Create a T-chart on the board with ***el/la/los/las*** on the left and ***más/menos*** on the right. Have the class brainstorm a list of nouns and adjectives to complete the chart. The *GramActiva* Video can serve as reinforcement.

13 Standards: 1.1

Resources: Answer Key: Student Edition, p. 81

Focus: Using superlatives to express opinions

Recycle: Objects and adjectives

Suggestions: Give students time to jot down adjectives to describe what's listed (***foto, libro,*** etc.). Have volunteers present questions and answers.

Answers will vary; questions are:

1. **—Para ti, ¿cuál es la posesión más importante?**
2. **¿... el disco compacto más popular?**
3. **¿... el video más gracioso?**
4. **¿... la foto más bonita?**
5. **¿... el videojuego más divertido?**
6. **¿... el libro más interesante?**

14 Standards: 1.1, 1.3

Focus: Personalizing superlatives

Recycle: Months of the year; leisure activities

Suggestions: Have each group decide on a presenter and a note taker. Make sure each student is participating.

Answers will vary.

Objectives

- Discuss and write about the best and worst
- Exchange information about bedrooms and colors
- Compare technology use in Spain to your class
- Identify flags from the Spanish-speaking world and design your own flag

Gramática

The superlative

To say that someone or something is the "most" or "least," use:

definite article **(el, la, los, las)** + noun + más / menos + adjective

La foto de mi familia es la posesión más importante para mí.

To say that someone or something is the "best" or the "worst," use:

definite article + mejor(es) / peor(es) + noun

Rojo y azul son los mejores colores para mi dormitorio.

Más ayuda realidades.com

***GramActiva* Video Tutorial:** Superlatives

***GramActiva* Activity**

13 Las casas de los ricos y famosos

Hablar

Un grupo de personas del programa de televisión "Las casas de los ricos y famosos" está en tu casa. Habla con el grupo sobre las cosas especiales en tu casa. Pregunta y contesta según el modelo.

Modelo

cuadro/bonito

A —*Para ti, ¿cuál es el cuadro más bonito?*
B —*Para mí, el cuadro más bonito es el cuadro de las flores rojas y amarillas.*

1. posesión / importante
2. disco compacto / popular
3. video / gracioso
4. foto / bonita
5. videojuego / divertido
6. libro / interesante

14 Los premios Héctor

Hablar • Escribir

1. En grupos de cuatro estudiantes, pregunta y contesta sobre las mejores y peores cosas del año. Decide el (la) mejor y el (la) peor de cada categoría de la lista y escribe una frase para cada una.

Modelo

el mes

A —*Para ti, ¿cuál es el mejor mes del año?*
B —*Para mí, el mejor mes del año es junio.*
A —*¿Y cuál es el peor mes del año?*
B —*El peor mes del año es enero.*

1. el programa de televisión
2. el video
3. el grupo musical
4. la película
5. el disco compacto

2. Prepara una presentación para la clase para dar un premio *(give a prize)* Héctor para las categorías indicadas.

Modelo

Nuestro grupo da el premio Héctor para el mejor mes del año a junio.
Nuestro grupo da el premio Héctor para el peor mes del año a enero.

DIFFERENTIATED INSTRUCTION

Students with Learning Difficulties

For *Actividades* 13–14, give students a copy of the *Modelos* with the words to be changed underlined.

Multiple Intelligences

Bodily/Kinesthetic: Have students play charades to act out what they think are the best music, songs, and television shows. Then have them discuss why they think they are the best.

15 Tus propias cosas 

Hablar • Escribir

1 Habla con otro(a) estudiante sobre las cosas que tienes en tu dormitorio. Pregunta y contesta según el modelo. Escribe las respuestas en una hoja de papel.

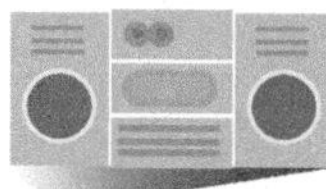

Modelo

A —*¿Tienes tu propio equipo de sonido?*
B —*Sí, tengo mi propio equipo de sonido. ¿Y tú?*
A —*No, pero puedo usar el equipo de sonido de mi familia.*

Estudiante A

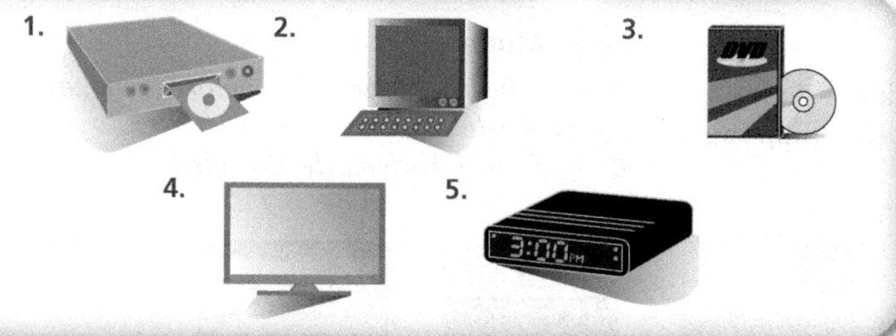

Estudiante B

Sí, tengo mi propio(a) . . .

No, pero comparto . . . con . . .

No, pero puedo usar . . . de mi familia.

No, no tengo . . .

2 Trabajen con otra pareja. Sumen *(Add together)* los resultados del paso *(step)* 1. Escriban frases para presentar los resultados a la clase. Compartan los resultados del grupo de ustedes con los otros grupos y sumen los resultados de toda la clase.

Modelo

Cuatro estudiantes tienen computadoras en sus casas.

3 Determinen un porcentaje *(percentage)* para cada aparato *(appliance)* tecnológico y creen *(create)* una gráfica para demostrar los resultados.

16 Cataluña y la tecnología 

Comparar • Escribir • Hablar

Estudia la gráfica y contesta las preguntas.

1. ¿Cuáles son los aparatos más populares en las casas en la región de Cataluña, en España?
2. Haz una encuesta en tu clase. Escribe frases para comparar los resultados de tu clase y la información de la gráfica.

Modelo

Nosotros tenemos más lectores DVD que . . .

Porcentaje de tecnología en las casas catalanas

Aparato	Porcentaje
Antena parabólica	22%
Lector DVD	64%
Acceso al Internet	73%
Teléfono móvil	83%
Computadora personal	100%
Televisión	100%

Practice and Communicate 6A

15 Standards: 1.1, 1.2, 1.3, 3.1

Resources: Answer Key: Student Edition, p. 81

Focus: Asking and answering questions about electronic equipment

Recycle: ***Tener; compartir***

Suggestions: Suggest that students keep a chart with responses. Items can be listed at the top and student names on the side. For part 2, have students write the results from other groups. For part 3, review how to calculate percentages.

Answers will vary but will include:

1. **lector DVD**
2. **computadora**
3. **videos**
4. **televisor**
5. **despertador digital**

BELLRINGER REVIEW

Show Voc. and Gram. Transparency 112. Have the class describe this bedroom choosing adjectives from this list: *bonito, ordenado, feo, desordenado, pequeño, verde, grande, azul, horrible, interesante.*

16 Standards: 1.1, 1.2, 4.1, 4.2

Resources: Answer Key: Student Edition, p. 82

Mapa global interactivo, Actividad 1 Explore the region of Catalonia in northeast Spain.

Focus: Interpreting a bar graph

Suggestions: Have students identify cognates on the graph. Provide phrases to guide them in their comparisons.

Answers:

1. **Los aparatos tecnológicos más populares en Cataluña son los televisores.**
2. **Answers will vary.**

Theme Project

Give students copies of the Theme Project outline and rubric from the *Teacher's Resource Book.* Explain the task to them, and have them perform Step 1. (For more information, see p. 270-b.)

ENRICH YOUR TEACHING

Culture Note

Cataluña consists of four provinces: Barcelona, Gerona, Lérida, and Tarragona. The area begins at the foot of the Pyrenees and includes much of the Mediterranean coast of Spain. Technology in this region is about as accessible and as frequently used as in the United States.

Teacher-to-Teacher

Have students work in groups and poll each other about their favorite color *(¿Cuál es tu color favorito?).* Then have them report back to the class and tally the results. Reveal the most popular color and ask the class to bring in as many objects as they can find in that color and / or wear clothing that color the next day.

17 Standards: 1.1, 1.3

Focus: Using colors and adjectives in a personalized context

Suggestions: If possible, bring to class colored paper to help stimulate ideas. Remind students to answer the last question about their personality.

Answers will vary.

Extension: Have students write a poem about themselves, their family, or school. They should include colors and adjectives from the exercise. Remind them that poems do not have to rhyme.

18 Standards: 1.1, 2.2

Resources: Voc. and Gram. Transparency 118

Focus: Describing flags of Spanish-speaking countries

Suggestions: You may want to provide students with additional vocabulary to describe the flags, such as ***el sol, las estrellas,*** and ***el escudo.***

Answers will vary.

Fondo cultural

Standards: 2.2, 4.2

Suggestions: Ask students what the stars and stripes on the United States flag represent. Have them use the Internet to do a keyword search of *United States state flags,* noting anything that is relevant to the history of any of the flags' designs.

Answers will vary.

Block Schedule

Have students choose a country from *Actividad* 18 and research the history of its flag. Ask them to replicate the flag on paper and present their reports to the class.

17 ¿De qué color es tu día?

Pensar • Escribir • Hablar

¿Cuáles son los colores que asocias con estas palabras? Escribe los colores.

Modelo

regular *gris*

1. contento
2. calor
3. artístico
4. horrible
5. reservado
6. triste
7. frío
8. sociable
9. gracioso
10. aburrido

Y para ti, ¿cuál es el color de tu personalidad?

18 Las banderas | 

Hablar

Identifica los colores de las banderas de los países *(countries)* o lugares de habla hispana. Trabaja con otro(a) estudiante.

Modelo

A —*La bandera tiene los colores rojo, amarillo y verde.*
B —*¿Es la bandera de Bolivia?*
A —*Sí.*

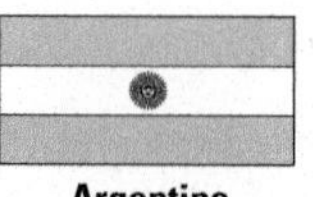
Argentina

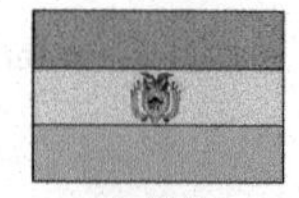
Bolivia

Chile

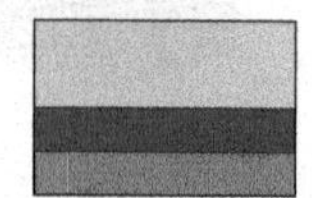
Colombia

Costa Rica

Cuba

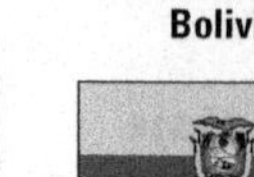
Ecuador

El Salvador

España

Guatemala

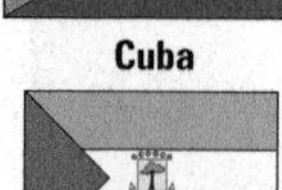
Guinea Ecuatorial

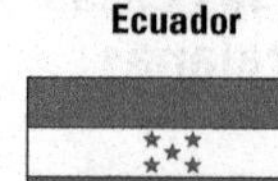
Honduras

Nicaragua

Panamá

Paraguay

Perú

Puerto Rico

República Dominicana

Uruguay

Venezuela

Fondo Cultural | México

La bandera mexicana has a fascinating history. According to tradition, the Aztecs were to build their capital city, Tenochtitlán, where they found an eagle perched on a cactus and devouring a serpent. This image is what you see in the center of the Mexican flag today.

- What flags can you identify in the United States that also contain a symbol with historical significance?

DIFFERENTIATED INSTRUCTION

Students with Learning Difficulties

Explain that there are no right or wrong answers for *Actividad* 17. For *Actividad* 18, review the names of the countries. You may want to help students find them on a world map.

Multiple Intelligences

Logical/Mathematical: Game of *Concentration:* Hand out 40 index cards. On 20 of them, write the name of a Spanish-speaking country. On the other cards, write the colors of each country's flag. Turn all the cards so that the blank side is facing upwards, *country cards* in one group, *color cards* in another. Students take turns matching a *color card* with a *country card.* Cards are removed when a match is found.

19 ¿Qué significan los colores?

Leer • Pensar • Escribir

En la psicología, hay un estudio de los significados *(meanings)* de diferentes colores en diferentes culturas. Lee las descripciones aquí para contestar las preguntas.

Conexiones | Las ciencias sociales

En muchas culturas, el verde significa buena salud, la primavera, las plantas y tranquilidad. Es un color de la paz.[1]

El blanco, en las culturas de las Américas, significa generalmente inocencia y paz. En ciertas culturas asiáticas, el blanco significa la muerte.[2]

El color que expresa energía, pasión y acción en muchas culturas diferentes es el rojo.

En muchas culturas, el amarillo significa atención, precaución, el sol y la energía. Es muy fácil ver el amarillo y se usa mucho para los taxis.

Un color que expresa protección, autoridad, confianza[3] y armonía es el azul. Vemos este color mucho en los uniformes de la policía y los militares.

[1]peace [2]death [3]confidence

Find words or expressions in the reading to explain the following uses of color:

- yellow traffic light
- green recycling symbol
- blue police uniform
- red roses for Valentine's Day

20 ¿Una bandera para ti

Escribir • Hablar

Imagina que vas a diseñar *(design)* una bandera para una organización, un club o un equipo *(team)*. ¿Qué colores vas a usar? ¿Por qué?

21 Y tú, ¿qué dices? | Talk!

Escribir • Hablar

1. ¿Cuáles son tus colores favoritos? ¿Qué posesiones tienes en tu dormitorio de estos colores?
2. Escribe una lista de cinco cosas que están en tu dormitorio y el color de cada cosa. Por ejemplo: *Tengo una lámpara anaranjada.*
3. ¿De qué colores son los libros y las carpetas que tienes para tus clases?

Más práctica GO

realidades.com | print

	realidades.com	print
Instant Check	✔	
Guided WB p. 191	✔	✔
Core WB p. 108	✔	✔
Comm. WB pp. 114, 118	✔	✔
***Hispanohablantes* WB** pp. 217, 219, 221		✔

Practice and Communicate 6A

19 Standards: 1.2, 1.3, 3.1, 4.1

Resources: Answer Key: Student Edition, p. 82

Focus: Reading about the significance of colors in various cultures

Suggestions: Do the reading as a class. Remind students to look for cognates.

Answers:

yellow traffic light—atención, precaución
green recycling symbol—buena salud, las plantas, tranquilidad
blue uniform—protección, autoridad
red roses—energía, pasión

Extension: Can students give examples of other colors that have "meaning"?

20 Standards: 1.1, 1.3

Focus: Identifying colors in a personalized context

Suggestions: Remind students to select colors that symbolize the values represented by their team or club.

Answers will vary.

21 Standards: 1.1, 1.2, 1.3

Focus: Using new vocabulary in a personalized context

Suggestions: Remind students about agreement: ***un libro rojo*** but ***una carpeta roja.*** You may want to give students the words for sheets, ***sábanas,*** pillow cases, ***fundas,*** and bedspread, ***colchón.***

Answers will vary.

Additional Resources

- Communication Wbk.: Audio Act. 8, p. 114
- Teacher's Resource Book: Audio Script, pp. 80–81
- Audio Program DVD: Cap. 6A, Track 11

ENRICH YOUR TEACHING

Teacher-to-Teacher

Have students draw or use a computer to design a music ad. For ideas, have them go to a Web site that sells music. Give them names of Spanish-speaking performers to search for. Ask them to look at the cover art and think about why the designer chose certain colors and what mood he or she was trying to convey.

21st Century Skills

Critical Thinking and Problem Solving

Working with a partner, have students choose two of the flags on page 282 and, using the information about colors on page 283, write a statement about what the color choices reveal about the country the flag represents.

ASSESSMENT

Prueba 6A-4 with Study Plan (online only)

Quiz: The superlative

- Prueba 6A-4: p. 152

6A Practice and Communicate

Gramática

Core Instruction

Standards: 4.1

Resources: Voc. and Gram. Transparency 117; Teacher's Resource Book: Video Script, p. 84; Video Program: Cap. 6A

INTERACTIVE WHITEBOARD
Grammar Activities 6A

Suggestions: Remind students that they already know some stem-changing verbs such as ***querer, preferir,*** and ***jugar.*** Use the *GramActiva* Video and / or the transparency to reinforce the similarity between ***poder, dormir,*** and ***jugar.***

22 Standards: 1.2, 1.3, 3.1

Resources: Answer Key: Student Edition, p. 82

Focus: Using ***dormir*** and solving a brain teaser

Suggestions: Have students set up the last question as a math problem.

Answers:

1. **dormimos**
2. **duerme**
3. **duerme**
4. **dormimos**
5. **dormimos**
6. **duermen**

Tomás duerme 6 horas. Catalina, 10 horas. Guillermo, 8 horas. Paco, 9 horas. Laura, 9 horas. Yo, 8 horas.

23 Standards: 1.1, 1.2, 1.3

Resources: Teacher's Resource Book: Audio Script, p. 81; Audio Program DVD: Cap. 6A, Track 12; Answer Key: Student Edition, p. 83

Focus: Listening comprehension with ***poder*** and ***dormir***

Suggestions: Give students time to read through the questions. Play the audio or read the script more than once.

Script and Answers:

1. **No pueden usar el equipo de sonido después de las ocho.** ***(Sí, pero no después de las ocho.)***
2. **Las chicas no pueden estar en los dormitorios de los chicos.** ***(las chicas)***
3. **No pueden tener televisores ni lectores DVD en el campamento.** ***(No.)***
4. **Pueden escuchar discos compactos pero sólo los domingos.** ***(sólo los domingos)***
5. **No pueden ni comer ni beber en las camas.** ***(No.)***
6. **No pueden dormir después de las siete de la mañana.** ***(No, sólo hasta las siete.)***

Gramática

Objectives

- Listen to, write, and discuss rules
- Read, write, and talk about sleep habits
- Describe objects to play a guessing game
- Design a dream bedroom for a classmate

Stem-changing verbs: *poder* and *dormir*

Like *jugar, poder* and *dormir* are stem-changing verbs. They have a change from *o* → *ue* in all forms except *nosotros* and *vosotros.* Here are the present-tense forms:

(yo)	**puedo**	(nosotros) (nosotras)	**podemos**
(tú)	**puedes**	(vosotros) (vosotras)	**podéis**
Ud. (él) (ella)	**puede**	Uds. (ellos) (ellas)	**pueden**

(yo)	**duermo**	(nosotros) (nosotras)	**dormimos**
(tú)	**duermes**	(vosotros) (vosotras)	**dormís**
Ud. (él) (ella)	**duerme**	Uds. (ellos) (ellas)	**duermen**

¿Recuerdas?

You use *puedo* and *puedes* to say what you can or cannot do:

—**¿Puedes** ir a la fiesta conmigo?
—No, no **puedo.**

Más ayuda realidades.com

- ***GramActiva*** **Video Animated Verbs**
- ***Canción de hip hop:*** *¡No podemos dormir!*
- ***GramActiva*** **Activity**

22 Rompecabezas

Leer • Escribir • Pensar

¿Cuántas horas duermen las personas en esta familia? Escribe la forma apropiada del verbo *dormir* para cada frase. Después contesta la pregunta.

¡Mis hermanos y yo __1.__ 50 horas al día! Es mucho, ¿no? Tomás, mi hermano mayor, __2.__ menos, seis horas al día. Catalina __3.__ más horas que todos—cuatro horas más que Tomás. Guillermo y yo __4.__ el mismo número de horas. Juntos *(Together)* nosotros __5.__ el mismo número de horas que Tomás y Catalina. Paco y Laura __6.__ el mismo número de horas. ¿Cuántas horas duerme cada persona (Tomás, Catalina, Guillermo, Paco, Laura y yo)?

Nota

When the forms of *poder* are followed by another verb, the second verb is in the infinitive form.

- Ana no **puede hablar** español.

23 El campamento Nadadivertido

Escuchar • Escribir • Hablar

Es el primer día en el campamento de verano Nadadivertido. Tu amigo(a) nunca escucha nada. Escucha las reglas *(rules)* del campamento y después contesta las preguntas de tu amigo(a).

1. ¿Podemos usar el equipo de sonido en la tarde?
2. ¿Quiénes no pueden ir a los dormitorios de los chicos?
3. ¿Podemos ver videos en los dormitorios?
4. ¿Cuándo podemos escuchar discos compactos?
5. ¿Podemos beber refrescos en la cama?
6. ¿Podemos dormir hasta *(until)* las nueve?

DIFFERENTIATED INSTRUCTION

Multiple Intelligences

Verbal/Linguistic: Have students compare themselves to another person (or thing). Encourage them to be creative and make it tongue-in-cheek, for example, saying they can swim faster than a fish. Point out that they should incorporate comparisons and ***poder.***

Heritage Language Learners

Have one student write what people can't do because of weather conditions. Another student will tell what he or she can do: *Hace fresco y Marta no puede tomar el sol. Pero puede ir al cine.*

24 Las reglas |  | 

Escribir • Hablar

Tienes que cuidar *(baby-sit)* a dos niños y no sabes las reglas de su casa. Primero escribe cinco preguntas para ellos. Después pregunta y contesta según el modelo. Aquí está una lista de verbos que puedes usar:

beber	escuchar	jugar
comer	ir	ver

Modelo

A —*¿Uds. pueden comer helado después de las siete?*
B —*No, nunca podemos comer helado después de las siete.*
o:—*¡Por supuesto! Siempre podemos comer helado después de las siete.*

25 ¡Podemos hacer muchas cosas! |  |

Hablar

Trabaja con otro(a) estudiante para decir qué pueden hacer diferentes personas con las posesiones que tienen.

Modelo

Marcos / sacar fotos
A —*¿Marcos puede sacar fotos?*
B —*¡Por supuesto! Tiene una cámara muy buena.*
o:—*No. No tiene una cámara.*

Estudiante A

1. Uds. / ver películas en casa
2. Raquel / hacer la tarea de álgebra
3. tu papá (o tu mamá) / usar el Internet
4. tú / escuchar discos compactos
5. Guille y Patricio / jugar videojuegos

Estudiante B

Pronunciación | |

The letters *r* and *rr*

Except at the beginning of a word or after *l* or *n*, the sound of the letter *r* is similar to the *dd* in the English word *ladder.* Listen to and say these words:

derecha	quiero	amarillo	bandera
pero	puerta	alfombra	morado

The sound of *rr* is similar to saying "batter, batter, batter" over and over again very quickly. Listen to and say these words:

perro	correr	guitarra	marrón
aburrido	arroz	pelirrojo	horrible

When *r* is the first letter of a word or comes after *l* or *n*, it is pronounced like the *rr*.

Roberto	Rita	Ricardo	rojo	regalo
rubio	radio	reloj	romper	Enrique

Try it out! Listen to and say this *trabalenguas:*

**Erre con erre cigarro,
erre con erre barril.
Rápido corren los carros,
cargados de azúcar del
ferrocarril.**

Practice and Communicate 6A

24 Standards: 1.1, 1.3

Focus: Asking and answering questions about rules
Recycle: Activities vocabulary
Suggestions: Review the *Nota*, p. 284. Before beginning the *Actividad*, encourage students to think about their own babysitting experiences.
Answers will vary.
Extension: In small groups, have students discuss their own house rules: ***En mi casa, no podemos....***

25 Standards: 1.1, 1.3

Resources: Answer Key: Student Edition, p. 83
Focus: Using ***poder*** to discuss use of electronic equipment
Recycle: ***Tener*** and activities vocabulary
Suggestions: Review the vocabulary words for the equipment pictured.
Answers will vary; questions are:

1. **¿Uds. pueden ver películas en casa?**
2. **¿Raquel puede hacer la tarea de álgebra?**
3. **¿Tu papá puede usar el Internet?**
4. **¿Tú puedes escuchar discos compactos?**
5. **¿Guille y Patricio pueden jugar videojuegos?**

Pronunciación
Core Instruction

Standards: 2.2, 4.1

Resources: Teacher's Resource Book: Audio Script, p. 81; Audio Program DVD: Cap. 6A, Track 13
Suggestions: Read the *Pronunciación* with students or use the audio. Model the two distinct sounds, exaggerating them somewhat for clarity. Have students repeat the words after you. Say the tongue twister and then ask volunteers to say it for the class.

ENRICH YOUR TEACHING

Teacher-to-Teacher

Do an Internet search using the keyword ***trabalenguas.*** Ask students to read them and write down the one that seems the hardest to say. Tell them not to worry too much if they don't understand the meaning because it is often a riddle. (You can review meanings in class.)

21st Century Skills

Technology Literacy Have students create an online survey to find out about the sleeping habits of the class. Have them compile the results and select "winners": who sleeps the most in a week, who the least, who gets up the earliest on the weekend, who sleeps the longest, etc. Have them post the results of the "sleep contest" on the class Web site.

26 Standards: 1.1, 1.2, 1.3, 4.1

Resources: Answer Key: Student Edition, p. 83

Focus: Reading comprehension about sleep

Suggestions: Have students look at the title of the article and the graphics to get an idea of what the article is about. Have them note cognates as they read. After some discussion, ask students to read and answer the questions.

Answers:

1. **El problema es que muchos adultos no duermen lo suficiente. 2. 68%; 3. sí; no; no; sí; 4. Answers will vary.**

Exploración del lenguaje

Core Instruction

Standards: 4.1

Resources: Answer Key: Student Edition, p. 84

Suggestions: Read with students. Brainstorm other words and roots they have learned. Post a list that students can add to.

Answers:

bebida; televisor; green fields; blue sky; a gray-haired old man

Fondo cultural

Standards: 1.2, 2.1, 4.2

Suggestions: Explain that when people take a ***siesta,*** the work day is no shorter; there's just a break in the middle and people work later into the evening. Put two columns on the board and ask the class to discuss the advantages and disadvantages of a ***siesta.***

Theme Project

Students can perform Step 2 at this point. Be sure students understand your suggestions. (See p. 270-b.)

Additional Resources

- Communication Wbk.: Audio Act. 9, p. 115
- Teacher's Resource Book: Audio Script, p. 81, Communicative Pair Activity BLM, pp. 88–89
- Audio Program DVD: Cap. 6A, Track 14

26 ¿Duermes bien?

Leer • Escribir • Hablar

Lee este artículo de una revista y contesta las preguntas.

1. Según el artículo, ¿cuál es el problema?
2. ¿Qué porcentaje de las personas duerme menos de ocho horas diarias durante la semana?
3. ¿El artículo presenta estas ideas? Contesta *sí* o *no.*

   Las personas que duermen poco . . .
   - . . . generalmente están más cansadas.
   - . . . trabajan mejor.
   - . . . juegan mucho y hacen ejercicio.
   - . . . son menos sociables.
4. Y tú, durante los fines de semana, ¿cuántas horas duermes en la noche?

¿Cuántas horas duermes por noche?

Un nuevo estudio indica que muchos adultos no duermen ni[1] seis horas por noche, y afecta mucho a su calidad de vida.[2]

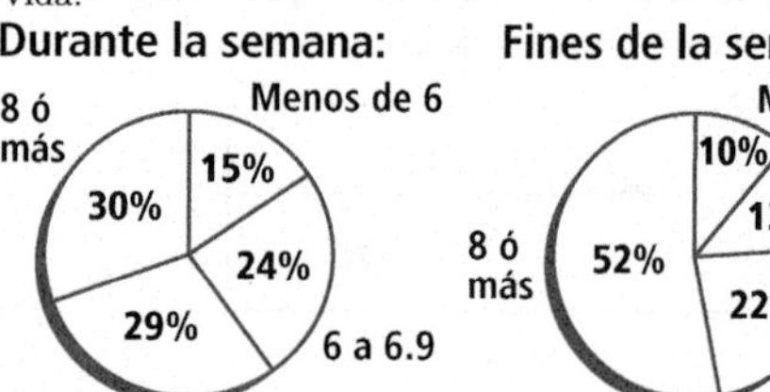

Las personas que duermen menos de seis horas por noche:

- Tienen más estrés y fatiga.
- Están más tristes y menos alertas.
- Hacen peor su trabajo.
- Sufren más lesiones[3].
- Tienen más problemas de relaciones interpersonales.
- Comen más de lo usual.
- Tienen menos energía.

[1]not even [2]quality of life [3]injuries

Exploración del lenguaje

Using root words

You can build your vocabulary, both in Spanish and in English, if you recognize the root of a word and know its meaning.

For example, because you know the root of one word, ***comer***, you can more easily learn another word, ***la comida.***

Try it out! Because you know the root of ***beber***, you can easily remember *la* ___?___. And since you know ***ver la televisión***, you can easily recognize *el* ___?___.

Once you learn another language, your mastery of your own language can increase. This is because you begin to use words from your second language to help you understand words in English that are new to you.

Try it out! Since you know *verde*, *azul,* and *gris,* what do you think these words mean?

verdant fields   *azure* sky   a *grizzled* old man

Fondo Cultural | El mundo hispano

La siesta, an afternoon nap after the large midday meal, has been observed in Spain and other Spanish-speaking countries for centuries. However, with modern-day pressures and in larger cities, many people no longer take off work for *la siesta.*

- What do you think would be some advantages and disadvantages of a *siesta* in your daily life?

En España, muchas tiendas se cierran entre las 14:00 y las 16:30 horas.

DIFFERENTIATED INSTRUCTION

Students with Learning Difficulties

Exploración del lenguaje: Review the concept of roots. Give several examples in English and then in Spanish. Teach students that this is an excellent strategy for learning new vocabulary words. Encourage them to keep a list of these words and suggest that they use a different color to write out the root.

Advanced Learners/Pre-AP*

Have students work together to compile a list of roots with examples. Ask them to type them up on a sheet of paper or create a poster.

27 Juego |  | 

Escribir • Hablar

Con otro(a) estudiante, describe tres cosas y escribe las descripciones. Lee las frases a otra pareja para ver si ellos pueden identificar las cosas.

 **Modelo**

A —*Es una cosa que toca música. Puede ser grande o pequeño. Está en muchas casas. ¿Qué es?*

B —*Es un equipo de sonido.*

> **Strategy**
>
> **Circumlocution**
>
> When you don't know or can't remember the word for something, you can describe it. You can tell what it is used for, what size it is, what color it is, where it is often found, and so on.

28 Y tú, ¿qué preguntas? |  | 

Escribir • Hablar • Dibujar

1. Escribe cinco preguntas que puedes hacer *(ask)* a otra persona. Puedes preguntar sobre las actividades que le gustan, cómo es, sus colores favoritos, sus intereses en música y deportes.
2. Haz tus preguntas a otro(a) estudiante. Escribe sus respuestas.
3. Dibuja un dormitorio especial para el (la) estudiante según sus respuestas a tus preguntas. Usa lápices de color. Presenta tu dibujo a tu compañero(a) y explica por qué el dormitorio es especial para él o ella.

Modelo

El dormitorio es especial para ti porque tus colores favoritos son azul y rojo.
Hay una foto de Rafael Nadal en la cómoda porque te gusta mucho el tenis.
Hay muchas fotos en las paredes porque sacas fotos de tus amigos también.
Tú eres muy gracioso y desordenado. Hay muchos videos y revistas en la cama.
Te gusta escuchar la música hip-hop. Aquí, en el estante, están tus discos compactos.

El español en la comunidad

In many communities in the United States, you can see the influence of Spanish-style architecture. Spanish-style buildings often have tile roofs, stucco exteriors, and interior courtyards or patios.

- Identify houses, buildings, or neighborhoods in your community that feature this style. Draw or take a picture of one example.

Más práctica

GO — realidades.com | print

	realidades.com	print
Instant Check	✔	
Guided WB pp. 193–194	✔	✔
Core WB p. 109	✔	✔
Comm. WB pp. 115, 119, 288	✔	✔
***Hispanohablantes* WB** pp. 218, 220		✔

ENRICH YOUR TEACHING

Culture Note

Antonio Gaudí (1852–1926), one of Spain's best-known architects, very much left his mark on his native city of Barcelona. He is known particularly for his *Iglesia de la Sagrada Familia,* which demonstrates his love of extravagance and ornateness. If possible, bring in books with samples of his work. Discuss his style and compare it to buildings that students are familiar with. Search online with the keywords ***Gaudí + Barcelona*** or ***Gaudí + Cathedral*** for images of the architect's most famous buildings to share with the class and to learn more about his life and work in Barcelona.

Practice and Communicate 6A

27 Standards: 1.1, 1.2, 1.3

Focus: Using circumlocutions

Recycle: Adjectives

Suggestions: Go over the *Strategy,* giving examples of circumlocutions in English and Spanish. Remind students to begin their description with *Es una cosa que . . .*

Answers will vary.

28 Standards: 1.1, 1.2, 1.3

Focus: Asking questions about preferences and demonstrating comprehension through drawing

Recycle: Adjectives; ***gustar***

Suggestions: Remind students that they will use the responses they receive to draw a bedroom.

Answers will vary.

Pre-AP* Support

- **Learning Objective:** Interpersonal Speaking
- **Activity 28:** Students practice informal speaking skills as they ask questions and use the information they learn.

El español en la comunidad

Core Instruction

Standards: 2.2, 4.2

Suggestions: After reading, ask students to discuss why patios and courtyards are common and the reason for using stucco. If there are no buildings in this style in your community encourage students to find pictures in magazines or on the Internet. When they bring in their pictures, ask them to label the colors.

ASSESSMENT

Prueba 6A-5 with Study Plan (online only)

Quiz: *poder* and *dormir*

- Prueba 6A-5: p. 153

Common Core: Reading

Lectura

Core Instruction

Standards: 1.1, 1.2, 1.3, 4.1

Focus: Reading comprehension, understanding cultural perspectives

Suggestions:

Pre-reading: Explain to students that they will be reading a letter to an advice columnist. Use their background knowledge to discuss what kinds of issues people typically send to these columnists. Direct students' attention to the *Strategy*, and find the words in the context of the story.

Reading: Have students read the passage silently before a volunteer reads it aloud. Students will probably create a mental image of the room. Pause between readings to have students share their images with the class.

Post-reading: Have students describe in their own words what is happening between the sisters and why one of them is asking for advice. Briefly discuss problems students may have with sharing a room with siblings.

Pre-AP* Support

- **Learning Objective:** Interpersonal Writing
- **Activity:** After students have read just the letter from Rosario to Magdalena, ask that they write an e-mail offering their own advice to Rosario. Then, have students read the response from Magdalena to Rosario on p. 289, and compare their recommendations to her own.
- ***Pre-AP* Resource Book:*** Comprehensive guide to Pre-AP* reading skill development, pp. 19–26

Block Schedule

Divide the class into groups of four or five and have them write and perform a skit about *El desastre en mi dormitorio.* They may follow the problems of Rosario or take a different direction. Tell them they all must help write the skit and appear in the production. If possible, make a video of the performances.

¡Adelante!

Objectives

- Read a letter and a response in an advice column
- Look for cognates to help you understand what you read
- Explore differences in technology use in the Spanish-speaking world

Lectura

El desastre en mi dormitorio

Lee esta carta *(letter)* a Querida Magdalena. Ella da soluciones a los problemas de los jóvenes en una revista.

Strategy

Using cognates
As you read the letter and response, look for cognates to help you better understand Rosario's problem. Try to guess the meaning of some of the cognates: *el desorden, la situación, recomendar, considerar.*

¿Qué debo hacer?

Con tu amiga Magdalena

"Querida Magdalena:

Mi problema tiene un nombre; es mi hermana Marta. Compartimos el mismo dormitorio y estoy desesperada. Todo en mi lado del dormitorio está en orden. Pero su lado es un desastre. Ella es la reina del desorden. Le encanta comer en el dormitorio. Hay pizza debajo de la cama. Hay botellas de agua en la mesita. Hay postre en el escritorio. Es horrible. Siempre deja[1] ropa,[2] videos y todas sus posesiones en el suelo,[3] en la mesita, en la cama. ¡No hay ni un libro en el estante!

Y ella no usa su propio equipo de sonido—¡no! Usa mi equipo y sin pedir[4] permiso. Y escucha música a toda hora (y a un volumen muy alto) y ¡yo no puedo dormir!

Las paredes en su lado del dormitorio son negras. Es el peor color y es feísimo. Mi color favorito es el amarillo, claro. Es más bonito que el negro, ¿no?

Estoy cansada de compartir el dormitorio con ella y su desorden.
¿Qué debo hacer?"

Rosario Molino
Montevideo, Uruguay

Mi problema tiene un nombre; es mi hermana, Marta.

[1]leaves [2]clothing [3]floor [4]asking for

DIFFERENTIATED INSTRUCTION

Students with Learning Difficulties

Brainstorm with students what Rosario might say in a letter complaining about her sister and what Magdalena might give for advice. Carefully read the passage with students, emphasizing cognates. Read the *¿Comprendes?* with students as well. You may need to provide them with a copy of these questions with key words and phrases underlined.

Advanced Learners

Ask students to write a letter to Magdalena with the opposite problem: Have students take the role of a messy person sharing a room with a brother or sister who could be considered too neat. Encourage them to be creative and write an original letter or use the one in the book as a model.

¡Es difícil compartir un dormitorio con otra persona!

Querida Rosario:

¡Qué problema! Es difícil compartir un dormitorio con otra persona, especialmente si la persona es tu hermana. Uds. son muy diferentes, ¿no? Tú eres más ordenada que ella. Ella cree que el color negro es el más bonito.

Necesitas hablar con tu hermana delante de tus padres. Tienes que explicar[5] la situación y recomendar unas soluciones. Es necesario encontrar[6] un punto intermedio.[7] Si la situación no es mejor después de unas semanas, tienes que considerar la posibilidad de separar el dormitorio con una cortina. ¡Pero no debe ser una cortina ni negra ni amarilla!

Tu amiga,
Magdalena

[5]explain [6]find [7]middle ground

¿Comprendes?

Lee las frases y decide quién dice *(says)* la frase. ¿Es Rosario, Marta o su madre?

1. "Pero me gusta comer en la cama y escuchar música".
2. "Soy una persona muy simpática y el color amarillo representa mi personalidad".
3. "Estoy muy ocupada y no tengo tiempo para 'un dormitorio perfecto'".
4. "Uds. tienen que respetar las posesiones de la otra".
5. "Mi color favorito es el negro. No me gustan los colores amarillo, anaranjado o azul".
6. "Ella debe pedir permiso para escuchar mis discos compactos".
7. "Tu hermana no es ordenada como tú. Tienes que ser más paciente".

Y tú, ¿qué dices?

¿Eres desordenado(a) como *(like)* Marta o eres ordenado(a) como Rosario? ¿En qué? Incluye dos ejemplos en tu respuesta.

Fondo Cultural | El mundo hispano

Los aparatos electrónicos In all Spanish-speaking countries, you will find the latest electronic devices, as well as a demand for instant communication and electronic media. However, access to some technologies, such as Internet, varies by country and even location within a country. While computer use in the Spanish-speaking world has grown, home computers are not as common as in the United States.

- Why do you think geographical location would be a factor in Internet access in Spanish-speaking countries? What reasons might influence home computer purchase and use?

Más práctica

realidades.com | print

Guided WB p. 195	✔	✔
Comm. WB p. 289	✔	✔
***Hispanohablantes* WB** pp. 222–223		✔
Cultural Reading Activity	✔	

ENRICH YOUR TEACHING

Culture Note

In the past, telephone systems throughout the Spanish-speaking world have often not functioned efficiently. It was at times difficult to reach someone by phone, or the connection was bad. Nowadays, however, these problems have been largely overcome by the availability of cell phones, which are widely used.

21st Century Skills

Communication Have students first compare and contrast the two girls (Marta and Rosario), using a Venn diagram. Then have them work in groups to prepare and present a conversation between the two girls and their parents, each girl explaining what she is like and why she can't live with the other girl. The parents should suggest some plausible solutions.

Reading 6A

¿Comprendes? Standards: 1.2, 1.3

Resources: Answer Key: Student Edition, p. 84

Focus: Reading comprehension

Suggestions: Have students close their books. Divide the room into two teams. Put the names ***Rosario, Marta,*** and ***su madre*** on the board. Read the lines dramatically and have team members take turns telling who said them. The team with the most correct answers wins.

Answers:
1. Marta
2. Rosario
3. Marta
4. su madre
5. Marta
6. Rosario
7. su madre

¿Y tú, qué dices?

Focus: Stating opinions

Suggestions: Model how to respond by comparing yourself with Rosario or Marta and giving examples. *Soy como Rosario. Pongo mis cosas en orden . . .*

Answers will vary.

BELLRINGER REVIEW

Have students tell a partner one problem they have with their bedroom. (Ex. *Mi dormitorio es muy pequeño.*)

Fondo cultural

Standards: 4.2

Suggestions: Write the question at the top of a transparency and draw two columns: *advantages* and *disadvantages*. Have students form small groups and discuss the impact technology has had on the culture of the United States. Then ask them to reflect on how it might conceivably impact other cultures.

Answers will vary.

For Further Reading

Student Resource: Realidades para hispanohablantes: Lectura 2, pp. 224–225

La cultura en vivo

Core Instruction

Standards: 2.1, 2.2, 3.1

Focus: Reading about and making ***luminarias***

Mapa global interactivo, Actividad 2 Look at the tradition of *luminarias* on both sides of the Rio Grande River.

Suggestions: If students are not familiar with them, introduce the concept of ***luminarias,*** lights used for special occasions to welcome people. Although once reserved for going to church, the tradition now extends to welcoming visitors to one's home. Direct students' attention to the text. Explain that today ***luminarias*** are more of a symbol than a practicality since most places have street lights, whereas in the early days of this tradition these probably were the only way to light a path.

Direct students to the *Try it out!* section. Help them make their own ***luminarias*** to display in the classroom.

Prepare supplies in advance. You may wish to make a template out of cardboard for the star as shown in the drawing. Have a completed ***luminaria*** ready so students have a model to work from. Students may have difficulties cutting out the design without cutting the shorter sides of the bag. Help them avoid this error.

Direct attention to the *Think about it!* section and have students discuss the questions.

Answers will vary.

Additional Resources

Student Resource: Realidades para hispanohablantes, p. 226

Pre-AP* Support

- **Learning Objective:** Presentational Speaking (Cultural Comparisons)
- **Background:** This task prepares students for the Spoken Presentational Communication tasks that focus on cultural comparisons in the exam.
- **Activity:** Have students prepare a two-minute (maximum) presentation on the following topic: Light-based decorations often signal holidays in different cultures. Think about the tradition of the *luminarias.* Then, think of an example of a similar use of light for special decoration in your own culture. Explain the similarities and differences between the two.

La cultura en vivo

Las luminarias 

Luminarias en Nuevo México

To celebrate Christmas in Mexico and the southwest United States, countless bags, tons of sand, and candles are transformed into flickering outdoor lanterns called *luminarias.* They are lined up along window ledges, walkways, and roofs and are lit to welcome visitors.

This tradition dates back more than 300 years, when villagers along the Río Grande built bonfires to light and warm their way to church on Christmas Eve. The luminarias used today go back to the 1820s, when traders introduced brown paper into the region and candles were set in sand in the bottom of the paper bags.

Try it out! Here's how you can make your own luminarias.

Materials

- 12" paper lunch bags
- sand
- small flashlights
- scissors

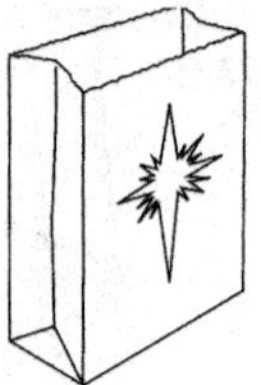

Figure 1

Figure 2

Figure 3

Directions

1 Trace a pattern on the side of the bag, leaving at least 4 inches at the top and 3 inches at the bottom. You may want to use the pattern in Fig. 1 or create your own.

2 Cut out the design, cutting through both sides of the bag. *(Fig. 1)*

3 Open the bag and fold down a 2" cuff around the top. *(Fig. 2)*

4 Fill the bag $\frac{1}{4}$ full of sand.

5 Place a flashlight in the sand. *(Fig. 3)*

6 Place the completed luminarias along your walkway, turn on the small flashlights, and enjoy these symbols of hope and joy for any special occasion.

Variations

1 Use white or brightly colored bags.

2 Paste or glue white or pastel tissue paper behind the cut-out design.

3 Cut a scalloped edge along the top of the bag instead of folding down the cuff.

4 Instead of sand, use soil, cat litter, or gravel to hold the flashlight in place.

Think about it! What kind of decorations do you use for special events? How is light used in different cultures to celebrate events?

DIFFERENTIATED INSTRUCTION

Multiple Intelligences

Visual/Spatial: Have students who finish early help those who may be having difficulties. They can also prepare for a class celebration that will display the ***luminarias*** by setting up the finished ones to light the way for visitors.

Heritage Language Learners

Ask students who are familiar with ***luminarias*** to share their personal experiences with the class. They should include what the occasion was and any particular celebrations that took place.

- Describe someone's personality based on his/her bedroom
- Use a word web to organize your ideas

Presentación oral 

La personalidad de un dormitorio

Task
You are studying how a bedroom reflects the personality of its owner(s). Use a photo or drawing of a bedroom and explain what its contents and colors tell about the owner's personality.

1 Prepare Bring in a photo, magazine picture, or drawing of a bedroom. Use this word web to think through what you want to say about the room and the personality of its owner. Then answer the questions.

- En tu opinión, ¿cómo es la persona que vive *(lives)* en el dormitorio? ¿Qué le gusta hacer?

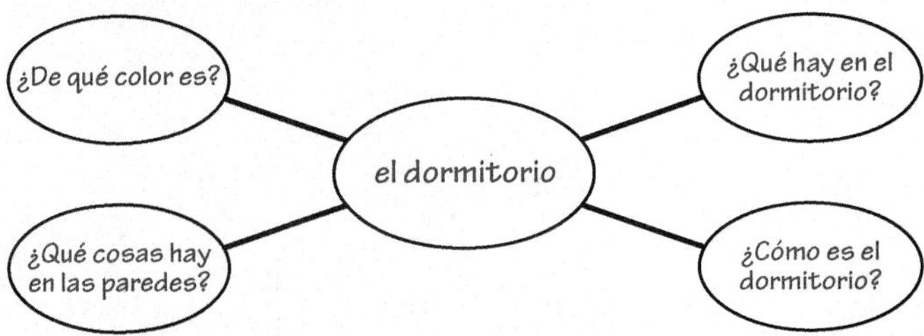

Strategy
Using graphic organizers
A word web can help you organize your thoughts for a presentation.

2 Practice Go through your presentation several times. You can use your notes to practice, but not to present. Try to:
- support your statements with examples
- use complete sentences
- speak clearly

3 Present Show your picture and give the information about the bedroom and the personality behind it.

4 Evaluation The following rubric will be used to grade your presentation.

Rubric	Score 1	Score 3	Score 5
Completeness of presentation	You describe the room, but have no visual.	You describe the room with a visual, but give no opinion.	You describe the room with a visual, and give your opinion.
Amount of information you communicate	You include two categories from the word web.	You include three categories from the word web.	You include all four categories from the word web.
How easily you are understood	You are extremely difficult to understand. Your teacher could only recognize isolated words and phrases.	You are understandable, but have frequent errors in vocabulary and/or grammar that hinder your comprehensibility.	You are easily understood. Your teacher does not have to "decode" what you are trying to say.

Speaking 6A

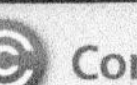 Common Core: Speaking

Presentación oral

Core Instruction

Standards: 1.3

Resources: Voc. and Gram. Transparency 119; Teacher's Resource Book: GramActiva BLM, p. 91

Focus: Speaking using vocabulary related to bedrooms

Suggestions: Review the task and steps with students. After reading the *Strategy,* model use of the graphic organizer. You may wish to provide students with a word web to fill in. Encourage them to articulate and to make eye contact during the presentation. Review the assessment rubric with the class to explain how you will grade the performance.

Pre-AP* Support
- **Learning Objective:** Presentational Speaking
- **Activity:** Remind students to focus on the presentational speaking skills used in this task such as fluency, pronunciation, and comprehensibility.
- ***Pre-AP* Resource Book:*** Comprehensive guide to Pre-AP* speaking skill development, pp. 39–50

Portfolio
Make video or audio recordings of student presentations in class, or assign the RealTalk activity so they can record their presentations online. Include the recording in their portfolios.

Additional Resources
Student Resources: Realidades para hispanohablantes, p. 227; Guided Practice: Presentación oral, p. 196

ENRICH YOUR TEACHING

21st Century Skills
Initiative and Self-Direction Have partners go through the practice steps and the rubric and evaluate each other's presentation. The partner should make sure that all the points listed in the practice step and in Score 5 of the rubric are being met as much as possible. Students should demonstrate improvement of their presentation based on partner feedback.

ASSESSMENT
Presentación oral
- Assessment Program: Rubrics, p. T31
  Go over the descriptions of the different levels of performance. After assessing students, help individuals understand how their performance could be improved.

Videomisterio

Core Instruction

Standards: 1.2, 1.3, 4.1, 5.2

Resources: Teacher's Resource Book: Video Script, pp. 84–85; Video Program: Cap. 6A; Video Program Teacher's Guide: Cap. 6A

Focus: Introducing the events and characters of this episode

Personajes importantes:

Lola Lago, detective
Paco, colega de Lola
Margarita, la secretaria de la oficina de Lola
Doña Lupe Aguirre, portera
Pedro Requena, nieto de doña Gracia Requena

Synopsis: Lola tells Paco about the incident on Sunday at her apartment building, but Paco is only interested in knowing if there is a case and a paying client. Lola believes that this case could lead to a client and she questions doña Lupe, who found doña Gracia on the floor. There are three mysteries at hand: (1) What caused doña Gracia's incident? (2) Where is her niece, María? (3) Where are doña Gracia's jewels? María, a professional model, spent three months in the hospital after a car accident. Doña Gracia's only other relative is her grandson, Pedro Requena, who lives in Italy. His father did not get along with doña Gracia's husband.

Suggestions:

Pre-viewing: Review with students the events of *Episodio* 2. The ambulance arrives for the victim, doña Gracia. Everyone is wondering where doña Gracia's niece, María, is. Inspector Gil questions Lola Lago, who saw two people leave doña Gracia's apartment the night before. Inspector Gil asks Lola to call if she has any further information.

Visual scanning: Direct students' attention to the first two photos and ask who they are (Paco and Margarita), and what relationship they have to Lola (they work in the same office). Before students read the *Resumen del episodio,* have them scan the text and find three cognates ***(importante, incidente, escena, describe, historia, familia)***. Then ask them to read the *Resumen* carefully. Ask students questions about what will happen in this episode.

Viewing: Show *Episodio* 3 to the class.

Objective

- **Understand the expanding plot of a mystery video set in Spain**

¿Eres tú, María?

Episodio 3

Antes de ver el video

Personajes importantes

Paco, quien trabaja en la oficina de Lola y la ayuda con las investigaciones

Margarita, la secretaria de la oficina

Nota cultural *El País* is probably Spain's most widely read and influential newspaper. You can consult an electronic version of *El País* on the Internet.

Resumen del episodio

Este episodio es muy importante. Lola le explica a Paco lo que pasó[1] en el incidente del domingo pasado.[2] En otra escena, Lola habla con doña Lupe quien le describe el incidente en el piso de doña Gracia. También doña Lupe le explica a Lola la historia de la familia de doña Gracia. ¿Por qué cree que María va a recibir toda la fortuna de doña Gracia?

[1]what happened [2]last Sunday

Palabras para comprender

dinero money
periodista newspaper reporter
¿Qué pasó . . .? What happened . . .?
No ve casi nada. She can hardly see anything.
abro I open
muerta dead
busco I'm looking for
¿Robaron . . .? Did they steal . . .?
las joyas jewels
accidente de coche car accident
Pasó antes de venir a vivir con doña Gracia. It happened before she came to live with doña Gracia.
Pasó tres meses . . . She spent three months . . .
el nieto grandson
No viene aquí nunca. He never comes here.
No conoce a su abuela. He doesn't know his grandmother.

DIFFERENTIATED INSTRUCTION

Heritage Language Learners

Have students read a daily edition of *El País* on the Internet. Ask them to write a summary of one news story paying attention to spelling and language usage.

Advanced Learners

Ask students to use the vocabulary from *Palabras para comprender* to tell what happened in this episode. Encourage them to use vocabulary from previous chapters.

La familia Requena

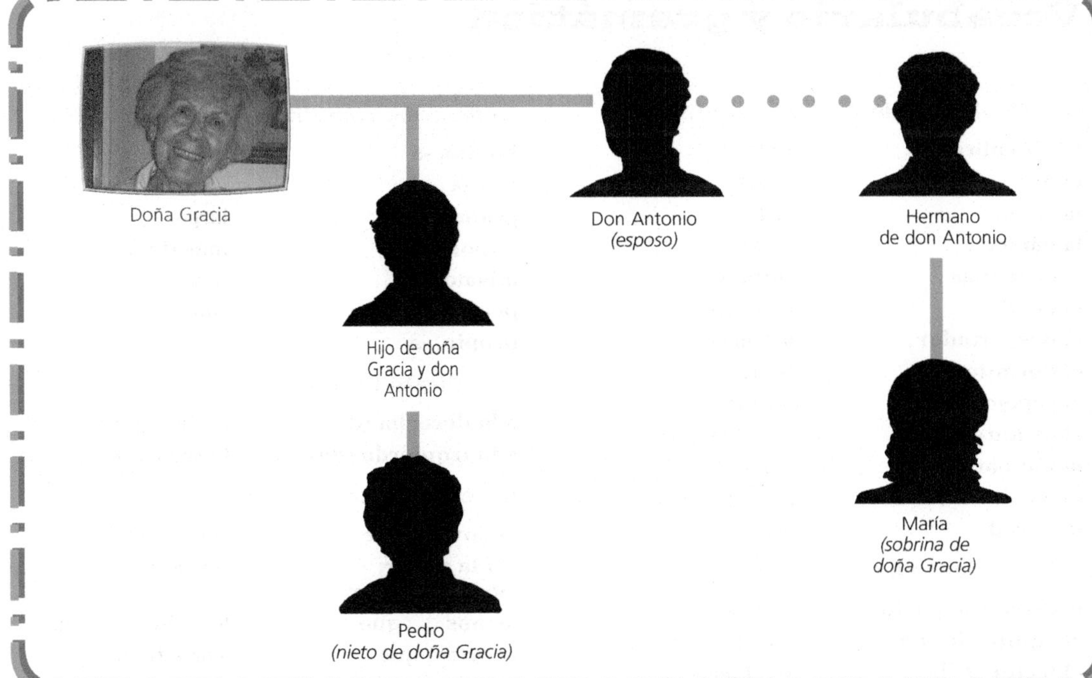

Después de ver el video

¿Comprendes?

Completa cada frase con la palabra apropiada del recuadro.

periodista	hija
fortuna	accidente de coche
joyas	conoce
dinero	sobrina

1. Según Paco, si no hay cliente, si no hay ____, entonces no hay nada.
2. Lola dice que trabaja para *El País,* un periódico importante en España, y es ____.
3. María es la ____ de Lorenzo Requena y la ____ de doña Gracia.
4. Doña Gracia es muy rica. Tiene una fortuna en dinero, ____ y arte.
5. Antes de venir a vivir con doña Gracia, a María le pasó un grave ____.
6. Pedro, el nieto de doña Gracia, vive en Italia y su abuela no lo ____
7. Según doña Lupe, María va a recibir la ____ de doña Gracia.

Más práctica GO

realidades.com | print

Actividades ✔

ENRICH YOUR TEACHING

Culture Note

There are many newspapers in Spain, each with its own political tendencies and views. There are many local newspapers, but there are national papers as well. Of the national newspapers, the best known include *El Mundo* and *El País.*

Teacher-to-Teacher

Have students look at Web sites that have the ***.es*** extension for Spain. These addresses change, but one example is *elmundo.es.* Students can try other words with the ***.es*** extension to see if they have successful hits.

Post-viewing: Have the class study the family tree at the top of the page and ask who can tell what the last names ***(apellidos)*** are of each person in the chart. You may need to explain that in Spanish people most often use two last names: the father's followed by the mother's maiden name. One example will come up in *Episodio* 4 (Dr. Sánchez Mata). When women marry, they keep their maiden name and add ***de*** plus their husband's last name: *Doña Gracia Salazar de Requena.*

Write the vocabulary presented with this episode on the board to help students create sentences for each important scene where a character is introduced. Direct attention to the *¿Comprendes?* section.

¿Comprendes? Standards: 1.2, 1.3

Resources: Answer Key: Student Edition, p. 84

Focus: Demonstrating comprehension; reviewing the plot

Suggestions: Ask students to read and answer the questions. Then, in pairs have them write their responses and work together to ensure that they both have the correct answers.

Answers:

1. **dinero**
2. **periodista**
3. **nieta; sobrina**
4. **joyas**
5. **accidente de coche**
6. **conoce**
7. **fortuna**

Theme Project

Students can perform Step 3 at this point. (For more information, see p. 270-b.)

Additional Resources

- *¿Eres tú, María?* Video Workbook, Episode 3
- *¿Eres tú, María?* Teacher's Video Guide: Answer Key

6A Review

Review Activities

To talk about things in a bedroom: Ask students to draw the shape of their bedrooms. Have them write the words from this list in the places where the items are located in their rooms. Then have them describe their rooms to their partners, using colors and other adjectives.

To talk about electronic equipment: Ask each student to put this list in the order of each item's importance to them. Have them put the list in the order in which they would like to buy items they do not own.

To indicate location: Have the class divide into pairs and use these phrases to describe the location of objects in their drawings of their rooms. Have students ask their partners to guess the object they are talking about. Model an example for the class: *Está a la derecha de la cama y a la izquierda de las cortinas.*

***Stem-changing verbs:* poder *and* dormir:** Student A will be the "child" asking if he or she can do some activity *(¿Puedo ir al cine?)*. Student B will be the "parent," telling Student A that he or she cannot do the activity, but suggesting another one. Students then reverse roles.

Portfolio

Invite students to review the activities they completed in this chapter, including written reports, posters or other visuals, recordings of oral presentations, or other projects. Have them select one or two items they feel best demonstrate their achievements in Spanish. Include these in students' portfolios. Have them include this with the Chapter Checklist and Self-Assessment Worksheet.

Additional Resources

Student Resources: Realidades para hispanohablantes, p. 228

Teacher Resources:

- Teacher's Resource Book: Situation Cards, p. 90, Clip Art, pp. 92–93
- Assessment Program: Chapter Checklist and Self-Assessment Worksheet, pp. T56–T57

Repaso | | |

Objectives

- Review the vocabulary and grammar
- Demonstrate you can perform the tasks on p. 295

Repaso del capítulo

Vocabulario y gramática

to talk about things in a bedroom

la alfombra	rug
el armario	closet
la cama	bed
la cómoda	dresser
las cortinas	curtains
el cuadro	painting
el despertador	alarm clock
el dormitorio	bedroom
el espejo	mirror
el estante	shelf, bookshelf
la lámpara	lamp
la mesita	night table
la pared	wall

to talk about electronic equipment

el disco compacto	compact disc
el equipo de sonido	sound (stereo) system
el lector DVD	DVD player
el televisor	television set
el video	video

to talk about colors

¿De qué color . . . ?	What color . . . ?
los colores	colors
amarillo, -a	yellow
anaranjado, -a	orange
azul	blue
blanco, -a	white
gris	gray
marrón	brown
morado, -a	purple
negro, -a	black
rojo, -a	red
rosado, -a	pink
verde	green

For *Vocabulario adicional,* see pp. 472–473.

to describe something

bonito, -a	pretty
feo, -a	ugly
grande	large
importante	important
mismo, -a	same
pequeño, -a	small
propio, -a	own

to indicate location

a la derecha (de)	to the right (of)
a la izquierda (de)	to the left (of)

to compare and contrast

mejor(es) que	better than
el / la mejor; los / las mejores	the best
menos . . . que	less, fewer . . . than
peor(es) que	worse than
el / la peor; los / las peores	the worst

other useful words

la cosa	thing
para mí	in my opinion, for me
para ti	in your opinion, for you
la posesión	possession

stem-changing verbs: *dormir* and *poder*

duermo	**dormimos**
duermes	**dormís**
duerme	**duermen**

puedo	**podemos**
puedes	**podéis**
puede	**pueden**

DIFFERENTIATED INSTRUCTION

Heritage Language Learners

Divide up the *Repaso del capítulo* sections and assign one to each heritage student. Ask them to write sentences for some of the words or phrases in the section. Then have students edit each other's work.

Students with Learning Difficulties

Have students check their vocabulary and grammar notebook sections against the list on this page. Have them add whatever they may have missed. Depending on student needs and abilities, an alternative assessment might need to be created or modifications made to the test. Provide students with a practice test so they can become familiar with the format.

Más repaso	GO	realidades.com | print
Instant Check	✔	
Puzzles	✔	
Core WB pp. 110–111		✔
Comm. WB pp. 290, 291–293	✔	✔

Preparación para el examen

On the exam you will be asked to . . .	Here are practice tasks similar to those you will find on the exam . . .	For review go to your print or digital textbook . . .
Interpretive		
 **1 Escuchar** Listen to and understand descriptions of bedrooms	You will be spending a month in a Spanish immersion camp. You go to the camp Web site and click on the audio descriptions of the student rooms. Which items are provided? Which items do you have to bring?	**pp. 272–275** *Vocabulario en contexto* **p. 276** Actividad 5 **p. 277** Actividad 7 **p. 281** Actividad 15
Interpersonal		
 **2 Hablar** Ask and answer questions about your bedroom and that of a classmate	You are asked to survey several classmates about their bedrooms to describe the "typical" teenage room for a class project. Ask a partner at least three questions including: a) information about the color of his or her room; b) whether or not there is a TV or sound system; c) whether he or she is able to study well in the room; d) what is on the walls.	**pp. 272–275** *Vocabulario en contexto* **p. 277** Actividad 7 **p. 281** Actividad 15
Interpretive		
 **3 Leer** Read and understand descriptions of bedroom colors that are associated with particular personality types	Decorators say that the colors of a room's walls should match the personality of the person living in it. Based on the descriptions of a "yellow personality" and a "blue personality," what kind of room best suits you? Why or why not? A las personas más sociables les gustan los dormitorios amarillos. Es el color más popular para los jóvenes a quienes les gusta hablar y hablar por teléfono. ¡Ellos son los mejores amigos! Al contrario, a las personas más serias les gustan los dormitorios azules. Ellos son los mejores estudiantes y los peores cómicos.	**p. 282** Actividad 17 **p. 283** Actividad 19 **pp. 288–289** *Lectura*
Presentational		
 **4 Escribir** Write a short paragraph comparing your bedroom to a friend's bedroom	After surveying classmates, you are asked to write a comparison of your room to that of one of the people you surveyed. Use the information from Task 2 to practice. You might compare: a) the colors; b) the sizes; c) the types of furniture; d) the number of different things on the walls.	**p. 277** Actividad 6 **p. 278** Actividad 10 **p. 291** *Presentación oral*
Cultures		
 **5 Pensar** Demonstrate an understanding of cultural perspectives regarding a celebration	Explain the historical significance of *las luminarias*. What is the history of other decorations used in the celebrations of different cultures?	**p. 290** *La cultura en vivo*

DIFFERENTIATED ASSESSMENT

CORE ASSESSMENT
- **Assessment Program:** Examen del capítulo 6A, pp. 154–161
- **Audio Program DVD:** Cap. 6A, Track 17
- **ExamView:** Chapter Test, Test Banks A and B

ADVANCED/PRE-AP*
- **ExamView: Pre-AP* Test Bank**
- **Pre-AP* Resource Book,** pp. 82–85

STUDENTS NEEDING EXTRA HELP
- **Alternate Assessment Program:** Examen del capítulo 6A
- **Audio Program DVD:** Cap. 6A, Track 17

HERITAGE LEARNERS
- **Assessment Program: Realidades para hispanohablantes:** Examen del capítulo 6A
- **ExamView: Heritage Learner Test Bank**

Performance Tasks

Standards: 5.2

Student Resource: Realidades para hispanohablantes, p. 229

Teacher Resources: Teacher's Resource Book: Audio Script, p. 81; Audio Program DVD: Cap. 6A, Track 16; Answer Key: Student Edition, p. 84

1. Escuchar

Suggestions: Use the audio or read the script.

Script and Answers:

¿Vas a pasar el verano con nosotros? Tenemos los mejores dormitorios. Después de un día de muchas actividades, puedes ver la tele o escuchar música. Hay un televisor y un equipo de sonido en todos los dormitorios.
(TVs and stereos are provided. Other answers will vary.)

2. Hablar

Suggestions: Have students write their questions and the answers to their partner's questions. Let them practice until they can perform without consulting their notes.

Answers will vary.

3. Leer

Suggestions: Point out that students will be asked about two personality types and their associated colors. If they have difficulty reading and understanding the text, refer them to the vocabulary list.

Answers will vary.

4. Escribir

Suggestions: Have students create a graphic organizer before they begin. Refer them to the chart on p. 278 for comparisons.

Answers will vary.

5. Pensar

Suggestions: Have students refer to the appropriate parts of the chapter. Reflect with them on the question.

Answers will vary.

6B ¿Cómo es tu casa?

AT A GLANCE

Objectives

- Listen to conversations about chores and read housing ads
- Talk about household chores and write a description of a house or apartment
- Exchange information while giving advice
- Understand cultural perspectives regarding homes and privacy
- Explain how houses in the Spanish-speaking world compare to those in the United States

Vocabulary

- Houses and apartments
- Rooms
- Household chores

Grammar

- Affirmative *tú* commands
- The present progressive tense

Culture

- *la arpillera,* p. 297
- *el patio,* p. 303
- Percentages of people living in houses and apartments in Caracas, Venezuela, p. 311
- The story of Cinderella, p. 313
- Cultural perspectives on architectural features, p. 314

Recycle ♻

- ***estar***
- ***ir*** + ***a*** + infinitive
- ***-ar, -er,*** and ***-ir*** verbs
- Comparatives
- Affirmative commands in direction lines
- Adjective agreement
- The present tense

RESOURCES

	FOR THE STUDENT	ONLINE	DVD	PRINT	FOR THE TEACHER	ONLINE	PREEXP	DVD	PRINT
Plan					Interactive TE and Resources DVD	•		•	
					Teacher's Resource Book, pp. 110–144	•		•	•
					Pre-AP* Resource Book, 82–85	•		•	•
					Lesson Plans	•			•
					Mapa global interactivo	•			
Introducción PP. **296–297**									
Present	Student Edition, pp. 296–297	•	•	•	Interactive TE and Resources DVD	•		•	
	DK Reference Atlas	•	•		Teacher's Resource Book, pp. 110–111	•		•	•
	Videocultura	•	•		Galería de fotos		•		
	Hispanohablantes WB, pp. 230–231			•	Map Transparencies, 12, 14–18, 20	•	•	•	
Vocabulario en contexto PP. **298–301**									
Present & Practice	Student Edition, pp. 298–301	•	•	•	Interactive TE and Resources DVD	•		•	
	Audio	•	•		Teacher's Resource Book, pp. 112–114, 117, 127–129	•		•	•
	Videohistoria	•	•		Vocabulary Clip Art	•	•	•	•
	Flashcards	•	•		Audio Program	•	•	•	
	Instant Check	•	•		Video Program: Videohistoria	•		•	
	Guided WB, pp. 197–206	•	•	•	Video Program Teacher's Guide: Cap. 6B	•		•	•
	Core WB, pp. 112–115	•	•	•	Vocabulary and Grammar Transparencies, 120–123	•	•	•	
	Comm. WB, pp. 120–123, 126	•	•	•	Answer Keys: Student Edition, pp. 85–86	•	•	•	
	Hispanohablantes WB, pp. 232–233			•	TPR Stories, pp. 77–91	•		•	•
Assess and Remediate					Prueba 6B–1: Assessment Program, pp. 162–163	•		•	•
					Assessment Program para hispanohablantes, pp. 162–163	•		•	•

	FOR THE STUDENT	ONLINE	DVD	PRINT	FOR THE TEACHER	ONLINE	PREEXP	DVD	PRINT
Vocabulario en uso PP. 302–304									
Present & Practice	Student Edition, pp. 302–304	•	•	•	Interactive Whiteboard Vocabulary Activities	•		•	
	Instant Check	•			Interactive TE and Resources DVD	•		•	
	Comm. WB, p. 123	•	•	•	Teacher's Resource Book, pp. 113–114, 120–121	•		•	•
	Hispanohablantes WB, pp. 234–235			•	Communicative Pair Activities, pp. 120–121	•		•	•
	Communicative Pair Activities	•			Audio Program	•	•	•	
					Videomodelos	•		•	
					Answer Keys: Student Edition, pp. 86–88	•	•	•	•
Assess and Remediate					Prueba 6B–2 with Study Plan	•			
					Prueba 6B–2: Assessment Program, pp. 164–165	•		•	•
					Assessment Program para hispanohablantes, pp. 164–165	•		•	•
Gramática PP. 305–311									
Present & Practice	Student Edition, pp. 305–311	•	•	•	Interactive Whiteboard Grammar Activities	•		•	
	Instant Check	•			Interactive TE and Resources DVD	•		•	
	Animated Verbs	•			Teacher's Resource Book, pp. 112, 114–115, 117–118, 122–123	•		•	•
	Tutorial Video: Grammar	•			Communicative Pair Activities, pp. 122–123	•		•	•
	Canción de hip hop	•			Audio Program	•	•	•	
	Guided WB, pp. 207–210	•	•	•	Videomodelos	•		•	
	Core WB, pp. 116–118	•	•	•	Video Program: GramActiva	•	•	•	
	Comm. WB, pp. 124–125, 127–128, 294	•	•	•	Vocabulary and Grammar Transparencies, 124–127	•	•	•	
	Hispanohablantes WB, pp. 236–241			•	Answer Keys: Student Edition, pp. 88–91	•	•	•	
	Communicative Pair Activities	•							
Assess and Remediate					Pruebas 6B–3 and 6B–4 with Study Plans	•			
					Pruebas 6B–3, 6B–4: Assessment Program, pp. 166, 167	•		•	•
					Assessment Program para hispanohablantes, pp. 166, 167	•		•	•
¡Adelante! PP. 312–317									
Application	Student Edition, pp. 312–317	•	•	•	Interactive TE and Resources DVD	•		•	
	Online Cultural Reading	•			Teacher's Resource Book, pp. 118–119	•		•	•
	Guided WB, pp. 211–212	•	•	•	Video Program: Videomisterio ¿Eres tú, María?	•		•	
	Comm. WB, pp. 129, 295	•	•	•	Video Program Teacher's Guide: Cap. 6B	•		•	
	Hispanohablantes WB, pp. 242–247			•	Videomisterio Quiz		•		
	¿Eres tú, María? Video WB, pp. 27–33	•	•	•	Answer Keys: Student Edition, p. 92	•	•	•	
Repaso del capítulo PP. 318–319									
Review	Student Edition, pp. 318–319	•	•	•	Interactive TE and Resources DVD	•		•	
	Online Puzzles and Games	•			Teacher's Resource Book, pp. 115, 124, 127–129	•		•	•
	Core WB, pp. 119–120	•	•	•	Audio Program	•	•	•	
	Comm. WB, pp. 296–299	•	•	•	Answer Keys: Student Edition, p. 92	•	•	•	
	Hispanohablantes WB, pp. 248–249			•					
	Instant Check	•							
Chapter Assessment									
Assess					Examen del capítulo 6B	•		•	•
					Assessment Program, pp. 168–174	•		•	•
					Alternate Assessment Program, pp. 63–68	•		•	•
					Assessment Program para hispanohablantes, pp. 168–174	•		•	•
					Audio Program, Cap. 6B, Examen	•		•	
					ExamView: Test Banks A and B questions only online	•		•	
					Heritage Learner Test Bank	•		•	
					Pre-AP* Test Bank	•		•	

REGULAR SCHEDULE (50 MINUTES)

DAY	Warm-up / Assess	Preview / Present / Practice / Communicate	Wrap-up / Homework Options
1	**Warm-up** (10 min.) • Return Examen del capítulo 6A	**Chapter Opener** (5 min.) • Objectives • Arte y cultura **Vocabulario en contexto** (30 min.) • Presentation: Vocabulario en contexto • Actividades 1, 2	**Wrap-up and Homework Options** (5 min.) • Core Practice 6B-1, 6B-2
2	**Warm-up** (5 min.) • Homework check	**Vocabulario en contexto** (40 min.) • Presentation: Videohistoria *Los quehaceres de Elena* • View: Videohistoria • Video Activities 1, 2, 3, 4 • Actividad 3	**Wrap-up and Homework Options** (5 min.) • Core Practice 6B-3, 6B-4 • Prueba 6B-1: Vocabulary recognition
3	**Warm-up** (10 min.) • Actividad 7 • Homework check ✔**Formative Assessment** (10 min.) • Prueba 6B-1: Vocabulary recognition	**Vocabulario en uso** (25 min.) • Interactive Whiteboard Vocabulary Activities • Actividades 4, 5, 6 • Fondo cultural • Audio Activities 5, 6	**Wrap-up and Homework Options** (5 min.) • Writing Activity 10 • Actividad 10
4	**Warm-up** (5 min.) • Homework check	**Gramática y vocabulario en uso** (40 min.) • Actividades 8, 9, 10 • Communicative Pair Activity • Presentation: Affirmative ***tú*** commands • View: GramActiva video • Interactive Whiteboard Grammar Activities • Actividades 11, 14, 15	**Wrap-up and Homework Options** (5 min.) • Core Practice 6B-5 • Actividad 13 • Prueba 6B-2 with Study Plan: Vocabulary production
5	**Warm-up** (10 min.) • Actividad 12 • Homework check ✔**Formative Assessment** (10 min.) • Prueba 6B-2 with Study Plan: Vocabulary production	**Gramática y vocabulario en uso** (25 min.) • Audio Activity 7 • Exploración del lenguaje • Presentation: The present progressive tense • View: GramActiva video • Interactive Whiteboard Grammar Activities • Actividades 16, 17, 18	**Wrap-up and Homework Options** (5 min.) • Writing Activities 11, 12, 13 • Actividades 21, 22 • Prueba 6B-3 with Study Plan: Affirmative ***tú*** commands
6	**Warm-up** (5 min.) • Homework check ✔**Formative Assessment** (10 min.) • Prueba 6B-3 with Study Plan: Affirmative ***tú*** commands	**Gramática y vocabulario en uso** (30 min.) • Actividades 19, 20 • Audio Activities 8, 9 • Communicative Pair Activity • Pronunciación	**Wrap-up and Homework Options** (5 min.) • Core Practice 6B-6, 6B-7 • Prueba 6B-4 with Study Plan: The present progressive tense
7	**Warm-up** (10 min.) • El español en el mundo del trabajo • Homework check ✔**Formative Assessment** (10 min.) • Prueba 6B-4 with Study Plan: The present progressive tense	**¡Adelante!** (25 min.) • Lectura • ¿Comprendes? • Fondo cultural • Presentación escrita: Steps 1, 5	**Wrap-up and Homework Options** (5 min.) • Presentación escrita: Step 2
8	**Warm-up** (5 min.) • Homework check	**¡Adelante!** (40 min.) • Presentación escrita: Step 3 • Perspectivas del mundo hispano	**Wrap-up and Homework Options** (5 min.) • Presentación escrita: Step 4 • Instant Check
9	**Warm-up** (5 min.) • Homework check	**¡Adelante!** (20 min.) • Videomisterio: *¿Eres tú, María?*, Episodio 4 **Repaso del capítulo** (20 min.) • Vocabulario y gramática • Preparación para el examen 1, 2, 3, 4, 5	**Wrap-up and Homework Options** (5 min.) • Core Practice 6B-8, 6B-9 • Instant Check • Examen del capítulo 6B
10	**Warm-up** (10 min.) • Homework check ✔**Summative Assessment** (40 min.) • Examen del capítulo 6B		

BLOCK SCHEDULE (90 MINUTES)

DAY	Warm-up / Assess	Preview / Present / Practice / Communicate	Wrap-up / Homework Options
1	**Warm-up** (10 min.) • Return Examen del capítulo 6A	**Chapter Opener** (5 min.) • Objectives • Arte y cultura **Vocabulario en contexto** (60 min.) • Presentation: Vocabulario en contexto • Actividades 1, 2 • Presentation: Videohistoria *Los quehaceres de Elena* • View: Videohistoria • Video Activities 1, 2, 3, 4 • Actividad 3 **Vocabulario en uso** (10 min.) • Interactive Whiteboard Vocabulary Activities • Actividades 4, 5, 6	**Wrap-up and Homework Options** (5 min.) • Core Practice 6B-1, 6B-2, 6B-3, 6B-4 • Prueba 6B-1: Vocabulary recognition
2	**Warm-up** (10 min.) • Homework check ✓**Formative Assessment** (10 min.) • Prueba 6B-1: Vocabulary recognition	**Gramática y vocabulario en uso** (65 min.) • Actividades 7, 8, 9, 10 • Fondo cultural • Audio Activities 5, 6 • Communicative Pair Activity • Presentation: Affirmative ***tú*** commands • View: GramActiva video • Interactive Whiteboard Grammar Activities • Actividades 11, 12	**Wrap-up and Homework Options** (5 min.) • Core Practice 6B-5 • Writing Activity 10 • Actividad 13 • Prueba 6B-2 with Study Plan: Vocabulary production
3	**Warm-up** (5 min.) • Audio Activity 7 • Homework check ✓**Formative Assessment** (10 min.) • Prueba 6B-2 with Study Plan: Vocabulary production	**Gramática y vocabulario en uso** (70 min.) • Actividades 14, 15 • Exploración del lenguaje • Audio Activity 7 • Presentation: The present progressive tense • View: GramActiva video • Interactive Whiteboard Grammar Activities • Actividades 16, 17, 18, 19, 20 • Audio Activities 8, 9 • Communicative Activity	**Wrap-up and Homework Options** (5 min.) • Core Practice 6B-6, 6B-7 • Writing Activities 11, 12, 13 • Pruebas 6B-3, 6B-4 with Study Plans: Affirmative ***tú*** commands, The present progressive tense
4	**Warm-up** (10 min.) • Actividad 16 • Homework check • El español en el mundo del trabajo ✓**Formative Assessment** (15 min.) • Pruebas 6B-3, 6B-4 with Study Plans: Affirmative ***tú*** commands, The present progressive tense	**Gramática y vocabulario en uso** (30 min.) • Pronunciación • Actividades 21, 22 **¡Adelante!** (30 min.) • Lectura • ¿Comprendes? • Fondo cultural • Presentación escrita: Steps 1, 5	**Wrap-up and Homework Options** (5 min.) • Presentación escrita: Step 2 • Lectura
5	**Warm-up** (5 min.) • Homework check	**¡Adelante!** (45 min.) • Presentación escrita: Step 3 • Perspectivas del mundo hispano **Repaso del capítulo** (35 min.) • Vocabulario y gramática • Preparación para el examen 1, 2, 3, 4, 5	**Wrap-up and Homework Options** (5 min.) • Presentación escrita: Step 4 • Core Practice 6B-8, 6B-9 • Instant Check • Examen del capítulo 6B
6	**Warm-up** (15 min.) • Homework check • Situation Cards **Repaso del capítulo** (10 min.) • Communicative Pair Activities ✓**Summative Assessment** (40 min.) • Examen del capítulo 6B	**¡Adelante!** (20 min.) • Videomisterio: *¿Eres tú, María?,* Episodio 4	**Wrap-up and Homework Options** (5 min.) • Videomisterio

Standards for *Capítulo* 6B

- To achieve the goals of the Standards, students will:

Communication

1.1 Interpersonal
- Talk about the locations of rooms in a house
- Talk about furniture found in homes
- Talk about household chores
- Give advice to another person

1.2 Interpretive
- Read and listen to information about rooms in a house
- Read and listen to information about household chores
- Read a picture-based story
- Listen to and watch a video about household chores
- Read an advertisement for an English language school
- Read a letter asking for personal advice
- Read a real estate advertisement
- Read about housing statistics in Venezuela
- Listen to and watch a video about household chores

1.3 Presentational
- Present information about household chores
- Present information about rooms in a house
- Write a letter giving advice
- Present information about housing in Venezuela

Culture

2.1 Practices and Perspectives
- Describe how architecture design promotes privacy in Spanish-speaking countries

2.2 Products and Perspectives
- Describe ***la arpillera*** patchwork appliqué in Chile
- Describe ***patios*** in Spain and the Americas
- Explain the use of home features such as patios

Connections

3.1 Cross-curricular
- Reinforce graphing and math skills

Comparisons

4.1 Language
- Talk about new vocabulary through the recognition of cognates
- Explain the use of ***tú*** commands
- Compare nouns formed from verbs as their roots
- Explain the progressive tense
- Explain the pronunciation of ***n*** and ***ñ***

4.2 Culture
- Compare crafts from different regions
- Compare idioms for names of house sections
- Compare types of patios
- Compare versions of "Cinderella" tales

Communities

5.1 Beyond the School
- Identify local increase in Spanish-language advertising

5.2 Lifelong Learner
- View a video mystery series

Capítulo

6B ¿Cómo es tu casa?

▾ Chapter Objectives

Communication

By the end of this chapter you will be able to:
- Listen to conversations about chores and read housing ads
- Talk about household chores and write a description of a house or apartment
- Exchange information while giving advice

Culture

You will also be able to:
- Understand cultural perspectives regarding homes and privacy
- Explain how houses in the Spanish-speaking world compare to those in the United States

You will demonstrate what you know and can do:
- Presentación escrita, p. 315
- Preparación para el examen, p. 319

You will use:

Vocabulary
- Houses and apartments
- Rooms
- Household chores

Grammar
- Affirmative *tú* commands
- The present progressive tense

Exploración del mundo hispano

Country Connection
Houses and Household Chores

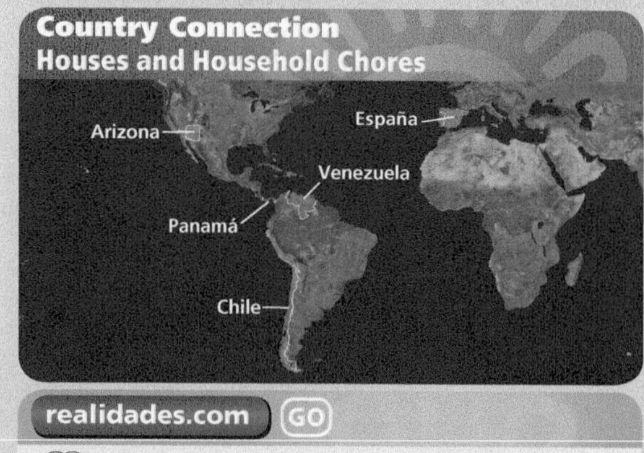

realidades.com GO

 Reference Atlas

 *Videocultura y actividad*

 *Mapa global interactivo*

Una casa en Tenerife, Islas Canarias, España

ENRICH YOUR TEACHING

Using Backward Design

Have students preview the sample performance tasks on *Preparación para el examen*, p. 319, and connect them to the Chapter Objectives. Explain to students that by completing the sample tasks they can self-assess their learning progress.

Mapa global interactivo

Download the *Mapa global interactivo* files for Chapter 6B and preview the activities. In Activity 1, you look at a small village in Chile. In Activity 2, you visit Seville, Spain, and in Activity 3 you compare neighborhoods in Caracas, Venezuela.

Arte y cultura | Chile

La arpillera is a popular textile folk art of rough patchwork appliqués created by women in Chile. Done in brilliant colors, the themes show the story of daily life, traditions, and values in the country.

- What other types of crafts have you seen that portray life in a region or country?

Arpillera de Chile ▶

PresentationExpress™
See pp. 296a–296b

Chapter Opener

Core Instruction

Resources: Map Transparencies 12, 14–18, 20

Suggestions: Introduce students to the chapter theme and review the objectives. Brainstorm a list of chores students must do in their homes. Point out to students that they will learn about cultural differences related to housing. The *Videohistoria* will present a comical episode about a sister who gets her little brother to do her household chores. And since students will be learning about chores, they'll learn how to give orders and tell what they're doing.

Videocultura View *La casa* with the class to learn how people in various Spanish-speaking countries live.

Arte y cultura

Standards: 2.2, 4.1

Suggestions: Point out that crafts are often a reflection of a country and its history. ***Arpilleras,*** named for their burlap backing, were first made as folk art by Chilean women to show the difficult conditions in which they lived. Wives of political prisoners or mothers who were trying to feed their families made and sold ***arpilleras.*** In addition to providing a small income, these bright designs were banners of hope.

Answers will vary but may include murals, primitive paintings, quilts, collages, and so forth.

Mapa global interactivo, Actividad 1 Look at a small village such as the ones on the *arpilleras* of Chile.

Teaching with Photos

Have students compare homes in their community with the home pictured. Ask: How is this home similar to homes you know? How is it different?

DIFFERENTIATED INSTRUCTION

Digital resources such as the ***Interactive Whiteboard*** activity banks, ***Videomodelos***, additional ***Online Activities, Study Plans***, automatically graded ***Leveled Workbook***, animated ***Grammar Tutorials, Flashcards***, and ***Vocabulary and Grammar Videos*** will help you reach students of different ability levels and learning styles.

STUDENTS NEEDING EXTRA HELP

Guided Practice Activities
- Flashcards, pp. 197–202
- Vocabulary Check, pp. 203–206
- Grammar Support, pp. 207–210

HERITAGE LEARNERS

Realidades para hispanohablantes
- Chapter Opener, pp. 230–231
- A primera vista, p. 232
- Videohistoria, p. 233
- Manos a la obra, pp. 234–241
- ¡Adelante!, pp. 242–247
- Repaso del capítulo, pp. 248–249

ADVANCED/PRE-AP*

Pre-AP* Resource Book,
- pp. 82–85

Communications Workbook
- Integrated Performance Assessment, p. 296

Vocabulario en contexto

Core Instruction

Standards: 1.2, 4.1

Resources: Teacher's Resource Book: Input Script, p. 112, Clip Art, pp. 127–129, Audio Script, p. 113; Voc. and Gram. Transparencies 120–121; TPR Stories Book, pp. 77–91; Audio Program DVD: Cap. 6B, Tracks 1–2

Focus: Presenting visualized vocabulary for rooms in a house and household chores; presenting verbs that tell someone to do something

Suggestions: Use the story in *TPR Stories Book* to present the new vocabulary and grammar or use the *Input Script* from the *Teacher's Resource Book.*

Present the vocabulary in three sets: the structure of a house, the rooms in a house, and household chores (including ***dar, lavar, poner***). Say each word on the transparencies, but wait to point to each picture until students point to the correct picture in the book. Have volunteers come up and point to pictures on the transparencies after you describe the picture (say who is in the room, what chore you are going to do, etc.).

Ask questions that require limited verbal response, such as: *¿Generalmente, la sala está en la planta baja? ¿Comes el desayuno en la cocina?*

Block Schedule

Create a large graphic organizer on the board with three columns labeled basement, ground floor, and upper floor. Have students come up and write under the headings one or two rooms that would logically be found on each floor. Write the names for furniture that they know on adhesive paper or on index cards. Place these on a table close to the board. Have volunteers place them under the appropriate rooms. Use tape to affix index cards to the board.

Vocabulario en contexto

Objectives

Read, listen to, and understand information about
- rooms in a house
- household chores
- how to tell someone to do something

la escalera

el despacho

el segundo piso

el primer piso

el baño

el garaje

la planta baja*

el comedor

la cocina

la sala

el sótano

el patio

*In most countries, Spanish speakers call the ground floor in a multi-story building *la planta baja,* the second floor *el primer piso,* the third floor *el segundo piso,* the fourth floor *el tercer piso,* and so on.

Se vende.
Casa particular de dos pisos y sótano. Sala grande, cocina moderna, comedor, despacho, 2 baños, 3 dormitorios, garaje.
Llama al 555-37-89.

—Me gustaría ver esta casa. Es grande y bonita.

—Sí, tiene tres dormitorios y un despacho. También tiene una cocina moderna, **si** te gusta cocinar.

SE VENDE
555-37-89

Más vocabulario

el apartamento	apartment
cerca (de)	close (to), near
lejos (de)	far (from)
bastante	enough, rather

DIFFERENTIATED INSTRUCTION

Heritage Language Learners

Have students pretend they are real estate agents. Have them create a flyer for a mansion they are selling. Encourage them to describe outrageous houses. After correcting the flyers, discuss any grammar and spelling concerns and have them make revisions as needed. Post the flyers and ask students to decide which house they would like to buy.

lavar los platos sucios

poner la mesa

pasar la aspiradora

dar de comer al perro

lavar la ropa

sacar la basura

cocinar

hacer la cama

arreglar el cuarto

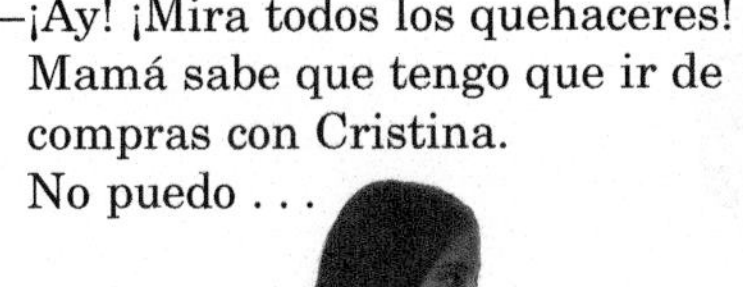

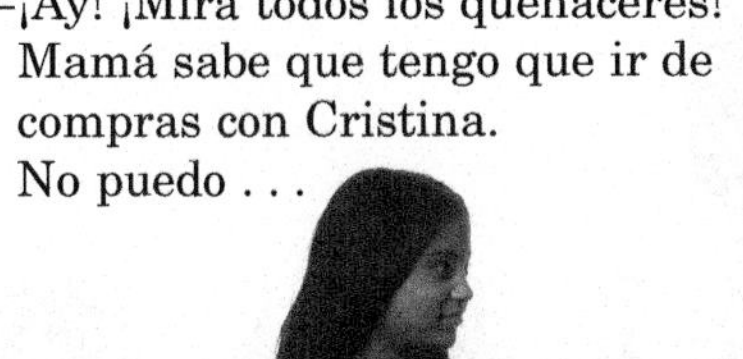

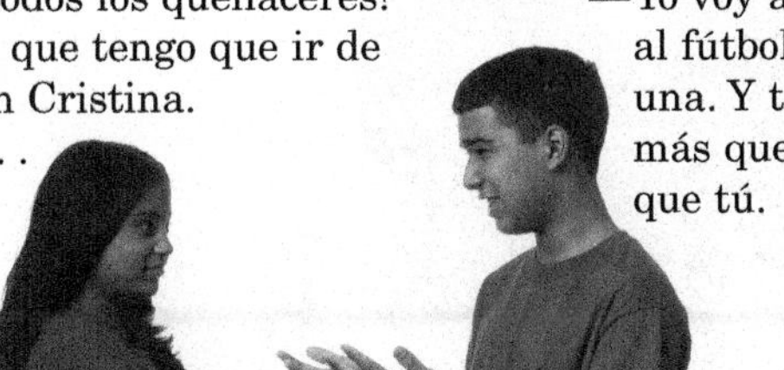

—¡Ay! ¡Mira todos los quehaceres! Mamá sabe que tengo que ir de compras con Cristina. No puedo . . .

—Yo voy a jugar al fútbol a la una. Y tengo más quehaceres que tú.

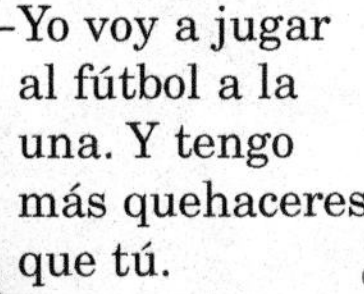

cortar el césped

lavar el coche

quitar el polvo

limpiar el baño

1 La casa de Elena

Escuchar

Escucha a Elena describir su casa. Señala cada cuarto que describe.

2 ¿Es lógico o no?

Escuchar

Escucha cada frase. Si es lógica, haz el gesto del pulgar hacia arriba *("thumbs-up" sign)*. Si no es lógica, haz el gesto del pulgar hacia abajo *("thumbs-down" sign)*.

Más práctica GO

realidades.com | print

Instant Check	✔	
Guided WB pp. 197–202	✔	✔
Core WB pp. 112–113	✔	✔
Comm. WB p. 126	✔	✔
***Hispanohablantes* WB** p. 232		✔

ENRICH YOUR TEACHING

Teacher-to-Teacher

Have groups draw floor plans on butcher paper. Have them draw or glue magazine photos on index cards to represent the chores and write sentences on the cards such as: *Tengo que dar de comer al perro.* Students select a card, read the sentence aloud, and place it in a room where the chore would be done.

21st Century Skills

Communication Have students use the announcement on page 298 as a model to create a For Sale ad for their own homes. Their ads should include information about the general layout of the house, number of rooms, and a contact number. After, have them choose one of the ads, and recreate the dialogue between a potential buyer and a real estate agent, who will try to sell the house to the buyer.

1 Standards: 1.2

Resources: Teacher's Resource Book: Audio Script, p. 113; Audio Program DVD: Cap. 6B, Track 3; Answer Keys: Student Edition, p. 85

Focus: Listening comprehension about chores and rooms in a house

Suggestions: Play the audio or read the script. Allow students to listen more than once. Pause to monitor students, making sure they are identifying the correct rooms.

Script and Answers:

1. **Mi casa tiene una cocina muy moderna.** *(la cocina)*
2. **El comedor está al lado de la cocina.** *(el comedor, la cocina)*
3. **El televisor está en la sala.** *(la sala)*
4. **Hay un baño en la planta baja.** *(el baño)*
5. **A veces mi mamá trabaja en casa en el despacho.** *(el despacho)*
6. **Tengo que poner la mesa en el comedor.** *(el comedor)*
7. **Mi dormitorio está en el primer piso.** *(el dormitorio)*
8. **No me gusta limpiar el sótano.** *(el sótano)*

BELLRINGER REVIEW

Have students say sentences about things they like to do on the weekends. Write a phrase like "*Los fines de semana me gusta* ________" on the board.

2 Standards: 1.2

Resources: Teacher's Resource Book: Audio Script, p. 113; Audio Program DVD: Cap. 6B, Track 4; Answer Keys: Student Edition, p. 85

Focus: Listening comprehension

Suggestions: Before doing the activity, have students decide which chores on p. 299 go with which rooms on p. 298. Use the audio or read the script aloud.

Script and Answers:

1. **Me gusta dormir en el comedor.** *(down)*
2. **Hago la cama en mi dormitorio.** *(up)*
3. **Paso la aspiradora en la sala.** *(up)*
4. **Lavo los platos sucios en el baño.** *(down)*
5. **Doy de comer al perro en la cocina.** *(up)*
6. **Tengo que cortar el césped en el garaje.** *(down)*
7. **Comemos la cena en el baño.** *(down)*
8. **Saco la basura en el garaje.** *(up)*

6B Language Input

Videohistoria

Core Instruction

Standards: 1.2

Resources: Voc. and Gram. Transparencies 122–123; Audio Program DVD: Cap. 6B, Track 5

Focus: Reading comprehension of contextualized vocabulary about chores

Suggestions:

Pre-reading: Using the transparencies, go panel by panel and ask students to predict the outcome. Direct students' attention to the Strategy and have them determine which chores Elena has to complete. Ask them to guess why Jorgito is in trouble.

Reading: Read the captions with students or use the audio. Using the transparencies and non-verbal clues, help students understand the new words in blue type. Point out the different forms of the verb ***dar*** in panels 3 and 4. Ask students the comprehension questions found on the transparencies.

Post-reading: Complete *Actividad* 3 to check comprehension.

Video

Core Instruction

Standards: 1.2

Resources: Teacher's Resource Book: Video Script, p. 117; Video Program: Cap. 6B; Video Program Teacher's Guide: Cap. 6B

Focus: Listening comprehension of contextualized vocabulary about chores

Suggestions:

Pre-viewing: Review the *Videohistoria* reading, and have students make a list of key ideas. Play an excerpt of the video with the sound down, and ask students to tell what panel of the *Videohistoria* it corresponds to.

Viewing: Show the video without pausing, then go back and show it again, pausing along the way to check for comprehension of new vocabulary. Ask students to discuss the bargaining between Elena and Jorgito. Is this something they do with their siblings?

Post-viewing: Complete the Video Activities in the *Communication Workbook.*

Los quehaceres de Elena

Elena no quiere hacer sus quehaceres. ¿Qué hace ella?

Strategy

Using language knowledge
You've just learned the infinitives for various household chores. Using what you know, what are the four activities that Elena tells Jorgito to do in Panel 5?

1

Elena: ¡Hola! Bienvenidos a mi casa. **Vivo** en el número 12 de la calle Apodaca. Vamos a entrar. Mi casa es su casa.

5

Jorgito: **¿Cuáles** son los quehaceres que necesito hacer?

Elena: **Pon** la mesa, lava los platos sucios en la cocina, **haz** la cama en mi dormitorio y da de comer al perro.

6

Mamá: Elena, ¡qué trabajadora eres!

Papá: ¡Cómo ayudas en casa! Das de comer al perro, lavas los platos, **pones** la mesa . . .

Elena: Ah, . . . **¿Recibo** mi dinero?

Mamá: **Un momento.** ¿Tu dormitorio está **limpio?**

7

Mamá: ¡Jorgito! ¡Qué perezoso eres! **¿Qué estás haciendo?**

Jorgito: Pero, . . . pero, . . .

Papá: Ni pero ni nada. ¡Jorgito, a tu dormitorio! Vamos a ver . . .

DIFFERENTIATED INSTRUCTION

Heritage Language Learners

Have students write a short paragraph about who among their siblings has household chores and who does the most work. They can include ways that family members try to get out of doing chores. When necessary, talk to students on an individual basis about spelling or grammatical errors they made in writing their paragraphs.

Students with Special Needs

Have students look at the photos and identify chores that need to be done. Highlight key words and phrases for them.

Elena: ¡Ay, no! Veo que tengo más quehaceres. Siempre lavo los platos sucios y **pongo** la mesa para la cena. ¡Y ahora necesito hacer más trabajo!

Elena: ¿Me **ayudas** con los quehaceres?

Jorgito: Quiero **dinero.**

Elena: No te **doy** dinero, pero puedes escuchar discos compactos en mi dormitorio.

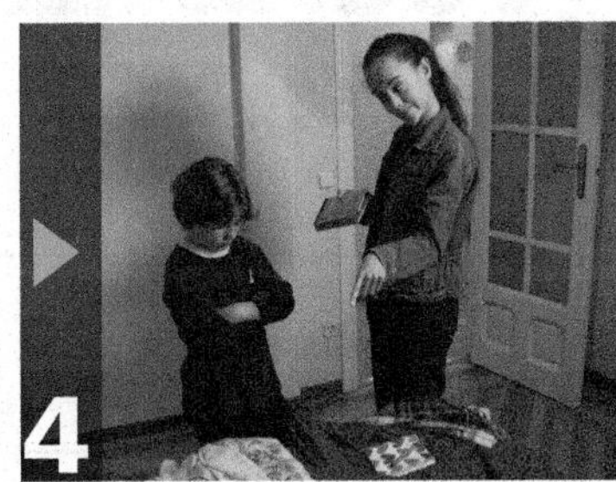

Jorgito: A ver. Si hago unos de los quehaceres, me **das** los discos y escucho música por una hora.

Elena: Media hora.

Jorgito: Cuarenta y cinco minutos.

Elena: Está bien.

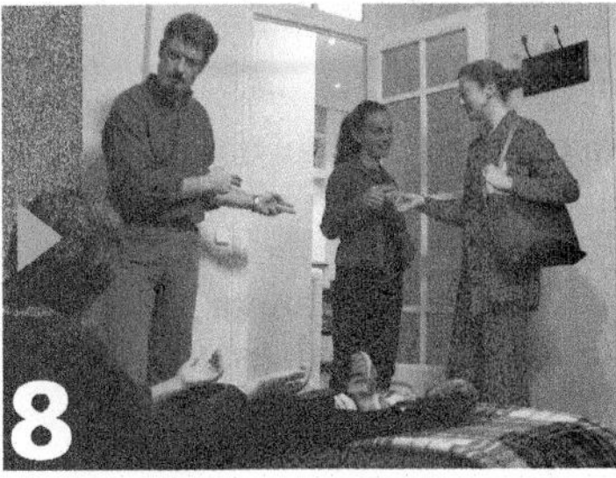

Mamá: Elena, tu dinero.

Elena: Gracias, mamá.

Papá: Jorgito, ¿cómo puedes vivir así? Tienes que arreglar tu cuarto, hijo: haz la cama, quita el polvo, pasa la aspiradora . . .

Jorgito: Pero, Elena . . .

Elena: ¡Adiós! ¡Voy al cine!

3 ¿Comprendes?

Escribir • Hablar

Lee las frases y escribe *cierta* si la frase es correcta o *falsa* si es incorrecta. Si la frase es incorrecta, escribe una frase nueva con la información correcta.

1. Elena siempre pone la mesa en su casa.
2. Jorgito está contento de escuchar los discos compactos.
3. Si hace unos de los quehaceres, Jorgito puede escuchar una hora de música.
4. Según los padres, Elena es muy trabajadora.
5. Según los padres, Jorgito es trabajador también.
6. Ahora Jorgito tiene mucho que hacer en su dormitorio.

Más práctica GO

realidades.com | print		
Instant Check	✔	
Guided WB pp. 203–206	✔	✔
Core WB pp. 114–115	✔	✔
Comm. WB pp. 120–122, 123	✔	✔
***Hispanohablantes* WB** p. 233		✔

3 Standards: 1.2, 1.3

Resources: Answer Keys: Student Edition, p. 86

Focus: Verifying understanding of the *Videohistoria*

Suggestions: Have students scan each sentence for key words that will help them understand the statement. When reviewing, ask that students point out where they found the information for the answer.

Answers:
1. **cierta**
2. **cierta**
3. **falsa: Si hace unos de los quehaceres, Jorgito puede escuchar cuarenta y cinco minutos de música.**
4. **cierta**
5. **falsa: Según los padres, Jorgito es perezoso.**
6. **cierta**

Pre-AP* Support

- **Learning Objective:** Presentational Writing and Speaking
- **Activity:** As a post-viewing activity, have teams of students rewrite the third frame of the scene, imagining that Jorgito and Elena agree on a different compensation for doing the chores. Then have them act out their new version of the fourth and fifth frames of the scene, changing the chores Jorgito must do.
- ***Pre-AP* Resource Book:*** Comprehensive guide to Pre-AP* vocabulary skill development, pp. 51–57

Additional Resources

- Communication Wbk.: Audio Act. 5, p. 123
- Teacher's Resource Book: Audio Script, p. 114
- Audio Program DVD: Cap. 6B, Track 7

ENRICH YOUR TEACHING

Teacher-to-Teacher

Use the vocabulary on chores to play charades with the students. Write the expressions on index cards, fold them up, and place them in a box. Ask volunteers to come to the front of the room, take a card from the box, and act out the chore. Other students will guess which chore the student is doing. Follow up their guesses with questions such as: *Y en tu casa, ¿quién pone la mesa?*

ASSESSMENT

Quiz: Vocabulary Recognition
- Prueba 6B-1: pp. 162–163

INTERACTIVE WHITEBOARD
Vocabulary Activities 6B

4 Standards: 1.2, 1.3

Resources: Teacher's Resource Book: Audio Script, p. 113; Audio Program DVD: Cap. 6B, Track 6; Answer Keys: Student Edition, p. 86

Focus: Listening comprehension about rooms in a house

Suggestions: Have students brainstorm a list of location words. They should look at each floor as if the side closest to the bottom of the page were the front of the house. Play the audio or read the script aloud.

Script

1. Está en la planta baja, al lado del comedor.
2. Está en el primer piso, a la derecha del baño.
3. Está a la derecha del dormitorio grande en el primer piso.
4. Está en la planta baja, detrás de la sala.
5. El coche está aquí.
6. Está delante del despacho en la planta baja.
7. La ropa sucia está aquí, debajo de la planta baja.
8. Está en la planta baja a la izquierda de la cocina.

Answers:

1. el despacho
2. el dormitorio
3. el baño
4. el comedor
5. el garaje
6. la cocina
7. el sótano
8. la sala

BELLRINGER REVIEW

Use the *Voc. and Gram. Transparencies.* Ask students to name the rooms on the ***planta baja, el primer piso,*** and ***el segundo piso.***

5 Standards: 1.1, 1.2, 1.3

Focus: Using contextualized vocabulary in written and oral formats

Suggestions: Model a true sentence and a false one. Have a volunteer provide correct information for the false statement.

Answers will vary.

Additional Resources

- Teacher's Resource Book: GramActiva BLM, p. 125

Manos a la obra

Vocabulario en uso

Objectives

- Listen to and write descriptions of a house
- Write about and discuss furniture and chores
- Exchange information about homes

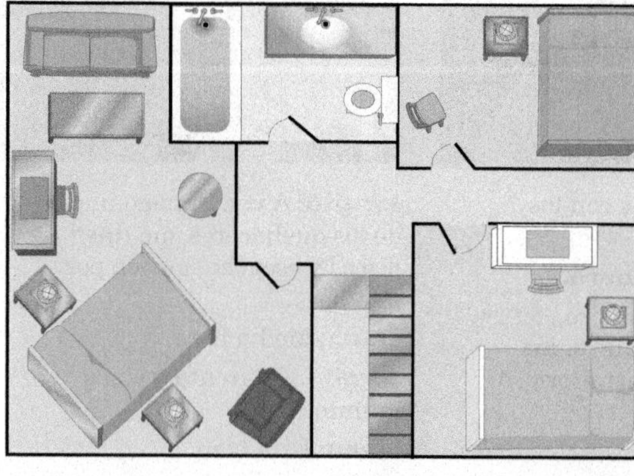

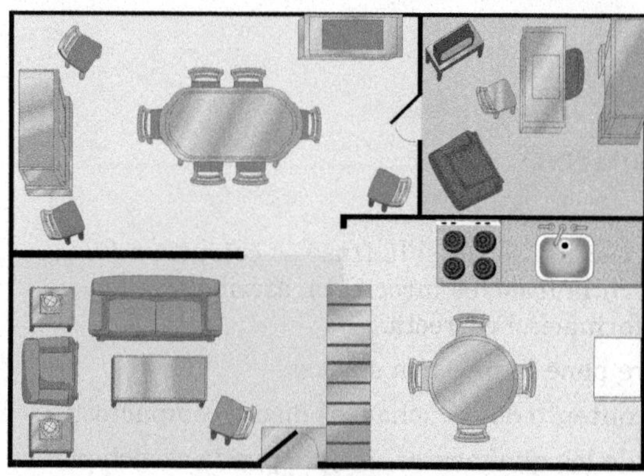

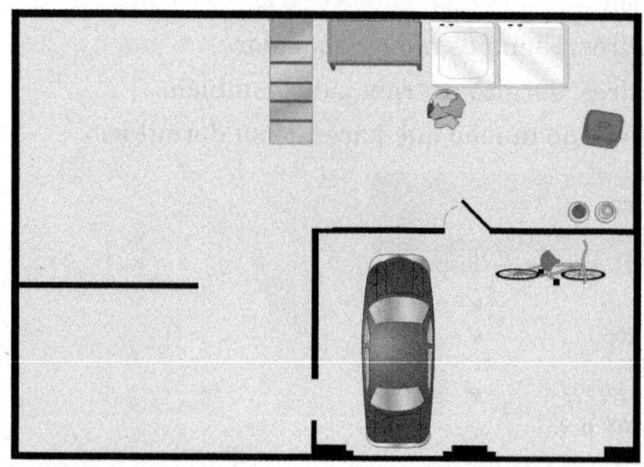

4 La casa de los Ramírez

Escuchar • Escribir

Los Ramírez van a comprar la casa que ves aquí. En una hoja de papel escribe los números del 1 al 8 y escribe el nombre de cada cuarto que describen.

Nota

Primero(a) and *tercero(a)* become *primer* and *tercer* before a masculine singular noun.

- Mi dormitorio está en el **primer** piso.
- Su apartamento está en el **tercer** piso.

5 ¿Cierto o falso?

Escribir • Escuchar • Hablar

Escribe cinco frases para indicar dónde están los cuartos en la casa de los Ramírez. Las frases pueden ser ciertas o falsas. Lee tus frases a otro(a) estudiante, quien va a indicar si son ciertas o falsas. Si son falsas, tiene que dar la información correcta.

Modelo

A —*La sala está en el primer piso.*
B —*Falso. La sala está en la planta baja.*

También se dice . . .

la sala = el salón *(muchos países),* el living *(España)*
el despacho = la oficina *(muchos países)*
el piso = la planta *(muchos países)*
el apartamento = el piso *(España),* el departamento *(muchos países)*

DIFFERENTIATED INSTRUCTION

Students with Learning Difficulties

Some students may have problems with the spatial representation on the activity. Point out that the visual represents three stories in a home.

6 ¿Dónde pongo la silla? |  | 

Hablar

Ayudas a la familia Ramírez a mudarse *(move)* a su nueva casa pero no sabes dónde poner sus cosas. Otro(a) estudiante te va a explicar dónde tienes que poner todo.

> **Nota**
>
> *Poner,* "to put," is also used in the expression *poner la mesa,* "to set the table." It has an irregular *yo* form: *pongo.*
>
> - En la mañana **pongo** la mesa.

Modelo

A —*¿Dónde pongo la silla?*
B —*Vamos a poner la silla en el comedor.*

Estudiante A

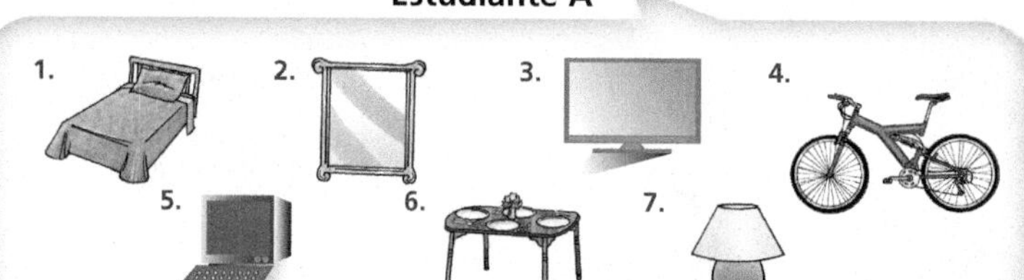

1. 2. 3. 4. 5. 6. 7.

Estudiante B

¡Respuesta personal!

7 ¿En qué cuarto?

Escribir

Ahora los Ramírez están muy contentos en su casa. ¿En qué cuarto hacen los Ramírez estos quehaceres? Escribe las frases.

Modelo
Sacan la basura en el garaje.

1. 
2.
3. 
4. 
5. 
6. 

Fondo Cultural | España

El patio in an apartment building in a large Spanish city is usually just an open area in the center of the building. In southern Spain, however, houses are often built around *patios,* which may have gardens as well as a fountain. The Moors brought this architectural style to Spain, and the Spaniards then carried it over to the Americas.

- How does the Spanish *patio* differ from what a patio is in your community? How is it similar?

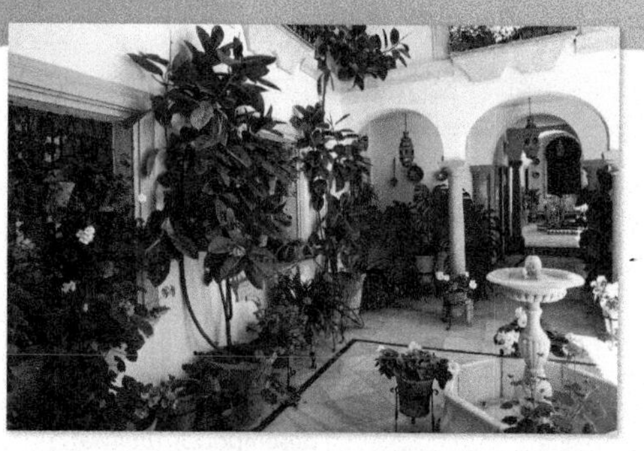

Un patio típico en Córdoba, España

ENRICH YOUR TEACHING

Culture Note

Because the climate of southern Spain is so warm throughout the year, many homes have a patio within the house that is open to the sky. These patios often contain a fountain, small pool, or garden to help cool the home. Usually this is a place for private relaxation, but every May the city of Córdoba has a festival during which each homeowner proudly displays his or her patio. Thousands of flowers and plants are used for decoration. People open their homes for several weeks so friends, neighbors, and tourists can come and enjoy their patios. A prize is awarded to the most beautiful patio.

6 Standards: 1.1

Resources: Answer Keys: Student Edition, p. 87

Focus: Re-entering familiar vocabulary in the context of rooms in a house

Recycle: Furnishings and electronics

Suggestions: Ask volunteers to read the model, and point out the different tenses used in each sentence.

Answers:

Student A
1. **¿Dónde pongo la cama?**
2. **¿Dónde pongo el espejo?**
3. **¿Dónde pongo el televisor?**
4. **¿Dónde pongo la bicicleta?**
5. **¿Dónde pongo la computadora?**
6. **¿Dónde pongo la mesa?**
7. **¿Dónde pongo la lámpara?**

Student B
Answers will vary.

7 Standards: 1.3

Resources: Answer Keys: Student Edition, p. 87

Focus: Practicing new vocabulary for chores and rooms of the house

Suggestions: Have a volunteer read the model, and point out that the verb is in the third person plural form because students are writing about ***los Ramírez,*** the Ramírez family.

Answers:
1. **Ponen la mesa en el comedor.**
2. **Hacen la cama en el dormitorio.**
3. **Lavan los platos sucios en la cocina.**
4. **Lavan la ropa en el sótano.**
5. **Quitan el polvo (de la lámpara) en la sala (el dormitorio, el despacho).**
6. **Pasan la aspiradora en el despacho (la sala, la cocina, el dormitorio).**

Fondo cultural

Standards: 2.2, 4.2

Suggestions: Explain that enclosed patios were often used by the Moors who occupied Spain for over 700 years. The Moors were Muslim and used patios as places for prayer. Have students discuss how they use patios and yards. Ask them to determine historical, cultural, or social variations that would lead to different uses of such areas.

Answers will vary.

Mapa global interactivo, Actividad 2 Visit Seville, Spain and learn about the tradition of *patios* in houses.

8 Standards: 1.1

Resources: Answer Keys: Student Edition, p. 88

Focus: Describing household chores

Suggestions: Point out that the question will use the familiar form of ***tener que*** + an infinitive, but Student B will have to conjugate the verb pictured. Ask volunteers to model a negative response from Student B: *No, no lavo nunca el coche.*

Answers: 1. ¿Tienes que cocinar?; 2. ¿... cortar el césped?; 3. ¿... dar de comer al perro?; 4. ¿... lavar los platos sucios?; 5. ¿... hacer la cama?; 6. ¿... quitar el polvo?; Student B answers will vary; verbs should be in the *yo* form.

9 Standards: 1.1, 1.3

Focus: Writing and speaking about the location of one's home

Recycle: Places in the community

Suggestions: Refer students to the *Más vocabulario*, p. 298. Brainstorm a list of place names to use as a word bank. Have two volunteers read the model and then repeat it, substituting the name of a movie theater in your community.

Answers will vary.

10 Standards: 1.2, 1.3

Focus: Writing and speaking about household chores in a personalized context

Answers will vary but verbs should be in the *yo* form.

Additional Resources

- Communication Wbk.: Audio Act. 6, p. 123
- Teacher's Resource Book: Audio Script, p. 114, Communicative Pair Activity BLM, pp. 120–121
- Audio Program DVD: Cap. 6B, Track 8

ASSESSMENT

Prueba 6B-2 with Study Plan (online only)

Quiz: Vocabulary Production

- Prueba 6B-2: pp. 164–165

8 ¿Cómo ayudas en casa?

Hablar

¿Ayudas mucho en casa? Habla de tus quehaceres con otro(a) estudiante.

Modelo

A —*¿Tienes que lavar el coche?*
B —*Sí, lavo el coche todos los sábados.*

Nota

Dar means "to give" and is used in the expression *dar de comer,* "to feed." It has an irregular *yo* form: *doy.*

- En mi casa **doy** de comer al perro.

Estudiante A

1.  
2. 
3. 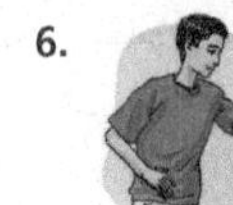
4.
5. 
6. 

Estudiante B

a veces
mucho
todos los días
todos los (sábados)
en el (verano)
los fines de semana
nunca

9 ¿Dónde vives?

Escribir • Hablar

Escribe una lista de cinco lugares en tu comunidad, como la escuela, el centro comercial, la biblioteca, etc. Pregunta a otro(a) estudiante si vive cerca o lejos de estos lugares.

Modelo

El cine Rex
A —*¿Vives cerca del cine Rex?*
B —*Sí, vivo bastante cerca del cine.*
o: —*No, vivo muy lejos.*

También se dice . . .

cocinar = guisar *(España)*
cortar el césped = cortar la hierba, cortar el pasto *(muchos países),* cortar el zacate *(México)*
lavar los platos = fregar los platos *(España)*
quitar el polvo = sacudir los muebles *(México)* desempolvar *(Bolivia)*

10 Y tú, ¿qué dices?

Escribir • Hablar

1. ¿Ayudas mucho o poco en casa? ¿Cuáles son tus quehaceres?
2. ¿Generalmente tu cuarto está sucio o limpio?
3. En tu casa, ¿quién pasa la aspiradora? ¿Quién saca la basura?
4. Para ti, ¿cuáles son los tres peores quehaceres? ¿Y los mejores?
5. Imagina que eres padre o madre. ¿Cuánto dinero recibe tu hijo(a) si hace sus quehaceres?
6. ¿Vives cerca o lejos de tu escuela?

DIFFERENTIATED INSTRUCTION

Advanced Learners/Pre-AP*

Have students model affirmative ***tú*** commands by writing and acting out a dialogue between either teacher and student or brother and sister. Another variation would be a dialogue between parent and son or daughter. In the dialogue, one person should be giving orders, and the other should be responding. Suggest that students write at least five lines. Encourage humor and creativity!

Gramática

▼ Objectives

- Listen to, follow, and write instructions and recommendations
- Read and respond to a letter and a survey
- Explain what has to be done around the house

Affirmative *tú* commands

When you tell friends, family members, or young people to do something, you use an affirmative *tú* command. To give these commands, use the same present-tense forms that you use for *Ud., él, ella.*

Infinitive	*Ud. / él / ella*	Affirmative *tú* commands
hablar	habla	¡Habla!
leer	lee	¡Lee!
escribir	escribe	¡Escribe!

- Certain verbs, like *poner* and *hacer,* have irregular command forms.

Jorgito, ¡**pon** la mesa! Jorgito, ¡**haz** tu cama!

¿Recuerdas?

In the direction lines of many activities, you have already seen many affirmative commands.

- **Habla** con otra persona.
- **Lee** las frases.
- **Escribe** la palabra apropiada.

Más ayuda realidades.com

 **GramActiva Video Tutorial:** Formation of regular *tú* commands

 ***Canción de hip hop:*** *Cenicienta*

 **GramActiva Activity**

11 "Simón dice . . ."

Escuchar • GramActiva

Escucha y sigue *(follow)* las instrucciones de tu profesor(a) o de otro(a) estudiante. Si no dicen *"Simón dice,"* no debes hacer la acción.

12 ¡Habla bien!

Escribir

Un(a) amigo(a) quiere hablar bien el español. ¿Qué recomiendas? Escribe el mandato *(command)* de los siguientes verbos.

Modelo

usar: *usa*
Usa un buen diccionario.

1. estudiar
2. ver
3. escuchar
4. escribir
5. hacer
6. hablar con
7. leer
8. practicar

Instituto de inglés

Aprende con nosotros
¡Cursos de verano!

Nuestro sistema cubre las cuatro habilidades esenciales:
Hablar ✶ *Comprender* ✶ *Leer* ✶ *Escribir*
Grupos reducidos • Cuotas accesibles

Tel/Fax: 212-1234

Gramática

Core Instruction

Standards: 4.1

Resources: Voc. and Gram. Transparency 124; Teacher's Resource Book: Video Script, p. 117; Video Program: Cap. 6B

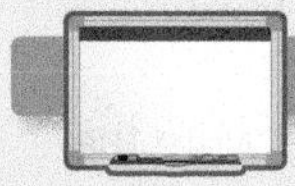
INTERACTIVE WHITEBOARD
Grammar Activities 6B

Suggestions: Direct attention to the *¿Recuerdas?* Ask what form of the verb the words in bold type resemble. Build upon students' knowledge of English grammar to discuss the meanings of these words. Use the transparency to reinforce the affirmative ***tú*** commands. Remind students to use this form only with friends and family. Use the *GramActiva* Video either as an introduction to the structure or as a follow-up.

11 Standards: 1.2

Focus: Listening to affirmative ***tú*** commands and following directions

Recycle: Activities

Suggestions: Prepare a set of commands before beginning the activity. As you give the first command, pantomime the activity.

Script

Simón dice... escribe tu nombre.
Simón dice... baila.
Simón dice... tócate la cabeza.
... toca la silla.

Answers will vary.

12 Standards: 1.2, 1.3

Resources: Answer Keys: Student Edition, p. 88

Focus: Writing affirmative ***tú*** commands

Suggestions: Have students come up with a list of other words that could be used to encourage someone to study and practice speaking a new language.

Answers will vary but will include:

1. **Estudia...**
2. **Ve...**
3. **Escucha...**
4. **Escribe...**
5. **Haz...**
6. **Habla con...**
7. **Lee...**
8. **Practica...**

ENRICH YOUR TEACHING

Teacher-to-Teacher

Ask students if someone could borrow a dollhouse from a younger sibling and bring it to the classroom. Use the dollhouse as a visual aid when practicing vocabulary.

21st Century Skills

Initiative and Self-Direction Remind students that may be having difficulty understading affirmative commands of the digital tools available for grammar review of this point in **realidades.com,** such as the *GramActiva* video, the online tutorial, and the *Canción de hip hop.*

6B Practice and Communicate

13 Standards: 1.2, 1.3

Resources: Answer Keys: Student Edition, p. 89

Focus: Reading comprehension; writing accuracy with ***tú*** commands and vocabulary

Recycle: Vocabulary for food and drink; vocabulary for exercise; adjectives describing feeling

Suggestions: When students write the response, encourage them to use other verbs and recommendations in addition to those in the box.

Answers will vary but should include:

Bebe...	**Haz ejercicio...**
Come...	**Levanta pesas...**
Corre...	**Juega...**
Duerme...	

BELLRINGER REVIEW

Have students list suggestions for how to be healthy, including advice on eating, sleeping, and exercising.

14 Standards: 1.1, 1.3

Resources: Answer Keys: Student Edition, p. 89

Focus: Practicing conversation

Recycle: Vocabulary for food and drink; vocabulary for exercise; adjectives describing feeling

Suggestions: Refer students to the *¿Recuerdas?* and point out that there are two parts to the activity. First, they must identify what is dirty. Then, they must form an affirmative command to tell their sibling to clean the item.

Answers:

1. **La alfombra está sucia. Pasa la aspiradora, por favor.**
2. **El espejo está sucio. Limpia el espejo, por favor.**
3. **El cuarto (dormitorio) está sucio (desordenado). Arregla el cuarto (dormitorio), por favor.**
4. **Las ventanas están sucias. Limpia las ventanas, por favor.**
5. **La ropa está sucia. Lava la ropa, por favor.**
6. **La cocina está sucia. Saca la basura, por favor.**

Block Schedule

Have students work in groups to create their own commercials for a household product, using affirmative ***tú*** commands as well as new vocabulary. Students can make or bring in props for their commercial.

13 ¿Qué debo hacer?

Leer • Escribir

Tu amiga Carmen tiene un problema y te escribe una carta. Lee su carta y escribe tus recomendaciones en otra carta, usando los verbos de la lista.

Modelo

Mi querida Carmen,
Aquí están mis recomendaciones:
Come menos dulces, . . .

¡Hola!

Tengo un problema grande. Quisiera estar mejor de salud. No estoy muy enferma pero tampoco estoy en buena forma. Siempre tengo mucho sueño y poca energía. Si camino a la escuela, estoy muy cansada. Si hago muchos quehaceres por la casa, también estoy cansada. ¡Y no quiero estar cansada! ¿Qué debo hacer?

Tu amiga desesperada,

Carmen

beber	dormir	jugar
comer	hacer ejercicio	¡Respuesta personal!
correr	levantar pesas	

14 Muchos quehaceres

Hablar

Debes hacer muchos quehaceres en casa, pero no quieres. ¡A ver si tu hermanito(a) puede hacer todo! Primero di *(say)* lo que está sucio (o lo que no está limpio). Luego di lo que tiene que hacer.

Modelo

Los platos no están limpios. Lava los platos, por favor.

¿Recuerdas?

Adjectives agree in number and gender with the nouns they modify.

- **La casa está sucia.**
- **Los platos están limpios.**

1. 
2. 
3. 
4.
5. 
6. 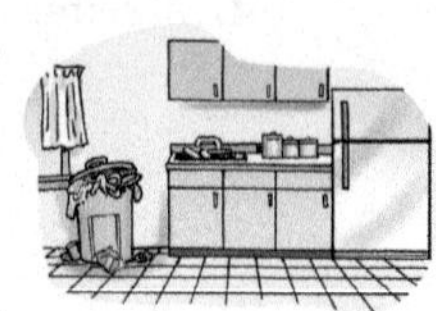

DIFFERENTIATED INSTRUCTION

Students with Learning Difficulties

Have students make a three-column chart to use as a reference. They should put the infinitive in the first column, the present-tense form used for ***Ud., él,*** and ***ella*** in the second column, and the affirmative ***tú*** command in the third column. They can add to the chart and use it as a reference throughout the chapter.

15 ¿Quién hace los quehaceres?

Leer • Escribir • Hablar

Un artículo de la revista española *Muy interesante* explica quién hace la mayoría de *(most of)* los quehaceres de la casa. Estudia las gráficas a la derecha y haz comparaciones entre *(between)* las mujeres y los hombres españoles. Después, explica si las mujeres hacen los siguientes quehaceres mucho más, un poco más o menos que los hombres.

Modelo

lavar los platos
Las mujeres lavan los platos mucho más que los hombres.

1. comprar cosas para la familia cada día
2. preparar la comida y la cena
3. cuidar *(take care of)* el coche
4. cuidar a las personas enfermas de la familia
5. lavar y planchar *(iron)* la ropa
6. ir al banco
7. limpiar la casa

*Together

Exploración del lenguaje

The endings *-dor* and *-dora*

Every day you use appliances and devices such as computers, calculators, and dryers. Many of these English words add the ending *-er* or *-or* to a verb, as in *toast* → *toaster*. Spanish follows a similar pattern. Identify the pattern in **despertador, computadora, calculadora,** and **aspiradora.** Can you guess what the corresponding verbs are and what they mean?

Try it out! Read each statement and decide which appliance is needed.

1. Tengo calor.
2. ¿Dónde está el pan tostado?
3. Mi ropa está sucia.
4. Necesito leche para el cereal.

a. Está en la tostadora.
b. Ponla en la lavadora.
c. Está en el refrigerador.
d. Necesitas el ventilador.

Más práctica GO realidades.com | print

Instant Check	✔	
Guided WB pp. 207–208	✔	✔
Core WB p. 116	✔	✔
Comm. WB pp. 124, 127	✔	✔
***Hispanohablantes* WB** pp. 234–237		✔

ENRICH YOUR TEACHING

Culture Note

Although many Spanish-speaking countries have warm climates, air-conditioning in homes is not as common as in the United States. Many homes have an open floor plan with a central patio and lots of windows and fans to circulate fresh air. Building materials such as adobe and ceramic tiles help keep walls and floors cool in warm weather.

21st Century Skills

Social and Cross-Cultural Skills Using the chart on Activity 15 as a starting point, have students work in small groups to discuss who does the chores mentioned in the chart in their own households. Have students keep track of the results, and compare with the data from Spain. Are there any similarities and differences between the results?

15 Standards: 1.1, 1.2, 1.3

Resources: Voc. and Gram. Transparency 126; Answer Keys: Student Edition, p. 90

Focus: Reading comprehension and writing accuracy with verbs describing household chores

Recycle: Numbers 1–80

Suggestions: Ask students to look at the graphs. They will need to use these comparisons in their answers.

Answers:

1. **Las mujeres compran cosas para la familia mucho más que los hombres.**
2. **Las mujeres preparan la comida y la cena mucho más que los hombres.**
3. **Las mujeres cuidan el coche mucho menos que los hombres.**
4. **Las mujeres cuidan a las personas enfermas de la familia un poco más que los hombres.**
5. **Las mujeres lavan y planchan la ropa mucho más que los hombres.**
6. **Las mujeres van al banco un poco más que los hombres.**
7. **Las mujeres limpian la casa mucho más que los hombres.**

Exploración del lenguaje
Core Instruction

Standards: 4.1

Resources: Answers on Tranparencies, p. 90

Suggestions: Have students brainstorm a list of other English words whose noun form ends in *-er* or *-or* (*teacher, actor, painter, operator, vendor,* etc.). Ask students to match the answers for *Try it out!* at their seats before you review them as a class.

Answers:

1. d; 2. a; 3. b; 4. c

Additional Resources

- Communication Wbk.: Audio Act. 7, p. 124
- Teacher's Resource Book: Audio Script, p. 112
- Audio Program DVD: Cap. 6B, Track 9

ASSESSMENT

Prueba 6B-3 with Study Plan (online only)

Quiz: Affirmative *tú* commands

- Prueba 6B-3: p. 166

Gramática

Core Instruction

Standards: 4.1

Resources: Voc. and Gram. Transparency 125; Teacher's Resource Book: Video Script, p. 118; Video Program: Cap. 6B

INTERACTIVE WHITEBOARD

Grammar Activities 6B

Suggestions: Direct attention to the *¿Recuerdas?* Be sure students understand that the present tense in Spanish already includes the meaning of doing something now. However, the present progressive tense puts stronger emphasis on the fact that the action is taking place as one speaks. Use the transparency to reinforce the forms of the present progressive tense. Use the *GramActiva* Video as an introduction to the structure or as a follow-up after your own grammar explanation.

16 Standards: 1.3

Focus: Using present progressive tense in writing

Recycle: ***-ar, -er,*** and ***-ir*** verbs

Suggestions: Point out that students can make sentences negative by putting ***no*** before the form of ***estar.*** Point out the spelling change in the present participle of ***leer,*** which is noted under the *Gramática* chart.

Answers will vary.

17 Standards: 1.2, 1.3

Resources: Teacher's Resource Book: Audio Script, p. 114; Audio Program DVD: Cap. 6B, Track 10; Answer Keys: Student Edition, p. 90

Focus: Listening comprehension and writing accuracy

Suggestions: Use the audio or read the script aloud. Have students listen to the script once without writing. Encourage students to use the art to help them.

Script and Answers:

—Hijos, ¿están haciendo sus quehaceres?
—Un momento. Estamos jugando videojuegos.
—No puedo. Estoy escribiendo un cuento.
—Lo siento. Estoy comiendo un sándwich.

Gramática

Objectives

- Listen to a conversation about chores
- Talk and write about what people are doing
- Read and respond to a housing ad and a survey

The present progressive tense

When you want to emphasize that an action is happening *right now*, you use the present progressive tense.

Paco está lavando los platos.	*Paco is washing dishes* (now).
Estoy haciendo la cama.	*I'm making the bed* (right now).

To form the present progressive tense, use the present-tense forms of *estar* + the present participle. The present participle is formed by dropping the ending of the infinitive and adding *-ando* for *-ar* verbs or *-iendo* for *-er* and *-ir* verbs.

(yo)	estoy	lavando comiendo escribiendo	(nosotros) (nosotras)	estamos	lavando comiendo escribiendo
(tú)	estás	lavando comiendo escribiendo	(vosotros) (vosotras)	estáis	lavando comiendo escribiendo
Ud. (él) (ella)	está	lavando comiendo escribiendo	Uds. (ellos) (ellas)	están	lavando comiendo escribiendo

Leer has an irregular spelling in the present participle: *leyendo.*

¿Recuerdas?

You use the present tense to talk about an action that regularly takes place, or that is happening now.

- Paco lava los platos.
  Paco ***washes*** *the dishes.*
  OR
  Paco ***is washing*** *the dishes.*

Más ayuda realidades.com

GramActiva **Video**
Tutorial: Formation of the present progressive

GramActiva **Activity**

16 ¿Qué están haciendo ahora?

Escribir

Escribe cinco frases para explicar lo que están haciendo varias personas en tu sala de clases.

Modelo

La profesora está escribiendo algo.

17 Escucha y escribe

Escuchar • Escribir

Estos hermanos tienen muchos quehaceres. Escucha y escribe la pregunta de la madre y las excusas de los hijos.

DIFFERENTIATED INSTRUCTION

Multiple Intelligences

Visual/Spatial: Have students take pictures, or cut out pictures from magazines, of people doing chores or other activities. Have students give a name to each person, and underneath each photo use the present progressive to write what he or she is doing. Display their work for the class to enjoy.

Students with Learning Difficulties

Use index cards as manipulatives to help students practice the present progressive. Make cards with the forms of ***estar*** and the endings ***-ando,*** and ***-iendo*** written on them. Make additional cards showing verbs with their infinitive endings removed. Students can use these cards to practice this new tense.

18 Un momento, por favor |  |

Hablar • Escribir

A veces no podemos hacer los quehaceres porque estamos haciendo otras cosas. Trabaja con otro(a) estudiante para dar un mandato y una excusa.

Modelo

A —*Por favor, da de comer al perro.*
B —*No puedo. Estoy estudiando para un examen.*

Estudiante A

1. 
2.  
3. 
4.
5.
6. 

Estudiante B

Un momento . . .	beber
No puedo . . .	comer
Lo siento . . .	escribir
Me gustaría	escuchar
pero . . .	estudiar
	hablar
	hacer
	jugar
	tocar

¡Respuesta personal!

19 Juego | |

Escribir • Hablar • GramActiva

1. En una hoja de papel *(sheet of paper)*, escribe una frase para explicar lo que está haciendo una persona (usa la forma *tú*). En otra hoja de papel, escribe una frase para explicar lo que están haciendo dos personas (usa la forma *Uds.*).

Modelo

Estás levantando pesas.
Uds. están esquiando.

2. Todas las frases van boca abajo *(face down)* encima de una mesa. Toma una frase. Si la frase usa la forma *tú*, haz la acción solo(a). Si la frase usa la forma *Uds.*, haz la acción con otro(a) estudiante. Los compañeros tienen que adivinar *(guess)* lo que estás (están) haciendo.

20 ¿Qué están haciendo todos? | |

Escribir • Hablar • GramActiva

Haz un dibujo de tres personas que están haciendo diferentes actividades. En otra hoja de papel, escribe dos preguntas sobre lo que está haciendo cada persona. Trabaja en un grupo de tres. Da tu dibujo a los otros estudiantes y lee tus preguntas. Tus compañeros tienen que contestar.

Modelo

A —*¿Qué está haciendo la chica?*
B/C —*Está lavando los platos sucios.*

Más práctica GO

realidades.com | print

Instant Check	✔	
Guided WB pp. 209–210	✔	✔
Core WB pp. 117–118	✔	✔
Comm. WB pp. 124–125, 128, 294	✔	✔
***Hispanohablantes* WB** pp. 238–239		✔

ENRICH YOUR TEACHING

Teacher-to-Teacher

Have students prepare a dialogue of a phone call in which a telemarketer is on the line, wishing to speak to anyone available. The person who answers should use the present progressive tense to make excuses for everyone else in the house, saying what they're doing at the moment. Ask students to add details, such as where they are in the house, or who they're with. If possible, have students record their conversations to play for the class.

Practice and Communicate 6B

18 Standards: 1.1, 1.3

Resources: Answer Keys: Student Edition, p. 91

Focus: Using ***tú*** commands and present progressive tense in writing and speaking

Recycle: Leisure activities

Suggestions: Remind students to use affirmative ***tú*** commands when they are Student A and the present progressive tense when Student B.

Answers:

Student A: 1. —Por favor, pon la mesa. 2. ..., lava el coche. 3. ..., pasa la aspiradora. 4.—..., haz la cama. 5. —..., saca la basura. 6.—..., corta el césped. Student B: Answers will vary.

19 Standards: 1.1, 1.3

Focus: Using the present progressive tense

Recycle: Leisure activities

Suggestions: Brainstorm activities that students can write on their papers.

Answers will vary.

20 Standards: 1.1, 1.3

Focus: Reading comprehension

Suggestions: Point out that student drawings can be stick drawings and set a time limit for preparing them.

Answers will vary.

Additional Resources

- Communication Wbk.: Audio Act. 8–9, pp. 124–125
- Teacher's Resource Book: Audio Script, p. 115, Communicative Pair Activity BLM, pp. 122–123
- Audio Program DVD: Cap. 6B, Tracks 11–12

ASSESSMENT

Prueba 6B-4 with Study Plan (online only)

Quiz: Present Progressive

- Prueba 6B-4: p. 167

21 Standards: 1.2

Resources: Voc. and Gram. Transparency 127; Answer Keys: Student Edition, p. 91

Focus: Reading comprehension

Recycle: Items found in the home; family members

Suggestions: Have students read silently, then ask volunteers to read the passages aloud. Assign small groups to focus on one of the people looking for a house. Each group should discuss the ad and decide if the house suits the needs of that person. Have students justify their answers, and have groups present their findings to the class.

Answer: Dora Peña

Extension: Have students write a short paragraph telling what their requirements for a house are. Suggest that they use the passages in the activities as models.

Pronunciación

Core Instruction

Standards: 4.1

Resources: Teacher's Resource Book: Audio Script, p. 115; Audio Program DVD: Cap. 6B, Track 13

Suggestions: Read the *Pronunciación* with the students or use the audio. Model the two distinct sounds, exaggerating them somewhat for clarity. Have students repeat the words after you. Say the tongue twister and then ask volunteers to say it for the class.

Theme Project

Students can perform Step 4 at this point. Be sure they understand your corrections and suggestions. (For more information, see p. 270-b.)

21 ¿Qué casa están buscando?

Leer • Pensar

En Santiago, Chile, tres personas están buscando *(looking for)* una nueva casa y leen el anuncio a la derecha. ¿Quién crees que va a comprar *(buy)* la casa?

José Guzmán: "Quiero vivir bastante cerca de mi trabajo. Para mi esposa es importante tener una cocina equipada. Prefiero una casa con sólo un piso porque mis padres van a vivir con nosotros y las escaleras son muy difíciles para ellos".

Alejandro Lara: "Mis padres y yo vivimos en un apartamento ahora. Quiero una casa con tres dormitorios porque mis primos vienen a nuestra casa a veces. No quiero una casa muy grande porque no me gusta ni pasar la aspiradora ni limpiar los baños".

Dora Peña: "Mi familia y yo estamos buscando una casa nueva. Tenemos dos hijas y mi mamá vive con nosotros. Quiero una casa con un dormitorio un poco separado para mi mamá. Prefiero tener alfombra en los dormitorios porque nuestras hijas juegan mucho allí".

Chile

LAS MEJORES CASAS
EN LA AVENIDA LA FLORIDA

CASA VENECIA: 310 m² 3 PISOS
DESDE CHP[1] 40.000.000

Planta baja: Amplia sala • Comedor separado • Cocina y baño de visitas
Primer piso: Dormitorio principal, más 2 dormitorios y otro baño
Segundo piso: Amplio dormitorio con baño completo y una gran sala de estar

«VISITE NUESTRA OFICINA Y COMPRE HOY MISMO»

- Cerámica en el primer piso
- Alfombra en dormitorios
- Cocina equipada
- Papel vinílico en paredes
- Armarios terminados
- Ventanas de aluminio
- Amplio jardín

¡Llame hoy! 232 9980

[1] Peso chileno

Pronunciación

The letters *n* and *ñ*

In Spanish, the letter *n* sounds like the *n* in "no." Listen to and say these words:

anaranjado	nieva	nadar	joven	desayuno
necesito	encantado	número	nombre	donde

However, the sound changes when there is a tilde (~) over the *n*. The *ñ* then sounds like the *-ny-* of the English word *canyon*. Listen to and say these words:

señor	otoño	español	enseñar	año
montañas	niña	mañana	piñata	cumpleaños

Try it out! Listen to this *trabalenguas* and then try to say it.

El señor Yáñez come ñames[1] en las mañanas con el niño.

[1]yams

DIFFERENTIATED INSTRUCTION

Heritage Language Learners

Point out that when one is writing, it is very important to include language-specific punctuation such as the tilde (~). Remind students that the meaning of a word is often dependent on these marks, and leaving them out can change the meaning, as in ***uña*** ("fingernail") and ***una*** ("a/an").

Advanced Learners

Ask students to use the Internet or other resources to find information on how living arrangements in Spanish-speaking countries differ between rural areas and urban ones. Suggest that students compare their findings to trends in the United States. Have students present their information to the class.

22 ¿Dónde viven?

Leer • Pensar

En la capital de Venezuela, Caracas, analizaron *(they analyzed)* dónde viven algunos habitantes. Según los estudios, ¿viven más personas en casas o en apartamentos? ¿Viven en casas y apartamentos grandes o pequeños? Estudia las gráficas y luego contesta las preguntas.

Venezuela

Nota

Do you see the pattern in the following numbers?

100,000 = cien mil
200,000 = doscientos mil
300,000 = trescientos mil

But watch out for 500,000:

542,656 = quinientos cuarenta y dos mil seiscientos cincuenta y seis

1,000,000 = un millón

Conexiones | Las matemáticas

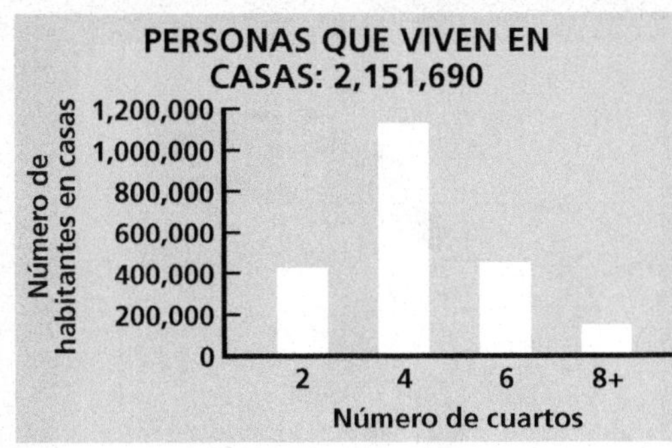

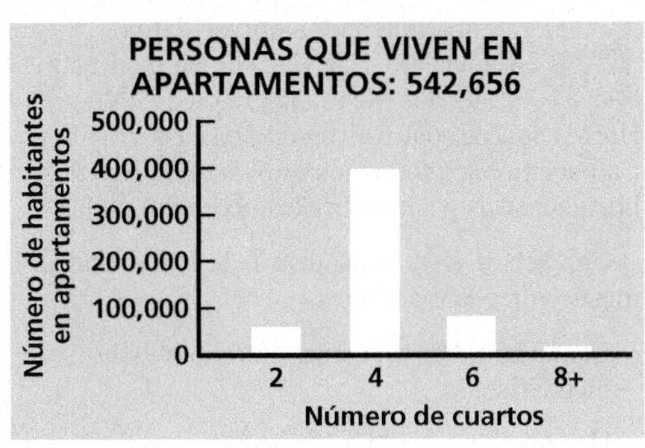

1. ¿Cuántas personas viven en una casa con dos cuartos? ¿Cuántas viven en un apartamento con dos cuartos?
2. ¿Cuántas personas viven en una casa con ocho o más cuartos? ¿Cuántas viven en un apartamento con ocho o más cuartos?
3. Calcula el porcentaje de personas que viven en una casa con cuatro cuartos. Calcula el porcentaje de personas que viven en un apartamento con cuatro cuartos.

El español en el mundo del trabajo

As the number of Hispanic homebuyers in the United States has grown, the demand for Spanish speakers in professions related to housing has also increased.

- Look for ads in Spanish in the real estate section of your local newspaper or at a local house and garden store. How would knowledge of Spanish be helpful for real estate agents, architects, builders, and retailers?

La Casa J. Knox Corbett en el distrito histórico de Tucson, Arizona

Practice and Communicate 6B

22 Standards: 1.2, 1.3, 3.1

Resources: Answer Keys: Student Edition, p. 91

Mapa global interactivo, Actividad 3 Compare neighborhoods in Caracas, Venezuela.

Focus: Reading comprehension; cultural understanding

Recycle: Numbers

Suggestions: Point out the *Nota* and work with students to practice forming these large numbers. Have students scan the graphs to predict what the activity is about. Then read the activity aloud and review the statistics. Discuss the answers to the questions. Ask students to compare these statistics with what they know about urban living arrangements in the United States. Then ask them to compare these statistics with what they can find out about their own community.

Answers:

1. **Más de 400,000; 50,000**
2. **100,000; 10,000**
3. **Casas con cuatro cuartos 51%; Apartamentos con cuatro cuartos 73.7% (74%)**

El español en el mundo del trabajo

Core Instruction

Standards: 5.1

Suggestions: Write the expressions ***se vende*** and ***se alquila*** on the board, and explain them or ask students to guess what these words mean.

Pre-AP* Support

- **Learning Objective:** Presentational Writing
- **Activity:** Have students prepare a brief paragraph describing their dream home. Encourage them to be creative in their description of their fantasy house, and to give details such as location (town *vs.* city), amenities, etc. Have them exchange paragraphs with a partner, and comment on their respective ideas.
- ***Pre-AP* Resource Book:*** Comprehensive guide to Pre-AP* communication skill development, pp. 10–57

Theme Project

Students can perform Step 5 at this point. Record their presentations for inclusion in their portfolios. (For more information, see p. 270-b.)

ENRICH YOUR TEACHING

Teacher-to-Teacher

Have students create their own ads for a newspaper listing. They can write an ad for a house or an apartment. Have them refer to sample ads in the textbook or, if possible, bring in some from a Spanish-language newspaper. You may be able to find ads on the Internet as well. Place student ads on the bulletin board.

21st Century Skills

Critical Thinking and Problem Solving To expand the suggestion for Activity 22, guide students on a brief investigation about urban living arrangements in their own city or community. Have them discuss the results with a partner and compare living habits (apartment vs. family home) between their own community, and the city of Caracas.

6B Reading

Common Core: Reading

Lectura

Core Instruction

Standards: 1.2

Focus: Reading comprehension of a Cinderella-like story using vocabulary for household chores

Suggestions:

Pre-reading: Read the *Strategy* aloud. Students may want to briefly discuss the plot of "Cinderella" before they begin skimming. Have students skim the story to look for a "Cinderella" story line and dialogue.

Reading: Have students read the selection. Point out that familiarity with the story line will help them understand the story, although there are differences. As they read, have them take brief notes about ***Cantaclara*** to compare her with Cinderella.

Post-reading: Have the class list comparisons between the two stories as you write them on the board. Then, have students re-read the last paragraph on p. 312. How does this story deviate from that of Cinderella? Ask students if they can explain the pun in ***Cantaclara's*** name (***Cantaclara*** = "sings clearly").

Extension: Have students write a different ending to the story: After ***Cantaclara's*** stepmother and stepsisters see her on television, what happens next?

BELLRINGER REVIEW

Have students pantomime several of the household chores as you say them using the ***tú*** command form.

Pre-AP* Support

- **Learning Objective:** Interpretive: Print
- **Activity:** As a class pre-reading activity, have students brainstorm a list of possible descriptive sentences for each of the illustrations and put the list on the board. Then have students tell a mini-story to a partner. Set a time limit for the narrations.
- ***Pre-AP* Resource Book:*** Comprehensive guide to Pre-AP* reading skill development, pp. 19–26

Objectives

- Read a version of "Cinderella"
- Skim to find characters and dialogue to aid comprehension
- Analyze the "Cinderella" story across cultures

Lectura

Cantaclara

Lee esta historia sobre una joven que se llama Cantaclara.

Strategy

Skimming
This reading is based on the story of Cinderella. Quickly skim the story and find characters and dialogue that remind you of Cinderella.

Hay una muchacha que se llama Cantaclara. Ella vive con su madrastra y sus dos hermanastras, Griselda y Hortencia. Las cuatro viven en una casa grande y Cantaclara hace todos los quehaceres. Sus dos hermanastras y su madrastra no hacen nada.

—Cantaclara, saca la basura. Y después, pon la mesa —dice la madrastra.

—Cantaclara, haz mi cama y limpia el baño —dice Griselda.

—Haz mi cama también —dice Hortencia.

—Un momento. Estoy lavando los platos ahora mismo —dice Cantaclara.

¡Pobre[1] Cantaclara! Hace todos los quehaceres y cuando trabaja, ella canta. Tiene una voz[2] muy clara y le encanta cantar.

Un día, Cantaclara entra en el dormitorio de Griselda para hacer la cama. Ve en la televisión un anuncio[3] para un programa muy popular que se llama *La estrella[4] del futuro*. En la televisión hay un señor que dice: "¡Hola, amigos! ¿Tienen talento? ¿Cantan bien? ¿Por qué no cantan para nosotros? ¡Pueden tener un futuro fantástico y recibir muchísimo dinero!"

Cantaclara está muy contenta. Ella puede cantar. Ella quiere un futuro fantástico. En este momento, ella decide cantar para el programa *La estrella del futuro*.

[1]Poor [2]voice [3]ad [4]star

DIFFERENTIATED INSTRUCTION

Heritage Language Learners

Have students write a brief summary of one of their favorite fairy tales or tall tales, using the present tense and the present progressive. Encourage students to include pictures or drawings.

Students with Learning Difficulties

Point out that in Spanish, dialogue is set off by dashes, whereas in English, dialogue is set off by quotation marks. Speaker tags are used similarly: sometimes they are provided, sometimes they are not. Work through the story with students and help them see where speakers change.

Es la noche del programa. Después de hacer todos los quehaceres, Cantaclara está saliendo[5] de casa cuando su madrastra le habla.

—Cantaclara, ¿adónde vas?

—Quiero salir por unas horas, madrastra. ¿Está bien?

—Ahora no. Tienes que limpiar la cocina —contesta la madrastra. —Está muy sucia.

—Pero, madrastra, tengo que . . .

—¡No importa, Cantaclara! ¡Limpia la cocina!

Cantaclara mira su reloj. Sólo tiene una hora. Va a la cocina y limpia todo. Trabaja muy rápidamente. Después de cuarenta y cinco minutos, termina el trabajo.

Cantaclara llega[6] al programa y canta su canción favorita. ¡Por supuesto ella canta mejor que todos![7] Ella va a tener un futuro fantástico y va a recibir muchísimo dinero.

Son las ocho de la noche. La madrastra y las dos hermanastras están en la sala y ven su programa favorito. Pero, ¿qué es esto? ¡Ven a Cantaclara en la pantalla!

—Mira, mamá. ¡Es Cantaclara! —dice Hortencia.

—¡Oh, no! Si Cantaclara es la nueva estrella del futuro, ¿quién va a hacer los quehaceres? —pregunta Griselda.

[5]is leaving [6]arrives [7]anyone else

¿Comprendes?

Pon las frases en orden según la historia.

1. Ella decide cantar en el programa *La estrella del futuro.*
2. Cantaclara es la persona que canta mejor en el programa.
3. Ella está lavando los platos.
4. Ella tiene que limpiar la cocina.
5. Ve el anuncio para *La estrella del futuro.*
6. Griselda no sabe quién va a hacer los quehaceres.
7. Cantaclara vive en una casa grande con su madrastra y sus dos hermanastras.
8. Son las ocho de la noche y la madrastra y las hermanastras están viendo la tele.

Fondo Cultural | El mundo hispano

La Cenicienta The story of Cinderella is perhaps the best-known fairy tale in the world. Almost every culture seems to have its own version and there may be over 1,500 variations. The tale appears to date back to a Chinese story from the ninth century, "Yeh-Shen."

- What aspects of the story might change from culture to culture?

Más práctica 

realidades.com | print

Guided WB p. 211	✔	✔
Comm. WB pp. 129, 295	✔	✔
***Hispanohablantes* WB** pp. 240–243		✔
Cultural Reading Activity	✔	

ENRICH YOUR TEACHING

Teacher-to-Teacher

Write a brief summary of "*Caperucita Roja*" ("Little Red Riding Hood") or another familiar fairy tale, leaving out the title. Make it as simple and comprehensible as possible, though some unfamiliar words are fine. Distribute copies to students and read the passage as a class. Have students guess which fairy tale they are reading. For a variation of this activity, have students act out the fairy tale or use a cloze passage to fill in the reading.

¿Comprendes? Standards: 1.2, 1.3

Resources: Answer Keys: Student Edition, p. 92

Focus: Reading comprehension

Suggestions: Have students read all the statements. Ask them to say whether each sentence they read takes place in the beginning, the middle, or the end of the story. Then, have them put each section of the story in order to get their finished product, which will be a summary of the story.

Answers:

(7) Cantaclara vive en una casa grande con su madrastra y sus dos hermanastras. (3) Ella está lavando los platos. (5) Ve el anuncio para *La estrella del futuro.* (1) Ella decide cantar en el programa *La estrella del futuro.* (4) Ella tiene que limpiar la cocina. (2) Cantaclara es la persona que canta mejor en el programa. (8) Son las ocho de la noche y la madrastra y las hermanastras están viendo la tele. (6) Griselda no sabe quién va a hacer los quehaceres.

Fondo cultural

Standards: 4.2

Suggestions: Point out to students that the name for Cinderella in Spanish is ***Cenicienta.*** (It is interesting to note that in most European versions, the girl's name includes something about ashes or cinders.) Use the question to have students predict how the variation of the fairy tale may be different. Have them research variations of the tale on the Internet or in the library.

Answers will vary but may include the culture in which the story is set, the tasks the young girl does, or the reward she earns.

For Further Reading

Student Resource: Realidades para hispanohablantes: Lectura 2, pp. 244–245

Perspectivas del mundo hispano

Core Instruction

Standards: 2.1, 2.2, 4.2

Focus: Reading about homes in Spanish-speaking countries

Suggestions: Tell students that there are many types and styles of architecture but that buildings usually have a form that is functional. One thing that influences the form is the local climate. An example is slanted roofs in places where it snows a lot. This lets the snow fall off, instead of building up and threatening a collapse from the weight.

Have students read the text. Discuss how the climate in many Spanish-speaking countries is warm enough to allow an outdoor patio where meals are often served. Discuss how the patio fits into the social aspects of the culture. It is private, yet open and relaxed. Note that acquaintances are not usually entertained in the home. Discuss other privacy-oriented characteristics of homes in Spanish-speaking countries, such as tall walls and bars on windows. Have students complete the *Check it out!* section and discuss the question with the class.

Students may have difficulty envisioning the patios in Spanish-speaking countries. Although uncovered, they are nonetheless inside the house. The rest of the house is built around the patio, and many rooms will have a door leading to it. Remind students that in many countries the climate is warm, and going outdoors to eat and socialize is pleasant.

Direct attention to the *Think about it!* section and have students discuss the questions.

Answers will vary.

Additional Resources

Student Resource: Realidades para hispanohablantes, p. 246

Perspectivas del mundo hispano

¿Cómo son las casas en el mundo hispano?

In many Spanish-speaking countries the architectural features of houses are very different from those in the United States. Houses tend to be separated from the outside by a barrier such as a tall wall or fence. The owner would open a gate to enter the property where there may be a carport or small outside area. In many communities, the outside wall of the house is located directly on the sidewalk and the front windows may contain bars or *rejas.* The doors may be large wooden or metal doors. A plain walled exterior gives no hints about what may be a beautiful, comfortable interior.

Inside, a home will often have an open space in the middle called the *patio.* Many rooms of the house open onto the *patio,* and it is a place for the family to meet, eat meals, talk, and spend time together. Privacy is valued, and the home and family activities are shielded from view from the outside.

El patio de una casa en Córdoba, España

Homes in Spanish-speaking countries are used for the family and to entertain very close relatives and friends. It is unusual to invite non-family members such as coworkers or casual friends into the home. Parties often take place in restaurants or small reception halls.

Check it out! Look around your neighborhood. How does the architecture of houses compare with the design of houses in the Spanish-speaking world?

Think about it! If architectural features of houses in Spanish-speaking countries imply a desire for privacy, what do the architectural features of houses in the United States imply? How does the concept of a *patio* compare in these cultures?

Una casa en Santo Domingo de Silos, España

DIFFERENTIATED INSTRUCTION

Advanced Learners

Have students choose a Spanish-speaking country and research the style of the houses. They should find out if the houses usually have a patio and the origins of the style of architecture. Have them share their findings with the class, showing pictures if possible.

Students with Learning Difficulties

Students may have difficulty understanding the basic layout of the homes described here. Show pictures or diagrams, but if using diagrams, make sure students understand the perspective.

Presentación escrita

- Create a flyer advertising a house or apartment
- Identify and answer key questions to find ideas

Se vende casa o apartamento

Task
Design a flyer in Spanish to promote the sale of your family's house or apartment. Create an attractive flyer that will make your home (or dream house) appealing to a potential buyer.

1. **Prewrite** Think about the information you want to include, then jot down your answers to these questions.
   - En general, ¿cómo es la casa o el apartamento?
   - ¿Qué cuartos hay? ¿Cómo son? ¿De qué colores son?
   - ¿Hay algo especial en la casa (piscina, cuarto especial)?
   - Incluye *(Include)* otra información importante como la dirección *(address)* y el precio *(price)*.

Strategy
Using key questions
Answering key questions can help you think of ideas for writing.

2. **Draft** Use the ad on p. 310 and your Prewrite answers to design the flyer. Include illustrations and other features to make it attractive. Begin with *Se vende casa / apartamento*.
3. **Revise** Read your ad to see that you have included all the information a potential buyer might want. Check for correct spelling. Share your flyer with a partner, who will check the following:
   - Is the flyer neat and attractive? Does it include a visual?
   - Is the key information provided?
   - Does it make you want to look at the property?
4. **Publish** Write a final copy, making any necessary changes. You may want to include it in a class collection called *Se vende* or in your portfolio.
5. **Evaluation** The following rubric will be used to grade your flyer.

Una casa típica, Coclé, Panamá

Rubric	Score 1	Score 3	Score 5
Neatness and attractiveness	You use no visual and your ad contains visible error corrections and smudges.	You use a visual, but your ad contains visual error corrections and smudges.	You use a visual, have no error correction or smudges, and your ad is attractive.
Use of vocabulary expressions	You use very little variation of vocabulary and have frequent usage errors.	You use limited vocabulary, with some usage errors.	You use an extended variety of vocabulary with very few usage errors.
Amount of information provided	You only describe rooms.	You describe rooms plus special features.	You describe rooms, special features, and provide price and address.

Common Core: Writing

Presentación escrita

Persuasive

Standards: 1.3

Focus: Writing using vocabulary related to homes

Suggestions: Review the task and the 5-step approach with students. Point out that there are key ideas that the flyer must include, such as number of bedrooms and baths, size, location, etc. Review the rubric with the class to explain how you will grade the flyers. Make a flyer of your own as a model or bring in flyers from a local realtor.

Extension: Have students present their flyers to the class. Students can decide which house would be the most expensive, the most modern, etc.

Pre-AP* Support

- **Learning Objective:** Interpersonal Writing
- **Activity:** Imagine you are buying a house. Turn the information from the flyer you created into an e-mail to a friend summarizing the specifics about this house. Ask the addressee for his or her opinion about the house.
- ***Pre-AP* Resource Book:*** Comprehensive guide to Pre-AP* writing skill development, pp. 27–38

Portfolio

Invite students to review the activities they completed in this chapter. Have them select one or two items that they feel best demonstate their achievements in Spanish to include in their portfolios.

Additional Resources

Student Resources: Realidades para hispanohablantes, p. 247; Guided Practice: Presentación escrita, p. 212

ENRICH YOUR TEACHING

21st Century Skills

Technology Literacy Encourage students to make their flyers electronic, combining online images, audio, and video. As part of their pre-writing task, have them ask and answer the questions with a partner, to make sure they include as much pertinent information as possible with accuracy.

ASSESSMENT

Presentación escrita

- Assessment Program: Rubrics, p. T32

  Go over the descriptions of the different levels of performance. After assessing students, help individuals understand how their performance could be improved.

Videomisterio

Core Instruction

Standards: 1.2, 4.1, 5.2

Resources: Teacher's Resource Book: Video Script, pp. 118–119; Video Program: Cap. 6B; Video Program Teacher's Guide: Cap. 6B

Focus: Introducing the events and vocabulary; scanning and reading the episode summary

Personajes importantes:
Lola Lago, detective
Paco, colega de Lola
Margarita, la secretaria de la oficina de Lola
Doña Lupe Aguirre, portera
Carmela, una buena amiga de Lola
Pedro Requena, nieto de doña Gracia Requena

Synopsis: Lola visits doña Lupe to find out more news about doña Gracia, who is getting better at the hospital. Doña Gracia does not remember anything about the incident. Then Lola meets her best friend, Carmela, at a café. Lola explains the events that led doña Gracia to the San Carlos hospital. Carmela has a friend, Rosalinda, who works at the hospital. Lola and Carmela agree to meet the next morning in the hospital to ask Rosalinda for information. Later, Lola meets Pedro as he inquires about his grandmother in the hospital. Lola offers her services as a detective, and gives him her card.

Suggestions:

Pre-viewing: Review with students the events of the previous episode. Lola questioned doña Lupe, who found doña Gracia on the floor. There are three mysteries at hand: (1) What caused doña Gracia's incident? (2) Where is her niece, María? (3) Where are doña Gracia's jewels? María, a professional model, spent three months in the hospital after a car accident. Doña Gracia's only other relative is her grandson, Pedro Requena, who lives in Italy. His father did not get along with doña Gracia's husband.

Review the *Nota cultural* with the class. You may want to show a picture, if available, of a ***tapa,*** such as a piece of *tortilla española.* Point out the *Palabras para comprender*, saying examples in context and writing the sentences on the board. Remind students that these words are only used to help them understand the episode and they are not responsible for that vocabulary.

Videomisterio

Objective

- Understand the expanding plot of a mystery video set in Spain

¿Eres tú, María?

Episodio 4

Antes de ver el video

Personajes importantes

Carmela, una buena amiga de Lola

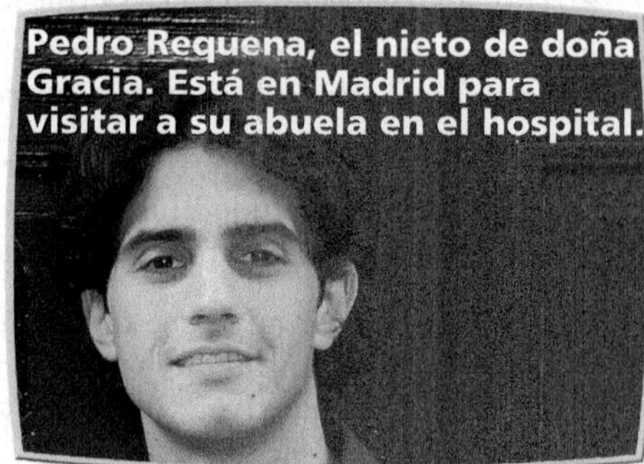

Pedro Requena, el nieto de doña Gracia. Está en Madrid para visitar a su abuela en el hospital.

Nota cultural *Tapas* are popular appetizers in Spain. *Tapas* come in small servings called *raciones,* and can be almost anything: olives, fish, meat, cheese, vegetables, shellfish, or any dish the chef cares to prepare. Eating *tapas* is a social event. Friends eat, drink, and relax as they talk. When you are done, you are charged according to how many platefuls of *tapas* you ate.

Resumen del episodio

Doña Gracia está mucho mejor y puede ir a casa en unos días. Pero no recuerda mucho del incidente. Lola llama por teléfono a su buena amiga, Carmela. Las dos van a un café para hablar y Carmela le dice a Lola que una de sus amigas, Rosalinda, trabaja en el hospital San Carlos. Es el hospital donde está doña Gracia. Deciden ir al hospital para hablar con Rosalinda y ver a doña Gracia. A la mañana siguiente, Lola habla con Pedro Requena.

Palabras para comprender

fui a visitarla I went to visit her
¿Habló del incidente? Did she talk about the incident?
¿Sabe . . .? Does she know . . .?
Lo único que recuerda . . . The only thing she remembers . . .
un golpe hit, blow
ahora mismo right away
preguntar por to ask about
los churros fried dough pastries
No estoy pensando en . . . I'm not planning to . . .
Voy a pensarlo. I'll think about it.

DIFFERENTIATED INSTRUCTION

Heritage Language Learners

Ask students to use the vocabulary from *Palabras para comprender* to tell what happened in this episode. Encourage them to go back and use vocabulary from previous chapters.

"Lo único que recuerda es un golpe aquí, en la cabeza. ¿La verdad? No sabe nada".

"Soy Pedro Requena. Exacto, el nieto de la Sra. Gracia Requena. Voy ahora mismo para el hospital".

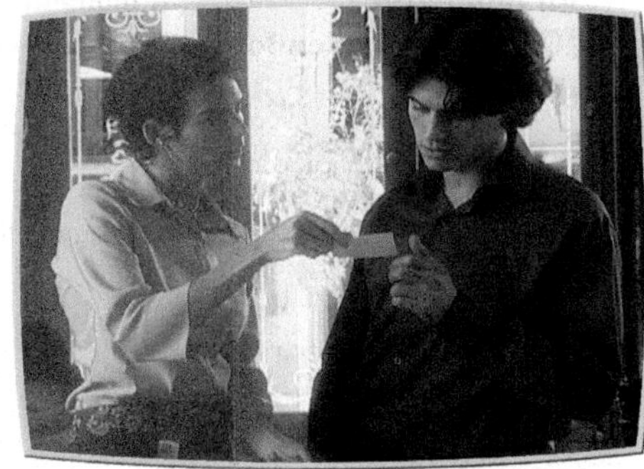

—Si necesita más información, aquí tiene mi número de teléfono.
—Gracias, señorita. Voy a pensarlo.

Después de ver el video

¿Comprendes?

A. Lee las frases y ponlas *(put them)* en orden cronológico.

1. Pedro no sabe si quiere contratar a una detective.
2. Lola y Carmela van al café a comer unas tapas.
3. Lola habla con Pedro y le da su número de teléfono.
4. Paco y Lola hablan en la oficina.
5. Pedro Requena habla por teléfono con el Dr. Sánchez Mata.
6. Doña Lupe dice que fue al hospital y habló con doña Gracia.
7. Carmela dice que su amiga, Rosalinda, trabaja en el hospital San Carlos.

B. Lee las frases y escribe el nombre de la persona que dice cada frase: Pedro, Carmela, Lola, doña Lupe o Paco.

1. No podemos trabajar si no hay cliente y no hay dinero.
2. Buenas noticias. Doña Gracia está mejor.
3. ¿Quieres tomar un café conmigo?
4. Mi amiga trabaja allí. Puedes hablar con doña Gracia.
5. No estoy pensando en contratar a un detective.

Video 6B

Visual scanning: Direct students' attention to the two photos on p. 316 and ask who they are (Carmela and Pedro) and what relationship they have to Lola (Lola's best friend and a potential client). Before students read the *Resumen del episodio,* have them scan the text and find three cognates ***(teléfono, café, hospital, deciden)***. Then ask them to read the *Resumen del episodio* carefully and ask questions about what will happen in this episode.

Viewing: If there is time after viewing the full episode, select some key moments that you wish to highlight, such as the scene in which Lola introduces herself to Pedro.

Post-viewing: Have the students look at the pictures at the top of the page and use them to summarize the scenes in this episode. Write the vocabulary presented in this episode on the board to help students create sentences for each important scene that adds new information to the plot. Direct students' attention to the *¿Comprendes?* section.

¿Comprendes? Standards: 1.2, 1.3

Resources: Answer Keys: Student Edition, p. 92

Focus: Verifying comprehension by answering questions; reviewing the plot

Suggestions: For part A, have students read all the sentences, then show the video again, pausing to allow them to make sentences as events occur. For part B, tape large photocopies of the characters' faces on the board and have volunteers point to the correct image.

Answers:

Part A: Sequence of events is 4, 6, 2, 7, 5, 1, 3.
Part B: 1. Paco; 2. D. Lupe; 3. Lola; 4. Carmela; 5. Pedro

Additional Resources

- *¿Eres tú, María?* Video Workbook, Episode 4
- *¿Eres tú, María?* Teacher's Video Guide: Answer Key

ENRICH YOUR TEACHING

Culture Note

Spaniards usually have a light breakfast, sometimes just coffee. Then they may have a mid-morning snack, which is called ***almuerzo.*** The early afternoon meal—the largest of the day—is ***la comida.*** Spaniards sometimes go out to eat ***tapas*** as dinner. Otherwise, ***la cena*** is a light meal.

21st Century Skills

Initiative and Self-Direction Direct students to do the online practice for this page. Then have them work with a partner to discuss the characters and plot of the video, making sure they understand and retain all the pertinent details. Have them develop their own system for keeping up with the plot as the *videomisterio* story progresses.

Review Activities

To talk about houses or apartments: Student A can draw a house plan and write the vocabulary words in English. Student A points to the room, and Student B says the word in Spanish. Have students exchange roles.

To name household chores: Students work in pairs to make sketches of household chores on note cards. Have them shuffle the cards and take turns saying the chore in Spanish, including a sentence about who does that chore in their house. Students may have "time trials" to see who can answer the fastest.

Affirmative tú commands and present progressive tense: After practicing household chores, Student A will be the "parent" and use commands to tell Student B to clean. Student B will have an excuse and must use the present progressive tense in the reply. Students then reverse roles.

Portfolio

Invite students to review the activities they completed in this chapter, including written reports, posters or other visuals, recordings of oral presentations, or other projects. Have them select one or two items that they feel best demonstrate their achievements in Spanish to include in their portfolios. Have them include this with the Chapter Checklist and Self-Assessment Worksheet.

Teacher-to-Teacher

Careers: *Tema* 6 has focused on houses. Have students work in small groups to talk about a career in the construction business. Have them write a list of words and expressions they have learned that would be useful for discussing the construction of a new home or apartment. Ask groups to share their lists.

Additional Resources

Student Resources: Realidades para hispanohablantes, p. 248

Teacher Resources:

- Teacher's Resource Book: Situation Cards, p. 124; Clip Art, pp. 127–129
- Assessment Program: Chapter Checklist and Self-Assessment Worksheet, pp. T56–T57

Repaso

Objectives

- Review the vocabulary and grammar
- Demonstrate you can perform the tasks on p. 319

Repaso del capítulo

Vocabulario y gramática

to talk about where someone lives

cerca (de)	close (to), near
lejos (de)	far (from)
vivir	to live

to talk about houses or apartments

el apartamento	apartment
el baño	bathroom
la cocina	kitchen
el comedor	dining room
el cuarto	room
el despacho	home office
la escalera	stairs, stairway
el garaje	garage
el piso	story, floor
la planta baja	ground floor
el primer piso	second floor
la sala	living room
el segundo piso	third floor
el sótano	basement

to name household chores

arreglar el cuarto	to straighten up the room
ayudar	to help
cocinar	to cook
cortar el césped	to cut the lawn
dar (yo doy, tú das)	to give
dar de comer al perro	to feed the dog
hacer la cama	to make the bed
lavar (el coche, los platos, la ropa)	to wash (the car, the dishes, the clothes)
limpiar el baño	to clean the bathroom
pasar la aspiradora	to vacuum
poner (yo pongo, tú pones)	to put, place
poner la mesa	to set the table
los quehaceres	chores
quitar el polvo	to dust
sacar la basura	to take out the trash

to describe household items

limpio, -a	clean
sucio, -a	dirty

other useful words

bastante	enough; rather
¿Cuáles?	which (ones)
el dinero	money
un momento	a moment
¿Qué estás haciendo?	What are you doing?
recibir	to receive
si	if, whether

affirmative *tú* commands

For regular verbs, use the *Ud./él/ella* form:

-ar:	**habla**
-er:	**lee**
-ir:	**escribe**

For *hacer* and *poner:*

hacer	**haz**
poner	**pon**

present progressive tense

Use the present-tense forms of *estar* + the present participle to say that you are doing something right now.

present participles:

-ar:	stem + **-ando** → **lavando**
-er:	stem + **-iendo** → **comiendo**
-ir:	stem + **-iendo** → **escribiendo**

For *Vocabulario adicional,* see pp. 472–473.

DIFFERENTIATED INSTRUCTION

Advanced Learners

Have students discuss when they do their chores, naming specific days of the week and times. Have them compare their workload with that of a sibling.

Students with Learning Difficulties

Give students the format of the actual test and the point values of different parts. This will help take much of the stress out of the testing situation. Help them decide which parts they need to study most. Consider study sessions in class or at a special time.

Más repaso GO realidades.com | print

Instant Check	✔	
Puzzles	✔	
Core WB pp. 119–120		✔
Comm. WB pp. 296, 297–299	✔	✔

Preparación para el examen

On the exam you will be asked to . . .	Here are practice tasks similar to those you will find on the exam . . .	For review go to your print or digital textbook . . .
Interpretive		
 **1 Escuchar** Listen to and understand teenagers' excuses for not doing a particular chore at the moment they are asked to do it	As you listen to a teenager explain to his mother why he can't do a particular chore at the moment, identify: a) what the mother wants the teenager to do; b) what the teenager says he is busy doing.	**pp. 298–301** *Vocabulario en contexto* **p. 303** Actividad 7 **p. 304** Actividad 8 **p. 308** Actividad 17 **p. 309** Actividad 18
Interpersonal		
 **2 Hablar** Give advice to someone about how to be successful in school	Your school counselors have asked you to participate in an orientation for new Spanish-speaking students. Offer each student in the group a piece of advice. For example, you might say *Escucha bien en clase* or *Haz la tarea.*	**p. 305** Actividad 12 **p. 306** Actividad 13
Interpretive		
 **3 Leer** Read and understand ads for apartments that you might find in the classified section of a Spanish-language newspaper	A friend is moving to Spain and asks you to help find an apartment. He wants a two-bedroom, two-bath apartment with a small kitchen. He wants to live near a gym and a library. Read this ad and answer the following: a) Is this a good apartment for him? b) How many of his requested features does it have? c) What other features that are mentioned might he like? Este maravilloso apartamento tiene todo. Está cerca de un parque y un gimnasio moderno. Tiene una cocina pequeña, pero totalmente equipada. Tiene dos dormitorios con estantes y un baño muy grande. También tiene televisión por satélite y un garaje privado. No se permiten animales.	**pp. 298–301** *Vocabulario en contexto* **p. 302** Actividades 4–5 **p. 310** Actividad 21 **p. 315** *Presentación escrita*
Presentational		
 **4 Escribir** Write a list of household chores that you are willing to do	You and your classmates are offering to do chores to earn money for your Spanish club. Make a list of at least eight chores that you would be willing to do.	**pp. 298–301** *Vocabulario en contexto* **p. 303** Actividades 6–7 **p. 304** Actividad 8 **p. 306** Actividad 14 **p. 307** Actividad 15
Cultures • Comparisons		
 **5 Pensar** Demonstrate an understanding of cultural perspectives regarding houses	Explain how the architectural features of many homes in the Spanish-speaking world reflect the importance the owners place on privacy. How do these features compare to those in homes in the United States?	**p. 303** *Fondo cultural* **p. 314** *Perspectivas del mundo hispano*

DIFFERENTIATED ASSESSMENT

CORE ASSESSMENT
- **Assessment Program:** Examen del capítulo 6B, pp. 168–174
- **Audio Program DVD:** Cap. 6B, Track 16
- **ExamView:** Chapter Test, Test Banks A and B

ADVANCED/PRE-AP*
- **ExamView: Pre-AP* Test Bank**
- **Pre-AP* Resource Book,** pp. 82–85

STUDENTS NEEDING EXTRA HELP
- **Alternate Assessment Program:** Examen del capítulo 6B
- **Audio Program DVD:** Cap. 6B, Track 16

HERITAGE LEARNERS
- **Assessment Program: Realidades para hispanohablantes:** Examen del capítulo 6B
- **ExamView: Heritage Learner Test Bank**

Performance Tasks

Standards: 1.1, 1.2, 1.3, 2.2, 4.2

Student Resource: Realidades para hispanohablantes, p. 249

Teacher Resources: Teacher's Resource Book: Audio Script, p. 115; Audio Program DVD: Cap. 6B, Track 15; Answer Keys: Student Edition, p. 92

1. Escuchar

Suggestions: Use the audio or read the script.

Script:

—Miguel, da de comer al perro. Son las siete de la tarde y el pobre Capitán no tiene comida.
—Mamá, el perro está jugando con el gato. No quiere comer ahora. Y yo estoy estudiando para mi examen de matemáticas. No puedo dar de comer a Capitán ahora.

Answers: **a) She tells Miguel to feed the dog.; b) He says he is studying for a math exam.**

2. Hablar

Suggestions: Remind students that their advice should use affirmative ***tú*** commands.

Answers will vary.

3. Leer

Suggestions: Students should make two columns on a sheet of paper. One side will have the friend's criteria, the other will be a list of what the apartment has.

Answers: **a. yes; b. 3; c. satellite television, private garage**

4. Escribir

Suggestions: Have students number their chores. They can include how much each chore will cost and make a small poster.

Answers will vary.

5. Pensar

Suggestions: Have students re-read the appropriate *Fondos culturales* and the *Perspectivas del mundo hispano* and look at the photos throughout the chapter.

Answers will vary.

Tema

7 De compras

7A ¿Cuánto cuesta?

- **Shopping and clothing**

Vocabulary: clothing; shopping; numbers 200–1,000

Grammar: stem-changing verbs: ***pensar, querer,*** and ***preferir;*** demonstrative adjectives

Cultural Perspectives: shopping

7B ¡Qué regalo!

- **Buying gifts and places to shop**

Vocabulary: places to shop; gifts; accessories; buying and selling

Grammar: preterite of ***-ar, -car,*** and ***-gar*** verbs; direct object pronouns ***lo, la, los, las***

Cultural Perspectives: gift-giving

THEME SUPPORT

Bulletin Boards

Theme: *De compras*

Ask students to cut out, copy, or download photos of clothing, accessories, currencies, and different types of storefronts and markets in Spanish-speaking countries. Cluster photos in three groups: clothing and accessories, currencies, and places to shop.

Hands-on Culture

Craft: *Pulseras de amistad*

Materials for one bracelet:

4 30" strands of yarn of different colors

Directions:

1. Join the four strands of yarn together, and make an overhand knot 8° from one end. Tie the end to the strap of a backpack or the back of a chair.
2. Hold the first strand of yarn in one hand (Color 1) and the second strand (Color 2) in the other. Wrap Color 1 over and under Color 2, then pull the end of Color 1 through the loop.
3. Hold Color 2 so that it doesn't move. Pull up on Color 1 to form a knot.
4. Repeat Steps 2 and 3 to do a second knot.
5. Let go of Color 2 and pick up the third strand of yarn (Color 3). Repeat Steps 2–4 with Colors 1 and 3. Let go of Color 3 and pick up the fourth strand of yarn (Color 4). Repeat Steps 2–4 with Colors 1 and 4.
6. To make the next row in the bracelet, repeat Steps 2–5, making the knots with Color 2. (Knot Color 2 over Color 3, Color 4, then Color 1.) Continue until the bracelet has reached the desired length, then tie an overhand knot. Trim the ends and tie the bracelet around your wrist.

Game

¿Qué vas a comprar?

Play this game in *Capítulo* 7B, after students have learned definite object pronouns.

Players: the whole class

Materials: index cards, two for each student

Rules:

1. Count out two index cards for each student. Divide the cards into two sets. Write an article of clothing, accessory, or gift on each index card in the first set. Write the corresponding places where each item can be purchased on the second set of cards. Shuffle each set of cards separately.
2. Give each student one card from each set. Divide students into two teams.
3. To find a match to their cards, students circulate, asking their classmates what they are going to buy and where they are going to buy it.
   Student 1: ¿Qué vas a comprar?
   Student 2: Voy a comprar unos zapatos.
   Student 1: ¿Dónde vas a comprarlos?
   Student 2: Voy a comprarlos en la zapatería. ¿Sabes dónde está?
   If Student 1 does not have the card: No, no sé dónde está.
   If Student 1 has the card: Está aquí. (The student hands over the card.)
4. After students get rid of their shopping location card, they must wait to be approached to match their item card. When a match is made, they sit down. Call time after four to five minutes. The winner is the team with the most members sitting down.

Variation: Make one set of cards, with two cards depicting the same items. Give each student a card. Students circulate, asking their classmates if they have the item on their card.

Student 1: ¿Tienes los zapatos?
Student 2: Sí, los tengo, *or* No, no los tengo.

THEME PROJECT

Catálogo de ventas por correo

Overview: Students create two pages from a mail-order catalog featuring magazine photos of three clothing items and three gift items, each accompanied by a brief description. Students present their catalog to the class, describing each item in complete sentences.

Resources: online or print clothing and accessory catalogs and fashion magazines; image editing and page layout software, and/or scissors, glue, markers, construction paper

Sequence: (suggestions for when to do each step appear throughout the chapters)

7A **STEP 1.** Review instructions so students know what is expected of them. Hand out the "Theme 7 Project Instructions and Rubric" from the *Teacher's Resource Book.*

STEP 2. Students look through mail-order catalogs for layout ideas, price ranges, and sizes. They then submit a rough sketch of their two-page layout. Return the drafts with your suggestions.

STEP 3. Students create their two-page layout, leaving room for their descriptions. Teach students the following vocabulary for sizes: ***talla*** ("size"), ***pequeño*** ("small"), ***mediano*** ("medium"), ***grande*** ("large").

7B **STEP 4.** Students submit a draft of their clothing and gift descriptions. Note your corrections and suggestions, then return drafts to students. Students partner to practice their catalog presentations.

STEP 5. Students present their catalog pages to the class, describing each item on the pages in complete sentences.

Options:

1. Students use a different currency and metric sizes in their catalogs, looking up conversions on the Internet.
2. Students feature only clothing or only gift items in their catalogs.

Assessment:

Here is a detailed rubric for assessing this project:

Theme 7 Project: *Catálogo de ventas por correo*

RUBRIC	Score 1	Score 3	Score 5
Evidence of planning	You didn't submit a sketch and draft.	You submitted the sketch and draft, but didn't correct them.	You submitted and corrected your draft and layout.
Use of illustrations	You didn't include any photos.	You included photos for most items. Your layout was somewhat effective.	You included photos for all items. Your layout was effective.
Presentation	You listed items, but didn't describe them. You rarely use complete sentences.	You described some but not all items completely. You included some incomplete sentences.	You described each item completely, using complete sentences.

21st Century Skills

Look for tips throughout *Tema* 7 to enrich your teaching by integrating 21st Century Skills. Suggestions for the Theme Project and Theme Culture follow below.

Theme Project

Modify the Theme Project with one or more of these suggestions:

Increase Collaboration

Have students work together in groups of three to increase their collaboration skills. Provide them with the handout "Work in teams" to help them organize their group and divide the tasks.

Develop Media Literacy

The instructions for the Theme Project give students the option to do their research online. Provide students with the handout "Analyze Media Content" to help them analyze Web sites. Tell students to think about what makes a Web site attractive and how the design of a site affects its message.

Support Critical Thinking and Problem Solving

As students plan their project, tell them to consider the following questions: Who are the potential buyers of your clothing? What kinds of items will you offer? What will be the price range and why?

Theme Culture

Foster Social and Cross-Cultural Skills

Help students bridge cultural differences by offering opportunities for them to discuss the culture highlighted throughout the chapter. Use the teaching suggestions for the *Fondo cultural* on page 321 to support discussion of cultural perspectives about fashion and clothing.

Videocultura View *Los mercados* online with the class to learn more about shopping in Spanish-speaking countries.

AT A GLANCE

Objectives

- **Listen to conversations and read about clothes and shopping**
- **Talk and write about shopping plans and gifts**
- **Exchange information while purchasing an item of clothing**
- **Understand the role of *molas* in the Kuna culture**
- **Compare the significance of crafts and clothing in Panama and the United States**

Vocabulary

- Shopping
- Clothing
- Prices and numbers

Grammar

- Stem-changing verbs: ***pensar, querer,*** and ***preferir***
- Demonstrative adjectives

Culture

- Joan Miró, p. 321
- Fernando Botero, p. 327
- Currencies of the
- Spanish-speaking world, p. 328
- Nonverbal language, p. 333
- Carolina Herrera, p. 335
- Traditional clothing of Panama, pp. 336–337
- ***Carnaval,*** p. 337
- Make a ***mola,*** p. 338

Recycle ♻

- ***quiero, quieres*** *and*
- ***prefiero, prefieres***
- ***me gusta(n), me encanta(n)***
- Places
- Colors
- Activities
- Infinitives
- Numbers

RESOURCES

	FOR THE STUDENT	ONLINE	DVD	PRINT	FOR THE TEACHER	ONLINE	PREEXP	DVD	PRINT
Plan					Interactive TE and Resources DVD	•		•	
					Teacher's Resource Book, pp. 146–183	•		•	•
					Pre-AP* Resource Book, pp. 86–89	•		•	•
					Lesson Plans	•			•
					Mapa global interactivo	•			
Introducción PP. **320–321**									
Present	Student Edition, pp. 320–321	•	•	•	Interactive TE and Resources DVD	•		•	
	DK Reference Atlas	•	•		Teacher's Resource Book, pp. 146–149	•		•	•
	Videocultura	•	•		Galería de fotos		•		
	Hispanohablantes WB, pp. 250–251			•	Fine Art Transparencies, 39	•	•	•	
					Map Transparencies, 12–18, 20	•	•	•	
Vocabulario en contexto PP. **322–325**									
Present & Practice	Student Edition, pp. 322–325	•	•	•	Interactive TE and Resources DVD	•		•	
	Audio	•	•		Teacher's Resource Book, pp. 151–153, 156, 164–168	•		•	•
	Videohistoria	•	•		Vocabulary Clip Art	•	•	•	•
	Flashcards	•	•		Audio Program	•	•	•	
	Instant Check	•			Video Program: Videohistoria	•		•	
	Guided WB, pp. 213–222	•	•	•	Video Program Teacher's Guide: Cap. 7A	•		•	•
	Core WB, pp. 121–124	•	•	•	Vocabulary and Grammar Transparencies, 128–131	•	•	•	
	Comm. WB, pp. 130–133, 136	•	•	•	Answer Keys: Student Edition, pp. 93–94	•	•	•	
	Hispanohablantes WB, pp. 252–253			•	TPR Stories, pp. 92–106	•		•	•
Assess and Remediate					Prueba 7A–1: Assessment Program, pp. 175–176	•		•	•
					Assessment Program para hispanohablantes, pp. 175–176	•		•	•

RESOURCES

	FOR THE STUDENT	ONLINE	DVD	PRINT	FOR THE TEACHER	ONLINE	PREEXP	DVD	PRINT
Vocabulario en uso PP. **326–329**									
Present & Practice	Student Edition, pp. 326–329	•	•	•	Interactive Whiteboard Vocabulary Activities	•		•	
	Instant Check	•			Interactive TE and Resources DVD	•		•	
	Comm. WB, pp. 133, 300	•	•	•	Teacher's Resource Book, pp. 153, 158–159	•		•	•
	Hispanohablantes WB, pp. 254–255			•	Communicative Pair Activities, pp. 158–159	•		•	•
	Communicative Pair Activities	•			Audio Program	•	•	•	
					Videomodelos	•		•	
					Fine Art Transparencies, 8	•	•	•	
					Answer Keys: Student Edition, pp. 94–95	•	•	•	•
Assess and Remediate					Prueba 7A–2 with Study Plan	•			
					Prueba 7A–2: Assessment Program, pp. 177–178	•		•	•
					Assessment Program para hispanohablantes, pp. 177–178	•		•	•
Gramática PP. **330–335**									
Present & Practice	Student Edition, pp. 330–335	•	•	•	Interactive Whiteboard Grammar Activities	•		•	
	Instant Check	•			Interactive TE and Resources DVD	•		•	
	Animated Verbs	•			Teacher's Resource Book, pp. 154–157, 160–161	•		•	•
	Tutorial Video: Grammar	•			Communicative Pair Activities, pp. 160–161	•		•	•
	Canción de hip hop	•			Audio Program	•	•	•	
	Guided WB, pp. 223–226	•	•	•	Videomodelos	•		•	
	Core WB, pp. 125–127	•	•	•	Video Program: GramActiva	•	•	•	
	Comm. WB, pp. 134–135, 137–138, 300	•	•	•	Vocabulary and Grammar Transparencies, 132–135	•	•	•	
	Hispanohablantes WB, pp. 256–261			•	Answer Keys: Student Edition, pp. 96–97	•	•	•	
	Communicative Pair Activities	•							
Assess and Remediate					Pruebas 7A–3 and 7A–4 with Study Plans	•			
					Pruebas 7A–3, 7A–4: Assessment Program, pp. 179, 180	•		•	•
					Assessment Program para hispanohablantes, pp. 179, 180	•		•	•
¡Adelante! PP. **336–341**									
Application	Student Edition, pp. 336–341	•	•	•	Interactive TE and Resources DVD	•		•	
	Online Cultural Reading	•			Teacher's Resource Book, p. 157	•		•	•
	Guided WB, pp. 227–228	•	•	•	Video Program: Videomisterio ¿Eres tú, María?	•		•	
	Comm. WB, pp. 139, 301	•	•	•	Video Program Teacher's Guide: Cap. 7A	•		•	
	Hispanohablantes WB, pp. 262–267			•	Videomisterio Quiz		•		
	¿Eres tú, María? Video WB, pp. 34–40	•	•	•	Map Transparencies, 13	•	•	•	
					Answer Keys: Student Edition, p. 98	•	•	•	
Repaso del capítulo PP. **342–343**									
Review	Student Edition, pp. 342–343	•	•	•	Interactive TE and Resources DVD	•		•	
	Online Puzzles and Games	•			Teacher's Resource Book, pp. 155, 162, 164–165	•		•	•
	Core WB, pp. 128–129	•	•	•	Audio Program	•	•	•	
	Comm. WB, pp. 302–305	•	•	•	Answer Keys: Student Edition, p. 99	•	•	•	
	Hispanohablantes WB, pp. 268–269			•					
	Instant Check	•							
Chapter Assessment									
Assess					Examen del capítulo 7A	•		•	•
					Assessment Program, pp. 181–187	•		•	•
					Alternate Assessment Program, pp. 69–73	•		•	•
					Assessment Program para hispanohablantes, pp. 181–187	•		•	•
					Audio Program, Cap. 7A, Examen	•		•	
					ExamView: Test Banks A and B questions only online	•		•	
					Heritage Learner Test Bank	•		•	
					Pre-AP* Test Bank	•		•	

REGULAR SCHEDULE (50 MINUTES)

DAY	Warm-up / Assess	Preview / Present / Practice / Communicate	Wrap-up / Homework Options
1	**Warm-up** (10 min.) • Return Examen del capítulo 6B	**Chapter Opener** (5 min.) • Objectives • Arte y cultura **Vocabulario en contexto** (30 min.) • Presentation: Vocabulario en contexto • Actividades 1, 2	**Wrap-up and Homework Options** (5 min.) • Core Practice 7A-1, 7A-2
2	**Warm-up** (5 min.) • Homework check	**Vocabulario en contexto** (40 min.) • Presentation: Videohistoria *Una noche especial* • View: Videohistoria • Video Activities 1, 2, 3, 4 • Actividad 3	**Wrap-up and Homework Options** (5 min.) • Core Practice 7A-3, 7A-4 • Prueba 7A-1: Vocabulary recognition
3	**Warm-up** (10 min.) • Actividades 4, 8 • Homework check ✓**Formative Assessment** (10 min.) • Prueba 7A-1: Vocabulary recognition	**Vocabulario en uso** (25 min.) • Interactive Whiteboard Vocabulary Activities • Actividades 5, 6, 7 • Fondo cultural • Audio Activities 5, 6 • Communicative Pair Activity	**Wrap-up and Homework Options** (5 min.) • Writing Activity 10 • Prueba 7A-2 with Study Plan: Vocabulary production
4	**Warm-up** (10 min.) • Actividad 9 • Homework check ✓**Formative Assessment** (10 min.) • Prueba 7A-2 with Study Plan: Vocabulary production	**Gramática y vocabulario en uso** (25 min.) • Actividades 10, 11 • Communicative Pair Activity • Presentation: Stem-changing verbs: ***pensar, querer,*** and ***preferir*** • View: GramActiva video • Interactive Whiteboard Grammar Activities • Actividades 13, 14	**Wrap-up and Homework Options** (5 min.) • Actividades 12, 15 • Writing Activity 11
5	**Warm-up** (10 min.) • Fondo cultural • Homework check	**Gramática y vocabulario en uso** (35 min.) • Pronunciación • Actividad 16 • Audio Activity 7 • Presentation: Demonstrative adjectives • View: GramActiva video • Interactive Whiteboard Grammar Activities • Actividad 18	**Wrap-up and Homework Options** (5 min.) • Core Practice 7A-5 • Actividad 17 • Writing Activity 13 • Prueba 7A-3 with Study Plan: Stem-changing verbs: ***pensar, querer,*** and ***preferir***
6	**Warm-up** (5 min.) • Homework check ✓**Formative Assessment** (10 min.) • Prueba 7A-3 with Study Plan: Stem-changing verbs: ***pensar, querer,*** and ***preferir***	**Gramática y vocabulario en uso** (30 min.) • Audio Activities 8, 9 • Actividad 19 • Exploración del lenguaje • Actividades 20, 21, 22	**Wrap-up and Homework Options** (5 min.) • Core Practice 7A-6, 7A-7 • Prueba 7A-4 with Study Plan: Demonstrative adjectives
7	**Warm-up** (10 min.) • Writing Activity 12 • Homework check ✓**Formative Assessment** (10 min.) • Prueba 7A-4 with Study Plan: Demonstrative adjectives	**Gramática y vocabulario en uso** (20 min.) • Communicative Pair Activity • Pronunciación • Fondo cultural • El español en la comunidad **¡Adelante!** (5 min.) • Presentación oral: Step 1	**Wrap-up and Homework Options** (5 min.) • La cultura en vivo • Presentación oral: Step 2
8	**Warm-up** (5 min.) • Homework check	**¡Adelante!** (30 min.) • Presentación oral: Step 3 **Repaso del capítulo** (10 min.) • Vocabulario y gramática • Preparación para el examen 1, 2	**Wrap-up and Homework Options** (5 min.) • Preparación para el examen 3, 4, 5 • Instant Check
9	**Warm-up** (5 min.) • Homework check	**¡Adelante!** (40 min.) • Lectura • ¿Comprendes? • Fondo cultural • Videomisterio: *¿Eres tú, María?,* Episodio 5	**Wrap-up and Homework Options** (5 min.) • Core Practice 7A-8, 7A-9 • Lectura • Videomisterio • Examen del capítulo 7A
10	**Warm-up** (10 min.) • Homework check • Answer questions ✓**Summative Assessment** (40 min.) • Examen del capítulo 7A		

BLOCK SCHEDULE (90 MINUTES)

DAY	Warm-up / Assess	Preview / Present / Practice / Communicate	Wrap-up / Homework Options
1	**Warm-up** (10 min.) • Return Examen del capítulo 6B	**Chapter Opener** (5 min.) • Objectives • Arte y cultura **Vocabulario en contexto** (50 min.) • Presentation: Vocabulario en contexto • Actividades 1, 2 • Presentation: Videohistoria *Una noche especial* • View: Videohistoria • Video Activities 1, 2, 3, 4 • Actividad 3 **Vocabulario en uso** (20 min.) • Interactive Whiteboard Vocabulary Activities • Actividades 4, 5, 6, 7 • Fondo cultural	**Wrap-up and Homework Options** (5 min.) • Core Practice 7A-1, 7A-2, 7A-3, 7A-4 • Prueba 7A-1: Vocabulary recognition
2	**Warm-up** (10 min.) • Actividad 8 • Homework check ✓**Formative Assessment** (10 min.) • Prueba 7A-1: Vocabulary recognition	**Gramática y vocabulario en uso** (65 min.) • Actividad 9 • Fondo cultural • Actividades 10, 11 • Audio Activities 5, 6 • Pronunciación • Audio Activity 7 • Communicative Pair Activity • Presentation: Stem-changing verbs: ***pensar, querer,*** and ***preferir*** • View: GramActiva video • Interactive Whiteboard Grammar Activities • Actividades 13, 14	**Wrap-up and Homework Options** (5 min.) • Core Practice 7A-5 • Writing Activity 10 • Actividades 12, 15 • Prueba 7A-2 with Study Plan: Vocabulary production
3	**Warm-up** (5 min.) • Homework check ✓**Formative Assessment** (10 min.) • Prueba 7A-2 with Study Plan: Vocabulary production	**Gramática y vocabulario en uso** (70 min.) • Writing Activity 11 • Actividad 16 • Presentation: Demonstrative adjectives • View: GramActiva video • Interactive Whiteboard Grammar Activities • Actividades 18, 19 • Exploración del lenguaje • Actividades 20, 21, 22 • Writing Activity 12	**Wrap-up and Homework Options** (5 min.) • Actividad 17 • Writing Activity 13 • Core Practice 7A-6, 7A-7 • Pruebas 7A-3, 7A-4 with Study Plans: Stem-changing verbs: ***pensar, querer,*** and ***preferir,*** Demonstrative adjectives
4	**Warm-up** (10 min.) • Homework check ✓**Formative Assessment** (15 min.) • Pruebas 7A-3, 7A-4 with Study Plans: Stem-changing verbs: ***pensar, querer,*** and ***preferir;*** Demonstrative adjectives	**Gramática y vocabulario en uso** (25 min.) • Audio Activities 8, 9 • Communicative Pair Activity • Fondo cultural • El español en la comunidad **¡Adelante!** (35 min.) • Presentación oral: Step 1 • La cultura en vivo	**Wrap-up and Homework Options** (5 min.) • Presentación oral: Step 2
5	**Warm-up** (5 min.) • Homework check	**¡Adelante!** (50 min.) • Lectura • ¿Comprendes? • Fondo cultural • Presentación oral: Step 3 **Repaso del capítulo** (30 min.) • Vocabulario y gramática • Preparación para el examen 1, 2, 3, 4, 5	**Wrap-up and Homework Options** (5 min.) • Core Practice 7A-8, 7A-9 • Instant Check • Lectura • Examen del capítulo 7A
6	**Warm-up** (15 min.) • Homework check • Situation Cards **Repaso del capítulo** (10 min.) • Communicative Pair Activities ✓**Summative Assessment** (40 min.) • Examen del capítulo 7A	**¡Adelante!** (20 min.) • Videomisterio: *¿Eres tú, María?,* Episodio 5	**Wrap-up and Homework Options** (5 min.) • Videomisterio

Standards for *Capítulo* 7A

- To achieve the goals of the Standards, students will:

Communication

1.1 Interpersonal
- Talk about shopping and clothes
- Talk about preferences and plans
- Talk about traditional clothing of Panama
- Discuss the plot of a video mystery series

1.2 Interpretive
- Read and listen to information about shopping and clothes
- Read a picture-based story
- Listen to and watch a video about shopping and clothes
- Read about preferences and plans
- Read an advertisement for a variety store
- Read about traditional clothing of Panama
- View a video mystery series

1.3 Presentational
- Present information about shopping and clothes
- Write about Botero's painting "En Familia"
- Present information about money and currency
- Present information about preferences and plans

Culture

2.1 Practices and Perspectives
- Explain etiquette of dress at social functions
- Describe the growing influence of Latin American fashion designers
- Describe traditional Panamanian festivals
- Describe ***Carnaval*** in Latin American Countries

2.2 Products and Perspectives
- Discuss Joan Miró and his painting
- Discuss the ***garibaldina***
- Discuss Fernando Botero, his painting and sculpture
- Discuss currency in Spanish-speaking countries
- Discuss traditional Panamanian festival costumes
- Discuss the fabric artwork style ***mola***

Connections

3.1 Cross-curricular
- Discuss important artists and their work: Miró, Botero, Herrera
- Reinforce mathematics skills
- Discuss fashion designer Carolina Herrera
- Reinforce knowledge of geography

3.2 Target Culture
- Read a poem of Puerto Rico, "En la puerta del cielo"

Comparisons

4.1 Language
- Explain the pronunciation of the letter ***z***
- Discuss verbs ***pensar, querer,*** and ***preferir***
- Discuss demonstrative adjectives
- Discuss a non-verbal expression for "That's expensive!"

4.2 Culture
- Compare changing fashions
- Compare artwork and symbolism of currency
- Compare celebrations in the United States to ***Carnaval***
- Compare personalized decorative clothing

Communities

5.1 Beyond the School
- Identify local stores that sell products from Spanish-speaking countries

5.2 Lifelong Learner
- View a video mystery series

Capítulo

7A ¿Cuánto cuesta?

Chapter Objectives

Communication

By the end of this chapter you will be able to:
- Listen to conversations and read about clothes and shopping
- Talk and write about shopping plans and gifts
- Exchange information while purchasing an item of clothing

Culture

You will also be able to:
- Understand the role of *molas* in the Kuna culture
- Compare the significance of crafts and clothing in Panama and the United States

You will demonstrate what you know and can do:
- Presentación oral, p. 339
- Preparación para el examen, p. 343

You will use:

Vocabulary
- Shopping
- Clothing
- Prices and numbers

Grammar
- Stem-changing verbs: *pensar, querer,* and *preferir*
- Demonstrative adjectives

Exploración del mundo hispano

Country Connection
Clothing and Shopping

realidades.com GO

Reference Atlas

Videocultura y actividad

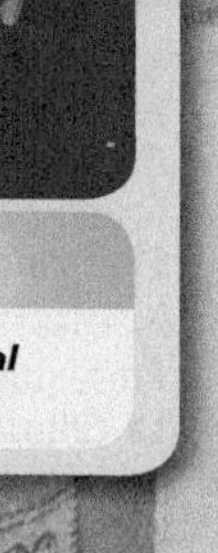

Mapa global interactivo

Mercado de artesanías, Playa del Carmen, México

ENRICH YOUR TEACHING

Using Backward Design

Have students preview the sample performance tasks on *Preparación para el examen,* p. 343, and connect them to the Chapter Objectives. Explain to students that by completing the sample tasks they can self-assess their learning progress.

Mapa global interactivo

Download the *Mapa global interactivo* files for Chapter 7A and preview the activities. Activity 1 takes you to Barcelona, Spain. In Activity 2, visit the Islas de San Blas and the Panama Canal.

Arte y cultura | España

Joan Miró (1893–1983) was born near Barcelona, Spain. He painted this self-portrait in 1919, when he was 26 years old. Here he portrays himself wearing a *garibaldina*, or cardigan, a collarless sweater or jacket that buttons in the front. *Garibaldinas* were popular at the time, and they were usually red, a color that makes this portrait even more intense.

- How do fashions change across time, or from culture to culture? Give three examples.

"El joven de la garibaldina roja" (autorretrato) (1919), Joan Miró ▶

DIFFERENTIATED INSTRUCTION

Digital resources such as the ***Interactive Whiteboard*** activity banks, ***Videomodelos***, additional ***Online Activities, Study Plans***, automatically graded ***Leveled Workbook***, animated ***Grammar Tutorials, Flashcards***, and ***Vocabulary and Grammar Videos*** will help you reach students of different ability levels and learning styles.

STUDENTS NEEDING EXTRA HELP

Guided Practice Activities
- Flashcards, pp. 213–218
- Vocabulary Check, pp. 219–222
- Grammar Support, pp. 223–226

HERITAGE LEARNERS

Realidades para hispanohablantes
- Chapter Opener, pp. 250–251
- A primera vista, p. 252
- Videohistoria, p. 253
- Manos a la obra, pp. 254–261
- ¡Adelante!, pp. 262–267
- Repaso del capítulo, pp. 268–269

ADVANCED/PRE-AP*

Pre-AP* Resource Book,
- pp. 86–89

Communications Workbook
- Integrated Performance Assessment, p. 302

PresentationExpress™
See pp. 320c–320d

Chapter Opener

Core Instruction

Resources: Map Transparencies 12–18, 20

Suggestions: Explain that students will learn how to talk about clothing, shopping, and prices. Brainstorm a list of words and expressions they think they will need in order to talk about shopping. Have them keep the list and check off the items covered in *Capítulo* 7A. The video story is about teenagers helping their friend dress appropriately for a party.

Videocultura View *Los mercados* online with the class to learn more about shopping in Spanish-speaking countries.

Arte y cultura

Standards: 2.2, 3.1, 4.2

Resources: Fine Art Transparencies, p. 39

Mapa global interactivo, Actividad 1 Explore Barcelona, Spain, home of the Miró Museum.

Suggestions: Talk about how clothes are often worn as a statement. Why are some articles of clothing popular? Who sets clothing trends? Ask if students could imagine someone wearing a ***garibaldina*** today. Are there regional differences in dress in the United States?

Answers might include the following: Clothing styles have become less formal and more comfortable over time. Possible examples include the wearing of jeans and men wearing suits and ties less frequently.

TEACHING WITH ART

Resources: Fine Art Transparencies, p. 39

Have students study the painting, then ask: How old is the person in the painting? What is he wearing? Why do you think the artist dressed himself in red for his self-portrait? What would students wear if they were to paint a self-portrait?

Vocabulario en contexto

Core Instruction

Standards: 1.2

Resources: Teacher's Resource Book: Input Script, p. 151, Clip Art, pp. 164–168, Audio Script, p. 152; Voc. and Gram. Transparencies 128–129; TPR Stories Book, pp. 92–106; Audio Program DVD: Cap. 7A, Tracks 1–2

Focus: Presenting new vocabulary about clothes and shopping

Suggestions: Use the story in the *TPR Stories Book* to present the new vocabulary and grammar or use the Input Script from the *Teacher's Resource Book*. Present the vocabulary in four sets: ***ropa deportiva, ropa elegante, ¿Cómo me queda?,*** and ***precios.*** Substitute the various clothing articles in the dialogues, using the transparencies as cues. Say each word on the transparencies, but wait to point to each picture until students point to the correct picture in the book. Have students write the words ***ropa elegante*** in large, red letters on one sheet of paper and ***ropa deportiva*** in blue letters on another. As you mention items, have students hold up the appropriate paper. Have volunteers point to clothing articles that they or classmates are wearing as you mention items. If you prefer, bring in examples of each article of clothing and set up your own "store" in which you are the clerk selling items to student customers.

BELLRINGER REVIEW

Have students review numbers by counting aloud in unison from 10 to 100 by tens.

Block Schedule

Write different events on index cards (a wedding, a rock concert, the first day of school, a day at an amusement park). Divide the class into groups and give each group a card. Each group will prepare a chart listing the *do's* and *don't's* of what to wear for the event on their card.

A primera vista

▼ Objectives

Read, listen to, and understand information about
- shopping for clothes
- plans, desires, and preferences

Vocabulario en contexto

—Buenos días. **¿En qué puedo servirle?**

—Necesito **comprar** una blusa. Y también **busco** unos jeans **nuevos.**

—**¿Prefiere** Ud. **llevar** una blusa deportiva o elegante?

—¡Me encantan las blusas deportivas!

DIFFERENTIATED INSTRUCTION

Advanced Learners

Have students choose a Spanish-speaking country and locate an example or picture of its currency. They can use reference books, the Internet, or call a currency exchange or bank. Have students copy or draw an example of one of the bills and tape it to a map, with a string stretching from the bill to the appropriate country.

Heritage Language Learners

Give each student a photograph cut from a magazine of people dressed either casually or formally. Have students write complete descriptions of the outfits. Encourage the use of descriptive adjectives. Check agreements carefully.

—¿Qué **piensas** comprar hoy?
—Necesito comprar un abrigo. Me gusta **ese** abrigo. **¿Entramos** en **la tienda?**

—¡Uf! **Me queda mal.**
—**Tienes razón.** Es demasiado grande.

—**¿Cómo me queda** este abrigo?
—**Te queda bien.** Me gusta. ¿Qué piensas?
—Me gusta también. **¿Cuánto cuesta?**
—A ver . . . Cuesta ochocientos pesos. Es un buen **precio,** ¿no?

doscientos pesos

trescientos **pesos**

cuatrocientos **pesos**

quinientos **pesos**

seiscientos **pesos**

setecientos pesos

ochocientos **pesos**

novecientos **pesos**

mil **pesos**

1 ¿Qué ropa llevan?

Escuchar

Escucha qué ropa llevan hoy diferentes personas. Señala en la foto o en los dibujos cada artículo de ropa que escuchas.

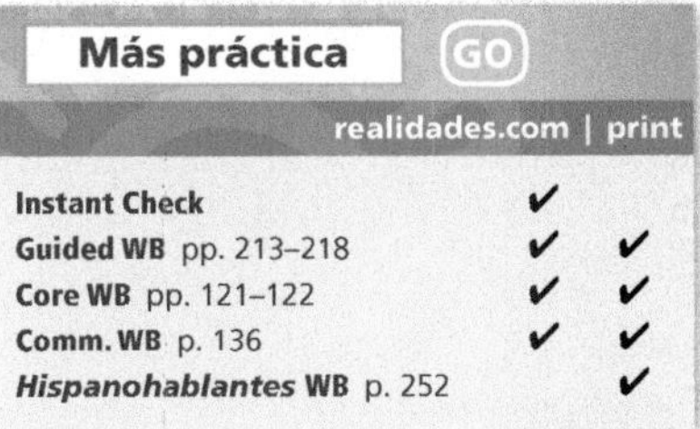

Más práctica GO

realidades.com | print

	realidades.com	print
Instant Check	✔	
Guided WB pp. 213–218	✔	✔
Core WB pp. 121–122	✔	✔
Comm. WB p. 136	✔	✔
***Hispanohablantes* WB** p. 252		✔

2 ¿Verano o invierno?

Escuchar

On a sheet of paper, draw a snowman on one side and the sun on the other. If a statement you hear is most logical for winter, hold up the snowman. If it is most logical for summer, hold up the sun.

Language Input 7A

Suggestions: Bring in articles of clothing. Put price tags on them, explaining that different countries use different currencies. Mention that depending on what monetary unit a country uses, the number might be quite large. Give students a supply of paper money. Play the role of the clerk quoting prices. Students demonstrate comprehension by handing you the appropriate number of bills.

1 Standards: 1.2

Resources: Teacher's Resource Book: Audio Script, p. 152; Audio Program DVD: Cap. 7A, Track 3; Answer Keys: Student Edition, p. 93

Focus: Listening comprehension of clothing vocabulary

Suggestions: Pause to monitor that students are pointing to the correct pictures.

Script and Answers:

1. **El profesor Ramírez lleva un traje. *(suit)***
2. **Leonardo lleva una gorra. *(cap)***
3. **Gerardo lleva pantalones cortos. *(shorts)***
4. **La dependienta lleva una falda azul. *(skirt)***
5. **Los zapatos que lleva José son negros. *(shoes)***
6. **Hace calor y Carlos lleva una camiseta. *(T-shirt)***
7. **Carmen lleva unas botas muy bonitas. *(boots)***
8. **Mi hermana lleva unos jeans nuevos. *(jeans)***

2 Standards: 1.2

Resources: Teacher's Resource Book: Audio Script, p. 152; Audio Program DVD: Cap. 7A, Track 4; Answer Keys: Student Edition, p. 93

Focus: Listening comprehension of seasonal clothing vocabulary

Suggestions: Ask students to draw their pictures large enough so you will be able to see them. If the students draw the snowman in blue and the sun in orange you can spot errors easily.

Script and Answers:

1. **¿Dónde está tu suéter? *(winter)***
2. **Necesito comprar un traje de baño nuevo. *(summer)***
3. **¿Por qué llevas pantalones cortos? *(summer)***
4. **Voy a llevar una sudadera hoy. *(winter)***
5. **¿Cuánto cuesta el abrigo? *(winter)***
6. **Mamá, ¿dónde está mi camiseta amarilla? *(summer)***
7. **Las botas son muy pequeñas. *(winter)***

ENRICH YOUR TEACHING

Teacher-to-Teacher

Have groups of students draw an outfit and ask them to label each piece of clothing with an estimated price in dollars. Then have them do an Internet search for the term "currency converter." Have students go to one of the sites and find out how much the outfit they created would cost in the currency of the Spanish-speaking country of their choice.

21st Century Skills

Creativity and Innovation Have students plan clothing they will need to spend a year in a Spanish-speaking country, listing items for each season in an e-mail to their host family. They should explain what they plan to bring and ask for feedback. Follow up with a role-play between "student" and "host-country parent."

Videohistoria

Core Instruction

Standards: 1.2, 2.1

Resources: Voc. and Gram. Transparencies 130–131; Audio Program DVD: Cap. 7A, Track 5

Focus: Presenting contextualized vocabulary and grammar; previewing the video

Suggestions:

Pre-reading: Discuss the pre-reading questions. Direct students' attention to the *Strategy* and have them read the *¿Comprendes?* questions. Point out that this strategy allows students to read with a purpose. Using the transparencies, go panel by panel and ask students to summarize the events. Ask students to identify problem(s) the characters encounter.

Reading: Read the captions with students or play the audio. Using the transparencies and nonverbal clues, help students understand the new words in blue type. Use the pictures to help students understand the difference between ***esta*** and ***esa,*** which will be explained later in the chapter.

Post-reading: Complete *Actividad* 3 to check comprehension.

Video

Core Instruction

Standards: 1.2, 2.1

Resources: Teacher's Resource Book: Video Script, p. 156; Video Program: Cap. 7A; Video Program Teacher's Guide: Cap. 7A

Focus: Comprehending a story about culturally appropriate clothing

Suggestions:

Pre-viewing: Ask students if they worry about what they wear to parties. Explain that the video deals with this dilemma.

Viewing: Show the video without the sound, stopping to ask what information students have learned from the images. Before playing the video with sound, remind students that they will not understand every word, but that they should listen and watch for overall understanding. Show the video once without pausing. Show it again, stopping to check comprehension.

Post-viewing: Complete the Video Activities in the *Communication Workbook*.

Una noche especial

¿Por qué necesita ir de compras Teresa? Lee la historia.

Strategy

Reading for key information
Reading the questions at the end of the *Videohistoria* before viewing or reading it will help you focus on key information.

1

Teresa: Esta falda no me queda bien y **este** vestido no me gusta. No sé qué llevar para la fiesta.

Claudia: Pues, puedes comprar ropa nueva. Hay una tienda de ropa aquí cerca y tienen ropa muy bonita.

Teresa: Sí, **quizás** una falda nueva . . . ¡**Vamos**!

5

Manolo: Ramón, son las ocho. La fiesta es a las nueve, ¿recuerdas?

Ramón: Sí, sí, tienes razón. Vamos.

6

Berta: Ramón, ¿tú piensas llevar esa ropa a la fiesta de Teresa? ¡**Esos** jeans y esa camiseta y . . . esa gorra! No, no puedes.

Ramón: ¿Y por qué no?

Berta: Umm . . . Pues, aquí en México no llevamos esa ropa a las fiestas.

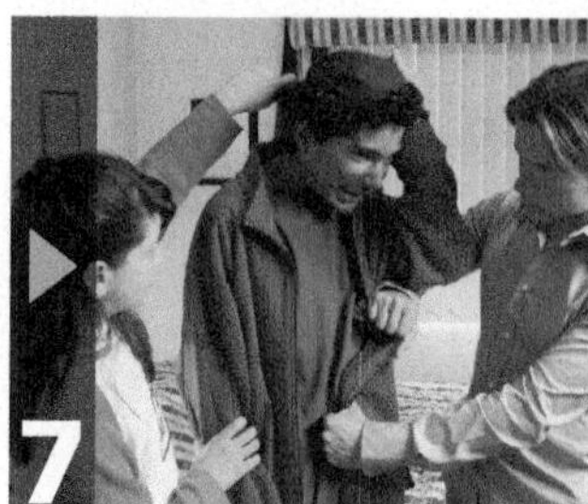

Ramón: ¡Yo quiero llevar mi gorra favorita, y me gustan **estos** jeans!

Manolo y Berta: Te ayudamos

DIFFERENTIATED INSTRUCTION

Heritage Language Learners

Have students continue the story by writing the conversation Ramón and Claudia would have if Ramón had not changed into nice clothing. Students can brainstorm the conversation and write the dialogue together. They could record their scenes to include in their portfolios.

Claudia: ¡Mira esta tienda!
Teresa: Mmmm . . . No sé. No tengo mucho dinero y **esa** ropa es muy cara.
Claudia: ¡Vamos! **¡Queremos** ver qué tienen!

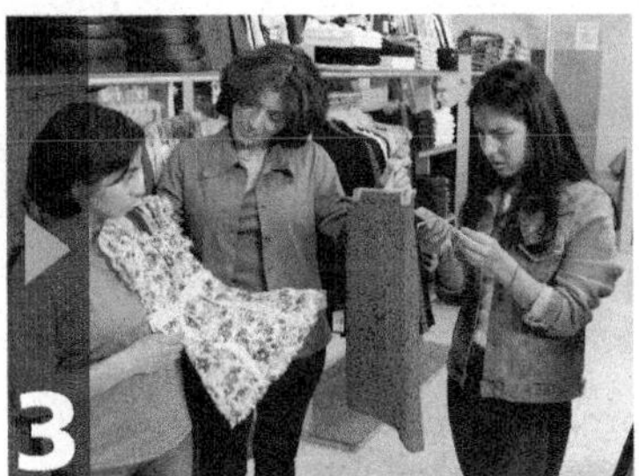

Teresa: Perdón, ¿señora?
Dependienta: ¿Sí? ¿En qué puedo servirle, señorita?
Teresa: Busco ropa para llevar a una fiesta. Me gustaría comprar esta falda y esta blusa.
Claudia: A ver . . . ¿**Cuánto cuestan?**
Teresa: ¡Seiscientos pesos! Pero, ¡es mucho dinero!

Dependienta: Bueno, aquí hay ropa que no cuesta **tanto.**
Claudia: Mira, Teresa. Esta falda cuesta trescientos pesos. ¿Qué piensas?
Teresa: ¡Genial! Y este suéter cuesta doscientos pesos. **Los dos** no cuestan tanto.

Teresa: ¡Hola! Buenas noches. Pero, ¿dónde está la gorra?

3 ¿Comprendes?

Hablar • Escribir

1. ¿Por qué no está contenta Teresa? ¿Adónde va ella?
2. Según Claudia, ¿qué puede hacer Teresa?
3. ¿Adónde van las dos?
4. ¿Tiene Teresa mucho o poco dinero?
5. ¿Por qué no compra Teresa la primera falda y blusa?
6. ¿Cuánto cuestan la segunda falda y blusa?
7. ¿Qué quiere llevar Ramón a la fiesta?
8. Cuando Ramón entra en la casa de Teresa, ¿qué lleva?

Más práctica GO

realidades.com | print		
Instant Check	✔	
Guided WB pp. 219–222	✔	✔
Core WB pp. 123–124	✔	✔
Comm. WB pp. 130–132, 133	✔	✔
***Hispanohablantes* WB** p. 253		✔

3 Standards: 1.1, 1.3

Resources: Answer Keys: Student Edition, p. 94

Focus: Reading for understanding

Suggestions: Remind students to search for key words in the questions. For example, if they see ***adónde,*** they need to look for a location. Have them work in groups of three or four to check their answers.

Answers:

1. **No está contenta porque no sabe qué llevar. Va a una fiesta.**
2. **Puede comprar ropa (una falda) nueva.**
3. **Van a una tienda de ropa.**
4. **Teresa no tiene mucho (tiene poco) dinero.**
5. **Porque cuestan mucho.**
6. **Cuestan quinientos pesos.**
7. **Quiere llevar su ropa favorita, unos jeans y una gorra.**
8. **Lleva una camisa y pantalones y tiene su gorra.**

Pre-AP* Support

- **Learning Objective:** Presentational Writing and Speaking
- **Activity:** As a post-viewing activity, have groups of students rewrite the sixth frame of the scene, imagining that Ramón is dressed too formally instead of too casually. Then have them act out their new version of the sixth, seventh, and eighth frames of the scene. You may want to make a video of the new scene to share with other classes.
- ***Pre-AP* Resource Book:*** Comprehensive guide to Pre-AP* vocabulary skill development, pp. 51–57

Additional Resources

- Communication Wbk.: Audio Act. 5, p. 133
- Teacher's Resource Book: Audio Script, p. 153
- Audio Program DVD: Cap. 7A, Track 8

ENRICH YOUR TEACHING

Culture Note

It is common in many Spanish-speaking countries for young adults to dress more formally than do young people in the United States. This applies not only to special events but also to instances not normally associated with dressing up, such as concerts, walks in the park, or just visiting family.

21st Century Skills

Social and Cross-Cultural Skills Have students talk with a native Spanish speaker or an exchange student from a Spanish-speaking country about this video. Have them summarize what happened and discuss what the event says about different cultural attitudes toward clothing for social events.

ASSESSMENT

Quiz: Vocabulary Recognition

- Prueba 7A-1: pp. 175–176

INTERACTIVE WHITEBOARD
Vocabulary Activities 7A

BELLRINGER REVIEW

Go around the room and point to different items students are wearing. Ask students to name them.

4 Standards: 1.3

Focus: Writing about clothing in a personalized context

Recycle: Leisure activities

Suggestions: Have students consider the activities for each location to help them decide what to wear.

Answers will vary.

Common Errors: Not correctly matching indefinite article to nouns in number and gender. Before beginning, have students give the article for each item of clothing.

5 Standards: 1.2

Resources: Teacher's Resource Book: Audio Script, p. 153; Audio Program DVD: Cap. 7A, Track 6; Answer Keys: Student Edition, p. 94

Focus: Listening comprehension; writing accurately using shopping vocabulary

Recycle: Adjectives; ***me gusta***

Suggestions: Clarify the use of the (+) and (–) signs.

Script and Answers:

1. **Esta blusa me queda muy bien. *(+)***
2. **Esta camisa cuesta demasiado. *(-)***
3. **Tienes razón. Estas botas son muy bonitas. *(+)***
4. **Estos zapatos me quedan mal. *(-)***
5. **No sé. Vamos a otra tienda. *(-)***
6. **Quizás, pero no me gusta mucho. *(-)***

6 Standards: 1.1

Focus: Using vocabulary in a conversation; practicing making clothing purchases

Recycle: ***Me gustaría;*** colors; present progressive

Suggestions: Practice the model with a student volunteer. Students can take turns being the salesperson and the customer. Help students with adjective use.

Answers will vary.

Manos a la obra

Vocabulario en uso

Objectives

- Listen to shoppers and clerks comment on clothes and prices
- Write and talk about the clothes you wear and buy
- Describe the clothes in a painting
- Discuss how clothes fit and how much they cost

4 ¿Qué piensas llevar?

Escribir

¡Es importante llevar ropa diferente en diferentes ocasiones! ¿Qué ropa piensas llevar a estos lugares o actividades? Escribe las frases.

Modelo

la casa de un amigo
Pienso llevar unos jeans y una camiseta.

1. la playa
2. un baile elegante
3. un concierto
4. las montañas
5. un partido de béisbol

5 Escucha y escribe

Escuchar • Escribir

Trabajas en una tienda de ropa y escuchas los comentarios de diferentes personas que buscan ropa. Escribe los números del 1 al 6 en una hoja de papel y escribe las frases que escuchas. Después indica con (+) o (-) si piensas que las personas van a comprar la ropa.

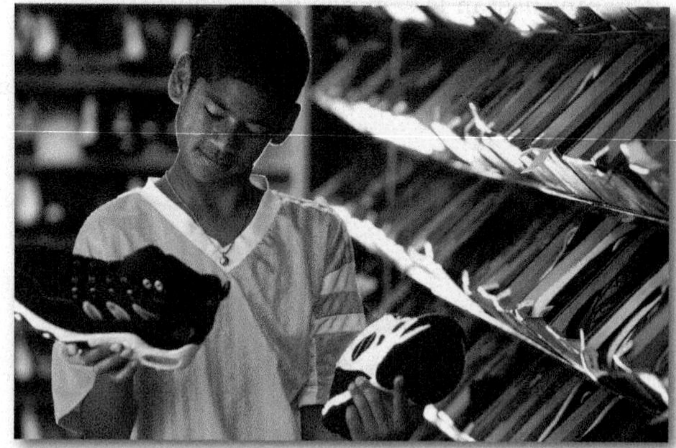

También se dice . . .

la camiseta = la playera *(México)*; la polera *(Chile)*; la remera *(Argentina)*

la chaqueta = la chamarra *(México, Bolivia)*; la campera *(Argentina, Chile, Paraguay, Uruguay)*

los jeans = los mahones *(el Caribe)*; las mezclillas *(México)*; los vaqueros *(Argentina, España)*; el pantalón vaquero *(España)*

el suéter = el jersey *(España)*; la chompa *(Bolivia, Ecuador, Paraguay, Perú, Uruguay)*

DIFFERENTIATED INSTRUCTION

Students with Learning Difficulties

Some students will have more success with *Actividad* 4 if you use the Clip Art from the *Teacher's Resource Book*. Give them pictures of the items that they can physically sort into piles according to the events listed.

Multiple Intelligences

Visual/Spatial: Have students draw or cut out magazine pictures of clothing to create flash cards. Students then present the pictures to small groups of classmates, naming each item of clothing, a suggested price, and the color. Have students quiz classmates, asking questions, such as: *¿Te gusta(n) ___? ¿Cuesta(n) mucho o poco? ¿Te gusta el color?*

6 ¿En qué puedo servirle? |  |

Hablar

Tú y tu compañero(a) van de compras. Pregunta y contesta según el modelo. Escoge cinco cosas.

Modelo

A —*¿En qué puedo servirle, señor (señorita)?*
B —*Me gustaría comprar una camisa nueva.*
A —*¿De qué color?*
B —*Estoy buscando una camisa blanca.*

7 Juego |  |

Escribir • Hablar

1. Escribe una descripción de la ropa de una persona en tu clase. Incluye dos o más cosas que lleva y los colores de la ropa.
2. Juega con otro(a) estudiante. Lee tu descripción. Tu compañero(a) tiene que identificar a la persona que describes. Antes de decir *(Before saying)* su nombre, él o ella tiene que hacer tres preguntas para saber más cosas. Por ejemplo: *¿Lleva una sudadera azul? ¿Tiene zapatos negros? ¿Sus calcetines son blancos? ¿Es Mateo?*

8 ¿Qué ropa llevan en el cuadro? | 

Escribir

Escribe cuatro o más frases que describen la ropa que lleva la familia en este cuadro de Fernando Botero.

Modelo

La madre lleva . . .

Fondo Cultural | Colombia

Fernando Botero (1932–) is a very famous artist from Medellín, Colombia. His paintings and sculptures feature people and objects that are puffed up to an exaggerated size. The figures celebrate life while at the same time making fun of what they represent

- What statement might an artist like Botero be making when his artwork presents humorous portrayals of politicians and prominent people?

"En familia" (1983), Fernando Botero ▶

Practice and Communicate 7A

7 Standards: 1.1, 1.3

Focus: Writing a description of what classmates are wearing

Recycle: Colors; adjective agreement

Suggestions: Write an example on the board and have students ask questions to guess the student's identity.

Answers will vary.

8 Standards: 1.3

Resources: Answer Keys: Student Edition, p. 95

Focus: Writing a description using clothing vocabulary

Recycle: Colors

Suggestions: Encourage students to brainstorm before they write. Have students write their responses for homework.

Answers:

la madre: **un vestido negro, zapatos negros; *el padre:* un traje marrón, una camisa blanca, zapatos negros; *el hijo:* pantalones cortos marrones, zapatos blancos, calcetines azules, un suéter rosado; *la hija:* una falda verde, un suéter amarillo, una blusa blanca, calcetines azules, zapatos marrones**

Fondo cultural

Standards: 2.2, 3.1

Resources: Fine Art Transparencies, p. 8

Suggestions: Bring in political cartoons and discuss what the artist is saying about the personal qualities of the politician through caricature.

Answers will vary but might include the idea that prominent people tend to take themselves very seriously and make themselves appear larger than life. The artist shows that these "important" people are human, too.

ENRICH YOUR TEACHING

Teacher-to-Teacher

Have students imagine that the family in Botero's painting will be starring in a new animated television series. Have them come up with names for all the family members, a description of each member's personality, and a brief synopsis of the first episode of the series. The student's descriptions and synopsis can be added to their portfolios for assessment purposes.

BELLRINGER REVIEW

Use Transparency 134 to quickly review clothing items in a personalized context.

9 Standards: 1.1, 1.2

Resources: Answer Keys: Student Edition, p. 95

Focus: Reading for comprehension

Suggestions: Have students read all the choices the ***joven*** has. Once students have made their matches, have them practice the conversation, then reverse roles.

Answers:

1. c
2. e
3. f
4. a
5. d
6. b

10 Standards: 1.2, 1.3

Resources: Teacher's Resource Book: Audio Script, p. 153; Audio Program DVD: Cap. 7A, Track 7; Answer Keys: Student Edition, p. 95

Focus: Listening for comprehension; writing numbers accurately

Suggestions: Have students read about Uruguay on p. xxvii.

Script and Answers:

1. **La camiseta cuesta 336 pesos.**
2. **¿Cuánto cuesta la blusa? 1.260 pesos.**
3. **El traje de baño sólo cuesta 980 pesos.**
4. **El suéter cuesta 1.568 pesos.**
5. **¿Cuánto cuesta el vestido? 1.680 pesos.**
6. **La chaqueta cuesta 1.764 pesos.**

Fondo cultural

Standards: 1.2, 1.3

Suggestions: Help students with the discussion question by asking them who appears on the one-, five-, ten-, twenty-, fifty-, and one hundred-dollar bills.

Answers: Boliva, Peru, Costa Rica, and the United States all honor people important to their history and culture. In the United States, we usually honor presidents on our money. We also honor our history, as on the state quarters.

9 En la tienda |  | 

Pensar • Leer • Hablar

Con otro(a) estudiante lee la conversación entre un(a) dependiente(a) y un(a) joven. Empareja lo que dice el (la) dependiente(a) con lo que contesta el (la) joven.

el (la) dependiente(a)

1. Buenas tardes. ¿En qué puedo servirle?
2. ¿Qué color prefiere Ud.?
3. Pues, estos pantalones son muy populares.
4. Sólo 50 dólares.
5. Pues, hay otros pantalones que no cuestan tanto.
6. Creo que le quedan muy bien.

el (la) joven

a. Perdón . . . ese precio es demasiado para mí.
b. Entonces voy a comprar estos pantalones.
c. Quiero comprar unos pantalones nuevos.
d. Son bonitos. A ver si me quedan bien.
e. No sé—quizás negro.
f. Me gustan. ¿Cuánto cuestan?

10 ¿Cuánto cuesta en Montevideo?

Escuchar • Escribir

Estás comprando ropa en Montevideo, Uruguay. Escucha los precios en pesos uruguayos. Escribe en tu hoja de papel el precio que escuchas.

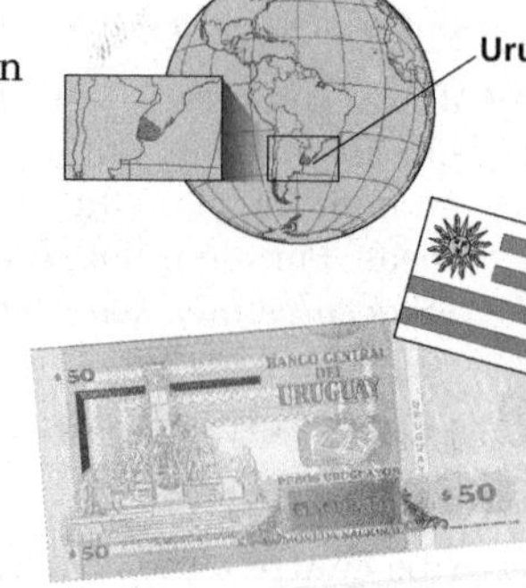

Modelo

los zapatos
Escuchas: *Los zapatos cuestan mil ochocientos veinte pesos.*
Escribes: *1820 pesos*

1. la camiseta
2. la blusa
3. el traje de baño
4. el suéter
5. el vestido
6. la chaqueta

Fondo Cultural | Bolivia | Costa Rica | Perú

The currencies of Bolivia, Peru, and Costa Rica are all different. Latin American countries have special names for their national currency and use different symbols as abbreviations. In Bolivia, the official currency is the *boliviano* (abbreviated *BOB*). The *nuevo sol* (abbreviated *s/*) is the official currency of Peru. Costa Rica's money is called the *colón*, and its symbol is a ¢ placed in front of the amount, as in ¢100 (meaning 100 *colones*). Cents are either *céntimos* or *centavos* in most Latin American countries. The images on the printed money honor each country's history and culture.

- How do the images on these currencies compare to those on bills and coins in the United States?

DIFFERENTIATED INSTRUCTION

Heritage Language Learners

Ask students to bring in money from their country of origin or find images of the currency. Before giving the presentation, have students tell how much money it is and what they can buy with it in their country of origin: *Son cien pesos. Puedes comprar un refresco.*

Advanced Learners

Tell students they have $100.00 to spend on clothes. Ask them to write sentences telling what items they would like to buy and their cost.

11 ¿Cómo me queda? | 

Hablar

Estás en una tienda de ropa. Te pruebas *(You're trying on)* la ropa y necesitas la opinión honesta de tu amigo(a). Tu amigo(a) siempre te hace *(gives you)* comentarios. Escoge dos artículos de ropa.

Nota

Me / te queda(n) follows the same pattern as *me / te gusta(n).*

- La camisa **me** queda bien pero los jeans **me** quedan mal.

Modelo

A —¿*Me queda* bien *el traje*? ¿Qué piensas?
B —*Te queda bien*. ¡*Qué guapo estás!*

Estudiante A

Estudiante B

Te queda(n) bien / mal.

Es / son muy / bastante / demasiado . . .

¡Qué guapo / bonita estás!

(No) me gusta(n) mucho.

Pronunciación |

The letter *z*

In most Spanish-speaking countries, the letter *z* sounds like the *s* in *see.* Listen to and say these words:

zapato	zanahoria	haz	almuerzo	quizás	nariz
izquierda	arroz	azul	razón	cabeza	perezoso

In many parts of Spain, however, the letter *z* is pronounced like the *th* in *think.* Listen to the words as a Spaniard says them and practice saying them as if you were in Spain.

Try it out! Listen to *"En la puerta del cielo"* ("At Heaven's Gate"), a traditional poem from Puerto Rico. Then say the poem aloud.

En la puerta del cielo,
venden zapatos
para los angelitos
que andan descalzos.

12 Y tú, ¿qué dices? | 

Escribir • Hablar

1. ¿Qué ropa llevas en el verano? ¿Y en el invierno? Incluye tres artículos de ropa para cada estación.
2. ¿Cuáles son tres artículos de ropa que te gustaría comprar? ¿Cuánto cuesta cada uno? ¿Cuál es el total?
3. Describe alguna ropa nueva que tienes.

ENRICH YOUR TEACHING

Culture Note

Tell students that ***colón,*** the name for many Spanish-speaking countries' currency, comes from the name Christopher Columbus ***(Cristóbal Colón),*** who had a profound impact on the Americas.

Teacher-to-Teacher

Ask students to bring unwanted clothing items. Make fake bills and give each student 20 ***pesos*** (or other currency). Auction off a few items, then ask a student to be the auctioneer. Describe the item: *Es una corbata roja. Cuesta tres pesos. ¿Quién da más?* Point out that *¿Quién da más?* means "Who will bid more?" Have the class donate the clothes to charity.

11 Standards: 1.1

Focus: Using ***quedar*** to express opinions about how clothing looks and fits

Suggestions: Point out the *Nota.* Students will need this structure when they give their opinion about friends' clothing. Be sure students understand the options they have in giving their opinions.

Answers will vary.

Pronunciación

Core Instruction

Standards: 4.1, 3.2

Resources: Audio Program DVD: Cap. 7A, Track 10

Suggestions: Have students read the words aloud twice to practice pronouncing the *z* both ways. Then say a word and ask students to tell you whether the word is pronounced as it would be in Spain or not. Exaggerate the sounds at first. Before reading the poem, have students identify the words that have the *s* sound.

12 Standards: 1.1, 1.3

Focus: Using clothing vocabulary in a personalized context

Recycle: Seasons

Suggestions: Inform students if answers should be complete sentences.

Answers will vary.

Additional Resources

- Communication Wbk.: Audio Act. 6, p. 133
- Teacher's Resource Book: Audio Script, p. 153, Communicative Pair Activity BLM, pp. 158–159
- Audio Program DVD: Cap. 7A, Track 9

ASSESSMENT

Prueba 7A-2 with Study Plan (online only)

Quiz: Vocabulary Production

- Prueba 7A-2: pp. 177–178

Gramática

Core Instruction

Standards: 4.1

Resources: Voc. and Gram. Transparency 132; Teacher's Resource Book: Video Script, p. 156; Video Program: Cap. 7A

INTERACTIVE WHITEBOARD
Grammar Activities 7A

Suggestions: Direct attention to the *¿Recuerdas?* Use the transparency to introduce the structure and a highlighter to demonstrate stem changes. The *GramActiva* Video can serve as a reinforcement of your explanation.

13 Standards: 1.2, 1.3

Resources: Teacher's Resource Book: Audio Script, p. 154; Audio Program DVD: Cap. 7A, Track 11; Answer Keys: Student Edition, p. 96

Focus: Listening for comprehension; writing with accuracy

Recycle: Leisure activities; plans

Suggestions: Have students skip a line between each sentence to leave space for Step 2. Remind students to conjugate the verb ***pensar*** in Step 2.

Script and Answers:

1. El sábado mis amigos y yo pensamos ir a la playa.
2. Esta tarde Elena piensa jugar al tenis con su hermano.
3. Juan y Felipe quieren ir a las montañas para esquiar.
4. Carlos y su familia piensan ir a un partido de béisbol.
5. Rosa quiere buscar un trabajo en el centro comercial.
6. Fernando y yo queremos jugar al fútbol esta tarde.

Part 2 Answers will vary.

Extension: Have students write what they are thinking of wearing to the following places: ***el gimnasio, la escuela, el campo, la playa, una fiesta.***

14 Standards: 1.1

Focus: Using ***pensar*** + **infinitive** in a personalized context

Recycle: Time expressions; leisure activities

Suggestions: Brainstorm with students a list of activities for Student B and write them on the board for reference.

Answers will vary.

Manos a la obra

Gramática

Objectives

- Listen to clothing choices and write about shopping plans
- Exchange information while discussing what you and others plan and want to do

Stem-changing verbs: *pensar, querer,* and *preferir*

Verbs like *pensar* ("to think," "to plan"), *querer* ("to want"), and *preferir* ("to prefer") are *e→ie* stem-changing verbs. The *-e-* of the stem changes to *-ie-* in all forms except *nosotros* and *vosotros*. Here are the forms:

(yo)	pienso quiero prefiero	(nosotros) (nosotras)	pensamos queremos preferimos
(tú)	piensas quieres prefieres	(vosotros) (vosotras)	pensáis queréis preferís
Ud. (él) (ella)	piensa quiere prefiere	Uds. (ellos) (ellas)	piensan quieren prefieren

¿Recuerdas?

You have used *quiero / quieres* and *prefiero / prefieres* to say what you want or prefer.

Use the infinitive for any verb that follows *pensar, querer,* or *preferir.*

¿Piensas comprar esa blusa?
Do you plan to buy *that blouse?*

Más ayuda realidades.com

GramActiva Video
Tutorial: *Querer*
Animated Verbs

Canción de hip hop: *¿Quieres ir de compras?*

GramActiva **Activity**

13 ¿Qué prefieren llevar?

Escuchar • Escribir

1. En una hoja de papel escribe los números del 1 al 6. Escucha lo que quieren o piensan hacer diferentes personas y escribe las frases.
2. Escribe otra frase para decir qué piensan llevar las personas para sus actividades.

Modelo

Mis primas quieren ir a un baile el viernes.
Piensan llevar una falda y una blusa.

14 ¿Qué piensas hacer?

Hablar

Habla con otro(a) estudiante sobre qué piensas hacer tú y qué piensan hacer otras personas.

Modelo

tu amigo(a) / después de las clases
A —*¿Qué piensa hacer tu amigo después de las clases?*
B —*Mi amigo David piensa montar en monopatín.*

Estudiante A

1. tus amigos(as) / mañana
2. tu familia / este fin de semana
3. tus amigos y tú / esta tarde
4. tú / el domingo
5. tu amigo(a) / esta noche

Estudiante B

¡Respuesta personal!

DIFFERENTIATED INSTRUCTION

Heritage Language Learners

Ask students to write six sentences telling what young people usually want, plan, or prefer to do on weekends and after school in their home country. Have them use the *Gramática* chart to guide them in grammar and writing accuracy. Have students read their work aloud.

Advanced Learners/Pre-AP*

Have students invent a dialogue in which they go shopping. They can describe what they plan to buy, what clothes their parents prefer, and what kinds of clothes they prefer to wear. Their shopping partner can provide opinions about fit and cost.

15 ¿Qué quieren comprar?

Escribir

Después de dos semanas de trabajo, todos los jóvenes tienen dinero y quieren ir de compras. Escribe frases para decir qué prefieren comprar y cuándo piensan ir de compras.

Modelo

Catalina quiere ir de compras. Prefiere comprar unos pantalones cortos. Piensa ir a la tienda de ropa el sábado.

Catalina / el sábado

1. Isidoro y Lorenzo / esta tarde

2. Julia y yo / mañana

3. Javier / este fin de semana

4. yo / ¿ ?

16 ¿Qué piensan hacer Uds.?

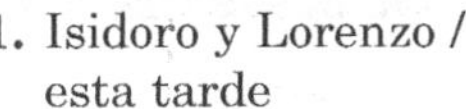

Escribir • Hablar

1. Copia la gráfica en una hoja de papel y escribe los nombres de tres personas con quienes vas a salir. ¿Adónde quieren ir Uds. y qué piensan hacer?

¿Con quién?	¿Adónde?	¿Qué?
Pepe	el gimnasio	levantar pesas

2. Dile *(Tell)* a otro(a) estudiante adónde quieren ir tú y la otra persona. Tu compañero(a) va a adivinar *(guess)* qué piensan hacer Uds. Puede continuar adivinando hasta *(until)* decir la actividad correcta.

Modelo

A —*Pepe y yo queremos ir al gimnasio.*
B —*¿Uds. piensan jugar al básquetbol?*
A —*No, no pensamos jugar al básquetbol.*
B —*¿Uds. piensan levantar pesas?*
A —*Sí, tienes razón. Pensamos levantar pesas.*

Pensamos comprar algo en el mercado.

Más práctica GO

realidades.com | print

	realidades.com	print
Instant Check	✔	
Guided WB pp. 223–224	✔	✔
Core WB p. 125	✔	✔
Comm. WB pp. 134, 137, 300	✔	✔
Hispanohablantes WB pp. 254–257		✔

Practice and Communicate 7A

15 Standards: 1.3

Resources: Answer Keys: Student Edition, p. 96

Focus: Using ***pensar, querer,*** and ***preferir*** to express what people would like to buy

Suggestions: Write the model on the board and underline the parts students will need to fill in. Remind students to conjugate the verbs ***pensar, querer,*** and ***preferir*** in their sentences.

Answers:

1. Isidoro y Lorenzo quieren ir de compras. Prefieren comprar unas gorras. Piensan ir a la tienda de ropa esta tarde.
2. queremos / preferimos ... zapatos / pensamos
3. quiere / prefiere ... un suéter / piensa
4. quiero / prefiero ... / pienso

Common Errors: Students might be confused by the ***yo*** in the second item. Make sure they understand that they should use the ***nosotros(as)*** form.

16 Standards: 1.1, 1.3

Focus: Exchanging information using ***con quién, adónde,*** and ***qué***

Recycle: Places and leisure activities

Suggestions: Draw the chart on the board and fill in the information for three students. Allow students to ask two questions to guess the correct activity in Step 2.

Answers will vary.

Theme Project

Give students copies of the Theme Project outline and rubric from the *Teacher's Resource Book.* Explain the task to them, and have them perform Step 1. (For more information, see p. 320-b.)

Additional Resources

- Communication Wbk.: Audio Act. 7, p. 134
- Teacher's Resource Book: Audio Script, p. 154
- Audio Program DVD: Cap. 7A, Track 12

ASSESSMENT

Prueba 7A-3 with Study Plan (online only)

Quiz: Stem-changing verbs: *pensar, querer,* and *preferir*

- Prueba 7A-3: p. 179

ENRICH YOUR TEACHING

Culture Note

Tell students that Spain's most famous department store is ***El Corte Inglés.*** Have students locate the store's Web site, or find it yourself before class and print copies of some of the pages. Ask students to compare and contrast the ads on the Web site with those of department stores in the United States.

Teacher-to-Teacher

Have students imagine that they are taking a trip to the coast of Mexico for three days. They can take only a very small suitcase (***una maleta***) that is about the size of their backpacks. What do they pack and why?

Gramática

Core Instruction

Standards: 4.1

Resources: Voc. and Gram. Transparency 133; Teacher's Resource Book: Video Script, pp. 156–157; Video Program: Cap. 7A

INTERACTIVE WHITEBOARD
Grammar Activities 7A

Suggestions: Discuss usage of *this, that, these,* and *those* in English. Remind students that demonstrative adjectives come before the noun and must have the same gender and number as the nouns that follow them. Use the *GramActiva* Video to reinforce your presentation. Practice the concept by placing similar objects in different parts of the room, pointing to an object, and asking students to bring it to you. (*Quiero esta gorra* or *Quiero esa gorra.)*

17 Standards: 1.2, 1.3

Resources: Answer Keys: Student Edition, p. 97

Focus: Reading for comprehension; using demonstrative adjectives in a guided context

Suggestions: Remind students that they will only be using ***este(a)*** and ***estos(as).*** They should identify the clothing items in each sentence, then determine if they are masculine or feminine, singular or plural.

Answers:

1. Estas
2. estos
3. esta
4. Este
5. esta
6. Estos

Pre-AP* Support

- **Learning Objective:** Presentational Speaking
- **Activity:** Have students bring in a family photo or an illustration from a magazine or the Internet that shows several people in the foreground and the background. Have them describe the scene in front of the class, contrasting the people and using demonstrative adjectives.
- ***Pre-AP* Resource Book:*** Comprehensive guide to Pre-AP* speaking skill development, pp. 39–50

Gramática

Objectives

- Point out items of clothing
- Read and discuss a clothing ad
- Exchange information while discussing prices and planning a fashion show

Demonstrative adjectives

You use demonstrative adjectives to point out nouns: ***this*** *cap,* ***these*** *socks,* ***that*** *shirt,* ***those*** *shoes.* Notice that "this" and "these" refer to things that are close to you, while "that" and "those" refer to things that are at some distance from you.

Here are the corresponding demonstrative adjectives in Spanish. Like other adjectives, demonstrative adjectives agree in gender and number with the nouns that follow them.

	"this," "these"	*"that," "those"*
SINGULAR	este suéter esta falda	ese vestido esa chaqueta
PLURAL	estos suéteres estas faldas	esos vestidos esas chaquetas

Strategy

Using rhymes to remember meaning
To remember the difference between these demonstrative adjectives that are spelled very similarly, memorize this rhyme:
"This" and "these" both have t's, "that" and "those" don't.

Más ayuda realidades.com

***GramActiva* Video**
Tutorial: Demonstrative adjectives

***GramActiva* Activity**

17 En la tienda de ropa

Leer • Escribir

Carmen está en una tienda y habla con su amiga sobre la ropa que se están probando *(trying on)*. Escribe la forma correcta de *este(a)* o *estos(as)* para cada número.

Carmen: __1.__ botas son bonitas, ¿no?
Mariel: Sí, pero creo que __2.__ zapatos son bastante feos.
Carmen: ¿Qué piensas de __3.__ blusa? A mí me gusta mucho.
Mariel: A mí también. __4.__ suéter es demasiado grande, ¿no?
Carmen: Tienes razón. Y pienso que __5.__ falda es muy larga también.
Mariel: Quizás. __6.__ jeans no cuestan mucho. ¡Qué bueno!

DIFFERENTIATED INSTRUCTION

Students with Learning Difficulties

Many students will benefit from physical demonstrations of the spatial distinctions between the demonstrative adjectives. Use actual items such as clothing or classroom objects. Stand directly beside students and point with them to nearby and faraway items that are the same, while using the demonstratives. Exaggerated pointing for ***ese*** will help reinforce the idea. Have pairs of students do the same thing until they begin to grasp the distinction.

18 ¡Un día con tu hermanito! 

Hablar

Tienes que cuidar *(take care of)* a tu hermanito. Tus padres tienen toda la ropa para él encima de la cama, ¡pero tu hermanito tiene sus propias ideas!

Modelo

A (tú)—*Tienes que llevar esta ropa.*
B (tu hermanito)—*¡No! No quiero llevar esa ropa. Prefiero esta ropa que está en el armario.*

19 Juego

Escribir • Hablar

¿Quién en tu clase sabe mejor cuánto cuestan diferentes cosas?

1. Trabaja con otro(a) estudiante. Escojan un objeto o una foto de un objeto. Puede ser ropa, algo de la casa, algo de la escuela, etc. Escriban una descripción de ese objeto y determinen cuánto cuesta.

Modelo

Este suéter azul y amarillo es . . . . Puedes llevar este suéter a . . . . Puedes comprar este suéter en . . . . ¿Cuánto cuesta este suéter? (Cuesta 55 dólares.)

2. Ahora, trabajen en grupos de cuatro parejas (ocho estudiantes). Lean la descripción de su objeto sin decir cuánto cuesta. La pareja que da el precio más aproximado *(closest)* sin exceder *(without exceeding)* el precio, gana.

Modelo

—Pensamos que el suéter cuesta 50 dólares.
—Daniel y Eva, Uds. ganan. El suéter cuesta 55 dólares.

Exploración del lenguaje

Nonverbal language

You've learned about the gesture *¡Ojo!*, which means "be careful." Another common gesture used by Spanish speakers conveys the meaning of "a lot of money." This gesture is made by holding the hand palm-up and rubbing the fingertips together. It is often accompanied by expressions such as *¡Cuesta muchísimo!* or *Es mucho dinero.* It can even be used when you're describing someone who is rich.

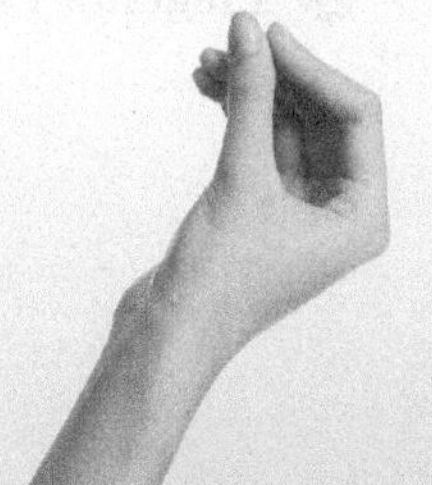

18 Standards: 1.1

Resources: Answer Keys: Student Edition, p. 97

Focus: Using demonstrative adjectives

Suggestions: Remind the students what adjectives to use for nearby objects and those that are far away.

Answers:

1. **estos pantalones / esos / estos**
2. **esta camiseta / esa / esta**
3. **estos calcetines / esos / estos**
4. **este suéter / ese / este**
5. **estos zapatos / esos / estos**

Extension: Have students create similar dialogues in which they try to get the little brother to eat various foods.

19 Standards: 1.1, 1.3

Focus: Using demonstrative adjectives and numbers in creative context

Recycle: Numbers; school supplies

Suggestions: Model the activity for students and have them guess the price of an object. After partners complete their descriptions, break the class into groups for Step 2.

Answers will vary.

Pre-AP* Support

- **Learning Objective:** Presentational Speaking
- **Activity 19:** Have students focus on the presentational speaking skills used in this task such as fluency, pronunciation, and comprehensibility.

Exploración del lenguaje
Core Instruction

Standards: 4.1

Suggestions: Demonstrate the gesture and have students imitate it. Hold up various articles and say: *¡Ay! ¡¿Trescientos dólares?! ¡Es mucho!* Then make the gesture. To apply it to people, say: *(El Sr. Bill Gates) tiene mucho, mucho dinero,* and make the gesture. Have students make up their own examples.

Additional Resources

- Voc. and Gram. Transparency 134

ENRICH YOUR TEACHING

Culture Note

For over 130 years, Spain used the ***peseta*** as its currency. In 2002, the euro replaced the ***peseta*** as Spain joined eleven other members of the European Union to create a common currency. Euros are similar to dollars in that 100 cents make one euro or one dollar, respectively. A euro coin or bill can be spent in any E.U. country.

21st Century Skills

Communication Have students who are having difficulty with the concept of demonstrative adjectives work with the *GramActiva* video, and the online tutorials. Then have each student bring five small objects or pictures to class and work with a group to place the objects in different places, ask questions about them, and identify them, using the demonstrative adjectives.

20 Standards: 1.1

Focus: Practicing buying gifts; using vocabulary in contextualized conversation

Recycle: Family vocabulary; colors

Suggestions: Be sure that Student A understands that he or she must choose an item that is shown in the clothing ad. Remind Student B to specify the clothing item and its color. Then have students reverse roles.

Answers will vary.

Extension: Bring in an authentic ad from an English- or Spanish-language clothing catalogue or newspaper and repeat the activity.

21 Standards: 1.1, 3.1

Resources: Answer Keys: Student Edition, p. 97

Focus: Cross-curricular math activity

Suggestions: Ask volunteers to explain about percentages and calculate one based on the information in the clothing ad for *Actividad* 20. Suggest that students calculate the discount to all items before they begin their conversations.

Answers will vary, but percentages are:

1. **falda marrón: 30%**
2. **blusa morada: 34%**
3. **sudadera gris: 40%**
4. **camisa blanca: 32%**
5. **camiseta azul: 39%**
6. **suéter rosado: 29%**
7. **pantalones cortos verdes: 33%**
8. **gorra roja: 43%**

Theme Project

Students can perform Step 2 at this point. Be sure students understand your corrections and suggestions. (For more information, see p. 320-b.)

Teacher-to-Teacher

Have students create labels and price tags in Spanish for items in the school store. You might have them create a conversion chart for the different currencies used in Spanish-speaking countries.

20 ¡Muchos regalos!

Leer • Hablar

Muchas personas en tu familia y unos amigos tienen cumpleaños este mes y tienes que comprar regalos. Tú y un(a) compañero(a) miran este anuncio de una tienda de ropa. Habla con tu compañero(a) sobre qué necesitas comprar.

Modelo

tu tía o tío

A —*Necesito un regalo para mi tía. Voy a buscar un suéter para ella.*

B —*Buena idea. ¿Te gusta este suéter rosado? Sólo cuesta 32 dólares.*

A —*Sí. Vamos a la tienda a buscar este suéter.*

1. tu hermano o amigo
2. tu hermana o amiga
3. tu abuelo o abuela
4. tu mamá o papá

21 En la tienda

Pensar • Hablar

Conexiones | Las matemáticas

Estás ahora en la tienda de ropa Perfección de la Actividad 20. Hablas con un(a) dependiente(a) sobre los descuentos que hay en la ropa hoy.

1. Calcula el porcentaje de descuento de la ropa en el anuncio.
2. Pregunta y contesta según el modelo.

Modelo

A —*Perdón, señor (señorita). ¿Cuánto cuesta ese suéter rosado?*

B —*Hoy este suéter cuesta sólo 32 dólares. Es un descuento del 29 por ciento.*

A —*¡Genial! Quiero comprar el suéter. ¡Qué buen precio!*

DIFFERENTIATED INSTRUCTION

Students with Learning Difficulties

If students have a difficult time with math, provide them with the percentages so that they can focus on the Spanish.

Multiple Intelligences

Visual/Spatial: Have students study fashion magazines and browse in stores to learn about the newest fashions, styles, and colors. Have them create an ad for an article of clothing to appear in a teen magazine or catalog. Have students think about what appeals to them and how much it costs. They can invent a brand name for their clothing and perhaps create a logo.

22 Un desfile de modas

Escribir • Hablar

Trabajen en grupos de tres. Una persona de los tres va a ser el (la) modelo en un desfile de modas *(fashion show)*. Decidan qué va a llevar el (la) modelo. En una hoja de papel, describan tres o más cosas que lleva el (la) modelo. Pueden incluir los colores, cuánto cuesta, dónde pueden comprar la ropa y en qué ocasión o estación pueden llevar la ropa.

Su modelo va a participar con los otros modelos de la clase en el desfile de modas. Los otros dos leen la descripción de la ropa.

Para decir más . . .

cómodo, -a	comfortable
elegante	elegant
de algodón	cotton
de lana	wool
de seda	silk

Modelo

El (La) modelo que entra en este momento lleva . . .

Fondo Cultural | Venezuela

Carolina Herrera is one of the world's leading fashion designers. This Venezuelan designer makes clothes, perfume, and accessories for women and cologne for men. She is one of many creative Spanish-speaking designers who are making their mark in the fashion world.

- Think of the names of some fashion designers from the United States. In what ways do you think they influence everyday culture?

El español en la comunidad

Locate a store in your community or on the Internet that sells products from Spanish-speaking countries. Visit the store or Web site and list the types of items you find there. Are they similar to the items listed in the ad? Bring your list to class and compare it with other students' lists. What are the most common types of items found in these stores?

Más práctica GO

realidades.com | print		
Instant Check	✔	
Guided WB pp. 225–226	✔	✔
Core WB pp. 126–127	✔	✔
Comm. WB pp. 134–135, 138	✔	✔
***Hispanohablantes* WB** pp. 258–261		✔

Practice and Communicate 7A

22 Standards: 1.1, 1.3

Focus: Writing and speaking in a contextualized situation

Recycle: Events and places

Suggestions: To create enthusiasm for this activity, bring in outrageous clothes. Direct students to the *Para decir más....* If possible, record the fashion shows.

Fondo cultural

Standards: 3.1, 2.1

Suggestions: Ask how many students have heard of Carolina Herrera and Oscar de la Renta (see *Culture Note* below). If students are not familiar with the names, show magazine photos of celebrities wearing outfits by these designers.

Answers will vary but may include that fashion designers influence everyday culture by suggesting through TV and magazine ads what people should be wearing. Because they continually change what is "in" and "out," they affect how people spend their money on clothing.

El español en la comunidad

Core Instruction

Standards: 1.2, 5.1

Resources: Voc. and Gram. Transparency 135

Suggestions: Help students come up with ideas for finding stores in your area or online.

Additional Resources

- Communication Wbk.: Audio Act. 8–9, pp. 134–135
- Teacher's Resource Book: Audio Script, pp. 154–155, Communicative Pair Activity BLM, pp. 160–161
- Audio Program DVD: Cap. 7A, Tracks 13–14

ENRICH YOUR TEACHING

Culture Note

One of the best-known names in fashion design in the United States is Oscar De La Renta. He was born in 1932 in Santo Domingo, the capital city of the Dominican Republic. He moved to the United States and, in 1965, formed his own business. He is one of the top Spanish-speaking fashion designers in the world.

Teacher-to-Teacher

Have students find an ad in a newspaper or magazine. They will create a similar ad in Spanish and add discount prices. The ad should include a small paragraph stating why the items are on sale and giving reasons for shopping at the store. Students may need to use a dictionary to find a few new words (***descuentos, gangas, barato***).

ASSESSMENT

Prueba 7A-4 with Study Plan (online only)

Quiz: Demonstrative Adjectives

- Prueba 7A-4: p. 180

Common Core: Reading

Lectura

Core Instruction

Standards: 1.1. 1.2, 2.1, 2.2, 3.1

Resources: Map Transparency 13

Mapa global interactivo, Actividad 2 Visit Panama's Islas de San Blas and the Canal.

Focus: Reading for comprehension and cultural perspectives

Suggestions:

Pre-reading: Read the information in the *Strategy* with students. Have them read the title and connect it with the photos and their prediction of what the reading is about. Ask them to focus their reading on discovering if their prediction was correct or not. Remind them that they need not understand all the details to do this.

Reading: Have student volunteers read sections of the article aloud. Stop after major sections and have students discuss what they have read. Students should try to get the main idea from the context and cognates. When they come across words they do not know, encourage them to look at surrounding words.

Post-reading: Have students review their predictions and see how accurate they were. Have them identify five words they think they have learned by using context clues.

Pre-AP* Support

- **Learning Objective:** Interpretive: Print
- **Activity:** Have all students follow along as you read the selection aloud. Then assign pairs of students one reading section. For their section, ask each pair to write a brief summary of the main points. Then, they should share decoding strategies for any unfamiliar vocabulary. Finally, they should create two multiple-choice questions. Once students have finished their preparations, go around the room asking each pair, in order, to share their summary.
- ***Pre-AP* Resource Book:*** Comprehensive guide to Pre-AP* reading skill development, pp. 19–26

Block Schedule

Have students choose another country and research its traditional clothing.

Objectives

- Read about traditional clothing in Panama
- Use maps and photos to predict content
- Compare and contrast *carnaval* celebrations to those in your community

Lectura

Strategy

Predicting
Look at the maps and photos on these pages and read the title to predict what the reading will be about. This will help you anticipate the types of words and expressions you will encounter as you read.

Tradiciones de la ropa panameña

Panamá

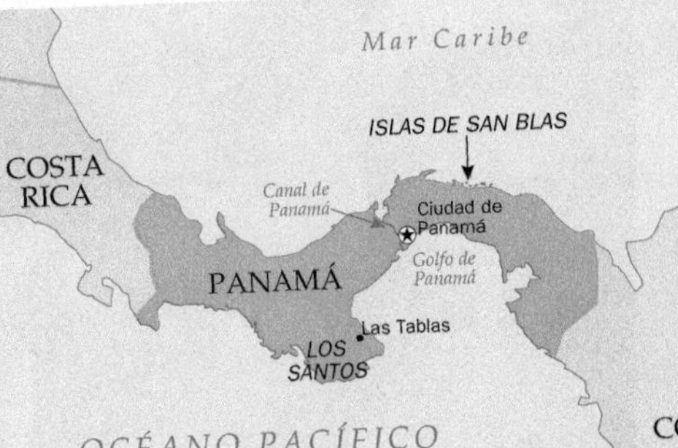

Una tradición panameña de mucho orgullo[1] es llevar el vestido típico de las mujeres, "la pollera". Hay dos tipos de pollera, la pollera montuna[2] y la pollera de gala, que se lleva en los festivales. La pollera de gala se hace a mano y cuesta muchísimo por la cantidad de joyas[3] que adornan el vestido. ¿Cuánto cuesta una pollera de gala? Puede costar unos 1.850 dólares americanos, y requiere aproximadamente siete meses de trabajo. La pollera es tan importante que en la ciudad de Las Tablas celebran el Día Nacional de La Pollera el 22 de julio.

Si quieres celebrar con los panameños, puedes visitar la ciudad de Las Tablas en la provincia de Los Santos. Las Tablas es famosa por ser el mejor lugar para celebrar los carnavales. Durante el carnaval y en otros festivales, puedes admirar los vestidos y los bailes tradicionales.

El canal de Panamá conecta el océano Pacífico con el mar Caribe y el océano Atlántico.

El istmo de Panamá es la conexión entre dos continentes, y tiene costas sobre el océano Pacífico y el mar Caribe. Es famoso por el canal en el que navegan barcos[4] de todo el mundo. El folklore panameño es muy variado. La música, los bailes y los vestidos son importantes en la vida[5] social, especialmente en las provincias del centro del país.

[1]pride [2]from the mountains [3]jewels [4]ships [5]life

336

DIFFERENTIATED INSTRUCTION

Heritage Language Learners

Have students write a paragraph about a tradition from their heritage country and whether they continue celebrating it here. Have them read their paragraphs in small groups and talk about why they think they will or will not continue the tradition.

Otro tipo de ropa auténtica de Panamá viene de los indios Kuna, un grupo de indígenas que viven en las islas de San Blas. Las mujeres llevan una blusa hecha[6] de molas. Las molas son paneles decorativos que forman la parte de adelante y de atrás de las blusas. Las mujeres demuestran[7] su talento y expresión personal con los diseños[8] originales de las molas. Los diseños representan formas humanas y animales. Hoy día, puedes ver y admirar molas como objetos de arte en muchos museos y colecciones.

Molas de colores brillantes con formas de animales

[6]made [7]demonstrate [8]designs

¿Comprendes?

1. ¿Por qué es importante Panamá en el comercio global?
2. ¿Cuáles son las dos formas de ropa auténtica de Panamá en el artículo?
3. ¿Qué puedes celebrar si visitas Las Tablas?
4. ¿Cuánto puede costar una pollera de gala? En tu opinión, ¿es mucho o poco dinero?
5. ¿Cómo se llama el grupo de indígenas que viven en las islas de San Blas?
6. ¿Quiénes llevan las molas, los hombres o las mujeres?
7. ¿Por qué es diferente cada mola?

Más práctica GO

	realidades.com	print
Guided WB p. 227	✔	✔
Comm. WB pp. 139, 301	✔	✔
***Hispanohablantes* WB** pp. 262–263		✔
Cultural Reading Activity	✔	

Fondo Cultural | El mundo hispano

Carnaval is a traditional celebration in many Latin American countries. It takes place in the weeks before the season of Lent. *Carnaval* normally includes the coronation of a beauty queen, parades, elaborate costumes, street music, and dancing. The *Carnaval* in Las Tablas, a town near the Pacific coast in Panama, is very popular and attracts thousands of visitors every year.

- What traditional parades or celebrations take place in your community? How do they compare to the celebration of *carnaval*?

ENRICH YOUR TEACHING

Culture Note

Very few human endeavors have changed the face of the planet as did the successful completion of the Panama Canal in 1914. None had ever aspired to accomplish something so incredible as splitting two continents. The Panama Canal soon became a vital link for the entire world. Where others had failed, the United States overcame numerous difficulties to build what remains one of the great engineering marvels of the world.

¿Comprendes? Standards: 1.2, 1.3

Resources: Answer Keys: Student Edition, p. 98

Focus: Demonstrating reading comprehension

Suggestions: Ask students to review the questions before reading.

Answers:

1. **Porque conecta el océano Pacífico con el mar Caribe y el océano Atlántico.**
2. **La pollera montuna y la pollera de gala.**
3. **Los carnavales y el Día Nacional de la Pollera.**
4. **Puede costar unos 1.850 dólares. Answers will vary.**
5. **Se llaman los indios Kuna.**
6. **Las mujeres.**
7. **Porque son originales.**

Fondo cultural

Standards: 2.1, 4.2

Suggestions: Ask students if they have ever heard of or participated in the Mardi Gras (French for "Fat Tuesday") celebration in New Orleans. Explain that ***Carnaval*** is a celebration that ends on the Tuesday before the Christian observance of Lent, which begins on Ash Wednesday and continues for 40 days of solemn preparation for Easter.

Answers will vary.

Teaching with Photos

Have students carefully examine the photos on pp. 336–337. Ask if certain colors are used more than others and if these are light or dark colors. Ask about the subjects of the ***molas,*** e.g., designs, animals, etc. Then ask how these traditional clothes are different from everyday dress in both students' heritage countries and the United States.

Theme Project

Students can perform Step 3 at this point. (For more information, see p. 320-b.)

For Further Reading

Student Resource: Realidades para hispanohablantes: Lectura 2, pp. 264–265

La cultura en vivo

Core Instruction

Standards: 2.2, 4.2

Resources: Teacher's Resource Book: GramActiva BLM, p. 163

Focus: Reading about ***molas*** and learning the process of creating one

Suggestions: Before class, gather the supplies, making sure you have two pencils for each project and a lot of brightly colored construction paper. Direct attention to the photo. Ask the class to describe the clothing and have them comment on the colors and designs. Ask them if they have any idea of the process used and how long they think it takes. Then explain that making a ***mola*** can take up to 100 hours.

Have students work in pairs or individually. Monitor the steps you think might be troublesome, such as cutting out all spaces not between the double lines and creating borders of different colors. Show an example of a contrasting background.

Ask students to show their work to the class. Direct attention to the *Think about it!* section and have students discuss the questions.

Answers will vary.

BELLRINGER REVIEW

Have students refer to pp. xviii–xxxi and have them mention each country represented, its capital, and the color of the flag.

Additional Resources

Student Resource: Realidades para hispanohablantes, p. 266

Pre-AP* Support

- **Learning Objective:** Presentational Speaking (Cultural Comparisons)
- **Background:** This task prepares students for the Spoken Presentational Communication tasks that focus on cultural comparisons in the exam.
- **Activity:** Have students prepare a two-minute (maximum) presentation in English (or Spanish, if possible), on how clothing can showcase the beliefs and values of a culture. Think of how *molas* reflect the Kuna Indians' culture. Compare this with an example of how clothing represents the values of your own culture.
- ***Pre-AP* Resource Book:*** Comprehensive guide to Pre-AP* speaking skill development, pp. 39–50

¡Adelante!

La cultura en vivo

Las molas

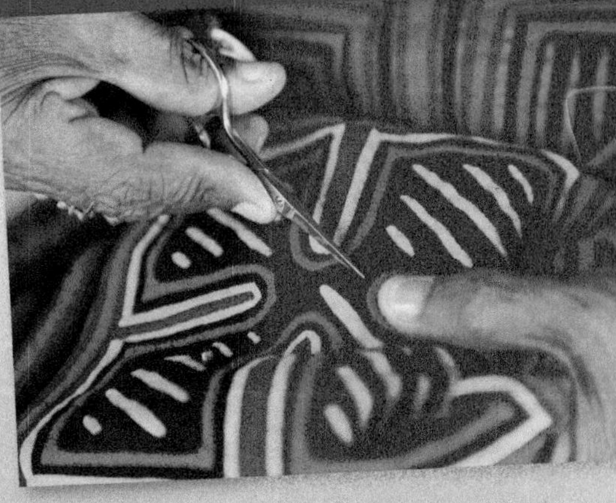

Molas are the bright fabric artwork created by the Kuna Indians of the San Blas Islands, a group of islands off the Panama coast in the Caribbean Sea. *Mola* is a Kuna word meaning "blouse." This art form was originally used to make clothing, but today the term *mola* refers to any piece of fabric made using this method.

Kuna women cut out a cloth pattern and sew it onto layers of cloth that have been sewn together. Pieces of the upper layers are cut away to expose the underlying colors and create a design. Later, the women embroider details. Many designs on *molas* represent nature or animals. Each *mola* may take many weeks to complete.

Try it out! Here's how you can make *molas* out of paper.

Materials

- 2 pencils
- rubber bands
- construction paper
- paste or glue
- scissors

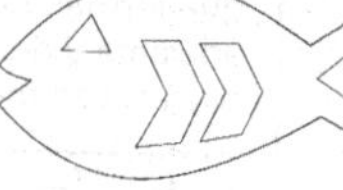

Figure 1

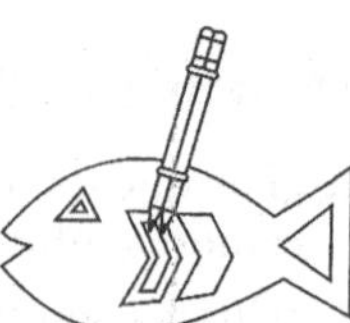

Figure 2

Directions

1 Your teacher will provide a pattern to trace on a piece of construction paper. You may prefer to trace around a cookie cutter or draw a simple design found in nature (for example, a leaf, flower, or fir tree). *(Fig. 1)*

2 Double all the lines by drawing with two pencils fastened together with rubber bands. *(Fig. 2)*

3 Cut out all spaces that do NOT fall between the double lines. *(Fig. 3)*

4 Paste or glue the cutout figure onto construction paper of a contrasting color.

5 Cut around the pasted or glued figure, leaving a border of the second color. *(Fig. 4)*

6 Paste or glue this cutout figure onto another piece of construction paper and cut around it, leaving a border of the new color. Paste the entire piece on a contrasting background.

Figure 3

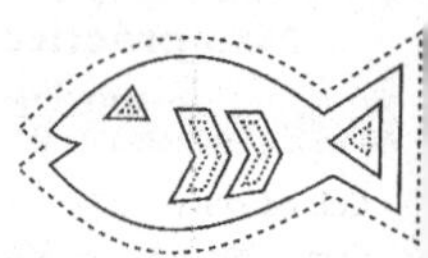

Figure 4

Think about it! Do you or anyone in your family practice a traditional handicraft? Do you have any clothes or outfits that you have made or customized to express your interests or personality?

DIFFERENTIATED INSTRUCTION

Students with Special Needs

You may need to provide construction paper already traced or cut out to accommodate some students.

Students with Learning Difficulties

If students have difficulty following these directions, you might provide models of each stage of production so they can see what their own version should look like. You might also create your own ***mola*** along with students, circulating so they can see how you are doing it.

Presentación oral 

- Demonstrate how to buy and sell clothing in a store
- Use feedback from your partner to improve your performance

¿En qué puedo servirle?

Task

You and a partner will play the roles of a customer and a salesclerk in a clothing store. You will ask and answer questions about the articles of clothing sold in the store. The customer will then decide whether or not to buy the articles.

1. **Prepare** Work with a partner to prepare the skit. One of you will play the role of the salesperson, and the other will be the shopper. Be prepared to play both roles. Decide the type of clothing the store will sell and bring to class articles of clothing or pictures from a magazine. Give the store a name.

   Cliente: Make a list of expressions and questions you can use to ask about, describe, and say whether you will buy an article of clothing.

   Dependiente(a): Make a list of expressions and questions you can use to help your client, answer his or her questions, and show him or her the clothing.

2. **Practice** Work with your partner and practice both roles. You might want to review *A primera vista,* the *Videohistoria,* and Actividad 9 for ideas. You can use your written notes when you practice, but not during the actual role play.

3. **Present** Your teacher will assign the roles. The clerk will begin the conversation. Keep talking until the customer has made a decision to buy or not to buy the article of clothing.

4. **Evaluation** The following rubric will be used to grade your presentation.

Rubric	Score 1	Score 3	Score 5
How well you sustain a conversation	You provide no conversational response or follow-up to what your partner says.	You provide frequent responses or follow-up to what your partner says.	You always respond to your partner, listen and ask follow-up questions, or volunteer additional information.
Completeness of presentation	You only describe the clothing.	You describe the clothing and price.	You describe the clothing, price, and the decision to purchase.
Use of new and previously learned vocabulary	You use very limited and repetitive vocabulary.	You use only recently acquired vocabulary.	You use recently acquired and previously learned vocabulary.

Strategy

Seeking feedback
As you practice with a partner, seek his or her feedback to correct errors you have made and to improve your overall performance.

ENRICH YOUR TEACHING

21st Century Skills

Leadership and Responsibility After completing the activities in this chapter, have students organize a fundraising event to help members of the community. Students should provide items for sale, organize and photograph them for a catalog, write descriptions, decide on prices, and then come up with an advertising campaign.

 Common Core: Speaking

Presentación oral

Core Instruction

Standards: 1.3

Focus: Practicing buying or selling clothing in a personalized context

Suggestions: Review the task and steps with students. After reading the *Strategy,* model how to give specific advice instead of only positive or negative comments. Review the rubric with the class to explain how you will grade the performance task.

Portfolio

Make video or audio recordings of student presentations in class, or assign the RealTalk activity so they can record their presentations online. Include the recording in their portfolios.

Pre-AP* Support

- **Learning Objective:** Presentational Speaking
- **Activity:** Remind students to focus on the presentational speaking skills used in this task such as fluency, pronunciation, and comprehensibility.
- ***Pre-AP* Resource Book:*** Comprehensive guide to Pre-AP* speaking skill development, pp. 39–50

Additional Resources

Student Resources: Realidades para hispanohablantes, p. 267; Guided Practice: Presentación oral, p. 228

ASSESSMENT

Presentación oral

- Assessment Program: Rubrics, p. T32

  Go over the descriptions of the different levels of performance. After assessing students, help individuals understand how their performance could be improved.

Videomisterio

Core Instruction

Standards: 1.2, 1.3, 5.1

Resources: Teacher's Resource Book: Video Script, p. 157; Video Program: Cap. 7A; Video Program Teacher's Guide: Cap. 7A

Focus: Introducing the events and characters of this episode

Personajes importantes: Lola Lago, detective; Carmula, Lola's best friend; Rosalinda, Carmela's friend who works at the San Carlos Hospital

Synopsis: Lola and Carmela meet at the San Carlos hospital, where they ask Rosalinda for help in getting information about María Requena, who spent three months in the hospital as a result of a car accident. Mysteriously, the medical record cannot be found. They inquire about María's friend, Julia, who was also in the accident. Julia died in the hospital, but her file cannot be found, either.

Suggestions:

Pre-viewing: Review with students the events of the previous episode. Doña Gracia was getting better at the hospital, although she did not remember anything about the incident that put her there. Then Lola met her best friend, Carmela, at a café. Lola explained the events that led to doña Gracia being in the San Carlos hospital. Carmela's friend, Rosalinda, works at the hospital so Carmela and Lola met the next morning in the hospital to ask Rosalinda for information. Later, Lola met Pedro as he inquired about his grandmother in the hospital. Lola offered her services as a detective and gave him her card.

Point out the *Palabras para comprender* to the class, saying examples in context and writing the sentences on the board. Remind students that these words are only used to help them understand the episode, and otherwise they are not responsible for that vocabulary.

Visual scanning: Direct students' attention to the picture on p. 340 and ask who this character is (Rosalinda), what relationship she has to Lola (a friend of Carmela, Lola's best friend), and where she works (hospital San Carlos). Before students read the *Resumen del episodio,* have them scan the text and find at least three cognates *(hospital, accidente, ocurrió, clínicos, problema).*

Objective

- Understand the expanding plot of a mystery video set in Spain

¿Eres tú, María?

Episodio 5

Antes de ver el video

Personaje importante

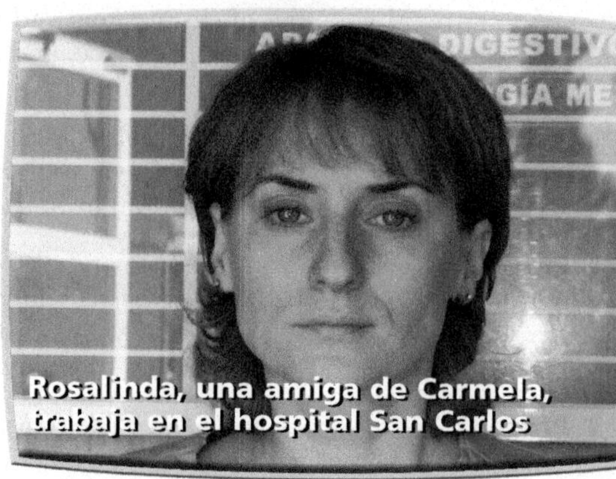

Rosalinda, una amiga de Carmela, trabaja en el hospital San Carlos

Resumen del episodio

Lola y Carmela van al hospital para hablar con Rosalinda sobre doña Gracia y María. Aprenden más sobre el accidente de coche de María. Ocurrió entre María y otra joven, Julia. Las dos fueron llevadas[1] al Hospital San Carlos. Desafortunadamente,[2] Julia murió. Rosalinda va a los archivos para buscar los historiales clínicos de Julia y María. Pero hay un problema. . . .

[1] were brought [2] unfortunately

Palabras para comprender

Estuvo aquí . . . She was here . . .
¿Te acuerdas de ella? Do you remember her?
Sí, me acuerdo de María. Yes, I remember María.
Dos coches chocaron . . . Two cars crashed . . .
la carretera highway
murió died
Les ayudó a las dos. He helped the two of them.
No viene a trabajar. He hasn't been coming to work.
el archivo records
los historiales clínicos medical records
los visitantes visitors

DIFFERENTIATED INSTRUCTION

Advanced Learners

Have students talk in groups about the investigative skills the characters use to gather evidence and understand what really happened. Remind them to use a variety of phrases to describe the characters, such as: ***Ella puede...*** or ***Ella sabe....***

Heritage Language Learners

Have students write sentences or a short paragraph in which they use at least six of the *Palabras para comprender*. You might do this after watching the episode, and have students create a narrative in which they describe what happened.

"Primero, quiero hablar de una paciente que se llama María Requena. Estuvo aquí, en el hospital".

"Pues, no está su historial clínico. Ni un papel. Nada, absolutamente nada sobre María Requena".

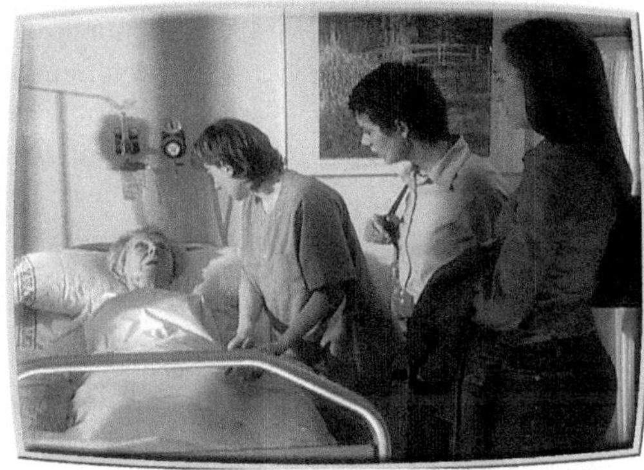

"¿Eres tú, María?"

Después de ver el video

¿Comprendes?

Lee las frases. Decide a quién(es) describe cada frase: Lola, Rosalinda, Carmela, doña Gracia, Julia, María o Luis Antonio.

1. Dos coches y dos chicas. Fue muy triste.
2. Ella murió en el accidente.
3. Hay un enfermero que ayudó a las dos.
4. Es muy simpática tu amiga.
5. No hay nada sobre ellas en los archivos.
6. Está bastante mal.
7. Las amigas de Carmela son amigas mías.

Nota gramatical Rosalinda uses two *vosotros* commands when she is talking with Carmela and Lola: *esperad* ("wait") and *venid* ("come"). You will hear this verb form often if you go to Spain.

ENRICH YOUR TEACHING

Culture Note

Most hospitals in Spain are state-run. Doctors take a national examination at the end of their studies to be selected as certified professionals to work in the national health system.

21st Century Skills

Critical Thinking and Problem Solving Encourage students to continue to record what happened in previous episodes in a format that works for them—for example, a table, chart, or timeline that shows the events, the characters, and the relationship between the characters. Students can use this information to understand, summarize and answer questions about the video story.

Then ask them to read the *Resumen del episodio* carefully and ask them questions about what they think will happen in this episode.

Viewing: Play *Episodio* 5 for the class. If there is time after viewing the full episode, select some key moments that you wish to highlight, such as the scene in which Rosalinda tells Lola that María's medical records cannot be found.

Post-viewing: Have the students look at the pictures and captions at the top of the page, and use them to summarize the scenes in this episode. Write the vocabulary presented in this episode on the board to help students write sentences for each important scene that adds new information to the plot. Also in this episode, one of the characters' lines is the title of the *Videomisterio*. Can students recall who asked, *"¿Eres tú, María?"*

Point out the *Nota gramatical*. You may want to write some examples of ***vosotros*** verb forms on the board. Then direct students' attention to the *¿Comprendes?* questions.

¿Comprendes? Standards: 1.2, 1.3

Resources: Answer Keys: Student Edition, p. 98

Focus: Demonstrating comprehension; identifying characters' roles

Suggestions: Have a volunteer dramatize the sentences. Then ask students to identify the character who says each line. Ask others what happened before or after each line was spoken.

Answers:

1. Julia / María
2. Julia
3. Luis Antonio
4. Rosalinda
5. Julia / María
6. Doña Gracia
7. Rosalinda

Additional Resources

- *¿Eres tú, María?* Video Workbook, Episode 5
- *¿Eres tú, María?* Teacher's Video Guide: Answer Key

Review Activities

To talk about shopping: Have students ask each other questions that incorporate these terms and useful expressions. For example, Student A might ask: *¿Qué dice el dependiente de la tienda?* Student B responds, *¿En qué puedo servirle?*

To talk about clothing: Have Student A draw a stick figure. Student B will name a piece of clothing. Student A draws the item on the stick figure. When the figure is dressed, have students reverse roles.

To talk about prices: Have Student A point to items and ask: *¿Cuánto cuesta(n)?* Student B answers with a price, which Student A writes down. Student B then checks the spelling and says, *Sí, tienes razón* or *No, no tienes razón.*

To indicate specific items: Bring to class objects such as different colored pens and pencils. Go to students' desks and put the objects in different proximity to them. Ask questions using demonstrative adjectives. For example, *¿Te gusta este lápiz o ese lápiz?*

Portfolio

Invite students to review the activities they completed in this chapter, including written reports, posters or other visuals, recordings of oral presentations, or other projects. Have them select one or two items that they feel best demonstrate their achievements in Spanish to include in their portfolios. Have them include this with the Chapter Checklist and Self-Assessment Worksheet.

Additional Resources

Student Resources: Realidades para hispanohablantes, p. 268

Teacher Resources:

- Teacher's Resource Book: Situation Cards, p. 162, Clip Art, pp. 164–165
- Assessment Program: Chapter Checklist and Self-Assessment Worksheet, pp. T56–T57

Repaso | | |

Objectives

- Review the vocabulary and grammar
- Demonstrate you can perform the tasks on p. 343

Repaso del capítulo

Vocabulario y gramática

to talk about shopping

buscar	to look for
comprar	to buy
el dependiente, la dependienta	salesperson
¿En qué puedo servirle?	How can I help you?
entrar	to enter
la tienda	store
la tienda de ropa	clothing store

to talk about clothing

el abrigo	coat
la blusa	blouse
las botas	boots
los calcetines	socks
la camisa	shirt
la camiseta	T-shirt
la chaqueta	jacket
la falda	skirt
la gorra	cap
los jeans	jeans
los pantalones	pants
los pantalones cortos	shorts
la sudadera	sweatshirt
el suéter	sweater
el traje	suit
el traje de baño	swimsuit
el vestido	dress
los zapatos	shoes
¿Cómo me / te queda(n)?	How does it (do they) fit (me / you)?
Me / te queda(n) bien / mal.	It fits (They fit) me / you well / poorly.
llevar	to wear
nuevo, -a	new

other useful words

quizás	maybe
Perdón.	Excuse me.
¡Vamos!	Let's go!

to talk about prices

¿Cuánto cuesta(n) . . . ?	How much does (do) . . . cost?
costar *(o → ue)*	to cost
el precio	price
tanto	so much
doscientos, -as	two hundred
trescientos, -as	three hundred
cuatrocientos, -as	four hundred
quinientos, -as	five hundred
seiscientos, -as	six hundred
setecientos, -as	seven hundred
ochocientos, -as	eight hundred
novecientos, -as	nine hundred
mil	a thousand

to indicate if someone is correct

tener razón	to be correct

to indicate specific items

los / las dos	both
este, esta	this
estos, estas	these
ese, esa	that
esos, esas	those

pensar *to think, to plan*

pienso	pensamos
piensas	pensáis
piensa	piensan

preferir *to prefer*

prefiero	preferimos
prefieres	preferís
prefiere	prefieren

querer *to want*

quiero	queremos
quieres	queréis
quiere	quieren

For *Vocabulario adicional*, see pp. 472–473.

DIFFERENTIATED INSTRUCTION

Multiple Intelligences

Logical/Mathematical: Have advanced learners go online to the Web site for a department store or mail-order business and print out the order forms. Ask them to choose clothing items within a specific budget and to fill out the form. Then have them tell you what they plan to buy or want to buy.

Students with Learning Difficulties

Have students use the Organizer from the *Practice Workbook* to create a study list and to solidify their knowledge of the chapter's vocabulary and grammar.

Más repaso GO realidades.com | print

Instant Check	✔	
Puzzles	✔	
Core WB pp. 128–129		✔
Comm. WB pp. 302, 303–305	✔	✔

Preparación para el examen

On the exam you will be asked to . . .	Here are practice tasks similar to those you will find on the exam . . .	For review go to your print or digital textbook . . .

Interpretive

1 Escuchar Listen and understand why people are returning clothing items

Listen as people explain to the clerk in a department store why they are returning or exchanging clothing they received as gifts. Try to decide if the reason is: a) it doesn't fit well; b) it's the wrong color or style; c) it's too expensive; d) they just didn't like it.

pp. 322–325 *Vocabulario en contexto*
p. 326 Actividad 5
p. 328 Actividad 10
p. 329 Actividad 11
p. 332 Actividad 17

Interpersonal

2 Hablar Describe what you are planning to buy with gift certificates from your favorite clothing store

You got gift certificates from your favorite clothing store for your birthday. Describe at least four items you would like to buy. You could say something like: *Me gustaría comprar un suéter rojo. Prefiero esos suéteres que me quedan grandes.*

pp. 322–325 *Vocabulario en contexto*
p. 327 Actividad 6
p. 328 Actividad 9
p. 329 Actividad 12
p. 330 Actividad 13
p. 331 Actividad 15
p. 334 Actividad 20
p. 339 *Presentación oral*

Interpretive

3 Leer Read and understand an online order form for a popular department store

You want to apply for a job at a department store. They need someone who understands Spanish to interpret the online orders that come in. Read the entries to see if you can tell them: a) the description of the item ordered; b) the color; c) the price.

	Artículo	Color	Precio
A.	sudadera	rojo/azul	355 pesos
B.	abrigo	negro	801 pesos
C.	falda	blanco/marrón/verde	506 pesos

pp. 322–325 *Vocabulario en contexto*
p. 328 Actividad 10
p. 334 Actividad 20

Presentational

4 Escribir Fill in an order form for specific clothing items you might purchase as gifts

Order the following items using the online order form: a) black boots for your sister, who is very little; b) a blue-and-white baseball cap for your brother, who would need a small size; c) three pairs of gray socks for your dad, who has VERY big feet!

Artículo	Color	Tamaño

pp. 322–325 *Vocabulario en contexto*
p. 327 Actividades 7–8
p. 329 Actividad 12
p. 331 Actividad 15

Cultures

5 Pensar Demonstrate an understanding of cultural perspectives on crafts and clothing

Think about something you would consider to be American folk art that has been passed on from one generation to another. How would it be similar to or different from the *molas* made by the Kuna Indians?

pp. 336–337 *Lectura*
p. 338 *La cultura en vivo*

DIFFERENTIATED ASSESSMENT

CORE ASSESSMENT

- **Assessment Program:** Examen del capítulo 7A, pp. 181–187
- **Audio Program DVD:** Cap. 7A, Track 17
- **ExamView:** Chapter Test, Test Banks A and B

ADVANCED/PRE-AP*

- **ExamView: Pre-AP* Test Bank**
- **Pre-AP* Resource Book,** pp. 86–89

STUDENTS NEEDING EXTRA HELP

- **Alternate Assessment Program:** Examen del capítulo 7A
- **Audio Program DVD:** Cap. 7A, Track 17

HERITAGE LEARNERS

- **Assessment Program: Realidades para hispanohablantes:** Examen del capítulo 7A
- **ExamView: Heritage Learner Test Bank**

Performance Tasks

Standards: 1.1, 1.2, 1.3, 2.2, 4.2

Student Resource: Realidades para hispanohablantes, p. 269

Teacher Resources: Teacher's Resource Book: Audio Script, p. 155; Audio Program DVD: Cap. 7A, Track 16; Answer Keys: Student Edition, p. 99

1. Escuchar

Suggestions: Use the audio or read the script.

Script:

SALESCLERK: Buenas tardes, señora.
SEÑORA: Buenas tardes, señor. Esta falda no me queda bien. Yo soy baja, y la falda es demasiado larga.
SALESCLERK: No hay problema, señora. Un momento. [pause] Aquí hay otra más corta.

Answer:

a) It doesn't fit well.

2. Hablar

Suggestions: Remind students to use adjectives to describe items and to make the adjectives agree with the nouns.

Answers will vary.

3. Leer

Suggestions: Students may need to review colors.

Answers:

a) sweatshirt; red and blue; 355 pesos
b) overcoat; black; 801 pesos
c) skirt; white, brown, and green; 506 pesos

4. Escribir

Suggestions: Have students try this activity without consulting the vocabulary list.

Answers:

a)	unas botas	negro	pequeño
b)	una gorra	azul y blanco	pequeño
c)	tres calcetines	gris	grande

5. Pensar

Suggestions: Have students refer to the appropriate parts of the chapter. Reflect with them on the question.

Answers will vary.

AT A GLANCE

Objectives

- **Listen to and read about gifts and gift stores**
- **Talk and write about items you've bought and their price**
- **Exchange information about gifts and price**
- **Compare cultural perspectives about shopping malls in Chile and the United States**
- **Explain the role of markets and specialty stores in Spanish-speaking countries**
- **Compare the significance of gifts in a Mexican festival and in holidays in the United States**

Vocabulary

- Stores and online shopping
- Gifts and clothing
- Expressions to describe past events

Grammar

- The preterite of ***-ar*** verbs
- The preterite of verbs ending in ***-car*** and ***-gar***

Culture

- ***ñandutí,*** p. 345
- ***Museo del Oro*** in Bogotá, p. 356
- Song, ***"El coquí"***, p. 357
- Zapotecs, p. 362
- Guelaguetza festival, p. 362
- Shopping habits in Spanish-speaking countries, p. 350
- ***El Rastro,*** p. 363
- ***artesanías,*** p. 365
- Chilean and United States consumer practices, p. 366

Recycle ♻

- Prepositions of location
- Information given in verb endings
- ***-ar*** verbs
- Verbs that end in ***-car*** and ***-gar***
- ***tener***
- Family members

RESOURCES

	FOR THE STUDENT	ONLINE	DVD	PRINT	FOR THE TEACHER	ONLINE	PREEXP	DVD	PRINT
Plan					Interactive TE and Resources DVD	•		•	
					Teacher's Resource Book, pp. 184–215	•		•	•
					Pre-AP* Resource Book, pp. 86–89	•		•	•
					Lesson Plans	•			•
					Mapa global interactivo	•			
Introducción PP. **344–345**									
Present	Student Edition, pp. 344–345	•	•	•	Interactive TE and Resources DVD	•		•	
	DK Reference Atlas	•	•		Teacher's Resource Book, pp. 184–185	•		•	•
	Videocultura	•	•		Galería de fotos		•		
	Hispanohablantes WB, pp. 270–271			•	Map Transparencies, 12–18, 20	•	•	•	
Vocabulario en contexto PP. **346–349**									
Present & Practice	Student Edition, pp. 346–349	•	•	•	Interactive TE and Resources DVD	•		•	
	Audio	•	•		Teacher's Resource Book, pp. 186–188, 191, 200–201	•		•	•
	Videohistoria	•	•		Vocabulary Clip Art	•	•	•	•
	Flashcards	•	•		Audio Program	•	•	•	
	Instant Check	•			Video Program: Videohistoria	•		•	
	Guided WB, pp. 229–236	•	•	•	Video Program Teacher's Guide: Cap. 7B	•		•	•
	Core WB, pp. 130–133	•	•	•	Vocabulary and Grammar Transparencies, 136–139	•	•	•	
	Comm. WB, pp. 140–143, 146	•	•	•	Answer Keys: Student Edition, pp. 100–101	•	•	•	
	Hispanohablantes WB, pp. 272–273			•	TPR Stories, pp. 92–106	•		•	•
Assess and Remediate					Prueba 7B–1: Assessment Program, pp. 188–189	•		•	•
					Assessment Program para hispanohablantes, pp. 188–189	•		•	•

RESOURCES

	FOR THE STUDENT	ONLINE	DVD	PRINT	FOR THE TEACHER	ONLINE	PREEXP	DVD	PRINT
Vocabulario en uso PP. **350–353**									
Present & Practice	Student Edition, pp. 350–353	•	•	•	Interactive Whiteboard Vocabulary Activities	•		•	
	Instant Check	•			Interactive TE and Resources DVD	•		•	
	Comm. WB, p. 143	•	•	•	Teacher's Resource Book, pp. 187–188, 194–195	•		•	•
	Hispanohablantes WB, pp. 274–275, 277			•	Communicative Pair Activities, pp. 194–195	•		•	•
	Communicative Pair Activities	•			Audio Program	•	•	•	
					Videomodelos	•		•	
					Answer Keys: Student Edition, pp. 102–103	•	•	•	•
Assess and Remediate					Prueba 7B–2 with Study Plan	•			
					Prueba 7B–2: Assessment Program, pp. 190–191	•		•	•
					Assessment Program para hispanohablantes, pp. 190–191	•		•	•
Gramática PP. **354–363**									
Present & Practice	Student Edition, pp. 354–363	•	•	•	Interactive Whiteboard Grammar Activities	•		•	
	Instant Check	•			Interactive TE and Resources DVD	•		•	
	Animated Verbs	•			Teacher's Resource Book, pp. 188–192, 196–197, 199	•		•	•
	Tutorial Video: Grammar	•			Communicative Pair Activities, pp. 196–197	•		•	•
	Canción de hip hop	•			Audio Program	•	•	•	
	Guided WB, pp. 237–240	•	•	•	Videomodelos	•		•	
	Core WB, pp. 134–136	•	•	•	Video Program: GramActiva	•	•	•	
	Comm. WB, pp. 144–145, 147–148, 306	•	•	•	Map Transparencies, 12–14, 20	•	•	•	
	Hispanohablantes WB, pp. 276–281			•	Vocabulary and Grammar Transparencies, 140–141	•	•	•	
	Communicative Pair Activities	•			Answer Keys: Student Edition, pp. 104–107	•	•	•	
Assess and Remediate					Pruebas 7B–3 to 7B–5 with Study Plans	•			
					Pruebas 7B–3 to 7B–5: Assessment Program, pp. 192–194	•		•	•
					Assessment Program para hispanohablantes, pp. 192–194	•		•	•
¡Adelante! PP. **364–369**									
Application	Student Edition, pp. 364–369	•	•	•	Interactive TE and Resources DVD	•		•	
	Online Cultural Reading	•			Teacher's Resource Book, p. 192–193	•		•	•
	Guided WB, pp. 241–242	•	•	•	Video Program: Videomisterio ¿Eres tú, María?	•		•	
	Comm. WB, pp. 149, 307	•	•	•	Video Program Teacher's Guide: Cap. 7B	•		•	
	Hispanohablantes WB, pp. 282–287			•	Videomisterio Quiz		•		
	¿Eres tú, María? Video WB, pp. 41–49	•	•	•	Answer Keys: Student Edition, p. 107	•	•	•	
Repaso del capítulo PP. **370–371**									
Review	Student Edition, pp. 370–371	•	•	•	Interactive TE and Resources DVD	•		•	
	Online Puzzles and Games	•			Teacher's Resource Book, pp. 190, 198, 200–201	•		•	•
	Core WB, pp. 137–138	•	•	•	Audio Program	•	•	•	
	Comm. WB, pp. 308–311	•	•	•	Answer Keys: Student Edition, p. 108	•	•	•	
	Hispanohablantes WB, pp. 288–289			•					
	Instant Check	•							
Chapter Assessment									
Assess					Examen del capítulo 7B	•		•	•
					Assessment Program, pp. 195–200	•		•	•
					Alternate Assessment Program, pp. 74–78	•		•	•
					Assessment Program para hispanohablantes, pp. 195–200	•		•	•
					Audio Program, Cap. 7B, Examen	•		•	
					ExamView: Test Banks A and B questions only online	•		•	
					Heritage Learner Test Bank	•		•	
					Pre-AP* Test Bank	•		•	

7B Lesson Plans

REGULAR SCHEDULE (50 MINUTES)

DAY	Warm-up / Assess	Preview / Present / Practice / Communicate	Wrap-up / Homework Options
1	**Warm-up** (10 min.) • Return Examen del capítulo 7A	**Chapter Opener** (5 min.) • Objectives • Arte y cultura **Vocabulario en contexto** (30 min.) • Presentation: Vocabulario en contexto • Actividades 1, 2	**Wrap-up and Homework Options** (5 min.) • Core Practice 7B-1, 7B-2
2	**Warm-up** (5 min.) • Homework check	**Vocabulario en contexto** (40 min.) • Presentation: Videohistoria *Un regalo especial* • View: Videohistoria • Video Activities 1, 2, 3, 4 • Actividad 3	**Wrap-up and Homework Options** (5 min.) • Core Practice 7B-3, 7B-4 • Prueba 7B-1: Vocabulary recognition
3	**Warm-up** (10 min.) • Actividad 5 • Homework check ✓**Formative Assessment** (10 min.) • Prueba 7B-1: Vocabulary recognition	**Vocabulario en uso** (25 min.) • Interactive Whiteboard Vocabulary Activities • Actividades 4, 7, 8 • Fondo cultural • Audio Activities 5, 6	**Wrap-up and Homework Options** (5 min.) • Writing Activity 10 • Actividades 6, 9, 10 • Prueba 7B-2 with Study Plan: Vocabulary production
4	**Warm-up** (5 min.) • Homework check ✓**Formative Assessment** (10 min.) • Prueba 7B-2 with Study Plan: Vocabulary production	**Gramática y vocabulario en uso** (30 min.) • Communicative Pair Activity • Exploración del lenguaje • Presentation: The preterite of *-ar* verbs • View: GramActiva video • Interactive Whiteboard Grammar Activities • Actividades 11, 12, 13	**Wrap-up and Homework Options** (5 min.) • Core Practice 7B-5 • Writing Activity 11 • Prueba 7B-3 with Study Plan: The preterite of *-ar* verbs
5	**Warm-up** (10 min.) • Actividad 14 • Homework check ✓**Formative Assessment** (10 min.) • Prueba 7B-3 with Study Plan: The preterite of *-ar* verbs	**Gramática y vocabulario en uso** (25 min.) • Audio Activity 7 • Communicative Pair Activity • Presentation: The preterite of verbs ending in *-car* and *-gar* • View: GramActiva video • Interactive Whiteboard Grammar Activities • Actividad 16 • Writing Activity 12 • Pronunciación	**Wrap-up and Homework Options** (5 min.) • Core Practice 7B-6 • Actividades 15, 17, 18 • Prueba 7B-4 with Study Plan: The preterite of verbs ending in *-car* and *-gar*
6	**Warm-up** (10 min.) • Fondo cultural • Audio Activity 8 • Homework check ✓**Formative Assessment** (10 min.) • Prueba 7B-4 with Study Plan: The preterite of verbs ending in *-car* and *-gar*	**Gramática y vocabulario en uso** (25 min.) • Presentation: Direct object pronouns • View: GramActiva Video • Interactive Whiteboard Grammar Activities • Actividades 21, 23, 24 • Audio Activity 9	**Wrap-up and Homework Options** (5 min.) • Core Practice 7B-7 • Actividades 19, 20 • Writing Activity 13 • Prueba 7B-5 with Study Plan: Direct object pronouns
7	**Warm-up** (10 min.) • Actividad 22 • Homework check ✓**Formative Assessment** (10 min.) • Prueba 7B-5 with Study Plan: Direct object pronouns	**Gramática y vocabulario en uso** (10 min.) • Fondos culturales • El español en el mundo del trabajo **¡Adelante!** (15 min.) • Presentación escrita: Steps 1, 5 • Perspectivas del mundo hispano	**Wrap-up and Homework Options** (5 min.) • Presentación escrita: Step 2
8	**Warm-up** (5 min.) • Homework check	**¡Adelante!** (25 min.) • Presentación escrita: Step 3 **Repaso del capítulo** (15 min.) • Vocabulario y gramática • Preparación para el examen 1, 2	**Wrap-up and Homework Options** (5 min.) • Presentación escrita: Step 4 • Preparación para el examen 3, 4, 5 • Instant Check
9	**Warm-up** (5 min.) • Homework check	**¡Adelante!** (40 min.) • Lectura • ¿Comprendes? • Fondo cultural • Videomisterio: *¿Eres tú, María?*, Episodio 6	**Wrap-up and Homework Options** (5 min.) • Core Practice 7B-8, 7B-9 • Lectura • Videomisterio • Examen del capítulo 7B
10	**Warm-up** (10 min.) • Homework check ✓**Summative Assessment** (40 min.) • Examen del capítulo 7B		

DAY	BLOCK SCHEDULE (90 MINUTES)		
	Warm-up / Assess	**Preview / Present / Practice / Communicate**	**Wrap-up / Homework Options**
1	**Warm-up** (10 min.) • Return Examen del capítulo 7A	**Chapter Opener** (5 min.) • Objectives • Arte y cultura **Vocabulario en contexto** (55 min.) • Presentation: Vocabulario en contexto • Actividades 1, 2 • Presentation: Videohistoria *Un regalo especial* • View: Videohistoria • Video Activities 1, 2, 3, 4 • Actividad 3 **Vocabulario en uso** (15 min.) • Interactive Whiteboard Vocabulary Activities • Actividades 4, 5, 6	**Wrap-up and Homework Options** (5 min.) • Core Practice 7B-1, 7B-2, 7B-3, 7B-4 • Prueba 7B-1: Vocabulary recognition
2	**Warm-up** (10 min.) • Homework check ✓**Formative Assessment** (10 min.) • Prueba 7B-1: Vocabulary recognition	**Gramática y vocabulario en uso** (65 min.) • Actividades 7, 8 • Fondo cultural • Audio Activities 5, 6 • Communicative Pair Activity • Exploración del lenguaje • Presentation: The preterite of ***-ar*** verbs • View: GramActiva video • Interactive Whiteboard Grammar Activities • Actividades 11, 12, 13	**Wrap-up and Homework Options** (5 min.) • Core Practice 7B-5 • Writing Activities 10, 11 • Actividades 9, 10 • Pruebas 7B-2, 7B-3 with Study Plans: Vocabulary production, The preterite of ***-ar*** verbs
3	**Warm-up** (10 min.) • Homework check • Actividad 14 ✓**Formative Assessment** (15 min.) • Pruebas 7B-2, 7B-3 with Study Plans: Vocabulary production, The preterite of ***-ar*** verbs	**Gramática y vocabulario en uso** (60 min.) • Audio Activity 7 • Presentation: The preterite of verbs ending in ***-car*** and ***-gar*** • View: GramActiva video • Interactive Whiteboard Grammar Activities • Actividades 15, 16 • Writing Activity 12 • Fondo cultural • Audio Activity 8 • Presentation: Direct object pronouns • View: GramActiva video • Interactive Whiteboard Grammar Activities • Actividades 21, 23, 24 • Audio Activity 9	**Wrap-up and Homework Options** (5 min.) • Core Practice 7B-6, 7B-7 • Actividades 15, 17, 18, 19, 20 • Writing Activity 13 • Pruebas 7B-4, 7B-5 with Study Plans: The preterite of verbs ending in ***-car*** and ***-gar,*** Direct object pronouns
4	**Warm-up** (10 min.) • Homework check • Actividad 22 ✓**Formative Assessment** (15 min.) • Pruebas 7B-4, 7B-5 with Study Plans: The preterite of verbs ending in ***-car*** and ***-gar,*** Direct object pronouns	**Gramática y vocabulario en uso** (25 min.) • Pronunciación • Fondos culturales • El español en el mundo del trabajo **¡Adelante!** (35 min.) • Presentación escrita: Steps 1, 5 • Lectura • ¿Comprendes? • Fondo cultural	**Wrap-up and Homework Options** (5 min.) • Presentación escrita: Step 2 • Lectura • Instant Check
5	**Warm-up** (5 min.) • Homework check	**¡Adelante!** (45 min.) • Perspectivas del mundo hispano • Presentación escrita: Step 3 **Repaso del capítulo** (35 min.) • Vocabulario y gramática • Preparación para el examen 1, 2, 3, 4, 5	**Wrap-up and Homework Options** (5 min.) • Presentación escrita: Step 4 • Core Practice 7B-8, 7B-9 • Examen del capítulo 7B • Instant Check
6	**Warm-up** (15 min.) • Homework check • Situation Cards **Repaso del capítulo** (10 min.) • Communicative Pair Activities ✓**Summative Assessment** (40 min.) • Examen del capítulo 7B	**¡Adelante!** (20 min.) • Videomisterio: *¿Eres tú, María?,* Episodio 6	**Wrap-up and Homework Options** (5 min.) • Videomisterio

Standards for *Capítulo* 7B

- To achieve the goals of the Standards, students will:

Communication

1.1 Interpersonal

- Talk about shopping and gifts
- Talk about stores and malls
- Talk about leisure activities, work, and chores
- Talk about historical events and dates
- Talk about things using direct object pronouns
- Talk about United States Hispanic commercial centers

1.2 Interpretive

- Read and listen to information about stores and malls
- Read and listen to information about shopping and gifts
- Read a picture-based story
- Listen to and watch a video about shopping and gifts
- Read a jewelry store advertisement
- Listen to information about work and chores
- Read about historical events and dates
- Read about Hispanic commercial centers in the United States
- View a video mystery series

1.3 Presentational

- Present information about shopping and gifts
- Present information about historical events and dates
- Present information about stores and malls
- Present information about activities, work, and chores

Culture

2.1 Practices and Perspectives

- Explain contrast of specialty shops and malls
- Discuss the Zapotec ***Guelaguetza*** festival
- Explain using ***tutear*** to invite informal address

2.2 Products and Perspectives

- Discuss ***ñandutí*** weavings of Paraguay
- Discuss ***El Museo del Oro***
- Discuss Madrid's flea market, ***El Rastro***
- Discuss ***las artesanías*** of Spanish-speaking countries
- Discuss that the Euro is the currency of Spain

Connections

3.1 Cross-curricular

- Read about Hispanic communities and commercial centers in United States cities
- Discuss historical events and dates

Comparisons

4.1 Language

- Talk about vocabulary through the recognition of cognates
- Discuss nouns that end in ***-ería***
- Explain forming the preterite tense of ***-ar*** verbs
- Discuss the preterite of verbs ending in ***-car*** and ***-gar***
- Discuss the pronunciation of ***gue***, ***gui***, ***que***, and ***qui***
- Discuss about direct object pronouns

4.2 Culture

- Compare selections of shopping destinations
- Compare museums and artifacts
- Compare local flea markets to ***El Rastro***
- Compare gift-giving festivals
- Compare attitudes about shopping mall experiences

Communities

5.1 Beyond the School

- Discuss opportunities for Spanish-speaking international buyers

5.2 Lifelong Learner

- View a video mystery series

Capítulo

7B ¡Qué regalo!

Chapter Objectives

Communication

By the end of this chapter you will be able to:

- Listen to and read descriptions of gifts and gift stores
- Talk and write about items you've bought and their price
- Exchange information while comparing gifts and price

Culture

You will also be able to:

- Compare cultural perspectives about shopping malls in Chile and the United States
- Explain the role of markets and specialty stores in Spanish-speaking countries
- Compare the significance of gifts in a Mexican festival and in holidays in the United States

You will demonstrate what you know and can do:

- Presentación escrita, p. 367
- Preparación para el examen, p. 371

You will use:

Vocabulary

- Stores and online shopping
- Gifts and clothing accessories
- Expressions to describe past events

Grammar

- The preterite of *-ar* verbs
- The preterite of verbs ending in *-car* and *-gar*
- Direct object pronouns

Exploración del mundo hispano

Country Connection
Shopping for Gifts

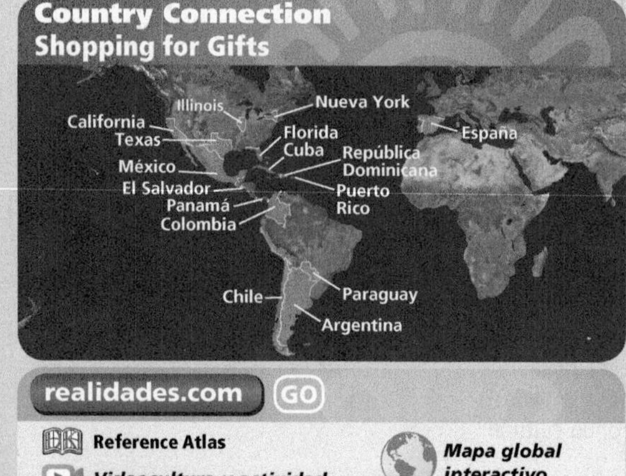

Reference Atlas
Videocultura y actividad
Mapa global interactivo

El centro comercial Galerías Pacífico, Buenos Aires, Argentina

344 trescientos cuarenta y cuatro
Tema 7 • De compras

ENRICH YOUR TEACHING

Using Backward Design

Have students preview the sample performance tasks on Preparación para el examen, p. 371, and connect them to the Chapter Objectives. Explain to students that by completing the sample tasks they can self-assess their learning progress.

Mapa global interactivo

Download the *Mapa global interactivo* files for Chapter 7B and preview the activities. Activity 1 takes you to San Luis Potosí, Mexico. In Activity 2, you look at several of the states in Mexico. In Activity 3, explore El Rastro in Madrid, Spain. In Activity 4, visit shopping areas in New York, Miami, Los Angeles, and San Antonio.

Arte y cultura | Paraguay

Ñandutí, which means "spider web" in the Guaraní language, refers to the fine lace weavings from the small South American country of Paraguay. Wall hangings and table linens are just a few of the intricately woven and multicolored items made from this fabric. *Ñandutí* looms are routinely found outside the doorways of houses in Itauguá, a small town where much of the country's *ñandutí* is made.

- Handmade items are usually more expensive than mass-produced ones. Why do you think some people are willing to pay more for these items?

Mantel *(Tablecloth)* de ñandutí, Itauguá, Paraguay

PresentationExpress™
See pp. 344a–344b

Chapter Opener

Core Instruction

Resources: Map Transparencies 12–18, 20

Suggestions: Brainstorm a list of things that teenagers buy when they go shopping. Prompt students to include accessories and gift items. The video in this chapter is about a teenage boy who needs help shopping for a birthday present. The GramActiva videos will help students learn the preterite of ***-ar*** verbs, verbs ending in ***-car*** and ***-gar,*** and direct object pronouns.

Videocultura View *Los mercados* online with the class to learn more about shopping in Spanish-speaking countries.

Arte y cultura

Standards: 2.1

Suggestions: Discuss the tradition of making crafts and clothing by hand. Point out that many such crafts are taught within a community and passed on from one generation to the next. Ask if there are any types of crafts or artwork that are typical of their community or region or of particular ethnic groups who live there.

Answers will vary but may include the following: People are more willing to buy handmade items at a higher price because, unlike mass-produced products, they are one-of-a-kind. They may also be of higher quality and reflect traditional craftsmanship.

Teaching with Photos

How does *Galerías Pacífico* compare to shopping centers you have visited? Take a few minutes to make a list of similarities and differences. What attracts you in the photo? What don't you like about this shopping center?

DIFFERENTIATED INSTRUCTION

Digital resources such as the ***Interactive Whiteboard*** activity banks, ***Videomodelos***, additional ***Online Activities, Study Plans***, automatically graded ***Leveled Workbook***, animated ***Grammar Tutorials, Flashcards***, and ***Vocabulary and Grammar Videos*** will help you reach students of different ability levels and learning styles.

STUDENTS NEEDING EXTRA HELP

Guided Practice Activities
- Flashcards, pp. 229–232
- Vocabulary Check, pp. 233–236
- Grammar Support, pp. 237–240

HERITAGE LEARNERS

Realidades para hispanohablantes
- Chapter Opener, pp. 270–271
- A primera vista, p. 272
- Videohistoria, p. 273
- Manos a la obra, pp. 274–281
- ¡Adelante!, pp. 282–287
- Repaso del capítulo, pp. 288–289

ADVANCED/PRE-AP*

Pre-AP* Resource Book,
- pp. 86–89

Communications Workbook
- Integrated Performance Assessment, p. 308

Vocabulario en contexto

Core Instruction

Standards: 1.2

Resources: Teacher's Resource Book: Input Script, p. 186, Clip Art, pp. 200–201, Audio Script, p. 187; Voc. and Gram. Transparencies 136–137; TPR Stories Book, pp. 92–106; Audio Program DVD: Cap. 7B, Tracks 1–2

Focus: Learning vocabulary about stores and shopping for gifts and accessories

Suggestions: Use the *TPR Stories Book* to present the new vocabulary and grammar, or use the Input Script from the *Teacher's Resource Book*. Present the vocabulary in three parts: specialty stores, gifts and accessories, and buying and selling. You might bring in some of the gift items and dramatize the two dialogues using the props. Use gestures and a calendar to help convey ***hace una semana*** and ***pagué.***

Extension: Make logical and illogical statements about items you are going to buy and the store where you will buy them. Have students give a "thumbs-up" sign for logical statements *(Voy a comprar un collar en la joyería.)* and a "thumbs-down" sign for illogical ones *(Voy a comprar unos zapatos en la tienda de electrodomésticos.).*

BELLRINGER REVIEW

Have students complete this sentence to suggest a good gift choice for one member of their family or a friend, then share with the class.

Un regalo bueno para ________ *es un/una* ________.

Teacher-to-Teacher

Have students extend their vocabularies by creating an ad with pictures of other gift items and accessories cut from magazines. Have them research the Spanish names of the items, using dictionaries and the Internet. Students can peer-teach the new vocabulary to their classmates in small groups.

Objectives

Read, listen to, and understand information about
- stores
- shopping for gifts and accessories
- things done in the past

Vocabulario en contexto

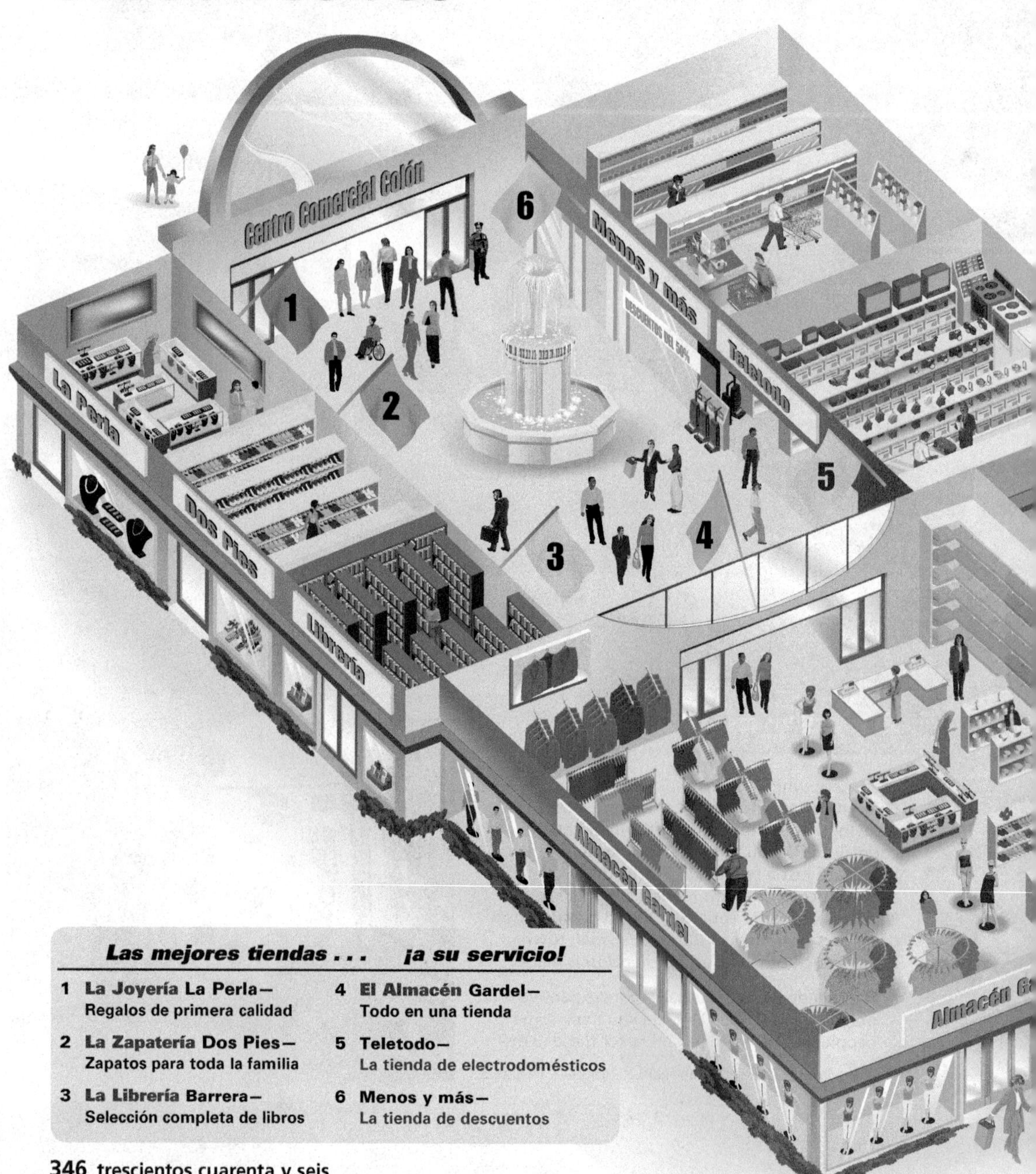

DIFFERENTIATED INSTRUCTION

Heritage Language Learners

Have students write a paragraph in which they describe their ideal birthday gift. They should include details such as who bought it, what it looks like, and what they plan to do with it. Allow students to turn in a rough draft first and determine if they want to include the paragraph in their portfolio.

Students with Learning Difficulties

Provide students with a copy of the ***centro comercial*** illustration on this page so that they can write store labels directly on it. Have them keep this in their notebooks for future reference.

—¡**Mira!** Todo cuesta menos aquí. ¡Qué **barato!**

—¡No puede ser! Yo **compré** esta cartera en el Almacén Gardel **hace una semana** y **pagué** mucho más. **¡Uf!**

la cartera
la corbata
los anteojos de sol
el llavero
los guantes
el bolso
el perfume

—Mi **novio** necesita un reloj pulsera.

—¿Por qué no **lo** compras? Cuesta 30 dólares. No es muy **caro**.

—¡Buena idea! Vamos a entrar.

la cadena
el reloj pulsera
el collar
la pulsera
los aretes
el anillo

1 ¿Qué vas a hacer?

Escuchar

Estás de compras con tu hermana en un centro comercial. Tu hermana te está diciendo todo lo que quiere hacer, o lo que necesita en el centro comercial. Para cada cosa que dice, señala dónde en el centro comercial tiene que ir.

2 ¿Dónde lo llevas?

Escuchar

Escucha cada una de estas frases. Señala la parte del cuerpo en la que una persona lleva cada artículo que se menciona.

Más práctica GO

realidades.com | print

Instant Check	✔	
Guided WB pp. 229–232	✔	✔
Core WB pp. 130–131	✔	✔
Comm. WB p. 146	✔	✔
***Hispanohablantes* WB** p. 272		✔

ENRICH YOUR TEACHING

Culture Note

One of the largest shopping centers in Spain is *Diagonal Mar* in Barcelona. Built within sight of the Mediterranean for the 1992 Olympic Games, it contains 220 shops and houses a 20-screen movie theater. Because the parking lot is so large, complimentary golf carts are available to drive shoppers to their cars.

Teacher-to-Teacher

Second-hand stores and garage sales are a great source for finding inexpensive costume jewelry and other props to use while presenting the vocabulary of this chapter.

1 Standards: 1.2

Resources: Teacher's Resource Book: Audio Script, p. 187; Audio Program DVD: Cap. 7B, Track 3; Answer Keys: Student Edition, p. 100

Focus: Listening comprehension of specialty shop vocabulary

Suggestions: Play the audio or read the script aloud. Brainstorm items sold in each store pictured.

Script and Answers:

1. **Primero necesito comprar unos aretes. *(Joyería La Perla)***
2. **Quiero comprar un televisor nuevo. *(Teletodo)***
3. **Necesito comprar ropa, unos zapatos y cosas para la casa y quiero ir a sólo una tienda. *(Almacén Gardel)***
4. **Busco un libro para mamá. *(Librería Barrera)***
5. **Necesito unas botas para el invierno. *(Zapatería Dos Pies)***
6. **Quiero comprar algo muy barato para Miguelito. *(Menos y más)***
7. **Tengo que comprar un vestido nuevo. *(Almacén Gardel)***
8. **¿Dónde puedo comprar unos anteojos de sol muy baratos? *(Menos y más)***

2 Standards: 1.2

Resources: Teacher's Resource Book: Audio Script, p. 187; Audio Program DVD: Cap. 7B, Track 4; Answer Keys: Student Edition, p. 101

Focus: Listening to identify on what part of the body one wears accessories

Suggestions: Make sure students understand the task. Say one of the gifts; have students repeat it and point to the part of the body where it is worn. Play the audio or read the script.

Script and Answers:

1. **¡Qué bonito es este anillo! *(finger)***
2. **Mira estos aretes que compré anoche. *(ears)***
3. **¿Qué piensas de la corbata azul? *(neck)***
4. **Ese reloj pulsera es demasiado caro. *(wrist)***
5. **Vamos a mirar los anteojos de sol en esa tienda. *(eyes)***
6. **¡Sólo pagué 15 dólares por estos guantes! *(hands)***
7. **Un collar es un regalo perfecto. *(neck)***
8. **Mira la pulsera que compré hace una semana. *(wrist)***

Videohistoria

Core Instruction

Standards: 1.2

Resources: Voc. and Gram. Transparencies 138–139; Audio Program DVD: Cap. 7B, Track 5

Focus: Learning contextualized vocabulary and grammar; previewing the video

Suggestions:

Pre-reading: Direct attention to the *Strategy.* Using the transparencies, go panel by panel, asking students to guess what is happening. Direct attention especially to panel 6. Do students see that there are two identical bags, and that Claudia is not picking up the one closet to her?

Reading: Read the captions or play the audio. Using the transparencies and nonverbal clues, help students understand the new words. Point out that they will be talking about the past.

Post-reading: Complete *Actividad* 3 to check comprehension.

Video

Core Instruction

Standards: 1.2

Resources: Teacher's Resource Book: Video Script, p. 191; Video Program: Cap. 7B; Video Program Teacher's Guide: Cap. 7B

Focus: Comprehending a story about buying a gift

Suggestions:

Pre-viewing: Ask students if they've ever received someone else's gift by mistake. If so, what happened? Explain that as they watch the video there will be references to the past, so they will need to pay close attention to the sequence of events.

Viewing: Remind students that they will not understand every word, but they should listen and watch for overall meaning. Play the video once without pausing, then again, stopping to check comprehension. Show it a third time without pausing. See the *Teacher's Resource Book* for additional ideas.

Post-viewing: Complete the Video Activities in the *Communication Workbook.*

Un regalo especial

¿Qué pasó cuando Manolo compró un regalo para su tía? Lee la historia.

Strategy

Using visuals
Look at the pictures as you read to help you understand the story.

Can you guess what happens at the end of the story?

Manolo: Necesito comprar un regalo para mi tía. Mañana es su cumpleaños.

Claudia: ¿Qué compraste **el año pasado?**

Manolo: Compré un libro. Quizás otro libro.

Claudia: ¡Qué aburrido! Vamos al centro comercial . . .

Claudia y Manolo están esperando el autobús. Tienen el regalo para la tía. A su derecha hay otra chica con un perro y otro regalo también.

Manolo: ¡Vamos, Claudia! Aquí viene el autobús.

Claudia: Bueno . . . bueno.

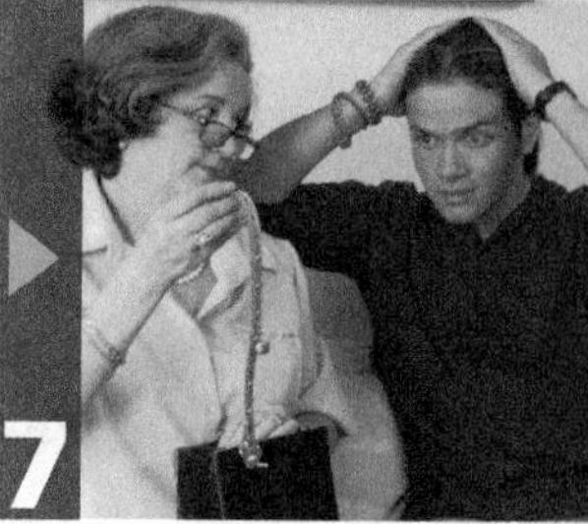

Manolo: ¡Feliz cumpleaños, tía! Te compré este regalo **ayer.**

Tía: ¿Para mí? Ah, es muy bonito, pero . . . sabes que no tenemos perro.

Manolo: ¡No entiendo . . . !

DIFFERENTIATED INSTRUCTION

Heritage Language Learners

Have students write a sequel to the *Videohistoria*, featuring the dog. Have them think about how receiving the beautiful "collar" affects the dog's life. Encourage humor and creativity. For example, students might suggest that the collar has magic power or belonged to someone famous who is looking for it.

Multiple Intelligences

Visual/Spatial: Have students work independently or in small groups to draw their ideal mall. It should include their favorite stores, as well as any desirable extras (indoor ice-skating rinks, movie theaters, etc.). Have them label the specialty shops and window displays in Spanish.

2

Manolo: Aquí **venden** guantes, corbatas . . .

Claudia: ¿Corbatas para tu tía? ¿No tienes otra idea? Mira, aquí hay otras cosas . . .

3

Manolo: ¡Ah! Tengo una idea. **Anoche** compré un videojuego **en la Red** con mi computadora. ¿Quizás podemos comprar **software?**

Claudia: Para un amigo, sí, pero para tu tía, ¡no!

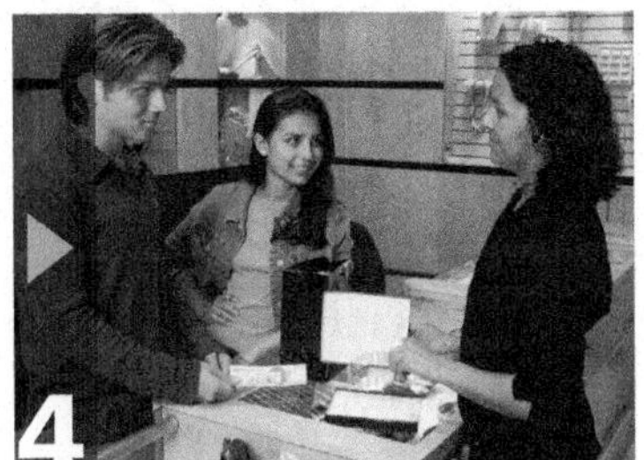

4

Claudia: Yo prefiero la joyería: una pulsera, un collar, un anillo. A ver. Señorita, ¿cuánto cuesta ese collar?

Dependienta: Cuesta 200 pesos con el descuento.

Claudia: ¡Qué barato! **La semana pasada** yo **pagué** 300 pesos por un collar.

8

Perro: ¡Me gusta mucho este collar nuevo! Me queda bien, ¿no crees?

3 ¿Comprendes?

Escribir • Hablar

1. ¿Por qué van de compras Manolo y Claudia?
2. ¿Qué compró Manolo para su tía el año pasado?
3. ¿Qué piensa Claudia de comprar otro libro?
4. A Claudia, ¿qué regalos le gustan más?
5. ¿Qué regalo compran y cuánto pagan?
6. ¿A la tía le gusta el collar? ¿Por qué?
7. Al fin *(At the end)*, ¿quién tiene el mejor collar?

Más práctica GO

	realidades.com	print
Instant Check	✔	
Guided WB pp. 233–236	✔	✔
Core WB pp. 132–133	✔	✔
Comm. WB pp. 140–142, 143	✔	✔
***Hispanohablantes* WB** p. 273		✔

3 Standards: 1.2, 1.3

Resources: Answer Keys: Student Edition, p. 101

Focus: Reading for understanding

Suggestions: Have students work in small groups to read the questions. Verify that each group has correctly interpreted each question, then have students work independently to write their answers. Be sure to clarify if you would like them to write brief answers or complete sentences.

Answers:

1. Porque Manolo necesita comprar un regalo para su tía.
2. un libro
3. Es muy aburrido.
4. las joyas
5. un collar, 200 pesos
6. Sí, le gusta, pero dice que no tienen un perro.
7. el perro

Block Schedule

Have students write and act out a conversation in which Manolo goes with Claudia to buy a present for his brother's birthday. This time, however, Manolo buys things for himself because of the low prices. When he finally finds something for his brother, he realizes he doesn't have enough money.

Pre-AP* Support

- **Learning Objective:** Interpersonal Speaking
- **Activity:** Have students create a short conversation based on Scene 4 in this video. One student will assume the role of the client. The other student will be the vendor. In the new scene, the client needs to buy something other than *el collar.*
- ***Pre-AP* Resource Book:*** Comprehensive guide to Pre-AP* vocabulary skill development, pp. 51–57

Additional Resources

- Communication Wbk.: Audio Act. 5, p. 143
- Teacher's Resource Book: Audio Script, p. 188
- Audio Program DVD: Cap. 7B, Track 7

ENRICH YOUR TEACHING

Culture Note

Although bargaining once was common in the United States, it is used less today. But it is still widely used in Latin America. In a marketplace, you can ask for ***una rebaja*** if you want the vendor to lower the price. However, in a mall, you are expected to pay the set price just as in the United States.

Teacher-to-Teacher

Have students find and write all examples of ***comprar*** in the past tense from the *Videohistoria* ***(compré, compraste)***. Write the verbs ***hablar*** and ***estudiar*** on the board and tell students that these ***-ar*** verbs follow the same pattern in the past. See if they can figure out how to say *I spoke Spanish with Manolo,* and *Did you study yesterday?*

ASSESSMENT

Quiz: Vocabulary Recognition

- Prueba 7B-1: pp. 188–189

7B Practice and Communicate

INTERACTIVE WHITEBOARD
Vocabulary Activities 7B

4 Standards: 1.1, 1.3

Resources: Teacher's Resource Book: Audio Script, pp. 187–188; Audio Program DVD: Cap. 7B, Track 6; Answer Keys: Student Edition, p. 102

Focus: Listening comprehension about stores

Suggestions: Play the audio or read the script. For part 2, have students draw on personal shopping experiences.

Step 1: Script and Answers:

1. **La ropa es más barata en una tienda de descuentos.**
2. **Prefiero un almacén porque venden muchas cosas diferentes.**
3. **Después de las clases voy a la librería con una amiga.**
4. **Me encanta mirar las cosas bonitas en una joyería.**
5. **Prefiero ir a una tienda de electrodomésticos.**
6. **Siempre puedo buscar algo en una zapatería.**

Step 2: **Answers will vary.**

5 Standards: 1.1, 1.3

Resources: Answer Keys: Student Edition, p. 102

Focus: Writing and talking about specialty shops

Recycle: clothing; electronics

Suggestions: Have students draw a two-column chart, listing name and type of store in the first column, and items sold in the second. For part 2, make sure students understand that Student B will guess the store described by Student A.

Answers will vary but may include:

1. **libros, revistas**
2. **ropa, joyas, discos compactos, etc.**
3. **aspiradoras, equipos de sonido, lectores DVD, televisores**
4. **cadenas, collares, relojes pulsera, pulseras, anillos, aretes**
5. **ropa, joyas, perfumes, corbatas, guantes, etc.**
6. **zapatos, botas, calcetines, bolsos**

Fondo cultural

Standards: 2.1, 4.2

Suggestions: Ask what kinds of stores students like. Discuss the differences between shopping in a specialty store and a mall. Do students know of any family-owned stores in their community?

Answers will vary.

Mapa global interactivo, Actividad 1 Visit a specialty store in San Luis Potosí, Mexico.

Vocabulario en uso

Objectives

- Listen to comments about stores and talk about where you shop
- Write about and discuss stores, gifts, and shopping trips
- Read and analyze an ad for a jewelry store
- Exchange information about shopping malls and gifts

4 Escucha y escribe

Escuchar • Escribir

1. Vas a escuchar lo que unos jóvenes dicen de algunas tiendas. En una hoja de papel escribe los números del 1 al 6. Escribe lo que escuchas.
2. Escribe frases para describir lo que crees que van a comprar los jóvenes en cada tienda.

Modelo

Creo que él (ella) va a comprar . . .

5 En tu comunidad

Escribir • Hablar

1. Para cada tienda de la lista, piensa en una que está en tu comunidad. Escribe una frase para describir dos o más cosas que venden allí.

Modelo

una tienda de ropa
En la tienda de ropa Moda, venden camisas, pantalones y corbatas.

1. una librería
2. una tienda de descuentos
3. una tienda de electrodomésticos
4. una joyería
5. un almacén
6. una zapatería

2. Trabaja con otro(a) estudiante. Lee lo que venden en cada tienda sin decir qué tipo de tienda es. Tu compañero(a) debe identificar qué tipo de tienda es.

Modelo

A —*Venden camisas, pantalones y corbatas allí.*
B —*¿Es una tienda de ropa?*

Fondo Cultural | El mundo hispa

Los centros comerciales and grandes almacenes are popular in Spanish-speaking countries, but many people still shop in traditior specialty stores. These stores are often owned ar operated by families, and customer loyalty is bui over generations.

- Why do you think small specialty stores contin to survive when large, one-stop superstores ar malls are very popular? Where do you prefer t shop? Why?

¿Qué venden en esta sombrería de Barcelona, España?

DIFFERENTIATED INSTRUCTION

Heritage Language Learners

Ask students to write a commercial for a specialty shop owned by a family member or friend. They should name the store and the products they sell and tell why people should shop there. If possible, have students record their commercials.

Students with Learning Difficulties

For *Actividad* 5 have students share with you, in English, some stores they are familiar with and what they sell. Allow students to use their vocabulary and grammar notebook sections, and encourage them to use their imaginations.

6 ¿Dónde está el almacén La Galería? 

Dibujar • Escribir • Hablar

Habla con otro(a) estudiante sobre dónde están las tiendas en un centro comercial.

1. Haz un dibujo de un centro comercial. En el dibujo incluye *(include)*:

   una zapatería, un almacén, un restaurante, una librería, una tienda de descuentos, una tienda de regalos, una tienda de ropa, una tienda de electrodomésticos

   ¡Respuesta personal!

2. Inventa un nombre para cada tienda y el restaurante. Escribe los nombres en tu dibujo.
3. Muestra *(Show)* tu dibujo a otro(a) estudiante. Haz seis preguntas sobre el centro comercial. Tu compañero(a) debe contestar.

Modelo

A —*¿Dónde está el restaurante La Mariposa?*
B —*Está detrás de la zapatería y la librería.*
A —*¿Por qué quieres ir allí?*
B —*Quiero comer con mi amigo.*

¿Recuerdas?

To tell the location of something, use *está . . . :*

a la derecha de
a la izquierda de
al lado de
cerca de
delante de
detrás de
lejos de

Para decir más . . .

entre between
enfrente de across from

vas / voy a . . .
quieres / quiero . . .
necesitas / necesito . . .
te / me gustaría . . .
piensas / pienso . . .
comer . . .
buscar . . .
comprar . . .
mirar . . .

7 Un buen regalo  

Hablar

Habla con otro(a) estudiante sobre los buenos regalos para diferentes personas.

Modelo

un señor que trabaja en una oficina
A —*¿Cuál es un buen* regalo para un señor que trabaja en una oficina?*
B —*Creo que una corbata es el mejor regalo para él.*
A —*¿Sabes dónde venden corbatas?*
B —*Por supuesto. En la tienda de ropa.*

Estudiante A

1. un(a) joven que no es puntual
2. un(a) joven que trabaja en un almacén
3. tu hermano(a) mayor (menor)
4. tu mejor amigo(a)
5. tu novio(a)
6. tu abuelo(a)

Estudiante B

¡Respuesta personal!

**Buen* is used in front of a masculine singular noun.

ENRICH YOUR TEACHING

Culture Note

One neighborhood store that can be found in nearly all small South American towns is the ***panadería.*** It is sometimes located in a family's home and provides fresh baked bread for the community.

Teacher-to-Teacher

Have students bring catalogs to class. Arrange them around the room, simulating shops in a mall. Have some students be store clerks. Have other students pair off and walk around the room to "shop." They should discuss what they are shopping for, who it is for, and how much they want to spend.

Practice and Communicate 7B

6 Standards: 1.1, 1.2, 1.3

Focus: Writing and speaking about malls

Recycle: locations; ***estar***

Suggestions: Supply colored pencils or markers for the students' drawings. For part 2, encourage them to think of creative names for their shops that indicate what items are sold there. Use one of the student drawings to introduce the new location expressions in *Para decir más....* Practice the model for part 3 with a volunteer, using his or her drawing.

Answers will vary.

Extension: Have students prepare an advertisement for one of the stores. They should include the store's name, what is on sale, store hours, and location. You may want to post their advertisements in the classroom.

BELLRINGER REVIEW

Show Vocabulary and Grammar Transparency 137 and have the students unscramble these three words for items found in either of the display windows.

veallor *meferpu* *daacen*

(**Answers:** *llavero, perfume, cadena*)

7 Standards: 1.1

Focus: Exchanging information about gift ideas

Recycle: Clothing vocabulary

Suggestions: Begin a discussion about gift ideas. Ask what things students consider when buying a gift. Do they tend to think more about what they like or what the person they are buying the gift for likes? Have them use this information to answer the questions. When asking questions in items 3–6, Student A might use the possessive ***tu*** instead of ***mi*** in the first speaking line. Clarify that students should be asking about their own friends or family members.

Answers will vary.

8 Standards: 1.1

Resources: Answer Keys: Student Edition, p. 103

Focus: Communicating about shopping

Suggestions: Role-play the model with a volunteer. Tell students that ***lo*** is a direct object pronoun. It replaces ***suéter*** and in this sentence means "it." Indicate its placement before the verb. Tell them they will learn more about how to use direct object pronouns later in the chapter.

Answers will vary but items are:

1. reloj pulsera
2. anillo
3. software
4. llavero
5. perfume
6. videojuego

Common Errors: Go around the room making sure that Student B is stressing the second syllable in the past tense forms ***compré*** and ***pagué.***

Extension: Have pairs of students repeat the activity, taking turns playing each role and asking about each other's school supplies.

9 Standards: 1.1, 1.2, 1.3, 4.1

Resources: Voc. and Gram. Transparency 142; Answer Keys: Student Edition, p. 103

Focus: Reading authentic material for comprehension

Recycle: Expressing preferences; using cognates

Suggestions: Have one volunteer read the *Strategy* and another read the jewelry ad. Students should note unknown words, look for cognates, and use context clues to guess their meaning. Suggest that students think about jewelry stores they may have visited to help them answer item 3.

Answers

1. relojes variados y todo tipo de joyas
2. Cuestan poco.
3. instalación de baterías de reloj; reparaciones de joyas y cadenas; arreglos de pulseras
4. Answers will vary.

Teacher-to-Teacher

Bring in copies of ads for specialty shops from Spanish-language newspapers or magazines. Distribute the ads and have each student write five questions based on the one they receive. Let students exchange ads and write answers to each others questions.

8 ¡Qué barato! ¡Qué caro!

Hablar

El fin de semana pasado compraste muchas cosas. Ahora un(a) amigo(a) quiere saber dónde compraste todas las cosas y cuánto pagaste.

Modelo

A —*¿Dónde compraste tu suéter nuevo?*
B —*Lo compré en la tienda de ropa.*
A —*¿Cuánto pagaste?*
B —*Pagué 25 dólares.*
A —*¡Qué barato!*
o: *¡Uf! ¡Qué caro!*

Estudiante A

1. 
2. 
3. 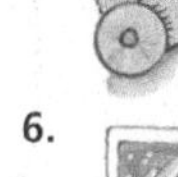
4. 
5.
6. 

Estudiante B

¡Respuesta personal!

9 Vamos a la joyería

Leer • Escribir • Hablar

Lee el anuncio de una joyería en Tegucigalpa, Honduras, y luego contesta las preguntas.

1. ¿Qué venden en la tienda?
2. Según el anuncio, ¿las cosas que venden en la tienda cuestan mucho o poco?
3. Además de *(In addition to)* vender, ¿qué otros servicios hay en la joyería?
4. Pregunta a dos personas diferentes:
   - ¿Qué te gustaría comprar en una joyería?
   - ¿Qué joyas tienes?

Strategy

Using cognates and context clues
Try to figure out the meanings of unknown words by looking for cognates or by seeing how other words are used in the sentence.

- Can you guess the meanings of *bajos, diamantes, piedras preciosas, baterías,* and *arreglos* in this ad?

JOYERÍA HERMANOS SILVA

Vendemos relojes variados y todo tipo de joyas para toda ocasión

- Anillos y collares de diamantes y otras piedras preciosas
- Baterías de reloj, incluyendo instalación
- Hacemos reparaciones y joyas nuevas de su oro* viejo
- Reparación de cadenas y arreglos de pulseras

Abierto lunes a sábado de 10:00 hs. a 18:00 hs.

¡Precios bajos todos los días!

MENCIONE ESTE ANUNCIO Y RECIBA UN DESCUENTO DEL 10%

*gold

DIFFERENTIATED INSTRUCTION

Heritage Language Learners

Explain such advertising tactics as bandwagon ("Everybody drinks Super Soda!"), snob appeal ("Super Soda, for the sophisticated!"), and expert opinion ("Take it from me, Joe Football-Player, Super Soda is the best!"). Have students find such ads in Spanish-language magazines.

Multiple Intelligences

Musical/Rhythmic: Have students create a short radio or TV ad for a jewelry store. The ad may contain a jingle to be sung or chanted.

▼ Exploración del lenguaje

Nouns that end in *-ería*

The Spanish word ending, or suffix, *-ería* usually indicates a place where something is sold, made, or repaired. This suffix is added to a form of the word that names the specialty item. For example, if you know that *una joya* is a piece of jewelry, you understand that you can buy jewelry at *la joyería.*

Try it out! You will often see these signs over stores. Tell what each one sells.

heladería	librería	pastelería
papelería	panadería	zapatería

Modelo

joyería
En la joyería venden joyas como anillos, pulseras y collares.

Venden flores para todas las ocasiones en esta florería en España.

Esta joyería vende pulseras, anillos y collares.

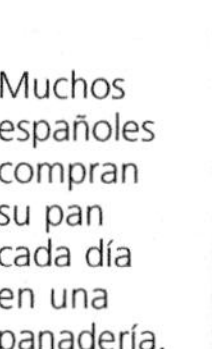

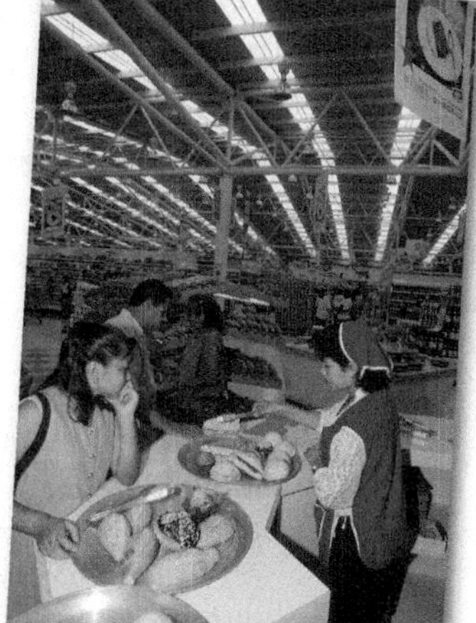

Muchos españoles compran su pan cada día en una panadería.

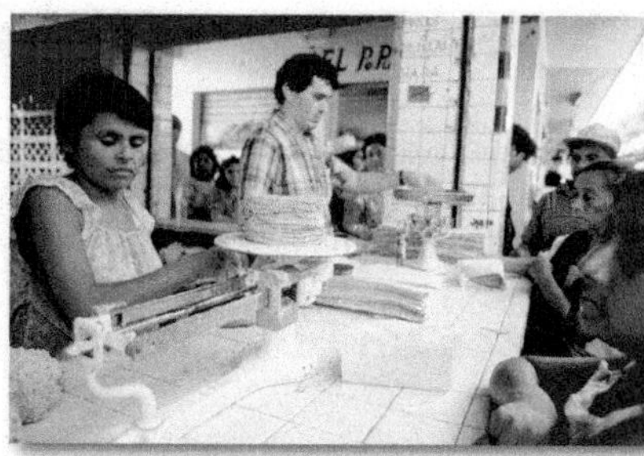

Muchos mexicanos compran tortillas frescas en una tortillería cerca de su casa.

▼10 Y tú, ¿qué dices? | Talk!

Escribir • Hablar

1. ¿A qué tiendas vas de compras? ¿Qué te gusta comprar?
2. ¿Para quiénes compras regalos? ¿Qué tipo de regalos compras?
3. ¿Qué regalo compraste recientemente? ¿Cuándo y dónde compraste el regalo? ¿Pagaste mucho o poco dinero?

ENRICH YOUR TEACHING

Culture Note

Mexico is well-known for its jewelry. For centuries, vast quantities of silver and gold have been unearthed there. Many gems and minerals are also prevalent: amethyst, topaz, turquoise, opals. This is one reason why the ***joyerías*** of Mexico have such a wide selection.

21st Century Skills

Information Literacy Have students locate Web sites for department stores in both the United States and in some Spanish-speaking countries. After they review the sites, have them comment on similarities and differences between the samples in terms of presentation, format, or content. Are similar strategies used to present the information? What may account for this?

Exploración del lenguaje

Core Instruction

Standards: 4.1

Resources: Answer Keys: Student Edition, p. 103

Suggestions: Tell students that in the context of shopping, when they see the ending ***-ería*** they can substitute the word *shop* or *store*. They should look at the root of each listed word in *Try it out!* to determine the kind of shop.

Answers: En la heladería venden helados; En la papelería venden papel; En la librería venden libros; En la panadería venden pan; En la pastelería venden pasteles; En la zapatería venden zapatos.

BELLRINGER REVIEW

Review the expression ***ir de compras*** and the preterite- and present-tense of ***comprar*** before *Actividad* 10.

10 Standards: 1.1, 1.3

Focus: Communicating about shopping habits

Suggestions: If students are hesitant to discuss their shopping habits, ask them to make up this information.

Answers will vary.

Pre-AP* Support

- **Learning Objective:** Presentational Speaking
- **Activity:** Have pairs of students create a story using a picture on this page. They should prepare for 30 seconds and talk for 30 seconds.

Additional Resources

- Communication Wbk.: Audio Act. 6, p. 143
- Teacher's Resource Book: Audio Script, p. 187, Communicative Pair Activity BLM, pp. 194–195
- Audio Program DVD: Cap. 7B, Track 8

ASSESSMENT

Prueba 7B-2 with Study Plan (online only)

Quiz: Vocabulary Production

- Prueba 7B-2: pp. 190–191

Gramática

Core Instruction

Standards: 4.1

Resources: Voc. and Gram. Transparency 140; Teacher's Resource Book: Video Script, p. 191; Video Program: Cap. 7B

INTERACTIVE WHITEBOARD

Grammar Activities 7B

Suggestions: Call students' attention to the *¿Recuerdas?* Use the transparency to introduce the structure. The *GramActiva* video can serve as reinforcement. Point out that students must look for context clues to tell whether the ***nosotros*** forms are in the present or preterite.

11 Standards: 1.2

Resources: Teacher's Resource Book: Audio Script, p. 188; Audio Program DVD: Cap. 7B, Track 9; Answer Keys: Student Edition, p. 104

Focus: Listening to and identifying present and past verb tenses

Recycle: Household chores

Suggestions: Play the audio or read the script. Remind students to listen for verb endings and context clues such as ***la semana pasada*** and ***ayer.***

Script and Answers:

1. **Ella cocina para la familia cada día. *(presente)***
2. **Mis padres trabajan todos los días excepto los fines de semana. *(presente)***
3. **Corté el césped después de las clases. *(pasado)***
4. **¿Ayudaste mucho a tus padres la semana pasada? *(pasado)***
5. **Mis hermanos limpiaron el baño y yo lavé los platos. *(pasado)***
6. **Mi hermano y yo lavamos el coche ayer. *(pasado)***
7. **Siempre arreglo mi cuarto en la mañana. *(presente)***
8. **Mi abuela arregló el sótano hace un mes. *(pasado)***

12 Standards: 1.1, 1.3

Resources: Answer Keys: Student Edition, p. 104

Focus: Using the preterite to write and speak about buying

Suggestions: Point out that students are using only ***comprar.***

Answers:

1. **compró unos aretes**
2. **compraron un videojuego**
3. **compró una cartera**
4. **compraste un collar**
5. **compraron una pulsera**
6. **compramos perfume**

Manos a la obra

Objectives

- Listen to a description of family activities
- Write and talk about what you and others did
- Interview a classmate about activities last week

Gramática

The preterite of *-ar* verbs

To talk about actions that were completed in the past, you use the preterite tense. To form the preterite tense of a regular *-ar* verb, add the preterite endings to the stem of the verb. Here are the preterite forms of *comprar:*

(yo)	compré	(nosotros) (nosotras)	compramos
(tú)	compraste	(vosotros) (vosotras)	comprasteis
Ud. (él) (ella)	compró	Uds. (ellos) (ellas)	compraron

Notice the accent marks on the endings *-é* and *-ó*.

The *nosotros* form is the same in the present and preterite tenses. You will need to look for other context clues to tell which tense is intended.

¿Recuerdas?

In Spanish, the endings of verbs identify both who is performing the action (the subject) and when it is being performed (the tense).

Más ayuda realidades.com

***GramActiva* Video**
Tutorials: Past tense, Tense, *Hacer* in time expressions, Preterite

Canción de hip hop: *¿Qué compraste ayer?*

***GramActiva* Activity**

11 ¿El presente o el pasado?

Escuchar

En una hoja de papel escribe los números del 1 al 8. Vas a escuchar ocho frases que describen los quehaceres de una familia. ¿Ocurren los quehaceres en el presente o el pasado *(past)*? Escribe *presente* o *pasado*.

12 El dinero es un buen regalo

Escribir • Hablar

Tus abuelos les regalaron *(gave)* a todos dinero y cada uno compró algo. Explica lo que compraron todos y cuándo compraron las cosas.

Modelo

Mi hermano ___ hace una semana.
Mi hermano compró un reloj pulsera hace una semana.

1.  Mi madre ___ ayer.
2. Mis primos ___ anoche.
3.  Mi papá ___ el año pasado.
4.  Tú ___ hace tres días.
5.  Mis tíos ___ hace un mes.
6.  Mi hermana y yo ___ ayer.

DIFFERENTIATED INSTRUCTION

Heritage Language Learners

Have students write a short paragraph describing a special gift they bought for someone in the past. Meet with individuals to review the spelling and grammar in their paragraphs.

Practice and Communicate 7B

13 Juego

Hablar • GramActiva

1. Tu profesor(a) va a enseñar a todos cómo deben señalar *(point to)* a diferentes personas *ella, nosotros, tú, ellos,* etc. Practica con tu profesor(a).

2. Trabaja en un grupo de cuatro. Una persona es líder y dice un infinitivo de la lista y un sujeto *(subject)*. Por ejemplo: *cantar / ella*. Los otros tienen que señalar a la persona, o a las personas, y decir el verbo en el pretérito: *ella cantó*. Continúa así con tres sujetos más y el mismo verbo. Después, cambia de *(change)* líderes.

¿Recuerdas?

arreglar	hablar
bailar	lavar
caminar	levantar
cantar	limpiar
cocinar	montar
cortar	nadar
dibujar	pasar
escuchar	patinar
esquiar	trabajar
estudiar	usar

14 Hace una semana

Escribir • Hablar

Usa el pretérito para escribir y hablar de tus actividades.

1. Copia la tabla en una hoja de papel. Usa los verbos de la lista de la Actividad 13 para escribir seis actividades que hiciste *(you did)* en el pasado. Indica cuándo hiciste cada actividad.

¿Qué?	*¿Cuándo?*
patiné	la semana pasada

Nota

To say when something happened, use *hace* + a time expression. It's like saying "ago."

- Compré la pulsera **hace un año.** *I bought the bracelet **a year ago**.*

2. Usa la información de la tabla para escribir frases sobre tus actividades. Incluye información para contestar *¿dónde?* y *¿con quién?* Después, lee tus frases a otro(a) estudiante y pregunta: *¿Y tú?* Tu compañero(a) debe contestar. Escribe la respuesta de tu compañero(a).

Modelo

A —*Patiné en el parque con mis amigos la semana pasada. ¿Y tú?*

B —*Monté en monopatín con mi hermana la semana pasada.*

3. Escribe tres frases con la información del paso 2.

Modelo

Patiné en el parque con mis amigos la semana pasada, pero Luisa montó en monopatín con su hermana.

Más práctica 

realidades.com | print

Instant Check	✔	
Guided WB pp. 237–238	✔	✔
Core WB p. 134	✔	✔
Comm. WB pp. 144, 147	✔	✔
***Hispanohablantes* WB** pp. 274–277		✔

13 Standards: 1.1

Focus: Talking about what people did

Recycle: Sports and activities; chores

Suggestions: Review subject pronouns and write a list of them on the chalkboard. Use three volunteers to demonstrate how to do part 2. Monitor groups as they work.

Answers will vary.

14 Standards: 1.1

Focus: Writing and speaking about activities in the past

Recycle: Sports, leisure activities, and household chores

Suggestions: Write a sample chart on the board. Students should raise their hands when they have completed part 1. Check their work and allow them to make revisions. Remind them to use ***hace* + *period of time*** when appropriate. Ask volunteers for the first item and time they listed. Use the information to model writing sentences that answer ***¿dónde?*** and ***¿con quién?***

Answers will vary.

Pre-AP* Support

- **Learning Objective:** Interpersonal Writing
- **Activity 14:** Use the information from Step 1 to write an e-mail to a friend talking about at least three activities you did over the weekend.
- ***Pre-AP* Resource Book:*** Comprehensive guide to Pre-AP* writing skill development, pp. 27–38

Additional Resources

- Communication Wbk.: Audio Act. 7, p. 144
- Teacher's Resource Book: Audio Script, p. 189
- Audio Program DVD: Cap. 7B, Track 10

ENRICH YOUR TEACHING

Culture Note

There are many different customs involving gifts in South America. For example, Colombians do not generally unwrap a gift when they receive it so as not to appear greedy, but in Chile gifts are usually opened immediately.

Culture Note

In Latin America and Spain, if you are invited to someone's home for dinner, it is customary to bring a simple gift, such as flowers or chocolates. If you are visiting from another country, it is thoughtful to give a gift that is a product of your homeland.

ASSESSMENT

Prueba 7B-3 with Study Plan (online only)

Quiz: The preterite of *-ar* verbs

- Prueba 7B-3: p. 192

7B Practice and Communicate

Gramática

Core Instruction

Standards: 4.1

Resources: Teacher's Resource Book: Video Script, pp. 191–192; Video Program: Cap. 7B

INTERACTIVE WHITEBOARD
Grammar Activities 7B

Focus: Presenting preterite of verbs ending in ***-car*** and ***-gar***

Suggestions: Direct students' attention to the *¿Recuerdas?* Use the transparency to introduce the structure. Tell students that the ***u*** is added to keep the "hard" sounds of the ***c*** and ***g***, and that the ***u*** is not pronounced. Point out that verbs that have a stem change in the present do *not* have a stem change in the preterite. The *GramActiva* video can serve as reinforcement.

15 Standards: 1.3

Resources: Answer Keys: Student Edition, p. 105

Focus: Writing verbs in the preterite

Suggestions: Remind students to read each sentence carefully to determine the subject and to read the entire passage before writing their answers.

Answers

1. jugaron
2. jugué
3. toqué
4. tocó
5. jugamos
6. sacó
7. pagaron
8. saqué

Common Errors: Remind students that ***jugar*** is used for games and ***tocar*** for musical instruments.

Fondo cultural

Standards: 2.2, 4.2

Suggestions: Brainstorm items commonly found in museums and have students discuss the importance of these items. Then have students read the *Fondo cultural,* study the photo, and discuss the questions in class. Lead a discussion about conserving objects from the past.

Answers will vary.

Teaching with Photos

Ask students to name ways we use gold today. Then discuss why people place so much value on something that is mainly used for jewelry and decoration.

Gramática

Objectives

- Write and talk about what you and others did
- Discuss gifts you bought
- Read a timeline to write and talk about historical events

The preterite of verbs ending in *-car* and *-gar*

Verbs that end in *-car* and *-gar* have a spelling change in the *yo* form of the preterite.

buscar: c → qu yo bus*qué*

Silvia y Rosa bus*caron* aretes pero yo bus*qué* un collar.

pagar: g → gu yo pa*gué*

¿Cuánto pa*gaste* por tu cadena? Pa*gué* 13 dólares.

Verbs such as *jugar* that have a stem change in the present tense do not have a stem change in the preterite.

El sábado pasado **jugué** al tenis.
Mis hermanos **jugaron** al básquetbol.

¿Recuerdas?

You know these verbs that end in *-car* and *-gar:*

buscar	**practicar**
jugar	**sacar**
pagar	**tocar**

Más ayuda realidades.com

***GramActiva* Video Tutorial:** Preterite

***GramActiva* Activity**

15 El viernes pasado

Escribir • Leer

El viernes pasado Juan invitó a unos amigos a su casa. Completa la descripción de sus actividades con la forma apropiada del pretérito de los verbos *jugar, pagar, sacar* y *tocar.*

El viernes pasado mis amigos pasaron tiempo conmigo en mi casa. Tomás y Fernando __1.__ videojuegos en mi dormitorio pero yo no __2.__ con ellos. Yo __3.__ la guitarra en la sala y todos cantamos. Jorge __4.__ el piano un poco también. Después de cantar, nosotros __5.__ al vóleibol. Mi amiga Ana __6.__ fotos de nosotros. ¡Qué graciosas son las fotos! A las nueve fuimos por pizza y ¡mis padres __7.__ la cuenta! ¡Qué bueno porque nunca tengo mucho dinero! Yo __8.__ fotos de todos mis amigos en la pizzería. ¡Qué bien lo pasamos nosotros!

Fondo Cultural | Colombia

El Museo del Oro in Bogotá, Colombia, houses over 33,000 objects of gold, emeralds, and other precious stones made by pre-Columbian cultures—cultures that existed long before the arrival of Columbus in the Americas. These ancient civilizations viewed gold as life-giving energy from the sun.

- What kinds of specialized museums have you visited in your community or in other locations? What did you learn from the types of objects that were included there?

El Museo del Oro en Bogotá, Colombia

DIFFERENTIATED INSTRUCTION

Heritage Language Learners

Have students write a paragraph about a sports competition or a musical performance in which they participated. If they want, they can create a fictitious event. Have them include as many of the past tense forms of the ***-car*** and ***-gar*** verbs from the *¿Recuerdas?* as they can.

Students with Learning Difficulties

For *Actividad* 15, remind students of the meanings of the four verbs used. Provide a copy of the paragraph so students can write directly on it. Consider providing the infinitive forms of the verbs that belong in the spaces. Modify the activity based on student needs and abilities.

Pronunciación

The letter combinations *gue, gui, que,* and *qui*

You know that when the letter *g* appears before the letters *a, o,* or *u,* it is pronounced like the *g* in "go," and that *g* before *e* and *i* is pronounced like the *h* in "he."

To keep the sound of the *g* in "go" before *e* and *i*, add the letter *u*: *gue, gui.* Don't pronounce the *u*. Listen to and say these words:

Guillermo	guitarra	espaguetis
guisantes	hamburguesa	Miguel

You also know that the letter *c* before *a, o,* or *u* is pronounced like the *c* in "cat," while the *c* before *e* and *i* is usually pronounced like the *s* in "Sally."

To keep the sound of the *c* in "cat" before *e* and *i*, words are spelled with *qu*: *que, qui.* The *u* is not pronounced. Listen to and say these words:

queso	quince	quieres	riquísimo
quehacer	quinientos	quisiera	querer

Try it out! Listen to the first verse of this traditional song from Puerto Rico entitled *"El coquí." El coquí* is a little tree frog found in Puerto Rico, named for the *coquí, coquí* sound that it makes at night. Say the verse.

El coquí, el coquí siempre canta.
Es muy suave el cantar del coquí.
Por las noches a veces me duermo
con el dulce cantar del coquí.
Coquí, coquí, coquí, quí, quí, quí,
coquí, coquí, coquí, quí, quí, quí.

16 Juego

Escribir • Escuchar • Hablar • GramActiva

1. Escribe en una hoja de papel una o dos frases para indicar qué regalo compraste, para quién es, dónde lo compraste y cuánto pagaste.

Modelo

Compré un collar para mi novia en la Red. Pagué 45 dólares.

2. Trabaja con un grupo de cuatro. Pon tu hoja de papel en una bolsa *(bag)* con las otras hojas del grupo. Cada uno toma una hoja, que debe ser de otro(a) estudiante del grupo. Cambia una parte de la frase y lee la nueva frase al grupo. ¿Quién puede identificar el cambio?

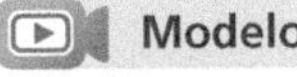

Modelo

A —*Esta persona compró un collar para su madre en la Red. Pagó 45 dólares.*
B —*No es cierto. Compré un collar para mi novia.*

ENRICH YOUR TEACHING

Culture Note

The ***Museo del Oro Banco Central*** in San José, Costa Rica, houses an impressive collection of pre-Columbian gold objects. This museum is complemented by a jade museum—***Museo de Jade Marco Fidel Tristán.*** Both jade and gold were precious items to the pre-Columbian peoples and these museums demonstrate some of their remarkable craftsmanship.

Teacher-to-Teacher

Have students conduct an Internet search for the types of Latin American products that can be bought online. For example, they might look for handicrafts or jewelry unique to a country, town, or region. They should report the names of businesses, the products they sell, how much they cost, and how long shipping takes. Have students share their research with the class.

Pronunciación
Core Instruction

Standards: 4.1

Resources: Teacher's Resource Book: Audio Script, p. 189; Audio Program DVD: Cap. 7B, Tracks 11–12

Suggestions: Read the *Pronunciación* section with the students or play the audio. Remind students that there are subtle pronunciation differences of these sounds and they may vary from region to region. Have students repeat the words after you. Pair students to say the verse aloud. Have them record their presentations.

BELLRINGER REVIEW

Use the Vocabulary and Grammar Transparencies to review the gift vocabulary students will use in *Actividad* 16.

16 Standards: 1.1, 1.2, 1.3

Focus: Writing and talking about gifts purchased in the past

Suggestions: Encourage students to include unique details in their sentences for Step 1, as another student will be changing the details in Step 2. Remind students to remember what they wrote.

Answers will vary.

17 Standards: 1.1, 1.2, 1.3, 3.1

Resources: Map Transparencies, 12–14, 20; Answer Keys: Student Edition, p. 105

Focus: Interpreting maps and timelines; using the preterite to describe historical events

Suggestions: Tell students to look first at the timeline, find the corresponding number on the map, and identify that location. You may want to provide them with a photocopy of the map with the locations written on it. After that, they need to find the event in the list that took place at that location. They may need to use a history book to make sure their information is accurate. Finally, they should use this information and the preterite tense of the infinitives to describe the events.

Answers:

1. **En 1492 Cristóbal Colón llegó a la República Dominicana.**
2. **En 1513 Juan Ponce de León exploró la Florida.**
3. **En 1540 Francisco Vázquez de Coronado buscó las siete ciudades de Cibola en el suroeste de los Estados Unidos.**
4. **En 1769 Fray Junípero Serra fundó la misión de San Diego de Alcalá.**
5. **En 1848 el presidente James K. Polk y los Estados Unidos pagaron 15 millones de dólares a México según el Tratado de Guadalupe Hidalgo.**
6. **En 1898 el presidente William McKinley y los Estados Unidos ayudaron a Cuba y Puerto Rico a declarar su independencia de España.**
7. **En 1904 el presidente Theodore Roosevelt y los Estados Unidos empezaron la construcción del Canal de Panamá.**

Block Schedule

Have students write five sentences about local or state historical events. They may need to research historical figures or make a trip to the library. Gather all the information and have the class make a mural timeline.

17 Una lección de historia

Leer • Pensar • Escribir • Hablar

Estudia la línea cronológica *(timeline),* los eventos y el mapa. Luego usa el pretérito para emparejar estos eventos históricos con las personas en la línea cronológica.

Modelo

1. *En 1492, Cristóbal Colón llegó* (arrived) *a la República Dominicana.*

Nota

Here is how you say dates:

- **1500** mil quinientos
- **1898** mil ochocientos noventa y ocho
- **2005** dos mil cinco

Conexiones | La historia

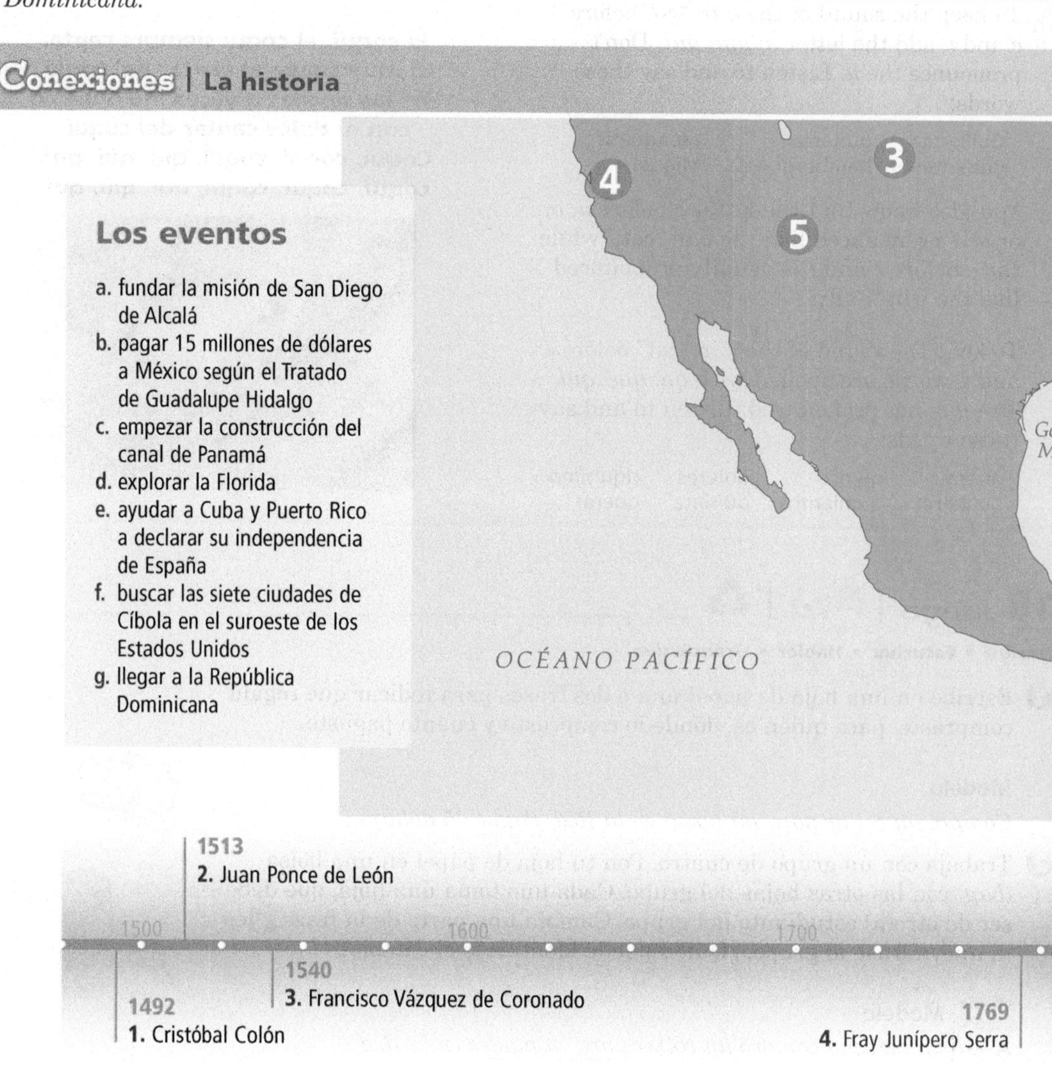

Los eventos

a. fundar la misión de San Diego de Alcalá
b. pagar 15 millones de dólares a México según el Tratado de Guadalupe Hidalgo
c. empezar la construcción del canal de Panamá
d. explorar la Florida
e. ayudar a Cuba y Puerto Rico a declarar su independencia de España
f. buscar las siete ciudades de Cíbola en el suroeste de los Estados Unidos
g. llegar a la República Dominicana

1492 1. Cristóbal Colón
1513 2. Juan Ponce de León
1540 3. Francisco Vázquez de Coronado
1769 4. Fray Junípero Serra

1500 — 1600 — 1700

DIFFERENTIATED INSTRUCTION

Students with Learning Difficulties

You may want to provide students with a timeline that contains all of the events in *Actividad* 17 in English. Providing them with this background knowledge will make the task less intimidating.

Advanced Learners/Pre-AP*

Have students write five sentences about local or state historical events. They may need to make a trip to the library. Gather all the information and have the class make a mural timeline.

El edificio más antiguo de los Estados Unidos está en San Agustín, en la Florida.

La misión de San Diego de Alcalá, en California, fue fundada en 1769.

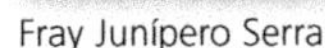

Fray Junípero Serra

OCÉANO ATLÁNTICO

Mar Caribe

2 6 1 6 7

1848
5. El presidente James K. Polk y los Estados Unidos

1900

1898
6. El presidente William McKinley y los Estados Unidos

1904
7. El presidente Theodore Roosevelt y los Estados Unidos

18 Y tú, ¿qué dices?

Escribir • Hablar

1. ¿Qué deportes practicaste el año pasado?
2. ¿Jugaste algún partido de tenis o de fútbol el mes pasado? ¿Cómo jugaste?
3. ¿Tocaste un instrumento musical ayer? ¿Cuál? Si no, ¿te gustaría saber tocar algún instrumento? ¿Cuál?
4. ¿Sacaste fotos durante tus vacaciones? Si no, ¿quién las sacó? ¿De qué?
5. Para el cumpleaños de tu mejor amigo(a), ¿qué compraste? ¿Cuánto pagaste?

Más práctica GO

	realidades.com	print
Instant Check	✔	
Guided WB p. 239	✔	✔
Core WB p. 135	✔	✔
Comm. WB pp. 144, 148, 306	✔	✔
***Hispanohablantes* WB** p. 278		✔

Practice and Communicate 7B

18 Standards: 1.1, 1.3

Resources: Answer Keys: Student Edition, p. 106

Focus: Using the preterite to talk about past activities

Recycle: Sports; musical instruments

Suggestions: Remind students that they can invent answers if the question does not apply to them or if they do not remember the answer.

Answers will vary but should include:

1. **practiqué**
2. **jugué**
3. **toqué**
4. **saqué**
5. **compré, pagué**

Common Errors: Some students might simply write ***Sí*** or ***No*** for items 2–4. Make sure they understand the follow-up questions for these items.

Teaching with Photos

Have students compare and contrast the two buildings in the photos. Point out the rounded archways and the freestanding exterior walls that form a courtyard. Point out that these are features of Spanish architecture and can be found in homes and buildings in Florida and California and throughout the Southwest.

Theme Project

Students can perform Step 4 at this point. Be sure they understand your corrections and suggestions. (For more information, see p. 320-b.)

Additional Resources

- Communication Wbk.: Audio Act. 8, p. 144
- Teacher's Resource Book: Audio Script, p. 189
- Audio Program DVD: Cap. 7B, Track 13

ASSESSMENT

Prueba 7B-4 with Study Plan (online only)

Quiz: The preterite of verbs ending in *-car* and *-gar*

- Prueba 7B-4: p. 193

ENRICH YOUR TEACHING

Culture Note

Ask students to name as many cities as they can that begin with ***San.*** Tell them that it is the shortened form of ***santo,*** the masculine word for "saint." Tell students that many of these cities began as missions and were named for saints. Point out that ***Santa*** is used before a female saint's name. Ask them to name cities in the United States that begin with ***Santa.***

21st Century Skills

Critical Thinking and Problem Solving Have students research a time period in the history of their city or state, decide which events are the most important ones, and create a timeline for those events. Have them compare their timeline with others and establish if similar events were selected to include in the timeline.

Gramática

Core Instruction

Standards: 4.1

Resources: Voc. and Gram. Transparency 141; Teacher's Resource Book: Video Script, p. 192; Video Program: Cap. 7B

INTERACTIVE WHITEBOARD

Grammar Activities 7B

Focus: Presenting direct object pronouns

Suggestions: Bring in items to use as a demonstration. On the chalkboard, write the words for these items with the definite article underlined. Say: *Yo compré el libro. Lo compré anoche*. Hold up the item as you say the second sentence. Point out that the direct object pronoun is different from the definite article only in the masculine singular form. Use the transparency to introduce the structure. Review object pronouns in English to help students understand the concept. The *GramActiva* video can serve as reinforcement of your explanation.

19 Standards: 1.3

Resources: Answer Keys: Student Edition, p. 106

Focus: Writing sentences using direct object pronouns

Suggestions: Emphasize that direct object pronouns have the same gender and number as the nouns they replace.

Answers:

1. **Ayer Juanita miró un bolso pero no lo compró.**
2. **Ayer los novios miraron un anillo pero no lo compraron.**
3. **Ayer tú miraste unos llaveros pero no los compraste.**
4. **Ayer nosotros miramos unos aretes pero no los compramos.**
5. **Ayer el señor Miró miró unos anteojos de sol pero no los compró.**
6. **Ayer yo miré unas pulseras pero no las compré.**

Extension: Have students write a sentence on a note card about something they looked at while shopping *(Ayer miré una corbata.)*. Students will exchange cards and ask one another if they bought the item or items they specified. *(¿La compraste?)* Student B will answer ***sí*** or ***no*** *(No, no la compré.)*.

Common Errors: Students use ***a*** after ***mirar.*** Remind students that ***mirar*** means "to look at" and there is no need for a preposition in Spanish.

Gramática

Objectives

- Write and talk about what people bought, where, and when
- Exchange information to guess who has different items
- Role-play conversations about shopping

Direct object pronouns

A direct object tells who or what receives the action of the verb.

Busco una cadena.

Compré unos guantes.

To avoid repeating a direct object noun, you can replace it with a direct object pronoun.

¿Dónde compraste tus aretes?
Where did you buy your earrings?

Los compré en la joyería Sánchez.
I bought them at Sánchez Jewelry.

Direct object pronouns agree in gender and number with the nouns they replace.

¿Tienes mi pulsera? No, no la tengo.

¿Tienes mis anillos? No, no los tengo.

	SINGULAR		PLURAL	
M.	lo	*it*	los	*them*
F.	la	*it*	las	*them*

A direct object noun *follows* the conjugated verb. A direct object pronoun comes *before* the conjugated verb.

When an infinitive follows a conjugated verb, the direct object pronoun can either be placed before the conjugated verb or be attached to the infinitive.

¿Quieres comprar el llavero?

Sí, lo quiero comprar.

o: Sí, quiero comprarlo.

Más ayuda realidades.com

GramActiva **Video Tutorial:** Direct object pronouns

GramActiva **Activity**

19 ¡No compraron nada!

Escribir

Ayer muchas personas fueron *(went)* al centro comercial y miraron muchas cosas pero ¡no compraron nada! Escribe lo que no compraron.

Modelo

Carlos 

Ayer Carlos miró unas carteras pero no las compró.

1. Juanita 
2. los novios 
3. tú
4. nosotros 
5. el señor Miró 
6. yo 

También se dice . . .

el anillo = la sortija *(muchos países)*

los aretes = los pendientes *(España);* los aros *(Argentina, Uruguay)*

la pulsera = el brazalete *(muchos países)*

el bolso = la cartera *(Argentina, Bolivia);* la bolsa *(Chile, México)*

los anteojos de sol = las gafas de sol *(Argentina, España)*

la cartera = la billetera *(Argentina, Uruguay, Bolivia)*

DIFFERENTIATED INSTRUCTION

Multiple Intelligences

Logical/Mathematical: Have students work in groups to create logic puzzles like the one in *Actividad* 20. They could use store names and gift items, or they could use school schedules and subjects, chores and rooms of the house, or any other set of previously learned vocabulary. Collect, copy, and redistribute the puzzles.

Students with Learning Difficulties

Write sentences on the board, circling object nouns and underlining object pronouns. Allow students to use their vocabulary notebook section for *Actividad* 19. Break the activity into parts: Part 1: *Ayer Carlos miró unas carteras;* Part 2: *pero no las compró.* For *Actividad* 20, you may want to limit the task by having students focus only on items 1, 3, 6, and 7.

20 ¿Quién compró qué?

Leer • Pensar • Escribir

¿Te gusta ser detective? ¡Vamos a ver si puedes descubrir lo que compraron las personas, dónde compraron las cosas y cuánto costó cada cosa!

1. Lee las pistas *(clues)*. Luego copia la tabla en una hoja de papel y completa la tabla.

Las pistas

1. José gastó *(spent)* $35 en la joyería.
2. El software costó $45.
3. Paco no compró la novela.
4. Isabel fue *(went)* de compras a la tienda de electrodomésticos.
5. Luisa gastó $20 en la librería.
6. Los guantes costaron $25.
7. Paco fue de compras al almacén, pero no compró el collar.

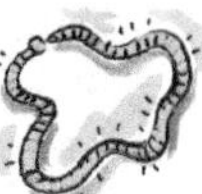

Nombre	¿Qué compró?	¿Dónde lo compró?	¿Cuánto costó?

2. Usa la información de la tabla y escribe tus frases completas.

Modelo

José compró . . . . Los (Las / Lo / La) compró en . . . . Costaron (Costó) . . . .

21 ¡Demasiadas preguntas! |  | 

Hablar

Tu hermanito te hace muchas preguntas. Trabaja con otro(a) estudiante y contesta todas sus preguntas con mucha paciencia.

1. ¿Vas a comprar perritos calientes?
2. ¿Quieres leer este libro?
3. ¿Tienes que hacer la tarea?
4. ¿Quieres jugar videojuegos conmigo?
5. ¿Puedo comer este pastel?
6. ¿Vas a hacer mi cama?

Modelo

A —*¿Necesito llevar mis botas en el invierno?*
B —*Sí, necesitas llevarlas.*
o: —*No, no necesitas llevarlas.*

Practice and Communicate 7B

20 Standards: 1.2, 1.3

Resources: Teacher's Resource Book: GramActiva BLM, p. 199; Answer Keys: Student Edition, p. 106

Focus: Reading and writing using past tense and direct object pronouns

Suggestions: Students may not know where to begin to unravel the mystery. Have them copy the chart and suggest that they begin by writing each person's name and the store where he or she shopped. Then have them write the logical item that could be bought at each store. Indicate that the art also provides clues. Before they begin writing, review the *Modelo*, filling in the information for José as a class.

Answers:

José compró un collar. Lo compró en la joyería. Costó $35. Isabel compró el software. Lo compró en la tienda de electrodomésticos. Costó $45. Paco compró unos guantes. Los compró en el almacén. Costaron $25. Luisa compró una novela. La compró en la librería. Costó $20.

21 Standards: 1.1

Resources: Answer Keys: Student Edition, p. 107

Focus: Using direct object pronouns

Suggestions: Write the *Modelo* on the chalkboard and have students identify the direct object noun ***(botas)***. Ask which direct object pronoun should be used ***(las)***. Remind students to attach the pronoun to the infinitive.

Answers may vary but will include:

1. **...voy a comprarlos.**
2. **...quiero leerlo.**
3. **...tengo que hacerla.**
4. **...quiero jugarlos contigo.**
5. **...puedes comerlo.**
6. **...voy a hacerla.**

ENRICH YOUR TEACHING

Teacher-to-Teacher

Have students do research about a Spanish-speaking community in the United States. See if they can find pictures or descriptions of the small shops, such as ***tortilla*** shops ***(tortillerías)***, bookstores, record stores, butcher shops, and so forth. Students can present their reports to the class.

21st Century Skills

Critical Thinking and Problem Solving As an extension of Activity 20, have pairs of students research on the Internet stores in their area (such as jewelry stores or bookstores) where these individuals could purchase similar items. Do any of these stores serve the Spanish-speaking community? Have students report their findings to the class.

22 Standards: 1.1, 1.3

Focus: Writing and conversing using direct object pronouns

Suggestions: Tell students they may write about family members and friends, or they can make up the information for part 1. Practice the *Modelo* with a volunteer before students begin part 2.

Answers: will vary.

Common Errors: In part 2, make sure Student A understands that he or she should not read the complete sentence, but should omit when the item was bought.

23 Standards: 1.1

Focus: Practicing direct object pronouns in a guessing game

Suggestions: Make sure that each group has five objects to put in the center. Tell students to remember what the five objects are so that they will know which one is missing. You may want to give small prizes to the winners.

Answers will vary.

Fondo cultural

Standards: 2.1, 4.2

Suggestions: Read the paragraph with students and have them study the photo. Guide their response to the question by directing their attention to the meaning of the word ***Guelaguetza.*** Tell students that the offering or gift was originally to the gods whom the indigenous people worshipped. They wanted to show the gods their gratitude for rain and bountiful crops.

Answers will vary but might include Thanksgiving.

Mapa global interactivo, Actividad 2 Look at several of the states in Mexico.

Theme Project

Students can perform Step 5 at this point. (For more information, see p. 320-b.)

22 ¿Cuándo los compró? 

Escribir • Hablar

1. Escribe cuatro frases para indicar lo que compró una persona y cuándo lo compró.

Modelo

Mi padre compró unos guantes la semana pasada.

2. Lee tus frases a otro(a) estudiante sin decir cuándo la persona compró el artículo. Tu compañero(a) va a preguntar cuándo lo compró.

Modelo

A —*Mi padre compró unos guantes.*
B —*¿Cuándo los compró?*
A —*Los compró la semana pasada.*

23 Juego

Hablar • GramActiva

Play this game in groups of five.

1. Each student in a group of five puts an object in the center of the group. The objects must be items for which you have learned the name in Spanish. One student turns around while another hides one of the objects.

2. The student who turned around now guesses who has the object. Correct first guesses are worth five points; correct second guesses are worth three. If the second guess is wrong, the student who has the object must say that he or she has it. All take turns being the "guesser."

Modelo

A —*Marta, ¿tienes el llavero?*
B —*No, no lo tengo.*
A —*Carlos, ¿tienes el llavero?*
C —*No, no lo tengo.*
A —*¿Quién tiene el llavero?*
D —*¡Yo lo tengo!*

Fondo cultural | México

The Zapotecs and other indigenous groups in the Mexican state of Oaxaca have their own languages and cultures. However, every July they all gather to celebrate the *Guelaguetza*, a Zapotec word that means "offering" or "gift." The *Guelaguetza* was first celebrated more than 3,000 years ago with music, dance, and food products. Today the festivities last two weeks and celebrate regional dances, music, costumes, and foods.

- What celebration in your culture is similar?

La fiesta de la Guelaguetza en Oaxaca, México ▶

DIFFERENTIATED INSTRUCTION

Heritage Language Learners

Ask students to give a presentation on a traditional dance, type of music, or costume from their heritage culture. Encourage them to talk with family members about this. They may choose to bring in examples or to teach a song or dance to the rest of the class.

Multiple Intelligences

Visual/Spatial: Have students do research and create posters on the history and traditions of the *Guelaguetza* and Oaxaca. Display their posters in the room.

24 Pero mamá, necesito . . . |

Hablar

Quieres ir de compras, pero primero debes hablar con tu madre o padre. Explica lo que necesitas y ¡pide *(ask for)* dinero! Tu madre o padre va a explicar por qué no necesitas comprar nada. Tu profesor(a) te dará el papel *(will assign the role)* que vas a hacer.

1. **Hijo(a):** Piensa en lo que quieres comprar y cómo vas a convencer *(convince)* a tu padre o madre.

   Padre (Madre): Tienes que decir a tu hijo(a) que no necesita lo que pide. Piensa en razones *(reasons)* para convencerle de esto.
2. Practica el drama con otro(a) estudiante.
3. Presenta el drama a tus compañeros. Ellos van a decidir quién tiene las mejores razones: los padres o los hijos.

Fondo Cultural | España

Madrid's *El Rastro* is said to be the world's largest flea market. Located in one of the oldest sections of the city, *El Rastro* attracts thousands of visitors every Sunday of the year. Vendors line the streets with their stalls and offer everything from blue jeans to fine art. Bargain hunters as well as serious antique collectors bargain for the best prices.

- Have you ever gone to a flea market in your community or state? What kinds of things did you find there? How do you think they would differ from the things found in Madrid's *El Rastro?*

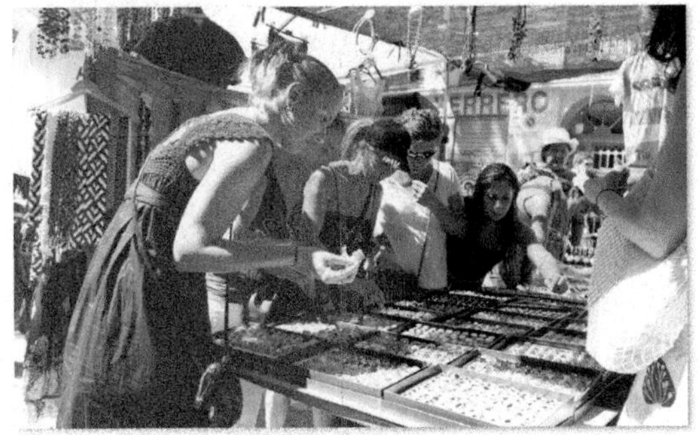

El Rastro, en Madrid, España

El español en el mundo del trabajo

Large stores and mail-order companies employ buyers who search the world over for goods to offer their customers. Buyers often need to rely on their language skills when looking for products in places where English may not be spoken, and when negotiating prices.

- What stores in your community might employ buyers who travel the world (or the Internet) in search of products from Spanish-speaking countries?

Más práctica GO

realidades.com | print

	realidades.com	print
Instant Check	✔	
Guided WB p. 240	✔	✔
Core WB p. 136	✔	✔
Comm. WB p. 145	✔	✔
***Hispanohablantes* WB** pp. 279–281		✔

Practice and Communicate 7B

24 Standards: 1.1

Focus: Using direct object pronouns in authentic speaking situations

Suggestions: Tell students to make a list of the things they want to buy. Have them think about reasons their parents might give for not being able to buy something. Encourage them to use direct object pronouns in their skits.

Answers will vary.

Fondo cultural

Standards: 2.2, 4.2

Suggestions: Before reading the *Fondo cultural,* ask students to discuss the advantages and disadvantages of shopping at flea markets. Ask why they think flea markets are popular.

Answers will vary.

Mapa global interactivo, Actividad 3 Explore El Rastro in Madrid, Spain.

Teaching with Photos

Have students write in Spanish items they see in the photo. Tell them to list the jewelry, clothing and accessories.

El español en el mundo del trabajo

Core Instruction

Standards: 5.1

Suggestions: List types of specialty shops on the chalkboard and have volunteers give the names of some of those types of shops in your community.

Additional Resources

- Communication Wbk.: Audio Act. 9, p. 145
- Teacher's Resource Book: Audio Script, pp. 189–190, Communicative Pair Activity BLM, pp. 196–197
- Audio Program DVD: Cap. 7B, Track 13

ASSESSMENT

Prueba 7B-5 with Study Plan (online only)

Quiz: Direct object pronouns
- Prueba 7B-5: p. 194

ENRICH YOUR TEACHING

Culture Note

La Lagunilla in Mexico City is another enormous open-air market. For five centuries people have come there to enjoy bargaining over the many goods available. Though it is open every day, Sunday is considered the best day to visit because the market expands to cover several blocks.

Teacher-to-Teacher

If there is a large Spanish-speaking population in your community, find out if there are any outdoor markets with Spanish-speaking vendors. If so, give students the assignment of visiting the market and reporting back on the products available there. Or you might schedule a field trip and go as a class.

Common Core: Reading

Lectura

Core Instruction

Standards: 1.1, 1.2, 3.1

Focus: Reading for comprehension; cultural perspectives

Mapa global interactivo, Actividad 4 Visit shopping areas in New York, Miami, Los Angeles, and San Antonio.

Suggestions: Direct students' attention to the objectives to preview goals for this section.

Pre-reading: Read the *Strategy* aloud and have students provide examples of how their prior experience has helped them with reading an unfamiliar text, listening to a news broadcast, or talking with a friend. For this assignment, they will need to think about a trip, shopping, and unique shopping items.

Reading: Have volunteers read the article aloud. After each paragraph, have students summarize what they have read. Then, have them think of an experience they have had that may be similar.

Post-reading: Ask students to share similar stories. Perhaps some have visited these locations. Discuss the *¿Comprendes?* questions in class, with students writing their answers as homework.

Extension: Have students write a paragraph telling which shopping site they would like to visit and why.

BELLRINGER REVIEW

Show the transparency of the map of the United States. As a class, locate these cities: *Nueva York, Miami, Los Ángeles, San Antonio.* Ask several students, *¿Visitaste una de estas ciudades el verano pasado?*

Block Schedule

Have students visit the library or use the Internet to research one of the shopping sites mentioned in the article. Ask them to write a report on the products sold and any events or festivals that are held there.

Objectives

- Read about shopping in four Hispanic communities in the United States
- Use prior experience to understand what you read
- Consider the relationship between handicrafts and artwork

Lectura 

¡De compras!

Lee este artículo de una revista. A Luisa le encanta ir de compras. ¿Qué puede comprar en cada ciudad?

Strategy

Using prior experience
Think about a trip that you took to another city. Did you go shopping? What items did you find that were unique to that city?

De COMPRA$
con Luisa, la compradora

¡Me encanta ir de compras! Hay muchos lugares donde me gusta ir de compras en los vecindarios[1] hispanos. Siempre es una experiencia divertida. Hay cosas que uno puede comprar que son muy baratas y que no hay en otros lugares. Voy a hablar de mis aventuras por las comunidades hispanas de Nueva York, Miami, Los Ángeles y San Antonio.

En el Barrio de Nueva York, en la calle[2] 116, venden ropa, comida típica del Caribe, discos compactos, libros y mucho más. Allí compré una camiseta con la bandera de Puerto Rico. En junio siempre hay una celebración grande que se llama el Festival de la calle 116. ¡Me encanta Nueva York!

La calle 116, en Nueva York

La Pequeña Habana y la calle Ocho son el corazón[3] de la comunidad cubana en Miami. Hay bodegas[4] que venden productos típicos cubanos: frijoles[5] negros y frutas tropicales como el maguey y la papaya. Allí compré pasta de guayaba, un dulce delicioso que los cubanos comen con queso blanco. ¡Qué rico!

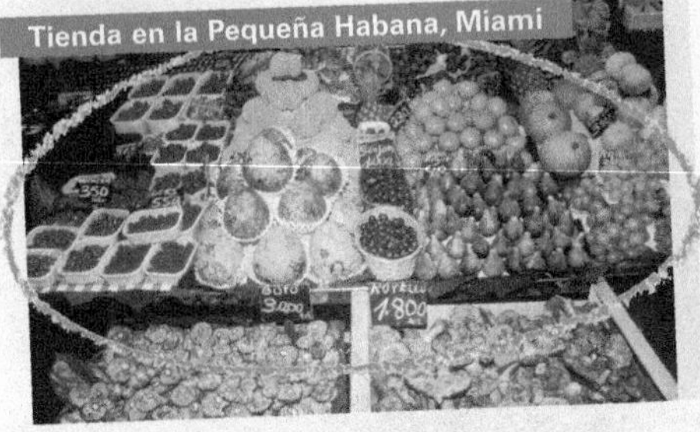
Tienda en la Pequeña Habana, Miami

Pasta de guayaba

[1]neighborhoods [2]street [3]heart
[4]grocery stores [5]beans

DIFFERENTIATED INSTRUCTION

Heritage Language Learners

Ask students to write a paragraph comparing shopping at a flea market and shopping at a mall. Have them refer to marketplaces in their heritage country or in the community.

Advanced Learners

Have students write five sentences about a souvenir they or someone they know bought while on a trip. They can share their stories with a small group or set up displays for their stories. Have them bring the souvenir to class, if possible.

De compras en la calle Olvera, Los Ángeles

El Mercado en San Antonio, Texas

La calle Olvera es la calle más antigua[6] de la ciudad de Los Ángeles y allí uno puede ver la cultura mexicana. Hay muchos restaurantes y muchos lugares para comprar artesanías.[7] Me encanta ir de compras en las joyerías porque las joyas me fascinan. En las joyerías de la calle Olvera, venden joyas de plata:[8] aretes, collares, anillos y mucho más. En una joyería de allí compré una pulsera muy bonita a un precio muy bajo.

¡Ahora vamos a hablar de San Antonio! ¡Qué compras! En esta ciudad bonita de Texas, hay tiendas de artesanías mexicanas que son fabulosas. Mis favoritas están en el Mercado o como dicen en inglés, *Market Square*. Allí compré una piñata para mi hermano, una blusa bordada[9] para mi madre, una cartera para mi padre y un sarape[10] para decorar mi dormitorio...¡y no pagué mucho!

[6]oldest [7]handicrafts [8]silver [9]embroidered [10]shawl; blanket

¿Comprendes?

1. De los cuatro lugares en *¡De compras!*, ¿adónde debe ir cada persona?

   Ana: Me gustaría comprar algo de Puerto Rico.

   Lorenzo: A mí me fascinan las artesanías mexicanas.

   Miguel: ¿Mi almuerzo favorito? El sándwich cubano.

2. ¿Qué compró Luisa en cada lugar?

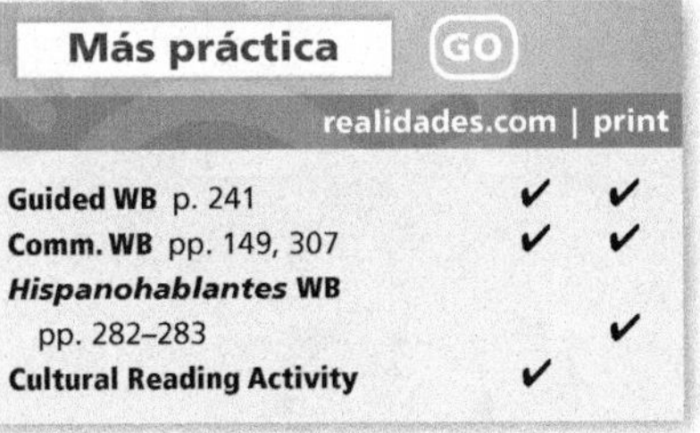

Más práctica GO

	realidades.com	print
Guided WB p. 241	✔	✔
Comm. WB pp. 149, 307	✔	✔
***Hispanohablantes* WB** pp. 282–283		✔
Cultural Reading Activity	✔	

Fondo Cultural | El mundo hispano

Las artesanías Handicrafts from Puerto Rico, Mexico, and other Spanish-speaking countries have been popular for years among tourists looking for gift ideas. Now these handicrafts are receiving recognition as museum quality artwork. At the Mexican Fine Arts Center Museum in the Pilsen neighborhood of Chicago, visitors can see permanent collections of paintings, weavings, sculpture, pottery, and silver jewelry from all over Mexico. Other types of handmade items are for sale in the museum's gift shop.

- Do you think that handicrafts should be displayed in museums along with fine art? Why or why not?

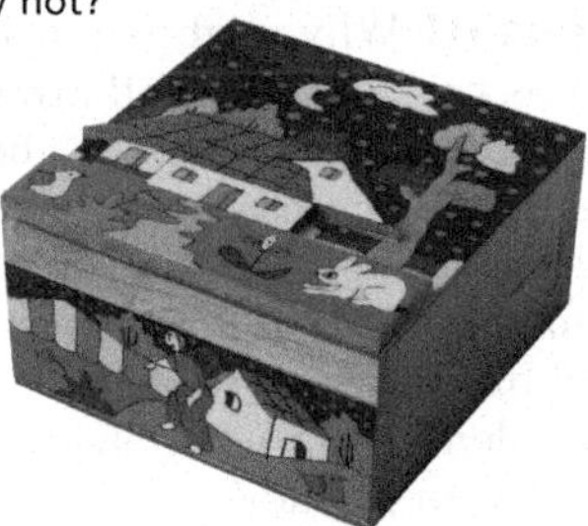

Una caja pintada de El Salvador

ENRICH YOUR TEACHING

Culture Note

The first two weekends in December, Puerto Rico highlights its native crafts with a huge cultural fair at which artisans set up booths to exhibit their work. Paintings, woodcarvings, embroidery, and ceramics are some of the crafts that are displayed.

21st Century Skills

Social and Cross-Cultural Skills Have students research a large shopping district in a Spanish-speaking country and find out about special events or celebrations held there. Have them create a print or electronic calendar providing information about all those events (dates, descriptions, what one can do or purchase there) on the appropriate month. Have them compare the celebrations to similar ones in the United States.

¿Comprendes? Standards: 1.2, 1.3

Resources: Answer Keys: Student Edition, p. 107

Focus: Demonstrating reading comprehension

Suggestions: Have students answer the questions. Ask volunteers to read the questions, give their answers, and tell the key words in each question that helped them find the answers in the reading.

Answers:

1. **Ana: La calle 116 en Nueva York**
   Lorenzo: El Mercado en San Antonio, Texas
   Miguel: Tienda en la Pequeña Habana, Miami
2. **Nueva York: camiseta con la bandera de Puerto Rico**
   Miami: pasta de guayaba
   Los Ángeles: pulsera
   San Antonio: piñata, blusa bordada, cartera, sarape

Fondo cultural

Standards: 2.2

Suggestions: Read the paragraph and the question aloud. Lead a discussion comparing fine art and handicrafts. Ask if students think there should be a distinction and to give reasons to support their opinions.

Answers will vary.

Pre-AP* Support

- **Learning Objective:** Interpretive: Print and Audio
- **Activity:** Write the names of the four cities highlighted in this article on the board. After reading the article, read teacher-made statements about each of the cities and have students indicate which city is being described.
- ***Pre-AP* Resource Book:*** Comprehensive guide to Pre-AP* reading skill development, pp. 19–26

For Further Reading

Student Resource: Realidades para hispanohablantes: Lectura 2, pp. 284–285

Perspectivas del mundo hispano

Core Instruction

Standards: 4.2

Focus: Reading about shopping malls and how people use them

Suggestions: Discuss with students their reasons for going to the mall. Point to the photo and have them compare it to malls they have been to. Have them read the text. Compare the reasons people from Chile and from the United States go to malls.

Direct attention to the *Think about it!* section and have students discuss the questions.

Answers will vary.

Mention that some adults in the United States complain about young people hanging around in the mall. Ask students if this is a valid complaint, and based on what they have read, if they think it would be an issue in Chile.

Have students complete the *Check it out!* section for homework. Discuss the answers at a later date.

Teacher-to-Teacher

e-amigos: Have students e-mail their *e-amigos* to ask about recent gifts they have purchased. Have them print out or e-mail you the questions and responses.

Additional Resources

Student Resource: Realidades para hispanohablantes, p. 286

Perspectivas del mundo hispano

¿Por qué vas al centro comercial?

Why do people go to the mall? Note the differences between consumers in Chile and the United States.

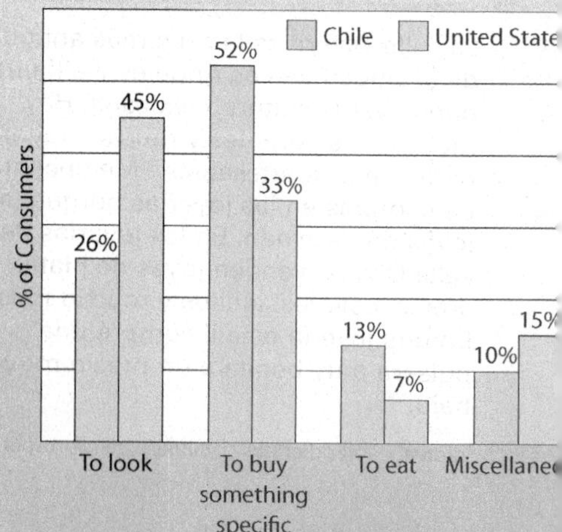

In the United States many people go to the mall to see what merchandise is available and to spend time. In Chile, many people go to the mall because they want to make a specific purchase. They decide where to go according to the merchandise they need to buy.

For many in the United States, going to the mall is more than going shopping. The mall offers an opportunity to eat and to spend time with friends. For 50% of United States consumers the atmosphere of a mall is very important. Only 13% of Chilean consumers think that atmosphere is important.

Although their motivation for going to the mall is different, 80% of both Chilean and United States consumers make a purchase once they are in the stores.

Check it out! Interview at least three people your age and at least three adults that you know and find out what their main reasons for going to a mall are, how they decide which mall to go to, and if they usually make a purchase while at the mall. Compare what you find out with the results above for shoppers in the United States and Chile.

Think about it! Why might shoppers in the United States consider the mall atmosphere an important factor in their decision about where to shop? Given what you have read about the reasons Chileans go shopping, what do you think a store clerk in a mall in Chile might expect you to do if you entered his or her store? How might a Chilean exchange student feel if he or she went to the mall with you and your friends?

En el centro comercial Galerías Pacífico, en Buenos Aires, Argentina

DIFFERENTIATED INSTRUCTION

Advanced Learners

Have students research malls in Spanish-speaking countries and in the United States. Ask them to prepare a visual comparison, using photos.

Heritage Language Learners

Have students conduct informal interviews of family or friends from their heritage country to find out when and why people go to malls. Do they go to spend time or only for a specific purchase?

Objectives

Aplicación

- Write a letter about a gift for a relative
- Decide on a format and organize information before writing

Presentación escrita

Un regalo para mi . . .

Task
You recently bought a gift for a family member. Write a letter to a relative about the gift so that he or she will not buy the same item.

1. **Prewrite** A family member is celebrating a birthday. Think about the gift you bought. Answer the questions to organize your thoughts.
   - ¿Para quién es el regalo?
   - ¿Qué compraste y por qué?
   - ¿Dónde lo compraste? ¿Cuánto pagaste?
   - ¿Cuándo es la fiesta de cumpleaños?

2. **Draft** Use your Prewrite answers to write a first draft. Begin your letter with *Querido(a)... or Hola...,* and close it with *Tu primo(a)...* or *Saludos,* or *Hasta pronto.*

3. **Revise** Read the letter and check spelling, vocabulary choice, verb forms, and agreement. Share the letter with your partner, who will check the following:
   - Is the letter easy to read and understand?
   - Does it provide all the necessary information?
   - Did you use appropriate letter form?
   - Are there any errors?

4. **Publish** Rewrite the letter, making any necessary changes or additions. Share your letter with your teacher. You may also want to add it to your portfolio.

5. **Evaluation** The following rubric will be used to grade your letter.

Rubric	Score 1	Score 3	Score 5
How easily the letter is understood	Only a little of what you have written is comprehensible to others.	Most of what you have written is comprehensible.	All of what you have written is comprehensible to others.
Amount of information provided	You only give information about the gift and where it was purchased.	You give information about the gift, where you bought it, and why.	You provide all gift information and information about the party.
Appropriate greeting and closing are used	You use only a greeting or closing.	You use both a greeting and closing, but there are errors.	You use both a greeting and closing accurately.
Accurate use of the preterite	You use many incorrect verb forms.	You use incorrect verb forms.	You use very few incorrect verb forms.

Strategy

Organizing information
Thinking about the correct format and necessary information beforehand will help you write a better letter.

Querido Mauricio:

Compré un reloj pulsera para el abuelito. Lo compré en el almacén Génova que está en el centro comercial Plaza del Río. No pagué mucho por él. Creo que al abuelito le va a gustar. Voy a ver a toda la familia el dos de octubre para la fiesta de cumpleaños del abuelito.

Tu primo,

Luis

Writing 7B

Common Core: Writing

Presentación escrita

Expository

Standards: 1.3

Focus: Writing a letter to describe a gift

Suggestions: Review the task and the steps with students. After reading the *Strategy,* suggest how they might organize information for a letter. Review the rubric to explain how you will grade their letters. Explain what is necessary for a top-scoring presentation, and have them use the model as a guide. Encourage students to write about a gift that was special, not necessarily expensive. Help them to work through each step of the writing process.

Portfolio

Have students add this activity to their portfolios.

Pre-AP* Support

- **Learning Objective:** Interpersonal Writing
- **Activity:** Have students use the information in the letter they wrote to draft a reply e-mail from the recipient of the gift. Have them imagine the family member has received the gift and writes an e-mail thanking the gift-giver and saying how much they enjoy the present.
- ***Pre-AP* Resource Book:*** Comprehensive guide to Pre-AP* writing skill development, pp. 27–38

Additional Resources

Student Resources: Realidades para hispanohablantes, p. 287; Guided Practice: Presentación escrita, p. 242

ENRICH YOUR TEACHING

Teacher-to-Teacher

Careers: *Tema* 7 has focused on shopping. Have students work in small groups to talk about a career in retail. Ask students to generate a list of words, expressions, or sentences they have learned that would be useful for working in or managing a clothing store. Ask different groups to share their lists.

21st Century Skills

Flexibility and Adaptability Using the letter on this page as a model, have students first discuss how the letter would be different if they wrote to a younger brother, to an older relative, or to a teacher. How would those changes affect the tone, the content, and the language of the letter?

ASSESSMENT

Presentación escrita

- Assessment Program: Rubrics, p. T32

Go over the descriptions of the different levels of performance. After assessing students, help individuals understand how their performance could be improved.

Videomisterio

Core Instruction

Standards: 1.2, 2.1, 2.2, 5.2

Resources: Teacher's Resource Book: Video Script, pp. 192–193; Video Program: Cap. 7B; Video Program Teacher's Guide: Cap. 7B

Focus: Introducing the events and vocabulary of this episode; scanning and reading the episode summary

Personajes importantes:

Lola Lago, detective
Margarita, secretaria de Lola
Paco, colega de Lola
Pedro, nieto de doña Gracia

Synopsis: Pedro Requena decides to hire Lola to investigate what caused the incident at his grandmother's house that sent her to the hospital and who stole doña Gracia's jewels from her apartment. Inspector Gil suspects María, since she has disappeared. Lola accepts the job and they come to an agreement on the cost of her services.

Suggestions:

Pre-viewing: Review the events of the previous episode. Lola and Carmela met at the San Carlos hospital where they asked Rosalinda for help in getting information about María Requena, who spent three months there as a result of a car accident. But her medical record cannot be found. They inquired about María's friend, Julia, who also was in the accident. Julia died in the hospital, but her file cannot be found either.

Review the *Nota cultural* with the class. You may want to ask students if they know when it is appropriate to use or switch from ***usted*** to the informal ***tú.*** Point out the *Palabras para comprender,* saying examples in context and writing the sentences on the chalkboard. Remind students that these words are to help them understand the episode and that they are not responsible for learning them.

Visual scanning: Direct students' attention to the pictures and ask who these characters are (Lola and Pedro), what their relationship is (he is Lola's client), and where they meet (at Lola's detective agency). Before students read the *Resumen,* have them scan the text and find three cognates. **(*oficina, detective, privado, preciosas, problema, robó*)** Then ask them to read the *Resumen* carefully and ask questions about what they think will happen in this episode.

Objective

- Understand the expanding plot of a mystery video set in Spain

¿Eres tú, María? Episodio 6

Antes de ver el video

Resumen del episodio

Lola llega a su oficina y hay un recado de Pedro Requena. Él viene a hablar con ella sobre su abuela, doña Gracia. Necesita un detective privado y quiere la ayuda de Lola y Paco. Pedro explica que su abuela es una mujer muy rica y que tiene joyas preciosas. Pero hay un problema. Las joyas de doña Gracia no están en el piso. Pedro cree que un ladrón robó las joyas. Pero, ¿cómo sabe el ladrón que hay joyas en el piso de doña Gracia?

Nota cultural Lola quotes Pedro a price for her agency's services in euros. The euro is the currency in Spain and many other countries in Europe that are part of the European Union.

Nota cultural In Spain, it is customary for adults to speak to new acquaintances using the formal *Ud.* In most cases, the other person will then invite you to address them informally using the *tú* form. This is called *tutear.* In this scene, Pedro invites Lola to speak to him informally. When you visit Spain, you should address new adult acquaintances in the *Ud.* form and wait to be invited to *tutear.*

Palabras para comprender

un recado a message
una cita an appointment
Acabo de venir del hospital. I just came from the hospital.
Vi a su abuela. I saw your grandmother.
necesito saber . . . I need to know . . .
el ladrón robó the burglar stole
nosotros cobramos we charge

DIFFERENTIATED INSTRUCTION

Advanced Learners

Have students write three sentences summarizing the episode. They should include at least four new vocabulary words from this chapter and write the sentences using preterite ***-ar*** verbs.

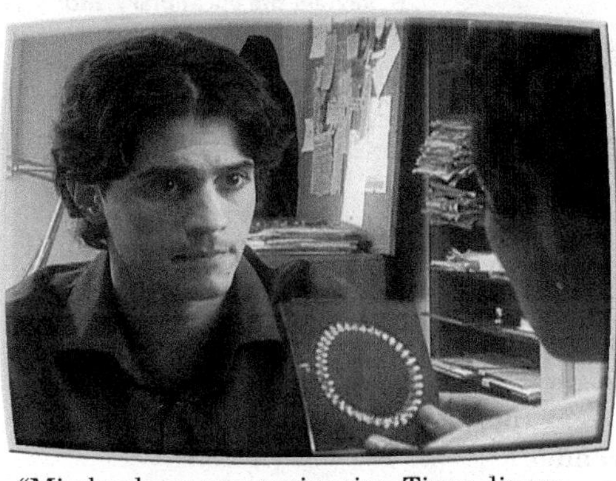

"Mi abuela es una mujer rica. Tiene dinero y joyas de valor. Son de la familia".

"María va a recibir todo el dinero, todas las joyas, todo de mi abuela".

"Pedro, vamos a buscar las joyas".

Después de ver el video

¿Comprendes?

Termina las frases con la palabra más apropiada del recuadro.

fotos	recado
joyas	dinero
sobrina	abuela
teléfono	nieto

1. Lola, hay un _____ para ti de un tal Pedro Reteña, Resqueña o Retena. Algo así.
2. El _____ de doña Gracia viene a la una y media.
3. ¡Qué bueno! Un cliente con _____.
4. Acabo de venir del hospital. Vi a su _____.
5. Aquí tengo unas _____ de ella.
6. Mira, las _____ no están en el piso.
7. Aquí está el número de _____: 318 18 02.

Más práctica GO

realidades.com | print

Actividades ✔

ENRICH YOUR TEACHING

Teacher-to-Teacher

English does not have formal and informal subject pronouns, but we do have definite levels of formal and informal language. Discuss the concept of "register" in order to develop student awareness of appropriate and inappropriate language in different situations in Spanish. Just as in English, the choice of formal versus informal words is another way Spanish speakers signal the form of address they expect from their counterparts in conversation.

Viewing: Play *Episodio* 6 for the class. If there is time after viewing the full episode, replay key moments that you wish to highlight, such as the scene in which Pedro explains to Lola that it is important to find the jewels because María is going to inherit everything from her aunt.

Post-viewing: Point out the list of words that appear in the box. Then have the students look at the pictures and the captions and summarize the scenes in this episode. Write the new words used in the episode on the chalkboard to help students create sentences for each important scene that adds new information to the plot. Then direct students' attention to the *¿Comprendes?*

¿Comprendes? Standards: 1.2, 1.3

Resources: Answer Keys: Student Edition, p. 107

Focus: Verifying comprehension by answering questions; reviewing the plot

Suggestions: Remind students to read all of the sentences before choosing the best word from the box to fill in the blank.

Answers:

1. **recado**
2. **nieto**
3. **dinero**
4. **abuela**
5. **fotos**
6. **joyas**
7. **teléfono**

Extension: Have students work in pairs to prepare who, what, when, where, and why comprehension questions about the reading. Give them an example.

Additional Resources

- *¿Eres tú, María?* Video Workbook, Episode 6
- *¿Eres tú, María?* Teacher's Video Guide: Answer Key

7B Review

Review Activities

To talk about about places where you shop: Let students work in pairs to quiz each other on the vocabulary. They can create flashcards, writing the Spanish word on one side and the English word on the other. They can also include drawings to help them remember the words.

To talk about gifts you might buy: Let students work in pairs and ask what gifts they have purchased, where they bought them, and how much they cost. This will also allow for practice of the preterite of ***comprar.*** Have students reverse roles.

To talk about buying and selling: Have students interview different pairs who have been practicing together to find out if their purchases were cheap or expensive and for whom they bought the gift. Students should use the preterite of ***buscar, comprar,*** and ***pagar.***

Direct object pronouns: Have students write five sentences about an item they bought. For each item, they must write where they purchased it and use a direct object pronoun. Example: *Compré un anillo para mi novia. Lo compré en la joyería.*

Portfolio

Invite students to review the activities they completed in this chapter, including written reports, posters or other visuals, recordings of oral presentations, or other projects. Have them select one or two items that they feel best demonstrate their achievements in Spanish to include in their portfolios. Have them include this with the Chapter Checklist and Self-Assessment Worksheet.

Additional Resources

Student Resources: Realidades para hispanohablantes, p. 288

Teacher Resources:

- Teacher's Resource Book: Situation Cards, p. 198, Clip Art, pp. 200–201
- Assessment Program: Chapter Checklist and Self-Assessment Worksheet, pp. T56–T57

Repaso | | |

▼ Objectives

- Review the vocabulary and grammar
- Demonstrate you can perform the tasks on p. 371

Repaso del capítulo

Vocabulario y gramática

to talk about places where you shop

el almacén *pl.* **los almacenes**	department store
en la Red	online
la joyería	jewelry store
la librería	bookstore
la tienda de descuentos	discount store
la tienda de electrodomésticos	household appliance store
la zapatería	shoe store

to talk about gifts you might buy

el anillo	ring
los anteojos de sol	sunglasses
los aretes	earrings
el bolso	purse
la cadena	chain
la cartera	wallet
el collar	necklace
la corbata	tie
los guantes	gloves
el llavero	key chain
el perfume	perfume
la pulsera	bracelet
el reloj pulsera	watch
el software	software

to talk about who might receive a gift

el novio	boyfriend
la novia	girlfriend

For *Vocabulario adicional*, see pp. 472–473.

to talk about buying or selling

barato, -a	inexpensive, cheap
caro, -a	expensive
mirar	to look (at)
pagar (por)	to pay (for)
vender	to sell

to talk about time in the past

anoche	last night
el año pasado	last year
ayer	yesterday
hace + *time expression*	ago
la semana pasada	last week

other useful expressions

¡Uf!	Ugh! Yuck!

preterite of regular *-ar* verbs

compré	**compramos**
compraste	**comprasteis**
compró	**compraron**

preterite of *-car* and *-gar* verbs

These verbs have a spelling change in the *yo* form of the preterite.

buscar *c* → *qu*	yo busqué
pagar *g* → *gu*	yo pagué
jugar *g* → *gu*	yo jugué

direct object pronouns

	SINGULAR	PLURAL
M.	**lo** *it*	**los** *them*
F.	**la** *it*	**las** *them*

DIFFERENTIATED INSTRUCTION

Students with Special Needs

Depending on each student's abilities and needs, a modified assessment will need to be created. If possible, give students a practice test so they are familiar with the structure of the assessment.

Heritage Language Learners

Have students write a guide for Spanish-speaking tourists visiting your community. They should include in their guide the best places to shop for the items from this chapter.

Más repaso GO realidades.com | print

Instant Check	✔	
Puzzles	✔	
Core WB pp. 137–138		✔
Comm. WB pp. 308, 309–311	✔	✔

Preparación para el examen

On the exam you will be asked to . . .	Here are practice tasks similar to those you will find on the exam . . .	For review go to your print or digital textbook . . .
Interpretive		
 **1 Escuchar** Listen as someone describes what she bought as a gift and where she bought it	As a teenager tells what she bought for her friend's *quinceañera,* see if you can tell: a) what she bought; b) where she bought it; c) how much she paid for it.	**pp. 346–349** *Vocabulario en contexto* **p. 347** Actividad 1 **p. 350** Actividad 4
Interpersonal		
 **2 Hablar** Exchange opinions about whether certain items are expensive or inexpensive	Think about a gift you've bought. Tell your partner what you bought, for whom you bought it, and how much you paid. Then ask your partner whether he or she thinks the gift was expensive or inexpensive. Your partner will then share the same information and ask the same questions about a gift that he or she bought.	**p. 350** Actividad 5 **p. 351** Actividades 6–7 **p. 352** Actividad 8 **p. 354** Actividad 12
Interpretive		
 **3 Leer** Read and understand an online advertisement for a store you might find on the Internet	While shopping online, you find a Web site for a discount store in Mexico City. Can you list at least two advantages for customers who shop here?	**pp. 346–349** *Vocabulario en contexto* **p. 352** Actividad 9

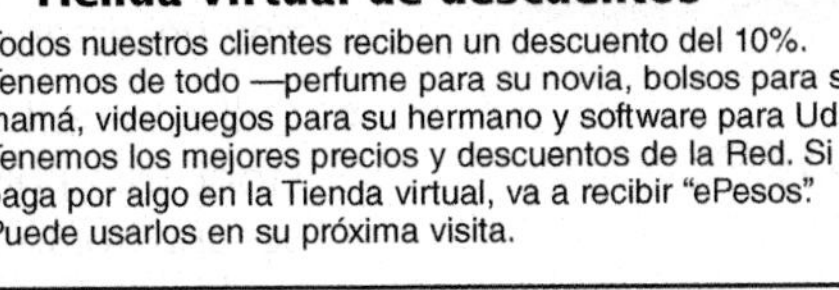

Presentational		
 **4 Escribir** Write a short explanation about some items that you have bought this school year with your own money	As an entry for your class journal, explain how you spent your money last month. Describe: a) at least two new clothing items or accessories you bought; b) where you bought the items; c) how much you paid for them.	**p. 354** Actividad 12 **p. 357** Actividad 16 **p. 360** Actividad 19 **p. 361** Actividad 20 **p. 362** Actividad 22 **p. 367** *Presentación escrita*
Cultures		
 **5 Pensar** Demonstrate an understanding of cultural perspectives regarding shopping	Think about what you do when you go to a shopping mall. Based on what you've learned in this chapter, would these be the same things that Chileans do? What similarities and differences would you expect to see in shopping malls and in attitudes of shoppers in both countries?	**p. 366** *Perspectivas del mundo hispano*

Review 7B

Performance Tasks

Standards: 1.1, 1.2, 1.3, 4.2

Student Resource: Realidades para hispanohablantes, p. 289

Teacher Resources: Teacher's Resource Book: Audio Script, p. 190; Audio Program DVD: Cap. 7B, Track 16; Answer Keys: Student Edition, p. 108

1. Escuchar

Suggestions: Use the audio or read the script. Students may want to create three columns on their papers: *¿Qué compró? ¿Dónde lo compró? ¿Cuánto costó?*

Script:

Yo compré este llavero para ella. Lo busqué en un almacén la semana pasada y pagué doscientos pesos. Es muy bonito, ¿no?

Answers: a) The person bought a key ring; b) The person bought it in a department store; c) The person paid 200 pesos.

2. Hablar

Suggestions: Give students time to think first. They can make up prices for different items to use both ***barato*** and ***caro.***

Answers will vary.

3. Leer

Suggestions: Have students read the ad silently, then have a volunteer read it aloud. Remind students that cognates can help them understand it.

Answers: 1. You can get a 10% discount; 2. You can accumulate "ePesos."

4. Escribir

Suggestions: Have students pre-write and write answers to a–c. Then they can flesh out their notes and write a paragraph. Encourage them to use some adjectives to describe the items.

Answers will vary.

5. Pensar

Suggestions: Have students refer to the *Perspectivas del mundo hispano* on p. 366.

Answers will vary.

DIFFERENTIATED ASSESSMENT

CORE ASSESSMENT
- **Assessment Program:** Examen del capítulo 7B, pp. 195–200
- **Audio Program DVD:** Cap. 7B, Track 17
- **ExamView:** Chapter Test, Test Banks A and B

ADVANCED/PRE-AP*
- **ExamView: Pre-AP* Test Bank**
- **Pre-AP* Resource Book,** pp. 86–89

STUDENTS NEEDING EXTRA HELP
- **Alternate Assessment Program:** Examen del capítulo 7B
- **Audio Program DVD:** Cap. 7B, Track 17

HERITAGE LEARNERS
- **Assessment Program: Realidades para hispanohablantes:** Examen del capítulo 7B
- **ExamView: Heritage Learner Test Bank**

Tema

8 Experiencias

8A De vacaciones

- **Travel, vacations, and past events**

Vocabulary: vacation places and activities; modes of transportation

Grammar: preterite of ***-er*** and ***-ir*** verbs; preterite of ***ir;*** the personal ***a***

Cultural Perspectives: travel and vacations

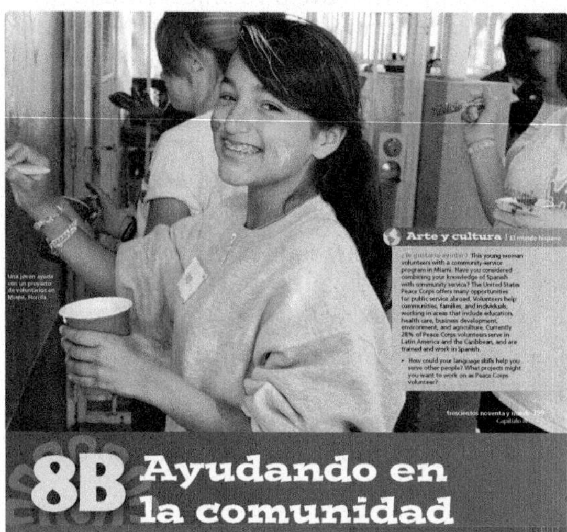

8B Ayudando en la comunidad

- **Volunteer work, community service tasks, what people do to help others**

Vocabulary: recycling and volunteer work; places in a community

Grammar: the verb ***decir;*** indirect object pronouns; preterite of ***hacer*** and ***dar***

Cultural Perspectives: volunteer work

THEME SUPPORT

Bulletin Boards

Theme: *Experiencias*

Ask students to cut out, copy, or download photos of famous tourist destinations and attractions from around the world, and of people engaged in recreational and volunteer activities. Cluster photos according to the three above-mentioned themes.

Hands-on Culture

Chant: *Invito a...*

Jumping rope is a popular pastime, while on vacation or at home, of children throughout the Spanish-speaking world. The following is a chant sung by the person jumping rope to invite someone else to jump with him or her.

Invito a... (the name of the person).
—*¿A qué?* —*A un pastel.*
—*¿A qué hora?* —*A las tres.*
Que una, que dos, que tres.

The person who has been invited jumps in.

Suggestions for using the chant:

1. Teach students the jumping chant, and explain how the game is played.
2. Bring in a long jump-rope. Ask two volunteers to swing the jump-rope and a third volunteer to jump.
3. Have the volunteer jumping begin the chant, then ask the class to join in on the second line.
4. Have the class clap out a rhythm for the jumpers after they say the last line of the chant until one of the jumpers steps on the rope, and is out.
5. Play again, until everyone who wants to take a turn has had one.

Game

¡Cuéntame!

Play this game to review the material from *Capítulo* 8A.

Players: the whole class

Materials: index cards

Rules:

1. On index cards, write vocabulary words and expressions from *Capítulo* 8A as well as other ***-er*** and ***-ir*** verbs students have learned. Place the cards in a box.
2. Have every student draw an index card from the box.
3. Ask for a volunteer to begin a story, using the word on his or her card in a sentence. Write the student's sentence on the board or a transparency. Ask the class to make any necessary corrections.
4. Call on another volunteer to continue the story, using his or her word. Write the second volunteer's sentence on the board, and have the class make any necessary corrections. Continue in this manner until the class feels the story has reached a logical conclusion. If every student has not had the chance to contribute to the story, begin a second story.

Student 1: (drew ***zoológico***) *Ayer visité el zoológico.*
Student 2: (drew ***autobús***) *Fui al zoológico en autobús.*
Student 3: (drew ***animal***) *Hay muchos animales en el zoológico.*

Variation: Play the game at the end of *Capítulo* 8B, writing only verbs on the index cards. Have students tell the story in the preterite tense.

THEME PROJECT

Diario ilustrado

Overview: On construction paper, or using layout software, students create illustrated journal entries for an imaginary one-week volunteer vacation they took. They then present their journals to the class, describing how they traveled, where they went, and what they did.

Resources: magazines, scissors, glue, markers, colored pencils or crayons, construction paper, or electronic layout/markup tools

Sequence: (suggestions for when to do each step appear throughout the chapters)

8A **STEP 1.** Review instructions so students know what is expected of them. Hand out the "Theme 8 Project Instructions and Rubric" from the *Teacher's Resource Book.*

STEP 2. Students submit an outline and sketch of their journal entries. Return the drafts with your suggestions.

STEP 3. Students cut out or draw the illustrations they need, then create the layout for their journals on construction paper or using electronic tools. Encourage students to think their ideas through before they lay them out.

8B **STEP 4.** Students submit drafts of their journal entries. Note your corrections and suggestions, then return drafts to students. Students correct their drafts, then partner to describe their trips.

STEP 5. Students present their journals to the class, describing where they went, what they did, and how they traveled.

Options:

1. Students present a slide show of a volunteer vacation, using transparencies or a computer.
2. Students create an illustrated itinerary of a real or imaginary vacation.

Assessment:

Here is a detailed rubric for assessing this project:

Theme 8 Project: *Diario ilustrado*

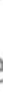

RUBRIC	Score 1	Score 3	Score 5
Evidence of planning	You didn't submit a sketch and draft.	You submitted the sketch and draft, but didn't correct them.	You submitted and corrected your sketch and draft.
Use of illustrations	You didn't include photos / illustrations.	You included photos / illustrations for most entries.	You included photos / illustrations for all entries.
Presentation	You listed places, activities, and transport; you had no description or complete sentences.	You listed places, activities, and transport; some description; some complete sentences.	You listed and described places, activities, and transport; you had complete sentences.

21st Century Skills

Look for tips throughout *Tema* 8 to enrich your teaching by integrating 21st Century Skills. Suggestions for the Theme Project and Theme Culture follow below.

Theme Project

Modify the Theme Project with these suggestions:

Develop Technology Literacy
To meet the goal of creating a journal that is not only informative but also appealing and attractive, have students enhance their journals by combining print, audio, and video images.

Encourage Collaboration
Have students work in small groups to compare their volunteer vacations. The group will choose the best proposal to present to the class, which then chooses a plan to take on as a class project. The handout "Make Decisions" will guide the team in choosing the best proposal.

Support Critical Thinking and Problem-Solving
As students evaluate their classmates' proposals, ask them to consider the following questions: What elements make for the strongest or most interesting projects? Impact of the volunteer work on the community? Location? Community need?

Theme Culture

Foster Social and Cross-Cultural Skills
Have students act as travel agents whose job it is to find a suitable vacation spot for a family that cannot decide between going to Mexico or to Peru. After reviewing the cultural information about both countries in the chapter, have students prepare a helpful report for their clients.

Videocultura View *Las vacaciones* with the class to learn about places to visit in Spanish-speaking countries.

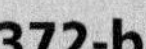

8A De vacaciones

AT A GLANCE

Objectives
- Listen to and read about trips and vacations
- Talk and write about favorite and imaginary trips
- Talk about and describe your best vacation
- Explain the tradition of the *ojo de Dios* and compare it to crafts in the United States
- Identify places of geographical and historical importance in Spanish-speaking countries and compare them to places in the United States

Vocabulary
- Vacation destinations and activities
- Modes of transportation
- Attractions, parks, and animals
- Expressions to talk about a trip or vacation

Grammar
- The preterite of ***-er*** and ***-ir*** verbs
- The preterite of ***ir***
- The personal ***a***

Culture
- Joaquín Sorolla, p. 373
- El Yunque National Park, p. 378
- Song ***"Cielito Lindo"*** p. 380
- Places in Mexico City, p. 382
- Public transportation in Mexico City, p. 382
- Patagonia, p. 384
- Geographic facts about the Americas, p. 388
- Cuzco, Machu Picchu, Lake Titicaca, Nazca lines, pp. 390–391
- ***El ojo de Dios,*** p. 392

Recycle ♻
- The preterite of ***-ar*** verbs
- Direct object pronouns ***lo, la, los, las***
- Question words
- ***-er*** and ***-ir*** verbs
- ***estar***
- ***ir; ir a*** + infinitive
- ***me gusta(n)***

RESOURCES

	FOR THE STUDENT	ONLINE	DVD	PRINT	FOR THE TEACHER	ONLINE	PREEXP	DVD	PRINT
Plan					Interactive TE and Resources DVD	•		•	
					Teacher's Resource Book, pp. 218–253	•		•	•
					Pre-AP* Resource Book, pp. 90–93	•		•	•
					Lesson Plans	•			•
					Mapa global interactivo	•			
Introducción PP. **372–373**									
Present	Student Edition, pp. 372–373	•	•	•	Interactive TE and Resources DVD	•		•	
	DK Reference Atlas	•	•		Teacher's Resource Book, pp. 218–221	•		•	•
	Videocultura	•	•		Galería de fotos		•		
	Hispanohablantes WB, pp. 290–291			•	Fine Art Transparencies, 18	•	•	•	
					Map Transparencies, 12–16, 18	•	•	•	
Vocabulario en contexto PP. **374–377**									
Present & Practice	Student Edition, pp. 374–377	•	•	•	Interactive TE and Resources DVD	•		•	
	Audio	•	•		Teacher's Resource Book, pp. 222–223, 227, 236–237	•		•	•
	Videohistoria	•	•		Vocabulary Clip Art	•	•	•	•
	Flashcards	•	•		Audio Program	•	•	•	
	Instant Check	•			Video Program: Videohistoria	•		•	
	Guided WB, pp. 243–252	•	•	•	Video Program Teacher's Guide: Cap. 8A	•		•	•
	Core WB, pp. 139–142	•	•	•	Vocabulary and Grammar Transparencies, 143–146	•	•	•	
	Comm. WB, pp. 150–153, 156	•	•	•	Answer Keys: Student Edition, pp. 109–111	•	•	•	
	Hispanohablantes WB, pp. 292–293			•	TPR Stories, pp. 107–121	•		•	•
Assess and Remediate					Prueba 8A–1: Assessment Program, pp. 201–202	•		•	•
					Assessment Program para hispanohablantes, pp. 201–202	•		•	•

RESOURCES

	FOR THE STUDENT	ONLINE	DVD	PRINT	FOR THE TEACHER	ONLINE	PREEXP	DVD	PRINT
Vocabulario en uso PP. **378–382**									
Present & Practice	Student Edition, pp. 378–382	•	•	•	Interactive Whiteboard Vocabulary Activities	•		•	
	Instant Check	•			Interactive TE and Resources DVD	•		•	
	Comm. WB, p. 153	•	•	•	Teacher's Resource Book, pp. 223–224, 230–231	•		•	•
	Hispanohablantes WB, pp. 294–295			•	Communicative Pair Activities, pp. 230–231	•		•	•
	Communicative Pair Activities	•			Audio Program	•	•	•	
					Videomodelos	•		•	
					Vocabulary and Grammar Transparencies, 149	•	•	•	
					Answer Keys: Student Edition, pp. 111–113	•	•	•	•
Assess and Remediate					Prueba 8A–2 with Study Plan	•			
					Prueba 8A–2: Assessment Program, pp. 203–204	•		•	•
					Assessment Program para hispanohablantes, pp. 203–204	•		•	•
Gramática PP. **383–389**									
Present & Practice	Student Edition, pp. 383–389	•	•	•	Interactive Whiteboard Grammar Activities	•		•	
	Instant Check	•			Interactive TE and Resources DVD	•		•	
	Animated Verbs	•			Teacher's Resource Book, pp. 224–225, 228, 232–233	•		•	•
	Tutorial Video: Grammar	•			Communicative Pair Activities, pp. 232–233	•		•	•
	Canción de hip hop	•			Audio Program	•	•	•	
	Guided WB, pp. 253–256	•	•	•	Videomodelos	•		•	
	Core WB, pp. 143–145	•	•	•	Video Program: GramActiva	•	•	•	
	Comm. WB, pp. 154–155, 157–158, 312	•	•	•	Vocabulary and Grammar Transparencies, 147–148	•	•	•	
	Hispanohablantes WB, pp. 296–301			•	Answer Keys: Student Edition, pp. 114–117	•	•	•	
	Communicative Pair Activities	•							
Assess and Remediate					Pruebas 8A–3, 8A–4, and 8A–5 with Study Plans	•			
					Pruebas 8A–3, 8A–4, and 8A–5: Assessment Program, pp. 205–207	•		•	•
					Assessment Program para hispanohablantes, pp. 205–207	•		•	•
¡Adelante! PP. **390–395**									
Application	Student Edition, pp. 390–395	•	•	•	Interactive TE and Resources DVD	•		•	
	Online Cultural Reading	•			Teacher's Resource Book, pp. 228–229	•		•	•
	Guided WB, pp. 257–258	•	•	•	Video Program: Videomisterio ¿Eres tú, María?	•		•	
	Comm. WB, pp. 159, 313	•	•	•	Video Program Teacher's Guide: Cap. 8A	•		•	
	Hispanohablantes WB, pp. 302–307			•	Videomisterio Quiz		•		
	¿Eres tú, María? Video WB, pp. 50–57	•	•	•	Vocabulary and Grammar Transparencies, 150	•		•	
					Map Transparencies, 15	•	•	•	
					Answer Keys: Student Edition, p. 117	•	•	•	
Repaso del capítulo PP. **396–397**									
Review	Student Edition, pp. 396–397	•	•	•	Interactive TE and Resources DVD	•		•	
	Online Puzzles and Games	•			Teacher's Resource Book, pp. 226, 234, 236–237	•		•	•
	Core WB, pp. 146–147	•	•	•	Audio Program	•	•	•	
	Comm. WB, pp. 314–318	•	•	•	Answer Keys: Student Edition, p. 117	•	•	•	
	Hispanohablantes WB, pp. 308–309			•					
	Instant Check	•							
Chapter Assessment									
Assess					Examen del capítulo 8A	•		•	•
					Assessment Program, pp. 208–214	•		•	•
					Alternate Assessment Program, pp. 79–84	•		•	•
					Assessment Program para hispanohablantes, pp. 208–214	•		•	•
					Audio Program, Cap. 8A, Examen	•		•	
					ExamView: Test Banks A and B questions only online	•		•	
					Heritage Learner Test Bank	•		•	
					Pre-AP* Test Bank	•		•	

REGULAR SCHEDULE (50 MINUTES)

DAY	Warm-up / Assess	Preview / Present / Practice / Communicate	Wrap-up / Homework Options
1	**Warm-up** (10 min.) • Return Examen del capítulo 7B	**Chapter Opener** (5 min.) • Objectives • Arte y cultura **Vocabulario en contexto** (30 min.) • Presentation: Vocabulario en contexto • Actividades 1, 2	**Wrap-up and Homework Options** (5 min.) • Core Practice 8A-1, 8A-2
2	**Warm-up** (5 min.) • Homework check	**Vocabulario en contexto** (35 min.) • Presentation: Videohistoria *¿Qué te pasó?* • View: Videohistoria • Video Activities 1, 2, 3, 4 • Actividad 3 **Vocabulario en uso** (5 min.) • Actividad 5	**Wrap-up and Homework Options** (5 min.) • Core Practice 8A-3, 8A-4 • Actividad 7 • Prueba 8A-1: Vocabulary recognition
3	**Warm-up** (10 min.) • Actividad 4 • Homework check ✔**Formative Assessment** (10 min.) • Prueba 8A-1: Vocabulary recognition	**Vocabulario en uso** (25 min.) • Interactive Whiteboard Vocabulary Activities • Actividades 6, 8, 10 • Audio Activities 5, 6 • Pronunciación	**Wrap-up and Homework Options** (5 min.) • Actividades 9, 12 • Writing Activity 10 • Prueba 8A-2 with Study Plan: Vocabulary production
4	**Warm-up** (10 min.) • Actividad 11 • Homework check ✔**Formative Assessment** (10 min.) • Prueba 8A-2 with Study Plan: Vocabulary production	**Gramática y vocabulario en uso** (30 min.) • Communicative Pair Activity • Presentation: The preterite of ***-er*** and ***-ir*** verbs • View: GramActiva video • Interactive Whiteboard Grammar Activities • Actividades 13, 15 • Fondos culturales • Audio Activity 7 • Communicative Pair Activity	**Wrap-up and Homework Options** (5 min.) • Core Practice 8A-5 • Writing Activity 11 • Prueba 8A-3 with Study Plan: The preterite of ***-er*** and ***-ir*** verbs
5	**Warm-up** (5 min.) • Actividad 14 • Homework check ✔**Formative Assessment** (10 min.) • Prueba 8A-3 with Study Plan: The preterite of ***-er*** and ***-ir*** verbs	**Gramática y vocabulario en uso** (30 min.) • Presentation: The preterite of ***ir*** • View: GramActiva video • Interactive Whiteboard Grammar Activities • Actividades 16, 17, 18 • Communicative Pair Activity	**Wrap-up and Homework Options** (5 min.) • Core Practice 8A-6 • Writing Activity 12 • Prueba 8A-4 with Study Plan: The preterite of ***ir***
6	**Warm-up** (5 min.) • Audio Activity 8 • Homework check ✔**Formative Assessment** (10 min.) • Prueba 8A-4 with Study Plan: The preterite of ***ir***	**Gramática y vocabulario en uso** (25 min.) • Presentation: The personal ***a*** • View: GramActiva video • Interactive Whiteboard Grammar Activities • Actividades 19, 20, 21 • Audio Activities 9	**Wrap-up and Homework Options** (5 min.) • Core Practice 8A-7 • Writing Activity 13 • Prueba 8A-5 with Study Plan: The personal ***a***
7	**Warm-up** (5 min.) • Actividad 22 • Homework check ✔**Formative Assessment** (10 min.) • Prueba 8A-5 with Study Plan: The personal ***a***	**Gramática y vocabulario en uso** (15 min.) • Exploración del lenguaje • El español en la comunidad • Situation Cards **¡Adelante!** (10 min.) • Presentación oral: Step 1 • La cultura en vivo	**Wrap-up and Homework Options** (5 min.) • Presentación oral: Step 2 • La cultura en vivo
8	**Warm-up** (5 min.) • Homework check	**¡Adelante!** (30 min.) • Presentación oral: Step 3 **Repaso del capítulo** (10 min.) • Vocabulario y gramática • Preparación para el examen 1, 2	**Wrap-up and Homework Options** (5 min.) • Preparación para el examen 3, 4, 5 • Instant Check
9	**Warm-up** (5 min.) • Homework check	**¡Adelante!** (40 min.) • Lectura • ¿Comprendes? • Videomisterio: *¿Eres tú, María?*, Episodio 7	**Wrap-up and Homework Options** (5 min.) • Core Practice 8A-8, 8A-9 • Lectura • Videomisterio • Examen del capítulo 8A
10	**Warm-up** (5 min.) • Homework check • Answer questions ✔**Summative Assessment** (40 min.) • Examen del capítulo 8A		

BLOCK SCHEDULE (90 MINUTES)

DAY	Warm-up / Assess	Preview / Present / Practice / Communicate	Wrap-up / Homework Options
1	**Warm-up** (10 min.) • Return Examen del capítulo 7B	**Chapter Opener** (5 min.) • Objectives • Arte y cultura **Vocabulario en contexto** (55 min.) • Presentation: Vocabulario en contexto • Actividades 1, 2 • Presentation: Videohistoria *¿Qué te pasó?* • View: Videohistoria • Video Activity 1, 2, 3, 4 • Actividad 3 **Vocabulario en uso** (15 min.) • Interactive Whiteboard Vocabulary Activities • Actividades 4, 5	**Wrap-up and Homework Options** (5 min.) • Core Practice 8A-1, 8A-2, 8A-3, 8A-4 • Actividad 7 • Prueba 8A-1: Vocabulary recognition
2	**Warm-up** (10 min.) • Homework check ✓**Formative Assessment** (10 min.) • Prueba 8A-1: Vocabulary recognition	**Gramática y vocabulario en uso** (65 min.) • Actividades 6, 8, 10, 11 • Pronunciación • Audio Activities 5, 6 • Communicative Pair Activity • Presentation: The preterite of ***-er*** and ***-ir*** verbs • View: GramActiva video • Interactive Whiteboard Grammar Activities • Actividades 13, 15 • Fondos culturales • Audio Activity 7 • Communicative Pair Activity	**Wrap-up and Homework Options** (5 min.) • Core Practice 8A-5 • Actividades 9, 12 • Writing Activities 10, 11 • Pruebas 8A-2, 8A-3 with Study Plans: Vocabulary production, The preterite of ***-er*** and ***-ir*** verbs
3	**Warm-up** (10 min.) • Homework check • Actividad 14 ✓**Formative Assessment** (15 min.) • Pruebas 8A-2, 8A-3 with Study Plans: Vocabulary production, The preterite of ***-er*** and ***-ir*** verbs	**Gramática y vocabulario en uso** (60 min.) • Presentation: The preterite of ***ir*** • View: GramActiva video • Interactive Whiteboard Grammar Activities • Actividades 16, 17, 18 • Communicative Pair Activity • Presentation: The personal ***a*** • View: GramActiva video • Interactive Whiteboard Grammar Activities • Actividades 19, 20, 21	**Wrap-up and Homework Options** (5 min.) • Core Practice 8A-6, 8A-7 • Writing Activity 12 • Pruebas 8A-4, 8A-5 with Study Plans: The preterite of ***ir***, The personal ***a***
4	**Warm-up** (15 min.) • Audio Activities 8, 9 • Homework check • Actividad 22 ✓**Formative Assessment** (15 min.) • Pruebas 8A-4, 8A-5 with Study Plans: The preterite of ***ir***, The personal ***a***	**Gramática y vocabulario en uso** (25 min.) • Writing Activity 13 • Exploración del lenguaje • El español en la comunidad **¡Adelante!** (30 min.) • Presentación oral: Step 1 • La cultura en vivo	**Wrap-up and Homework Options** (5 min.) • Presentación oral: Step 2 • La cultura en vivo
5	**Warm-up** (5 min.) • Homework check • Presentación oral: Step 2	**¡Adelante!** (50 min.) • Presentación oral: Step 3 • Lectura • ¿Comprendes? **Repaso del capítulo** (30 min.) • Vocabulario y gramática • Preparación para el examen 1, 2, 3, 4, 5	**Wrap-up and Homework Options** (5 min.) • Core Practice 8A-8, 8A-9 • Examen del capítulo 8A • Instant Check • Lectura
6	**Warm-up** (15 min.) • Homework check • Situation Cards **Repaso del capítulo** (10 min.) • Communicative Pair Activities ✓**Summative Assessment** (40 min.) • Examen del capítulo 8A	**¡Adelante!** (20 min.) • Videomisterio: *¿Eres tú, María?*, Episodio 7	**Wrap-up and Homework Options** (5 min.) • Videomisterio

Standards for *Capítulo* 8A

- To achieve the goals of the Standards, students will:

Communication

1.1 Interpersonal
- Talk about: travel and vacation activities; a scuba diving school; leisure activities, work, and chores; historical events and dates; leisure activities; local attractions of their community

1.2 Interpretive
- Read and listen to information about: travel and vacations; past events; El Yunque, Puerto Rico
- Read a picture-based story
- Listen to and watch a video about Sarapiquí, Costa Rica
- Read: about the río Paraná; an advertisement for a scuba diving school; a version of "Goldilocks and the Three Bears"; a traditional rhyme; journal entries about a trip to Perú
- View a video mystery series

1.3 Presentational
- Present information about: a trip to Sarapiquí; El Yunque, Puerto Rico; local attractions; history and geography of Perú
- Write about a scuba diving school
- Recite a traditional rhyme

Culture

2.1 Practices and Perspectives
- Discuss Perú's Independence Day celebrations
- Explain Spain's method of writing addresses

2.2 Products and Perspectives
- Discuss: Joaquín Sorolla and his painting; Mexico's transportation system; Machu Picchu, Nazca Lines and Titicaca; history and geography of Perú; the ***ojos de Dios*** weaving of Mexico

Connections

3.1 Cross-curricular
- Discuss important artists and their work: Joaquín Sorolla; the history and geography of Perú
- Read about the Patagonia region of Argentina
- Reinforce geography skills

Comparisons

4.1 Language
- Talk about vocabulary through the recognition of cognates; the preterite of ***-er*** and ***-ir*** verbs
- Explain: the irregular preterite form of the verb ***ir***, ***-ar*** verbs
- Talk about: the personal ***a***; nouns that end in ***-io*** and ***-eo***; diphthongs

4.2 Culture
- Compare ***ojos de Dios*** to traditional handicrafts of the United States

Communities

5.1 Beyond the School
- Talk about services available to Spanish-speakers at local tourist attractions

5.2 Lifelong Learner
- View a video mystery series

Capítulo

8A De vacaciones

▾ Chapter Objectives

Communication
By the end of this chapter you will be able to:
- Listen to and read descriptions of trips and vacations
- Talk and write about favorite and imaginary trips
- Exchange information while describing your best vacation

Culture
You will also be able to:
- Explain the tradition of the *ojo de Dios* and compare it to crafts in the United States
- Identify places of geographical and historical importance in Spanish-speaking countries and compare them to places in the United States

You will demonstrate what you know and can do:
- Presentación oral, p. 393
- Preparación para el examen, p. 397

You will use:

Vocabulary
- Vacation destinations and activities
- Modes of transportation
- Attractions, parks, and animals
- Expressions to talk about a trip or vacation

Grammar
- The preterite of *-er* and *-ir* verbs
- The preterite of *ir*
- The personal *a*

Exploración del mundo hispano

Country Connection
Travel and Vacations

realidades.com GO

Reference Atlas
Videocultura y actividad
Mapa global interactivo

ENRICH YOUR TEACHING

Using Backward Design
Have students preview the sample performance tasks on *Preparación para el examen,* p. 397, and connect them to the Chapter Objectives. Explain to students that by completing the sample tasks they can self-assess their learning progress.

Mapa global interactivo
Download the *Mapa global interactivo* files for Chapter 8A and preview the activities. In Activity 1, visit Valencia, Spain. In Activity 2, you travel to Argentina and in Activity 3, to the Dominican Republic. Activity 4 takes you to Mexico City. In Activity 5, you explore Peru.

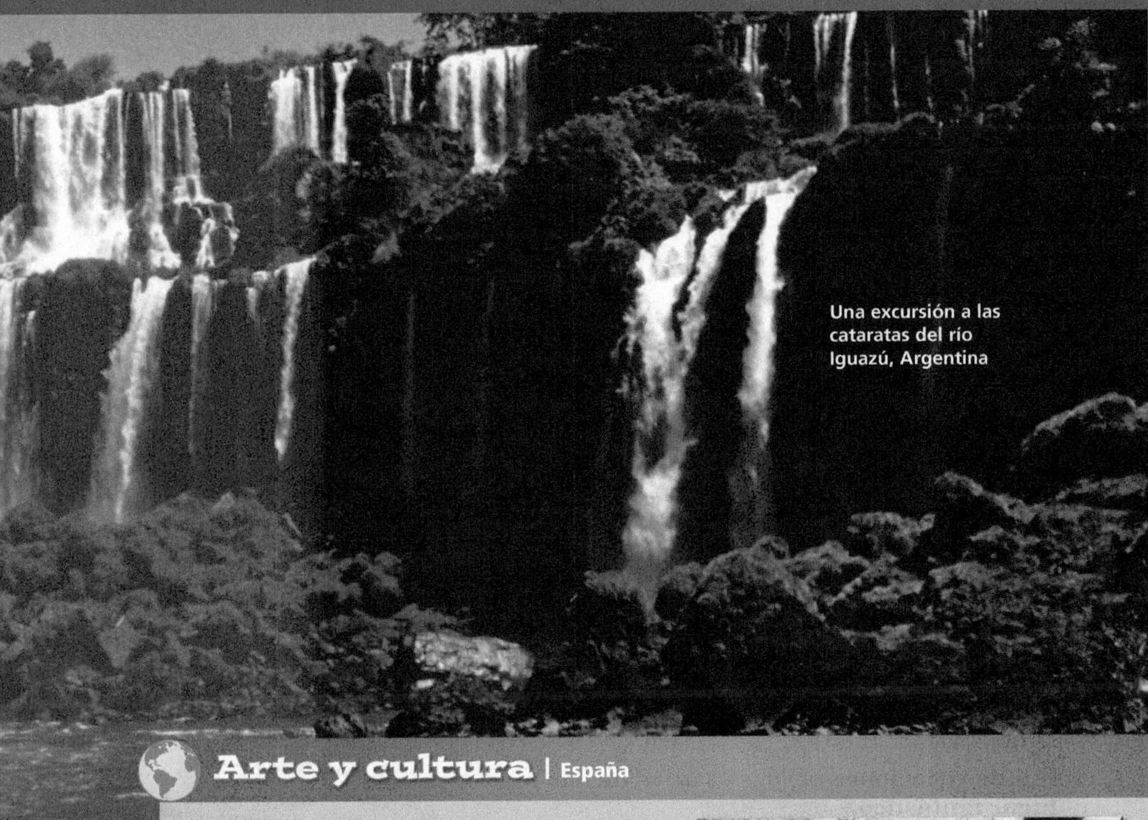

Una excursión a las cataratas del río Iguazú, Argentina

Arte y cultura | España

Spanish artist **Joaquín Sorolla y Bastida** (1863–1923) was famous for his paintings of the sea and coastline. Known as *el pintor de la luz* (the painter of light), Sorolla was a master at capturing the movement and reflection of light and water in sea and sky. He did many portraits of beachgoers along the coast of his native Valencia. The city of Valencia continues to be a destination for Spaniards and international tourists, who visit the beautiful towns and beaches of the Costa Blanca.

- What would you highlight if you were painting your town or city?

"La hora del baño, Valencia" (1909), Joaquín de Sorolla y Bastida ▶

La hora del baño, Valencia (1909). O/L-1,50x1,505. Sorolla, Joaquín.

DIFFERENTIATED INSTRUCTION

Digital resources such as the ***Interactive Whiteboard*** activity banks, ***Videomodelos***, additional ***Online Activities***, ***Study Plans***, automatically graded ***Leveled Workbook***, animated ***Grammar Tutorials***, ***Flashcards***, and ***Vocabulary and Grammar Videos*** will help you reach students of different ability levels and learning styles.

STUDENTS NEEDING EXTRA HELP

Guided Practice Activities
- Flashcards, pp. 243–248
- Vocabulary Check, pp. 249–252
- Grammar Support, pp. 253–256

HERITAGE LEARNERS

Realidades para hispanohablantes
- Chapter Opener, pp. 290–291
- A primera vista, p. 292
- Videohistoria, p. 293
- Manos a la obra, pp. 294–301
- ¡Adelante!, pp. 302–307
- Repaso del capítulo, pp. 308–309

ADVANCED/PRE-AP*

Pre-AP* Resource Book,
- pp. 90–93

Communications Workbook
- Integrated Performance Assessment, p. 314

Preview 8A

PresentationExpress™
See pp. 372c–372d

Chapter Opener

Core Instruction

Resources: Map Transparencies 12–16, 18

Suggestions: Have students predict the type of vocabulary words that might be introduced for talking about vacations. Discuss the kinds of activities they do while on vacation. Inform them that this chapter's *Videohistoria* presents a journey to Sarapiquí, a national park in Costa Rica.

Tell students that upon completion of the chapter, they will be able to talk about events that happened in the past, using the preterite tense of ***-er*** and ***-ir*** verbs.

Videocultura View *Las vacaciones* with the class to learn about places to visit in Spanish-speaking countries.

Arte y cultura

Standards: 2.2, 3.1

Resources: Fine Art Transparencies p. 18

Mapa global interactivo, Actividad 1 Visit Valencia, Spain, home of the artist Joaquín Sorolla.

Suggestions: Joaquín Sorolla is best known for his landscapes and portraits, and for beach scenes of his native Valencia. Have students notice the relationship between light and shadow in the painting *La hora del baño* (1909)—the light on the water, and the shadows at the women's feet. Mention that Sorolla was an Impressionist painter, and that this movement is characterized partly by such attention to light effects.

Answers will vary.

TEACHING WITH ART

Have students look at the painting by Sorolla and make a list of 10 words, expressions, or descriptions that come to mind. Have students share their lists.

Vocabulario en contexto

Core Instruction

Standards: 1.2, 4.1

Resources: Teacher's Resource Book: Input Script, p. 222, Clip Art, pp. 236–237, Audio Script, p. 223; Voc. and Gram. Transparencies 143–144; TPR Stories Book, pp. 107–121; Audio Program DVD: Cap. 8A, Tracks 1–2

Focus: Presenting vocabulary for places to visit and things to see and do on vacation; vocabulary to talk about travel; preterite of ***-er*** and ***-ir*** verbs and of the verb ***ir***

Suggestions: Use the Input Script from the *Teacher's Resource Book* or the story in the *TPR Stories Book* to present this new vocabulary and grammar. You may wish to present the vocabulary in three groups: places to visit, things to do, and ways to travel. Use the audio to introduce the dialogues. Guide the presentation using the transparencies. Cue the idea of "past" by gesturing back over your shoulder. Ask short-answer questions to check comprehension: *¿Vas de vacaciones con tu familia? ¿Adónde vas? ¿Qué te gusta hacer cuando estás de vacaciones? ¿Te gusta más ir al parque de diversiones o al museo?*

BELLRINGER REVIEW

Show Voc. and Grammar Transparency 81. Name an activity and ask volunteers to tell you the place where they would do each activity.

Block Schedule

Have students choose one of the places shown and create an advertisement for it. It should include a proper name for the place (for example, *El Museo Principal*), the address and phone number, and a list of three things for tourists to see and do there. Some choices may require that you provide students with additional vocabulary. Distribute poster board or construction paper for students to do a final copy. Display the ads in the room.

A primera vista

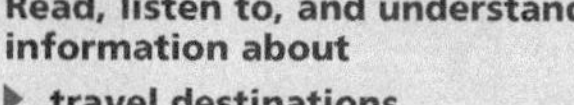

▼ Objectives

Read, listen to, and understand information about
- travel destinations
- vacation activities
- past events

Vocabulario en contexto

—**Dime,** ¿adónde **fuiste** el mes pasado?

—**Fui de vacaciones** con mis padres a **un lugar fantástico.**

—¿Qué lugar **visitaste?**

—Fui a Barcelona. Me gusta mucho **viajar** a otros **países como** México, España, Guatemala . . .

—¿Qué **hiciste?**

—Pues, fui al zoológico con mi familia.

—¿**Te gustó?** ¿Qué **viste?**

—**Fue** fantástico. **Vi** muchos **animales** como os y monos y también muchas otras **atraccione** También compré **unos recuerdos:** una camiseta, unos aretes y un llavero.

DIFFERENTIATED INSTRUCTION

Students with Learning Difficulties

Remind students that using what they already know is very important when beginning a new lesson. If they think of all the activities that can be done at each of the places shown, it will be easier for them to understand the vocabulary. Reinforce this by asking general questions about vacation spots and activities as you proceed.

—Y **¿saliste de la ciudad?**

—¡Por supuesto! **Salí*** muy **temprano** para ir al mar. **Durante** el día **aprendí a** bucear. Fue muy divertido. **Regresamos** al **hotel** muy **tarde,** como a las diez de la noche.

*The verb *salir* has an irregular *yo* form in the present tense: *salgo.*

el avión

el barco

el tren

el autobús

—¿Cómo prefieres viajar?

—**En avión.**

1 El viaje de María Luisa

Escuchar

Vas a escuchar a María Luisa describir su viaje. Señala en tu libro cada lugar que ella menciona.

Más práctica GO

realidades.com | print

Instant Check	✔	
Guided WB pp. 243–248	✔	✔
Core WB pp. 139–140	✔	✔
Comm. WB p. 156	✔	✔
***Hispanohablantes* WB** p. 292		✔

2 ¿Qué piensas? ¿Sí o no?

Escuchar

Vas a escuchar diez frases. Si la frase es lógica, haz el gesto del pulgar hacia arriba *("thumbs-up" sign)*. Si es ilógica, haz el gesto del pulgar hacia abajo *("thumbs-down" sign)*.

ENRICH YOUR TEACHING

Teacher-to-Teacher

If you have traveled in Spanish-speaking countries, reinforce the new vocabulary by sharing photos, printed materials, or souvenirs from places you have visited. If you have not, request brochures with photos from a travel agent or download pictures from the Internet to print or project for the class.

21st Century Skills

Communication After students have practiced the vocabulary with the eText embedded audio files and have done the auto scored online practice, have them interview each other about things they do when they go on vacation.

1 Standards: 1.2

Resources: Teacher's Resource Book: Audio Script, p. 223; Audio Program DVD: Cap. 8A, Track 3; Answer Keys: Student Edition, p. 109

Focus: Listening comprehension

Suggestions: Be sure students see that the answers may be on either page.

Script and Answers:

1. **Fui al mar a nadar y tomar el sol. *(ocean)***
2. **Visité el zoológico y vi muchos animales. *(zoo)***
3. **Fui al lago a pasear en bote. *(lake)***
4. **Vi una obra de teatro en el Teatro Nacional. *(theater)***
5. **El parque de diversiones fue muy divertido. *(amusement park)***
6. **Vi un monumento grande en el parque. *(park)***
7. **Me gustó mucho ver el partido de fútbol en el estadio. *(stadium)***

2 Standards: 1.2

Resources: Teacher's Resource Book: Audio Script, p. 223; Audio Program DVD: Cap. 8A, Track 4; Answer Keys: Student Edition, p. 110

Focus: Listening comprehension

Suggestions: Make a "thumbs-up" or "thumbs-down" sign, without always being correct, and have students agree or disagree.

Script and Answers:

1. **Nado en el mar. *(up)***
2. **Hay un parque de diversiones en la cafetería. *(down)***
3. **Paseamos en bote en el hotel. *(down)***
4. **Voy a un concierto con los monos del zoológico. *(down)***
5. **Me gusta tomar el sol cuando voy al lago. *(up)***
6. **Hago mi tarea en el parque de diversiones. *(down)***
7. **Aprendo a bucear en el museo. *(down)***
8. **Saco fotos del monumento. *(up)***
9. **Voy a la escuela en avión. *(down)***
10. **En el mar viajo en barco. *(up)***

Teacher-to-Teacher

Throughout the activities in this chapter, be sensitive to the fact that some students' families do not have the luxury of travel and vacation. Tell all students that they may talk about ideal trips in any activity that calls for personal experiences.

8A Language Input

Videohistoria

Core Instruction

Standards: 1.2

Resources: Voc. and Gram. Transparencies 145–146; Audio Program DVD: Cap. 8A, Track 5

Focus: Presenting additional contextualized vocabulary

Suggestions:

Pre-reading: Direct attention to the *Strategy.* Using the transparencies, ask students to guess who is having problems.

Reading: While volunteers read the roles, have the others make a list of unfamiliar words. Help students determine the meaning of new words by using visual cues and context. Have a new group reread the text or play the audio.

Post-reading: Have students compare their predictions with what actually happened. Complete *Actividad* 3 to check comprehension.

Video

Core Instruction

Standards: 1.2

Resources: Teacher's Resource Book: Video Script, p. 227; Video Program: Cap. 8A; Video Program Teacher's Guide: Cap. 8A

Focus: Listening comprehension of contextualized vocabulary

Suggestions:

Pre-viewing: Have students recall main ideas of the *Videohistoria*.

Viewing: Show the video once without pausing; then show it again, stopping periodically to check comprehension. Point out that Gloria uses the word ***aves*** to refer to birds. Do students see the connection to the English word "aviation"?

Post-viewing: Have students complete Video Activity 1 in the *Communication Workbook.*

¿Qué te pasó?

¿Qué le pasó a Tomás durante su visita al parque nacional Sarapiquí en Costa Rica?

Strategy

Using visuals to make predictions
Before you read the story, look at the pictures to try to predict what will happen. After you finish reading, see how your predictions compared with what you read.

Raúl: Aquí están **los boletos** para el autobús.
Tomás: ¿Cuánto dura **el viaje**
Gloria: El parque está a 82 kilómetros de San José. Es un viaje de hora y media.

Gloria: Va a ser una foto fantástica, Tomás. Un momento . . . un poco más a la izquierda.
Tomás: ¿Aquí?
Gloria: No, un poco más. Uno, dos . . .
Tomás: ¡Ay!
Raúl: Tomás, ¿dónde estás? ¿Estás bien?

Gloria: Lo siento, Tomás. ¿Quieres regresar a casa?
Raúl: ¿Quieres **descansar** un poco?
Tomás: No. Estoy bien. ¡Vamos a la catarata* La Paz!

*waterfall

Tomás: Quiero una foto de la catarata. ¡Es **tremenda, impresionante!** Uno puede estar muy cerca de ella.
Raúl: No, creo que estar un poco lejos de ella es mejor. Voy a ayudarte, Tomás.
Gloria: Un poco más hacia atrás* y a la derecha . . .

*towards the back

DIFFERENTIATED INSTRUCTION

Advanced Learners

Have students research and prepare a report about Sarapiquí National Park in Costa Rica. Students may use drawings or pictures from the Internet for their presentations.

Students with Special Needs

You may wish to provide hearing-impaired students with a copy of the script so that they may follow along and engage in post-viewing activities.

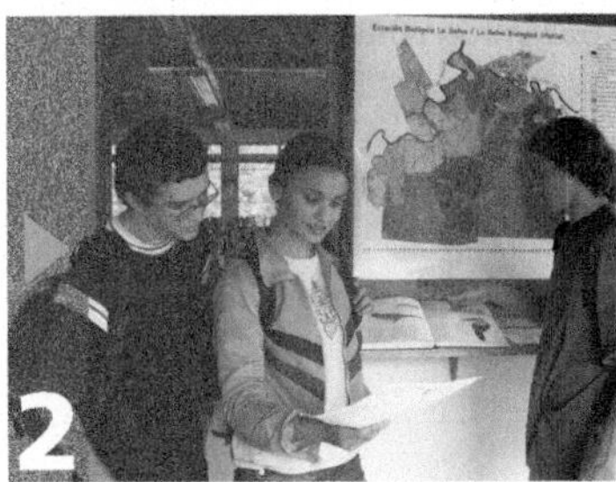

Gloria: Mira este mapa del **parque nacional.** Es mi parque favorito y lo llamamos "bosque lluvioso".* No hace ni frío ni calor, pero llueve mucho.

Tomás: Aquí hay un libro sobre los animales del parque.

*rain forest

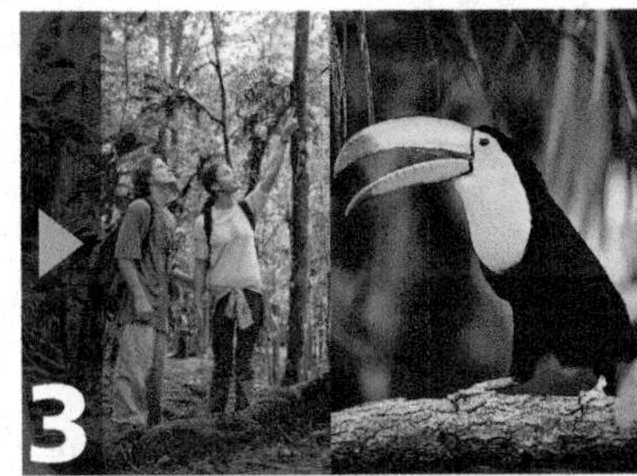

Gloria: ¿Lo viste? Allí en **el árbol.**

Tomás: No, no lo vi. ¿Qué es?

Gloria: Es **un pájaro.** Es un tucán. Hay más de cuatrocientas especies de pájaros en el parque.

Raúl: Tomás, **¿qué te pasó?**

Tomás: ¡Hay agua en las palmas! Eh . . . ¡no es nada divertido!

Raúl: Pero, Tomás, es un bosque lluvioso y llueve todo el tiempo. Siempre hay agua en las palmas. Pero sólo es un poco de agua.

Gloria: Estás aprendiendo muchas cosas, ¿verdad?

Mamá: ¡Tomás! **¿Cómo lo pasaste?** ¿Qué te pasó?

Gloria: Pobre* Tomás . . . **fue un desastre.**

Tomás: No fue tan malo. **Me gustó.** Aprendí mucho y vi muchas cosas nuevas. ¡Pero hay mucha agua en el bosque lluvioso y en la catarata!

*Poor

3 ¿Comprendes?

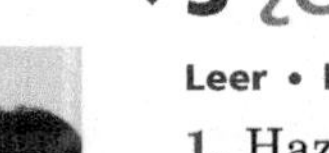

Leer • Escribir

1. Haz una lista de cinco cosas que aprendiste sobre el bosque lluvioso Sarapiquí.
2. ¿A quién se refiere cada frase: a Tomás, a Gloria o a Raúl?
   - a. Compró los boletos para el autobús.
   - b. Sacó fotos de los otros.
   - c. No vio el pájaro.
   - d. Sarapiquí es su parque favorito.
   - e. Ayudó a Tomás delante de la catarata La Paz.
   - f. Vio un libro sobre los animales del parque.
   - g. Decidió no descansar.
   - h. Cree que el viaje a Sarapiquí fue un desastre.

Más práctica GO

realidades.com | print

	realidades.com	print
Instant Check	✔	
Guided WB pp. 249–252	✔	✔
Core WB pp. 141–142	✔	✔
Comm. WB pp. 150–152, 153	✔	✔
***Hispanohablantes* WB** p. 293		✔

3 Standards: 1.2, 1.3

Resources: Answer Keys: Student Edition, p. 111

Focus: Checking comprehension of the *Videohistoria*

Suggestions: As you review students' answers for item 1, have them reread the correct excerpt from the story. For item 2, suggest they make a chart with each person's name and write the letter of each sentence in the appropriate space.

Answers:

1. **Answers will vary but may include: Está a 82 kilómetros de San José. No hace ni frío ni calor. Llueve mucho. Hay más de cuatrocientas especies de pájaros. Hay una catarata.**
2. **a. Raúl** **e. Raúl**
   b. Gloria **f. Tomás**
   c. Tomás **g. Tomás**
   d. Gloria **h. Gloria**

Pre-AP* Support

- **Learning Objective:** Presentational Speaking
- **Activity:** Prepare large clip art flashcards of the places presented in this chapter. Have pairs of students come to the front of the class and randomly select one of the flashcards from the stack. Then have the pair re-read to the class one of the dialogs presented on pp. 374–375, making the appropriate substitutions to go along with the flashcard they have drawn.
- ***Pre-AP* Resource Book:*** Comprehensive guide to Pre-AP* vocabulary skill development, pp. 51–57

Teacher-to-Teacher

Restatement is a good means of assessing comprehension. Display the transparencies for the *Videohistoria* and have students give summaries in their own words.

Additional Resources

- Communication Wbk.: Audio Act. 5, p. 153
- Teacher's Resource Book: Audio Script, p. 223
- Audio Program DVD: Cap. 8A, Track 9

ASSESSMENT

Quiz: Vocabulary Recognition

- Prueba 8A-1: pp. 201–202

ENRICH YOUR TEACHING

Culture Note

Central and South America are destinations for ecotourism vacations. Ecotourism involves travel to natural areas to study and enjoy the wild plants and animals, as well as the cultural aspects of the areas. Costa Rica has thousands of visitors every year who explore the rich biodiversity of its rain forests, cloud forests, and wetlands.

21st Century Skills

Leadership and Responsibility Have groups of students research on the Internet the current status of one of the rain forests in Central America or South America and propose a possible long term solution for protecting it. Have each group present its solutions to the class, so that they can select the best plan and post it on the class Web site.

INTERACTIVE WHITEBOARD
Vocabulary Activities 8A

BELLRINGER REVIEW

Have students identify the activities pictured in the art for *Actividad* 4. Ask: *¿Qué hace(n)?*

4 Standards: 1.3

Focus: Rating and talking about vacation activities

Suggestions: For part 1, tell students that if they have not done the activity they may simply say ***no me gustaría.*** For part 2, remind Student A to choose from all ten possible choices, not only from the items that he or she liked.

Answers will vary.

5 Standards: 1.2, 1.3

Resources: Teacher's Resource Book: Audio Script, p. 223; Audio Program DVD: Cap. 8A, Track 6; Answer Keys: Student Edition, p. 111

Focus: Listening and writing about a vacation in Puerto Rico

Suggestions: Play the audio or read the script once without stopping. Then play or read the script a second time, pausing to allow students to write the sentences. Finally, allow students to hear it a third time to check their answers.

Script and Answers:

1. **El verano pasado fui a Puerto Rico con mi familia.**
2. **Fue mi primer viaje en avión y me gustó mucho.**
3. **Puerto Rico es un país impresionante y fantástico.**
4. **Puedes bucear, descansar y tomar el sol en la playa.**
5. **También puedes visitar El Yunque para ver pájaros, árboles y flores.**
6. **Quiero regresar a Puerto Rico. Compro mi boleto hoy.**

Common Errors: Students may forget to write accent marks. Write words with accents on the board, using colored chalk to mark the accents.

Block Schedule

Have each student think of a vacation spot that others will know and make a list of five related words. In groups of three or four, have students read their clues while others guess what their vacation spot is.

Objectives

- Write and talk about trips and vacation activities
- Listen to a description of a trip
- Read and write about boating and scuba-diving vacations
- Exchange information while comparing favorite trips

Vocabulario en uso

4 Una lista de actividades

Escribir • Hablar

1. ¿Qué actividades te gusta hacer cuando vas de vacaciones? ¿Qué actividades no te gusta hacer? En una hoja de papel, haz tres columnas y escribe *me gusta mucho, me gusta* y *no me gusta nada*. Debajo de cada expresión, escribe estas actividades en la columna apropiada.

ver . . .

visitar . . .

sacar fotos de . . .

ir a . . .

ir a . . .

comprar . . .

2. Usa tu lista de actividades y habla con otro(a) estudiante. Pregunta y contesta según el modelo. Haz por lo menos *(at least)* cuatro preguntas.

Modelo

A —*Cuando vas de vacaciones, ¿qué te gusta más: ver una obra de teatro o ir al zoológico?*
B —*Me gusta más ir al zoológico.*

5 Escucha y escribe

Escuchar • Escribir

Vas a escuchar a una persona describir su viaje a Puerto Rico. Uno de los lugares que visitó es El Yunque. En una hoja de papel escribe los números del 1 al 6 y escribe las frases que escuchas.

El Yunque, un parque nacional de Puerto R

DIFFERENTIATED INSTRUCTION

Advanced Learners

Have students research the region of the Paraná River delta using the Internet or other available resources. Suggest they find geographical information about the region, as well as its impact on the local tourism and other economies. Have them present their findings upon completion of *Actividad* 7.

Heritage Language Learners

Have students research an interesting or important natural area or national park in their heritage country and report on it. Have them write its name, show its location on a map, and tell about distinctive features such as unusual animals, plant life, and scenery.

6 ¿Qué te gustaría hacer? 

Hablar

Habla con otro(a) estudiante sobre adónde les gustaría ir de vacaciones.

Modelo

A —*Dime, ¿te gustaría ir de vacaciones a una ciudad?*
B —*Sí, porque en una ciudad puedes ir de compras y comer en restaurantes fantásticos.*
o:—*No. Me gustaría más ir a un parque nacional porque puedes ir de cámping.*

Estudiante A

1. una ciudad
2. un parque nacional
3. un lago
4. el mar

Estudiante B

¡Respuesta personal!

7 El delta del río[1] Paraná 

Leer • Escribir

Lee la descripción del delta del río Paraná, a 30 kilómetros de Buenos Aires, y completa las frases con las palabras correctas de los recuadros. Después contesta las preguntas.

tren	ciudad	país	lugar

Al norte de la __1.__ de Buenos Aires, Argentina, está el delta del río Paraná, un laberinto de islas y canales con más de 2.500 kilómetros navegables. Es un __2.__ favorito de los habitantes de Buenos Aires para ir de excursión. Para ir de Buenos Aires al delta, muchas personas viajan en __3.__ hasta[2] el Tigre, un pueblo[3] pequeño.

descansar	regresar	pasear	montar

Aquí las personas pueden __4.__ en bote por los canales, __5.__ y tomar el sol en la orilla[4], __6.__ a caballo o practicar el esquí acuático.

recuerdos	lagos	pájaros	árboles

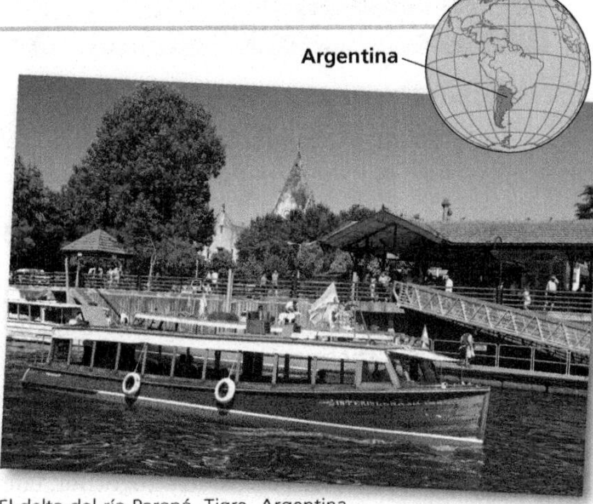

El delta del río Paraná, Tigre, Argentina

También pueden comprar comida y __7.__ turísticos en los mercados[5]. Las personas siempre tienen sus cámaras en las excursiones al delta porque hay muchos tipos de animales y __8.__ que viven en los __9.__ muy altos.

- Para ti, ¿es el delta del río Paraná un buen lugar para ir de vacaciones? ¿Por qué?
- ¿Qué actividades te gustaría hacer en este lugar?

[1]river [2]as far as [3]town [4]riverbank [5]markets

Practice and Communicate 8A

6 Standards: 1.1

Focus: Talking about vacation preferences

Suggestions: Have students make a four-column chart using the locations in the Estudiante A box as the headings. Tell students to brainstorm activities they associate with each location and to write them in the appropriate columns. Practice the Modelo with a student volunteer and explain how students can use their notes to communicate with their partners.

Answer will vary.

7 Standards: 1.2, 1.3

Resources: Answer Keys: Student Edition, p. 112

Mapa global interactivo, Actividad 2 Follow the Paraná River on its course through Argentina.

Focus: Reading for comprehension

Suggestions: Have students begin by reading the article silently, without filling in the blanks. Encourage them to read for meaning, rather than stopping whenever they encounter an unfamiliar word. Have them read again, one paragraph at a time. Point out that the questions at the end are asking them to apply the facts they learned to form an opinion about whether they would like to spend time in this area.

Answers:

1. ciudad
2. lugar
3. tren
4. pasear
5. descansar
6. montar
7. recuerdos
8. pájaros
9. árboles

Pre-AP* Support

- **Learning Objective:** Presentational Writing
- **Activity 7:** Have students write a short paragraph to expand on their answer to the first of the two questions after the reading, defending their choice, and suggesting an alternative, if needed.
- ***Pre-AP* Resource Book:*** Comprehensive guide to Pre-AP* writing skill development, pp. 27–38

ENRICH YOUR TEACHING

Culture Note

The Paraná River drains a larger land area than any other river system in South America, except the Amazon. It flows southwest from Brazil and travels along part of the border between Argentina and Paraguay. Large ships are able to travel up the Paraná into Argentina.

21st Century Skills

Social and Cross-Cultural Skills If there are exchange students in your school from Central America or South America, have students interview them about how people in their country feel about the rain forests. Have them compare their findings to attitudes toward such natural resources in the United States.

8 Standards: 1.1

Focus: Using vocabulary to talk about different places and modes of transportation

Recycle: ***me gustaría; poder***

Suggestions: Refer students to the maps on pp. xviii–xxxi. Have them choose two destinations. If students choose a country whose vocabulary is listed in the *También se dice...*, they may wish to use the culturally appropriate word.

Answers will vary.

Pronunciación

Core Instruction

Standards: 4.1

Resources: Teacher's Resource Book: Audio Script, pp. 223–224; Audio Program DVD: Cap. 8A, Tracks 7–8

Suggestions: Use the audio or read the *Pronunciación* with students. Remind them that the vowel sounds in diphthongs should blend together. Have students practice with each other, first saying the list of words with diphthongs and then the list of words with the vowels pronounced as separate sounds.

Play the recording of *"Cielito lindo"* from the audio. Have students with musical ability record their own version of the song.

Block Schedule

Have students prepare itineraries for travel to or within Spanish-speaking countries. They can use the Internet or a local travel agent for information. Have them include the mode of transportation, the date and time of travel (using the 24-hour clock), and departure and arrival locations. Create a bulletin board with illustrations of the destinations students chose and post their itineraries.

8 Cómo puedes viajar |  | 

Hablar

Mira los mapas al principio del libro. Dile a tu compañero(a) que te gustaría viajar de un lugar o país a otro. Tu compañero(a) debe decir cómo puedes viajar entre los dos lugares.

Modelo

A —*Me gustaría viajar de la República Dominicana a Puerto Rico.*

B —*Pues, entonces, puedes viajar en barco o en avión.*

También se dice . . .

el autobús =
el camión *(México);*
el colectivo, el ómnibus *(Argentina, Bolivia);* la guagua *(Puerto Rico, Cuba);* el micro *(Perú, Chile)*

Estudiante A

¡Respuesta personal!

Estudiante B

Pronunciación

Diphthongs

In Spanish, there are two groups of vowels: "strong" *(a, e* and *o)* and "weak" *(i* and *u)*.

When a weak vowel is combined with any other vowel, the individual vowel sounds become blended to form a single sound called a diphthong *(un diptongo)*. Listen to and say these words:

limpiar	*baile*	*siete*	*seis*	*estadio*	*ciudad*
fuimos	*cuarto*	*juego*	*aire*	*piensas*	*autobús*

When two strong vowels are together, each vowel is pronounced as a separate sound. Listen to and say these words:

teatro	*museo*	*pasear*	*bucear*
cereal	*video*	*leer*	*zoológico*
traer	*idea*	*tarea*	*cumpleaños*

If there is an accent mark over a weak vowel, it causes that letter to be pronounced as though it were a strong vowel. Listen to and say these words:

día	*frío*	*tíos*	*zapatería*
joyería	*país*	*esquío*	*gustaría*

Try it out! Listen to some of the lines of *"Cielito lindo,"* a song from Mexico that is very popular with mariachi bands. Can you identify the diphthongs in the lyrics? Try saying the words and then singing the song.

De la sierra morena,
cielito lindo, vienen bajando
un par de ojitos negros,
cielito lindo, de contrabando.
¡Ay, ay, ay, ay!
Canta y no llores,
porque cantando se alegran,
cielito lindo, los corazones.

DIFFERENTIATED INSTRUCTION

Heritage Language Learners

Have students bring in lyrics to a song traditional to their heritage country. Type the lyrics and distribute them to the rest of the class. Have the entire class look for examples of diphthongs as they read the lyrics to the song.

Students with Special Needs

If students with fine motor skill difficulties cannot make the appropriate gestures for part 2 of *Actividad* 9, have them point to the correct illustration as they tell its meaning.

9 ¿Quieres aprender a bucear? 

Leer • Escribir • Hablar

Lee el anuncio y contesta las preguntas.

Escuela de buceo "Flor del mar"

Puerto Plata, República Dominicana

Cursos de buceo "Flor del mar"

¡Aprende a bucear en sólo tres cursos!
Ve peces impresionantes y otros animales del mar.
Practica un deporte interesante y divertido.
Pasa tiempo con amigos en un lugar fantástico.

Señales de buceo

Hay un lenguaje especial que permite a los buzos comunicarse en el agua con señales. En los cursos de buceo, puedes aprender estas señales. Así no vas a tener ningún problema practicando este deporte. Algunas de las señales más importantes son:

Si quieres información sobre un curso de buceo en la República Dominicana, comunícate al 555-19-19 con la Dra. María Elena Santos o al 555-02-28 con Marcos Morelos.

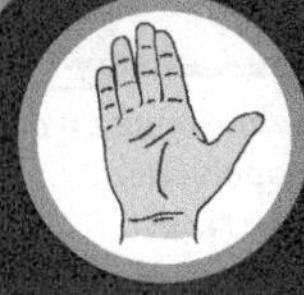
Alto

Ir hacia arriba

Ir hacia abajo

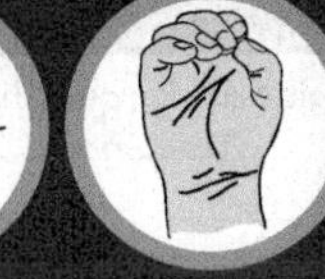
Preguntar si estás bien

Contestar OK o sí

Hay un problema

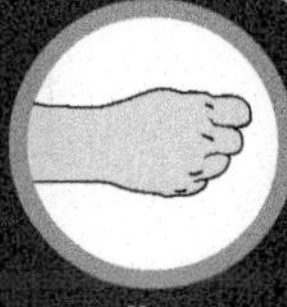
¡Peligro!

1. ¿Por qué debes estudiar cursos de buceo en la escuela "Flor del mar"?
2. Practica las señales con otro(a) estudiante. ¿Qué puedes comunicar?

10 ¿Dónde aprendiste a bucear?   

Hablar

Habla con otro(a) estudiante sobre dónde aprendió a hacer las actividades de la lista.

1. bucear
2. montar a caballo
3. esquiar
4. montar en bicicleta
5. patinar
6. tocar la guitarra

Modelo

nadar

A —*¿Dónde aprendiste a nadar?*
B —*Aprendí a nadar en California.*
o: —*No aprendí a nadar nunca pero me gustaría aprender.*
o: —*No aprendí a nadar nunca y no quiero aprender.*

9 Standards: 1.2

Resources: Voc. and Gram. Transparency 149; Answer Keys: Student Edition, p. 112

Mapa global interactivo, Actividad 3 Locate Puerto Plata in the Dominican Republic.

Focus: Reading, writing, and speaking about scuba diving

Suggestions: Point out the two basic themes of the advertisement—reasons why one should take the *Flor del mar* course and important safety signals. Before students do item 2, practice the signals as a class. Have volunteers communicate messages to share with the class and have other students interpret them.

Answers will vary but may include:

1. **Porque puedo aprender a bucear con sólo tres cursos, puedo ver peces impresionantes y otros animales del mar, o puedo practicar un deporte interesante y divertido.**
2. **Answers will vary.**

Extension: Have students create an ad for another activity taught in this chapter, such as ***montar a caballo, pasear en bote, tomar el sol,*** or ***ver una obra de teatro.***

10 Standards: 1.1

Focus: Communicating about different activities

Recycle: Leisure activities

Suggestions: Have student volunteers read the model various times, so as to include all possible options. Point out the preterite forms ***aprendiste*** and ***aprendí.*** Remind students to switch roles.

Answers will vary.

Additional Resources

- Communication Wbk.: Audio Act. 6, p. 153
- Teacher's Resource Book: Audio Script, p. 224 Communicative Pair Activity BLM, pp. 230–231
- Audio Program DVD: Cap. 8A, Track 10

ENRICH YOUR TEACHING

Culture Note

Two excellent locations for scuba diving are Belize and Monterey, California. Belize, located south of Mexico and north of Guatemala, is tiny in size but has over 200 islands off its mainland and is encircled by Belize reef, which is nearly 200 miles long. The bright blue waters provide excellent visibility for viewing colorful coral, parrot fish, angel fish, barracuda, eels, spider crabs, lobsters, nurse sharks, and other marine life. Although Monterey Bay is colder than Belize, it is recognized as one of the best diving locations in America. Rare kelp forests are found in the Monterey Bay and Aquatic Reserve.

8A Practice and Communicate

11 Standards: 4.1

Resources: Answer Keys: Student Edition, p. 113

Focus: Communicating about a vacation in Mexico City

Recycle: Question words

Suggestions: Point out that ***fui, fuiste,*** and ***fue*** are the first-, second-, and third-person preterite forms of ***ir;*** and that ***vi*** and ***viste*** are the first- and second-person preterite forms of ***ver.*** Also point out that ***a + el*** becomes ***al.*** Before students begin, have them study the pictures and the captions they will use.

Answers:

Student A
—¿Adónde fuiste?
—¿Qué viste?
—¿Cómo lo pasaste allí? ¿Te gustó?

Student B

1. **—Fui al Museo de Arte de Frida Kahlo.**
   —Vi muchos cuadros interesantes.
   —¡Fue fantástico!
2. **—Fui al Zoológico del Parque Chapultepec.**
   —Vi animales como osos y monos.
   —¡Fue tremendo!
3. **—Fui al parque de diversiones en el Parque Chapultepec.**
   —Vi muchas atracciones.
   —¡Fue muy divertido!
4. **—Fui al Teatro del Auditorio.**
   —Vi una obra de teatro.
   —¡Fue fenomenal!
5. **—Fui al Estadio.**
   —Vi un partido de fútbol.
   —¡Fue genial!

12 Standards: 1.1, 1.3

Focus: Writing and speaking about vacations

Suggestions: You might assign this activity as homework. Suggest that students read all the questions and think about their answers before they write.

Answers will vary.

ASSESSMENT

Prueba 8A-2 with Study Plan (online only)

Quiz: Vocabulary Production
- Prueba 8A-2: pp. 203–204

11 ¿Adónde fuiste?

Hablar

La primavera pasada fuiste de vacaciones a la Ciudad de México. Ahora tienes tus fotos y hablas con otro(a) estudiante. En la Ciudad de México viste estas cosas:

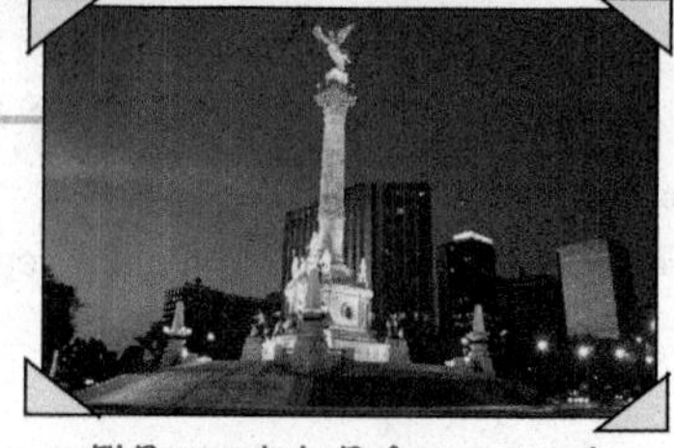

El Paseo de la Reforma con el monumento del Ángel de la Independencia
¡Impresionante!

un partido de fútbol muchas atracciones una obra de teatro el monumento del Ángel de la Independencia animales como osos y monos muchos cuadros interesantes

Modelo

A —*¿Adónde fuiste?*
B —*Fui al Paseo de la Reforma.*
A —*¿Qué viste?*
B —*Vi el monumento del Ángel de la Independencia.*
A —*¿Cómo lo pasaste allí? ¿Te gustó?*
B —*Fue impresionante. Me gustó mucho.*

1.

Museo de arte de Frida Kahlo
¡Fantástico!

2.

El Zoológico del Parque Chapultepec
¡Tremendo!

3.
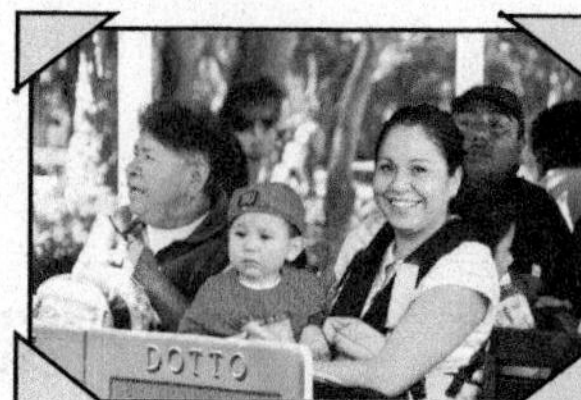
El parque de diversiones en el Parque Chapultepec
¡Muy divertido!

4.

El Teatro del Auditorio
¡Fenomenal!

5.

El Estadio Azteca
¡Genial!

12 Y tú, ¿qué dices?

Escribir • Hablar

1. ¿Adónde te gustaría ir de vacaciones en los Estados Unidos? ¿Cómo quieres viajar? ¿Qué te gustaría hacer?
2. ¿Qué ciudades te gustaría visitar? ¿Qué lugares en esas ciudades quieres ver?
3. Cuando viajas, ¿prefieres salir temprano o tarde?
4. Durante un viaje, ¿descansas mucho o regresas a casa muy cansado(a)?

DIFFERENTIATED INSTRUCTION

Multiple Intelligences

Bodily/Kinesthetic: Encourage small groups of students to act out the events of *Ricitos de Oro y los tres osos* while you or a student volunteer reads the story aloud. You may wish to bring in props for the story, such as a blond wig, bowls, and spoons.

Students with Learning Difficulties

In *Actividad* 11, remind students that only the underlined sections of the model will change.

Manos a la obra

▼ Objectives

- Read and complete a fairy tale
- Write about and discuss what you and others did on vacation

Gramática

The preterite of *-er* and *-ir* verbs

Regular *-er* and *-ir* verbs are similar to one another in the preterite. Here are the preterite forms of *aprender* and *salir.* Notice the accent marks on the endings *-í* and *-ió:*

(yo)	aprend**í**	(nosotros) (nosotras)	aprend**imos**
(tú)	aprend**iste**	(vosotros) (vosotras)	aprend**isteis**
Ud. (él) (ella)	aprend**ió**	Uds. (ellos) (ellas)	aprend**ieron**

(yo)	sal**í**	(nosotros) (nosotras)	sal**imos**
(tú)	sal**iste**	(vosotros) (vosotras)	sal**isteis**
Ud. (él) (ella)	sal**ió**	Uds. (ellos) (ellas)	sal**ieron**

¿Recuerdas?

You have already learned to talk about completed past actions using regular *-ar* verbs.

The verb *ver* is regular in the preterite but does not have accent marks in any of its forms:

vi viste vio vimos visteis vieron

Más ayuda realidades.com

***GramActiva* Video**
Animated Verbs
Tutorials: Preterite, Preterite of regular verbs

***GramActiva* Activity**

13 Ricitos de Oro y los tres osos 

Leer • Escribir

Escribe los verbos apropiados en el pretérito para completar cada frase del cuento *Ricitos de Oro y los tres osos.*

Un día los tres osos 1. *(salir / beber)* temprano de su casa para caminar. Ricitos de Oro, una chica muy bonita, 2. *(comer / ver)* la casa de los tres osos y 3. *(recibir / abrir)* la puerta. Ella no 4. *(ver / comprender)* que era[1] la casa de los tres osos y 5. *(comer / aprender)* toda la comida del oso chiquito. Luego ella 6. *(beber / decidir)* dormir un poco. Poco después, los tres osos regresaron a su casa, 7. *(abrir / salir)* la puerta y 8. *(deber / ver)* a Ricitos de Oro en la cama del osito. Cuando Ricitos de Oro 9. *(viajar / ver)* a los osos, 10. *(abrir / salir)* de la casa rápidamente. 11. *(Comer / Correr)* hasta llegar[2] a su propia casa.

[1]it was [2]until she arrived

Fondo Cultural | México

Mexico City's *Metro* is one of the most advanced subway systems in the world. It is fast, modern, and very inexpensive. In addition, an extensive bus service crosses the whole city. Smaller green and gray minibuses, called *peseros,* also serve passengers along major routes.

- Why do you think Mexico City has such an advanced and varied public transportation system?

ENRICH YOUR TEACHING

Culture Note

The Frida Kahlo Museum was the home of the artist Frida Kahlo. She later lived there with her husband, the muralist Diego Rivera, who donated the house to the people of Mexico upon Kahlo's death in 1954. The museum gives visitors a glimpse into the lives of these two talented, sometimes controversial, artists.

21st Century Skills

Creativity and Innovation Working in small groups, have students create a new version of the *Ricitos de Oro* tale in Activity 13. Have them imagine the host of a news program interviews *Ricitos de Oro* and one of the bears. Have students prepare a script, and teams of volunteers present their versions to the class. Remind students to pay attention to their use of the preterite.

Gramática

Core Instruction

Standards: 4.1

Resources: Voc. and Gram. Transparency 147; Teacher's Resource Book: Video Script, p. 228; Video Program: Cap. 8A

INTERACTIVE WHITEBOARD
Grammar Activities 8A

Suggestions: Ask students to scan the *Gramática,* and recall where they may have seen any of these verb forms. Use the transparencies and the *GramActiva* Video to reinforce your presentation. Point out the accent marks and stress their importance.

13 Standards: 1.3

Resources: Answer Keys: Student Edition, p. 114

Focus: Conjugating ***-er*** and ***-ir*** verbs in the preterite, in a story context

Recycle: Various ***-er*** and ***-ir*** infinitives

Suggestions: Have students identify the story title before beginning. Remind them that their background knowledge of the story can help them determine the meanings of unfamiliar words.

Answers:

1. salieron
2. vio
3. abrió
4. comprendió
5. comió
6. decidió
7. abrieron
8. vieron
9. vio
10. salió
11. Corrió

Fondo cultural

Standards: 2.2

Suggestions: Tell students that Mexico City has the largest population of any city in the Spanish-speaking world. Car owners are limited to specific days they can drive, in an effort to reduce pollution.

Answers will vary but may include the fact that many people in large cities do not own cars, or that people need to commute into and around the central city for work.

Mapa global interactivo, Actividad 4 Visit sites along the Metro in Mexico City.

Theme Project

Give students copies of the Theme Project outline and rubric from the *Teacher's Resource Book.* Explain the task to them, and have them perform Step 1. (For more information, see p. 372-b.)

BELLRINGER REVIEW

Write the preterite forms of *-er* and *-ir* on the board to review.

14 Standards: 1.3

Focus: Writing about activities in the past

Recycle: Leisure activities

Suggestions: Have students choose and conjugate the verbs before completing their sentences. Students will need their answers for *Actividad* 15.

Answers will vary.

15 Standards: 1.1, 1.3

Focus: Writing verbs in the preterite

Recycle: Leisure activities

Suggestions: Remind students that effective comparisons include both similarities and differences.

Answers will vary.

Fondo cultural

Standards: 3.1

Suggestions: Help students locate Patagonia on a map or globe. Explain that Patagonia contains the largest desert in the Americas but also contains areas of mountains, cliffs, and beaches. Winter temperatures range from 16° to –27° F, and summer temperatures often exceed 100° F.

Answers will vary but will probably include references to regions such as Arizona, Nevada, or Alaska, and to animals such as coyotes or reptiles.

Additional Resources

- Communication Wbk.: Audio Act. 7, p. 154
- Teacher's Resource Book: Audio Script, pp. 224–225
- Audio Program DVD: Cap. 8A, Track 11

ASSESSMENT

Prueba 8A-3 with Study Plan (online only)

Quiz: Preterite of *-er* and *-ir* verbs

- Prueba 8A-3: p. 205

14 Durante las vacaciones

Escribir

Escribe seis frases para decir qué hicieron *(did)* estas personas durante sus vacaciones. Usa las palabras de la lista.

comer en . . .
compartir una casa en . . .
escribir . . .
correr en . . .
aprender a . . .
ver . . .
salir de casa temprano para . . .
salir con . . .

Modelo

Durante las vacaciones, mi hermana y yo corrimos en la playa de Santa Mónica.

1. mi familia y yo
2. mis amigos
3. yo
4. mis padres
5. mi hermano(a)
6. mi amigo(a) *(nombre)*

15 Tú y yo

Escribir • Hablar

1. Trabaja con otro(a) estudiante. Lee una frase de la Actividad 14. Tu compañero(a) va a contestar si tiene una idea similar en su hoja de papel.

Modelo

A —*Mi hermana y yo corrimos en la playa de Santa Mónica.*
B —*Mi amigo y yo también corrimos, pero nosotros corrimos en un estadio.*
o: —*Yo no corrí en las vacaciones. Escribí cuentos todos los días.*

2. Escribe seis frases para comparar lo que hicieron tú y tu compañero(a) durante las vacaciones.

Modelo

Adela y yo corrimos durante las vacaciones.
Ella corrió en un estadio con su amigo.
Yo corrí en la playa con mi hermana.

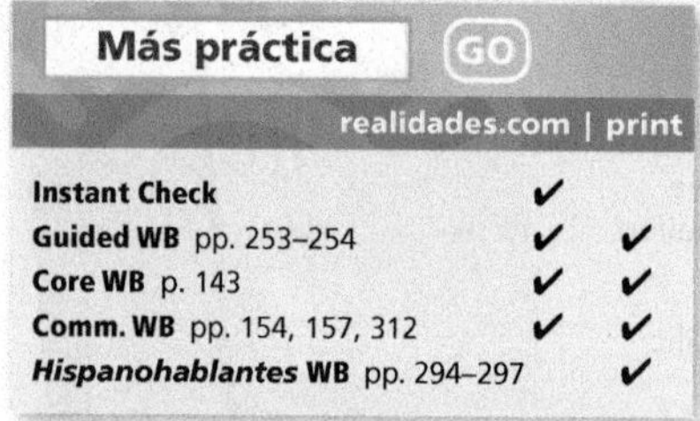

Más práctica GO

realidades.com | print

	realidades.com	print
Instant Check	✔	
Guided WB pp. 253–254	✔	✔
Core WB p. 143	✔	✔
Comm. WB pp. 154, 157, 312	✔	✔
Hispanohablantes WB pp. 294–297		✔

Fondo Cultural | Argentina | Chile

La Patagonia is a vast, windy region of diverse climates and terrains at the southern tip of South America. It lies east of the Andes and spans parts of Chile and nearly a quarter of Argentina. A sparsely populated area, it is home to many species, including a large colony (325,000 breeding pairs) of Magellanic penguins, whose breeding grounds are the eastern and western coasts of Chile and Argentina, as well as offshore islands.

- What regions of the United States can be compared to Patagonia? What types of animals live in those regions?

Pingüinos de la Patagonia

DIFFERENTIATED INSTRUCTION

Advanced Learners/Pre-AP*

Have students use their notes from *Actividades* 14 and 15 to create a short travel journal. They may describe a real trip or an imaginary one. They should tell where they went, with whom they traveled, what they did, and what they saw.

Multiple Intelligences

Visual/Spatial: Students may find that it is easier to organize their information for *Actividades* 14 and 15 if they create a Venn diagram. The first oval should contain information about themselves, and the second should have information about their friend. Have students highlight the sentences that overlap and need to be put in the ***nosotros(as)*** form.

Gramática

▼ Objectives

- Write about and discuss where you and others went on vacation and what you did
- Exchange information about past trips while playing a game

The preterite of *ir*

Ir is irregular in the preterite. Notice that the preterite forms of *ir* do not have accent marks:

(yo) **fui**	(nosotros) (nosotras) **fuimos**
(tú) **fuiste**	(vosotros) (vosotras) **fuisteis**
Ud. (él) (ella) **fue**	Uds. (ellos) (ellas) **fueron**

The preterite of *ir* is the same as the preterite of *ser*. The context makes the meaning clear.

José **fue** a Barcelona. *José went to Barcelona.*
El viaje **fue** un desastre. *The trip was a disaster.*

Strategy

Using memory devices
Here's a memory tip to help you remember the subjects of *fui* and *fue:*

The "I" form ends in *-i (fui).*

The "he" and "she" form ends in *-e (fue).*

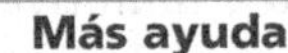

Más ayuda realidades.com

***GramActiva* Video**
Animated Verbs

Canción de hip hop: *¿Adónde fuiste?*

***GramActiva* Activity**

▼16 ¿Adónde fueron? 

Hablar

Con otro(a) estudiante, di adónde y cómo fueron estas personas a estos lugares.

Óscar y Lourdes

Modelo

A —*¿Adónde fueron Óscar y Lourdes?*
B —*Fueron al teatro.*
A —*¿Cómo fueron?*
B —*Fueron en coche.*

1. 
los Sánchez

2. 
tus amigos y tú

3. 
Liliana

4. 

Uds.

5. 
Gregorio

6. **¡Respuesta personal!**
tú

Gramática

Core Instruction

Standards: 4.1

Resources: Voc. and Gram. Transparency 148; Teacher's Resource Book: Video Script, p. 228; Video Program: Cap. 8A

INTERACTIVE WHITEBOARD
Grammar Activities 8A

Suggestions: Have students scan the *Gramática*. Point out that the preterite forms of ***ir*** do not have accent marks. Use the *Strategy* to discuss the use of memory devices. Play the *GramActiva* Video either as an initial introduction or as a follow-up to your grammar explanation.

16 Standards: 1.1

Resources: Answer Keys: Student Edition, p. 115

Focus: Communicating about travel using the preterite of ***ir***

Suggestions: Point out that some of the pictures are of specific places, while others will require that students use general vocabulary words.

Answers:

1. —¿Adónde fueron los Sánchez?
—Fueron al parque de diversiones.
—¿Cómo fueron?
—Fueron en coche.
2. —¿Adónde fueron tus amigos y tú?
—Fuimos a la ciudad.
—¿Cómo fueron?
—Fuimos en tren.
3. —¿Adónde fue Liliana?
—Fue a Puerto Rico.
—¿Cómo fue?
—Fue en barco.
4. —¿Adónde fueron Uds.?
—Fuimos a Chile.
—¿Cómo fueron?
—Fuimos en avión.
5. —¿Adónde fue Gregorio?
—Fue al estadio.
—¿Cómo fue?
—Fue en autobús.
6. —¿Adónde fuiste tú?
—Answers will vary.
—¿Cómo fuiste?
—Answers will vary.

ENRICH YOUR TEACHING

Teacher-to-Teacher

Fill your classroom with travel posters, advertisements, banners, souvenirs, ticket stubs, and anything you can find to correspond with the theme of vacation places and activities. Provide students with a library of Spanish-language travel magazines and books to browse through. This linguistically and culturally rich environment will enhance learning.

17 Standards: 1.1, 1.3

Focus: Playing a game to create and revise illogical sentences

Recycle: Places and modes of transportation

Suggestions: Point out that in part 2, students have to decide which of their sentences is the silliest and then correct it.

Answers will vary.

18 Standards: 1.1, 1.3

Focus: Talking and writing about past vacations

Recycle: Leisure activities

Suggestions: Have students fill out their charts before they begin speaking. Group students in threes and remind them to take turns asking and answering questions. Encourage students to recycle activities and place names from previous chapters, in addition to using the current vocabulary.

Answers will vary.

Common Errors: Students may overgeneralize accent rules for the preterite of ***-ir*** by accenting the ***i*** in ***fui.*** Remind them that ***fui*** and ***fue*** do not need accents.

Pre-AP* Support

- **Learning Objective:** Interpersonal Speaking
- **Activity 18:** Students practice informal speaking as they describe past vacations to one another.

Portfolio

Have students include their description from *Actividad* 18 in their portfolio.

Additional Resources

- Communication Wbk.: Audio Act. 8, p. 154
- Teacher's Resource Book: Audio Script, p. 225
- Audio Program DVD: Cap. 8A, Track 12

ASSESSMENT

Prueba 8A-4 with Study Plan (online only)

Quiz: The preterite of *ir*

- Prueba 8A-4: p. 206

17 Juego

Escribir • Hablar • GramActiva

1. Play in groups of four. Each person cuts a sheet of paper to form a perfect square. Fold that square into four smaller squares. Unfold the paper and label the squares *a, b, c,* and *d.* Follow Step a below for the *a* square. Fold the corner of that little square so it covers what you have written. Pass the paper to the person on your left. Follow Step b for the *b* square on the paper you receive from the person on your right, fold down the corner, and pass it to your left. Continue until all the squares have been filled. Do not look at what is written on the paper you receive. Write all of your answers in Spanish.
   - **a.** Write a subject plus the correct preterite form of *ir.*
   - **b.** Write a destination or place *(a / al / a la . . .).*
   - **c.** Write a mode of transportation.
   - **d.** Write a reason *(para* + infinitive) for going somewhere.

a. Mis amigos fueron	al estadio
c. en barco	para ver una obra de teatro

2. When you get your original paper back, unfold each square and read the complete sentence to your group. Let the group decide, *¿Cuál es la frase más tonta* (silly)? Read your silliest sentence to the class. Then make changes to the sentence so it makes sense.

18 Tus vacaciones pasadas

Escribir • Hablar

1. Piensa en un lugar donde fuiste de vacaciones. Copia la tabla y escribe el lugar, dos o más actividades que hiciste y una descripción del viaje.

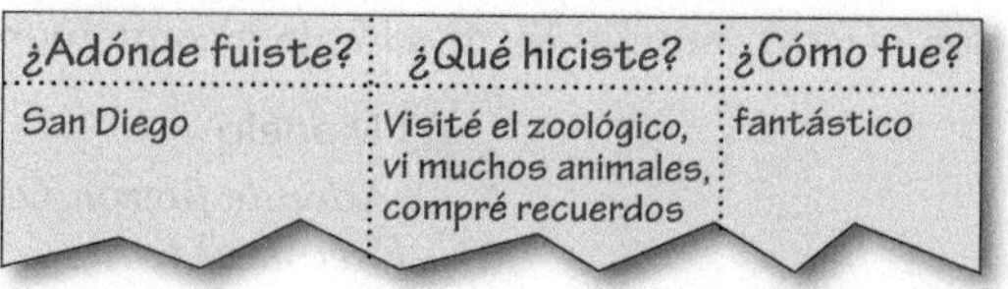

¿Adónde fuiste?	¿Qué hiciste?	¿Cómo fue?
San Diego	Visité el zoológico, vi muchos animales, compré recuerdos	fantástico

2. Habla con dos estudiantes sobre sus vacaciones.

Modelo

A —*¿Adónde fuiste de vacaciones?*
B —*Fui a San Diego.*
A —*¿Qué hiciste allí?*
B —*Visité el zoológico y vi muchos animales. Compré recuerdos también.*
A —*¿Cómo lo pasaste? ¿Te gustó?*
B —*Fue fantástico.*

3. Escribe una descripción de los viajes de los dos estudiantes con quienes hablaste.

Modelo

Pedro fue a San Diego. Visitó el zoológico. Vio muchos animales y compró recuerdos. Su viaje fue fantástico. Miguel fue a . . .

Más práctica GO

realidades.com | print

Instant Check	✔	
Guided WB p. 255	✔	✔
Core WB p. 144	✔	✔
Comm. WB pp. 154, 158	✔	✔
***Hispanohablantes* WB** p. 298		✔

DIFFERENTIATED INSTRUCTION

Multiple Intelligences

Verbal/Linguistic: For *Actividad* 17, have groups of students collect all of the illogical sentences and compile them into a story. Remind them that they may have to adapt some of the sentences to make them fit better, but the goal is to be silly and entertaining. Encourage them to include illustrations and share their writing with the class.

Students with Learning Difficulties

Have students use the chart in *Actividad* 18 to take notes when they listen to other students describing their trips.

Gramática

▼ Objectives

- Read and represent a traditional children's rhyme
- Identify geographical features of some Spanish-speaking countries
- Write about and discuss whom you saw and what you visited on a trip

The personal *a*

You know that the direct object is the person or thing that receives the action of a verb. When the direct object is a person or group of people, you usually use the word *a* before the object. This is called the "personal *a*."

Visité a mi abuela.	*I visited my grandmother.*
Vimos a Juan y Gloria.	*We saw Juan and Gloria.*

You can also use the personal *a* when the direct object is a pet.

Busco a mi perro, Capitán.

To ask who receives the action of a verb, use *¿A quién?*

¿A quién visitaron Uds.?

Más ayuda realidades.com

***GramActiva* Video**
Tutorial: Personal *a*

19 Don Pepito y don José  

Leer • Escribir • Hablar

1. Lee esta rima tradicional.

—Hola, don Pepito.
—Hola, don José.
—¿Pasó* Ud. por mi casa?
—Por su casa no pasé.
—¿Vio Ud. a mi abuela?
—A su abuela no la vi.
—Adiós, don Pepito.
—Adiós, don José.

* Did (you) stop by

2. Ahora escribe las líneas *¿Vio Ud. a mi abuela?* y *A su abuela no la vi* y sustituye estos miembros de la familia por "abuela". Usa el pronombre *(pronoun)* apropiado.

1. tíos **2.** hermano **3.** primas **4.** hermanita

3. Con otro(a) estudiante, lee la rima. Un(a) estudiante va a ser don Pepito y el (la) otro(a), don José. Lean la rima cuatro veces, cada vez con un miembro diferente de la familia.

Nota

You have learned the direct object pronouns *lo*, *la*, *los*, and *las*. These direct object pronouns can refer to people as well as to things. Note that the direct object pronouns do not take the personal *a*.

—¿Viste **a tus primos** durante tus vacaciones?

—Sí, **los** vi.

En Barcelona, España

ENRICH YOUR TEACHING

Culture Note

The use of the titles ***don*** and ***doña*** in the Spanish-speaking world is a gesture of courtesy today. These titles were originally used to display a high level of respect and formality. The words come from the Latin words ***dominus*** (male) or ***domina*** (female) meaning "lord" or "master." In centuries past, only people of high rank and nobility were referred to as ***don*** or ***doña.***

Teacher-to-Teacher

Encourage more musically-inclined students to put the rhyme about don Pepito and don José to music. Let them play or sing their compositions to the class.

Gramática

Core Instruction

Standards: 4.1

Resources: Teacher's Resource Book: Video Script, p. 228; Video Program: Cap. 8A

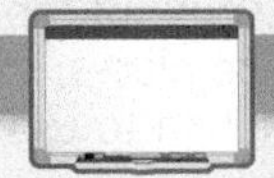

INTERACTIVE WHITEBOARD
Grammar Activities 8A

Suggestions: On the board, write a sentence in Spanish that has a *subject + verb + direct object* structure. Have students identify the direct object. Write another sentence in which the direct object is a person. Once students have identified the direct object in the second example, proceed with the presentation of the use of the personal **a** before a person or animal. Use the *GramActiva* Video either as an initial introduction to the structure or as a follow-up after your own grammar explanation.

19 Standards: 1.2, 1.3

Resources: Answer Keys: Student Edition, p. 116

Focus: Reading, writing, and speaking using the personal ***a***

Recycle: Family members

Suggestions: Explain to students that in part 2, they must change the family member, the form of the possessive adjectives (***mi*** and ***su***) and the pronouns. Point out the *Nota* to prevent students from overgeneralizing the personal ***a*** rule. If students ask why there is both a direct object noun ***(abuela)*** and a pronoun ***(la)***, explain that when a direct object noun precedes a verb, the pronoun is also used.

Answers:

1. **—¿Vio Ud. a mis tíos?**
   —A sus tíos no los vi.
2. **—¿Vio Ud. a mi hermano?**
   —A su hermano no lo vi.
3. **—¿Vio Ud. a mis primas?**
   —A sus primas no las vi.
4. **—¿Vio Ud. a mi hermanita?**
   —A su hermanita no la vi.

Extension: Have students write two sentences naming people they would like to visit and two sentences naming places they would like to visit.

20 Standards: 1.1

Resources: Answer Keys: Student Edition, p. 116

Focus: Asking and answering questions with and without personal ***a***

Recycle: Direct object pronouns

Suggestions: Point out that some of the items are people and others are places, so students will need to decide when to use the personal ***a.***

Answers:

Student A

1. —¿Visitaste a tus abuelos durante las vacaciones?
2. —¿Visitaste a un(a) amigo(a) que no vive aquí...?
3. —¿Visitaste un parque de diversiones...?
4. —¿Visitaste a tus primos...?
5. —¿Visitaste otra ciudad...?
6. —¿Visitaste el museo de arte...?

Student B: Answers will vary.

21 Standards: 3.1

Resources: Answer Keys: Student Edition, p. 116

Focus: Reading about geography

Recycle: Comparison of adjectives

Suggestions: Encourage students to refer to the maps on pp. xviii–xxxi as they work to identify each country.

Answers:

1. Nicaragua
2. Ecuador
3. México
4. Brasil
5. Colombia

Extension: Have students each write one clue about one of the countries on the list that wasn't used in the activity. As each student reads the clue, the class will guess the country being described.

Theme Project

Students can perform Step 2 at this point. Be sure they understand your corrections and suggestions. (For more information, see p. 372-b.)

Book Schedule

Have students choose a city in a Spanish-speaking country and write a short paragraph about what tourists can see there. They can use sources such as magazines, library books, and the Internet to gather information and illustrations.

20 De visita | 

Hablar

Pregunta a otro(a) estudiante si visitó a diferentes personas o diferentes lugares durante las vacaciones.

Modelo

tus tíos

A —*¿Visitaste a tus tíos durante las vacaciones?*

B —*Sí, los visité.*

o: —*No, no los visité.*

Estudiante A

1. tus abuelos
2. un(a) amigo(a) que no vive aquí
3. un parque de diversiones
4. tus primos
5. otra ciudad
6. el museo de arte

Estudiante B

¡Respuesta personal!

21 Juego de geografía: Las Américas

Leer • Pensar

¿Conoces[1] bien los países de las Américas? Empareja las descripciones con los países apropiados.

Conexiones | La geografía

1. Este país es el más grande de América Central. En el suroeste hay un lago muy grande que tiene el mismo nombre que el país. El lago está muy cerca de la frontera[2] con Costa Rica. En el este del país está el mar Caribe donde el clima es tropical y llueve mucho.
2. Este país pequeño tiene dos regiones tropicales, en el este y en el oeste, con montañas en el centro. Un cuarto de las personas en el país son de origen indígena y hablan quechua, el idioma[3] de los incas. Su nombre viene de la línea imaginaria que cruza el país.
3. Las ciudades más grandes de este país, como la capital, están en el centro del país donde hay montañas y volcanes. En el norte hay desiertos extensos y en el sur hay selvas[4] tropicales. Este país comparte una frontera con los Estados Unidos.
4. Este país es el más grande de América del Sur, con el río más grande del mundo[5]. Una gran parte del país es selva tropical con miles de especies de plantas, árboles y animales como monos, jaguares y tucanes. No hablan español aquí; hablan portugués.
5. Es el único[6] país de América del Sur que tiene playas en el mar Caribe y el océano Pacífico. Es un país famoso por su café, que viene de los valles fértiles.

México
El Salvador
Nicaragua
Colombia
Brasil
Uruguay
Chile
Bolivia
Ecuador
Cuba

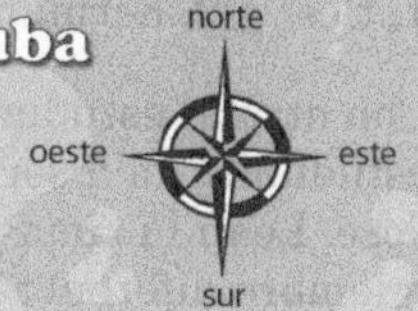

[1]Do you know [2]border [3]language [4]forests [5]world [6]only

DIFFERENTIATED INSTRUCTION

Heritage Language Learners

Have students create clues like those in *Actividad* 21 about their heritage country. To guide them, ask questions about the climate, the land formations, the bodies of water, the capital, and the largest cities. Correct their work, then use the clues to extend the *Actividad.*

Exploración del lenguaje

Nouns that end in *-io* and *-eo*

Latin words for buildings and places have carried into many modern languages, including Spanish. In many place names, the Latin ending *-um* (which remains in a number of words in English today) changed to an *-io* or *-eo* in Spanish. You know some of these words: *el estadio, el museo, el gimnasio.*

El acuario de Valencia, España

Try it out! Based on your knowledge of English and what you have learned about Spanish place names from Latin, match the definitions with the Spanish words in the list.

1. where you stand to deliver a speech
2. usually found in a cemetery
3. where you can see all kinds of sea life
4. where you sit when you see school plays or concerts
5. where you go to learn about stars and planets
6. where the ancient Romans went to see sporting events

a. el auditorio
b. el podio
c. el acuario
d. el planetario
e. el coliseo
f. el mausoleo

22 Y tú, ¿qué dices? 

Escribir • Hablar

1. ¿Qué puedes visitar en tu comunidad? ¿Hay museos, parques de diversiones o monumentos? ¿Cuál prefieres visitar?
2. El año pasado, ¿fuiste a ver una obra de teatro en tu comunidad o en tu escuela? ¿Te gustó? ¿Por qué? ¿Cuestan mucho los boletos de teatro?
3. El año pasado, ¿visitaste un museo o un zoológico en tu comunidad? ¿Cómo lo pasaste?
4. ¿Prefieres viajar a otros países o ciudades, o prefieres visitar lugares en tu comunidad?

El español en la comunidad

POR FAVOR NO LE DE COMIDA A LOS ANIMALES

Your community may have some of the tourist destinations you learned about in this chapter, such as *un museo, un teatro, un zoológico,* or *un parque de diversiones.* Think of different opportunities to use your Spanish at each of the locations. As you learn more Spanish, perhaps you could provide tours to visitors who speak Spanish. You could help write brochures and maps in Spanish to assist Spanish-speaking visitors. Can you think of other opportunities?

- Visit one of these locations in person or online and see what written resources are available in Spanish. Bring these materials to class to share with other students.

Más práctica GO | realidades.com | print

	realidades.com	print
Instant Check	✔	
Guided WB p. 256	✔	✔
Core WB p. 145	✔	✔
Comm. WB p. 155	✔	✔
Hispanohablantes WB pp. 299–301		✔

ENRICH YOUR TEACHING

Teacher-to-Teacher

Have students work in groups to create a vacation brochure for Spanish-speakers who visit your community. Students should include places to visit, things to see and do, and the best way to travel. You might submit copies of the best brochures to the local visitor's bureau.

21st Century Skills

Technology Literacy Remind students of the various digital tools available in **realidades.com** that target different types of learners and will help them learn and practice the grammar points in the chapter: eText with embedded audio, tutorials, *Canción de hip-hop,* and online grammar practice.

Exploración del lenguaje

Core Instruction

Standards: 4.1

Resources: Answer Keys: Student Edition, p. 117

Suggestions: Before beginning, ask students to brainstorm a list of English words ending in *-um.* Compare their list with the list in *Try it out!*

Answers:

1. b
2. f
3. c
4. a
5. d
6. e

22 Standards: 1.1, 1.2

Focus: Writing and talking about places to visit in your community

Suggestions: Arrange students in small groups to discuss each question. When reviewing answers, be sure you ask a student about others in his or her group.

Answers will vary.

El español en la comunidad

Core Instruction

Standards: 5.1

Suggestions: If you live in a small community, encourage students to think about a larger city near you or one that they have visited.

Additional Resources

- Communication Wbk.: Audio Act. 9, p. 155
- Teacher's Resource Book: Audio Script, p. 225, Communicative Pair Activity BLM, pp. 232–233
- Audio Program DVD: Cap. 8A, Track 13

ASSESSMENT

Prueba 8A-5 with Study Plan (online only)

Quiz: The personal *a*

- Prueba 8A-5: p. 207

Common Core: Reading

Lectura

Core Instruction

Standards: 1.2, 1.3, 2.1, 2.2, 3.1

Resources: Map Transparency 15

Mapa global interactivo, Actividad 5 Explore ancient and modern-day Peru.

Focus: Reading comprehension of journal entries about a trip to Peru

Suggestions:

Pre-reading: Direct students' attention to the *Strategy* and model how familiar words in a sentence can help determine the meaning of unfamiliar words. Have students write the words from the *Strategy* on a sheet of paper and identify each word as they encounter it in the journal entries.

Reading: Have students read *Álbum de mi viaje al Perú* silently. When they have finished, have student volunteers reread the journal entry aloud. After each entry, ask students to give a brief summary of the day's events.

Post-reading: Ask students to tell what context clues or familiar words they used to determine the meaning of the words from the *Strategy*. Have students identify the main locations in Peru—Cuzco, Lima, Machu Picchu, Lago Titicaca, and Nazca. Use the *¿Comprendes?* questions to check comprehension.

Pre-AP* Support

- **Learning Objective:** Presentational Writing
- **Activity:** Have students bring to class a picture of a historical place they have visited or would like to visit. Have them write two entries for activities they did or might have done on those days, crafted as e-mails to friends or blog posts for an online trip diary.
- ***Pre-AP* Resource Book:*** Comprehensive guide to Pre-AP* reading skill development, pp. 27–38

BELLRINGER REVIEW

Show the Map Transparency 15 of *La América del Sur* to locate these places. *Cuzco, Lima, Machu Picchu, Lago Titicaca, las Líneas de Nazca.*

Objectives

- Read journal entries about a trip to Peru
- Use context clues to understand new words

Lectura

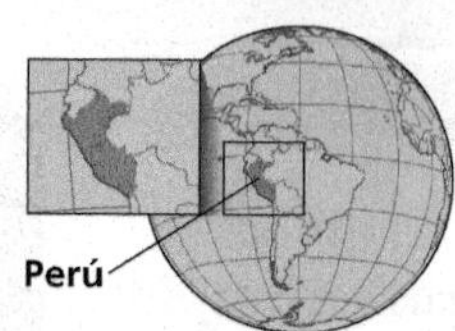

Álbum de mi viaje al Perú

Por Sofía Porrúa

Strategy

Using context clues
If you don't recognize a word, use the other words in the sentence to guess its meaning. Can you guess the meaning of *antigua, altura, construyeron,* and *nivel?*

domingo, 25 de julio
Estoy en el Perú con mis amigos Beto y Carmen. Vamos en autobús a Cuzco, antigua capital del imperio inca. Hoy día es una ciudad pequeña y una atracción turística. Beto está sacando muchas fotos con su cámara digital. Carmen está dibujando todo lo que ve. Las montañas son fantásticas.

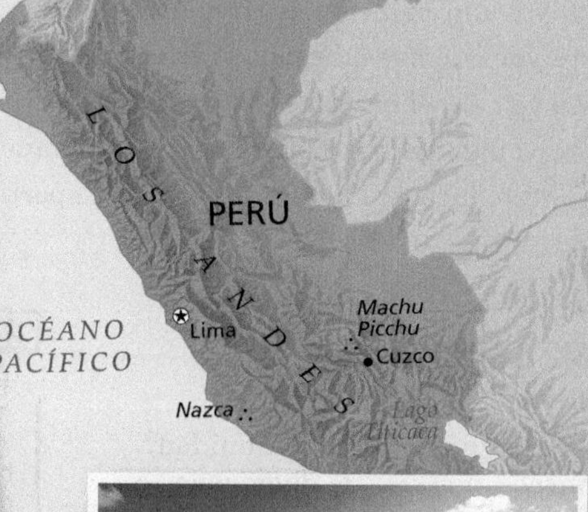

miércoles, 28 de julio
Hoy es el Día de la Independencia peruana. En esta fecha en 1821, José de San Martín proclamó la independencia del Perú. En Lima, gran ciudad moderna y capital del país, hay grandes celebraciones.

jueves, 29 de julio
Hoy estamos en Machu Picchu, ruinas impresionantes de una ciudad antigua de los incas. A más de 2.000 metros de altura en los Andes, los incas construyeron calles, casas, acueductos, palacios, templos y terrazas para cultivar. Hiram Bingham, un arqueólogo de la Universidad de Yale, descubrió[1] Machu Picchu en 1911.

[1]discovered

DIFFERENTIATED INSTRUCTION

Advanced Learners

Have students research a location they would go to if they could only visit one of the places described in the journal. Students should find additional information about the location and write a short description about it. The paragraph could be written in a journal style and might include a drawing or magazine picture as illustration.

Heritage Language Learners

Have students use the graphic organizer on p. 391 to research and note information about a country of their choice. Then have them write journal entries that include their findings, using the *Lectura* as a model.

sábado, 31 de julio
Estamos paseando en bote por el lago Titicaca, en la frontera del Perú y Bolivia. Es el lago más grande de estos países y el más alto del mundo.[2] ¡Estamos a más de 3.800 metros sobre el nivel del mar!

miércoles, 4 de agosto
Ahora estamos en un avión pequeño. Sobre la tierra[3] podemos ver algo muy misterioso: hay un desierto donde vemos enormes dibujos de animales y figuras geométricas. Estos dibujos se llaman las Líneas de Nazca. Miden[4] más de 300 metros y tienen más de dos mil años. ¿Quiénes los dibujaron, y por qué? Es necesario estar en un avión para verlos. ¿Cómo dibujaron los artistas algo tan[5] grande sin poder verlo?

Mañana regresamos al Cuzco y el domingo salimos de Perú. ¡Un viaje muy interesante! Beto tiene sus fotos y Carmen, sus dibujos. Yo no soy ni fotógrafa ni artista, por eso voy a comprar tarjetas postales como recuerdos.

[2]world [3]ground [4]They measure [5]so

¿Comprendes?

1. ¿Cómo va a recordar Sofía su viaje al Perú? ¿Y Beto y Carmen?
2. Pizarro y los españoles descubrieron muchas de las ciudades de los incas. ¿Por qué piensas que no descubrieron Machu Picchu? ¿Quién la descubrió?
3. Para muchos turistas que visitan el lago Titicaca es difícil caminar y respirar *(breathe)*. ¿Por qué piensas que tienen estos problemas?
4. ¿Cuáles son los misterios de las Líneas de Nazca?
5. Copia la tabla en una hoja de papel. Usa la información de la lectura para comparar Perú con los Estados Unidos.

	Perú	Estados Unidos
a. Dos lugares históricos y turísticos		
b. Día de la Independencia		
c. Año de la proclamación de la independencia		
d. Capital del país hoy		
e. Héroe nacional		

Más práctica GO

realidades.com | print

	realidades.com	print
Guided WB p. 257	✔	✔
Comm. WB pp. 159, 313	✔	✔
***Hispanohablantes* WB** pp. 302–303		✔
Cultural Reading Activity	✔	

¿Comprendes? Standards: 1.2, 1.3

Resources: Answer Keys: Student Edition, p. 117

Focus: Reading comprehension of facts about Peru and the United States

Suggestions: Suggest that students read the questions first, and then reread the passage to find the correct answer. If necessary, suggest that they use their history books or other reference materials for additional information about the United States.

Answers:

1. **Sofía escribe en su álbum. Beto saca fotos. Carmen dibuja.**
2. **Porque está a más de 2.000 metros de altura. Lo descubrió Hiram Bingham, un arqueólogo de la Universidad de Yale.**
3. **Porque está a 3.800 metros sobre el nivel del mar.**
4. **¿Quiénes las dibujaron y por qué? ¿Cómo dibujaron los artistas algo tan grande sin poder verlo?**
5. **Answers will vary.**

Theme Project

Students can perform Step 3 at this point. (For more information, see p. 372-b.)

Teacher-to-Teacher

Careers: *Capítulo* 8A has focused on travel. Have students work in small groups to talk about a career in the travel industry. Ask them to generate a list of words, expressions, and sentences they have learned that would be useful in giving Spanish tours of their community. Ask groups to share their lists.

For Further Reading

Student Resource: Realidades para hispanohablantes: Lectura 2, pp. 304–305

ENRICH YOUR TEACHING

Culture Note

In southwestern Peru, ancient geometric symbols and depictions of animals are etched into the surface of the barren plain near Nazca. Known as the "Nazca Lines," the artwork spans an area of approximately 200 square miles and includes representations of a hummingbird, monkey, heron, whale, and spider.

21st Century Skills

Information Literacy Have students research Web sites for a Spanish-speaking country and, using the criteria they developed earlier to evaluate them, use the Web sites with the most accurate and best organized information to create an electronic photo album similar to the one on pp. 390–391.

La cultura en vivo

Core Instruction

Standards: 2.2, 4.2

Focus: Reading about and creating an ***ojo de Dios***

Suggestions: Begin a brief discussion about good-luck charms. Point out some common ones, such as rabbits' feet and four-leaf clovers. Tell students that they will learn about and make a kind of good-luck charm that dates back hundreds of years.

Have them read the two paragraphs. Point out that ***ojos de Dios*** are a form of artwork. Remind them that before machines and electricity existed, people made things by hand. Many of these handmade items have become important forms of artwork that help keep traditions alive. Direct attention to the woman in the photo. She is from one of the indigenous groups of Mexico that still make the ***ojos de Dios*** today. Have students look at the photo of the ***ojo de Dios.*** Ask why this might be considered an "eye."

Popsicle sticks or cut dowels will work well for this. Make your own ***ojo de Dios*** in advance to estimate the amount of time and yarn needed and for use as a model. Also make a partial one, stopping at Step 2, so that students can use it as a guide for getting started.

Prior to class, gather enough materials for each student. Have a variety of colors of yarn, and if possible have more than one ball of each color to make sharing easier. Make sure your colors include white for those who wish to represent the white of an eye. Have students read the steps before beginning. Answer any questions. Go through the steps slowly and circulate to give assistance as needed.

You may wish to have students bring in feathers, beads, or tassels for decoration.

Direct attention to *Think about it!* and have students discuss the questions.

Answers will vary.

Additional Resources

Student Resource: Realidades para hispanohablantes, p. 306

¡Adelante!

La cultura en vivo

El ojo de Dios

Mujer tarahumara en San Rafael, México

Traveling in the Spanish-speaking world you will encounter a marvelous variety of artwork and crafts, many of which have their origins in the time before the Spaniards came to the Americas. One form of art that is popular among visitors to parts of Mexico is the *ojo de Dios.*

The *ojo de Dios* is a diamond-shaped weaving. As a gift, it symbolizes good wishes from one person to another. *Ojos de Dios* may have originated in Peru about 300 B.C. The people best known for making these today are the Indians of Mexico's Sierra Madre region. The Cora, Huichol, Tarahumara, and Tepehuane all make and use these weavings in their daily lives.

How to make an *ojo de Dios*

Materials

- yarn
- scissors
- two sticks of the same size
- optional: feathers, beads, or tassels for finishing touches

Figure 1

Figure 2

Directions

1 Tie the sticks together to form a cross. *(Fig. 1)*

2 Tie the end of the yarn to the center of the cross.

3 Weave the yarn over and around each stick, keeping the yarn pulled tight. *(Fig. 2)* To change color, knot together two ends of different-colored yarn. The knot should fall on the back side. Continue wrapping until the sticks are covered with yarn. Tie a small knot at the back and leave enough yarn to make a loop for hanging.

4 You may want to add feathers, beads, or tassels to the ends of the sticks. Hang your decorative piece for everyone to enjoy.

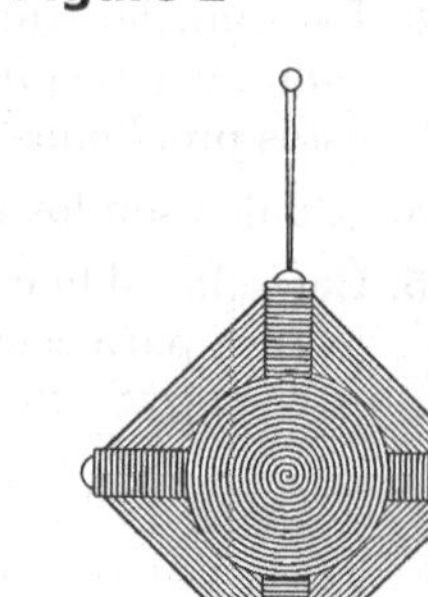
Figure 3

Think about it! What are some of the traditional handicrafts in the United States? What is the ethnic heritage of these crafts?

DIFFERENTIATED INSTRUCTION

Multiple Intelligences

Visual/Spatial: Students may pick this up quickly. If so, encourage them to add finishing touches to personalize their ***ojo de Dios.*** They may also be able to help others who are having difficulties with the process.

Students with Special Needs

Students may have difficulties getting the two sticks to stay together as in Figure I. If so, you may prepare the sticks for them, or ask a more adept student to help out. Some may also have trouble wrapping the yarn. If so, provide a model and demonstrate for them a few times. Students may benefit from working in pairs.

Objectives | Aplicación

- Describe a trip you took
- Use a word web to organize your ideas

Presentación oral 

Mi viaje

Task
Tell a friend about a trip you took. It could be a vacation, a visit to family, or an imaginary trip. Use photos or drawings to make your talk more interesting.

1 Prepare Use the word web to think about what you did on your trip. Include information and events in each circle. Use photos or pictures to illustrate each part of the trip noted on the word web. Design an appealing illustration of your trip.

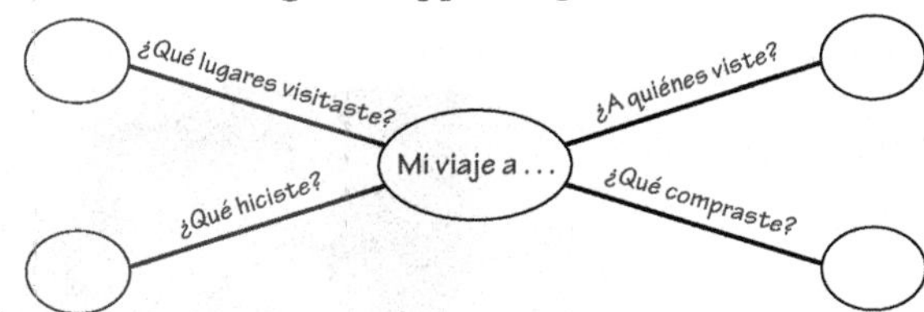

Strategy

Using graphic organizers
Using a graphic organizer such as a word web will help you think through what you want to say in your presentation.

2 Practice Use the information in your word web to tell a partner about your trip. Go through your story several times using the photographs or illustrations. Use your notes in practice, but not when you present. End by saying how you felt about the trip.

Modelo
En marzo, fui a la Florida para visitar a mis primos. Tomamos el sol en la playa y nadamos mucho. Aprendí a bucear y vi animales muy interesantes en el mar. La Florida es un lugar fantástico. El viaje fue muy divertido.

3 Present Talk about your trip to a small group or the whole class. Use your photos or drawings to help you.

4 Evaluation The following rubric will be used to grade your presentation.

Rubric	Score 1	Score 3	Score 5
Amount of information provided	You include two categories from the word web.	You include three categories from the word web.	You include all four categories from the word web.
Use of photographs or visuals	You include only two visuals that clearly connect to trip.	You include three visuals that clearly connect to trip.	You include four visuals that clearly connect to trip.
How easily you are understood	You are extremely difficult to understand. Your teacher could only recognize isolated words and phrases.	You are understandable, but have frequent errors in vocabulary and/or grammar that hinder your comprehensibility.	You are easily understood. Your teacher does not have to "decode" what you are trying to say.

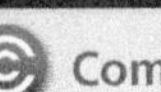 Common Core: Speaking

Presentación oral

Core Instruction

Standards: 1.1, 1.3

Resources: Voc. and Gram. Transparency 150; Teacher's Resource Book: GramActiva BLM, p. 235

Focus: Communicating about vacations in a personalized context

Suggestions: Review the task and the four-step approach with students. Review the rubric with the class to explain how you will grade the performance task. Emphasize that it is quality, not length, which is most important. Do a presentation of your own to model a top-scoring presentation.

Remind students that a successful presentation begins with good planning. Students should work on their word webs and incorporate their visual aids as they speak. Remind them to practice with a partner before they present.

Portfolio

Make video or audio recordings of student presentations in class, or assign the RealTalk activity so they can record their presentations online. Include the recording in their portfolios.

Pre-AP* Support

- **Learning Objective:** Presentational Speaking
- **Activity:** Remind students to focus on the presentational speaking skills used in this task such as fluency, pronunciation, and comprehensibility.
- ***Pre-AP* Resource Book:*** Comprehensive guide to Pre-AP* speaking skill development, pp. 39–50

Additional Resources

Student Resources: Realidades para hispanohablantes, p. 307; Guided Practice, p. 258

ENRICH YOUR TEACHING

Teacher-to-Teacher

To create the *Mi viaje* presentation, have students use the photos, illustrations, and information they have used in creating other class projects for this chapter, or souvenirs collected from vacations they have taken. Have them think of an illustration for each of the word web questions.

21st Century Skills

Critical Thinking and Problem Solving Have students interview family members to find out what kind of vacation they would like to take in the summer. Have them use a Venn diagram to compare and contrast two vacation sites they have learned about in this chapter. By looking at the similarities and differences, they can make an informed decision about where to go with the family.

ASSESSMENT

Presentación oral

- Assessment Program: Rubrics, p. T33

Go over the descriptions of the different levels of performance. After assessing students, help individuals understand how their performance could be improved.

Videomisterio

Core Instruction

Standards: 1.2, 2.1, 5.2

Resources: Teacher's Resource Book: Video Script, pp. 228–229; Video Program: Cap. 8A; Video Program Teacher's Guide: Cap. 8A

Focus: Introducing the episode, scanning, and reading the summary

Personajes importantes:

Lola Lago, detective

Rosalinda, nurse

Pedro, Doña Gracia's grandson

Synopsis: Rosalinda finds out Julia Romero's address and calls Lola to let her know. Then Pedro and Lola meet at doña Gracia's apartment. There they find a postcard sent to María from Luis Antonio Llamas, a former secretary to doña Gracia's husband. By chance, the name of one of the nurses that cared for Julia in the hospital was Luis Antonio. Next they go to Julia Romero's apartment. They discover that she no longer lives there, but the new tenant has a box of Julia's belongings. In the box they find several letters from Luis Antonio.

Suggestions:

Pre-viewing: Review with students the events of the previous episode. Pedro Requena decides to hire Lola to investigate what caused the incident at his grandmother's house that sent her to the hospital and who stole doña Gracia's jewels from her apartment. Inspector Gil suspects María, since she has disappeared.

When discussing the *Nota cultural,* ask students how addresses in Spain are different from those in the United States. Provide examples of the *Palabras para comprender* in context and write them on the board. Remind students that these words are only used to help them understand the episode and they are not responsible for that vocabulary.

Objective

- Understand the expanding plot of a mystery video set in Spain

¿Eres tú, María?

Episodio 7

Antes de ver el video

Resumen del episodio

Lola y Pedro visitan el piso elegante de doña Gracia. Entran en la habitación[1] de María. Hay ropa, libros, unas fotos y una tarjeta postal. Lola y Pedro leen algo muy interesante en la tarjeta postal. Después, van al piso de Julia. Allí vive un hombre que no conoce a Julia. Pero antes vivía[2] una chica en el piso. Todavía hay unas cosas de esa chica: ropa, unas cartas y unos papeles. ¿Y qué más?

[1] bedroom [2] used to live

"Lola, te llamo porque tengo información sobre la otra chica en el accidente. Tengo la dirección de su piso. Es Calle Norte, 23, 1°, D".

Nota cultural Addresses in Spain are written differently than in the United States. For example, the name of Julia's street is Calle Norte. The building number is 23. The 1° *(primero)* indicates the apartment is on the first floor (not the ground floor, but what we would call the second floor), and Julia lives in apartment D.

Palabras para comprender

¡Suerte! Good luck!

No la conozco. I don't know her.

tenía un secretario had a secretary

tuvo problemas con él had problems with him

¡Qué casualidad! What a coincidence!

DIFFERENTIATED INSTRUCTION

Advanced Learners

Have advanced learners explain what they think the relationship is between Luis Antonio and Julia. How did Pedro know who Luis Antonio was?

Heritage Language Learners

In this episode, Pedro and Lola speak of several coincidences as ***una casualidad,*** which is a false cognate. "Casualty" in English is equivalent to ***muerto*** or ***pérdida*** in Spanish. Ask students to mention other false cognates they know or have noticed, such as "resume" and ***resumen*** ("resume" translates as ***volver a empezar*** or ***comenzar de nuevo***).

"¿A quién buscáis? Antes aquí vivía una chica . . .".

"Mira esta tarjeta postal. Interesante, ¿no?"

"¿Sabes, Pedro? En mi profesión la casualidad no existe".

Después de ver el video

¿Comprendes?

Pon las frases en orden según el episodio.

1. Pedro recuerda el nombre de Luis Antonio Llamas, un secretario de su papá.
2. Leen la tarjeta postal de Luis Antonio.
3. Pedro llama a Lola para invitarla a visitar el piso de su abuela.
4. El joven en el piso de Julia no está nada contento.
5. Rosalinda llama a Lola para darle la dirección de Julia.
6. Quieren ver la habitación de María.
7. Deciden visitar el piso de Julia.

Nota gramatical In this episode you will hear a few more examples of the *vosotros* form: *queréis, sois, podéis, buscáis.* Remember that in Spain you use *vosotros* or *vosotras* when talking to more than one person whom you would address individually as *tú.*

ENRICH YOUR TEACHING

Teacher-to-Teacher

The ***vosotros*** form, such as in ***queréis, sois, podéis,*** and ***buscáis*** presented in the *Nota grammatical,* is formed by adding the endings ***-áis, -éis,*** and ***-ís*** to ***-ar, -er,*** and ***-ir*** verbs. Write on the board a few of the verbs presented so far, using the corresponding ***vosotros*** endings. Remind students that ***vosotros*** is used to speak to a group of people whom you would address as ***tú*** individually.

Video 8A

Visual scanning: Discuss who is pictured before students read the *Resumen del episodio.* Have them scan the text and find three cognates ***(visitan, fotos, interesante).***

Viewing: If there is time after viewing the full episode, go back and replay some key moments that you wish to highlight, such as the scene in which Lola and Pedro visit doña Gracia's apartment.

Post-viewing: Point out the *Nota gramatical.* Write the vocabulary presented in this episode on the board to help students create sentences for each important scene that adds new information to the plot. Then have students do the *¿Comprendes?* activity.

¿Comprendes? Standards: 1.1, 1.3

Resources: Answer Keys: Student Edition, p. 117

Focus: Verifying comprehension; reviewing the plot

Suggestions: Have students read through all the statements before placing them in order. Tell them the pictures on pp. 394–395 do not represent the sequence in the video.

Answers:

5, 4, 2, 7, 1, 3, 6

Additional Resources

- *¿Eres tú, María?* Video Workbook, Episode 7
- *¿Eres tú, María?* Teacher's Video Guide: Answer Key

Review Activities

To talk about places to visit and things to see on vacation: Have students work in pairs to quiz each other on the vocabulary. Students can create flashcards, writing the Spanish word on one side of an index card and the English word on the other.

To talk about things to do on vacation: Have students name a location from the previous section, and then ask one another *¿Qué viste?* or *¿Qué aprendiste?*

To talk about ways to travel: Have one student name a vacation place. The other student will suggest an appropriate way to get there.

To talk about your vacation and to express time: Have students create a cloze passage in which they leave out vocabulary words and expressions. They should provide a word bank and exchange their passages with another student.

Portfolio

Invite students to review the activities they completed in this chapter, including written reports, posters or other visuals, recordings of oral presentations, or other projects. Have them select one or two items that they feel best demonstrate their achievements in Spanish to include in their portfolios. Have them include this with the Chapter Checklist and Self-Assessment Worksheet.

Additional Resources

Student Resources: Realidades para hispanohablantes, p. 308

Teacher Resources:

- Teacher's Resource Book: Situation Cards, p. 234, Clip Art, pp. 236–237
- Assessment Program: Chapter Checklist and Self-Assessment Worksheet, pp. T56–T57

Repaso | | |

Objectives

- Review the vocabulary and grammar
- Demonstrate you can perform the tasks on p. 397

Repaso del capítulo

Vocabulario y gramática

to talk about places to visit on vacation

la ciudad	city
el estadio	stadium
el lago	lake
el lugar	place
el mar	sea
el monumento	monument
el museo	museum
el país	country
el parque de diversiones	amusement park
el parque nacional	national park
el teatro	theater
la obra de teatro	play
el zoológico	zoo

to talk about things to see on vacation

el animal	animal
el árbol	tree
la atracción *pl.* **las atracciones**	attraction(s)
el mono	monkey
el oso	bear
el pájaro	bird

to talk about things to do on vacation

aprender (a)	to learn
bucear	to scuba dive / snorkel
(comprar) recuerdos	(to buy) souvenirs
descansar	to rest, to relax
montar a caballo	to ride horseback
pasear en bote	to go boating
tomar el sol	to sunbathe
visitar	to visit

to talk about ways to travel

en	by
el autobús	bus
el avión	airplane
el barco	boat, ship
el tren	train

to talk about your vacation

el boleto	ticket
como	like, such as
¿Cómo lo pasaste?	How was it (for you)?
dime	tell me
fantástico, -a	fantastic
Fue un desastre.	It was a disaster.
el hotel	hotel
impresionante	impressive
ir de vacaciones	to go on vacation
Me gustó.	I liked it.
¿Qué hiciste?	What did you do?
¿Qué te pasó?	What happened to you?
regresar	to return
salir	to leave, to go out
¿Te gustó?	Did you like it?
tremendo, -a	tremendous
vi	I saw
¿viste . . . ?	Did you see . . . ?
viajar	to travel
el viaje	trip

to express time

durante	during
tarde	late
temprano	early

preterite of *-er* and *-ir* verbs

aprendí **salí**	**aprendimos** **salimos**
aprendiste **saliste**	**aprendisteis** **salisteis**
aprendió **salió**	**aprendieron** **salieron**

preterite of *ir*

fui	**fuimos**
fuiste	**fuisteis**
fue	**fueron**

For *Vocabulario adicional,* see pp. 472–473.

DIFFERENTIATED INSTRUCTION

Heritage Language Learners

Have students write a ten-sentence paragraph describing a trip. The sentences must use the preterite of ***-er*** and ***-ir*** verbs, and of ***ir***. Encourage them to use different subject pronouns as they tell the story. Have them check their spelling and verb forms carefully.

Multiple Intelligences

Logical/Mathematical: Give students a blank grid on which to create a word search puzzle. Have them choose fifteen vocabulary words or expressions and write them into the grid. Ask them to fill in the remaining blocks with random letters. Underneath the grid, have students write how many words are hidden in the puzzle. Have them exchange puzzles.

Más repaso GO realidades.com | print

	realidades.com	print
Instant Check	✔	
Puzzles	✔	
Core WB pp. 146–147		✔
Comm. WB pp. 314, 315–318	✔	✔

Preparación para el examen

On the exam you will be asked to . . .	Here are practice tasks similar to those you will find on the exam . . .	For review go to your print or digital textbook . . .
Interpretive		
 **1 Escuchar** Listen to and understand what someone says he did and where he went during his last vacation	As part of a presentation in Spanish class, a student talked about his last vacation. As you listen, see if you can determine: a) where he went; b) one thing he did; c) one thing he saw.	**pp. 374–377** *Vocabulario en contexto* **p. 375** Actividad 1 **p. 378** Actividades 4–5
Interpersonal		
 **2 Hablar** Tell about your best trip or vacation	Find out where your partner went on his or her best vacation, and what he or she did and saw. As you listen, make a drawing that includes details of the trip. Then your partner will ask you to describe your best vacation. Do your drawings match the descriptions?	**p. 379** Actividad 6 **p. 380** Actividad 8 **p. 382** Actividad 11 **p. 385** Actividad 16 **p. 386** Actividad 18 **p. 393** *Presentación oral*
Interpretive		
 **3 Leer** Read and understand a vacation postcard	Read the postcard Javier sent to his friend last summer during his family vacation. Which things does he say he liked? Was there anything he didn't like? *¡Hola! Salí de vacaciones la semana pasada y ahora estamos aquí en Puerto Rico. Visitamos a nuestra tía en San Juan. Ayer fuimos al Viejo San Juan, donde vi muchos monumentos. También vi El Morro, un lugar muy famoso. ¡Fue fabuloso! Hoy fui a la playa de Luquillo y tomé el sol. Los otros bucearon por tres horas, pero a mí no me gusta el mar. Después, comimos arroz con pollo en un restaurante. ¡Uf! ¡Siempre arroz con pollo aquí! Regreso el sábado. ¡Hasta luego! Javier*	**p. 379** Actividad 7 **p. 381** Actividad 9 **p. 388** Actividad 21 **pp. 390–391** *Lectura*
Presentational		
 **4 Escribir** Write a brief narrative about an imaginary character's trip	You have been asked by a first-grade teacher to write a story in Spanish for her students. She has a stuffed bear in her room, *el Oso Teo,* so you decide to write the story about him and his trip. Tell where he went, what he did, what he saw, and what he ate. Begin with something like, *"El Oso Teo fue de viaje a su parque favorito . . ."*	**p. 378 Actividad 4** **p. 384** Actividades 14–15 **p. 386** Actividad 18 **p. 389** Actividad 22 **pp. 390–391** *Lectura*
Cultures • Comparisons		
 **5 Pensar** Demonstrate an understanding of cultural perspectives regarding artwork and crafts	Think about a gift you might give someone to symbolize good luck and good fortune in our culture. Compare it to a traditional craft from Mexico that is given for the same reason. Describe its significance and history in the Spanish-speaking world.	**p. 392** *La cultura en vivo*

Performance Tasks

Standards: 1.1, 1.2, 1.3, 2.1, 3.1

Student Resource: Realidades para hispanohablantes, p. 309

Teacher Resources: Teacher's Resource Book: Audio Script, p. 226; Audio Program DVD: Cap. 8A, Track 15; Answer Keys: Student Edition, p. 117

1. Escuchar

Suggestions: Students may want to create three columns on their paper: Where they went; What they did; What they saw.

Script:

Oye. Todo fue tremendo. Fuimos de vacaciones al parque nacional por una semana. Monté a caballo con mis primos y paseé en bote con mi padre. ¡Vi unos árboles más grandes que una casa!

Answers: a) They went to the national park. b) They went horseback riding. c) They saw trees bigger than houses.

2. Hablar

Suggestions:

Encourage students to draw quickly while they listen, sketching out the main idea rather than focusing on drawing with a lot of detail.

Answers will vary.

3. Leer

Suggestions: Encourage students to make a list of pros and cons to determine what Javier liked about his trip and what he didn't like.

Answers: What Javier liked: San Juan, monuments, and El Morro What Javier didn't like: the sea, *arroz con pollo.*

4. Escribir

Suggestions: Have students organize their thoughts by taking notes to answer these questions: Who? Where? What did he do? What did he see? What did he eat?

5. Pensar

Suggestions: Refer students to the reading on pp. 390–391 to prepare them.

Answers will vary.

DIFFERENTIATED ASSESSMENT

CORE ASSESSMENT
- **Assessment Program:** Examen del capítulo 8A, pp. 208–214
- **Audio Program DVD:** Cap. 8A, Track 16
- **ExamView:** Chapter Test, Test Banks A and B

ADVANCED/PRE-AP*
- **ExamView: Pre-AP* Test Bank**
- **Pre-AP* Resource Book,** pp. 90–93

STUDENTS NEEDING EXTRA HELP
- **Alternate Assessment Program:** Examen del capítulo 8A
- **Audio Program DVD:** Cap. 8A, Track 16

HERITAGE LEARNERS
- **Assessment Program: Realidades Para Hispanohablantes:** Examen del capítulo 8A
- **ExamView: Heritage Learner Test Bank**

8B Ayudando en la comunidad

AT A GLANCE

Objectives

- Listen to and read about community service
- Talk and write about volunteer activities and recycling
- Exchange information about volunteering
- Compare perspectives about volunteer activities in Spanish-speaking countries to your community
- Compare environmental efforts in Spain, Costa Rica, and other Spanish-speaking countries to programs in your community

Vocabulary

- Recycling
- Places in a community
- Volunteer work

Grammar

- The present tense of ***decir***
- Indirect object pronouns
- The preterite of ***hacer*** and ***dar***

Culture

- Peace Corps, p. 399
- Recycling in Spain, p. 405
- Blown glass art in Mexico, p. 406
- The doctors of Interplast, p. 407
- Protected natural areas of Costa Rica, p. 407
- Conservation efforts in Puerto Rico, p. 409
- ***Hospital de la Caridad,*** Spain, p. 412
- ***las tortugas tinglar,*** p. 415
- ***Hábitat para la Humanidad,*** pp. 416–417
- Cultural perspectives on volunteer work, p. 418

Recycle ♻

- Direct object pronouns ***lo, la, los, las***
- Expressions ***¿Cómo se dice?*** and ***Y tú ¿qué dices?***
- ***¿Qué hiciste?***
- ***tener*** idioms
- ***poder***
- ***me gusta(n), me encanta(n)***
- Adjectives
- ***dar***
- ***ir a*** + infinitive
- Preterite of ***-ar, -er,*** and ***-ir*** verbs

RESOURCES

	FOR THE STUDENT	ONLINE	DVD	PRINT	FOR THE TEACHER	ONLINE	PREEXP	DVD	PRINT
Plan					Interactive TE and Resources DVD	•		•	
					Teacher's Resource Book, pp. 254–286	•		•	•
					Pre-AP* Resource Book, pp. 90–93	•		•	•
					Lesson Plans	•			•
					Mapa global interactivo	•			
Introducción PP. **398–399**									
Present	Student Edition, pp. 398–399	•	•	•	Interactive TE and Resources DVD	•		•	
	DK Reference Atlas	•	•		Teacher's Resource Book, pp. 254–255	•		•	•
	Videocultura	•	•		Galería de fotos		•		
	Hispanohablantes WB, pp. 310–311			•	Map Transparencies, 12–15, 18	•	•	•	
Vocabulario en contexto PP. **400–403**									
Present & Practice	Student Edition, pp. 400–403	•	•	•	Interactive TE and Resources DVD	•		•	
	Audio	•	•		Teacher's Resource Book, pp. 257–259, 262, 270–271	•		•	•
	Videohistoria	•	•		Vocabulary Clip Art	•	•	•	•
	Flashcards	•	•		Audio Program	•	•	•	
	Instant Check	•			Video Program: Videohistoria	•		•	
	Guided WB, pp. 259–268	•	•	•	Video Program Teacher's Guide: Cap. 8B	•		•	•
	Core WB, pp. 148–151	•	•	•	Vocabulary and Grammar Transparencies, 151–154	•	•	•	
	Comm. WB, pp. 160–163, 166	•	•	•	Answer Keys: Student Edition, pp. 118–119	•	•	•	
	Hispanohablantes WB, pp. 312–313			•	TPR Stories, pp. 107–121	•		•	•
Assess and Remediate					Prueba 8B–1: Assessment Program, pp. 215–216	•		•	•
					Assessment Program para hispanohablantes, pp. 215–216	•		•	•

RESOURCES

	FOR THE STUDENT	ONLINE	DVD	PRINT	FOR THE TEACHER	ONLINE	PREEXP	DVD	PRINT
Vocabulario en uso PP. **404–407**									
Present & Practice	Student Edition, pp. 404–407	•	•	•	Interactive Whiteboard Vocabulary Activities	•		•	
	Instant Check	•			Interactive TE and Resources DVD	•		•	
	Comm. WB, p. 163	•	•	•	Teacher's Resource Book, pp. 258–259, 264–265	•		•	•
	Hispanohablantes WB, pp. 314–315, 320–321			•	Communicative Pair Activities, pp. 264–265	•		•	•
	Communicative Pair Activities	•			Audio Program	•	•	•	
					Videomodelos	•		•	
					Map Transparencies, 13	•	•	•	
					Answer Keys: Student Edition, pp. 119–121	•	•	•	•
Assess and Remediate					Prueba 8B–2 with Study Plan	•			
					Prueba 8B–2: Assessment Program, pp. 217–218	•		•	•
					Assessment Program para hispanohablantes, pp. 217–218	•		•	•
Gramática PP. **408–415**									
Present & Practice	Student Edition, pp. 408–415	•	•	•	Interactive Whiteboard Grammar Activities	•		•	
	Instant Check	•			Interactive TE and Resources DVD	•		•	
	Animated Verbs	•			Teacher's Resource Book, pp. 259–263, 266–267	•		•	•
	Tutorial Video: Grammar	•			Communicative Pair Activities, pp. 266–267	•		•	•
	Canción de hip hop	•			Audio Program	•	•	•	
	Guided WB, pp. 269–272	•	•	•	Videomodelos	•		•	
	Core WB, pp. 152–154	•	•	•	Video Program: GramActiva	•	•	•	
	Comm. WB, pp. 164–165, 167–168, 319	•	•	•	Vocabulary and Grammar Transparencies, 155–158	•	•	•	
	Hispanohablantes WB, pp. 316–321			•	Answer Keys: Student Edition, pp. 121–123	•	•	•	
	Communicative Pair Activities	•							
Assess and Remediate					Pruebas 8B–3, 8B–4, and 8B–5 with Study Plans	•			
					Pruebas 8B–3, 8B–4, and 8B–5 with Study Plans: Assessment Program, pp. 219–221	•		•	•
					Assessment Program para hispanohablantes, pp. 219–221	•		•	•
¡Adelante! PP. **416–421**									
Application	Student Edition, pp. 416–421	•	•	•	Interactive TE and Resources DVD	•		•	
	Online Cultural Reading	•			Teacher's Resource Book, p. 263	•		•	•
	Guided WB, pp. 273–274	•	•	•	Video Program: Videomisterio ¿Eres tú, María?	•		•	
	Comm. WB, pp. 169, 320	•	•	•	Video Program Teacher's Guide: Cap. 8B	•		•	
	Hispanohablantes WB, pp. 322–327			•	Videomisterio Quiz		•		
	¿Eres tú, María? Video WB, pp. 58–66	•	•	•	Map Transparencies, 13	•	•	•	
					Answer Keys: Student Edition, p. 124	•	•	•	
Repaso del capítulo PP. **422–423**									
Review	Student Edition, pp. 422–423	•	•	•	Interactive TE and Resources DVD	•		•	
	Online Puzzles and Games	•			Teacher's Resource Book, pp. 261, 268, 270–271	•		•	•
	Core WB, pp. 155–156	•	•	•	Audio Program	•	•	•	
	Comm. WB, pp. 321–324	•	•	•	Answer Keys: Student Edition, p. 125	•	•	•	
	Hispanohablantes WB, pp. 328–329			•					
	Instant Check	•							
Chapter Assessment									
Assess					Examen del capítulo 8B	•		•	•
					Assessment Program, pp. 222–228	•		•	•
					Alternate Assessment Program, pp. 85–89	•		•	•
					Assessment Program para hispanohablantes, pp. 222–228	•		•	•
					Audio Program, Cap. 8B, Examen	•		•	
					ExamView: Test Banks A and B questions only online	•		•	
					Heritage Learner Test Bank	•		•	
					Pre-AP* Test Bank	•		•	

8B Lesson Plans

DAY	REGULAR SCHEDULE (50 MINUTES)		
	Warm-up / Assess	**Preview / Present / Practice / Communicate**	**Wrap-up / Homework Options**
1	**Warm-up** (10 min.) • Return Examen del capítulo 8A	**Chapter Opener** (5 min.) • Objectives • Arte y cultura **Vocabulario en contexto** (30 min.) • Presentation: Vocabulario en contexto • Actividades 1, 2	**Wrap-up and Homework Options** (5 min.) • Core Practice 8B-1, 8B-2
2	**Warm-up** (5 min.) • Homework check	**Vocabulario en contexto** (40 min.) • Presentation: Videohistoria *Cómo ayudamos a los demás* • View: Videohistoria • Video Activities 1, 2, 3, 4 • Actividad 3	**Wrap-up and Homework Options** (5 min.) • Core Practice 8B-3, 8B-4 • Prueba 8B-1: Vocabulary recognition
3	**Warm-up** (10 min.) • Actividad 6 • Homework check ✓**Formative Assessment** (10 min.) • Prueba 8B-1: Vocabulary recognition	**Vocabulario en uso** (25 min.) • Interactive Whiteboard Vocabulary Activities • Actividades 4, 5, 8 • Fondos culturales • Audio Activities 5, 6	**Wrap-up and Homework Options** (5 min.) • Writing Activity 10 • Actividad 7 • Prueba 8B-2 with Study Plan: Vocabulary production
4	**Warm-up** (5 min.) • Homework check ✓**Formative Assessment** (10 min.) • Prueba 8B-2 with Study Plan: Vocabulary production	**Gramática y vocabulario en uso** (30 min.) • Communicative Pair Activity • Exploración del lenguaje • Presentation: The present tense of ***decir*** • View: GramActiva video • Interactive Whiteboard Grammar Activities • Actividades 9, 11, 12	**Wrap-up and Homework Options** (5 min.) • Core Practice 8B-5 • Writing Activity 11 • Prueba 8B-3 with Study Plan: The present tense of ***decir***
5	**Warm-up** (10 min.) • Actividad 10 • Homework check ✓**Formative Assessment** (10 min.) • Prueba 8B-3 with Study Plan: The present tense of ***decir***	**Gramática y vocabulario en uso** (25 min.) • Audio Activity 7 • Presentation: Indirect object pronouns • View: GramActiva video • Interactive Whiteboard Grammar Activities • Actividades 13, 14 • Communicative Pair Activity	**Wrap-up and Homework Options** (5 min.) • Core Practice 8B-6 • Writing Activity 12 • Actividad 16 • Prueba 8B-4 with Study Plan: Indirect object pronouns
6	**Warm-up** (10 min.) • Actividad 15 • Audio Activity 8 • Homework check ✓**Formative Assessment** (10 min.) • Prueba 8B-4 with Study Plan: Indirect object pronouns	**Gramática y vocabulario en uso** (25 min.) • Presentation: The preterite of ***hacer*** and ***dar*** • View: GramActiva video • Actividades 17, 18, 19 • Interactive Whiteboard Grammar Activities • Fondo cultural • Audio Activity 9	**Wrap-up and Homework Options** (5 min.) • Core Practice 8B-7 • Writing Activity 13 • Prueba 8B-5 with Study Plan: The preterite of ***hacer*** and ***dar***
7	**Warm-up** (10 min.) • Actividad 20 • Homework check ✓**Formative Assessment** (10 min.) • Prueba 8B-5 with Study Plan: The preterite of ***hacer*** and ***dar***	**Gramática y vocabulario en uso** (15 min.) • Pronunciación • Actividad 21 • El español en el mundo del trabajo **¡Adelante!** (10 min.) • Presentación escrita: Steps 1, 5 • Perspectivas del mundo hispano	**Wrap-up and Homework Options** (5 min.) • Actividad 22 • Presentación escrita: Step 2
8	**Warm-up** (5 min.) • Homework check	**¡Adelante!** (25 min.) • Presentación escrita: Step 3 • Perspectivas del mundo hispano **Repaso del capítulo** (15 min.) • Vocabulario y gramática • Preparación para el examen 1, 2	**Wrap-up and Homework Options** (5 min.) • Presentación escrita: Step 4 • Preparación para el examen 3, 4, 5 • Instant Check
9	**Warm-up** (5 min.) • Homework check	**¡Adelante!** (40 min.) • Lectura • ¿Comprendes? • Fondo cultural • Videomisterio: *¿Eres tú, María?*, Episodio 8	**Wrap-up and Homework Options** (5 min.) • Core Practice 8B-8, 8B-9 • Videomisterio • Lectura • Examen del capítulo 8B
10	**Warm-up** (10 min.) • Homework check ✓**Summative Assessment** (40 min.) • Examen del capítulo 8B		

<table>
<tr><th colspan="4">BLOCK SCHEDULE (90 MINUTES)</th></tr>
<tr><th>DAY</th><th>Warm-up / Assess</th><th>Preview / Present / Practice / Communicate</th><th>Wrap-up / Homework Options</th></tr>
<tr><td>1</td><td>Warm-up (10 min.)
• Return Examen del capítulo 8A</td><td>Chapter Opener (5 min.)
• Objectives
• Arte y cultura
Vocabulario en contexto (55 min.)
• Presentation: Vocabulario en contexto
• Actividades 1, 2
• Presentation: Videohistoria Cómo ayudamos a los demás
• View: Videohistoria
• Video Activities 1, 2, 3, 4
• Actividad 3
Vocabulario en uso (15 min.)
• Interactive Whiteboard Vocabulary Activities
• Actividades 4, 5</td><td>Wrap-up and Homework Options (5 min.)
• Core Practice 8B-1, 8B-2, 8B-3, 8B-4
• Prueba 8B-1: Vocabulary recognition</td></tr>
<tr><td>2</td><td>Warm-up (10 min.)
• Actividad 6
• Fondo cultural
• Homework check
✓Formative Assessment (10 min.)
• Prueba 8B-1: Vocabulary recognition</td><td>Gramática y vocabulario en uso (65 min.)
• Actividad 8
• Fondos culturales
• Audio Activities 5, 6
• Communicative Pair Activity
• Exploración del lenguaje
• Presentation: The present tense of decir
• View: GramActiva video
• Interactive Whiteboard Grammar Activities
• Actividades 9, 10, 12</td><td>Wrap-up and Homework Options (5 min.)
• Core Practice 8B-5
• Actividad 7
• Writing Activities 10, 11
• Pruebas 8B-2, 8B-3 with Study Plans: Vocabulary production, The present tense of decir</td></tr>
<tr><td>3</td><td>Warm-up (10 min.)
• Actividad 11
✓Formative Assessment (15 min.)
• Pruebas 8B-2, 8B-3 with Study Plans: Vocabulary production, The present tense of decir</td><td>Gramática y vocabulario en uso (60 min.)
• Audio Activity 7
• Presentation: Indirect object pronouns
• View: GramActiva video
• Interactive Whiteboard Grammar Activities
• Actividades 13, 14
• Communicative Pair Activity
• Presentation: The preterite of hacer and dar
• View: GramActiva video
• Interactive Whiteboard Grammar Activities
• Actividades 17, 18, 19
• Fondo cultural
• Audio Activity 9</td><td>Wrap-up and Homework Options (5 min.)
• Core Practice 8B-6, 8B-7
• Writing Activity 12
• Actividades 15, 16
• Writing Activity 13
• Pruebas 8B-4, 8B-5 with Study Plans: Indirect object pronouns, The preterite of hacer and dar</td></tr>
<tr><td>4</td><td>Warm-up (5 min.)
• Audio Activity 8
• Homework check
• Actividad 20
✓Formative Assessment (15 min.)
• Pruebas 8B-4, 8B-5 with Study Plans: Indirect object pronouns, The preterite of hacer and dar</td><td>Gramática y vocabulario en uso (30 min.)
• Pronunciación
• Actividad 21
• El español en el mundo del trabajo
• Presentación escrita: Steps 1, 5
• Perspectivas del mundo hispano
¡Adelante! (35 min.)
• Lectura
• ¿Comprendes?
• Fondo cultural</td><td>Wrap-up and Homework Options (5 min.)
• Actividad 22
• Presentación escrita: Step 2
• Lectura
• Instant Check</td></tr>
<tr><td>5</td><td>Warm-up (5 min.)
• Homework check</td><td>¡Adelante! (45 min.)
• Presentación escrita: Step 3
Repaso del capítulo (35 min.)
• Vocabulario y gramática
• Preparación para el examen 1, 2, 3, 4, 5</td><td>Wrap-up and Homework Options (5 min.)
• Presentación escrita: Step 4
• Core Practice 8B-8, 8B-9
• Instant Check
• Examen del capítulo 8B</td></tr>
<tr><td>6</td><td>Warm-up (15 min.)
• Homework check
• Situation Cards
Repaso del capítulo (10 min.)
• Communicative Pair Activities
✓Summative Assessment (40 min.)
• Examen del capítulo 8B</td><td>¡Adelante! (20 min.)
• Videomisterio: ¿Eres tú, María?, Episodio 8</td><td>Wrap-up and Homework Options (5 min.)
• Videomisterio</td></tr>
</table>

Standards for *Capítulo* 8B

- To achieve the goals of the Standards, students will:

Communication

1.1 Interpersonal
- Talk about: volunteer work; community service; recycling and conservation; gifts and gift-giving; past activities in which people engaged; prestigious awards people have received

1.2 Interpretive
- Read and listen to information about: volunteer work; community service; recycling
- Read: a picture-based story; about protected areas of Costa Rica; a public service announcement about recycling; about Habitat for Humanity in Guatemala
- Listen to and watch a video about recycling and volunteer work
- Listen to information about tinglar tortoise protection
- View a video mystery series

1.3 Presentational
- Present information about: recycling; volunteer work; community service; tinglar tortoise protection
- Write about: past activities in which people engaged; prestigious awards people have received

Culture

2.1 Practices and Perspectives
- Discuss: recycling in Spain; ***la Asociación conservacionista de Monteverde*** in Costa Rica; ***la Hermandad de la Caridad*** in Seville
- Explain student volunteerism in Spanish-speaking countries

2.2 Products and Perspectives
- Describe Mexico's glass art made from recyclables

Connections

3.1 Cross-curricular
- Read about protected areas of Costa Rica
- Reinforce math skills
- Discuss recycling and environmental issues; Americorps

Comparisons

4.1 Language
- Talk about: vocabulary through the recognition of cognates; noun endings ***-dad, -tad, -ción,*** and ***-sión;*** the present tense of the verb ***decir;*** the pronunciation of ***gue, gui, que,*** and ***qui;*** the preterite of the verbs ***hacer*** and ***dar;*** the pronunciation of the letter ***x***
- Explain indirect object pronouns

4.2 Culture
- Compare: Spain's recycling program to local programs; reuse of recyclable materials in other products; involvement in volunteerisim projects; local programs in place to help the needy

Communities

5.1 Beyond the School
- Identify: ways to apply Spanish to volunteerism; opportunities for Spanish-speakers in the non-profit sector

5.2 Lifelong Learner
- View a video mystery series

Capítulo 8B Ayudando en la comunidad

Chapter Objectives

Communication

By the end of this chapter you will be able to:
- Listen to and read about community service
- Talk and write about volunteer activities and recycling
- Exchange information about volunteering

Culture

You will also be able to:
- Compare perspectives about volunteer activities in Spanish-speaking countries to your community
- Compare environmental efforts in Spain, Costa Rica, and other Spanish-speaking countries to programs in your community

You will demonstrate what you know and can do:
- Presentación escrita, p. 419
- Preparación para el examen, p. 423

You will use:

Vocabulary
- Recycling
- Places in a community
- Volunteer work

Grammar
- The present tense of *decir*
- Indirect object pronouns
- The preterite of *hacer* and *dar*

Exploración del mundo hispano

Country Connection
Helping in Your Community

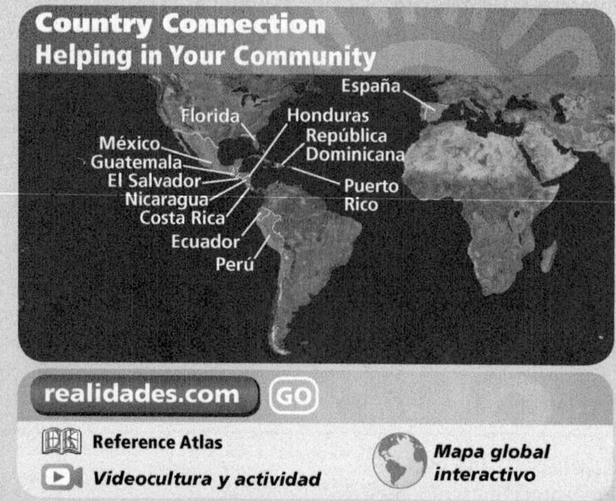

realidades.com GO

Reference Atlas

Videocultura y actividad

Mapa global interactivo

Una joven ayuda con un proyecto de voluntarios en Miami, Florida.

398 trescientos noventa y ocho
Tema 8 • Experiencias

ENRICH YOUR TEACHING

Using Backward Design

Have students preview the sample performance tasks on *Preparación para el examen,* p. 423, and connect them to the Chapter Objectives. Explain to students that by completing the sample tasks they can self-assess their learning progress.

Mapa global interactivo

Download the *Mapa global interactivo* files for Chapter 8B and preview the activities. Activity 1 looks at Peace Corps projects in Latin America. Activity 2 visits the Cloud Forest of Costa Rica, and Activity 3 looks at tortoise habitats in the Dominican Republic, Puerto Rico, and Costa Rica.

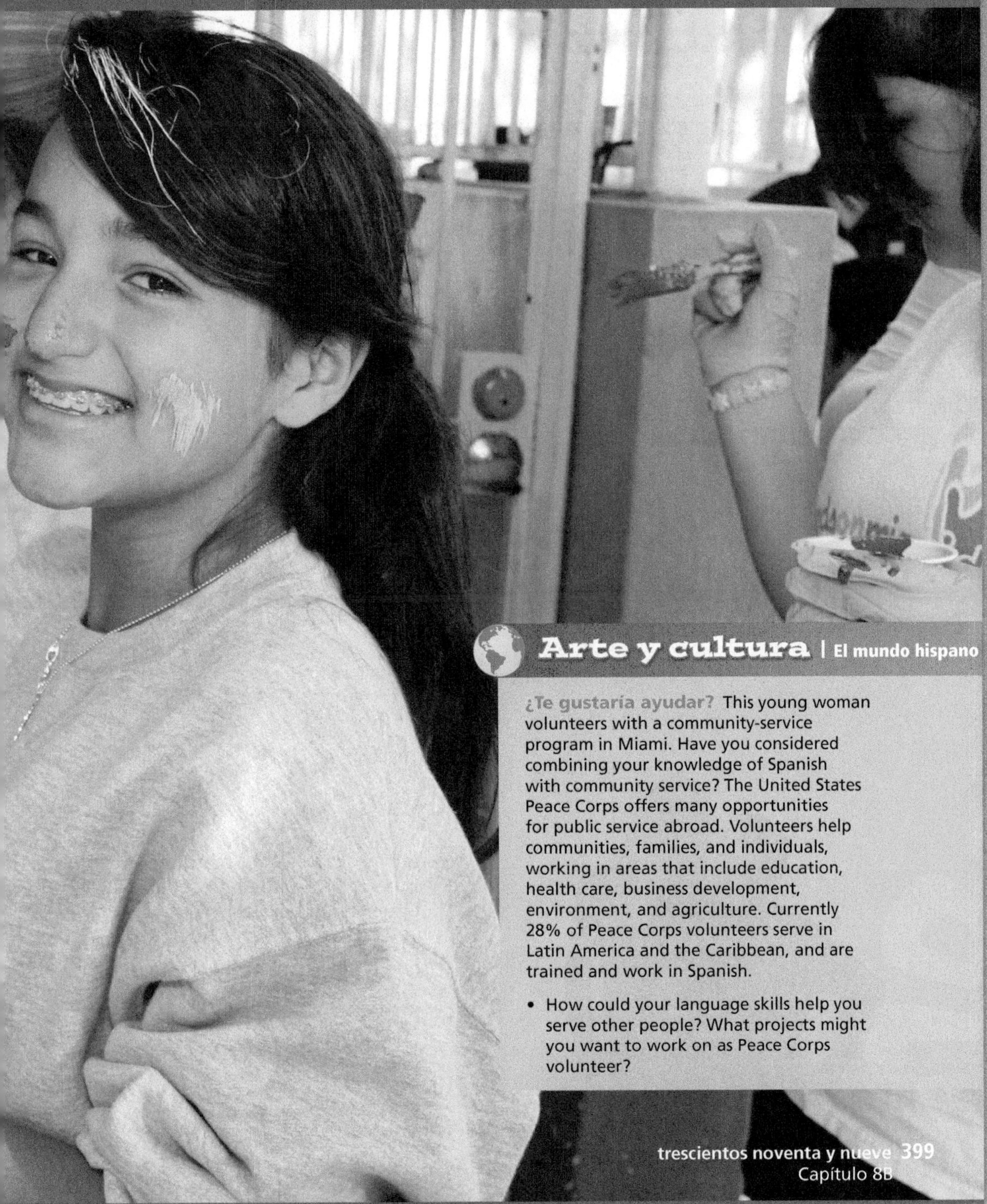

Arte y cultura | El mundo hispano

¿Te gustaría ayudar? This young woman volunteers with a community-service program in Miami. Have you considered combining your knowledge of Spanish with community service? The United States Peace Corps offers many opportunities for public service abroad. Volunteers help communities, families, and individuals, working in areas that include education, health care, business development, environment, and agriculture. Currently 28% of Peace Corps volunteers serve in Latin America and the Caribbean, and are trained and work in Spanish.

- How could your language skills help you serve other people? What projects might you want to work on as Peace Corps volunteer?

DIFFERENTIATED INSTRUCTION

Digital resources such as the ***Interactive Whiteboard*** activity banks, ***Videomodelos***, additional ***Online Activities, Study Plans***, automatically graded ***Leveled Workbook***, animated ***Grammar Tutorials, Flashcards***, and ***Vocabulary and Grammar Videos*** will help you reach students of different ability levels and learning styles.

STUDENTS NEEDING EXTRA HELP

Guided Practice Activities
- Flashcards, pp. 259–264
- Vocabulary Check, pp. 265–268
- Grammar Support, pp. 269–272

HERITAGE LEARNERS

Realidades para hispanohablantes
- Chapter Opener, pp. 310–311
- A primera vista, p. 312
- Videohistoria, p. 313
- Manos a la obra, pp. 314–321
- ¡Adelante!, pp. 322–327
- Repaso del capítulo, pp. 328–329

ADVANCED/PRE-AP*

Pre-AP* Resource Book,
- pp. 90–93

Communications Workbook
- Integrated Performance Assessment, p. 321

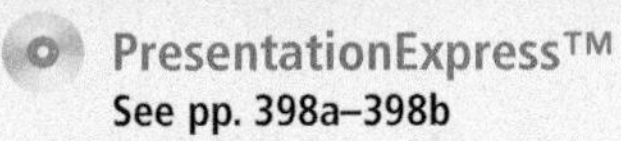

PresentationExpress™
See pp. 398a–398b

Chapter Opener

Core Instruction

Resources: Map Transparencies 12–15, 18

Suggestions: Have students tell you what activities they participate in that help the community. Ask them to name volunteer organizations at your school. Tell students that the *Videohistoria* for this chapter deals with the various volunteer projects being done by students. Remind students that they will continue to work with the past tense of verbs as they discuss how people helped others. Students will also learn about volunteer organizations. Discuss which organizations they are familiar with and tell what the aim of each group is.

Videocultura View *Las vacaciones* with the class to learn about places to visit in Spanish-speaking countries.

Arte y cultura

Standards: 5.1

Suggestions: Point out to students that volunteer organizations such as the Peace Corps are great launching places for careers in medicine, education, health care, and engineering. Volunteers get to travel and experience new cultures while making a contribution to humanity. Discuss whether or not they would be interested in joining the Peace Corps or a similar organization.

Answers will vary.

Mapa global interactivo, Actividad 1 Explore Peace Corps projects in Latin America.

Teaching with Photos

What is the mood of the photo? (Light and happy.) These people seem to be having a good time while performing a valuable service for their community. How might working side by side with others help a language learner improve their second language skills?

Vocabulario en contexto

Core Instruction

Standards: 1.2

Resources: Teacher's Resource Book: Input Script, p. 257, Clip Art, pp. 270–271, Audio Script, p. 258; Voc. and Gram. Transparencies 151–152; TPR Stories Book, pp. 107–121; Audio Program DVD: Cap. 8B, Tracks 1–2

Focus: Presenting new vocabulary for volunteer work, places in the community and recycling; the verb ***decir;*** the preterite of ***dar*** and ***hacer***

Suggestions: Use transparencies to present the vocabulary in three sections: people and places for volunteer work, recycling vocabulary, and names of in a community. Use the story in the *TPR Stories Book* to present the new vocabulary and grammar.

Have students scan the text to predict what the students' conversations are about. Then, while volunteers act out the dialogue, have other students make a list of unfamiliar words. Use visual cues or context to guide students to the meanings of the words on their list.

BELLRINGER REVIEW

Show Voc. and Gram. Transparency 121. Have students share with the class an activity that they do to help around the house.

Block Schedule

Bring in at least two of each of the recyclable items shown in the illustration on p. 401, and two recycling bins (use boxes if the bins are unavailable). Have students work in groups to write the vocabulary word for a recyclable item on an index card. Collect the index cards and put them in a bag. Divide the class into two teams and, as you pick out a vocabulary word, give them the command *¡Reciclen la lata!* As you say the command, have students get the appropriate item and put it into the correct box. The first team to correctly "recycle" gets a point, and the team with the most points wins.

▼ Objectives

Read, listen to, and understand information about
- volunteer work
- community-service tasks
- what people did to help others

Vocabulario en contexto

¿Quieres ayudar a los demás?

¡Trabaja como voluntario en tu comunidad!

ayudar en un jardín de verduras

trabajar en un proyecto de construcción

¡Habla con los Amigos del barrio hoy! ¡Tú puedes ser la diferencia!

hacer trabajo voluntario en una escuela primaria

trabajar en un campamento de deportes

—Mira el cartel. Hay **problemas*** en nuestra comunidad. Debemos trabajar como voluntarios.

—Tienes razón. ¿Cómo puedes **decidir** qué hacer? Es la primera **vez** que trabajo como voluntario.

—Quiero enseñar**les** a **los niños** a leer. **Es necesario** poder leer, ¿no crees?

*Even though *problema* ends in -a, it is a masculine noun: *Tengo un problema.*

DIFFERENTIATED INSTRUCTION

Multiple Intelligences

Naturalist: Have students create recycling bins for the school. Give them a box and have them illustrate and label items that should and should not be placed in the box. This is a good way for students to practice spelling and to reinforce meaning. Leave one recycling bin in your room and share the others with various staff members to display in their classrooms or offices.

—¿Me ayudas a **reciclar** la basura del río y de las calles? Son cosas que se pueden usar **otra vez. Dicen** que tenemos que **separarlas.**

—Bueno, te ayudo. ¿Adónde vamos a **llevarlas?**

—Al centro de reciclaje en la calle Bolívar.

1 El trabajo voluntario

Escuchar

Gloria investiga *(is researching)* los trabajos voluntarios en la comunidad. Señala cada lugar que ella menciona.

2 ¿Qué puedes reciclar?

Escuchar

Estás separando unos artículos en dos cajas: una es para el papel y la otra es para todos los demás artículos. Levanta una mano si debes poner el artículo en la caja para papel. Levanta dos manos si debes ponerlo en la otra caja.

Más práctica GO

	realidades.com	print
Instant Check	✔	
Guided WB pp. 259–264	✔	✔
Core WB pp. 148–149	✔	✔
Comm. WB p. 166	✔	✔
***Hispanohablantes* WB** p. 312		✔

1

Standards: 1.2

Resources: Teacher's Resource Book: Audio Script, p. 258; Audio Program DVD: Cap. 8B, Track 3; Answer Keys: Student Edition, p. 118

Focus: Listening to identify places to volunteer

Suggestions: Play the audio or read the script. Pause between each sentence to monitor students' answers.

Script and Answers:

1. **Me gustaría trabajar en una escuela primaria. *(escuela primaria)***
2. **Es importante recoger basura del río. *(al lado del río)***
3. **Mucha gente ayuda en los proyectos de construcción. *(proyecto de construcción)***
4. **Puedo ayudar en el centro de reciclaje. *(centro de reciclaje)***
5. **Me gustan las flores. Puedo ayudar en un jardín. *(un jardín)***
6. **Es importante recoger basura del lado de la calle. *(la calle)***

2

Standards: 1.2

Resources: Teacher's Resource Book: Audio Script, p. 258; Audio Program DVD: Cap. 8B, Track 4; Answer Keys: Student Edition, p. 118

Focus: Listening to identify recyclables

Suggestions: Play the audio or read the script. As a variation of this activity, have students draw two bins on a sheet of paper and label one ***papel,*** and the other ***otro.*** Then, have them write in the correct box the vocabulary word that they hear in each sentence. This may be useful in larger classes, where it may be difficult to monitor students' hand-raising.

Script and Answers:

1. **Aquí están los periódicos. *(una mano)***
2. **¿Dónde pongo la botella? *(dos manos)***
3. **¿Y las latas? *(dos manos)***
4. **Tengo unas revistas. *(una mano)***
5. **¿Y estos papeles? *(una mano)***
6. **Hay muchos vasos de vidrio aquí. *(dos manos)***

ENRICH YOUR TEACHING

Culture Note

Over the past 20 years, the United States has increased its recycling rate because many neighborhoods have increased their recycling. Paper is the largest waste product in the United States and represents about 30% of all our garbage. In 2009, for the first time, more than 60% of waste paper in the U.S. was recycled. For each ton of recycled paper, 17 trees and a considerable amount of energy resources are conserved.

Teacher-to-Teacher

Start a bulletin board display with the title: *¿Quieres ayudar a los demás?* As you go through the chapter, gradually add students' work to the display. Encourage students to look for appropriate materials in Spanish about recycling and volunteering to post on the bulletin board.

Videohistoria

Core Instruction

Standards: 1.2

Resources: Voc. and Gram. Transparencies 153–154; Audio Program DVD: Cap. 8B, Track 5

Focus: Presenting new vocabulary and grammar in the context of the story; previewing the language video

Suggestions:

Pre-reading: Have students point to pictures of volunteer work that they have done. Then, direct their attention to the *Strategy* and remind them to consider the possible volunteer jobs available as they read.

Reading: Play the audio and allow students to follow along in their books. Using the transparencies and pantomime, help students understand the new words in blue type.

Post-reading: Complete *Actividad* 3 to check comprehension.

Video

Core Instruction

Standards: 1.2

Resources: Teacher's Resource Book: Video Script, p. 262; Video Program: Cap. 8B; Video Program Teacher's Guide: Cap. 8B

Focus: Comprehending new vocabulary and grammar in authentic visual context

Suggestions:

Pre-viewing: Have students quickly scan the panels and captions to identify cognates that will help them understand the video.

Viewing: Remind students that they do not need to understand every word in the video to understand what is happening, but they should consider the context of the video and what they read in the *Videohistoria* reading to guide their comprehension. Show the video once without pausing; then show it again, stopping to check comprehension.

Post-viewing: Complete the Video Activities in the *Communication Workbook*.

Cómo ayudamos a los demás

Gloria, Raúl y Tomás hacen trabajo voluntario. ¿Por qué les gusta ser voluntarios?

Strategy

Activating prior knowledge
Before you read this selection, think about what you know about the topic of volunteer work. In what ways can one volunteer in your community?

Gloria: Raúl y yo trabajamos como voluntarios en **el Hospital** Nacional de Niños. ¿Quieres venir con nosotros?

Tomás: Sí. Me encanta el trabajo voluntario. Es **increíble** la satisfacción que **nos** da cuando ayudamos a los demás.

5

Raúl: El año pasado yo trabajé en un centro para **ancianos.** Pasé mucho tiempo con ellos.

6

Tomás: Soy miembro de un club que se llama "Casa Latina". El año pasado recogimos ropa **usada.** ¿Sabes que **hay que** separar la ropa y después lavarla?

Gloria: **¿Qué más hicieron** Uds.?

Tomás: Luego le **dimos** la ropa a **la gente pobre.**

Raúl: Aquí podemos reciclar el papel y las botellas.

Gloria: Mira, para el plástico, el papel y el vidrio.

Tomás: En mi comunidad también reciclamos.

DIFFERENTIATED INSTRUCTION

Multiple Intelligences

Interpersonal/Social: Have students create a flier to promote a canned food drive. Then copy the fliers to distribute to the entire class and to other classes. If possible, have these students set up a table in the school cafeteria to collect canned goods for a local food bank. Another option is to have them organize a clothing drive for a community organization.

Students with Learning Difficulties

Read through the *¿Comprendes?* sentences with students. Highlight the key words and phrases you want students to pay particular attention to when reading or listening to the *Videohistoria*.

á: Un momento. ¿Pueden
. reciclar este papel y
s botellas?
ás: ¡Por supuesto! Dame la
a de plástico.

3

Tomás: ¿Y qué hacen Uds. en el hospital?

Gloria: Ayudamos con los niños. Leemos libros y cantamos y jugamos con ellos. **A menudo** les traemos **juguetes.**

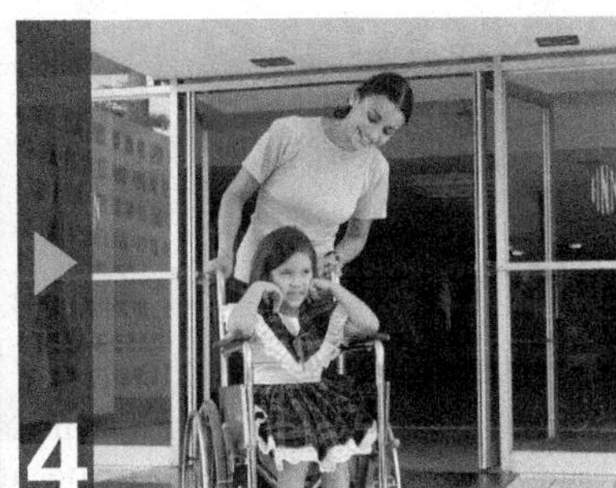

4

Gloria: A veces es difícil porque los niños están muy enfermos. Pero es **una experiencia inolvidable.**

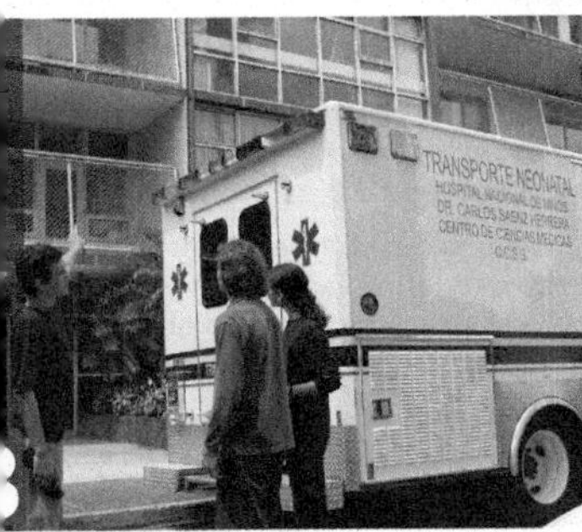

l: Mira. Aquí está el
pital. ¿Entramos?

3 ¿Comprendes?

Leer • Hablar

¿A quién describe cada frase: a Gloria, a Tomás o a Raúl? ¡Ojo! Una frase puede describir a más de una persona.

1. "Me gusta mucho el trabajo voluntario".
2. "Trabajo en un hospital para niños".
3. "Ayudar a los demás me da mucha satisfacción".
4. "Trabajo con los niños y les traigo juguetes".
5. "Me gusta pasar tiempo con los ancianos. Les leo el periódico y hablo con ellos".
6. "Recojo* la ropa usada".
7. "Es importante reciclar las botellas y latas".

**Recoger* is a regular *-er* verb with a spelling change in the *yo* form of the present tense: *recojo.*

Más práctica GO

	realidades.com	print
Instant Check	✔	
Guided WB pp. 265–268	✔	✔
Core WB pp. 150–151	✔	✔
Comm. WB pp. 160–162, 163	✔	✔
***Hispanohablantes* WB** p. 313		✔

3 Standards: 1.2, 1.1

Resources: Answer Keys: Student Edition, p. 119

Focus: Verifying understanding of the *Videohistoria*

Suggestions: Point out to students the *¡Ojo!* note and make sure they understand that a sentence can describe more than one person. When reviewing the answers, have students identify the panel that supports their answer.

Answers:

1. Gloria, Tomás y Raúl
2. Gloria y Raúl
3. Tomás y Gloria
4. Gloria y Raúl
5. Raúl
6. Tomás
7. Gloria, Tomás y Raúl

Extension: Have students read the sentences again to determine which ones they could use to describe themselves. Invite students to share their answers with a partner or in a small group.

Pre-AP* Support

- **Learning Objective:** Presentational Writing and Speaking
- **Activity:** As a post-viewing activity, have students work in small groups to write a short additional scene for the video. Have them imagine they go into the hospital and meet the Volunteer Services Coordinator. The coordinator greets them and asks if they have any previous volunteer experience. The students playing Gloria, Tomás and Raúl introduce themselves and briefly describe their past experiences, according to the information in video. Have volunteers act out their new scene in front of the class.
- ***Pre-AP* Resource Book:*** Comprehensive guide to Pre-AP* vocabulary skill development, pp. 51–57

Additional Resources

- Communication Wbk.: Audio Act. 5, p. 163
- Teacher's Resource Book: Audio Script, pp. 258–259
- Audio Program DVD: Cap. 8B, Track 7

ENRICH YOUR TEACHING

Culture Note

Amigos de las Américas is an international volunteer organization. All volunteers need to be able to speak Spanish before they travel to one of 15 countries in Central or South America. Volunteers help in many ways. Particular areas of emphasis are education and public health.

Teacher-to-Teacher

Invite representatives from a local volunteer organization or the Peace Corps to talk about volunteer opportunities. Ask the representative to talk about how speaking Spanish or another language other than English can be an advantage for working in almost any profession.

ASSESSMENT

Quiz: Vocabulary Recognition

- Prueba 8B-1: pp. 215–216

INTERACTIVE WHITEBOARD
Vocabulary Activities 8B

4 Standards: 1.2, 1.3

Resources: Teacher's Resource Book: Audio Script, p. 258; Audio Program DVD: Cap. 8B, Track 6; Answer Keys: Student Edition, p. 119

Focus: Listening to and writing sentences about recycling

Recycle: Colors

Suggestions: Play the audio or read the script. Allow students to listen once before they begin to write. For part 2, tell students that if they do not know what kind of recycling program exists in your community, they can write about an ideal program.

Script and Answers:

1. **Las personas llevan su basura en bolsas de plástico al centro de reciclaje.**
2. **En el centro hay cuatro cajas diferentes.**
3. **La primera caja es para la basura regular.**
4. **Hay que separar el vidrio. Lo ponemos en la caja verde.**
5. **Es necesario reciclar el papel. Usamos la caja azul para el papel.**
6. **La caja amarilla es para el plástico y las latas.**

Answers to part 2 will vary.

BELLRINGER REVIEW

Draw four recycling bins on the board. As a class activity, ask students to suggest a label for the outside of each bin and then brainstorm several items to be placed in each bin.

5 Standards: 1.1

Resources: Answer Keys: Student Edition, p. 120

Focus: Communicating about recycling

Suggestions: Remind students to pay attention to the gender and number of the item pictured so that they can use the correct direct object pronoun.

Answers:

Student A

1. **¿Hay que reciclar las latas?**
2. **¿... el periódico (los periódicos)?**
3. **¿... el plástico?**
4. **¿... las botellas?**
5. **¿... las cajas?**
6. **¿... las revistas?**

Student B

Answers will vary but direct object pronouns should be:

1. las	**3. lo**	**5. las**
2. los	**4. las**	**6. las**

Manos a la obra

Vocabulario en uso

Objectives

- Listen and write about a recycling program
- Talk and write about community service
- Discuss recycling in your community
- Read about Costa Rican and Spanish conservation efforts and compare them to programs in the United States

4 Escucha y escribe

Escuchar • Escribir

En la región de Cataluña en España, hay un sistema para reciclar que usan muchas personas.

España

1. En una hoja de papel, escribe los números del 1 al 6. Escucha la descripción de este sistema y escribe las frases.
2. Escribe tres frases para describir el sistema de reciclaje que usan, o que deben usar, en tu comunidad o barrio. Si quieres, usa las frases sobre Cataluña como modelo.

También se dice . . .

la lata = el bote *(España, Puerto Rico)*

En la Costa del Sol, España

5 El reciclaje 

Hablar

Habla con otro(a) estudiante sobre el reciclaje.

Modelo

A —*En nuestra comunidad, ¿hay que reciclar el papel?*
B —*¡Por supuesto! Lo separamos y lo ponemos en la caja azul.*
o: —*No sé. Nosotros no lo reciclamos.*

¿Recuerdas?

The direct object pronouns *lo, la, los,* and *las* replace nouns. They have the same gender and number as the nouns they replace.

1. 
2. 
3.
4.  
5. 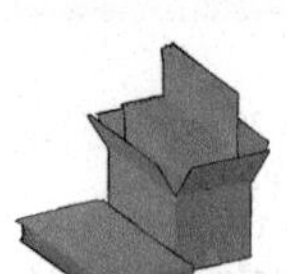
6. 

DIFFERENTIATED INSTRUCTION

Advanced Learners

Have students create profiles, like the ones for *Actividad* 6 on p. 405, giving their opinions on volunteer work. Give them colored paper to write their final copies on and suggest that they include a photo. Post the profiles in the classroom.

Heritage Language Learners

Ask students to use the pictures to compare the Spanish recycling system to that of their home country. Is recycling important there? How is the recycling system organized? If possible, have students compare with the one in your community.

6 El trabajo voluntario

Leer • Pensar • Escribir • Hablar

Según las preferencias de los jóvenes de las fotos, explica dónde debe trabajar cada uno de ellos.

Modelo

Samuel debe trabajar en un hospital.

Teresa: Prefiero los trabajos al aire libre* como un proyecto de construcción. Me encanta trabajar con las manos.

Rafael: Mi trabajo voluntario favorito es estar con niños en un campamento o una escuela primaria. Para mí es una experiencia inolvidable ver cómo aprenden tanto.

Samuel: Me gusta mucho ayudar a la gente pobre o a las víctimas de los desastres. Sus problemas son muy importantes para mí.

Bárbara: Me gusta mucho pasar tiempo con los ancianos. Son muy interesantes y simpáticos y me enseñan muchas cosas.

*outdoors

1. 
2. 
3. 
4.
5.
6. 

Fondo Cultural | España

El reciclaje Spain is one of the leading European countries in recycling. Spain's glass recycling program is called *Ecovidrio,* from the Spanish words for ecology *(ecología)* and glass *(vidrio). Ecovidrio* started in the 1990s and has been very successful. Glass recycling is an excellent way of reducing waste and protecting the environment.

- How do efforts in your community compare to glass recycling in Spain? What other efforts are available in your community?

Reciclaje de vidrio en Andalucía, España

Practice and Communicate 8B

6 Standards: 1.1, 1.2, 1.3

Resources: Answer Keys: Student Edition, p. 120

Focus: Writing and speaking about volunteer opportunities in a community

Suggestions: Remind students that some people have interests that would make them suitable to work at more than one location.

Answers will vary but may include:

1. **Rafael debe trabajar en un campamento.**
2. **Teresa debe trabajar en un jardín.**
3. **Bárbara debe trabajar en un centro para ancianos.**
4. **Teresa debe trabajar en un centro de reciclaje.**
5. **Samuel debe trabajar en un centro de protección civil.**
6. **Teresa debe ayudar a recoger basura al lado del río.**

Fondo cultural

Standards: 2.1, 4.2

Suggestions: Remind students that when they are answering the second question, they should consider all recyclables, not just glass. Refer them to the picture in *Actividad* 4 to point out the various types of recycling.

Answers will vary but may include the fact that many people take their recyclables directly to the plant, or that recyclable materials are picked up with other garbage.

ENRICH YOUR TEACHING

Teacher-to-Teacher

Have students promote recycling and Spanish in school by creating reminders for people to recycle. Post them in the school cafeteria, library, classrooms, and copy room.

21st Century Skills

Leadership and Responsibility Divide the class into four teams to research volunteer organizations in their area dedicated to one of the relief tasks mentioned in Activity 6. Have them focus their search on organizations that provide services in the Spanish-speaking community. Based on their findings, have each group report on opportunities available for volunteer work and propose a plan for class participation.

8B Practice and Communicate

Exploración del lenguaje
Core Instruction

Standards: 4.1

Resources: Answer Keys: Student Edition, p. 121

Suggestions: Before beginning, have students make a list of three words that end in *-ty* and three that end in *-sion*. Encourage them to predict what the Spanish word might be, and then to use their glossary or a Spanish-English dictionary to see if they are correct.

Answers:

generosity	**communication**
responsibility	**commission**
variety	**vegetation**
tranquility	**information**
liberty	**organization**
university	**presentation**

Fondo cultural

Standards: 2.2, 4.2

Suggestions: Direct students' attention to the examples of glassware in the photo. What differences do they notice between this glassware and items that are mass produced?

Answers will vary, buy may include stationery and other paper products, and bottles and jars.

7 Standards: 1.1, 1.3

Focus: Writing and speaking about recycling and volunteering

Suggestions: Before asking students to answer orally in a whole-class setting, let them discuss the questions in pairs.

Answers will vary.

Exploración del lenguaje

Nouns that end in *-dad, -tad, -ción,* and *-sión*

You know that *actividad* means "activity" and that *comunidad* means "community." In Spanish, nouns that end in *-dad* or *-tad* usually correspond to nouns in English that end in *-ty*. Nouns that end in *-dad* or *-tad* are feminine.

In a similar way, nouns in Spanish that end in *-ción* or *-sión* frequently correspond to nouns in English that end in *-tion* or *-sion*. These nouns are also feminine. You know that *construcción* means "construction" and that *posesión* means "possession."

Try it out! Figure out the meanings of these Spanish words.

la generosidad	*la comunicación*
la responsabilidad	*la comisión*
la variedad	*la vegetación*
la tranquilidad	*la información*
la libertad	*la organización*
la universidad	*la presentación*

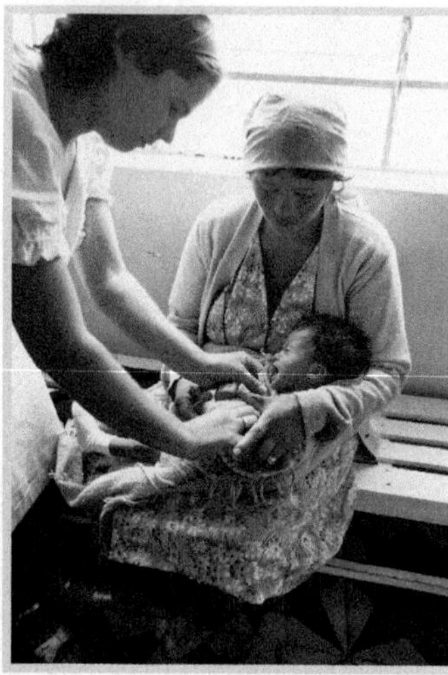

Una enfermera asiste a un bebé en una clínica de salud en Honduras.

Fondo Cultural | México

El arte de vidrio Mexico is known for its production of beautiful glassware. Many of these works of art—including a wonderful variety of drinking glasses, bowls, and vases—are made from recycled bottles or car windshields. The glass is melted and hand-blown into new forms. Artisans also make trays and decorative windows by cutting different pieces of colored glass into a collage, then melting them together into a single piece. Each recycled glass artwork is unique.

- What everyday items or art objects are you familiar with that are made from recycled materials?

Arte de vidrio de México

7 Y tú, ¿qué dices? | Talk!

Escribir • Hablar

1. ¿Qué cosas reciclas en casa? ¿Y en la escuela? ¿Qué más podemos reciclar?
2. ¿Qué puede hacer la gente para tener un barrio más limpio?
3. ¿Qué tipo de trabajo voluntario te gustaría hacer?
4. Escribe dos recomendaciones sobre cómo debemos ayudar a los demás.
5. ¿Qué organizaciones en tu comunidad reciben ropa usada o juguetes como donación? ¿Qué más podemos darles a las personas que necesitan ayuda?

DIFFERENTIATED INSTRUCTION

Multiple Intelligences

Visual/Spatial: Have students create and write captions for a collage that demonstrates the benefits of recycling or another environmental conservation effort. Students can post their collages in the classroom and give a brief presentation about them.

Students with Learning Difficulties

For *Actividad* 8, on p. 407, provide students with this formula to help them calculate the percentage: $\frac{\text{áreas protegidas}}{\text{área total}} \times 100$. On the board, demonstrate a simple example ($\frac{8}{10}$ is equal to .8 or 80%). Then, point out that the concept is the same. Students must divide 19,652 into 4,459 to find the percentage of protected land.

8 La protección de las áreas naturales

Leer • Hablar • Escribir

Costa Rica es un país increíble con mucha vegetación y una gran variedad de animales. La conservación de estas áreas naturales del país es muy importante. Por eso hay muchas áreas protegidas[1] en el país.

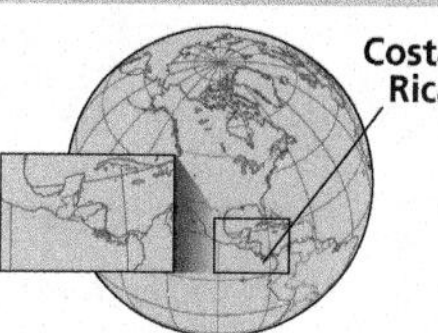

Conexiones | Las matemáticas

1. Mira el mapa de Costa Rica. Las áreas protegidas (como parques nacionales y reservas) están indicadas en verde. Estima qué porcentaje del área total del país es el área protegida.
2. Mira la tabla que compara las áreas protegidas con el área total del país. Trabaja con otro(a) estudiante para:
   - calcular qué porcentaje del área total es el área protegida.
   - comparar la respuesta con las estimaciones que hicieron Uds.

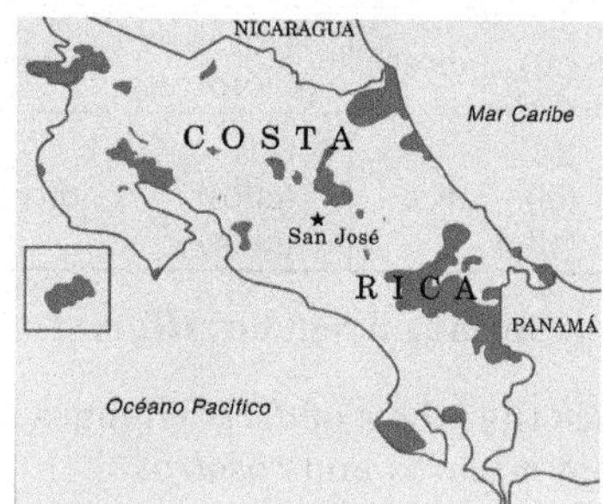

Áreas protegidas	Área total
4.656 millas cuadradas	19.730 millas cuadradas

3. Averigua[2] cuántas millas cuadradas tienen los Estados Unidos y cuántas de estas millas son parques nacionales o estatales y, por lo tanto[3], áreas protegidas. Busca la información en una enciclopedia o en el Internet.
4. Calcula qué porcentaje del área total de los Estados Unidos son estos parques. Preparen un informe sobre los resultados.

Modelo

El área total de los Estados Unidos es de ___ millas cuadradas.
___ millas cuadradas son parques nacionales o estatales.
Estos parques representan el ___ por ciento del país.

[1] protected [2] Figure out [3] therefore

Fondo cultural | Costa Rica

La Asociación Conservacionista de Monteverde in Costa Rica helps protect the rain forest in the Monteverde Cloud Forest Preserve. Young people from around the world come to help preserve the natural forest. Volunteers maintain trails and help in preservation projects.

- What programs in your community or state are similar to the program in Costa Rica?

Entrada a la Reserva Bosque Nuboso, Monteverde, Costa Rica

ENRICH YOUR TEACHING

Culture Note

Rotaplast International and Interplast are non-profit agencies that help children with congenital defects. Rotaplast is a group effort of North and South American surgeons, anesthelogists, and nurses. The doctors operate free of charge on children with cleft lips or palates. Local volunteers organize travel from the children's rural hometowns to the cities for surgery.

21st Century Skills

Technology Literacy Have students first research volunteer opportunities in the school or community that require knowledge of Spanish. Have each student who wants to be a volunteer submit a list of his or her skills and interests, along with a digital photo, so that an electronic volunteer directory can be created.

Practice and Communicate 8B

8 Standards: 1.2, 1.3, 3.1

Resources: Map Transparencies, 13; Answer Keys: Student Edition, p. 121

Focus: Using vocabulary to communicate about conservation

Suggestions: For Step 2, guide students through completion of the calculations by giving them a formula to work with. Refer to the map of Costa Rica and ask students whether or not the percentage they get seems logical based on the amount of shaded area. For Step 3, guide students to the information on national parks in the United States by using the keyword *National Park Service.*

Answers:

1. **Answers will vary.**
2. **El área protegida es 23,6 por ciento del área total del país.**

3-4. **El área total de los Estados Unidos es de 3.794.083 millas cuadradas.**
131.622,5 millas cuadradas son parques nacionales o estatales.
Estos parques representan el 3,5 por ciento del país.

Fondo cultural

Standards: 2.1, 3.1, 4.2

Suggestions: Help students answer the question by asking them what areas in your community or state are or should be protected. Once students identify places, they may be able to name the appropriate organizations.

Answers will vary.

Mapa global interactivo, Actividad 2 Visit the Cloud Forest of Costa Rica.

Additional Resources

- Communication Wbk.: Audio Act. 6, p. 163
- Teacher's Resource Book: Audio Script, p. 259, Communicative Pair Activity BLM, pp. 264–265
- Audio Program DVD: Cap. 8B, Track 8

ASSESSMENT

Prueba 8B-2 with Study Plan (online only)

Quiz: Vocabulary Production

- Prueba 8B-2: pp. 217–218

Gramática

Core Instruction

Standards: 4.1

Resources: Voc. and Gram. Transparency 155; Teacher's Resource Book: Video Script, p. 262; Video Program: Cap. 8B

INTERACTIVE WHITEBOARD
Grammar Activities 8B

Suggestions: Read through the *Gramática* box with students, noting that the ***yo*** form of ***decir*** is irregular. Point out that there is an ***e*** / ***i*** stem change in all forms of the verb except the ***nosotros*** and ***vosotros*** forms. Direct students' attention to the *¿Recuerdas?* Show the *GramActiva* Video, either as an introduction to the structure or as a follow-up after your own grammar explanation.

9 Standards: 1.2, 1.3

Resources: Answer Keys: Student Edition, p. 121

Focus: Conjugating the verb ***decir***

Suggestions: Point out the information in the *Nota* for question 2. Remind students that they will be using these sentences again in *Actividad* 10.

Answers:

1. **dicen**
2. **dice**
3. **dicen**
4. **dice**
5. **decimos**
6. **digo**
7. **dices**

Common Errors: Students sometimes apply the stem change to the ***nosotros*** form, producing ***dicimos.*** Remind them that stem changes do not apply to the ***nosotros*** and ***vosotros*** forms. Tell them that only stressed syllables have a stem change.

10 Standards: 1.2, 1.3

Focus: Writing about recycling using forms of ***decir***

Suggestions: Point out that students will change all of the sentences to the ***yo*** form. Remind students that these sentences will be used again in *Actividad* 11.

Answers will vary.

Manos a la obra

Objectives

- Summarize what people say about volunteering
- Read and write about recycling in Puerto Rico
- Exchange information while comparing opinions about environmentalism

Gramática

The present tense of *decir*

The verb *decir* means "to say" or "to tell." Here are all its present-tense forms:

(yo)	digo	(nosotros) (nosotras)	decimos
(tú)	dices	(vosotros) (vosotras)	decís
Ud. (él) (ella)	dice	Uds. (ellos) (ellas)	dicen

The *yo* form is irregular: ***digo.***

Notice that the *e* of *decir* changes to *i* in all forms except *nosotros* and *vosotros.*

¿Recuerdas?

You have used forms of *decir* in the questions *¿Cómo se dice?* and *Y tú, ¿qué dices?*

Más ayuda realidades.com

GramActiva **Video**
Tutorial: *Decir*
Animated Verbs
GramActiva **Activity**

9 Hay que reciclar

Escribir

Escribe las formas apropiadas del verbo *decir* para completar las opiniones de diferentes personas sobre cómo tener una comunidad limpia.

1. Mis padres ____ que es necesario recoger la basura en las calles.
2. La gente ____ que es importante llevar los periódicos a un centro de reciclaje.
3. Las personas en mi comunidad ____ que tenemos que separar la basura.
4. Mi profesor de biología ____ que es necesario reciclar el vidrio y el plástico.
5. Nosotros ____ que debemos limpiar nuestro barrio y comunidad.
6. Yo ____ que el reciclaje es muy importante.
7. ¿Qué ____ tú?

Nota

Use the *él / ella* form of the verb with *la gente.*

To tell *what* people say, use ***que*** after *decir.*

- La gente **dice que** . . .

10 ¿Qué dices tú?

Leer • Escribir

Lee las frases del 1 al 5 de la Actividad 9. Escribe otras para decir si haces estas mismas actividades a menudo, a veces o nunca.

Más práctica GO

realidades.com | prin

Instant Check	✔	
Guided WB p. 269	✔	✔
Core WB p. 152	✔	✔
Comm. WB pp. 164, 167	✔	✔
Hispanohablantes **WB** pp. 314–316		✔

DIFFERENTIATED INSTRUCTION

Advanced Learners/Pre-AP*

Have students write a short newspaper article about recycling in their community. In the article, students should use the verb ***decir,*** quoting what experts and officials say about the topic. As a variation, have students use presentation software to create a PowerPoint presentation for the class.

Students with Learning Difficulties

Before students begin work on *Actividad* 9, have them read through the sentences and correctly identify the subject of each one.

11 ¿Cómo debemos participar más?

Escribir • Hablar

1. Forma un grupo con cuatro estudiantes. Comparen las frases que escribieron para la Actividad 10 y digan con qué frecuencia *(how often)* todos hacen las cosas. Cada grupo va a presentar sus frases a la clase.
2. Cada estudiante debe anotar las respuestas de todos los grupos.

Modelo

En nuestro grupo, una persona dice que recoge la basura en las calles a menudo. Tres personas dicen que no la recogen nunca.

3. Después de escuchar y anotar las frases de todos los grupos, calcula el porcentaje de estudiantes que hacen estas actividades a menudo, a veces o nunca. Escribe frases sobre los resultados.

Modelo

En esta clase, el 10 por ciento de las personas dicen que recogen la basura en las calles a menudo; el 70 por ciento dicen que la recogen a veces; y el 20 por ciento dicen que no la recogen nunca.

12 Las 3 Rs

Leer • Hablar • Escribir

Lee el anuncio que está abajo *(below)*. Habla de Puerto Rico y la importancia de la conservación. Luego contesta las preguntas.

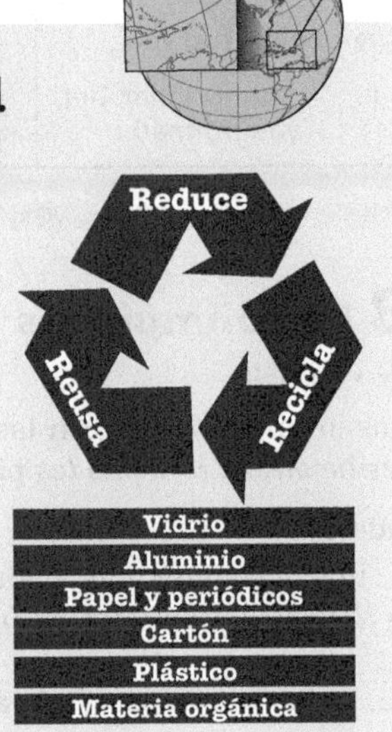

¡Tú puedes ser parte de la solución del problema de la basura en nuestra isla!

Recuerda esta guía práctica de las 3Rs

Reduce: Cuando vas de compras, decide no comprar cosas que no son necesarias.

Reusa: Usa un producto, objeto o material varias veces[1]. No debes tirar[2] a la basura las cosas que puedes usar otra vez.

Recicla: Usa los mismos materiales otra vez o usa un proceso natural o industrial para hacer el mismo o nuevos productos.

Lo que compras, comes, cultivas o tiras puede ser la diferencia entre un buen futuro o un futuro de destrucción para Puerto Rico.

[1]several times [2]throw away

1. ¿Cómo puedes "reducir"? ¿Qué cosas compras o usas a veces que no son necesarias?
2. ¿Cómo puedes reciclar o reusar cosas en casa o en la escuela?
3. Según las frases que escribiste para la Actividad 11, escribe tres recomendaciones para cuidar *(take care of)* más tu comunidad.

ENRICH YOUR TEACHING

Culture Note

The island of Puerto Rico has diverse ecosystems and valuable resources but it is sometimes difficult to implement recycling programs because of limited landfill options. This is due to the fact that Puerto Rico's population of almost 4 million people inhabit an island that is only about 100 miles long and 35 miles wide.

Teacher-to-Teacher

Look online for information about volunteer and environmental groups in Spanish-speaking countries. Download information about the groups. Keep these authentic materials in the classroom to share with your students.

11 Standards: 1.1, 1.2, 1.3, 3.1

Focus: Writing and speaking about recycling

Suggestions: Provide students with a table to fill in as they listen. Across the top of the table, write the words ***a menudo, a veces,*** and ***nunca*** in three columns. Use the suggestions from *Actividad* 9 and make a row for each one. As they listen, have students tally the names of their classmates on the table. Remind them that to calculate the percentage, they should take the number of students in each box on their table and divide that number by the total number of students in the class.

Answers will vary.

Pre-AP* Support

- **Learning Objective:** Interpersonal Writing
- **Activity 11:** Have students turn the group's answers into an e-mail to you, the teacher, summarizing their findings.

12 Standards: 1.1, 1.2, 1.3, 4.1

Resources: Voc. and Gram. Transparency 158; Answer Keys: Student Edition, p. 122

Focus: Reading and writing about recycling

Suggestions: Have students recall where they see the recycling symbol in their everyday lives. Brainstorm what kinds of products are commonly labeled with the symbol. Point out the cognates before students read. After students finish the reading, ask a volunteer to summarize.

Answers will vary but may include:

1. **Puedo comprar sólo las cosas que son necesarias.**
2. **Puedo llevar los productos usados a un centro de reciclaje.**
3. **Answers will vary.**

Additional Resources

- Communication Wbk.: Audio Act. 7, p. 164
- Teacher's Resource Book: Audio Script, p. 259
- Audio Program DVD: Cap. 8B, Track 9

ASSESSMENT

Prueba 8B-3 with Study Plan (online only)

Quiz: The present tense of *decir*
- Prueba 8B-3: p. 219

Gramática

Core Instruction

Standards: 4.1

Resources: Voc. and Gram. Transparency 156; Teacher's Resource Book: Video Script, pp. 262–263; Video Program: Cap. 8B

INTERACTIVE WHITEBOARD
Grammar Activities 8B

Suggestions: Have two volunteers role-play one person giving something to the other. As the students do this, narrate their action using indirect object pronouns. Have the other students provide sample sentences in English that contain indirect object pronouns. Remind students that, unlike in English, prepositions such as "for" or "to" are not necessary when using indirect object pronouns in Spanish. Use the *GramActiva* Video either as an introduction to the structure or as a follow-up after your own grammar explanation.

13 Standards: 1.3

Resources: Answer Keys: Student Edition, p. 122

Focus: Using indirect object pronouns

Suggestions: Point out to students that they need to know what the indirect object is before they can choose the correct indirect object pronoun. Remind them that the indirect object follows the word ***a*** in each sentence.

Answers:

1. Les
2. Le
3. Les
4. Les
5. Nos
6. Me
7. Nos

Common Errors: Students often confuse direct object pronouns ***(lo, los, la, las)*** with indirect object pronouns. Remind them that ***le*** and ***les*** are the indirect object pronouns.

Theme Project

Students can perform Step 4 at this point. Be sure they understand your corrections and suggestions. (For more information, see p. 372-b.)

Gramática

Objectives

- Write about and discuss what you and others do for people in the community
- Play a listening comprehension game with classmates

Indirect object pronouns

An indirect object tells *to whom* or *for whom* an action is performed. Indirect object pronouns are used to replace an indirect object noun.

Les doy dinero.	*I give money to them.*
Te llevo el vidrio y las latas.	*I'll bring you the glass and the cans.*
¿Nos reciclas estas botellas, por favor?	*Will you please recycle these bottles for us?*

The indirect object pronoun comes right before the conjugated verb. Here are the different indirect object pronouns:

SINGULAR		PLURAL	
me	(to / for) me	nos	(to / for) us
te	(to / for) you	os	(to / for) you
le	(to / for) him, her; you *(formal)*	les	(to / for) them; you *(formal)*

When an infinitive follows a conjugated verb, the indirect object pronoun can be attached to the infinitive or be placed before the conjugated verb.

Quiero darle un juguete al niño.
o: Le quiero dar un juguete al niño.

Because *le* and *les* have more than one meaning, you can make the meaning clear, or show emphasis, by adding *a* + the corresponding name, noun, or pronoun.

Les damos lecciones **a Miguel y a Felipe.**
Les damos lecciones **a los niños.**
Les damos lecciones **a ellos.**

Más ayuda realidades.com

- ***GramActiva* Video Tutorials:** Indirect object pronouns, Indirect objects
- ***Canción de hip hop:*** *Experiencia inolvidable*
- ***GramActiva* Activity**

13 Las Olimpíadas Especiales

Leer • Escribir

Unos jóvenes ayudan con las Olimpíadas Especiales. Escribe *me, te, le, nos* o *les* para completar cada frase.

Modelo

___ llevan comida a los padres de los niños.
Les llevan comida a los padres de los niños.

1. ___ dan naranjas y jugo a los participantes.
2. ___ hacen una donación a la señora que organizó el evento.
3. ___ traen agua a mis compañeros porque tienen sed.
4. ___ dan lecciones de varios deportes a los participantes.
5. ___ dicen a nosotros que debemos preparar los concursos *(contests)*.
6. ___ traen a mí un sándwich porque tengo hambre.
7. ___ dicen a nosotros que necesitan más ayuda.

Voluntarios y atletas en las Olimpíadas Especiales, Miami

DIFFERENTIATED INSTRUCTION

Heritage Language Learners

Have students write a short composition in which they use at least six examples of indirect object pronouns. You might want to give them topics such as a gift exchange, a mix-up, or a family gathering, all of which might easily elicit the use of the pronouns. Once students have written their rough drafts, have them peer-edit the compositions and prepare a final draft.

Students with Learning Difficulties

Many students have difficulty learning the correct word order for sentences with indirect object pronouns. To help them, write a sentence on index cards, putting each word on a separate card. Mix up the cards. Groups of students can then practice reassembling the cards in the correct order to form the sentences.

14 Juego

Hablar • GramActiva

1. Tu profesor(a) va a dividir a los estudiantes en grupos de cinco. Cada grupo forma una fila *(line)*. Las primeras personas de cada fila van al frente de la clase y el (la) profesor(a) les dice una frase.
2. Las personas regresan a sus grupos y le dicen a la primera persona de la fila, *"Me dice que . . . "* y repite la frase del (de la) profesor(a). Luego la primera persona repite la frase a la segunda persona de la fila.
3. Cada grupo continúa hasta decir la frase a la última *(last)* persona. Esta persona escribe la frase que escucha en una hoja de papel. El grupo más rápido y que dice la frase más correcta gana *(wins)* el juego.

15 ¿Cómo ayuda la gente a los demás?

Escribir

Escribe frases para decir cómo la gente ayuda a los demás. Usa las palabras de las listas y *a menudo, a veces* o *nunca*.

dar	dinero	ropa usada	los pobres
enseñar	flores	juguetes	los niños
comprar	cuentos	periódicos	las personas enfermas
llevar	comida	revistas	los ancianos
leer	una lección de . . .		

Modelo

A veces la gente les lleva comida a los ancianos.

16 Regalos

Escribir • Hablar

1. En una hoja de papel, haz dos listas. En la primera, escribe los nombres de cinco personas. En la segunda, escribe un regalo para cada una de estas personas.
2. Habla con otro(a) estudiante sobre los regalos que vas a comprar.

Modelo

A —*¿A quién vas a comprar un regalo?*
B —*Le voy a comprar un regalo a mi abuela.*
A —*¿Qué le vas a comprar?*
B —*Le voy a comprar flores.*

Más práctica GO

realidades.com | print

	realidades.com	print
Instant Check	✔	
Guided WB pp. 270–271	✔	✔
Core WB p. 153	✔	✔
Comm. WB pp. 165, 168	✔	✔
Hispanohablantes WB pp. 317–318		✔

14 Standards: 1.2

Focus: Reviewing indirect object pronouns

Recycle: *Decir*

Suggestions: Remind students to use the indirect object pronouns as they pass the message through the line.

Answers will vary.

Extension: Play the game again, letting the winning group choose a leader to come up with a secret sentence with which to begin the game.

15 Standards: 1.3

Focus: Writing about helping others

Recycle: Expressions of frequency

Suggestions: To personalize the activity, have students use themselves, family members, and people in their school as the subjects of their sentences.

Answers will vary.

16 Standards: 1.1, 1.3

Focus: Writing and speaking about giving gifts

Recycle: Gift items

Suggestions: Brainstorm a list of possible gifts that students could mention. Remind students to take turns being Student A and Student B.

Answers will vary.

Additional Resources

- Communication Wbk.: Audio Act. 8, p. 165
- Teacher's Resource Book: Audio Script, pp. 259–260
- Audio Program DVD: Cap. 8B, Track 10

ENRICH YOUR TEACHING

Culture Note

Founded in the United States in 1968, the Special Olympics have grown steadily over the years. Now over 150 countries participate in the various tournaments that take place. The most important tournaments are the Special Olympics World Summer and World Winter Games, which are held at alternating four-year intervals. Special Olympics events attract more than one milion athletes worldwide. All Spanish-speaking countries are involved with Special Olympics. In Central and South America, there are over 60,000 athletes who participate.

ASSESSMENT

Prueba 8B-4 with Study Plan (online only)

Quiz: Indirect Object Pronouns

- Prueba 8B-4: p. 220

Gramática

Core Instruction

Standards: 4.1

Resources: Voc. and Gram. Transparency 157; Teacher's Resource Book: Video Script, p. 263; Video Program: Cap. 8B

INTERACTIVE WHITEBOARD
Grammar Activities 8B

Suggestions: To present the lesson, write commands for giving something to another person. Randomly distribute these to students as they enter the room and, when you give them a signal, have them perform the action shown. Guide the presentation by narrating the actions: *¿Qué hizo Jon? Él le dio el libro a ella.* You may wish to give various students the same action to elicit various forms of the verbs. Remind students that there are no accent marks on either verb. Use the *GramActiva* Video either as an introduction to the structure or as a follow-up.

17 Standards: 1.2, 1.3

Resources: Answer Keys: Student Edition, p. 122

Focus: Writing in the preterite

Recycle: Preterite of *-ar, -er* and *-ir* verbs and *ir*

Suggestions: Have students read the paragraph once before trying to fill in the blanks. Reproduce the text on a transparency for review and have volunteers provide the correct answers.

Answers:

1. decidimos
2. hicimos
3. llevamos
4. dio
5. visitamos
6. dimos
7. hablaron
8. dieron
9. hice

Fondo cultural

Standards: 2.1, 4.2

Suggestions: As students discuss the question, remind them that a person "in need" does not have to be poor or old. They should also consider community programs designed to help youths and adults in social or educational areas.

Answers will vary but may include *Meals on Wheels* and *Big Brother/Big Sister* organizations.

Gramática

Objectives

- Listen to a description of disaster-relief efforts
- Exchange information and write about what you and others did
- Read and write about a program to protect sea turtles

The preterite of *hacer* and *dar*

Hacer and *dar* are irregular verbs in the preterite. Notice that these verbs do not have any accent marks in the preterite.

- The preterite stem for *hacer* is *hic-*. In the *Ud./él/ella* form, the *-c-* changes to a *-z-* so that it keeps the "s" sound: *hizo.*
- The preterite stem for *dar* is *di-*. The same stem is used for all the preterite forms.

(yo)	hice	(nosotros) (nosotras)	hicimos
(tú)	hiciste	(vosotros) (vosotras)	hicisteis
Ud. (él) (ella)	hizo	Uds. (ellos) (ellas)	hicieron

(yo)	di	(nosotros) (nosotras)	dimos
(tú)	diste	(vosotros) (vosotras)	disteis
Ud. (él) (ella)	dio	Uds. (ellos) (ellas)	dieron

¿Recuerdas?

You used the preterite *tú* form of *hacer* when you asked, *¿Qué hiciste?*

Más ayuda realidades.com

GramActiva Video Animated Verbs

GramActiva Activity

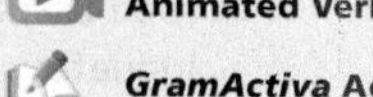

17 En un hospital

Leer • Escribir

Una joven habla de su experiencia como voluntaria en un hospital. Escribe los verbos en el pretérito para completar las frases.

Mis amigos y yo __1.__ *(dar / decidir)* hacer un trabajo voluntario en un hospital. Nosotros __2.__ *(ir / hacer)* dibujos para los ancianos en el hospital. La semana pasada una amiga y yo __3.__ *(llevar / hablar)* los dibujos al hospital. La enfermera[1] nos __4.__ *(dar / decidir)* permiso para entrar en los cuartos de varios ancianos. Nosotros __5.__ *(llevar / visitar)* a los ancianos y les __6.__ *(decidir / dar)* los dibujos. Los ancianos nos __7.__ *(hablar / llevar)* de sus familias y nos __8.__ *(decidir / dar)* abrazos.[2] Ésta fue la primera vez que yo __9.__ *(hacer / llevar)* un trabajo voluntario. Fue una experiencia inolvidable para nosotros. Vamos a regresar al hospital otra vez.

[1] nurse [2] hugs

Fondo Cultural | España

El Hospital de la Caridad, a hospice in Seville, Spain, was founded in the 1600s by the monks of *la Hermandad de la Caridad* (Charity Brotherhood). Today, the brothers still look after people who are old or poor, as part of a long tradition of caring for the needy.

- What programs in your community provide support for people in need?

El Hospital de la Caridad en Sevilla, España

DIFFERENTIATED INSTRUCTION

Advanced Learners

Have students prepare a pamphlet that outlines volunteering options in the community. For each organization that they name, have students obtain contact information and write the duties of the volunteers.

Heritage Language Learners

Have students write a mission statement for a real or fictitious community organization. You may wish to provide them with a copy of a sample mission statement, such as the one for your school, as an example.

18 Las donaciones

Escuchar • Escribir

Vas a escuchar cómo varias personas y organizaciones, como la Cruz Roja, ayudaron a las víctimas de un desastre en El Salvador. En una hoja de papel, escribe los números del 1 al 6. Escribe las frases que escuchas.

La Cruz Roja ayuda en El Salvador.

19 ¿Qué hicieron el sábado pasado?

Escribir • Hablar

1. Escribe lo que hicieron estas personas el fin de semana pasado.

tu mejor amigo(a)	tu madre (padre)
tú y tus amigos	tu profesor(a) de . . .
tus amigos(as)	tú

2. Habla con otro(a) estudiante sobre lo que hicieron las personas.

Modelo

tus amigos

A —*¿Qué hicieron tus amigos el fin de semana pasado?*

B —*Mis amigos fueron al río. Y tus amigos, ¿qué hicieron ellos?*

A —*Vieron una película en el cine.*

o: —*No sé qué hicieron ellos.*

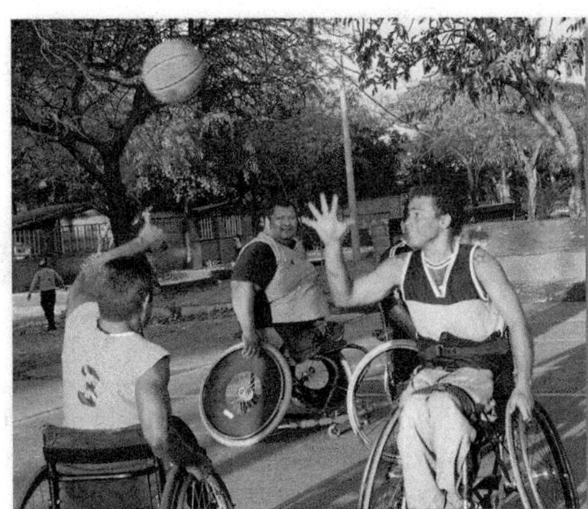

Un grupo de amigos juegan al básquetbol en Managua, Nicaragua.

20 Y tú, ¿qué dices?

Escribir • Hablar

1. ¿Qué hiciste el viernes pasado? ¿Qué hicieron tus amigos?
2. ¿Qué hizo tu familia el verano pasado?
3. ¿Qué les diste a tus hermanos o a tus amigos para su cumpleaños? ¿Qué te dieron a ti?
4. ¿Qué hizo la gente de tu comunidad el año pasado para ayudar a los pobres o a las víctimas de un desastre?
5. ¿Hizo tu barrio algo para ayudar a los ancianos o a los niños? ¿Qué?

Más práctica GO

realidades.com | print

	realidades.com	print
Instant Check	✔	
Guided WB p. 272	✔	✔
Core WB p. 154	✔	✔
Comm. WB pp. 165, 319	✔	✔
Hispanohablantes WB pp. 319–321		✔

ENRICH YOUR TEACHING

Teacher-to-Teacher

To practice the preterite structures, have students keep a journal. Provide students with two or three questions at the start of each class to respond to in their journal. For more advanced groups, allow students to write to the best of their ability without prompts. When you collect the journals, write responses to the students, and ask them follow-up questions to keep the dialogue going.

Practice and Communicate 8B

18 Standards: 1.2, 1.3

Resources: Teacher's Resource Book: Audio Script, p. 260; Audio Program DVD: Cap. 8B, Track 11; Answer Keys: Student Edition, p. 123

Focus: Listening and writing about how people helped others

Suggestions: Play the audio or read the script aloud several times so that students may review their answers.

Script and Answers:

1. **Los voluntarios hicieron mucho para ayudar a las personas.**
2. **Muchos estudiantes en los Estados Unidos dieron dinero.**
3. **Otras personas les dieron ropa y zapatos usados.**
4. **Nosotros les dimos botellas de agua y comida.**
5. **La Cruz Roja les dio camas a muchas personas.**
6. **Una familia de mi comunidad trabajó como voluntaria allí.**

19 Standards: 1.1, 1.3

Focus: Writing and speaking about the past

Recycle: Leisure activities, sports

Suggestions: Have students brainstorm a list of activities that they, their families, or their friends did over the weekend.

Answers will vary.

20 Standards: 1.1, 1.3

Focus: Writing and speaking about past events

Suggestions: You may want to have students write these answers in their notebooks in the form of a journal entry.

Additional Resources

- Communication Wbk.: Audio Act. 9, p. 165
- Teacher's Resource Book: Audio Script, pp. 260–261, Communicative Pair Activity BLM, pp. 266–267
- Audio Program DVD: Cap. 8B, Track 13

ASSESSMENT

Prueba 8B-5 with Study Plan (online only)

Quiz: The preterite of *hacer* and *dar*

- Prueba 8B-5: p. 221

21 Standards: 1.1, 1.3

Resources: Teacher's Resource Book: GramActiva BLM, p. 269

Focus: Writing questions to use vocabulary and grammar in context

Suggestions: Provide students with copies of popular magazines or have them use the Internet if they cannot name enough people from memory.

Answers will vary.

Pronunciación

Core Instruction

Standards: 4.1

Resources: Teacher's Resource Book: Audio Script, p. 260; Audio Program DVD: Cap. 8B, Track 12

Suggestions: After you model the typical pronunciation of the letter ***x*** for students, point out the exception noted in the right-hand column. Read the picture caption to demonstrate the difference. Remind students that they are not only reading the questions for the *Try it out!* but they should also answer in a way that will practice pronunciation of the letter ***x***.

Pre-AP* Support

- **Learning Objective:** Interpretive: Print and Audio
- **Activity:** Distribute Clip Art to groups of four students and have them use ***dar*** + **indirect object pronouns** using the clip art as props; e.g., *Yo te doy una manzana.* Have them pose questions in the third person such as *¿Quién le dio una manzana a ...?*
- ***Pre-AP* Resource Book:*** Comprehensive guide to Pre-AP* communication skill development, pp. 10–57

Block Schedule

Have students use the results of *Actividad* 21 to have an awards ceremony. In groups of four or five, have students prepare a short skit in which two of them are the hosts of the ceremony, and the others play the roles of celebrities accepting the prizes. Encourage humor and creativity.

21 Juego

Escribir • Hablar

1. En grupos de cuatro, deben pensar en diferentes premios *(prizes)* que reciben las personas: por ejemplo, el premio Nobel, el Heisman, el Óscar, el Emmy, el Golden Globe o el Grammy. Cada uno escribe una pregunta que tu grupo va a hacerle a otro grupo sobre los premios que dieron el año pasado.
2. Tu grupo debe leer una de las preguntas a otro grupo, que tiene 30 segundos para contestarla. Si el grupo contesta bien la primera vez, recibe tres puntos. Si contesta bien la segunda vez, recibe un punto. Si contesta mal, tu grupo debe decirles la respuesta.

Modelo

A —*¿A quién le dieron el Óscar por ser la mejor actriz el año pasado?*
B —*Le dieron el premio a . . .*

Para decir más . . .

la actriz	actress
el actor	actor
el / la cantante	singer
el / la atleta	athlete

Al autor colombiano Gabriel García Márque le dieron el premio Nobel de Literatura.

Pronunciación

The letter *x*

The letter *x* is pronounced several ways. When it is between vowels or at the end of a word, it is pronounced /ks/. Listen to and say these words:

examen	*taxi*	*aproximadamente*
exactamente	*dúplex*	*éxito*

When the *x* is at the beginning of a word, it is usually pronounced /s/. At the end of a syllable, the *x* can be pronounced /s/, /ks/, or /gs/. Listen to and say these words:

xilófono	*explicar*	*experiencia*
exploración	*experimento*	*experto*

Try it out! Work with a partner to ask and answer these questions, paying special attention to how you pronounce the letter *x*.

1. ¿En qué clase son más difíciles los exámenes?
2. ¿Qué clase tienes durante la sexta hora?
3. ¿En qué clase haces experimentos? ¿Qué tipo de experimentos haces?
4. ¿En qué clase hablas o escribes mucho de tus experiencias personales?

In the 1500s, the *x* represented the "h" sound of the Spanish letter *j*. That is why you see some words, like México, Oaxaca, and Texas written with *x*, even though the *x* is pronounced like the letter *j*. In words from indigenous languages of Mexico and Central America, the *x* has the /sh/ sound, as with the Mayan cities of Xel-há and Uxmal.

Una familia en Xochimilco, México

DIFFERENTIATED INSTRUCTION

Multiple Intelligences

Interpersonal/Social Intelligence: Have students think of awards that they could present to other students in the class. They should write a short introduction about each award winner that explains why he or she is getting the award. Encourage students to use indirect object pronouns and the verb ***dar*** in their presentations.

Heritage Language Learners

Let pairs or small groups work together to make up tongue twisters that the class can use to practice the pronunciation of words with the letter ***x***. Then, have them teach the tongue twisters to the class.

22 Las tortugas tinglar

Leer • Escribir • Hablar

Lee esta información sobre las tortugas tinglar. Luego contesta las preguntas.

¡La tortuga tinglar es enorme! Es la tortuga marina más grande del mundo[1]. Los tinglares adultos pueden ser de hasta siete pies de largo y pesar[2] hasta 1.400 libras[3]. Cada año, entre febrero y julio, esta tortuga sale del mar en la noche y pone sus huevos en playas tropicales, como las de la República Dominicana, Costa Rica o de la isla de Culebra cerca de Puerto Rico. Después regresa a aguas frías.

Desde 1970 el tinglar está en peligro[4] de extinción. Por eso, en la primavera voluntarios de diferentes países van a las playas como las de la isla de Culebra. Llevan trajes de baño, jeans, sudaderas, camisetas, cámaras, binoculares, linternas[5], repelente contra mosquitos y muchas ganas de[6] ayudar a las tortugas. Patrullan[7] las playas buscando las tortugas.

Después que las tortugas ponen los huevos, los voluntarios los llevan a un nido artificial. Aproximadamente 60 días después, las tortuguitas salen de los huevos. Los voluntarios llevan a las tortuguitas al mar donde nadan continuamente por unas 28 horas. Estos voluntarios son muy importantes para la preservación de la tortuga tinglar.

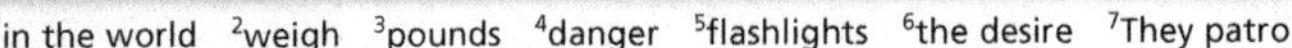

[1]in the world [2]weigh [3]pounds [4]danger [5]flashlights [6]the desire [7]They patrol

1. Para ti, ¿cuáles son los hechos *(facts)* más increíbles sobre la tortuga tinglar?
2. Escribe una lista, en orden, del trabajo que hacen los voluntarios en la playa.
3. ¿Te gustaría trabajar como voluntario en una de las playas donde están las tortugas tinglar? ¿Por qué?

Protegiendo a las tortugas en las Islas Cayman

El español en el mundo del trabajo

There may be community service organizations in your neighborhood where knowing Spanish is helpful. These organizations include medical clinics, food kitchens, senior centers, career counseling and job training, and after-school programs. Volunteering your skills for these agencies is the first step to finding out if you would be interested in pursuing work in the nonprofit sector.

- Check with local agencies to find out which ones offer services in Spanish (or in other languages). Develop a class list of volunteer opportunities in your community in which you could use your Spanish skills.

ENRICH YOUR TEACHING

Culture Note

Other endangered species found in Spanish-speaking countries are the great harpy eagle, which can be found in Central and South America, the short-tailed chinchilla in Peru, Argentina, Chile, and Bolivia, the yellow-tailed woolly monkey in Peru, and the Bolivian blue-throated macaw.

Teacher-to-Teacher

Have students research another endangered animal from Latin America and create a poster that includes facts about the animal and describes efforts to protect it and its habitat.

Practice and Communicate 8B

22

Standards: 1.2, 1.3

Resources: Answer Keys: Student Edition, p. 123

Mapa global interactivo, Actividad 3 Look at tortoise nesting sites in the Dominican Republic, Puerto Rico, and Costa Rica.

Focus: Reading for comprehension

Suggestions: Have students look at the photos and predict what the text will be about. Ask students to read the article silently and then have a volunteer read it aloud. To check comprehension, have volunteers provide summaries of each paragraph. For item 2, have students create a visual such as a flowchart to show the process that the volunteers go through with the newborn turtles.

Answers will vary but may include:

1. **Que es la más grande del mundo; pueden ser de hasta siete pies de largo y pesar hasta 1.400 libras.**
2. **Los voluntarios van a las playas de la Isla de Culebra; Patrullan las playas buscando tortugas; Llevan los huevos a un nido artificial; Llevan las tortuguitas al mar.**
3. **Answers will vary.**

Extension: Read several sentences about the turtles and the volunteers from the article. Leave out the subject of the sentence as you read it: *Llevan las tortuguitas al mar.* Have students write ***tortuga*** or ***voluntario*** on their papers.

Pre-AP* Support

- **Learning Objective:** Interpretive: Print
- **Activity 22:** Students use reading comprehension skills to learn about the leatherback turtle.

El español en el mundo del trabajo

Core Instruction

Standards: 5.1

Suggestions: After they read the passage, provide students with local directories of community service organizations to expose them to these agencies.

Theme Project

Students can perform Step 5 at this point. Record their presentations for inclusion in their portfolios. (For more information, see p. 372-b.)

8B Reading

Common Core: Reading

Lectura

Core Instruction

Standards: 1.2, 4.1, 1.3

Resources: Map Transparency 13

Focus: Reading an article about an international volunteer organization

Suggestions:

Pre-reading: Ask students if they are familiar with Habitat for Humanity. If so, ask volunteers to provide whatever background information they have.

Reading: Have students read the article silently all the way through and make a list of cognates they encounter while they read. Then have volunteers read the selection aloud or listen to the audio. Stop after each paragraph and ask students to summarize the main idea.

Post-reading: Have students complete the *¿Comprendes?* questions or give a summary of the text to check comprehension.

Pre-AP* Support

- **Learning Objective:** Interpretive: Print and Audio
- **Activity:** For the first paragraph of the reading selection, have students read one sentence at a time, looking up after each sentence. Ask a quick, one-word-answer question about that sentence. Have students read the second paragraph silently. Then read several true/false statements to the class for response. Working in pairs, have one student read aloud the final section to a partner. Then have a partner write a one-sentence summary to share with the class.
- ***Pre-AP* Resource Book:*** Comprehensive guide to Pre-AP* reading skill development, pp. 19–26

BELLRINGER REVIEW

Start this activity by mentioning an important year in recent history. Then review numbers by asking students to tell the class in what year they were born.

Block Schedule

If possible, have students write questions to ask a former Habitat for Humanity volunteer. Compile the questions, and e-mail the organization. If you receive responses, copy them to share with the class.

Objectives

- Read about an international volunteer organization
- Use cognates to increase comprehension
- Identify benefits of volunteer work

Lectura

Lee este artículo sobre una organización que hace proyectos de construcción en muchos países del mundo.

Strategy

Recognizing cognates
Recognizing cognates in the following article can help improve your understanding of the reading.

Hábitat para la Humanidad Internacional

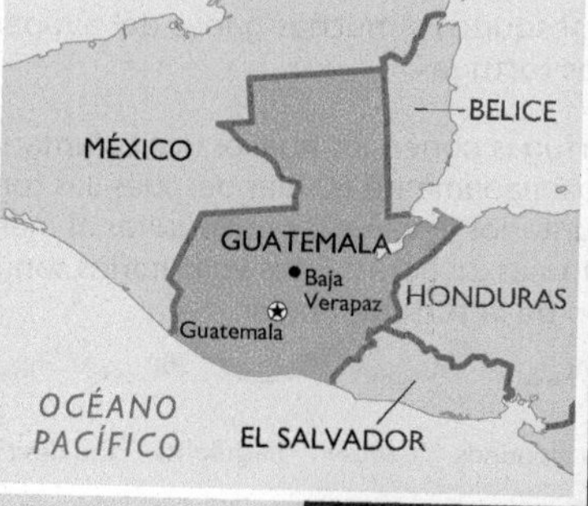

Hábitat es una organización internacional que ayuda a la gente pobre a tener casa. Su objetivo es construir casas seguras[1] que no cuestan mucho para las personas que no tienen mucho dinero. Hábitat trabaja con las familias pobres, con los grupos de voluntarios y con las personas que les dan dinero. Esta organización tiene más de 2.500 proyectos en muchas comunidades de los Estados Unidos y otros 1.600 proyectos en más de 83 países diferentes. Hábitat ha construido[2] unas 250.000 casas en todo el mundo.

Guatemala tiene quince afiliados de Hábitat. Cada afiliado tiene su propio dinero y hace su plan de construcción y sus proyectos. Los afiliados de Guatemala tienen mucho éxito[3]. Han construido más de 10.000 casas y tienen planes para construir 15.000 más en los años que vienen. Según Hábitat, las personas pobres tienen que ayudar a construir sus casas. Es una manera positiva de ayudar a los demás. Hábitat les da los materiales de construcción y los trabajadores voluntarios. Cuando la casa está construida, el nuevo propietario[4] paga una pequeña hipoteca[5] cada mes. Después, los nuevos propietarios tienen que ayudar a otros futuros propietarios a construir sus casas.

[1] safe [2] has built [3] success [4] owner [5] mortgage

Un proyecto de Hábitat para la Humanidad Internacional

DIFFERENTIATED INSTRUCTION

Heritage Language Learners

Have students research other Spanish-speaking countries in which Habitat for Humanity has assisted in building homes. The Internet is a good source of information. Students can find statistics, stories about volunteers, and even view pictures of houses in many stages of construction. Have students write a brief newspaper article about a specific project or report back to the class on their findings.

Para todos, es una experiencia increíble.

Trabajadores de Hábitat para la Humanidad Internacional

—Ayer fue mi cumpleaños y recibí el mejor regalo de mi vida, mi propia casa —dijo una señora de la comunidad de Baja Verapaz.

La mayoría[6] del dinero viene de donaciones privadas y del trabajo voluntario de muchísimas personas.

¿Sabes que el ex-presidente Jimmy Carter y su esposa Rosalynn son dos de los primeros miembros voluntarios de Hábitat? Los grupos de voluntarios son una parte fundamental del éxito de la organización.

—Es una experiencia inolvidable para ayudar a los demás —dijo un voluntario en Guatemala.

[6] the majority

¿Comprendes?

1. ¿Qué hace Hábitat?
2. ¿Con quiénes trabaja Hábitat?
3. ¿En cuántos países está Hábitat?
4. ¿Cuántas casas construyeron los afiliados de Guatemala?
5. ¿Qué tienen que pagar los nuevos propietarios?
6. ¿Qué tienen que hacer los nuevos propietarios?
7. ¿De dónde viene el dinero para construir las casas?
8. Y a ti, ¿te gustaría trabajar con Hábitat? ¿Por qué?

Más práctica GO

realidades.com | print

	realidades.com	print
Guided WB p. 273	✔	✔
Comm. WB pp. 169, 320	✔	✔
Hispanohablantes WB pp. 322–323		✔
Cultural Reading Activity	✔	

Fondo Cultural | Estados Unidos

El trabajo voluntario AmeriCorps is an organization of volunteers who work in urban and rural communities throughout the United States. They teach children to read, assist victims of natural disasters, and participate in other activities that benefit needy people.

One of the advantages of serving as an AmeriCorps volunteer is learning skills that can be used later in the workplace.

- What are some of the skills a volunteer might learn? Why are they important?

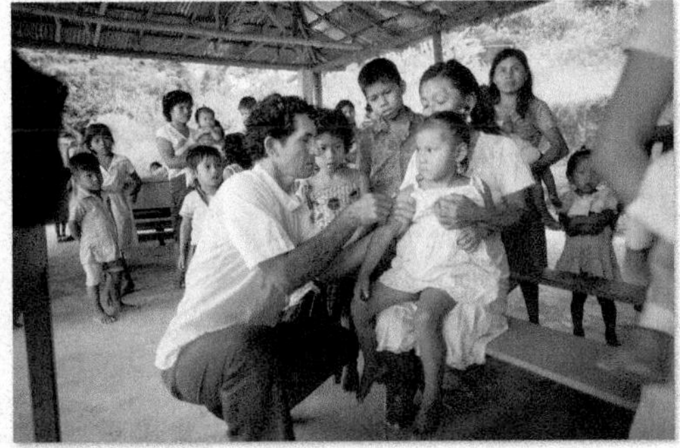

Doctores de las Naciones Unidas en Santa Cruz, Perú

¿Comprendes? Standards: 1.2, 1.3

Resources: Answer Keys: Student Edition, p. 124

Focus: Demonstrating reading comprehension by answering questions about the article

Suggestions: Discuss the questions in class, asking students to identify information from the article that supports their answers.

Answers:

1. **Ayuda a la gente pobre a tener casa.**
2. **Trabaja con las familias pobres.**
3. **Hábitat está en más de 83 países.**
4. **Construyeron más de 10.000 casas.**
5. **Tienen que pagar una pequeña hipoteca cada mes.**
6. **Tienen que ayudar a futuros propietarios a construir sus casas.**
7. **El dinero viene de las donaciones privadas y del trabajo voluntario de muchas personas.**
8. **Answers will vary.**

Fondo cultural

Standards: 3.1

Suggestions: Brainstorm ways teens can help in their community. Ask how volunteer work can help students prepare for the future. Arrange the class in groups to answer the questions.

Answers will vary.

For Further Reading

Student Resource: Realidades para hispanohablantes: Lectura 2, pp. 324–325

ENRICH YOUR TEACHING

Teacher-to-Teacher

If your school allows fundraising activities, you might want to have your students design a T-shirt. Have students write a message in Spanish about the importance of helping others. You can send the design to a local silk-screener and sell the shirts to raise money to donate to Habitat for Humanity or another charity.

21st Century Skills

Productivity and Accountability Have students prepare for a day with *Hábitat para la Humanidad* in a Spanish-speaking community by making sure they know all the vocabulary and expressions necessary to communicate with the people in an effective way. Assist them as needed to teach each other any vocabulary they may be lacking (such as tools, actions, items found in construction).

Perspectivas del mundo hispano

Core Instruction

Standards: 2.1

Focus: Reading about volunteer organizations and activities

Suggestions: Discuss opportunities for volunteering. Help students see that both the volunteer and the community benefit. It is a good way to gain hands-on experience, and sometimes volunteers discover that they want to pursue a career in that field. Have students read the text. Discuss the different types of volunteer work students in Spanish-speaking countries do. Have students answer the *Check it out!* questions. You may wish to tally the number of students and the types of work on the board.

Discuss different types of volunteer work. Using the examples cited in the text, ask students if the same types of work could be done in their community. What other types of volunteer work might be available? Help students understand that communities always have a need for volunteers, but that some positions may be needed more than others.

Direct students' attention to the *Think about it!* section and have them discuss the question.

Answers will vary.

Teacher-to-Teacher

Have students display the posters they made for the *Presentación escrita* around the school for other students to read.

Additional Resources

Student Resource: Realidades para hispanohablantes, p. 326

Pre-AP* Support

- **Learning Objective:** Presentational Speaking (Cultural Comparisons)
- **Background:** This task prepares students for the Spoken Presentational Communication tasks that focus on cultural comparisons in the exam.
- **Activity:** Have students interview their peers and/or use the Internet to help them prepare a two-minute (maximum) presentation in English or Spanish, if possible, on attitudes toward volunteer activities among teenagers in different cultures. Have them summarize the information described in the reading and compare it with what they know and have learned, explaining similarities and differences.
- ***Pre-AP* Resource Book:*** Comprehensive guide to Pre-AP* speaking skill development, pp. 39–50

Perspectivas del mundo hispano

¿Trabajas como voluntario?

Throughout the Spanish-speaking world students are involved in volunteer activities and organizations. In many private schools students are encouraged to serve their community for two to three hours per week to help them learn responsibilities that will make them good citizens. Community service also provides a good occasion to explore different professions such as education, medicine, or social work. For example, many young people work with local branches of the *Cruz Roja* (Red Cross) and learn how to respond in times of emergency. Courses are offered by the organization, and some students even study for a degree in health services.

In many Spanish-speaking countries, students are involved in causes dealing with the environment. In these countries, the natural beauty of the land is not only a source of national pride, it is also an economic resource and important to the well-being of the country. Students work at recycling centers collecting paper, glass, and plastic and collect trash along roadsides and in parks.

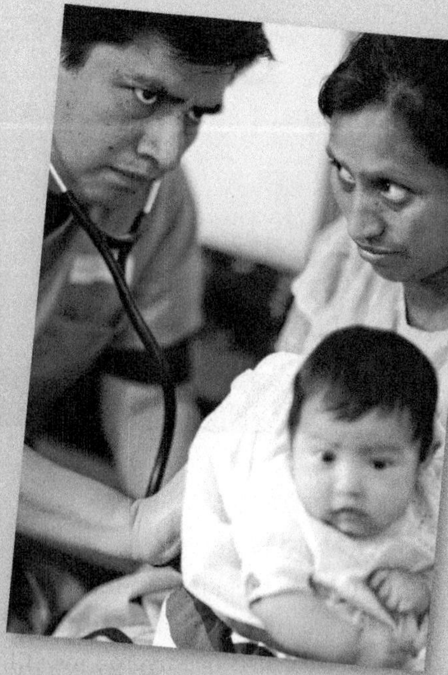

Un médico voluntario en una clínica de Guatemala

Check it out! Survey the students in your class. Who does volunteer work? What kind of work do they do? How often are they involved in community service activities?

Think about it! How does the involvement in volunteerism among teenagers in many Spanish-speaking countries compare with the involvement of teenagers in your community?

En la Reserva Ecológica El Ángel, en el Ecuador

DIFFERENTIATED INSTRUCTION

Heritage Language Learners

Have students learn about the ***Cruz Roja*** or another community-based organization in a Spanish-speaking country of their choice. Ask them to prepare a short report on what the organization does.

- Design a poster promoting community service
- Use key questions to cover important ideas

Presentación escrita

¿Puedes ayudarnos?

Task
Your school wants to organize a clean-up campaign for a park, recreation center, playground, or other place in your community. Make a poster announcing the project and inviting students to participate.

1. **Prewrite** Answer the following questions about your project.
   - ¿Qué van a limpiar y qué tienen que hacer?
   - ¿Dónde está el lugar?
   - ¿Cuándo y cuántas horas van a trabajar?
   - ¿Quién(es) puede(n) participar?

2. **Draft** Use the answers to the questions to prepare a first draft. Organize the information logically. Remember that you want students to stop and read the poster.

3. **Revise** Check your draft for spelling, accent marks, punctuation, and vocabulary usage. Share your work with a partner, who will check the following:
   - Is the information presented clearly and arranged logically?
   - Is there anything that you should add or change?
   - Are there any errors?

4. **Publish** Prepare a final version, making any necessary changes. Add visuals to make the poster appealing. Display it in the classroom, cafeteria, or school library, or add it to your portfolio.

5. **Evaluation** The following rubric will be used to grade your presentation.

Rubric	Score 1	Score 3	Score 5
Completeness of information	You provide only the name of your project.	You provide the name and location of your project.	You provide your project name, location, plus when, for how long, and who.
Accuracy of language	You use little variation of vocabulary with many grammar errors.	You use limited vocabulary with some grammar errors.	You use a variety of vocabulary with very few grammar errors.
Visual presentation	Your only visual on the poster is the title.	You provide the title and one visual on your poster, in color.	You provide the title and two or more visuals on your poster, in color.

Strategy

Using key questions
Answering key questions can help you think of ideas for writing.

Writing 8B

Common Core: Writing

Presentación escrita

Persuasive
Standards: 1.3, 1.2

Focus: Communicating about a community-service project in a personalized context

Suggestions: Review the rubric with the class. Bring in a sample poster from a local organization. Point out that the key parts of a successful poster are the answers to the questions listed in Step 1. Encourage students to make their posters visually attractive as well as persuasive.

Portfolio

Include the final poster in students' portfolios.

Pre-AP* Support

- **Learning Objective:** Presentational Writing
- **Activity:** You've announced a worthwhile community event and invited people to attend. Now, write a brief, persuasive paragraph defending community service in general. Who benefits from these activities? Why should every student participate?
- ***Pre-AP* Resource Book:*** Comprehensive guide to Pre-AP* writing skill development, pp. 27–38

Additional Resources

Student Resources: Realidades para hispanohablantes, p. 327; Guided Practice: Presentación escrita, p. 274

ENRICH YOUR TEACHING

Teacher-to-Teacher

Careers: *Cap.* 8B has focused on volunteerism. Have students work in small groups to talk about a career in community service. Ask them to write a list of words, expressions, and sentences they have learned that would be helpful in creating promotional materials in Spanish to recruit volunteers for a food bank. Ask groups to share their lists.

21st Century Skills

Technology Literacy Have students participate in a real event in the community and make an electronic poster advertising the event, combining video, audio, and digital images. Have them get permission to show the poster to other Spanish classes or even in the community, at places where Spanish is spoken.

ASSESSMENT

Presentación escrita

- Assessment Program: Rubrics, p. T33

Go over the descriptions of the different levels of performance. After assessing students, help individuals understand how their performance could be improved.

Videomisterio

Core Instruction

Standards: 1.2, 1.3, 5.2

Resources: Teacher's Resource Book: Video Script, p. 263; Video Program: Cap. 8B; Video Program Teacher's Guide: Cap. 8B

Focus: Introducing the events and vocabulary of this episode; scanning and reading the episode summary

Personajes importantes:

Lola Lago, detective
Pedro, Doña Gracia's grandson
Carmela, Lola Lago's friend
Julia Romero, María's friend who died in the hospital
Inspector Gil, police officer

Synopsis: Pedro and Lola discuss the clues they have so far. They do not know where María may be, but now they know that she went to Julia Romero's apartment. Lola sees María in front of doña Gracia's apartment. Lola calls Inspector Gil to let him know that she has seen María.

Suggestions: Review with students the events of *Episodio* 7: Rosalinda finds out Julia Romero's address and calls Lola to let her know. Then Pedro and Lola meet at doña Gracia's apartment. There they find a postcard sent to María from Luis Antonio Llamas, a former secretary to doña Gracia's husband. By chance, the name of one of the nurses that cared for Julia in the hospital was Luis Antonio. Next they go to Julia Romero's apartment. They discover that she no longer lives there, but the new tenant has a box of Julia's belongings. In the box they find several letters from Luis Antonio.

Point out the *Palabras para comprender* to the class, saying examples in context and writing the sentences on the board. Remind students that these words are only used to help them understand the episode and they are not responsible for that vocabulary.

Objective

- Understand the expanding plot of a mystery video set in Spain

¿Eres tú, María?

Episodio 8

Antes de ver el video

"A ver. Esta foto. Yo conozco a este hombre. Pero no sé de qué. ¡Qué problema!"

Resumen del episodio

Después de visitar el piso de Julia, Lola y Pedro van a un café a tomar unos refrescos. Hablan de las cosas de Julia que el joven acaba de darles:[1] la ropa, las fotos, los papeles. Cuando Lola llega a su piso en la noche, ve que una mujer entra en el edificio número 8. Lola cree que es María. Sale rápidamente de su piso y espera[2] enfrente. Una mujer sale del edificio y Lola le pregunta, "¿Eres tú, María?"

[1] just gave them [2] waits

Palabras para comprender

María tenía las llaves. María had the keys.
Ella las perdió. She lost them.
¡No me sigas! Don't follow me!
Acabo de ver . . . I just saw . . .
Acabo de hablar con . . . I just spoke with . . .

DIFFERENTIATED INSTRUCTION

Advanced Learners

Ask students to prepare questions to test the class's comprehension of the reading. Have them work in pairs or small groups to ask *who, what, when, where,* and *why* questions. Provide them with a model.

Heritage Language Learners

Have students write a creative continuation of the episode. Tell them to include information on what happens to each character in the video.

—¿Eres María Requena?
—¿Por qué quieres saberlo?

—Acabo de hablar con María Requena delante del piso de doña Gracia.

—Srta. Lago, esto es cosa de la policía.

Después de ver el video

¿Comprendes?

A. ¿Quién lo dice: Lola, Carmela, Pedro, el Inspector Gil, la camarera o María?

1. ¿Qué desean Uds.?
2. Y yo, un agua mineral.
3. ¿Cómo es que tienes las llaves del piso de Julia?
4. ¿Sabes algo más sobre el caso de doña Gracia?
5. Las diez y media. ¡Por fin!
6. ¿Qué quieres? ¿Quién eres?
7. ¡No me sigas! ¡No me sigas!
8. Acabo de ver a María Requena.
9. Ahora trabajo para Pedro Requena, el nieto de doña Gracia.
10. Hay que decirlo todo a la policía.

B. Escribe dos frases que describan cada foto de esta página.

Video 8B

Visual scanning: Direct students' attention to the pictures and ask who these characters are. Before students read the *Resumen del episodio,* have them scan the text and find three cognates. ***(visitar, café, fotos, edificio)*** Then ask them to read the *Resumen del episodio* carefully and ask questions about what they think will happen in this episode.

Viewing: Play *Episodio* 8 to the class. If necessary, rewind and replay parts of the video that give important information about the story.

Post-viewing: Complete the *¿Comprendes?* questions in class.

¿Comprendes? Standards: 1.2, 1.3

Resources: Answer Keys: Student Edition, p. 124

Focus: Verifying comprehension by answering questions; reviewing the plot

Suggestions: After each item, verify the correct answer by playing the appropriate section of the video. For part B, have students write the sentences in the form of a summarizing paragraph.

Answers:

Part A

1. **Lo dice la camarera.**
2. **Lo dice Lola.**
3. **Lo dice Pedro.**
4. **Lo dice Carmela.**
5. **Lo dice Lola.**
6. **Lo dice María.**
7. **Lo dice María.**
8. **Lo dice Lola.**
9. **Lo dice Lola.**
10. **Lo dice el Inspector Gil.**

Part B answers will vary.

Additional Resources

- *¿Eres tú, María?* Video Workbook, Episode 8
- *¿Eres tú, María?* Teacher's Video Guide: Answer Key

ENRICH YOUR TEACHING

Teacher-to-Teacher

To help students better understand the stories, have them identify the elements of a plot for the *Videomisterio*. Review the meanings of each element: ***el enredo o complicación*** ("set-up or introduction"), ***el punto culminante*** ("climax"), and ***el desenredo*** or ***la resolución*** ("outcome").

Review Activities

To talk about recycling and places in a community: Have students make a sketch of a recyclable item. Then, line students up in two rows, facing each other. Have students say the recyclable item. Have the students rotate in the line for variation.

To talk about possibilities for volunteer work: Have students work in pairs. Student A tells Student B what his or her interests are and Student B recommends a place in the community where Student A can volunteer his or her time. Have students exchange roles.

To practice* decir*, the preterite of* dar *and* hacer*, and indirect object pronouns: Have students write five sentences telling what different people say about recycling and volunteer work. Students should try to include the past tense of ***dar*** and ***hacer*** and use indirect object pronouns. Have students review each other's sentences and then read them aloud.

Example: *Mi profesora dice que ella le dio ropa a los niños en su comunidad.*

Portfolio

Invite students to review the activities they completed in this chapter, including written reports, posters or other visuals, recordings of oral presentations, or other projects. Have them select one or two items that they feel best demonstrate their achievements in Spanish to include in their portfolios. Have them include this with the Chapter Checklist and Self-Assessment Worksheet.

Additional Resources

Student Resources: Realidades para hispanohablantes, p. 328

Teacher Resources:

- Teacher's Resource Book: Situation Cards, p. 268, Clip Art, pp. 270–271
- Assessment Program: Chapter Checklist and Self-Assessment Worksheet, pp. T56–T57

Repaso | | |

Objectives

- Review the vocabulary and grammar
- Demonstrate you can perform the tasks on p. 423

Repaso del capítulo

Vocabulario y gramática

to talk about recycling

la bolsa	bag, sack
la botella	bottle
la caja	box
el cartón	cardboard
el centro de reciclaje	recycling center
la lata	can
llevar	to take; to carry
el periódico	newspaper
el plástico	plastic
reciclar	to recycle
recoger	to collect; to gather
separar	to separate
usado, -a	used
el vidrio	glass

to talk about places in a community

el barrio	neighborhood
la calle	street, road
la comunidad	community
el jardín	garden, yard
el río	river

to discuss possibilities for volunteer work

los ancianos	older people
el anciano	older man
la anciana	older woman
el campamento	camp
los demás	others
la escuela primaria	primary school
la gente	people
el hospital	hospital
el juguete	toy
los niños	children
el niño	young boy
la niña	young girl
pobre	poor
el problema	problem
el proyecto de construcción	construction project
el trabajo voluntario	volunteer work
el voluntario, la voluntaria	volunteer

other useful expressions

a menudo	often
decidir	to decide
Es necesario.	It's necessary.
la experiencia	experience
Hay que . . .	One must . . .
increíble	incredible
inolvidable	unforgetable
¿Qué más?	What else?
la vez *pl.* **las veces**	time
otra vez	again

decir *to say, to tell*

digo	**decimos**
dices	**decís**
dice	**dicen**

indirect object pronouns

SINGULAR	PLURAL
me (to / for) me	**nos** (to / for) us
te (to / for) you	**os** (to / for) you
le (to / for) him, her; you *(formal)*	**les** (to / for) them; you *(formal)*

preterite of *dar*

di	**dimos**
diste	**disteis**
dio	**dieron**

preterite of *hacer*

hice	**hicimos**
hiciste	**hicisteis**
hizo	**hicieron**

For *Vocabulario adicional,* see pp. 472–473.

DIFFERENTIATED INSTRUCTION

Heritage Language Learners

Have students write a letter to the editor about a problem in their community. Students should describe the situation and offer a solution to the problem. Remind them to include indirect object pronouns and the preterite forms of ***dar*** and ***hacer.***

Students with Learning Difficulties

Have students use the Organizer from the *Practice Workbook* to create a study list and to reinforce their knowledge of the chapter's vocabulary and grammar.

Más repaso GO realidades.com | print

	realidades.com	print
Instant Check	✔	
Puzzles	✔	
Core WB pp. 155–156		✔
Comm. WB pp. 321, 322–324	✔	✔

Preparación para el examen

On the exam you will be asked to . . .	Here are practice tasks similar to those you will find on the exam . . .	For review go to your print or digital textbook . . .
Interpretive		
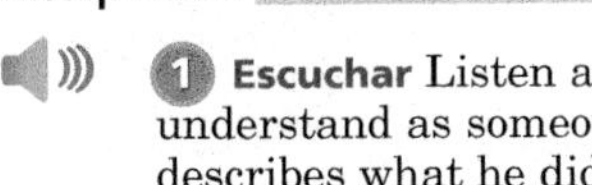 **1 Escuchar** Listen and understand as someone describes what he did in his community	A radio station is sponsoring a contest to encourage people to help in the community. Listen as a teen tells the announcer what he did. Identify whether he: a) helped older people; b) worked on a recycling project; c) contributed money; d) volunteered in a hospital or school.	**pp. 400–403** *Vocabulario en contexto* **p. 401** Actividades 1–2 **p. 404** Actividad 4 **p. 413** Actividad 18
Interpersonal		
 **2 Hablar** Ask and answer questions about what you or someone you know did to help others in the past few months	Many organizations offer scholarships to students who help others. With a partner, practice asking and answering the following questions for the scholarship interviews with a local agency that works in the Spanish-speaking community: a) What did you do to help others? b) Why did you decide to do volunteer work?	**p. 404** Actividad 5 **p. 405** Actividad 6 **p. 406** Actividad 7
Interpretive		
 **3 Leer** Read and understand what people gave as donations to various people or groups	The Spanish Club treasurer's report about charitable contributions is ready for the members. Read one line item from the report. Indicate whether the member(s) donated: a) cash; b) lessons for an individual or group; c) clothing; d) furniture. For example, you might read: *Scott y Jamie le dieron una cama y una cómoda a una familia pobre.*	**p. 412** Actividad 17 **p. 415** Actividad 22 **pp. 416–417** *Lectura*
Presentational		
 **4 Escribir** Write a list of things teenagers can do to help in your community	To encourage your classmates to participate in *La semana de la comunidad,* make a poster for your classroom with at least five suggestions for activities. For example: *Recicla las botellas. Ayuda a los niños de la escuela primaria.*	**p. 408** Actividades 9–10 **p. 409** Actividad 12 **p. 410** Actividad 13 **p. 411** Actividad 15 **p. 412** Actividad 17 **p. 419** *Presentación escrita*
Cultures		
 **5 Pensar** Demonstrate an understanding of cultural perspectives regarding volunteer work	Think about the volunteer activities in which you and your friends participate. Based on what you've learned in this chapter, compare these to the type of work teenage volunteers do in Spanish-speaking countries.	**pp. 400–403** *Vocabulario en contexto* **p. 407** *Fondo cultural* **pp. 416–417** *Lectura* **p. 417** *Fondo cultural* **p. 418** *Perspectivas del mundo hispano*

DIFFERENTIATED ASSESSMENT

CORE ASSESSMENT
- **Assessment Program:** Examen del capítulo 8B, pp. 222–228
- **Audio Program DVD:** Cap. 8B, Track 16
- **ExamView:** Chapter Test, Test Banks A and B

ADVANCED/PRE-AP*
- **ExamView: Pre-AP* Test Bank**
- **Pre-AP* Resource Book,** pp. 90–93

STUDENTS NEEDING EXTRA HELP
- **Alternate Assessment Program:** Examen del capítulo 8B
- **Audio Program DVD:** Cap. 8B, Track 16

HERITAGE LEARNERS
- **Assessment Program: Realidades para hispanohablantes:** Examen del capítulo 8B
- **ExamView: Heritage Learner Test Bank**

Performance Tasks

Standards: 1.1, 1.2, 1.3, 4.2

Student Resource: Realidades para hispanohablantes, p. 329

Teacher Resources: Teacher's Resource Book: Audio Script, p. 261; Audio Program DVD: Cap. 8B, Track 15; Answer Keys: Student Edition, p. 125

1. Escuchar

Suggestions: Play the audio or read the script aloud.

Script:

Ayer yo fui al hospital para pasar tiempo con los niños de cinco y seis años. Les leí unos cuentos y les traje juguetes y libros. Fue increíble la satisfacción que me dio cuando ayudé a los niños.

Answers:

a) no **c) no**
b) no **d) yes**

2. Hablar

Suggestions: Assign students fictitious volunteer jobs to describe for the purpose of variation or for students who have not done volunteer work.

Answers will vary.

3. Leer

Suggestions: Point out to students that they are only reading one line from the report, which is included here.

Answers: d

4. Escribir

Suggestions: Have students begin each suggestion with a command—***recicla, ayuda, recoge,*** etc. Encourage students to vary their vocabulary words for each of the suggestions.

Answers will vary.

5. Pensar

Suggestions: Have students brainstorm ideas and write them on the board or on an overhead transparency.

Answers will vary.

Tema 9

Medios de comunicación

9A El cine y la televisión

- **Movies, television, and recent events**

Vocabulary: television shows; movie genres; giving opinions

Grammar: ***acabar de*** **+ infinitive;** ***gustar*** and similar verbs

Cultural Perspectives: movies and television; common gestures

9B La tecnología

- **Computers and the Internet**

Vocabulary: computers; communication; computer-related activities

Grammar: the verbs ***pedir*** and ***servir; saber*** and ***conocer***

Cultural Perspectives: the use of technology

THEME SUPPORT

Bulletin Boards

Theme: ***Medios de comunicación***

Ask students to cut out, copy, or download photos of movies and television shows from around the world, as well as photos of computers and computer-related items. Cluster photos to reflect the three categories just mentioned.

Hands-on Culture

Art: ***Pintar un mural***

Murals decorate many public buildings in Mexico and the Spanish-speaking communities of the United States. They often celebrate the culture of the local community by communicating the history and accomplishments of its residents, thus serving as an important ***medio de comunicación.***

Materials: butcher paper, pencils, paint brushes, paint of different colors, tape

1. Divide students into four or five groups. Ask each group to brainstorm a list of important events in the history of their community or state. Have groups then choose one event to depict in their mural.
2. Students discuss what to include, then draw their mural in pencil on two large pieces of butcher paper that have been taped together.
3. Students paint their mural.
4. Display the murals in the classroom. Have each group explain its mural.

Game

Te voy a explicar

This game practices the skill of circumlocution. Play it to review the vocabulary from *Capítulo* 9B.

Players: the whole class, playing in pairs

Materials: index cards, timer or stopwatch

Rules:

1. Divide the class into two teams, A and B. Have students from Team A partner with students from Team B to write all the new verbs and nouns from *Capítulo* 9B on index cards.
2. Ask partners to shuffle their cards and place them face down in two piles, one in front of each student.
3. Set your timer or stopwatch for 30 seconds. When you call ***"Empieza,"*** one student turns over a card. He or she then describes or explains the word to his or her partner without saying the word itself. If the partner guesses the word before the 30 seconds is up, he or she receives three points.
   Student A: Es una cosa. Sirve para tomar fotos. Después, bajas las fotos en la computadora.
   Student B: La cámara digital
4. Have partners switch roles to repeat Step 3. Students should write on a sheet of paper how many points they received in this round.
5. Have the members of Team A move to work with a different partner from Team B.
6. Repeat Steps 3–5 until all the vocabulary has been practiced. At the end of play, ask each team to tally its cumulative points. Check each team's math. The team with the most points wins.

Variation: Have only one player from each team play each round while the rest of the class watches.

THEME PROJECT

Cápsula de información

Overview: Students create time capsules that would show someone from the future what life is like today. They should include short descriptions accompanied by illustrations of popular movies, television shows, music videos, computer programs and / or Web sites, how people spend their time, and so on. Students then present their time capsules to the class, explaining why they included each time.

Resources: colored pencils or crayons, pens, blank paper, paper-towel tubes, or other containers to serve as time capsules

Sequence: (suggestions for when to do each step are found throughout the chapters)

STEP 1. Review instructions so students know what is expected of them. Hand out the "Theme 9 Project Instructions and Rubric" from the *Teacher's Resource Book*.

STEP 2. Students submit a list of items / activities and sketches of the illustrations they wish to include in their time capsule. Return the lists and visuals with your suggestions.

STEP 3. Students create layouts for the pages to go in the time capsule. Each page contains a description and an illustration of one of the items from the student's list.

9B

STEP 4. Students submit a draft of their descriptions for each item on their list. Note your corrections and suggestions, then return drafts to students. Students correct their drafts, then partner to describe their time capsules.

STEP 5. Students present their time capsules to the class, explaining why they chose each item they included.

Options:

1. Students research another time period and create a time capsule for that era.
2. Students create a list of the year's best and worst media: television shows, movies, songs, computer programs, Web sites, etc.

Assessment:

Here is a detailed rubric for assessing this project:

Theme 9 Project: *Cápsula de información*

RUBRIC	Score 1	Score 3	Score 5
Evidence of planning	You didn't submit a list, sketches, or draft.	You submitted the draft and layout but didn't correct them.	You submitted and corrected your draft and layout.
Use of illustrations	You didn't include any illustrations.	You included Illustrations for most items.	You included Illustrations for all items.
Presentation	You listed items to be included in the capsule, but did not adequately describe them or explain why they were chosen.	You briefly described items to be included in the capsule, but did not adequately explain why they were chosen.	You briefly described items to be included in the time capsule and explained why they were chosen.

21st Century Skills

Look for tips throughout *Tema* 9 to enrich your teaching by integrating 21st Century Skills. Suggestions for the Theme Project and Theme Culture follow below.

Theme Project

Modify the Theme Project with one or more of these suggestions:

Develop Technology Literacy
Have students include in the time capsule an electronic representation of their activities as a class, to post on the class Web site. Have different groups of students prepare video explanations of the various activities during the year, including why they organized the events and what they learned from them.

Encourage Collaboration
Have students work in small groups to look more in depth at the individual choices in each category. Together, the group should make a decision about which DVD, Web site, etc., best represents today's world. Have students work with the handout "Analyze Media Content" for guidelines.

Foster Productivity and Accountability
Have students work with the rubric for this assignment and figure out what they need to do to make the best grade possible. Have students evaluate each other's choices, presentations, etc. with the rubric in mind and make suggestions for improvement.

Theme Culture

Support Critical Thinking and Problem Solving
Have students do Internet research of a TV network in two Spanish-speaking countries, discussing similarities and differences. They then compare those networks to similar networks in the United States.

Videocultura View *Medios de comunicación* with the class to learn about Spanish media in the United States and the world.

9A El cine y la televisión

AT A GLANCE

Objectives

- **Listen to and read different opinions about television**
- **Talk and write about television programs and movies**
- **Exchange information while sharing opinions about television and film**
- **Understand and use common gestures in Spanish-speaking countries, and compare them to ones you use**
- **Compare popular television programs in Spanish-speaking countries with programs in the U.S.**

Vocabulary

- Television programs
- Movies
- Words and expressions to give opinions

Grammar

- ***Acabar de*** + infinitive
- ***Gustar*** and similar verbs

Culture

- Alfonso Cuarón, p. 424
- Luis Buñuel, Salvador Dalí, p. 425
- ***Telenovelas,*** p. 431
- Average numbers of hours people watch television in different countries, p. 433
- ***Sábado gigante,*** p. 434
- Influences of Greek and Arabic on Spanish, p. 435
- Spanish-language television networks, p. 437
- TV-watching habits of teens, pp. 440–441
- Gestures, p. 442

Recycle ♻

- Adverbs
- ***me gusta(n), me encanta(n)***
- Adjective agreement
- ***dar***
- Question words
- Infinitives

RESOURCES

	FOR THE STUDENT	ONLINE	DVD	PRINT	FOR THE TEACHER	ONLINE	PREEXP	DVD	PRINT
Plan					Interactive TE and Resources DVD	•		•	
					Teacher's Resource Book, pp. 288–323	•		•	•
					Pre-AP* Resource Book, pp. 94–97	•		•	•
					Lesson Plans	•			•
					Mapa global interactivo	•			
Introducción PP. **424–425**									
Present	Student Edition, pp. 424–425	•	•	•	Interactive TE and Resources DVD	•		•	
	DK Reference Atlas	•	•		Teacher's Resource Book, pp. 288–291	•		•	•
	Videocultura	•	•		Galería de fotos		•		
	Hispanohablantes WB, pp. 330–331			•	Fine Art Transparencies, 13	•	•	•	
					Map Transparencies, 12, 15–16, 18, 20	•	•	•	
Vocabulario en contexto PP. **426–429**									
Present & Practice	Student Edition, pp. 426–429	•	•	•	Interactive TE and Resources DVD	•		•	
	Audio	•	•		Teacher's Resource Book, pp. 293–295, 298, 306–307	•		•	•
	Videohistoria	•	•		Vocabulary Clip Art	•	•	•	•
	Flashcards	•	•		Audio Program	•	•	•	
	Instant Check	•			Video Program: Videohistoria	•		•	
	Guided WB, pp. 275–284	•	•	•	Video Program Teacher's Guide: Cap. 9A	•		•	•
	Core WB, pp. 157–160	•	•	•	Vocabulary and Grammar Transparencies, 159–162	•	•	•	
	Comm. WB, pp. 170–173, 176	•	•	•	Answer Keys: Student Edition, pp. 126–127	•	•	•	
	Hispanohablantes WB, pp. 332–333			•	TPR Stories, pp. 122–133	•		•	•
Assess and Remediate					Prueba 9A–1: Assessment Program, pp. 229–230	•		•	•
					Assessment Program para hispanohablantes, pp. 229–230	•		•	•

RESOURCES

	FOR THE STUDENT	ONLINE	DVD	PRINT	FOR THE TEACHER	ONLINE	PREEXP	DVD	PRINT
Vocabulario en uso PP. **430–433**									
Present & Practice	Student Edition, pp. 430–433	•	•	•	Interactive Whiteboard Vocabulary Activities	•		•	
	Instant Check	•			Interactive TE and Resources DVD	•		•	
	Comm. WB, p. 173	•	•	•	Teacher's Resource Book, pp. 230–231, 294–296	•		•	•
	Hispanohablantes WB, pp. 334–335, 341			•	Communicative Pair Activities, pp. 300–301	•		•	•
	Communicative Pair Activities	•			Audio Program	•	•	•	
					Videomodelos	•		•	
					Vocabulary and Grammar Transparencies, 164	•	•	•	
					Answer Keys: Student Edition, pp. 128–129	•	•	•	•
Assess and Remediate					Prueba 9A–2 with Study Plan	•			
					Prueba 9A–2: Assessment Program, pp. 231–232	•		•	•
					Assessment Program para hispanohablantes, pp. 231–232	•		•	•
Gramática PP. **434–439**									
Present & Practice	Student Edition, pp. 434–439	•	•	•	Interactive Whiteboard Grammar Activities	•		•	
	Instant Check	•			Interactive TE and Resources DVD	•		•	
	Animated Verbs	•			Teacher's Resource Book, pp. 296–299, 302–303	•		•	•
	Tutorial Video: Grammar	•			Communicative Pair Activities, pp. 302–303	•		•	•
	Canción de hip hop	•			Audio Program	•	•	•	
	Guided WB, pp. 285–288	•	•	•	Videomodelos	•		•	
	Core WB, pp. 161–163	•	•	•	Video Program: GramActiva	•	•	•	
	Comm. WB, pp. 174–175, 177–178, 325	•	•	•	Vocabulary and Grammar Transparencies, 2, 163	•	•	•	
	Hispanohablantes WB, pp. 336–341			•	Answer Keys: Student Edition, pp. 130–131	•	•	•	
	Communicative Pair Activities	•							
Assess and Remediate					Pruebas 9A–3 and 9A–4 with Study Plans	•			
					Pruebas 9A–3, 9A–4: Assessment Program, pp. 233, 234	•		•	•
					Assessment Program para hispanohablantes, pp. 233, 234	•		•	•
¡Adelante! PP. **440–445**									
Application	Student Edition, pp. 440–445	•	•	•	Interactive TE and Resources DVD	•		•	
	Online Cultural Reading	•			Teacher's Resource Book, pp. 299, 305	•		•	•
	Guided WB, pp. 289–290	•	•	•	Video Program: Videomisterio ¿Eres tú, María?	•		•	
	Comm. WB, pp. 179, 326	•	•	•	Video Program Teacher's Guide: Cap. 9A	•		•	
	Hispanohablantes WB, pp. 342–347			•	Videomisterio Quiz		•		
	¿Eres tú, María? Video WB, pp. 67–73	•	•	•	Vocabulary and Grammar Transparencies: 165	•	•	•	
					Answer Keys: Student Edition, pp. 131–132	•	•	•	
Repaso del capítulo PP. **446–447**									
Review	Student Edition, pp. 446–447	•	•	•	Interactive TE and Resources DVD	•		•	
	Online Puzzles and Games	•			Teacher's Resource Book, pp. 297, 304, 306–307	•		•	•
	Core WB, pp. 164–165	•	•	•	Audio Program	•	•	•	
	Comm. WB, pp. 327–330	•	•	•	Answer Keys: Student Edition, p. 133	•	•	•	
	Hispanohablantes WB, pp. 348–349			•					
	Instant Check	•							
Chapter Assessment									
Assess					Examen del capítulo 9A	•		•	•
					Assessment Program, pp. 235–238	•		•	•
					Alternate Assessment Program, pp. 91–95	•		•	•
					Assessment Program para hispanohablantes, pp. 235–238	•		•	•
					Audio Program, Cap. 9A, Examen	•		•	
					ExamView: Test Banks A and B questions only online	•		•	
					Heritage Learner Test Bank	•		•	
					Pre-AP* Test Bank	•		•	

REGULAR SCHEDULE (50 MINUTES)

DAY	Warm-up / Assess	Preview / Present / Practice / Communicate	Wrap-up / Homework Options
1	**Warm-up** (10 min.) • Return Examen del capítulo 8B	**Chapter Opener** (5 min.) • Objectives • Arte y cultura **Vocabulario en contexto** (30 min.) • Presentation: Vocabulario en contexto • Actividades 1, 2	**Wrap-up and Homework Options** (5 min.) • Core Practice 9A-1, 9A-2
2	**Warm-up** (5 min.) • Homework check	**Vocabulario en contexto** (40 min.) • Presentation: Videohistoria *¿Qué dan en la tele?* • View: Videohistoria • Video Activities 1, 2, 3, 4 • Actividad 3	**Wrap-up and Homework Options** (5 min.) • Core Practice 9A-3, 9A-4 • Prueba 9A-1: Vocabulary recognition
3	**Warm-up** (10 min.) • Actividad 5 • Homework check ✔**Formative Assessment** (10 min.) • Prueba 9A-1: Vocabulary recognition	**Vocabulario en uso** (25 min.) • Interactive Whiteboard Vocabulary Activities • Actividades 4, 6, 7 • Fondo cultural • Audio Activities 5, 6	**Wrap-up and Homework Options** (5 min.) • Actividad 9 • Writing Activity 10 • Prueba 9A-2 with Study Plan: Vocabulary production
4	**Warm-up** (10 min.) • Actividad 8 • Homework check ✔**Formative Assessment** (10 min.) • Prueba 9A-2 with Study Plan: Vocabulary production	**Gramática y vocabulario en uso** (25 min.) • Actividades 10, 11 • Communicative Pair Activity • Presentation: *Acabar de* + infinitive • View: GramActiva video • Interactive Whiteboard Grammar Activities • Actividad 13	**Wrap-up and Homework Options** (5 min.) • Actividad 12 • Writing Activity 11
5	**Warm-up** (10 min.) • Fondo cultural • Homework check	**Gramática y vocabulario en uso** (35 min.) • Exploración del lenguaje • Audio Activity 7 • Communicative Pair Activity • Presentation: *Gustar* and similar verbs • View: GramActiva video • Interactive Whiteboard Grammar Activities • Actividades 14, 15 • Fondo cultural	**Wrap-up and Homework Options** (5 min.) • Core Practice 9A-5 • Actividad 16 • Prueba 9A-3 with Study Plan: *Acabar de* + infinitive
6	**Warm-up** (5 min.) • Homework check ✔**Formative Assessment** (10 min.) • Prueba 9A-3 with Study Plan: *Acabar de* + infinitive	**Gramática y vocabulario en uso** (30 min.) • Audio Activities 8, 9 • Actividades 17, 18	**Wrap-up and Homework Options** (5 min.) • Core Practice 9A-6, 9A-7 • Writing Activity 13 • Prueba 9A-4 with Study Plan: *Gustar* and similar verbs
7	**Warm-up** (10 min.) • Writing Activity 12 • Homework check ✔**Formative Assessment** (10 min.) • Prueba 9A-4 with Study Plan: *Gustar* and similar verbs	**Gramática y vocabulario en uso** (10 min.) • Communicative Pair Activity • Pronunciación • El español en la comunidad **¡Adelante!** (15 min.) • Presentación oral: Step 1 • La cultura en vivo	**Wrap-up and Homework Options** (5 min.) • Presentación oral: Step 2
8	**Warm-up** (5 min.) • Presentación oral: Step 2	**¡Adelante!** (30 min.) • Presentación oral: Step 3 **Repaso del capítulo** (10 min.) • Vocabulario y gramática • Preparación para el examen 1, 2	**Wrap-up and Homework Options** (5 min.) • Preparación para el examen 3, 4, 5 • Instant Check
9	**Warm-up** (5 min.) • Homework check	**¡Adelante!** (40 min.) • Lectura • ¿Comprendes? • Y tú, ¿qué dices? • Videomisterio: *¿Eres tú, María?*, Episodio 9	**Wrap-up and Homework Options** (5 min.) • Core Practice 9A-8, 9A-9 • Lectura • Videomisterio • Examen del capítulo 9A
10	**Warm-up** (10 min.) • Homework check • Answer questions ✔**Summative Assessment** (40 min.) • Examen del capítulo 9A		

BLOCK SCHEDULE (90 MINUTES)

DAY	Warm-up / Assess	Preview / Present / Practice / Communicate	Wrap-up / Homework Options
1	**Warm-up** (10 min.) • Return Examen del capítulo 8B	**Chapter Opener** (5 min.) • Objectives • Arte y cultura **Vocabulario en contexto** (50 min.) • Presentation: Vocabulario en contexto • Actividades 1, 2 • Presentation: Videohistoria *¿Qué dan en la tele?* • View: Videohistoria • Video Activities 1, 2, 3, 4 • Actividad 3 **Vocabulario en uso** (20 min.) • Interactive Whiteboard Vocabulary Activities • Actividades 4, 5, 6, 7 • Fondo cultural	**Wrap-up and Homework Options** (5 min.) • Core Practice 9A-1, 9A-2, 9A-3, 9A-4 • Prueba 9A-1: Vocabulary recognition
2	**Warm-up** (10 min.) • Actividad 8 • Homework check ✓**Formative Assessment** (10 min.) • Prueba 9A-1: Vocabulary recognition	**Gramática y vocabulario en uso** (65 min.) • Audio Activities 5, 6 • Actividades 10, 11 • Communicative Pair Activity • Presentation: *Acabar de* + infinitive • View: GramActiva video • Interactive Whiteboard Grammar Activities • Actividad 13 • Audio Activity 7 • Fondo cultural	**Wrap-up and Homework Options** (5 min.) • Core Practice 9A-5 • Writing Activity 10 • Actividades 9, 12 • Prueba 9A-2 with Study Plan: Vocabulary production
3	**Warm-up** (5 min.) • Homework check ✓**Formative Assessment** (10 min.) • Prueba 9A-2 with Study Plan: Vocabulary production	**Gramática y vocabulario en uso** (70 min.) • Exploración del lenguaje • Writing Activity 11 • Communicative Pair Activity • Presentation: *Gustar* and similar verbs • View: GramActiva video • Interactive Whiteboard Grammar Activities • Actividades 14, 15, 17, 18 • Fondo cultural • Writing Activities 12, 13	**Wrap-up and Homework Options** (5 min.) • Core Practice 9A-6, 9A-7 • Actividad 16 • Pruebas 9A-3, 9A-4 with Study Plans: *Acabar de* + infinitive, *Gustar* and similar verbs
4	**Warm-up** (10 min.) • Homework check ✓**Formative Assessment** (15 min.) • Pruebas 9A-3, 9A-4 with Study Plans: *Acabar de* + infinitive, *Gustar* and similar verbs	**Gramática y vocabulario en uso** (30 min.) • Audio Activities 8, 9 • Communicative Pair Activity • Fondo cultural • Pronunciación • El español en la comunidad **¡Adelante!** (30 min.) • Presentación oral: Step 1 • La cultura en vivo	**Wrap-up and Homework Options** (5 min.) • Presentación oral: Step 2
5	**Warm-up** (5 min.) • Presentación oral: Step 2	**¡Adelante!** (50 min.) • Presentación oral: Step 3 • Lectura • ¿Comprendes? • Y tú, ¿qué dices? **Repaso del capítulo** (30 min.) • Vocabulario y gramática • Preparación para el examen 1, 2, 3, 4, 5	**Wrap-up and Homework Options** (5 min.) • Core Practice 9A-8, 9A-9 • Instant Check • Lectura • Examen del capítulo 9A
6	**Warm-up** (15 min.) • Homework check • Situation Cards **Repaso del capítulo** (10 min.) • Communicative Pair Activities ✓**Summative Assessment** (40 min.) • Examen del capítulo 9A	**¡Adelante!** (20 min.) • Videomisterio: *¿Eres tú, María?*, Episodio 9	**Wrap-up and Homework Options** (5 min.) • Videomisterio

Standards for *Capítulo* 9A

- To achieve the goals of the Standards, students will:

Communication

1.1 Interpersonal
- Talk about movies and television
- Talk about opinions about the media
- Talk about likes and dislikes

1.2 Interpretive
- Read and listen to information about movies and television
- Read and listen to opinions about the media
- Read a picture-based story
- Listen to and watch a video about television choices
- View a video mystery series

1.3 Presentational
- Present information about movies and television
- Present information about opinions about the media
- Write about household chores

Culture

2.1 Practices and Perspectives
- Talk about the popularity of ***Sábado Gigante***

2.2 Products and Perspectives
- Discuss Mexican-born film director Alfonso Cuarón
- Discuss Spanish-born film director Luis Buñuel
- Discuss Salvador Dalí and his painting
- Discuss the popularity and style of ***telenovelas***
- Discuss the variety show ***Sábado Gigante***

Connections

3.1 Cross-curricular
- Discuss important artists and their work: Cuarón, Buñuel, Dalí
- Reinforce math skills

Comparisons

4.1 Language
- Talk about vocabulary through the recognition of cognates
- Talk about the use of ***acabar de*** + ***infinitive*** for recent events
- Explain the influence of Greek, Latin, and Arabic on the Spanish language
- Explain ***gustar*** and similar verbs
- Discuss linking words
- Discuss and compare communicative gestures

4.2 Culture
- Compare avant garde film makers
- Compare ***las telenovelas*** to soap operas
- Compare ***Sábado Gigante*** to other long-running shows

Communities

5.1 Beyond the School
- Identify local Spanish language television programming

5.2 Lifelong Learner
- View Latin American cable or satellite television
- View a video mystery series

Capítulo 9A El cine y la televisión

Chapter Objectives

Communication

By the end of this chapter you will be able to:
- Listen to and read different opinions about television
- Talk and write about television programs and movies
- Exchange information while sharing opinions about television and film

Culture

You will also be able to:
- Understand and use common gestures in Spanish-speaking countries, and compare them to ones you use
- Compare popular television programs in Spanish-speaking countries with programs in the United States

You will demonstrate what you know and can do:
- Presentación oral, p. 443
- Preparación para el examen, p. 447

You will use:

Vocabulary
- Television programs
- Movies
- Words and expressions to give opinions

Grammar
- *Acabar de* + infinitive
- *Gustar* and similar verbs

Exploración del mundo hispano

Country Connection
Movies and Television

realidades.com GO

Reference Atlas

Videocultura y actividad

Mapa global interactivo

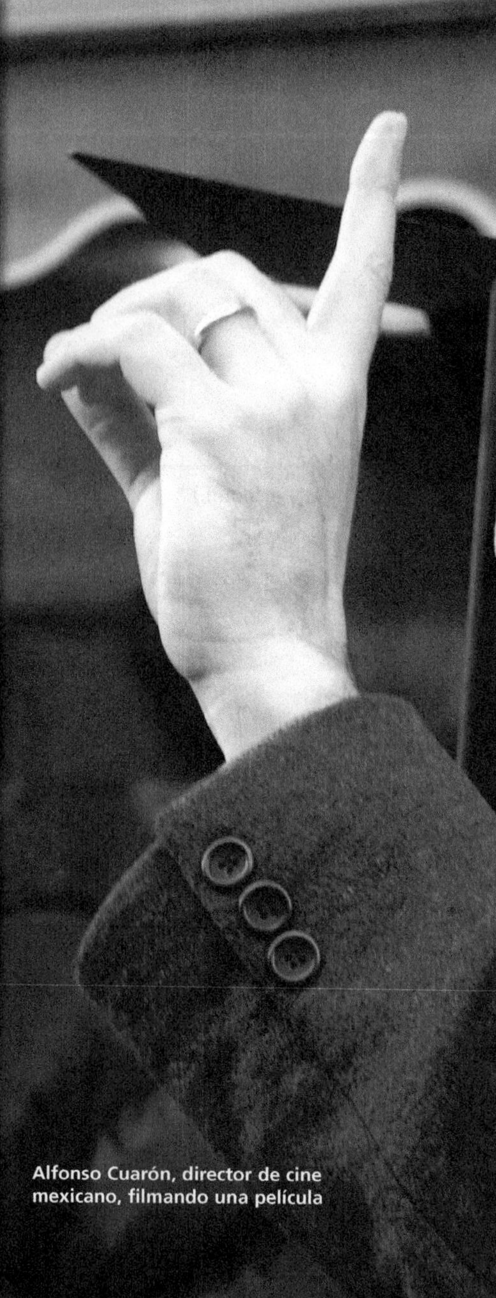

Alfonso Cuarón, director de cine mexicano, filmando una película

ENRICH YOUR TEACHING

Using Backward Design

Have students preview the sample performance tasks on *Preparación para el examen,* p. 447, and connect them to the Chapter Objectives. Explain to students that by completing the sample tasks they can self-assess their learning progress.

Mapa global interactivo

Download the *Mapa global interactivo* files for Chapter 9A and preview the activity. In this activity, you discover Andalusia and Granada.

Arte y cultura | España

Portrait of Luis Buñuel Luis Buñuel (1900–1983) was a Spanish-born film director. He made films in Spain, the United States, Mexico, and France. His films were often controversial because of their strong imagery and difficult topics. Buñuel made two surrealist films with artist Salvador Dalí (1904–1989), Spain's most famous surrealist painter. The films mixed reality and dreams. This portrait of Buñuel was painted by Dalí in 1924 when the painter was 20 years old and Buñuel was 24.

- Who are some young film directors today whose films are considered to be "cutting edge"?

"Retrato de Luis Buñuel" (1924), Salvador Dalí ▶

DIFFERENTIATED INSTRUCTION

Digital resources such as the ***Interactive Whiteboard*** activity banks, ***Videomodelos***, additional ***Online Activities, Study Plans***, automatically graded ***Leveled Workbook***, animated ***Grammar Tutorials, Flashcards***, and ***Vocabulary and Grammar Videos*** will help you reach students of different ability levels and learning styles.

STUDENTS NEEDING EXTRA HELP

Guided Practice Activities
- Flashcards, pp. 275–280
- Vocabulary Check, pp. 281–284
- Grammar Support, pp. 285–288

HERITAGE LEARNERS

Realidades para hispanohablantes
- Chapter Opener, pp. 330–331
- A primera vista, p. 232
- Videohistoria, p. 333
- Manos a la obra, pp. 334–341
- ¡Adelante!, pp. 342–347
- Repaso del capítulo, pp. 348–349

ADVANCED/PRE-AP*

Pre-AP* Resource Book,
- pp. 94–97

Communications Workbook
- Integrated Performance Assessment, p. 327

PresentationExpress™
See pp. 424c–424d

Chapter Opener

Core Instruction

Resources: Map Transparencies 12, 15–16, 18, 20

Suggestions: Explain that students will learn how to talk about movies and television. Brainstorm a list of different types of movies and television shows. Have students give one example for each category and a short description. The video story is about a group of friends who try to agree on what to watch on television.

Videocultura View *Medios de comunicación* with the class to learn about Spanish media in the United States and the world.

Arte y cultura

Standards: 2.2, 4.2

Resources: Fine Art Transparencies, p. 13

Suggestions: Explain the concept of surrealism. Refer students to the painting of Luis Buñuel and ask them if they think this painting exemplifies this artistic movement.

Answers will vary but may include Sofia Coppola, and Robert Rodríguez.

Teaching with Photos

By the time Alfonso Cuarón was 12 years old, he already knew a lot about filmmaking. His hobbies were watching films at home or in theaters, and making Super 8 films, using his siblings as actors. Have students imagine that they are behind the camera, directing a film. What subject would they choose? How would they go about making their movie?

Culture Note

Alfonso Cuarón was born in Mexico City, but his success is international, and he has directed films in English and Spanish. His *Harry Potter and the Prisoner of Azkaban* won a BAFTA Award in 2011, for Kid's Vote for Film of the Decade. Cuarón has also directed film adaptations of novels by Frances Hodson and Charles Dickens, and received numerous awards for his acclaimed film, *Children of Men*.

9A Language Input

Vocabulario en contexto

Core Instruction

Standards: 1.2, 4.2

Resources: Teacher's Resource Book: Input Script, p. 293, Clip Art, pp. 306–307, Audio Script, p. 294; Voc. and Gram. Transparencies 159–160; TPR Stories Book, pp. 122–133; Audio Program DVD: Cap. 9A, Tracks 1–2

Focus: Presenting new vocabulary about television shows

Suggestions: Use the story in the *TPR Stories Book* to present the new vocabulary and grammar or use the Input Script from the *Teacher's Resource Book.*

Explain to the students that they will be reading about television shows that can be seen on *Canal 9.* Before they start the reading, have them look at the pictures and guess what kind of shows are offered.

When presenting the different types of movies, use videos or DVDs from the library and have students tell you what kind of films they are and describe the movies.

BELLRINGER REVIEW

Have students copy and complete the following sentences from the board:

1) *Mi clase de inglés empieza a las ____ y termina a las ____.*
2) *El almuerzo empieza a las ____ y termina a las ____.*
3) *Mi mamá sale de la casa a las ____ y vuelve a las ____.*

Block Schedule

Use the Internet to search for Spanish titles of recent Hollywood movies. Have students try to guess what the title of the movie is in English. If they get it on the first try, have them explain what kind of movie it is. If they don't get it from the title, give them hints by explaining what type of film it is, who the major actors and actresses are, and so on. You can also use Spanish titles of popular TV shows from the United States.

A primera vista

Objectives

Read, listen to, and understand information about
- movies and television programs
- opinions on media entertainment

Vocabulario en contexto

¿Qué le interesa? Un programa...

¿...de entrevistas?

Entre tú y yo
Pablo Ramírez habla con personas fascinantes.

¿...educativo?

Nuestro planeta
Explora el mundo de los animales.

¿...de concursos?

¡Una fortuna para ti!
¡Los participantes pueden recibir mucho dinero!

¿...de noticias?

Las noticias de hoy
Presentamos todo lo que necesita saber del mundo en 30 minutos.

¿...deportivo?

Fútbol hoy
Hay fútbol, fútbol y más fútbol.

¿...una telenovela?

Secretos de amor
¿Qué va a pasar con Rosario y Felipe en este programa emocionante?

¿...musical?

Ritmos latinos
Le presenta música de más de 20 países diferentes.

¿...de dibujos animados?

Patito y Paquito
Una presentación cómica para todos los niños.

—¿Qué quieres ver en la tele?

—¿La verdad? **Me aburre** la televisión. No me interesan nada los programas que **dan.**

—No estoy de acuerdo. Pienso que la televisión presenta muchos programas interesantes y divertidos.

DIFFERENTIATED INSTRUCTION

Multiple Intelligences

Visual/Spatial: Have students create their own movie posters. Encourage them to use their imaginations when thinking of titles.

Heritage Language Learners

Have students write a short paragraph describing a recent movie. Students should include the name of the movie and the type of movie it is. They should also tell when the movie begins using the 24-hour clock. Point out that the 24-hour clock is often used when referring to movie schedules.

—¿Qué dan en el Cine Florida?

—Hay seis películas. Mis amigos dicen que esta película policíaca es muy **violenta.** No quiero verla. Me interesan más las películas románticas como *Antonio y Ana.*

—Yo también quiero verla. ¿A qué hora va a **empezar?**

—**Empieza** a las cuatro y media, y **termina antes de** las seis. **Dura menos de** una hora y **media.**

—**¿De veras?** Son **casi** las cuatro. ¡Vamos ahora!

Más práctica GO

realidades.com | print

	realidades.com	print
Instant Check	✔	
Guided WB pp. 275–280	✔	✔
Core WB pp. 157–158	✔	✔
Comm. WB p. 176	✔	✔
***Hispanohablantes* WB** p. 332		✔

1 ¿Qué dan en la tele hoy?

Escuchar

Vas a escuchar información sobre ocho programas del Canal 9. Señala cada tipo de programa en tu libro.

2 ¿Qué película vamos a ver?

Escuchar

Vas a escuchar siete frases sobre las películas que dan en el Cine Florida. Si una frase es lógica, haz el gesto del pulgar hacia arriba. Si no es lógica, haz el gesto del pulgar hacia abajo.

ENRICH YOUR TEACHING

Teacher-to-Teacher

Have students find information on the Internet about a television program from a Spanish-speaking country. Tell them to get an idea of what type of show it is by looking at images and skimming any text. Ask them to write a short description of the show.

21st Century Skills

Communication Have students learn and practice the vocabulary using the embedded audio files of the eBook and the online vocabulary practice. Then have them use the flashcards to quiz each other about TV preferences.

Language Input 9A

1 Standards: 1.2

Resources: Teacher's Resource Book: Audio Script, p. 294; Audio Program DVD: Cap. 9A, Track 3; Answer Keys: Student Edition, p. 126

Focus: Listening comprehension about television shows

Suggestions: Play the audio or read the script aloud. Pause to monitor that students are selecting the correct television program.

Script and Answers:

1. **¡Puede ganar un televisor nuevo si contesta esta pregunta! *(de concursos)***
2. **Hoy vamos a hablar sobre diferentes animales que podemos ver en el zoológico. *(educativo)***
3. **¡Qué partido! Fue fantástico. Los Leones ganaron seis a tres. Son los mejores de la liga. *(deportivo)***
4. **Hola amigos. Me llamo Pepita Lupita. ¿Quieres cantar conmigo? ¡La-la-la-la! *(de dibujos animados)***
5. **—Hoy estoy hablando con el actor principal de la película romántica *Antonio y Ana.* Hola, Pedro. ¿Cómo está Ud.?**
   —Bien, gracias. Me encanta estar aquí. *(de entrevistas)*
6. **Muy buenas noches. Habla Ramón Montes. Hoy en Washington, el presidente dice que la situación económica está mejor. *(de noticias)***
7. **¡No puede ser! Por favor, María. Te necesito. Te quiero. Eres la más importante para mí. *(una telenovela)***
8. **¡Ahora aquí para cantar con nosotros, el grupo El Mariachi Michoacán! *(musical)***

2 Standards: 1.2

Resources: Teacher's Resource Book: Audio Script, p. 294; Audio Program DVD: Cap. 9A, Track 4; Answer Keys: Student Edition, p. 127

Focus: Listening comprehension

Suggestions: Remind students to base their reponses on the movie list from *Cine Florida.*

Script and Answers:

1. **La película policíaca es muy violenta. *(thumbs-up)***
2. **¡Ay! No dan una película romántica esta semana. *(thumbs-down)***
3. **Dan un drama muy bueno esta tarde. ¿Por qué no vamos a verlo? *(thumbs-up)***
4. ***Antonio y Ana* es una película de ciencia ficción. *(thumbs-down)***
5. **Vamos con mi hermanito a ver *El terror en el castillo.* Es una comedia muy divertida. *(thumbs-down)***
6. **Esta semana dan la película *La tragedia de Laura* en el Cine Florida. *(thumbs-up)***
7. ***Mi tío tonto* es una película de ciencia ficción. Vamos a verla. *(thumbs-down)***

Videohistoria

Core Instruction

Standards: 1.2

Resources: Voc. and Gram. Transparencies 161–162; Audio Program DVD: Cap. 9A, Track 5

Focus: Presenting additional contextualized vocabulary and grammar; previewing the video

Suggestions:

Pre-reading: Brainstorm a list of words or phrases used to express agreement or disagreement. Have students compare the words and expressions on their lists with the words they find in the *Videohistoria*.

Reading: Read the captions with students or play the audio. Using transparencies and non-verbal clues helps students understand the new words in blue type.

Post-reading: Complete *Actividad* 3 to check comprehension.

Video

Core Instruction

Standards: 1.2

Resources: Teacher's Resource Book: Video Script, p. 298; Video Program: Cap. 9A; Video Program Teacher's Guide: Cap. 9A

Focus: Comprehending a story about deciding which television show to watch

Suggestions:

Pre-viewing: Ask students if it is difficult to decide what to watch on television. Ask them who gets to decide what shows to watch when they watch television with their friends and family.

Viewing: Remind students that body language and facial expressions can help them understand what people are saying. Show the video once without pausing. Show it again, pausing to check for comprehension.

Post-viewing: Complete the Video Activities in the *Communication Workbook*.

¿Qué dan en la tele?

¿Qué programa de televisión van a ver los chicos? Lee la historia.

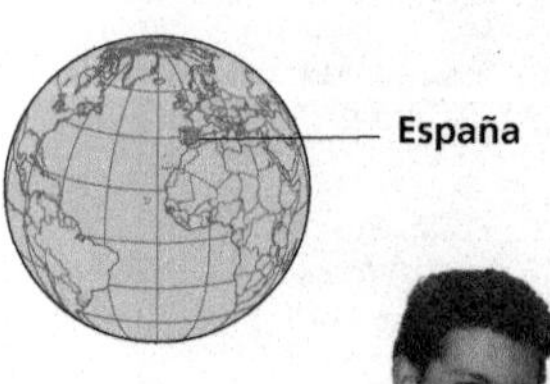

Strategy

Scanning
Looking for details prior to reading can help with comprehension. Scan the reading and look for instances in which one or more people disagree about something. What do they disagree about and what are some expressions used?

Ignacio: ¿Qué dan en la televisión? Elena, ¿dónde está el mando a distancia?*

Elena: Está encima de la mesita, al lado de la lámpara.

Ignacio: ¡Ah, sí! Lo veo. Vamos a ver lo que hay . . .

*remote control

5

Ignacio: No me gustan estos programas **infantiles.** ¿Qué más hay?

Elena: Un momento . . . este programa de entrevistas es mi favorito. Hablan de todo. Ohhh, **¡acaban de** hablar con mi actor favorito!

Ignacio: Sí, y ya terminaron. **Por eso** no tenemos que verlo.

Ignacio: Podemos ver un programa de concursos.

Javier: ¿O un programa educativo? ¿O las noticias?

Todos: ¡Nooo!

Ignacio: ¡Tantos canales y no hay nada que ver!

Ana: ¿Por qué no vamos al cine?

Ana: Quiero ver una comedia.

Elena: Yo prefiero ver una película romántica.

Ignacio: No, son tontas. ¿Qué tal una película de ciencia ficción?

Todos: ¡Nooo!

Javier: Dan un drama nuevo en el Cine Tamayo.

Todos: ¡Nooo!

DIFFERENTIATED INSTRUCTION

Heritage Language Learners

Have students write a persuasive paragraph to convince their classmates that they should watch a particular television show. Be sure students include a thesis statement, at least two sentences about why someone should watch their show, and a summary statement.

Students with Learning Difficulties

Have students create a T-chart. On one side of their papers have students write ***los programas que quieren ver*** along with a list of the kinds of television programs that are discussed in the *Videohistoria*. On the other side they should write ***las películas que quieren ver*** with a list of the kinds of movies Elena and her friends talk about.

2

Ana: ¡Fabuloso! Mi telenovela favorita.

Elena: Sí, me encanta. Es muy emocionante. **El actor** y **la actriz** principales son muy guapos.

Ignacio: ¡No! Me aburren las telenovelas. Vamos a ver otro canal.

Ana y Elena: Ignacio, ¡nuestra telenovela, por favor!

3

Elena: ¿Qué más hay? Mmmm. **¿Qué clase de** programa es éste?

Ana: Es **un programa de la vida real.** Es muy realista.

Ignacio: No son realistas. Pienso que son **tontos.** ¿Verdad, Javier?

Javier: Pues, no sé mucho **sobre** esta clase de programas.

4

Jorgito: Elena, quiero ver dibujos animados. **Ya** son las cuatro.

Elena: Jorgito, ¿no ves que estoy con mis amigos? Tú puedes ver la tele más tarde. Mira, puedes escuchar música en mi dormitorio.

Jorgito: Está bien, pero sólo hoy.

Todos: Adiós, Jorgito.

8

Jorgito: Ahora puedo ver los dibujos animados, **especialmente** mi favorito, *Rin, ran, run.* ¡Qué bien!

3 ¿Comprendes?

Escribir • Hablar

¿A quién(es) se refiere *(refers)* cada frase: Ana, Elena, Ignacio, Javier o Jorgito? Una frase puede referirse a más de una persona.

1. No me interesan nada las telenovelas.
2. No veo mucho los programas de la vida real.
3. Me encanta este programa. Hablan con actores.
4. Me encantan las telenovelas.
5. Voy a escuchar música.
6. Yo prefiero ver una película romántica.
7. Ahora no hay nadie aquí. Puedo ver mi programa favorito.

Más práctica GO

realidades.com | print

	realidades.com	print
Instant Check	✔	
Guided WB pp. 281–284	✔	✔
Core WB pp. 159–160	✔	✔
Comm. WB pp. 170–172, 173	✔	✔
***Hispanohablantes* WB** p. 333		✔

3 Standards: 1.1, 1.3

Resources: Answer Keys: Student Edition, p. 127

Focus: Reading for understanding

Suggestions: Have students work in pairs. Tell them to cover the statements in the book so that they can't read them. Read each statement aloud and have students scan the *Videohistoria* to find the correct answer. The first pair to raise their hands and give the correct answer receives a point. The pair with the most correct answers wins.

Answers:

1. Ignacio
2. Javier
3. Elena
4. Ana y Elena
5. Jorgito
6. Elena
7. Jorgito

Pre-AP* Support

- **Learning Objective:** Interpersonal Speaking
- **Activity:** Have students create a short conversation based on Scene 7 of this video. Ask them to change the types of movies the friends are discussing, and to finish the dialogue by proposing one movie all the characters agree to go see.
- ***Pre-AP* Resource Book:*** Comprehensive guide to Pre-AP* vocabulary skill development, pp. 51–57

Additional Resources

- Communication Wbk.: Audio Act. 5, p. 173
- Teacher's Resource Book: Audio Script, p. 295
- Audio Program DVD: Cap. 9A, Track 8

ENRICH YOUR TEACHING

Culture Note

Point out that in the past many Spanish-speaking celebrities were not as well known in the United States as they are today. Ask students if they have heard of Desi Arnaz and explain that he was one of the first actors from a Spanish-speaking country to succeed on American television. Ask them to name Spanish speakers they have seen on television shows or in movies.

21st Century Skills

Critical Thinking and Problem Solving Have students discuss in small groups the differences between soap operas and reality TV shows. Have them draw conclusions about why one type of show might be more popular than the other in some countries.

ASSESSMENT

Quiz: Vocabulary Recognition

- Prueba 9A-1: pp. 229–230

INTERACTIVE WHITEBOARD
Vocabulary Activities 9A

4 Standards: 1.1, 1.2, 1.3

Resources: Teacher's Resource Book: Audio Script, pp. 294–295; Audio Program DVD: Cap. 9A, Track 6; Answer Keys: Student Edition, p. 128

Focus: Listening comprehension; giving your opinion about television shows

Suggestions: Play the audio or read the script aloud. Before students get together with a partner to do Step 2, have them check their answers to Step 1.

Script:

Step 1

1. **Siempre vemos los programas educativos porque son realistas. *(educativos / realistas)***
2. **¿Los programas de dibujos animados? ¡No! Son demasiado infantiles. *(los dibujos animados / infantiles)***
3. **Uy, me aburren los programas de entrevistas. Son muy tontos. *(de entrevistas / tontos)***
4. **Me encantan las telenovelas. ¡Qué emocionantes son! *(las telenovelas / emocionantes)***
5. **No veo los programas de concursos porque generalmente son aburridos. *(de concursos / aburridos)***
6. **Me interesan los programas de la vida real. Son fascinantes. *(de la vida real / fascinantes)***

Step 2
Answers will vary.

BELLRINGER REVIEW

Have volunteers tell the class the type of movie or program being illustrated in *Actividad* 5.

5 Standards: 1.3

Focus: Writing about movies and television shows in a personalized context

Suggestions: Be sure students understand what type of show each of the pictures represents. Remind students to save their work for *Actividad* 6.

Answers will vary.

Manos a la obra

Vocabulario en uso

Objectives

- Listen to and write descriptions of different television programs
- Read about and discuss opinions of and preferences for programs and movies
- Exchange information about the amount of television you and others watch

4 Muchas opiniones

Escuchar • Escribir • Hablar

Un programa de radio les pregunta a sus oyentes *(listeners)* qué piensan de los diferentes programas de televisión.

1. En una hoja de papel copia la tabla y escribe los números del 1 al 6. Vas a escuchar las opiniones de unas personas. Escribe la clase de programa en la primera columna y la descripción en la segunda columna. Luego escribe frases para expresar tu opinión.

Programa de televisión	Descripción
1. las comedias	muy cómicas

Modelo
Me encantan las comedias porque son muy cómicas.

2. Habla con otro(a) estudiante. Di si estás de acuerdo con sus opiniones.

Modelo
Estoy de acuerdo. Las comedias son muy cómicas.
o:—*No estoy de acuerdo. Las comedias son muy tontas.*

5 Buenos ejemplos

Escribir

Escoge seis de los siguientes programas de televisión. Luego escribe frases para dar un buen ejemplo de los diferentes programas.

Modelo
Pirates of the Caribbean *es una comedia.*

DIFFERENTIATED INSTRUCTION

Students with Special Needs

Using the script for Step 1 in *Actividad* 4, create a cloze passage for hearing impaired students. Leave out the adjectives and have students choose the correct answer from a word bank.

Students with Learning Difficulties

For *Actividad* 5, assign individual students a specific type of television program. Have them read their examples aloud and create a master list on the board for students to use in *Actividad* 6.

6 ¿Te gustaría ver . . . ?

Hablar

Usa la información que escribiste en la Actividad 5 y habla con otro(a) estudiante sobre qué clase de programas le gustaría ver. Él o ella puede usar las siguientes palabras.

me aburren	tontos, -as	fascinantes
me gustan	emocionantes	cómicos, -as
me interesan	violentos, -as	infantiles
me encantan	realistas	**¡Respuesta personal!**

Modelo

A —*¿Te gustaría ver una comedia como Pirates of the Caribbean?*
B —*¡Uf! Me aburren las comedias. Son tontas.*
o: —*¡Por supuesto! Me encantan las comedias. Son cómicas.*

7 Escucha y escribe

Escuchar • Escribir

Escucha y luego escribe en una hoja de papel lo que dice un joven sobre un programa de televisión que ve.

8 ¿Qué programa ves tú?

Escribir • Hablar

1. Usa la descripción del programa de televisión de la Actividad 7 como modelo y escribe sobre un programa que tú ves. No debes nombrar el programa en la descripción.
2. Lee tu descripción a otros(as) estudiantes de la clase. Ellos deben identificar el programa que describes.

Fondo Cultural | Argentina | España | México | Venezuela

Las telenovelas Venezuela, Mexico, Argentina, and Spain produce many soap operas that are popular with people of all ages. Unlike soap operas in the United States that continue for years with the same characters, the *telenovelas* frequently last only a matter of months. They are then replaced with new shows and different characters.

- What are the advantages of stories that continue for years versus stories that are new every several months? Which would you prefer?

Los actores practican para la telenovela *Cuidado con el ángel*.

6 Standards: 1.1

Focus: Using contextualized vocabulary with a model conversation; stating opinions about television programs

Recycle: Likes and dislikes

Suggestions: Remind Student A to use *¿Te gustaría ver...?* and a specific program from *Actividad* 5. Point out that Student B should use the words and phrases in the box.

Answers will vary.

Common Errors: Forgetting to make the adjective agree in number and gender with the noun. Remind students to make adjectives agree with the nouns they describe.

7 Standards: 1.2, 1.3

Resources: Teacher's Resource Book: Audio Script, p. 295; Audio Program DVD: Cap. 9A, Track 7; Answer Keys: Student Edition, p. 128

Focus: Listening for comprehension; writing with accuracy

Suggestions: Use the audio or read the script aloud. Have students correct their writing and save it to use in *Actividad* 8.

Script and Answers:

A menudo veo la telenovela que se llama *Un día más*. Dura una hora. Empieza a las seis de la tarde y termina a las siete. Lo dan en el Canal 11. Me gustan las telenovelas. Para mí, son muy emocionantes.

8 Standards: 1.1, 1.3

Focus: Writing in a personalized context about watching television

Suggestions: Review the paragraph students wrote in *Actividad* 7. Point out that ***empezar*** means "to begin" and is an ***e → ie*** stem-changing verb.

Answers will vary.

Fondo cultural

Standards: 2.2, 4.2

Suggestions: Before beginning the reading, direct students' attention to the photo and have them guess what kind of program *Cuidado con el ángel* is. Ask students to name soap operas that they have seen.

Answers will vary.

ENRICH YOUR TEACHING

Culture Note

This photo was taken on the set of the Mexican soap opera *Cuidado con el ángel* at the Televisa studios in Mexico City. Mexican actress Maite Perroni and Cuban actor William Levy (the man standing to the left of the crib) rehearse for the show as the director, Victor M. Foulloux, stands between them, giving them instructions.

21st Century Skills

Productivity and Accountability Have students watch several types of Spanish TV programs and then discuss in pairs or small groups which type of program would interest them most to work in as a career, if they were in this field. Have them think about what it would take to have such a career and develop a plan to accomplish that.

9 Standards: 1.2, 1.1

Resources: Voc. and Gram. Transparency 164; Answer Keys: Student Edition, p. 129

Focus: Reading comprehension of movie reviews; asking questions in a personalized context

Recycle: Asking questions

Suggestions: Review question words with students. Remind them that all question words have accent marks. Point out that in questions, the subject often comes after the verb. You may want to use the transparency. Begin by asking students to predict what the article is about by reading the title and opening question. Direct students' attention to the ratings key. What do the stars indicate? Have students scan the article and tell you how many movies are reviewed and which one received the worst rating.

Students should take turns being Student A and Student B switching roles after each movie. After talking about all three films, students should decide which movie they want to see.

Answers will vary but should include:

Cuando el amor llega: **Es una película romántica; es sobre un joven rico enamorado de una chica pobre; el amor de los jóvenes es imposible; dura dos horas y media; los actores principales son Cristina Campos y Rafael Montenegro.**

Mis padres son de otro planeta: **Es una película de comedia y ciencia ficción; es fascinante y cómica; unos chicos descubren que sus padres son originarios de otro planeta; dura más de tres horas; los actores principales son Javier Zaragoza y Miguel Vilar.**

Mi perro es mi héroe: **Es un drama; no es violenta, es realista y divertida; el perro le salva la vida a toda la familia; dura menos de dos horas; los actores principales son Ana Jiménez y Antonio Barrera.**

Block Schedule

Have students work in pairs to write a movie review column for a newspaper. Have them use the questions in *Actividad* 9 to help them begin. If your school has a newspaper, you may want to submit some of the reviews to be published.

9 ¿Qué dicen los críticos?  

Leer • Hablar

Lee el artículo de abajo que escribieron los críticos Guillo y Nadia. Luego trabaja con otro(a) estudiante para decidir qué película van a ver. Contesta las preguntas en el recuadro.

Nota

Use *más / menos* **de** with numbers.

- más **de** tres horas
- menos **de** diez personas

Modelo

A —*Acabo de leer un artículo sobre la película . . . ¿Te gustaría verla?*

B —*¿Qué clase de película es?*

¿Qué clase de película es?	¿Cuánto tiempo dura?
¿De veras? ¿Cómo es?	¿Quiénes son los actores principales?
¿Sí? ¿Qué pasa en la película?	Pues, ¿quieres verla?

En nuestra opinión

¿Piensas ir al cine este fin de semana? Nadia y Guillo te dan sus impresiones de tres nuevas películas . . .

Guillo

Nadia

★★★ recomendable
★★ más o menos
★ no la recomiendo

Cuando el amor llega Con Cristina Campos y Rafael Montenegro. Una película romántica sobre un joven rico enamorado de una chica pobre. Ante la oposición de sus padres, el amor de los jóvenes es imposible. Esta película, de dos horas y media, es similar a las viejas fórmulas de las telenovelas—un poco tonta y aburrida. Los protagonistas son buenos, pero los actores secundarios son demasiado dramáticos. Recomendable para personas que no tienen nada que hacer.(★)

Mis padres son de otro planeta Unos chicos descubren que sus padres son originarios de otra galaxia y que están en este planeta para explorar y planear una invasión. Una producción para toda la familia que combina elementos de comedia y ciencia ficción. Es tan fascinante y cómica que no puedes creer que estás en el cine por más de tres horas. Los actores principales, Javier Zaragoza y Miguel Vilar, son fantásticos. (★★★)

Mi perro es mi héroe Un drama para toda la familia—no es violenta y es bastante realista. Un poco infantil, pero con mucha acción y emoción. El mejor amigo del hombre, el perro, con inteligencia y valor, le salva la vida* a toda la familia. La película es divertida pero un poco corta (menos de dos horas). Tiene muy buenos actores, como Ana Jiménez y Antonio Barrera. Es una buena película. (★★★)

*saves the life

DIFFERENTIATED INSTRUCTION

Heritage Language Learners

Have students write a movie critique about a film produced in their heritage country or a film featuring their favorite Spanish-speaking actor or actress.

Students with Learning Difficulties

To help students calculate averages for *Actividad* 10, create a worksheet for them. Be sure to include the formula and blank spaces for their personal responses. Allow students to use a calculator.

10 ¿Cuántas horas de tele?

Pensar • Hablar • Escribir

Vas a calcular el promedio *(average)* de horas que tus compañeros ven la tele.

Conexiones | Las matemáticas

1. Escribe el número de horas que viste la tele cada día de la semana pasada. Suma *(Add up)* estas horas. Calcula el promedio de horas para cada día.

   ____ *(total de horas)* dividido por 7

2. Trabaja con un grupo de cuatro personas. Pregunta a tus compañeros(as) el tiempo promedio que vieron la televisión cada día. Escribe la información que recibes de tu grupo.

Modelo

A —*Como promedio, ¿cuántas horas viste la tele cada día?*

B —*La vi casi dos horas cada día.*

3. Calcula el promedio de horas que tu grupo vio la tele cada día la semana pasada. Escribe una frase para presentar la información a la clase.

11 La tele en tu vida

Pensar • Leer • Hablar

En un estudio reciente, se dio a conocer que, como promedio, las personas de los Estados Unidos ven ocho horas de tele al día. ¡La suma de estas horas equivale a casi cuatro meses al año frente a la televisión!

1. Usa el promedio de horas de tu grupo de la Actividad 10 y calcula el número total de horas que vieron la tele en un año.
   - 365 días al año por *(promedio de horas)* son *(total de horas)* al año

2. Usa el total de horas al año para contestar estas preguntas. *(Nota: Hay aproximadamente 720 horas en un mes.)*
   1. ¿Tu grupo ve la tele más de un mes al año o menos?
   2. ¿La ven Uds. más que el promedio de personas en los Estados Unidos o menos? ¿Y de las personas en los otros países de la gráfica?
   3. ¿Crees que las personas en los países de la gráfica ven demasiada tele? ¿Por qué?

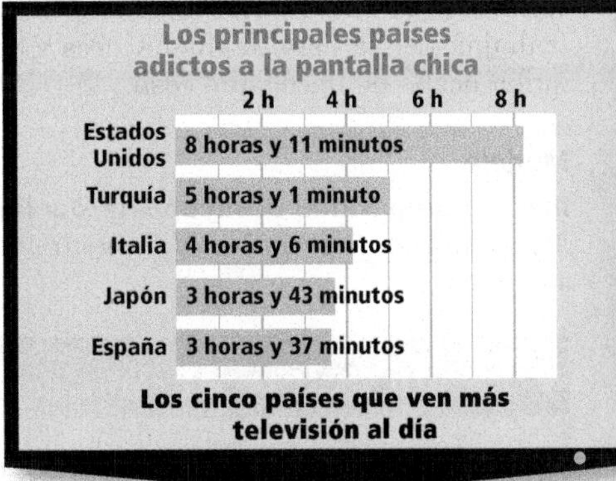

Source: Organisation for Economic Co-Operation and Development

ENRICH YOUR TEACHING

Teacher-to-Teacher

Have the class create a bar graph. Tell them to number one axis from 1 to 24 and to write activities such as ***hacer la tarea, comer la cena, practicar deportes,*** and ***dormir*** on the other axis. Have students complete the graph to show how many hours per day they do each activity. Ask students to compare the time they spend watching television with the time they spend on other activities. When students have completed their graphs, have them calculate the class average.

Practice and Communicate 9A

10 Standards: 1.1, 1.3, 3.1

Focus: Using mathematics

Recycle: Numbers

Suggestions: Write an example of how to calculate an average. Remind students to save this information for *Actividad* 11.

Answers will vary.

Common Errors: Using the incorrect preterite forms of ***ver.*** Review the preterite of ***ver*** before beginning the *Actividad.*

11 Standards: 1.1, 1.2, 1.3, 3.1

Focus: Comparing and discussing information about television-viewing habits

Suggestions: Before beginning the activity, direct students' attention to the transparency or to the graph in the book. Tell students to look for cognates.

Write the math formulas on the board.

Answers will vary.

Extension: Ask students to calculate the percentage of time they spend watching specific types of television shows.

Pre-AP* Support

- **Learning Objective:** Interpersonal Writing
- **Activity 9:** Have students choose one of the three movies reviewed in the activity and, based on the information, draft an e-mail inviting a friend to watch it and describing it briefly. Conversely, have them use the information to write the e-mail to a friend describing how good (or bad!) the movie, which they have just seen, was.
- ***Pre-AP* Resource Book:*** Comprehensive guide to Pre-AP* writing skill development, pp. 27–38

Additional Resources

- Communication Wbk.: Audio Act. 6, p. 173
- Teacher's Resource Book: Audio Script, pp. 295–296, Communicative Pair Activity BLM, pp. 300–301
- Audio Program DVD: Cap. 9A, Track 9

ASSESSMENT

Prueba 9A-2 with Study Plan (online only)

Quiz: Vocabulary Production

- Prueba 9A-2: pp. 231–232

Gramática

Core Instruction

Standards: 4.1

Resources: Teacher's Resource Book: Video Script, p. 298; Video Program: Cap. 9A

INTERACTIVE WHITEBOARD

Grammar Activities 9A

Suggestions: Point out that just as students used the present tense of ***ir* + *a* + infinitive** to indicate an action taking place in the future, they can use the present tense of ***acabar de* + infinitive** to indicate an action that recently took place. You may want to use the *GramActiva* video to introduce the structure or as a follow-up to your presentation.

12 Standards: 1.3

Resources: Answer Keys: Student Edition, p. 130

Focus: Writing sentences about recently performed activities

Recycle: Household chores and leisure activities

Suggestions: Remind students that in a complete sentence they need to capitalize the first word of the sentence and provide punctuation.

Answers:

1. **Mamá acaba de preparar el desayuno de sus hijos.**
2. **Carlitos acaba de comer el desayuno.**
3. **Mariel acaba de limpiar su dormitorio.**
4. **Ezequiel acaba de sacar la basura.**
5. **Ezequiel, Carlitos y Mariel acaban de terminar su tarea.**
6. **Papá acaba de pasar la aspiradora en la sala.**
7. **Elena acaba de dar de comer al gato.**
8. **Todos acaban de buscar sus abrigos.**

Fondo cultural

Standards: 2.1 2.2

Suggestions: Point out that *Sábado Gigante* incorporates a variety of different programming in one show. Ask students to name the diffent kinds of programming included in the show and have them give examples of other variety shows in the United States. Explain that *Sábado Gigante* has aired on *Univisión* since 1986.

Answers will vary.

Manos a la obra

Gramática

Objective

- Write about and discuss activities that you and others have just done

Acabar de + infinitive

When you want to say that something just happened, use the present tense of *acabar de* + infinitive.

Acabo de ver un programa musical.	*I just saw a music program.*
Mis padres acaban de ir al cine.	*My parents just went to the movies.*
Acabamos de hablar de esa película.	*We just talked about that movie.*

Although the action took place in the past, the present-tense forms of *acabar* are used.

Más ayuda realidades.com

- *GramActiva* Video Tutorial: *Acabar de* + infinitive
- *GramActiva* Activity

12 ¡Acaban de hacer muchas cosas!

Escribir

La familia Martínez acaba de hacer muchas cosas esta mañana antes de ir a estudiar y trabajar. Lee la lista de quehaceres y escribe quién acaba de hacer qué cosa.

Modelo

mamá / preparar el desayuno de sus hijos
Mamá <u>acaba de preparar</u> el desayuno de sus hijos.

Quehaceres . . .

1. mamá / preparar el desayuno de sus hijos
2. Carlitos / comer el desayuno ✓
3. Mariel / limpiar su dormitorio ✓
4. Ezequiel / sacar la basura ✓
5. Ezequiel, Carlitos y Mariel / terminar su tarea ✓
6. papá / pasar la aspiradora en la sala ✓
7. Elena / dar de comer al gato ✓
8. todos / buscar sus abrigos ✓

Fondo Cultural | El mundo hispano

Sábado gigante is one of the longest running shows in television history. Its popular host, Don Francisco, started this unique variety program in his native Chile in 1962. It now airs from Miami every Saturday night and brings comedy, celebrity guests, musical performances, games, and contests to more than 100 million viewers in 42 countries. In the past decade, the program has celebrated its 1000th episode and 20th anniversary on the Miami-based Univisión network.

- What television shows do you know that have enjoyed continued success over the years?

El famosísimo Don Francisco ▲

DIFFERENTIATED INSTRUCTION

Multiple Intelligences

Verbal/Linguistic: Ask students to write three sentences about what they just did in their last class. Have them read their sentences aloud while other students try to guess which class is being described.

Heritage Language Learners

Ask students if they or anyone they know watches *Sábado Gigante*. What is their opinion of the show? If Spanish-language programming is available in your area, ask students to watch *Sábado Gigante* or a similar program in Spanish and write a short description of the show.

13 Acabo de ver . . .

Escribir • Hablar

1. Copia la gráfica en una hoja de papel. Escribe tres clases de programas de televisión, obras de teatro o películas que acabas de ver. Da el nombre y haz una descripción.

Acabo de ver . . .	Nombre	Descripción
Una película romántica	*¡No puedo vivir sin ti!*	*demasiado triste*

2. Trabaja con otro(a) estudiante para hablar sobre lo que acaban de ver.

Modelo

A —*Acabo de ver una película romántica.*
B —*¿De veras? ¿Cómo se llama?*
A —*¡No puedo vivir sin ti!*
B —*¿Te gustó?*
A —*No, no me gustó porque es demasiado triste.*

¿Recuerdas?

Some adverbs you can use in descriptions are:

bastante muy
demasiado un poco

Más práctica GO

realidades.com | print

Instant Check	✔	
Guided WB pp. 285–286	✔	✔
Core WB p. 161	✔	✔
Comm. WB pp. 177, 325	✔	✔
***Hispanohablantes* WB** pp. 333–337		✔

Exploración del lenguaje

Words of Greek and Arabic origin

Languages change when regions and nations interact with, or are conquered or colonized by, people who speak a different language. Long before the Romans brought Latin to Spain, certain Greek words had entered the Latin language. Words like *el problema, el programa,* and *el drama* originally were masculine nouns in Greek. When they came into Latin and then Spanish, they kept their masculine gender even though they end in *a.*

Try it out! Which of these new words would you use in the following sentences?

el clima el sistema el poema

1. No comprendo _____ de clasificación de películas en ese país.
2. Me gustaría visitar Panamá porque _____ allí es tropical.
3. Me gusta _____ que acabo de leer.

Arabic also had a large influence on Spanish. Around A.D. 700 the Arabic-speaking Moors invaded Spain from northern Africa. They ruled for 800 years and played a major role in the development of the Spanish language and culture. Words that came from Arabic often begin with the letters *al-*. Many words in Spanish that have a *z* or a *j* in them are also of Arabic origin. You know these words that came from Arabic: *alfombra, azúcar, naranja.*

Try it out! You also know these words that are from Arabic. Fill in the missing letters.

a_ul __macén _anahoria

ENRICH YOUR TEACHING

Culture Note

Spanish has also been influenced by indigenous cultures in North America, South America, Central America, and the Caribbean. For example, the words ***chocolate, aguacate,*** and ***tomate*** come from Náhuatl while ***papa*** is from Quechua. The word ***huracán*** is borrowed from Taino.

Teacher-to-Teacher

Have students look up information on Spanish-language television stations in their area. Ask them to find a listing on a station's Web site and describe the kind of programs that are offered. Ask if the station carries the show *Sábado Gigante.*

BELLRINGER REVIEW

Give students two words and have them tell you the type of movie or television show you are describing. For example you say: ***triste/novios*** and the students respond: ***una película romántica.***

13 Standards: 1.1, 1.3

Resources: Voc. and Gram. Transparency 163

Focus: Describing movies and television shows; using ***acabar de* + infinitive**

Recycle: Adverbs

Suggestions: Direct students' attention to the *¿Recuerdas?* Explain that adverbs describe verbs or adjectives and therefore do not change in number or gender.

Answers will vary.

Exploración del lenguaje
Core Instruction

Standards: 4.1

Resources: Answer Keys: Student Edition, p. 130

Mapa global interactivo, Actividad Discover Andalusia and Granada.

Suggestions: Have students identify Spain, Italy, and Greece on a map. Point out that modern-day maps do not reflect the time periods in the reading.

Answers: **1. el sistema; 2. el clima; 3. el poema azul; almacén; zanahoria**

Theme Project

Give students copies of the Theme Project outline and rubric from the *Teacher's Resource Book*. Explain the task to them, and have them perform Step 1. (For more information, see p. 424-b.)

Additional Resources

- Communication Wbk.: Audio Act. 7, p. 174
- Teacher's Resource Book: Audio Script, p. 296
- Audio Program DVD: Cap. 9A, Track 10

ASSESSMENT

Prueba 9A-3 with Study Plan (online only)

Quiz: ***Acabar de*** **+ Infinitive**

- Prueba 9A-3: p. 233

Gramática

Core Instruction

Standards: 4.1

Resources: Teacher's Resource Book: Video Script, pp. 298–299; Video Program: Disc 18, Cap. 9A

INTERACTIVE WHITEBOARD

Grammar Activities 9A

Suggestions: Review the indirect object pronouns and objects of prepositions with students. Point out that ***mí*** and ***ti*** follow a preposition, not ***yo*** and ***tú.*** Use the transparency to review the structure and play the *GramActiva* video as reinforcement.

BELLRINGER REVIEW

Show Voc. and Gram. Transparency 160. As you point to different types of movies, ask students to respond to whether they like or don't like each type.

14 Standards: 1.2, 1.3

Resources: Teacher's Resource Book: Audio Script, p. 296; Audio Program DVD: Cap. 9A, Track 11; Answer Keys: Student Edition, p. 131

Focus: Listening to opinions; writing with accuracy

Suggestions: Ask students what programs their family members typically like to watch. Play the audio or read the script aloud.

Script and Answers:

1. **A mi hermana le encantan las telenovelas.**
2. **A mis padres no les gustan nada los programas de la vida real.**
3. **A nosotros nos interesan mucho los programas deportivos.**
4. **A mí me aburren los programas de entrevistas.**
5. **A mi hermanito le interesan los programas educativos sobre los animales.**
6. **A ti te gustan los programas musicales, ¿no?**

Extension: Have students say if they agree with the opinions of the Linares family or not. Ask them to explain why they agree or disagree.

Gramática

Objectives

- Listen to a family's comments about programs
- Discuss and write opinions about television and movies
- Create an ideal television programming schedule

Gustar and similar verbs

Even though we usually translate the verb *gustar* as "to like," it literally means "to please." So when you say, *Me gustan los programas deportivos,* you're actually saying, "Sports programs are pleasing to me." *Programas deportivos* is the subject of the sentence, and *me* is the indirect object. Here's the pattern:

indirect object + form of *gustar* + subject

The subject in a sentence with *gustar* usually follows the verb. You need to know if the subject is singular or plural to know which form of *gustar* to use. If the subject is singular, use *gusta.* If it's plural, use *gustan.* If it's an infinitive, use *gusta.*

Me gusta **el actor** en la telenovela pero no me gustan **las actrices.**

A mis amigos les gusta **ver** películas.

To emphasize or clarify *who* is pleased, you can use an additional *a* + pronoun:

A mí me gustan los dibujos animados, pero **a él** no le gustan.

Here are the other verbs you know that are similar to *gustar:*

aburrir	A mí **me aburren** las películas románticas.
doler *(o→ue)*	A Fernando **le duelen** los pies.
encantar	A mis padres **les encanta** el teatro.
faltar	**Me faltan** un cuchillo y un tenedor.
interesar	**Nos interesan** mucho los programas musicales.
quedar	¿No **te queda** bien el vestido?

¿Recuerdas?

You have used *me gusta(n), te gusta(n),* and *le gusta(n)* to talk about what a person likes.

- A mí **me gusta** el cine pero a mi hermano **le gusta** más la televisión.

Más ayuda realidades.com

- *GramActiva* **Video Tutorial:** *Gustar* and similar verbs
- ***Canción de hip hop:*** *¿Qué te interesa?*
- ***GramActiva Activity***

14 Escucha y escribe

Escuchar • Escribir

Escucha las opiniones de la familia Linares sobre los programas que dan en la televisión. En una hoja de papel, escribe los números del 1 al 6 y escribe las frases que escuchas.

Nos gustan las películas cómicas.

DIFFERENTIATED INSTRUCTION

Heritage Language Learners

Ask students if they have a favorite soccer team from their heritage country. Have them write a short paragraph expressing their opinions about soccer and the World Cup. Encourage them to use phrases ***me aburre, me interesa, me gusta,*** and ***me encanta.***

15 A mí y a ti

Escribir • Hablar

1. Trabaja con otro(a) estudiante. Copia el diagrama Venn en una hoja de papel. Escribe el nombre de tu compañero(a) encima del óvalo a la derecha. En el óvalo indicado con *A mí* escribe cinco clases de películas o programas de televisión que te gustan.

2. Pregunta a tu compañero(a) si le gustan las clases de programas y películas que tú escribiste. Si a él o a ella le gusta la clase de programa o película, escribe el nombre en el óvalo de la derecha. (Vas a usar el diagrama Venn en la Actividad 16.)

Modelo

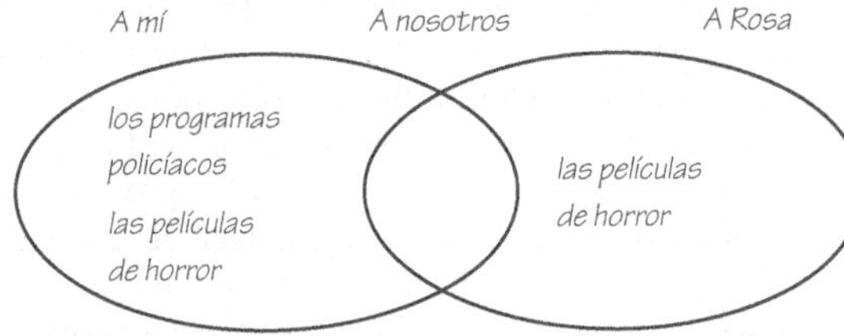

Modelo

A —*¿Te gustan los programas policíacos?*
B —*A ver . . . no, no me gustan mucho.*
A —*Pues, ¿te gustan las películas de horror?*
B —*Sí, me gustan mucho.*

16 A nosotros nos gusta . . .

Escribir

Compara los dos lados de tu diagrama. Escribe las clases de programas y películas que a los dos les gustan en el centro de ese diagrama. Escribe al menos cinco frases completas para describir qué les gusta a Uds.

Modelo

A nosotros nos gustan las películas de horror.
A mí me gustan los programas policíacos pero a Rosa no le gustan.

Modelo

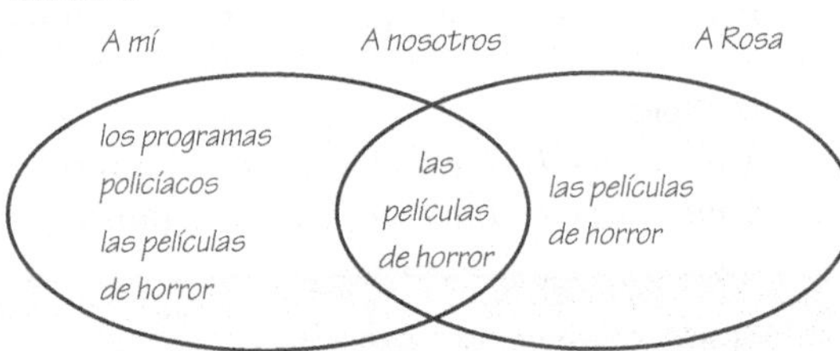

Fondo Cultural | El mundo hispano

Cable television The cable and satellite television industry in Latin America has grown tremendously. Hundreds of channels are available to viewers. Some cable channels specialize in news or sports, and offer their programming to other countries as well. Among the sports, soccer is the one that attracts the most viewers. The World Cup is enormously popular in Latin America and around the world.

- What Latin American programs can you find in your local cable or satellite listings? Watch some of them to find out where these programs are produced.

Practice and Communicate 9A

BELLRINGER REVIEW

Use Transparency 163 to quickly review opinions about television programs.

15 Standards: 1.1, 1.3

Resources: Voc. and Gram. Transparency 2

Focus: Talking about likes and dislikes in a personalized context

Suggestions: Give students a copy of a blank Venn diagram. Before students get together with their partners, have them brainstorm a list of five types of movies and write the ones they like in the first oval of the diagram.

Answers will vary.

Common Errors: Using the ***yo*** form of the verb ***gustar.*** Before you begin the exercise, review the use of ***gustar*** with indirect object pronouns.

16 Standards: 1.3

Resources: Voc. and Gram. Transparency 2

Focus: Expressing similarities and differences in likes and dislikes

Suggestions: You may want to have some of the groups use the words ***aburrir, interesar,*** or ***encantar*** instead of ***gustar.*** Encourage students to use words like ***pero, también,*** and ***tampoco*** when writing their sentences.

Answers will vary.

Extension: Have students repeat the activity using actors and actresses as the focus.

Fondo cultural

Standards: 5.2

Suggestions: Direct students' attention to the photo. Ask students what kind of television show is being shown.

Answers will vary.

ENRICH YOUR TEACHING

Teacher-to-Teacher

Have students search for television listings for various Spanish-speaking countries. Assign each student a different location. Ask students to list at least two programs that they would want to watch and two programs that they would not want to watch and to explain why.

21st Century Skills

Critical Thinking and Problem Solving Have students create survey questions about TV preferences using their responses to Activities 15 and 16 as a model. Have them take home their surveys to find out which shows people in the family prefer. Have them discuss the results in class and analyze preferences among different groups.

17 Standards: 1.1, 1.3

Focus: Practicing with verbs similar to ***gustar***

Recycle: Vocabulary for body parts, clothes, classes, and meals

Suggestions: Before beginning the activity, brainstorm examples of things that might interest or bore students. Encourage students to use vocabulary from previous chapters as well as from this chapter.

Answers will vary.

Pronunciación

Core Instruction

Standards: 4.1

Resources: Teacher's Resource Book: Audio Script, p. 297; Audio Program DVD: Cap. 9A, Track 14

Suggestions: Have students provide examples in English in which their words flow together. Remind students that the ***h*** in Spanish is silent. Have students practice reading the sentences and record their final version.

Theme Project

Students can perform Step 2 at this point. Be sure students understand your corrections. (For more information, see p. 424-b.)

17 Juego

Escribir • Hablar • GramActiva

1. Trabaja en grupos de cuatro personas. Necesitas 20 tarjetas de tres colores. Debes tener cinco tarjetas de un color para la columna 1, cinco de otro color para la columna 2 y diez del tercer color para la columna 3. En cada tarjeta, escribe una de las palabras o expresiones de las dos primeras columnas. Para la tercera columna, escribe dos palabras para cada categoría (por ejemplo, para "cuerpo" puedes escribir *el brazo* en una tarjeta, y *la pierna* en otra).

a mí	encanta(n)	cuerpo
a mi amigo(a)	duele(n)	películas
a nosotros	interesa(n)	clases
a mis amigos	aburre(n)	ropa
a Uds.	queda(n) bien	comidas

2. Baraja *(Shuffle)* las tarjetas de cada columna y ponlas boca abajo *(face down)* en sus tres grupos. Toma una tarjeta de cada grupo, forma una frase completa y di la frase. *Importante:* Para las palabras del primer grupo, vas a tener que escoger una de estas palabras: *me, te, le, nos, les.* Si tu grupo decide que la gramática de tu frase es correcta, recibes 1 punto. Recibes otro punto si la frase es lógica. Si puedes cambiar la frase para hacerla lógica, recibes 2 puntos.

duele(n)
a mi amigo(a)
el pescado

Modelo

A mi amigo le duele el pescado. (1 punto)
A mi amigo le duele la pierna. (2 puntos)

Pronunciación

Linking words

In Spanish just as in English, you don't pronounce a sentence as completely separate words. Instead, the words flow together in phrases. That is why it often seems that phrases or sentences sound as if they are one long word.

How the words flow together depends on the last sound of a word and the beginning sound of the following word. The flow of sounds is usually created by two of the same vowels, two different vowels, or a consonant followed by a vowel. Listen to and say these word combinations:

me‿encanta	de‿entrevistas	le‿aburre
nos‿interesa	dibujos‿animados	de‿horror

Try it out! Listen to and say these sentences. Be careful not to break the flow of sound where you see "‿".

Me‿interesa‿ese programa de‿entrevistas.
A‿Ana le‿aburre‿ese programa‿educativo.
La película de‿horror dura‿una‿hora‿y media.
Vamos‿a ver lo que‿hay‿en la tele.
Me‿encanta‿el actor de‿esa telenovela.

DIFFERENTIATED INSTRUCTION

Heritage Language Learners

Have students listen to *Try it out!* and write the sentences they hear, without looking at the book. Point out any spelling errors they make, such as leaving out the initial ***h*** in a word.

Students with Special Needs

Have groups with students who are colorblind cut their cards into different shapes to differentiate the columns in *Actividad* 17.

18 ¿Qué hay en la tele?

Escribir • Hablar

A veces decimos, "¡Hay tantos canales y programas en la tele pero no hay nada interesante!". Ahora tienes la oportunidad de planear seis horas de televisión para el sábado, desde las 17.00 horas hasta las 23.00 horas, para un concurso que se llama "Tus propias seis horas en la tele".

1. Trabaja en un grupo de tres. Escriban una lista de programas o películas que les gustaría incluir *(include)* en las seis horas. Den esta información para cada programa o película:
   - la clase de programa
   - el nombre
   - cómo es
   - cuánto tiempo dura
   - para quiénes es recomendable
   - por qué le va a interesar al público
2. Preparen una presentación para la clase. Pueden hacer algo visual para acompañar su presentación.
3. Después de escuchar a los diferentes grupos, cada grupo va a votar por la mejor presentación. ¡No pueden votar por la suya *(your own)*! Los grupos tienen que escribir cuatro frases para explicar su decisión. El grupo que recibe más votos gana el concurso.

Modelo

Nosotros votamos por la presentación del grupo de Ana, David y Kathy. Tienen muchos programas que nos interesan a nosotros.

El español en la comunidad

While many television networks are losing viewers, the number of viewers watching Spanish-language networks is growing. Choose a Spanish-language network such as *Univisión, Telemundo, Azteca América,* or *Telefutura* and look online at their program listings. Find the name of a program for each kind of show on p. 426. Watch a few minutes of one of the programs. Although you might find it difficult to understand, tune in from time to time. You'll be amazed at how much you'll learn!

- How are the listings similar to or different from those for the networks you usually watch? Write your impressions of the television show you watched.

Más práctica GO

realidades.com | print

	realidades.com	print
Instant Check	✔	
Guided WB pp. 287–288	✔	✔
Core WB pp. 162–163	✔	✔
Comm. WB pp. 174–175, 178	✔	✔
***Hispanohablantes* WB** pp. 338–341		✔

Practice and Communicate 9A

18 Standards: 1.1, 1.2, 1.3

Focus: Describing television shows and movies as a group project

Recycle: Adjectives and adverbs

Suggestions: Have students prepare Step 1 in class. Tell them to decide who will present each television show and have them prepare their presentations for homework. Set aside time before beginning the presentations for students to finalize their projects as a group. After each presentation, give students time to ask questions.

Answers will vary.

Pre-AP* Support

- **Learning Objective:** Presentational Speaking
- **Activity 18:** Students practice formal speaking skills as they present recommendations for television programming to the class.

El español en la comunidad

Core Instruction

Standards: 5.1

Suggestions: Arrange for students to view a Spanish-language television show in class. Point out that some speakers may be easier to understand than others.

Answers will vary.

Extension: Have students write a short description of a Spanish-language show.

Additional Resources

- Communication Wbk.: Audio Act. 8–9, pp. 174–175
- Teacher's Resource Book: Audio Script, pp. 296–297
- Audio Program DVD: Cap. 9A, Tracks 12–13

ASSESSMENT

Prueba 9A-4 with Study Plan (online only)

Quiz: *Gustar* and similar verbs

- Prueba 9A-4: p. 234

ENRICH YOUR TEACHING

Culture Note

Spanish-speaking countries often consider it important to have a mixture of local and foreign television programming. This allows each country's citizens to experience things such as foreign films while preserving their national and cultural identity. Ask students if they think this is a good idea. Also ask how they feel television could influence a culture.

Teacher-to-Teacher/Pre-AP*

Have students make crossword puzzles like the ones found in most television guides. Have them give the clues using the vocabulary from this chapter. Tell them to use ***horizontal*** and ***vertical*** for "up" and "down." Make copies of students' crossword puzzles and distribute them as a vocabulary review.

Common Core: Reading

Lectura

Core Instruction

Standards: 1.2, 1.3

Focus: Reading for comprehension and cultural perspectives

Suggestions:

Pre-reading: Direct students' attention to the *Strategy*. Remind them that they use this strategy when they read in English. Have them look at the title and the photos and predict what the reading is about.

Reading: Have students read the text without stopping and ask them to summarize the reading. After they finish the summary, have them read the text a second time and tell them to make a list of the words that they do not know. Have them use a Spanish-English dictionary to figure out the meaning of the words. Tell students to read the *Lectura* a third time using their list of defined words and have them check the accuracy of their summary.

Post-reading: Have students write a list of reasons why watching too much television is not healthy. Tell them to base their list on the *Lectura*. Ask students to tell whether they agree or disagree with these reasons.

Pre-AP* Support

- **Learning Objective:** Interpretive: Print and Audio
- **Activity:** As a pre-reading activity, divide the article into two parts—the first two paragraphs and the last three paragraphs. Divide the class in half and give each group one of the reading sections. Have them read their section and then write two multiple-choice questions for the segment they were assigned. Collect the questions and redistribute them to the opposite group of students. Ask students to take a few moments to read the questions that they received. Next, read aloud (or play a teacher-made recording of) each segment. The students with the multiple-choice questions listen for the correct answers, while the students who wrote the questions follow along with the article as it is being read.
- ***Pre-AP* Resource Book:*** Comprehensive guide to Pre-AP* reading skill development, pp. 19–26

Objectives

- Read about TV-watching habits of teens
- Read without stopping to understand unknown words

Lectura

Una semana sin televisión

Strategy

Reading for comprehension
Read without stopping at unknown words. Then go back, decide if the words are important, and see if you can guess their meanings.

¿Sabes que los niños estadounidenses pasan más horas al año pegados a la pantalla de su televisión que haciendo cualquier otra cosa, a excepción de dormir?

Hay estudios que dicen que ver demasiado la televisión puede causar malos hábitos de comida, falta de ejercicio y obesidad. En cuatro horas de dibujos animados el sábado por la mañana los niños pueden ver 202 anuncios sobre refrescos, dulces y cereales azucarados. Esta comida combinada con las horas frente a la pantalla resulta en que uno de cada seis niños estadounidenses tenga exceso de peso.

También hay estudios que dan nuevas pruebas de la relación entre la televisión y la violencia. Uno de estos estudios indica que niños que ven más de una hora de televisión al día tienen más probabilidad de ser violentos y agresivos de adultos.

DIFFERENTIATED INSTRUCTION

Multiple Intelligences

Interpersonal/Social: Have students create a flier for a ***semana sin televisión*** campaign. Ask them to try to convince students in Spanish classes at your school to pledge to refrain from television for a week. Ask students who make the pledge to keep a journal of the activities that they do to replace watching television.

Heritage Language Learners

Have students interview family members or friends who speak Spanish and ask them what interesting activities they can do to replace watching television. Ask them to write a report quoting each person they interviewed.

¿Quieres participar en una solución? Durante el mes de abril millones de personas en más de treinta países apagan la tele por una semana. En vez de ver la tele los participantes van con sus familias o con amigos al campo, o a caminar, montar en bicicleta o visitar un parque.

¿Y qué pasa después de unos días sin televisión? Una niña de diez años dice: —¿Para qué necesito la tele? Hay muchas cosas más interesantes que puedo hacer.

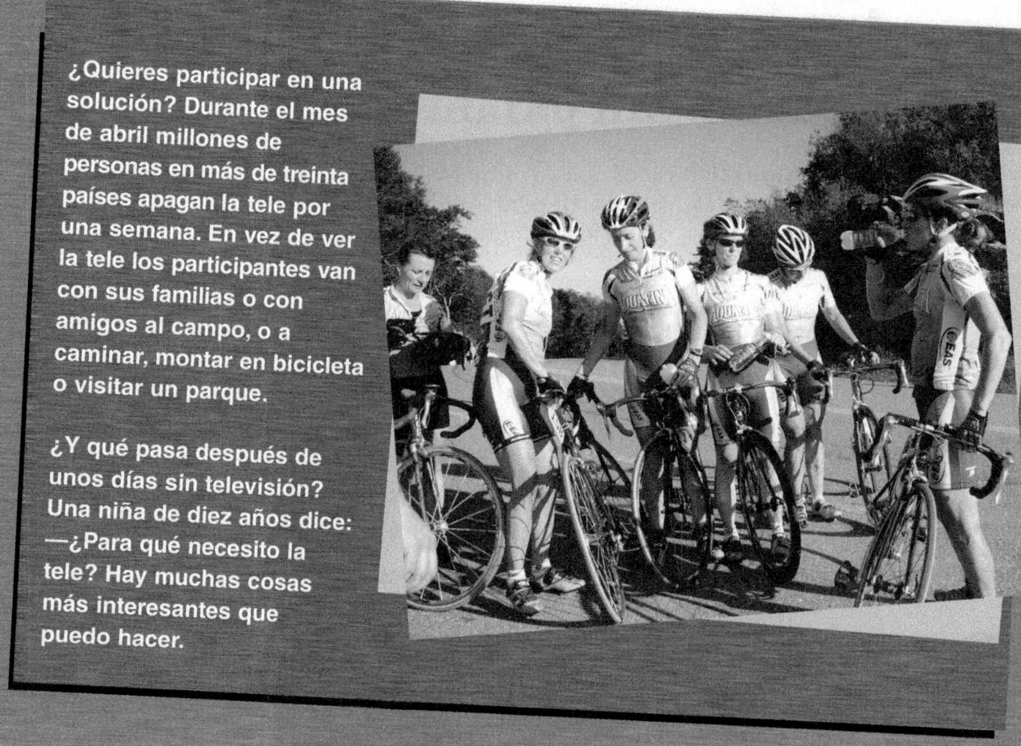

¿Comprendes?

Prepara información para un debate sobre la cuestión: ¿Es bueno o malo ver la televisión?

1. Escribe una lista de cuatro razones *(reasons)* a favor de no ver la tele. Usa información que leíste en el artículo.
2. Escribe una lista de cuatro razones a favor de ver la tele.

Y tú, ¿qué dices? 

1. Usa la información en tu lista para expresar tu opinión: ¿Es bueno o malo ver la televisión? ¿Por qué?
2. Para ti, ¿va a ser fácil o difícil pasar una semana sin ver la televisión? ¿Por qué?
3. En Chile, a una persona que ve mucha televisión se le llama "un(a) tevito(a)". ¿Qué puedes decirle a un(a) tevito(a) para persuadirlo(a) a hacer otras cosas que son mejores para la salud?

Más práctica GO

	realidades.com	print
Guided WB p. 289	✔	✔
Comm. WB pp. 179, 326	✔	✔
***Hispanohablantes* WB** pp. 342–343		✔
Cultural Reading Activity	✔	

¿Comprendes? Standards: 1.2, 1.3

Resources: Answer Keys: Student Edition, p. 131

Focus: Demonstrating reading comprehension

Suggestions: Before students answer the questions, brainstorm a list of reasons for and against watching television.

Answers will vary but may include:

1. **Puede causar malos hábitos de comida, falta de ejercicio, obesidad y violencia. Uno puede hacer muchas cosas más interesantes.**
2. **Answers will vary.**

BELLRINGER REVIEW

Have students brainstorm in pairs to write three activities that are good for your health that they could do outside. Share with the class.

Y tú, ¿qué dices? Standards: 1.2, 1.3

Focus: Answering questions about television.

Answers will vary.

Extension: Arrange desks in a way that facilitates holding a debate. Divide students into two groups: those who support watching television and those who are against it. Have students use information from the reading and their notes, to defend their positions.

For Further Reading

Student Resource: Realidades para hispanohablantes: Lectura 2, pp. 344–345

ENRICH YOUR TEACHING

Teacher-to-Teacher

Ask students to verify the information in the reading by watching one hour of cartoons on television and reporting on the commercials that are shown. Have them write the name(s) of the cartoon(s) and keep a log of the advertisements. Tell them to include the name of each product, the kind of product being advertised *(**cereales, juguetes, dulces,** and so forth),* and the length of each commercial. Ask them to write their opinion about whether or not the ads could cause bad habits or otherwise negatively influence young viewers.

La cultura en vivo

Core Instruction

Standards: 4.1

Focus: Reading about using gestures to communicate

Suggestions: Before beginning the activity, discuss body language and gestures to make sure students know what they are. Demonstrate some familiar gestures, such as nodding and shaking the head, and waving your hand; ask students to say what they mean. Explain that all cultures use gestures, but that a given gesture does not always mean the same thing in all cultures. It is important to find out what gestures mean in other cultures before doing them. They could have rude meanings.

Direct students' attention to the photos. Ask which, if any, of the gestures mean the same as in the United States.

Have students work in pairs to practice the gestures. Keep the focus on positive, pleasant gestures. Ask pairs of students to present their skits to the class.

Direct attention to the *Think about it!* section and have students discuss the questions.

Answers will vary.

Additional Resources

Student Resource: Realidades para hispanohablantes, p. 346

La cultura en vivo

Comunicación sin palabras

Every culture has gestures that communicate a message. You've already seen gestures for *¡ojo!* and *más o menos.* Here are a few more gestures used in many Spanish-speaking countries to communicate a message.

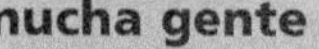

mucha gente

¡Hay mucha gente en la fiesta!

(Place your fingertips together, then open your hand. Repeat this motion in a rhythmic gesture.)

un poco

Por favor, un poquito de postre.

¡a comer!

¡Vamos a comer!

(With your fingertips bunched, bring your hand up close to your mouth, then extend it forward, bending your arm at the elbow. Repeat the motion two or three times.)

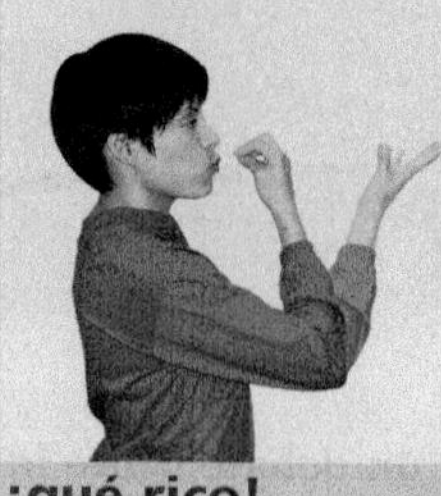

¡qué rico!

¡Este plato está muy rico!

(Kiss the bunched fingertips of one hand, then quickly push your hand away, extending your fingers.)

no sé

No sé dónde está el libro.

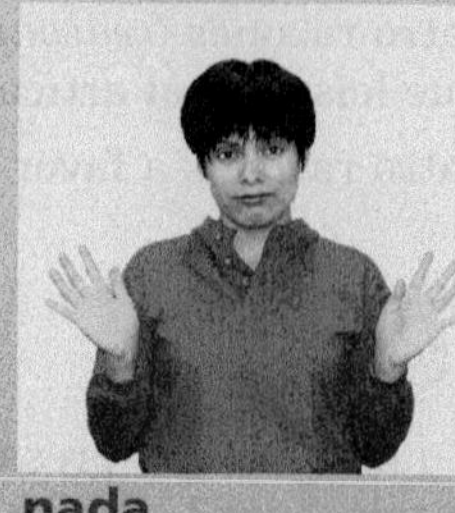

nada

No tengo nada.

Try it out! Work with a partner and create a short skit in which you use one of these gestures. Present it for the class.

Think about it! What gestures do you use most often? Do you ever use gestures that are the same as or similar to the ones shown on this page? Do you think you would understand some of the gestures on this page even without an explanation?

DIFFERENTIATED INSTRUCTION

Advanced Learners

Students may pick these gestures up quickly. If so, have them research additional gestures used in a Spanish-speaking country of their choice. Gestures may be found on the Internet under the category of "body language."

Heritage Language Learners

Students may be familiar with these and other gestures. Allow them to present a short skit to the class using a socially acceptable different gesture from their heritage countries (pre-approved by you), and have the class guess its meaning.

Presentación oral 

¿Qué dan esta semana?

Objectives

- Present a review of a recent movie or television show
- Use a chart to organize key information

Task

You are reviewing a movie or television show you have just seen for your school's closed-circuit TV system. Prepare a summary of the movie or show.

1 Prepare Choose a movie or TV show, then download or cut out ads or photos about it. Copy the chart below and provide the information for the movie or show you have chosen.

Nombre		Cómo es	
Clase de película o programa		Cuánto tiempo dura	
Actor / actores		Para quiénes es	
Actriz / actrices		Tus impresiones	

Strategy

Using charts
Create a chart to help you think through the key information you will want to talk about. This will help you speak more effectively.

2 Practice Use your notes from the chart for your presentation. Create a poster with the visuals you have collected. Go through your presentation several times. You may use your notes in practice, but not when you present. Try to:

- provide all key information about the film or show
- use complete sentences in your presentation
- speak clearly

3 Present Present your chosen movie or television show to a small group or the class. Use your poster to help guide you.

4 Evaluation The following rubric will be used to grade your presentation.

Rubric	Score 1	Score 3	Score 5
Completeness of presentation	Your only visual on the poster is the title.	You included the title and one visual on the poster, in color.	You include the title plus two or more visuals on the poster, in color.
Amount of information you communicate	You only include the movie or TV show and actors.	You provide descriptions of the movie or TV show plus actors.	You provide elements shown to the left, plus personal impressions.
How easily you are understood	You are extremely difficult to understand. Your teacher could only recognize isolated words and phrases.	You are understandable, but with frequent errors in vocabulary and/or grammar that hinder your comprehensibility.	You are easily understood. Your teacher does not have to "decode" what you are trying to say.

Common Core: Speaking

Presentación oral

Core Instruction

Standards: 1.3

Resources: Voc. and Gram. Transparency 165; Teacher's Resource Book: GramActiva BLM, p. 305

Focus: Presenting a review of a movie or television show

Suggestions: Review the task and steps with students. After reading the *Strategy,* point out the chart in Step 1 and explain to students how to use it to organize information. Help students understand the chart by choosing a movie or television show that students are familiar with and brainstorming answers for each category. Review the rubric with the class to explain how you will grade the perfomance task.

Portfolio

Make video or audio recordings of student presentations in class, or assign the RealTalk activity so they can record their presentations online. Include the recording in their portfolios.

Pre-AP* Support

- **Learning Objective:** Presentational Speaking
- **Activity:** Remind students to focus on the presentational speaking skills used in this task such as fluency, pronunciation, and comprehensibility.
- ***Pre-AP* Resource Book:*** Comprehensive guide to Pre-AP* speaking skill development, pp. 39–50

Additional Resources

Student Resources: Realidades para hispanohablantes: p. 347; Guided Practice: Presentación oral, p. 290

ASSESSMENT

Presentación oral

- Assessment Program: Rubrics, p. T33

Go over the descriptions of the different levels of performance. After assessing students, help individuals understand how their performance could be improved.

ENRICH YOUR TEACHING

Teacher-to-Teacher

e-amigos: Ask students to write to their *e-amigos* about their favorite television show. Have them base their exchanges on their *Presentación oral* summaries. Have them print out or e-mail you their questions and answers.

21st Century Skills

Creativity and Innovation Have students play the role of an agent, pitching the show to a group of investors. They can make a traditional or an electronic presentation of the show, using either print, or digital materials. Part of the presentation should be to explain why the show is so good and why the investors should choose it.

Videomisterio

Core Instruction

Standards: 1.2, 4.1, 5.2

Resources: Teacher's Resource Book: Video Script, p. 299; Video Program: Cap. 9A; Video Program Teacher's Guide: Cap. 9A

Focus: Introducing the events and characters of this episode

Personajes importantes:

Lola Lago, detective
Paco, Lola Lago's colleague
Margarita, Lola Lago's secretary
Julia Romero, María's friend
Inspector Gil, police officer

Synopsis: Lola calls her office to ask Margarita and Paco to help her follow two people. Margarita overhears that the person Lola thinks is María is really Julia. When the two strangers leave, Paco follows them to the train station. Then, Lola calls Inspector Gil to ask him to meet her at the train station right away.

Suggestions:

Pre-viewing: Review with students the events of the previous episode. Pedro and Lola discuss the clues that they have so far. They do not know where María may be, but now they know that she went to Julia Romero's apartment. Lola sees María in front of doña Gracia's apartment. Lola calls Inspector Gil to let him know that she has seen María.

Point out the *Nota gramatical.* Direct students' attention to the *Palabras para comprender* and give them examples in context. Remind students to use these words to help them understand the episode.

Visual scanning: Direct students' attention to the picture and ask who each of the characters are. Before students read the *Resumen del episodio,* have them scan the text and find three cognates. For example, ***café, talentos, detective, evidente,*** and ***misterioso.***

Extension: Ask students to prepare questions about the reading. Have them work in pairs and ask the questions in a trivia game show format. Have them ask *who, what, when, where,* and *why* questions.

Objective

- Understand the expanding plot of a mystery video set in Spain

¿Eres tú, María?

Episodio 9

Antes de ver el video

"Paco, te digo que te necesito ahora mismo. Por favor, rápido. Y a Margarita, también".

Nota gramatical What's a good mystery without an expression like "Follow her!"? In this episode you'll hear several uses of the verb to follow: *seguir.*

sigo	seguimos
sigues	seguís
sigue	siguen

Resumen del episodio

Al día siguiente Lola va a su trabajo, cuando ve a María. ¡Qué suerte! Lola la sigue y llama a Paco y a Margarita. Ella necesita a los dos ahora mismo para ayudarla. Vigilan[1] a María y a un hombre en el café, y Margarita muestra[2] sus talentos de detective. Es evidente que María y el hombre no están nada contentos. Pero, ¿quién es este hombre misterioso y por qué quiere irse de Madrid?

[1]They watch [2]shows

Palabras para comprender

¡Venid! Come!
ve a sentarte go sit
aparece appears
quiere irse wants to go away
vengan en seguida come right away
sigue vigilando continue watching

DIFFERENTIATED INSTRUCTION

Advanced Learners

Have students read the captions under each of the photos and continue the conversations based on what they know so far about the *Videomisterio*. Have students work in pairs to practice their dialogues. Call on volunteers to present their dialogues to the class.

Heritage Language Learners

Point out the ***vosotros(as)*** command forms of the verb ***venir.*** Explain that these are used when talking to a group of people whom individually you would address as ***tú.*** Ask students to compare the ***vosotros(as)*** command forms with what is used in their heritage countries.

—¡Ay de mí!
—Cálmate, Lola.

"Lola, ¿quién es ese hombre? ¿De qué están hablando?"

"Ahora lo comprendo todo. Voy a llamar al Inspector Gil".

Después de ver el video

¿Comprendes?

A. Contesta las preguntas.

1. ¿Quiénes ayudan a Lola con la investigación?
2. ¿Quién va al café para escuchar a María y al hombre?
3. ¿Está Lola tranquila o nerviosa? ¿Por qué?
4. Según Lola, ¿quién es el hombre en el café?
5. Según Margarita, ¿quién es la chica en el café?
6. Según Margarita, ¿el hombre quiere quedarse *(stay)* en Madrid o quiere irse?

B. Lola dice, "Ahora lo comprendo todo". En tu opinión, ¿qué comprende Lola? ¿Cuál es la solución del misterio?

Más práctica GO

realidades.com | print

Actividades	✔	✔

ENRICH YOUR TEACHING

Culture Note

There are two main train stations that service Madrid: Chamartín and Atocha. The Atocha train station, a nineteenth-century style building, was renovated to include an indoor park with plants and cafés. *RENFE (Red Nacional de los Ferrocarriles Españoles)* is the agency in charge of running trains in Spain.

21st Century Skills

Collaboration After students do the Internet activity to test their comprehension, have them work in groups to review the video episodes and make predictions about how the video will end. Each person in the group should come up with one idea, and they should all support their predictions with clues from the actual video story.

Video 9A

Viewing: Play *Episodio* 9 to the class. If there is time after viewing the full episode, select some key moments that you wish to highlight, such as the scene in which Margarita reports to Lola on what she heard in the conversation between the two strangers.

Post-viewing: Have students look at the pictures and the captions at the top of the page and use them to summarize the scenes in this episode. Brainstorm a list of vocabulary in this episode that is used to add new information to the plot.

Direct students' attention to the *¿Comprendes?*

¿Comprendes?

Resources: Map Transparency 18; Answer Keys: Student Edition, p. 132

Focus: Verifying comprehension by answering questions; reviewing the plot

Suggestions:

For part B, have students write a short paragraph about what Lola really knows and what they think is the answer to the mystery. Have them present their ideas to the class and ask the other students to say why they agree or disagree.

Answers:

Part A

1. **Paco y Margarita ayudan a Lola con la investigación.**
2. **Margarita va al café para escuchar la conversación.**
3. **Lola está nerviosa porque no quiere ser descubierta.**
4. **Según Lola, el hombre en el café es Luis Antonio Llamas, un hombre de Barcelona.**
5. **Según Margarita, la chica en el café no es María; es Julia.**
6. **Según Margarita, el hombre quiere irse.**

Part B
Answers will vary.

Theme Project

Students can perform Step 3 at this point. (For more information, see p. 424-b.)

Additional Resources

- *¿Eres tú, María?* Video Workbook, Episode 9
- *¿Eres tú, María?* Teacher's Video Guide: Answer Key

Review Activities

To talk about television shows: Play a version of charades. Divide students into four or five teams. Have volunteers from one team pantomime a television show. Give team members a point if they correctly guess the kind of show and the name of the program.

To talk about movies: Continue the game of charades, changing the topic to movies.

To give your opinion of a movie or a program: Divide students into pairs. Ask them to brainstorm a list of seven movie titles. While one reads the titles, the other says an adjective that describes each movie. Have them switch roles.

To ask and tell about movies or programs: Ask students to describe the last movie they saw. Tell them to say the title, what kind of movie it was, the main actor and actress, where they saw the film, when it started, and how long it lasted.

Verbs similar to* gustar:** On twelve index cards, have students write ***-n, me, te, le, nos, les, aburre, duele, encanta, falta, interesa, and ***queda.*** Write ***a*** + prepositional pronoun along with a noun and have students complete the sentence. For example: ***a mí / las películas cómicas.*** Remind them to use ***-n*** for plural subjects.

Portfolio

Invite students to review the activities they completed in this chapter, including written reports, posters or other visuals, recordings of oral presentations, or other projects. Have them select one or two items that they feel best demonstrate their achievements in Spanish to include in their portfolios.

Additional Resources

Student Resources: Realidades para hispanohablantes, p. 348

Teacher Resources:

- Teacher's Resource Book: Situation Cards, p. 304, Clip Art, pp. 306–307
- Assessment Program: Chapter Checklist and Self-Assessment Worksheet, pp. T56–T57

Objectives

- Review the vocabulary and grammar
- Demonstrate you can perform the tasks on p. 447

Repaso del capítulo

Vocabulario y gramática

to talk about television shows

el canal	channel
el programa de concursos	game show
el programa deportivo	sports show
el programa de dibujos animados	cartoon show
el programa de entrevistas	interview program
el programa de la vida real	reality program
el programa de noticias	news program
el programa educativo	educational program
el programa musical	musical program
la telenovela	soap opera

to talk about movies

la comedia	comedy
el drama	drama
la película de ciencia ficción	science fiction movie
la película de horror	horror movie
la película policíaca	crime movie, mystery
la película romántica	romantic movie

to give your opinion of a movie or program

cómico, -a	funny
emocionante	touching
fascinante	fascinating
infantil	for children; childish
realista	realistic
tonto, -a	silly, stupid
violento, -a	violent
me aburre(n)	it bores me (they bore me)
me interesa(n)	it interests me (they interest me)

to ask and tell about movies or programs

el actor	actor
la actriz	actress
dar	to show
durar	to last
empezar *(e → ie)*	to begin
terminar	to end
más / menos de	more / less than
medio, -a	half
¿Qué clase de . . . ?	What kind of . . . ?

to talk about what has just happened

acabar de + *infinitive*	to have just . . .

verbs similar to *gustar*

aburrir	to bore
doler *(o → ue)*	to hurt, to ache
encantar	to please very much, to love
faltar	to be missing
interesar	to interest
quedar	to fit

other useful expressions

antes de	before
casi	almost
¿De veras?	Really?
especialmente	especially
por eso	therefore, for that reason
sobre	about
ya	already

For *Vocabulario adicional,* see pp. 472–473.

DIFFERENTIATED INSTRUCTION

Students with Learning Difficulties

Have students review the *Repaso del capítulo* and create flashcards for any words that they do not know. Pair them with a student who is more confident with the vocabulary to practice. Before the test, provide students with a practice test, so they can become comfortable with the format.

Heritage Language Learners

Have students write a few paragraphs telling about their perfect birthday celebration: Where are they going to have it? Whom are they going to invite? What food are they going to eat? What kind of music are they going to play? Encourage them to use as many vocabulary words from this chapter as they can.

Más repaso GO realidades.com | print

	realidades.com	print
Instant Check	✔	
Puzzles	✔	
Core WB pp. 164–165		✔
Comm. WB pp. 327, 328–330	✔	✔

Preparación para el examen

On the exam you will be asked to . . .	Here are practice tasks similar to those you will find on the exam . . .	For review go to your print or digital textbook . . .
Interpretive		
 **1 Escuchar** Listen and understand as people express opinions about movies and TV programs	Listen as you hear a phone pollster ask people about TV programs they have watched on the new Spanish-language cable station. For each viewer, decide if the shows were: a) boring; b) interesting; c) too violent; d) too childish or silly.	**pp. 426–429** *Vocabulario en contexto* **p. 430** Actividad 4 **p. 431** Actividades 6–7 **p. 435** Actividad 13
Interpersonal		
 **2 Hablar** Ask and answer questions about the types of movies and TV programs people prefer	Tell your partner about a movie or TV program you just saw and express your opinion about it. Ask if your partner saw the same thing and what he or she thought of it. If your partner didn't see it, ask him or her to tell about something he or she just saw. You might say: *Acabo de ver una película fantástica con Tom Cruise . . .*	**pp. 426–429** *Vocabulario en contexto* **p. 430** Actividad 4 **p. 431** Actividad 6 **p. 432** Actividad 9 **p. 435** Actividad 13 **p. 437** Actividad 15 **p. 443** Presentación oral
Interpretive		
 **3 Leer** Read and understand what an entertainment critic writes about a new TV program	Before class begins, you grab a Spanish-language magazine and turn to the entertainment section. After reading part of the entertainment critic's review, see if you can determine his opinion of a new soap opera series, *Mi secreto*. Does he like it? Why or why not? En el primer episodio de **Mi secreto**, nos aburren con una historia infantil y con actores sin talento que quieren ser emocionantes pero no pueden. ¡Pienso que este programa es para las personas que no tienen nada que hacer!	**pp. 426–429** *Vocabulario en contexto* **p. 432** Actividad 9
Presentational		
 **4 Escribir** Write about a movie you recently saw	You are keeping a journal to practice writing in Spanish. Today you are going to write about a movie you saw recently. Mention the name of the movie, the type of movie it is, and what you liked or disliked about it.	**p. 431** Actividad 8 **p. 435** Actividad 13 **p. 437** Actividades 15–16 **p. 443** *Presentación oral*
Cultures • Comparisons		
5 Pensar Demonstrate an understanding of common gestures	You have learned that almost all cultures can communicate without words. With a partner, see if you can demonstrate the six gestures you have learned in this chapter from the Spanish-speaking world. Are these gestures similar to those in our culture?	**p. 442** *La cultura en vivo*

Review 9A

Performance Tasks

Standards: 1.1, 1.2, 1.3, 4.1

Student Resource: Realidades para hispanohablantes, p. 349

Teacher Resources: Teacher's Resource Book: Audio Script, p. 297; Audio Program DVD: Cap. 9A, Track 16; Answer Keys: Student Edition, p. 133

Focus: Preparing for the exam

1. Escuchar

Suggestions: Play the audio or read the script.

Script and Answers:

1. **A nosotros no nos gusta el programa *Paco Payaso.* Debe ser un programa educativo para niños, pero es demasiado infantil. Mi hijo tiene ocho años y a él no le gusta cantar una canción del alfabeto. *(too childish)***
2. **Pienso que los programas de la vida real son ridículos. Me aburren mucho. No me importan ni me interesan. *(boring)***
3. **Me gustan mucho los programas de entrevistas. Me encanta el programa *Miguel.* Él es muy cómico y tiene entrevistas muy interesantes. *(interesting)***

2. Hablar

Suggestions: Have students create a chart like the one on p. 443 to organize their ideas.

Answers will vary.

3. Leer

Suggestions: Before beginning the reading, have students discuss their opinions of soap operas.

Answers will vary but may include:

No le gusta nada el programa. Es infantil y aburrido.

4. Escribir

Suggestions: Have students do this activity for homework and write an entry about the television shows they watch that night.

Answers will vary.

5. Pensar

Suggestions: Be sure to monitor students for appropriate gestures.

Answers will vary.

DIFFERENTIATED ASSESSMENT

CORE ASSESSMENT
- **Assessment Program:** Examen del capítulo 9A, pp. 235–238
- **Audio Program DVD:** Cap. 9A, Track 17
- **ExamView:** Chapter Test, Test Banks A and B

ADVANCED/PRE-AP*
- **ExamView: Pre-AP* Test Bank**
- **Pre-AP* Resource Book,** pp. 94–97

STUDENTS NEEDING EXTRA HELP
- **Alternate Assessment Program:** Examen del capítulo 9A
- **Audio Program DVD:** Cap. 9A, Track 17

HERITAGE LEARNERS
- **Assessment Program: Realidades para hispanohablantes:** Examen del capítulo 9A
- **ExamView: Heritage Learner Test Bank**

9B La tecnología

AT A GLANCE

Objectives
- Listen to and read conversations about computers
- Talk about the Internet and write a Web profile
- Exchange information about Internet use and the benefits of computers
- Identify the impact of the Internet on the Spanish language
- Compare computer use in Spanish-speaking countries with your own use of technology

Vocabulary
- Communication
- Computer-related activities
- Internet and digital products

Grammar
- The present tense of ***pedir*** and ***servir***
- ***saber*** and ***conocer***

Culture
- Pablo Picasso, p. 449
- ***La Real Academia Española,*** p. 455
- Internet use in Spain, p. 456
- Inventions, p. 463
- Impact of the Internet on the Spanish Language, pp. 464–465
- Cultural perspectives on computer use, pp. 466

Recycle ♻
- Greetings
- Preterite of ***hacer***
- ***ir a*** + infinitive
- Indirect object pronouns
- ***tener***
- ***sé, sabes***
- Direct object pronouns
- Personal ***a***

RESOURCES

	FOR THE STUDENT	ONLINE	DVD	PRINT	FOR THE TEACHER	ONLINE	PREEXP	DVD	PRINT
Plan					Interactive TE and Resources DVD	•		•	
					Teacher's Resource Book, pp. 324–355	•		•	•
					Pre-AP* Resource Book, pp. 94–97	•		•	•
					Lesson Plans	•			•
					Mapa global interactivo	•			
Introducción PP. **448–449**									
Present	Student Edition, pp. 448–449	•	•	•	Interactive TE and Resources DVD	•		•	
	DK Reference Atlas	•	•		Teacher's Resource Book, pp. 324–325	•		•	•
	Videocultura	•	•		Galería de fotos		•		
	Hispanohablantes WB, pp. 350–351			•	Fine Art Transparencies, 45	•	•	•	
					Map Transparencies 12, 18–20	•	•	•	
Vocabulario en contexto PP. **450–453**									
Present & Practice	Student Edition, pp. 450–453	•	•	•	Interactive TE and Resources DVD	•		•	
	Audio	•	•		Teacher's Resource Book, pp. 326–328, 331, 340–341	•		•	•
	Videohistoria	•	•		Vocabulary Clip Art	•	•	•	•
	Flashcards	•	•		Audio Program	•	•	•	
	Instant Check	•			Video Program: Videohistoria	•		•	
	Guided WB, pp. 291–298	•	•	•	Video Program Teacher's Guide: Cap. 9B	•		•	•
	Core WB, pp. 166–169	•	•	•	Vocabulary and Grammar Transparencies, 166–169	•	•	•	
	Comm. WB, pp. 180–183, 185	•	•	•	Answer Keys: Student Edition, pp. 134–135	•	•	•	
	Hispanohablantes WB, pp. 352–353			•	TPR Stories, pp. 122–133	•		•	•
Assess and Remediate					Prueba 9B–1: Assessment Program, pp. 241–242	•		•	•
					Assessment Program para hispanohablantes, pp. 241–242	•		•	•

	FOR THE STUDENT	ONLINE	DVD	PRINT	FOR THE TEACHER	ONLINE	PREEXP	DVD	PRINT
Vocabulario en uso PP. **454–457**									
Present & Practice	Student Edition, pp. 454–457	•	•	•	Interactive Whiteboard Vocabulary Activities	•		•	
	Instant Check	•			Interactive TE and Resources DVD	•		•	
	Comm. WB, p. 183	•	•	•	Teacher's Resource Book, pp. 254–255, 327–328, 339	•		•	•
	Hispanohablantes WB, pp. 354–355, 360			•	Communicative Pair Activities, pp. 254–255	•		•	•
	Communicative Pair Activities	•			Audio Program	•	•	•	
					Videomodelos	•		•	
					Vocabulary and Grammar Transparencies, 172	•	•	•	
					Answer Keys: Student Edition, pp. 135–136	•	•	•	•
Assess and Remediate					Prueba 9B–2 with Study Plan	•			
					Prueba 9B–2: Assessment Program, pp. 243–244	•		•	•
					Assessment Program para hispanohablantes, pp. 243–244	•		•	•
Gramática PP. **458–463**									
Present & Practice	Student Edition, pp. 458–463	•	•	•	Interactive Whiteboard Grammar Activities	•		•	
	Instant Check	•			Interactive TE and Resources DVD	•		•	
	Animated Verbs	•			Teacher's Resource Book, pp. 256–257, 328–329, 331–332	•		•	•
	Tutorial Video: Grammar	•			Communicative Pair Activities, pp. 256–257	•		•	•
	Canción de hip hop	•			Audio Program	•	•	•	
	Guided WB, pp. 299–302	•	•	•	Videomodelos	•		•	
	Core WB, pp. 170–172	•	•	•	Video Program: GramActiva	•	•	•	
	Comm. WB, pp. 183–184, 186–187, 331	•	•	•	Vocabulary and Grammar Transparencies, 170–171	•	•	•	
	Hispanohablantes WB, pp. 356–361			•	Answer Keys: Student Edition, pp. 137–140	•	•	•	
	Communicative Pair Activities	•							
Assess and Remediate					Pruebas 9B–3 and 9B–4 with Study Plans	•			
					Pruebas 9B–3, 9B–4: Assessment Program, pp. 245, 246	•		•	•
					Assessment Program para hispanohablantes, pp. 245, 246	•		•	•
¡Adelante! PP. **464–469**									
Application	Student Edition, pp. 464–469	•	•	•	Interactive TE and Resources DVD	•		•	
	Online Cultural Reading	•			Teacher's Resource Book, pp. 332–333	•		•	•
	Guided WB, pp. 303–304	•	•	•	Video Program: Videomisterio ¿Eres tú, María?	•		•	
	Comm. WB, pp. 188, 332	•	•	•	Video Program Teacher's Guide: Cap. 9B	•		•	
	Hispanohablantes WB, pp. 362–367			•	Videomisterio Quiz		•		
	¿Eres tú, María? Video WB, pp. 76–81	•	•	•	Answer Keys: Student Edition, pp. 140–141	•	•	•	
Repaso del capítulo PP. **470–471**									
Review	Student Edition, pp. 470–471	•	•	•	Interactive TE and Resources DVD	•		•	
	Online Puzzles and Games	•			Teacher's Resource Book, pp. 329–330, 338, 340–341	•		•	•
	Core WB, pp. 173–174	•	•	•	Audio Program	•	•	•	
	Comm. WB, pp. 333–336	•	•	•	Answer Keys: Student Edition, p. 142	•	•	•	
	Hispanohablantes WB, pp. 368–369			•					
	Instant Check	•							
Chapter Assessment									
Assess					Examen del capítulo 9B	•		•	•
					Assessment Program, pp. 247–250	•		•	•
					Alternate Assessment Program, pp. 96–100	•		•	•
					Assessment Program para hispanohablantes, pp. 247–250	•		•	•
					Audio Program, Cap. 9B, Examen	•		•	
					ExamView: Test Banks A and B questions only online	•		•	
					Heritage Learner Test Bank	•		•	
					Pre-AP* Test Bank	•		•	

REGULAR SCHEDULE (50 MINUTES)

DAY	Warm-up / Assess	Preview / Present / Practice / Communicate	Wrap-up / Homework Options
1	**Warm-up** (10 min.) • Return Examen del capítulo 9A	**Chapter Opener** (5 min.) • Objectives • Arte y cultura **Vocabulario en contexto** (30 min.) • Presentation: Vocabulario en contexto • Actividades 1, 2	**Wrap-up and Homework Options** (5 min.) • Core Practice 9B-1, 9B-2
2	**Warm-up** (5 min.) • Homework check	**Vocabulario en contexto** (40 min.) • Presentation: Videohistoria *¿Cómo se comunica?* • View: Videohistoria • Video Activities 1, 2, 3, 4 • Actividad 3	**Wrap-up and Homework Options** (5 min.) • Core Practice 9B-3, 9B-4 • Prueba 9B-1: Vocabulary recognition
3	**Warm-up** (10 min.) • Actividad 6 • Homework check ✔**Formative Assessment** (10 min.) • Prueba 9B-1: Vocabulary recognition	**Vocabulario en uso** (25 min.) • Interactive Whiteboard Vocabulary Activities • Actividades 4, 5, 7, 8 • Fondos culturales	**Wrap-up and Homework Options** (5 min.) • Writing Activity 10 • Actividad 9
4	**Warm-up** (5 min.) • Homework check	**Gramática y vocabulario en uso** (40 min.) • Audio Activities 5, 6 • Communicative Pair Activity • Exploración del lenguaje • Presentation: The present tense of *pedir* and *servir* • View: GramActiva video • Interactive Whiteboard Grammar Activities • Actividades 11, 12, 13	**Wrap-up and Homework Options** (5 min.) • Core Practice 9B-5 • Actividad 14 • Prueba 9B-2 with Study Plan: Vocabulary production
5	**Warm-up** (10 min.) • Actividad 10 • Homework check ✔**Formative Assessment** (10 min.) • Prueba 9B-2 with Study Plan: Vocabulary production	**Gramática y vocabulario en uso** (25 min.) • Audio Activity 7 • Communicative Pair Activity • Presentation: *Saber* and *conocer* • View: GramActiva video • Interactive Whiteboard Grammar Activities • Actividades 15, 16	**Wrap-up and Homework Options** (5 min.) • Writing Activities 11, 12, 13 • Actividad 18 • Prueba 9B-3 with Study Plan: The present tense of *pedir* and *servir*
6	**Warm-up** (5 min.) • Homework check ✔**Formative Assessment** (10 min.) • Prueba 9B-3 with Study Plan: The present tense of *pedir* and *servir*	**Gramática y vocabulario en uso** (30 min.) • Actividades 17, 19 • Audio Activities 8, 9 • Pronunciación • El español en el mundo del trabajo	**Wrap-up and Homework Options** (5 min.) • Core Practice 9B-6, 9B-7 • Prueba 9B-4 with Study Plan: *Saber* and *conocer*
7	**Warm-up** (5 min.) • Homework check ✔**Formative Assessment** (10 min.) • Prueba 9B-4 with Study Plan: *Saber* and *conocer*	**¡Adelante!** (30 min.) • Lectura • ¿Comprendes? • Presentación escrita: Steps 1, 5	**Wrap-up and Homework Options** (5 min.) • Presentación escrita: Step 2 • Lectura
8	**Warm-up** (5 min.) • Homework check	**¡Adelante!** (40 min.) • Presentación escrita: Step 3 • Perspectivas del mundo hispano	**Wrap-up and Homework Options** (5 min.) • Presentación escrita: Step 4 • Instant Check
9	**Warm-up** (5 min.) • Homework check	**¡Adelante!** (20 min.) • Videomisterio: *¿Eres tú, María?*, Episodio 10 **Repaso del capítulo** (20 min.) • Vocabulario y gramática • Preparación para el examen 1, 2, 3, 4, 5	**Wrap-up and Homework Options** (5 min.) • Core Practice 9B-8, 9B-9 • Instant Check • Videomisterio • Examen del capítulo 9B
10	**Warm-up** (10 min.) • Homework check ✔**Summative Assessment** (40 min.) • Examen del capítulo 9B		

BLOCK SCHEDULE (90 MINUTES)

DAY	Warm-up / Assess	Preview / Present / Practice / Communicate	Wrap-up / Homework Options
1	**Warm-up** (10 min.) • Return Examen del capítulo 9A	**Chapter Opener** (5 min.) • Objectives • Arte y cultura **Vocabulario en contexto** (55 min.) • Presentation: Vocabulario en contexto • Actividades 1, 2 • Presentation: Videohistoria *¿Cómo se comunica?* • View: Videohistoria • Video Activities 1, 2, 3, 4 • Actividad 3 **Vocabulario en uso** (15 min.) • Interactive Whiteboard Vocabulary Activities • Actividades 4, 5	**Wrap-up and Homework Options** (5 min.) • Core Practice 9B-1, 9B-2, 9B-3, 9B-4 • Prueba 9B-1: Vocabulary recognition
2	**Warm-up** (10 min.) • Actividad 6 • Homework check ✔**Formative Assessment** (10 min.) • Prueba 9B-1: Vocabulary recognition	**Gramática y vocabulario en uso** (65 min.) • Fondos culturales • Actividades 7, 8 • Audio Activities 5, 6 • Communicative Pair Activity • Exploración del lenguaje • Presentation: The present tense of *pedir* and *servir* • View: GramActiva video • Interactive Whiteboard Grammar Activities • Actividades 11, 12, 13	**Wrap-up and Homework Options** (5 min.) • Core Practice 9B-5 • Writing Activity 10 • Actividad 9 • Prueba 9B-2 with Study Plan: Vocabulary production
3	**Warm-up** (5 min.) • Actividad 10 • Homework check ✔**Formative Assessment** (10 min.) • Prueba 9B-2 with Study Plan: Vocabulary production	**Gramática y vocabulario en uso** (70 min.) • View: GramActiva video • Actividad 14 • Audio Activity 7 • Communicative Pair Activity • Presentation: *Saber* and *conocer* • View: GramActiva video • Interactive Whiteboard Grammar Activities • Actividades 15, 16, 17, 18, 19 • Writing Activities 11, 12, 13	**Wrap-up and Homework Options** (5 min.) • Core Practice 9B-6, 9B-7 • Pruebas 9B-3, 9B-4 with Study Plans: The present tense of *pedir* and *servir, Saber* and *conocer*
4	**Warm-up** (15 min.) • Actividad 19 • Homework check ✔**Formative Assessment** (15 min.) • Pruebas 9B-3, 9B-4 with Study Plans: The present tense of *pedir* and *servir, Saber* and *conocer*	**Gramática y vocabulario en uso** (25 min.) • Audio Activities 8, 9 • Pronunciación • El español en el mundo del trabajo • Situation Cards **¡Adelante!** (30 min.) • Lectura • ¿Comprendes? • Presentación escrita: Steps 1, 5	**Wrap-up and Homework Options** (5 min.) • Presentación escrita: Step 2 • Lectura
5	**Warm-up** (5 min.) • Homework check	**¡Adelante!** (45 min.) • Presentación escrita: Step 3 • Perspectivas del mundo hispano **Repaso del capítulo** (35 min.) • Vocabulario y gramática • Preparación para el examen 1, 2, 3, 4, 5	**Wrap-up and Homework Options** (5 min.) • Presentación escrita: Step 4 • Core Practice 9B-8, 9B-9 • Instant Check • Examen del capítulo 9B
6	**Warm-up** (10 min.) • Homework check • Situation Cards **Repaso del capítulo** (10 min.) • Communicative Pair Activities ✔**Summative Assessment** (45 min.) • Examen del capítulo 9B	**¡Adelante!** (20 min.) • Videomisterio: *¿Eres tú, María?*, Episodio 10	**Wrap-up and Homework Options** (5 min.) • Videomisterio

Standards for *Capítulo* 9B

- To achieve the goals of the Standards, students will:

Communication

1.1 Interpersonal

- Talk about computers and technology
- Talk about asking for and describing things
- Talk about ordering at restaurants
- Talk about what activities different people can do
- Talk about knowledge of people and places

1.2 Interpretive

- Read and listen to information and opinions about computers and technology
- Read and listen to information about communication
- Read a picture-based story
- Listen to and watch a video about communications technology
- Read a survey about computer use, skills, and attitudes
- View a video mystery series

1.3 Presentational

- Present information about computers and the Internet
- Present information about communication
- Present information about technology
- Write about ordering at restaurants
- Write descriptions of objects
- Present information about knowledge of people and places
- Perform a scene from a video mystery series

Culture

2.1 Practices and Perspectives

- Discuss ***La Real Academia de la Lengua***
- Explain how technology is altering users' adherence to pure Spanish
- Learn about the rise in use of ***cibercafés***

2.2 Products and Perspectives

- Discuss Picasso and his painting

Connections

3.1 Cross-curricular

- Discuss important artists and their work: Picasso
- Read about ***las cuevas de Altamira***
- Talk about the evolution of communications technology

Comparisons

4.1 Language

- Talk about vocabulary through the recognition of cognates
- Explain how to use ***-mente*** to form an adverb
- Talk about the verbs ***pedir*** and ***servir***
- Explain how and when to use ***saber*** and ***conocer***
- Pronounce words by dividing them into syllables
- Discuss ***la invasión del ciberspanglish***

4.2 Culture

- Compare frequency of Internet usage
- Compare public access to computers and the Internet

Communities

5.1 Beyond the School

- Identify ways Spanish-speaking ability is valuable in the communications industry

5.2 Lifelong Learner

- Investigate use of Spanish-language Internet for study and pleasure
- View a video mystery series

Capítulo

9B La tecnología

Chapter Objectives

Communication

By the end of this chapter you will be able to:

- Listen to and read conversations about computers
- Talk about the Internet and write a Web profile
- Exchange information about Internet use and the benefits of computers

Culture

You will also be able to:

- Identify the impact of the Internet on the Spanish language
- Compare computer use in Spanish-speaking countries with your own use of technology

You will demonstrate what you know and can do:

- Presentación escrita, p. 467
- Preparación para el examen, p. 471

You will use:

Vocabulary

- Communication
- Computer-related activities
- Internet and digital products

Grammar

- The present tense of *pedir* and *servir*
- *Saber* and *conocer*

Exploración del mundo hispano

Country Connection
Technology and Communication

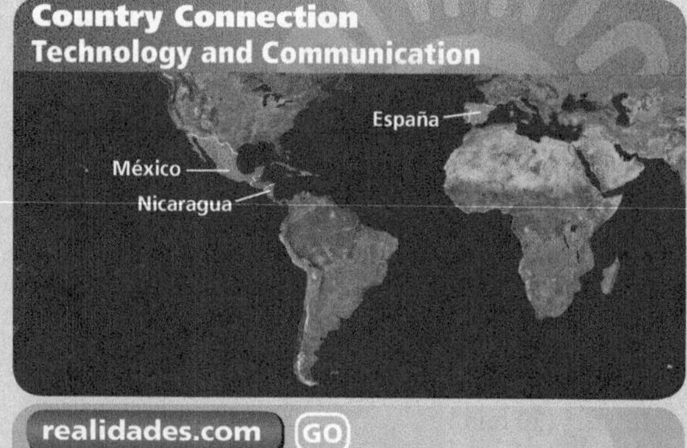

realidades.com GO

Reference Atlas

Videocultura y actividad

Mapa global interactivo

Estudiantes nicaragüenses con sus computadoras nuevas, Tipitapa, Nicaragua

ENRICH YOUR TEACHING

Using Backward Design

Have students preview the sample performance tasks on *Preparación para el examen,* p. 471, and connect them to the Chapter Objectives. Explain to students that by completing the sample tasks they can self-assess their learning progress.

Mapa global interactivo

Download the *Mapa global interactivo* files for Chapter 9B and preview the activity. The activity takes you to the prehistoric caves of Altamira in Spain.

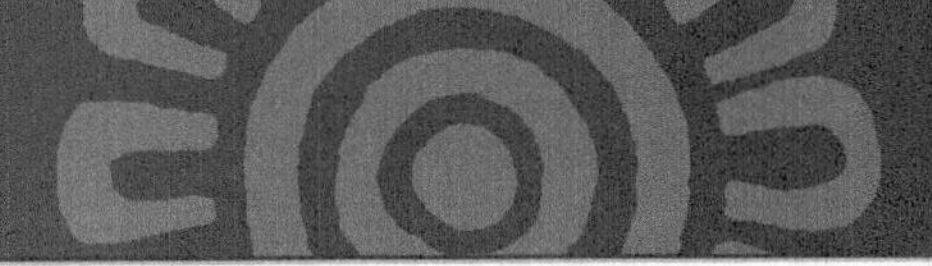

Arte y cultura | España

"Reading the Letter" is from Picasso's Neo-Classical period, when he was influenced by Roman sculpture. The heavy lines and statue-like shapes highlight the seriousness of the moment shown. In 1921, mail was the main form of communication, and telephone use was limited. Today initiatives such as One Laptop per Child, shown in the photo, help students in developing countries connect with the global community.

- How do you and your friends communicate? How can equal access to technology change communication worldwide?

"Reading the Letter" (1921), Pablo Picasso ▶

Oil on canvas, 184 X 105 cm. © 2009 Estate of Pablo Picasso/Artists Rights Society (ARS), New York. Photo: Réunion des Musées Nationaux/Art Resource, NY.

PresentationExpress™
See pp. 448a–448b

Chapter Opener

Core Instruction

Resources: Map Transparencies 12, 18, 20

Suggestions: Introduce students to the chapter theme and review the objectives. Point out that they will learn technical terms related to computers. The *A primera vista* video will include a story about teenagers helping one another learn to communicate by computer. Remind students that although they may be current with the latest trends in technology, not everyone feels the same enthusiasm.

Videocultura View *Medios de comunicación* with the class to learn about Spanish media in the United States and the world.

Arte y cultura

Standards: 2.2, 3.1

Resources: Fine Art Transparencies, p. 45

Suggestions: Ask students to study the painting carefully, including the subjects and their relationship to each other. Can they see clues, such as the posture, hands, and facial expressions that help inform viewers of the contents of the letter? Ask students if they think the letter contains good news or bad news. Show other examples of Picasso's work from his Neo-Classical period.

Answers will vary.

Culture Note

Tell students that by 2010, the One Laptop per Child Organization (OLPC) had provided 17,000 laptops to public school students and suburban neighborhoods throughout Nicaragua. The students pictured are from the Miguel Larreynaga School, in Tipitapa, a town 27 km north of Managua. Point out that some features of these laptops make them especially useful: They are portable, wireless, and durable.

DIFFERENTIATED INSTRUCTION

Digital resources such as the ***Interactive Whiteboard*** activity banks, ***Videomodelos***, additional ***Online Activities, Study Plans***, automatically graded ***Leveled Workbook***, animated ***Grammar Tutorials, Flashcards***, and ***Vocabulary and Grammar Videos*** will help you reach students of different ability levels and learning styles.

STUDENTS NEEDING EXTRA HELP

Guided Practice Activities
- Flashcards, pp. 291–294
- Vocabulary Check, pp. 295–298
- Grammar Support, pp. 299–302

HERITAGE LEARNERS

Realidades para hispanohablantes
- Chapter Opener, pp. 350–351
- A primera vista, p. 352
- Videohistoria, p. 353
- Manos a la obra, pp. 354–361
- ¡Adelante!, pp. 362–367
- Repaso del capítulo, pp. 368–369

ADVANCED/PRE-AP*

Pre-AP* Resource Book,
- pp. 94–97

Communications Workbook
- Integrated Performance Assessment, p. 333

9B Language Input

Vocabulario en contexto

Core Instruction

Standards: 1.2

Resources: Teacher's Resource Book: Input Script, p. 326, Clip Art, pp. 340–341, Audio Script, p. 327; Voc. and Gram. Transparencies 166–167; TPR Stories Book, pp. 122–133; Audio Program DVD: Cap. 9B, Tracks 1–2

Focus: Introducing new vocabulary; using visualized vocabulary and cognates about computer uses and ways to communicate

Suggestions: Use the story in the *TPR Stories Book* to present the new vocabulary and grammar or use the Input Script from the *Teacher's Resource Book.*

Present the vocabulary in three sets: words to talk about communication, computer-related activities, and computer-generated products (including ***pedir, servir, saber,*** and ***conocer***). With their books closed, tell students that you are going to name various computer functions. They should guess what the function is and picture how they might do that function. Then show the transparencies and have students look at the visualized vocabulary in the book.

BELLRINGER REVIEW

Have students unscramble the words and conjugate the verb to make logical sentences.

1) *usar/la computadora/Mario y Graciela/ en el laboratorio*
2) *Paula/en la clase de arte/dibujar*
3) *escribir/una composición/nosotros/en la clase de inglés*

A primera vista

Objectives

Read, listen to, and understand information about
- computers and computer use
- ways to communicate

Vocabulario en contexto

"En **el laboratorio** en nuestra escuela, los estudiantes **saben** usar las computadoras para hacer muchas cosas. A muchos estudiantes les gusta . . .

. . . **crear documentos** o escribir **una composición,**

. . . hacer **gráficos,**

. . . y preparar **presentaciones** con diapositivas.

Otros estudiantes **están en línea** para **navegar en la Red.** Pueden **buscar un sitio Web** o **bajar información** para **un informe.**

A otros les interesa **grabar un disco compacto.** Esta chica graba canciones".

DIFFERENTIATED INSTRUCTION

Advanced Learners

Using the new vocabulary and phrases, have students develop a survey with at least six ***sí/no*** questions about computer use. Invite them to create the survey on a computer and insert clip art beside each question. Have them survey a small group and tally the results and summarize them in writing.

Heritage Language Learners

Have students work in pairs or small groups to discuss which tasks mentioned on pp. 450–451 they know how to do. Students should also ask each other how they prefer to communicate with friends and family members.

1 ¿Sí o no?

Escuchar

Vas a escuchar siete frases. Si una frase es cierta, haz el gesto del pulgar hacia arriba. Si una frase es falsa, haz el gesto del pulgar hacia abajo.

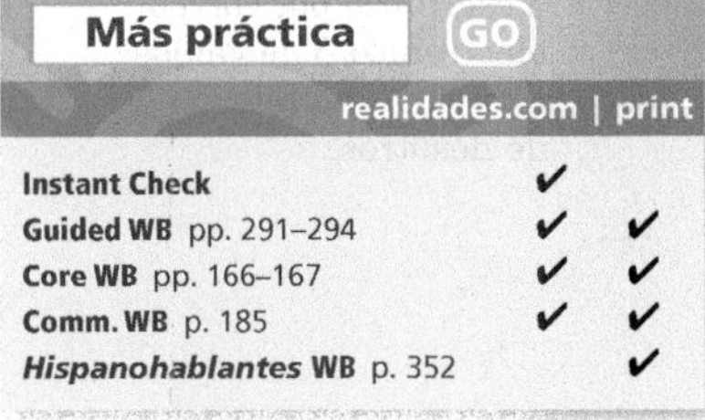

Más práctica		
realidades.com | print		
Instant Check	✔	
Guided WB pp. 291–294	✔	✔
Core WB pp. 166–167	✔	✔
Comm. WB p. 185	✔	✔
Hispanohablantes WB p. 352		✔

2 ¿Es lógico?

Escuchar

Primero lee las respuestas. Luego escucha cada conversación y escoge el comentario más lógico.

1. a. Al papá le gusta usar la Red.
   b. El papá no sabe usar la Red.
2. a. El estudiante quiere grabar un disco compacto.
   b. El estudiante quiere bajar información.
3. a. Va a enviarle una carta.
   b. Va a enviarle una tarjeta.

ENRICH YOUR TEACHING

Teacher-to-Teacher

Play a form of *Pictionary* using the words and phrases from pp. 450–451. Divide students into teams and give each team a large sheet of paper. Ask a member from each group to come to you for a word to draw for his or her group. Write it down and make sure that the student does not say it aloud. Have the student go back to the group and silently draw the word until someone guesses it. The group must spell it correctly in order to gain points.

1 Standards: 1.2

Resources: Teacher's Resource Book: Audio Script, p. 327; Audio Program DVD: Cap. 9B, Track 3; Answer Keys: Student Edition, p. 134

Focus: Listening comprehension; identifying new vocabulary

Suggestions: Play the audio or read the script. Allow students to listen more than once. Pause to monitor students. Give them several chances to listen and give a "thumbs-up" or "thumbs-down" sign.

Script and Answers:

1. **Necesito una computadora para comunicarme cara a cara con mis amigos. *(down)***
2. **Para navegar en la Red necesito estar en línea. *(up)***
3. **No es posible jugar juegos en la Red. *(down)***
4. **No podemos preparar una presentación con diapositivas en una computadora portátil. *(down)***
5. **Tengo que estar en la Red para crear gráficos y documentos. *(down)***
6. **Es posible enviar una foto por correo electrónico. *(up)***
7. **No es posible enviar una tarjeta por correo electrónico. *(down)***

2 Standards: 1.2

Resources: Teacher's Resource Book: Audio Script, p. 327; Audio Program DVD: Cap. 9B, Track 4; Answer Keys: Student Edition, p. 134

Focus: Listening comprehension

Suggestions: Have students read the sentences carefully and note the differences. In item 2, ***grabar*** and ***bajar*** sound very similar. Make sure students can differentiate.

Script and Answers:

1. **—Hijo, no me gusta nada navegar en la Red.**
   —Pero, papá, no es complicado. *(b)*
2. **—Necesito bajar información de la Red para un informe.**
   —Muy bien. Tienes que estar en línea. *(b)*
3. **—Tu tía va a celebrar su cumpleaños en una semana.**
   —¿Por qué no le envías una tarjeta? *(b)*

Videohistoria

Core Instruction

Standards: 1.2, 4.1

Resources: Voc. and Gram. Transparencies 168–169; Audio Program DVD: Cap. 9B, Track 5

Focus: Presenting additional vocabulary and grammar in the context of the story; previewing the language video

Suggestions:

Pre-reading: Using the Transparencies, go panel by panel and ask students to predict the storyline. Direct students' attention to the *Strategy* and have them skim the reading and list cognates. Ask them what they think the boy might learn to do.

Reading: Read the captions with students or use the audio. Using the transparencies and nonverbal clues, help students understand the new words in blue type. Ask if the list of cognates helped them with comprehension. Remind students that in panel 4, ***ordenador*** means ***computadora.*** Ask the comprehension questions found on the transparencies.

Post-reading: Complete *Actividad* 3 to check comprehension.

Video

Core Instruction

Standards: 1.2, 4.1

Resources: Teacher's Resource Book: Video Script, p. 331; Video Program: Cap. 9B; Video Program Teacher's Guide: Cap. 9B

Focus: Comprehending new vocabulary and grammar in authentic visual context

Suggestions:

Pre-viewing: Review the *Videohistoria* reading and have students make a list of key ideas. Play an excerpt of the video with the sound down and ask students to tell which panel in the *Videohistoria* it corresponds to.

Viewing: Have students pay attention to the intonation of questions and answers. Ask if Ana is patient with Javier's questions. Is it easy to teach someone how to use a computer? Show the video once without pausing. Then show it again, stopping to check comprehension.

Post-viewing: Complete the Video Activities in the *Communication Workbook.*

¿Cómo se comunica?

Ana sabe usar una cámara digital y una computadora. Ella puede navegar en la Red y tiene su propia página Web. ¿Qué le va a enseñar a Javier?

Strategy

Recognizing cognates
Recognizing cognates in the following dialogue can help improve your understanding. Skim the reading and make a list of the cognates.

España

1

Javier: Hola, Ana. ¿Cómo estás?

Ana: Muy bien, ¿y tú? Mira. Acabo de comprar esta **cámara digital.** Es fascinante. ¿La **conoces?**

Javier: A ver. No **conozco** ese tipo de cámara. ¡Qué interesante!

5

Ana: Aquí puedes navegar en la Red o **visitar salones de chat.** Mira, mi **página Web.** Yo la hice.

Javier: ¿Tú la hiciste? ¡Qué bien! Pero . . . **¿para qué sirve?**

Ana: El Internet **sirve para** mucho. Puedes **escribir por** correo electrónico, buscar información, jugar juegos . . .

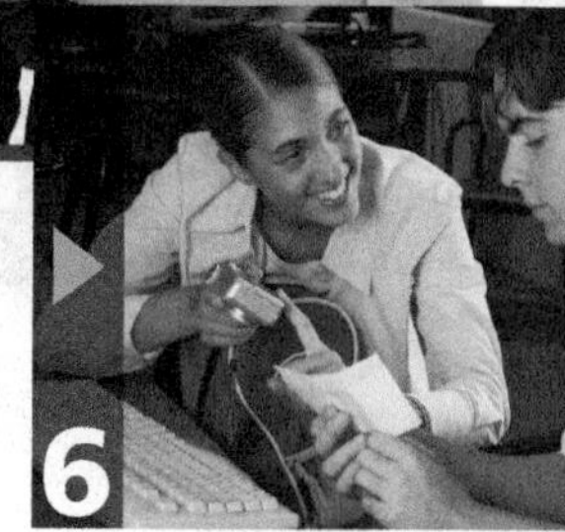

Ana: Tengo una idea. Tu amigo Esteban tiene **dirección electrónica,** ¿no?

Javier: Creo que sí. ¡Ah! Aquí está en su carta.

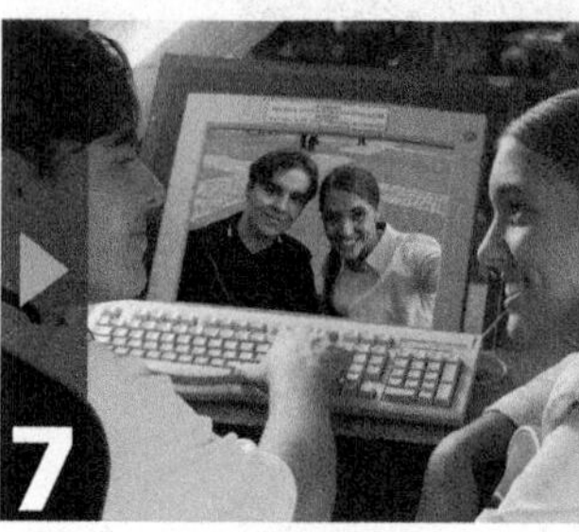

Javier: Hola, Esteban. Saludos desde un cibercafé en Madrid . . .

Ana: ¡Eso es! Tú vas a escribirle por correo electrónico. Y le vamos a enviar esta foto de nosotros.

DIFFERENTIATED INSTRUCTION

Students with Learning Difficulties

Remind students how they can be helped by using cognates to support reading comprehension. Point out that many terms in Spanish related to computers and ways of communication are cognates of English words. Explain that, because they are cognates, their correct pronunciation will require extra attention. Provide students with additional pronunciation practice of the cognates found in the *Videohistoria.*

Ana: ¿Adónde vas?

Javier: Voy a enviar una tarjeta a Esteban, mi amigo en San Antonio. Mira, tengo una foto de él.

Ana: Mmmm. Es muy simpático, ¿no? Si quieres, te acompaño.

Ana: Vamos, Javier. Uno, dos, tres. Y mira, aquí estás. **¿Qué te parece?**

Javier: Muy bien. Sacaste las fotos muy **rápidamente**. Veo que no es complicado.

Javier: Un momento, voy a enviar mi tarjeta.

Ana: ¿Por qué no te comunicas con Esteban por correo electrónico?

Javier: Porque no tengo ordenador.

Ana: No importa. En Madrid hay muchos cibercafés. Vamos a uno.

Javier: . . . y aquí estoy con mi buena amiga, Ana. ¿Qué tal la familia? Y el cumpleaños de Cristina, ¿cómo lo pasaste?

Esteban: Es evidente que Javier está muy contento en Madrid.

También se dice . . .

la computadora = el ordenador *(España)*

3 ¿Comprendes?

Leer • Escribir

En cada frase hay un error. Lee la frase y después escribe la frase con la información correcta.

1. Ana acaba de comprar una computadora portátil.
2. Javier quiere enviarle a Esteban una carta.
3. Javier no le escribe por correo electrónico porque no le gusta usar las computadoras.
4. Javier saca las fotos con la cámara digital.
5. Según Ana, la Red no sirve para mucho.
6. Ana le escribe a Esteban por correo electrónico.
7. Javier le pregunta a Esteban sobre el cumpleaños de Angélica.

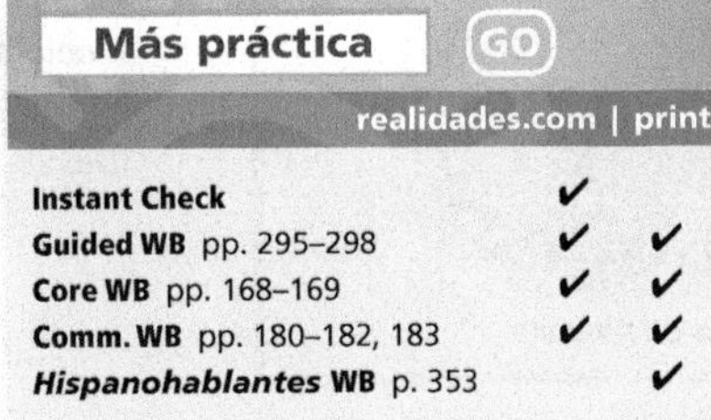

Más práctica GO

realidades.com | print

Instant Check	✔	
Guided WB pp. 295–298	✔	✔
Core WB pp. 168–169	✔	✔
Comm. WB pp. 180–182, 183	✔	✔
Hispanohablantes WB p. 353		✔

3 Standards: 1.2, 1.3

Resources: Answer Keys: Student Edition, p. 135

Focus: Reading comprehension; writing to verify understanding

Suggestions: Encourage students to first attempt to correct the sentences without looking back at the conversation on the page. Ask volunteers to read their corrected sentences aloud.

Answers:

1. **Ana acaba de comprar una cámara digital.**
2. **Javier quiere enviarle a Esteban una tarjeta.**
3. **Esteban no le escribe por correo electrónico porque no tiene computadora.**
4. **Ana saca las fotos con la cámara digital.**
5. **Según Ana, el Internet (la Red) sirve para mucho.**
6. **Javier le escribe a Esteban por correo electrónico.**
7. **Javier le pregunta a Esteban sobre el cumpleaños de Cristina.**

Extension: Have students look at the *También se dice....* Ask students to use ***ordenador*** instead of ***computadora*** in the first and third sentences of the activity, making the necessary changes to any modifying words.

Pre-AP* Support

- **Learning Objective:** Interpersonal Writing
- **Activity:** Have students work in pairs to write the whole text of Javier's e-mail to Esteban. Have students imagine Esteban tells his friend about his adventures in Madrid, including details about his experience in the cibercafé in Madrid.
- ***Pre-AP* Resource Book:*** Comprehensive guide to Pre-AP* vocabulary skill development, pp. 51–57

Additional Resources

- Communication Wbk.: Audio Act. 5, p. 183
- Teacher's Resource Book: Audio Script, pp. 327–328
- Audio Program DVD: Cap. 9B, Track 7

ASSESSMENT

Quiz: Vocabulary Recognition

- Prueba 9B-1: pp. 241–242

ENRICH YOUR TEACHING

Culture Note

An increasing number of Spanish speakers have found that the use of the Internet has enhanced their personal relationships with others. Not only can they remain in contact with friends and relatives in their heritage country, but many have also found new friendships on the Web.

21st Century Skills

Social and Cross-Cultural Skills Have students interview native speakers or exchange students to find out if the methods young people use to communicate are the same in their country as in the United States. If those students use text messaging, have your students find out some typical text messages and share them with the class.

9B Practice and Communicate

INTERACTIVE WHITEBOARD
Vocabulary Activities 9B

BELLRINGER REVIEW

Create printouts of computer graphics, Web pages, and presentation software slides. Have students identify them using the new vocabulary.

4 Standards: 1.1, 1.2, 1.3

Resources: Voc. and Gram. Transparency 172; Teacher's Resource Book: GramActiva BLM, p. 339

Focus: Reading and responding to a survey about computer skills

Recycle: ***Deber***

Suggestions: After students read the quiz aloud and review vocabulary, have them read the questions silently and write the letter of each response. Make sure they know how to add up their points. Use yourself as a model by telling them what you scored and what computer course you should take.

Answers will vary.

Common Errors: Students often confuse the ***yo*** and ***tú*** verb forms when conversing with a partner. Review the ***yo*** and ***tú*** forms of ***deber*** before you begin Step 2.

Extension: Create a model exercise that students can do in pairs. Student A: *¿Qué aprendiste en la clase básica?* Student B: *Aprendí a crear documentos.*

Pre-AP* Support

- **Learning Objective:** Interpretive: Print
- **Activity** 4: Students use reading comprehension skills as they read and respond to a survey.

Fondo cultural

Standards: 3.1

Suggestions: Ask students why they think people drew pictures on cave walls. What other unique forms of communication can they think of? Then read the paragraph and question about cave dwellers' art.

Answers will vary.

Mapa global interactivo, Actividad Explore the prehistoric caves of Altamira in Spain.

Vocabulario en uso

Objectives

- Read and exchange information about how you and others use computers and the Internet
- Listen to and express opinions about computers and communication

4 La computadora y tú

Leer • Pensar • Hablar

1. Toma esta prueba *(test)* sobre cómo usas la computadora. Determina tu evaluación y lee la recomendación del Centro de Computación.
2. Pregunta a otro(a) estudiante qué curso debe tomar según los resultados de la prueba. Tiene que darte tres razones *(reasons)* para justificar el curso.

Modelo

A —*¿Qué curso debes tomar?*
B —*Debo tomar un curso avanzado.*
A —*¿Por qué?*
B —*Porque ya navego en la Red y busco sitios Web. Sé crear un sitio Web.*

La computadora y t

1. ¿Cómo te comunicas más con otras persona
   a. Les hablo cara a cara.
   b. Les envío cartas o tarjetas.
   c. Les escribo por correo electrónico.
   d. Visito salones de chat.
2. ¿Cómo buscas información cuando escribes informes?
   a. Voy a la biblioteca por un libro.
   b. Les pido ayuda a mis amigos.
   c. Navego en la Red y busco sitios Web.
   d. Bajo documentos que me sirven mucho.
3. ¿Qué sabes hacer en la computadora?
   a. Sé encender* la computadora.
   b. Sé escribir una composición.
   c. Sé crear una presentación usando diapositivas.
   d. Sé crear un sitio Web.
4. ¿Para qué te sirve la computadora?
   a. No me sirve para nada.
   b. Me sirve para jugar juegos.
   c. Me sirve para navegar en la Red.
   d. Me sirve para buscar y bajar información.
5. ¿Cuál es tu opinión de las computadoras?
   a. Tengo miedo de las computadoras.
   b. Las computadoras son demasiado complicadas.
   c. Las computadoras me ayudan a hacer cosas más rápidamente.
   d. Las computadoras son necesarias para la comunicación.

Evaluación
Cada a = 1 punto
Cada b = 3 puntos
Cada c = 4 puntos
Cada d = 6 puntos

El Centro de Computación tiene cursos ideales para ti. Según el resultado de la prueba, debes tomar uno de estos cursos:

Puntos	Tu curso ideal
de 5 a 10	Básico 1
de 11 a 16	Básico 2
de 17 a 23	Intermedio
de 24 a 30	Avanzado

*to turn on

Fondo Cultural | España

Las cuevas de Altamira Long before people were able to write, they drew pictures on cave walls. These are the first records we have of communication. Spectacular paintings of bison, deer, horses, and wild boars were discovered in 1879 in the caves of Altamira in northern Spain. These drawings are more than 14,000 years old.

- Why do you think the cave dwellers drew pictures of animals? What would you draw?

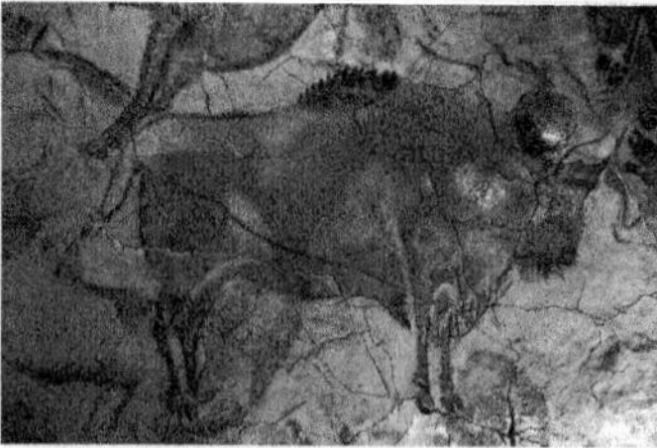

Un bisonte en las cuevas de Altamira

DIFFERENTIATED INSTRUCTION

Advanced Learners

Have students research the Altamira caves on the Internet. Have them create a brief software slide show or print it out. Divide the class into pairs or groups to write a short report on one aspect of the caves.

Heritage Language Learners

Have students type in the words *Real Academia Española* in a search engine. Tell them to locate and explore the dictionary and look up some of the recent vocabulary words they have learned. Have students research the history of the *Real Academia Española*. When was it founded? What was its mission?

5 Opiniones diferentes

Escuchar • Escribir

1. Vas a escuchar las opiniones de cuatro personas sobre cómo prefieren comunicarse. En una hoja de papel, escribe los números del 1 al 4 y escribe lo que escuchas.
2. Después de escuchar sus opiniones, indica si crees que las personas que tienen estas opiniones están en la sala o en el laboratorio de computadoras.

6 Definiciones

Leer • Escribir

Lee las definiciones y escribe la palabra correspondiente.

Modelo

Es como enviar una carta por computadora.
el correo electrónico

1. Es una foto que podemos proyectar durante una presentación.
2. Es una composición musical que podemos cantar.
3. Es una forma de comunicación que usa bolígrafo y papel. *(Hay dos posibilidades.)*
4. Es un lugar en la Red que da información sobre una organización o una persona.
5. Es una computadora pequeña que puedes llevar a diferentes lugares.
6. Es un lugar en la escuela donde hay muchas computadoras que los estudiantes pueden usar.
7. Es una forma de comunicación bonita o cómica que le envías* a una persona para su cumpleaños.
8. Es algo visual que puedes crear o ver en la computadora.
9. Es algo que escribes sobre un tema para una clase. *(Hay dos posibilidades.)*

*Enviar has an accent mark on the í in all present-tense forms except *nosotros* and *vosotros*.

Fondo Cultural | España

La Real Academia Española was founded in Spain in 1713 with a mission to preserve the quality, elegance, and purity of the Spanish language. There are now *Academias* in all the Spanish-speaking countries, including the Philippines and the United States. Today the *Academias* ensure that changes in Spanish reflect the needs of its more than 360 million native speakers. La Real Academia Española publishes the most complete, authoritative dictionary of the Spanish language.

- Why do you think that it's important to preserve the quality and purity of a language?

La Real Academia Española en Madrid

ENRICH YOUR TEACHING

Culture Note

Since 1780, the *Real Academia Española* has been improving and updating a definitive dictionary of the Spanish Language. The *Academia Norteamericana de la Lengua Española,* located in New York City, is the most recent ***academia*** to join the *Asociación de Academias.* Founded in 1973, it became part of the *Asociación de Academias* in 1980. By contrast, the *Academia Mexicana de la Lengua* was founded in 1875 and the *Academia Peruana de la Lengua* in 1887.

Practice and Communicate 9B

5 Standards: 1.2, 1.3

Resources: Teacher's Resource Book: Audio Script, p. 327; Audio Program DVD: Cap. 9B, Track 6; Answer Keys: Student Edition, p. 135

Focus: Listening comprehension; writing with accuracy; stating an opinion in a personalized context

Suggestions: Play the audio or read the script. Allow students plenty of time to write. For Step 2, students will decide which room is applicable to each individual.

Script and Answers:

1. **Me gusta más hablar cara a cara con mis amigos. No los visito en los salones de chat. *(sala)***
2. **No me gusta ir a la biblioteca por libros. Prefiero estar en línea en casa buscando información. *(sala)***
3. **Me interesa más crear una presentación usando gráficos. Es fácil bajar los gráficos y ponerlos en un documento o archivo. *(laboratorio)***
4. **No me comunico con mis amigos por correo electrónico. Les hablo por teléfono o les escribo cartas. *(sala)***

6 Standards: 1.2, 1.3

Resources: Answer Keys: Student Edition, p. 136

Focus: Reading definitions of new vocabulary; writing with accuracy

Suggestions: Allow students to work with a partner. Suggest that they first write down as many terms as they can on their own, and then consult the book for help in finding the remaining words and verifying spelling.

Answers:

1. **la diapositiva**
2. **la canción**
3. **la carta, la tarjeta**
4. **el sitio Web**
5. **la computadora portátil**
6. **el laboratorio**
7. **la tarjeta**
8. **los gráficos, el sitio Web, la página Web**
9. **el informe, el documento**

Fondo cultural

Standards: 2.1

Suggestions: Explain that in the United States there is no single authority on proper English that is equivalent to the *Real Academia Española*. Discuss how the English language changes rapidly, especially with new technology terms.

Answers will vary but may include that communication among generations, even those separated by long periods of time, is easier when the quality and purity of a language have been preserved.

9B Practice and Communicate

BELLRINGER REVIEW

Use the Transparency to review the conversation and visualized vocabulary on p. 451.

7 Standards: 1.1, 1.2, 1.3

Resources: Answer Keys: Student Edition, p. 136

Focus: Writing reasons for using various means of communication

Suggestions: Review the *¿Recuerdas?* and provide examples of ***les*** in the context of a few sentences. Tell students that their sentences should tell some fact about the form of communication and state why it is used. Make sure each group keeps a tally of their preferences by having a representative from the group write this information on the board.

Answers will vary but should include:

1. **escribir por correo electrónico**
2. **hablar cara a cara**
3. **escribir tarjetas**
4. **escribir cartas**

Common Errors: Using the direct object pronouns ***los*** or ***las*** instead of the indirect object pronoun ***les.*** Call attention to the *¿Recuerdas?* and tell students to use ***les*** in this activity.

8 Standards: 1.2, 1.3, 4.2

Resources: Answer Keys: Student Edition, p. 136

Focus: Reading and interpreting statistics; answering questions in writing about Internet use and sharing those answers in small groups

Suggestions: Before reading the ad aloud, have students review the questions to guide their reading. Point out that students will have to use the information given to figure out the answers to item 1. After they write the remaining answers, have them share their work in small groups.

Answers:

1. **los estadounidenses más que los españoles; los groenlandeses más que los estadounidenses**

2.–3. Answers will vary.

7 ¿Cómo te comunicas?

Escribir • Hablar

¿Recuerdas?

You use the indirect object pronoun *les* to mean "to them" or "for them."

Para decir más . . .

eficiente efficient

íntimo, -a personal

rápido, -a quick, fast

1. Mira cada dibujo y escribe qué forma de comunicación es. Luego escribe por qué se usa esta forma de comunicación.

Modelo

hablar por teléfono
Casi todos tienen teléfonos. Es fácil.

1. 

2. 

3. 

4. 

2. Trabaja con un grupo de cinco personas y pregunta a tus compañeros cómo se comunican con otras personas y por qué. Escriban sus respuestas.

Modelo

A —*¿Cómo te comunicas con otras personas?*
B —*Les hablo por teléfono.*
A —*¿Por qué?*
B —*Porque casi todos tienen teléfonos y es fácil*

3. Una persona de cada grupo va a escribir en la pizarra la forma preferida de comunicación de su grupo. Según esta información, ¿cuál es la forma de comunicación preferida de la clase?

8 ¿Quiénes están en línea?

Leer • Escribir • Hablar

Lee el anuncio y luego contesta estas preguntas.

1. ¿Quiénes usan más el Internet: los estadounidenses o los españoles? ¿Los estadounidenses o los groenlandeses?
2. ¿Usas tú el Internet a menudo, a veces o nunca?
3. Entre *(Among)* las personas que conoces, ¿quién usa más el Internet? ¿Para qué lo usa?

¡A sus teclados[1], listos . . . a navegar!

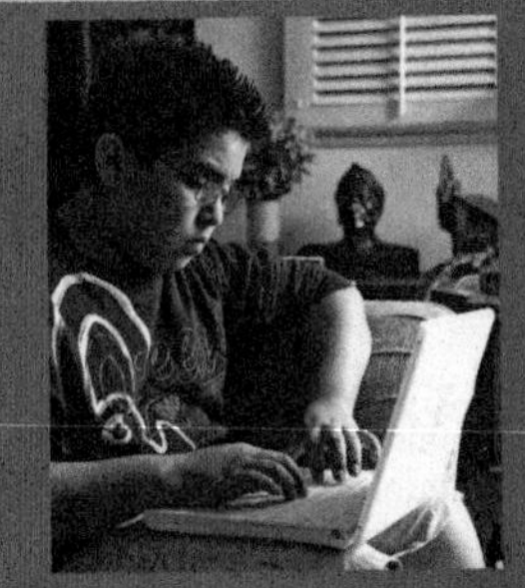

¿Usas el Internet? En el mundo hay más de mil millones de internautas. El récord lo tienen los groenlandeses:[2] nueve de cada diez personas usan la Red. En los Estados Unidos, siete de cada diez estadounidenses[3] la usan. En España la gente está lejos de esa cifra.[4] Sólo seis de cada diez españoles están conectados al Internet.

[1]keyboards [2]Greenlanders [3]Americans [4]figure

DIFFERENTIATED INSTRUCTION

Heritage Language Learners

Have students brainstorm a short set of questions as a group and individually interview a Spanish-speaking person about the Internet and e-mail, asking him or her about the influence of English words. Make sure they ask about the difficulty of including accent marks in e-mail. Have students report responses to the class.

Advanced Learners

Have students e-mail you a link to their favorite Web site and explain why they like it. Compile these into one e-mail and either send it to your student list or post it on the class homepage.

9 Y tú, ¿que dices?

Escribir • Hablar

1. ¿Tienes tú, o tiene tu familia o un(a) amigo(a), una computadora portátil? ¿Qué te parece?
2. ¿A veces tienes miedo de las computadoras? ¿Por qué?
3. ¿Tienes tu propia dirección electrónica? Crea una nueva dirección electrónica "inolvidable" para las personas que nunca recuerdan *(remember)* tu dirección.
4. ¿Qué sabes crear en la computadora?
5. ¿Qué sitio Web conoces mejor? ¿Qué te parece?

Exploración del lenguaje

Using *-mente* to form an adverb

Adverbs are words that describe verbs. They often tell *how* an action is performed. Many adverbs in English end in the letters *-ly*: *slowly, frequently, happily,* and so on. To form similar adverbs in Spanish, add the ending *-mente* to the feminine singular form of an adjective. This *-mente* ending is equivalent to the *-ly* ending in English.

rápida → rápidamente	fácil → fácilmente	general → generalmente
práctica → prácticamente	feliz → felizmente	especial → especialmente

Note that if the adjective has a written accent, as with *rápida, fácil,* and *práctica,* the accent appears in the same place in the adverb form.

Try it out! Give the adverb for each of the adjectives in the list. Then use each adverb in one of the sentences. Some sentences have more than one possible answer.

normal total completo frecuente reciente

1. El laboratorio de nuestra escuela es ____ nuevo.
2. ____ les escribo a mis amigos por correo electrónico pero hoy les envío una carta.
3. ____ mis padres nos compraron una nueva computadora.
4. Mi hermano está ____ contento cuando está usando la computadora.
5. ____ grabamos canciones en un disco compacto.

9 Standards: 1.1, 1.3

Focus: Writing and speaking about computer use in a personalized context

Suggestions: After students write their answers, divide the class into small groups and have them share their answers.

Answers will vary.

Exploración del lenguaje

Core Instruction

Standards: 4.1

Suggestions: Begin by discussing the function of adverbs. Remind students that knowing and recognizing patterns of language similarities between Spanish and English will help them learn and use new vocabulary quickly. Have students practice saying the adjectives and adverbs aloud.

Answers will vary but may include:

1. **completamente, totalmente**
2. **Frecuentemente**
3. **Recientemente**
4. **totalmente, completamente**
5. **Normalmente**

Additional Resources

- Communication Wbk.: Audio Act. 6, p. 183
- Teacher's Resource Book: Audio Script, p. 328, Communicative Pair Activity BLM, pp. 254–255
- Audio Program DVD: Cap. 9B, Track 8

ENRICH YOUR TEACHING

Teacher-to-Teacher

Have students create a class Web page together. Work with the media specialist at your school and assign different tasks to different groups. Get ideas for content and layout from the class as a whole before giving specific assignments to small groups. Ask students who have already made a page to help the others. Develop the content, such as Spanish projects, in your class. One of the many advantages of having a class Web page is that you can publish student writing online for others to read and post information or assignments for the class.

ASSESSMENT

Prueba 9B-2 with Study Plan (online only)

Quiz: Vocabulary Production

- Prueba 9B-2: pp. 243–244

Gramática

Core Instruction

Standards: 4.1

Resources: Voc. and Gram. Transparency 170; Teacher's Resource Book, Video Script, p. 331; Video Program: Cap. 9B

INTERACTIVE WHITEBOARD
Grammar Activities 9B

Suggestions: Ask students what the rule is for conjugating ***pensar, querer,*** and ***preferir.*** Have them compare the charts on p. 330 with the ones on p. 458 to see how the verbs change from ***e*** to ***ie*** or ***e*** to ***i.*** Show the *GramActiva* Video.

BELLRINGER REVIEW

Remind students that ***servir*** also means "to be useful for." Point out that in this activity they will use the verb in this sense in the phrase ***sirve para....***

10 Standards: 1.3, 4.1

Resources: Answer Keys: Student Edition, p. 137

Focus: Using ***pedir*** and other verbs to write about computer-related tasks

Suggestions: Review the model with students, making sure they understand the structure they will be writing. Have them refer to the chart above the activity.

Answers:

1. **Mario le pide ayuda al profesor porque no sabe grabar un disco compacto.**
2. **Nosotros le pedimos ayuda al profesor porque no comprendemos por qué hay un error.**
3. **Tú le pides ayuda al profesor porque quieres crear una canción.**
4. **Marisol y Elena le piden ayuda al profesor porque no pueden abrir el documento.**
5. **Yo le pido ayuda al profesor porque deseo enviar una foto por correo electrónico.**
6. **Vicente y yo le pedimos ayuda al profesor porque no podemos crear nuestro sitio Web.**

Common Errors: Students may omit the indirect object pronoun ***le*** before the verb. Before beginning the activity, tell students that they will use ***le*** in every sentence.

Theme Project

Students can perform Step 4 at this point. Be sure they understand your corrections and suggestions. (For more information, see p. 424-b.)

Manos a la obra

Gramática

Objectives

- Talk and write about asking for help
- Discuss what your favorite restaurant serves and give advice about ordering
- Discuss an object's use while playing a game

The present tense of *pedir* and *servir*

Pedir and *servir* are stem-changing verbs in which the *e* in the stem of the infinitive changes to *i* in all forms except *nosotros* and *vosotros.*

Here are the present-tense forms of *pedir* and *servir:*

(yo)	pido	(nosotros) (nosotras)	pedimos
(tú)	pides	(vosotros) (vosotras)	pedís
Ud. (él) (ella)	pide	Uds. (ellos) (ellas)	piden

(yo)	sirvo	(nosotros) (nosotras)	servimos
(tú)	sirves	(vosotros) (vosotras)	servís
Ud. (él) (ella)	sirve	Uds. (ellos) (ellas)	sirven

Pedir means "to ask for."

Juan **pide** la dirección electrónica.
Pedimos más información sobre la Red.

Servir means "to serve" or "to be useful for."

Servimos refrescos después de la clase.
Las computadoras **sirven** para mucho.

Más ayuda 

realidades.com

 ***GramActiva* Video Animated Verbs**

 ***GramActiva* Activity**

10 En la clase de tecnología

Escribir

En la clase de tecnología hay muchas cosas que los estudiantes no pueden hacer. Por eso le piden ayuda al profesor. Escribe las frases.

Modelo

Fernando (no poder / bajar los gráficos)
Fernando le pide ayuda al profesor porque no puede bajar los gráficos.

1. Mario (no saber / grabar un disco compacto)
2. nosotros (no comprender / por qué hay un error)
3. tú (querer / crear una canción)
4. Marisol y Elena (no poder / abrir el documento)
5. yo (desear / enviar una foto por correo electrónico)
6. Vicente y yo (no poder / crear nuestro sitio Web)

Nota

In English you say that you ask *for* help. In Spanish, "for" is implied in the meaning of *pedir* and a separate word is *not* used.

DIFFERENTIATED INSTRUCTION

Advanced Learners

As a long-term project, have students go online and create a list of Web sites that provide information about Spanish lessons or exchange programs that they might be interested in. Have students preview the sites and rate them. Students can share their results with the class.

Multiple Intelligences

Bodily/Kinesthetic: Have students write a skit about going to a restaurant and ordering a meal. Have them bring in some props and perform the skit for the class or, if possible, record it and show it to the class.

11 ¿Pides muchas cosas? |  | ♻

Hablar

Habla con otro(a) estudiante sobre las cosas que les pides a diferentes personas.

¿Recuerdas?

The indirect object pronouns *le* and *les* mean "to him, her, you *(pl.)*, them." With *pedir*, they refer to the person whom you ask for something.

Modelo

dinero

A —*¿A quién le pides dinero?*

B —*Le pido dinero a mi mejor amiga, Luisa.*

o: —*Les pido dinero a mis padres.*

1. ropa nueva
2. tiempo libre sin tarea
3. ayuda con . . .
4. tu propio(a) . . .
5. tiempo libre sin quehaceres
6. **¡Respuesta personal!**

12 Los mejores restaurantes |  | ♻

Hablar • Escribir

1. Piensa en los restaurantes que conoces. ¿Qué sirven allí que te gusta? Con otro(a) estudiante, habla sobre los restaurantes y la comida que sirven.

Modelo

A —*¿En qué restaurante comes?*

B —*Como en el restaurante . . . . A menudo pido . . . allí. Es muy . . . . Lo sirven con . . . .*

2. Ahora hablen con otra pareja de los restaurantes donde Uds. comen, lo que piden y con qué sirven las comidas. Preparen tres o más recomendaciones de restaurantes para presentar a la clase.

Modelo

Si Uds. quieren comer bien, recomendamos el restaurante Las Palmeras. Siempre pedimos el pescado . . . ¡es delicioso! Lo sirven con arroz. . . .

13 Juego |  | ♻

Escribir • Hablar

Con otro(a) estudiante, escriban descripciones de tres cosas y expliquen para qué sirven. Lean las frases a otra pareja para ver si ellos pueden identificar las cosas.

Modelo

A —*Es una cosa bastante pequeña. Puede estar en tu mochila o pupitre. No cuesta mucho dinero.*

B —*¿Para qué sirve?*

A —*Sirve para escribir cartas o composiciones.*

B —*Es un bolígrafo.*

14 Y tú, ¿qué dices? | Talk!

Escribir • Hablar

1. ¿A quién le pides ayuda con la computadora? ¿Le pides ayuda a menudo o sólo a veces?
2. ¿Qué haces cuando tus amigos te piden ayuda con la computadora? ¿Para qué cosas te piden ayuda?

Más práctica GO

realidades.com | print

	realidades.com	print
Instant Check	✔	
Guided WB pp. 299–300	✔	✔
Core WB p. 170	✔	✔
Comm. WB pp. 183, 186, 331	✔	✔
***Hispanohablantes* WB** pp. 354–357		✔

Practice and Communicate 9B

11 Standards: 1.1

Focus: Practicing the present tense of ***pedir*** in pairs

Recycle: Indirect object pronouns

Suggestions: Remind students to use a different person for each item and to use ***le*** and ***les***.

Answers will vary.

12 Standards: 1.1, 1.3

Focus: Using pedir to talk and write about restaurants and ordering food

Recycle: Food vocabulary

Suggestions: Have partners brainstorm a list of restaurants and the food they like. For Step 2, point out the plural verb forms.

Answers will vary.

13 Standards: 1.1, 1.3

Focus: Writing and describing objects

Recycle: Present tense of ***servir***

Suggestions: Circulate among students, correcting their descriptions as they write them. If the pair identifying the object has difficulty, have the other pair give three possible answers, one of which is correct.

Answers will vary.

14 Standards: 1.1, 1.3

Focus: Answering questions using ***pedir***

Suggestions: Make sure that students understand the questions.

Additional Resources

- Communication Wbk.: Audio Act. 7, p. 183
- Teacher's Resource Book: Audio Script, p. 328
- Audio Program DVD: Cap. 9B, Track 9

ENRICH YOUR TEACHING

Teacher-to-Teacher

Have students play a different version of the game in *Actividad* 13. Ask them to write descriptions of local restaurants instead of objects. Encourage them to include in their descriptions what they order and what is served at the restaurant. The other pair will try to identify the restaurant.

21st Century Skills

Technology Literacy Remind students of the digital tools available online to help them learn and practice this grammar concept: the eText with embedded audio, the *GramActiva* video, the animated verbs, and the additional grammar practice.

ASSESSMENT

Prueba 9B-3 with Study Plan (online only)

Quiz: *Pedir* and *servir*

- Prueba 9B-3: p. 245

Gramática

Gramática

Core Instruction

Standards: 4.1

Resources: Voc. and Gram. Transparency 171; Teacher's Resource Book: Video Script, pp. 331–332; Video Program: Cap. 9B

INTERACTIVE WHITEBOARD
Grammar Activities 9B

Suggestions: Remind students that ***saber*** is used to talk about knowing facts or information. Although ***conocer*** is primarily used to talk about people and places, it can be used with objects when discussing familiarity. Use the *GramActiva* Video to reinforce the difference between the two verbs.

15 Standards: 1.1

Resources: Answer Keys: Student Edition, p. 138

Focus: Using ***saber*** to talk about what people know how to do

Recycle: Leisure activities

Suggestions: Practice the *Modelo* with a volunteer. Remind students to tell how often the person does the activity (e.g., ***todos los días, después de las clases, a veces, los fines de semana***).

Answers:

Student A
1. —¿Quién sabe jugar al tenis?
2. —¿... sabe grabar un disco compacto?
3. —¿... sabe tocar la guitarra?
4. —¿... sabe usar la computadora (crear documentos)?
5. —¿... sabe hacer gráficos (preparar presentaciones con diapositivas)?
6. —¿... sabe tocar música en la computadora?

Student B
Answers will vary.

Common Errors: Students often want to insert ***cómo*** between the conjugated form of ***saber*** and the infinitive. Remind them that *how* is included in the meaning of ***saber*** so there is no need for the word ***cómo.***

Extension: Have students use the *Modelo* and ask their partner about other activities.

Theme Project

Students can perform Step 5 at this point. Record their presentations for inclusion in their portfolios. (For more information, see p. 424-b.)

Objectives
- Discuss and write about people you know and what you know how to do
- Read a timeline and write about technological inventions

Saber and *conocer*

Sé and *sabes* come from the verb *saber,* "to know." There is another verb in Spanish that also means "to know": *conocer.* Use *conocer* to talk about people, places, and things that you are familiar with.

Here are the present-tense forms of *saber* and *conocer.* Except for the *yo* forms, they are regular in the present tense.

¿Recuerdas?

You have used *(yo) sé* and *(tú) sabes* to talk about knowing a fact and to say what you know how to do.
- **¿Sabes** dónde está la biblioteca?
- Yo **sé** esquiar bastante bien.

(yo)	sé	(nosotros) (nosotras)	sabemos
(tú)	sabes	(vosotros) (vosotras)	sabéis
Ud. (él) (ella)	sabe	Uds. (ellos) (ellas)	saben

(yo)	conozco	(nosotros) (nosotras)	conocemos
(tú)	conoces	(vosotros) (vosotras)	conocéis
Ud. (él) (ella)	conoce	Uds. (ellos) (ellas)	conocen

- *Conocer* is followed by the personal *a* when the direct object is a person. Direct object pronouns can also be used with *conocer.*

¿Conocen Uds. a la señora que trabaja en el laboratorio?
Sí, la conocemos bien. ¿Quieres conocerla?

Más ayuda realidades.com

***GramActiva* Video**
Tutorials: Adverbs, Adverbial clauses
Animated Verbs

Canción de hip hop: *Tecnología*

***GramActiva* Activity**

15 Lo que sabemos hacer

Hablar

Habla con otro(a) estudiante sobre quiénes saben hacer las diferentes actividades en los dibujos.

Modelo
A —*¿Quién sabe esquiar?*
B —*Mario sabe esquiar. Lo hace a menudo.*

1. 
2. 
3. 
4. 
5. 
6. 

DIFFERENTIATED INSTRUCTION

Heritage Language Learners

Have students write five sentences about what their family members know how to do *(**saber**)* and five sentences about people and places that they know *(**conocer**)*. Have these students read what they wrote to small groups.

Advanced Learners/Pre-AP*

Divide students into small groups to play a game. Have one student in each group write down two things that they can do and one that they cannot do. Then have them convincingly say that they can do all three things. After asking indirect but related questions, other group members try to guess which was the lie *(**la mentira**)*.

16 ¿Qué lugares conoces? ¿Y a qué personas?

Escribir • Hablar

Si una persona visita tu comunidad y tu escuela, ¿puedes ayudarla a conocer a diferentes personas y lugares? Escribe frases completas con las formas apropiadas del verbo *conocer* y la información necesaria. Después lee tus frases a otro(a) estudiante. ¿Conocen Uds. a las mismas personas y los mismos lugares?

¿Conoces la Plaza de España en Sevilla?

España

1. (Yo) ____ a muchos de los estudiantes en la clase de . . .
2. Mis amigos y yo (no) ____ a la secretaria de la escuela. Es la Sra. . . .
3. Mi hermano(a) / amigo(a) ____ bastante bien al (a la) profesor(a) de . . .
4. Mis amigos ____ bien el parque de diversiones . . .
5. (Yo) ____ la tienda . . . donde me gusta comprar . . .
6. Mi madre (padre) ____ bien *(un lugar en tu ciudad)* . . .
7. Si la persona necesita usar la computadora, nosotros ____ el programa de software . . .

17 ¿Saber o conocer?

Hablar

Trabaja con otro(a) estudiante para ver lo que sabe y conoce.

Modelo

la persona que trabaja en la biblioteca de la escuela
A —*¿Conoces a la persona que trabaja en la biblioteca de la escuela?*
B —*Sí, la conozco. Es la Sra. Wilton. Es muy simpática.*
o: —*No, no la conozco.*

bailar salsa
A —*¿Sabes bailar salsa?*
B —*Sí, sé bailar salsa. Me encanta.*
o: —*No, no sé bailar salsa.*

1. la hermana de . . .
2. bajar información de la Red
3. el nombre de una canción en español
4. las cámaras digitales
5. España o México
6. la dirección electrónica de . . .
7. un sitio Web interesante
8. enviar fotos por la Red

ENRICH YOUR TEACHING

Teacher-to-Teacher

Have students develop ideas for a virtual tour of their community or school. Have them take photos and insert them into a presentation software program. Add a sentence explaining each photo.

21st Century Skills

Creativity and Innovation After students work with the *GramActiva* video, animated verbs, and the *Canción de hip-hop,* have them work in groups to create a song, poem, or skit highlighting the difference between *saber* and *conocer*.

Practice and Communicate 9B

16 Standards: 1.3

Resources: Answer Keys: Student Edition, p. 138

Focus: Completing sentences with ***conocer*** in a personalized context; comparing experiences

Recycle: Places and classroom vocabulary

Suggestions: Complete the first item with students, modeling how they must supply their own words.

Answers:

People and place names will vary.

1. conozco
2. conocemos
3. conoce
4. conocen
5. conozco
6. conoce
7. conocemos

Extension: Ask students to describe interesting places in their community for tourists. (Ex. *Conozco un parque bonito cerca de mi casa.)*

BELLRINGER REVIEW

Write several sentences on the board or on a transparency, a few of which contain ***saber*** and most of which contain ***conocer.*** Ask students to underline the things that are *known* in each sentence so that they can see how ***conocer*** is about familiarity with people, places, and things. Also, have them circle the personal ***a*** when it appears.

17 Standards: 1.1

Resources: Answer Keys: Student Edition, p. 139

Focus: Expressing familiarity with and knowledge of people, places, things, and activities

Suggestions: Practice both models with students, then divide the class into pairs. Have students decide whether to use ***saber*** or ***conocer*** to ask the question. Circulate to make sure they are selecting the correct verb.

Answers:

Student A

1. —¿Conoces a la hermana de ...?
2. —¿Sabes bajar información de la Red?
3. —¿Sabes el nombre de una canción en español?
4. —¿Conoces las cámaras digitales?
5. —¿Conoces España o México?
6. —¿Sabes la dirección electrónica de ...?
7. —¿Conoces un sitio Web interesante?
8. —¿Sabes enviar fotos por la Red?

Student B

Answers will vary.

Pronunciación

Core Instruction

Standards: 4.1

Resources: Teacher's Resource Book: Audio Script, p. 329; Audio Program DVD: Cap. 9B, Track 12; Answer Keys: Student Edition, p. 139

Suggestions: Have students divide the English word *collar* into syllables *(col-lar)*. Then outline on the board the rules presented on this page and write examples for each one. To reinforce your teaching, play the audio.

Have students work in pairs to complete the *Try it out!* activity. Ask them to write their answers on the board and to pronounce each word.

Answers:

1. e-mo-cio-nan-te
2. rá-pi-da-men-te
3. com-pu-ta-do-ra
4. a-na-ran-ja-do
5. e-lec-tró-ni-co
6. co-mu-ni-ca-mos

Extension: On the board, write a few words. Have students quietly clap as they say each syllable. Have volunteers divide the words into syllables.

18 Standards: 1.2, 1.3

Resources: Answer Keys: Student Edition, p. 140

Focus: Reading an advertisement for a telephone caller ID option and writing opinions about the issue

Suggestions: Have the class note the title of the activity, read the ad, and discuss the humor of including a picture of the "Three Little Pigs" and the "Big Bad Wolf." Ask students if they think the ad is effective and if they feel that the product is worthwhile. After students write down their answers, encourage partners to help each other with spelling and grammar. When students have revised their writing, tell them to include this work in their portfolios.

Answers will vary but may include:

1. Sí, lo conocen y saben lo que quiere.
2.–4. Answers will vary.

Extension: Invite pairs of students to use another fairy tale to advertise a different fictional product.

Pronunciación

Dividing words into syllables

Knowing how to divide words into syllables will help you sound out a new word. Just as in English, all syllables in Spanish include a vowel. When there is a consonant between two vowels, you divide the word into syllables before the consonant. The letter combinations *ch, ll,* and *rr* are never divided in Spanish.

Listen to and say these words:

ju-gar	pá-gi-na	la-bo-ra-to-rio	na-ve-gar
ca-lle	no-ti-cias	co-mu-ni-dad	a-bu-rri-do

When there are two consonants between vowels, you divide the word between the consonants. Exceptions are the blends *pr, pl, br, bl, fr, fl, tr, dr, cr, cl, gr,* and *gl.* These blends are never divided and go with the following vowel: *pro-ble-ma.* Listen to and say these words:

car-ta	in-fan-til	con-cur-sos	jar-dín
par-que	a-bri-go	des-can-sar	pa-dres

When there are three or more consonants between vowel sounds, the first two go with the vowel that precedes them and the third goes with the vowel that follows them: *trans-por-te.* When the second and third consonants form a blend, however, the first consonant goes with the vowel before it and the other consonants go with the vowel that follows them: *en-tre.*

Listen to and say these words:

es-cri-to-rio	com-pli-ca-do
en-tre-vis-tas	com-pras-te

Try it out! See if you can separate the following words into the correct syllables.

1. emocionante
2. rápidamente
3. computadora
4. problema
5. electrónico
6. comunicamos

18 Los tres cerditos

Leer • Escribir

Lee el anuncio y contesta las preguntas.

1. ¿Conocen los cerditos a la "persona" que está en la ventana? ¿Saben ellos lo que quiere?
2. ¿Tiene tu familia un servicio de identificación de llamadas en su teléfono? ¿Te gusta este servicio, o te gustaría tener este servicio? ¿Por qué?
3. ¿Te parece bien saber quién llama por teléfono? ¿Por qué?
4. ¿Te gusta hablar por teléfono? ¿Con quién te gusta hablar más?

¿Sabes quién es?

Pide el servicio de identificación de llamadas.
Si eres cliente de Teléfonos Caribe, es completamente gratis.

Así, siempre vas a saber quién está llamando.
¡Pídelo hoy! Llama al teléfono 20-05-617.

DIFFERENTIATED INSTRUCTION

Heritage Language Learners

Have students speak to relatives about technology use in their heritage country. Then ask them to write down one form of communication per index card or sheet of paper. Make sure they include ***los teléfonos celulares.*** On the back of the card, students should write who uses the form of communication more, using ***más que*** and ***menos que*** *(La gente de los Estados Unidos usa los teléfonos celulares más que la gente de...).*

19 ¿Qué inventos conoces?

Leer • Pensar • Escribir • Dibujar

Mucho antes de la invención de la computadora personal, había *(there were)* otros inventos que nos ayudaron a comunicarnos y que seguimos *(keep)* usando. Mira la línea cronológica y lee la lista de inventos. Luego contesta las preguntas.

Conexiones | Las tecnologia

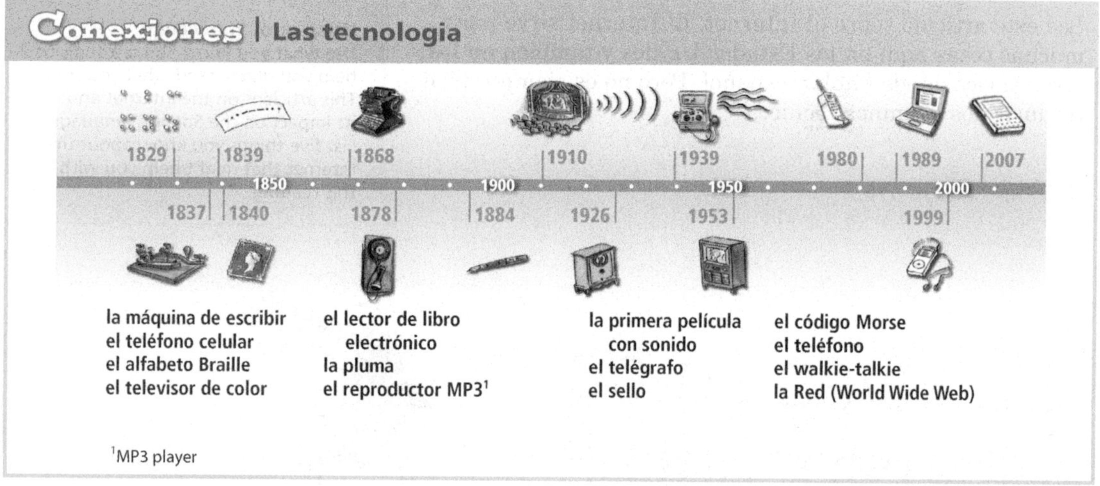

la máquina de escribir el teléfono celular el alfabeto Braille el televisor de color	el lector de libro electrónico la pluma el reproductor MP3[1]	la primera película con sonido el telégrafo el sello	el código Morse el teléfono el walkie-talkie la Red (World Wide Web)

[1]MP3 player

1. Identifica cada invento según el año en que se inventó y explica qué impacto tiene sobre la comunicación.
2. Busca información en la Red o en la biblioteca para identificar los inventores de cada invento de la lista.
3. ¿Cuál de estos inventos te parece el más importante? ¿Por qué?
4. Piensa en un invento que quieres hacer. ¿Para qué sirve? Escribe un párrafo y haz un dibujo para explicar tu invento.

El español en el mundo del trabajo

The ability to share information is crucial in the 21st century. Innovations from medicine, science, technology, engineering, manufacturing, and social services need to be communicated across the globe. With a partner, make a list of six ways in which information can be spread. For each, tell how knowing Spanish would be beneficial. Share your ideas with the class.

Más práctica GO

realidades.com | print

	realidades.com	print
Instant Check	✔	
Guided WB pp. 301–302	✔	✔
Core WB pp. 171–172	✔	✔
Comm. WB pp. 184, 187	✔	✔
***Hispanohablantes* WB** pp. 358–361		✔

ENRICH YOUR TEACHING

Teacher-to-Teacher

Play a version of the game "Telephone." Create several teams whose average language ability is similar. Show one member of each team the same sentence, which he or she should silently read. Have those students return to their seats, write the sentence from memory, and then briefly show what they wrote to the next person on the team, who writes the sentence from memory, and so on. The team that finishes first gets a point. The team that ends up with a sentence that is closest to the original (determined by the teacher) gets one point also. After playing a few rounds, you might have students play the original Telephone game by whispering sentences.

Practice and Communicate 9B

19 Standards: 1.2, 1.3, 3.1

Resources: Answer Keys: Student Edition, p. 140

Focus: Reading a timeline of inventions; developing an idea for an invention

Suggestions: Discuss the timeline and inventions. Have students work with a partner or in small groups. Schedule time for students to research and present their inventions.

Answers:

1. la maquina de escribir—1868; el teléfono celular—1980; el alfabeto Braille—1829; el televisor—1926; el televisor de color—1953; la pluma—1884; el reproductor MP3—1999; la primera película con sonido—1910; el telégrafo—1837; el sello—1840; el código Morse—1839; el teléfono—1878; el walkie-talkie—1939; la Red—1989;
2–4. Answers will vary.

Extension: Vote for the most creative, expensive, and useful inventions.

El español en el mundo del trabajo

Core Instruction

Standards: 5.1

Suggestions: Before students read the information, ask them how knowing Spanish would be beneficial in the business world.

Pre-AP* Support

- **Learning Objective:** Interpretive: Print and Audio
- **Activity:** In pairs, have students write the names of several students and teachers and what each person knows how to do. As a class activity, have volunteers read the names asking *"¿Conoces a _____?"* The response is *"Sí, él/ella, (ellos/ellas) sabe jugar al ajedrez."*

Additional Resources

- Communication Wbk.: Audio Act. 8–9, p. 184
- Teacher's Resource Book: Audio Script, pp. 328–329, Communicative Pair Activity BLM, pp. 256–257
- Audio Program DVD: Cap. 9B, Tracks 10–11

ASSESSMENT

Prueba 9B-4 with Study Plan (online only)

Quiz: ***saber* and *conocer***

- Prueba 9B-4: p. 246

9B Reading

Common Core: Reading

Lectura

Core Instruction

Standards: 1.2, 1.3, 2.1, 4.1

Focus: Reading for comprehension; understanding cultural perspectives

Suggestions:

Pre-reading: Read the *Strategy* aloud and have students write a list of five things they know about the Internet. Make sure they keep this list to use later. Direct them to the title and ask them what they think it means. Ask students to skim the *Lectura* to get a general idea of what it is about.

Reading: As students read the selection, have them focus on information about how the Internet impacts the Spanish language. Have them also look for advantages and disadvantages of the Internet.

Post-reading: Ask students the following questions: Do you think the idea expressed in the title is true or not? In what ways has technology affected the Spanish language? Why do you think many terms are in English? What advantages or disadvantages does the Internet have for Spanish speakers and Spanish-language learners?

BELLRINGER REVIEW

Have students unscramble these words for projects that can be completed on a computer:

sacubr minicórofan
bragar nu cisod pactocom
careh cágrofis

(**Answers:** buscar información; grabar un disco compacto; hacer gráficos)

Block Schedule

Have students work in pairs to write a matching "quiz" for the computer terms on p. 465. When all are finished, have them close their books and exchange "quizzes" with other pairs. Find out how many knew most of the answers and which terms were the most difficult.

Objectives

- Read about the impact of the Internet on the Spanish language
- Use prior knowledge to understand what you read

Lectura

La invasión del ciberspanglish

Lee este artículo sobre el Internet. El Internet sirve para muchas cosas aquí en los Estados Unidos y también en los otros países donde hablan español. Pero no es siempre fácil traducir[1] los términos técnicos.

Strategy

Using prior knowledge
Use what you know about a topic to help you understand what you read. This article is on the Internet and its impact on the Spanish language. List five things you know about the Internet that might help you with this reading.

La invasión del ciberspanglish

¿Te gusta usar el Internet? Actualmente[2] hay gente en todos los países del mundo que usa el Internet. Sirve para muchas cosas: para hacer compras, divertirse, educarse, trabajar, buscar información, hacer planes para un viaje y mucho más. Hoy en día uno no puede pensar en una vida sin computadoras o el Internet.

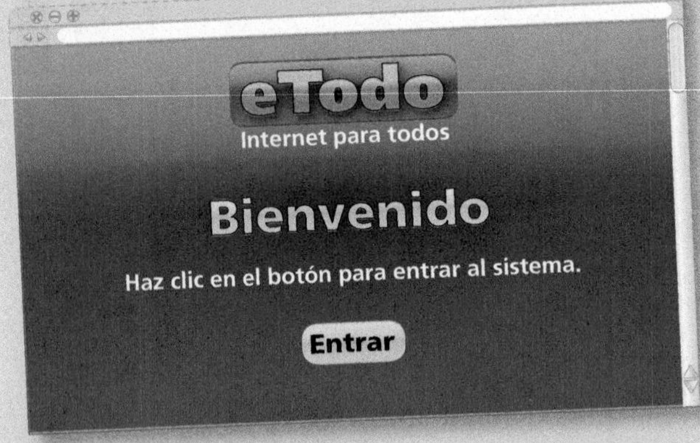

Si quieres explorar el Internet en español, hay una explosión de portales (sitios que sirven como puerta al Internet) en los Estados Unidos, España y América Latina. Como puedes imaginar, hay una rivalidad[3] grande entre estos portales para atraer[4] a los hispanohablantes. Algunos portales dan la misma información en inglés y español; sólo tienes que hacer clic para cambiarla.

[1]to translate [2]Nowadays [3]rivalry [4]to attract

DIFFERENTIATED INSTRUCTION

Heritage Language Learners

Have students read the list of words on p. 465. Have them make posters with helpful phrases related to technology that students might use in the computer lab. Before students make their posters, ask them to make a draft of the phrases they will display so that you can first review them for accuracy.

Multiple Intelligences

Visual/Spatial: Have students develop ideas for a virtual tour of their community or school. Have them take photos of places and of people working, and insert the photos into a presentation software program. Students can add captions that explain each photo.

Juntos,[5] el inglés y el español en el Internet dieron origen al "ciberspanglish". A algunas personas no les gusta nada este nuevo "idioma"[6]. Piensan que el español es suficientemente rico para poder traducir los términos del inglés. Hay otros que dicen que no hay problema con mezclar[7] los idiomas para comunicarse mejor. Piensan que el "ciberspanglish" es más fácil y lógico porque los términos técnicos vienen del inglés y expresarlos en español es bastante complicado.

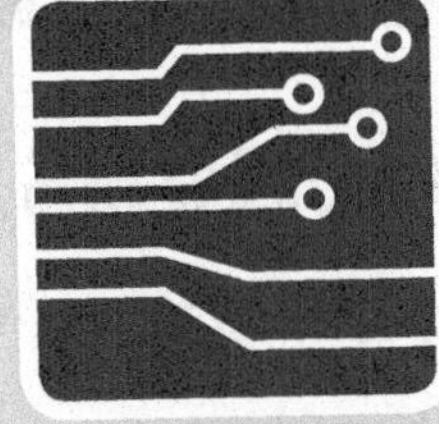

Éste es un debate que va a durar[8] mucho tiempo, y no presenta grises.

Términos de ciberspanglish	Términos en español
emailear	mandar por correo electrónico
espam	un bombardeo de grandes cantidades de correo electrónico
chatear	conversar
hacer clic	picar con el ratón
hacer doble clic	picar dos veces con el ratón
rebootear	rearrancar
linkear	enlazar con una página en Internet
crashear	quebrar o chocar
formatear	hacer un formato
programar	escribir un programa
escanear	rastrear o digitalizar
surfear	explorar o navegar
hacer un upgrade	actualizar o subir un grado
el clipart	dibujos artísticos
hacer un exit	salir
printear	imprimir

[5]Together [6]language [7]mixing [8]to last

¿Comprendes?

1. Look at the list you created for the Strategy "Using prior knowledge." Place a check mark next to any pieces of information mentioned in the article.
2. According to the article, how could the Internet help you learn more Spanish?
3. Summarize briefly the two sides of the argument related to *ciberspanglish.*
4. You have already learned that Spanish borrowed words from languages such as Greek and Arabic. Is *ciberspanglish* different? Why or why not?
5. What do you think the statement *Éste es un debate que . . . no presenta grises* means? Why is it appropriate as the closing statement for this article?

Más práctica GO

realidades.com | print

	realidades.com	print
Guided WB p. 303	✔	✔
Comm. WB pp. 188, 332	✔	✔
***Hispanohablantes* WB** pp. 362–363		✔
Cultural Reading Activity	✔	

ENRICH YOUR TEACHING

Culture Note

Technology and the Internet have brought about the creation of so many new terms in English that new Spanish technology dictionaries are being created. The purpose of these dictionaries is to promote the use of vocabulary that reflects the linguistic and cultural sensibilities of Spanish speakers.

21st Century Skills

Communication Have students debate the issue of "ciberspanglish" and the role it plays for Spanish speakers in communication. If possible, have students gather information and opinions from native speakers and exchange students from Spanish-speaking countries to help support their side of the debate. Students should also give examples to illustrate their points.

¿Comprendes? Standards: 2.1

Focus: Demonstrating reading comprehension

Suggestions: Have students check the lists they made before reading to see which of their ideas were mentioned in the article. Then discuss the other questions with students. If they need help with the fifth question, ask students what is meant by: *Things are not just black and white. There are shades of gray.*

Answers will vary but may include:

1. **Answers will vary.**
2. **One can find a lot of resources in Spanish, or in both English and Spanish, on the Internet.**
3. **Some people say it's easier to use "ciberspanglish" because technical terms come from English; others say that Spanish is rich enough for all definitions.**
4. **Answers will vary.**
5. **It means that it is a heated debate with two definite sides to the argument.**

Teacher-to-Teacher

Carefully evaluate a Spanish chat line that would be appropriate for your class. There are options such as bilingual, for those learning Spanish, and voice chat. You can also set up a chat or e-mail exchange with another class in your school or one in another country. Discuss guidelines to follow when using chat, such as not sharing personal information. Start by having students only read the exchanges on the chat line. Then, have students tell you what you should write. Finally, have them participate on the chat line, carefully monitoring the questions they receive from others.

Pre-AP* Support

- **Learning Objective:** Interpretive: Print and Audio
- **Activity:** Prepare a crossword puzzle using vocabulary words from the *Términos de ciberspanglish* column. Write the equivalent *Términos en español* for each puzzle entry on a separate index card. Then create a set of cards for each group. Divide students into groups, giving each group a blank puzzle and a set of equivalents. Students must explain their words to the rest of the group without using the words themselves. The group members must determine the word being described and write it in the appropriate space on the puzzle.
- ***Pre-AP* Resource Book:*** Comprehensive guide to Pre-AP* reading skill development, pp. 19–26

For Further Reading

Student Resource: Realidades para hispanohablantes: Lectura 2, pp. 364–365

Perspectivas del mundo hispano

Core Instruction

Standards: 2.1, 4.2

Focus: Reading about computer usage

Suggestions: Discuss how computers are used. Point out that today they are found in private homes, libraries, offices, hospitals, schools—just about everywhere. Not long ago they were only used in businesses, and the Internet didn't exist. Mention that in most Latin American countries, computers are not as widespread as in the United States. Have students read the text and discuss the reasons why this is true. Talk about what people use the computer for. How does that compare to usage here? Discuss ***cibercafés*** and how young people from Spanish-speaking countries use them. Have students complete the *Check it out!* section and discuss the question in class.

For many students, the primary use of computers is Internet access. Discuss how they use the Internet. Guide students to see that in Spanish-speaking countries, ***cibercafés*** are a modern way to socialize.

Direct attention to the *Think about it!* section and have students discuss it.

Answers will vary.

Additional Resources

Student Resource: Realidades para hispanohablantes, p. 366

Perspectivas del mundo hispano

¿Para qué usas una computadora?

In many Spanish-speaking countries, the use of computers and access to the Internet are often not as widespread as in the United States. Some homes don't have telephones, computers cost more money, and in some cases, the Internet is not as accessible. Schools and libraries may not have computers or the same access to the Internet as they often do in most communities in the United States. For these reasons, many cybercafés have opened. Cybercafés are nice places for students to meet after school and work on assignments, do research, or e-mail friends. They offer very inexpensive access to the Internet.

Usando computadoras para estudiar, México

In recent years, the number of *portales* (portals) that serve as access points to the Internet has increased and many of these are offered in Spanish as well as English. The number of *buscadores* (search engines) has also increased, making it easier for Spanish speakers to search for information or just surf the Internet.

Haciendo la tarea en la computadora

Check it out! Survey your friends. Over the course of one week, how much time do they spend using a computer and for what reasons?

Think about it! Name three ways that you think Spanish-language Internet sites could help you learn more Spanish and understand the perspectives of Spanish speakers.

DIFFERENTIATED INSTRUCTION

Advanced Learners

Have students use a Spanish-language Web site of their choice to answer the *Think about it!* section. Have them present their findings to the class.

Heritage Language Learners

Have students use a Spanish-language Web site of their choice to find out about computer usage in their heritage country or in another Spanish-speaking country.

| Objectives | Aplicación

Presentación escrita

La computadora en mi vida

- Write an e-mail about your computer use
- Use examples to support a persuasive argument

Task
Your parents think you spend too much time on the computer. You disagree. Send an e-mail to your best friend in Mexico explaining your position and how you plan to defend your computer use.

1. **Prewrite** In a chart, list at least three ways you use computers and the benefit *(la ventaja)* to you.

Cómo uso la computadora	La ventaja
Busco información para mis clases en Internet.	Aprendo mucho y es muy interesante.

2. **Draft** Use the information from the chart to write the first draft of your e-mail. Here are some expressions you might include:
   pienso que . . . tengo que . . .
   creo que . . . primero (segundo, tercero), . . .

3. **Revise** Check for spelling, accent marks, verb forms, pronouns, and vocabulary use. Share the e-mail with a partner. Your partner should check the following:
   - Is the paragraph easy to read and understand?
   - Does it provide good support for your position?
   - What could you add to give more information, or change to make it clearer?
   - Are there any errors?

4. **Publish** Rewrite the e-mail, making necessary changes. Share with your teacher and add it to your portfolio.

5. **Evaluation** The following rubric will be used to grade your e-mail.

Rubric	Score 1	Score 3	Score 5
Amount of information you provided	You list one way and benefit.	You list two ways and benefits.	Your list of ways and benefits is complete.
Presentation of reason and benefit	Your reason and support for your position lack clarity.	Your reasons and support for your position are clear, but not forceful.	You are clear and persuasive in your reasons and support for your position.
Vocabulary, spelling, grammar	Your vocabulary use is limited with several errors in spelling and grammar.	Your vocabulary use is somewhat extensive, but you have many errors in spelling and grammar.	You have very few errors in spelling and grammar and use varied vocabulary.

Strategy

Using supporting examples
When preparing a persuasive argument, you should first clearly state your position and then provide examples to support it. Making a list of your arguments will help you make a strong statement.

Writing 9B

Common Core: Writing

Presentación escrita

Persuasive

Standards: 1.3

Focus: Writing a defense of frequent use of the computer

Suggestions: Review the task and the five-step approach with students. After reading the *Strategy* with them, have students write a position statement and list three reasons to support it. They can write these statements in a chart or use some other graphic organizer. Review the rubric with the class to explain how you will grade the performance task. Have students work through each step of the writing process.

Portfolio

Have students save their finished work for inclusion in their portfolios.

Pre-AP* Support

- **Learning Objective:** Presentational Writing
- **Activity:** Let's hear the other side of the story. Based on the e-mail you wrote to your friend in Mexico, take the side of your parents. Why do you think they are trying to restrict your access to the Internet? Write a brief paragraph, to "you," from your folks, explaining the parental positions.
- ***Pre-AP* Resource Book:*** Comprehensive guide to Pre-AP* writing skill development, pp. 27–38

Additional Resources

Student Resources: Realidades para hispanohablantes, p. 367; Guided Practice: Presentación escrita, p. 304

ENRICH YOUR TEACHING

Teacher-to-Teacher

If you have not done so already, create a class Web page so that you can collect links to sites that augment your lessons. Investigate and select a number of interactive Web sites. Make sure they cover an array of your students' learning styles. Have your e-mail address on the page so students can write to tell you which of the Web sites they liked and why, and what they learned.

21st Century Skills

Media Literacy In order to make their case to their parents, have students examine appropriate Web sites that contain information about the importance of computers in today's world so that their arguments are as strong as possible. In order to make their case, have students create an interesting and informative presentation that combines print, video, audio, and images.

ASSESSMENT

Presentación escrita

- Assessment Program: Rubrics, p. T34
  Go over the descriptions of the different levels of performance. After assessing students, help individuals understand how their performance could be improved.

Videomisterio

Core Instruction

Standards: 1.3, 5.2

Resources: Teacher's Resource Book: Video Script, pp. 332–333; Video Program: Cap. 9B; Video Program Teacher's Guide: Cap 9B

Focus: Introducing the events and vocabulary of this episode; scanning and reading the episode summary

Personajes importantes:

Lola Lago, detective
Paco, Lola Lago's colleague
Margarita, Lola Lago's secretary
Julia Romero, María's friend
Inspector Gil, police officer
Luis Antonio Llamas, Julia's boyfriend
Pedro, Doña Gracia's grandson
Doña Gracia, Pedro's grandmother

Synopsis: The police arrive at the train station and they arrest the person Lola thought was María. It is really Julia. Then the police arrest Luis Antonio and they find doña Gracia's jewels in his suitcase. Inspector Gil and Lola figure out how Luis Antonio convinced Julia to steal María's identity when María died in the hospital. It was a coincidence that Luis Antonio was a nurse in the same hospital after María's car accident. In the end, Pedro meets his grandmother, who is happy to meet him.

Suggestions:

Pre-viewing: Review the events of the previous episode. Lola calls her office to ask Margarita and Paco to help her follow two people. Margarita overhears that the person Lola thought to be María is really Julia. When the two strangers leave, Paco follows them to the train station. Lola calls Inspector Gil to ask him to meet her at the train station right away.

Point out the *Palabras para comprender,* saying examples in context and writing the sentences on the board. Remind students that these words are only used to help them understand the episode and they are not active vocabulary.

Objective

- Understand the conclusion of a mystery video set in Spain

¿Eres tú, María?

Episodio 1

Antes de ver el video

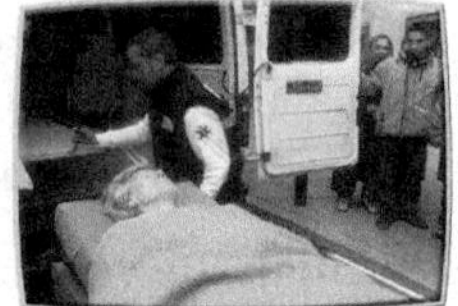

Resumen del episodio

Es el último episodio y Lola y el Inspector Gil van a solucionarlo todo. En realidad, ¿quién es María? ¿Qué importancia tiene Luis Antonio? ¿Quién tiene las joyas? ¿Cómo y por qué ocurrió el crimen? ¿Quién va a la cárcel? ¿Quién va a necesitar un buen abogado? ¿Qué pasa cuando Pedro ve a su abuela por primera vez?

Palabras para comprender

Deténgala. Arrest her.
No quería. I didn't want to.
las reconoció recognized them
los novios boyfriend and girlfriend
tomó took
mucha suerte a lot of luck
robarlas to steal them
no quería esperar didn't want to wait
Parece que . . . It seems like . . .
la cárcel jail
un abogado lawyer

DIFFERENTIATED INSTRUCTION

Heritage Language Learners

Ask students to use the vocabulary from *Palabras para comprender* to tell what happened in this episode. Encourage them to go back and use vocabulary from previous chapters.

Advanced Learners

Have students write down possible answers to the questions in the *Resumen del episodio.* After they watch the episode, have them return to their answers to see how many they got right. Have them discuss how their responses differed from what really happened.

Y tú, ¿qué piensas?

¿Sabes lo que va a pasar en este episodio? Escribe tus respuestas a las preguntas en el Resumen del episodio. Ahora, mira el episodio y compara tus respuestas con lo que pasó. ¿Tenías razón?

Después de ver el video

¿Comprendes?

A. ¿A quién(es) describe cada frase: Lola, María, Julia, Luis Antonio, Pedro o doña Gracia?

1. Pues, señorita, es evidente que Ud. sabe mucho.
2. Las reconoció en el hospital.
3. Es evidente en la foto que son novios.
4. Murió en el hospital.
5. No puede ver muy bien.
6. Viene a Madrid para vivir con ella.
7. Tiene ochenta y cinco años y está de buena salud.
8. Entra en el piso y ataca a la señora.
9. Ud. no va a París, señor. Ud. va a la cárcel.
10. La mejor detective de Madrid.

B. Con un grupo de tres o cuatro estudiantes, escoge una escena del video. Tu profesor(a) les va a dar el guión *(script)* de la escena. Representen la escena para la clase. Hay que aprender de memoria el papel *(the part)*, llevar la ropa del personaje y representar la escena de una manera bien profesional.

ENRICH YOUR TEACHING

Teacher-to-Teacher

Divide the class into four groups and ask each to come up with an alternate ending to the story. You may want to select one group of students (different from those selected for part B of *¿Comprendes?)*, assign character roles to each of them, and have them perform the new ending for the class.

Video 9B

Visual scanning: Direct students' attention to the photos and ask who these characters are. Before students read the *Resumen del episodio,* have them scan the text and find three cognates *(episodio, inspector, solucionar, importancia, crimen).* Then ask them to read the *Resumen del episodio* carefully and ask questions about what will happen in this episode. Ask them to look for the answers as they view this episode.

Post-viewing: Have students look at the photo and tell or guess what happened or will happen in the last scenes of this episode. Write the vocabulary presented in this episode on the board to help students create sentences for each important scene that adds new information to the plot.

¿Comprendes? Standards: 1.2, 1.3

Resources: Answer Keys: Student Edition, p. 141

Suggestions: For part B, have students write two to five sentences about what Lola understands now and about the solution to the mystery. Ask students to use the vocabulary presented in this episode.

Answers:

Part A

1. Lola
2. Luis Antonio
3. Luis Antonio y Julia
4. María
5. doña Gracia
6. Julia
7. doña Gracia
8. Luis Antonio
9. Luis Antonio
10. Lola

Teacher-to-Teacher

Careers: *Tema* 9 has focused on technology. Have students work in small groups to talk about a career in technology support and services. Ask them to write a list of words and expressions they have learned that would be helpful in training people to use technology. Ask groups to share their lists.

Additional Resources

¿Eres tú, María? Video Workbook, Episode 10

¿Eres tú, María? Teacher's Video Guide: Answer Key

Review Activities

To talk about communication: Write *¿Cómo te comunicas?* on the board. Ask students to answer the question orally using items from the section.

To talk about computer-related activities: On a worksheet or on the board, create a chart with the following three headings: *los documentos, la Red, los gráficos.* Ask students to write each item from this section under the heading to which it best relates. If an item could go under more than one heading, have students decide which heading is most appropriate.

Other useful expressions: Use items from this section to create a list of questions and a separate list of responses. Have students work in pairs. Student A selects a question and Student B selects an appropriate answer from the response list.

Portfolio

Invite students to review the activities they completed in this chapter, including written reports, posters or other visuals, recordings of oral presentations, or other projects. Have them select one or two items that they feel best demonstrate their achievements in Spanish to include in their portfolios. Have them include this with the Chapter Checklist and Self-Assessment Worksheet.

Additional Resources

Student Resources: Realidades para hispanohablantes, p. 368

Teacher Resources:

- Teacher's Resource Book: Situation Cards, p. 338, Clip Art, pp. 340–341
- Assessment Program: Chapter Checklist and Self-Assessment Worksheet, pp. T56–T57

Repaso

▼ Objectives

- Review the vocabulary and grammar
- Demonstrate you can perform the tasks on p. 471

Repaso del capítulo

Vocabulario y gramática

to talk about communication

cara a cara	face-to-face
la carta	letter
comunicarse **(yo) me comunico** **(tú) te comunicas**	to communicate (with)
enviar	to send
la tarjeta	card

to talk about computer-related activities

bajar	to download
buscar	to search (for)
la cámara digital	digital camera
la canción, *pl.* **las canciones**	song
la composición, *pl.* **las composiciones**	composition
la computadora portátil	laptop computer
crear	to create
el curso **tomar un curso**	course to take a course
la diapositiva	slide
la dirección electrónica	e-mail address
el documento	document
escribir por correo electrónico	to send an e-mail message
estar en línea	to be online
grabar un disco compacto	to burn a CD
los gráficos	graphics
la información	information
el informe	report
el laboratorio	laboratory
navegar en la Red	to surf the Web
la página Web	Web page
la presentación, *pl.* **las presentaciones**	presentation
el sitio Web	Web site
visitar salones de chat	to visit chat rooms

other useful expressions

complicado, -a	complicated
¿Para qué sirve?	What's it (used) for?
¿Qué te parece?	What do you think?
rápidamente	quickly
Sirve para . . .	It's used for . . .
tener miedo (de)	to be afraid (of)

pedir (e → i) *to ask for*

pido	**pedimos**
pides	**pedís**
pide	**piden**

servir (e → i) *to serve, to be useful for*

sirvo	**servimos**
sirves	**servís**
sirve	**sirven**

saber *to know (how)*

sé	**sabemos**
sabes	**sabéis**
sabe	**saben**

conocer *to know, to be acquainted with*

conozco	**conocemos**
conoces	**conocéis**
conoce	**conocen**

For *Vocabulario adicional*, see pp. 472–473.

DIFFERENTIATED INSTRUCTION

Students with Learning Difficulties

Have students review the *Repaso del capítulo* and create flashcards for any words that they do not know. Pair them with a student who is more confident with the vocabulary to practice. Before the test, provide students with a practice test, so they can become comfortable with the format.

Heritage Language Learners

Have students write a few paragraphs telling about their perfect birthday celebration: Where are they going to have it? Whom are they going to invite? What food are they going to eat? What kind of music are they going to play? Encourage them to use as many vocabulary words from this chapter as they can.

Más repaso GO realidades.com | print

Instant Check	✔	
Puzzles	✔	
Core WB pp. 173–174		✔
Comm. WB pp. 333, 334–336	✔	✔

Preparación para el examen

On the exam you will be asked to . . .	Here are practice tasks similar to those you will find on the exam . . .	For review go to your print or digital textbook . . .
Interpretive		
 **1 Escuchar** Listen and understand as people talk about how they use computers	You overhear some people expressing their opinions about computers. Tell whether each person likes or dislikes using computers.	**pp. 450–454** *Vocabulario en contexto* **p. 451** Actividades 1–2 **p. 455** Actividad 5
Interpersonal		
 **2 Hablar** Ask and answer questions about what you know about computers and the Internet	A local Internet company wants to interview you to work as a telephone tech support assistant. To prepare, you and your partner take turns interviewing each other. Ask if your partner: a) knows how to surf the Web; b) is familiar with Web sites for teens; c) knows how to use the computer to create music; d) knows how to make graphics. Then switch roles.	**pp. 450–454** *Vocabulario en contexto* **p. 454** Actividad 4 **p. 457** Actividad 9 **p. 459** Actividad 14 **p. 460** Actividad 15 **p. 461** Actividad 17
Interpretive		
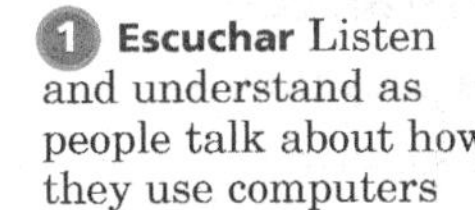 **3 Leer** Read and understand part of an online conversation in a chat room	A teen in the chat room *Mis padres y yo* is upset. According to the teenager, what do his parents not understand? What is his parents' opinion? *¡Yo soy muy impaciente! Para hacer la tarea, me gusta tener la información que necesito rápidamente. Mis padres dicen que puedo ir a la biblioteca y buscar libros allí para hacer mi tarea, pero me gustaría tener mi propia computadora. Ellos piensan que las computadoras sólo sirven para jugar videojuegos. ¿Qué hago?*	**pp. 450–454** *Vocabulario en contexto* **p. 454** Actividad 4 **p. 455** Actividad 6 **p. 456** Actividad 8 **pp. 464–465** *Lectura*
Presentational		
 **4 Escribir** Write your personal profile *(perfil)* for a Web survey	You are completing a Web survey online for *MundoChat*. Provide answers to the following questions: a) what you like to do; b) your favorite Web site; c) how often you visit chat rooms; d) how much time you spend online each day.	**p. 458** Actividad 10 **p. 459** Actividad 14 **p. 461** Actividad 16 **p. 467** *Presentación escrita*
Cultures • Comparisons		
 **5 Pensar** Demonstrate an understanding of cultural perspectives regarding technology	Explain why cybercafés are so popular in many Spanish-speaking countries. Compare how you use computers to the way in which teenagers might use them in these countries. If you were to live in one of these countries, how might you approach homework differently?	**p. 466** *Perspectivas del mundo hispano*

DIFFERENTIATED ASSESSMENT

CORE ASSESSMENT
- **Assessment Program:** Examen del capítulo 9B, pp. 247–250
- **Audio Program DVD:** Cap. 9B, Track 15
- **ExamView:** Chapter Test, Test Banks A and B

ADVANCED/PRE-AP*
- **ExamView: Pre-AP* Test Bank**
- **Pre-AP* Resource Book,** pp. 94–97

STUDENTS NEEDING EXTRA HELP
- **Alternate Assessment Program:** Examen del capítulo 9B
- **Audio Program DVD:** Cap. 9B, Track 15

HERITAGE LEARNERS
- **Assessment Program: Realidades para hispanohablantes:** Examen del capítulo 9B
- **ExamView: Heritage Learner Test Bank**

Performance Tasks

Standards: 1.1, 1.2, 1.3, 4.2

Student Resource: Realidades para hispanohablantes, p. 369

Teacher Resources: Teacher's Resource Book: Audio Script, pp. 329–330; Audio Program DVD: Cap. 9B, Track 14; Answer Keys: Student Edition, p. 142

1. *Escuchar*

Suggestions: Use the audio or read the script. You may wish to play or read the entire script aloud first and then start over again, stopping after each person's statement.

Script and Answers:

1. **A mí me gusta más hablar cara a cara con mis amigos. Así, puedo ver si están aburridos, interesados o impacientes. No puedo verlos si uso la computadora. *(doesn't like using computers)***
2. **Prefiero usar mi computadora para escribir correos electrónicos a mis amigas. Es más rápido y económico. *(likes using computers)***
3. **Con las computadoras puedo buscar información para mis presentaciones en clase. Es más práctico que ir a la biblioteca. *(likes using computers)***
4. **A veces las computadoras no funcionan bien o hay muchas personas en el laboratorio. Me gusta más escribir las composiciones en mi cuaderno. *(doesn't like using computers)***

2. *Hablar*

Suggestions: If students have difficulty expressing their opinions orally, they can write them first, using model phrases from the chapter. Have them practice their answers until they can say them without consulting their notes.

Answers will vary.

3. *Leer*

Suggestions: Students can create a T-chart, listing the parents' opinion on one side and the teen's opinion on the other.

Answers will vary but may include:
His parents don't understand that computers can be used for doing research. They think computers are just for entertainment.

4. *Escribir*

Suggestions: Have students try this activity without consulting the chapter.

Answers will vary.

5. *Pensar*

Suggestions: Have students reread the *Perspectivas del mundo hispano*. Reflect with them on the questions asked here.

Answers will vary.

Vocabulario adicional

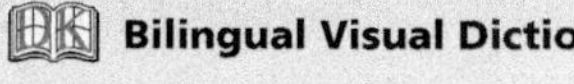

Tema 1

Las actividades

coleccionar sellos / monedas to collect stamps / coins
jugar al ajedrez to play chess
patinar sobre hielo to ice-skate
practicar artes marciales *(f.)* to practice martial arts
tocar to play *(an instrument)*
- **el bajo** bass
- **la batería** drums
- **el clarinete** clarinet
- **el oboe** oboe
- **el saxofón** *pl.* **los saxofones** saxophone
- **el sintetizador** synthesizer
- **el trombón** *pl.* **los trombones** trombone
- **la trompeta** trumpet
- **la tuba** tuba
- **el violín** *pl.* **los violines** violin

Tema 2

Las clases

el alemán German
el álgebra *(f.)* algebra
el anuario yearbook
la banda band
la biología biology
el cálculo calculus
el drama drama
la fotografía photography
el francés French
la geografía geography
la geometría geometry
el latín Latin
la química chemistry
la trigonometría trigonometry

Las cosas para la clase

la grapadora stapler
las grapas staples
el sacapuntas *pl.* **los sacapuntas** pencil sharpener
el sujetapapeles *pl.* **los sujetapapeles** paper clip
las tijeras scissors

Tema 3

Las comidas

Las frutas

el aguacate avocado
la cereza cherry
la ciruela plum
el coco coconut
el durazno peach
la frambuesa raspberry
el limón *pl.* **los limones** lemon
el melón *pl.* **los melones** melon
la pera pear
la sandía watermelon
la toronja grapefruit

Las verduras

el apio celery
el brócoli broccoli
la calabaza pumpkin
el champiñón *pl.* **los champiñones** mushroom
la col cabbage
la coliflor cauliflower
los espárragos asparagus
las espinacas spinach
el pepino cucumber

La carne

la chuleta de cerdo pork chop
el cordero lamb
la ternera veal

Los condimentos

la mayonesa mayonnaise
la mostaza mustard
la salsa de tomate ketchup

Otro tipo de comidas

los fideos noodles

Tema 4

Los lugares y actividades

el banco bank
el club club
el equipo de . . . ___ team
la farmacia pharmacy
la oficina office
la práctica de . . . ___ practice
la reunión *pl.* **las reuniones de . . .** ___ meeting
el supermercado supermarket

Tema 5

Los animales

el conejillo de Indias guinea pig
el conejo rabbit
el gerbo gerbil
el hámster *pl.* **los hámsters** hamster
el hurón *pl.* **los hurones** ferret
el loro parrot
el pez *pl.* **los peces** fish
la serpiente snake
la tortuga turtle

Los miembros de la familia

el bisabuelo, la bisabuela great-grandfather, great-grandmother
el nieto, la nieta grandson, granddaughter
el sobrino, la sobrina nephew, niece

Las descripciones de personas

llevar anteojos to wear glasses

ser

- **calvo, -a** bald
- **delgado, -a** thin
- **gordo, -a** fat

tener

- **la barba** beard
- **el bigote** moustache
- **las pecas** freckles
- **el pelo lacio** straight hair
- **el pelo rizado** curly hair
- **las trenzas** braids

Tema 6

Las partes de la casa y cosas en la casa

el balcón *pl.* **los balcones** balcony

la estufa stove

el jardín *pl.* **los jardines** garden

el lavadero laundry room

la lavadora washing machine

el lavaplatos *pl.* **los lavaplatos** dishwasher

el microondas *pl.* **los microondas** microwave oven

los muebles furniture

el patio patio

el refrigerador refrigerator

la secadora clothes dryer

el sillón *pl.* **los sillones** armchair

el sofá sofa

el tocador dressing table

Los quehaceres

quitar

- **la nieve con la pala** to shovel snow
- **los platos de la mesa** to clear the table

rastrillar las hojas to rake leaves

Los colores

(azul) claro light (blue)

(azul) marino navy (blue)

(azul) oscuro dark (blue)

Tema 7

Las expresiones para las compras

ahorrar to save

el dinero en efectivo cash

gastar to spend

la(s) rebaja(s) sale(s)

regatear to bargain

se vende for sale

La ropa

la bata bathrobe

el chaleco vest

las pantimedias pantyhose

el paraguas *pl.* **los paraguas** umbrella

el pijama pajamas

la ropa interior underwear

el saco loose-fitting jacket

los tenis tennis shoes

las zapatillas slippers

los zapatos atléticos athletic shoes

los zapatos de tacón alto high-heeled shoes

Tema 8

Las expresiones para los viajes

el aeropuerto airport

la agencia de viajes travel agency

los cheques de viajero travelers' checks

el equipaje luggage

hacer una reservación to make a reservation

el lugar de interés place of interest

el pasaporte passport

volar *(o → ue)* to fly

Los animales del zoológico

el ave *(f.) pl.* **las aves** bird

el canguro kangaroo

la cebra zebra

el cocodrilo crocodile

el delfín *pl.* **los delfines** dolphin

el elefante elephant

la foca seal

el gorila gorilla

el hipopótamo hippopotamus

la jirafa giraffe

el león *pl.* **los leones** lion

el oso bear

el oso blanco polar bear

el pingüino penguin

el tigre tiger

Tema 9

Las expresiones para las computadoras

la búsqueda search

comenzar *(e → ie)* **la sesión** to log on

el disco duro hard disk

la impresora printer

imprimir to print

el marcapáginas *pl.* **los marcapáginas** bookmark

multimedia multimedia

la página inicial home page

la tecla de borrar delete key

la tecla de intro enter key

Resumen de gramática

Grammar Terms

Adjectives describe nouns: *a **red** car.*

Adverbs usually describe verbs; they tell when, where, or how an action happens: *He read it **quickly**.* Adverbs can also describe adjectives or other adverbs: ***very** tall, **quite well**.*

Articles are words in Spanish that can tell you whether a noun is masculine, feminine, singular, or plural. In English, the articles are ***the, a,*** and ***an***.

Commands are verb forms that tell people to do something: ***Study!, Work!***

Comparatives compare people or things.

Conjugations are verb forms that add endings to the stem in order to tell who the subject is and what tense is being used: *escrib**o**, escrib**iste**.*

Conjunctions join words or groups of words. The most common ones are ***and, but,*** and ***or***.

Direct objects are nouns or pronouns that receive the action of a verb: *I read the **book**. I read **it**.*

Gender in Spanish tells you whether a noun, pronoun, or article is masculine or feminine.

Indirect objects are nouns or pronouns that tell you to whom / what or for whom / what something is done: *I gave **him** the book.*

Infinitives are the basic forms of verbs. In English, infinitives have the word "to" in front of them: ***to walk***.

Interrogatives are words that ask questions: ***What** is that? **Who** are you?*

Nouns name people, places, or things: ***students, Mexico City, books.***

Number tells you if a noun, pronoun, article, or verb is singular or plural.

Prepositions show relationship between their objects and another word in the sentence: *He is **in** the classroom.*

Present tense is used to talk about actions that always take place, or that are happening now: *I always **take** the bus; I **study** Spanish.*

Present progressive tense is used to emphasize that an action is happening *right now: I **am doing** my homework; he **is finishing** dinner.*

Preterite tense is used to talk about actions that were completed in the past: *I **took** the train yesterday; I **studied** for the test.*

Pronouns are words that take the place of nouns: ***She** is my friend.*

Subjects are the nouns or pronouns that perform the action in a sentence: ***John** sings.*

Superlatives describe which things have the most or least of a given quality: *She is the **best** student.*

Verbs show action or link the subject with a word or words in the predicate (what the subject does or is): *Ana **writes**; Ana **is** my sister.*

Nouns, Number, and Gender

Nouns refer to people, animals, places, things, and ideas. Nouns are singular or plural. In Spanish, nouns have gender, which means that they are either masculine or feminine.

Singular Nouns	
Masculine	**Feminine**
libro	carpeta
pupitre	casa
profesor	noche
lápiz	ciudad

Plural Nouns	
Masculine	**Feminine**
libros	carpetas
pupitres	casas
profesores	noches
lápices	ciudades

Definite Articles

El, la, los, and *las* are definite articles and are the equivalent of "the" in English. *El* is used with masculine singular nouns; *los* with masculine plural nouns. *La* is used with feminine singular nouns; *las* with feminine plural nouns. When you use the words *a* or *de* before *el,* you form the contractions *al* and *del: Voy **al** centro; Es el libro **del** profesor.*

Masculine	
Singular	Plural
el libro	los libros
el pupitre	los pupitres
el profesor	los profesores
el lápiz	los lápices

Feminine	
Singular	Plural
la carpeta	las carpetas
la casa	las casas
la noche	las noches
la ciudad	las ciudades

Indefinite Articles

Un and *una* are indefinite articles and are the equivalent of "a" and "an" in English. *Un* is used with singular masculine nouns; *una* is used with singular feminine nouns. The plural indefinite articles are *unos* and *unas.*

Masculine	
Singular	Plural
un libro	unos libros
un escritorio	unos escritorios
un baile	unos bailes

Feminine	
Singular	Plural
una revista	unas revistas
una mochila	unas mochilas
una bandera	unas banderas

Pronouns

Subject pronouns tell who is doing the action. They replace nouns or names in a sentence. Subject pronouns are often used for emphasis or clarification: *Gregorio escucha música. **Él** escucha música.*

A direct object tells who or what receives the action of the verb. To avoid repeating a direct object noun, you can replace it with a *direct object pronoun*. Direct object pronouns have the same gender and number as the nouns they replace: *¿Cuándo compraste **el libro? Lo** compré ayer.*

An indirect object tells to whom or for whom an action is performed. *Indirect object pronouns* are used to replace an indirect object noun: ***Les** doy dinero. (I give money to them.)* Because *le* and *les* have more than one meaning, you can make the meaning clear, or show emphasis, by adding *a* + the corresponding name, noun, or pronoun: ***Les** doy el dinero a **ellos.***

After most prepositions, you use *mí* and *ti* for "me" and "you." The forms change with the preposition *con: conmigo, contigo.* For all other persons, you use subject pronouns after prepositions.

The personal a

When the direct object is a person, a group of people, or a pet, use the word *a* before the object. This is called the "personal *a*": *Visité **a** mi abuela. Busco **a** mi perro, Capitán.*

Subject Pronouns		Direct Object Pronouns		Indirect Object Pronouns		Objects of Prepositions	
Singular	Plural	Singular	Plural	Singular	Plural	Singular	Plural
yo	nosotros, nosotras	me	nos	me	nos	(para) mí, conmigo	nosotros, nosotras
tú	vosotros, vosotras	te	os	te	os	(para) ti, contigo	vosotros, vosotras
usted (Ud.)	ustedes (Uds.)	lo, la	los, las	le	les	Ud.	Uds.
él, ella	ellos, ellas					él, ella	ellos, ellas

Adjectives

Words that describe people and things are called adjectives. In Spanish, most adjectives have both masculine and feminine forms, as well as singular and plural forms. Adjectives must agree with the noun they describe in both gender and number. When an adjective describes a group including both masculine and feminine nouns, use the masculine plural form.

Masculine	
Singular	Plural
alto	altos
inteligente	inteligentes
trabajador	trabajadores
fácil	fáciles

Feminine	
Singular	Plural
alta	altas
inteligente	inteligentes
trabajadora	trabajadoras
fácil	fáciles

Shortened Forms of Adjectives

When placed before masculine singular nouns, some adjectives change into a shortened form.

bueno	buen chico
malo	mal día
primero	primer trabajo
tercero	tercer plato
grande	gran señor

One adjective, ***grande,*** changes to a shortened form before any singular noun: *una* ***gran*** *señora, un* ***gran*** *libro.*

Possessive Adjectives

Possessive adjectives are used to tell what belongs to someone or to show relationships. Like other adjectives, possessive adjectives agree in number with the nouns that follow them.

Only *nuestro* and *vuestro* have different masculine and feminine endings. *Su* and *sus* can have many different meanings: *his, her, its, your,* or *their.*

Singular	Plural
mi	mis
tu	tus
su	sus
nuestro, -a	nuestros, -as
vuestro, -a	vuestros, -as
su	sus

Demonstrative Adjectives

Like other adjectives, demonstrative adjectives agree in gender and number with the nouns that follow them. Use *este, esta, estos, estas* ("this" / "these") before nouns that name people or things that are close to you. Use *ese, esa, esos, esas* ("that" / "those") before nouns that name people or things that are at some distance from you.

Singular	Plural
este libro	estos libros
esta casa	estas casas

Singular	Plural
ese niño	esos niños
esa manzana	esas manzanas

Interrogative Words

You use interrogative words to ask questions. When you ask a question with an interrogative word, you put the verb before the subject. All interrogative words have a written accent mark.

¿Adónde?	¿Cuándo?	¿Dónde?
¿Cómo?	¿Cuánto, -a?	¿Por qué?
¿Con quién?	¿Cuántos, -as?	¿Qué?
¿Cuál?	¿De dónde?	¿Quién?

Comparatives and Superlatives

Comparatives Use ***más . . . que*** or ***menos . . . que*** to compare people or things: *más interesante que . . . , menos alta que . . .*

When talking about number, use *de* instead of *que: Tengo **más de** cien monedas en mi colección.*

Superlatives Use this pattern to express the idea of "most" or "least."

el
la + noun + más / menos + adjective
los
las

Es la chica más seria de la clase.
Son los perritos más pequeños.

Several adjectives are irregular when used with comparatives and superlatives.

older	mayor
younger	menor
better	mejor
worse	peor

Affirmative and Negative Words

To make a sentence negative in Spanish, *no* usually goes in front of the verb or expression. To show that you do not like either of two choices, use *ni . . . ni.*

Alguno, alguna, algunos, algunas and *ninguno, ninguna* match the number and gender of the noun to which they refer. *Ningunos* and *ningunas* are rarely used. When *alguno* and *ninguno* come before a masculine singular noun, they change to *algún* and *ningún.*

Affirmative	Negative
algo	nada
alguien	nadie
algún	ningún
alguno, -a, -os, -as	ninguno, -a, -os, -as
siempre	nunca
también	tampoco

Adverbs

To form an adverb in Spanish, *-mente* is added to the feminine singular form of an adjective. This *-mente* ending is equivalent to the "-ly" ending in English. If the adjective has a written accent, such as *rápida, fácil,* and *práctica,* the accent appears in the same place in the adverb form.

general → generalmente
especial → especialmente
fácil → fácilmente
feliz → felizmente
rápida → rápidamente
práctica → prácticamente

Verbos

Regular Present and Preterite Tenses

Here are the conjugations for regular *-ar, -er,* and *-ir* verbs in the present and preterite tense.

Infinitive	Present		Preterite	
estudiar	estudio estudias estudia	estudiamos estudiáis estudian	estudié estudiaste estudió	estudiamos estudiasteis estudiaron
correr	corro corres corre	corremos corréis corren	corrí corriste corrió	corrimos corristeis corrieron
escribir	escribo escribes escribe	escribimos escribís escriben	escribí escribiste escribió	escribimos escribisteis escribieron

Present Progressive

When you want to emphasize that an action is happening *right now,* you use the present progressive tense.

estudiar	estoy estudiando estás estudiando está estudiando	estamos estudiando estáis estudiando están estudiando
correr	estoy corriendo estás corriendo está corriendo	estamos corriendo estáis corriendo están corriendo
escribir	estoy escribiendo estás escribiendo está escribiendo	estamos escribiendo estáis escribiendo están escribiendo

Affirmative tú Commands

When telling a friend, a family member, or a young person to do something, use an affirmative *tú* command. To give these commands for most verbs, use the same present-tense forms that are used for *Ud., él, ella.* Some verbs have an irregular affirmative *tú* command.

Regular	Irregular	
¡Estudia!	decir	di
¡Corre!	hacer	haz
¡Escribe!	ir	ve
	poner	pon
	salir	sal
	ser	sé
	tener	ten
	venir	ven

Stem-changing Verbs

Here is an alphabetical list of the stem-changing verbs. Next year, you will learn the preterite verb forms that are shown here in italic type.

Infinitive and Present Participle	Present		Preterite	
costar (o → ue) costando	cuesta	cuestan	costó	costaron
doler (o → ue) doliendo	duele	duelen	dolió	dolieron
dormir (o → ue) *durmiendo*	duermo duermes duerme	dormimos dormís duermen	dormí dormiste *durmió*	dormimos dormisteis *durmieron*
empezar (e → ie) empezando	empiezo empiezas empieza	empezamos empezáis empiezan	*empecé* empezaste empezó	empezamos empezasteis empezaron
jugar (u → ue) jugando	juego juegas juega	jugamos jugáis juegan	jugué jugaste jugó	jugamos jugasteis jugaron
llover (o → ue) lloviendo	llueve		llovió	
nevar (e → ie) nevando	nieva		nevó	
pedir (e → i) *pidiendo*	pido pides pide	pedimos pedís piden	pedí pediste *pidió*	pedimos pedisteis *pidieron*
pensar (e → ie) pensando	pienso piensas piensa	pensamos pensáis piensan	pensé pensaste pensó	pensamos pensasteis pensaron
preferir (e → ie) *prefiriendo*	prefiero prefieres prefiere	preferimos preferís prefieren	preferí preferiste *prefirió*	preferimos preferisteis *prefirieron*
sentir (e → ie) *sintiendo*	*See* preferir			
servir (e → i) *sirviendo*	*See* pedir			

479

Spelling-changing Verbs

These verbs have spelling changes in different tenses. The spelling changes are indicated in black.

Next year, you will learn the preterite verb forms that are shown here in italic type.

Infinitive and Present Participle	Present		Preterite	
buscar (c → qu) buscando	*See regular verbs*		**busqué** buscaste buscó	buscamos buscasteis buscaron
comunicarse (c → qu) *comunicándose*	*See reflexive verbs*		*See reflexive verbs and* **buscar**	
conocer (c → zc) conociendo	**conozco** conoces conoce	conocemos conocéis conocen	*See regular verbs*	
creer (i → y) *creyendo*	*See regular verbs*		creí creíste ***creyó***	creímos creísteis ***creyeron***
empezar (z → c) empezando	*See stem-changing verbs*		**empecé** empezaste empezó	empezamos empezasteis empezaron
enviar (i → í) enviando	**envío** **envías** **envía**	enviamos enviáis **envían**	*See regular verbs*	
esquiar (i → í) esquiando	*See* **enviar**		*See regular verbs*	
jugar (g → gu) jugando	*See stem-changing verbs*		**jugué** jugaste jugó	jugamos jugasteis jugaron
leer (i → y) leyendo	*See regular verbs*		*See* **creer**	
pagar (g → gu) pagando	*See regular verbs*		*See* **jugar**	
parecer (c → zc) pareciendo	*See* **conocer**		*See regular verbs*	
practicar (c → qu) practicando	*See regular verbs*		*See* **buscar**	
recoger (g → j) recogiendo	**recojo** recoges recoge	recogemos recogéis recogen	*See regular verbs*	
sacar (c → qu) sacando	*See regular verbs*		*See* **buscar**	
tocar (c → qu) tocando	*See regular verbs*		*See* **buscar**	

Irregular Verbs

These verbs have irregular patterns. Next year, you will learn the preterite verb forms that are shown here in italic type.

Infinitive and Present Participle	Present		Preterite	
dar dando	doy das da	damos dais dan	di diste dio	dimos disteis dieron
decir *diciendo*	digo dices dice	decimos decís dicen	*dije* *dijiste* *dijo*	*dijimos* *dijisteis* *dijeron*
estar estando	estoy estás está	estamos estáis están	*estuve* *estuviste* *estuvo*	*estuvimos* *estuvisteis* *estuvieron*
hacer haciendo	hago haces hace	hacemos hacéis hacen	hice hiciste hizo	hicimos hicisteis hicieron
ir *yendo*	voy vas va	vamos vais van	fui fuiste fue	fuimos fuisteis fueron
poder *pudiendo*	puedo puedes puede	podemos podéis pueden	*pude* *pudiste* *pudo*	*pudimos* *pudisteis* *pudieron*
poner poniendo	pongo pones pone	ponemos ponéis ponen	*puse* *pusiste* *puso*	*pusimos* *pusisteis* *pusieron*
querer queriendo	quiero quieres quiere	queremos queréis quieren	*quise* *quisiste* *quiso*	*quisimos* *quisisteis* *quisieron*
saber sabiendo	sé sabes sabe	sabemos sabéis saben	*supe* *supiste* *supo*	*supimos* *supisteis* *supieron*
salir saliendo	salgo sales sale	salimos salís salen	salí saliste salió	salimos salisteis salieron
ser siendo	soy eres es	somos sois son	fui fuiste fue	fuimos fuisteis fueron
tener teniendo	tengo tienes tiene	tenemos tenéis tienen	*tuve* *tuviste* *tuvo*	*tuvimos* *tuvisteis* *tuvieron*

Irregular Verbs (continued)

Next year, you will learn the preterite verb forms that are shown here in italic type.

Infinitive and Present Participle	Present		Preterite	
traer *trayendo*	traigo traes trae	traemos traéis traen	*traje* *trajiste* *trajo*	*trajimos* *trajisteis* *trajeron*
venir *viniendo*	vengo vienes viene	venimos venís vienen	*vine* *viniste* *vino*	*vinimos* *vinisteis* *vinieron*
ver viendo	veo ves ve	vemos veis ven	vi viste vio	vimos visteis vieron

Reflexive Verbs

Next year, you will learn the preterite verb forms that are shown here in italic type.

Infinitive and Present Participle	Present	
comunicarse *comunicándose*	me comunico te comunicas *se comunica*	*nos comunicamos* *os comunicáis* *se comunican*
Affirmative Familiar (*tú*) Command	**Preterite**	
comunícate	me comuniqué te comunicaste *se comunicó*	*nos comunicamos* *os comunicasteis* *se comunicaron*

Expresiones útiles para conversar

The following are expressions that you can use when you find yourself in a specific situation and need help to begin, continue, or end a conversation.

Greeting Someone

Buenos días. Good morning.

Buenas tardes. Good afternoon.

Buenas noches. Good evening. Good night.

Making Introductions

Me llamo . . . My name is . . .

Soy . . . I'm . . .

¿Cómo te llamas? What's your name?

Éste es mi amigo *m.* **. . .** This is my friend . . .

Ésta es mi amiga *f.* **. . .** This is my friend . . .

Se llama . . . His / Her name is . . .

¡Mucho gusto! It's a pleasure!

Encantado, -a. Delighted.

Igualmente. Likewise.

Asking How Someone Is

¿Cómo estás? How are you?

¿Cómo andas? How's it going?

¿Cómo te sientes? How do you feel?

¿Qué tal? How's it going?

Estoy bien, gracias. I'm fine, thank you.

Muy bien. ¿Y tú? Very well. And you?

Regular. Okay. Alright.

Más o menos. More or less.

(Muy) mal. (Very) bad.

¡Horrible! Awful!

¡Excelente! Great!

Talking on the Phone

Aló. Hello.

Diga. Hello.

Bueno. Hello.

¿Quién habla? Who's calling?

Habla . . . It's [name of person calling].

¿Está . . . , por favor? Is . . . there, please?

¿De parte de quién? Who is calling?

¿Puedo dejar un recado? May I leave a message?

Un momento. Just a moment.

Llamo más tarde. I'll call later.

¿Cómo? No le oigo. What? I can't hear you.

Making Plans

¿Adónde vas? Where are you going?

Voy a . . . I'm going to . . .

¿Estás listo, -a? Are you ready?

Tengo prisa. I'm in a hurry.

¡Date prisa! Hurry up!

Sí, ahora voy. OK, I'm coming.

Todavía necesito . . . I still need . . .

¿Te gustaría . . . ? Would you like to . . . ?

Sí, me gustaría . . . Yes, I'd like to . . .

¡Claro que sí (no)! Of course (not)!

¿Quieres . . . ? Do you want to . . . ?

Quiero . . . I want to . . .

¿Qué quieres hacer hoy? What do you want to do today?

¿Qué haces después de las clases? What do you do after school (class)?

¿Qué estás haciendo? What are you doing?

Te invito. It's my treat.

¿Qué tal si . . . ? What about . . . ?

Primero . . . First . . .

Después . . . Later . . .

Luego . . . Then . . .

Making an Excuse

Estoy ocupado, -a. I'm busy.

Lo siento, pero no puedo. I'm sorry, but I can't.

¡Qué lástima! What a shame!

Ya tengo planes. I already have plans.

Tal vez otro día. Maybe another day.

Being Polite

Con mucho gusto. With great pleasure.

De nada. You're welcome.

Disculpe. Excuse me.

Lo siento. I'm sorry.

Muchísimas gracias. Thank you very much.

Te (Se) lo agradezco mucho. I appreciate it a lot.

Muy amable. That's very kind of you.

Perdón. Pardon me.

¿Puede Ud. repetirlo? Can you repeat that?

¿Puede Ud. hablar más despacio? Can you speak more slowly?

Keeping a Conversation Going

¿De veras? Really?

¿Verdad? Isn't that so? Right?

¿En serio? Seriously?

¡No lo puedo creer! I don't believe it!

¡No me digas! You don't say!

Y entonces, ¿qué? And then what?

¿Qué hiciste? What did you do?

¿Qué dijiste? What did you say?

¿Crees que . . . ? Do you think that . . .?

Me parece bien. It seems alright.

Perfecto. Perfect.

¡Qué buena idea! What a good idea!

¡Cómo no! Of course!

De acuerdo. Agreed.

Está bien. It's all right.

Giving a Description When You Don't Know the Name of Someone or Something

Se usa para . . . It's used to / for . . .

Es la palabra que significa . . . It's the word that means . . .

Es la persona que . . . It's the person who . . .

Ending a Conversation

Bueno, tengo que irme. Well, I have to go.

Chao. (Chau.) Bye.

Hasta pronto. See you soon.

Hasta mañana. See you tomorrow.

Vocabulario español–inglés

The *Vocabulario español–inglés* contains all active vocabulary from the text, including vocabulary presented in the grammar sections.

A dash (—) represents the main entry word. For example, **pasar la —** after **la aspiradora** means **pasar la aspiradora.**

The number following each entry indicates the chapter in which the word or expression is presented. The letter *P* following an entry refers to the *Para empezar* section.

The following abbreviations are used in this list: *adj.* (adjective), *dir. obj.* (direct object), *f.* (feminine), *fam.* (familiar), *ind. obj.* (indirect object), *inf.* (infinitive), *m.* (masculine), *pl.* (plural), *prep.* (preposition), *pron.* (pronoun), *sing.* (singular).

A

a to *(prep.)* (4A)

— ...le gusta(n) he/she likes (5A)

— ...le encanta(n) he/she loves (5A)

— casa (to) home (4A)

— la derecha (de) to the right (of) (6A)

— la izquierda (de) to the left (of) (6A)

— la una de la tarde at one (o'clock) in the afternoon (4B)

— las ocho de la mañana at eight (o'clock) in the morning (4B)

— las ocho de la noche at eight (o'clock) in the evening / at night (4B)

— menudo often (8B)

— mí también I do (like to) too (1A)

— mí tampoco I don't (like to) either (1A)

¿— qué hora? (At) what time? (4B)

— veces sometimes (1B)

— ver Let's see (2A)

el abrigo coat (7A)

abril April (P)

abrir to open (5A)

la abuela, el abuelo grandmother, grandfather (5A)

los abuelos grandparents (5A)

aburrido, -a boring (2A)

me aburre(n) it bores me (they bore me) (9A)

aburrir to bore (9A)

acabar de + *inf.* to have just ...(9A)

el actor actor (9A)

la actriz *pl.* **las actrices** actress (9A)

acuerdo:

Estoy de —. I agree. (3B)

No estoy de —. I don't agree. (3B)

¡Adiós! Good-bye! (P)

¿Adónde? (To) where? (4A)

agosto August (P)

el agua *f.* water (3A)

ahora now (5B)

al *(a + el),* **a la,** to the (4A)

al lado de next to (2B)

la alfombra rug (6A)

algo something (3B)

¿— más? Anything else? (5B)

allí there (2B)

el almacén *pl.* **los almacenes** department store (7B)

el almuerzo lunch (2A)

en el — for lunch (3A)

alto, -a tall (5B)

amarillo, -a yellow (6A)

el amigo male friend (1B)

la amiga female friend (1B)

anaranjado, -a orange (6A)

la anciana, el anciano older woman, older man (8B)

los ancianos older people (8B)

el anillo ring (7B)

el animal animal (8A)

anoche last night (7B)

los anteojos de sol sunglasses (7B)

antes de before (9A)

el año year (P)

el — pasado last year (7B)

¿Cuántos años tiene(n) ...? How old is/are ...? (5A)

Tiene(n) ... años. He/She is / They are ... (years old). (5A)

el apartamento apartment (6B)

aprender (a) to learn (to) (8A)

aquí here (2B)

el árbol tree (8A)

los aretes earrings (7B)

el armario closet (6A)

arreglar el cuarto to straighten up the room (6B)

el arroz rice (3B)

el arte:

la clase de — art class (2A)

artístico, -a artistic (1B)

asco:

¡Qué —! How awful! (3A)

la atracción *pl.* **las atracciones** attraction(s) (8A)

atrevido, -a daring (1B)

el autobús *pl.* **los autobuses** bus (8A)

el avión *pl.* **los aviones** airplane (8A)

¡Ay! ¡Qué pena! Oh! What a shame/pity! (4B)

ayer yesterday (7B)

ayudar to help (6B)

el azúcar sugar (5B)

azul blue (6A)

B

bailar to dance (1A)

el baile dance (4B)

bajar (información) to download (9B)

bajo, -a short (5B)

la bandera flag (2B)

el baño bathroom (6B)

el traje de — swimsuit (7A)

barato, -a inexpensive, cheap (7B)

el barco boat, ship (8A)

el barrio neighborhood (8B)

el básquetbol: jugar al — to play basketball (4B)

bastante enough, rather (6B)

beber to drink (3A)

las bebidas beverages (3B)

béisbol: jugar al — to play baseball (4B)

la biblioteca library (4A)

bien well (P)

el bistec steak (3B)

blanco, -a white (6A)

la blusa blouse (7A)

la boca mouth (P)

el boleto ticket (8A)

el bolígrafo pen (P)

la bolsa bag, sack (8B)

el bolso purse (7B)

bonito, -a pretty (6A)

las botas boots (7A)

el bote: pasear en — to go boating (8A)

la botella bottle (8B)

el brazo arm (P)

bucear to scuba dive, to snorkel (8A)

bueno (buen), -a good (1B)

Buenas noches. Good evening. (P)

Buenas tardes. Good afternoon. (P)

Buenos días. Good morning. (P)

buscar to look for (7A); to search (for) (9B)

C

el caballo: montar a — to ride horseback (8A)

la cabeza head (P)

cada día every day (3B)

la cadena chain (7B)

el café coffee (3A); café (4A)

la caja box (8B)

los calcetines socks (7A)

la calculadora calculator (2A)

la calle street, road (8B)

calor:

Hace —. It's hot. (P)

tener — to be warm (5B)

la cama bed (6A)

hacer la — to make the bed (6B)

la cámara camera (5A)

la — digital digital camera (9A)

el camarero, la camarera waiter, waitress (5B)

caminar to walk (3B)

la camisa shirt (7A)

la camiseta T-shirt (7A)

el campamento camp (8B)

el campo countryside (4A)

el canal (TV) channel (9A)

la canción *pl.* **las canciones** song (9B)

canoso: pelo — gray hair (5B)

cansado, -a tired (4B)

cantar to sing (1A)

cara a cara face-to-face (9B)

la carne meat (3B)

caro, -a expensive (7B)

la carpeta folder (P)

la — de argollas three-ring binder (2A)

la carta letter (9B)

el cartel poster (2B)

la cartera wallet (7B)

el cartón cardboard (8B)

la casa home, house (4A)

a — (to) home (4A)

en — at home (4A)

casi almost (9A)

castaño: pelo — brown (chestnut) hair (5B)

catorce fourteen (P)

la cebolla onion (3B)

celebrar to celebrate (5A)

la cena dinner (3B)

el centro:

el — comercial mall (4A)

el — de reciclaje recycling center (8B)

cerca (de) close (to), near (6B)

el cereal cereal (3A)

los cereales grains (3B)

cero zero (P)

la chaqueta jacket (7A)

la chica girl (1B)

el chico boy (1B)

cien one hundred (P)

las ciencias:

la clase de — naturales science class (2A)

la clase de — sociales social studies class (2A)

cinco five (P)

cincuenta fifty (P)

el cine movie theater (4A)

la ciudad city (8A)

la clase class (2A)

la sala de clases classroom (P)

¿Qué — de...? What kind of ...? (9A)

el coche car (6B)

la cocina kitchen (6B)

cocinar to cook (6B)

el collar necklace (7B)

el color *pl.* **los colores** (6A)

¿De qué — ...? What color ...? (6A)

la comedia comedy (9A)

el comedor dining room (6B)

comer to eat (3A)

cómico, -a funny, comical (9A)

la comida food, meal (3A)

como like, as (8A)

¿cómo?:

¿— eres? What are you like? (1B)

¿— es? What is he/she like? (1B)

¿— está Ud.? How are you? *formal* (P)

¿— estás? How are you? *fam.* (P)

¿— lo pasaste? How was it (for you)? (8A)

¿— se dice ...? How do you say ...? (P)

¿— se escribe ...? How is ... spelled? (P)

¿— se llama? What's his/her name? (1B)

¿— te llamas? What is your name? (P)

¿— te queda(n)? How does it (do they) fit you? (7A)

la cómoda dresser (6A)

compartir to share (3A)

complicado, -a complicated (9B)

la composición *pl.* **las composiciones** composition (9B)

comprar to buy (7A)

comprar recuerdos to buy souvenirs (8A)

comprender to understand (3A)

la computadora computer (2B)

la — portátil laptop computer (9B)

usar la — to use the computer (1A)

comunicarse to communicate (9B)

(tú) te comunicas you communicate (9B)

(yo) me comunico I communicate (9B)

la comunidad community (8B)

con with (3A)

— mis/tus amigos with my/your friends (4A)

¿— quién? With whom? (4A)

el concierto concert (4B)

conmigo with me (4B)

conocer to know, to be acquainted with (9B)

contento, -a happy (4B)

contigo with you (4B)

la corbata tie (7B)

correr to run (1A)

cortar el césped to cut/to mow the lawn (6B)

las cortinas curtains (6A)

corto, -a short (5B)

los pantalones cortos shorts (7A)

la cosa thing (6A)

costar (o → ue) to cost (7A)

¿Cuánto cuesta(n) ...? How much does (do) ... cost? (7A)

crear to create (9B)

creer to think (3B)

Creo que ... I think ... (3B)

Creo que no. I don't think so. (3B)

Creo que sí. I think so. (3B)

el cuaderno notebook (P)

el cuadro painting (6A)

¿Cuál? Which?, What? (3A)

¿— es la fecha? What is the date? (P)

¿Cuándo? When? (4A)

¿cuánto?: ¿— cuesta(n) ... ? How much does (do) ... cost? (7A)

¿cuántos, -as? how many? (P)

¿Cuántos años tiene(n) ...? How old is/are ...? (5A)

cuarenta forty (P)

el cuarto room (6B)

cuarto, -a fourth (2A)

y — *(time)* quarter past (P)

menos — *(time)* quarter to (P)

cuatro four (P)

cuatrocientos, -as four hundred (7A)

la cuchara spoon (5B)

el cuchillo knife (5B)

la cuenta bill (5B)

el cumpleaños birthday (5A)

¡Feliz —! Happy birthday! (5A)

el curso: tomar un curso to take a course (9B)

D

dar to give (6B)

— + *movie or TV program* to show (9A)

— de comer al perro to feed the dog (6B)

de of (2B); from (4A)

¿— dónde eres? Where are you from? (4A)

— la mañana/la tarde/la noche in the morning /afternoon / evening (4B)

— nada. You're welcome. (5B)

— plato principal as a main dish (5B)

— postre for dessert (5B)

¿— qué color ...? What color ...? (6A)

¿— veras? Really? (9A)

debajo de underneath (2B)

deber should, must (3B)

decidir to decide (8B)

décimo, -a tenth (2A)

decir to say, to tell (8B)

¿Cómo se dice ...? How do you say ...? (P)

dime tell me (8A)

¡No me digas! You don't say! (4A)

¿Qué quiere — ...? What does ... mean? (P)

Quiere — ... It means ... (P)

Se dice ... You say ... (P)

las decoraciones decorations (5A)

decorar to decorate (5A)

el dedo finger (P)

delante de in front of (2B)

delicioso, -a delicious (5B)

los demás, las demás others (8B)

demasiado too (4B)

el dependiente, la dependienta salesperson (7A)

deportista sports-minded (1B)

derecha: a la — (de) to the right (of) (6A)

el desayuno breakfast (3A)

en el — for breakfast (3A)

descansar to rest, to relax (8A)

los descuentos: la tienda de — discount store (7B)

desear to wish (5B)

¿Qué desean (Uds.)? What would you like? (5B)

desordenado, -a messy (1B)

el despacho office (home) (6B)

el despertador alarm clock (6A)
después afterwards (4A)
después (de) after (4A)
detrás de behind (2B)
el día day (P)
Buenos —s . Good morning. (P)
cada — every day (3B)
¿Qué — es hoy? What day is today? (P)
todos los —s every day (3A)
la diapositiva slide (9B)
dibujar to draw (1A)
el diccionario dictionary (2A)
diciembre December (P)
diecinueve nineteen (P)
dieciocho eighteen (P)
dieciséis sixteen (P)
diecisiete seventeen (P)
diez ten (P)
difícil difficult (2A)
digital: la cámara — digital camera (9B)
dime tell me (8A)
el dinero money (6B)
la dirección electrónica e-mail address (9B)
el disco compacto compact disc (6A)
grabar un disco compacto to burn a CD (9B)
divertido, -a amusing, fun (2A)
doce twelve (P)
el documento document (9B)
doler (o → ue) to hurt (9A)
domingo Sunday (P)
dónde:
¿—? Where? (2B)
¿De — eres? Where are you from? (4A)
dormir (o → ue) to sleep (6A)
el dormitorio bedroom (6A)
dos two (P)
los/las dos both (7A)
doscientos, -as two hundred (7A)
el drama drama (9A)
los dulces candy (5A)
durante during (8A)
durar to last (9A)

E

la educación física: la clase de — physical education class (2A)
el ejercicio: hacer — to exercise (3B)
el the *m. sing.* (1B)
él he (1B)
los electrodomésticos: la tienda de — household appliance store (7B)
electrónico, -a: la dirección — e-mail address (9B)
ella she (1B)
ellas they *f. pl.* (2A)
ellos they *m. pl.* (2A)
emocionante touching (9A)
empezar (e → ie) to begin, to start (9A)
en in, on (2B)
— + *vehicle* by, in, on (8A)
— casa at home (4A)
— la ... hora in the ... hour (class period) (2A)
— la Red online (7B)
¿— qué puedo servirle? How can I help you? (7A)
encantado, -a delighted (P)
encantar to please very much, to love (9A)
a él/ella le encanta(n) he/she loves (5A)
me/te encanta(n) ... I/you love ... (3A)
encima de on top of (2B)
enero January (P)
enfermo, -a sick (4B)
la ensalada salad (3A)
la — de frutas fruit salad (3A)
enseñar to teach (2A)
entonces then (4B)
entrar to enter (7A)
enviar (i → í) to send (9B)
el equipo de sonido sound (stereo) system (6A)
¿Eres...? Are you ...? (1B)
es is (P); (he/she/it) is (1B)
— el *(number)* **de** *(month)* it is the ... of ... *(in telling the date)* (P)
— el primero de *(month)*. It is the first of ... (P)
— la una. It is one o'clock. (P)
— necesario. It's necessary. (8B)
— un(a) ... it's a ... (2B)
la escalera stairs, stairway (6B)
escribir:
¿Cómo se escribe ...? How is ... spelled? (P)
— cuentos to write stories (1A)
— por correo electrónico to write e-mail (9B)
Se escribe ... It's spelled ... (P)
el escritorio desk (2B)
escuchar música to listen to music (1A)
la escuela primaria primary school (8B)
ese, esa that (7A)
eso: por — that's why, therefore (9A)
esos, esas those (7A)
los espaguetis spaghetti (3B)
el español: la clase de — Spanish class (2A)
especialmente especially (9A)
el espejo mirror (6A)
la esposa wife (5A)
el esposo husband (5A)
esquiar (i → í) to ski (1A)
la estación *pl.* **las estaciones** season (P)
el estadio stadium (8A)
el estante shelf, bookshelf (6A)
estar to be (2B)
¿Cómo está Ud.? How are you? *formal* (P)
¿Cómo estás? How are you? *fam.* (P)

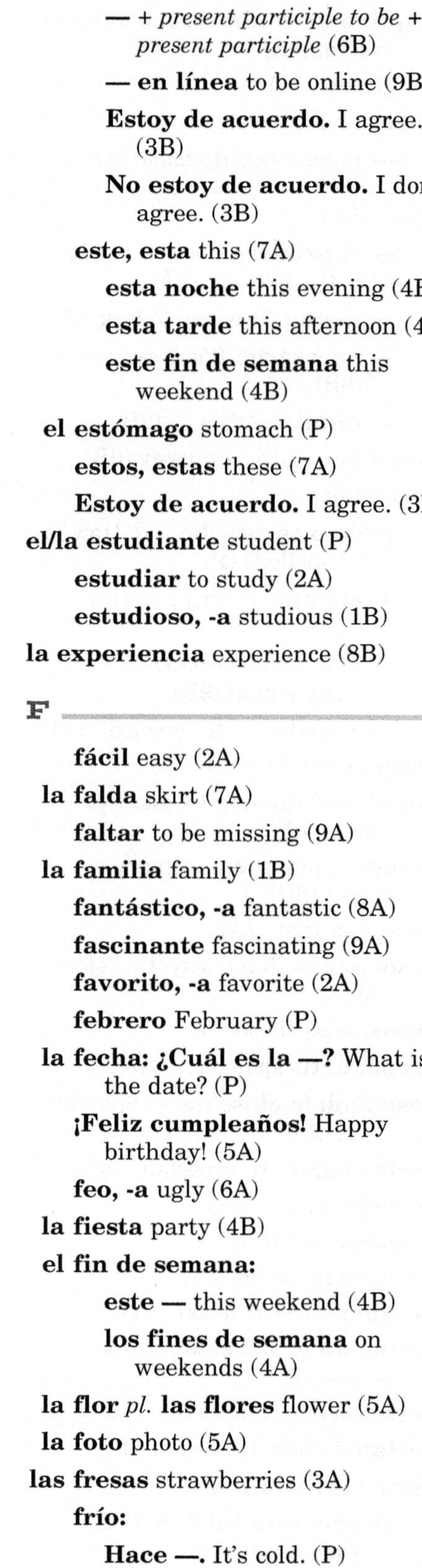

— + *present participle to be + present participle* (6B)

— en línea to be online (9B)

Estoy de acuerdo. I agree. (3B)

No estoy de acuerdo. I don't agree. (3B)

este, esta this (7A)

esta noche this evening (4B)

esta tarde this afternoon (4B)

este fin de semana this weekend (4B)

el estómago stomach (P)

estos, estas these (7A)

Estoy de acuerdo. I agree. (3B)

el/la estudiante student (P)

estudiar to study (2A)

estudioso, -a studious (1B)

la experiencia experience (8B)

F

fácil easy (2A)

la falda skirt (7A)

faltar to be missing (9A)

la familia family (1B)

fantástico, -a fantastic (8A)

fascinante fascinating (9A)

favorito, -a favorite (2A)

febrero February (P)

la fecha: ¿Cuál es la —? What is the date? (P)

¡Feliz cumpleaños! Happy birthday! (5A)

feo, -a ugly (6A)

la fiesta party (4B)

el fin de semana:

este — this weekend (4B)

los fines de semana on weekends (4A)

la flor *pl.* **las flores** flower (5A)

la foto photo (5A)

las fresas strawberries (3A)

frío:

Hace —. It's cold. (P)

tener — to be cold (5B)

fue it was (8A)

— un desastre. It was a disaster. (8A)

el fútbol: jugar al — to play soccer (4B)

el fútbol americano: jugar al — to play football (4B)

G

la galleta cookie (3A)

el garaje garage (6B)

el gato cat (5A)

generalmente generally (4A)

¡Genial! Great! (4B)

la gente people (8B)

el gimnasio gym (4A)

el globo balloon (5A)

el golf: jugar al — to play golf (4B)

la gorra cap (7A)

grabar un disco compacto to burn a CD (9B)

gracias thank you (P)

gracioso, -a funny (1B)

los gráficos computer graphics (9B)

grande large (6A)

las grasas fats (3B)

gris gray (6A)

los guantes gloves (7B)

guapo, -a good-looking (5B)

los guisantes peas (3B)

gustar:

a él/ella le gusta(n) he/she likes (5A)

(A mí) me gusta ... I like to ... (1A)

(A mí) me gusta más ... I like to ... better (I prefer to ...) (1A)

(A mí) me gusta mucho ... I like to ... a lot (1A)

(A mí) no me gusta ... I don't like to ... (1A)

(A mí) no me gusta nada ... I don't like to ... at all. (1A)

Le gusta ... He/She likes ... (1B)

Me gusta ... I like ... (3A)

Me gustaría ... I would like ... (4B)

Me gustó. I liked it. (8A)

No le gusta ... He/She doesn't like ... (1B)

¿Qué te gusta hacer? What do you like to do? (1A)

¿Qué te gusta hacer más? What do you like better (prefer) to do? (1A)

Te gusta ... You like ... (3A)

¿Te gusta ...? Do you like to ...? (1A)

¿Te gustaría ...? Would you like ... ? (4B)

¿Te gustó? Did you like it? (8A)

H

hablar to talk (2A)

— por teléfono to talk on the phone (1A)

hacer to do (3B)

hace + *time expression* ago (7B)

Hace calor. It's hot. (P)

Hace frío. It's cold. (P)

Hace sol. It's sunny. (P)

— ejercicio to exercise (3B)

— la cama to make the bed (6B)

— un video to videotape (5A)

haz *(command)* do, make (6B)

¿Qué hiciste? What did you do? (8A)

¿Qué tiempo hace? What's the weather like? (P)

(yo) hago I do (3B)

(tú) haces you do (3B)

hambre: Tengo —. I'm hungry. (3B)

la hamburguesa hamburger (3A)

hasta:

— luego. See you later. (P)

— mañana. See you tomorrow. (P)

Hay There is, There are (P, 2B)

— que one must (8B)

el helado ice cream (3B)

el hermano, la hermana brother, sister (5A)

el hermanastro, la hermanastra stepbrother, stepsister (5A)

os hermanos brothers; brother(s) and sister(s) (5A)

el hijo, la hija son, daughter (5A)

os hijos children; sons (5A)

la hoja de papel sheet of paper (P)

¡Hola! Hello! (P)

el hombre man (5B)

la hora:

en la ... — in the ... hour (class period) (2A)

¿A qué hora? At what time? (4B)

el horario schedule (2A)

horrible horrible (3B)

el horror: la película de — horror movie (9A)

el hospital hospital (8B)

el hotel hotel (8A)

hoy today (P)

os huevos eggs (3A)

I

la iglesia church (4A)

igualmente likewise (P)

impaciente impatient (1B)

importante important (6A)

impresionante impressive (8A)

increíble incredible (8B)

infantil childish (9A)

la información information (9B)

el informe report (9B)

el inglés: la clase de — English class (2A)

inolvidable unforgettable (8B)

inteligente intelligent (1B)

interesante interesting (2A)

interesar to interest (9A)

me interesa(n) it interests me (they interest me) (9A)

el invierno winter (P)

ir to go (4A)

— a + *inf.* to be going to + *verb* (4B)

— a la escuela to go to school (1A)

— de cámping to go camping (4B)

— de compras to go shopping (4A)

— de pesca to go fishing (4B)

— de vacaciones to go on vacation (8A)

¡Vamos! Let's go! (7A)

izquierda: a la — (de) to the left (of) (6A)

J

el jardín *pl.* **los jardines** garden, yard (8B)

los jeans jeans (7A)

el joven, la joven young man, young woman (5B)

joven *adj.* young (5B)

la joyería jewelry store (7B)

las judías verdes green beans (3B)

jueves Thursday (P)

jugar (a) (u → ue) to play (games, sports) (4B)

— al básquetbol to play basketball (4B)

— al béisbol to play baseball (4B)

— al fútbol to play soccer (4B)

— al fútbol americano to play football (4B)

— al golf to play golf (4B)

— al tenis to play tennis (4B)

— al vóleibol to play volleyball (4B)

— videojuegos to play video games (1A)

el jugo:

— de manzana apple juice (3A)

— de naranja orange juice (3A)

el juguete toy (8B)

julio July (P)

junio June (P)

L

la the *f. sing.* (1B); it, her *f. dir. obj. pron.* (7B)

el laboratorio laboratory (9B)

lado: al — de next to, beside (2B)

el lago lake (8A)

la lámpara lamp (6A)

el lápiz *pl.* **los lápices** pencil (P)

largo, -a long (5B)

las the *f. pl.* (2B); them *f. dir. obj. pron.* (7B)

— dos, los dos both (7A)

la lata can (8B)

lavar to wash (6B)

— el coche to wash the car (6B)

— la ropa to wash the clothes (6B)

— los platos to wash the dishes (6B)

le (to/for) him, her, *(formal)* you *sing. ind. obj. pron.* (8B)

— gusta ... He/She likes ... (1B)

— traigo ... I will bring you ... (5B)

No — gusta ... He/She doesn't like ... (1B)

la lección *pl.* **las lecciones de piano** piano lesson (class) (4A)

la leche milk (3A)

la lechuga lettuce (3B)

el lector DVD DVD player (6A)

leer revistas to read magazines (1A)

lejos (de) far (from) (6B)

les (to/for) them, *(formal)* you *pl. ind. obj. pron.* (8B)

levantar pesas to lift weights (3B)

la librería bookstore (7B)

el libro book (P)

la limonada lemonade (3A)

limpiar el baño to clean the bathroom (6B)

limpio, -a clean (6B)

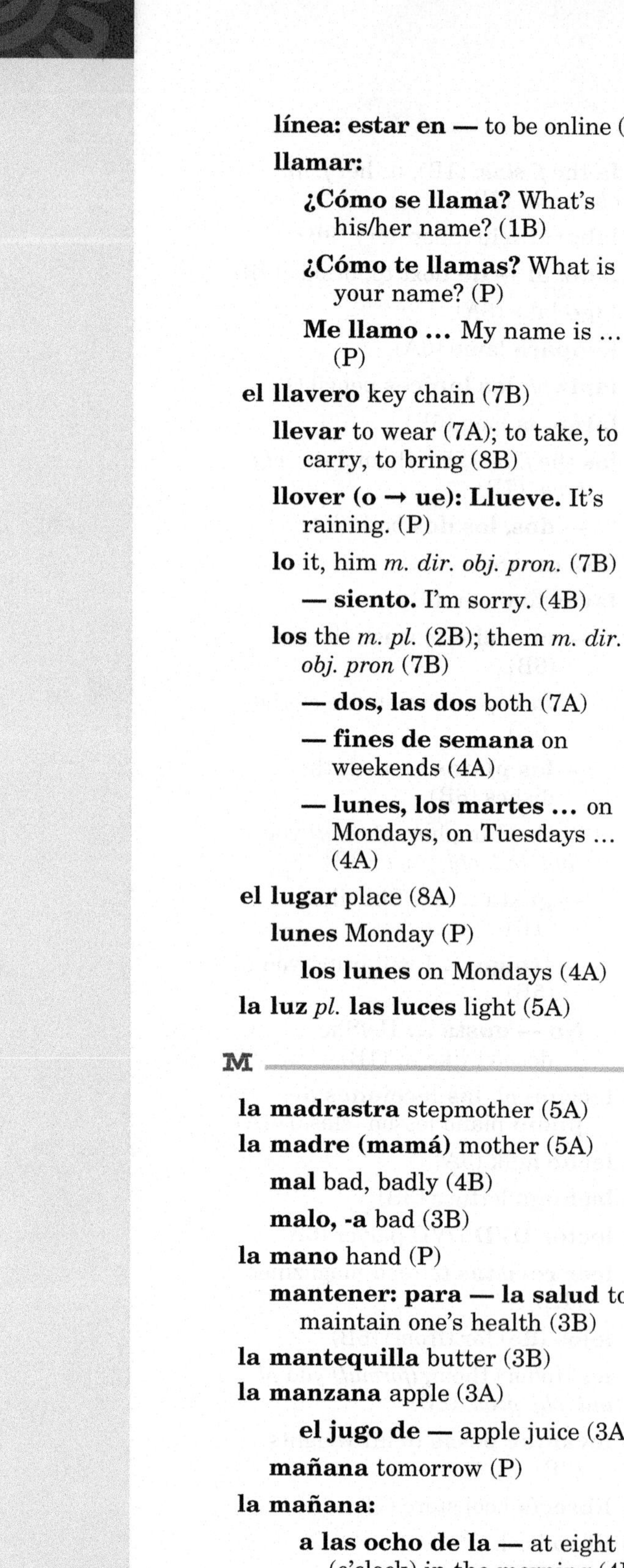

línea: estar en — to be online (9B)
llamar:
¿Cómo se llama? What's his/her name? (1B)
¿Cómo te llamas? What is your name? (P)
Me llamo ... My name is ... (P)
el llavero key chain (7B)
llevar to wear (7A); to take, to carry, to bring (8B)
llover (o → ue): Llueve. It's raining. (P)
lo it, him *m. dir. obj. pron.* (7B)
— siento. I'm sorry. (4B)
los the *m. pl.* (2B); them *m. dir. obj. pron* (7B)
— dos, las dos both (7A)
— fines de semana on weekends (4A)
— lunes, los martes ... on Mondays, on Tuesdays ... (4A)
el lugar place (8A)
lunes Monday (P)
los lunes on Mondays (4A)
la luz *pl.* **las luces** light (5A)

M

la madrastra stepmother (5A)
la madre (mamá) mother (5A)
mal bad, badly (4B)
malo, -a bad (3B)
la mano hand (P)
mantener: para — la salud to maintain one's health (3B)
la mantequilla butter (3B)
la manzana apple (3A)
el jugo de — apple juice (3A)
mañana tomorrow (P)
la mañana:
a las ocho de la — at eight (o'clock) in the morning (4B)
de la — in the morning (4B)
el mar sea (8A)
marrón *pl.* **marrones** brown (6A)
martes Tuesday (P)
los martes on Tuesdays (4A)
marzo March (P)
más:
¿Qué —? What else? (8B)
— ... que more ... than (2A)
— de more than (9A)
— o menos more or less (3A)
las matemáticas: la clase de — mathematics class (2A)
mayo May (P)
mayor older (5A)
me (to/for) me *ind. obj. pron.* (8B)
— aburre(n) it/they bore(s) me (9A)
— falta(n) ... I need ... (5B)
— gustaría I would like (4B)
— gustó. I liked it. (8A)
— interesa(n) it/they interest(s) me (9A)
— llamo ... My name is ... (P)
— queda(n) bien/mal. It/They fit(s) me well/poorly. (7A)
— quedo en casa. I stay at home. (4A)
¿— trae ...? Will you bring me ...? (5B)
media, -o half (P)
y — thirty, half-past (P)
mejor:
el/la —, los/las —es the best (6A)
—(es) que better than (6A)
menor younger (5A)
menos:
más o — more or less (3A)
— ... que less/fewer ... than (6A)
— de less/fewer than (9A)
el menú menu (5B)
menudo: a — often (8B)
el mes month (P)
la mesa table (2B)
poner la — to set the table (6B)
la mesita night table (6A)
la mezquita mosque (4A)
mi, mis my (2B, 5A)
mí:
a — también I do (like to) too (1A)
a — tampoco I don't (like to) either (1A)
para — in my opinion, for me (6A)
miedo: tener — (de) to be scared (of), to be afraid (of) (9B
miércoles Wednesday (P)
mil a thousand (7A)
mirar to look (at) (7B)
mismo, -a same (6A)
la mochila bookbag, backpack (2B)
el momento: un — a moment (6B)
el mono monkey (8A)
las montañas mountains (4A)
montar:
— a caballo to ride horseback (8A)
— en bicicleta to ride a bicycle (1A)
— en monopatín to skateboard (1A)
el monumento monument (8A)
morado, -a purple (6A)
mucho a lot (2A)
— gusto pleased to meet you (P)
muchos, -as many (3B)
la mujer woman (5B)
el museo museum (8A)
muy very (1B)
— bien very well (P)

N

nada nothing (P)
(A mí) no me gusta — ... I don't like to ... at all. (1A)
De —. You're welcome. (5B)
nadar to swim (1A)
la naranja: el jugo de — orange juice (3A)

la nariz *pl.* **las narices** nose (P)
navegar en la Red to surf the Web (9B)
necesario: Es —. It's necessary. (8B)
necesitar:
(yo) necesito I need (2A)
(tú) necesitas you need (2A)
negro, -a black (6A)
el pelo — black hair (5B)
nevar (e → ie) Nieva. It's snowing. (P)
ni ... ni neither ... nor, not ... or (1A)
el niño, la niña young boy, young girl (8B)
los niños children (8B)
No estoy de acuerdo. I don't agree. (3B)
¡No me digas! You don't say! (4A)
no soy I am not (1A)
noche:
a las ocho de la — at eight (o'clock) in the evening, at night (4B)
Buenas —s. Good evening. (P)
de la — in the evening, at night (4B)
esta — this evening (4B)
nos (to/for) us *ind. obj. pron.* (8B)
¡— vemos! See you later! (P)
nosotros, -as we (2A)
novecientos, -as nine hundred (7A)
noveno, -a ninth (2A)
noventa ninety (P)
noviembre November (P)
el novio, la novia boyfriend, girlfriend (7B)
nuestro(s), -a(s) our (5A)
nueve nine (P)
nuevo, -a new (7A)
nunca never (3A)

O

o or (1A)
la obra de teatro play (8A)
ochenta eighty (P)
ocho eight (P)
ochocientos, -as eight hundred (7A)
octavo, -a eighth (2A)
octubre October (P)
ocupado, -a busy (4B)
el ojo eye (P)
once eleven (P)
ordenado, -a neat (1B)
os (to/for) you *pl. fam. ind. obj. pron.* (8B)
el otoño fall, autumn (P)
otro, -a other, another (5B)
otra vez again (8B)
¡Oye! Hey! (4B)

P

paciente patient (1B)
el padrastro stepfather (5A)
el padre (papá) father (5A)
los padres parents (5A)
pagar (por) to pay (for) (7B)
la página Web Web page (9B)
el país country (8A)
el pájaro bird (8A)
el pan bread (3A)
el — tostado toast (3A)
la pantalla (computer) screen (2B)
los pantalones pants (7A)
los — cortos shorts (7A)
las papas potatoes (3B)
las — fritas French fries (3A)
el papel picado cut-paper decorations (5A)
la papelera wastepaper basket (2B)
para for (2A)
— + *inf.* in order to + *inf.* (4A)
— la salud for one's health (3B)
— mantener la salud to maintain one's health (3B)
— mí in my opinion, for me (6A)
¿ — qué sirve? What's it (used) for? (9B)
— ti in your opinion, for you (6A)
la pared wall (6A)
el parque park (4A)
el — de diversiones amusement park (8A)
el — nacional national park (8A)
el partido game, match (4B)
pasar:
¿Cómo lo pasaste? How was it (for you)? (8A)
— la aspiradora to vacuum (6B)
— tiempo con amigos to spend time with friends (1A)
¿Qué pasa? What's happening? (P)
¿Qué te pasó? What happened to you? (8A)
pasear en bote to go boating (8A)
el pastel cake (5A)
los pasteles pastries (3B)
patinar to skate (1A)
pedir (e → i) to order (5B); to ask for (9B)
la película film, movie (9A)
la — de ciencia ficción science fiction movie (9A)
la — de horror horror movie (9A)
la — policíaca crime movie, mystery (9A)
la — romántica romantic movie (9A)
ver una — to see a movie (4A)
pelirrojo, -a red-haired (5B)
el pelo hair (5B)
el — canoso gray hair (5B)
el — castaño brown (chestnut) hair (5B)
el — negro black hair (5B)
el — rubio blond hair (5B)
pensar (e → ie) to plan, to think (7A)
peor:
el/la —, los/las —es the worst (6A)

—(es) que worse than (6A)
pequeño, -a small (6A)
Perdón. Excuse me. (7A)
perezoso, -a lazy (1B)
el **perfume** perfume (7B)
el **periódico** newspaper (8B)
pero but (1B)
el **perrito caliente** hot dog (3A)
el **perro** dog (5A)
la **persona** person (5A)
pesas: levantar — to lift weights (3B)
el **pescado** fish (3B)
el **pie** foot (P)
la **pierna** leg (P)
la **pimienta** pepper (5B)
la **piñata** piñata (5A)
la **piscina** pool (4A)
el **piso** story, floor (6B)
primer — second floor (6B)
segundo — third floor (6B)
la **pizza** pizza (3A)
la **planta baja** ground floor (6B)
el **plástico** plastic (8B)
el **plátano** banana (3A)
el **plato** plate, dish (5B)
de — principal as a main dish (5B)
el — principal main dish (5B)
la **playa** beach (4A)
pobre poor (8B)
poco: un — (de) a little (4B)
poder (o → ue) to be able (6A)
(yo) puedo I can (4B)
(tú) puedes you can (4B)
policíaca: la película — crime movie, mystery (9A)
el **pollo** chicken (3B)
poner to put, to place (6B)
pon *(command)* put, place (6B)
— la mesa to set the table (6B)
(yo) pongo I put (6B)
(tú) pones you put (6B)

por:
— eso that's why, therefore (9A)
— favor please (P)
¿— qué? Why? (3B)
— supuesto of course (3A)
porque because (3B)
la **posesión** *pl.* **las posesiones** possession (6A)
el **postre** dessert (5B)
de — for dessert (5B)
practicar deportes to play sports (1A)
práctico, -a practical (2A)
el **precio** price (7A)
preferir (e → ie) to prefer (7A)
(yo) prefiero I prefer (3B)
(tú) prefieres you prefer (3B)
preparar to prepare (5A)
la **presentación** *pl.* **las presentaciones** presentation (9B)
la **primavera** spring (P)
primer (primero), -a first (2A)
— piso second floor (6B)
el **primo,** la **prima** cousin (5A)
los **primos** cousins (5A)
el **problema** problem (8B)
el **profesor,** la **profesora** teacher (P)
el **programa** program, show (9A)
el — de concursos game show (9A)
el — de dibujos animados cartoon (9A)
el — de entrevistas interview program (9A)
el — de la vida real reality program (9A)
el — de noticias news program (9A)
el — deportivo sports program (9A)
el — educativo educational program (9A)
el — musical musical program (9A)

propio, -a own (6A)
el **proyecto de construcción** construction project (8B)
puedes: (tú) — you can (4B)
puedo: (yo) — I can (4B)
la **puerta** door (2B)
pues well *(to indicate pause)* (1A)
la **pulsera** bracelet (7B)
el reloj — watch (7B)
el **pupitre** student desk (P)

Q

que who, that (5A)
qué:
¿Para — sirve? What's it (used) for? (9B)
¡— + adj.! How ...! (5B)
¡— asco! How awful! (3A)
¡— buena idea! What a good/nice idea! (4B)
¿— clase de ...? What kind of ... ? (9A)
¿— desean (Uds.)? What would you like? (5B)
¿— día es hoy? What day is today? (P)
¿— es esto? What is this? (2B)
¿— hiciste? What did you do? (8A)
¿— hora es? What time is it? (P)
¿— más? What else? (8B)
¿— pasa? What's happening? (P)
¡— pena! What a shame/pity! (4B)
¿— quiere decir ... ? What does ... mean? (P)
¿— tal? How are you? (P)
¿— te gusta hacer? What do you like to do? (1A)
¿— te gusta más? What do you like better (prefer) to do? (1A)
¿— te parece? What do you think (about it)? (9B)
¿— te pasó? What happened to you? (8A)

¿— tiempo hace? What's the weather like? (P)

quedar to fit (7A), to stay (4A)

¿Cómo me queda? How does it fit (me)? (7A)

Me / te queda bien. It fits me / you well. (7A)

Me quedo en casa. I stay home. (4A)

el quehacer (de la casa) (household) chore (6B)

querer (e → ie) to want (7A)

¿Qué quiere decir ...? What does ... mean? (P)

Quiere decir ... It means ... (P)

quisiera I would like (5B)

(yo) quiero I want (4B)

(tú) quieres you want (4B)

el queso cheese (3A)

¿Quién? Who? (2A)

quince fifteen (P)

quinientos, -as five hundred (7A)

quinto, -a fifth (2A)

quisiera I would like (5B)

quitar el polvo to dust (6B)

quizás maybe (7A)

R

rápidamente quickly (9B)

el ratón *pl.* **los ratones** (computer) mouse (2B)

razón: tener — to be correct (7A)

realista realistic (9A)

recibir to receive (6B)

reciclar to recycle (8B)

recoger (g → j) to collect, to gather (8B)

los recuerdos souvenirs (8A)

comprar recuerdos to buy souvenirs (8A)

la Red:

en la — online (7B)

navegar en la — to surf the Web (9B)

el refresco soft drink (3A)

el regalo gift, present (5A)

regresar to return (8A)

regular okay, so-so (P)

el reloj clock (2B)

el — pulsera watch (7B)

reservado, -a reserved, shy (1B)

el restaurante restaurant (4A)

rico, -a rich, tasty (5B)

el río river (8B)

rojo, -a red (6A)

romántico, -a: la película — romantic movie (9A)

romper to break (5A)

la ropa: la tienda de — clothing store (7B)

rosado, -a pink (6A)

rubio, -a blond (5B)

S

sábado Saturday (P)

saber to know (how) (9B)

(yo) sé I know (how to) (4B)

(tú) sabes you know (how to) (4B)

sabroso, -a tasty, flavorful (3B)

el sacapuntas pencil sharpener (2B)

sacar:

— fotos to take photos (5A)

— la basura to take out the trash (6B)

la sal salt (5B)

la sala living room (6B)

la sala de clases classroom (P)

la salchicha sausage (3A)

salir to leave, to go out (8A)

la salud:

para la — for one's health (3B)

para mantener la — to maintain one's health (3B)

el sándwich de jamón y queso ham and cheese sandwich (3A)

sé: (yo) — I know (how to) (1B)

sed: Tengo —. I'm thirsty. (3B)

según according to (1B)

— mi familia according to my family (1B)

segundo, -a second (2A)

— piso third floor (6B)

seis six (P)

seiscientos, -as six hundred (7A)

la semana week (P)

este fin de — this weekend (4B)

la — pasada last week (7B)

los fines de — on weekends (4A)

señor (Sr.) sir, Mr. (P)

señora (Sra.) madam, Mrs. (P)

señorita (Srta.) miss, Miss (P)

separar to separate (8B)

septiembre September (P)

séptimo, -a seventh (2A)

ser to be (3B)

¿Eres ...? Are you ...? (1B)

es he/she is (1B)

fue it was (8A)

no soy I am not (1B)

soy I am (1B)

serio, -a serious (1B)

la servilleta napkin (5B)

servir (e → i) to serve, to be useful (9B)

¿En qué puedo servirle? How can I help you? (7A)

¿Para qué sirve? What's it (used) for? (9B)

Sirve para ... It's used for ... (9B)

sesenta sixty (P)

setecientos, -as seven hundred (7A)

setenta seventy (P)

sexto, -a sixth (2A)

si if, whether (6B)

sí yes (1A)

siempre always (3A)

siento: lo — I'm sorry (4B)

siete seven (P)

la silla chair (2B)

simpático, -a nice, friendly (1B)

sin without (3A)

la sinagoga synagogue (4A)
el sitio Web Web site (9B)
sobre about (9A)
sociable sociable (1B)
el software software (7B)
el sol:
Hace —. It's sunny. (P)
los anteojos de — sunglasses (7B)
tomar el — to sunbathe (8A)
sólo only (5A)
solo, -a alone (4A)
Son las ... It's ... *(time)* (P)
la sopa de verduras vegetable soup (3A)
el sótano basement (6B)
soy I am (1B)
su, sus his, her, your *formal,* their (5A)
sucio, -a dirty (6B)
la sudadera sweatshirt (7A)
sueño: tener — to be sleepy (5B)
el suéter sweater (7A)
supuesto: por — of course (3A)

T

tal: ¿Qué — ? How are you? (P)
talentoso, -a talented (1B)
también also, too (1A)
a mí — I do (like to) too (1A)
tampoco: a mí — I don't (like to) either (1A)
tanto so much (7A)
tarde late (8A); afternoon (4B)
a la una de la — at one (o'clock) in the afternoon (4B)
Buenas —s. Good afternoon. (P)
de la tarde in the afternoon (4B)
esta — this afternoon (4B)
la tarea homework (2A)
la tarjeta card (9B)
la taza cup (5B)
te (to/for) you *sing. ind. obj. pron.* (8B)
¿— gusta ...? Do you like to ... ? (1A)
¿— gustaría ...? Would you like ...? (4B)
¿— gustó? Did you like it? (8A)
el té tea (3A)
el — helado iced tea (3A)
el teatro theater (8A)
el teclado (computer) keyboard (2B)
la tecnología technology/computers (2A)
la clase de — technology/ computer class (2A)
la telenovela soap opera (9A)
el televisor television set (6A)
el templo temple; Protestant church (4A)
temprano early (8A)
el tenedor fork (5B)
tener to have (5A)
(yo) tengo I have (2A)
(tú) tienes you have (2A)
¿Cuántos años tiene(n) ...? How old is/are ... ? (5A)
— calor to be warm (5B)
— frío to be cold (5B)
— miedo (de) to be scared (of), to be afraid (of) (9B)
— razón to be correct (7A)
— sueño to be sleepy (5B)
Tengo hambre. I'm hungry. (3B)
Tengo que ... I have to ... (4B)
Tengo sed. I'm thirsty. (3B)
Tiene(n) ... años. He/She is/ They are ... years old. (5A)
el tenis: jugar al — to play tennis (4B)
tercer (tercero), -a third (2A)
terminar to finish, to end (9A)
ti you *fam. after prep.*
¿Y a —? And you? (1A)
para — in your opinion, for you (6A)
el tiempo:
el — libre free time (4A)
pasar — con amigos to spend time with friends (1A)
¿Qué — hace? What's the weather like? (P)
la tienda store (7A)
la — de descuentos discount store (7B)
la — de electrodomésticos household appliance store (7B)
la — de ropa clothing store (7A)
Tiene(n) ... años. He/She is / They are ... (years old). (5A)
el tío, la tía uncle, aunt (5A)
los tíos uncles; aunt(s) and uncle(s) (5A)
tocar la guitarra to play the guitar (1A)
el tocino bacon (3A)
todos, -as all (3B)
— los días every day (3A)
tomar:
— el sol to sunbathe (8A)
— un curso to take a course (9B)
los tomates tomatoes (3B)
tonto, -a silly, stupid (9A)
trabajador, -a hardworking (1B)
trabajar to work (1A)
el trabajo work, job (4A)
el — voluntario volunteer work (8B)
traer:
Le traigo ... I will bring you ... (5B)
¿Me trae ...? Will you bring me ...? (5B)
el traje suit (7A)
el — de baño swimsuit (7A)
trece thirteen (P)
treinta thirty (P)
treinta y uno thirty-one (P)
tremendo, -a tremendous (8A)
el tren train (8A)
tres three (P)

trescientos, as three hundred (7A)

triste sad (4B)

tu, tus your (2B, 5A)

tú you *fam.* (2A)

U

Ud. (usted) you *formal sing.* (2A)

Uds. (ustedes) you *formal pl.* (2A)

¡Uf! Ugh!, Yuck! (7B)

un, una a, an (1B)

un poco (de) a little (4B)

la una: a la — at one o'clock (4B)

uno one (P)

unos, -as some (2B)

usado, -a used (8B)

usar la computadora to use the computer (1A)

usted (Ud.) you *formal sing.* (2A)

ustedes (Uds.) you *formal pl.* (2A)

las uvas grapes (3B)

V

las vacaciones: ir de — to go on vacation (8A)

¡Vamos! Let's go! (7A)

el vaso glass (5B)

veinte twenty (P)

veintiuno (veintiún) twenty-one (P)

vender to sell (7B)

venir to come (5B)

la ventana window (2B)

ver to see (8A)

a — ... Let's see (2A)

¡Nos vemos! See you later! (P)

— la tele to watch television (1A)

— una película to see a movie (4A)

el verano summer (P)

veras: ¿De —? Right? (9A)

¿Verdad? Right? (3A)

verde green (6A)

el vestido dress (7A)

la vez, *pl.* **las veces** time (8B)

a veces sometimes (1B)

otra — again (8B)

vi I saw (8A)

viajar to travel (8A)

el viaje trip (8A)

el video video (5A)

los videojuegos: jugar — to play video games (1A)

el vidrio glass (8B)

viejo, -a old (5B)

viernes Friday (P)

violento, -a violent (9A)

visitar to visit (8A)

— salones de chat to visit chat rooms (9B)

¿Viste? Did you see? (8A)

vivir to live (6B)

el vóleibol: jugar al — to play volleyball (4B)

el voluntario, la voluntaria volunteer (8B)

vosotros, -as you *pl.* (2A)

vuestro(s), -a(s) your (5A)

Y

y and (1A)

¿— a ti? And you? (1A)

— cuarto quarter past (P)

— media thirty, half-past (*in telling time*) (P)

¿— tú? And you? *fam.* (P)

¿— usted (Ud.)? And you? *formal* (P)

ya already (9A)

yo I (1B)

el yogur yogurt (3A)

Z

las zanahorias carrots (3B)

la zapatería shoe store (7B)

los zapatos shoes (7A)

el zoológico zoo (8A)

English-Spanish Vocabulary

The *English-Spanish Vocabulary* contains all active vocabulary from the text, including vocabulary presented in the grammar sections.

A dash (—) represents the main entry word. For example, **to play —** after **baseball** means **to play baseball.**

The number following each entry indicates the chapter in which the word or expression is presented. The letter *P* following an entry refers to the *Para empezar* section.

The following abbreviations are used in this list: *adj.* (adjective), *dir. obj.* (direct object), *f.* (feminine), *fam.*(familiar), *ind. obj.* (indirect object), *inf.* (infinitive), *m.* (masculine), *pl.* (plural), *prep.* (preposition), *pron.* (pronoun), *sing.* (singular).

A

a, an un, una (1B)
a little un poco (de) (4B)
a lot mucho, -a (2A)
a thousand mil (7A)
able: to be — poder (o → ue) (6A)
about sobre (9A)
according to según (1B)
— my family según mi familia (1B)
acquainted: to be — with conocer (9B)
actor el actor (9A)
actress la actriz *pl.* las actrices (9A)
address: e-mail — la dirección electrónica (9B)
afraid: to be — (of) tener miedo (de) (9B)
after después (de) (4A)
afternoon:
at one (o'clock) in the afternoon a la una de la tarde (4B)
Good —. Buenas tardes. (P)
in the — de la tarde (4B)
this — esta tarde (4B)
afterwards después (4A)
again otra vez (8B)
ago hace + *time expression* (7B)
agree:
I —. Estoy de acuerdo. (3B)
I don't —. No estoy de acuerdo. (3B)
airplane el avión *pl.* los aviones (8A)
alarm clock el despertador (6A)
all todos, -as (3B)
almost casi (9A)
alone solo, -a (4A)
already ya (9A)
also también (1A)
always siempre (3A)
am:
I — (yo) soy (1B)
I — not (yo) no soy (1B)
amusement park el parque de diversiones (8A)
amusing divertido, -a (2A)
and y (1A)
¿— you? ¿Y a ti? *fam.* (1A); ¿Y tú? *fam.* (P); ¿Y usted (Ud.)? *formal* (P)
animal el animal (8A)
another otro, -a (5B)
Anything else? ¿Algo más? (5B)
apartment el apartamento (6B)
apple la manzana (3A)
— juice el jugo de manzana (3A)
April abril (P)
Are you ...? ¿Eres ...? (1B)
arm el brazo (P)
art class la clase de arte (2A)
artistic artístico, -a (1B)
as como (8A)
— a main dish de plato principal (5B)
to ask for pedir (e → i) (9B)
at:
— eight (o'clock) a las ocho (4B)
— eight (o'clock) at night a las ocho de la noche (4B)
— eight (o'clock) in the evening a las ocho de la noche (4B)
— eight (o'clock) in the morning a las ocho de la mañana (4B)
— home en casa (4A)
— one (o'clock) a la una (4B)
— one (o'clock) in the afternoon a la una de la tarde (4B)
— what time? ¿A qué hora? (4B)
attraction(s) la atracción *pl.* las atracciones (8A)
August agosto (P)
aunt la tía (5A)
aunt(s) and uncle(s) los tíos (5A)
autumn el otoño (P)

B

backpack la mochila (2B)
bacon el tocino (3A)
bad malo, -a (3B); mal (4B)
badly mal (4B)
bag la bolsa (8B)
balloon el globo (5A)
banana el plátano (3A)
baseball: to play — jugar al béisbol (4B)
basement el sótano (6B)
basketball: to play — jugar al básquetbol (4B)
bathroom el baño (6B)
to be ser (3B); estar (2B)
He/She is / They are ... years old. Tiene(n) ... años. (5A)
How old is/are ...? ¿Cuántos años tiene(n) ...? (5A)
to — + *present participle* estar + *present participle* (6B)
to — able poder (o → ue) (6A)
to — acquainted with conocer (9B)
to — afraid (of) tener miedo (de) (9B)
to — cold tener frío (5B)
to — correct tener razón (7A)
to — going to + *verb* ir a + *inf.* (4B)
to — online estar en línea (9B)

to — scared (of) tener miedo (de) (9B)

to — sleepy tener sueño (5B)

to — useful servir (e → i) (9B)

to — warm tener calor (5B)

beach la playa (4A)

bear el oso (8A)

because porque (3B)

bed la cama (6A)

to make the — hacer la cama (6B)

bedroom el dormitorio (6A)

beefsteak el bistec (3B)

before antes de (9A)

o begin empezar (e → ie) (9A)

behind detrás de (2B)

best: the — el/la mejor, los/las mejores (6A)

better than mejor(es) que (6A)

beverages las bebidas (3B)

bicycle: to ride a — montar en bicicleta (1A)

bill la cuenta (5B)

binder: three-ring — la carpeta de argollas (2A)

bird el pájaro (8A)

birthday el cumpleaños (5A)

Happy —! ¡Feliz cumpleaños! (5A)

black negro (6A)

black hair el pelo negro (5B)

blond hair el pelo rubio (5B)

blouse la blusa (7A)

blue azul (6A)

boat el barco (8A)

boating: to go — pasear en bote (8A)

book el libro (P)

bookbag la mochila (2B)

bookshelf el estante (6A)

bookstore la librería (7B)

boots las botas (7A)

o bore aburrir (9A)

it/they —(s) me me aburre(n) (9A)

boring aburrido, -a (2A)

both los dos, las dos (7A)

bottle la botella (8B)

box la caja (8B)

boy el chico (1B)

—friend el novio (7B)

young — el niño (8B)

bracelet la pulsera (7B)

bread el pan (3A)

to break romper (5A)

breakfast el desayuno (3A)

for — en el desayuno (3A)

to bring traer (5B); llevar (8B)

I will — you ... Le traigo ... (5B)

Will you — me ...? ¿Me trae ...? (5B)

brother el hermano (5A)

brothers; brother(s) and sister(s) los hermanos (5A)

brown marrón *pl.* marrones (6A)

— (chestnut) hair el pelo castaño (5B)

to burn a CD grabar un disco compacto (9B)

bus el autobús *pl.* los autobuses (8A)

busy ocupado, -a (4B)

but pero (1B)

butter la mantequilla (3B)

to buy comprar (7A)

to — souvenirs comprar recuerdos (8A)

by + *vehicle* en + *vehicle* (8A)

C

café el café (4A)

cake el pastel (5A)

calculator la calculadora (2A)

camera la cámara (5A)

digital — la cámara digital (9B)

camp el campamento (8B)

can la lata (8B)

can:

I — (yo) puedo (4B)

you — (tú) puedes (4B)

candy los dulces (5A)

cap la gorra (7A)

car el coche (6B)

card la tarjeta (9B)

cardboard el cartón (8B)

carrots las zanahorias (3B)

to carry llevar (8B)

cartoon el programa de dibujos animados (9A)

cat el gato (5A)

CD: to burn a CD grabar un disco compacto (9B)

to celebrate celebrar (5A)

cereal el cereal (3A)

chain la cadena (7B)

chair la silla (2B)

channel (TV) el canal (9A)

cheap barato, -a (7B)

cheese el queso (3A)

chicken el pollo (3B)

childish infantil (9A)

children los hijos (5A); los niños (8B)

chore: household — el quehacer (de la casa) (6B)

church la iglesia (4A)

Protestant — el templo (4A)

city la ciudad (8A)

class la clase (2A)

classroom la sala de clases (P)

clean limpio, -a (6B)

to clean the bathroom limpiar el baño (6B)

clock el reloj (2B)

close (to) cerca (de) (6B)

closet el armario (6A)

clothing store la tienda de ropa (7A)

coat el abrigo (7A)

coffee el café (3A)

cold:

It's —. Hace frío. (P)

to be — tener frío (5B)

to collect recoger (g → j) (8B)

color:

What — ...? ¿De qué color ...? (6A)

—s los colores (6A)

to come venir (5B)

comedy la comedia (9A)

comical cómico, -a (9A)

to communicate comunicarse (9B)

I — (yo) me comunico (9B)

you — (tú) te comunicas (9B)

community la comunidad (8B)

compact disc el disco compacto (6A)

to burn a — grabar un disco compacto (9B)

complicated complicado, -a (9B)

composition la composición *pl.* las composiciones (9B)

computer la computadora (2B)

— graphics los gráficos (9B)

— keyboard el teclado (2B)

— mouse el ratón (2B)

— screen la pantalla (2B)

—s/technology la tecnología (2B)

laptop — la computadora portátil (9B)

to use the — usar la computadora (1A)

concert el concierto (4B)

construction project el proyecto de construcción (8B)

to cook cocinar (6B)

cookie la galleta (3A)

correct: to be — tener razón (7A)

to cost costar (o → ue) (7A)

How much does (do) ... — ? ¿Cuánto cuesta(n)? (7A)

country el país (8A)

countryside el campo (4A)

course: to take a course tomar un curso (9B)

cousin el primo, la prima (5A)

—s los primos (5A)

to create crear (9B)

crime movie la película policíaca (9A)

cup la taza (5B)

curtains las cortinas (6A)

to cut the lawn cortar el césped (6B)

cut-paper decorations el papel picado (5A)

D

dance el baile (4B)

to dance bailar (1A)

daring atrevido, -a (1B)

date: What is the —? ¿Cuál es la fecha? (P)

daughter la hija (5A)

day el día (P)

every — todos los días (3A); cada día (3B)

What — is today? ¿Qué día es hoy? (P)

December diciembre (P)

to decide decidir (8B)

to decorate decorar (5A)

decorations las decoraciones (5A)

delicious delicioso, -a (5B)

delighted encantado, -a (P)

department store el almacén *pl.* los almacenes (7B)

desk el pupitre (P); el escritorio (2B)

dessert el postre (5B)

for — de postre (5B)

dictionary el diccionario (2A)

Did you like it? ¿Te gustó? (8A)

difficult difícil (2A)

digital camera la cámara digital (9B)

dining room el comedor (6B)

dinner la cena (3B)

dirty sucio, -a (6B)

disaster: It was a — . Fue un desastre. (8A)

discount store la tienda de descuentos (7B)

dish el plato (5B)

as a main — de plato principal (5B)

main — el plato principal (5B)

to do hacer (3B)

— *(command)* haz (6B)

— you like to ...? ¿Te gusta ...? (1A)

I — (yo) hago (3B)

What did you —? ¿Qué hiciste? (8A)

you — (tú) haces (3B)

document el documento (9B)

dog el perro (5A)

to feed the — dar de comer al perro (6B)

door la puerta (2B)

to download bajar (información) (9B)

drama el drama (9A)

to draw dibujar (1A)

dress el vestido (7A)

dresser la cómoda (6A)

to drink beber (3A)

during durante (8A)

to dust quitar el polvo (6B)

DVD player el lector DVD (6A)

E

e-mail:

— address la dirección electrónica (9B)

to write an — message escribir por correo electrónico (9B)

early temprano (8A)

earrings los aretes (7B)

easy fácil (2A)

to eat comer (3A)

educational program el programa educativo (9A)

eggs los huevos (3A)

eight ocho (P)

eight hundred ochocientos, -as (7A)

eighteen dieciocho (P)

eighth octavo, -a (2A)

eighty ochenta (P)

either tampoco (1A)

I don't (like to) — a mí tampoco (1A)

eleven once (P)

else:

Anything —? ¿Algo más? (5B)

What —? ¿Qué más? (8B)

to end terminar (9A)

English class la clase de inglés (2A)

enough bastante (6B)

to enter entrar (7A)

especially especialmente (9A)

evening:

Good —. Buenas noches. (P)

in the — de la noche (4B)

this — esta noche (4B)

every day cada día (3B); todos los días (3A)

Excuse me. Perdón. (7A)

to exercise hacer ejercicio (3B)

expensive caro, -a (7B)

experience la experiencia (8B)

eye el ojo (P)

F

face-to-face cara a cara (9B)

fall el otoño (P)

family la familia (1B)

fantastic fantástico, -a (8A)

far (from) lejos (de) (6B)

fascinating fascinante (9A)

fast rápidamente (9B)

father el padre (papá) (5A)

fats las grasas (3B)

favorite favorito, -a (2A)

February febrero (P)

to feed the dog dar de comer al perro (6B)

fewer:

— … than menos … que (6A)

— than … menos de … (9A)

fifteen quince (P)

fifth quinto, -a (2A)

fifty cincuenta (P)

film la película (9A)

finger el dedo (P)

to finish terminar (9A)

first primer (primero), -a (2A)

fish el pescado (3B)

to go —ing ir de pesca (4B)

to fit:

How does it (do they) fit me / you? ¿Cómo me / te queda(n)? (7A)

It / They —(s) me well / poorly. Me queda(n) bien / mal. (7A)

five cinco (P)

five hundred quinientos, -as (7A)

flag la bandera (2B)

flavorful sabroso, -a (3B)

floor el piso (6B)

ground — la planta baja (6B)

second — el primer piso (6B)

third — el segundo piso (6B)

flower la flor *pl.* las flores (5A)

folder la carpeta (P)

food la comida (3A)

foot el pie (P)

football: to play — jugar al fútbol americano (4B)

for para (2A)

— breakfast en el desayuno (3A)

— lunch en el almuerzo (3A)

— me para mí (6A)

— you para ti (6A)

fork el tenedor (5B)

forty cuarenta (P)

four cuatro (P)

four hundred cuatrocientos, -as (7A)

fourteen catorce (P)

fourth cuarto, -a (2A)

free time el tiempo libre (4A)

French fries las papas fritas (3A)

Friday viernes (P)

friendly simpático, -a (1B)

from de (4A)

Where are you —? ¿De dónde eres? (4A)

fruit salad la ensalada de frutas (3A)

fun divertido, -a (2A)

funny gracioso, -a (1B); cómico, -a (9A)

G

game el partido (4B)

— show el programa de concursos (9A)

garage el garaje (6B)

garden el jardín *pl.* los jardines (8B)

to gather recoger (g → j) (8B)

generally generalmente (4A)

gift el regalo (5A)

girl la chica (1B)

—friend la novia (7B)

young — la niña (8B)

to give dar (6B)

glass el vaso (5B); el vidrio (8B)

gloves los guantes (7B)

to go ir (4A)

Let's —! ¡Vamos! (7A)

to be —ing to + *verb* ir a + *inf.* (4B)

to — boating pasear en bote (8A)

to — camping ir de cámping (4B)

to — fishing ir de pesca (4B)

to — on vacation ir de vacaciones (8A)

to — shopping ir de compras (4A)

to — to school ir a la escuela (1A)

to — out salir (8A)

golf: to play — jugar al golf (4B)

good bueno (buen), -a (1B)

— afternoon. Buenas tardes. (P)

— evening. Buenas noches. (P)

— morning. Buenos días. (P)

Good-bye! ¡Adiós! (P)

good-looking guapo, -a (5B)

grains los cereales (3B)

grandfather el abuelo (5A)

grandmother la abuela (5A)

grandparents los abuelos (5A)

grapes las uvas (3B)

graphics los gráficos (9B)

gray gris (6A)

— hair el pelo canoso (5B)

Great! ¡Genial! (4B)

green verde (6A)

— beans las judías verdes (3B)

ground floor la planta baja (6B)

guitar: to play the — tocar la guitarra (1A)

gym el gimnasio (4A)

H

hair el pelo (5B)

black — el pelo negro (5B)

blond — el pelo rubio (5B)

brown (chestnut) — el pelo castaño (5B)

gray — el pelo canoso (5B)

half media, -o (P)

— -past y media (P)

ham and cheese sandwich el sándwich de jamón y queso (3A)

hamburger la hamburguesa (3A)

hand la mano (P)

happy contento, -a (4B)

— birthday! ¡Feliz cumpleaños! (5A)

hardworking trabajador, -a (1B)

to have tener (5A)

to — just … acabar de + *inf.* (9A)

I — to … tengo que + *inf.* (4B)

he él (1B)

he/she is es (1B)

He/She is / They are … years old. Tiene(n) … años. (5A)

head la cabeza (P)

health:

for one's — para la salud (3B)

to maintain one's — para mantener la salud (3B)

Hello! ¡Hola! (P)

to help ayudar (6B)

How can I — you? ¿En qué puedo servirle? (7A)

her su, sus *possessive adj.* (5A); la *dir. obj. pron.* (7B); le *ind. obj. pron.* (8B)

here aquí (2B)

Hey! ¡Oye! (4B)

him lo *dir. obj. pron.* (7B); le *ind. obj. pron.* (8B)

his su, sus (5A)

home la casa (4A)

at — en casa (4A)

— office el despacho (6B)

(to) — a casa (4A)

homework la tarea (2A)

horrible horrible (3B)

horror movie la película de horror (9A)

horseback: to ride — montar a caballo (8A)

hospital el hospital (8B)

hot:

— dog el perrito caliente (3A)

It's —. Hace calor. (P)

hotel el hotel (8A)

hour: in the … — en la … hora (class period) (2A)

house la casa (4A)

household:

— chore el quehacer (de la casa) (6B)

— appliance store la tienda de electrodomésticos (7B)

how:

— + *adj.*! ¡Qué + *adj.*! (5B)

— awful! ¡Qué asco! (3A)

how? ¿cómo? (P)

— are you? ¿Cómo está Ud.? *formal* (P); ¿Cómo estás? *fam.* (P); ¿Qué tal? *fam.* (P)

— can I help you? ¿En qué puedo servirle? (7A)

— do you say … ? ¿Cómo se dice …? (P)

— does it (do they) fit (you)? ¿Cómo te queda(n)? (7A)

— is … spelled? ¿Cómo se escribe …? (P)

— many? ¿cuántos, -as? (P)

— much does (do) … cost? ¿Cuánto cuesta(n) …? (7A)

— old is/are … ? ¿Cuántos años tiene(n) …? (5A)

— was it (for you)? ¿Cómo lo pasaste? (8A)

hundred: one — cien (P)

hungry: I'm —. Tengo hambre. (3B)

to hurt doler (o → ue) (9A)

husband el esposo (5A)

I

I yo (1B)

— am soy (1B)

— am not no soy (1B)

— do too a mí también (1A)

— don't either a mí tampoco (1A)

— don't think so. Creo que no. (3B)

— stay at home. Me quedo en casa. (4A)

— think … Creo que … (3B)

— think so. Creo que sí. (3B)

— will bring you … Le traigo … (5B)

— would like … Me gustaría (4B); quisiera (5B)

—'m hungry. Tengo hambre. (3B)

—'m sorry. Lo siento. (4B)

—'m thirsty. Tengo sed. (3B)

ice cream el helado (3B)

iced tea el té helado (3A)

if si (6B)

impatient impaciente (1B)

important importante (6A)

impressive impresionante (8A)

in en (P, 2B)

— front of delante de (2B)

— my opinion para mí (6A)

— order to para + *inf.* (4A)

— the … hour en la … hora (class period) (2A)

— your opinion para ti (6A)

incredible increíble (8B)

inexpensive barato, -a (7B)

information la información (9B)

intelligent inteligente (1B)

to interest interesar (9A)

it/they interest(s) me me interesa(n) (9A)

interesting interesante (2A)

interview program el programa de entrevistas (9A)

is es (P)

he/she — es (1B)

it la, lo *dir. obj. pron.* (7B)

— fits (they fit) me well/poorly. Me queda(n) bien/mal. (7A)

— is ... Son las *(in telling time)* (P)

— is one o'clock. Es la una. (P)

— is the ... of ... Es el *(number)* de *(month) (in telling the date)* (P)

— is the first of ... Es el primero de *(month)*. (P)

— was fue (8A)

— was a disaster. Fue un desastre. (8A)

—'s a ... es un/una ... (2B)

—'s cold. Hace frío. (P)

—'s hot. Hace calor. (P)

—'s necessary. Es necesario. (8B)

—'s raining. Llueve. (P)

—'s snowing. Nieva. (P)

—'s sunny. Hace sol. (P)

J

jacket la chaqueta (7A)

January enero (P)

jeans los jeans (7A)

jewelry store la joyería (7B)

job el trabajo (4A)

juice:

apple — el jugo de manzana (3A)

orange — el jugo de naranja (3A)

July julio (P)

June junio (P)

just: to have — (done something) acabar de + *inf.* (9A)

K

key chain el llavero (7B)

keyboard (computer) el teclado (2B)

kind: What — of ... ? ¿Qué clase de ...? (9A)

kitchen la cocina (6B)

knife el cuchillo (5B)

to know saber (4B, 9B); conocer (9B)

I — (yo) conozco (9B)

I — (how to) (yo) sé (4B)

you — (tú) conoces (9B)

you — (how to) (tú) sabes (4B)

L

laboratory el laboratorio (9B)

lake el lago (8A)

lamp la lámpara (6A)

laptop computer la computadora portátil (9B)

large grande (6A)

last:

— night anoche (7B)

— week la semana pasada (7B)

— year el año pasado (7B)

to last durar (9A)

late tarde (8A)

later: See you — ¡Hasta luego!, ¡Nos vemos! (P)

lazy perezoso, -a (1B)

to learn aprender (a) (8A)

to leave salir (8A)

left: to the — (of) a la izquierda (de) (6A)

leg la pierna (P)

lemonade la limonada (3A)

less:

less ... than menos ... que (6A)

less than menos de (9A)

Let's go! ¡Vamos! (7A)

Let's see A ver ... (2A)

letter la carta (9B)

lettuce la lechuga (3B)

library la biblioteca (4A)

to lift weights levantar pesas (3B)

light la luz *pl.* las luces (5A)

like como (8A)

to like:

Did you — it? ¿Te gustó? (8A)

Do you — to ...? ¿Te gusta ...? (1A)

He/She doesn't — ... No le gusta ... (1B)

He/She —s ... Le gusta ... (1B); A él/ella le gusta(n) ... (5A)

I don't — to ... (A mí) no me gusta ... (1A)

I don't — to ... at all. (A mí) no me gusta nada ... (1A)

I — ... Me gusta ... (3A)

I — to ... (A mí) me gusta ... (1A)

I — to ... a lot (A mí) me gusta mucho ... (1A)

I — to ... better (A mí) me gusta más ... (1A)

I —d it. Me gustó. (8A)

I would — Me gustaría (4B); quisiera (5B)

What do you — better (prefer) to do? ¿Qué te gusta más? (1A)

What do you — to do? ¿Qué te gusta hacer? (1A)

What would you —? ¿Qué desean (Uds.)? (5B)

Would you —? ¿Te gustaría? (4B)

You — ... Te gusta ... (3A)

likewise igualmente (P)

to listen to music escuchar música (1A)

little: a — un poco (de) (4B)

to live vivir (6B)

living room la sala (6B)

long largo, -a (5B)

to look:

to — (at) mirar (7B)

to — for buscar (7A)

lot: a — mucho, -a (2A)

to love encantar (9A)

He/She —s ... A él/ella le encanta(n) ... (5A)

I/You — ... Me/Te encanta(n)... (3A)

lunch el almuerzo (2A)

for — en el almuerzo (3A)

M

madam (la) señora (Sra.) (P)

main dish el plato principal (5B)

as a — de plato principal (5B)
to maintain one's health para mantener la salud (3B)
make *(command)* haz (6B)
to make the bed hacer la cama (6B)
mall el centro comercial (4A)
man el hombre (5B)
older — el anciano (8B)
many muchos, -as (3B)
how — ¿cuántos, -as? (P)
March marzo (P)
match el partido (4B)
mathematics class la clase de matemáticas (2A)
May mayo (P)
maybe quizás (7A)
me me *ind. obj. pron* (8B)
for — para mí (6A), me (8B)
— too a mí también (1A)
to — me (8B)
with — conmigo (4B)
meal la comida (3A)
to mean:
It —s ... Quiere decir ... (P)
What does ... — ? ¿Qué quiere decir ... ? (P)
meat la carne (3B)
menu el menú (5B)
messy desordenado, -a (1B)
milk la leche (3A)
mirror el espejo (6A)
miss, Miss (la) señorita (Srta.) (P)
missing: to be — faltar (9A)
moment: a — un momento (6B)
Monday lunes (P)
on Mondays los lunes (4A)
money el dinero (6B)
monkey el mono (8A)
month el mes (P)
monument el monumento (8A)
more:
— ... than más ... que (2A)
— or less más o menos (3A)
— than más de (9A)
morning:
Good —. Buenos días. (P)
in the — de la mañana (4B)
mosque la mezquita (4A)
mother la madre (mamá) (5A)
mountains las montañas (4A)
mouse (computer) el ratón (2B)
mouth la boca (P)
movie la película (9A)
to see a — ver una película (4A)
— theater el cine (4A)
to mow the lawn cortar el césped (6B)
Mr. (el) señor (Sr.) (P)
Mrs. (la) señora (Sra.) (P)
much: so — tanto (7A)
museum el museo (8A)
music:
to listen to — escuchar música (1A)
—al program el programa musical (9A)
must deber (3B)
one — hay que (8B)
my mi (2B); mis (5A)
— name is ... Me llamo ... (P)
mystery la película policíaca (9A)

N

name:
My — is ... Me llamo ... (P)
What is your —? ¿Cómo te llamas? (P)
What's his/her —? ¿Cómo se llama? (1B)
napkin la servilleta (5B)
national park el parque nacional (8A)
near cerca (de) (6B)
neat ordenado, -a (1B)
necessary: It's —. Es necesario. (8B)
necklace el collar (7B)
to need
I — necesito (2A)
I — ... Me falta(n) ... (5B)
you — necesitas (2A)
neighborhood el barrio (8B)
neither ... nor ni ... ni (1A)
never nunca (3A)
new nuevo, -a (7A)
news program el programa de noticias (9A)
newspaper el periódico (8B)
next to al lado de (2B)
nice simpático, -a (1B)
night:
at — de la noche (4B)
last — anoche (7B)
night table la mesita (6A)
nine nueve (P)
nine hundred novecientos, -as (7A
nineteen diecinueve (P)
ninety noventa (P)
ninth noveno, -a (2A)
nose la nariz *pl.* las narices (P)
not ... or ni ... ni (1A)
notebook el cuaderno (P)
nothing nada (P)
November noviembre (P)
now ahora (5B)

O

o'clock:
at eight — a las ocho (4B)
at one — a la una (4B)
It's one —. Es la una. (P)
It's ... — Son las ... (P)
October octubre (P)
of de (2B)
— course por supuesto (3A)
office (home) el despacho (6B)
often a menudo (8B)
Oh! What a shame/pity! ¡Ay! ¡Qué pena! (4B)
okay regular (P)
old viejo, -a (5B)
He/She is / They are ... years —. Tiene(n) ... años. (5A)
How — is/are ... ? ¿Cuántos años tiene(n) ... ? (5A)
—er mayor (5A)
—er man el anciano (8B)

—er people los ancianos (8B)
—er woman la anciana (8B)
on en (2B)
— Mondays, on Tuesdays ... los lunes, los martes ... (4A)
— top of encima de (2B)
— weekends los fines de semana (4A)
one uno (un), -a (P)
at — (o'clock) a la una (4B)
one hundred cien (P)
one must hay que (8B)
onion la cebolla (3B)
online en la Red (7B)
to be — estar en línea (9B)
only sólo (5A)
to open abrir (5A)
opinion:
in my — para mí (6A)
in your — para tí (6A)
or o (1A)
orange anaranjado, -a (6A)
— juice el jugo de naranja (3A)
to order pedir (e → i) (5B)
other otro, -a (5B)
others los/las demás (8B)
our nuestro(s), -a(s) (5A)
own propio, -a (6A)

P

painting el cuadro (6A)
pants los pantalones (7A)
paper: sheet of — la hoja de papel (P)
parents los padres (5A)
park el parque (4A)
amusement — el parque de diversiones (8A)
national — el parque nacional (8A)
party la fiesta (4B)
pastries los pasteles (3B)
patient paciente (1B)
to pay (for) pagar (por) (7B)
peas los guisantes (3B)
pen el bolígrafo (P)
pencil el lápiz *pl.* los lápices (P)
— sharpener el sacapuntas (2B)
people la gente (8B)
older — los ancianos (8B)
pepper la pimienta (5B)
perfume el perfume (7B)
person la persona (5A)
phone: to talk on the — hablar por teléfono (1A)
photo la foto (5A)
to take —s sacar fotos (5A)
physical education class la clase de educación física (2A)
piano lesson (class) la lección *pl.* las lecciones de piano (4A)
pink rosado, -a (6A)
piñata la piñata (5A)
pizza la pizza (3A)
place el lugar (8A)
to place poner (6B)
to plan pensar (e → ie) (7A)
plastic el plástico (8B)
plate el plato (5B)
play la obra de teatro (8A)
to play jugar (a) (u → ue) (4B); tocar (1A)
to — baseball jugar al béisbol (4B)
to — basketball jugar al básquetbol (4B)
to — football jugar al fútbol americano (4B)
to — golf jugar al golf (4B)
to — soccer jugar al fútbol (4B)
to — sports practicar deportes (1A)
to — tennis jugar al tenis (4B)
to — the guitar tocar la guitarra (1A)
to — video games jugar videojuegos (1A)
to — volleyball jugar al vóleibol (4B)
please por favor (P)
to please very much encantar (9A)
pleased to meet you mucho gusto (P)
pool la piscina (4A)
poor pobre (8B)
possession la posesión *pl.* las posesiones (6A)
poster el cartel (2B)
potatoes las papas (3B)
practical práctico, -a (2A)
to prefer preferir (e → ie) (7A)
I — (yo) prefiero (3B)
I — to ... (a mí) me gusta más ... (1A)
you — (tú) prefieres (3B)
to prepare preparar (5A)
present el regalo (5A)
presentation la presentación *pl.* las presentaciones (9B)
pretty bonito, -a (6A)
price el precio (7A)
primary school la escuela primaria (8B)
problem el problema (8B)
program el programa (9A)
purple morado, -a (6A)
purse el bolso (7B)
to put poner (6B)
I — (yo) pongo (6B)
— *(command)* pon (6B)
you — (tú) pones (6B)

Q

quarter past y cuarto (P)
quarter to menos cuarto
quickly rápidamente (9B)

R

rain: It's —ing. Llueve. (P)
rather bastante (6B)
to read magazines leer revistas (1A)
realistic realista (9A)
reality program el programa de la vida real (9A)
Really? ¿De veras? (9A)
to receive recibir (6B)
to recycle reciclar (8B)
recycling center el centro de reciclaje (8B)

red rojo, -a (6A)

—-haired pelirrojo, -a (5B)

to relax descansar (8A)

report el informe (9B)

reserved reservado, -a (1B)

to rest descansar (8A)

restaurant el restaurante (4A)

to return regresar (8A)

rice el arroz (3B)

rich rico, -a (5B)

to ride:

to — a bicycle montar en bicicleta (1A)

to — horseback montar a caballo (8A)

right: to the — (of) a la derecha (de) (6A)

Right? ¿Verdad? (3A)

ring el anillo (7B)

river el río (8B)

road la calle (8B)

romantic movie la película romántica (9A)

room el cuarto (6B)

to straighten up the — arreglar el cuarto (6B)

rug la alfombra (6A)

to run correr (1A)

S

sack la bolsa (8B)

sad triste (4B)

salad la ensalada (3A)

fruit — la ensalada de frutas (3A)

salesperson el dependiente, la dependienta (7A)

salt la sal (5B)

same mismo, -a (6A)

sandwich: ham and cheese — el sándwich de jamón y queso (3A)

Saturday sábado (P)

sausage la salchicha (3A)

to say decir (8B)

How do you —? ¿Cómo se dice? (P)

You — ... Se dice ... (P)

You don't —! ¡No me digas! (4A)

scared: to be — (of) tener miedo (de) (9B)

schedule el horario (2A)

science:

— class la clase de ciencias naturales (2A)

— fiction movie la película de ciencia ficción (9A)

screen: computer — la pantalla (2B)

to scuba dive bucear (8A)

sea el mar (8A)

to search (for) buscar (9B)

season la estación *pl.* las estaciones (P)

second segundo, -a (2A)

— floor el primer piso (6B)

to see ver (8A)

Let's — A ver ... (2A)

— you later! ¡Nos vemos!, Hasta luego. (P)

— you tomorrow. Hasta mañana. (P)

to — a movie ver una película (4A)

to sell vender (7B)

to send enviar (i → í) (9B)

to separate separar (8B)

September septiembre (P)

serious serio, -a (1B)

to serve servir (e → i) (9B)

to set the table poner la mesa (6B)

seven siete (P)

seven hundred setecientos, -as (7A)

seventeen diecisiete (P)

seventh séptimo, -a (2A)

seventy setenta (P)

to share compartir (3A)

she ella (1B)

sheet of paper la hoja de papel (P)

shelf el estante (6A)

ship el barco (8A)

shirt la camisa (7A)

T- — la camiseta (7A)

shoe store la zapatería (7B)

shoes los zapatos (7A)

short bajo, -a; corto, -a (5B)

shorts los pantalones cortos (7A)

should deber (3B)

show el programa (9A)

to show + *movie or TV program* dar (9A)

shy reservado, -a (1B)

sick enfermo, -a (4B)

silly tonto, -a (9A)

to sing cantar (1A)

sir (el) señor (Sr.) (P)

sister la hermana (5A)

site: Web — el sitio Web (9B)

six seis (P)

six hundred seiscientos, -as (7A)

sixteen dieciséis (P)

sixth sexto, -a (2A)

sixty sesenta (P)

to skate patinar (1A)

to skateboard montar en monopatín (1A)

to ski esquiar (i → í) (1A)

skirt la falda (7A)

to sleep dormir (o → ue) (6A)

sleepy: to be — tener sueño (5B)

slide la diapositiva (9B)

small pequeño, -a (6A)

to snorkel bucear (8A)

snow: It's —ing. Nieva. (P)

so much tanto (7A)

so-so regular (P)

soap opera la telenovela (9A)

soccer: to play — jugar al fútbol (4B)

sociable sociable (1B)

social studies class la clase de ciencias sociales (2A)

socks los calcetines (7A)

soft drink el refresco (3A)

software el software (7B)

some unos, -as (2B)

something algo (3B)

sometimes a veces (1B)
son el hijo (5A)
—s; —(s) and daughter(s) los hijos (5A)
song la canción *pl.* las canciones (9B)
sorry: I'm —. Lo siento. (4B)
sound (stereo) system el equipo de sonido (6A)
soup: vegetable — la sopa de verduras (3A)
souvenirs los recuerdos (8A)
to buy — comprar recuerdos (8A)
spaghetti los espaguetis (3B)
Spanish class la clase de español (2A)
to spell:
How is ... spelled? ¿Cómo se escribe ... ? (P)
It's spelled ... Se escribe ... (P)
to spend time with friends pasar tiempo con amigos (1A)
spoon la cuchara (5B)
sports:
to play — practicar deportes (1A)
— -minded deportista (1B)
— show el programa deportivo (9A)
spring la primavera (P)
stadium el estadio (8A)
stairs, stairway la escalera (6B)
to start empezar (e → ie) (9A)
to stay: I — at home. Me quedo en casa. (4A)
stepbrother el hermanastro (5A)
stepfather el padrastro (5A)
stepmother la madrastra (5A)
stepsister la hermanastra (5A)
stereo system el equipo de sonido (6A)
stomach el estómago (P)
store la tienda (7A)
book— la librería (7B)
clothing — la tienda de ropa (7A)
department — el almacén *pl.* los almacenes (7B)
discount — la tienda de descuentos (7B)
household appliance — la tienda de electrodomésticos (7B)
jewelry — la joyería (7B)
shoe — la zapatería (7B)
story el piso (6B)
stories: to write — escribir cuentos (1A)
to straighten up the room arreglar el cuarto (6B)
strawberries las fresas (3A)
street la calle (8B)
student el/la estudiante (P)
studious estudioso, -a (1B)
to study estudiar (2A)
stupid tonto, -a (9A)
sugar el azúcar (5B)
suit el traje (7A)
summer el verano (P)
to sunbathe tomar el sol (8A)
Sunday domingo (P)
sunglasses los anteojos de sol (7B)
sunny: It's —. Hace sol. (P)
to surf the Web navegar en la Red (9B)
sweater el suéter (7A)
sweatshirt la sudadera (7A)
to swim nadar (1A)
swimming pool la piscina (4A)
swimsuit el traje de baño (7A)
synagogue la sinagoga (4A)

T

T-shirt la camiseta (7A)
table la mesa (2B)
to set the — poner la mesa (6B)
to take llevar (8B)
to — a course tomar un curso (9B)
to — out the trash sacar la basura (6B)
to — photos sacar fotos (5A)
talented talentoso, -a (1B)
to talk hablar (2A)
to — on the phone hablar por teléfono (1A)
tall alto, -a (5B)
tasty sabroso, -a (3B); rico, -a (5B)
tea el té (3A)
iced — el té helado (3A)
to teach enseñar (2A)
teacher el profesor, la profesora (P)
technology/computers la tecnología (2A)
technology/computer class la clase de tecnología (2A)
television: to watch — ver la tele (1A)
television set el televisor (6A)
to tell decir (8B)
— me dime (8A)
temple el templo (4A)
ten diez (P)
tennis: to play — jugar al tenis (4B)
tenth décimo, -a (2A)
thank you gracias (P)
that que (5A); ese, esa (7A)
—'s why por eso (9A)
the el, la (1B); los, las (2B)
— best el/la mejor, los/las mejores (6A)
— worst el/la peor, los/las peores (6A)
theater el teatro (8A)
movie — el cine (4A)
their su, sus (5A)
them las, los *dir. obj. pron.* (7B); les *ind. obj. pron.* (8B)
then entonces (4B)
there allí (2B)
— is/are hay (P, 2B)
therefore por eso (9A)
these estos, estas (7A)
they ellos, ellas (2A)
thing la cosa (6A)
to think creer (3B)
pensar (e → ie) (7A)
I don't — so. Creo que no. (3B)
I — ... Creo que ... (3B)

I — so. Creo que sí. (3B)

What do you — (about it)? ¿Qué te parece? (9B)

third tercer (tercero), -a (2A)

third floor el segundo piso (6B)

thirsty: I'm —. Tengo sed. (3B)

thirteen trece (P)

thirty treinta (P); y media *(in telling time)* (P)

thirty-one treinta y uno (P)

this este, esta (7A)

— afternoon esta tarde (4B)

— evening esta noche (4B)

— weekend este fin de semana (4B)

What is — ? ¿Qué es esto? (2B)

those esos, esas (7A)

thousand: a — mil (7A)

three tres (P)

three hundred trescientos, -as (7A)

three-ring binder la carpeta de argollas (2A)

Thursday jueves (P)

ticket el boleto (8A)

tie la corbata (7B)

time la vez *pl.* las veces (8B)

At what —? ¿A qué hora? (4B)

free — el tiempo libre (4A)

to spend — with friends pasar tiempo con amigos (1A)

What — is it? ¿Qué hora es? (P)

tired cansado, -a (4B)

to a *(prep.)* (4A)

in order — para + *inf.* (4A)

— the a la, al (4A)

— the left (of) a la izquierda (de) (6A)

— the right (of) a la derecha (de) (6A)

toast el pan tostado (3A)

today hoy (P)

tomatoes los tomates (3B)

tomorrow mañana (P)

See you —. Hasta mañana. (P)

too también (1A); demasiado (4B)

I do (like to) — a mí también (1A)

me — a mí también (1A)

top: on — of encima de (2B)

touching emocionante (9A)

toy el juguete (8B)

train el tren (8A)

to travel viajar (8A)

tree el árbol (8A)

tremendous tremendo, -a (8A)

trip el viaje (8A)

Tuesday martes (P)

on —s los martes (4A)

TV channel el canal (9A)

twelve doce (P)

twenty veinte (P)

twenty-one veintiuno (veintiún) (P)

two dos (P)

two hundred doscientos, -as (7A)

U

Ugh! ¡Uf! (7B)

ugly feo, -a (6A)

uncle el tío (5A)

uncles; uncle(s) and aunt(s) los tíos (5A)

underneath debajo de (2B)

to understand comprender (3A)

unforgettable inolvidable (8B)

us: (to/for) — nos *ind. obj. pron.* (8B)

to use:

to — the computer usar la computadora (1A)

What's it —d for? ¿Para qué sirve? (9B)

used usado, -a (8B)

useful:

to be — servir (9B)

is — for sirve para (9B)

V

vacation: to go on — ir de vacaciones (8A)

to vacuum pasar la aspiradora (6B)

vegetable soup la sopa de verduras (3A)

very muy (1B)

— well muy bien (P)

video el video (5A)

video games: to play — jugar videojuegos (1A)

to videotape hacer un video (5A)

violent violento, -a (9A)

to visit visitar (8A)

to — chat rooms visitar salones de chat (9B)

volleyball: to play — jugar al vóleibol (4B)

volunteer el voluntario, la voluntaria (8B)

— work el trabajo voluntario (8B)

W

waiter, waitress el camarero, la camarera (5B)

to walk caminar (3B)

wall la pared (6A)

wallet la cartera (7B)

to want querer (e → ie) (7A)

I — (yo) quiero (4B)

you — (tú) quieres (4B)

warm: to be — tener calor (5B)

was fue (8B)

to wash lavar (6B)

to — the car lavar el coche (6B)

to — the clothes lavar la ropa (6B)

to — the dishes lavar los platos (6B)

wastepaper basket la papelera (2B)

watch el reloj pulsera (7B)

to watch television ver la tele (1A)

water el agua *(f.)* (3A)

we nosotros, -as (2A)

to wear llevar (7A)

weather: What's the — like? ¿Qué tiempo hace? (P)

Web:

to surf the — navegar en la Red (9B)

— page la página Web (9B)

— site el sitio Web (9B)

Wednesday miércoles (P)

week la semana (P)

last — la semana pasada (7B)

weekend:

on —s los fines de semana (4A)

this — este fin de semana (4B)

welcome: You're —. De nada. (5B)

well bien (P); pues ... *(to indicate pause)* (1A)

very — muy bien (P)

what? ¿cuál? (3A)

— are you like? ¿Cómo eres? (1B)

(At) — time? ¿A qué hora? (4B)

— color ... ? ¿De qué color ... ? (6A)

— day is today? ¿Qué día es hoy? (P)

— did you do? ¿Qué hiciste? (8A)

— do you like better (prefer) to do? ¿Qué te gusta hacer más? (1A)

— do you like to do? ¿Qué te gusta hacer? (1A)

— do you think (about it)? ¿Qué te parece? (9B)

— does ... mean? ¿Qué quiere decir ... ? (P)

— else? ¿Qué más? (8B)

— happened to you? ¿Qué te pasó? (8A)

— is she/he like? ¿Cómo es? (1B)

— is the date? ¿Cuál es la fecha? (P)

— is this? ¿Qué es esto? (2B)

— is your name? ¿Cómo te llamas? (P)

— kind of ... ? ¿Qué clase de...? (9A)

— time is it? ¿Qué hora es? (P)

— would you like? ¿Qué desean (Uds.)? (5B)

—'s happening? ¿Qué pasa? (P)

—'s his/her name? ¿Cómo se llama? (1B)

—'s it (used) for? ¿Para qué sirve? (9B)

—'s the weather like? ¿Qué tiempo hace? (P)

what!:

— a good/nice idea! ¡Qué buena idea! (4B)

— a shame/pity! ¡Qué pena! (4B)

When? ¿Cuándo? (4A)

Where? ¿Dónde? (2B)

— are you from? ¿De dónde eres? (4A)

(To) —? ¿Adónde? (4A)

whether si (6B)

which? ¿cuál? (3A)

white blanco, -a (6A)

who que (5A)

Who? ¿Quién? (2A)

Why? ¿Por qué? (3B)

wife la esposa (5A)

Will you bring me ... ? ¿Me trae ... ? (5B)

window la ventana (2B)

winter el invierno (P)

with con (3A)

— me conmigo (4B)

— my/your friends con mis/tus amigos (4A)

— whom? ¿Con quién? (4A)

— you contigo (4B)

without sin (3A)

woman la mujer (5B)

older woman la anciana (8B)

work el trabajo (4A)

volunteer — el trabajo voluntario (8B)

to work trabajar (1A)

worse than peor(es) que (6A)

worst: the — el/la peor, los/las peores (6A)

Would you like ...? ¿Te gustaría ...? (4B)

to write:

to — e-mail escribir por correo electrónico (9B)

to — stories escribir cuentos (1A)

Y

yard el jardín *pl.* los jardines (8B)

year el año (P)

He/She is / They are ... —s old. Tiene(n) ... años. (5A)

last — el año pasado (7B)

yellow amarillo, -a (6A)

yes sí (1A)

yesterday ayer (7B)

yogurt el yogur (3A)

you fam. *sing.* tú (2A); *formal sing.* usted (Ud.) (2A); *fam. pl.* vosotros, -as (2A); *formal pl.* ustedes (Uds.) (2A); *fam. after prep.* ti (1A); *sing. ind. obj. pron.* te (8B); *pl. fam. ind. obj. pron.* os (8B); *ind. obj. pron.* le, les (8B)

And — ? ¿Y a ti? (1A)

for — para ti (6A)

to/for — *fam. pl.* os (8B)

to/for — *fam. sing.* te (8B)

with — contigo (4B)

— don't say! ¡No me digas! (4A)

— say ... Se dice ... (P)

You're welcome De nada (5B)

young joven (5B)

— boy/girl el niño, la niña (8B)

— man el joven (5B)

— woman la joven (5B)

—er menor (5A)

your *fam.* tu (2B); *fam.* tus, vuestro(s), -a(s) (5A); *formal* su, sus (5A)

Yuck! ¡Uf! (7B)

Z

zero cero (P)

zoo el zoológico (8A)

Grammar Index

Structures are most often presented first in *A primera vista*, where they are practiced lexically. They are then explained later in a *Gramática* section or a *Nota*. Light-face numbers refer to the pages where structures are initially presented or, after explanation, where student reminders occur. **Bold-face numbers** refer to pages where structures are explained or are otherwise highlighted.

Acknowledgments

Maps All maps created by XNR Productions.

Photographs Every effort has been made to secure permission and provide appropriate credit for photographic material. The publisher deeply regrets any omission and pledges to correct errors called to its attention in subsequent editions.

Unless otherwise acknowledged, all photographs are the property of Pearson Education, Inc.

Photo locators denoted as follows: Top (T), Center (C), Bottom (B), Left (L), Right (R), Background (Bkgd)

Cover (L) Ron Levine/Getty Images; (CL) iStockphoto; (CR) Jeff Greenberg/Alamy Images; (R) Chris Cheadle/Alamy

Front Matter v (TR) Kuttig - Travel - 2/Alamy Images, (TL) Art Resource, NY, (BR) digital vision/Getty Images, (BL) Getty Images; **vii** (TR) Alamy, (BR, BC) NASA, (BL) StockTrek/SuperStock; **xvii** (C) Bettmann/Corbis, (Bkgd) José Fusta Raga/Corbis; **xix** (BR) ©Phil Schermeister/Corbis; **xx** (Bkgd) Danny Lehman/Corbis; **xxii** (Bkgd) ©David Zimmerman/Corbis, (BL) Exactostock/SuperStock; **xxiv** (Bkgd) Shutterstock; **xxvi** (Bkgd) Michael Hilton/Alamy Images; **xxviii** (Bkgd) ©Paul Hardy/Corbis, (BL) ©Mark L. Stephenson; **xxix** (BR) ©José Fuste Raga/Corbis; **xxx** (Bkgd) ©Craig Tuttle/Corbis, (B) ©Strauss/Curtis/Corbis; **xxxi** (BR) ©Ron Watts/Corbis, (BL) Corbis

1 ©Philip Scalia/Alamy Images; **3** PhotoEdit Spencer Grant/SB: olopes/Fotolia (TC), M. Ferguson/PhotoEdit PhotoEdit: Rido/Fotolia (B); **5** (TR) Rido/Fotolia; **8** (BR) SuperStock; **11** PhotoEdit; **13** Bridgeman Art Library; **15** Morton Beebe/Corbis; **16** (BR) ©Pedro Armestre/Getty Images; **17** ©DK Images; **18** (BR, BL, BCL, BCR) SuperStock; **19** (L) ©Gordon R. Gainer, (CL) Getty Images, (CR) Photo Researchers, Inc., (R) ©Ramon Berk/Shutterstock; **20** (TR) ©Sharon Day/Shutterstock, (TL) Comstock/Thinkstock, (BR, BL) DDB Stock Photography, NASA; **24** (Bkgd) ©Imagestate Media Partners Limited - Impact Photos/Alamy Images; **25** (Inset) Art Resource, NY; **28** (B) Bettmann/Corbis, (T) Roberto M. Arakaki/ImageState; **29** (C) Buddy Mays/ImageState, (T) SuperStock; **31** (R) Alamy Images; **34** (C) Museo Bellapart; **35** (TL) ©Bonnie Kamin/PhotoEdit, (TR) Blaine Harrington Photo, (C) Latin Focus, (BL) Niko Guido/Getty Images, (BR) ZUMApress/NewsCom; **40** (BC) Marisol Díaz/Latin Focus, (T) Hola Images/Corbis; **41** (TR) Jimmy Dorantes/Latin Focus, (B) PhotoEdit; **42** (L) Alamy Images; **43** (TR) Daemmrich Photography, (BR) Kathy Ferguson-Johnson/PhotoEdit; **44** (Bkgd) Bettmann/Corbis; **45** (TL, CR) Bettmann/Corbis, (BL) José Fuste Raga/Corbis; **48** (Bkgd) ©imagebroker/Alamy Images; **49** (Inset) Art Resource, NY; **51** Panos Pictures; **57** Blend Images/Alamy; **58** Simón Bolívar (1783–1830) (chromolitho)/Private Collection/Archives Charmet/Bridgeman Art Library; **62** ©Gary Bogdon/NewSport/Corbis; **65** Cindy Miller Hopkins/NewsCom; **66** (CL) micromonkey/Fotolia, (CR) DDB Stock Photography, Tony Arruza/Tony Arruza; **68** (Bkgd) Bettmann/Corbis; **69** (T, B) Bettmann/Corbis, (CR) Linda Whitwam/©DK Images; **72** (Bkgd) ©dbimages/Alamy Images; **73** (Inset) Courtesy Marlborough Gallery, NY; **80** Jeff Greenberg/PhotoEdit; **81** (BR) NewsCom; **83** (BCR) ©Andy Dean/Fotolia, (CR) ©Bill Bachmann/Alamy Images, (TCL) ©holbox/Shutterstock, (CL) ©Tetra Images/Getty Images, (TCR) Rob/Fotolia, (BL) Creatas/Thinkstock, (C) Panos Pictures; **85** DDB Stock Photography; **86** (BR) Paul Conklin/PhotoEdit; **88** Panos Pictures; **89** Corbis Bridge/Alamy Images; **90** (B) Bettemann/Corbis, (Inset) Martin Shields/Alamy Images; **91** (BR) ©National Geographic Image Collection/Alamy Images, (TC) ©Ron Niebrugge/Alamy Images; **92** (T) ©Hector Rio/EFE/NewsCom, (BR) ©John Vizcaino/Reuters/Landov LLC; **93** (BR) Jeff Greenberg/PhotoEdit; **94** (Bkgd) José Fuste Raga/Corbis; **95** (BR) ©Randy Faris/Corbis, (CR) Danny Lehman/Corbis, (TR) Lindsay Hebberd/Corbis; **98** (Bkgd) Carlos S. Pereyra/DDB Stock Photography; **99** SUN/NewsCom; **104** DDB Stock Photography; **106** (CR) ©flashover/Alamy Images; **108** DDB Stock Photography; **111** ©Spencer Grant/PhotoEdit; **112** (T) ©Jan Halaska/Photo Researchers, Inc.; **113** (B) ©Keith Dannemiller/Alamy Images, (T) Getty Images; **114** (BR) Jeremy Horner/Panos Pictures, (CL) National Geographic Image Collection/Alamy Images; **115** (BR) Jean-Leo Dugast/Panos Pictures, (TL) Jeremy Horner/Panos Pictures, (BC) Jon Spaull/Panos Pictures, (BL) Panos Pictures, (TR) Sean Sprague/Panos Pictures; **116** (C) ©Bill Bachmann/Alamy Images, (BR) Carlos S. Pereyra/DDB Stock Photography; **117** (B) Alamy Images; **118** (Inset) Bettmann/Corbis, (Bkgd) Getty Images; **119** (BR) ©J. A. Murillo, (CL) Bettmann/Corbis, (TR) Corbis; **122** (Bkgd) ©Blend Images/SuperStock; **123** (Inset) Art Resource, NY; **132** (BR) ©Dorothy Alexander/Alamy Images, ©Ivonne Barreto/Latin Focus; **133** (BR) ©Corbis/SuperStock; **134** (BR) ©Slim Plantagenate/Alamy; **137** Cindy Miller Hopkins/NewsCom; **139** (BR) ©imagebroker/Alamy; **140** raptorcaptor/Fotolia; **141** (T) SuperStock; **142** (Bkgd) Bettmann/Corbis; **143** (TR, CL) Bettmann/Corbis, (BL) Corbis; **146** (Bkgd) ©imagebroker/SuperStock; **147** (Inset) The Great City of Tenochtitlán, detail of a woman selling vegetables, 1945 (mural), Rivera, Diego (1886–1957)/Palacio Nacional, Mexico City, Mexico/Giraudon/Bridgeman Art Library; **152** ©David R. Frazier Photolibrary, Inc./Alamy; **156** ImageState; **158** (CR) AGE Fotostock, (BR) eStock Photo; **160** (BL) ©Associated Press, (BL) Charles Rex Arbogast/©AP Photo, (TR) James Nelson/Getty Images; **163** (TL) ANTONIO SCORZA/AFP/Getty Images/NewsCom, (BR) NewsCom; **164** (TR) ©Alison Wright/Photo Researchers, Inc., (B) NewsCom; **165** (CR) ©Jimmy Dorantes/Latin Focus, (BR) DDB Stock Photography; **166** (Bkgd) Corbis; **167** (C) ©Prisma/SuperStock, (TR, BR) Bettmann/Corbis; **170** (Bkgd) ©imagebroker/Alamy Images; **171** (Inset) Art Resource, NY; **177** NewsCom; **179** Alamy Images; **180** (BR) AFP/Getty Images/NewsCom; **181** (BL) ©Jack Hollingsworth/Corbis, (TR, TC, CR) ©Jimmy Dorantes/Latin Focus; **185** AFP PHOTO/DOMINIQUE FAGET/NewsCom; **187** (T) Alamy Images, (B) PhotoLibrary Group, Inc.; **188** (BR) Jon Bursnall/Latin Focus; **189** (CR) ©Dave G. Houser/Corbis, (TL) Exactostock/SuperStock, Malcolm Fife/eStock Photo, (TR) NewsCom; **190** (TR) ©GoGo Images Corporation/Alamy; **191** (TR) ©Bill Bachmann/PhotoEdit, (BR) ©Jimmy Dorantes/Latin Focus; **192** (CR) ©Randy Faris/Corbis, (TC) Medioimages/Photodisc/

Thinkstock; **193** (Bkgd) Alamy, (BL) Bettmann/Corbis; **196** (Bkgd) Getty Images; **197** (Inset) Getty Images; **205** (BR) Secretaría de Turismo y Desarrollo/Latin Focus; **207** (TR) ©Tony Savino/The Image Works, Inc., (C) Shutterstock; **208** (CL) Chris Trotman/DUOMO/©PCN Photography, (TCL) ©Image of Sportcom Image of Sport Photos/NewsCom, (TCR) ©D. Lippitt/Einstein/NBAE/Getty Images, (R, BR) NewsCom; **209** ©Reuters NewMedia Inc./Corbis; **210** (CL) NewsCom, (BL) PhotoEdit; **211** (L) ©Michael Taylor/Lonely Planet Images; **212** Chris Trotman/Duomo/©PCN Photography; **213** (T) Cspa/CSPA/Cal Sport Media/ZUMAPRESS/NewsCom, (BR) Darrell Walker/UTHM/Icon SMI/NewsCom; **214** (BR) ©Jimmy Dorantes/Latin Focus; **215** ZUMA Press,Inc./Alamy; **216** (Bkgd) ©Nik Wheeler/Corbis, (C) NASA; **217** (CR) Bettmann/Corbis, (TR) Kevin Fleming/Corbis; **220** (Bkgd) ©Blend Images/SuperStock; **221** (Inset) Carmen L. Garza; **226** Carmen L. Garza; **227** (TR) ©Gardel Bertrand/PhotoLibrary Group, Ltd.; **229** eStock Photo; **230** AFP/Getty Images; **231** (TL) Art Resource, NY, (BR) Bridgeman Art Library; **235** ©DK Images; **236** (CR) Art Resource, NY, (BL) DDB Stock Photography; **237** (CR) ©Felipe Rodríguez/Alamy Images; **238** (BR) ©Corbis/SuperStock; **239** (TL) ©Corbis/SuperStock; **240** ©David Seawell/Corbis; **241** (C) SuperStock; **246** (Bkgd) ©Gary Latham/Alamy Images; **247** (Inset) ©Erich Lessing/Art Resource, NY; **253** Alamy Images; **254** DDB Stock Photography; **255** (CL) ©Danita Delimont/Alamy Images; **259** (C) Jimmy Dorantes/Latin Focus, (TR) michaeljung/Fotolia; **260** eStock Photo; **261** (BR) ImageState; **262** ©Megan Bowers/Latin Focus; **263** (TR) Bettmann/Corbis, (CR) Danny Lehman/Corbis; **264** (CR) NewsCom; **265** (BR) ©Rob Wilson/Shutterstock; **270** (Bkgd) ©William Panzer/Alamy Images; **271** (Inset) Peter Horree/Alamy Images; **286** (CR) ©GoGo Images Corporation/Alamy, ©Jimmy Dorantes/Latin Focus; **287** Travis Houston/Shutterstock; **290** SuperStock; **291** ©B2M Productions/Getty Images; **296** (Bkgd) ©Greg Balfour Evans/Alamy Images; **303** SuperStock; **311** ©DK Images; **314** (BR) ©Mark Boulton/Alamy Images, (T) SuperStock; **315** (T) SuperStock; **320** (Bkgd) ©John Mitchell/Alamy Images; **321** (BL) Art Resource, NY; **326** (B) Getty Images; **327** Courtesy Marlborough Gallery, NY; **328** (C, BR, BC) ©Jimmy Dorantes/Latin Focus, (CR) ©Jimmy Durantes/Latin Focus; **331** Rubberball/Corbis; **335** (BR) Alamy Images, (CR) NewsCom, (BL) Shutterstock; **336** (BL) ©Alberto Lowe/Reuters/Landov LLC, (CR) ©Dixon Hamby/Alamy, (BR) ©IFA Bilderteam/eStock Photo; **337** (BR) ©Stringer/Xinhua/Photoshot/NewsCom, (TL) eStock Photo; **338** Alamy Images; **339** (TR) ©Javier Larrea/AGE Fotostock; **344** (Bkgd) ©Chad Ehlers/Alamy Images; **345** (Inset) JTB Photo Communications, Inc/Alamy Images; **350** Alamy Images; **353** (CR) ©Ilene MacDonald/Alamy, (CL) ©Peter Titmuss/Alamy Images, (BL) DDB Stock Photography, (BR) PhotoEdit; **356** Alamy Images; **357** Shutterstock; **359** (TL) ©itsallgood/Fotolia, (C) ©San Diego Historical Society Photo Collection, (TR) SuperStock; **362** (BR) ©age fotostock/Robert Harding World Imagery; **363** (BL) Alamy Images; **364** (CL, BR) PhotoEdit; **365** (TL) ©David Zanzinger/Alamy Images, (TR) ©M. Timothy O'Keefe/Alamy Images; **366** (BR) ©John Arnold Images Ltd./Alamy Images; **367** Glenda Powers/Fotolia; **372** (Bkgd) ©Jordi Cami/Alamy Images; **373** (Inset) NewsCom; **378** Bettmann/Corbis; **379** (CR) ©David R. Frazier Photolibrary, Inc./Alamy Images; **380** DDB Stock Photography; **381** ImageState; **382** (CR) ©Dorothy Alexander/Alamy Images, (BR) ©Russell Gordon/Danita Delimont, Agent, (CL, BL) ©Salatiel Barragán/Latin Focus, (CC) ©Stringer/Mexico/Reuters/Landov LLC, (TR) Bettmann/Corbis; **383** (BR) ©Nina Raingold/Getty Images; **384** Shutterstock; **387** ©Bly Photography; **389** ©Jimmy Dorantes/Latin Focus, SuperStock; **390** (CL) ©Kirill Trifonov/Shutterstock, (CL) ©Michele Burgess, (BL) Alamy Images; **391** (TR) ©Gavin Hellier/Getty Images, Alamy Images; **392** ©Bly Photography; **393** (T) Corbis; **398** (Bkgd) ©Jeff Greenberg/Alamy Images; **404** AGE Fotostock; **405** (TC) ©Michael Newman/PhotoEdit, (TR, TL) lunamarina/Fotolia, (C) Rido/Shutterstock, (BR) SuperStock; **406** (BL) ©Jenny Matthews/Alamy Images, (CR) ©Jimmy Dorantes/Latin Focus; **407** SuperStock; **409** (BC) ©Puerto Rico Conservation Foundation; **410** Alamy Images; **412** ©Fernando Alda/Corbis; **413** (CR) ©Jenny Matthews/Alamy Images, (TR) National Geographic Image Collection; **414** (TR) ©Marcelo Salinas/Latin Focus, (BR) SuperStock; **415** (BL) DDB Stock Photography, (BR) PhotoEdit, (CR) Shutterstock; **416** Mite Kuzevski/Demotix/Demotix/Corbis; **417** (TL) ©A. Ramey/PhotoEdit, (BR) SuperStock; **418** (TR) ©Tina Manley/Alamy Images, (BR) Chuck Place Photography; **419** (TR) PhotoEdit; **424** (Bkgd) ©Universal Pictures/Strike ENT/Beacon Communications LLC/Album/NewsCom; **425** (Inset) Art Resource, NY; **432** (CR, C) Felix Mizioznikov/Fotolia; **434** Bettmann/Corbis; **436** (BR) Alamy; **437** epa european pressphoto agency b.v./Alamy; **439** ©Associated Press; **440** (BR) ©Michel Bussy/Getty Images, (CR) ImageState; **441** (TR) ©Andre Jenny/Alamy Images; **443** (CR) ©Danita Delimont/Alamy Images, (TR) ©David R. Frazier Photolibrary, Inc./Alamy Images; **448** (Bkgd) ©Elmer Martínez/AFP/Getty Images/NewsCom; **449** (Inset) Art Resource, NY; **454** ©MELBA PHOTO AGENCY/Alamy; **455** ©MELBA PHOTO AGENCY/Alamy; **456** ©Michael Newman/PhotoEdit, Inc.; **461** Hect/Shutterstock; **463** (C) ©John Vachon/Corbis, (BL) Fancy/Alamy; **466** (BR) ©i love images/Alamy; **467** (TR) ©James Davis/ImageState

Text

Bayard Presse SA

"A sus teclados, listos…¡a navegar!" Text by Anne-Laure Fournier–Le Ray © Images Doc/Reportero Doc, Bayard Jeunesse, 2002. Reprinted by permission.

La Fundación Puertorriqueña de Conservación

"Reduce - Reusa - Recicla" from LA FUNDACIÓN PUERTORRIQUEÑA DE CONSERVACIÓN & Logo of LA FUNDACIÓN PUERTORRIQUEÑA DE CONSERVACIÓN, Copyright © 2001. Used by permission of La Fundación Puertorriqueña de Conservación.

Muy Interesante

"¿Quién hace las tareas?" by Matilde de la Vara from *Muy Interesante* – Marzo 2002 No. 250. Published by GyJ España Ediciones, S.L. S en C. Used by permission.

PARS International Corporation

"¡Apágala!" from *Time for Kids,* April 12, 2002, Vol. 7, No. 22. Copyright © 2002 Time Inc. Used under license.

Note: Every effort has been made to locate the copyright owner of material reproduced in this component. Omissions brought to our attention will be corrected in subsequent editions.